Encyclopedia of

Library and Information Sciences, Fourth Edition

Volume 2

Encyclopedias from the Taylor & Francis Group

Print	Online

Agriculture

Encyclopedia of Agricultural, Food, and Biological Engineering, 2nd Ed., 2 Vols. — Pub'd. 10/21/10
K10554 (978-1-4398-1111-5) K11382 (978-1-4398-2806-9)

Encyclopedia of Animal Science, 2nd Ed., 2 Vols. — Pub'd. 2/1/11
K10463 (978-1-4398-0932-7) K10528 (978-0-415-80286-4)

Encyclopedia of Biotechnology in Agriculture and Food — Pub'd. 7/16/10
DK271X (978-0-8493-5027-6) DKE5044 (978-0-8493-5044-3)

Business and Computer Science

Encyclopedia of Computer Science & Technology, 2nd Ed., 2 Vols. — Pub'd 12/21/2016
K21573 (978-1-4822-0819-1) K21578 (978-1-4822-0822-1)

Encyclopedia of Information Assurance, 4 Vols. — Pub'd. 12/21/10
AU6620 (978-1-4200-6620-3) AUE6620 (978-1-4200-6622-7)

Encyclopedia of Information Systems and Technology, 2 Vols. — Pub'd. 12/29/15
K15911 (978-1-4665-6077-2) K21745 (978-1-4822-1432-1)

Encyclopedia of Library and Information Sciences, 4th Ed. — Publishing 2017
K15223 (978-1-4665-5259-3) K15224 (978-1-4665-5260-9)

Encyclopedia of Software Engineering, 2 Vols. — Pub'd. 11/24/10
AU5977 (978-1-4200-5977-9) AUE5977 (978-1-4200-5978-6)

Encyclopedia of Supply Chain Management, 2 Vols. — Pub'd. 12/21/11
K12842 (978-1-4398-6148-6) K12843 (978-1-4398-6152-3)

Encyclopedia of U.S. Intelligence, 2 Vols. — Pub'd. 12/19/14
AU8957 (978-1-4200-8957-8) AUE8957 (978-1-4200-8958-5)

Encyclopedia of Wireless and Mobile Communications, 2nd Ed., 3 Vols. — Pub'd. 12/18/12
K14731 (978-1-4665-0956-6) KE16352 (978-1-4665-0969-6)

Chemistry, Materials and Chemical Engineering

Encyclopedia of Chemical Processing, 5 Vols. — Pub'd. 11/1/05
DK2243 (978-0-8247-5563-8) DKE499X (978-0-8247-5499-0)

Encyclopedia of Chromatography, 3rd Ed. — Pub'd. 10/12/09
84593 (978-1-4200-8459-7) 84836 (978-1-4200-8483-2)

Encyclopedia of Iron, Steel, and Their Alloys, 5 Vols. — Pub'd. 1/6/16
K14814 (978-1-4665-1104-0) K14815 (978-1-4665-1105-7)

Encyclopedia of Plasma Technology, 2 Vols. — Pub'd 12/12/2016
K14378 (978-1-4665-0059-4) K21744 (978-1-4822-1431-4)

Encyclopedia of Supramolecular Chemistry, 2 Vols. — Pub'd. 5/5/04
DK056X (978-0-8247-5056-5) DKE7259 (978-0-8247-4725-1)

Encyclopedia of Surface & Colloid Science, 3rd Ed., 10 Vols. — Pub'd. 8/27/15
K20465 (978-1-4665-9045-8) K20478 (978-1-4665-9061-8)

Engineering

Dekker Encyclopedia of Nanoscience and Nanotechnology, 3rd Ed., 7 Vols. — Pub'd. 3/20/14
K14119 (978-1-4398-9134-6) K14120 (978-1-4398-9135-3)

Environment (continued from top right)

Encyclopedia of Energy Engineering and Technology, 2nd Ed., 4 Vols. — Pub'd. 12/1/14
K14633 (978-1-4665-0673-2) KE16142 (978-1-4665-0674-9)

Encyclopedia of Optical and Photonic Engineering, 2nd Ed., 5 Vols. — Pub'd. 9/22/15
K12323 (978-1-4398-5097-8) K12325 (978-1-4398-5099-2)

Environment

Encyclopedia of Environmental Management, 4 Vols. — Pub'd. 12/13/12
K11434 (978-1-4398-2927-1) K11440 (978-1-4398-2933-2)

Encyclopedia of Environmental Science and Engineering, 6th Ed., 2 Vols. — Pub'd. 6/25/12
K10243 (978-1-4398-0442-1) KE0278 (978-1-4398-0517-6)

Encyclopedia of Natural Resources, 2 Vols. — Pub'd. 7/23/14
K12418 (978-1-4398-5258-3) K12420 (978-1-4398-5260-6)

Medicine

Encyclopedia of Biomaterials and Biomedical Engineering, 2nd Ed. — Pub'd. 5/28/08
H7802 (978-1-4200-7802-2) HE7803 (978-1-4200-7803-9)

Encyclopedia of Biomedical Polymers and Polymeric Biomaterials, 11 Vols. — Pub'd. 4/2/15
K14324 (978-1-4398-9879-6) K14404 (978-1-4665-0179-9)

Concise Encyclopedia of Biomedical Polymers and Polymeric Biomaterials, 2 Vols. — Pub'd. 8/14/17
K14313 (978-1-4398-9855-0) KE42253 (978-1-315-11644-0)

Encyclopedia of Biopharmaceutical Statistics, 3rd Ed. — Pub'd. 5/20/10
H100102 (978-1-4398-2245-6) HE10326 (978-1-4398-2246-3)

Encyclopedia of Clinical Pharmacy — Pub'd. 11/14/02
DK7524 (978-0-8247-0752-1) DKE6080 (978-0-8247-0608-1)

Encyclopedia of Dietary Supplements, 2nd Ed. — Pub'd. 6/25/10
H100094 (978-1-4398-1928-9) HE10315 (978-1-4398-1929-6)

Encyclopedia of Medical Genomics and Proteomics, 2 Vols. — Pub'd. 12/29/04
DK2208 (978-0-8247-5564-5) DK501X (978-0-8247-5501-0)

Encyclopedia of Pharmaceutical Science and Technology, 4th Ed., 6 Vols. — Pub'd. 7/1/13
H100233 (978-1-84184-819-8) HE10420 (978-1-84184-820-4)

Routledge Encyclopedias

Encyclopedia of Public Administration and Public Policy, 3rd Ed., 5 Vols. — Pub'd. 11/6/15
K16418 (978-1-4665-6909-6) K16434 (978-1-4665-6936-2)

Routledge Encyclopedia of Modernism — Pub'd 5/11/16
Y137844 (978-1-135-00035-6)

Routledge Encyclopedia of Philosophy Online — Pub'd. 11/1/00
RU22334 (978-0-415-24909-6)

Routledge Performance Archive — Pub'd. 11/12/12
Y148405 (978-0-203-77466-3)

Encyclopedia of

Library and Information Sciences, Fourth Edition

Volume 2

From: *Cataloging* To: *Engineering Literatures and Their Uses*

Encyclopedia Edited By

John D. McDonald

and

Michael Levine-Clark

CRC Press
Taylor & Francis Group
Boca Raton London New York

CRC Press is an imprint of the
Taylor & Francis Group, an **informa** business

First published 2018 by CRC Press

Published 2019 by CRC Press
Taylor & Francis Group
6000 Broken Sound Parkway NW, Suite 300
Boca Raton, FL 33487-2742

First issued in paperback 2020

© 2018 by Taylor & Francis Group, LLC
CRC Press is an imprint of the Taylor & Francis Group, an informa business

No claim to original U.S. Government works

ISBN-13: 978-1-4665-5259-3 (HB Set)
ISBN-13: 978-0-8153-8625-4 (Vol. 2) (hbk)

ISBN 13: 978-0-3675-7010-1 (PB Set)
ISBN 13: 978-0-3675-7017-0 (Vol. 2) (pbk)

Visit the Taylor & Francis Web site at
http://www.taylorandfrancis.com

and the CRC Press Web site at
http://www.crcpress.com

Encyclopedia of Library and Information Sciences, Fourth Edition

Brief Contents

v

Encyclopedia of Library and Information Sciences, Fourth Edition

Editors-in-Chief

John D. McDonald
Analytics and Assessment, EBSCO Information Services

Michael Levine-Clark
University of Denver Libraries, Denver, Colorado

Editorial Advisory Board

Contributors

June Abbas / *School of Library and Information Studies, University of Oklahoma, Norman, Oklahoma, U.S.A.*

Richard Abel / *Portland, Oregon, U.S.A.*

Eileen G. Abels / *College of Information Science and Technology, Drexel University, Philadelphia, Pennsylvania, U.S.A.*

Tia Abner / *American Medical Informatics Association (AMIA), Bethesda, Maryland, U.S.A.*

Donald C. Adcock / *Dominican University, River Forest, Illinois, U.S.A.*

Kendra S. Albright / *School of Library and Information Science, University of South Carolina, Columbia, South Carolina, U.S.A.*

Mikael Alexandersson / *University of Gothenburg, Gothenburg, Sweden*

Joan M. Aliprand / *Cupertino, California, U.S.A.*

Jacqueline Allen / *Dallas Museum of Art, Dallas, Texas, U.S.A.*

Romano Stephen Almagno / *International College of St. Bonaventure, Rome, Italy*

Connie J. Anderson-Cahoon / *Southern Oregon University Library, Ashland, Oregon, U.S.A.*

Karen Anderson / *Archives and Information Science, Mid Sweden University, ITM, Härnösand, Sweden*

Rick Anderson / *University of Utah, Salt Lake City, Utah, U.S.A.*

Silviu Andrieş-Tabac / *Institute of Cultural Heritage, Moldova Academy of Sciences, Chişinău, Republic of Moldova*

Peng Hwa Ang / *Wee Kim Wee School of Communication and Information, Nanyang Technological University, Singapore*

Hermina G.B. Anghelescu / *School of Library and Information Science, Wayne State University, Detroit, Michigan, U.S.A.*

Leah Arroyo / *American Association of Museums, Washington, District of Columbia, U.S.A.*

Terry Asla / *Senior Lifestyles Researcher, Seattle, U.S.A.*

Shiferaw Assefa / *University of Kansas, Lawrence, Kansas, U.S.A.*

Ilse Assmann / *Radio Broadcast Facilities, SABC, Johannesburg, South Africa*

Maija-Leena Aulikki Huotari / *University of Oulu, Oulu, Finland*

Henriette D. Avram / *Library of Congress, Washington, District of Columbia, U.S.A.*

Sven Axsäter / *Department of Industrial Management and Logistics, Lund University, Lund, Sweden*

Murtha Baca / *Getty Research Institute, Los Angeles, California, U.S.A.*

Roger S. Bagnall / *Institute for the Study of the Ancient World, New York University, New York, New York, U.S.A.*

Nestor Bamidis / *GSA-Archives of Macedonia, Thessaloniki, Greece*

Franz Barachini / *Business Innovation Consulting—Austria, Langenzersdorf, Austria*

Rebecca O. Barclay / *Rensselaer Polytechnic Institute, Troy, New York, U.S.A.*

Judit Bar-Ilan / *Department of Information Science, Bar-Ilan University, Ramat Gan, Israel*

Alex W. Barker / *Museum of Art and Archaeology, University of Missouri, Columbia, Missouri, U.S.A.*

John A. Bateman / *University of Bremen, Bremen, Germany*

Marcia J. Bates / *Department of Information Studies, Graduate School of Education and Information Studies, University of California, Los Angeles (UCLA), Los Angeles, California, U.S.A.*

Philippe Baumard / *School of Engineering, Stanford University, Stanford, California, U.S.A., and University Paul Cézanne, Aix-en-Provence, France*

David Bawden / *City, University of London, London, U.K.*

Jennifer Bawden / *Museum Studies Program, Faculty of Information Studies, University of Toronto, Toronto, Ontario, Canada*

David Bearman / *Archives & Museum Informatics, Toronto, Ontario, Canada*

William K. Beatty / *Northwestern University Medical School, Chicago, Illinois, U.S.A.*

A.R. Bednarek / *University of Florida, Gainesville, Florida, U.S.A.*

Clare Beghtol / *Faculty of Information Studies, University of Toronto, Toronto, Ontario, Canada*

Lori Bell / *Alliance Library System, East Peoria, Illinois, U.S.A.*

Danna Bell-Russel / *Library of Congress, Washington, District of Columbia, U.S.A.*

William Benedon / *Benedon & Associates, Encino, California, U.S.A.*

Anna Bergaliyeva / *Kazakhstan Institute of Management, Economics and Strategic Research (KIMEP), Almaty, Kazakhstan*

Sidney E. Berger / *Phillips Library, Peabody Essex Museum, Salem, Massachusetts, U.S.A.*

Andrew J. Berner / *University Club of New York, New York, New York, U.S.A.*

Sean F. Berrigan / *Policy, Library and Archives Canada, Ottawa, Ontario, Canada*

John W. Berry / *NILRC: Network of Illinois Learning Resources in Community Colleges, Dominican University, River Forest, Illinois, U.S.A.*

Michael W. Berry / *Department of Electrical Engineering and Computer Science, University of Tennessee, Knoxville, Tennessee, U.S.A.*

Suresh K. Bhavnani / *Center for Computational Medicine and Bioinformatics, University of Michigan, Ann Arbor, Michigan, U.S.A.*

Tamara Biggs / *Chicago History Museum, Chicago, Illinois, U.S.A.*

Frank Birkebæk / *Roskilde Museum, Roskilde, Denmark*

Ann P. Bishop / *Graduate School of Library and Information Science, University of Illinois at Urbana-Champaign, Urbana, Illinois, U.S.A.*

Julia Blixrud / *Association of Research Libraries, Washington, District of Columbia, U.S.A.*

Gloria Bordogna / *Italian National Research Council, Institute for the Dynamics of Environmental Processes, Dalmine, Italy*

Steve Bosch / *Administration Department, University of Arizona, Tucson, Arizona, U.S.A.*

Kimberly S. Bostwick / *Ecology and Evolutionary Biology, Cornell University Museum of Vertebrates, Ithaca, New York, U.S.A.*

Natalia T. Bowdoin / *University of South Carolina Aiken, Aiken, South Carolina, U.S.A.*

Patrick J. Boylan / *Department of Cultural Policy and Management, City University, London, U.K.*

Amy E. Brand / *CrossRef, Lynnfield, Massachusetts, U.S.A.*

Judy Brooker / *Australian Library and Information Association, Deakin, Australian Capital Territory, Australia*

Terrence Brooks / *iSchool, University of Washington, Seattle, Washington, U.S.A.*

Vanda Broughton / *School of Library, Archive and Information Studies, University College London, London, U.K.*

Cecelia Brown / *School of Library and Information Studies, University of Oklahoma, Norman, Oklahoma, U.S.A.*

Jos de Bruijn / *Digital Enterprise Research Institute, University of Innsbruck, Innsbruck, Austria*

Steve Bryant / *BFI National Archive, Herts, U.K.*

Alan Bryden / *International Organization for Standardization, Geneva, Switzerland*

Jeff E. Bullard / *Free Library of Philadelphia, Philadelphia, Pennsylvania, U.S.A.*

Kathleen Burns / *Beinecke Rare Book and Manuscript Library, Yale University, New Haven, Connecticut, U.S.A.*

Brenda A. Burton / *Library, Kirkland & Ellis LLP, Chicago, IL, U.S.A.*

E. Burton Swanson / *Anderson School of Management, University of California, Los Angeles, Los Angeles, California, U.S.A.*

Donald I. Butcher / *Canadian Library Association, Ottawa, Ontario, Canada*

Kevin Butterfield / *Wolf Law Library, College of William and Mary, Williamsburg, Virginia, U.S.A.*

Alex Byrne / *University of Technology, Sydney—Sydney, New South Wales, Australia*

Brian Byrne / *Discipline of Psychology, School of Behavioural, Cognitive and Social Sciences, University of New England, Armidale, New South Wales, Australia, Australian Research Council Centre of Excellence in Cognition and its Disorder, Australia, and National Health and Medical Research Council Centre of Research Excellence in Twin Research, Australia*

Bernadette G. Callery / *School of Information Sciences, University of Pittsburgh, Pittsburgh, Pennsylvania, U.S.A.*

Paul D. Callister / *Leon E. Bloch Law Library, University of Missouri-Kansas City School of Law, Kansas City, Missouri, U.S.A.*

Perrine Canavaggio / *International Council on Archives, Paris, France*

Sarah R. Canino / *Dickinson Music Library, Vassar College, Poughkeepsie, New York, U.S.A.*

Robert Capra / *School of Information and Library Science, University of North Carolina, Chapel Hill, North Carolina, U.S.A.*

Nicholas Carroll / *Hastings Research, Inc., Las Vegas, Nevada, U.S.A.*

Ben Carterette / *Department of Computer and Information Sciences, University of Delaware, Newark, Delaware, U.S.A.*

Vittorio Castelli / *T.J. Watson Research Center, IBM, Yorktown Heights, New York, U.S.A.*

Jane Rosetta Virginia Caulton / *Library of Congress, Washington, District of Columbia, U.S.A.*

Richard Cave / *Formerly at the Public Library of Science, San Francisco, California, U.S.A.*

Roderick Cave / *Loughborough University, Loughborough, U.K.*

Marcel Caya / *Department of History, University of Quebec at Montreal (UQAM), Montreal, Quebec, Canada*

Frank Cervone / *Purdue University Calumet, Hammond, Indiana, U.S.A.*

Leslie Champeny / *Alaska Resources Library and Information Services (ARLIS), Anchorage, Alaska, U.S.A.*

Lois Mai Chan / *School of Library and Information Science, University of Kentucky, Lexington, Kentucky, U.S.A.*

Sergio Chaparro-Univazo / *Graduate School of Library and Information Science, Simmons College, Boston, Massachusetts, U.S.A.*

Mary K. Chelton / *Graduate School of Library and Information Studies, Queens College Flushing, New York, U.S.A.*

Hsinchun Chen / *Department of Management Information Systems, University of Arizona, Tucson, Arizona, U.S.A.*

Jianhua Chen / *Computer Science Department, Louisiana State University, Baton Rouge, Louisiana, U.S.A.*

Eric R. Childress / *OCLC, Dublin, Ohio, U.S.A.*

Michael A. Chilton / *Department of Management, Kansas State University, Manhattan, Kansas, U.S.A.*

TzeHuey Chiou-Peng / *Spurlock Museum, University of Illinois at Urbana-Champaign, Urbana, Illinois, U.S.A.*

Hyun-Yang Cho / *Department of Library and Information Science, Kyonggi University, Suwon, South Korea*

Jae-Hwang Choi / *Department of Library and Information Science, Kyungpook National University, Daegu, South Korea*

Carol E.B. Choksy / *School of Library and Information Science, Indiana University, Bloomington, Indiana, U.S.A.*

Su Kim Chung / *University Libraries, University of Nevada–Las Vegas, Las Vegas, Nevada, U.S.A.*

James Church / *University Libraries, University of California, Berkeley, Berkeley, California, U.S.A.*

Barbara H. Clubb / *Ottawa Public Library, Ottawa, Ontario, Canada*

Arlene Cohen / *Pacific Islands Library Consultant, Seattle, Washington, U.S.A.*

Barbara Cohen-Stratyner / *New York Public Library for the Performing Arts, New York, U.S.A.*

Edward T. Cokely / *Center for Adaptive Behavior and Cognition, Max Planck Institute for Human Development, Berlin, Germany*

Arthur H. Cole / *Harvard University, Cambridge, Massachusetts, U.S.A.*

John Y. Cole / *Center for the Book, Library of Congress, Washington, District of Columbia, U.S.A.*

Patrick Tod Colegrove / *DeLaMare Science & Engineering Library, University Libraries, University of Nevada, Reno, Reno, Nevada, U.S.A.*

Edwin T. Coman, Jr. / *University of California, Riverside, California, U.S.A.*

Nora T. Corley / *Arctic Institute of North America, Montreal, Quebec, Canada*

Sheila Corrall / *Department of Information Studies, University of Sheffield, Sheffield, U.K.*

Erica Cosijn / *Department of Information Science, University of Pretoria, Pretoria, South Africa*

Richard J. Cox / *School of Computing and Information, University of Pittsburgh, Pittsburgh, Pennsylvania, U.S.A.*

Barbara M. Cross / *Records and Information Management, Sony Pictures Entertainment, Culver City, California, U.S.A.*

Kevin Crowston / *School of Information Studies, Syracuse University, Syracuse, New York, U.S.A.*

Adrian Cunningham / *National Archives of Australia (NAA), Canberra, Australian Capital Territory, Australia*

Judith N. Currano / *University of Pennsylvania, Philadelphia, Pennsylvania, U.S.A.*

Susan Curzon / *University Library, California State University–Northridge, Northridge, California, U.S.A.*

Ingetraut Dahlberg / *Bad Koenig, Germany*

Nan Christian Ploug Dahlkild / *Royal School of Library and Information Science, Copenhagen, Denmark*

Jay E. Daily / *University of Pittsburgh, Pittsburgh, Pennsylvania, U.S.A.*

Kimiz Dalkir / *Graduate School of Library and Information Studies, McGill University, Montreal, Quebec, Canada*

Prudence W. Dalrymple / *Drexel University College of Computing & Informatics, Philadelphia, Pennsylvania, U.S.A.*

Marcel Danesi / *Department of Anthropology, University of Toronto, Toronto, Ontario, Canada*

Xuan Hong Dang / *Computer Vision and Image Understanding, Institute for Infocomm, A* STAR, Singapore*

Yan Dang / *Department of Management Information Systems, University of Arizona, Tucson, Arizona, U.S.A.*

Evelyn Daniel / *School of Information and Library Science, University of North Carolina at Chapel Hill, Chapel Hill, North Carolina, U.S.A.*

Richard A. Danner / *School of Law, Duke University, Durham, North Carolina, U.S.A.*

Regina Dantas / *Museu Nacional, HCTE, Universidade Federal do Rio de Janeiro, Rio de Janeiro, Brazil*

Daniel C. Danzig / *Consultant, Pasadena, California, U.S.A.*

Robert Allen Daugherty / *University Library, University of Illinois at Chicago, Chicago, Illinois, U.S.A.*

Charles H. Davis / *Indiana University, Bloomington, IN, U.S.A., and School of Library and Information Science, Indiana University, Bloomington, Indiana, U.S.A.*

Gordon B. Davis / *Carlson School of Management, University of Minnesota, Minneapolis, Minnesota, U.S.A.*

Mary Ellen Davis / *American Library Association, Chicago, Illinois, U.S.A.*

Peter Davis / *International Centre for Cultural and Heritage Studies, Newcastle University, Newcastle upon Tyne, U.K.*

Sheryl Davis / *University Library, University of California, Riverside, Riverside, California, U.S.A.*

Ronald E. Day / *School of Library and Information Science, Indiana University, Bloomington, Indiana, U.S.A.*

Cheryl Dee / *School of Library and Information Science, University of South Florida, Tampa, Florida, U.S.A.*

Robert DeHart / *Department of History, Middle Tennessee State University, Murfreesboro, Tennessee, U.S.A.*

Brenda Dervin / *School of Communication, Ohio State University, Columbus, Ohio, U.S.A.*

Brian Detlor / *Information Systems, McMaster University, Hamilton, Ontario, Canada*

Don E. Detmer / *American Medical Informatics Association (AMIA), Bethesda, Maryland, U.S.A.*

Stella G. Dextre Clarke / *Information Consultant, Oxfordshire, U.K.*

Catherine Dhérent / *National Library of France, Paris, France*

Anne R. Diekema / *Gerald R. Sherratt Library, Southern Utah University, Cedar City, Utah, U.S.A.*

Susan S. DiMattia / *DiMattia Associates, Stamford, Connecticut, U.S.A.*

Gloria Dinerman / *The Library Co-Op, Inc., Edison, New Jersey, U.S.A.*

Jesse David Dinneen / *School of Information Studies, McGill University, Montreal, Quebec, Canada*

Bernard Dione / *School of Librarianship, Archivists Information Science (EBAD), Cheikh Anta Diop University, Dakar, Senegal*

Dieyi Diouf / *Central Library, Cheikh Anta Diop University of Dakar, Dakar, Senegal*

Keith Donohue / *National Historical Publications and Records Commission, Washington, District of Columbia, U.S.A.*

Ann Doyle / *X̱wi7xwa Library, First Nations House of Learning, University of British Columbia, Vancouver, British Columbia, Canada*

Carol D. Doyle / *Government Documents Department and Map Library, California State University, Fresno, California, U.S.A.*

Marek J. Druzdzel / *School of Information Sciences and Intelligent Systems Program, University of Pittsburgh, Pittsburgh, Pennsylvania, U.S.A., and Faculty of Computer Science, Bialystok Technical University, Bialystok, Poland*

Kathel Dunn / *National Library of Medicine, Bethesda, Maryland, U.S.A.*

Luciana Duranti / *School of Library, Archival and Information Studies, University of British Columbia, Vancouver, British Columbia, Canada*

Joan C. Durrance / *School of Information, University of Michigan, Ann Arbor, Michigan, U.S.A.*

Maria Economou / *Department of Communication and Cultural Technology, University of the Aegean, Mytilini, Greece*

Gary Edson / *Center for Advanced Study in Museum Science and Heritage Management, Museum of Texas Tech University, Lubbock, Texas, U.S.A.*

Mary B. Eggert / *Library, Kirkland & Ellis LLP, Chicago, IL, U.S.A.*

Daniel Eisenberg / *Florida State University, Tallahassee, Florida, U.S.A.*

Innocent I. Ekoja / *University Library, University of Abuja, Abuja, Nigeria*

Sarah Elliott / *International Centre for Cultural and Heritage Studies, Newcastle University, Newcastle upon Tyne, U.K.*

David Ellis / *Department of Information Studies, Aberystwyth University, Wales, U.K.*

Jill Emery / *Portland State University Library, Portland, Oregon, U.S.A.*

Zorana Ercegovac / *InfoEN Associates, Los Angeles, California, U.S.A.*

Timothy L. Ericson / *School of Information Science, University of Wisconsin-Milwaukee, Milwaukee, Wisconsin, U.S.A.*

Elena Escolano Rodríguez / *National Library of Spain, Madrid, Spain*

Leigh S. Estabrook / *Graduate School of Library and Information Science, University of Illinois at Urbana- / Champaign, Champaign, Illinois, U.S.A.*

Mark E. Estes / *Alameda County Law Library, Oakland, California, U.S.A.*

Beth Evans / *Library, Brooklyn College, City University of New York, Brooklyn, New York, U.S.A.*

Joanne Evans / *Centre for Organisational and Social Informatics, Monash University, Melbourne, Victoria, Australia*

Dominic J. Farace / *Grey Literature Network Service, TextRelease/GreyNet, Amsterdam, The Netherlands*

David Farneth / *Special Collections and Institutional Records, Getty Research Institute, Los Angeles, California, U.S.A.*

Sharon Fawcett / *Office of Presidential Libraries, National Archives and Records Administration, College Park, Maryland, U.S.A.*

Dieter Fensel / *Institute of Computer Science, University of Innsbruck, Innsbruck, Austria, and National University of Ireland, Galway, Galway, Ireland*

Thomas L. Findley / *Leo A. Daly/Architects & Engineers, Omaha, Nebraska, U.S.A.*

Karen E. Fisher / *Information School, University of Washington, Seattle, Washington, U.S.A.*

Nancy Fjällbrant / *Chalmers University of Technology Library, International Association of Technological University Libraries, Gothenburg, Sweden*

Julia Flanders / *Brown University, Providence, Rhode Island, U.S.A.*

Nancy Flury Carlson / *Westinghouse Electric Corporation, Pittsburgh, Pennsylvania, U.S.A.*

Roger R. Flynn / *School of Information Sciences and Intelligent Systems Program, University of Pittsburgh, Pittsburgh, Pennsylvania, U.S.A.*

Helen Forde / *Department of Information Studies, University College London, London, U.K.*

Douglas J. Foskett / *University of London, London, U.K.*

Susan Foutz / *Institute for Learning Innovation, Edgewater, Maryland, U.S.A.*

Christopher Fox / *Department of Computer Science, James Madison University, Harrisonburg, Virginia, U.S.A.*

Carl Franklin / *Consultant, Columbus, Ohio, U.S.A.*

Jonathan A. Franklin / *Gallagher Law Library, University of Washington, Seattle, Washington, U.S.A.*

Thomas J. Froehlich / *School of Library and Information Science, Kent State University, Kent, Ohio, U.S.A.*

Steve Fuller / *Department of Sociology, University of Warwick, Coventry, U.K.*

Crystal Fulton / *School of Information and Communication Studies, University College Dublin, Dublin, Ireland*

Carla J. Funk / *Medical Library Association, Chicago, Illinois, U.S.A.*

Jonathan Furner / *Department of Information Studies University of California, Los Angeles, Los Angeles, California, U.S.A.*

Dennis Galletta / *Katz Graduate School of Business, University of Pittsburgh, Pittsburgh, Pennsylvania, U.S.A.*

D. Linda Garcia / *Communication Culture and Technology, Georgetown University, Washington, District of Columbia, U.S.A.*

Holly Gardinier / *Honnold/Mudd Library, Libraries of The Claremont Colleges, Claremont, California, U.S.A.*

Sally Gardner Reed / *Association of Library Trustees, Advocates, Friends and Foundations (ALTAFF), Philadelphia, Pennsylvania, U.S.A.*

Janifer Gatenby / *Online Computer Library Center (OCLC), Leiden, The Netherlands*

Ramesh C. Gaur / *Kalanidhi Division, Indira Gandhi National Centre for the Arts (IGNCA), New Delhi, India*

Lee Anne George / *Association of Research Libraries, Washington, District of Columbia, U.S.A.*

David E. Gerard / *College of Librarianship Wales, Cardiganshire, Wales, U.K.*

Malcolm Getz / *Department of Economics, Vanderbilt University, Nashville, Tennessee, U.S.A.*

Mary W. Ghikas / *American Library Association, Chicago, Illinois, U.S.A.*

Nicholas Gibbins / *School of Electronics and Computer Science, University of Southampton, Southampton, U.K.*

Gerd Gigerenzer / *Center for Adaptive Behavior and Cognition, Max Planck Institute for Human Development, Berlin, Germany*

Tommaso Giordano / *Library, European University Institute, Florence, Italy*

Lilian Gisesa / *Kenya National Archives, Nairobi, Kenya*

Edward A. Goedeken / *Iowa State University, Ames, Iowa, U.S.A.*

Warren R. Goldmann / *National Technical Institute for the Deaf, Rochester Institute of Technology, Rochester, New York, U.S.A.*

David Gordon / *Milwaukee Art Museum, Milwaukee, Wisconsin, U.S.A.*

David B. Gracy II / *School of Information, University of Texas at Austin, Austin, Texas, U.S.A.*

Karen F. Gracy / *School of Library and Information Science, Kent State University, Kent, Ohio, U.S.A.*

Renny Granda / *Universidad Central de Venezuela, Caracas, Venezuela*

Paul Gray / *School of Information Systems and Technology, Claremont Graduate University, Claremont, California, U.S.A.*

Jane Greenberg / *Metadata Research Center, School of Information and Library Science, University of North Carolina at Chapel Hill, Chapel Hill, North Carolina, U.S.A.*

Karen Greenwood / *American Medical Informatics Association (AMIA), Bethesda, Maryland, U.S.A.*

Jill E. Grogg / *Libraries, University of Alabama, Tuscaloosa, Alabama, U.S.A.*

Melissa Gross / *School of Information, Florida State University, Tallahassee, Florida, U.S.A.*

Andrew Grove / *Guest Faculty, Information School, University of Washington, Seattle, Washington, U.S.A.*

Dinesh K. Gupta / *Department of Library and Information Science, Vardhaman Mahaveer Open University, 3 Kota, India*

Laurel L. Haak / *Open Researcher and Contributor ID, Inc. (ORCID), U.S.A.*

Kate Hagan / *American Association of Law Libraries, Chicago, Illinois, U.S.A.*

Kathleen Hall / *Leon E. Bloch Law Library, University of Missouri-Kansas City School of Law, Kansas City, Missouri, U.S.A.*

Virginia M.G. Hall / *Center for Educational Resources, The Sheridan Libraries, Johns Hopkins University, Baltimore, Maryland, U.S.A.*

Wendy Hall / *Intelligence, Agents, Multimedia Group, University of Southampton, Southampton, U.K.*

Stuart Hamilton / *International Federation of Library Associations and Institutions, The Hague, The Netherlands*

Maureen L. Hammer / *Knowledge Management, Batelle Memorial Institute, Charlottesville, Virginia, U.S.A.*

Jong-Yup Han / *Research Information Team, KORDI, Seoul, South Korea*

Debra Gold Hansen / *School of Library and Information Science, San Jose State University, Yorba Linda, California, U.S.A.*

Derek L. Hansen / *University of Maryland, College Park, Maryland, U.S.A.*

Eugene R. Hanson / *Shippensburg State College, Shippensburg, Pennsylvania, U.S.A.*

Jane Hardy / *Australian Library and Information Association, Deakin, Australian Capital Territory, Australia*

Julie Hart / *American Association of Museums, Washington, District of Columbia, U.S.A.*

Hiroyuki Hatano / *Surugadai University, Saitama, Japan*

Robert M. Hayes / *Department of Information Studies, University of California, Los Angeles, Los Angeles, California, U.S.A.*

Caroline Haythornthwaite / *Graduate School of Library and Information Science, University of Illinois at Urbana- / Champaign, Champaign, Illinois, U.S.A.*

Penny Hazelton / *Gallagher Law Library, University of Washington, Seattle, Washington, U.S.A.*

P. Bryan Heidorn / *Graduate School of Library and Information Science, University of Illinois at Urbana-Champaign, Champaign, Illinois, U.S.A.*

Helen Heinrich / *Collection Access and Management Services, California State University–Northridge, Northridge, California, U.S.A.*

Doris S. Helfer / *Collection Access and Management Services, California State University– Northridge, Northridge, California, U.S.A.*

Markus Helfert / *School of Computing, Dublin City University, Dublin, Ireland*

Jean Henefer / *School of Information and Communication Studies, University College Dublin, Dublin, Ireland*

Steven L. Hensen / *Rare Book, Manuscript and Special Collections Library, Duke University, Durham, North Carolina, U.S.A.*

Pamela M. Henson / *Archives, Smithsonian Institution, Washington, District of Columbia, U.S.A.*

Peter Hernon / *Graduate School of Library and Information Science, Simmons College, Boston, Massachusetts, U.S.A.*

Dorothy H. Hertzel / *Case Western Reserve University, Cleveland, Ohio, U.S.A.*

Francis Heylighen / *Free University of Brussels, Brussels, Belgium*

Randolph Hock / *Online Strategies, Annapolis, Maryland, U.S.A.*

Theodora L. Hodges / *Berkeley, California, U.S.A.*

Sara S. Hodson / *Huntington Library, San Marino, California, U.S.A.*

Judy C. Holoviak / *American Geophysical Union, Washington, District of Columbia, U.S.A.*

Aleksandra Horvat / *Faculty of Philosophy, University of Zagreb, Zagreb, Croatia*

Ali Houissa / *Olin Library, Cornell University, Ithaca, New York, U.S.A.*

Pamela Howard-Reguindin / *Library of Congress Office, Nairobi, Kenya*

Han-Yin Huang / *International Centre for Cultural and Heritage Studies, Newcastle University, Newcastle upon Tyne, U.K.*

Kathleen Hughes / *American Library Association, Chicago, Illinois, U.S.A.*

Betsy L. Humphreys / *National Library of Medicine, Bethesda, Maryland, U.S.A.*

Charlene S. Hurt / *University Library, Georgia State University, Atlanta, Georgia, U.S.A.*

Sue Hutley / *Australian Library and Information Association, Deakin, Australian Capital Territory, Australia*

John P. Immroth / *University of Pittsburgh, Pittsburgh, Pennsylvania, U.S.A.*

Peter Ingwersen / *Royal School of Library and Information Science, University of Copenhagen, Copenhagen, Denmark*

Vanessa Irvin / *Library and Information Science Program, Information and Computer Sciences Department, University of Hawaii at Mānoa, Honolulu, Hawaii, U.S.A.*

Karla Irwin / *University Libraries, University of Nevada–Las Vegas, Las Vegas, Nevada, U.S.A.*

October R. Ivins / *Ivins eContent Solutions, Sharon, Massachusetts, U.S.A.*

Kalervo Järvelin / *School of Information Science, University of Tampere, Tampere, Finland*

Jean Frédéric Jauslin / *Federal Department of Home Affairs (FDHA), Swiss Federal Office of Culture, Bern, Switzerland*

V. Jeyaraj / *Hepzibah Institute of Conversion, Chennai, India*

Scott Johnston / *McPherson Library, University of Victoria, Victoria, British Columbia, Canada*

Trevor Jones / *Mountain Heritage Center, Western Carolina University, Cullowhee, North Carolina, U.S.A.*

William Jones / *Information School, University of Washington, Seattle, Washington, U.S.A.*

Jay Jordan / *OCLC Online Computer Library Center, Inc., Dublin, Ohio, U.S.A.*

Corinne Jörgensen / *School of Information Studies, Florida State University, Tallahassee, Florida, U.S.A.*

Gene Joseph / *Aboriginal Library Consultant, Langley, British Columbia, Canada*

Daniel N. Joudrey / *School of Library and Information Science, Simmons College, Boston, Massachusetts, U.S.A.*

Heidi Julien / *Library and Information Studies, State University of New York–Buffalo, Buffalo, New York, U.S.A.*

Janet Kaaya / *Department of Information Studies, University of California, Los Angeles, California, U.S.A.*

Philomena Kagwiria Mwirigi / *Kenya National Library Service (KNLS), Nairobi, Kenya*

Athanase B. Kanamugire / *Library Consultant, Dhahran, Saudi Arabia*

Paul B. Kantor / *School of Communication and Information, Rutgers University, New Brunswick, New Jersey, U.S.A.*

Sofia Kapnisi / *International Federation of Library Associations and Institutions, The Hague, the Netherlands*

Nelson Otieno Karilus / *Kenya National Library Service (KNLS), Nairobi, Kenya*

Amy M. Kautzman / *University of California, Berkeley, Berkeley, California, U.S.A.*

Karalyn Kavanaugh / *Account Services Manager, EBSCO Information Services, Birmingham, Alabama, U.S.A.*

Caroline Kayoro / *Kenya National Library Service (KNLS), Nairobi, Kenya*

Andreas Kellerhals / *Federal Department of Home Affairs (FDHA), Swiss Federal Archives, Bern, Switzerland*

John M. Kennedy / *Indiana University, Bloomington, Indiana, U.S.A.*

Kristen Kern / *Portland State University, Portland, Oregon, U.S.A.*

Christopher S.G. Khoo / *School of Communication and Information, Nanyang Technological University, Singapore*

Tapan Khopkar / *University of Michigan, Ann Arbor, Michigan, U.S.A.*

Irene Muthoni Kibandi / *Kenya National Library Service (KNLS), Nairobi, Kenya*

Ruth E. Kifer / *Dr. Martin Luther King, Jr. Library, San Jose State University, San Jose, California, U.S.A.*

Seong Hee Kim / *Department of Library and Information Science, Chung-Ang University, Seoul, South Korea*

Pancras Kimaru / *Kenya National Library Service (KNLS), Nairobi, Kenya*

Karen E. King / *Washington, District of Columbia, U.S.A.*

William R. King / *University of Pittsburgh, Pittsburgh, Pennsylvania, U.S.A.*

Susan K. Kinnell / *Consultant, Santa Barbara, California, U.S.A.*

Laurence J. Kipp / *Harvard University, Cambridge, Massachusetts, U.S.A.*

Thomas G. Kirk, Jr. / *Earlham College Libraries, Earlham College, Richmond, Indiana, U.S.A.*

Breanne A. Kirsch / *Library, Emerging Technologies, University of South Carolina Upstate, Spartanburg, South Carolina, U.S.A.*

Vernon N. Kisling, Jr. / *Marston Science Library, University of Florida, Gainesville, Florida, U.S.A.*

Adam D. Knowles / *San Diego, California, U.S.A.*

Rebecca Knuth / *Library and Information Science Program, University of Hawaii, Honolulu, Hawaii, U.S.A.*

Michael Koenig / *College of Information and Computer Science, Long Island University, Brookville, New York, U.S.A.*

Jesse Koennecke / *Cornell University Library, Cornell University College of Arts and Sciences, Ithaca, New York, U.S.A.*

Jes Koepfler / *Museum Studies Program, Faculty of Information Studies, University of Toronto, Toronto, Ontario, Canada*

Amelia Koford / *Blumberg Memorial Library, Texas Lutheran University, Seguin, Texas, U.S.A.*

Toru Koizumi / *Library, Rikkyo University, Tokyo, Japan*

Josip Kolanović / *Croatian State Archives, Zagreb, Croatia*

Sjoerd Koopman / *International Federation of Library Associations and Institutions, The Hague, the Netherlands*

Donald Kraft / *Department of Computer Science, U.S. Air Force Academy, Colorado Springs, Colorado, U.S.A.*

Allison Krebs / *University of Arizona, Tucson, Arizona, U.S.A.*

Judith F. Krug / *Office for Intellectual Freedom, American Library Association, Chicago, Illinois, U.S.A.*

D.W. Krummel / *Emeritus, Graduate School of Library and Information Science, University of Illinois at Urbana-Champaign, Champaign, Illinois, U.S.A.*

Carol Collier Kuhlthau / *Department of Library and Information Science, Rutgers University, New Brunswick, New Jersey, U.S.A.*

Krishan Kumar / *Former Head, Department of Library and Information Science, University of Delhi, New Delhi, India*

Sanna Kumpulainen / *Library, Tampere University of Technology, Tampere, Finland*

Michael J. Kurtz / *National Archives at College Park, U.S. National Archives and Records Administration, College Park, Maryland, U.S.A.*

Zhenhua Lai / *Department of Management Information Systems, University of Arizona, Tucson, Arizona, U.S.A.*

Mounia Lalmas / *Department of Computing Science, University of Glasgow, Glasgow, U.K.*

Heather M. Lamond / *Massey University Library, Palmerston North, New Zealand*

F.W. Lancaster / *Graduate School of Library and Information Science, University of Illinois at Urbana-Champaign, Urbana, Illinois, U.S.A.*

Ronald L. Larsen / *School of Information Sciences, University of Pittsburgh, Pittsburgh, Pennsylvania, U.S.A.*

Ray R. Larson / *School of Information, University of California—Berkeley, Berkeley, California, U.S.A.*

Jesús Lau / *Library Services Unit USBI Veracruz (USBI VER), University of Veracruz, Veracruz, Mexico*

Judith V. Lechner / *Department of Educational Foundations, Leadership, and Technology, Auburn University, Auburn, Alabama, U.S.A.*

Christopher A. Lee / *School of Information and Library Science, University of North Carolina at Chapel Hill, Chapel Hill, North Carolina, U.S.A.*

Janet Lee / *University of Denver, Denver, Colorado, U.S.A, and Regis University, Denver, Colorado, U.S.A.*

Catherine Leekam / *Museum Studies Program, Faculty of Information Studies, University of Toronto, Toronto, Ontario, Canada*

Kjell Lemström / *Department of Computer Science, University of Helsinki, Helsinki, Finland*

Timothy F. Leslie / *Department of Geography and Geoinformation Science, George Mason University, Fairfax, Virginia, U.S.A.*

Noémie Lesquins / *Scientific Mission (DSR), National Library of France, Paris, France*

Rosalind K. Lett / *Information-2-Knowledge, Atlanta, Georgia, U.S.A.*

Allison V. Level / *Colorado State University, Fort Collins, Colorado, U.S.A.*

Michael Levine-Clark / *Penrose Library, University of Denver, Denver, Colorado, U.S.A.*

Anany Levitin / *Department of Computing Sciences, Villanova University, Villanova, Pennsylvania, U.S.A.*

Marjorie Lewis / *Canaan, New York, U.S.A.*

Elizabeth D. Liddy / *School of Information Studies, Syracuse University, Syracuse, New York, U.S.A.*

Silje C. Lier / *Software & Information Industry Association, Washington, District of Columbia, U.S.A.*

Jane E. Light / *Dr. Martin Luther King, Jr. Library, San Jose Public Library, San Jose, California, U.S.A.*

Paul M. Lima / *Canadian Heritage Information Network (CHIN), Gatineau, Quebec, Canada*

Louise Limberg / *Swedish School of Library and Information Science, University of Borås and University of Gothenburg, Borås, Sweden*

Shin-jeng Lin / *Department of Business Administration, Le Moyne College, Syracuse, New York, U.S.A.*

Sarah Lippincott / *Educopia Institute, Atlanta, Georgia, U.S.A.*

Peter Johan Lor / *School of Information Studies, University of Wisconsin-Milwaukee, Milwaukee, Wisconsin, U.S.A., and Department of Information Science, University of Pretoria, Pretoria, South Africa*

Beth Luey / *Fairhaven, Massachusetts, U.S.A.*

Joseph Luke / *Kazakhstan Institute of Management, Economics and Strategic Research (KIMEP), Almaty, Kazakhstan*

Claudia Lux / *Central and Regional Library of Berlin (ZLB), Berlin, Germany*

Marianne Lykke / *Information Interaction and Architecture, Royal School of Library and Information Science, Aalborg, Denmark*

Elena Macevičiūtė / *Faculty of Communication, Vilnius University, Vilnius, Lithuania, and Swedish School of Library and Information Science, University of Borås, Borås, Sweden*

Juan D. Machin-Mastromatteo / *Universidad Central de Venezuela, Caracas, Venezuela*

Barbara A. Macikas / *American Library Association, Chicago, Illinois, U.S.A.*

Leslie Madsen-Brooks / *Boise State University, Boise, Idaho, U.S.A.*

William J. Maher / *Archives, University of Illinois at Urbana-Champaign, Urbana, Illinois, U.S.A.*

Thomas Mann / *Library of Congress, Washington, District of Columbia, U.S.A.*

Sylva Natalie Manoogian / *Department of Information Studies, University of California, Los Angeles, Los Angeles, California, U.S.A.*

Daniel Marcu / *Information Sciences Institute, University of Southern California, Marina del Rey, California, U.S.A.*

James W. Marcum / *Fairleigh Dickinson University, Madison, New Jersey, U.S.A.*

Francesca Marini / *School of Library, Archival and Information Studies, University of British Columbia, Vancouver, British Columbia, Canada*

Johan Marklund / *Department of Industrial Management and Logistics, Lund University, Lund, Sweden*

Dian I. Martin / *Small Bear Technical Consulting, LLC, Thorn Hill, Tennessee, U.S.A.*

Susan K. Martin / *Lauinger Library, Georgetown University, Washington, District of Columbia, U.S.A.*

Paul F. Marty / *College of Communication and Information, Florida State University, Tallahassee, Florida, U.S.A.*

Dan Marwit / *Lee H. Skolnick Architecture + Design Partnership, New York, New York, U.S.A.*

Laura Matzer / *Arizona Museum for Youth, Mesa, Arizona, U.S.A.*

Robert L. Maxwell / *Special Collections and Metadata Catalog Department, Brigham Young University, Provo, Utah, U.S.A.*

Hope Mayo / *Houghton Library, Harvard University, Cambridge, Massachusetts, U.S.A.*

Sally H. McCallum / *Network Development and MARC Standards Office, Library of Congress, Washington, District of Columbia, U.S.A.*

Gavan McCarthy / *eScholarship Research Centre, University of Melbourne, Melbourne, Victoria, Australia*

Ian McGowan / *Former Librarian, National Library of Scotland, Edinburgh, U.K.*

Roger McHaney / *Department of Management, Kansas State University, Manhattan, Kansas, U.S.A.*

I.C. McIlwaine / *University College London, School of Library, Archive and Information Studies, London, U.K.*

Sue McKemmish / *Centre for Organisational and Social Informatics, Monash University, Melbourne, Victoria, Australia*

Marie E. McVeigh / *JCR and Bibliographic Policy, Thomson Reuters - Scientific, Philadelphia, Pennsylvania, U.S.A.*

Linda Mboya / *National Museums of Kenya, Nairobi, Kenya*

Judith Adams Meadows / *State Law Library of Montana, Helena, Montana, U.S.A.*

K. van der Meer / *Faculty of Electrical Engineering, Mathematics and Computer Science, Delft University, the Netherlands; Information and Library Science, IOIW, Antwerp University, Belgium; and D-CIS, Delft, The Netherlands*

Bharat Mehra / *School of Information Sciences, University of Tennessee, Knoxville, Tennessee, U.S.A.*

Margaret Ann Mellinger / *OSU Libraries & Press, Oregon State University, Corvallis, Oregon, U.S.A.*

Elizabeth E. Merritt / *American Association of Museums, Washington, District of Columbia, U.S.A.*

David Millman / *Academic Information Systems, Columbia University, New York, U.S.A.*

Jack Mills / *North-Western Polytechnic, London, U.K.*

Kevin L. Mills / *National Institute of Standards and Technology, Gaithersburg, Maryland, U.S.A.*

Staša Milojević / *Department of Information Studies, University of California, Los Angeles, Los Angeles, California, U.S.A.*

Marla Misunas / *Collections Information and Access, San Francisco Museum of Modern Art, San Francisco, California, U.S.A.*

Joan S. Mitchell / *OCLC Online Computer Library Center, Inc., Dublin, Ohio, U.S.A.*

Yoriko Miyabe / *Rikkyo University, Tokyo, Japan*

Diane Mizrachi / *University Libraries, University of California–Los Angeles, Los Angeles, California, U.S.A.*

William Moen / *Texas Center for Digital Knowledge, University of North Texas, Denton, Texas, U.S.A.*

Abdul Moid / *University of Karachi, Karachi, Pakistan*

Hermann Moisl / *Center for Research in Linguistics, University of Newcastle upon Tyne, Newcastle upon Tyne, U.K.*

Ole Magnus Mølbak Andersen / *Danish State Archives, Copenhagen, Denmark*

Mavis B. Molto / *Utah State University, Logan, Utah, U.S.A.*

Philip Mooney / *Heritage Communications, Coca-Cola Company, Atlanta, Georgia, U.S.A.*

Reagan W. Moore / *San Diego Supercomputer Center, University of North Carolina at Chapel Hill, Chapel Hill, North Carolina, U.S.A.*

Mersini Moreleli-Cacouris / *Department of Library Science and Information Systems, Technological Educational Institute (TEI) of Thessaloniki, Sindos, Greece*

Paul K. Moser / *Department of Philosophy, Loyola University Chicago, Chicago, Illinois, U.S.A.*

Clara C. Mosquera / *Library, Kirkland & Ellis LLP, Chicago, IL, U.S.A.*

David J. Muddiman / *Leeds Metropolitan University, Leeds, U.K.*

Nancy C. Mulvany / *Bayside Indexing Service, Fort Collins, Colorado, U.S.A.*

Sue Myburgh / *School of Communication, University of South Australia, Adelaide, South Australia, Australia*

Elli Mylonas / *Brown University, Providence, Rhode Island, U.S.A.*

Jeremy Myntti / *J. Willard Marriott Library, Salt Lake City, Utah, U.S.A.*

Jacob Nadal / *ReCAP: The Research Collections and Preservation Consortium, Princeton, New Jersey, U.S.A.*

Diane Nahl / *Information and Computer Sciences Department, University of Hawaii, Honolulu, Hawaii, U.S.A.*

Robert Nardini / *Vice President, Library Services, ProQuest Books, La Vergne, Tennessee, U.S.A.*

Arnold vander Nat / *Department of Philosophy, Loyola University Chicago, Chicago, Illinois, U.S.A.*

Charles M. Naumer / *Information School, University of Washington, Seattle, Washington, U.S.A.*

Sophie Ndegwa / *Kenya National Library Service (KNLS), Nairobi, Kenya*

Dixie Neilson / *University of Florida, Gainesville, Florida, U.S.A.*

Sarah Beth Nelson / *School of Information and Library Sciences, University of North Carolina at Chapel Hill, Chapel Hill, North Carolina, U.S.A.*

Stuart J. Nelson / *National Library of Medicine, Bethesda, Maryland, U.S.A.*

Stephanie Nemcsok / *Museum Studies Program, Faculty of Information Studies, University of Toronto, Toronto, Ontario, Canada*

Ken Neveroski / *College of Information and Computer Science, Long Island University, Brookville, New York, U.S.A.*

Jennifer Ng / *Museum Studies Program, Faculty of Information Studies, University of Toronto, Toronto, Ontario, Canada*

Melissa Niiya / *Portland Public Schools, Portland, Oregon, U.S.A.*

Angela Noseworthy / *Museum Studies Program, Faculty of Information Studies, University of Toronto, Toronto, Ontario, Canada*

Barbara E. Nye / *Ictus Consulting, LLC, Pasadena, California, U.S.A.*

Charles Nzivo / *Kenya National Library Service (KNLS), Nairobi, Kenya*

Dennis O'Brien / *Maps and Wayfinding, LLC, Mystic, Connecticut, U.S.A.*

Karen Lynn O'Brien / *American Library Association, Chicago, Illinois, U.S.A.*

Kieron O'Hara / *Intelligence, Agents, Multimedia Group, University of Southampton, Southampton, U.K.*

Elizabeth O'Keefe / *Morgan Library and Museum, New York, U.S.A.*

Denise I. O'Shea / *Fairleigh Dickinson University, Teaneck, New Jersey, U.S.A.*

Douglas W. Oard / *College of Information Studies, University of Maryland, College Park, Maryland, U.S.A.*

Maria Oldal / *Morgan Library and Museum, New York, U.S.A.*

Lorne Olfman / *School of Information Systems and Technology, Claremont Graduate University, Claremont, California, U.S.A.*

Bette W. Oliver / *Austin, Texas, U.S.A.*

Annette Olson / *Biological Resources Division, U.S. Geological Survey, Reston, Virginia, U.S.A.*

Hope A. Olson / *School of Information Studies, University of Wisconsin-Milwaukee, Milwaukee, Wisconsin, U.S.A.*

Lawrence J. Olszewski / *OCLC Library, Dublin, Ohio, U.S.A.*

Kok-Leong Ong / *School of Information Technology, Deakin University, Burwood, Victoria, Australia*

Tim Owen / *Chartered Institute of Library and Information Professionals (CILIP), London, U.K.*

John C. Paolillo / *School of Informatics and School of Library and Information Science, Indiana University, Bloomington, Indiana, U.S.A.*

Eun Bong Park / *Library Service Department, National Library of Korea, Seoul, South Korea*

Soyeon Park / *Department of Library and Information Science, Duksung Womens University, Seoul, South Korea*

Gabriella Pasi / *Department of Informatics, Systems and Communication, University of Studies of Milano Bicocca, Milan, Italy*

Norman Paskin / *Tertius Ltd., Oxford, U.K.*

Christiane Paul / *Whitney Museum of American Art, New York, U.S.A.*

Ellen Pearlstein / *Information Studies and UCLA / Getty Program in the Conservation of Ethnographic and Archaeological Materials, University of California, Los Angeles, Los Angeles, California, U.S.A.*

Kathleen de la Peña McCook / *School of Library and Information Science, University of South Florida, Tampa, Florida, U.S.A.*

Steve Pepper / *Department of Linguistics, University of Oslo, Oslo, Norway*

Manuel A. Pérez-Quiñones / *Department of Software and Information Systems, University of North Carolina, Charlotte, North Carolina, U.S.A.*

Paul Evan Peters / *University of Pittsburgh, Pittsburgh, Pennsylvania, U.S.A.*

Jakob Heide Petersen / *Danish Agency for Libraries and Media, Copenhagen, Denmark*

Mary Jane Petrowski / *American Library Association, Chicago, Illinois, U.S.A.*

Katharine J. Phenix / *Northglenn Branch, Rangeview Library District, Northglenn, Colorado, U.S.A.*

Robert B. Pickering / *Gilcrease Museum, and Museum Science and Management Program, University of Tulsa, Tulsa, Oklahoma, U.S.A.*

Janice T. Pilch / *Rutgers University Libraries, Rutgers University, New Brunswick, New Jersey, U.S.A.*

Thomas E. Pinelli / *Langley Research Center, National Aeronautics and Space Administration (NASA) Hampton, Virginia, U.S.A.*

Daniel Pitti / *Alderman Library, Institute for Advanced Technology in the Humanities, University of Virginia, Charlottesville, Virginia, U.S.A.*

Elena Ploşniţă / *Science Department, National Museum of Archaeology and History of Moldova, Chisinau, Republic of Moldova*

Gabriela Podušelová / *Slovak National Museum, Bratislava, Slovak Republic*

Danny C.C. Poo / *School of Computing, Department of Information Systems, National University of Singapore, Singapore*

Martine Poulain / *Department of Libraries and Documentation, National Institute for the History of Art (INHA), Paris, France*

Tammy Powell / *National Library of Medicine, Bethesda, Maryland, U.S.A.*

Stephen Prine / *Library of Congress, Washington, District of Columbia, U.S.A.*

Mary Jo Pugh / *Editor, American Archivist, Walnut Creek, California, U.S.A.*

Ajit K. Pyati / *University of Western Ontario, London, Ontario, Canada*

Aimée C. Quinn / *Government Publications Services, Brooks Library, Central Washington University, Ellensburg, Washington, U.S.A.*

Jennie Quiñónez-Skinner / *University Library, California State University–Northridge, Northridge, California, U.S.A.*

Debbie Rabina / *School of Library and Information Science, Pratt Institute, New York, New York, U.S.A.*

Katalin Radics / *Research Library, University of California—Los Angeles, Los Angeles, California, U.S.A.*

Carl Rahkonen / *Harold S. Orendorff Music Library, Indiana University of Pennsylvania, Indiana, Pennsylvania, U.S.A.*

Jocelyn Rankin / *Centers for Disease Control and Prevention Library, Atlanta, Georgia, U.S.A.*

Samuel J. Redman / *Department of History, University of California, Berkeley, Berkeley, California, U.S.A.*

Thomas C. Redman / *Navesink Consulting Group, Little Silver, New Jersey, U.S.A.*

Barbara Reed / *Recordkeeping Innovation, Sydney, New South Wales, Australia*

Marcia Reed / *Getty Research Institute, Los Angeles, CA, U.S.A.*

CarrieLynn D. Reinhard / *Department of Communication, Business, and Information Technologies, Roskilde University, Roskilde, Denmark*

Harold C. Relyea / *Congressional Research Service, Library of Congress, Washington, District of Columbia, U.S.A.*

Steve Ricci / *Department of Information Studies/Film and Television, University of California–Los Angeles, Los Angeles, California, U.S.A.*

Ronald E. Rice / *Department of Communication, University of California–Santa Barbara, Santa Barbara, California, U.S.A.*

John V. Richardson, Jr. / *Department of Information Studies, University of California, Los Angeles, Los Angeles, California, U.S.A.*

Soo Young Rieh / *School of Information, University of Michigan, Ann Arbor, Michigan, U.S.A.*

Kevin S. Rioux / *Division of Library and Information Science, St. John's University, Queens, New York, U.S.A.*

Julian Roberts / *Wolfson College, University of Oxford, Oxford, U.K.*

Lyn Robinson / *City, University of London, London, U.K.*

Diane Robson / *University Libraries, Media Library, University of North Texas, Denton, Texas, U.S.A.*

Michael Rodriguez / *Michigan State University Libraries, East Lansin, Michigan, U.S.A.*

Juraj Roháč / *Department of Archival Science and Auxiliary Historical Sciences, Comenius University in, Bratislava, Slovak Republic*

Mark Roosa / *Pepperdine University, Malibu, California, U.S.A.*

Jonathan Rose / *Department of History, Drew University, Madison, New Jersey, U.S.A.*

Howard Rosenbaum / *School of Library and Information Science, Indiana University, Bloomington, Indiana, U.S.A.*

Catherine Sheldrick Ross / *Faculty of Information and Media Studies, University of Western Ontario, London, Ontario, Canada*

Shannon Ross / *Canadian Heritage Information Network (CHIN), Gatineau, Quebec, Canada*

Richard Rubin / *School of Library and Information Science, Kent State University, Kent, Ohio, U.S.A.*

Lynne M. Rudasill / *University of Illinois at Urbana-Champaign, Champaign, Illinois, U.S.A.*

Michael Rush / *Beinecke Rare Book and Manuscript Library, Yale University, New Haven, Connecticut, U.S.A.*

Mariza Russo / *Faculty of Administration and Accounting Sciences (FACC), Federal University of Rio de Janeiro, Rio de Janeiro, Brazil*

Athena Salaba / *Kent State University, Kent, Ohio, U.S.A.*

Romelia Salinas / *California State University, Los Angeles, Los Angeles, California, U.S.A.*

Airi Salminen / *Department of Computer Science and Information Systems, University of Jyväskylä, Jyväskylä, Finland*

Michael J. Salvo / *Department of English, Purdue University, West Lafayette, Indiana, U.S.A.*

Robert J. Sandusky / *University Library, University of Illinois at Chicago, Chicago, Illinois, U.S.A.*

Tefko Saracevic / *School of Communication and Information, Rutgers University, New Brunswick, New Jersey, U.S.A.*

Chris Sauer / *Said Business School, University of Oxford, Oxford, U.K.*

Rejéan Savard / *School of Library and Information Science, University of Montreal, Montreal, Quebec, Canada*

Reijo Savolainen / *School of Information Sciences, University of Tampere, Tampere, Finland*

Barbara Schaefer / *Geneseo, New York, U.S.A.*

Silvia Schenkolewski-Kroll / *Department of Information Science, Bar-Ilan University, Ramat Gan, Israel*

Lael J. Schooler / *Center for Adaptive Behavior and Cognition, Max Planck Institute for Human Development, Berlin, Germany*

Joachim Schöpfel / *Department of Library and Information Sciences (IDIST), GERiico Laboratory Charles de Gaulle University Lille 3, Villeneuve d'Ascq, France*

Catherine F. Schryer / *Department of English Language and Literature, University of Waterloo, Waterloo, Ontario, Canada*

Marjorie Schwarzer / *Museum Studies Department, John F. Kennedy University, Berkeley, California, U.S.A.*

Jo Ann Secor / *Lee H. Skolnick Architecture + Design Partnership, New York, New York, U.S.A.*

Sara Selwood / *Department of Cultural Policy and Management, City University, London, U.K.*

Frank B. Sessa / *University of Pittsburgh, Pittsburgh, Pennsylvania, U.S.A.*

Mark Sgambettera / *Bronx County Historical Society, Bronx, New York, U.S.A.*

Ayman Shabana / International Institute, University of California, Los Angeles, Los Angeles, California, U.S.A.

Nigel Shadbolt / *School of Electronics and Computer Science, University of Southampton, Southampton, U.K.*

Kalpana Shankar / *School of Informatics, Indiana University, Bloomington, Indiana, U.S.A.*

Debora Shaw / *School of Library and Information Science, Indiana University, Bloomington, Indiana, U.S.A.*

Conrad Shayo / *Department of Information and Decision Sciences, California State University—San Bernardino, San Bernardino, California, U.S.A.*

Elizabeth Shepherd / *Department of Information Studies, University College London, London, U.K.*

Beverly K. Sheppard / *Institute for Learning Innovation, Edgewater, Maryland, U.S.A.*

Ross Shimmon / *Faversham, U.K.*

Snunith Shoham / *Department of Information Science, Bar-Ilan University, Ramat Gan, Israel*

Lyudmila Shpilevaya / *New York Public Library, New York, New York, U.S.A.*

David Shumaker / *School of Library and Information Science, Catholic University of America, Washington, District of Columbia, U.S.A.*

Judith A. Siess / *Information Bridges International, Inc., Champaign, Illinois, U.S.A.*

John Edward Simmons / *Museologica, Bellefonte, Pennsylvania, U.S.A.*

Anestis Sitas / *Aristotle University of Thessaloniki, Thessaloniki, Greece*

Roswitha Skare / *Institute of Culture and Literature, UiT The Arctic University of Norway, Tromsø, Norway*

Katherine Skinner / *Educopia Institute, Atlanta, Georgia, U.S.A.*

Lee H. Skolnick / *Lee H. Skolnick Architecture + Design Partnership, New York, New York, U.S.A.*

Mette Skov / *Department of Communication and Psychology, Aalborg University, Aalborg, Denmark*

Bobby Smiley / *Vanderbilt University, Heard Libraries, Nashville, Tennessee, U.S.A.*

Linda C. Smith / *School of Information Sciences, University of Illinois at Urbana-Champaign, Champaign, Illinois, U.S.A.*

Lois Smith / *Human Factors and Ergonomics Society, Santa Monica, California, U.S.A.*

Lori Smith / *Linus A. Sims Memorial Library, Southeastern Louisiana University, Hammond, Louisiana, U.S.A.*

Patricia A. Smith / *Colorado State University, Fort Collins, Colorado, U.S.A.*

Scott A. Smith / *Langlois Public Library, Langlois, Oregon, U.S.A.*

A. Patricia Smith-Hunt / *Science Library, Preservation Services, University of California, Riverside, Riverside, California, U.S.A.*

Karen Smith-Yoshimura / *Online Computer Library Center (OCLC), San Mateo, California, U.S.A.*

Diane H. Sonnenwald / *University College Dublin, Dublin, Ireland*

Nour Soufi / *Library Cataloging and Metadata Center, University of California, Los Angeles, Los Angeles, California, U.S.A.*

Barbara M. Spiegelman / *Churchill Associates, Pittsburgh, Pennsylvania, U.S.A.*

Robert P. Spindler / *Department of Archives and Manuscripts, Arizona State University, Tempe, Arizona, U.S.A.*

Joie Springer / *Information Society Division, UNESCO, Paris, France*

Suresh Srinivasan / *National Library of Medicine, Bethesda, Maryland, U.S.A.*

Guy St. Clair / *Knowledge Management and Learning, SMR International, New York, New York, U.S.A.*

Cheryl L. Stadel-Bevans / *National Archives and Records Administration, College Park, Maryland, U.S.A.*

Jill Stein / *Institute for Learning Innovation, Edgewater, Maryland, U.S.A.*

Marcia K. Stein / *Museum of Fine Arts, Houston, Houston, Texas, U.S.A.*

Jela Steinerová / *Department of Library and Information Science, Comenius University in, Bratislava, Slovak Republic*

Dick Stenmark / *Department of Applied IT, IT University of Gothenburg, Gothenburg, Sweden*

Andy Stephens / *OBE, Board Secretary, Head of International Engagement, The British Library, London, U.K.*

Margaret Stieg Dalton / *School of Library and Information Studies, University of Alabama, Tuscaloosa, Alabama, U.S.A.*

Katina Strauch / *Addlestone Library, College of Charleston, Charleston, South Carolina, U.S.A.*

Robert D. Stueart / *Graduate School of Library and Information Science, Simmons College, Boston, Massachusetts, U.S.A.*

Paul F. Stuehrenberg / *Yale Divinity Library, New Haven, Connecticut, U.S.A.*

Brian William Sturm / *School of Information and Library Sciences, University of North Carolina at Chapel Hill, Chapel Hill, North Carolina, U.S.A.*

Anna Suorsa / *University of Oulu, Oulu, Finland*

Brett Sutton / *Aurora University, Aurora, Illinois, U.S.A.*

Sarah Sutton / *Mary and Jeff Bell Library, Texas A&M University-Corpus Christi, Corpus Christi, Texas, U.S.A.*

Destinee Kae Swanson / *Adams Museum & House, Inc., Deadwood, South Dakota, U.S.A.*

H.L. Swanson / *GSOE, University of California, Riverside, California, U.S.A.*

Miriam E. Sweeney / *School of Library and Information Studies, University of Alabama, Tuscaloosa, Alabama, U.S.A.*

Shelley Sweeney / *University of Manitoba, Winnipeg, Manitoba, Canada*

Jean Tague-Sutcliffe / *Graduate School of Library and Information Science, University of Western Ontario, London, Ontario, Canada*

Masaya Takayama / *National Archives of Japan, Tokyo, Japan*

Sanna Talja / *Department of Information Studies and Interactive Media, University of Tampere, Tampere, Finland*

G. Thomas Tanselle / *Vice President, John Simon Guggenheim Memorial Foundation, New York, New York, U.S.A.*

Ivan Tanzer / *Museum Studies Program, Faculty of Information Studies, University of Toronto, Toronto, Ontario, Canada*

Melissa Terras / *UCL Department of Information Studies, UCL Centre for Digital Humanities, University College London, London, U.K.*

Mike Thelwall / *School of Computing and Information Technology, University of Wolverhampton, Wolverhampton, U.K.*

Lynne M. Thomas / *Rare Books and Special Collections, Northern Illinois University, DeKalb, Illinois, U.S.A.*

Lawrence S. Thompson / *University of Kentucky, Lexington, Kentucky, U.S.A.*

Jens Thorhauge / *Danish Agency for Libraries and Media, Copenhagen, Denmark*

Anne Thurston / *International Records Management Trust, London, U.K.*

Michael Tiemann / *Open Source Initiative, Chapel Hill, North Carolina, U.S.A.*

Christinger Tomer / *School of Information Sciences, University of Pittsburgh, Pittsburgh, Pennsylvania, U.S.A.*

Elaine G. Toms / *Faculty of Management, Dalhousie University, Halifax, Nova Scotia, Canada*

Jack Toolin / *Whitney Museum of American Art, New York, U.S.A.*

Jennifer Trant / *Archives & Museum Informatics, Toronto, Ontario, Canada*

Barry Trott / *Williamsburg Regional Library, Williamsburg, Virginia, U.S.A.*

Alice Trussell / *Hale Library, Kansas State University, Manhattan, Kansas, U.S.A.*

John Mark Tucker / *Abilene Christian University, Abilene, Texas, U.S.A.*

James M. Turner / *School of Library and Information Sciences, University of Montreal, Montreal, Quebec, Canada*

Louise Tythacott / *Centre for Museology, University of Manchester, Manchester, U.K.*

George Tzanetakis / *Department of Computer Science, University of Victoria, Victoria, British Columbia, Canada*

Franklyn Herbert Upward / *Centre for Organisational and Social Informatics, Monash University, Melbourne, Victoria, Australia*

Richard Urban / *Graduate School of Library and Information Science, University of Illinois, Champaign, Illinois, U.S.A.*

Rachel E. Vacek / *University of Michigan, Ann Arbor, Michigan, U.S.A.*

Ron Van den Branden / *Centre for Scholarly Editing and Document Studies, Royal Academy of Dutch Language and Literature, Gent, Belgium*

Sydney C. Van Nort / *The City College of New York, The City University of New York, New York, U.S.A.*

Edward Vanhoutte / *Centre for Scholarly Editing and Document Studies, Royal Academy of Dutch Language and Literature, Gent, Belgium*

Rebecca Vargha / *Information and Library Science Library, University of North Carolina at Chapel Hill, Chapel Hill, North Carolina, U.S.A.*

Jana Varlejs / *School of Communication, Information and Library Studies, Rutgers University, New Brunswick, New Jersey, U.S.A.*

Jason Vaughan / *Library Technologies, University of Nevada, Las Vegas University Libraries, Las Vegas, Nevada, U.S.A.*

Dale J. Vidmar / *Southern Oregon University Library, Ashland, Oregon, U.S.A.*

Diane Vizine-Goetz / *OCLC Online Computer Library Center, Inc., Dublin, Ohio, U.S.A.*

Ellen M. Voorhees / *Information Technology Laboratory, National Institute of Standards and Technology, Gaithersburg, Maryland, U.S.A.*

Sharon L. Walbridge / *Libraries Washington State University, Pullman, Washington, U.S.A.*

Stephanie Walker / *Brooklyn College, City University of New York, Brooklyn, New York, U.S.A.*

Virginia A. Walter / *Department of Information Studies, University of California, Los Angeles, Los Angeles, California, U.S.A.*

Mark Warschauer / *School of Education, University of California, Irvine, CA, U.S.A.*

Nigel M. Waters / *Department of Geography and Geoinformation Science, George Mason University, Fairfax, Virginia, U.S.A.*

Kathryn M. Wayne / *Art History/Classics Library, University of California, Berkeley, California, U.S.A.*

Frank Webster / *City University, London, U.K.*

Jeff Weddle / *School of Library and Information Studies, University of Alabama, Tuscaloosa, Alabama, U.S.A.*

Judith Weedman / *School of Library and Information Science, San Jose State University, Fullerton, California, U.S.A.*

Stuart L. Weibel / *Office of Research and Special Projects, OCLC Research, Dublin, Ohio, U.S.A.*

Jennifer Weil Arns / *School of Library and Information Science, University of South Carolina, Columbia, South Carolina, U.S.A.*

Bella Hass Weinberg / *Division of Library and Information Science, St. John's University, Queens, New York, New York, U.S.A.*

Volker M. Welter / *Department of the History of Art and Architecture, University of California, Santa Barbara, Santa Barbara, California, U.S.A.*

Caryn Wesner-Early / *ASRC Aerospace & Defense, US Patent & Trademark Office, Alexandria, Virginia, U.S.A.*

Lynn Westbrook / *School of Information, University of Texas at Austin, Austin, Texas, U.S.A.*

Howard D. White / *College of Computing and Informatics, Drexel University, Philadelphia, PA, U.S.A., and College of Information Science and Technology, Drexel University, Philadelphia, Pennsylvania, U.S.A.*

Layna White / *San Francisco Museum of Modern Art, San Francisco, California, U.S.A.*

Michael J. White / *Engineering and Science Library, Queen's University, Kingston, Ontario, Canada*

Sarah K. Wiant / *School of Law, Washington and Lee University, Lexington, Virginia, U.S.A.*

Stephen E. Wiberley, Jr. / *University of Illinois at Chicago, Chicago, Illinois, U.S.A.*

Gunilla Widén-Wulff / *Information Studies, Åbo Akademi University, Åbo, Finland*

Bradley J. Wiles / *Hill Memorial Library, Louisiana State University, Baton Rouge, Louisiana, U.S.A.*

Mary I. Wilke / *Center for Research Libraries, Chicago, Illinois, U.S.A.*

Barratt Wilkins / *Retired State Librarian of Florida, Tallahassee, Florida, U.S.A.*

Peter Willett / *Department of Information Studies, University of Sheffield, Sheffield, U.K.*

Kate Williams / *University of Illinois at Urbana-Champaign, Champaign, Illinois, U.S.A.*

Kirsty Williamson / *Caulfield School of IT, Monash University, Caulfield, Victoria, Australia and School of Information Studies, Charles Sturt University, Wagga Wagga, New South Wales, Australia*

Concepción S. Wilson / *School of Information Systems, Technology and Management, University of New South Wales, Sydney, New South Wales, Australia*

Ian E. Wilson / *Librarian and Archivist of Canada 2004–2009, Ottawa, Ontario, Canada*

Kristen Wilson / *North Carolina State University Libraries, Raleigh, North Carolina, U.S.A.*

Thomas D. Wilson / *Publisher/Editor in Chief, Information Research, U.K.*

Catherine C. Wilt / *PALINET, Philadelphia, Pennsylvania, U.S.A.*

Charles Wilt / *Association for Library Collections and Technical Services (ALCTS), Chicago, Illinois, U.S.A.*

Niels Windfeld Lund / *Institute of Culture and Literature, UiT The Arctic University of Norway, Troms , Norway*

Michael F. Winter / *Shields Library, University of California, Davis, California, U.S.A.*

Erica Wiseman / *Graduate School of Library and Information Studies, McGill University, Montreal, Quebec, Canada*

Steve W. Witt / *University of Illinois at Urbana-Champaign, Champaign, Illinois, U.S.A.*

Blanche Woolls / *iSchool, San Jose State University, San Jose, California, U.S.A.*

Louisa Worthington / *Public Library Association, Chicago, Illinois, U.S.A.*

Jadwiga Woźniak-Kasperek / *Institute of Information and Book Studies, University of Warsaw, Warsaw, Poland*

Judith Wusteman / *School of Information and Communication Studies, University College Dublin, Dublin, Ireland*

Iris Xie / *School of Information Studies, University of Wisconsin–Milwaukee, Milwaukee, Wisconsin, U.S.A.*

Yiyu Yao / *Department of Computer Science, University of Regina, Regina, Saskatchewan, Canada, and International WIC Institute, Beijing University of Technology, Beijing, China*

Janis L. Young / *Library of Congress, Washington, District of Columbia, U.S.A.*

Priscilla C. Yu / *University Library, University of Illinois at Urbana-Champaign, Urbana, Illinois, U.S.A.*

Jana Zabinski / *American National Standards Institute, New York, New York, U.S.A.*

Lisl Zach / *iSchool, Drexel University, Philadelphia, Pennsylvania, U.S.A.*

Olga Zaitseva / *Kazakhstan Institute of Management, Economics and Strategic Research (KIMEP), Almaty, Kazakhstan*

Marcia Lei Zeng / *School of Library and Information Science, Kent State University, Kent, Ohio, U.S.A.*

Yi Zeng / *International WIC Institute, Beijing University of Technology, Beijing, China*

Višnja Zgaga / *Museum Documentation Center, Zagreb, Croatia*

Jun Zhang / *Pitney Bowes, Shelton, Connecticut, U.S.A.*

Yulei Zhang / *Department of Management Information Systems, University of Arizona, Tucson, Arizona, U.S.A.*

Kai Zheng / *Department of Health Management and Policy, University of Michigan, Ann Arbor, Michigan, U.S.A.*

Ning Zhong / *Department of Life Science and Informatics, Maebashi Institute of Technology, Maebashi-City, Japan, and International WIC Institute, Beijing University of Technology, Beijing, China*

Maja Žumer / *University of Ljubljana, Slovenia*

Vladimir Zwass / *Computer Science and Management Information Systems, Fairleigh Dickinson University, Teaneck, New Jersey, U.S.A.*

Encyclopedia of Library and Information Sciences, Fourth Edition

Contents

Volume I

Volume I (*cont'd.*)

Volume I (*cont'd.*)

Volume II

Volume II (*cont'd.*)

Decision Sciences / *Sven Axsäter and Johan Marklund* 1192

Decision Support Systems / *Marek J. Druzdzel and Roger R. Flynn* 1200

Demand-Driven Acquisition/Patron-Driven Acquisition / *Michael Levine-Clark* 1209

Denmark: Libraries, Archives, and Museums / *Jens Thorhauge, Jakob Heide Petersen and Ole Magnus Mølbak Andersen* 1215

Descriptive Cataloging Principles / *Elena Escolano Rodríguez* 1229

Design Science in the Information Sciences / *Judith Weedman* 1242

Dewey Decimal Classification (DDC) / *Joan S. Mitchell and Diane Vizine-Goetz* 1256

Digital Content Licensing / *Paul D. Callister and Kathleen Hall* 1267

Digital Divide and Inclusion / *Mark Warschauer and Melissa Niiya* 1279

Digital Humanities / *Julia Flanders and Elli Mylonas* 1286

Digital Humanities and Academic Libraries / *Bobby Smiley and Michael Rodriguez* 1298

Digital Images / *Melissa Terras* 1307

Digital Millennium Copyright Act of 1998 / *Jonathan A. Franklin* 1316

Digital Object Identifier (DOI®) System / *Norman Paskin* 1325

Digital Preservation / *Jacob Nadal* 1332

Diplomatics / *Luciana Duranti* 1338

Disaster Planning and Recovery for Cultural Institutions / *Sheryl Davis, A. Patricia Smith-Hunt and Kristen Kern* 1347

Document Information Systems / *K. van der Meer* 1360

Document Theory / *Niels Windfeld Lund and Roswitha Skare* 1372

Document Type Definition (DTD) / *Judith Wusteman* 1381

Dublin Core Metadata Initiative (DCMI): A Personal History / *Stuart L. Weibel* 1390

Economics Literature: History *[ELIS Classic]* / *Arthur H. Cole and Laurence J. Kipp* 1399

Electronic Records Preservation / *Robert P. Spindler* 1413

Electronic Resources & Libraries (ER&L) / *Jesse Koennecke* 1419

Encoded Archival Description / *Daniel Pitti and Michael Rush* 1423

Engineering Literatures and Their Users *[ELIS Classic]* / *Thomas E. Pinelli, Ann P. Bishop, Rebecca O. Barclay and John M. Kennedy* 1433

Volume III

Volume III (*cont'd.*)

Volume III (*cont'd.*)

Volume IV

Volume IV (*cont'd.*)

Volume V

Volume V (*cont'd.*)

Volume VI

Volume VI (*cont'd.*)

Volume VI (*cont'd.*)

Volume VII

Volume VII (*cont'd.*)

Introduction to the Encyclopedia of Library and Information Sciences, Fourth Edition

How to Use This Encyclopedia

Entries are arranged alphabetically in this encyclopedia (see end papers for alphabetical list). The editors of this edition (ELIS-4) have decided to forego the Topical Table of Contents that was provided in ELIS-3 by editors Marcia Bates and Mary Niles Maack. At the time of publication of ELIS-3, the Topical TOC was crucial for readers to get a sense of how subjects were grouped and an understanding of the field or subfield through the clustering of categorical entries in the print edition. ELIS-4 is envisioned as a primarily online reference work where a Topical TOC does not serve the same purpose. The print edition is served well by the main TOC as well as the detailed index, while entries in the online version are easily discoverable through title, author, keyword, and full text searches.

In sum, relevant entries can be found by

1. Entry title (alphabetical arrangement of entries in the encyclopedia or listing in the end papers)
2. Specific name or keyword, including the index at the end of each volume

If the first name or keyword searched is not found, try several more variations—either different words or a different order of words. Most topics are described in several ways in the literature of a discipline, and the first term or phrase that comes to mind may not be the one used here.

Scope of the Encyclopedia

The title of the third edition, *Encyclopedia of Library and Information Sciences*, ended with the letter "s" because the encyclopedia was broadened to cover a spectrum of related and newly emerging information disciplines, including archival science, document theory, informatics, and records management, among others. The fourth edition continues this trend but with an extensive focus on the aspects of library and information sciences that have been heavily impacted by the adoption and reliance on online information distribution. This focus is reflected in the inclusion of numerous new entries such as digital preservation, altmetrics, web-scale discovery services, demand-driven acquisitions, and global open knowledgebases. Alongside these entries based on entirely new topics, the expanded use of the Internet for information has led to new treatment of traditional LIS topics such as resource description and access (RDA) that reflects the adoption of new standards for cataloging.

ELIS-4 also seeks to build upon the description of professional practice to round out the theoretical perspective that previous editions covered very well. Both current editors are academic research librarians and thus, focused heavily on addressing gaps in the encyclopedia related to academic research information while still relying heavily on the structure established by editors of ELIS-3. For example, ELIS-3 introduced country profiles and ELIS-4 builds upon that with new entries for New Zealand and a third on Brazil, in addition to revisions for Slovakia, Netherlands, Canada, Belarus, Kazakhstan, and Brazil among others. This edition also expands the number of entries for named cultural and information entities that did not appear in previous editions, such as the National Library of Medicine, North American Serials Interest Group (NASIG), the International Association of Scientific, Technical and Medical Publishers (STM), and ASLIB, as well as entities like the HathiTrust that have been established since the last edition was published. A number of new entries describing important information conferences such as the Acquisitions Institute at Timberline, the Charleston Conference, and Electronic Resources in Libraries (ER&L) also help round out the encyclopedia and further the description of the current state of academic research librarianship.

ELIS-4 also continues the tradition of designating important entries of historical or theoretical importance as "ELIS Classics." These are entries by major figures in the library and information sciences or those that describe core concepts in LIS theory, practice, or education that appeared in earlier editions of the encyclopedia. The current editors preserved the approximately 40 previous "ELIS Classics" and designated 13 previous entries as new "ELIS Classics."

There are more than 550 entries, of which more than 20 are new, another 93 are revisions to prior entries that have been brought up to date by their authors or by new authors, about 30 are ELIS Classics, and about 400 are reprinted from an earlier edition since they have remained relevant to the present. It is important to note that the editors also had to make some choices related to retiring entries that were no longer relevant—due to the passage of time and the development of the field, the technologies and theories described in those entries were deemed to be out of scope for the new edition and thus not revised or reprinted.

Encyclopedia Authors

As in past editions, the authors writing for the encyclopedia are major researchers, librarians and practitioners, and leaders in the fields and subfields in the disciplines in which they are writing. Noted scholars are well represented, and a number of authors are former leaders in LIS associations, including the American Library Association (ALA), the Association for College and Research Libraries (ACRL), the International Federation of Library Associations and Institutions (IFLA), the American Society for Information Science and Technology (ASIS&T), and the American Association of Library and Information Science Education (ALISE). In addition, there are many contributors who are current or former directors of major institutions. As in past editions, the editors are very proud of the range and diversity of authors who have written these entries for the encyclopedia and we thank them for sharing their expertise with the current and future readers and researchers in the field.

Finally, the editors for ELIS-4 have grappled with the challenges of entry generation that was noted by previous editors in nearly every edition: that not all ideas, topics, and potential entries were able to be completed for publication in this edition. While we made a valiant attempt to include entries identified by ELIS-3 editors but not secured for publication in that edition, we sometimes could not find authors willing to take those topics on. Similarly, we were sometimes unable to secure revisions to entries from new authors when previous authors were unable to perform that task. To the greatest extent possible, we endeavored to replace authors when entries were deemed important enough to appear in ELIS-4 but initial or previous authors had to decline or defaulted. No doubt, the editors of ELIS-5 will also pick up the mantle and attempt to round out the encyclopedia with entries for anything that ELIS-4 missed. As noted by editors Bates and Niles Maack in ELIS-3, this problem of missing topics was also acknowledged by Allen Kent, editor of the first edition of ELIS. Kent stated in 1973, "I have prepared this presentation to make sure the lessons of Diderot-d'Alembert are recalled in terms of encyclopedia-making as an exercise in the art of the possible."

Background and Development of the Encyclopedia

The first edition of ELIS, under the editorship principally of Allen Kent and Harold Lancour, was published between 1968 and 1982. The 33 volumes of the first edition were published in alphabetical sequence during those years. After the "Z" volume appeared in 1982, a number of supplements were published at roughly the rate of two per year, up to and including volume 73, which appeared in 2003. Miriam Drake was appointed editor for the second edition, which appeared in 2003, both online and in paper. The second edition came out at one time in four large-format volumes, with a supplement in 2005 [3]. Kent and Lancour covered a wide range of librarianship, information science, and some computer science topics. Drake, an academic library director, emphasized academic libraries, and the ELIS-2 volumes contained many profiles of major academic libraries and professional library associations.

The third edition, under the editorship of Marcia Bates and Mary Niles Maack, reflected a growing convergence among the several disciplines that concern themselves with information and the cultural record. As information science educators and noted researchers in the field, their focus was on growing the encyclopedia in the theoretical fields of information sciences as well as drawing together the associated information and cultural disciplines such as archival sciences and museum studies within the overall field of LIS.

For this edition, we have focused on developing the encyclopedia to reflect the changing nature of information production and consumption through online and digital forms. We have also endeavored to fill in gaps in the description of important people, places, and theories in the information sciences, and further enhanced the description of important concepts related to the provision of research information and the field's major institutions.

We continue to see the audience for the encyclopedia just as previous editors have: as principally consisting of 1) the educated lay person interested in one or more of its topics, 2) students learning about a topic, and 3) professionals and researchers in the several fields who want to learn about something new, or to be refreshed on a familiar topic.

We honored the previous editors by reengaging their superb Editorial Advisory Board with significant new additions of experts known to the current editors. (See listing in the front matter.) These leaders and experts from as many disciplines as are in the encyclopedia provided excellent guidance and feedback for the editors as they began the process of new topic generation, evaluation of previous entries, and offering to author or review numerous entries throughout the process of publication.

All new and revised entries were reviewed by one or more outside expert reviewer as well as one or more of the editors. Referees provided invaluable feedback to authors, including noting errors or omissions as well as making suggestions on additional aspects of the topic to cover. While we made every reasonable attempt through this process to check the accuracy of every entry and every fact, undoubtedly readers will find some topics explained more thoroughly or accurately than others. Indeed, due to the time frame from the beginning of the generation of the fourth edition and the time of publication, readers will reasonably note that some topics have been quickly superseded due to this passage of time, so the date of acceptance of the entry will be noted on each entry since several years may have passed since the writing of the entry and the publication of this edition.

Acknowledgments

This edition of the encyclopedia was possible only through the countless hours that the editors, John McDonald and Michael Levine-Clark, spent reviewing the previous encyclopedia entries, outlining the topics that were missing or that were newly emerging in the field, and identifying appropriate expert authors to write those new entries. In addition, the editors devoted extensive time to corresponding with previous authors encouraging them to revise their entries, and finding replacement authors for important entries that needed revisions but whose original authors were unavailable.

Both editors wish to acknowledge the expertise of each other and their knowledge of our field, their extensive network of contacts, and their ability to work closely together to ensure the success of this encyclopedia. Neither of them could have completed this project alone.

They acknowledge and thank the Taylor & Francis Group editors, Claire Miller and Rich O'Hanley, as well as Susan Lee, who passed away at the early stages of the preparation of this edition, and more recently, Alexandra Torres, who supported and kept the editors and authors on track over the course of the years of work on this edition of the encyclopedia.

The editors thank the authors who wrote and revised entries, and the huge number of reviewers who refereed the entries. Without their dedication, expertise, and willingness to share their knowledge with others, there would be no encyclopedia. They also wish to thank the Editorial Advisory Board for their advice, suggestions of topics and authors, their hours spent writing or reviewing for the final edition. They also wish to thank the previous editors, Marcia Bates and Mary Niles Maack, whose organization and structure for ELIS-3 provided an excellent blueprint for ELIS-4.

Encyclopedia of Library and Information Sciences, Fourth Edition

Volume 2

Pages 723–1454

Cataloging–Chartered

Chemistry–China

Circulation–College

Communication–
Corporate Art

Corporate Information–
Custody

Data–Dewey

Digital–Disaster

Document–Engineering

Cataloging

Daniel N. Joudrey
School of Library and Information Science, Simmons College, Boston, Massachusetts, U.S.A.

Abstract
Bibliographic control, the larger field of which cataloging is a part, is discussed in order to provide the context for cataloging. A major product of the process of cataloging, the catalog, is explained in order to underscore why cataloging is needed. The processes for completing original cataloging are delineated, followed by a brief look at cooperative and copy cataloging. Methods for encoding metadata records for online storage and display are outlined.

INTRODUCTION

The purpose of this entry is twofold: 1) to set the context in which cataloging takes place and 2) to introduce the basic concepts of cataloging. The discussion begins with an introduction to the realm of bibliographic control and a brief exploration of where cataloging fits within that realm. Catalogs are discussed in terms of their forms, functions, and components. An overview of the entire process of cataloging—descriptive cataloging, subject analysis, and authority control—is then given, followed by a look at cooperative and copy cataloging that make original cataloging of all materials for every collection unnecessary. Finally, there is mention of the formats of bibliographic records in catalogs and some emerging trends in the twenty-first century related to encoding and sharing bibliographic metadata.

BIBLIOGRAPHIC CONTROL

Cataloging is a subset of the larger field that is sometimes called *bibliographic control* or *information organization*, and it is helpful to view it in that context. Bibliographic control is defined by Elaine Svenonius as "the skill or art... of organizing knowledge (information) for retrieval."[1] Richard P. Smiraglia defines it as a process that encompasses "the creation, storage, manipulation, and retrieval of bibliographic data."[2] In other words, bibliographic control is the process of describing information resources and providing name, title, and subject access to the descriptions, resulting in records that serve as surrogates for the actual items of recorded information. These surrogate records (sometimes called *entries*, *bibliographic records*, or simply *metadata*) are then placed into information retrieval tools, where the records act as pointers to the actual information resources. The comprehensive descriptions found in the records provide users with

enough information to determine the potential value of the resources without actually having to view the items directly. Surrogate records are stored in a variety of retrieval tools including bibliographies, catalogs, indexes, finding aids, museum registers, bibliographic databases, and search engines.

The concept of bibliographic control is applied to all types of information resources including books, journal articles, corporate records, physical objects, digital images, and myriad other formats, and it includes both human-based and machine-derived metadata creation. While it includes activities such as bibliography, indexing, archival description, etc., the presence of the root word *biblio* suggests to some that bibliographic control focuses primarily on books, a resource type most commonly associated with libraries and library cataloging. Consequently, in recent years another phrase—*information organization* (or sometimes *organization of information*)—has been used increasingly to refer to the overarching concept of bibliographic control (i.e., describing all types of information resources for the purpose of retrieval). Arlene G. Taylor, in *The Organization of Information*, points out that "retrieval of information is dependent upon its having been organized." She goes on to note that in addition to retrieval, the "organization of information also allows us to keep a usable record of human endeavors for posterity."[3]

In the universe of all knowledge, including knowledge that cannot necessarily be expressed verbally (e.g., music, and art), there is a certain amount of that knowledge that has been recorded in some way (e.g., written down, digitized, and painted). This subset is often referred to as the *bibliographic universe*. Taylor describes the bibliographic universe as "all instances of recorded knowledge," and goes on to state, "Only the bibliographic universe can be controlled."[4] Such control is maintained through the use of retrieval tools in which each discrete information resource is represented by a surrogate record. Anyone

Encyclopedia of Library and Information Sciences, Fourth Edition DOI: 10.1081/E-ELIS4-120053411

who has attempted to maintain a list of references to articles, a collection of books, or a set of bookmarks for web resources on a particular subject (or by a particular artist or author) has practiced bibliographic control over a very small part of the bibliographic universe. For such projects to succeed, it is necessary to decide what data elements to record about each resource; for example, it may be decided that creator(s), title, subject keywords, a standard identifier, and the location of the resource should be included in the description. The data elements that are recorded to describe a resource are referred to as *metadata*—a term that is often defined as "data about data," but is more usefully understood as a set of important attributes of a resource that assist in finding, identifying, selecting, obtaining, and managing the resource. As the collection grows, so does the complexity of storing, managing, and retrieving needed information. When this occurs, the art and skills of organizing information become essential for the successful creation, maintenance, and use of the collection. In traditional library settings, the art and skills of bibliographic control are referred to as *cataloging*, and the result of these activities is a retrieval tool called a *catalog*.

CATALOGS

A catalog is an organized set of bibliographic records that represents the holdings of a particular collection and/or resources accessible in a particular location. It may be arranged by classification notation, alphabetically by names, titles, or subjects, and in various other ways. A collection may consist of any of several types of materials—books, periodicals, maps, coins, sound recordings, paintings, musical scores, to name just a few. Traditionally, the collection represented by a catalog has been located in one place or at least in different parts of the same institution. Increasingly, however, catalogs may represent the holdings of more than one library, as libraries form consortia or otherwise link their catalogs for the purposes of interlibrary sharing. (Such catalogs are sometimes called *union catalogs*.) In addition, catalogs may include surrogate records for resources that are not owned by the institution, but to which the library can provide access, including websites, online subscription databases, e-books, online journals, and digital library collections.

Why prepare catalogs? Catalogs are necessary whenever a collection of resources grows too large to be remembered item for item. A small private library or a classroom library has little need for a formal catalog; the user can recall each book, sound recording, map, or other such item by author, title, subject, the item's shape, its color, or its position on a particular shelf. When such a collection becomes a little larger, an informal arrangement, such as grouping the items by subject categories, provides access to them. When a collection becomes too large for such a simple approach, a formal record of the collection is necessary. There are two major reasons to make such a formal record of larger collections: for retrieval and for inventory purposes. In addition to being unable to remember what is in a large collection for access purposes, it also becomes impossible for the owner to remember what has been acquired, lost, replaced, etc. A catalog can serve as a record of what is owned as well as a retrieval tool.

Forms of Catalogs

Historically, library catalogs have appeared in various forms. In ancient times, papyrus scrolls and clay tablets were all the rage, but in today's library the catalog primarily appears in one of four distinct formats: book catalogs, microform catalogs, card catalogs, and online public access catalogs (OPACs). While book, microform, and card catalogs are still used in many places around the world, the OPAC has become the most commonly used form of catalog in the Western world. Of these four forms of catalogs, the book catalog is the oldest. In its earliest appearances, the book catalog contained handwritten entries, but by the end of the nineteenth century, the printed book catalog was the most common form of catalog in Western libraries. Today, they are still used in some libraries that cannot or have chosen not to automate access to their collections and in other libraries for some parts of their collections. Because printed book catalogs were rather expensive to produce and quickly became outdated, they were gradually replaced by card catalogs.

Until the late twentieth century, the card catalog was the library catalog most often found around the world. In a card catalog, each information resource is represented by a set of standard 7.5 × 12.5 cm cards (roughly 3 × 5 in.), although in the beginning of the card era the size was not always standard. Multiple cards are prepared in order to represent the various access points needed in the catalog (i.e., a card for each author, a card for the title of the work, a card for each subject represented in the work, a card for a series, etc.). Cards were at first handwritten before the typewriter came into standard use. Typeset cards were available from the Library of Congress (LC) beginning in 1901. Later, cards were often prepared by photo-reproduction of a printed or typed original. Cards are now most often computer-produced from machine-readable catalog records. The card catalog is still found in libraries throughout the world (it is sometimes difficult to remember that in some places, electricity is not always reliably present—making online catalogs impractical). In the United States, card catalogs can still be found in small libraries that cannot afford the software and equipment necessary to switch to an online catalog. They are also used in some larger libraries for specific parts of the collection, perhaps for older materials or special collections.

Microform catalogs became popular with the development of computer output microform (COM) in the mid-to-late twentieth century. COM catalogs could be produced in either microfilm or microfiche. With this form of catalog, it was feasible to provide a completely integrated new catalog every 3 months or so, rather than providing supplements to be used with a main catalog as was needed with printed book catalogs. COM catalogs did require the use of microfiche or microfilm readers—bulky pieces of equipment that took up a great deal of space and were not portable. While COM catalogs were useful from the perspective of librarians, microform catalogs were not popular with users.

The online catalog, often referred to as an *OPAC*, has rapidly become the catalog of choice among librarians and users. The OPAC is usually one component of a larger automated system called an *integrated library system* (ILS)—a computer system that includes various modules to perform different functions in a library while sharing access to the same database. Other modules in the ILS may exist for cataloging, authority control, acquisitions, serials management, circulation, course reserves, and interlibrary loan functions. In the OPAC, the public interface to the ILS, bibliographic records stored in the ILS database are displayed on a screen in response to requests from users. Until the 1990s, such integrated systems were costly, and only very large libraries could afford them. Now, systems have been developed for use on every size computer and have become more affordable, including some that are available freely as open source software. In the beginning of the twenty-first century, as technology continues to progress, some difficulties associated with integrated library systems are becoming more evident. Often, the online catalog is negatively compared to web interfaces for popular online bookstores or to major Internet search engines, suggesting that catalogs are no longer a favored retrieval tool among users. In an attempt to satisfy users and create a more friendly search environment, new innovations in system design (i.e., the inclusion of meta-searching, faceted browsing, cover art, user tagging, tag clouds, and user reviews) are starting to appear in both OPACs and *discovery environments*, which are a user interfaces that work in coordination with the OPAC to provide alternate views of the metadata contained within. For example, a large set of results from a keywords search may be browsed using classification, creators, genre, subjects, dates, and various other facets as guideposts. Most recently, a number of library automation vendors have been offering new products, sometimes referred to as *library services platforms*, which go beyond the tradition ILS in their "engagement with electronic and digital content. In their own distinctive ways, these recently announced or delivered systems aim to break free of the models of automation centered mostly on print materials deeply embodied by the incumbent line of integrated library systems... to handle all the different forms of content."[5]

Functions of Catalogs

Catalogs, whatever their form, have four basic functions. The first is the *identifying* function. All retrieval tools aim at allowing a user, who has a citation or has a particular resource in mind, to match that known item with an entry in the tool—limited, of course, by the scope of the retrieval tool. The scope of a library catalog, for example, is often the items owned or made accessible by the institution; therefore, the user should be able to match or identify or find an entry for a known item that the library owns, or for an item to which the local institution can provide access.

The second function is the *collocating* or *gathering* function. Collocation is a means for bringing together in the catalog like and closely related entities; for example, resources about dinosaurs are grouped together under the subject heading *Dinosaurs*. The subject heading in this case acts as a gathering point for all resources about this topic. In many cases, a particular work is shown in relation to a larger group of connected works. For example, the bibliographic record for a play based upon Mark Twain's *Huckleberry Finn* should be found with records for editions of *Huckleberry Finn*, which in turn can be found with records for other works of Mark Twain. The most common way of accomplishing collocation is through the process of *authority control*—using a unique character string (or some other form of identifier) to represent each name, work, or subject in order to achieve consistency within the catalog or other retrieval tool. If entries for *Huckleberry Finn* are sometimes found under *H* (for *Huckleberry Finn*) and sometimes under *A* (for *Adventures of Huckleberry Finn*) with no connecting references, collocation has not been accomplished.

The third function of catalogs is the *evaluating* or *selecting* function. This function allows a user to choose from among many different records the one that best seems to represent the information or specific physical resource desired. For example, a user looking for a particular edition of *Huckleberry Finn* should be able to select it from among several, if it is one of those listed in the catalog; or, given a choice between a spoken recording on a cassette tape or in the form of an MP3 file, a user could choose the one most appropriate for his or her circumstances, such as the resource that can be used with the equipment available to that user. It can be seen that the first three functions, first described by Charles A. Cutter as his "objects" of the catalog,[6] are somewhat interdependent.

An additional function of a catalog is that of *locating* or *obtaining* resources, a function not always served by other bibliographic tools. One can tell from a library catalog whether the library contains a certain resource and, if so, where it is physically located. This is true even of union catalogs in the sense that the catalog identifies which libraries house particular items, although one may need more detail to know where in a particular library to find an item. With many catalogs, the circulation system is linked, making it possible for the user to learn whether or not an item is available for use. Virtual locations of online resources are provided in catalogs through their uniform resource locators (URLs).

Components of Catalog Systems

Basically, there are three components comprising a whole catalog: a public access catalog, a shelflist, and an authority file or files. In printed catalogs, these are separate physical components. In online catalogs, the OPAC and shelflist are really different ways to search the same file; the authority file is actually a separate file. The public access catalog is the main component, giving access to bibliographic records via author, title, subject, or keyword. This is the catalog component readily available for the use of library patrons. Increasingly, OPACs include links to enhancements held outside the bibliographic records, such as online versions of the resource, tables of contents, and publisher blurbs and reviews.

A shelflist is a record of the holdings of a library; entries are arranged in the order of the items on the shelf—hence the name *shelflist*. With the cataloging of datasets, software, and web resources, for which there is often not a physical item to be placed on a shelf, the name is less descriptive. Records of a library's holdings for such entities may be placed in order by classification notation, acquisition number, or some other device. A shelflist record usually contains a record of ownership of numbers of copies and/or volumes held, as well as information about locations of copies, especially when a library is made up of several collections. Shelflists in print form have traditionally been kept in areas not accessible to the public. There have been notable exceptions to this, however, especially in situations where the areas in which materials are shelved (called *stacks*) are not open to the public. In these situations, browsing the shelflist can substitute for browsing in the stacks. Another change in the availability of shelflists has occurred with online catalogs. When classification is an access point in the catalog, the results of classification notation searches are displayed in shelflist (i.e., classification) order, essentially making the shelflist available to everyone. In addition, most online catalogs provide copy and location information at all access points.

Authority files contain records of the forms of names, titles, and subjects that have been chosen as the standardized forms to use as *authorized access points* (AAPs) in a catalog. An AAP is the exact string of characters used to represent an entity consistently. Authority records also contain lists of references made in the public catalog from unauthorized to authorized forms, so that users do not have to know the actual authorized forms of name, title, or subject in order to retrieve the needed information from the catalog. Traditionally, authority files, like shelflists, have been kept in areas inaccessible to the public. Again, online catalogs have changed this. In some systems, authority files serve as indexes to the catalog.

Online catalogs usually contain all three of these components, but they are not always as distinctly separate as they are in printed catalogs. Authority files still are nonexistent in some online catalogs, and in others, they are unlinked files. Increasingly, however, links between the authority files and the bibliographic files are established so that the authority files may serve as the index(es) to the access points used in the catalog, and in some cases they serve to alert catalogers automatically to inconsistencies in the authority-controlled metadata. In addition, a number of other components have been added to online catalogs. Acquisitions and in-process records are available to the public in many systems, and circulation information is available in virtually every system.

CATALOGING

The means by which catalogs are prepared is through the process called *cataloging*. This process usually begins with descriptive cataloging, including access point choice and creation, and then moves into subject analysis. Additionally, authority control and the encoding of the metadata are mixed into the process.

Foundations of Twenty-First-Century Cataloging

In the early years of the twenty-first century, the international cataloging community has worked to create new standards and models to inform information organization activities. These included the design and elaboration of sound theoretical models to illustrate the bibliographic universe and its components, such as *Functional Requirements for Bibliographic Records* (FRBR) and *Functional Requirements for Authority Data* (FRAD), both developed by the International Federation of Library Associations and Institutions (IFLA). These efforts also included the formation of principles to guide the cataloging process, which resulted in the *Statement of International Cataloguing Principles* developed through a series of IFLA Meetings of Experts on an International Cataloging Code (IME ICC). More recently, these foundational documents supported the development of a new set of cataloging instructions: *RDA: Resource Description & Access* (RDA), an international cataloging standard grounded in Anglo-American cataloging traditions.

FRBR, published by IFLA in 1998, is a conceptual model of the various entities found in the bibliographic universe and the relationships among them.[7] In other words, it is an entity-relationship model—an approach commonly used in modeling relational databases—which attempts to describe users' requirements for bibliographic systems. The FRBR model is thus concerned with the entities found in the bibliographic universe and how those entities interact (i.e., the relationships among the entities). The bibliographic entities are broken into three groups in the FRBR model. Group 1 includes resource-based entities and the hierarchical levels represented in them. These include two abstract levels, *works* and *expressions*, and two concrete levels, *manifestations* and *items*. The first entity, *work*, exists only in the mind of its creator, but the second entity, *expression*, is the articulation of the work's ideas or concepts through spoken words, alphanumeric symbols, choreographic notation, musical notation, or some other method of communication. A *manifestation* is a physical embodiment of an expression of a work. It is a material object or electronic representation of the expressed work in the form of books, video recordings, web pages, sound recordings, paintings, and so on. An *item* is a single, specific instance of a manifestation; that is, it is the exact copy that is owned or accessed by a user. Group 2 represents those entities responsible for the establishment of group 1 entities. These include *persons*, *families*, and *corporate bodies*. These entities have several roles related to group 1 entities; for example, a person may create a work or help to realize an expression, a corporate body may produce a manifestation, or a family may own a particular item. The entity *family* is included in group 2, even though it is not found in the FRBR model, because it is discussed in FRBR's companion document, FRAD.[8] Group 3 entities include subject entities described as *concepts*, *objects*, *places*, and *events*, as well as the group 1 and group 2 entities (which may also be used as subjects). The FRBR model presents ways to describe the entities with their attributes and also ways to relate various entities to each other. FRBR also reminds us that users want to find, identify, select, and obtain information in the resources that we catalog. A number of libraries and ILS vendors have experimented with systems that can make use of the FRBR model, and FRBR and FRAD are two foundations for the new set of descriptive cataloging guidelines, RDA. In 2016, a world-wide review of the FRBR-Library Reference Model (FRBR-LRM) began. The FRBR-LRM was developed to harmonize the separate "Functional Requirements" conceptual models into a single standard covering all aspects of bibliographic, subject, and authority metadata.[9] At the time of this writing, significant changes in cataloging's underlying conceptual model are expected as a result of these revisions.

After a series of five meetings held between 2003 and 2007, the IME ICC disseminated in 2009 their *Statement of International Cataloguing Principles* (ICP). The purpose of the IME ICC meetings was to update the Paris Principles, which were agreed upon in 1961 and underlay all the major cataloging codes used throughout the world. The meetings' discussions were the basis for international agreement on an updated set of cataloging principles and a glossary of terminology. These principles emphasize convenience for users, stating, for example, that metadata

should be available in languages and scripts that users can read. In addition to discussing 10 basic objectives that guide the construction of cataloging codes (i.e., convenience, accuracy, standardization, etc.), the statement addresses six major principles related to entities, attributes, and relationships; functions of the catalog; bibliographic description; access points; authority records; and foundations for search capabilities. In 2015, IFLA's ICP was revised, and a world-wide review began in 2016. Some additions to the general principles are expected after the revisions are complete.[10]

RDA, published in 2010, is a set of cataloging rules constructed by the RDA Steering Committee (RSC) to supersede the last version of *Anglo-American Cataloging Rules* (AACR). It is solidly based on FRBR, FRAD, and the IME ICC's *Statement of International Cataloguing Principles*. The goals of the RSC were to overcome the inconsistencies and inadequate structure of AACR and to provide rules for meaningful metadata for multiple types of resources that can be used by a wider audience than just the Anglo-American cataloging community. At the time of this writing, it appears that RDA is becoming an international standard for cataloging; it has been translated into Chinese, Finnish, French, German, Italian, and Spanish, and it has been adopted by over a dozen national libraries from around the world, with more expected to adopt it in the future. It is hoped that by providing a more all-encompassing set of rules for description and access, greater cooperation between libraries and other information communities may be developed.[11] Whether this occurs or not is one of the main issues to be resolved in the realm of bibliographic control.

Encoding

Unless catalog cards are typed manually, encoding permeates the entire cataloging process. The results of each of the descriptive, subject, and authority processes are entered into a machine-readable form that is compatible with the online system in which the catalog record will be used. In the current cataloging environment, the most commonly used encoding standard is the MAchine-Readable Cataloging (MARC) bibliographic format, or in the case of authority records, the MARC authorities format. Increasingly other forms of encoding—often in the form of schemas established in the eXtensible Markup Language (XML)—are being found in integrated library systems, discovery environments, and library services platforms. At the time of this writing, a project to develop an alternative approach for sharing metadata, the Bibliographic Framework Initiative (BIBFRAME), is being headed by the Library of Congress.[12]

Descriptive Cataloging

Descriptive cataloging is the phase of the cataloging process that is concerned with the identification and description of a resource, the recording of this information in the form of a cataloging record, the selection of name and title access points the formation of AAPs for the names and titles, and the encoding of these data elements so that they will be machine-readable. Descriptive cataloging describes the makeup of a resource and identifies the persons or institutions responsible for the intellectual contents. Descriptive cataloging is concerned with both the carrier and the content of a resource, but does not address the topical contents of the resource, which are the province of subject cataloging.

Description

Identification and description are interrelated processes in descriptive cataloging. Identification consists of the choice of conventional elements, guided by a set of rules based on agreed-upon international standards. When the cataloger has properly identified the conventional elements, they are described in a catalog record in such a fashion that the description is unique and can be applied to no other entity in the collection. In other words, each resource should be distinguished from everything with which it could be confused. Elements considered essential for this purpose in describing physical resources are usually title, statement of responsibility, edition information, standard numbers, and publication, distribution, or production information. Physical description—extent and size of the resource—and series metadata are often essential to this purpose as well. Components essential for describing virtual resources (e.g., Internet documents) are title, statement of responsibility, version information (if present), date information, and location information (e.g., URL). In addition, the cataloger gives elements of description that may be helpful to a user in evaluating the potential use of the resource, such as whether it is illustrated, its intended audience, what equipment is needed to use it, any restrictions there may be on use, or its mode of access. Such descriptive metadata may be part of the conventional elements or may be contained within (sometimes extensive) notes in the catalog record.

Access

After describing a resource, the cataloger selects particular names and titles to be access points. Names of persons, families, and corporate bodies associated with the creation of a work are chosen according to the cataloging rules used. Title access points also are chosen—in addition to the obvious main title (called *title proper*) there may be alternative titles, variant titles, series titles, and titles of other works related in some way to the work being cataloged. The names and titles chosen are then formatted as AAPs, constructed in a form that will make them readily accessible in the catalog and will enhance collocation of related resources. This is done using cataloging instructions and through reference to the authority file (ensuring that the authorized form of name is used consistently), thus continuing the process of authority control.

In earlier cataloging practices, one access point was chosen as the *main entry* or *primary access point*. The main entry was typically the person or entity primarily responsible for the creation of a work. Because one access point was considered to be the main entry, the remaining access points were referred to as *added entries*. Both types of entries allowed for the retrieval of resources in the catalog, but the main entry had an additional function of identifying the work embodied in the resource being cataloged. A combination of main entry and title was the most common way of referring to a work in the realm of cataloging. In RDA, the terms *main entry* and *added entries* are not used, but the work-identification function of main entry is still needed. Catalogers require a consistent name for a work and the most logical one is the through the creation of an access point comprising the AAP for the principal (or first-named) creator along with the preferred title for the work (e.g., Shakespeare, William, 1564–1616. Hamlet).

Subject Analysis

The subject analysis process begins with determining the *aboutness* of the work, that is, what subject concepts are covered by the intellectual or artistic content of a work, and in the case of some creative works, the form or genre represented by the resource. Once these have been determined, the concepts are then translated into one or more forms of controlled vocabulary. Controlled vocabularies can take a verbal approach (i.e., subject headings or descriptors from a thesaurus) or a notational approach (i.e., symbols from a classification scheme) to subject representation. When taking a verbal approach, as many subject headings as are appropriate are chosen from a standard list to represent the topics of the work. Again, an authority file must be consulted if the works are to be properly collocated into the catalog with other works covering the same or related subject concepts. Verbal subject representation may take the form of single terms assigned individually to a work to represent a single concept, or it may take the form of strings of terms to represent multiple facets of a topic, if the controlled vocabulary allows this type of heading construction.

When using the notational approach, symbols from the classification scheme used by the library are assigned to the resource. Traditionally in the United States, classification serves both as a means for bringing an item in close proximity with other like items in the catalog and, in the case of tangible resources, as the first element of the *call number*, a device used to identify and locate a particular item on library shelves. The cataloger, therefore, must choose the one best place in the classification scheme for the item. In other parts of the world, however, or in nontraditional collections, more than one classification notation may be assigned to a resource to represent multiple topics or multiple aspects of subjects found in the content. These multiple classification numbers may be used as searchable access points in the catalog, but with only one being chosen to represent the shelf location of the item.

Authority Control

Authority control is the result of the process of maintaining consistency in the verbal forms of names, titles, and subjects terms used to represent an entity, and the further process of showing the relationships that exist among those names, works, and subjects. It is accomplished through use of descriptive cataloging instructions (in the case of names and titles), use of a controlled vocabulary (for subject headings and descriptors), and reference to an authority file to create an authorized character string. An authority file is a group of records for the names, titles, or subjects chosen for use in a catalog. Each authority record in an authority file may contain, in addition to the form chosen for use as the AAP, a list of variant forms or terms that may be used as references. More recently, additional metadata elements reflecting attributes of persons, families, corporate bodies, and works have been added to authority records to provide more understanding of the entity being described in the record. Elements such as place and date associated with the entity, gender, field of activity, associated language, occupation, associated group, and the like provide greater context for the entity. A carefully prepared authority record also contains a list of sources consulted in the process of deciding upon the authorized form of name or term, the variant forms to use as references, and additional data elements to include. It is possible to practice authority control by letting the catalog itself serve as the authority file, that is, by assuming that the form of heading used in the catalog is correct. In larger catalogs, this has proved to be difficult, and it is very challenging to keep track of references without an authority file.

It is authority control that makes cataloging more than just a process of creating a series of bibliographic records to represent discrete works, because authority control allows the cataloger to create AAPs for names, titles, and subjects that show the relationships among the works cataloged. It means that the AAP for a particular name, when used in different records, is always consistent so that bibliographic records for all works by and about the same person or family, or emanating from the same corporate body, can be displayed together. An AAP for a work (formerly called a *uniform title*), which often consists of the name of the principal author followed by a standardized title, can be consistently presented so that bibliographic records for all editions, translations, sound or video recordings, adaptations, abridgements, etc., of a work can be displayed together. The subject heading or descriptor that is used to represent the same topic or concept in different works can be used in one form so that to the extent that works are identified as being about the same

subject concept, all such works can be displayed together collocated under the authorized subject term. Authority control of subject terminology also makes it possible to refer users from terms not used (e.g., Haplorhini) to those that are used (e.g., Monkeys), as well as from terms that are used (e.g., City dwellers) to broader terms (e.g., Persons) and/or narrower terms (e.g., Yuppies) and from terms that are used (e.g., Cooking) to other related terms that may be of interest (e.g., Gastronomy).

As we move more and more into the international arena, virtual authority control connecting national authority files with each other is becoming essential. Creators of catalogs in various countries using various languages need to be able to designate their own "authorized" forms of names, while at the same time recognizing variant names for the same person or other entity in other languages. International catalogs should not be required to use the English-language authorized forms, but should be able to link users to entities they seek, regardless of the language used in their searches.

Cooperative and Copy Cataloging

The process of cataloging described earlier is often referred to as *original cataloging*. Fortunately, it is not necessary for every information resource in every library to be cataloged originally in that library. Because libraries acquire copies of many of the same items, or decide to catalog the same online resources, their catalogers can share metadata by adapting a copy of the original cataloging created by another library for their own catalogs, a process commonly called *copy cataloging*.[13] This is related to the idea of *cooperative cataloging*, the working together of independent institutions to share network memberships or to create cataloging that can be used by others.

In the United States, cooperative and copy cataloging efforts began in earnest in the early part of the twentieth century, when LC started selling its standard printed catalog cards to libraries in 1901. H. W. Wilson entered the field in the 1930s with simplified catalog cards for sale. A number of other companies created and sold catalog cards from the 1950s into the 1970s. In addition, LC book catalogs were available in large libraries, and methods were devised for photocopying entries from them for adaptation and use in local catalogs. With the development of the MARC format in the late 1960s, cooperative cataloging took a new turn. At first, the companies selling cards simply loaded LC's MARC tapes into their computers and printed cards from them. But the beginning of bibliographic networks based on MARC not only changed the availability of cards but also introduced the truly cooperative availability of cataloging data. The first bibliographic network was OCLC—at first the Ohio College Library Center, but now OCLC Online Computer Library Center, Inc. Libraries can become members (either individually or through regional networks) and contribute original cataloging to the system. Any member library then can use records found in the system contributed by LC, other national libraries, or other member libraries. At first, the OCLC cataloging system was used only for the production of cards. Once the appropriate technology became available, libraries realized that making changes to an online record is much easier than trying to adjust photocopies or preprinted cards. Now, most libraries simply download MARC records directly into their local online systems for use in their OPACs. In recent years, SkyRiver was created as an alternative to OCLC. In addition to OCLC and SkyRiver, smaller regional and local networks exist in large numbers.

The amount of original cataloging remaining after use of cooperative cataloging depends upon the type and size of library. The more specialized the library, the more original cataloging it has. Specialized collections can require a high percentage of original cataloging, even though the collection or library may be quite small. There is now increased interest in cataloging more of the unique materials (e.g., local history, digitized materials, rare foreign language resources, and genealogy materials) that local libraries may have in order to make these essentially hidden resources available to wider audiences.

In the mid-1990s, there was a movement toward outsourcing both original and copy cataloging in some libraries. Outsourcing involves contracting with vendors outside the library to do some of the cataloging (or occasionally all the cataloging) for the library. The move has both advantages and disadvantages, and much has been written on this subject.[14,15]

In addition, vendors may provide metadata alongside the resources being sold or leased to libraries and other information institutions. In some cases, complete or nearly complete sets of records may be provided to the institution to be loaded directly into its catalog. Although it may be provided for individual resources, this type of service is more useful when dealing with large resources sets, particularly electronic resources (e.g., a collection of 5,000 streaming videos). The quality of such metadata, however, varies among vendors. Some catalog record sets may require little to no manipulation, but others may need to be enhanced or customized before being used by the institution.

FORMATS OF BIBLIOGRAPHIC RECORDS IN CATALOGS

In order for them to be displayed in retrieval tools, the surrogates created for each information resource must be encoded for machine processing or printing. The cataloging process, therefore, requires the encoding of the bibliographic records in the format of the system being used. Uniformity of display is very desirable so that patrons can

know how to read a record and where to expect to see certain metadata elements. In printed catalogs, the display of metadata was quite standard. Most libraries and card production sources followed the LC pattern, because LC-printed cards were so extensively used and because the order of elements devised by LC made a logical presentation of data. That order was codified by the various versions of the AACR.[16]

Today, the vast majority of catalog records are created using one of the MARC formats. The first MARC format was developed at LC around 1965. The version used in the United States was, for many years, referred to as USMARC to distinguish it from the versions used in other countries (e.g., IBERMARC and danMARCAACR). The latest version, published in 1999, is called *MARC 21*. It is a "harmonization" of CAN/MARC and USMARC, and the name is meant to show that it is ready for the twenty-first century. Because many national versions of MARC exist, exchanging bibliographic data across international boundaries might be difficult, were it not for UNIMARC, created in 1977, which acts as a crosswalk or a translator between different versions of MARC and can be used as an encoding scheme itself. A general discussion of MARC and several other encoding standards can be found in Taylor and Joudrey's *Organization of Information* and Joudrey, Taylor, and Miller's Introduction to Cataloging and Classification.[17,18]

MARC is not the only way to encode library metadata. In recent years, other approaches to encoding have been explored because some catalogers and information technologists have seen its limitations. A frequent criticism of MARC is its lack of interoperability with nonlibrary computer networks and systems. Not only does the MARC format limit the ability of libraries to interact with other forms of data, but also library metadata cannot easily be shared with other communities. The Library of Congress Working Group on the Future of Bibliographic Control stated that the library community needs to recognize that "the World Wide Web is both our technology platform and the appropriate platform for the delivery of our standards," and "people are not the only users of the data we produce in the name of bibliographic control, but so too are machine applications that interact with those data in a variety of ways."[19] It is with these concerns in mind that libraries began exploring alternatives to the MARC format.

XML (ISO 8879) is a subset of the Standard Generalized Markup Language (SGML). In recent years, it has been used to store and share structured data on the World Wide Web. Like any markup language, XML is used to describe the various features and attributes found in documents, but unlike Hyper Text Markup Language (HTML)—which is also derived from SGML and is currently the language of the web—it is not focused on displaying text. Instead, XML focuses on identifying the various pieces or components of a text. For example,

HMTL allows users to manipulate the size and look of the text (using bold, larger font sizes, etc.); XML allows users to identify elements such as a document's title, its creator, relationships among the elements, what elements are required, etc. As the web has grown, HTML has been criticized because it is too simplistic to provide for many desirable applications. Some thought for a while that full support of SGML on the web was the answer. However, SGML is fairly complex and has features that make the programming involved complicated and lengthy. XML was developed as an answer to these problems. It is essentially a version of SGML that can be used on the web. Its components are the same: entities, elements, and attributes. XML is referred to as *extensible* because it allows its users to develop their own descriptive tags; it is very flexible and can be used to support many different types of web applications.

XML is touted by its developers as being just as easy to use on the web as HTML, but at the same time being as powerful as SGML.[20] Although XML uses the same basic components as SGML, XML does not require a document type definition (DTD) or an XML schema. Schemas and DTDs are mechanisms used to define the elements and attributes used when describing documents. When attempting to consistently and fluidly share data of a particular type, in a particular community, or for a particular purpose, a defined set of tags and elements become essential for interoperability. In the library community, a MARCXML schema and DTD have been created in order to share MARC metadata with a wider community.[21] Both mimic the content designation structure of the MARC21 bibliographic format, but encoding is in XML syntax. For example, instead of finding a title proper encoded as

```
245  14  $a  The  title  is  here  /  $c  by
         Annie  Author.
```

in the MARCXML schema, the title element would appear as:

```
<datafield tag="245" ind1="1" ind2="4">
   <subfield code="a">The title is here /
   </subfield>
   <subfield code="c">by Annie Author.
   </subfield>
</datafield>
```

Other XML-based approaches to library metadata include Metadata Object Description Schema, a schema for a bibliographic element set that uses natural language tags instead of the numerical MARC content designators;[22] Metadata Authority Description Schema, a schema for an authority data element set that may be used to provide metadata about agents, events, and terms;[23] and the Metadata Encoding & Transmission Standard, a schema for encoding descriptive, administrative, and structural metadata for digital library objects.[24]

These approaches to encoding cataloging data, however, may not be sufficient for the type of sharing that is of interest and of concern at the time of this writing. Another project to develop a replacement for the MARC bibliographic format has been initiated by the Library of Congress. It is the aforementioned BIBFRAME, and it is meant to move cataloging data from the record structure found in the silos of traditional OPACs to the open linked data environment of the Semantic Web. This project, while still in early stages, has great potential to change the way resources are retrieved and connected.

CONCLUSION

Despite the changes in the field that have occurred over the past decade, cataloging will continue to evolve. Economics, developing technology, and the rapidly growing number of information resources in the bibliographic universe will guarantee this. Despite the current developments described earlier, the ways in which change will occur is not completely predestined. While many have tried to predict the trajectory of library cataloging throughout the centuries, many have gotten it wrong. In the 1904 edition of his *Rules for a Dictionary Catalog*, Charles Cutter stated that he could not "help thinking that the golden age of cataloging is over, and the difficulties and discussions which have furnished an innocent pleasure to so many will interest them no more. Another lost art."[25] In this particular case, Cutter was wrong, because more than a century later, many are still passionately discussing the difficulties and future directions of the art. While cataloging will change, what will remain constant is the desire of information institutions to maintain bibliographic control over their information resources for retrieval and historical purposes.

REFERENCES

1. Svenonius, E. Directions for research in indexing, classification, and cataloging. *Library Resources & Technical Services*. **1981**, 25 (1), 88.
2. Smiraglia, R.P. Bibliographic control theory and nonbook materials. In *Policy and Practice in Bibliographic Control of Nonbook Media*; Intner, S.S., Smiraglia, R.P., Eds.; American Library Association: Chicago, IL, 1987; 15.
3. Taylor, A.G. *The Organization of Information*, Library and Information Science Text Series, 2nd Ed.; Libraries Unlimited: Westport, CT, 2004; 2.
4. Taylor, A.G. *Introduction to Cataloging and Classification*, Library and Information Science Text Series, 10th Ed.; Libraries Unlimited: Westport, CT, 2006; 4.
5. Breeding, M. A cloudy forecast for libraries. *Information Today*. **2011**, 31 (7). http://www.infotoday.com/cilmag/sep11/breeding.shtml (accessed March 17, 2016).

6. Cutter, C.A. *Rules for a Dictionary Catalog*, 4th Ed.; GPO: Washington, DC, 1904; 12.

7. International Federation of Library Associations and Institutions (IFLA). *Functional Requirements for Bibliographic Records*; K.G. Saur: München, Germany, 1998. http://www.ifla.org/publications/functional-requirements-for-bibliographic-records (accessed March 17, 2016).

8. IFLA. *Functional Requirements for Authority Data: A Conceptual Model*; K.G. Saur: München, Germany, 2009. http://www.ifla.org/publications/ifla-series-on-bibliographic-control-34 (accessed March 17, 2016).

9. IFLA FRBR Review Group. World-wide review of the FRBR-Library Reference Model, a consolidation of the FRBR, FRAD and FRSAD conceptual models. http://www.ifla.org/node/10280 (accessed March 17, 2016).

10. IFLA. *Statement of International Cataloguing Principles*; K.G. Saur: München, Germany, 2009. http://www.ifla.org/publications/statement-of-international-cataloguing-principles (accessed March 17, 2016).

11. RDA Steering Committee. *RSC RDA Steering Committee Website*. http://www.rda-rsc.org/ (accessed March 17, 2016).

12. Library of Congress. Bibliographic Framework Initiative. http://www.loc.gov/bibframe/ (accessed March 17, 2016).

13. Taylor, A.G. *Cataloging with Copy: A Decision-Maker's Handbook*, 2nd Ed.; Libraries Unlimited: Englewood, CO, 1988.

14. Benaud, C.; Bordeianu, S. *Outsourcing Library Operations in Academic Libraries: An Overview of Issues and Outcomes*; Libraries Unlimited: Englewood, CO, 1998.

15. Colver, M.; Wilson, K. *Outsourcing Technical Services Operations*; American Library Association: Chicago, IL, 1997.

16. American Library Association. *Anglo-American Cataloguing Rules*, 2nd Ed., 2002 Revision; American Library Association: Chicago, IL, 2002, prepared under the direction of the Joint Steering Committee for Revision of AACR; [and earlier editions].

17. Taylor, A.G.; Joudrey, D.N. *The Organization of Information*, Library and Information Science Text Series, 3rd Ed.; Libraries Unlimited: Westport, CO, 2009; 129–155.

18. Joudrey, D. N.; Taylor, A.G.; Miller, D.P. *Introduction to Cataloging and Classification*, Library and Information Science Text Series; 11th Ed.; Libraries Unlimited/ABC-CLIO: Santa Barbara, CA, 2015; 795–886.

19. Library of Congress Working Group on the Future of Bibliographic Control. On the Record. 2008. http://www.loc.gov/bibliographic-future/ (accessed March 17, 2016).

20. World Wide Web Consortium (W3C). Extensible Markup Language (XML). 2015. http://www.w3.org/XML/ (accessed March 17, 2016).

21. Library of Congress. MARCXML MARC 21 XML Schema Official Web Site. 2015. http://www.loc.gov/standards/marcxml/ (accessed March 17, 2016).

22. Library of Congress. MODS Metadata Object Description Schema Official Web Site. 2016. http://www.loc.gov/standards/mods/ (accessed March 17, 2016).

23. Library of Congress. MADS Metadata Authority Description Schema Official Web Site. 2013. http://www.loc.gov/standards/mads/ (accessed March 17, 2016).

24. Library of Congress. METS Metadata Encoding & Transmission Standard Official Web Site. 2016. http://www.loc.gov/standards/mets/ (accessed March 17, 2016).

25. Cutter, C.A. *Rules for a Dictionary Catalog*, 4th Ed.; GPO: Washington, DC, 1904; 5.

Cataloging Cultural Objects (CCO)

Elizabeth O'Keefe
Maria Oldal
Morgan Library and Museum, New York, U.S.A.

Abstract

The entry provides an overview of the data content standard, *Cataloging Cultural Objects* (CCO), developed by the Visual Resources Association (VRA), and published in 2006 by the American Library Association (ALA). CCO fills a gap in the array of descriptive standards by providing guidelines for visual resources curators, museum documentation specialists, archivists, librarians, or anyone engaged in the documentation of works of art and architecture, objects of material culture, and their images. The entry begins by placing CCO within the context of object and visual image cataloging and the broader framework of data content standards. Following the organization of the guide, which is divided into three parts, General Guidelines, Elements, and Authorities, it summarizes the main features of CCO. Finally, it evaluates CCO in terms of its suitability for use by the metadata communities that form its intended audience, and its sustainability.

INTRODUCTION

Cataloging Cultural Objects (CCO) is a data content standard for the description of art and cultural objects and their visual surrogates. CCO was developed by the Visual Resources Association (VRA) to provide guidance to visual resources curators, museum documentation specialists, librarians, archivists, and anyone engaged in describing works of art and architecture, objects of material culture, and their images. It was published in 2006 by the American Library Association (ALA).

The entry begins by placing CCO in the context of object and visual image cataloging, and within the broader framework of data content standards. Following the organization of the guide, which is divided into three parts—General Guidelines, Elements, and Authorities—it summarizes the main features of CCO. Finally, it evaluates CCO in terms of its suitability for use by the metadata communities that form its intended audience, and its sustainability.

HISTORICAL CONTEXT OF CCO

CCO was developed to answer the need for standards appropriate to the description of art and cultural works, as opposed to textual materials. (For a more in-depth discussion of the difference between a work in the bibliographic sense and a unique work of art or material culture, see the entry for "Work of Art.") Data standards for the description of art and cultural objects have lagged considerably behind those used for textual materials. This can be ascribed partly to the fact that textual materials usually exist in multiples. When many libraries own a copy of the same publication,

shared cataloging becomes cost-effective, and this in turn leads to a demand for common data standards.

Long before the introduction of the computer, libraries had developed common cataloging rules, and were sharing bibliographic records through published union catalogs and catalog card distribution programs. The advent of computerization accelerated this process, leading to the development in the 1960s of Machine Readable Cataloging (MARC),[1] a defined set of data elements that facilitated the exchange of bibliographic information and fostered the creation of modern online library catalogs and union catalogs such as Online Computer Library Center (OCLC) WorldCat.

Art and cultural objects are usually unique, which eliminates the greatest economic incentive for data standardization. As a result, museum guidelines for the documentation of objects were developed and implemented locally, and tailored to local needs, rather than based on a broader conceptual framework. The emergence of computing technology and the digital revolution kindled new interest in data standards. Although records for unique objects cannot be shared in the same way as records for copies of the same book, use of a common set of data elements and of controlled access points formulated according to agreed-upon rules facilitates other types of information sharing, such as the pooling of records in union catalogs or electronic catalogs raisonnés. Early efforts by the museum community to share collection information were hampered by incompatible formats and content,[2] making it evident that standards were a prerequisite for meaningful data exchange and sharing.

The visual resources community has long been aware of the advantages of data sharing, since there is considerable overlap in the objects depicted in image collections.

Encyclopedia of Library and Information Sciences, Fourth Edition DOI: 10.1081/E-ELIS4-120044175

Several projects tested the viability of pooling records for art images (p. 11);[2] the disparities and inconsistencies in cataloging brought to light when records for the same work were aggregated provided convincing proof of the need for common data standards.

The museum and visual resources communities considered, but ultimately rejected, adoption of library data standards. There was a consensus that rules developed primarily for textual materials and/or material issued through a formal publication process could not provide adequate guidance for the description of unique objects. Unlike published works, objects are non-self-describing; the cataloger must supply most of the information required to document the object, so the emphasis in library cataloging rules on transcription of information appearing on the item, and the elaborate hierarchy of preferred sources of information was not applicable to object cataloging. Moreover, the physical characteristics of objects are far more varied than those of a book, and far more important for description and retrieval. One has only to consider the fact that a bibliographic record for a book routinely omits several pieces of information required for object cataloging—the object type (book), the support (paper), the medium (ink), and the technique (printing)—to realize that library cataloging rules are inadequate for object cataloging.

Early efforts to develop standards for object cataloging focused on data format definition. The International Committee for Documentation of the International Council of Museums (CIDOC) Conceptual Reference Model,[3] and Categories for the Description of Works of Art (CDWA)[4] represent attempts by the museum community to articulate conceptual frameworks for the description of objects. CIDOC covers all types of material collected by museums and related institutions,[5] while CDWA is limited to "works of art, architecture, other material culture, groups and collections of works, and related images."[6] The Visual Resources Association's VRA Core[7] was influenced by CDWA, but it expanded on areas not initially covered by CDWA, eliminated most of the elements defined for administrative data needed for managing museum objects, and added elements needed to describe images.

These standards satisfied the need for an agreed-upon set of data elements. Still lacking was a standard for defining the content of the data elements. CCO is intended to supply the missing piece. Although CCO was developed by the VRA to complement VRA Core, it is intentionally data-format neutral, and can be applied within the framework of MARC, CDWA, CIDOC, Encoded Archival Description (EAD),[8] or any other format designed for encoding cultural heritage information.

DEVELOPMENT OF CCO

Work on CCO formally began in 2001, with the formation of a five-person editorial team drawn from the VRA Data Standards Committee and the Getty Standards Program.[9] Primary funding was supplied by the Getty Foundation and the Digital Library Federation, supplemented by the Andrew W. Mellon Foundation. After reviewing and evaluating existing data content standards and practices, the team developed a conceptual structure for the publication. The first draft was subjected to extensive criticism and review by an advisory committee that included members of the visual resources, museum, library, and archives communities. A Web-based beta version of CCO was posted in November 2003; 35 experts conducted an additional formal review in 2004. The guidelines were published in 2006 by the ALA on behalf of the VRA.

ORGANIZATION OF CCO

CCO is organized in three sections: General Guidelines, Elements, and Authorities. These sections are preceded by an introduction that defines its purpose, audience, scope, and methodology, and followed by a select bibliography, glossary, and index. Throughout CCO, there are copious examples illustrating individual rules, as well as sample Work records and Authority records.

Part 1, General Guidelines

Part 1 of CCO provides a conceptual framework and general guidelines for the cataloging of cultural objects and their visual surrogates. Some of the topics covered in this section are applicable to any type of cataloging: for example, issues of minimal description, item- and collection-level cataloging, indexing depth and consistency, and the use of controlled vocabularies and authority files. Other issues pertain to the special characteristics of cultural material or to the environment in which object cataloging customarily takes place. These include the following.

What are you cataloging?

This question refers not to the identification of the object (is it a painting? a sculpture? a church?) but to the focus of the record:

> Before beginning the task of descriptive cataloguing, a cataloguer must ask a basic but potentially complex question: What am I cataloguing? This question refers to the relationship between a work and its parts, and between a work and the images that represent it.[10]

The item described may consist of a single object produced at a discrete point in time or one reworked over the years by several different hands. It may be a single work composed of many different parts, such as a building or an altarpiece. Or it may be multiple works within a series, a set, an archival group, or a collection. In each case, the cataloger must determine the focus of the description, and decide how many records are needed. Separate records should be created whenever there is enough unique information pertaining to a part to warrant it.

Further complications arise when the item being described is an image of an object, and therefore at one remove from the object. The image may consist of a view of the entire work, a detail of the work, or several works:

> ... imagine a photograph intended to document an original two-dimensional painting (i.e., a photograph that contains the entire work and nothing more).... Now imagine that the photographer had stepped back fifteen feet, expanded the perspective, and instead of a photograph of a painting, it becomes a photograph of a painting on a wall of a building with a sculpture in the foreground. The photograph is no longer a simple image of a single work; the photograph now represents a complex layer of information open to subjective interpretation (pp. 3–4).[10]

Related works

Since many objects are physically complex, or related to other works, CCO discusses relationships between works in some detail. Related works are defined as "works that have an important conceptual relationship to each other" (p. 377).[10] These relationships may be intrinsic or extrinsic. Intrinsic relationships take the form of whole-part relationships: for example, the relationship between a triptych and its component panels or between a building and the various rooms, the relationship between a collection and the individual items within it, or the relationship between a series and its individual members. CCO recommends recording all intrinsic relationships. Extrinsic relationships should be noted whenever possible, especially those that are not otherwise apparent in the description, for example, when one work is preparatory for or copied from another.

Relationship between the work and the image

An image has its own characteristics, such as the medium (photograph, slide, digital file), the angle or view at which it was taken, and the date of image capture. All of these need to be recorded, but kept distinct from the description of the work depicted. In order to make a clear distinction between a work and its visual surrogate, CCO recommends creating separate work and image records, and linking the records.

Database design

In Part 1 and throughout the publication, CCO offers a great deal of guidance on database design. It is tacitly assumed that users of CCO will have a significant role in either creating the database or influencing its design, since

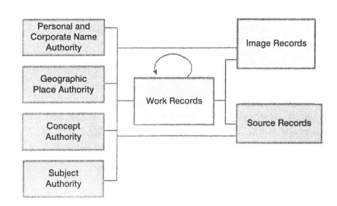

Fig. 1 Entity relationship diagram for CCO.
Source: From Baca.[10] Fig. 1 (p. 20).

most visual resources collections and museum collections are managed using locally designed databases or customized versions of purchased or open source software. Although CCO may be applied in a variety of database settings, a relational database is recommended because of "the complexity of cultural information and the importance of Authority Records." The entity relationship diagram reproduced here illustrates relationships between works, authorities, and images in a relational database implementation of CCO (Fig. 1).

Display and indexing

CCO makes a clear distinction between display data and indexing data. Its recommendations regarding the treatment of data for indexing purposes are similar to those made in library cataloging guidelines: for example, creator names that are presented in direct order in free text should be inverted for indexing purposes, and dates should be normalized to facilitate machine processing. Its discussion of display or free-text data illustrates a major difference between the cataloging environments of the object cataloger and the book cataloger. Since object catalogers must usually supply the description of the item being cataloged, rather than being obliged, as book catalogers are, to transcribe the information appearing on the item, they have much greater discretion about how to word the information. Moreover, the information in object records is more likely than the bibliographic records in a library catalog to be repurposed in multiple ways. CCO concentrates, therefore, not on giving rules for transcription but on providing guidance on recording display data in a form easily understood by the end user in a variety of different contexts, from slide labels to wall panels to Web sites.

Part 2, Elements

Part 2 describes the nine data areas that appear in Work and Image records.

Entry 1: Object Naming (Work Type and Title)
Entry 2: Creator Information
Entry 3: Physical Characteristics
Entry 4: Stylistic, Cultural, and Chronological Information
Entry 5: Location and Geography
Entry 6: Subject
Entry 7: Class
Entry 8: Description
Entry 9: View Information

Each entry begins with a definition of the element and subelements covered in that entry, information on whether it is controlled, repeatable, or required, and a list of recommended sources of terminology. The bulk of each entry is devoted to cataloging rules. These rules, which are illustrated with numerous examples, cover syntax, suggested terminology for subelements in various media or subcategories, choice of singular versus plural (where relevant), capitalization, abbreviation, preferred language, and how to deal with ambiguity and uncertainty. The rules are followed by sections on presentation of the data (free text vs. controlled fields) and on the relationship between the work record and authority record. Each entry closes with sample work records and associated authority records.

Part 2: Entry 1, object naming

Object Naming includes two elements: Work Type and Title. Work Type identifies the work or works being cataloged and establishes the logical focus of the record. Work Type is usually based on physical form (e.g., statuette, hanging scroll, skyscraper), function (e.g., storage jar, presentation drawing, cathedral), medium or technique (e.g., engraving, watercolor, mosaic), or content (e.g., manuscript, sampler). Work Type, which is required, is recorded in a repeatable, controlled vocabulary field. In the case of multiple Work Types, one should be flagged as preferred. Work Type terms appear in the singular, unless the record describes a group of items, in which case the plural form is used.

The Title element comprises titles, identifying phrases, or names given to a work. Object titles take many forms: owner's titles (e.g., Wrigley Building), creator's titles (e.g., Hanging Spider), inscribed titles, titles referring to the owner, location, or history of the work (e.g., British Museum Harley 2788 or Bayeux Tapestry), and descriptive titles. Descriptive titles may refer to historical or religious subjects (e.g., Allegory of Music), works, places, or figures (e.g., Studies of a Female Nude); if the work is nonrepresentative, the title may simply repeat the work type (e.g., Silver Chocolate Pot). As the examples illustrate, CCO follows museum documentation practice rather than library cataloging rules by recommending the capitalization of all significant words in titles.

Unlike printed books and journal articles, many works of art or architecture are not self-describing. Catalogers must look for titles beyond the work; when no title can be found, the cataloger must construct one that indicates what the work is or what it depicts. CCO instructs catalogers to record all significant titles associated with the work, and to flag one title as preferred. A Title Type (e.g., preferred, inscribed, repository), taken from a controlled list, should be supplied for every title.

Part 2: Entry 2, creator information

Creator Information includes the name and role of every "individual, group of individuals, corporate body, cultural group, or other entity that contributed to creating, designing, producing, manufacturing, or altering the work."[15] An art or cultural work may be produced by multiple creators performing multiple roles, all of which should be recorded.

Creator names and roles are required. Since works of art signed by the artist are the exception rather than the rule, CCO makes provision for recording the source on which the attribution is based, and the degree of certainty (e.g., probable, doubtful, etc.) Possible sources include the work itself, stylistic analysis, traditional ascriptions, inventories, or other evidence. Former attributions should also be recorded, since art information is extremely fluid, and users may seek a work under a previous attribution.

CCO's instructions for recording information about unknown creators are based on art historical practice, which has developed an elaborate, nuanced terminology for unknown creators. Sometimes a work of art can be assigned to an anonymous creator, that is, "one whose hand is identified and whose oeuvre is established, but whose name is not known (for example, Master of The Dido Panels)" (p. 91).[10] When no creator can be identified, but the style of the work suggests a relationship between the work and a known artist or group of artists, art historians express gradations of certainty by combining the known artist's name with a qualifier: "School of Rembrandt" or "Follower of Hokusai." If the work cannot be associated with any known artist, it should be attributed to a nationality or a culture: "Unknown, French" or "Unknown, Maya."

CCO recommends the use of standardized forms of creator names and roles. It provides a list of useful sources for names and role types as well as guidelines for formulating names for indexing and for display. For indexing purposes the inverted form of the name, followed by the role, is used. For displays, which in museum settings customarily contain brief biographical information about the creator, CCO recommends including the creator's name, nationality, birth and death dates, and role(s) in natural language order (e.g., sculpted by . . .).

Part 2: Entry 3, physical characteristics

Elements discussed in Physical Characteristics include Measurements, Materials and Techniques, State and Edition, and Additional Physical Characteristics, such as inscriptions and facture. CCO offers detailed guidance on recording the physical characteristics of the work types likely to be found in collections of art and cultural objects. Since these include paintings, drawings and watercolors, prints, sculpture and other three-dimensional works, books and manuscripts, furniture and architectural detail, ceramics and glass works, jewelry and utilitarian works, architecture, textiles and clothing, performance art and installations, film and video, and electronic and digital media, it is not surprising that Entry 3 is by far the longest entry in Part 2. The instructions in this entry are particularly helpful to library catalogers, who are unlikely to think of recording characteristics such as weight (for coins or megalithic monuments), size (for articles of clothing), or shape (for an oval painting). CCO recommends that the amount of detail be appropriate to an institution's needs: museums and other repositories that manage collections of physical objects will require more detailed descriptions than visual resources collections, which manage only the visual surrogates.

Measurement is a required element. Measurement types and units vary, depending on the nature of the object. CCO provides instructions on recording a bewildering variety of different types of measurement, including height and width, depth, diameter and circumference, shape, weight, volume and area, size, format, running time, scale, and structural dimensions. Measurements should be recorded in both a controlled field (to facilitate machine processing) and a user-friendly free-text display field. Here is an example for a carved gem:

Measurements display: 31 mm (1 1/8 inch) (diameter), 7.32 g (.2354 troy ounce)

Controlled fields:

Value: 31; Unit: mm; Type: diameter

Value: 7.32; Unit: gram; Type: weight (p. 113)[10]

The Materials and Techniques element, which is also required, includes information about the creation processes (engraving, painting, photography), media (ink, oil paint), and support (paper, canvas, marble) of the work. The State and Edition element is used for works produced in multiples, such as prints (e.g., first of three states), or books (e.g., 2nd edition). The Additional Physical Characteristics element comprises features such as inscriptions and markings and facture. CCO briefly discusses condition and examination history and conservation history, but refers users to fuller treatment of these topics in Categories for the Description of Works of Art.

Part 2: Entry 4, stylistic, cultural, and chronological information

The data elements covered in Entry 4 have little in common with library descriptive cataloging standards. Style and culture have no real parallel in library cataloging, but are extremely important for cultural materials, since they provide a way to study a work in the context of other works created in the same style or in the same culture. The chronological information covered by CCO pertains to the creation, revision, and destruction of physical objects, while library cataloging focuses on the publication and copyright dates of manifestations of works.

CCO defines Style as the element that identifies "the named, defined style, historical or artistic period, movement, group, or school whose characteristics are represented in the work being cataloged" (p. 156).[10] Stylistic terms may be based on a technique (Red-Figure) or on an artistic movement (Surrealist), or they may be related to a specific chronological period (Ming Dynasty, Renaissance). Culture is defined as the element that contains "the name of the culture, people, or nationality from which the work originated" (p. 157).[10] Chronological information refers to "the date or range of dates associated with the creation, design, production, presentation, performance, construction, or alteration of the work or its components" (p. 157).[10] A date may be a single point in time or a range as broad as several thousand years.

CCO offers guidance on the choice of terms for style and culture, and provides lists of controlled vocabularies. Considerable space is devoted to the syntax and presentation of dates, especially uncertain and approximate dates. Most objects do not bear a date; those by known artists can sometimes be dated by internal or external evidence, or at least assigned to a date during the artist's known years of activity. Dating for works by unknown artists is largely done through stylistic analysis; since some styles are associated with chronological periods occupying hundreds or thousands of years, date spans are necessarily very broad.

Part 2: Entry 5, location and geography

CCO defines the Location and Geography element as covering four different categories of location associated with art and cultural works: Current Location, Creation Location, Discovery Location, and Former Locations. (Topical location information is recorded in the Subject element, discussed in Entry 6.) The Current Location of an object may consist solely of a geographic place name, or a combination of the name of the owning institution and its geographic location, e.g., Florence (Italy), Galleria degli Uffizi. CCO instructs catalogers to treat the accession or inventory numbers which museums use to identify objects as Current Location information. Although it may seem superfluous to include Current Location information in a repository's local catalog, it facilitates data exchange and retrieval in union catalogs or federated searches. If the Current Location is unknown, CCO instructs catalogers to record the last known location.

The Creation Location of a work is often unknown. Since users often search for material by this parameter, the geographic place, nationality, or culture elements in authority records for persons and corporate bodies associated with the work are often substituted for Creation Location in queries. Discovery Location becomes especially meaningful when little else is known about a work or its creation. Former Locations may refer to a work's ownership and collecting history, or be related to its exhibition, loan, conservation, or historical context. CCO also provides a list of published sources for place names, repositories, and buildings.

Part 2: Entry 6, subject

CCO defines the Subject element as "an identification, description, or interpretation of what is depicted in and by a work or image" (p. 207).[10] This is not always easy to determine, and the difficulty is compounded by the fact that subject encompasses both what the work is about (its iconographical, narrative, thematic, or symbolic meaning), and what is actually depicted in the work (plants, animals, human figures, buildings, etc.) CCO recommends identifying both types of subject, at the level of detail appropriate to end users.

The universe of possible subjects is virtually unlimited. It may include "things, places, activities, abstract shapes, decorations, stories, and events from literature, mythology, religion, or history ... [p]hilosophical, theoretical, symbolic, and allegorical themes and concepts" (p. 207),[10] and human beings. The Subject element is required for all works. When a work is nonrepresentational, CCO suggests recording the form or function of the work as its subject; for example, the subject of a rug with no patterns or decoration would be "rug."

Subject information should be presented in two ways: as controlled indexing terms and as free-text description, which allows for interpretation as well as indicating ambiguity and uncertainty. A list of useful vocabularies, organized by type (e.g., event, fictional characters, plants, etc.) is provided, with the warning that subject indexing of art generally requires multiple vocabularies as well as locally supplied terms.

CCO recommends that the choice of singular or plural for subject terms reflect the number of entities depicted in the work: for example, if the work depicts one chair, the indexing term would be "chair," while "chairs" would be used for the depiction of several chairs. This is a departure from the practice of thesauri and controlled lists used in libraries, which customarily prefer the plural form of a common noun.

Part 2: Entry 7, class

The Class element is used to relate a specific work to other works with similar characteristics, such as "material, form, shape, function, region of origin, cultural context, or historical or stylistic period" (p. 235).[10] It is generally based on the organizational scheme of a particular repository or collection, and is intended for local use only. The Class element bears a resemblance to library classification numbers, in that it facilitates browsing through groupings of similar works. But unlike library classification numbers, the Class element is not based on subject, and it is not used to arrange physical collections, but to facilitate conceptual browsing.

CCO recommends that Class terminology be less specific than the terminology used for the Object Name element, since Class is intended to place the work in a hierarchy. For example, the Class element for a Brewster chair would be "furniture," or, if greater specificity is required, "chairs." Plural terms are preferred, since classifications represent groups of similar items, rather than an individual item. The Class element is the only CCO element for which a free-text version is not recommended; if desired, the controlled terms may be concatenated for display purposes. For example, the hierarchy of classification for a painted Chinese screen could be displayed as Asian art, furniture, and paintings.

Part 2: Entry 8, description

The Description element is a note that elucidates the content and context of a work. It takes the form of a concise and coherent essay-like text that elaborates on the subject, function, or significance of the work, comments on information in the other elements, and records uncertain or disputed points. Although Description is a free-text note, consistent style, grammar, and sentence structure are recommended. CCO encourages brevity, and prescribes natural word order and complete sentences. Description can be treated as a separate element within the record, or attached to the relevant fields. In either case, CCO recommends adding the source of information (usually a bibliographic citation that comes from a source authority record) and the location within the source (usually a page number). Repositories of art and cultural objects may need additional notes about the physical description, condition, conservation, or provenance of the work. Some of these notes are inappropriate for public display and may be suppressed from public view.

Part 2: Entry 9, view information

The View Information element describes how an object is depicted in an image. View Information helps users, many of whom have access to a work only through a surrogate, to understand the nature of the original. It also helps distinguish between different images of the same work. View Information appears only in the Image record, which is linked to the Work record for the object. The Image record also contains administrative and technical metadata such as the image control number, type (slide, photography, digital file), size or dimensions, format (Cibachrome, jpeg), source, and rights information. These fields are described briefly in Part 1, but CCO does not attempt to provide exhaustive coverage of this type of data.

View Description, Type, Subject, and Date are subelements of View Information. View Description, a freetext field, and View Type, a controlled vocabulary field, both describe the "spatial, chronological or contextual aspects of the work as captured in the image view" (p. 263).[10] These aspects include the portion or extent of the work depicted in the image, the range or position (distant or close-up), the angle or perspective, whether the image depicts the interior or exterior of a built work, cardinal directions for built works, environment, or lighting, and positional attributes for three-dimensional works (e.g., a profile view of a face).

View Subject describes subject matter specific to an image, for example, the subject of an image depicting a close-up of the hands of the Mona Lisa would be "hands" or "female hands." View Date includes any date or range of dates associated with the capture of the image, as opposed to the creation of the object, which is recorded in the Work record, or the generation of derivative images, which is treated as administrative data within the Image record. View Date information is particularly useful for works that have been damaged, lost, or altered, or for images taken during the production or creation of a work. Both subelements may be presented as free-text and as controlled fields.

Part 3, Authorities

Part 3 of CCO is devoted to authorities. CCO recommends using controlled vocabularies whenever possible, and documenting preferred terms and variants in authority files. The authorities should be linked to Work and Image records in order to facilitate cataloging, searching, and retrieval. Five different categories of authority are defined: source (a standardized bibliographic reference used for citing sources from which information is derived),[11] personal and corporate name, geographic place, concept, and subject. This categorization differs in two respects from the way authorities are treated in the library data format, MARC. Within MARC, concept is subsumed under subject, instead of being treated as a separate category, and an authority record is created for a work whenever a controlled access point is needed for the work. In CCO, authority records are created in the source authority only for titles of secondary material; the Work record functions

as the equivalent of an authority record for the object described in it.

General characteristics of the entries on authority files

The organization of the entry on authorities follows the same model as the entries on the CCO elements. Each entry begins with a definition of the authority type, discusses its special characteristics, gives guidance on dealing with ambiguity and uncertainty, discusses how the information should be organized, lists required elements, and provides suggestions for sources of controlled vocabulary. The "Editorial Rules" that follow cover some of the topics covered by "Cataloging Rules" in Part 2, such as capitalization, abbreviation, and preferred language; but also include guidance on the choice of preferred term, the inclusion of additional information appropriate to the authority type, and the provision of links based on associative and hierarchical relationships to other entities documented in the authority files. Each entry ends with a discussion of data presentation issues, such as indexing and display, and sample authority records.

CCO prescribes much more detail in authority records than is customary in the library world, where the rule is to include only as much information as is needed to identify the entity being described. Like the recommendation to include contextual and critical information about the object in the work record, this reflects the tendency in museums and visual resources collections to use the catalog as a vehicle for outreach and for dissemination of scholarly research. By contrast, librarians make a sharp distinction between the roles of the cataloger, the bibliographer, and the literary critic or historian, with the catalog serving chiefly as a pointer to the works themselves and to other sources of information about them.

Personal and Corporate Name Authority: CCO recommends creating personal and corporate name authority records for persons and corporate bodies associated with works of art and cultural objects. The relationship may take the form of creative responsibility, patronage, or current or former ownership, or it may be a topical relationship, when a person is depicted in a work. Authority records should be made for unknown creators identified in the Creator element as "unknown [culture or nationality]"; however, qualifiers such as "workshop of" or "school of," which denote an unknown creator associated with a known artist, should be recorded in the Work record instead of the authority record. CCO recommends using published sources for personal and corporate names, but provides guidance on how to formulate names not found in standard sources, and how to choose among variants when standard sources offer conflicting forms. Catalogers are instructed to record variant names, and two forms of the preferred name: one in natural order for display purposes, the other in inverted order for indexing. In addition to documenting authorized name forms, authority records should provide biographical and historical information such as birth and death dates and places, life roles, culture, race, ethnicity, and gender for persons, and start and end dates, national affiliation, functions, and location for corporate bodies.

Geographic Place Authority: Geographic Place Authorities include physical features, such as islands, rivers, and mountains, and administrative geographic entities or inhabited places, such as states, ecclesiastical governing bodies, and cities. Terms may be very broad, denoting whole continents or general regions such as the Middle East, or very narrow, denoting a street address within a city or a trench within an archaeological dig. Both current and historical places, such as archaeological sites, deserted settlements, and former nations are represented; however, fictional places such as Oz or Narnia must be entered in the Subject Authority file.

A list is provided of authoritative sources for geographic names. CCO also provides guidance on formulating place names not found in standard sources, and choosing a preferred form among variants. In addition to preferred and variant forms of the names, CCO requires recording place type (e.g., river, county) and broader context information. Broader context information consists of the next level of geographic subdivision; the broader context for Burgundy would be France. A thesaurus structure is recommended for the file, in order to allow retrieval and display by geographic hierarchies; this is particularly useful for research on art and cultural objects, since it allows contextual study on various hierarchical levels.

Concept Authority: Terms in the Concept authority file contain information about generic concepts, as opposed to proper nouns or names. Concept terms are used to describe the work type, material, processes used in creating the work, style, period, culture, creator and life roles, physical attributes of the object, and abstractions such as theoretical and critical concerns, ideologies, attitudes, and social or cultural movements. These terms appear mainly in nonsubject fields, but could be used to index subject elements of a work, for example, when a painting contains a depiction of a bronze urn.

Subject Authority: The subject authority file should be reserved for

> iconographical terminology, including proper names of literary, mythological, or religious characters or themes, historical events and themes, and any other terminology needed for subjects that falls outside the scope of the other three authorities

(p. 352). Terms from the other authority files may be used to index persons, corporate bodies, places, concepts, and objects depicted in works (Figs. 2 and 3).

ASSESSMENT OF CCO

Although CCO was developed by the VRA, it is aimed at and draws upon the expertise of numerous metadata communities in addition to visual resources professionals. Members of the visual resources and museum communities shared their understanding of the nature of the materials described, and their familiarity with existing descriptive practices. Librarians and archivists contributed their knowledge of their own communities' cataloging practices as well as insights derived from bibliographic and archival control: a principles-based approach to cataloging, the value of sharing data, and the importance of standardization and of controlled vocabularies. The confluence of these cataloging traditions makes CCO a more versatile guide, and optimizes its chances of being adopted as either a primary cataloging code or a complement to other codes.

CCO is likely to have the widest acceptance in the visual resources community, from which it originates, and which forms its core user group. The array of works covered by CCO—fine arts, cultural objects, works in the built environment—coincides with the works depicted in visual resources collections. Many of CCO's provisions reflect descriptive and organizational practices in visual resources cataloging, and the detailed guidance on database design reflects the do-it-yourself database environment in which most visual resources curators operate. Although individual descriptive practices in various visual resources collections may vary considerably, CCO might be the unifying tool the community needs to bring their descriptive practices closer together, foster best practices, and pave the way to a shared cataloging environment.

In the world of museum object documentation, there is an increasing awareness of the need for and advantages of conforming to standards. CCO draws heavily on descriptive practices in museums, and it is eminently suitable for use in a museum environment, though it would have to be supplemented by CDWA for certain types of administrative metadata. For museums electing to adopt a data content standard, CCO is the logical choice.

CCO will never become the main cataloging standard for the archives and library communities, since their collections contain too much material that falls outside its scope. But CCO could provide the necessary guidance for archivists faced with describing objects such as a writing tool, an article of clothing, or a coin, since *Describing Archives: A Content Standard* (DACS), the data content standard of the Society of American Archivists, deals chiefly with group- or collection-level cataloging, and focuses mainly on textual materials. Library catalogers faced with cataloging objects could also use CCO to complement AACR, the existing data content standard. Although CCO is not always compatible with AACR, it is seldom in open conflict with it. CCO does not dictate rules for formulating access points, leaving catalogers free

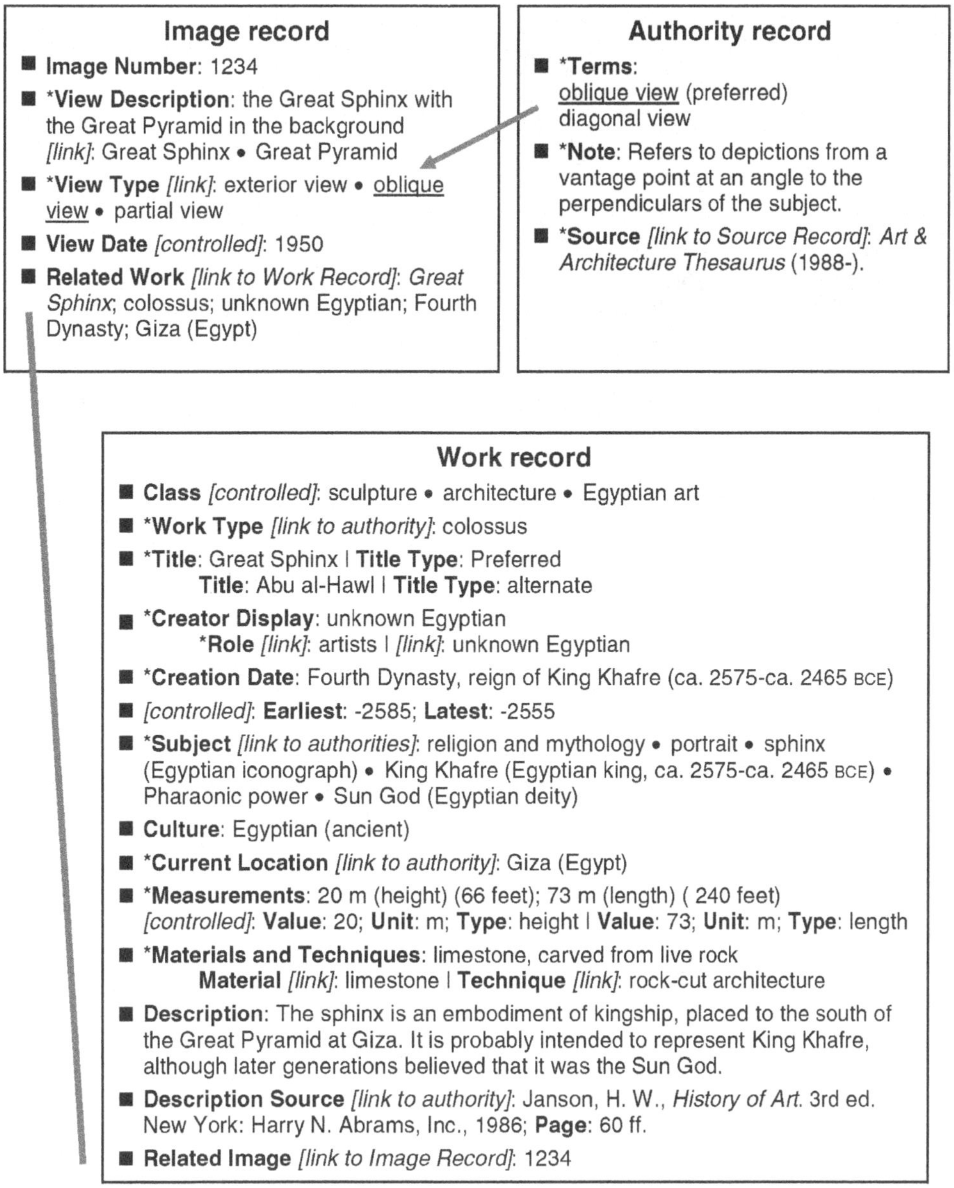

Image record

- ■ **Image Number**: 1234
- ■ ***View Description**: the Great Sphinx with the Great Pyramid in the background *[link]*: Great Sphinx • Great Pyramid
- ■ ***View Type** [link]*: exterior view • oblique view • partial view
- ■ **View Date** *[controlled]*: 1950
- ■ **Related Work** *[link to Work Record]*: *Great Sphinx*; colossus; unknown Egyptian; Fourth Dynasty; Giza (Egypt)

Authority record

- ■ ***Terms**:
  oblique view (preferred)
  diagonal view
- ■ ***Note**: Refers to depictions from a vantage point at an angle to the perpendiculars of the subject.
- ■ ***Source** [link to Source Record]*: *Art & Architecture Thesaurus* (1988-).

Work record

- ■ **Class** *[controlled]*: sculpture • architecture • Egyptian art
- ■ ***Work Type** [link to authority]*: colossus
- ■ ***Title**: Great Sphinx | **Title Type**: Preferred
  Title: Abu al-Hawl | **Title Type**: alternate
- ■ ***Creator Display**: unknown Egyptian
  ***Role** [link]*: artists | *[link]*: unknown Egyptian
- ■ ***Creation Date**: Fourth Dynasty, reign of King Khafre (ca. 2575-ca. 2465 BCE)
- ■ *[controlled]*: **Earliest**: -2585; **Latest**: -2555
- ■ ***Subject** [link to authorities]*: religion and mythology • portrait • sphinx (Egyptian iconograph) • King Khafre (Egyptian king, ca. 2575-ca. 2465 BCE) • Pharaonic power • Sun God (Egyptian deity)
- ■ **Culture**: Egyptian (ancient)
- ■ ***Current Location** [link to authority]*: Giza (Egypt)
- ■ ***Measurements**: 20 m (height) (66 feet); 73 m (length) (240 feet)
  [controlled]: **Value**: 20; **Unit**: m; **Type**: height | **Value**: 73; **Unit**: m; **Type**: length
- ■ ***Materials and Techniques**: limestone, carved from live rock
  Material *[link]*: limestone | **Technique** *[link]*: rock-cut architecture
- ■ **Description**: The sphinx is an embodiment of kingship, placed to the south of the Great Pyramid at Giza. It is probably intended to represent King Khafre, although later generations believed that it was the Sun God.
- ■ **Description Source** *[link to authority]*: Janson, H. W., *History of Art.* 3rd ed. New York: Harry N. Abrams, Inc., 1986; **Page**: 60 ff.
- ■ **Related Image** *[link to Image Record]*: 1234

Fig. 2 Image record linked to Work and Authority records: Egyptian monument. Required and recommended elements are marked with an asterisk.
Source: From Baca.[10] 276, Fig. 43.

to continue using AACR as their guide to formulating access points within object records, while incorporating the information recommended by CCO into free-text notes. The decision to remain format neutral means that CCO records can be accommodated in EAD, the data format used by archivists, and MARC, the data format used by librarians.

CCO's future prospects also depend on its sustainability. The VRA holds the copyright to CCO, and is responsible for supporting education and training in the use of the standard as well as its maintenance and dissemination. Even before its publication, the editorial team did yeoman's work publicizing the forthcoming standard, and

seeking comments; a section of the association's Web site was devoted to early drafts. After its release, VRA took a proactive role in arranging CCO-related presentations and workshops at conferences of the main professional organizations in the relevant metadata communities, publishing articles about the standard, and expanding the CCO Commons.[12] This area of the VRA Web site provides online support in the form of sample records, brief summaries of the rules, FAQs, training tools and presentations, and links to crosswalks, related data standards, and vocabularies. In late December 2006, two new committees were formed to provide a more formal structure for sustaining the code. The CCO Standing Committee is charged with

Fig. 3   The Great Sphinx at Giza, Egypt, with the Great Pyramid in the background.
Source: © 2002 Maria Oldal.

maintenance and dissemination, and the CCO Advisory Committee advises on education and works with the Standing Committee to encourage the use of this standard.

CONCLUSION

CCO fills a long-standing gap in the array of data content standards. Previous standards were developed largely for cataloging textual material; consequently, they did not address basic issues of cataloging art and cultural works, or provide guidance on describing the special characteristics of specific object types. CCO provides detailed guidelines for description, access, and subject cataloging of art and cultural materials and their visual surrogates. Clearly written, well-organized, and illustrated with numerous examples, it can be read with profit even by those who simply wish to learn more about the description of these materials. For information professionals charged with

creating descriptions of art and cultural materials, CCO seems likely to play the same role for object cataloging as AACR has long played for book cataloging: their basic cataloging tool.

REFERENCES

1. MARC. http://www.loc.gov/marc/ (accessed October 2007).
2. Elings, M.W.; Waibel, G. Metadata for all. VRA Bull. **2007**, *34*(1), 10–11.
3. http://cidoc.ics.forth.gr/official_release_cidoc.html.
4. http://www.getty.edu/research/conducting_research/standards/cdwa/.
5. http://cidoc.ics.forth.gr/docs/cidoc_crm_version_4.2.2.pdf Definition of the CIDOC conceptual reference model, version 4.2.2, August 2007, p. ii.
6. http://www.getty.edu/research/conducting_research/standards/cdwa/introduction.html.
7. http://www.vraweb.org/projects/vracore4/index.html.
8. http://www.loc.gov/ead/.
9. Lanzi, E.; McRae, L. Building through standards. VRA Bull. **2007**, *34*(1).
10. Baca, M. (Ed.) *Cataloging Cultural Objects: A Guide to Cultural Works and Their Images*; American Library Association: Chicago, IL, 2006; 3.
11. Unlike the other four authority types, each of which is discussed in a separate chapter in Part 3, the source authority is mentioned only in Part 1.
12. http://vraweb.org/ccoweb/cco/tools.html.

BIBLIOGRAPHY

1. *Cataloging Cultural Objects: A Guide to Cultural Works and Their Images*; American Library Association: Chicago, IL, 2006.
2. Creating shareable metadata: Cataloging Cultural Objects (CCO) and the standards landscape. Special issue of the VRA Bull. **2007**, *34*(1).

Catalogs and Cataloging: History *[ELIS Classic]*

Eugene R. Hanson
Shippensburg State College, Shippensburg, Pennsylvania, U.S.A.

Jay E. Daily
University of Pittsburgh, Pittsburgh, Pennsylvania, U.S.A.

Abstract

The catalog is the enduring means of access to information about the collection of a library. Without such information, use of a library would be limited to browsing the shelves in hopes of finding materials of interest. Hanson and Daily trace the development of catalogs from ancient times to the middle of the twentieth century. In parallel they also trace the history of cataloging rules and principles through the many codes of practice that have been developed over the years. The authors' speculation on what computerized catalogs *might* be like in the future, once developed, provides an interesting sidelight on the thinking of the era preceding the automation of catalogs.

—ELIS Classic, from 1970

INTRODUCTION

The story of catalogs and cataloging is only one phase of the broad panorama of library development. Traditionally the library has devoted its efforts to the acquisition, preservation, and promotion of graphic materials entailing the use of some system of bibliographic organization or control. Such organization is not unique to the library. History reveals the interrelationship between the activities of the bookseller, bibliographer, and librarian, all of whom sought to organize materials for effective location or retrieval. The methods employed are similar because they have a common goal, although they are inspired by relatively different purposes. Many attempts have been made to obtain some standardization of bibliographic entries among library catalogs, book trade publications, and published bibliographies. A substantial relationship exists between cataloging, designed to serve a definite library purpose, and bibliography, which has a more universal content and application. Cataloging in the United States has tended to be independent of book dealers' needs, while many European countries have coordinated bibliographic activities for centuries. Current efforts in international cataloging will no doubt serve to promote a closer working correlation of the two efforts. The Appendix lists the codes of cataloging rules in chronological order, their significance is the international character of standardization, still under way.

The library catalog is only one of the many forms of bibliography. It is generally defined as a list of books contained within a single library and is comprehensive rather than selective. In actual practice, although catalogs list the bulk of the monograph and at least part of the serial publications within a library, practices vary depending on the particular library. Jennette Hitchcock,[1] in a study conducted in 1939, estimated that subject headings could be omitted for four-fifths of the 90 different types of material. The results of her survey indicated that a significant number of libraries had followed this practice of omission. Librarians customarily tend to list only books in the catalog, influenced apparently by the traditional definition, although today library collections include a wide range of graphic materials. The reverence accorded the monograph perhaps was due in part to the dominance of the codex during the early periods; it was not seriously rivaled by other forms until the seventeenth century. The origin of learned societies as a result of the scholarly endeavors of the Renaissance led to the founding of the first scholarly periodicals in the 1660s. The increasing emphasis upon science encouraged the publication of serial publications, and by the eighteenth century they were the principal vehicles for the dissemination of scientific information. Other disciplines and agencies readily adopted the new form; this led to the proliferation of government documents, proceedings of Congresses, annual reports, and popular magazines evident during the nineteenth century and reaching an all-time high by the midpoint of the twentieth century. Libraries, with their roots planted in the humanistic spirit of the past, failed to respond sufficiently and rapidly enough to the growing variety and numbers of publications outside the realm of the monograph, and proved inadequate to fulfill the expected industrial and governmental needs that now tended to dominate the national scene. As a result, specialized groups became documentalists or information scientists in much the same way that librarianship and bibliography had separated years ago. The relationships were strong, but the methods and purposes varied to the point that each considered itself a separate discipline.

Encyclopedia of Library and Information Sciences, Fourth Edition DOI: 10.1081/E-ELIS4-120008972

The movement to gain bibliographic control of serials has traditionally been of secondary concern to most librarians, although the efforts of Poole, Cutter, and Billings indicated a growing awareness, which has continued to develop since their time. The number of periodical indexes from the nineteenth to the twentieth centuries attested to their dominant position in the bibliographic structure, even though librarians were confident that less effort was necessary and that bibliographic accuracy could be sacrificed in favor of more rapid processing.

The influence of the bibliographer on library cataloging was apparent as the position of librarian was generally relegated to a scholar or a man of letters. The librarian sought to organize the materials in a manner suitable to his needs or those of his immediate associates, without particular regard for ease of accessibility—this would come during the later years when the library was eventually recognized as an educational tool. With the rise of a pragmatic philosophy of education there came the rise of the librarian schooled in the technical aspects of practical organization rather than in bibliographical theories. The preparation of the catalog by the late nineteenth and early twentieth centuries ceased to be an immediate undertaking of the library administrator and was relegated to practitioners who were dependent upon codes and traditions rather than results. The problem, however, shortly became a concern of the total library, for the rising costs of cataloging forced both administrators and catalogers to reexamine their methods and question the need for bibliographic detail, with the hope of relying more upon the other available bibliographic tools. A period of reevaluation and technological change has brought about an increasingly pragmatic approach that attempts to fulfill the needs of the versatile user while minimizing the expense of processing time and effort.

The process of cataloging, in its narrowest sense, is the compilation of headings and bibliographic descriptions for use in the catalog. This could, perhaps, be considered the work of a pragmatic bibliographer, although catalogers are beginning to find other ways of determining the amount and kind of bibliographic descriptions necessary. In a broad sense the process encompasses descriptive cataloging that may include, in addition to bibliographic descriptions, the choice and form of author headings and subject cataloging, which results in the assignment of classification numbers and subject headings. Catalogs may be distinguished as to purpose by such designations as public catalog, which serves the patron; official catalog, which serves the cataloging staff; and union catalog, which is a list of holdings of many libraries. Format or physical form is also used as a basis of describing the catalog with the most common being card, printed book, sheaf (slip with loose leaf binder), guard book (slips mounted in a special book), computer, and visible file. The arrangement of the catalog is a third consideration. The three most popular approaches are the

dictionary, which files authors, titles, subjects, and references in one alphabet; the divided catalog, which separates some of these headings; and the classified, which utilizes a systematic arrangement of subject entries supplemented by author, subject, and title indexes in alphabetical order. Other less frequently encountered variations are alphabetico-classed for subject headings, a combination of the alphabetico-classed and the dictionary catalog, and a number of single or combined arrangements of subject alphabetical and/or author and name catalogs. To this may be added a wide variety of variations of the divided dictionary catalog based on a horizontal (chronological) arrangement as well as vertical (type of entry) arrangement resulting in a separation of subject headings from author and/or title. Other combinations are possible with the printed book catalog serving as a supplement to the card catalog or vice versa. The correlation of shelf list and/or bibliographies with a printed book or card catalog present other possibilities.

The functions of the early catalog were comparatively simple, serving as an inventory list with progressive patterns of arrangement based on the order of accession, chronologically by date of publication or period of author. From these evolved a wide variety of approaches and an expansion of the inventory idea to include retrieval. The subject catalog, which employs a system of conceptual terms to depict the content of the material, has been the major outcome of centuries of development. The derivation of subject terms or headings may be dependent upon the title or content of the book and may be standardized through the use of a classification scheme or a specially prepared list. Cutter believed that

the ideal catalog would give under every subject its complete bibliography, not only mentioning all the monographs on the subject, but all works which in any way illustrate it, including all parts of books, magazine articles, and the best encyclopedias that treat of it; in short, the catalog would lay out just that course of reading which a man who thoroughly studied the subject, with a view not only to learn it, but to master the history of its treatment by others, would be obliged to pass through.[2]

He continued by admonishing that "this can rarely be done because it is beyond the ability of librarians and the means of libraries." In addition, in *Rules for a Dictionary Catalog*, Cutter contended that the purpose or objects of the catalog were as follows:[3]

1. To enable a person to find a book of which either is known: author, title, or subject.
2. To show what the library has by a given author, subject, or in a given kind of literature.
3. To assist in the choice of a book: as to its edition (bibliographically) or as to its character (literary or topical).

These were restated in the *International Conference on Cataloguing Principles* of the International Federation of Library Associations as follows:[4]

Functions of the catalog. The catalog should be an efficient instrument for ascertaining:

2.1   whether the library contains a particular book specified by
      (a)   its author and title, or
      (b)   if the author is not named in the book, its title alone, or
      (c)   if author and title are inappropriate or insufficient for identification, a suitable substitute for the title; and
2.2   (a)   which works by a particular author and
      (b)   which editions of a particular work are in a library.

The inventory list functioned as a catalog and only later developed into a retrieval device that became probably the most highly organized part of an interrelated bibliographic network. The expanding number of points of access in the catalog indicates the comprehensive approach now possible. As subject terminology is perfected and mechanized methods are developed and applied, new dimensions will further expand the catalog until the spectrum of organized knowledge will rest upon a combination of the total bibliographic force, not just one phase.

The catalog serves as the key to the functions of a library and is a communicative device based upon a long process of social habits, designed to provide methodical and effectual access to graphic materials.[5] Insight into the present practices can best be achieved by a survey of the catalogs of the past with particular attention to the developing forms and purposes that are reflected in our modern catalogs. Our major attention will be directed to the English-speaking countries, particularly Great Britain through the eighteenth century and the United States during the nineteenth and twentieth centuries.

AGE OF INVENTORY

Ancient Times

Primitive methods of bibliographical control have existed since the beginning of the first libraries. The original approaches were primitive, although Norris alleged that "the catalogs in use in the seventeenth century B.C. were very similar to those which are now in use in the twentieth century A.D."[6] The archeological excavations at Assurbanipal (1668–626 B.C.) revealed that bibliographic information was recorded on tablets that were similar to a press guide or a very rudimentary shelf list. These tablets served as a crude location device by recording title (occasionally

with opening words), number of tablets, number of lines, distinct subdivisions, and a location or classification symbol.[7] A similar method was employed at Edfu (200–300 B.C.), where a list of books was reputed to have been engraved on the wall.

The Alexandria Library supposedly had an extensive catalog compiled by Callimachus in the form of *Pinakes* in 250 B.C. There is, however, some element of doubt whether this was actually a catalog of the Alexandrian Library or merely a bibliography compiled by the celebrated first cataloger. Norris suggested the possibility that Hermippus, an assistant to Callimachus, may have actually compiled the catalog in 220 B.C.[6] It was described as a classified catalog complete in 120 books, but very few fragments exist.

Witty was able to trace only about five true fragments, which were in reality only quotations from the original. The other conjectured remnants were found to be "oblique references" by ancient authors to the bibliographical work of Callimachus.[8] The term *Pinakes* (singular: *Panax*) was first used by the Greeks to indicate the tablets placed above the library press that served as a guide to its content and later denoted a catalog.[8] The actual title was "Tables of those who were outstanding in every phase of culture and their writings—in 120 books."[8] The fragments reveal a newsy biobibliography of the works of the period with information more applicable for a biographical work than a catalog. Bibliographical information was comprised of a stoichiometric note (number of lines in text) and probably the first words of a work. The entries were subdivided by author or by chronological order.

The primal catalogs through the height of Greek civilization can be conjectured as quasiclassified with a broad subject and form arrangement that resembled an embryonic shelf list. The title concept was not firmly established so that opening words of text were of great importance and were always employed. The author was frequently cited without further reference, a practice that did not cause confusion in view of the paucity of works. As a result one of the most unique contributions of the Greeks may have been the first use of the author concept, for the traditional practice of the Orient has been under title.[9] The Tripitaka, the source of Buddhist scriptures, was organized only by title.

The Roman period was marked by scanty information regarding catalogs and cataloging. Public and private libraries were common during this period, depending largely upon the works of the Greeks, which were the foundation of Roman culture. Rolls were generally separated by Latin and Greek with general subject divisions used within both categories, and probably an attempt was made to retain all the works of a single author together under the relevant subjects. Two varieties of catalogs, the classified and the bibliographical lists, were prevalent with the former based on shelf arrangement and the latter seeking continuity through authors. Both ordinarily included titles and/or first lines, number of lines in work, and frequently appended biographical information. It was clear that the Romans continued the precedence as established by Callimachus adding nothing new to the art.[7] The beginnings of Christianity brought little change to the Roman conceptions of the library for the first seven centuries, except the addition of new works, and works of the church fathers supplementing or even supplanting the authors and philosophers of Greece and Rome.[10] Gradually, however, public or temple libraries began to decline, especially after the third century when Christianity became the state religion. In A.D. 336 with Constantinople now the center of the Roman empire, the libraries of Rome were rivaled by the collections assembled by a succession of emperors who as a whole supported libraries and scholarship until the conquest by the Turks in 1453. The great libraries of the empire slowly were dispersed or suffered the ravages of neglect. Few extant accounts actually depict the dispersal of the manuscripts and the razing of the temple structures.

Middle Ages: Early Period (Fifth Through Eleventh Centuries)

The fall of Rome in the sixth century brought about a decline in scholarship with the deliberate destruction and dispersion of the public or temple libraries as well as many private collections. The next 10 centuries for the libraries of the Western world would be characterized by small collections of surprisingly similar manuscripts in the many monasteries established in this period. The austere life of the monastic orders was not entirely new; the tradition existed among the Essenes during the early days of the Christian period. The place of books in the monastery was important, for monks were admonished to read, meditate, and copy for the glory of the afterlife. One of the outstanding monastic clerics to whom libraries owe a debt was Cassiodorus,[11] who after serving in public life retired and founded a monastery at Vivarium in Benevento (southern Italy). His respect for learning was clearly reflected in his famous *Institutiones*, which served as a scholarly model for the many orders and furnished an annotated guide to what he considered valuable.

These monasteries were the major instruments of education, such as it was, and were the primary vehicles in the preservation and production of books. The need for library catalogs, however, was limited during this early period, with efforts directed only toward an inventory record. One of the most elementary type was a list of books given by Gregory to the church of Saint Clements. It consisted of a marble tablet inscribed with an introduction or prayer and a few treasured Biblical works.[12] The poetical catalog composed by Alcuin of York in the eighth century was a unique form that was in reality a list of famous authors or a bibliography, although it was reputed by some to be a catalog of the York monastery. Another simple listing of

this period was Saint Augustine's *De Trinitate*. This was merely a list of works transcribed on the final flyleaf of a book.[9] Emperor Louis the Pious (814–840) actuated the compilation of catalogs when he decreed that monasteries and cathedrals should make a list of all the books they possessed.[13] These early catalogs or inventory lists were thus fashioned by the immediate need for a list of material possessions. The books were generally arranged not by author but by the importance of the work, with precedence given to the Bible and other religious works and with secular works placed last. In addition, these terse lists were not indicative of the full contents of the works included, because it was common practice during this period to bind several works by the same author, or treatises by various authors but on similar subjects, within one cover as an economy measure. Thus a small collection of 10 volumes may actually contain nearly double this number of distinct works. The purpose of the list was to identify the book rather than analyze the contents of the physical volumes. Fortunately, Armarians realized the value of a more complete analysis of at least the distinct works. Several catalogs of the ninth century provided a listing of the works within each volume and the "number of volumes or rolls in which each work was contained."[9]

One outstanding literary work, *The Myriobiblion*, is indicative of the bibliographic contribution of the period. It was compiled ca. A.D. 842–848 by Photius, patriarch of Constantinople. It bore a strong resemblance to the *Pinakes* of Callimachus and was a primitive but interesting review of approximately 280 works of the period with bibliographic, biographic, and critical information.[14] The Upper Rhineland monastery at Lorsch in the tenth century produced a more typical catalog in the following order: liturgical works, the Testaments, theological and patristic works, lives of the saints, and last poetry, with a few of the classic authors.[13] Catalog production between the ninth and eleventh centuries was suprisingly active. Gottlieb listed 24 catalogs from the ninth century, 17 from the tenth, and 30 from the eleventh.[15]

The period of the early monastic and cathedral library catalogs may be characterized as a period of rudimentary methods. The earliest catalogs were crude lists, frequently inscriptions, without apparent order or sequence, which later became parchment inventories placed near the book presses and further expanded into more distinctive works as the library grew. The manuscripts were arranged, or classified, by broad subjects. The most common order was: archives, scriptural texts and commentaries, constitutions, council and synodal proceedings, homilies and epistles of the fathers, lectionaries, and legends of martyrdom with secular literature frequently placed in a subsection divided by the seven liberal arts: grammar, rhetoric, logic, arithmetic, geometry, music, and astronomy.[13] This arrangement reflected a utilitarian as well as a philosophical aspect. As long as the collections were small the divisions were simple. Frequently, secondary arrangements were by order of acquisition or size. The widely varying catalogs of the early Christian period were most nearly like the modern shelf list and provided an inventory designed to facilitate record keeping while showing the location of the work.

Middle Ages: Late Period (Twelfth Through Fourteenth Centuries)

Twelfth century

Catalog arrangement of this century continued in the same casual manner. The extant portion of the 1158 catalog of the monastery at Prüfening indicated a chronological sequence for all books that were grouped after the Biblical works. The compiler was foresighted enough to provide space for the collection of later acquisitions.[13]

The Christchurch catalog, 1170, was the first to use a system of reference letters placed both within the catalog and the books.[16] The Lincoln Cathedral Library Catalog of ca. 1200 continued the practice of including opening words as well as the title and added another feature, an introduction.[6]

Although only a few catalogs have been discussed, the twelfth century was characterized by a large number produced on the continent with Gottlieb listing 62 examples.[15] The typical catalog, however, remained an inventory list compiled with a general lack of system on a two-column parchment page. The broad subject arrangement was the accepted pattern with titles generally subarranged in chronological order rather than alphabetical by author. Author's names served primarily as a means of identification with little attention given to form and accuracy. The information listed was extremely brief, composed of author's name and short title, frequently with the opening words of the work and occasional statements concerning physical conditions, color, or number of items in the volume. The addition of the beginning words of the text was necessary to aid in distinguishing anonymous works and works with identical or similar titles. As a whole the information included was so vague that it offered little aid outside the context of the individual library.

Thirteenth century

The thirteenth century found a continuation of the shelf or press arrangement with short titles and opening words. The Glastonbury catalog of 1247[6] employed a unique and remarkable classification. Books that were by obscure authors but yet valuable for subject information were placed under the subject. Those by well-known writers were placed under the author. This system, in effect, was an attempt to select an entry that would best serve the needs of the user. The beginnings of union catalogs can be traced to the *Registrum Librorum Angliae*, 1250–1296,

which was an unfinished attempt to record the holdings of 183 English monastic libraries.

The earliest information regarding the libraries of the universities came to light in the catalog of the Sorbonne at the University of Paris in 1289. It contained over 1017 Latin titles but only four in French, arranged by 10 major divisions: the seven liberal arts (or the trivium and quadrivium) plus theology, medicine, and law. Authors were arranged alphabetically within each division followed by the title and the beginning words of the text.[7]

Fourteenth century

The fourteenth century provided an abundance of examples although few new innovations. Subject arrangement was common; five of the seven catalogs described by Norris had this arrangement. The catalog of Christchurch, Canterbury, 1313–1331, was considered to be the first to adapt an alphabetical order under at least one subject heading, theology. In addition a system of press marks was present as well as an inept attempt to list the works of each volume.[6]

The Exeter Cathedral Library catalog of 1327 was an author catalog with only one subject heading. It listed the value of each book, as it was probably intended only for the inventory of church property.

The catalog of the Saint Martin's Priory at Dover of 1389 had an unusual three-part arrangement by location number. The first section was intended for the use of the librarian, consisting of a tabular shelf list; the second was a duplicate of the shelf list with enumeration of the individual works bound within each volume; and third was a crude alphabetical-analytical index designed to indicate the location of an individual treatise in a volume.[17] The addition of the author index to this inventory list added the dimension of a true catalog, which was not evident in many of the examples up to this time. The catalog of the Leicester Abbey in 1394 exhibited a similar characteristic with a double catalog of authors and subjects.[13]

The catalog of the Library of Meaux Abbey, 1396, was arranged by the location of the bookshelves, which were scattered about the abbey. It did have a more distinct feature, however, in its introductory remarks concerning the origins of the catalog; these were later to become an interesting addition to book catalogs as late as the nineteenth century.

The catalogs of the fourteenth century were the familiar inventory lists arranged by broad subjects with books assigned to a designated or fixed location on the shelves. In effect this was merely the classification of shelf space within the presses, which were marked as to content. This concept encouraged the use of press marks, which could readily be added to the books as an aid in reshelving. Each individual library devised a unique mark generally relying upon alphabetic characters and upon Roman and Arabic numbers. The Dover (1389) and Durham (1391) catalogs established the practice of recording the "opening words of the second leaf of each book," which was to become an almost universal method in the next few centuries.[16]

Modern Period

The fifteenth and sixteenth centuries were a period of sweeping sociological, economic, and cultural changes that reverberated throughout the whole social structure. The Reformation shifted the power from the old universal church to a wider range of authorities with secular organizations assuming more responsibility in many of the nations. In England, the decline of the monastic orders tended to shift the collections of books to the private, college, and university libraries, which was impelled by the suppression of the monasteries during the reign of Henry VIII, 1536–1539. The collegiate libraries were to suffer some of the same harassment in 1549 from the Commissioners of Edward VI, who sought to root out "superstitious literature." In spite of these difficulties the influence of the Renaissance on scholars, who were nurtured within the academic community, caused them to emphasize the collection and preservation of books as the mark of gentlemen and valuable assets for a nation. The beginning and rapid development of printing from movable type assured a wide distribution of multiple identical copies of a work, a technological advance hitherto unknown to the world. The expensive manuscript books with parchment pages, beautiful and unique, ceased to be the primary form of communication. Printed books were the beginning of a revolution with which bibliographic organization had to keep pace. No longer would the written word be controlled by a central authority that closely guarded the use and distribution of ideas. The existing few and soon numerous libraries, though still in monasteries, cathedrals, universities, and private palaces, began to acquire universality. The stagnation of the preceding centuries ended. The private libraries of the past had represented a broad range of tastes, but were limited in number due to the cost and paucity of the manuscript codices. The church had reluctantly retained the works of the ancients, primarily as a method of education rather than for their contribution to Christian ethics. The university libraries and expanding private libraries began to seek a wide representation of works and assumed the role of conveyors of human knowledge rather than the preserver of a few standard works. Leaders such as Naude and Dury recognized the value in retaining all types of works as the tools of the scholars and the links to the past. The printers and booksellers, albeit with large economic motivation, provided the substance of libraries as well as forging a major link in the bibliographic chain through the efforts of such giants as Maunsell. As the libraries developed, the methods of bibliographic organization slowly evolved despite poor communication, a lack of clear objectives and functions, minimal economic resources, traditionalism,

and the relegation of library usage to a selected few. By the end of the sixteenth century the dawn of the new era was at hand and blossomed fully in the next three centuries.

Fifteenth century

The beginning of the century brought the *Catalogus Scriptorum Ecclesiae* by John Boston, a monk at Bury Saint Edmunds. Apparently he intended to continue the *Registrum* of the previous century, as identical code numbers were employed in both.[18] He increased the list of authors' names from 85 to 700 and included additional libraries as well as biographical information.[17]

The catalog of the private library of Amplonius Ratinck de Berka, 1410–1412, which was later given to the University of Erfurt, represented one of the more carefully classified catalogs of the period. Arrangement was by broad subjects such as grammar, poetry, logic, rhetoric, mathematics, natural philosophy, metaphysics, moral philosophy, medicine, law, and theology, with the contents of each volume fully listed and frequently extending to 10 or more items.[19]

The collegiate catalog of Peterhouse Library, Cambridge, 1418, was arranged by the traditional subjects and indicated two distinct collections, one for reference, which consisted of chained books, and one for lending to the "fellows." Its unique feature lay in the use of the last word of the second folio in addition to the widely accepted practice of indicating the first words. This pattern was also followed by the Cambridge University Library catalog of 1424.[6]

The Vatican Library catalog of 1481 depicted the accepted practice of placing the books in bookcases by broad subject arrangement. The catalog was simply an inventory device to show the locations of the materials within the bookcases of the Latin, the Greek, and the Inner libraries, and the Bibliotheca Pontificia.[10]

The most outstanding catalog of this century was that of the Saint Augustine's Library of Canterbury, 1497. It was comprised of three parts: first, a location list indicating in tabular form the exact place where the books were located and/or the name of the borrower; second, an unfinished alphabetical listing of all books in the library with a reference to the page number of the catalog where the full entries and the press marks could be found; and third, the main section of the catalog.[6] The latter was a model of uniformity with the general title or that of the first treatise, the name of the donor, the contents (titles) of other works in the volume, the traditional first words of the second work, and the press mark.[17]

The alphabetical approach with its problem of interfiling was more common on the Continent than in England during this period. Several catalogs that originated in Austria and Germany revealed the efforts to achieve more logical points of access to the shelf arrangement. An alphabetical catchword index to the shelf list was formulated at an Austrian monastery at Aggsback; a list of authors, subject designations, and catch title anonymous works were employed as special indexes to the catalog at Melk Monastery in 1483; and dictionary-type catalogs with a multiple-entry approach through author and title catchword were reported at the monasteries of Rebdorf at Eichstaett and Aegidian at Nurënburg.[20]

The most obvious change during the fifteenth century was a break in the traditional bibliographic organization both within and outside the libraries. Generally, the university catalogs were not as well developed as those of the monasteries. The subject arrangement of the inventory was still the dominant order, but the finding list concept was slowly evolving through the addition of author indexes. Extent of description remained fairly constant with bibliographic comments at a minimum, but exceptions were evident in the Durham Catalog of 1416 which had such information as value, size, doubtful authorship, stolen books, and location.[6] Thompson reported that the earliest entry of the pages in a work appeared in 1465.[13] Press marks were used to some extent as in the fourteenth century while the use of the last word as well as the first of each treatise was an innovation. The Saint Augustine Catalog was perhaps the most outstanding product, with its analysis of the parts of volumes through the use of rather advanced cross references, which were given the status of entries.[18]

Before leaving this century some attention should be given to an important approach devised by Johann Tritheim, who began his bibliographic career with the reorganizing and cataloging of the German monastic library at Sponheim. While engaged in this undertaking, he apparently realized the vàlue of a bibliography of ecclesiastical writers, which he completed in 1494. The *Liber de scriptoribus ecclesiasticis* enumerated 277 works, recorded about 7000 books, and reflected a considerable amount of investigation.[19] The inclusion of an alphabetical index of authors, arranged by their Christian names, was appended to facilitate the use of the chronological arrangement and established a principle that was to continue as a bibliographical method for many centuries to come.[19] Thus recognition of multiple access to books was clearly emerging as standard bibliographic procedure with the finding list theory becoming a recognized element within the catalog.

Sixteenth century

The sixteenth century found a continuation of the concept of the inventory device. Some catalogs, such as Saint Martin's Priory of Dover, had gone beyond this by developing shelf lists and analytics. The value of analyzing each part of the physical volume was evident in many catalogs but was by no means universally accepted.

The entry had little resemblance to that of the modern catalog with only title and first words and perhaps last

words of each work. This, however, was to be modified somewhat during this century and substantially during the next as the printed book became relatively commonplace. Catalog production shifted from monasteries to collegiate and private collectors. The century was truly productive with some of the most positive influences for the catalog attributed to Gesner, Triflerus, and Maunsell. Their efforts stimulated a systematic approach rather than the individualistic methods of the past.

Only two monastic catalogs are of particular value during this century. First, the Syon catalog of 1526 was important because it was the first English catalog to incorporate the idea of Tritheim by including an alphabetical index of authors. It utilized a subject arrangement within the main section with letters of the alphabet denoting subjects. These were then combined with Arabic numbers, which represented accession numbers, to form a complete press mark. Donors and opening words of the second work in the volume are recorded as well as the traditional abbreviated entry. The second was the 1558 catalog of the library of the Bretton Monastery, which was the first to include in the entry the names of editors and translators.

One of the greatest contributions of this century, however, was made by Konrad Gesner, who in 1545 issued the first volume of a comprehensive international bibliographical dictionary entitled *Bibliotheca Universalis*. The work was divided into several distinct parts. First, the main section was comprised of a listing of all the Latin, Greek, and Hebrew authors that were known to the compiler. The arrangement was by the author's Christian name with an added "summary list" of author's names in inverted order.[19] The second volume was the *Pandectarum*, in which the works of the first volume were rearranged under 21 subject headings that were more extensive than ordinarily found in a typical library catalog up to this point; this represented a marked improvement. The scheme, however, gives the "...impression that it was drawn up empirically and then forced into a pseudo-logical system."[19] The use of copious subdivisions and an alphabetical index of headings were features that were truly remarkable. As an added bit of information for the book collector, Gesner provided instructions for arranging books in a library. He suggested that books be divided by size and then by some order on the shelves. A catalog of books in shelf order and an alphabetical author index were considered sufficient, although a record by accession number with acquisition and value was also contributory. In addition to these suggestions he pointed out that his *Bibliotheca* could be readily used as a catalog to any library by the addition of press marks.

Additional support for a logically organized library catalog was expounded in 1560 in a manual published in Augsburg by Florian Treflerus, a Benedictine monk. He stressed the value of a catalog and suggested that five catalogs were desirable: first, one arranged alphabetically by the name of the author; second, one arranged in classed order or shelf list order; third, one serving as a subject index to the various contents of all books; fourth, an alphabetical index to the third; and fifth, one intended to list books held in reserve because of age or condition. He suggested a shelf mark comprised of a letter designation for size, color, and subject. The first two were represented by abbreviations, but the subject scheme was delineated by the first 17 letters of the alphabet.[6]

The last provocative work of this century was done by Andrew Maunsell, a London bookseller who in 1595 compiled a bibliography of books published in English. He adopted new methods and shunned the examples of "the learned men that have written Latine Catalogues."[21] A dictionary arrangement was followed with a single alphabet of authors, limited added entries such as translators, and subject words. Individual entries were arranged alphabetically by author's surname rather than the Christian name, and the anonymous works were entered under title, subject, or sometimes both if it would facilitate location. When subject was used it was as a "see" reference to the main entry. This practice was continued in library catalogs and encouraged the custom of distinguishing the main entry. All Bibles or books of the Bible were listed together under the designation Bible to facilitate their location and no doubt influenced later use of uniform headings. The form of entry had a completeness of description lacking in most earlier library catalogs. It was composed of author's names, translator if present, sufficient name of printer or bookseller, imprint date, and type of format.

It is readily seen that this century witnessed great strides in bibliographical organization, with two of the most important contributions emanating from outside the library itself. The two library catalogs described were significant since they incorporated some of the concepts that were later suggested by Treflerus, Gesner, and Maunsell. Gesner and Treflerus clearly championed the need for several points of access through multiple indexes. Maunsell's direct and simple approach to the problems of entry word, arrangement, anonymous works, and completeness of description would have a decided influence upon the codes of the succeeding centuries. As the century closed it was clear that a recognition of the need for uniformity and a systematic approach to catalogs and cataloging would soon be a reality rather than just the vague promise of a few erudite bibliographers.

AGE OF THE FINDING LIST

Modern Period

Seventeenth century

The dawn of the seventeenth century found a continued lack of understanding regarding the nature and purpose of library cataloging. The familiar concepts persisted with shelf arrangement designed for administrative reasons rather than the needs of the patrons. The classification by size as well as subject gained in popularity. The finding list idea, however, was clearly established with author indexes widely advocated. The development of the printed catalog was a highlight of this century. The old manuscript catalog had been laboriously produced while the new lists lent themselves to extensive production if the need should arise.

The number of libraries continued to increase, but cataloging methods changed only slightly although there seemed to be some standardization during the first quarter of the century.[23] The gulf between the medieval and the modern methods of cataloging could be discerned in the precocious instructions given by Naude, Dury, Baillet, and the Bodleian Catalogue of 1674. The first general library catalog that served primarily as a finding list was the Bodleian Catalogue of 1620. The combined efforts of Thomas James and Sir Thomas Bodley produced a catalog that was arranged by the author's surnames and catchword titles for anonymous works. The functions of the catalog had finally come to the forefront, although it was in an unintentional manner. Bibliographers would continue to extend the points of access that would be valuable to students and scholars. The major philosophical issues involved in catalog construction were in the offing and only in the nineteenth century were they explored more fully.

The Bodleian catalogs were one of the dominant influences of the seventeenth century and would continue to affect all succeeding study of cataloging procedures. The principal figure behind the reorganization of the Oxford University Library was Sir Thomas Bodley, a retired English diplomat, who dominated the cataloging efforts of Thomas James, the first librarian. The initial printed catalog of 1605 was primarily a shelf list of printed books and manuscripts. The arrangement was typical of the sixteenth century, with groupings by the four academic disciplines of theology, medicine, law, and art. Size separated the books further with the folios chained to the reading desks and the quartos and octavos shelved in special locked cases. Individual entries were listed under subjects, alphabetically by the author when known. Anonymous and pseudononymous works were placed under the most significant word of the title or else under the first word. The entry was somewhat more complete, with author's name in natural order, title, place, date, size, and location, but lacking edition. To the main catalog was appended an alphabetical index of authors and lists of commentators. The original intent was to print the contents of a single shelf on one page, which would allow extra pages to be used as shelf guides. Recent additions were to be included within an appendix.[6]

In 1613 an alphabetical author catalog was compiled in manuscript form. It was never printed but rather formed the draft for the second catalog.

The 1620 catalog was a milestone in catalog arrangement, as it used a single sequence of authors' surnames (Christian name first), with anonymous works placed under the first or most striking word of the title. This in effect was our modern dictionary catalog in its embryonic stages without the benefit of uniform subject headings. The idea here, as in other earlier catalogs, was to provide a single entry for each book with the author considered the most logical approach. The anonymous works had created serious problems in other catalogs. Entries for them frequently were made under title, under form heading, or under the most striking word of the title. This catalog utilized the latter method, not in the sense of a systematic coverage of subject information but rather as an attempt to establish some assemblage of materials lacking authors by subject words or forms that might be remembered by the catalog user. The titles of the ancient works had never been a unique form of identification and even at this time were considered of doubtful value in their natural order. The catchword seemed to be the logical way to supplement the author list by serving to group materials of a like nature (form or subject) rather than to scatter them by title. Other practices were separation of author's name from title, books by several authors entered under each name, cross references used, and initial or pseudonym constituted an anonymous work.

The last Bodleian catalog of the century was issued in 1674 under the direction of Thomas Hyde; it kept the alphabetical sequence of authors with catch titles for anonymous works as well as making provisions for the assembling of literary units. The preface contained a number of rules that were the most innovative cataloging procedures formulated until the middle of the nineteenth century. Many of the rules had been previously followed in the earlier Bodleian catalogs, but now the rules for main entry clearly supported three continuing concepts. First, the literary unit principle was expressed by the fact that only one form of the author's name was selected for use in the catalog. Second, an assumed name with cross references was used if the author's name was not given. Translations were entered under original author. Finally, anonymous works were entered in one of four ways: 1) under selected form headings for widely used works, 2) under place or edition for less used works, 3) under biography referred to for biography, and 4) under the most striking or subject word of title.[6] The recognition and assemblage of authors known by different names, under a single form, constituted the first principle of modern cataloging.[22]

The catalog of the Lumley collection, compiled by Anthony Alcock in 1609, was a typical private library compilation. It was comprised basically of a classed catalog of 2500 printed books and 400 manuscripts that were arranged within eight classes ranging from theology to music, to which was appended an alphabetical index of authors.[23]

The catalog of the Sion College Library, 1650, was one of the early dictionary catalogs with names of authors and subjects filed in a single alphabet. Subject headings and authors' surnames were printed in italics, while guide letters were placed at the top of each column of a two-column page with press marks indicating press, shelf, and order of books on the shelf. The general practice of a single entry per book prevailed, with entry either under author or under subject for anonymous works, as used in the Bodleian Catalogue of 1620.[6]

In addition to the catalogs cited, the status of cataloging was depicted through the contribution of five authors of the period. Gabriel Naude included valuable hints to the librarian regarding the catalog in his *Instructions. . . .*[24] He commented on the desirability of the catalog and suggested the compilation of two: the first, arranged according to classes (morals, sciences, and devotion) and the faculties (theology, physics, law, mathematics, humanities, etc.) with subdivisions; and the second, an alphabetical author catalog.[24] He pointed out the need for a miscellaneous class, criticized the single access of some catalogs, and exalted the superiority of the systematic arrangement over the fixed location.

John Dury, a protestant clergyman and later Royal Librarian, in 1650 published in England a small pamphlet devoted to library economy. He contended that "the proper charge then of the Honorarie Libraric Keeper in an Universitie should bee thought upon, and the end of the Imploiment in my conception, is to keep the publick stock of learning which is in Books and Manuscripts, to increas it, and to propose it to others in the waie which may bee most useful unto all. . . ."[25] A catalog was the first step. It should be divided by sciences (subject or classes) and languages. He concluded that space on the shelves and in the printed catalog should allow for the "increase of number" and that a reference to the location of the book on the shelves be included. He spoke of the printed catalog as though it were commonplace and called for an annual supplement compiled for use in the library and "made common to those that are abroad," through printing every 3 years. He suggested other methods such as acquisition by exchange, faculty opinions in selection and cataloging, and the selective cataloging of doubtful publications through the use of an alphabetical author catalog with notes regarding subject. Treflerus in 1560 had suggested a similar list but limited it to books that had been superseded or that were worn.

Adrien Barillet, a French librarian and teacher, achieved two distinctions in the field of cataloging: first, the compilation of a catalog in 1682 of the library of Chretien-Francois de Lamoignon with an alphabetical subject index; and second, the formulation of a set of rules for the multientry, alphabetical catalog (subjects and titles for anonymous works). He advocated the use of major subject categories for shelf arrangement that could be further subdivided by chronological, geographic, or more minute subjects; upheld extensive use of cross references; lamented the traditional single-dimensional approach of the present shelf arrangements as being too restrictive; championed the subject index as the key to the collection through a multidimensional approach; supported the need for an alphabetical index of authors' surnames; and differentiated between the entry of biographical works under specific name or subject.[20] In general, his remarks exhibited a firm grasp of the value of the catalog for the location of all materials of the library.

Near the end of the century another provocative publication appeared on the construction of the library catalog. The author was a Danish book collector by the name of Frederic de Rostgaard. His somewhat complicated arrangement of a double page, divided into columns, which designated size and the chronological arrangement of entries within each column with accession number and a letter to designate the subject, provided a varying approach to the grouping of books. He also included instructions for an alphabetical index of subjects and authors arranged by surname with reference to size, accession number, and subject.

The seventeenth century was one of growth, experimentation, and expression. The catalog had progressed to the finding-list stage, but still was beset by an absence of universally accepted principles although the many manuals indicated a more systematic attempt. Cross references were now accepted practice and analytical entries were used, especially in the alphabetical subject catalogs as suggested by Baillet. The imprint was now a standard item of the catalog entry, although still limited to place and date. That the subject arrangement was becoming much more refined was due in part to the publication of Bacon's system of classification of human knowledge. The classification that had been used for centuries in the catalogs seemed necessitated by the shelf arrangement rather than by a proven need for a classified catalog forming a systematic arrangement of subjects to provide access to collections. Classification continued to play a more important role as knowledge became more systematized. The value of the subject and author indexes as a means of expanding the approach to the single-dimension shelf arrangement was recognized and discussed by the theorists of the period, but they continued to remain as adjuncts rather than an essential part of the catalog. The use of catchword titles for anonymous works added a limited subject dimension to the catalog, which would progress beyond its original intent. The use of the surname had largely replaced the archaic practice of entry by Christian name, although some vestige of the former remained with the Christian name frequently recorded before the surname. The question of arrangement was still in doubt, with a full range of possibilities. For example, the catalog of the Norwich City Library of 1658–1883 illustrated the shifting trends in concepts of arrangement. The initial catalog followed the subject method but shifted to the author approach in the eighteenth century, then adopted the division by language and size, and finally returned again to the author catalog in

the nineteenth century.[6] In addition to the question of arrangement, the use of the original language of the book for title, the treatment and analysis of composite works, indication of size, inclusion of eminent printer with date and place, designation of first edition or best edition, assemblage of different editions of every author together in chronological order, and designation of the value of the book were all problems that confronted the cataloger of the century according to Humphrey Wanley, an assistant librarian at the Bodleian.[6] Many problems would be answered only to be replaced by more perplexing ones brought on by an expanding society; however, the question of arrangement would persist to the present day. The cataloging process slowly developed from the evolutionary examples and rudimentary codes of this century to the more theoretical and logical efforts of the eighteenth and nineteenth centuries.

Eighteenth century

The eighteenth century was a time of stabilization rather than one of innovation. The expanding university and private collections, augmented by a few municipal libraries, grew in size but only slightly in organizational methods. The French code of 1791, which was the first national code, represented the only major contribution of the century toward a solidification of cataloging procedures. The arrangement of the catalog was still dominately by subject or by size, with the author approach gaining since the publication of the Bodleian of 1620. The spread of new ideas was slow as each individual library approached the preparation of a catalog greatly restricted by local conditions and attitudes. The printed catalog that became so abundant after the seventeenth century did allow for a distribution of examples highly susceptible to the apprenticeship status of the early bibliographers, who were ordinarily not too concerned with theory.

The inventory or shelf list approach had slowly yielded to a more erudite product, the catalog, although the persistent concern for books on the shelves, not the indexing of knowledge, inhibited the process. Some of the methods of classification developed beyond the simple arrangements of the past and expanded the major classes and subdivisions. The Philadelphia Library Company of 1789 exploited the suggestion of Naude, Baillet, and Dury by classifying under three major divisions and 31 classes, which were then subdivided by size. The purely artificial arrangement by size was frequently used during the seventeenth and eighteenth centuries in accord with the suggestions of Gesner and Rostgaard, and perpetuated the major concern for shelf arrangement. Size is still utilized today as a secondary shelf arrangement, although the storage libraries have recognized its value as well as the accession number approach.

The increased information included in the entry was evident in the catalog of the Friends' Library of 1708, which added place of birth and residence, time and place of death, edition information, and number of sheets in work. Although it was primarily an alphabetical catalog arranged by authors' surnames, a few subject and form divisions as well as titles for anonymous work were included.[6]

The fourth Bodleian Catalogue of 1738 continued the tradition of the alphabetical arrangement by author and catch title for anonymous titles subarranged in chronological order. The addition of the name of the printer indicated that one of the problems suggested by Wanley had been solved.

The catalog of the Sion College Library departed from its former alphabetical arrangement of 1650 and was reissued in classified order in 1724.[6] The artificial scheme was similar to many of the period, which was simply a designation of letters to represent not necessarily subjects, but rather book presses and their contents.

Compilers frequently contended that a catalog by shelf order was most suitable, as missing items could be readily detected and the donors could more quickly determine which presses needed books.[6] The latter reason was legitimate at that time and was reflected in the later library laws of Great Britain and in such American catalogs as that of Harvard, 1723.

The Chetham catalog of 1791 attempted to utilize a "judicious and scientific" arrangement under the divisions of theology, law, history, sciences and arts, and humanistic literature, which could in turn be subdivided as necessary. The lack of an index badly hampered its use until 1826, when some relief was afforded through the addition of an author index, which gave the title of anonymous works.[6]

Harvard College had the distinction of issuing the first printed library catalog in America in 1723. Its expressed purpose was not for the improved use of library facilities, but rather as a solicitation device to be circulated "to friends abroad." The catalog served as an inventory and was arranged by size with subdivision by author and catchword titles for anonymous works, although the later editions were in alphabetical order.

Twenty years later, in 1743, Yale produced an excellent catalog composed of three parts: a manuscript shelf list, an alphabetical list of authors, and a classified guide or index for student reading that was divided by approximately 23 major classes with appropriate subdivisions. Books were listed under as many as five subjects in order to bring out the various contents of the volume.[26]

Generally, the catalogs produced in America during the eighteenth century favored the size or author arrangement or a combination of both, with only three out of approximately 24 relying upon the subject approach. Of these, only the Philadelphia Library Company Catalogue of 1789, with its three divisions and 31 classes that were subarranged by size, and the Harvard catalog of 1790, with its 64 classes that chose subarrangement by author, are of particular significance. The use of the index was

slowly evolving as a valuable asset and was frequently found in the American catalogs. The catalogs of the Philadelphia Association Library Company of 1765 and the Library Company of Philadelphia, 1770, frequently made entries under the first or substantive word of the title in addition to the author,[26] which would later develop into accepted practice. The information contained in the entry was approximately the same as the British successors. In spite of the unique innovations that have been described, the early American catalogs as a whole could be characterized as rudimentary devices primarily serving as an inventory or index, arranged in a single sequence with generally only a single entry for each work.

Near the end of the century the French revolutionary government confiscated a large number of books and manuscripts from a countless number of institutional and private libraries. The code of 1791 was formulated to provide simple but comprehensive rules for organization, beginning with the assembling and numbering of the books and continuing through the mailing of the completed cards to Paris. Playing cards or slips of paper were suggested as a format, which was the first mention of such an approach in any code. The completed code was to contain an accession number, title exactly as recorded in the book unless extremely long, imprint (place, printer, date), size, and other exceptional features. The author's name, as it appeared on the title page or elsewhere in the work, or a word that was most indicative of the subject if anonymous, was underlined for emphasis. Cards were then arranged alphabetically and fastened together by a thread through the lower left-hand corner. The name of the parish or district was recorded at the bottom of the card. A copy was then made on ordinary paper for retention within the district, and the cards were forwarded to Paris. It was reported in 1794 that approximately one million cards had been compiled as a record for roughly three million volumes.[27]

The close of the century witnessed few new innovations in cataloging procedures. Author, size, and subject or a combination of any two dominated the arrangements with preference to author and size. A chronological subarrangement rather than alphabetical by title was frequently used in the author catalogs, although the size of the collection dictated the practice in this regard. Completeness of description varied, with the catalog of the Friends' Library being the first to use the number of sheets. Analytical entries continued to gain in popularity, as shown in the Yale catalog of 1743 and in the catalogs of the two society libraries of Philadelphia in 1765 and 1770. The inverted form of the author's name was now a reality, in spite of the use of the possessive form by some of the less progressive libraries.

Nineteenth century

At the beginning of the nineteenth century some vestige of the old inventory concept still persisted. Generally, the catalog was considered a finding list but occasionally was further refined to include the newest Bodleian concept of assembling literary units together. The purpose of the catalog had evolved through two distinct phases: first, the inventory or content of shelves, which was prevalent in the monastic period; second, the finding list, which began with the author indexes and attained recognition with the alphabetical catalog of the Bodleian in 1620. In addition, Akers[22] acknowledged a third state, that of assembling literary units, which was originally expressed and practiced in the Bodleian Catalogue of 1674. Akers further contended that the stage demanded a highly developed instrumentation with differentiation between author, subject, and title entries, with main entry determined by authorship, and with the finding list function assigned to secondary entries in the event that the main entries were inadequate for quick location of the book.[22] The catchword title continued to be used throughout this century, but was dominated by Edwards's statement that "of necessity such catalogues must deal rather with the phraseology of title pages than with the subject of book."[28] As a result of strict adherence to this and the idea of only one entry per book, the development of subject headings was retarded. Cutter very philosophically avowed that after the introduction of the title entries for anonymous books,

> . . .the next step was to make the title-entries not merely for anonymous books but for all which had any good word in the title from which to refer, the object being to provide a means by which anyone who had heard of the book could easily find it.[2]

Apparently catch titles were considered as an adjuvant means of grouping materials on certain subjects together, and were used by at least 19 catalogs in the United States between 1815 and 1854.[2] It should be pointed out that Cutter, in 1876, codified the practice of entry by author, subject, title, and form and refuted the notion that "a catalogue must of necessity confine itself to titles only of books."[2]

This was a century of codes, with 15 major works originating in Great Britain, France, and the United States, not to mention the individual rules as expounded in the introductions of countless catalogs. The number of catalogs produced during the first three-fourths of this century numbered over 1000 (including supplements) in the United States alone. This was the age of the printed book catalog, which was to continue until the waning years of the century, largely replaced by the card catalog in the early twentieth century only to be revived later.

Our discussion for this century will be directed mainly toward the American catalog and the codes developed by the British Museum, Jewett, and Cutter.

Considerable attention was devoted during this century and the early years of the twentieth to the relative merits of the alphabetical author, the dictionary, the classified, and the alphabetical-classified catalogs. The alphabetical author catalog consisted primarily of the surnames of the authors while anonymous titles were entered by one of the Bodleian code suggestions. Only one entry per book was considered necessary, although deviations from this occurred quite early in the Philadelphia Association Library Company catalog. The dictionary catalog evolved from the author catalog and is an alphabetical sequence of duplicate entries for authors, titles, subjects, and forms. Frequently the name is used in a narrow sense to apply only to a single alphabetical sequence, while in the broadest connotation it indicates the mere alphabetical arrangement of several separate files. The main distinction lies in the arrangement of specific subjects that are in alphabetical rather than systematic order.

The classified catalog is limited to subjects that are arranged in a systematic order so that related objects are grouped together or in close proximity. The subject-arranged catalogs discussed up to this point were habitually arranged in an unsystematic order so the value of a subject, author, and title index was readily seen although not always present at the preliminary stages. Just when the true classed catalog developed is open to debate, since the early subject arranged shelf lists were pseudoclassified. The assumption that the classified catalog developed before the alphabetical is misleading, for without the modern classification schemes and indexes of the twentieth-century classified catalog, it would fall far short in achieving the usability of the dictionary form.[29] The early works of Gesner, Naude, Dury, and later Brunet were instrumental in an attempt to systematize the approach to knowledge in the library catalog. The lack of suitable classification schemes retarded the full use of the classified catalog, but the nineteenth century brought some alleviation. For the sake of clarity, the term classed catalog rather than subject arrangement or subject catalog will be used in the discussion of the nineteenth and twentieth centuries. The term subject catalog in its broadest sense does not refer to the arrangement, but rather to the inclusion of subject entries.

The alphabetico-classed catalog, which became popular during the middle of the nineteenth century, was basically a merger of the best points of the dictionary and classed catalogs. Cutter indicated that ". . .the subjects are grouped in broad classes with numerous alphabetical subdivisions."[3] This definition was somewhat limited and has been expanded by Shera to include two possible arrangements: first, major divisions in alphabetical order with subdivisions classified in an "appropriate manner," or second, classified order for major divisions with subdivisions in alphabetical sequences.[30] The catalog of the New York Public Library was strongly influenced by the alphabetico-classed concept, although recent subject headings tend toward greater specificity.

In addition, the combined catalog mentioned by Cutter was composed first of a classified catalog and second of a dictionary catalog, with author and anonymous-title entries, subject entries, other title entries, and subject references to classed catalog.[2] This approach would be similar to the combined use of a dictionary catalog and shelf list.

In the early part of the century, the popularity of the alphabetical catalog continued despite the fact that the classified catalog was developing into a sophisticated device with systematic classification schemes and author and/or subject indexes. In 1810 (2nd ed., 1820), Jacques-Charles Brunet published a classified bibliography or *catalogue raisonné* of books for booksellers and private bibliophiles; it consisted of an alphabetical author index with full entry to which was appended a classified abbreviated entry catalog or *"table en forme de catalogue raisonné."*[29] The latter was devoid of a separate index, although it did have a brief summary outline that provided a cumbersome but nonetheless systematic access.

The *Catalogue of Printed Books* of the Society of Antiquaries of London, 1816, was reputed to be the first true dictionary catalog; it used the duplicate entry approach within a single alphabet, including catchword or subject word for anonymous works as well as for those the authors of which were known.[31] This practice, however, was followed to a limited extent in the Philadelphia Association Library Company Catalogue of 1765. Eight years later, Robert Watt issued the *Bibliotheca Britannica*, a two-part bibliography with one alphabetical sequence for authors and a second for subjects. His deviation from the phraseology of the title page as the only source of subject headings was to have a profound effect on indexing methods, ultimately producing a dictionary arrangement.[29] Panizzi acknowledged the influence of R. Watt's work on his proposed plan, but pointed out that insufficient information had been given "to the titles of books or to the index."[32]

As the purpose of the catalog became more clearly defined, libraries began to reintroduce the classified catalog, which incorporated such refinements as systematic classification schemes devised by Bacon, Horne, Brunet, and others. Indexes were not considered an essential part and were comprised primarily of authors, although the Providence Athenaeum catalog of 1837 included editors and translators.[2] Thus new means of access were evolving through the index, which served to provide added entries for the book catalog.

At the same time supporters of the alphabetical arrangement sought to improve the subject approach. The Andover Theological Seminary catalog, compiled by O.A. Taylor in 1838, was one of the best alphabetical catalogs of the period and was based on the German practice that provided for two separate alphabetical catalogs arranged by author and by subject. He managed to complete the author section but never finished the systematic index.[26] Taylor was aided by Charles Jewett, a student, who would later adapt his example at Brown University.

The subject index of 1843 to the author catalog of Brown was to serve as an alphabetical and a pseudoclassed index and was comprised of a single sequence of subjects or catchwords, broad subject entries, and specific entries.[26] Although Jewett only infrequently deviated from the phraseology of the title page, the departure from the traditional concept of Panizzi and Edwards was significant enough to foster a movement that would in time free the subject index from the restraint of title terminology. "The way was now open for the compilation of a full dictionary catalog."[26] Three years later a similar catalog was issued by the Linonian Society of Yale, using a single alphabet with author, title, and subject word.[2]

Another form of alphabetical catalog, issued in 1844 by the New York Mercantile Company, was comprised of an author catalog with an alphabetically classified index. The index was divided into 69 subjects arranged in alphabetical order, with individuals works listed beneath each heading in a similar arrangement.[26]

The first half of the nineteenth century was characterized by a variety of combinations of arrangements and indexes. The first major group was comprised of catalogs that were arranged primarily by subject or classified order. The most elementary form was by broad classes or subjects in a shelf list order, with works subarranged by accession and chronologically by imprint date, title, or author. An extension of this was close classification with classes or divisions subdivided into more minute facets by a systematic scheme. Both were considered indexes with single or variant combinations of author, title, or subject as optional features, but their presence became commonplace as librarians recognized the need for a multidimensional approach and stopped arguing about whether the patrons sought material primarily by author or subject. The classified approach was considered more difficult to use, which was true until the development of classification schemes and indexes. The problem of looking in two places, however, always will tend to be somewhat of a disadvantage of this arrangement.

The second broad group of catalogs had a primary arrangement in alphabetical order. They were in many cases indexes to a secondary classified order, but the major emphasis was placed upon the ready accessibility of an alphabetical, rather than a systematic, approach. In other words, both were complementary to one another, with a classified system being rather limited without an alphabetical index and the alphabetical system badly limited because of extreme dependency upon the occurrence of letters. Some of the most common types of arrangements in alphabetical order were: subject list or combinations of subject, author, and title to a classified catalog; subject list with works listed beneath each heading with possible indexes for author and/or title; classes with subdivisions in alphabetical order or classified order; and author list with appended subject list in alphabetical or classed order. Some of the more sophisticated types actually developed shortly after the turn of the century. It is easily seen that the distinctions are not always too clear. The recognition of the value of each type of arrangement precipitated some rather unusual combinations, which testify to the ingenuity of American bibliographers and librarians. The emergence of the dictionary catalog unquestionably demonstrates the growing influence of the public library in American society. The development of a new form, the card catalog, seemed to parallel the new arrangement during the second half of this century.

In 1853 in an introduction to a classified catalog compiled by Ezra Abbot for the Cambridge High School, the changing concepts of authorship were reflected in the placing of anonymous works under the first word of the title if not an article or preposition, societies under name, periodicals under title, and collections under editor.[33]

The continuing effort to utilize the key words of the title as a source of information slowly led toward the development of the dictionary catalog. In 1854, Sampson Low issued an *Index to the Titles* for the *British Catalogue of Books Published in 1854*. The former classified index with its 34 classes was now arranged in one alphabetical sequence. This new "concordance of titles," which supposedly presented the "author's own definition" of his book, was concerned not with subject information but rather with a more ready location device for the booksellers.[2] The idea was further developed in 1856 by Crestadoro, a former assistant to Low.

Frederick Poole, in 1854, compiled a dictionary catalog at the Boston Mercantile Library with a single sequence of authors, titles, and subjects. The use of subject words rather than independent subject headings continued the obedience to wording of the titles. The catalog was limited to a single line for each work and was one of the first condensed catalogs produced as an answer to the overwhelming costs of the comprehensive printed form. The lack of cross references was unfortunate, as the related subject words were further obscured just as failure to provide for multiple subjects of composite works further limited the subject value. The catalog continued the tradition as employed in Poole's *Index to Periodical Literature*, which was first begun at Yale for the libraries of the Linonian and Brothers' Society in 1848.

After leaving the Smithsonian, Jewett became librarian at the Boston Public Library in 1857 and 1 year later issued a catalog for the Lower Hall; it continued the title entry idea with synonymous words scattered but strengthened it with a wider variety of subject words employing duplicate entries to bring out the various aspects of polytopical books. It also included cross references, which were considered the "greatest improvement of all," from many subjects to others that were of a similar nature.[2] The authors' names were placed first under the headings, thus allowing for easy alphabetical arrangement and greater importance for subject emphasis. Jewett thus "...took the first steps, somewhat wavering steps, it is

true, in a different direction."[2] He recognized the informational purpose as well as the need for a specific citation and sought to bring about some distinction between subject and title entries. "The idea was not thoroughly carried out, but it had been conceived."[2] The prominence of the subject idea continued to develop in the later Bates Hall Index and its supplements. The dictionary catalog was now an immature but accepted method; however, the idea of specific entry was still in a formative stage though regimented by the title page.

Ezra Abbott entered the catalog scene once again in 1861 by embarking upon an alphabetico-classed card catalog for the Harvard University library, where cards had formed a "private card supplement" since 1833.[34] This practice was not entirely new, as libraries for years had maintained files of "slips" which were integrated into supplements or new editions of the printed or manuscript catalog and served the staff as a supplementary list. Their use was not an American innovation, as they were employed by Abbe Rozier in 1775 for the compilation of an index of publications of the Paris Academie des Sciences; again in 1791 as described in the French code; then by the Society of Telegraph Engineers in London in 1820; and continuously since 1827 by the Trinity College in Dublin.[35] The British Museum used an 11- by 4-inch slip, which formed the basis for a sheaf catalog begun in 1841.[35] The first catalog designed for public use within the United States was reputed to be at the Philadelphia Library Company in 1857.[36] Bates Hall at Boston Public Library instituted a public Card Catalog in 1871 with two rods across the top of each drawer to hold the cards securely.[35] The University of Rochester was reported to have used them temporarily as early as 1846.[2] In addition to the use of cards, the Harvard Catalog was the first time a librarian had undertaken a subject catalog that would include true subject headings for each book that were derived from the content of the book rather than the words of the title.[26] The subjects would not be scattered by accident of alphabet but rather would be grouped together under a common form. To Abbot, the most logical approach was to compile two separate catalogs or indexes, one for authors and one for subjects. The former would follow the usual pattern and be primarily intended as a finding list for determining the availability of a particular book. The second would be made up of subjects, arranged in alphabetical order, which were subdivided by various aspects in a second alphabetical sequence, thus allowing for some of the advantage of the classified catalog. In addition to entries for books, analytical entries for academy proceedings and periodicals were included. He reasoned that none of the three approaches presently used were feasible: first, the closely classified catalog required a knowledge of a complex classification scheme; second, the broadly classed catalog tended to be too general an approach; and third, the dictionary scattered materials in every part of the catalog.[26] Abbot's efforts were to have a decided effect upon the cataloging procedures, particularly upon the extensive application of cards. His suggested subject arrangement was not widely accepted, although it was in part adopted for the dictionary catalog with its many subdivisions, which became a part of the latter. Cutter commented that Abbot's system was "...best adopted for the thorough investigation of comprehensive subjects"; while the dictionary catalog was for "finding quickly what relates to a person, a place or other specific topic."[2]

The dictionary and classified catalogs were collocated in 1874 by J. Schwartz at the New York Apprentices Library;[37] he believed that the "abstract" information or "objects," which must be "viewed in their relations to other objects, or as parts," can best be located by the classified catalog, while "concrete" information or "objects," which "may be viewed as complete" in themselves, can best be located by the dictionary catalog. Thus the information supplied by both was equally valuable but "...both methods cannot be united without doing violence to the principles on which each is based." The ideal catalog could be obtained by the acceptance of "both as co-ordinate parts of one whole." The results were first a classified catalog of all books (imprints omitted) arranged by 24 classes, 216 possible divisions, and about 2000 subdivisions. This was prefixed by a synopsis of the classification scheme to facilitate ready location within each class. The second part was an alphabetical listing: authors and anonymous title entries with individual works subarranged alphabetically by title (complete with imprint); titles that do not clearly indicate subjects or topics "whether stated in title or only implied" followed by a list of all books thereon; class headings used as references to classified; and cross references. The subject headings adapted were frequently in inverted order with the noun or substantive first, then followed by an adjective. The catalog exemplified an attempt to use the best of both, but entailed a considerable effort to compile. The twentieth century would find a similar procedure being used with reference cards placed in the dictionary card catalog that directed the user to the shelf list for general and voluminous classes of information. This approach has never been extensively employed and certainly has great possibility for allowing more selective inclusion in the dictionary catalog while utilizing the ever-present shelf list as a systematic access.

The catalog of the Boston Athenaeum of 1874 was a monumental product of this period and embodied the most advanced thinking of Charles Cutter, who is most clearly identified with the dictionary catalog. The catalog was begun in 1856, the year that Poole assumed the post of librarian, and continued in various stages of development until Cutter became librarian in 1868. Cutter was visibly displeased with the preceding efforts, as he sought to achieve high standards with complete and carefully constructed entries. Author headings were meticulously established with full names and identity of authors of anonymous works if possible; otherwise they were entered under the first word of the title. Unique subject headings were employed without regard to phraseology of the title, which had become accepted, if not universal, practice by this time. Contents notes were added for each collected work with analytics made for these under author, title, and subject as well as entries for periodical articles and society publications. This was a tremendous feat, but he considered the catalog to be the key to the library collection. At the other end of the spectrum during this same year, Poole published a finding list at the Chicago Public Library that was simply a reproduction of the shelf list with brief bibliographic information. The popularity of such abbreviated lists persisted throughout the remainder of the century. The Boston Athenaeum catalog became the model of the period, with its dictionary arrangement by author, title, and subject with form occasionally denoted by references. The acceptance of the dictionary catalog was then almost universal within the United States, although a few classed catalogs were produced.

In addition to the publication of Cutter's *Rules* in 1876, four other events occurred that were to have an effect upon cataloging. First, the founding of the American Library Association (ALA) united and concentrated efforts in the direction of cataloging with discussion and activities centering around the advantages and disadvantages of the card or book catalog, the merits of the dictionary or classified catalog, analytic indexing of periodicals, indexes for government publications, potential use of bibliographies, and other issues concerning bibliographic organization. Maddox concluded that the most widely discussed library topics of the period, 1876–1885, were classification and cataloging.[38] The second was the publication of the Dewey Decimal Classification with subject index by the young Amherst librarian. This scheme was designed for a classified catalog and supplied a long-awaited standard index to subjects that would tend to solve one of its major disadvantages. Librarians quickly recognized the value of the scheme, utilizing it first for the classified catalog and later primarily as a shelf arrangement for the dictionary catalog. The third was the planned publication of the *American Library Journal*, which was to serve as "a periodical supplement" to the 1876 Report.[39] In addition, the editors solicited copies of catalog cards or slips to be used as examples of methods and catalogs in the many libraries and hinted at possible cooperative cataloging ventures by the *Journal* through the "printing of accurate titles of new books in such a way that they can be used for the card catalogs of libraries."[39] And the fourth was the founding of the Library Bureau, which both standardized the dimensions of the catalog card and later was one of the first organizations to offer printed catalog cards for sale.

The catalog of the Brooklyn Mercantile Library, 1880, was based on the alphabetico-classed concept which attempted to bring some semblance of order to the subject headings rather than scattering them throughout the dictionary catalog. It occurred at a period when the book catalog was beginning to wane and at a time when the Boston Athenaeum catalog overshadowed other contributions. S. B. Noyes, the compiler, sought a systematic approach to authors, titles, and subjects within a single alphabet by forming certain general classes or class lists, such as BIOGRAPHY (individual subjects), COUNTRIES (alphabetical arrangement), or FICTION (alphabetically by author and title), within the general alphabetical sequence. Specific headings were then grouped primarily under 30 such class lists, which were interspersed among authors, titles, and cross references in traditional alphabetical order. Topics that were too fragmentary, complex, or many-sided would be placed in the general alphabet rather than under the general classes for easy location. Analytics for collections, miscellaneous essays, and some periodical articles were included. The purpose of the catalog was aptly described by Noyes:

> The catalogue is designed to secure as far as possible, in one alphabet, an index to authors, titles, class headings, subject class headings, specific subjects and subheads, so that the inquirer may at once be directed to what he is in search of.[40]

Although it was well received, Cutter criticized the catalog as a "mixture of partial dictionary and incomplete classification...."[2] The user must know the degree of comprehensiveness of subject, which was generally a varying process as clearly pointed out by Oliver Lilley[41] in the next century. Cutter further contended that with such classes the arrangement was a "return to the dictionary plan by specific entry," and certain important classes were lacking which had for instance been used as subjects for a separately published class list for the Lower Hall at Boston Public Library. He conceded that perhaps this irregular selection of classes might "correspond to the public's unsystematic association of ideas" with the reader possibly looking "in the right place at first" and avoiding extensive use of cross references. He concluded that: "Never the less it may prove a most successful catalogue."[2] Nearly 80 years later the comment was made that "its (alphabetico-classed) possibilities have never been adequately explored."[30]

The Index-Catalogue of the Library of the Surgeon-General's Office, 1880–1895, compiled under the direction of John S. Billings, was another monumental product of the period, requiring over 20 years to complete. The title, "index-catalog," was used to denote the inclusion of books and periodicals. The consistent use of specific headings, which were independent of title words, and a systematic employment of aspect subheadings, which were separated by brackets rather than dashes, were outstanding features of this 16 volume classic.[29]

Centralized cataloging or the preparation of catalogs or cards by a centralized agency or library for distribution to other libraries was first suggested shortly after the middle of the century by William D. Cooley, an English geographer, and Charles Jewett, through the use of stereotyped plates. Photographic techniques were suggested in 1835 by Albert Blor[42] and again at the Librarians Conference in 1877 by Henry Stevens, who speculated that centrally produced cards might include a photographically reduced title page for each entry.[43] F. Max Müller, former librarian at the Bodleian, had suggested the use of printed slips that could be distributed with each book in an article in the *Times* (London) of March 1876. He contended that national libraries should assume the responsibility for cataloging publications produced within their borders and pointed out the desirability of requesting each author to compose a "proper slip of his own book." He also proposed that printed slips could be used to maintain three or four kinds of catalogs such as alphabetical by authors, chronological, local, and classified by subject.[44] Similar proposals regarding the use of printed slips had been made by Otis Robinson, librarian at the University of Rochester, 2 years previously, and in 1876 by Justin Winsor, the librarian of Harvard.[44] The first successful, but short-lived, attempt was by *Publishers' Weekly* in the form of slips that could be cut apart and pasted on cards. This was followed by a similar venture in 1887 by the American Library Association, which sought to supply cards. The Rudolph Indexing Company in 1893 planned to supply cards for over 100,000 volumes, but this failed to materialize.[45] The Library Bureau issued cards from 1893 through 1896 until the project was shifted to the American Library Association Publication Section, where it was quickly dropped, although efforts continued through the production of cards for serials and composite books. As the century ended, plans were in the offing to expand the publication of cards by the American Library Association but in July 1898, the Library of Congress began to print catalog cards for American copy-righted books. A short time later cards were exchanged with two or three large libraries, which were also printing catalog cards at that time. A printed card service has been available to all libraries since 1901. Failure of the early attempts at cooperative cataloging was largely attributed to the inability of librarians to accept such a radical innovation; failure of cards to conform to individual practices such as author headings, size of card, and bibliographic information; and the long delays in shipment.[45]

The early catalogs had occasionally utilized a supplementary alphabetical subject index, which was the forerunner of our present subject lists. After the freeing of subject words from the phraseology of the title, librarians quickly became conscious of the lack of uniformity among the subject headings selected by the various catalogs. The dictionary catalog made the problem even more acute, as now the subject headings were words that would be suggestive of content, not the title. It was soon observed that they must utilize a syndetic structure to be effective in covering the many possible approaches by the user. A committee was established in 1879 by the American Library Association to study the problem of an index to subject headings that would serve as an appendix to Cutter's *Rules*. Cutter, the chairman, reported 2 years later that an impasse had been reached as "we can't agree."[46] The efforts of the committee continued with numerous reports and membership changes attesting to the difficulties. In 1895 the project culminated in the publication of the *List of Subject Headings for Use in the Dictionary Catalogue*. The work was a composite listing of terms used by several large catalogs and other sources which had been carefully screened and was complete with "see" and "see also" references. It was considered a standard list for all types of libraries and found wide acceptance in three editions until the final issue in 1911, when it was largely replaced by the Library of Congress list of subject headings, which was issued in parts between 1909 and 1914. The popularity of the latter was assured by the widespread use of printed catalog cards. Its failure to include references until 1943 was a decided drawback, although supplements were a distinct asset in keeping up to date on new terminology.

Three other important bibliographic tools, which would affect catalogs, were issued during this period. The first was the third edition of *Poole's Index to Periodicals Literature*, which extended coverage to 1882. The second was the *A.L.A. Index* of 1893, which was designed to index collections and composite works and free the catalog of innumerable analytics for this type of material. The third was the *Catalog of the A.L.A. Library, 1893*, which was to serve as a selection aid, cataloging guide, and printed catalog. It is interesting to note that all three of these have continued to be issued, although under different names and publishers, until the present time.

Codes: British Museum.

Before the merging of the Royal Library with the Cottonian, Harleian, and Sloan collections in 1753, early individual cataloging attempts were as a whole poorly planned and executed. In 1759 the trustees expressed the desirability of a catalog and further suggested in 1807 that a separate alphabetical catalog for each collection be compiled as well as a general classed catalog.[6] These efforts culminated in the issuance of seven volumes between 1813 and 1819, during the tenure of Sir Henry H. Baber as Keeper of Printed Books.

The current emphasis on scientific classification was skillfully presented by Thomas H. Horne, who submitted his *Outline for the Classification of the Library* in 1825 to the trustees, who engaged Horne temporarily to accomplish such a catalog at the British Museum. Although the project came to an impasse, this proposal and his *Observations on the Manner in Which Titles of Books are to be Entered and Classed* were valuable additions to cataloging literature. The latter contained a few rules which pertained to bibliographic descriptions such as content notes, forms of authors' names, and the need for several indexes to the classified catalog.

The work on the classified catalog begun by Horne was suspended in 1834, at which time Mr. Baber proposed a plan for an alphabetical author catalog based on 16 rules that provided for uniform cataloging slips, entry under author if it appeared any place in the work, form of name taken from title page, anonymous works placed under "prominent or leading word" with name of possible author inserted at end of titles in brackets, pseudonymous works cataloged under pseudonym with real name inserted after title in brackets, entry under editor for collected works, and translations entered under original author.[47] In addition he proposed that Panizzi, an impetuous Italian political refugee, should be given the task of editing the new work. The proposal was rejected and then followed by committee studies in 1834 and 1836, during which time the arguments for the classified and alphabetical catalogs were vehemently expressed with few concrete results. In 1837 Panizzi was appointed the Keeper of the Printed Books in spite of strenuous objections. The work on the new catalog was authorized by the trustees in 1838 with a projected completion data of 1840, but with the stipulation that each letter of the alphabet was to be published individually instead of the original "shelf by shelf" plan of Baber and Panizzi.[6]

The so-called "Ninety-one Rules" employed in the compilation of this catalog were not the work of Panizzi alone but were accomplished by the unique method of having Edward Edwards, J.W. Jones, J.H. Parry, and Thomas Watts compile codes, which were then studied and criticized. The resultant code was thus formulated by the effort of five men who carefully collaborated to express the best in cataloging philosophy of the period. It was approved by the Board of Trustees in 1839 and published 2 years later.[6] The final product consisted of 91 rather than the originally suggested 79 rules and was decidedly inferior because of the meddling of the trustees.[48] Work on the catalog, however, was not progressing as smoothly with the first volume so marred by omissions that the printing was suspended in 1841, although the manuscript project continued. A rash of criticisms and investigations in 1847 ensued, with Panizzi defending the "Ninety-one Rules," but now questioning the feasibility of a printed catalog for such a large library. In 1849 a guard book catalog was devised with the entries copied on slips that were formed into a 150-volume catalog by 1851.[6]

The influence of Panizzi may have been overemphasized, although his impact upon modern cataloging was decisive. An assessment of his contribution is obscured somewhat by the fact that the "Ninety-one Rules" were a product of collaboration, although the testimony before the commissions was assumed to be an expression of his ideas. He was a fervent supporter of the author catalog, contending that this was the most natural approach by the user. An "index of matter" or title subject words, which were severely limited by the admonition that only the title page was to serve as a source, was appended. The authority of the title page was accepted as a means of attaining a consistent catalog in the typical tradition of the Bodleian Catalogue in 1674. The practice of using abbreviated references which guided the user to the main entry was considered a feasible method of gaining space in the book catalog and set a precedent that would be followed by future librarians even after the advent of the card catalog and the unit card should have negated such a concept. The treatment of anonymous works was a major concern and indicated Panizzi's feeling that the catalog must be more than a quickly prepared finding list. He sought to separate anonymous works into corporate bodies and form heading groups where possible, still leaving room for those entries that could only be called miscellaneous. The first were arranged in alphabetical order under the name of the country or place "from which they derive their denomination or for want of such denomination, under the name of the place from whence their acts are issued."[32] Organizations such as academies, universities, and learned societies were entered under the form heading ACADEMIES, and were subarranged by continent and then country. The second group was designed to place special types of material where form was apparently considered essential under such headings as PERIODICAL PUBLICATIONS, EPHEMERIDES, CATALOGUES, LITURGIES, and BIBLE. The final group was comprised of miscellaneous publications that lacked authors and were not covered in the other categories. They were listed in order of preference as possible alternatives: 1) enter under person if referred to in title, 2) enter under place if referred to in title, 3) enter under substantive if lacking both person or place, and 4) enter under first word if not substantive in title.

This elaborate structure clearly reflected the problem of anonymous publications, which included corporate and miscellaneous works lacking the name of a personal author on the title page. The rules were frequently divergent from Panizzi's opinions as revealed in the testimony by his preference for the first word that was not an article or a preposition rather than the first substantive,[32] by his belief that the reader was expected to know the title of the book just as readily as the author,[32] by his objection to class headings asserting that the most desirable situation would allow every title in its place without any other heading than "its own fixed and certain heading" with fewer titles under each entry,[32] and by his contention that a cataloger must take the title as it occurs rather than forming it to suit his convenience.[32] Many of his opponents advocated entry under the subject word rather than the first important word. One of the major contributions of the "Ninety-one Rules" was the concept of placing

corporate bodies under the country or place, although the names were derived from the title and could be construed to have the quality of a subject rather than a corporate author. The system of form headings was a secondary approach relegating special types of works to a consistent location which supposedly made them more accessible than a wide variety of non-descript titles. This approach persisted in British cataloging practices to the twentieth century and was evident in all of the codes including the 1967 Anglo-American code. The reluctance to utilize the conventional title as an entry was evinced by the final group of miscellaneous anonymous work, although it was not indicative of Panizzi's philosophy.

The "Ninety-one Rules" were a monumental achievement, as they represented the first attempt to codify the rules for the compilation of an author catalog with logical guides for cross references. Many of the basic concepts originated from the Bodleian and other leading libraries. The "Ninety-one Rules" were to form a basis for future codes and had a particular effect upon librarianship in the English-speaking countries.

Codes: Jewett, 1853. The first distinct code of cataloging rules issued in the United States was compiled by Charles C. Jewett, librarian of the Smithsonian Institution. Jewett sought primarily to provide a set of uniform rules established on principles, and supplemented by explanations and examples. The "principal object" of the rules was to secure uniformity; however, he cautioned that even the most elaborate rules were inadequate to "provide for every case of difficulty which may occur."[49] About one-third of the publication was devoted to a description of an ingenious system that had originally been proposed in 1850 at a meeting of the American Association for the Advancement of Science in New Haven and again at the Librarians Conference of 1853. Jewett's plan was truly remarkable for its day as it called for the compilation of a code of rules, the submission of catalog entries by individual libraries according to these rules, stereotyping of each single entry, and the production of catalogs according to demand by simply interfiling and printing. The project failed, however, as it was too far advanced for the period to achieve widespread support as well as being hampered by technical problems that developed in the material used for the stereotype plates. The advantages described by the author were: elimination of duplicate effort, source of location for books, useful bibliographic information, guide for exchange, increased uniformity, possible American bibliography, and a future universal bibliography. The possible list of American literature embodied the concept that was later used in the Library of Congress printed catalogs. He pointed out that copyright books were required by law to be deposited at the Smithsonian and that these could be listed in monthly bulletins, annual lists, and quinquennial catalogs that would form a record of American publications.

He asserted that a catalog was a list of titles of books that a library contained and was generally not expected to give any further information "than the author gives or ought to give in the title page, and the publisher, in the imprint, or colophon; except the designation of form which is almost universally added."[49] He admonished that

> ...the catalog is designed to show what books are contained in a particular collection, and nothing more. Persons in want of further information, are expected to seek for it in bibliographical dictionaries, literary histories, or similar works.[49]

The alphabetical catalog according to Jewett was the best type and he supported this with many of the arguments previously advanced by Panizzi. He proposed an alphabetical rather than a classified index as it was considered easier to use.

The rules themselves are basically those formulated by Panizzi but with a few changes such as the simplified treatment of anonymous works. The corporate concept was more clearly established in Rule 23 that placed all corporate bodies in one category and provided that they be entered under the name of the body. Cross references were to be made from "any important substantive or adjective, to the principal word."[49] U.S. government publications were to be placed under *United States*. To secure uniformity, anonymous works were to be entered under the first word of the title which was not an article with cross references made from other words that might be sought. The librarian would be relieved of problems and the reader would no longer have to search in two places for a book. "Any rule for selecting the most prominent word of a title, or for entering a book under the name of its subject, would be found fatal to uniformity...."[49] Pseudonymous works were to be placed under the assumed name followed by *pseud* but were not considered pseudonymous if the author had "...published any edition, continuation, or supplement under his name."[49]

The contribution of this small pamphlet should not be underestimated. The plea for uniformity would prove to be somewhat idealistic although the suggested rules were widely accepted, exerting a strong influence on future development of catalogs and codes.

Codes: Crestadoro, 1856. Four years after the publication of Jewett's rules, Andres Crestadoro issued an informative pamphlet[50] that advocated an extension of the subject word concept. He objected to the classified catalog because of its dependence upon an artificial arrangement and suggested a detailed entry catalog arranged by accession number that would be supplemented by a rather comprehensive alphabetical index of authors and subjects. He believed that the cataloger should add the author, subject, and "nature" or form of each book to the index even though the title failed to yield this information. An

extensive system of cross references was proposed to overcome the lack of standardized terminology by referring from as many terms of the title as necessary, by connecting synonymous terms, and by interrelating class headings with subordinate or "partially synonymous" terms. Title terminology was always preferred with supplied information, only as a last resort supplied by the cataloger. This would scatter similar subjects in several locations, although at least a recognition of the need for a subject approach was expounded.

Codes: Cutter, 1876. The most comprehensive rules formulated during this century were by Charles Cutter. They were issued as part two of the Bureau of Education Report *Public Libraries in the United States...*[2] The rules evinced the influence of Panizzi, Jewett, Perkins, Abbot, Poole, and other leading librarians of the century. The first edition was issued in 1876 and was continued through a fourth in 1904 that Cutter suggested was actually unnecessary in view of the success of Library of Congress cataloging.[3] The rules covered the full range of cataloging procedures including a section of definitions; another on entry (where to enter) that contained subsections pertaining to authors, title, subject, and form catalogs as well as analysis; a section on style (how to enter) which included aspects of descriptive cataloging such as headings, body of card, collation, contents, notes, capitalization, and punctuation; and other minor sections pertaining to other catalogs and cataloging of special materials. Some of the major points regarding entry were: entry under personal or corporate author or substitute for it, bodies of men considered as authors, corporate bodies under name, anonymous works entered under title including periodicals, entry under original title for anonymous works when variant titles appear in successive volumes, specific subject heading rather than inclusive class, and subject entry under words expressing content of book rather than under terminology of title.

The rules were the epitome of the cataloging "art" of the period and were complete with copious notes which discussed the problems and suggested possible alternatives. Cutter's pragmatic approach was based primarily upon three principles. First, was the principle of convenience and habit of the user. System and simplicity should be sacrificed when strict adherence to rules and uniformity create practices which are at odds with the "general and deeply rooted" habits of the public.[3] Second, was the principle of specific and consistent subject entries. Each term used was to be applicable to innumerable books as it was derived from the content and not the title. It should consist of a specific heading, not the class, to which it was subordinate. To this was added the syndetic structure to connect related and synonymous terms.[3] Third, the catalog was more than a mere finding list "for a given book by an author's name" and should facilitate the location of all books of an author by placing them together in one place.[3]

The rules for the subject catalog represented the first attempt at such a codification and were to serve as the basis of American subject cataloging practices until the present day. Although they were designed to establish principles and practices with alternative solutions, they reflected the occasional uncertainty of the author and are marred by inconsistencies that still haunt cataloging theoreticians today. The Vatican code of 1931 was the only other completed codification of rules for the subject catalog and included one section on general principles and forms and a second on specific areas of application.

Many of the problems of the present dictionary subject catalog may be attributed in part to the context in which Cutter compiled his rules. The book catalog was still the dominant tool although the card catalog was gaining stature and was recognized by his last edition of the *Rules* as the way of the future. The *Rules* were compiled for a book catalog, dependent upon the main entry concept, and were designed for the relatively small popular library with a collection of information sources in the traditionally monographic format rather than the highly specialized texts in varying forms, and promulgated the developing concept of subject analysis that was generally regarded as a convenience rather than a necessity.[41] The lack of direction that has persisted in the subject catalog may be attributed in part to the unquestioning adherence to Cutter's *Rules* and a failure to expand the few principles that were presented. Similar issues were still visible in the twentieth century when Frarey enumerated the eight major problems of the subject catalog: the principle of specific entry, terminology, form and structure of headings, choice among alternatives (place or subject), confusion of title and entry, size and complexity, reference structure, and maintenance.[51] Without a doubt, little progress had been made since the days of Cutter except the addition of a new obstacle, the size of the subject catalog that aims at thorough analysis.

The *Rules* as a whole proved to be a valuable addition to library literature and provided a codification of policies so badly needed by American libraries. Many of the issues raised by Cutter were to become the subject of intense debates in the next century. On the negative side the rules supplied a refuge for tradition and tended to reduce cataloging to a routine rather than make it the application of principles. Akers commented that since the 1876 issuance of the *Rules* "...there has been no further development in principles although an enormous amount of work has been done in amplifying, codifying, and clarifying rules, which has contributed to a needed uniformity of practice."[22]

The nineteenth century had been productive years in catalogs and in cataloging procedures. The beginning of the century found both the classified and alphabetical author catalog in use with a variety of subject arrangements and indexes. Panizzi and Jewett both proclaimed the author catalog the most usable and reasonable form.

The newly developing author catalogs eventually evolved into the dictionary form when subject headings were recognized as independent forms and no longer dependent upon the phraseology of the title page. In 1876 Poole reported that "the plan of the catalogue with references under authors and subjects, in one alphabetical arrangement, is the one which is now most universally used and is preferable to the classified plan."[52] By 1893 catalog arrangement was still divergent with the single alphabetical order for authors and subject dominating, although some libraries still separated authors and subjects in two distinct parts with the latter in dictionary-classified or alphabetico-classified order. In Europe the classified catalog tended to be more popular, although the subject catalog was never strongly advocated in Great Britain during this century. The Germanic countries tended to develop comprehensive catalogs divided into an alphabetical catalog of authors and anonymous titles and a separate subject catalog or "schlagwortkatalog" that was arranged alphabetically by subject or catchword or the "systematischer katalog" arranged in classified order (logically or alphabetically) by subject.

The form of the catalog was manuscript or printed book at the beginning of the century. The use of slip catalogs, which were maintained originally only for preparation of the printed catalog, slowly began to evolve beyond their original intent. Cards had originally been suggested and used by French libraries in the eighteenth century, but failed to achieve widespread application until expanding book production and changing concepts of bibliographic organization stimulated the need for increased flexibility. Slip catalogs were frequently only accessible to librarians, but the Boston Public Library and the Philadelphia Library Company opened their slip catalogs to public use during the 1850s,[53] while the former introduced a public card catalog in 1871. By 1893, Lane reported that the card catalog (43 reported) was the dominant form and was conceded a necessity although it infrequently served as a supplement for the printed book (13 reported). He also found that "most libraries still employ a running hand, generally preferring an upright and round to a slanted or angular one."[54] He reported that the typewriter was now being used by over 40 libraries and that printed cards from the Library Bureau were used by three. He ascertained that catalog cabinet drawers were generally designed for one instead of two rows of cards, which were divided in size between 12.5 × 7.5 cm. (U.S. Postal Card) and 12.5 × 5 cm. although other unusual sizes were in use.

The need for the catalog was now recognized with the subject cataloging evolving from the shelf inventories, to the anonymous title, to the subject word, and eventually the subject heading as advocated by Jewett, Abbot, and Cutter. Lane found a consensus that every book should have an author or title entry and that most should have subject cards. Out of 191 libraries surveyed, 171 reported subject catalogs in one form or another.[54] Subject headings were still a matter of catalog's choice and varied widely, but the subject approach to books aided by the syndetic structure was firmly established and awaited further development.

The form of author or title entry progressed considerably during the century. Anonymous works were originally treated by intricate form headings, subject or place entries, or a host of alternatives. Jewett and Cutter advocated the separation of corporate bodies from the anonymous category and established a simple and logical framework. By the end of the century corporate bodies tended to be entered primarily by first word of title or place depending upon the inclusion of the name within the title or whether it was a local British or American group.[54]

Varying opinions continued to govern pseudonyms at both the beginning and the end of the century.

The entry of descriptive elements had continued to increase. In the book catalog there are wide variations depending upon whether the entry was subject, author, or title as abbreviated forms were used to economize printing space. Lane determined this practice was still present in 1893 even though cards were now widely accepted.[54]

Throughout the eighteenth century the title page continued to be the basis for the description, with brackets later used to indicate supplied information. The publisher or printer was recognized as an important part of the imprint early in the century. The use of size continued to be standard procedure although methods varied somewhat. Inclusive paging began during the early years and was widely accepted by the end of the century. Editors, translators, and now artists were all recognized as essential parts of the bibliographic description.

By 1893 Lane discerned that libraries tended to agree on the following: diminishing use of capital letters but no uniform practice, Arabic rather than Roman numerals, compound names under last part for English and first part for others, English and French names under prefix, and periodicals under title unless too generic. The use of contents notes evolved more fully during this century and were widely used during the last quarter. Analytics also developed more widespread use as bibliographers sought to increase the usability of the catalog and included periodicals and society publications as in the Harvard card catalog of 1861 and in the Boston Athenaeum Catalog of 1874.

Codes were accepted during this century as the guides for cataloging compilation rather than the individualistic ideas that had dominated. Panizzi, Jewett, and Cutter were the major leaders of the century with Cutter's influence still dominating today's scene. Lane found that the majority of libraries used Cutter, with infrequent or supplemental use of codes by Linderfelt, Library School Rules (Dewey), and ALA.[54]

The nineteenth century was a period of prodigious growth in cataloging procedures and codification. This was the era of numerous catalogs beginning with initiatory inventories and finding lists and culminating in the monumental printed dictionary catalogs. American cataloging had passed through a pioneer period while Europeans experienced stabilization. The lack of rules for the construction of catalogs during the early years stimulated local ingenuity, and techniques were crude with uniformity at a minimum. The situation was greatly improved by mid-century, and codes have become a standard part of the cataloging process. The freedom from restraint during this century had nurtured innovative and conflicting ideas, pragmatic and idealistic approaches, and enhanced interest by bibliographers and scholars who slowly began to recognize the necessity for at least some semblance of bibliographic organization. Cataloging activities ceased to be the major concern of the administrators and were relegated to trained practitioners. The differentiation in staff assignments became more pronounced. Cataloging could be considered the first recognized specialization within libraries with Harvard establishing a distinct department devoted to this endeavor in 1859.[48] Personnel training and recruitment, however, were largely based on expediency for Poole suggested that "there are ladies in the eastern cities who have had much experience in cataloging, and who devote themselves to this speciality...."[52] The opening of the Columbia School of Library Economy in 1887 assisted development by supplying personnel with previous technical training.

AGE OF SOVEREIGNTY AND SCRUTINY

Modern Period

Twentieth century

The cataloging activities of the twentieth century may be divided into two distinct periods: first, a period of traditionalism which extended approximately to 1941; and second, a period of reevaluation and rebirth.

The survey of cataloging practices by Lane in 1893 was followed by a similar report in the opening years of the new century. He attempted to review some of the then current cataloging tendencies that faced the profession. He began by pointing out that the catalog had been a simple author list but now every library needed as perfect a subject catalog as possible. The debate over the relationship between subject bibliography and subject catalog persisted intermittently when Raynard Swank renewed the discussion in the 1940s. American librarians such as J.C.M. Hanson tended to seek wide coverage for the subject catalog while the European librarians frequently relied heavily upon subject lists. Lane was further concerned by the growing size of the catalog and suggested that certain sections of the catalog could be printed, that selected lists could be compiled for use by the general reader, and that existing bibliographies could be checked to denote library holdings and to provide for omission of older imprints by libraries attempting to compile a subject catalog. He maintained that classification was used basically as a shelf arrangement, was designed primarily for the popular library, and had contributed little to the subject catalog. He pointed out the values and problems of certain enriching devices of the catalog such as subject headings, annotations, and analytics. He concluded that the card catalog was here to stay although national libraries still relied upon the printed catalog, and that codes tended to "become longer the oftener they are revised," although the object was to seek simplicity and uniformity with specific instructions for more cases. Lane expressed hope for international uniformity in bibliographic matters and card publication by foreign governments, and he contended that the catalog was a finding list and not a bibliographic dictionary, but expressed the need for cooperation and centralization and described some of the cooperative projects such as printed cards and local union lists of periodicals.[55]

Two events that were to have a decided effect occurred during the early part of the twentieth century. The reorganization of the Library of Congress revitalized its cataloging department with an influx of qualified personnel such as James Christian Meinert Hanson and Charles Martel who later became leaders in the field of cataloging and classification. The second was the appointment of a committee by ALA in 1901 under the chairmanship of Hanson to revise the old 1883 catalog rules so that they were in accord with those of Library of Congress. A draft or advanced copy was issued a short time later and circulated for comments and criticisms. At the same time the Library Association (Great Britain) was also in the process of revising their cataloging rules and it occurred to Dewey that this was an opportune time to establish some uniformity among the English-speaking countries of the world. A committee was formed and in 1908 the code was completed and published in two separate editions although there were only eight rules upon which agreement could not be achieved. Within the United States the reconciliation of the rules with Library of Congress was not as complete as hoped for; the codification of their practices was still in the developmental stage and efforts had to be continued in this direction.[56]

Cooperative cataloging, which is defined as the compilation of catalog cards through a joint effort by a number of libraries in an effort to reduce duplication of operations,[57] continued during this century. The Library of Congress began the printing of catalog cards submitted by other government libraries in 1902, and this was further extended to include several large libraries outside the government structure in 1910. By 1932 the Cooperative Cataloging Committee of the ALA had opened an office at the Library of Congress with a subsidy from the General Education Board. Two years later the Cooperative Cataloging and Classification Service became a division of the

library and by 1941 it was largely absorbed by the Descriptive Cataloging Division.[58] Efforts at cooperative cataloging were never as intense as those directed toward centralization, which would afford more concentration of staff and tools, maximum standardization of procedures and codification of rules, and substantially improved supervision and administration.

The dictionary form of the catalog continued to dominate the scene with some exceptions such as the 1903 Classed Catalog of the Carnegie Library of Pittsburgh, which was compiled by Margaret Mann and was to be remembered not only for its arrangement but also for its printed format. The debate over the relative merits of the classified and dictionary catalog continued although the issue was largely closed in the United States. In 1905 Fletcher intimated that the dictionary catalog

> ...has the character of a superstition in so far as it is accepted and religiously carried out on grounds that are traditional, rather than on intelligent conviction that it meets present needs and is good for the future needs for which we must make provisions.

He warned that changes had occurred in the size of libraries, methods of administration, and the attitude toward the library patron that must be considered in catalog construction, and he suggested that the subject catalog be supplemented by the shelf list, bibliographies, reading lists, and indexes.[59] Rider later renewed the discussion, contending that librarians lacked imagination in approaching the problem of bibliographic organization and should examine such alternatives to the dictionary catalog as the classified catalog, microphotography, book catalogs, and smaller-sized catalog cards. He contended that a philosophy of the catalog was necessary and cited Hanson and Mudge as believing the catalog was an end in itself while Richardson and Currier believed it existed only to put the reader in contact with the library's holdings. He criticized the bibliographic method of cataloging as practiced by the Library of Congress, which was slavishly adhered to by the majority of the libraries in the U.S.[60] Interest in the classified catalog was somewhat stimulated at an institute on subject analysis of library materials in 1953 when Harry Dewey and Kanardy Taylor supported its excellence. Dewey succinctly outlined the ease of converting the dictionary catalog to the classified.[61] Kanardy Taylor contended that the alphabetical was best for public use while the classified was more adaptable to scientific research and concluded by agreeing with Gjelsness who contended in 1931 that "perhaps we have gone too far in accepting a standard product and applying it to all purposes" and called for a "universal reevaluation."[62]

Continued interest in the classified catalog in a few special libraries, the mounting pressures for improved bibliographic organization, experimentation with new approaches to classification, and the recognition of the underdeveloped potential of the classified catalog precipitated the publication of a manual in 1956 that sought to depict the functions, characteristics, and necessary procedures.[30] Although well done, this manual failed to stimulate the production of classified catalogs, as a survey made in 1962 listed only 16 classified catalogs in use in the United States and Canada.[63] Today exemplary classified catalogs are found at John Crerar, the Engineering Societies Library of New York, and Boston University Library, and the National Library of Canada. Some libraries did produce duplicate shelf lists, which were used as adjuncts to the dictionary catalog, but further development of the classified catalog in the United States must await another era.

Advocates of the dictionary catalog attempted to facilitate more rapid use and maintenance in the 1940s by separating the subject and form entries and the author and title entries into two distinct files, although other combinations were possible. The separation was reputed to alleviate searching by the user and to make filing by library personnel considerably easier. A number of college and university libraries, such as the University of Denver, adopted the divided catalog but interest was limited with only 24 divided catalogs found out of 457 academic libraries surveyed with the majority of them developing between 1938–1947.[64] Later the discussion shifted from the author-subject division of the catalog to the horizontal division by date of publication as large research libraries sought to devise a solution to the problem of the mass of entries under some headings.

Size became a topic of discussion as book production soared. The major virtue of the card catalog soon became a detriment as catalogers continued insertion of added entries in the form of analytics, numerous subject headings, title cards, series cards, and catch-titles as well as a host of references for both authors and subjects. Each new edition of the subject lists tended to multiply the number of references until librarians began to question their use. The traditional form of descriptive cataloging continued to necessitate the inclusion of items that some librarians thought should have been relegated to biographical and bibliographic sources outside the catalog.

Library administrators began to bewail high cataloging costs while catalogers struggled to evaluate their methods. As a whole, cataloging departments of the early twentieth century were poorly organized and administered, regimented by tradition rather than by objective analysis of the situation, and dependent upon Library of Congress cataloging practices. To complicate matters the number of catalogs also increased with duplicate cards filed in official, departmental, and union catalogs being maintained at unknown expense. Library of Congress cataloging policies continued to expand with supplementary rules or decisions printed on cards after 1911. Numerous special publications such as a guide for cataloging periodicals

issued in 1918[65] and another for serials in 1919[66] were characteristic of the growing complex of rules. The ever increasing arrearage at the Library of Congress, which was due in part to the mass of rules, precipitated an extensive study by Joeckel in 1940.[67] The survey clearly indicated that the proliferation of rules must be arrested and the present body reduced and simplified. This was followed by further studies during this decade which evinced the desired simplification of cataloging procedures and would reach its climax in the revision of the code a few years later. Librarians were beginning to demand that the principles of cataloging be recognized rather than attempting to provide rules for every situation.

Outside the Library of Congress the use of centrally prepared catalog cards was clearly a time saver, but the constant rechecking and adherence to minutia tended to keep the cataloging costs at a high level. In an effort to counteract the growing size of the card catalog, selective and simplified cataloging were suggested as possible solutions. Selective cataloging was suggested by Dury in 1649 and was thoroughly discussed by Van Hoesen in 1928.[68] Selective cataloging is an attempt to limit the number of catalog entries by designating library materials for varying degrees according to their potential use. Generally full cataloging is accorded reference works while at the other end of the scale pamphlets or government documents are usually completely excluded from the cataloging process. The economic feasibility of this method was recognized although the cataloger was required to be aware of the users' methods and demands. Simplified cataloging denotes an effort to omit or greatly simplify elements of the catalog card that are not considered essential. It is intended to achieve economy by an abbreviated entry, less effort for verification of author's name, fewer added entries, or similar steps that are not considered essential in a small public library or a childrens' collection. The Library of Congress instituted cataloging categories in 1947 and limited cataloging in 1951. Both are examples of selective and simplified cataloging as certain types of materials were relegated to full bibliographic description while others were described less fully. Added entries were made only after a careful scrutiny of their potential value. In spite of the objection by some catalogers that every book in the library should be subject to the same rules, all libraries practice some form of simplified or selective cataloging. Some innovations are the omission of subject entries for older works, limited use of added entries, and simplified entry for materials in storage. The widespread use of printed cards by commercial companies such as H.W. Wilson and *Library Journal* attest to the acceptance of simplified cataloging by public and school libraries.

The use of the card catalog was also a subject of discussion and represented an attempt to utilize empirical research in offering a more logical approach to one of Cutter's basic principles, the user. Early studies were primarily discussions of inadequacy, complexity, and organization of catalogs based on traditional impressions and theories of the user and his approach to the catalog.[69] During the 1930s the studies began to become more concerned with the user's point of view and continued to develop in outlook and method. A survey of 27 catalog use studies completed between 1930–1956 revealed some shortcomings in methodology and tended to relate only to the quantitative use of the catalog. Some of the more significant findings were: catalog used by 50–60% of all library users; nonspecialist tends to use catalog more than specialist; subject catalog infrequently used to find all material in library; English language material of recent date most widely sought; author, title, call number, and subject heading most widely used information; problem of use stems largely from lack of understanding and application of principle of specific entry, preferences for subject or place, and inability to deal with obsolete terminology; subject catalog considered effective about 70% of the time; need for better instruction in use of catalog; and possible modification into a more selective tool as some evidence supports dispensability in present form.[69]

Active revision of the 1908 code began in 1930 with the appointment of a committee on code revision by the ALA. The preliminary edition of the revised code was issued in 1941 and was divided into two sections: the first dealt with form of entry and heading, and the second was concerned with the description of the book. The code was received with a rash of complaints, largely due to the elaborate rules suggested in part two, which was dropped in the final publication of the second edition. It was immediately apparent that a reevaluation or reappraisal of cataloging policies was needed. This call for reevaluation marked the end of the traditional period and the beginning of the new.

In 1941 the "crisis in cataloging" was succinctly depicted by Andrew D. Osborn who called for an end to the slavish adherence to codes that tended to obscure reasons and principles and maintained that cataloging was an art that was based upon a few simple rules. He continued by discussing the four types of cataloging: legalist theory (an expanding complexity of rules); perfectionism (effort to catalog a book once and for all); bibliographic (cataloging molded into a branch of descriptive bibliography); and pragmatic theory (rules and decisions serving a practical purpose). He soundly condemned the continuance of the three tradition-bound methods and called for recognition of a need for the pragmatic cataloger. He contended that card catalogs frequently failed to achieve their goals because of meaningless practices, a need for three distinct grades of cataloging with the standard less detailed than advocated by the 1908 code, simplified rules even a necessity for the Library of Congress, self-cataloging methods advisable for little-used materials, high quality for essential items but little for nonessential, practical interpretation of any point, and a review of the treatment of serials, documents, and nondocuments to determine cataloging

needs. He concluded that the classical period was drawing to a close and that the change could be largely attributed to extreme systematization and standardization that had resulted from too much work.[70]

Five years later the report of Herman Henkle on descriptive cataloging by the Library of Congress clearly reflected the changing concepts and sought to develop functions and techniques.[71] The functions were aimed at presenting an accurate description of each book that would indicate its relationship to other editions and issues as well as entries for other books. The new rules, which were published in 1949, attempted to carry out the proposals of the study with brevity and simplicity.[72] They were intended as an adjunct to the *ALA Cataloging Rules for Author and Title Entries*, which were finally issued the same year. In spite of the years of discussion and the interest shown in the new codes, they tended to produce only a change in details, with the *ALA Rules* in particular tending to ignore the discussion, rather than reflecting it.[56] In any event, the period of discussion regarding the codes of 1949 tended to focus concern on the need to reevaluate the function of the catalog, to adapt time-saving methods within the cataloging department, to cope with mass acquisition, and to search for new approaches that would ensure a less pronounced growth of the card catalog.

Within a few years after the appearance of the "twin codes" a movement for the simplification of author and title entries was afoot. The need for guiding principles was examined by Seymour Lubetzky in his study of 1953 that has exerted a major influence upon the actions of the resulting committees.[73] As in the case of the 1908 code, the activities of the special committees appointed by the ALA were coordinated with a similar committee of the Library Association (Great Britain) and was further augmented by a committee of the Canada Library Association. International cooperation was afforded through the International Conference on Cataloging Principles, Paris, 1961.[4] The results of the conference were encouraging as a relatively uniform consensus of opinion resulted in a statement of principles pertaining to the function and structure of the catalog and to the choice, form, and structure of entries. These principles clearly reflected the influence of Lubetzky's critique as well as his unfinished draft of 1960[74] and were accepted by the Catalog Code Revision Committee in 1962. The Paris Principles "were seriously questioned by the large research libraries who were alarmed by the possible extensive recataloging as a result of their retrospective application." The Library of Congress conducted a detailed study of the "theoretical merits" of the statement and attempted to ascertain the proportion of change required in the retrospective application of the rules in its card catalog.[75] The results, as expected, provided support for the contention that the large research libraries were unable to accept the radical changes because of the heavy costs of revising the many catalog entries. The so called "Miami Compromise," which agreed to certain exceptions regarding the retention of the archaic entry under place rather than name of the corporate body, was approved and incorporated into the code Rules 98 and 99. The Library of Congress accepted the code only as it affects new author headings by adopting the practice of superimposition that allows the new rules to apply only in establishing entries not previously used while reverting to the old rules for all entries presently established in the catalog. As a whole the rules were a significant improvement for they were based upon a set of principles that freed them from some of the rigidity of the past. The inclusion of the rules for descriptive cataloging and for special material provided a single volume rather than the multiple works of the past.

Centralized cataloging became a primary concern during this century. Printed card production was largely limited to a few large public libraries and the Library of Congress. The card distribution service of the latter soon became recognized as a valuable asset with many libraries making extensive use of the somewhat limited number of available cards. In 1938 H.W. Wilson began the printing of catalog cards that were designed primarily for the needs of public and school libraries. The cards followed a simplified system, aimed at providing less bibliographic detail for the more popular titles with annotations and analytics adding another dimension for reading guidance.

The growing need for cataloging information and the dissatisfaction with the present services stimulated the movement for cataloging or processing centers that were occasionally established within large public libraries with small units contracting for services, or at the state level through the efforts of the state library commission, or at the regional level through an association of libraries.

Georgia was the first state library to initiate the distribution of printed cards in 1944. In the following years a number of similar centers were established as were commercial enterprises offering a variety of cataloging services. The major problems of availability and the delay in supplying cards stimulated a large amount of discussion which resulted in a number of cooperative plans such as the one suggested by Ralph Ellsworth in 1948 to assure the availability of printed cards for all books that were acquired by the Library of Congress and cooperating libraries.[76] In 1953 the Library of Congress inaugurated the All-The-Book Plan in an effort to increase the number of titles for which printed cards were available. The library hoped to solicit prepublication copies of current American imprints from the publishers so that cards would be produced as soon as possible. The Library of Congress order numbers were also supplied to the publishers who placed them on the verso of the title page to assure ready accessibility in ordering cards. The services were further improved in 1959 when R.W. Bowker Co. agreed to lend to the Library of Congress review copies received by them for listing in *Library Journal* and *Publishers' Weekly* in

exchange for cataloging information, which would be included in the latter. Wholesale book dealers and commercial processing centers such as Alanar cooperated by lending copies that were not readily available.[77] Through this program the bulk of the trade books now had printed catalog cards available. It was estimated that in 1965 Dewey numbers were available in 80% of all Library of Congress printed cards because of this expanded coverage.[77]

The Library Service Act of 1956 with its state plans and federal funds added further impetus to the development of centers such as the Southwest Missouri Library Services, Inc. in 1957. The trend was apparent for by 1965–1966 there were 63 identified cooperative processing centers in 41 states.[78]

School libraries enjoyed a similar interest with centralized processing, utilized as early as 1917 in one instance although by 1961 such services had expanded to include at least 3% of the elementary and 2% of the secondary schools.[79] The National Defense Act and the Elementary and Secondary Education Act of 1965 yielded increased book budgets that in turn actuated the need for cataloging services. Centralized centers for school libraries began to develop as did commercial services ranging from the *Library Journal* kits to complete processing. The charges for standard cataloging by the commercial centers in 1967 varied from $0.60 to $1.90, with custom or special cataloging costs much higher.[80] Card production at the centers and within individual libraries had developed extensively from the early heliotype method mentioned by Cutter in 1876.[2] A study completed in 1965 outlined the following methods of card procurement or production: purchase, manual typing, stencil duplication (postcard size), fluid duplication, stencil duplication (full size), offset, addressing machine (fiber or metal stencil), automatic typewriter, Diazo duplication, electrostatic copying (Xerox, etc.), defusion transfer copying, and projection photocopying.[81] To this list may be added the newest computer-produced cards, which are generated by individual libraries as well as being available commercially from the Catalogue Card Corporation of America. Efforts of college and university libraries have been devoted primarily toward improving the program at the Library of Congress although Colorado embarked upon a state processing center. Junior and small 4-year colleges frequently use commercial services in addition to the Library of Congress while infrequently relying upon the state and regional centers.

The Cataloging-in-Source experiment was the revival of a movement that was suggested and attempted during the nineteenth century and was designed to provide a copy of each catalog card within the book itself. The project was conducted by the Library of Congress between June 1958 and February 1959, with over 157 publishers cooperating through the provision of proof copies for 1203 publications.[42] The plan was well conceived but was hampered by a variety of factors such as a lack of cooperation by many publishers (only a little over 50% of those originally contacted actually participated) and dissatisfaction with the interrupted production schedules. Some reservations were also evident at the Library of Congress when the projected increases in staff and facilities were questioned in the light of the possible results. The results were well received by the libraries although an extensive consumer reaction survey failed to provide sufficient "clear cut evidence" of possible savings and of utilization of the information. The cataloging information contained in the *Publishers' Weekly* and SACAP, an acquisition and cataloging service instituted by Bro-Dart that would provide paper offset masters suitable for producing a sufficient number of catalog cards, were suggested as more economical methods of obtaining similar results. The project passed into oblivion with the following:

> In light of the experience gained through the experiment, it is concluded that neither a full nor a partial Cataloging-in-Source Program is desirable. The *Publishers' Weekly* and SACAP programs have suggested methods by which the potential promise of Cataloging-in-Source might be realized in a much more economical way. There should be no further experiments with Cataloging-in-Source. If the new programs fail to meet their objectives, further experiments should be conducted along the lines these programs have laid down.[42]

The Cards-with-Books-Program of 1961 was another attempt by the Library of Congress to get cards into the hands of librarians as quickly as possible. The major thrust of the program was to encourage publishers and book wholesalers to supply printed cards with their publications. Special arrangements were made at the Library of Congress to facilitate this operation and by 1967 over 96 wholesale distributors and publishers were annually distributing almost 10 million cards (about two million sets).[82] Many were still hesitant, however, in spite of the fact that libraries purchase approximately 80–85% of all current American trade books through wholesale book distributors and card sales at the Library of Congress indicate that about 80% of all cards sold are for current American imprints.[83]

Generally Library of Congress printed cards are available for only about 50% of the research library acquisitions with availability directly related to the acquisition and cataloging efforts of the Library of Congress and the cooperating libraries. The development of the Area Studies programs and the passage of PL 480 created an increased need for catalog cards in a wide variety of foreign languages that were simply beyond the capabilities of most cataloging departments. In 1962 a concerted effort was made to improve the availability of such cards by the Library of Congress adding several language sections to its descriptive cataloging division, with cooperative copy being supplied by large libraries such as Princeton, and

data sheets being compiled by personnel in the country of origin of each publication. A major step toward the systematization of centralized cataloging at the national and international level occurred in 1965 with the passage of the Higher Education Act, Title II-C. The Library of Congress was provided funds in 1966 to embark upon an unprecedented program of worldwide acquisition and centralized national cataloging aimed at alleviating the pressing needs of the research libraries.[82] The resulting National Program of Acquisitions and Cataloging, known in Europe as the Shared Cataloging Program, was to expedite acquisition through a carefully formulated plan of blanket orders and purchase arrangements. Cataloging operations were accelerated through the use of entries from national bibliographies that provide an international aspect although adjustments were made so that entries complied with existing standards. By the end of the first year of operations nine overseas offices were providing publications from 21 countries with cataloging information from 17 foreign sources.[82] Catalog cards for over 150,000 publications were supplied to over 92 cooperating libraries in America within the first 12 months of its existence.[82] The impact of the program will be widely felt by the cooperating libraries as a preliminary analysis of the availability of cards for foreign titles indicated a record high of 73% opposed to the former 50% expectancy while the total number of all titles processed at the Library of Congress rose 20%.[82] The magnitude of the cataloging operation at the Library of Congress is clearly shown by a reported sale of over 74 million printed cards to approximately 20,000 libraries throughout the world by the Card Division in 1967.[82]

Centralized cataloging operations were not confined to printed cards only, for in 1965 the Library of Congress published the first reports pertaining to a proposed plan for issuing cataloging information on magnetic tape. The first tapes for this experiment in Machine Readable Cataloguing Data (MARC) were issued in November, 1966, to 16 participating libraries and resulted in over 16,000 records for current English-language monographs being provided by the end of the fiscal year.[82] The results were carefully studied and a more highly developed standardized format was put into operational distribution under the MARC II designation.

Centralized cataloging has experienced tremendous growth during this century. The problems of individualism, time, and limited availability have tended to inhibit the universal acceptance although the situation improved considerably during the last decades. After over 100 years the visionary ideas of Jewett were nearing fruition.

The early 1930s witnessed the establishment of a number of local and regional union catalogs within the United States. The availability of personnel through the Work Project Administration exerted a strong influence upon their proliferation but the ensuing years proved difficult for many of them to endure because of soaring maintenance costs.

Three bibliographic centers at Philadelphia, Denver, and Seattle today attest to the feasibility of the concept. The major reason for the survival of the latter two was probably the establishment of a broad base of regional membership held together by a strong moral belief in the cooperative idea as well as a definite need for such a service within an area rather sparsely populated and without extensive state library collections.[84]

The most notable union catalog is the National Union Catalog that was established in 1901 at the Library of Congress to provide a listing of governmental libraries in Washington and important libraries outside the city. The reciprocal exchange of cards soon became a reality and depository catalogs were established in many of the major libraries. The growth of the catalog continued and by 1926 it contained more than two million entries. From 1927 to 1932 a grant from John D. Rockefeller, Jr. financed the "Project B" program that was designed to expand the catalog to contain the location of all important reference books in American libraries. After 25 years of administration the Card Division was relieved of the Union Catalog project in 1932 when it was established as a separate unit. Continued efforts by librarians, particularly those working through the ALA, focused attention upon the venture which in turn led to increased financial support so necessary for expansion. The official name, National Union Catalog, was adopted in 1948 and by 1964 over 15 million cards represented approximately eight million titles and editions.[85]

The pressing problem of maintaining the depository catalogs within the specially selected libraries and the need for wider distribution of cataloging information necessitated a more economical and feasible approach. The most logical solution lay in the revival of the book catalog that had continued as a standard in many national libraries in spite of abandonment by others. A *Catalog of Books Represented by Library of Congress Printed Cards Issued to July 31, 1942* was published in 1942–1946 in 167 volumes and was followed by a series of supplements for both authors and subjects. In 1956 the catalog was expanded to include the holdings of the National Union Catalog and the next issue was given a new title to reflect this increased coverage. The movement to encompass an extended retrospective period led to the publication of *The National Union Catalog, 1952, 1955 Imprints...* and the most recent, *The National Union Catalog, Pre-1956 Imrpints*, that is presently being published by Mansell Information Publishing Ltd. (England), and will contain over 16 million cards. Thus the whole spectrum of the National Union Catalog will now be available through the use of the printed book catalog.

The success of the Library of Congress book catalogs and the advent of electronic hardware had a decided effect upon the return of the book catalog. In 1953 the Lamont Library at Harvard produced a printed catalog that was designed for wide distribution to students and faculty.

The catalog was produced by a photo-offset lithographic process such as used by the Library of Congress catalogs, only each of the 40,000 titles were retyped, generally one line per title, in a classified order that was supplemented by an author index of approximately 60 pages and an index of the classification.

The Library and Information Service of Western Australia compiled a classified nonfiction book catalog in 1965 containing approximately 67,000 titles. The classified section was comprised of two volumes arranged by the Dewey Decimal System while the subject index was compiled from the Library of Congress subject headings that were carefully formulated into relative index entries. The entries were typed on strips that were then printed by a photolithographic process. Future revisions are planned by positioning new entries among the original strips.[86]

A variety of other printing techniques are presently used with varying degrees of success depending upon the desired results and the amount of economic support. The linotype slugs method, used by H.W. Wilson, can be revised simply by interfiling new slugs and removing obsolete ones. It is expensive but is especially well adapted to the cumulative indexing scheme.

The shingled card technique with offset is inexpensive and especially adaptable for the smaller operation. The process entails the photographing of overlapping cards arranged like shingles, preparation of an offset plate from a reduced negative, and final printing. The sequential camera is a refinement of this technique and consists of a special camera capable of photographing only a part of the catalog card as it is placed before the lens. This method was used successfully in 1959 by the National Library of Medicine for the production of its *Current List of Medical Literature*.

The early Library of Congress catalogs utilized a photo-offset process based upon a photographically reduced negative produced by assembling cards immediately after one another in columns. Later a special card was printed which eliminated the blank spaces at the bottom, thus expanding the contents of each page considerably. Another offset process that utilizes microfilm and electrostatic or xerographic reproductions for plate composition has been extensively used by G.K. Hall since 1959 for the reprinting of a wide variety of library catalogs for commercial distribution.

One of the first catalogs produced by tabulating machines was that of the King County Public Library, Seattle, in 1951 and issued on expendable IBM paper. The Los Angeles County Public Library employed a similar approach but went further and prepared multilith masters which were then used to print two extensive and carefully compiled catalogs in 1952 and 1954. The first was a four-volume children's catalog divided into separate alphabets for authors, titles, and subjects and an adult catalog of 37 volumes that was divided into separate alphabets for authors (8 volumes), titles (6 volumes), conventional subjects (18 volumes), fiction subjects (four volumes), and foreign books (one volume).[87]

The New York State Catalog of 1956–1960 was designed principally for interlibrary loan and was a single line entry checklist of books and ephemeral material in three broad subjects issued in separate parts. The catalog was produced by the use of a tabulating machine and photo-offset printing.

The Baltimore County Public Library Book Catalog, issued in 1965, was a completely computerized product containing approximately 55,000 titles with bimonthly and annual supplements. The shelf list was arranged in alphabetical order, then edited, and key punched on cards that were later transferred to magnetic tape for storage. The computer organized printout resulted in a divided catalog for authors, titles, and subjects. Simplified catalog-ing procedures were used as the main emphasis was a finding list rather than a bibliographic tool. Added entries were held to a minimum although no limit was placed on the number of subject headings.[88]

One computer-produced catalog appeared at Stanford University in 1966 with the first issue of an annual catalog containing about 25,000 titles arranged in a three-part format: author and title, subject, and shelf list. The source of information was the basic Library of Congress cards, which were keypunched and then converted to magnetic tape. The catalog sought to provide "…something more than reproductions of unit catalog cards" and rejected both the traditional main entry concept and unit card in an effort to gain space.[89] The final printouts were photo-graphically reduced and placed on offset masters for printing.

The contemporary book catalog made tremendous strides in the last two decades of its revitalization. Gener-ally production of the book catalogs falls into three cate-gories. First, the photo-offset method based on the production of a photographically reduced negative by shingling or grouping individual cards, by a sequential camera, or by the use of microfilm and electrostatic print-ing. Second, tabulating machines with punched cards or tape equipment are used to produce printouts or multilith masters. The former may be used as copy for the photo-offset while the latter is immediately available for print-ing. Third, the computer now is capable of organizing information for catalog production which results in print-outs for immediate use or for the production of photo-offset masters. Two other categories should be mentioned although they are an advance beyond the book catalog. First, the use of some form of microprint, suggested by Fremont Rider as early as 1940. Limited production of catalogs that utilize some form of microprint is available although accessibility has hampered extensive use. Another use is in such index-machines as Filmores, Flip, Fosdic, Media, Minicard, Rapid Selector, Verac, and Walnut.[90] Second, the futuristic computer-stored catalog as depicted by many current experiments may eventually

become economically feasible. Presently the computer imput necessary to produce a book catalog could readily be adapted to direct user access and several libraries are making provisions for on-line, real-time terminal inquiries.[91]

Catalogs and cataloging will continue as in the past to vary considerably from one library to another depending upon needs, former practices, personnel, and financial resources. History clearly indicates that new methods are not unique to this century. A review of some of the so-called recent innovations reveals our debt to the past. The KWIC Index is nothing more than the old subject word concept which was revered by Edwards and criti-cized by Cutter. The finding list or limited entry catalog was used and strongly supported over 100 years ago by Poole. Arrangement of books in order of accession was practiced even in the most ancient libraries. The use of broad rather than close classification was employed for years. Size classification, so useful in storage libraries, was suggested hundreds of years ago by Gesner. The past can play an important role in future development if new practices are based upon a rational approach stemming from empirical research rather than tradition. The failure to define the functions of the catalog has created a frame-work of mythology regarding the needs of the users that was further promulgated by Cutter and accepted verbatim by catalogers as gospel. The method used to determine these potential needs during the time of Cutter has never been clearly enumerated although his philosophy has prevailed for almost 100 years and before that was adum-brated by the Bodleian and British Museum Rules which enounced dogma in the same authoritative tones. At that time, however, the position of the library was decidedly different from today as literacy was low and only the gentry had access to printed materials. As the libraries grew and assumed a prominent place in the educational structure, the catalog retained the nineteenth century rules for construction of the printed book catalog while slowly being filled with twentieth century acquisitions. The prob-lem of determining the needs of the user is characterized by an infinite number of variables that are changing every day as the demands of society are modified. The few trends, which are discernible from extant studies, are diffi-cult to translate into action that will fulfill all the needs at reasonable cost. The solution seems to lie in the formula-tion of catalog-centered criteria, as suggested by Taube, that would provide evaluation based on size, compilation and maintenance costs, amount of appropriate and relevant material, number of access points, extent of information about each item, inclusion of many types of information for various purposes, and a low rate of growth.[41] These must then be assigned values with regard to the individual library in order to provide a statement of reasonable and attainable functions that can be interpreted into specific goals. The next step is the formulation of methods com-plete with suitable alternatives. These, however, are not an end in themselves but serve to carry out the specific goals and more inclusive functions.

It is impossible to foresee the many possible forms and methods which will characterize the catalog of the future because of the infinite variations existing from one library to another. General trends, however, may be conjectured upon the basis of events of the past although levels and extent of applications will vary widely.

The most advanced form of the catalog of the foretellable future will be the computerized catalog so aptly depicted by Swanson.[92,93] This catalog will consider 11 performance goals: user dialogues (programmed interrogation), aids to browsing, user-indexed library, access to in-depth information, wheat and chaff identification, national "network" of libraries, national network of bibliographic tools, instant information, remote interrogation and delivery, active dissemination, and quality control over library services (improved feedback).[92] The basic system would be comprised of two-way communication with a computer-stored catalog such as the National Union Catalog through the use of a console that would permit the user to progress from simple bibliographic or limited subject information through a series of heuristic steps to the actual text. Many of the more specialized works such as periodical articles could be obtained as printouts while the contents of monographs could be examined through a display of the table of contents or indexes by a type of cathode ray tube while the final examination would be dependent upon an actual physical perusal. The plan devotes sufficient attention to all of the performance goals. The cost, based on National Union Catalog size and use, is estimated at about $50 per minute, clearly prohibitive, with the primary problem created by the disproportionately large amount of information storage to that which is actually used.[93] The only solution seems to lie in the development of equipment that could economically surmount this problem and the utilization of more complex operations pertaining to subjects rather than simple descriptive searches involving the specific author, title, etc.[93] The potential use of the computer in providing access to technical reports, government documents, periodical articles, and other highly specialized information has been clearly demonstrated and may be the most economically feasible area of immediate development. The failure of the present subject catalog to go beyond a cursory analysis could be greatly improved through such an application. Libraries will continue to seek wider coverage and will no doubt strengthen their positions through a more thorough subject analysis rather than by concentrating on the traditional monographic sources. Research libraries may find it feasible to store bibliographic information for all sources within the computer and produce printed catalogs only for the monographic materials that will be sought by a large number of users, while the computer information would be available for serious researchers desiring comprehensive searches. The inclusion of actual textual materials would be limited primarily to the units of a more manageable length rather than attempting to convert to total text storage for extensive monographic material.

A more immediate and universal application of the computer will be the production of book catalogs and catalog cards. As costs are reduced wider application will result in increased regional and national cooperation with catalogs being produced from state or regional union lists in much the same way as from the National Union Catalog. Wide distribution of cataloging information will in turn stimulate more sophisticated methods of card reproduction for those who seek to retain the card catalog.

Aside from the computer, less sweeping but significant changes will probably take place in the immediate future and would be more generally applicable to a large number of libraries. It seems likely that the book catalog will slowly become the dominant manual system with the card catalog serving as a supplement analogous to the old slip catalogs. The dichotomy of expanding the catalog beyond the monograph and limiting it to a reasonable size will continue as a major source of debate. Where computers are available the problem will be a question of input and storage, while both systems will strive to provide more information organized in such a way that the whole file must not be searched for each request. Horizontal division by date will allow older materials to be printed in a separte sequence, and the use of bibliographies will continue to prove useful. The use of the shelf list (conventional or printed) will serve as a source for large blocks of information that can readily be connected by references. The classified catalog will continue to gain new converts like the National Library of Canada where the Library of Congress system is applied. Centrally produced subject indexes for the classified catalog would greatly add to this movement, with several now available through G.K. Hall from such libraries as Boston University and John Crerar although much more needs to be done in this area. Classification will continue to rise above the shelf-location status that it was originally accorded in the United States and serve as a flexible subject device within the catalog. The use of the shelf list will be expanded, serving as a basis for computerization and as an expanded approach to subjects in the manual systems. Terminology will be of primary concern in all types of catalogs with emphasis given to logical development by specialists. Classified subject lists, as suggested by Mostecky,[94] and thesauri will be prepared to replace the outmoded subject lists with complex and unsuitable terminology set in an illogical syndetic structure. Careful studies, such as those done by Daily, Lilley, and Pettus, all accentuate the need for a more realistic approach to the place of subject headings, descriptors, or indexing terms within the subject catalog. The intellectual process of converting a remote concept into a possible subject heading will be guided by improved lists with heuristic qualities rather than the chance inclusion of references. The present subject lists have been used to some extent as supplementary guides to the public catalog, but will be eventually replaced by the new lists that will convert the users concepts into catalog access points. The use of references within the catalog itself could be dropped with the lists serving as the first step to the subject approach. Libraries will continue to expand in-depth subject analysis within the manual systems. Analytics and wider coverage could be accomplished by separate indexes and bibliographies and by improvement of existing sources using a greater degree of more cooperative methods. The service basis approach by H.W. Wilson is indicative of the feasibility and economy of such action. Professional organizations have and should continue to make advances in this direction. Every possible effort should be made to extend cooperative indexing to its fullest potential so that it is available in usable formats, with reduced duplication and increased accessibility to the largest number of possible users. Professional organizations and the federal government will play an active role in such improvements with national planning developing far beyond present levels. Continued centralized efforts such as MEDLAR and MARC will be joined by a host of preparation centers to extend bibliographic control that is much less than popularly supposed. Use of centralized services and decentralized centers will combine a variety of approaches to produce and disseminate the guides to graphic materials. Regional cataloging centers will expand operations with the aid of centrally produced copy. Less deviation will be found between cataloging methods of the various libraries particularly in the areas of descriptive cataloging with a more pragmatic approach overcoming the traditionalism of the past. Major problems of the past will become minor ones of the future with the functions of the catalog clearly placed in a context of simplicity and usefulness.

The literary unit and main entry principle will undergo intensive study that will result in a restatement of their function within the context of the card catalog. The main entry and unit-card concepts have both been eliminated from the computerized catalog, resulting in a substantial saving of space. The literary unit principle will be carried out logically by added entries that may again be accorded new prominence particularly within the computerized catalog. The verification process of the old methods will be modified to meet with a minimum amount of effort. The catalog will perform as a finding list rather than a bio-bibliographical tool which seemed so desirable during the early part of the twentieth century.

Other minor innovations will include a return to the use of guide cards rather than typing subject headings on each card, photographic reproduction of title pages that could be reduced for inclusion on catalog cards or left full size and placed in a loose-leaf binder serving as a supplement, sequential arrangement of books on shelves, and achievement of the original intentions of the *Anglo-*

American Rules with names gaining precedence over locations. In regard to the arrangement of books, it is interesting to note that Dewey originally intended to provide classification numbers that would bring out other subjects of the book and suggested a sequential arrangement of books on the shelves rather than alphabetically by author.

The cataloging operation of the future will be based first upon a succinct statement of functions formulated in the light of needs; second, upon research, reevaluation, and experimentation that constantly provide alternative solutions and new methods; third, upon ideas, concepts, and machinery originating outside the library itself which will aid in the organizational process; fourth, upon professional personnel who plan, direct, develop, and evaluate the program and rely upon technicians who utilize the existing centralized services in the mechanical preparation of a catalog within a planned framework; and fifth, upon the combined cooperative effort of the professional, scholarly, and governmental units which benefit from increased bibliographic accessibility.

The twentieth century may be characterized as a period of growth and development of productivity. The emerging subject catalog developed within the context of the printed book catalog and retained many of the constraints until a new age of librarians began to rise above the technological phases of catalog production. Subject lists developed largely from existing library practices with the profession originating the quest in this direction only to be supplanted by the rather singular effort of the Library of Congress. The fate of the classified catalog was sealed in the United States when the Library of Congress adopted the dictionary catalog that resulted in the issuing of printed unit cards that set the pattern for the whole nation. Research was at a minimum with the appeal to authority exerting an over-powering influence. Catalogers followed the edict of Cutter and debated only his alternative suggestions. The lack of empirical research permitted the catalog to develop with regard only to the book although a secondary effort was given to the periodical indexes, which strangely enough seemed to be outside the realm of the cataloger. The rules employed in the construction of the book catalog were perpetuated in such outmoded practices as the main entry. The card catalog eventually faltered under the weight of the increased number of books being printed with book budgets stretching its size far beyond original expectations. The newly formed administrative librarian, who had only recently relinquished the task of catalog construction to the practitioners, began to complain about the costs of processing. Catalogers sought to evaluate their own procedures but were hampered by traditional functions, outlooks, and methods. The codes continued to grow with each edition until finally the discontents of the 1940s brought some simplification first within the realm of descriptive cataloging that by 1967 had been expanded to include more logical approaches to author headings.

Traditionalism and economic expediency once again caused some attrition but progress was made.

Cooperative and centralized cataloging were given impetus with expanding resources and federal funds largely responsible for their growth because the astute foresight of many librarians focused attention in this area.

The coming of the computer served to answer the immediate needs of the seeker of specialized information and is now being applied to conventional library situations with varying degrees of success. Its place in future development is apparent and is dependent upon pecuniary resources and logical applications.

By mid-century the subject catalog was the subject of considerable debate. User studies have failed to provide concrete answers for all situations but generally have indicated trends that aided in selecting methods. The role of the subject catalog, though generally recognized, has undergone more intensive study with its components, such as subject headings and the syndetic structure, receiving considerable attention. The results have been rewarding in a limited degree with some understanding gained through analytic studies of subject terminology and a burgeoning number of special subject lists or thesauri. Libraries, like other social institutions, have failed to keep up with new innovations and as a whole have retained old methods or hastily accepted practices that lead to unendurable problems. The subject catalog will continue to demand major emphasis during the remainder of the century that hopefully will be marked by scientifically sound experimentation and rational development.

CONCLUSION

The unfolding of the story of catalogs and cataloging has indicated general trends, which may be succinctly summarized. The ancient period was a time of crude inventory lists that served only as a listing of property rather than an index to the library. The contributions of Callimachus to the cataloging field were typical of the early bio-bibliographic endeavors that were prepared by scholars in order to preserve a record of the leading literary works of the period. This method was characteristic of the attempts of the ancient civilizations that sought to perpetuate the culture for ensuing generations. The concept of authorship and title was confusing, with listings frequently a combination of author names, titles, and/or first lines although the Greeks were probably responsible for the use of the author in reference to individual works. Chronology or order of accession were the primary orders of arrangement. The rise of Christianity shifted the centers of learning to the monasteries where the codex was used and reproduced for distribution to other religious houses. Books were an exceedingly valuable commodity which necessitated a record of the holdings of each collection. Slowly the lists began to reflect a utilitarian aspect with

books arranged not by the old chornological approach but by order of importance to the user that in turn led to broad subject and form arrangements persisting for many centuries and later forming the basis for the more systematic classification schemes. As these lists lacked author or subject, and title indexes, they were not catalogs in the modern sense of the word but rather resembled our shelf list in character and use.

In the thirteenth century the first union catalog was attempted and college and university libraries, which were to exert such an influence on later development, began to assemble comprehensive collections.

The fourteenth century brought the inclusion of an author index appended to an inventory list that could conceivably be designated as a true catalog.

The fifteenth century with the invention of movable metal type brought a new need for bibliographic organization with leaders such as Tritheim who appended an index of authors to his chronologically arranged bibliography of ecclesiastical writers and exhibited a concept of the main and added entry which was further developed by Gesner, Treflerus, Maunsell, and Sir Thomas Bodley.

The sixteenth century was marked by a number of leading bibliographies produced by Gesner and Maunsell who were joined by Treflerus in providing information on the construction of catalogs. Two astute bibliographers suggested that a bibliography could be pressed into service as a substitute for the catalog. Maunsell's use of the author's surname was indicative of the changing concepts regarding names. The addition of supplementary indexes was clearly emerging with the number of access points going far beyond the original inventory list and catalogs beginning to assume the retrieval function.

The seventeenth century brought the Bodleian catalogs. The author arrangement of the influential issue of 1620 advanced the concept of entry with considerable attention to the determination of the form of main entry and an expression of the literary unit principle. An early form of the dictionary catalog with authors and subjects filed in a single alphabet appeared although the single entry (author or title for anonymous) was the rule of the day. A number of codes of instructions by Naude, Dury, and Baillet indicated that interest in the catalog was increasing with methods taking on a few primitive signs of standardization.

The eighteenth century found a national cataloging project in France using cards as a basis of the catalog as well as a national cataloging code. Bibliographical description slowly increased and was assuming more of its modern aspects.

The nineteenth century was the high point of cataloging with a number of important codes produced, beginning with the British Museum and reaching a zenith in Cutter's *Rules* of 1876. Catalogs steadily developed under the concept of the subject word particularly within Germany and America as the single entry idea expanded beyond conventional application. The card catalog became more commonplace after 1860 and assumed a variety of arrangements reflecting a number of divergent opinions. The subject catalog was the major contribution of the era and was employed first in America by Jewett. Cutter was to provide the definitive work with the publication of his *Rules* in 1876, which were to serve for years as authoritative and final. The problem of catalog arrangement was still a controversial issue at this time and was never satisfactorily resolved, although, elements of the classified printed book catalog were readily adopted to the dictionary card form. The emergence of centralized cataloging at the Library of Congress, which was based upon a dictionary catalog, terminated serious debate and elevated the technological aspects of its catalog to a paramount place with little regard for its philosophical advantages over the classified systems.[41] Classification became not a tool of the catalog but rather a location symbol. The catalog was dependent upon an alphabetical order which was supported by a syndetic structure, serving as a systematic guide to subject terminology. Subject headings and cross references, however, grew not by design but rather by chance until the burgeoning size of the catalog brought forth a deluge of criticism against Cutter's answer to the classified catalog. The lack of an acceptable classification scheme no doubt influenced the rapid growth of the dictionary catalog, which came under close scrutiny during the twentieth century. The overemphasis on rules and a preoccupation with monographs in libraries stymied innovation to such an extent that seekers of specialized information and extraordinary services turned first to the documentalist and then to the information scientists. The mid-fifties produced a number of studies pertaining to the classified catalog, approaches and needs of the user, cost analysis, catalog division, book catalogs, and the relationship of bibliographies to the catalog. All of these reflected the failure to adequately study the fundamental design and purpose of the alphabetical subject catalog in card form.[41] By the end of the nineteenth century the pattern of catalog construction was well defined with subject headings, main entry, literary unit principle, dictionary catalog, classification, unit cards, added entries, and adequate bibliographical descriptions all well-developed elements. Cooperative cataloging was in its beginning stage with the first efforts directed toward an early type of cataloging-in-source, which advocated slips with the books.

The twentieth century brought an expansion of cooperative and centralized cataloging, three new cataloging codes for the English speaking world, numerous subject lists, and a general reevaluation of the cataloging process beginning with the descriptive phase. The junglelike growth in the size of library collections forced many librarians to seek simplified methods as well as expanding cooperative and centralized services.

Substantial sums of money have been used since the intervention of the federal government into the field of scientific information with primary efforts directed toward retrieval of specialized information but later expanding to encompass services of more immediate value to public and research libraries. The National Program of Acquisitions and Cataloging Program is one example of the concerted effort which will result in a more comprehensive coverage of printed cards for foreign titles and will stimulate international cooperation in bibliographic control.

Continued technological advancements such as the electric typewriter, electrostatic copying, telefacsimile transmission, and computers will expedite cataloging activities.

The present and future hold great promise for the development of catalogs into a more useful, more functional, and more comprehensive tool through the formulation of attainable goals, continued experimentation, empirical research, and cooperative effort. So far there is no indication that the need for catalogs will ever diminish or be replaced.

APPENDIX LIST OF CODES OF CATALOGING RULES

1791   *Instruction pour procéder a la confection du catalogue de chacune des bibliotheques sur lesquelles les Directoires ont dû ou doivent incessaminent apposer les scelles* Imprimerie nationale, Paris, 1791.

1841   *The British Museum code of ninety-one rules*, adopted by the Trustees in 1839.

1852   C.C. Jewett, *Smithsonian report on the construction of catalogues of libraries. . .and their publication by means of separate, stereotyped titles, with rules and examples.*

1876   C.A. Cutter, *Rules for a printed dictionary catalog.* (Revised in 1889, 1891, and 1904.)

1878   Cambridge University, *Rules to be observed in forming the alphabetical catalogue of printed books.* (Originally contained 49 Rules but enlarged to 64 in 1925.)

1878   *L'Instruction general erelative au service des bibliotheques universitaires.*

1883   American Library Association, *Condensed rules for an author and title-catalog.*

1883   Oxford, Bodleian Library. *Compendious cataloging rules for the author catalog.*

1883   Library Association, *Cataloguing rules.*

1884   F.B. Perkins, *San Francisco cataloguing for public libraries.*

1886   American Library Association, *Condensed rules for a card catalog.*

1886   K. Dziatzko, *Instruction fur die Ordnung der Titel im alphabetischen Zettelkatalog der Konigl, und Universitatsbibliothek zu Breslau.*

1888 M. Dewey, *Rules for author and classed catalogs as used in Columbia College Library.*

1889 L. Delisle, *Instructions elementaires et techniques pour la mise et le maintien en ordre des livres d'une bibliotheque.*

1889 M. Dewey, *Library school card catalog rules; with 52 facsimiles of sample cards for author and classed catalogs.*

1890 L. Delisle, *Instructions elementaires et techniques pour la mise et le maintien en ordre des livres d'une bibliotheque,* Lille, 1890.

1890 K. Linderfelt, *Eclectic card catalog rules; author and title entires based on Dziatzko's "Instruction" compared with the rules of the British Museum, Cutter, Dewey, Perkins and other authorities,* Boston, 1890.

1899 Prussia, *Instruktionen fur die alphabetischen Kataloge der preussischen Bibliotheken, vom 1899.* Zweite ausgabe, 1908.

1902 Spain, *Junta facultativa de archivos, bibliotecas y museos,* Madrid.

1905 United States, Library of Congress, Catalog division. *Supplementary rules on cataloguing.* (First published as a monograph but continued on cards.)

1908 American and British Library Associations, *Cataloguing rules; author and title entries.*

1909 *Instruktionen fur die alphabetischen Kataloge der preuszischen Bibliotheken vom 10. mai 1889. 2. ausg. in der fassung vom 10. August 1908.* Berlin.

1912 Association des Bibliothecaires Francais, *Regles et usages observes dans les principales bibliotheques de Paris...*

1912 French Library Association, *Regles et usages observés dans les principales bibliotheques de Paris pour la rédaction et le classement des catalogues d'auteurs et d'anonymes, 1912.*

1913 Association Des bibliothecaires francais, *...Regles et usages observés dans les principales bibliotheques de Paris pour la rédaction et le classement des catalogues d'auteurs et d'anonymes (1912)...,* Paris.

1916 Sweden, Kungliga biblioteket, *Katalogregler for Kungl, biblioteket samt anvisningar for anordnande av bokband,* Av riksbibliotekarien faststallda den 30 juni 1916, Stockholm.

1917 Denmark, Bogsamlingskomite, *Katalogisering; raad og regler til brug ved ordningen af bogsamlinger, udgivet af Statens bogsamlings-komite,* Copenhagen, 1917.

1921 Norway, Norsk bibliotekforening, *Forslag til katalogiseringsregler utarb. av Norsk bibliotekforenings katalogkomite,* Christiania, 1921.

1921 Vereinigung schweizerischer bibliothekare, *Entwurf zu einer Katalogisierungsinstruktion fur den schweizerischen Gesamtkatalog,* Zurich, 1921.

1922 Italy, Commissione incaricata di progorre un nuovo codice di regole (etc.), *Regole per la compilazi one del catalogo alfabetico,* Rome, 1922.

1922 Bayerische staabsbibliothek, *Katalogisierungsordnung. 2. ausg.,* Munich, 1922.

1922 Bodleian Library, *...Rules for the cataloguing of printed books published before 1920...,* Oxford, 1922.

1923 France, Bibliotheque nationale, *Usages suivis dans la redaction du Catalogue general des livers imprimes de la Bibliotheque nationale, recueillis et coordonnes par E.G. Ledos,* Paris, 1923.

1925 Norway, Norsk bibliotekforening, *Katalogiseringsregler for norske biblioteker utarb, av Norsk bibliotekforenings katalogkomite,* Oslo, 1925.

1929 Association des Bibliothecaires Francais, *Regles generales.*

1931 The Vatican code, *Norme per il catalogo degli stampati.*

1936 *Rules for compiling the catalogues of printed books, maps and music in the British Museum.* Revised edition.

1941 *A.L.A. Catalog rules: author and title entries,* prepared by the Catalog Code Revision Committee of the American Library Association, with the collaboration of a Committee of the (British) Library Association.

1949 *A.L.A. Cataloging rules for author and title,* 2nd ed., ALA, Chicago, 1949.

1949 U.S. Library of Congress, *Rules for descriptive cataloguing in the Library of Congress,* Government Printing Office, Washington, D.C., 1949.

1961 Germany (Federal Republic), Budestag, Bundestag, Bibliothek, *Instruktionen fur die Kataloge der Bibliothek des deutschen Bundestages,* 1961.

1961 U.S.S.R., *Glavone upravlenie kul'turno-prosvetitel' nykh uchrezhdenii. Edinye pravila opisaniia proizvedenii pechati dlia bibliotechnykh katalogov.* Chast' I. Vypusk 2. *Organizatsiia alfavitnogo Kataloga knig,* 2-e izdanie, ispravlennoe i dopolnennoe. (*Standard rules for the description of printed works for library catalogs. Pt. 1, Section 2; Arrangement of the alphabetical catalog of books.* 2nd ed., rev. enl.), Biblioteka im. Lenina, Moscow, 1961.

1964 Spain, Direccion General de Archivos y Bibliotecas, *Instrucciones para la redaccion del catálogo alfabético de autores y obras anónimas en las bibliotecas publicas del estado, dirigidas por el Cuerpo Facultativo de Archíveros, Bibliotecarios y Arqueólogos,* 3 ed. reformata, Dir. Gen. de Archivos y Bibliotecas, Madrid, 1964.

1965 Verein Deutscher Bibliothekar, Kommission fur alphabetische Katalogisierung, *Regeln fur die alphabetische Katalogisierung. Teilentwurf.*

Kolstermann, Frankfurt, 1965. (A partial compilation of a new German code with Part I pertaining to corporate authorship and Part II covering alphabetical arrangement. This work clearly indicates the Paris principles.)

1965　Japanese Library Association, *Nippon Cataloguing Rules*, 1965. (This extensive code was clearly influenced by the Paris principles.)

1965　Zentralinstitut fur Bibliothekswesen, *Titelaufnahme fur die Kataloge der allegemeinbildenden Bibliotheken*, 2nd rev. ed., Bibliographis-ches Institut, Leipzig, 1965. (The Paris principles have strongly influenced this code although corporate bodies are not recognized as main entries.)

1967　*Anglo-American cataloging rules*, prepared by the American Library Association, The Library of Congress, The Library Association and the Canadian Library Association, ALA, Chicago, 1967.

REFERENCES

1. Hitchcock, J. E. Subject coverage in University Library catalogs. Libr. Q. January **1940**, January *10*, 69–94.
2. Cutter, C. A. Library Catalogues. In *Public Libraries in the United States of America; Their History, Condition and Management*; U.S. Bureau of Education, Ed.; U.S. Department of Interior, Bureau of Education Special Report, Part I Government Printing Office: Washington, DC, 1876; 526–622 839 Chapter XXVII.
3. Cutter, C. A. *Rules for a Dictionary Catalog*, 4th Ed. U.S. Bureau of Education Special Report on Public Libraries, Part II Govt. Printing Office: Washington, D.C., 1904; 5–6 12–13 31 67 rewritten.
4. International Federation of Library Associations. *International Conference on Cataloguing Principles, Paris, 9th–18th October, 1961*; London, U.K., 1963; 26.
5. Jolley, L. *The Principles of Cataloguing*, Philosophical Library: New York, 1961; 6.
6. Norris, D. M. *A History of Cataloguing and Cataloguing Methods 1100–1850: With an Introductory Survey of Ancient Times*, Grafton: London, U.K., 1939; 2, 5, 20–22, 24, 29-30, 38, 78–87, 91-93, 113–114, 135, 136, 142–147, 151–153, 163, 178, 181–191, 193–195, 201, 207.
7. Johnson, E. D. *A History of Libraries in the Western World*, Scarecrow Press: New York, 1965; 25, 77, 122, 123.
8. Witty, F. J. Pinakes of Callimachus. Libr. J. April **1958**, *28*, 132–136.
9. Strout, R. F. The development of the catalog and cataloging codes. Libr. Q. October **1956**, *26*, 254–275.
10. Clark, J. W. *Care of Books*, Cambridge University Press: Cambridge, U.K., 1901; 43, 214-217.
11. Cassiodorus, M. A. In *An Introduction to Divine and Human Reading*; Jones, L. W., Ed.; Columbia University Press: New York, 1946; 43, 214–217.
12. Serverance, H. O. Three of the earliest book catalogues. Public Libr. **1905**, *10*, 116–117.
13. Thompson, J. W. *The Medieval Library*, Hafner: New York, 1957; 614–617, 620,621.
14. Condit, L. Bibliography in its prenatal existence. Libr. Q. October **1937**, 7, 564–576.
15. Gottlieb, T. *Über Mittelalterliche, Bibliotheken*, Harrassowitz: Leipzig, Germany, 1891. As quoted in Thompson[13].
16. *Medieval Libraries in Great Britain*, 2nd Ed.; Ker, N. R., Ed.; Offices of the Royal Historical Society: London, U.K., 1964; xix–xx.
17. Savage, E. *Old English Libraries, the Making, Collection and Use of Books During the Middle Ages*, Methesen: London, U.K., 1911; 58, 59, 104–106.
18. Strout, R. F. *Toward a Better Cataloguing Code;* Papers Presented Before the Twenty-first Annual Conference of the Graduate Library School of the University of Chicago, June 13–15, 1956, Univ. Chicago Press: Chicago, IL, 1957; 10–562 [Reprints of papers originally published in *Lib. Quart.*, 26 (October 1956)].
19. Besterman, T. *The Beginnings of Systematic Bibliography*, 2nd Rev. Ed. Oxford University Press; Milford: Oxford, U.K., 1936; 7, 8, 10, 15, 17.
20. Verner, M. Adrien Baillet (1649–1706) and his rules for an alphabetical subject catalog. Libr. Q. July **1968**, *38*, 217–230.
21. Maunsell, A. *The First Part of the Catalogue of English Printed Books: Which Concerneth Such Matters of Divinities as Both Bin Written in Our Own Tongue, or Translated Out of Anie Other Language*, J. Windet: London, U.K., 1595; v (The seconde parte, etc.).
22. Akers, S. G. *Simple Library Cataloging*, 5th Ed. Scarecrow Press: Metuchen, NJ, 1969; 58 286.
23. Jayne, S. *Library Catalogues of the English Renaissance*, University of California Press: Berkeley, CA, 1956; 37 140.
24. Naudeus, G. *Instructions Concerning Erecting of a Library Presented to My Lord the President De Mesme...*, Houghton Mifflin: Cambridge, MA, 1903; 74–75 80 translated by J. Evelyn (Originally printed in 1661.).
25. Dury, J. The reformed librarie keeper or two copies concerning the place and office of the library keeper, 1649. In *Literature of Libraries in the 17th and 18th Centuries*; Dana, J. C., Kent, H. W., Eds.; McClurg: Chicago, IL, 1906; Vol. 2, 45–46.
26. Ranz, J. *The Printed Book Catalogue in American Libraries: 1723–1900*, ACRL Monograph Number 26 American Library Association: Chicago, IL, 1964; 8–10 28–29 70–71.
27. Cole, G. W. An early French general catalogue. Libr. J. **1900**, *25*, 329–331.
28. Edwards, E. *Memoirs of Libraries; Including a Handbook of Library Economy*, Franklin: New York; Vol. 2, 155–156 (Reprint of 1859 ed., 2 vols. in 1.).
29. Metcalfe, J. *Alphabetical Subject Indication of Information*, Rutgers Series on Systems for the Intellectual Organization of Information Graduate School of Library Science, Rutgers State University: New Brunswick, NJ, 1965; Vol. 3, 29–31.
30. Shera, J. H. Egan, M. E. *The Classified Catalog, Basic Principles and Practices*, American Library Association: Chicago, IL, 1956; IX X 13.

31. Pettee, J. E. *Subject Headings; The History and Theory of the Alphabetical Subject Approach to Books*, Wilson: New York, 1946; 26–27.

32. British Museum, Parliament, House of Commons, *Report of the Commission Appointed to Inquire into the Constitution of the Museum*, Parliamentary Papers; London, U.K., 1850; Vol. 24, IX Questions #9869, #9692, #9754, #9736.

33. Rhees, W. J. *Manual of Public Libraries, Institutions and Societies in the United States and British Provinces of North America*, Lippincott: Philadelphia, PA, 1859; 133–134.

34. Fiske, J. The librarian's work. Atl. Mo. **1876**, *38*, 480–491.

35. James, M. S.R. The progress of the modern card catalog principle. In *The Library and Its Content*; Sawyer, H. P., Ed.; Classics in American Librarianship Wilson: New York, 1925; 331–338.

36. Heiss, R. M. The card catalog in libraries of the united states before 1876. Masters Thesis, Graduate School of Library Science, University of Illinois: Urbana. IL, 1938; 79 unpublished.

37. Schwartz, J. Catalogues and cataloguing, Pt. III. In *Public Libraries in the United States of America, Their History, Condition and Management*; U.S. Bureau of Education, Ed.; U.S. Department of Interior, Bureau of Education Special Report, Part I U.S. Government. Printing Office: Washington, DC, 1876; 651–660 Chapter XXVIII, Part III.

38. Maddox, L. Trends and Issues in American Librarianship as Reflected in the Papers and Proceedings of the American Library Association, 1876–1885. *Ph.D. Dissertation*, Department of Library Science, University of Michigan: Ann Arbor, MI, 1958; 1 unpublished.

39. U.S. Bureau of Education, *Public Libraries in the United States of America; Their History, Condition and Management*, U.S. Department of the Interior, Bureau of Education Special Report, Part I Government Printing Office: Washington, DC, 1876; XXIX.

40. Noyes, S. B. Catalogues and cataloguing, Part II. In *Public Libraries in the United States of America; Their History, Condition and Management*; U.S. Bureau of Education, Ed.; U.S. Department of Interior, Bureau of Education Special Report, Part I Government Printing Office: Washington, DC, 1876; 648–657 Chapter XXVIII.

41. Lilley, O. Evaluation of the subject catalog, criticisms and a proposal. Am. Doc. **1954**, *5*, 41–60.

42. U.S. Library of Congress, Processing Department, *Cataloging-in-Source Experiment, a Report to the Librarian of Congress by the Director of the Processing Department*, Library of Congress: Washington, DC, 1960; V–VI XI 52.

43. Stevens, H. Photo-bibliography: Or a central bibliographical clearinghouse. Libr. J. November–December **1877**, *2*, 162–173.

44. Robinson, O. H. College Library Administration. In *Public Libraries in the United States of America; Their History, Condition and Management*; U.S. Bureau of Education, Ed.; U.S. Department of Interior, Bureau of Education Special Report, Part I Government Printing Office: Washington, DC, 1876; 505–525 Chapter XXVI.

45. Jordon, F. P. History of printed catalogue cards. Public Libr. **1904**, *9*, 318–321.

46. American Library Association Committee on an index to subject headings, Report on subject headings by the Chairmen of the committee, Mr. Cutter. Libr. J. **1881**, *6*, 114–115.

47. Francis, F. C. A reconsideration of the british museum rules for compiling the Catalogues of Printed Books—I. In *Cataloging Principles and Practices; An Inquiry*; University of London, School of Librarianship and Archives, Ed.; The Library Association: London, U.K., 1954; 26–36 (edited with an introduction by M. Piggott) Chapter III.

48. Osborn, A. *Descriptive Cataloging*, 2nd Preliminary Ed. Univ. Pittsburgh Graduate School of Library and Information Sciences: Pittsburgh, PA, 1965; 7–8.

49. Jewett, C. C. *On the Construction of Catalogues of Libraries and Their Publication by Means of Separate, Stereotyped Titles with Rules and Examples*, 2nd Ed. Smithsonian Report Smithsonian Institution: Washington, DC, 1853; Vol. 10185;2 54–56.

50. Crestadoro, A. *The Art of Making Catalogues of Libraries*, The Literary Scientific and Artistic Reference Office: London, U.K., 1856. As quoted in Cutter[2].

51. Frarey, C. J. *Subject Headings*, The State of the Library Arts Graduate School of Library Service, Rutgers State University: New Brunswick, NJ, 1960; Vol. 1, Part 2, 31–47.

52. Poole, W. F. Organization and management of public libraries. In *Public Libraries in the United States, Their History, Condition and Management*; U.S. Bureau of Education, Ed.; U.S. Department of Interior, Bureau of Education Special Report, Part I Government Printing Office: Washington, DC, 1876; 476–504 Chapter XXV.

53. Baker, M. O. American library catalogs a hundred years ago. Wilson Libr. Bull. December **1958**, *33*, 284–285.

54. Lane, W. C. Cataloging. In *Papers Prepared for the Worlds Library Congress Held at the Columbian Exposition*; Dewey, M., Ed.; U.S. Bureau of Education, Chapter IX of Part II of the Report of the Commission of Education, 1892–1893 Government Printing Office: Washington, DC, 1896; 835–850.

55. Lane, W. C. Present tendencies of cataloguing practice. *Papers and Proceedings of the 26th Conference at the Louisiana Purchase Exposition, St. Louis*, American Library Association: Chicago, IL, October 1904; 134–143.

56. Jolley, L. Some recent developments in cataloguing in the U.S.A. J. Doc. June **1950**, *6*, 70–82.

57. American Library Association, *A.L.A. Glossary of Library Terms with a Selection of Terms in Related Fields*, American Library Association: Chicago, IL, 1943; 26 (compiled by Elizabeth H. Thompson).

58. Library of Congress, Descriptive Cataloging Division, *Cooperative Cataloging Manual for the Use of Contributing Libraries*, Government. Printing Office: Washington, DC, 1944; 8–9.

59. Fletcher, W. I. Future of the catalogue. Libr. J. **1905**, *30*, 141–144.

60. Rider, F. Alternatives for the present dictionary catalog. In *The Acquisition and Cataloging of Books*; Randall, W. M., Ed.; University Chicago Press: Chicago, IL, 1940; 133–162.

61. Dewey, H. Some special aspects of the classified catalog. In *The Subject Analysis of Library Materials*; Tauber, M. F.,

Ed.; Columbia University School of Library Service: New York, 1953; 114–129.

62. Taylor, K. L. Subject catalogs vs. classified catalogs. In *The Subject Analysis of Library Materials*; Tauber, M. F., Ed.; Columbia University School of Library Service: New York, 1953; 100–113.

63. American Library Association, Resources and Technical Services Division, Cataloging and Classification Section. Classification Committee, Classified Catalogs. Libr. Resour. Tech. Serv. **1962**, Summer *6*, 274–275.

64. Thom, I. W. The divided catalog in college and university libraries. Coll. Res. Libr. July **1949**, *10*, 236–241.

65. MacNair, M. *A Guide to the Cataloging of Periodicals*, 3rd Ed. Government Printing Office: Washington, DC, 1925.

66. Pierson, H. W. *A Guide to the Cataloging of Serial Publications of Societies and Institutions*, 2nd Ed. Government Printing Office: Washington, DC, 1931.

67. U.S. Library of Congress Librarian's Committee, *Report to the Librarian of Congress on the Processing Operations in the Library of Congress*, Library of Congress: Washington, DC, 1940.

68. Van Hoesen, H. B. *Selective Cataloging*, Wilson: New York, 1928.

69. Frarey, C. J. Studies of use of the subject catalog: Summary and evaluation. In *The Subject Analysis of Library Materials*; Tauber, M. F., Ed.; Columbia University School of Library Services: New York, 1953; 147–166.

70. Osborn, A. D. The crisis in cataloging. Libr. Q. October **1941**, *2*, 393–411.

71. U.S. Library of Congress, Processing Department, *Studies of Descriptive Cataloging: A Report to the Librarian of Congress by the Director of the Processing Department*, Govt. Printing Office: Washington, DC, 1946.

72. U.S. Library of Congress, *Rules for Descriptive Cataloging in the Library of Congress*, Government Printing Office: Washington, DC, 1949.

73. Lubetzky, S. *Cataloguing Rules and Principles: A Critique of the A.L.A. Rules for Entry and a Proposed Design for Their Revision Prepared for the Board on Cataloging Policy and Research of the A.L.A. Division of Cataloging and Classification*, Library of Congress, Processing Department: Washington, DC, 1953.

74. Lubetzky, S. *Code of Cataloging Rules, Author and Title Entry; An Unfinished Draft for a New Edition of Cataloging Rules Prepared for the Catalog Code Revision Committee*, American Library Association: Chicago, IL, 1960.

75. Spalding, C. S. Introduction. *Anglo-American Cataloging Rules*, American Library Association. Prepared by the American Library Association, The Library of Congress, The Library Association, and the Canadian Library Association: Chicago, IL, 1967; 1–6.

76. Ellsworth, R. E. Mr. Ellsworth's report. Libr. Congr. Inf. Bull. November **1948**, 16–22 Appendix.

77. U.S. Library of Congress, *Annual Report of the Librarian of Congress for the Fiscal Year Ending June 30, 1965*, Library of Congress: Washington, DC, 1966; 34 40.

78. Hiatt, P. Cooperative processing centers for public libraries. Libr. Trends. July **1967**, *16*, 67–84.

79. Darling, R. L. School library processing centers. Libr. Trends. July **1967**, *16*, 56 58–66.

80. Westby, B. M. School library processing centers. Libr. Trends. July **1967**, *16*, 46–57.

81. Fry (George) and Associates, Inc., *Catalog Card Reproduction*, Library Technology Projects Publication #9 American Library Association: Chicago, IL, 1965; 5.

82. U.S. Library of Congress, *Annual Report of the Librarian of Congress for the Fiscal Year Ending June 30, 1967*, Library of Congress: Washington, DC, 1968; 17–18 36 39 53.

83. Treyz, J. H. The cards-with-books program. Am. Libr. Assoc. Bull. May **1963**, *57*, 433–444.

84. Esterquest, R. T. Cooperation in library services. Libr. Q. **1961**, *31*, 71–89.

85. Cronin, J. W. The National Union and Library of Congress catalogs: Problems and prospects. Libr. Q. January **1964**, *34*, 77–98.

86. Sharr, F. A.; Creasey, V.; Drake, C. L. The production of a new book type catalogue in Australia. Libr. Resour. Tech. Serv. **1966**, Spring *10*, 143–154.

87. Shoemaker, R. Some American 20th century book catalogs: Their purpose, format and production techniques. Libr. Resour. Tech. Serv. **1960**, Summer *4*, 195–207.

88. Kieffer, P. The Baltimore county public library book, Catalog. Libr. Resour. Tech. Serv. **1966**, Spring *10*, 133–141.

89. Johnson, R. D. A book catalog at Stanford. J. Libr. Autom. March **1968**, *1*, 13–49.

90. Weber, C. D. The changing character of the catalog in Am. Libr. Q. **1964**, *34*, 20–33.

91. Weber, D. C. Book catalog trends in 1966. Libr. Trends. July **1967**, *16*, 149–164.

92. Swanson, D. R. Design requirements for a future library. In *Libraries and Automation Proceedings of the Conference on Libraries and Automation, held at Airlie Foundation, Warrenton, Virginia, May 26–30, under the sponsorship of the Library of Congress, National Science Foundation and Council on Library Resources, Inc.*; Markuson, B. E., Ed.; Library of Congress: Washington, DC, 1964; 11–21.

93. Swanson, D. R. Dialogues with a catalog. Libr. Q. January **1964**, *34*, 113–125.

94. Mostecky, V. Study of see also references structure in relation to the subject of international law. Am. Doc. **1956**, *7*, 294–314.

BIBLIOGRAPHY

1. Abbot, E. Statements Respecting the New Catalogues of the College Library. *Report of the Committee of the Overseers of Harvard College Appointed to Visit the Library for the Year 1863*. Harvard University: Boston, MA, 1864.

2. Avram, H. D. Knapp, J. F. Rather, L. J. *The MARC II Format, a Communications Format for Bibliographic Data*, Library of Congress Information Systems Office: Washington, DC, 1968.

3. Beck, F. Zur geschichte des schlagwortkatalogs. Prax. Theor. Zent.bl. Bibl.wes. **1923**, *40*, 495–496 As quoted in Verner.[20]

4. Becker, G. *Catalogi Bibliothecarum Antiqui Bonn, Max Cohen 1885*, as quoted in Thompson.[13]

5. Daily, J. E. The grammar of subject headings, a formulation of rules for subject headings based on a syntactical and morphological analysis of the library of congress list. PhD Dissertation; Columbia University. School of Library Service: New York, 1957 unpublished.

6. Irwin, R. R. Use of the card catalog in the public library. Master's Essay, Graduate Library School. University of Chicago: Chicago, IL, 1949 unpublished. As quoted in Frarey.[69]

7. Kingery, R. E. Building card catalogs for eventual migration into book forms. In *Book Catalogs*; Kingery, R. E., Tauber, M. F., Eds.; Scarecrow Press: New York, 1963; 93–122.

8. Lilley, O. How specific is 'specific'. J. Cat. Classif. January **1955**, *11*, 3–8.

9. Macray, W. D. *Annals of the Bodleian Library*, 2nd Ed. Clarendon Press: Oxford, U.K., 1890. As quoted in Ref. [6].

10. Metcalfe, J. *Subject Classifying and Indexing of Libraries and Literature*, Scarecrow Press: New York, 1959.

11. Morsch, L. Cooperation and centralization. Libr. Trends. October **1953**, *2*, 342–355.

12. Osborn, V. J. A History of cooperative cataloging in the United States. Master's Thesis, University of Chicago Graduate Library School, 1944 unpublished.

13. Pettee, J. E. The development of authorship entry and formulation of authorship rules as found in the Anglo American Code. Libr. Q. July **1936**, *6*, 270–290.

14. Pettus, C. *Subject Headings in Education, A Systematic List for Use in a Dictionary Catalog*, Wilson: New York, 1938.

15. Rostgaard, F. *Project d'une Nouvelle Methode Pour Dresser le Catalogue d'une Bibliotheque*, 2nd Ed.; Paris, France, 1698.

16. Runge, S. Some recent developments in subject cataloging in Germany. Libr. Q. January **1941**, *11*, 46–68.

17. Shores, L. *Origins of the American College Library, 1638–1800*, Shoe String Press: Hamden, CT, 1966.

18. Swank, R. C. Subject catalogs, classifications or bibliographies? A review of critical discussion, 1876–1942. Libr. Q. October **1944**, *14*, 316–322.

19. The National Union Catalogs. ALA Bull. January **1969**, *63*, 39–41.

Censorship and Content Regulation of the Internet

Peng Hwa Ang
Wee Kim Wee School of Communication and Information, Nanyang Technological University, Singapore,

Abstract
Censorship is defined as the intervention by a third party between the free exchange of a willing sender and a willing receiver of information; typically, censorship is repressive in that both sender and receiver do not want the intervention. Censorship of the Internet began clumsily from when it was made publicly available. Then governments were trying to reconcile the new medium with existing rules on traditional media. Since then, there have been two other overlapping and parallel waves of attempts to censor Internet content. Today's censorship of the Internet is more nuanced. Governments in general do not accept the argument that the Internet is difficult to censor. Among the methods used are simple denial of access to the Internet, passing punitive laws that would deter others when those who are caught are prosecuted, and using blocking technology. The most acceptable face of such censorship would be for the protection of minors and through filtering of the Internet. Censorship of the Internet will continue to exist because of the cultural differences that exist.

INTRODUCTION

For many years after it was introduced to the public, it was held as a self-evident truth that the Internet could not be censored or regulated. The sentiment was first pronounced by John Gilmore in 1993, before the Internet became widely available to the public, the "Net treats censorship as damage and routes around it."[1] It was reiterated by John Perry Barlow in his Declaration of Cyberspace that governments have no place in cyberspace.[2]

One of the reasons is that the Internet has a diffused packet-switching architecture that was absent any visible central governing body that regulated it on a daily operational basis. It seemed designed to evade government control. If there was a slogan then, it would have been "information wants to be free."[3]

Scholars such as David Johnson and David Post argued that the Internet could not be governed by existing legal regimes because it crossed borders.[4] The U.S. government under President Bill Clinton declared a hands-off approach to Internet communication and e-commerce because of its "decentralized nature and... tradition of bottom-up governance."[5]

The Internet has come a long way. As at November 2007, there were an estimated 1.3 billion users, almost 20% of all inhabitants on the planet, and the number is still rising.[6] The evidence is overwhelming today that neither the architecture nor the lack of a visible central governing body necessarily means the Internet is beyond government control.[7,8] The Final Report of the Working Group on Internet Governance shows that there is a need for a central body to at least coordinate the Internet for it to function.[9] This is the Internet Corporation for Assigned Names and Numbers (ICANN). While ICANN cannot be accused of censorship, the fact that it is located in the United States gave rise to the issue of what happens when the United States is at war with another country. What happens to the Internet in the other country? Before the war in Iraq, the operators of the Iraqi domain name .IQ, who were based in Texas, were arrested and charged with unauthorized sale of computer parts to fund terrorist groups. The operators were eventually convicted in 2005 and 2007.[10]

It was at the World Summit on the Information Society (WSIS) in Tunis to discuss the Report of the Working Group on Internet Governance (WGIG) that it was agreed by all the countries present, including the United States, that the country code top level domain (ccTLD) system would be managed only by the country themselves. In the case of the .AF domain name for Afghanistan, the private individual who held the right to operate it signed his right away to the new government in 2004.[11] The WSIS Declaration in Tunis implicitly recognizes the sovereignty of national government over the Internet. The long arm of national laws can reach into the realm of Web site content; it is possible, within limits, for governments to control the Internet.[12]

Another group that has shown interest in gaining some measure of control over the Internet is the private sector. If information ever wanted to be free, the providers did not. Increasingly, content is being copyrighted. Government regulation is necessary to balance the rights of individual to privacy and fair use of information with the desires of the private corporation.

DEFINITION OF CENSORSHIP

A working definition of censorship by this author is: the intervention by a third party between the free exchange of

Encyclopedia of Library and Information Sciences, Fourth Edition DOI: 10.1081/E-ELIS4-120044407

a willing sender and a willing receiver of information; typically, censorship is repressive in that both sender and receiver do not want the intervention.

There are a few points to note about the above definition. First, the definition of censorship is independent of the party. This is in contrast to the position in some countries, such as the United States under the First Amendment to its Constitution, the government shall "pass no law" abridging content. This means that in the United States and in countries that have similar phrasing in their constitutions, the governments cannot, subject to qualifications by the courts, censor content. Business, however, is not subject to the same restrictions place on government.

An example of such a divide would be, say, a song with lyrics calling the police "pigs." In many countries, such lyrics would be banned by law because they encourage the flouting of law and order. In the United States, however, such lyrics would be allowed but business may refuse to carry the music and other groups may encourage boycott of the singer of the song.

Second, it excludes such acts as editing, which seeks to improve the meaning and clarity of the message. The definition may or may not include gatekeeping functions, such as which messages should appear and in what order. In those instances, it is not always clear if there are legitimate grounds for gatekeeping or if it is censorship—in the sense of intervention with the primary intent of blocking the transmission and reception of the information.

Third, the definition includes what is sometimes called "pre-censorship." As practiced on traditional print and broadcast media, censorship involves the removal or deletion of forbidden material. With the Internet, it is often not possible to remove or delete material from a Web site. Instead, the most frequently used method is to deny, block, or filter access. To distinguish the act of removal, some call such denial of access "precensorship." The distinction, however, is not helpful and in fact disguises the fact that censorship is at its most egregious when the content is blocked even before it sees the light of day.

Sometimes, what may be censorship to one person is to another perfectly legitimate, perhaps even backed up by law. For example, the European Union lists as grounds for restricting information that are "potentially harmful or illegal contents or can be misused as a vehicle for criminal activities" the following:

- National security (instructions on bomb-making, illegal drug production, terrorist activities).
- Protection of minors (abusive forms of marketing, violence, pornography).
- Protection of human dignity (incitement to racial hatred or racial discrimination).
- Economic security (fraud, instructions on pirating credit cards).
- Information security (malicious hacking).

- Protection of privacy (unauthorized communication of personal data, electronic harassment).
- Protection of reputation (libel, unlawful comparative advertising).
- Intellectual property (unauthorized distribution of copyrighted works, e.g., software or music).[13]

That list includes restricting information that violates privacy, reputation, and intellectual property rights. In general, most countries around the world would consider the restrictions acceptable and be legal under law. The United States, because of its First Amendment, would be an outlier in this regard. For example, hate speech, such as the denial of the Holocaust, is allowed under the United States and the government would not be able to censor them on the Internet. In practice, however, there would be pressure from business and civil society exerted on the hosts to remove such offensive material. Often, such pressure can be effective.

HISTORY

Early Days

Since the diffusion of the Internet to the public, three overlapping and parallel "waves" of attempts to regulate Internet content may be discerned. The waves reflect the attempts of national governments and international agencies to wrestle with the Internet. In the first wave, from 1994 to 1997 in the early days of the Internet, the approach was to attempt to fit the Internet into the same mold as traditional mass media. That is, governments used legislation and existent executive powers and resources that most closely resembled that part of the Internet to regulate it. If that part of the Internet functioned like a newspaper, then newspaper laws applied; if another part functioned as a broadcasting station, then broadcast rules applied. This "functional approach" to regulating the Internet is understandable because lawyers and judges are trained to use precedents and analogies in their arguments.

In South Korea, the offline rules pertaining to national security were imported to apply to the Internet.[14] Under the National Security Law, any publication that praised North Korea would be banned. So when one page of the massive Geocities Web site praised the North Korean leader Kim Il Sung, South Korea blocked access to the entire Geocities site.[15] After a hailstorm of international criticism that followed that incident, South Korea removed that block and has not attempted a similar move.

When Singapore made Internet access publicly available, it was the first country in the world to develop a code of practice for Web site owners in 1996 but also the first to have an official government Web site (http://www.sg). It was, however, the code of practice that drew worldwide attention, because it was the first Internet-specific legislation aimed at regulating content. The code empowered the authorities to block for residential users some 100 mostly pornographic sites using a proxy server; experts said the proxy server could block up to 300 sites after which the user would notice the slowed access. The code also licensed Web site owners, in line with Singapore rules that require licensing of all who publish any periodicals. The license would be revoked if the terms for them were breached. In a nod that recognized the uniqueness of the Internet, licenses were automatically issued—that is one was given a license when one operated a Web site.[16] Why was this fiction of an automatic "class license" created when it is well-nigh possible to just have a law that criminalized the breach of the rules in the code? Functionally, the Singapore regulators were treating the Internet as a traditional mass medium: anyone who ran a mass medium in Singapore had to have a license.

Meanwhile in the West, governments were attempting to apply rules to the Internet to combat credit card fraud, pornography, etc concerning the Net, as was reported in the news then. It was as if Prometheus had brought back fire and all that the media covered were people getting burned by it. One incident that marked this feverish pitch was the *Time* magazine cover story of July 3, 1995, in which the magazine said that more than 80% of the images posted on Usenet newsgroups were pornographic.[17] The study was later discredited.

Inevitably, there was pressure on politicians "to do something." Laws were passed hastily. In the United States, the U.S. Supreme Court struck down a part of the Communications Decency Act in 1997.[18] Across the Atlantic, a similar fate befell a comparable law in France. In 1996, the French Constitutional Council struck down provisions of a new Telecommunications Law that empowered the Conseil Supérieur de la Télématique to make recommendations on what types of content was permissible.[14]

In short, between 1995 and 1996, it looked as if the Internet would never be regulated. Countries that were trying to regulate it were either failing before the courts or failing in practice. Singapore was giving it a shot but in essence, it was not really doing much. Laws in the United States and France were being struck down. In the conceptual space, scholars such as Post and Johnson suggested that the Internet needed a new legal regime and the United States said that it was taking a more hands-off approach to regulation.

Latter Days

Law enforcement, however, was not taking a similar approach. Australia, which had probably the soundest Internet policies at that time, conducted a sweep for consumer fraud in 1996. No new Internet laws were passed for the sweep. Instead, the consumer protection agency relied on existent laws. Since then, a number of countries, including the United States, have joined Australia in conducting such annual sweeps under an umbrella organization called International Consumer Protection and Enforcement Network (ICPEN).[19]

Similar sweeps have also been mounted against child pornography. Cyber libertarians say the Net is ungovernable because effective regulation requires international cooperation and such cooperation is difficult to come by. For example, what is a crime in one country may not be a crime in another. There is one offence that virtually all countries can agree upon—the use of children for pornography. (Japan had to pass child porn laws in May 1999 to be in line with international norms; until then, the Japanese drew no distinction between porn of children and adults.[20]) In a sweep called Operation Cathedral, police in 14 countries in the OECD cooperated to crack several child-porn rings.[21] Today, child porn is an area that police patrol.

On the legislative front, with direct regulation failing before constitutional challenges, attention turned toward self-regulation. It appeared that a prevalent notion was that self-regulation was *the only* way to regulate the Internet. In 1998, the Internet Law and Policy Forum, an independent and loose association formed mainly of lawyers, initiated an effort to look at self-regulation. Its Web site carried a bibliography that appeared to signal the start of a serious study on the subject of self-regulation.[22] Unfortunately, the study appeared to have been stuck at that starting line of 1998.

From 2000

Around the turn of the millennium, two trends toward regulation were discernable: self-regulation and direct regulation. The Internet industry has been reluctant to self-regulate. The U.S. Federal Trades Commission, after giving several one-year deadlines for the industry to regulate the privacy of children using the Net, passed the Children Online Privacy Protection Act in 2000.[23] In Australia, the Internet Industry Association emerged with a code of practice after five fruitless years when the Federal government passed a law that, among other things, compelled the development of the code.[24] The Federal law has forced some sites to move from Australia.[25]

In Europe, there has been some movement toward self-regulation. Internet Service Providers' associations have often developed codes to minimize their own liability as well as to self-regulate some aspects of business. This contrasts with the United States, which is suspicious of codes, and Asia, which lacks cohesive industry associations. The movement toward self-regulation in Europe has been aided by the work of the Bertelsmann Foundation.[26]

In 1999, the Foundation, started by one of the world's largest book publishing houses, brought together a group of experts to address the issue of content filtering. The Internet Content Rating Association (ICRA) filtering platform based on platform for Internet content selection (PICS) was launched a year later. ICRA, an effort with which the author was involved, aimed to empower parents with simple tools to filter contents of Web sites while addressing the charge of censorship. American civil libertarian groups such as the American Civil Liberties Union (ACLU) and the Center for Democracy and Technology (CDT) were among various bodies consulted during the development of the platform. ICRA's idea was simple: Web sites were to tag every page; users were then to decide what content they would allow. Although it did succeed in creating a filter that was acceptable for the most part by civil libertarians because tagging was not compulsory, ICRA did not succeed in getting the tool to be incorporated into Web browsers. An attempt to develop a plug-in failed. The result was that it was never in use. In February 2007, ICRA relaunched itself as the Family Online Safety Institute (FOSI).[27]

The Western European experiment in self-regulation is commendable but appears to have blunted by the reality that it is limited in practice. Nevertheless, Western Europe may well play a significant leadership role in the laws and policies of regulating the Internet. There are several reasons for this.

In general, many Western European countries acknowledge some degree of censorship of some media content. This position more closely resembles the situation in many parts of the world where censorship is present, varying only in degree.

On the other hand, many European countries also protect free expression under Article 10 of the Council of Europe's convention on human rights, more formally known as the Convention for the Protection of Human Rights and Fundamental Freedoms.[28] This protection resembles the U.S. First Amendment as well the culture of Internet users. In short, Europe has checks and balances on the competing interests of censorship and free expression.

Against this backdrop, there have been surprising developments in the Western European countries. In 2000, a French court ordered the Internet search-engine Yahoo to block French users from accessing a section of the site that auctioned Nazi memorabilia.[29] Although Yahoo initially objected, it later banned the sale of Nazi and hate-related material on its site.[30] To be sure, there are peculiarities in the case. First, Yahoo had used a French domain name—yahoo.fr. That gave the French a jurisdictional toehold on Yahoo. Second, Yahoo was targeting the French users through its advertising. So when Yahoo said it had no way to filter out users the judge was unconvinced: if French users could be directed to a French version of Yahoo, surely Yahoo could filter its users to deny them access to Nazi memorabilia. The information on which the judge based the findings had been given by a panel of experts that included Internet-pioneer Vinton

Cerf. The experts, however, did not agree with the conclusion of the judge on ideological (the Internet should be free) and pragmatic (the filtering was only about 70% effective anyway) grounds. The ideological ground is impossible to explain away. But the pragmatic ground reflects a deficient understanding of the purpose of censorship—it is not meant to be 100% effective.

This is a form of what economists call the "Nirvana fallacy"—something is not worth doing if it does not achieve perfect results. For example, an argument often made against censorship is that on the Internet, a user can always make an international phone call anyway. The argument misses the point. It has never been possible to reliably block anything, even at customs. The persistent will always find a way around the censors. The censor's goal is achieved if it is difficult for *most* users to access the material.

The French approach may be used in other countries. Korea has reportedly ordered its Internet service providers to block access to Korean-language pornographic sites hosted overseas that do not restrict access with an age-verification process.[31]

A major case regarding blocking access to the Internet is the dispute between Antigua and the United States over Internet gambling. In 2003, Antigua filed a formal complaint against United States with the World Trade Organization (WTO), arguing that the United States' restricting online gambling violated obligations that it had made in 1994 regarding international trade. The United States argued that it was blocking access to online gambling sites on moral grounds. In 2004, the WTO ruled in favor of tiny Antigua. The United States appealed and lost in 2005.[32] On December 2007, after long debates and many delays, the WTO finally ruled that Antigua won compensation of US$21 million per year from the United States. However, the United States continued to refuse to comply and at the time of writing, Antigua has threatened to abrogate all its intellectual property treaties with the United States and open itself to allow piracy of movies and music on the island.[33]

ARGUMENTS AGAINST CENSORSHIP

Problems of Internet Censorship

Even with traditional media, censorship has never been 100% effective 100% of the time. With the Internet, it is even more difficult to censor.

The root of the problem for censors is that the Internet combines characteristics of the newspaper, telephone, the radio, the television, and the computer. Each of these inventions alone has contributed to an increase in the transmission and reception of information. Combined, they offer a surfeit of information for censors.

Second, the reach of the Internet ranges the spectrum from one-to-one (e-mail)—which is usually uncensored—to one-to-many (Web sites) and many-to-many (Usenet groups)—which tends to attract some form of censorship. No technology before has had such a combination of reach. E-mail is generally viewed in most countries as private communication, an "e" version of regular mail. But it is possible to conduct mass mailings and some discussion groups are conducted through such mailings. In short, e-mail, a private communication medium, has the potential to be a mass medium.

Theoretically, there is no reason that e-mail cannot be read and censored. It just takes a lot of work. Opening and reading e-mail, however, may well be the most effective means of turning users away and killing the growth of the Internet. In 1994, through a misunderstanding of a high-level official request, Internet accounts of an access provider in Singapore were scanned for .GIF files. Of 80,000 files scanned, five were found pornographic by Singapore standards and the users were warned. Although no non-GIF file was opened, users nevertheless were irate. Many expressed grave reservations about security and privacy on the system. In the end, the access provider had to assure its users that no such scanning will occur in the future.[16]

Third, there is the problem of regulatory paradigm. By combining the traits of traditional communication media and blurring their boundaries, the Internet poses the question of who is to regulate the content and by what standards even domestically.

Should the Internet be treated as a postal service because it has e-mail? Or would the capabilities of Internet Relay Chat and voice-telephony make it a telecommunication service? Then does the presence of electronic newspapers make it a print medium? Or should the availability of radio and television stations make it a broadcast medium? Should its use of the computer mean that the computer model of regulations applies?

In practice, regulators bypass these questions by treating the Internet based on its functions. That is, a Web-based newspaper is likely to be treated as a newspaper, an online radio station as a radio station. It means that there is no single regulatory paradigm. Such an approach, however, is not sustainable in the long run because it magnifies the regulatory problem of convergence where different rules and standards apply to convergent products and services. For example, is a news Web site that combines a newspaper with television news to be treated as a newspaper or a television station?

The fourth problem in Internet censorship is that the computer culture celebrates maximum (and sometimes anarchistic) freedom, not censorship. The early Internet operated with a loose, informal consensus. It arose from universally accepted technical protocols for carrying on electronic conversation from remote locations and times, and it gave birth to common language, culture, and norms.

No matter how system administrators at individual sites may restrict access to objectionable materials, savvy users can overcome the hurdles. Sites that are banned in one country are quickly relocated in another. Sites that are blocked are bypassed through anonymizing proxies. Ways and means to bypass censorship are published online.[34]

Fifth, the Internet highlights a major legal issue in global interconnectivity: which censorship standard applies? The issue extends beyond the classic "what is pornography" debate as first highlighted in a U.S. case where a bulletin board service (BBS) operator in California was convicted of delivering pornography to a resident in Tennessee.[35]

The Internet offers a myriad of material on subjects such as drug culture, bomb-making, murder, and anti-Semitism. Material that is illegal in one country and punishable with a heavy sentence may be wholly legal in another part of the world.

Germany's case of the Neo-Nazis frames the problem best. In January 1996, the German phone company Deutsche Telekom blocked users of its computer network from accessing the Web site of Ernst Zündel, a German-born activist living in Toronto, Canada, suspected of distributing Neo-Nazi and anti-Semitic material over the Internet.[36] Given the history of Germany, such a response is perhaps understandable.

However, in the United States several prestigious universities offered to mirror Zündel's site.[36] Similarly, when Germany tried to block access to a magazine called Radikal, 47 other sites all over the world mirrored the Radikal site.[37] Enforcement of this German law outside of Germany is practically impossible. Any attempt at censorship therefore also has to consider the international dimension.

Finally, the process of regulation tends to proceed piecemeal and almost always lags behind changes in technology. Censorship of any new medium today is most likely to come into play after the objectionable material has been sent. Until then, censors would not be aware of the possibility of circumvention or violation. In the interim, before the passage of any regulation, there is the gray area.

METHODS OF CENSORSHIP

Access Control

Negroponte has said that bits and bytes do not stop at borders.[38] Authoritarian regimes, however, can stop them. A 2001 study of the Internet in China and Cuba illustrated this point: the Internet does not automatically disempower authoritarian governments.[39] In Myanmar, modems, even those built into laptops, have to be licensed. Those who use unlicensed modems have been jailed.[40]

Slightly less draconian is the use of centralized access, typically through some form of state control. A number of states in the Middle East—such as Syria, Iran, and Iraq—use this approach. The fear of being caught accessing unauthorized material is the deterrent. However, the limited means of access discourages competition, which inhibits the diffusion of the Net.[41]

China regulates access in another way: by compelling Internet subscribers to register with the police.[42] Those who use the cybercafes have to show some identification before being able to access the Net. Lest the idea appear too wild, a similar notion of registering users has been proposed by Robert Cailliau,[43] the codeveloper of the World Wide Web with Tim Berners-Lee.

In Singapore, Internet access providers have to use proxy servers to block 100 "high-traffic" pornographic sites for home subscription plans.[44] The process of having to look up the blacklist does slow down access a little.[45] Such centralized controls have limited capabilities: at most, several hundred pornographic sites can be blocked in the face of hundreds of thousands others.

To block these hundreds of thousands of sites, companies have sprung up to offer regularly updated blacklists of pornographic sites. The names of these sites are then blocked from user access. Such a family-friendly Internet access plan is increasingly available throughout the world. However, because of the costs of installing and maintaining the list, subscribers have to pay more for such plans.

Passing Laws

A common misperception is that if there are no new rules for the Internet, it means the Internet is not regulated. This perception is misplaced because in the United States, Internet users have been convicted for violating pre-Internet state laws concerning pornography.[14]

In South Korea, a government official was quoted in the 1990s as saying: "A South Korean who meets by chance a North Korean on Internet had better report to the police within seven days."[14] South Korean security police in the 1990s have tracked down users who, in online debates, expressed opinions that could "benefit the enemy."[14] Such actions are authorized by the National Security Law. According to a civil rights activist, Kim Young Sik, president of the South Korean Civil Union Against Censorship, users have had their access restricted because of comments that were deemed to be in violation of the National Security Laws.[45]

How successfully existent laws can be applied to the Internet depends on how well an analogy can be drawn to the Internet. In Singapore, for example, Web sites of religious and political organizations, as well as online newspapers produced locally, have to be registered.[46] Although the law appears novel, it is essentially an adaptation of existing media laws in Singapore.

As regulators understand the Internet better, they have attempted to pass legislation to regulate content. However, passing Internet-specific laws does not necessarily imply a censorial intent. In many countries, it is necessary to pass Internet-specific laws because the medium is new. For example, without Internet-specific laws recognizing electronic evidence, it would be impossible to conduct e-commerce.[47]

That laws in the United States and France were struck down because they conflict with freedom of expression does not mean that it is not legally possible to censor the Internet. What it means is that legislators cannot simply rush the laws for political expedience. Initially, perhaps because the medium is so new, the laws appear not to have been well-thought out.

In the European Union, soon after publication of the EU paper on "Illegal and Harmful Content on the Internet,"[48] Internet service providers were, for a time, fearful of possible legislation that would make them liable for content for which they had not originated. Since then, Internet-specific immunity provisions have been written in a range of countries—Germany, United States, Singapore, India, Bermuda, France, Australia—so that intermediaries who do not originate content would not be held liable.[49] The immunity for intermediaries is an example where laws need not be restrictive of the Internet.

Using Technology

Laws, however, are blunt instruments for what is essentially a delicate task of picking and choosing content to be removed. Inevitably, the very technology that has enabled the spread of the information has been used to censor. However, the result has been mixed at best.

Probably the first program to censor the Internet was developed by medical researcher Richard DePew in 1993. Annoyed by anonymous messages on the Usenet groups he read, he developed a program he called Automated Retroactive Minimal Moderation (ARMM) to delete them. The program failed at first. Several versions later, when it succeeded, it affected the workings of other connected computers.[50]

Many Usenet readers disagreed with DePew's deletions because it deprived them of the messages. Since then, DePew has stopped using ARMM. Instead, he has developed a program called a bincancel-bot, which removes inappropriately placed binary files from Usenet groups. Such binary files tend to be large, usually contain either programs or images, and are often off-topic. This time, there was a more muted reaction.[51]

A similar "cancelbot" was first used spam sent by law firm, Canter and Siegel, who in 1994 sent to more than 1000 Usenet groups off-topic advertisements hawking their legal services. A 25-year-old Norwegian programmer, Arnt Gulbrandsen, developed a cancelbot that hunted down and deleted messages sent by the firm.[52] However, there is room for abuse. In September 1996, a computer user in the United States sent an unauthorized cancelbot to remove 25,000 messages from the Usenet.[53]

As might be expected, there are software circumvention tools to defeat censorship; they may be successful in varying degree, depending inversely on how earnest the censors are. It is a cat-and-mouse game. For example, China's censorship has become more sophisticated. In 2002, on a visit to Shanghai, the author saw that Google's search results were blocked for the actual site but not for the cached version. So it was easy to bypass the censorship. But a later year, access through the cache was also blocked.

Anonymising programs and proxies make it difficult for the censor to trace the user and thereby may be able to defeat a block. Tor and Psiphon software allow users to access the Internet through a computer with uncensored access. As might also be expected, there are sites giving advice on how to beat the censors.

Filtering[54]

Of all the technological means to censor the Internet, the most widespread is filtering by the end-user. The goal of filtering is to empower parents to block undesirable content to children, the only group for which censorship is internationally accepted. One category of filtering software resides in the user's computer. Much in the same way as antivirus software, such filtering program require regular updates for sites to be added. Another category of filters resides in the server and is a service provided by the Internet service provider; users subscribe to the service, usually on a monthly basis. Filtering software programs have been endorsed, at one time or another, by industry and governments in Europe, Australia, and the United States.

Such programs have improved in sophistication. Initially, some of the software blocked off sites merely for having words such as "breast" on its pages. There were concerns by civil libertarians that this meant blocking educational or medical sites. Today's filtering programs are more context sensitive. Nevertheless, they still suffer from two inherent limitations of such programs. First, filters have to balance the need to be accurate with the comprehensiveness of the filter. The more comprehensive the filter (the more offensive words it recognizes), the less accurate it will be in parsing context. The second limitation is that the filter software needs to be updated frequently.

TRENDS

A few years ago, it was easier to discern the trends: overall, the Internet would make countries freer.[55] After the September 11, 2001 attack, however, security has become a more important part of network policy. The freewheeling Internet has become less freewheeling.

Governments often point to a historical or cultural basis for censorship. In the classic case, Germany has had its memory-searing record of anti-Semitism. Singapore had a history of race riots in mid-1960s. South Korea has its fear of the North Korean invasion. And so the bias toward security and censorship, instead of openness, has a basis in historical events.

Some form of censorship, perhaps better phrased as content regulation, of the Internet is here to stay. The question is the degree and the form of censorship. In some ways, censorship of the Internet is more severe than censorship of traditional media. In the digital world, one either receives the content or not at all; a garbled message is usually unreadable. In the analog world, one may receive the content partially. A garbled message may be partially readable; a printed copy may be smudged or covered over but parts may be readable. Also, online censorship is often through a blocking mechanism, which is prior restraint. Legal doctrine views this as a more severe form of censorship than restriction after publication.

There are several areas where censorship is on the rise. A developing area of censorship is copyright. The early use of copyright was indeed for censorship. There is very little debate on this issue as rights are being extended by rights-holders, at the expense of society at large.[56]

U.S. companies such as Yahoo and Google face the question of the extent to which they should respect the laws of a foreign land when that law clashes with a fundamental value such as free expression. In Yahoo's case, the company has swung from ignoring the French government to being wholly compliant to the Chinese government's request for the name of a journalist, who was subsequently sentenced to 10 years imprisonment for disseminating "state secrets." Ironically, Yahoo was not legally bound to do so.[57] The European Union has issued a declaration urging companies that do business in repressive countries to develop a code of conduct to "put limits on the activities of companies in repressive countries."[58] Yahoo, Google, Microsoft, and a few others did attempt such a code but at Yahoo, it was rejected by the shareholders.[59] Reporters Without Borders in 2005 got 35 investment firms to sign a "Joint investor statement on freedom of expression and the Internet" and to "monitor the activities of Internet sector companies in repressive countries."[60] It is however, difficult to see how such a code would be implemented because it would mean disobeying the laws of a land that the business operates in censorship and trade.

CONCLUSION

Censorship tends to be more tolerated in times of crisis and war. At the time of writing, the war on terrorism in

Iraq, Afghanistan, and around the world was still raging. A greater degree of censorship and other retrenchment of civil liberties may therefore be expected. Temporarily, at least, the freedom and anarchy that the Internet vanguard had hoped for is likely to be curtailed from the West.

The future of freedom on the Net, however, is bright. Freedom House's study of Net freedom concludes that the large number of users alone will make it hard for governments to censor, and that thereby creates more space for public debate. Free speech has either won or will win any battle censors may put up over the Internet.

As the Internet has developed, it is also clear where the boundaries are for censorship. The one area that virtually all countries agree to censor is materials that go to the young. The United States has gone so far as to impose laws, such as the Children Online Privacy Protection Act, that have closed down Web sites. Other areas that developed countries are prepared to see regulated are child pornography and representations to consumers that spill over to become consumer fraud.

Apart from these areas, censorship laws become murky and harder to defend. Many people accept that countries do have a right to their own cultural identity. And certainly history plays a part. But not every one agrees how that culture and history should be treated. Hence the debate over censorship will continue. Especially on the Internet.

REFERENCES

1. Elmer-DeWitt, P. First nation in cyberspace. Time December 6, **1993**.
2. Barlow, J.P. *Cyberspace Independence Declaration*; Davos: Switzerland, February 8. WIRED 1996, 4.06.
3. Barlow J.P. The economy of ideas: A framework for patents and copyrights in the digital age. WIRED 1994, March, p. 83, 89. This credits the "information wants to be free" slogan to Stewart Brand.
4. Johnson, D.R.; Post, D.G. Law and Borders—The rise of law in cyberspace. Stanf. Law Rev. **1996**, *48* (2), 1367.
5. *Presidential Directive on Electronic Commerce*, 1997, July, http://www.technology.gov/digeconomy/presiden.htm (accessed March 28, 2008).
6. *World Internet Users and Population Stats*. http://www.internetworldstats.com/stats.htm (accessed March 28, 2008).
7. Lessig, L. *Code and Other Laws of Cyberspace*; Basic Books: New York, 1999.
8. Shapiro, A. *The Control Revolution: How the Internet Is Putting People in Charge and Changing the World We Know*; Public Affairs: New York, 1999.
9. Working Group on Internet Governance, 2005, final report.
10. McCarthy, K. Iraq domain owner convicted: Bayan Elashi and his four brothers face 10 years in U.S. jail. The Register July 9, **2004**. http://www.theregister.co.uk/2004/07/09/iraq_domain_owner_convicted/ (accessed March 28, 2008).
11. McCarthy, K. This is what is happening to Iraq's Internet domain. The Register June 30, **2004**. http://www.theregister.co.uk/2004/06/30/iraq_internet_domain/ (accessed March 28, 2008).
12. Goldsmith, J.; Wu, T. *Who Controls the Internet: Illusions of a Borderless World*; Oxford University Press: Oxford, U.K., 2006.
13. European Commission. *Illegal and Harmful Content on the Internet: Communication to the European Parliament, the Council, the Economic and Social Committee and the Committee of the Regions*, 1996. http://ec.europa.eu/archives/ISPO/legal/en/internet/communic.html (accessed March 28, 2008).
14. Ang, P.H. *How Countries Are Regulating Internet Content*; Internet Society Annual Conference, Kuala Lumpur, Malaysia, June 1997. http://www.isoc.org/isoc/whatis/conferences/inet/97/proceedings/B1/B1_3.HTM1997 (accessed March 28, 2008).
15. Brekke, D. South Korea blocks geocities. Wired News October 22 1997. http://www.wired.com/news/email/7896.html (accessed October 23, 1997 changed).
16. Ang, P.H.; Nadarajan, B. Censorship and the Internet: A Singapore perspective. CACM **1996**, *39* (6), 72–78.
17. Elmer-De Witt, P. On a screen near you: Cyberporn. Time July 3, **1995**, 38.
18. Shapiro, A. *The Control Revolution: How the Internet Is Putting People in Charge and Changing the World We Know*; Public Affairs: New York, 1999; 35–38.
19. Attorney General of the United States of America v. American Civil Liberties Union, et al. 117 S. Ct. 2329 138. L. Ed. 2d 874 (1997). http://www.law.cornell.edu/supct/html/96-511.ZO.html (accessed March 28, 2008).
20. The website is http://www.icpen.org/.
21. Japan: The darker side of cuteness. The Economist May 8, **1998**, 32.
22. How police smashed child porn club, CNN Worldwide, February 13, 2001. http://www3.cnn.com/2001/WORLD/europe/UK/02/13/paedophile.police/ (accessed March 28, 2008).
23. Working Group, Bibliography of Internet self regulation, *Internet Law and Policy Forum*, (undated. at http://www.ilpf.org/groups/bib4_15.htm (accessed March 28, 2008) (The original draft of the bibliography was credited to Matthew J. McCloskey and dated 1998).
24. Federal Trade Commission. *New Rule Will Protect Privacy of Children Online*, October 20, 1999. http://www.ftc.gov/opa/1999/10/childfinal.htm (accessed March 28, 2008).
25. ABA registers new codes of practice for Internet industry, Australian Broadcasting Authority, May 10, 2002. http://www.acma.gov.au/WEB/STANDARD/pc=PC_91318 (accessed March 28, 2008).
26. Taggart, S. Down under smut goes up over. Wired News February 2, 2000. http://www.wired.com/news/politics/0,1283,34043,00.html (accessed March 28, 2008).
27. Waltermann, J.; Machill, M., Eds. *Protecting Our Children On The Internet: Towards a New Culture of Responsibility*; Bertelsmann Foundation Publishers: Gutersloh, Germany, 2000.
28. More efforts at keeping kids safe online. CBS News February 15, 2007. http://www.cbsnews.com/stories/2007/02/15/

scitech/pcanswer/main2482273.shtml (accessed March 28, 2008).

29. http://conventions.coe.int/Treaty/en/Treaties/Html/005.htm (accessed March 28, 2008).

30. Yahoo! Ordered to bar the French from Nazi items, The Wall Street Journal, November 21, **1999**.

31. Yahoo! Will ban hate material and charge fees on auction sites. The Wall Street Journal, January 3, **2001**.

32. Creed, A. Korean government promises action against porn sites. Newsbytes April 11, **2001**. http://www.newsbytes.com/news/01/164417.html (accessed September 1, 2001, changed).

33. Rivlin, G. Gambling dispute with a tiny country puts U.S. in a bind. New York Times, August 23, **2007**. http://www.nytimes.com/2007/08/23/business/worldbusiness/23gamble.html?_r=2&th=&oref=slogin&emc=th&pagewanted=all&oref=slogin (accessed March 28, 2008).

34. Triplett, W. Antigua threatens to allow piracy: Gov't hopes to settle trade dispute with US, Variety, March 18, 2008. http://www.variety.com/article/VR1117982630.html?categoryid=amp;cs=/webaddress] (accessed 28 March, 2008).

35. How to do it: Circumventing the censors, 2007. Foreign Policy. October, http://www.foreignpolicy.com/story/cms.php?story_id=4022 (accessed 28 March, 2008).

36. USA vs Robert Alan Thomas and Carleen Thomas, 1996. FED App. 0032P (6th Cir.).

37. Censuring the censors: Azeem Azhar looks at hardening attempts to control the Internet, Guardian, February 8, **1996**.

38. McClellan, J. Germany calling. Guardian, September 25 **1996**.

39. Negroponte, N. *Being Digital*; Hodder & Stoughton: Great Britain, U.K., 1995.

40. Kalathil, S.; Boas, T.C. *Open Networks, Closed Regimes: The Impact of the Internet on Authoritarian Rule*; Carnegie Endowment for International Peace: Washington, DC, 2003.

41. Bardacke, T. High price to pay for Internet use in Burma. Financial Times October 5, **1996**.

42. Sussman, L.R. Censor dot Gov: The Internet and press freedom 2000. J. Govern. Inform. September/October, **2000**, 27 (5), 537–545.

43. Nebehay, S. Web co-inventor backs licensing. ZDNet November 29, 1999. http://news.zdnet.co.uk/story/0,s2075495,00.html (accessed 8 October, 2001, changed).

44. Singapore Broadcasting Authority. SBA's approach to the Internet June 2001. http://www.sba.gov.sg/work/sba/internet.nsf/ourapproach/1 (accessed October 8, 2001, changed).

45. Tong, M.C. Device to block out blacklisted web sites. Straits Times July 20, **1996**.

46. Kim, Y.S. Computer communication censorship in Korea. *Presentation at the MacBride Roundtable*, Seoul, South Korea, August, 1996.

47. The Singapore Broadcasting Authority (Class Licence) Notification, 1996, http://www.gov.sg/sba/netreg/regrel.htm (accessed October 8, 2001, changed).

48. Ang, P.H. Why Asia is losing the cyberspace race. Asian Wall Street Journal, April 14, **1999**.

49. European Commission. *Illegal and Harmful Content on the Internet: Communication to the European Parliament, the Council, the Economic and Social Committee and the Committee of the Regions*. 1996. http://ec.europa.eu/archives/ISPO/legal/en/internet/communic.html (accessed March 28, 2008).

50. Ang, P.H. *Ordering Chaos*; Thomson: Singapore, 2005.

51. Wilson, D.L. A computer program that can censor electronic messages sets off a furor, Chronicle of Higher Education, May 12, **1993**, A21.

52. Frauenfelder, M. Usenet's Etiquette-Enforcement Agency, Wired News July 17, **1997**. http://www.wired.com/news/topstories/0,1287,5262,00.html (accessed October 8, 2001). http://www.ecis.com/~alizard/usenspam.html (accessed March 28, 2008).

53. Lewis, P. Censors become a force on cyberspace frontier. New York Times, June 29, **1994**, A1.

54. Cancelbot attacks usenet. Wall Street Journal, September 27, **1996**, A13A.

55. A more detailed multi-country study. In *Access Denied: The Practice and Policy of Global Internet Filtering*; Deibert, R.J., Palfrey, J.G., Rohozinski, R., Zittrain, J., Eds.; MIT Press: Boston, MA, 2008.

56. Ang, P.H. Why the Internet will make Asia freer. Harvard Asia. **2001**, V (3), 48, http://www.fas.harvard.edu/~asiactr/haq/index.htm (accessed September 1, 2001).

57. Lessig, L. *Free Culture: How Big Media Uses Technology and the Law to Lock Down Culture and Control Creativity*; Penguin Press: New York, 2004.

58. Marquand, R. Yahoo, Chinese police, and a jailed journalist, Christian Science Monitor September 9, **2005**. http://www.csmonitor.com/2005/0909/p01s03-woap.html (accessed March 28, 2008).

59. European Parliament resolution on freedom of expression on the Internet, European Union, July 6, 2006. http://www.europarl.europa.eu/sides/getDoc.do?pubRef=-//EP//TEXT+TA+P6-TA-2006–0324+0+DOC+XML+V0//EN&language=EN (accessed March 28, 2008).

60. Yahoo's China policy rejected. BBC News June 12, **2007**. http://news.bbc.co.uk/2/hi/business/6747095.stm (accessed March 28, 2008).

61. Joint investor statement on freedom of expression and the Internet, Reporters without Borders, December 22, 2005. http://www.rsf.org/print.php3?id_article=16009 (accessed October 5, 2009).

62. Sussman, L.R. J. Gov. Inform. For a more detailed multi-country study. *Access Denied: The Practice and Policy of Global Internet Filtering*; Deibert, R.J., Palfrey, J.G., Rohozinski, R., Zittrain, J., Eds.; MIT Press: Boston, MA, 2008.

Center for Research Libraries

Mary I. Wilke
Center for Research Libraries, Chicago, Illinois, U.S.A.

Abstract
The Center for Research Libraries fosters and advances scholarly inquiry through cost-effective, cooperative programs that provide reliable access through traditional and electronic means to unique and unusual collections of library materials in all appropriate formats, international in scope, and comprehensive in disciplines.

INTRODUCTION

The Center for Research Libraries (CRL) is an international consortium of university, college, and independent research libraries. The CRL supports original research and inspired teaching in the humanities, sciences, and social sciences by preserving and making available to scholars a wealth of rare and uncommon primary source materials from all world regions.

CRL

History

The CRL was founded in 1949 as the Midwest Interlibrary Center by ten Midwestern research universities. The founding institutions were the University of Chicago, the Illinois Institute of Technology, the University of Illinois, the State University of Iowa, Indiana University, the University of Kansas, Michigan State College, the University of Minnesota, Northwestern University, and Purdue University. It arose following a decade of study and planning for a regional cooperative deposit library. As originally conceived, the CRL was to serve four programmatic purposes: cooperative storage of little-used materials, cooperative acquisitions, coordination of collecting policies, and centralized cataloging. Of these four functions, centralized cataloging and coordination of collecting policies proved unworkable at that time. The founding planners pursued, rather, the creation of a consortium whose role would be to develop and maintain a corpus of scholarly research materials, assembled cooperatively through deposits and purchases and to make those materials available to consortium members.

Construction of the storage and processing facility was completed in 1951, and the CRL opened in that year. In the ensuing half century, the consortium has grown to include more than 210 research universities and libraries from North America. In 2005, the University of Hong Kong became the CRL's first global member. Since then, the Max Planck Institute for Human Development in Germany and Nalanda University in India have joined as global members. The CRL now maintains a centralized collection facility and a corpus of research materials consisting of more than five million volumes and microform volume equivalents.

The need among academic libraries for cooperative solutions to acquisition and storage problems in the mid-twentieth century became, if anything, more pressing with the passage of time. In his article about the CRL in the first edition of the *Encyclopedia of Library and Information Science*, Ray Boylan stated that as "knowledge (and the publications containing it) has grown, researchers have had to become more specialized in order to master it."[1] Despite such adaptive behavior on the part of scholars, individual academic libraries were scarcely able to purchase, catalog, store, preserve, and make available all of the materials necessary to meet the specialized research needs of faculty and students. In the intervening years, the growth of scholarly resources has only accelerated. At the same time, the scope of scholarly inquiry has been enlarged as well, through the introduction of new disciplines and fields of study. The late-twentieth-century revolution in digital technology also expanded the array of media through which scholarly communications are transacted, thus raising the prospective costs of comprehensive collecting in those disciplines to higher levels while competing with the need to provide electronic access to resources. As the need has grown, so have the services, collections, and programs the CRL offers.

Global Resources Collaborations

To address the changing realities of humanities and social science research, the CRL has formed strategic partnerships with other organizations whose goals align with the CRL's mission. Through these partnerships, the CRL

Encyclopedia of Library and Information Sciences, Fourth Edition DOI: 10.1081/E-ELIS4-120053690

brings new expertise and resources to bear on its efforts to digitize, preserve, and provide access to published materials in four major domains.

Partnerships

Global Resources Agriculture Partnership–Project Ceres: The CRL works with the U.S. Agricultural Information Network and the Agriculture Network Information Center to support the ongoing preservation and digitization of historical collections in the field of agriculture. The CRL provides funding to libraries to digitize and commit to preserving print materials essential to the study of the history and economics of agriculture.

Global Resources Law Partnership: The CRL works with the Law Library Microform Consortium (LLMC) to expand access to legal and governmental primary source documents serving the research interests of the CRL's diverse library community. The CRL and LLMC identify, preserve, and provide digital access to important at-risk primary source documents in law and government from the United States and other national jurisdictions.

Global Resources Partnership in Science, Technology, and Engineering: In 2012, the CRL and the Linda Hall Library (LHL) of Science, Engineering, and Technology formed a strategic partnership to preserve, further develop, and provide access to historical research collections in the fields of science, technology, and engineering. The partnership builds upon the rich holdings of print serials in those fields assembled by the two institutions during the past six decades. The combined holdings of the two institutions constitute a premier library of global science. The CRL and LHL are pooling resources to promote the visibility of these collections worldwide, making them available electronically and through traditional interlibrary loan (ILL) and document delivery to researchers through the CRL libraries.

News: Access to news in its many forms requires coordination and participation of a variety of stakeholders. As one of the foremost news collections in North America and the world, the CRL works to systematically identify critical collections; establish consensus on preservation, archiving, and digitization needs; and negotiate licenses and partnerships to obtain access to materials available electronically. The CRL's partnership with Readex on the World Newspaper Archive supports the library community's efforts to preserve and provide persistent electronic access to historical newspapers from around the globe. Through its work with the International Coalition on Newspapers (ICON), the CRL partners with major news repositories around the world to preserve and improve access to historical news collections. ICON places increasing emphasis on assessment of sustainable digital news repositories, and the ICON database of newspapers is the most comprehensive source of information on digitized newspapers in trustworthy repositories.

Additionally, the CRL represents the interests of its members to obtain favorable terms of access to historical (digitized) and current (born-digital) news sources. The CRL establishes relationships with media organizations (such as the New York Times), commercial providers, and academic partners to ensure the persistence and accessibility of these resources.

Global Resources Programs

AFRINUL: The Cooperative African Newspapers Project seeks to enhance the utilization of newspapers as a source of information about Africa. The project has developed the African Newspapers Union List (AFRINUL), a centralized electronic database of holdings information for newspapers (all formats and all languages) published in sub-Saharan Africa.

CAMP: The Cooperative Africana Materials Project (CAMP) acquires, preserves, and maintains microform and digital collections of unique, rare, and bulky or voluminous Africana research materials for its members. CAMP emphasizes original preservation of newspapers, journals, government publications, archives, and the personal papers of scholars and government leaders.

CIFNAL: Collaborative Initiative for French Language Collections (CIFNAL), the Collaborative Initiative for French Language Collections, was founded in 2006 to promote and facilitate the cooperative exchange of ideas and resources between Francophone and North American research libraries. CIFNAL seeks to improve access to French and French-language resources through licensing, digitization, and institutional connections.

GNARP: The German–North American Resources Partnership (GNARP) supports the acquisition, sharing, and use of German-language materials among North American libraries and the fostering of closer collaboration with German research libraries.

HRADP: The Human Rights Archives and Documentation Program (HRADP) facilitates efforts by institutions to identify, preserve, and provide access to human rights–related archives and documentation by collecting and sharing information about the nature and status of at-risk materials and providing other technical, communications, and financial support for preserving and maintaining those materials.

ICON: ICON is a multi-institutional effort to promote the accessibility and preservation of international newspaper collections by gathering and providing data on physical and digital collections of newspapers from all world regions. The program supports the ICON Database of International Newspapers and conducts assessments of major newspaper digitization initiatives.

LAMP: LAMP (formerly known as the Latin American Microform Project) acquires, preserves, and maintains microform and digital collections of unique, rare, and bulky or voluminous Latin American research materials for its members. LAMP emphasizes original preservation, either through microfilming or digitization, of newspapers, journals, archives, and ephemeral material from Latin America and the Caribbean.

LARRP: The Latin Americanist Research Resources Project (LARRP) is a cooperative initiative that seeks to improve access to the array of research resources published in Latin America. LARRP supports collaborative projects that increase free and open access to information in support of learning and scholarship in Latin American studies and cultivates relationships within the academic library community.

MEMP: The Middle East Materials Project (MEMP) acquires, preserves, and maintains microform and digital collections of unique, rare, and bulky or voluminous research materials pertaining to the field of Middle Eastern studies for its members. MEMP emphasizes original preservation, either through microfilming or digitization, of newspapers, pamphlets, and ephemeral material from or about the Middle East and the Arab world.

PAN: The CRL sponsors the Print Archive Network Forum (PAN), a biannual meeting held in conjunction with ALA conferences, to share information, expertise, and best practices about strategic management of print archive programs. PAN invites libraries and consortia of all sizes to participate.

SAMP: The South Asia Materials Project (SAMP) acquires, preserves, and maintains microform and digital collections of unique, rare, and bulky or voluminous research materials in South Asian studies for its members. SAMP emphasizes original preservation, either through microfilming or digitization, of newspapers, journals, official publications, monographs, and ephemera in all languages of South Asia.

SEAM: The Southeast Asia Materials Project (SEAM) acquires, preserves, and maintains microform and digital collections of unique, rare, and bulky or voluminous research materials in Southeast Asian studies for its members. SEAM emphasizes original preservation, either through microfilming or digitization, of newspapers, archives, manuscripts, journals, and ephemera relating to all countries of Southeast Asia.

SEEMP: The Slavic and East European Materials Project (SEEMP) acquires, preserves, and maintains microform and digital collections of unique, rare, and bulky or voluminous research materials pertaining to the field of Slavic and East European studies for its members. SEEMP emphasizes original preservation, either through microfilming or digitization, of newspapers, journals, books, archives, pamphlets, and other relevant materials from the region.

TRAIL: Technical Report Archive and Image Library (TRAIL) works to ensure preservation, discoverability, and persistent open access to government technical publications regardless of form or format. TRAIL identifies, acquires, catalogs, digitizes, and provides persistent and free access to historical collections of federally funded technical research reports held by research libraries and other organizations.

The Collection

The CRL holds more than five million newspapers, journals, dissertations, archives, government publications, and other traditional and digital resources for research and teaching. Holdings include such diverse materials as 800,000 doctoral dissertations from outside the United States and Canada (including those of Albert Einstein, Dag Hammarskjöld, and other Nobel Laureates), some of the earliest African–American newspapers, and several human rights–related archives. Emphasis is on materials produced outside the United States, and the CRL has special strength in publications and archives from developing nations.

Resource Sharing

The CRL is committed to fast, accurate delivery of materials and digital content for faculty and student research. ILL provides a mechanism for access to CRL materials by members. One of the most important CRL ILL features is unlimited access to important research materials with extended loan periods: patrons from member libraries can make an unlimited number of requests, request any amount of material to be sent, and are allowed to use the CRL materials for as long as necessary. (The CRL will recall an item only if another patron from a member library requests the material.) The lengthy loan period is possible because the CRL collects material that is rarely used at single institutions. On-demand digitization of fragile and rare material, if possible after assessing condition, is also a service the CRL provides. The CRL staff has worked to improve discoverability of its tangible and digital resources by creating cross-links to the CRL OPAC and web-based collection guides from various open-access web resources developed by the CRL and its affiliates.

Cooperative Collection Development

Since its earliest days, cooperative collection development was accomplished in two ways: through the CRL's deposit service and through the CRL's purchase programs. Initially, many of the CRL's original members deposited material that was rarely used in their own libraries (Fig. 1). The depositing library gained shelf space in their own stacks for the acquisition of new materials. These deposits formed the core of many of the CRL's collections. The deposit program remains an important service for both the individual member library and for the larger community as the CRL continues to receive titles for its JSTOR print archives (JSTOR was the Andrew W. Mellon

Foundation's acronym for the "Journal Storage" Project). The CRL/JSTOR Print Archive Project provides assurance to the CRL members and to the library community that paper copy of all JSTOR titles will be available as an archive. More information about the CRL/JSTOR Print Archive Project is available at https://www.crl.edu/archiving-preservation/print-archives/crl-administered/jstor.

The second part of the CRL's cooperative collection program is its purchase programs. Material is purchased in four ways: subscriptions, demand purchases, purchase proposals, and shared purchases. From the CRL's inception, certain classes of materials had been identified as material the CRL should collect. Selected titles in these classes are acquired through subscriptions. In fact, when the CRL opened for business in 1951, it began with entering subscriptions to 40 newspapers. Along with the newspaper subscriptions, the CRL maintains subscriptions to various rarely held serial titles, such as the *Asian Journal of Chemistry*.

The Demand Purchase Program works with the classes of materials the CRL specifically collects: newspapers, foreign doctoral dissertations, and archival records. Each year, a percentage of the collection budget is set aside to purchase-on-demand materials in these classes if a patron from a member library so requests and the CRL does not presently own them. One example concerned a researcher studying the Berlin Airlift. Relevant material from Public Record Office files had recently been micropublished. The researcher was able to request the CRL to purchase this archival material using its Demand Purchase Program. The patron's library did not have to spend money and time on purchasing, cataloging, and storing the material. Other member libraries also benefited from the CRL's

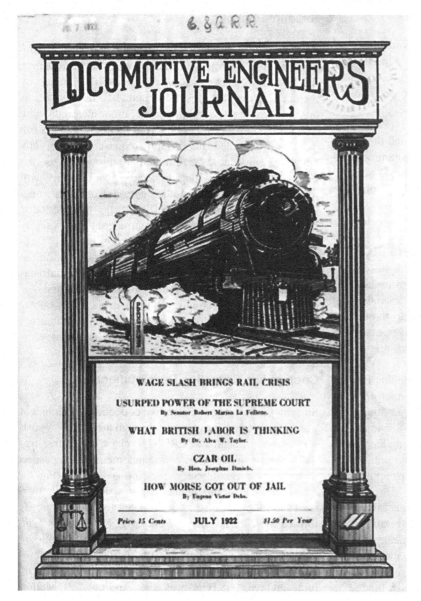

Fig. 1 Cover of *Locomotive Engineers Journal*, July 1922, Vol. 52.

acquisitions of this material, as they did not need to purchase the material for their own library.

A portion of each year's budget is set aside for the Purchase Proposal Program. Each year, representatives from member libraries propose titles for purchase through this program. If the proposals meet the specified criteria, the item is balloted. The criteria can be found at https://www.crl.edu/collections/cooperative-collection-building/purchase-proposal-program. Member libraries then rank items on the ballot and the CRL purchases as many of the approved titles as possible with the year's available pool of money. Many of the major microform sets the CRL owns were acquired through this program. Recent acquisitions of material through this program include "Church Missionary Society Archive. Section III: Central Records, Parts 12–22", "La Dépêche algérienne: journal politique quotidian (1885–1943)", and "Qing gong nei wu fu zou xiao dang."

How to Use CRL

As mentioned earlier, the use of the CRL's collections by patrons at its member institutions is free and unrestricted. As the CRL's collections are rarely held and used at any single institution, a researcher can often have the luxury of loan periods lasting years. The use of the CRL's collections, for those not affiliated with a CRL member institution, is provided on a cost recovery basis and subject to certain limitations. For more information, read the nonmember loan policies found at https://www.crl.edu/services/borrowing/non-member-lending.

The CRL's online public access catalog (http://catalog.crl.edu/) contains more than 1,300,000 records. However, many of the materials held by the CRL are uncataloged. Presently, the CRL is working to provide more access to these collections and more information can be found in the section "Other Collections" here: https://www.crl.edu/collections/crl-collecting-areas.

CONCLUSION

The CRL was founded at a time when individual university libraries realized they could not be self-sufficient. Time has shown that cooperative collection development and resource sharing remains essential for academic libraries. The CRL aims to realize a shared network of traditional and digital resources for scholarly research and teaching and to develop and manage these resources strategically for the benefit of the academic and independent research libraries community.

REFERENCE

1. Boylan, R. The center for research libraries. In *Encyclopedia of Library and Information Science*; 1st Ed.; Kent, A., Lancour, H., Nasri, W., Eds.; Marcel Dekker, Inc.: New York, 1968; 156–167. For more information on CRL collections, please see the overview page: https://www.crl.edu/collections.

Charleston Conference

Katina Strauch
Addlestone Library, College of Charleston, Charleston, South Carolina, U.S.A.

Abstract

This entry covers the history, founding, evolution, structure, values, and future directions of the Charleston Conference held annually in Charleston, South Carolina.

HISTORY AND FOUNDING

The Charleston Conference was begun in 1980 by Katina Strauch who was the then newly hired Head of Acquisitions at the College of Charleston's Robert S. Small Library. At that time the library had a small materials budget ($150,000) for all material acquisitions. The library also had no travel budget and little knowledge of acquisitions processing. However, the Library staff was a young, energetic, and innovative group. The Head of Special Collections at the time, Dr. Ralph Melnick, was planning an Antiquarian Book Fair, and the Head of Reference, Cerise Oberman-Soroka, was already running a highly successful conference for reference librarians on approaches to bibliographic instruction. The College also had hired a new continuing education director, Sue Sommer. Sue, Ralph, and Cerise encouraged Katina to start a conference connected with the Antiquarian Book Fair focused on acquisition of rare and out of print materials. Accordingly, the first Charleston Conference's speakers included, among others, Jake Chernofsky, Editor of *AB Bookman's Weekly for the specialist book world*, Bob Barrows from Arno Press, and Paul Koda, Rare Books Librarian, University of North Carolina (UNC)-Chapel Hill. There were approximately 25 attendees including Mike Markwith (Blackwell's), Corrie Marsh (Georgetown), John Ryland (Hampden-Sydney College), Bill Schenck (UNC-Chapel Hill), and Tom Leonhardt (Duke University). Several of the papers from that first meeting were published by Jake Chernofsky in *AB Bookman's Weekly*.

After the first Conference, word spread. Since there were no other conferences like this for acquisitions personnel, there was no need for organized publicity, just word of mouth. So a grassroots gathering of a handful of acquisitions librarians has grown over the ensuing three decades to over 1500 attendees in 2012. The timeline as created for the Conference's 25th anniversary is included at the end of this essay.

GUIDING TENETS AND EVOLUTION OVER TIME

Originally held in the spring and spanning two days, the Conference was moved to the first or second week of November because academic acquisitions librarians normally are too consumed by their local institution's budgetary issues in late spring. Based on attendees' recommendations, it was also lengthened a half day into Saturday, which allowed attendees to drink in the appeal of historic Charleston as a venue and to offer additional sessions to an audience of broader professional scope.

After the Conference was several years old and its attendance was growing, Katina felt the need to initiate more frequent communication with past attendees. Accordingly, and with the help of Steve Johnson, Head of Acquisitions at Clemson University who had his own beer lover's newsletter and helped with the layout, Katina and her husband Bruce launched *Against the Grain: Linking Publishers, Vendors, and Librarians* in March 1989. Originally conceived as a four-page mimeographed handout for Conference attendees only, *ATG* grew quickly.

The first issue was 10 pages long instead of four, and *ATG* issues now comprise a minimum of 88 pages. The first issues of *ATG* were distributed by Ballen Booksellers International and Alfred Jaeger, Inc. with help from Ambassador Books, Inc. Ads were not initially intended for the publication, but *Against the Grain* began to get requests for ad space. Edna Laughrey, former Head of Acquisitions at the University of Michigan, volunteered and became *ATG*'s first ads manager. Thus, Katina began to involve willing Conference attendees in increasing the reach of the Conference to the library and publishing world. Word of the Conference continued to spread, and attendance continued to grow.

The program for the first decade of Charleston Conferences was a series of consecutive plenary talks by a handful of speakers. However, in the 1990s, as the online, networked world began to expand, topics were too diverse to fit into a series of plenary talks given over only two and one-half days. Traditional lines of demarcation between

Encyclopedia of Library and Information Sciences, Fourth Edition DOI: 10.1081/E-ELIS4-120049485

the operations inside libraries have blurred and continue to blur, and the Charleston Conference has been able to stay not only current but be on the cutting edge of factors influencing change in information's allied professions.

The Conference is an organic, living organization. As such, Conference organizers began to plan concurrent presentation sessions to complement the generally broader-scope plenary presentations. These concurrent sessions tended to be subject or process focused and allowed more attendees to present their research findings to the professional information community. The 2015 Charleston Conference included over 300 such concurrent sessions.

Over time the original focus of the Conference on acquisitions applications in academic libraries has broadened to encompass a full range of ideas, problems, and opportunities faced by scholarly publishers, vendors, and libraries and the advancement, sharing, and preservation of knowledge. Topics such as copyright and compliance, standards, communication, digital rights, networking, technology advances, budgets, and archiving are germane to everyone in the information profession.

When Katina began the Conference, she had two caveats. First, she did not want concurrent sessions; she wanted everyone to hear the same paper at the same time and react to its content as a community. Second, she did not want exhibits as she felt the Conference should be about ideas and not become a commercial venue. Also, as a newly minted acquisitions librarian from an unknown academic library, she wanted to create a venue that wasn't just for the "big guys" and already-well-known librarians. She didn't want to exclude them, of course, but she wanted to be mindful of the little, insignificant guys, many coming from small academic institutions. The Conference has held true to the original attendee-inclusive objectives for thirty-six years.

Although as concurrent sessions became a necessity given the explosion of the virtual world and the growth of attendance, the Charleston Conference still gives opportunities for presentations, open questions, friendly repartee, and continued discussion to players from all types of academic libraries, interested public and special libraries, scholarly publishers, vendors and aggregators, consultants, students, etc. Unknown participants are frequently given special consideration when they are identified. A third caveat—Katina wanted to preserve informality, giving the opportunity for give and take during plenary. Microphones are opened to the audience after each plenary presentation, and anyone wishing to comment or question is encouraged to do so. The only requirement to speak is to first identify oneself.

Regarding the introduction of commercial exhibits, in 1999, after attending conferences with exhibits of all sorts of products, the organizers decided to trial a focused Vendor Showcase. This allowed companies with products of direct application and interest to collection developers, acquisitions librarians, serials librarians, digital services librarians, etc. to showcase their products for librarians to see firsthand, unencumbered by multiple products less applicable to the relevant information professional in attendance. The now successful Vendor Showcase is held prior to the main conference on Wednesday for an eight-hour period and does not conflict with programming on Thursday, Friday, and Saturday. The exhibits are kept simple; tables may be shared by more than one related vendor/publisher. The physical structure and short duration for the Vendor Showcase attains the informal feeling so characteristic of Charleston Conferences overall. Vendors do not have to staff exhibit booths during Conference presentations of interest to them. They are encouraged to send their most knowledgeable representatives to answer questions from Conference attendees and to interact openly in other sessions and social activities. A smorgasbord of refreshments set up in the middle of the Vendor Showcase area also adds to its pleasant and informal atmosphere.

ORGANIZATIONAL ISSUES AND DETAILS

As previously noted, a grassroots gathering of a handful of acquisitions librarians in 1980 grew to 1800 in 2015 and includes a mix of publishers, vendors, aggregators, consultants, students, and librarians. Spread over two and one-half days in early November—late Wednesday afternoon through mid-afternoon Saturday—broad, often controversial, topics of interest to the world of information professionals are explored in plenary sessions, which are interspersed with multiple concurrent "breakout" focused sessions exploring the practical, the novel, or the clever application to instruction and research. Speakers are drawn not only from the information professions of publishing, academic/public/research/government librarianship, vendors of information tools, and technology gurus but from the corporate world of the broader service industry sector, such as Google or Amazon. Prominent speakers, known for both their professional acumen and their presentation skills, are solicited, and expert panels providing opposing or complementary viewpoints are convened and are deftly moderated. A multisection, printed program offers not only the daily program schedule and a précis of each presentation but also the bios of all presenters and a list of those attendees who have preregistered along with their contact information.

The program itself is a feat of organization and information. The program is produced in hardcopy and in digital form available via the Conference website. When recently surveyed, attendees continue to want a printed program in addition to the online. Attendees can manage their own online Conference calendar. The Conference online program serves as a retrospective repository of sorts where presenters may add their slides postconference in addition to the abstracts of all presentations already available prior to the Conference. Recordings of all plenary sessions (when permitted by speakers) are made available free of charge on the Conference website as well.

Cognizant of travel budgets across academic libraries, online registration begins in early June before the end of most institutions' fiscal year. "Early bird" registration generally closes in early September, and regular registration generally is open through mid-October. On-site registration is possible but is not encouraged. The Conference secures blocks of rooms in several hotels—mostly those close to Marion Square in downtown Charleston. Shuttle buses are available between Conference hotels and venues on a limited schedule. The Charleston Area Convention and Visitors Bureau assists planners with hotel and restaurant information, and vendors can seek their assistance in planning ancillary entertainment.

The Francis Marion Hotel has served as the Conference's anchor hotel since the College of Charleston repurposed its adjoining Lightsey Center in 2001 where the Conference had been based for several years. Prior to the Lightsey Center, the Charleston Conference was held in several College of Charleston venues depending on availability and space required—a student commons room on campus, in the Education Center, and in the Sottile Theatre. Since relocating to the Francis Marion Hotel, which is too small to accommodate the entire Conference, the Conference has used several hotels and College of Charleston buildings in addition to the Francis Marion— the historic Embassy Suites hotel in downtown Charleston (the site of the old Citadel), the downtown Hampton Inn, the Marlene and Nathan Addlestone Library of the College of Charleston, the School of Sciences and Mathematics Building of the College of Charleston, and most recently the Marriott Courtyard (once a Holiday Inn). The Gaillard Center in downtown Charleston was renovated in 2015 and holds 1800 attendees. There are several additional hotels in the works in downtown Charleston, so the Conference planners are optimistic that downtown Charleston will continue to be a viable location for the Charleston Conferences.

The fact that the Charleston Conference is *not* sponsored by a professional association, such as ALA or AHA, contributes to its uniqueness. That no professional or corporate entity drives its focus gives Conference organizers the freedom to expand to where the action is, to predict where it will be, and nimbly go there first. Program design is in the hands of a small, unpaid leadership group providing continuity and structure. This contrasts positively against the design of programs for many professional association conferences where volunteer organizers come and go, and topics may be planned years in advance at a time when they are relevant, but relevance may have changed. Charleston Conference planners are able to put a program together with a shorter lead time; thus the programs offer immediate appeal and current relevance.

Regarding the Conference structure, seasoned attendees know what to expect of the day and when—lending calm to an otherwise frenetic schedule of presentations and associated activities. For those new to the Conference, a few "old-timers" serve as mentors to newbies by answering their questions emailed prior to the Conference and are also available for additional guidance during the Conference, staffing an information table near the registration area. The use of mentors was brokered by Pam Cenzer, then at the University of Florida, and Susan Campbell of York College, who suggested it. The mentors welcome first timers and orient them as needed. Mentors also serve a "concierge" function for all attendees by interpreting local maps, giving directions, suggesting restaurants, and advising on transportation choices. Being available for immediate problem-solving assistance adds to their overall usefulness.

THE CONFERENCE PROGRAM

Each year's Conference is organized around a catchy theme, which drives the content of the plenary sessions and many of the concurrent sessions.

Included here is a list of all of the conference themes:

2016: Roll With the Times or the Times Roll Over You
2015: Where Do We Go From Here
2014: The Importance of Being Earnest
2013: Too Much is Not Enough (tentative)
2012: Accentuate the Positive
2011: Something's Gotta Give!
2010: Anything Goes
2009: Necessity is the Mother of Invention
2008: The Best of Times, The Worst of Times
2007: What Tangled Webs We Weave
2006: Unintended Consequences
2005: Things Are Seldom What They Seem
2004: All the World's A Serial
2003: Games People Play
2002: Two Faces Have I: One For Books and One for Bytes
2001: The Trends They Are A'Changing
2000: Is Bigger Better?
1999: And the Beat Goes On
1998: We Want More For Less
1997: Learning From Our Mistakes
1996: Money Talks
1995: Still Crazy After All These Words
1994: The Savage Marketplace
1993: Bubble, Bubble Toil and Trouble
1992: The Medium is the Message
1991: And I Am Right, And You Are Right, Too-Loo-Ra-Lay
1990: The Pure and Simple Truth (each session of this conference was prefaced with a quotation from Oscar Wilde)
1989: Remembrance of Things Past
1988: Questioning Assumptions
1987: Plus Ça Change
1986: External Influences on Acquisitions and Collection Development

1985: More Than You Ever Wanted to Know About Finance

1984: Old Problems, New Solutions

1983: Collection Development in the 1980s

1982: Charleston Conference did not take place. (Katina's daughter Ileana was born.)

1980, 1981: no overlying themes yet

Invited speakers deliver plenary presentations in the Carolina Ballroom of the Francis Marion Hotel. These approximately 45-minute presentations are simultaneously transmitted for viewing to large audiences gathered in several other ballrooms and large meeting rooms across the Conference venues. Each venue has at least one moderator who interacts via microphone with a counterpart in the Carolina Ballroom allowing those remote from the physical speaker to feel intimately involved in "the action." Courtesy reigns in the Francis Marion ballroom even though contrarian views are encouraged. In 2015, plenary sessions were held in the Performance Hall of the Gaillard Center, which meant that all attendees were together in one venue.

Each year brings presentations of current interest, yet annual reprises of certain themes engender great audience anticipation. Recent favorites have been a panel discussion on recent—or anticipated—legislation and current court cases that affect the information landscape and a point-counterpoint debate on the future of the information industry. Speakers chosen as panelists speak to the multiple facets of a hot topic, recently the advance in technology and user acceptance of e-books. Individual plenary presentations may be delivered by prominent information professionals or by individuals prominent in advancing fields that impact the information professions.

Concurrent, smaller-audience, breakout sessions are more loosely organized, but several thematic tracks are offered for those interested in zeroing in on one facet of the information spectrum. Tracks such as budget/fundraising/allocation formulae, end users/use statistics/usability studies, management, and technology offer broadly targeted presentations. Individuals seeking to present choose the track where they feel their presentation would best fit, and Conference program organizers select from them to develop a balanced program. Location of the breakout session rooms across multiple venues is done differently from other conferences where a specialized group may hear presentations in the same room or two for the duration of the conference.

Theme tracks are less important in room choice than the size of the audience anticipated to attend. Room sizes at the several Conference venues vary widely and accommodate from 15 to 800.

The Charleston Conference is a dynamic community. Organizers welcome suggestions and ideas for innovations. Fast Tech Talks give companies a chance to showcase a product or service. Innovation Sessions allow participants to discuss or brainstorm new approaches. Poster Sessions give presenters the opportunity to display information regarding their department or library. Preconferences are designed to delve deeply into a subject when there is insufficient time during a plenary or concurrent session and the topic is deemed by the organizers to be important. Juried Product Development Forums allow companies to discuss possible future products, ideas, or innovations with a small group of interested librarians. Dine-Arounds on Friday nights give attendees an opportunity to meet each other and try out the culinary fare in a nearby restaurant. Each of these program innovations was suggested by conference attendees or members of the Charleston Conference planning group.

Concurrent presentations at midday, termed "Lively Lunches," allow attendees not to break their trend of concentration but to eat lunch in the meeting rooms during lunchtime presentations. With so many restaurants offering takeout in the immediate vicinity of Charleston's Marion Square, the Lively Lunches allow attendees to select their own fare with only a 30-minute recess. Over the past several years with more restaurant choices in the vicinity, more time has been allowed for attendees to get lunch and return to the sessions.

Breakout and Lively Lunch program choices are so varied that attendees must make their choices in advance. The sessions are kept small, and the number of concurrent sessions/Lively Lunches offered increases with the increasing number of Conference attendees. Questions are always encouraged in all sessions; microphones are also provided there as necessary. Members of the audience are encouraged to chime in with questions or to add their own experience/opinion. Often there is much give-and-take between presenter and audience to the benefit of all assembled. Most breakout sessions attract at least seven attendees, and some require extra chairs for forty or more. Sessions expected to draw the biggest crowd are scheduled in the larger conference rooms in the Francis Marion or the Marriott Courtyard—hotels located around the edge of Marion Square. Some sessions are held in the College of Charleston's Addlestone Library, which offers an opportunity to explore that lovely building opened in January 2005. Sessions have also been held in the College's School of Sciences and Mathematics Building across the street from Addlestone. Prior to 2001, the College of Charleston's Lightsey Center served as a venue. In 2015, many breakout rooms were made available at the opening of the Gaillard Center four blocks away.

The Gala Reception buffet on Thursday evening is included in the registration fee and has been held in various locations about town, for example, the South Carolina Aquarium, the Old Exchange & Provost Dungeon, the College of Charleston School of Sciences and Mathematics Courtyard, the William Blacklock House, and Rivers Green of the College of Charleston. A particularly memorable event was an oyster roast held at the city's Visitor Center. The city's stamp is continually intertwined into the culture of the Conference. For those attendees whose employers do not reimburse meals, this Conference does not send them back home hungry!

Late Wednesday afternoon's Juried Product Development Forum presentations, for which a limited number of noncorporate conference attendees may register in advance, allow vendors to test the market for a product or procedure in the development stage before introducing it to the market. Vendor submissions are reviewed by an anonymous panel, and the successful applicants must demonstrate that their product/process has been developed to the point where it can be judged; they cannot simply look to bounce an idea off the participant group. As a result, an interested and knowledgeable audience provides feedback in time for a revision, improvement, or extension.

The Conference's commitment to a responsive culture is demonstrated by a postconference Rump Session held on Saturday afternoon to immediately review the past days' events. All attendees are invited, and thinking begins for the next year's Conference. Conference critiques are requested from all registrants and are analyzed for their suggestions. Thus, the planning cycle begins anew.

CONFERENCE ADMINISTRATION

The Charleston Conference has several important working groups. The local arrangements group handles registrations, hotel logistics, communicates with registrants, and the like. This working group consists of three key people who keep everything in order. The Charleston Conference content planning group selects keynote speakers and concurrent session presentations. This group consists of librarians, publishers, and vendors from many areas. Members of the planning group stay involved as long as they are able. Additional members of the planning group are added every year. The Conference planners like continuity.

There is a primary leader of the Conference planning group. The first primary contact was Judy Webster, Head of Acquisitions at the University of Tennessee, who unfortunately passed away too early. The next primary contact was Rosann Bazirjian who was at Penn State University at the time and is now Dean of Libraries at UNC-Greensboro. Rosann has recently retired. The current primary program contact is Beth Bernhardt also at UNC-Greensboro.

Several key individuals contribute to the overall success of the Charleston Conference. Leah Hinds is the primary contact for the Conference overall. Leah oversees registration and is the Associate Director of the Charleston Conference. Leah works with Beth Bernhardt and the Conference planning group on the content of the program. Leah also manages the Conference website http:/charlestonlibraryconference.com and *Against the* Grain website the-grain.com, contacts potential advertisers and sponsors, and manages the publication of the Conference Proceedings by Purdue University Press.

Toni Nix handles the Vendor Showcase and *Against the Grain* advertising. Sharna Williams coordinates all registrations and manages the Juried Product Development Forums. Regina Semko retired as previous long-time registrar of the Conference. Regina was with the Conference for over ten years and saw many changes over her tenure with the Conference. And, of course, the founder, Katina Strauch, continues to be both behind and at front and center in the scene! Katina is now Assistant Dean for Technical Services and Collection Development at the Addlestone Library.

The content planning group at present, numbering over sixteen members and chaired by Beth Bernhardt for the past six years, consists of librarians, publishers, vendors, and consultants. The primary organization and content of the plenary sessions is decided by this group. Proposals for concurrent sessions are submitted online and a small group makes selections, at times consulting specific members of the content planning group. Members of the content planning group are mindful of the content and evaluations of both the plenary sessions and the concurrent sessions. The content planning group holds several regular conference calls during the year.

The Conference design offers opportunities for corporate sponsors, some of whom underwrite a morning or afternoon coffee break or the Southern—ham and biscuit—breakfast on Saturday. They often invite groups of their customers for dinner on Friday evening.

For those attendees not being feted by a vendor or publisher on Friday evening, the Conference sponsors group dinners, called Dine-Arounds, at several local restaurants with a sign-up sheet at the information booth. Those dinner groups meet in the Francis Marion lobby and are guided on a walk to their chosen restaurant. Dine-Arounds underscore that sense of community among Conference attendees, which is promoted by its very structure in a city famed for Southern hospitality. In the same spirit of community and friendliness, the Conference feted long-time attendees at its 25th anniversary in 2005 with a booklet featuring the career biographies of 50 individuals from all walks of the information profession who had influenced this Conference's long-term success.

Organizing committee members audit some of the breakout sessions and may report in *Against the Grain*, a publication emanating from the Conference, but not limited to Conference reporting. *Against the Grain* is mailed bimonthly to all Conference registrants for the year following a Conference and is available via www.against-the-grain.com/. For many years, Ramune Kubilius has managed the reports from Charleston Conferences for *Against the Grain*.

LEGACY AND PUBLICATIONS

Papers from the Charleston Conferences have always been considered worthy of publication and sharing. As noted earlier, several of the papers from the very first Charleston Conference were published in *AB Bookman's Weekly*.

Beginning in 1983, Scott Bullard, editor of *Library Acquisitions*: *Practice and Theory* published by Pergamon Press, began to publish many of the papers from the Charleston Conferences. *Against the Grain* published the proceedings in 2000 and Greenwood Publishing Group/ Libraries Unlimited published the proceedings from 2001 to 2009. In 2009 the Conference entered into an agreement with Purdue University Press to publish the future proceedings. Purdue University Press is also publishing a Charleston Insights monograph series building on important issues and trends from the Conferences. The first Charleston Insights monograph published in 2012 was by copyright guru Lolly N. Gasaway of UNC-Chapel Hill entitled *Copyright Questions and Answers for Information Professionals*. More volumes from the Charleston Insights are in the works.

In 1997, Mario Casalini, President of Casalini Libri in Fiesole, Italy, approached Katina about starting a conference like Charleston in Italy. The Fiesole Collection Development Retreats were begun in April, 1999, and many of the presentations are freely available at http:// libraries.casalini.it/retreat/.

In 2006, ABC-Clio began the annual Vicky Speck ABC-Clio Leadership Award. Vicky Speck edited many Charleston Conference proceedings with Rosann Bazirjian before her untimely death. Recipients of the Vicky Speck Award to date have been Anthony Watkinson, Jack Montgomery, Beth Bernhardt, Heather Miller, Eleanor Cook, Glenda Alvin, Ramune Kubilius, Leah Hinds, and Tony Horava.

Several companies give scholarships to help attendees defray the cost of attending the Conference. EBSCO, Harrassowitz Verlag, Swets, and IGI Global are among those frequent donors.

VALUES

The Charleston Conference's unique appeal lies in its relatively small size, broad-to-specific mix of presentation topics; close interactions between library-related professionals, scholarly publishers, aggregators, and vendors; no exhibits conflicting with sessions; compact venue; overall aura of informality; and a structure that fosters a "complete immersion" experience.

The Charleston Conference sticks to the set of values that the organizers consider essential to its operation. The atmosphere must be informal and welcoming so that people can say what they think. Allow *humor* and levity. ly said, "many a truth is said in jest." Humor goes a long way to create a lively and friendly atmosphere. The programming must be *flexible*, allowing time for last-minute, timely additions to the program. The structure must be *dynamic* so that changes can be made to the structure of the programming frequently. It is important to *surprise* attendees with

innovative programming. Avoid groupthink; peer review is good and necessary, but we all have a tendency to reward/ accept what is the conventional wisdom. Acknowledge that new and *good ideas can come from anywhere* and that a library technical assistant or a "low person on the totem pole" can have just as valid an idea or concept as the CEO or Library Dean. When sessions are suggested, evaluate the idea and work with the presenter to make his or her point in a way that will increase its understandability to the audience. *Try not to turn down ideas out of hand*. Remember— *everyone has a good idea. Take chances* with programming, plenary or concurrent. Try what other conferences won't do or can't do. Do not be overly bureaucratic. Be positive and smile at all times. The Conference founder tries to be *impartial*. Remember—"Nothing will ever be attempted if all possible objections must first be overcome" (Samuel Johnson, 1709–1784).

The added charm of the Charleston, South Carolina, setting featuring fine, moderately priced restaurants, obvious and extensive historical significance, and artistic and recreational opportunities plus sheer physical beauty buoys the Conference's appeal and contributes to its success. The vision and vigilant guidance of a single individual, Katina Strauch, aided by a coterie of hard-working assistants, has served to keep the Conference high on the desiderata list of most librarians—both in the United States and international.

THE FUTURE

The Charleston Conference began as an idea nurtured by a group of librarians, publishers, and vendors. It continues to be nurtured by those same categories of individuals who love books, libraries, information, and knowledge. What is certain is that it will continue to evolve. Long may it continue.

Editor's note: Many people have helped with this history of the Charleston Conference. Special thanks are extended to Julie Arnheim, Shirley Davidson, Leah Hinds, and Mike Markwith along with Katina Strauch, Charleston Conference Founder.

BIBLIOGRAPHY

1. The 27th annual Charleston Conference: What tangled webs we weave. Inf. Today **2008**, *25* (1), 31–34.
2. NewsMakers Hana Levay wins Swets scholarship. Inf. Today **2008**, *25* (11) (12), 25.
3. ALA looking ahead. ALCTS Newslett. Online **2005**, *16* (4) (08), 1.
4. Charleston Conference 1987, 1988. Libr. Acquisit. **1987**, *12* (2), 131–263.
5. Charleston Conference 1988. Issues in Book and Serial Acquisitions "Questioning Assumptions" Libr. Acquisit. **1989**, *13* (2), 87–197.

6. Charleston Conference 1988. Libr. Acquisit. **1986**, *10* (2), 87–128.

7. Highlights of the 2003 Charleston Conference. Libr. Hi Tech News **1989**, *21* (1) (01/01), 12.

8. Issues in Book and Serial Acquisitions: College of Charleston. Libr. Acquisit. **1985**, *9* (1), 1–78. May 17-18, 1984.

9. Panel presentation: Truth in vending. Libr. Acquisit. **1985**, *9* (1), 65–78.

10. Katina, P.S.; Sally, S.; Zappen, S.H., eds. Practical Issues in Collection Development and Collection access: The 1993 Charleston Conference, Routledge, 1995.

11. Profile: Katina Strauch. Serials **2006**, *19* (3), 71–72.

12. Seeking common ground (editorial). 1996. Choice (Dec.): 562.

13. Abel, R. Cost-plus pricing: an old nag with a second wind? Libr. Acquisit. **1988**, *9* (2), 201–202.

14. Abel, R. The librarian as synthesizer. Libr. Acquisit. **1988**, *12* (2), 139–147.

15. Abel, R. Players in the knowledge transfer enterprise. Libr. Acquisit. **1988**, *12* (2), 159–161.

16. Abel, R. Invisible colleges, information and libraries. Libr. Acquisit. **1991**, *15* (3), 271–277.

17. Abel, R. Contradictions in the scholarly enterprise and their effects on libraries. **1991**, *15* (3), 413–418.

18. Albanese, A. At Charleston, content is king. Libr. J. **1976**, *132* (20) (12), 18.

19. Albanese, A.; Kenney, B. Dual publication exposed at Emerald. Libr. J. **2004**, *129* (20) (12), 20.

20. Anderson, R. Charleston Conference 1998. Lib. Collect., Acquisit. Tech. Ser. **1999**, *23* (2), 183–190.

21. Arlen, S. Book review: Charleston Conference proceedings 2001. Coll. Res. Libr. **2004**, *65* (1) (01), 81–82.

22. Astle, D.L. With sci/tech journals, hidden costs cost a lot. Libr. Acquisit. **1988**, *12* (2), 163–167.

23. Astle, D.L. The scholarly journal: whence or wither. J. Acad. Libr. **1989**, *15* (7), 151–156.

24. Astle, D.L. Preservation issues and acquisitions. Libr. Acquisit. **1990**, *14* (3), 301–305.

25. Baker, C. Field trip. Libr. J. **1976**, *133* (11) (06/15), 46.

26. Baldwin, J.A. Why do we still buy books? Libr. Collect. Acquisit. Tech. Serv. **2000**, *24* (3), 403–404.

27. Barker, J.W. Acquisitions and collection development: 2001. Libr. Acquisit. **1988**, *12* (2), 243–248.

28. Barker, J.W.; Tonkery, D. Unbundling vendor costs. Libr. Acquisit. **1991**, *15* (3), 399–406.

29. Barker, J.W. Vendor studies redux: Evaluating the approval plan option from within. Libr. Acquisit. **1989**, *13* (2), 133–141.

30. Barnes, M.; Clayborne, J.; Palmer, S.S. Book pricing: Publisher, vendor, and library perspectives. Collect. Build. **2005**, *24* (3), 87–91.

31. Basch, N.B. Pricing. Libr. Acquisit. **1988**, *12* (2), 203–5.

32. Bazirjian, R. The mergers panel: Highlights of the Charleston Conference. Libr. Collect. Acquisit. Tech. Serv. **2000**, *24* (3), 412–413.

33. Bazirjian, R.; Speck, V.Charleston Conference on Issues in Book and Serial Acquisition. 2004. Charleston Conference proceedings 2003. USA: Libraries Unlimited.

34. Bernhardt, B.R.; Bazirjian, R.; Speck, V.Charleston Conference on Issues in Book and Serial Acquisition. 2006. Charleston Conference proceedings 2004 Libraries Unlimited.

35. Besara, R.; Kinsley, K. Academic libraries—Measuring up: Assessment and collaboration for student success. New Libr. World **2011**, *112* (9) (09), 416.

36. Bishop, J.; Smith, P.A.; Sugnet, C. Refocusing a gift program in an academic library. Libr. Collect. Acquisit. Tech. Serv. **2010**, *34* (4), 115–122.

37. Block, D. Issues in collection management: Librarians, booksellers, publishers. Serials Rev. **1996**, *22* (3), 141–3.

38. Bock, J.; Burgos-Mira, R. Navigating to the future: Understanding common tasks in a multi-campus environment in the dramatically changing acquisition world. J. Electron. Resour. Libr. **2010**, *22* (3), 113.

39. Boissonnas, C.M. Desperately seeking status: Acquisitions librarians in academic libraries. Libr. Acquisit. **1991**, *15* (3), 349–354.

40. Boissonnas, C.M. When we buy books we know what we pay for-or do we? Libr. Acquisit. **1989**, *13* (2), 87–101.

41. Boissonnas, C.M. The cost is more than that elegant dinner: Your ethics are at steak. Libr. Acquisit. **1987**, *11* (2), 145–152.

42. Boissonnas, C.M. What cost, automation? Libr. Acquisit. **1986**, *10* (2), 107–12.

43. Boissonnas, C.M. Katina's baby: the Charleston Conference at 15. Libr. Acquisit. Practice Theory **1996**, *20* (3), 281–299.

44. Boissy, R.W.; Taylor, T.N.; Stamison, C.M.; Henderson, K.S.; Okerson, A.; Van Rennes, R.; Dooley, J. Is the "Big deal" dying? Serial Rev. *38* (1) (3), 36–45.

45. Bonk, S.C. Will resource sharing live up to its potential? Libr. Acquisit. **1989**, *13* (2), 171–175.

46. Bonk, S.C. Rethinking the acquisition budget: Anticipating and managing change. Libr. Acquisit. **1986**, *10* (2), 97–106.

47. Bonk, S.C. Toward a methodology of evaluating serials vendors. Libr. Acquisit. **1985**, *9* (1), 51–60.

48. Botero, C.; Carrico, S.; Tennant, M.R. Using comparative online journal usage studies to assess the big deal. Libr. Resour. Tech. Serv. **2008**, *52* (2) 61, 62-68.

49. Britten, W.A. Building and organizing internet collections. Libr. Acquisit. Practice Theory **1995**, *19* (2), 243, 244–249.

50. Brown, D. On the circuit: Report from the Charleston Conference, USA 31 October–4 November 2002 [and other conferences]. Serials **2003**, *16* (1), 107.

51. Brown, L.B. 1998 Charleston Conference: Issues in Book and Serials Acquisition. Serials Rev. **1999**, *25* (2) (01/02), 108–117.

52. Brown, L.A. Useful or useless use statistics? A summary of conference presentations on usage data from the 22nd Annual Charleston Conference, Issues in Book and Serial Acquisition. Serials Rev. **2003**, *29* (2) (06), 145–150.

53. Brown, L.A. Approval vendor selection-what's best practice? Libr. Acquisit. Practice Theory **1998**, *22* (3), 341–351.

54. Bryant, E.; Lifer, E.S E-journals rule Charleston affair. *Library Journal* 122 (20) (12): 20. Libr. J. **1997**, *122* (20) (12), 20.

55. Calvert, P. Charleston Conference proceedings 2002. Online Information Review 28 (3) (01/03): 239-. Online Inf. Rev. **2004**, *28* (3) (01/03), 239.

56. Calvert, P.; Gelfand, J.; Riggs, C. Editorial. Libr. Hi Tech News **2002**, *19* (2), 1.

57. Campbell, N.F. Charleston Conference proceedings 200531 (4) (01/03): 109-10. Collect. Manage. **2006**, *31* (4) (01/03), 109–110.

58. Caraway, B.L. Gleanings from the whirl. 61 (3) (Oct): 454. Serials Libr. **2011**, *61* (3) (Oct), 454.

59. Caraway, B.L. Gleanings from the whirl. 61 (3) (Oct): 454. Serials Libr. **2011**, *61* (2) (Aug), 283.

60. Caraway, B.L. Serials report. Serials Librarian 59 (3) (Oct): 219. Serials report. Serials Libr. **2010**, *59* (3) (Oct), 219.

61. Caraway, B.L. Serials report. Serials Libr. **2009**, *57* (4) (Nov), 283.

62. Carlson, B.A. Book review: Practical issues in collection development and collection access: The 1993 Charleston Conference—15 selected papers from the conference by Strauch, Katina, Somers, S, Zappen, S, Jennings, A. Bull. Med. Libr. Assoc. **1996**, *84* (4) (Oct), 595–597.

63. Cassell, K.A. Report on the Charleston Conference 2006. Collect. Build. **2007**, *26* (2), 63–64.

64. Cassell, K.A. Charleston Conference 2004. Libr. Hi Tech News **2005**, *22* (1), 12–13.

65. Cassell, K.A. Report on the Charleston Conference. Collect. Building **2005**, *24* (2), 72–73.

66. Cassell, K.A. Editorial {Michael Keller presentation}. Collect. Build. **2005**, *24* (3), 79.

67. Cassell, K.A.; Mercado, M.I. Charleston Conference 2009. Libr. Hi Tech News **2010**, *27* (1), 1–3.

68. Cassell, K. Charleston Conference. Collect. Build. **2009**, *29* (2) (01/02), 77–78.

69. Cassell, K. Report on the 23rd annual Charleston Conference 2003. Collect. Build. **2004**, *23* (2) (01/02), 54–55.

70. Cassell, K.A.; Mercado, M.I. Conference report from the Charleston Conference 2006. Libr. Hi Tech News **2007**, *24* (1), 12–13.

71. Cenzer, P.S. Decentralized acquisitions-a future or a trend? Libr. Acquisit. **1985**, *9* (1), 37–40.

72. Chamberlain, C.E. Issues in book and serial acquisition: Old problems, new solutions. Serials Rev. **1984**, *10* (Winter), 94–95.

73. Chamberlain, C.E. The impact of institutional change: Opportunities for acquisitions. Libr. Acquisit. **1987**, *11* (2), 153–159.

74. Chamberlain, C.E. The gatekeeper and information. Libr. Acquisit. **1991**, *15* (3), 265–269.

75. Chapman, L. Book acquisitions in higher education libraries in England: Collection development or damage limitation. Libr. Acquisit. **1991**, *15* (3), 287–94.

76. Chapman, L. Divided by a common language, united by common problems: Buying foreign books for U.K academic libraries. Libr. Acquisit. **1991**, *15* (3), 447–451.

77. Clark, S.D.; Winters, B.A. Bidness as usual: The responsible procurement of library materials. Libr. Acquisit. **1990**, *14* (3), 265–274.

78. Clemens, R.G. Reports of conferences, institutes, and seminars {including 2008 Charleston Conference}. Bidness as usual: The responsible procurement of library materials. Serials Rev. **2009**, *35* (2) (6), 105–106.

79. Cohen, DK. The present state of education for acquisitions librarians. Libr. Acquisit. **1991**, *15* (3), 359–364.

80. Collins, C.S.; Walters, W.H. Open access journals in college library collections. Serials Libr. **2010**, *59* (2) (Aug), 194.

81. Collins, M. SERU: An alternative to licensing-an interview with Selden Durgom Lamoureux. Serials Review **2007**, *33* (2) (6), 122–128.

82. Cox, F.M.; Devine, D.M.; Harvell, G.G. The Charleston Conference: Informative, fun and informal. Libr. Hi Tech News **2001**, *18* (2), 21–24.

83. Cox, J. The global market: 1992 is watching us. Libr. Acquisit. **1991**, *15* (3), 345–347.

84. Creibaum, L. XXVIII Annual Charleston Conference. Serials Rev. **2009**, *35* (2) (06), 107–109.

85. Creibaum, L. Charleston Conference report. Arkansas Libr. **2006**, *63* (4) (12/15), 27–28.

86. Curtis, J. Publishing policies, off the top of my head. Libr. Acquisit. **1988**, *12* (2), 221–224.

87. Davis, H.; Day, A.; Orcutt, D. Further reflections on the WorldCat collection analysis tool. Collect. Manage. **2008**, *33* (3) (07), 236–245.

88. Davis, P.M. Fair publisher pricing, confidentiality clauses and a proposal to even the economic playing field. D-Lib Mag. **2004**, *10*(2).

89. Davis, S.; Siar, J.; Brown, L.A. Report of conferences, institutes, and seminars. Serials Rev. **2003**, *29* (2), 144–150.

90. Davis, S. Serials spoken here: Reports of conferences, institutes, and seminars. Serials Rev. **2001**, *27* (2) (8), 78.

91. Davis, S; Bustion, M; Tian, J; Bluh, P; Kirkland, K Serials spoken here: Reports on conferences, institutes and seminars. Serials Rev. **1998**, *24* (1), 111–129.

92. Davis, S.; Stevens, L. 20th Annual Charleston Conference, Issues in Book and Serial Acquisition: Is bigger better? *Serials Rev.* **2001**, *27* (2) (06), 81.

93. Davis, S.; Wilhite, M.; Brown, L. Serials spoken here: Reports of conferences, institutes, and seminars. Serials Rev. **1999**, *25* (2) (06), 103.

94. Desmarais, N. Electronic book and serial acquisitions: the medium is the message. Comput. Libr. **1993**, *13* (1), 25–7.

95. Devin, R.B. Who's using what? Libr. Acquisit. **1989**, *13* (2), 25–27.

96. Dole, W.V. Myth and reality: Using OCLC/Amigos collection analysis CD to measure collections against peer collections and against institutional priorities. Libr. Acquisitions **1994**, *18* (Summer), 179–182.

97. Dole, W.V. Librarians, publishers, and vendors: Looking for Mr. Goodbuy. Libr. Acquisit. **1987**, *11* (2), 125–134.

98. Dole, W.V. Acquisitions and collection development: 2001-the end user. Libr. Acquisit. **1988**, *12* (2), 249–253.

99. Dougherty, R.M. The Russian peasant and the bird: A moral keynote. Libr. Acquisit. **1989**, *13* (2), 187–192.

100. Downey, K. Managing selection for electronic resources: Kent State University develops a new system to automate selection. J. Electron. Resour. Libr. **2012**, *24* (2) (Apr), 127.

101. Duchin, D. The apparently automatic self-inflating price of books. Libr. Acquisit. **1989**, *13* (2), 115–118.

102. Dulaney, C.K.; Miller, A.; Nadeski, K.; Paiste, M.S.; Rathemacher, A.J.; Toranzo, V.; Blythe, K. Reports of conference, institutes, and seminars. Serials Rev. 2012 (in press).

103. Eberhart, G.M. The 25th Charleston Conference: Books and serials face an uncertain but exciting future. Am. Libr. **2005**, *36* (11) (12), 34–35.

104. Emery, J. Evaluating, selecting, and acquiring electronic resources: Part III—usage and other statistics. Serials Rev. **2001**, *27* (2) (8), 78–81.

105. Emery, J. He demand driven acquisitions pilot project by the Orbis Cascade Alliance: An interview with members of the demand driven acquisitions implementation team. Serials Rev. *38* (2), 132–136.

106. England, L.; Fu, L. Electronic resources evaluation central: Using off-the-shelf software, web 2.0 tools, and LibGuides to manage an electronic resources evaluation process. J. Electron. Resour. Libr. *23* (1) (Jan), 30.

107. Faigel, M. Methods and issues in collection evaluation today. Libr. Acquisit. **1985**, *9* (1), 21–35.

108. Farrell, K.T.; Truitt, M. Defining functional requirements for acquisitions records: Vendor metadata. Libr. Collect. Acquisit. Tech. Serv. **2004**, *28* (4), 473–487.

109. Farrell, K. Buying direct: the vendor perspective. Libr. Acquisit. **1990**, *14* (3), 285–287.

110. Fath, A.D. Things are seldom what they seem: 25th annual Charleston Conference. Serials Rev. **2006**, *32* (2) (6), 133–136.

111. Fenner, A. Fast times in technical services: Challenges and opportunities. Southeastern Libr. **2005**, *53* (3), 12.

112. Fidishun, D. {Charleston Conference proceedings 2001}. Libr. Collect. Acquisit. Tech. Serv. **2004**, *28* (3) (01/03), 354–355.

113. Flowers, J.L. Emotional intelligence in the workplace. Libr. Collect. Acquisit. Tech. Serv. **2000**, *24* (3), 431–433.

114. Flowers, J.L. Systems thinking about acquisitions and serials issues and trends: A report on the 1993 Charleston Conference. Libr. Acquisit. Practice Theory **1994**, *18* (2), 227–238.

115. Foster, C. Foreword: Revisiting open access: Anything new in four years? Serials Rev. **2008**, *34* (1) (3), 11–12.

116. Garofalo, D.A. Tips from the trenches. J. Electron. Resour. Libr. **2011**, *23* (3) (Jul), 274.

117. Gaynor, E. Literary texts in an electronic age: Scholarly implications and library services: Edited by Brett Sutton. Urbana-Champaign, IL: Graduate school of library and information science, University of Illinois at Urbana Champaign, 1994. 207p. $25.00. ISBN 0-87845096-3. J. Acad. Libr. **1996**, *22* (3), 226–227.

118. Geckle, B.J.; Fath, A.D.; Davis, S. Reports of conferences, institutes, and seminars. Serials Rev. **2006**, *32* (2), 131–133.

119. Gelfand, J.; Taylor, A. The Charleston Conference: 25th anniversary celebration of a meeting. Libr. Hi Tech News **2006**, *23* (1), 10–12.

120. Genoni, P. Charleston Conference proceedings 2002. Libr. Manage. **2004**, *25* (6/7), 321–322.

121. Graham, G. Publishers, librarians and the eternal triangle. Libr. Acquisit. **1991**, *15* (3), 261–264.

122. Gurshman, S.J. 1996 Charleston Conference: Issues in Book and Serials Acquisitions. Ser. Rev. **1997**, *23* (1), 65–71.

123. Hacken, R. The current state of European studies in North America and of scholarly publishing in Western Europe. J. Acad. Libr. **1998**, *24* (3) (5), 201–207.

124. Hadro, J. Competition heats up discovery marketplace. Libr. J. (1976) **2010**, *1351* (17) (10/16), 16–16.

125. Hamaker, C. Time series circulation data for collection development or: You can't Intuit that. Libr. Acquisit. Practice Theory **1995**, *19* (2), 191–195.

126. Hamaker, C. Library serials budgets: Publishers and the twenty percent effect. Libr. Acquisit. **1988**, *12* (2), 211–19.

127. Hannay, W.M. Antitrust aspects of unbundling vendor services. Libr. Acquisit. **1991**, *15* (3), 407–408.

128. Hannay, W.M. Antitrust aspects of book discounting in the library world. Libr. Acquisit. **1991**, *15* (3), 385–386.

129. Hannay, W.M. Antitrust issues in publishing. Libr. Acquisit. **1990**, *14* (3), 227–232.

130. Hanson, M. Buying time: Preservation and acquisitions. Libr. Acquisit. **1991**, *15* (3), 393–397.

131. Hardo, J. Charleston discovery face-off draws crowd. Libr. J. (1976) **2010**, *135* (20) (12), 24–26.

132. Hawkins, D.T. Necessity is the mother of invention: The 29th Charleston Conference. Inform. Today **2010**, *27* (1) (01), 25–26.

133. Hawkins, D.T. The 28th Charleston Conference: The best of times … the worst of times. Inform. Today **2009**, *26* (1) (01), 26–27.

134. Hawkins, D.T. The 27th annual Charleston Conference: What tangled webs we weave. Inform. Today **2008**, *25* (1) (01), 31–34.

135. Hawkins, D.T. Unintended consequences: The Charleston Conference. Inform. Today **2007**, *24* (1) (01), 25–27.

136. Hawkins, D.T. Major end-of-year conferences. 2006, Inform. Today **2012**, *23* (10) (11), 30–31.

137. Hawkins, D.T. Charleston Conference: Following industry trends. Inform. Today **2012**, *29* (1), 16.

138. Hawks, C.P. 1991 Conference scene: Predominant themes. Libr. Acquisit. **1992**, *16* (Fall), 247–255.

139. Hendrickson, K.H. Library vendors: How do they use us? Libr. Acquisit. **1989**, *13* (2), 121–123.

140. Hendrickson, K.H.; Strauch, K.P. Intellectual property rights and scholarly publishing in the twenty-first century. Libr. Acquisit. **1991**, *15* (3), 419–421.

141. Heroux, M.S. Anatomy and physiology of the publisher/vendor/librarian relationship: Borrowing from that old country classic, 'I may be a Christian, Lord, but I'm a woman too'. Libr. Acquisit. **1988**, *12* (2), 207–210.

142. Hitchcock-Mort, K.A. Collection management in the eighties-where are we now? Libr. Acquisit. **1985**, *9* (1), 3–12.

143. Hoffert, B. Meeting of the minds. Libr. J. (1976) **1992**, *117* (02/16), 129–130.

144. Hughes, C.A. The case for scholars' management of author rights. Portal : Libr. Acad. **April 2006**, *6* (2), 123–126.

145. Intner, S.S. Issues in collection management: Librarians, booksellers, publishers: Edited by Murray S. Martin (Foundations in library and information science, vol. 31). Greenwich, CT: JAI press, 1995. 193p. $73.25. ISBN 1-55938-608-6. J. Acad. Libr. **1996**, *22* (2), 226.

146. Ives, G.; Fallon, S. Stung if you do, stung if you don't-The good and the bad of the big deal. Serials Libr. **2009**, *56* (1-4), 163–167.

147. Ivins, A. Charleston Conference: Issues in Book and Serial Acquisition: Questioning Assumptions. Serials Rev. **October 1989**, *15* (1), 74–76.

148. Ivins, A. Charleston Conference: Issues in Book and Serial Acquisitions: Remembrance of Things Past. Serials Rev. **1989**, *15* (4), 68–69.

149. Ivins, A. Do subscription agents earn their service charges, and how can we tell? Libr. Acquisit. **1989**, *13* (2), 143–147.

150. James-Barnes, M. Charleston Conference report. Arkansas Libr. **2006**, *63* (4) (12,15), 25–26.

151. Johnson, K.G.; Miller, B.H.; McDonald, E.; Mi, J.; Roe, S.; Alan, R.; Slaughter, P.; Baker, G.; Wilkinson, F.C.; Lewis, L.K. The balance point: Jumping through the hoops: Serials librarians' reflections on tenure, reappointment, and promotion experiences in academia. Serials Rev. **2005**, *31* (1) (3), 39–53.

152. Jones, D. On-demand information delivery: Integration of patron-driven acquisition into a comprehensive information delivery system. J. Libr. Admin. **2011**, *51* (7 Oct, 764.

153. Kasprowski, R.; Butler, D.; Chatfield, C.; Massey, T.; Davis, S.K.; Hu, S.; Blythe, K. Reports of conferences, institutes, and seminars. Serials Rev. **2010**, *36* (2), 116–119.

154. Kenney, B. OpenURL, publishing models top the agenda at Charleston. **2003**, Libr. J. (1976) **2010**, *128* (20 (12), 27.

155. Kenney, B. More bytes than books in Charleston. Libr. J. (1976) **2002**, *127* (20 (12), 18, 2002.

156. Kelvil, L.H. The approval plan of smaller scope. Libr. Acquisit. **1985**, *14* (3), 13–20.

157. Kflu, T. Vendor performance evaluation: Numeric formula. Libr. Acquisit. **1990**, *14* (3), 301–312.

158. Kirkland, K.L. 1997 Charleston Conference: Issues in Book and Serials Acquisition. Serial Rev. **1998**, *24* (1) (04/15), 120–129.

159. Kruger, B. U.K. books and their U.S. imprints: A cost and duplication study. Libr. Acquisit. **1991**, *15* (3), 301–312.

160. Kaul, N. Charleston Conference keynote address: James T. Stephens. Libr. Acquisit. **1997**, *21* (3), 241.

161. Lassner, K. The buying direct view. Libr. Acquisit. **1990**, *14* (3), 283–284.

162. Lawson, K. Introduction. Ser. Libr. **2010**, *59* (2) (Aug), 137.

163. Lenzini, R. The trends they are a'changing. Serials **March 2002**, *15* (1), 65–66.

164. Leonhardt, T.W. Place of special collections in the acquisitions budget. AB Bookman's Weekly **1982**, *70* (07/05), 75–79.

165. Leonhardt, T.W. The acquisitions librarian as informed consumer: 'Mad as Hell and not going to take it anymore!'. Libr. Acquisit. **1988**, *12* (2), 149–154.

166. Leonhardt, T.W. Buying direct vs. third party buying. Libr. Acquisit. **1988**, *12* (2), 259–260.

167. Link, F.E. Do vendors cost too much for the service they provide? Libr. Acquisit. **1989**, *13* (2), 125–128.

168. Lippincott, S.K.; Brooks, S.; Harvey, A.; Ruttenberg, J.; Swindler, L.; Vickery, J. Librarian, publisher, and vendor perspectives on consortial E-book purchasing: The experience of the TRLN beyond print summit. **2012**, Serial Rev. **1989**, *38* (1) (3), 3–11.

169. Lockman, E.J. Is the customer always right: or, wait a minute, don't you want my business? Libr. Acquisit. **1987**, *11* (2), 121–123.

170. Lopez, J.S. The great leveler: The library budget. Libr. Acquisit. **1988**, *12* (2), 229–234.

171. Lowry, C.B. Year 2 of the 'great recession': Surviving the present by building the future. J. Libr. Admin. **2011**, *51* (1) (01), 37.

172. Lynden, F.C. Fund-raising tips. Libr. Acquisit. **1991**, *15* (3), 387–391.

173. Lynden, F.C. Prices and discounts. Libr. Acquisit. **1988**, *12* (2), 255–258.

174. Machovec, G.; Strauch, K. In the company of librarians. Searcher **2012**, *20* (1), 28–33. Jan.

175. MacIntyre, R.; Blackwell, L.S. Industry initiatives: What you need to know. Serials Librarian 60 (1-4) (01): 186. Serial Libr. **2011**, *60* (1–4) (01), 186.

176. Macomber, N. Charleston Conference proceedings 2005. J. Acad. Libr. **2007**, *33* (3 (05), 424.

177. MacRitchie, J. The devil in the detail. **2004**, Austr. Libr. J. *53* (3 (08.07), 326.

178. Maddux, J. Exchange rate and inflation. Libr. Acquisit. **1988**, *12* (2), 181–185.

179. Malanchuk, P. African Acquisitions: Strategies to locate and acquire current and retrospective Africana. Libr. Acquisit. **1991**, *15* (3), 453–461.

180. Marsh, C.V. Charleston Conference 1989. Library Acquisitions 14 (3): 317-. **1990**, Libr. Acquisit. *14* (3), 317.

181. Marsh, C.V. Charleston Conference 1989: Issues in book and serial acquisitions: Remembrance of things past. Libr. Acquisit. **1990**, *14* (3), 215–216.

182. Marsh, C.V. Charleston Conference peer data surveys. Libr. Acquisit. **1989**, *13* (2), 193–195.

183. Marsh, C.V. The business of library acquisitions: A consumer model. Libr. Acquisit. **1987**, *11* (2), 161–163.

184. Marsh, C.V.; Lockman, E.J. Net book pricing. Libr. Acquisit. **1988**, *11* (2), 167–176.

185. Martin, S.O. Charleston Conference (on) Issues in Book and Serial Acquisition: The Pure and Simple Truth. Serials Rev. **1991**, *17*, 33–35.

186. Massey, T.; Blythe, K. 2009 Charleston Conference: Issues in Book and Serial Acquisition: "Necessity is the mother of invention" Serials Rev. **2010**, *36* (2), 121–122.

187. Massey, T. 2003 Charleston Conference, University of South Carolina. Library Mosaics 15 (5) (09/08): 17-. Libr. Mosaics **2004**, *15* (5) (09/08), 17.

188. Mastejulia, R. Publisher policies and their impact on the market. Libr. Acquisit. **1987**, *11* (2), 139–144.

189. McCallister, M. Whither the book. **2006**, Charleston Conf. Proc. *2004* (01), 141–143.

190. McCune, S.M. What is the value of information? Libr. Acquisit. **1989**, *13* (2), 161–164.

191. McLaren, M. E-books: A report on the state of the market. **2000**, Libr. Collect. Acquisit. Tech. Serv. *24* (3) (Fall), 404–407.

192. McLaren, M. Full acquisitions systems. Libr. Acquisit. **1990**, *14* (3), 247–250.

193. McQuillan, B.; Fattig, K.M.; Kemp, R.; Stamison, C.; England, D. **2010**, Electronic resource management system integration strategies: Opportunity, challenge or promise? . Seial Libr. **Jan 1990**, *58* (1–4), 106.

194. Melkin, A. Third party buying vs. buying direct: John Wiley's marketing efforts to vendors and libraries. Libr. Acquisit. **1988**, *12* (2), 225–227.

195. Mercado, M.I. Highlights of the 2003 Charleston Conference. Libr. Hi Tech News **2004**, *21* (1), 12–13.

196. Merriman, J.B. Pricing updates. Libr. Acquisit. **1990**, *14* (3), 296.

197. Merriman, J.B. Subscription agents-are they worth their salt? Libr. Acquisit. **1989**, *13* (2), 149–152.

198. Meyers, B. What do you feed precocious dinosaurs so they'll stay healthy? Libr. Acquisit. **1996**, *20* (3), 351–353.

199. Miller, H.S. How not to buy books for libraries: Contracts, bids, and recent developments in New York State. Libr. Acquisit. **1990**, *14* (3), 275–281.

200. Moltke-Hansen, D. Don't you weep, don't you moan: A sermon in entrepreneurship for acquisitions librarians. Libr. Acquisit. **1991**, *15* (3), 365–369.

201. Moore, K.; Duggan, L. Transparency and publisher pricing models. Serials Libr. **1991**, *60* (1-4) (01), 98.

202. Moore, M. Keeping current with electronic resources and libraries. J. Electron. Resour. Med. Libr. **2011**, *8* (3), 263–271. Jul.

203. Muller, K. Charleston Conference 1992. **1948–1993**, ALCTS Newslett. *4* (1) (01), 3–5.

204. Nadeski, K.; Paiste, M.S.; Wiles-Young, S.; Yongvongpaibul, P.; Szabo, K.; Miller, A.; Ryan, C.E.; Rogers, T.; Blythe, K. Reports of conferences, institutes, and seminars. Serials Rev. **2011**, *37* (2), 123–127.

205. Newman, E.J. The emergence of European publishing. Libr. Acquisit. **1990**, *14* (3), 233–235.

206. Nicholas, D. Social media and research workflow: A Charleston Conference observatory survey. Charleston Advisor **2011**, *12* (4) (04), 65–66.

207. Nicholas, D.; Paul, H.; Maria, M.; Anthony, W.; Szabo, K. Engaging with scholarly digital libraries (publisher platforms): The extent to which 'added-value' functions are used. Inform. Process. Manage. **2006**, *42* (3) (5), 826–842.

208. Nicholas, D.; Huntington, P.; Watkinson, A. Scholarly journal usage: The results of deep log analysis. J. Doc. **2005**, *61* (2), 248–280.

209. Nicholas, D.; Rowlands, I.; Jubbs, M.; Jamali, R. The impact of the economic downturn on libraries: With special reference to university libraries. J. Acad. Libr. **2010**, *36* (5) (9), 376–382.

210. Nicholas, D.; Watkinson, A.; Rowlands, I.; Jubb, M. Social media, academic research and the role of university libraries. J. Acad. Libr. **2011**, *37* (5) (9), 373–375.

211. Nissley, M. Handle with care! delicate package! CD-ROMs and the acquisitions process. [presented at Charleston Conference 1989). Libr. Acquisit. **1990**, *14* (3), 251–256.

212. Oder, N. A bit of a downer in Charleston. Libr. J, **2008**, *133* (20) (12/1), 21.

213. Oder, N.; Lifer, E.St. Books and serials talk in Charleston. Libr. J. **1996**, *121* (20) (12), 20–22.

214. Ogburn, J.L. The value of acquisitions in the library of the future. Libr. Acquisit. **1991**, *15* (3), 355–358.

215. Ojala, M. Friending Charleston. Inf. Today **2009**, *26* (1) (01), 27–28.

216. Okerson, A.L. Married to the library. Lib. Acquisit. **1989**, *13* (2), 155–160.

217. Parkurst, T.S. Serial pricing and copyrights: prophecies, strategies and fallacies. Libr. Acquisit. **1990**, *14* (3), 223–6.

218. Parrillo, G. Fast facts. College Res. Libr. News **2010**, *71* (2) (02), 120.

219. Paul, S.K. The future of standards. Libr. Acquisit. **1988**, *12* (2), 235–238.

220. Polanka, S. Off the shelf: Ask the aggregators. Booklist **2011**, *107* (9) (1), 119.

221. Potter, W.G. The growing demand for electronic publishing. Libr. Acquisit. **1991**, *15* (3), 371–377.

222. Powell, A. Times of crisis accelerate inevitable change. J. Libr. Admin. **2011**, *51* (1) (01), 105.

223. Pritchard, E. Electronic ordering systems. Libr. Acquisit. **1990**, *14* (3), 245–246.

224. Quinn, M.E. Librarian's library. Charleston on my mind. Am. Libr. **January 2010**, *41* (1), 104–105.

225. Quinn, R.M.D. Trust and excellence. J. Am. Libr. *14* (6) (01), 343.

226. Rapp, D. Charleston Conference: Big ideas, big challenges. Libr. J. (1976) **2011**, *136* (20) (12), 22–24.

227. Rapp, D.; Williams, W.Charleston Conference: Big ideas, big challenges. Vol. 136; 130. [JOURNAL?]2005.

228. Rast, E. "Remembrance of things past;" - Charleston Conference 1989. NASIG Newslett. **1989**, *4* (6), 8–10.

229. Ray, R.L. 1992 Charleston Conference on Book and Serial Acquisitions A report. Libr. Acquisit. **1993**, *17* (3), 363–371.

230. Reid, M.T. A general overview of collection building. Libr. Acquisit. **1991**, *15* (3), 295–299.

231. Reilly, B.F. A report on the Charleston pre-conference "weighing the evidence: Evaluating major research databases. A general overview of collection building. Charleston Advisor **2012**, *13* (3), 54.

232. Richards, D.T. By your selection are ye known. Libr. Acquisiti. **1991**, *15* (3), 279–285.

233. Riddick, J.F. Serials automation: A look at financial considerations. Libr. Acquisiti. **1986**, *10* (20), 117–121.

234. Rogers, M.; Oder, N.; Schafer, J. Charleston focuses on E-journals. Libr. J. **2001**, *126* (20) (12), 18.

235. Romanansky, M. The chicken-pluckin' library market. Libr. Acquisit. **1988**, *12* (2), 197–200.

236. Rose, P.M. 1995 Charleston Conference report. Serials Rev. **1996**, *22* (07/15), 103–107.

237. Rose-Wiles, L. The high cost of science journals: A case study and discussion. J. Electron. Resour. Libr. **2011**, *23* (3) (Jul), 219.

238. Rowlands, I.; Nicholas, D.; Russell, B.; Canty, N.; Watkinson, A. Social media use in the research workflow. Learned Publishing **2011**, *24* (3)(07), 183–195.

239. Sales, D. Acquisitions and the South African experience. Collection Management **1995**, *19* (3-4) (01), 141–150.

240. Satisky, D.B. The global market: 1992 is watching the United States. Libr. Acquisit. **1991**, *15* (3), 341–343.

241. Schrift, L.B. After Thor, what's next: The Thor power tool decision and its impact on scholarly publishing. Libr. Acquisit. **1985**, *9* (1), 61–63.

242. Secor, J.R. Ignorance is bliss. Libr. Acquisit. **1991**, *15* (3), 379–383.

243. Secor, J.R. Bookselling in a changing environment. Libr. Acquisit. **1986**, *10* (2), 123–128.

244. Sexton, M.; Feldman, G. Problem solving in Charleston. Publishers Weekly **1991**, *238* (54) (12/13), 34–35.

245. Shelock, E.A. Wrap-up. Libr. Acquisit. **1990**, *14* (3), 217–221.

246. Shelock, E.A. Publisher counterpoint. Libr. Acquisit. **1990**, *14* (3), 237–239.

247. Sievers-Hill, A. Report on the 30th anniversary Charleston Conference: Issues in Book and Serial Acquisitions, "Anything goes", 3–6 November 2010, Charleston,

South Carolina, USA. New Libr. World **2011**, *112* (5) (06), 278.

248. Sievers-Hill, A. A review of "Charleston Conference proceedings 2007" Collection Management **2010**, *35* (1), 50–1. January.

249. Sill, L.A. Charleston Conference proceedings, 2002. Libr. Collect. Acquisit. Tech. Services **2005**, *29* (2) (01/02), 225.

250. Silva, J.L. A leap into the future: Serials literature of 2002. Serials Rev. **2004**, *30* (1), 33–41.

251. Skelley, E.; Waring, J. Obtaining books and journals from the USSR-and a bit of Eastern Europe. Libr. Acquisit. **1991**, *15* (3), 443–446.

252. Somers, S.W.Issues in Book and Serials Acquisition Conference: Charleston, SC, November 1988. Technical Services Quarterly 7 (1), 1989.

253. Somers, S.W. Vendor/Library relations: A perspective. Libr. Acquisit. **1989**, *11* (2), 135–138.

254. Somers, S.W. The exchange rate and inflation: A study of sacred cows, lemmings and other assorted things. Libr. Acquisit. **1988**, *12* (2), 177–180.

255. Somers, S.W. Issues in book and serials acquisition: All you never wanted to know about finances. Tech. Serv. Quart. **1986**, *4* (10/15), 69–73.

256. Steele, C. «Book to the future: 21st century models for the scholarly monograph». Paper presented at Charleston Conference on Issues in Books and Serial Acquisition 2005. 2006. http://hdl.handle.net/1885/43261.

257. Steinle, K.; Daniels, T.Charleston Conference on Issues in Book and Serial Acquisition. 2007. Charleston Conference proceedings 2006. Libraries Unlimited.

258. Steinle, K.; Daniels, T.; Bernhardt Eds, B.R.Charleston Conference proceedings 2005. Libraries Unlimited.

259. Steinle, K.; Daniels, T.; Bernhardt Eds, B.R.Charleston Conference proceedings 2007. Libraries Unlimited.

260. Stevens, L. 20th Annual Charleston Conference, Issues in Book and Serial Acquisition: Is bigger better? Serials Rev. **2001**, *27* (2) (01/02), 81–94.

261. Strauch, B.; Chesler, A. A licensing survival guide for librarians. J. Electron. Resour. Med. Libr. **2009**, *6* (2) (Apr), 123.

262. Strauch, K. Older is better. Libr. Acquisitions **1990**, *15* (3), 257–260.

263. Strauch, K. Remembrance of things past and Looking toward 1990. Libr. Acquisit. **1990**, *14* (3), 319–320.

264. Strauch, K. Charleston conference 1988: Issues in book and serial acquisition: Questioning assumptions. libr. acquisit. **1989**, *13* (2), 81–83.

265. Strauch, K. Issues in book and serial acquisitions: External influences on acquisitions and collection development. Libr. Acquisit. **1987**, *11* (2), 119–163.

266. Strauch, K.; Webster, J. And another thing… the Charleston phenomenon. LOGOS: Journal of World Book Community **1997**, *8* (3) (8), 165, 167, 169.

267. Sutherland, L. Practical issues in collection development and collection access: The 1993 Charleston Conference: Edited by Katina Strauch, Sally Somers, Susan Zappen, and Anne Jennings. New York: Haworth Press, 1995. 193p. $24.95. ISBN 1-56024-733-9.] Published also as Collection Management, 19, nos. 3/4.]. Serials Rev. **1996**, *22* (2), 96–97.

268. Szabo, K.; Blythe, K. The 30th anniversary Charleston Conference: Issues in Book and Serial Acquisition from a first-time attendee's perspective. Serials Rev. **2011**, *37* (2) (6), 129–132.

269. Tagler, J. What are the reasons for the current packaging of journals. Libr. Acquisit. **1989**, *13* (2), 109–13.

270. Tenopir, C. E-access changes everything. Libr. J. **1976**, *135* (1) (01), 26, 2010.

271. Tenopir, C. A new-old role for libraries. Libr. J. **1976**, 1*134* (2) (2), 24, 2009.

272. Tenopir, C. Ebooks arrive. Libr. J. **1976**, *133* (2) (02), 25, 2008.

273. Tenopir, C. Books are back!. Libr. J. **1976**, *130* (20) (12/21), 40, 2005.

274. Tenopir, C. Online serials heat up. Libr. J. *127* (16) (10), 36, 2002.

275. Terry, G. In a wider context: Research libraries within the university community. Libr. Acquisit. **1990**, *14* (3), 241–242.

276. Theus, P. Conference Report: Charleston 2001. Collect. Build. **2002**, *21* (2), 74.

277. Thibodeau, P.L.; Tagler, J. The Chicago collaborative. Serials Libr. **2010**, *58* (1-4), (Jan), 149.

278. Tonkery, D. EBSCO and serials solutions face off over search discovery. Inform. Today **2011**, *28* (1) (01), 20.

279. Toranzo, V. 2011 Charleston Conference. Serials Rev. **2012**, *38* (2), 147–148.

280. Tuttle, M. Magazine fulfillment centers: What they are, how they operate, and what we can do about them. Libr. Acquisit. **1985**, *9* (1), 41–49.

281. Tuttle, M. North American prices for British scholarly journals. Libr. Acquisit. **1986**, *10* (2), 89–96.

282. Tyler, D.C.Patron-driven purchase on demand programs for printed books and similar materials: A chronological review and summary of findings. Libr. Philos. Practice (Jun 2011): 1–19, 2011.

283. Warzala, M. Acquisition of monographic series: Approval plan versus standing order. Libr. Acquisit. **1991**, *14*, 313–327.

284. Webster, J.D.; Strauch, K.P. Review of the history of the library/jobber/publisher relationship. Libr. Acquisit. **1991**, *15*, 409–411.

285. Weir, R.O. Trimming the library materials budget: Communication and preparation as key elements. Serials Rev. **2010**, *36* (3) (9), 147–151.

286. Williams, W. Charleston Conference proceedings 2003. Libr. J. **2005**, *130* (3) (02/15), 164.

287. Williams, W. Charleston Conference proceedings 2001 (book). Libr. J. **2003**, *128* (8) (5), 161.

288. Williams, W. Popular Charleston meeting grows up: More attendees ponder information's future medium: Print or electronic? Libr. J. **1992**, *117* (12), 24.

289. Wittenberg, R.C. The approval plan: An idea whose time has gone? and come again? Libr. Acquisit. **1988**, *12* (2), 239–242.

290. Wolverton, R.E.; Davidson, K. E-resource round up. J. Electron. Resour. Libr. **2011**, *23* (2), (Apr), 174.

291. Young, P.R. Serials pricing update. Libr. Acquisit. **1990**, *14* (3), 297–299.

292. Zappen, S.H. Are the methods working? Where do we go from here? Collect. Manage. **1995**, *19* (3–4) (01), 17.

Chartered Institute of Library and Information Professionals (CILIP)

Tim Owen
Chartered Institute of Library and Information Professionals (CILIP), London, U.K.

Abstract

The Chartered Institute of Library and Information Professionals (CILIP) is the leading professional body for librarians, information specialists, and knowledge managers in the United Kingdom. It has members both in the UK and in approximately 100 countries throughout the world. Its members work in all sectors, including business and industry, science and technology, further and higher education, schools, local and central government, the health service, the voluntary sector, national and public libraries. CILIP was formed in April 2002 as a result of the unification of the Library Association (founded in 1877) and the Institute of Information Scientists. CILIP is the only body in the United Kingdom to accredit university courses in library and information studies, and its Royal Charter empowers it to award Chartered professional status to Members who fulfill its professional criteria.

CILIP is governed by a Council and an Executive Board, supported by a number of special Committees, Panels, and Boards. It provides a full range of services to its members, details of which can be found on its web site at http://www.cilip.org.uk. In 2008 CILIP included approximately 21,000 members and offered its services to approximately 15,000 people engaged in library and information work who are regular customers of CILIP Enterprises.

INTRODUCTION

The Chartered Institute of Library and Information Professionals (CILIP) is the leading professional body for librarians, information specialists, and knowledge managers in the United Kingdom. It has approximately 21,000 members, both in the United Kingdom and in around 100 countries. Its Members work in all sectors, including business and industry, science and technology, further and higher education, schools, local and central government, the health service, the voluntary sector, national and public libraries. CILIP was formed in April 2002 as a result of the unification of the Library Association and the Institute of Information Scientists.

CILIP's goals are to position the profession at the heart of the information revolution; develop and enhance the role and skills of all its Members; present and champion those skills, together with new ones that will be acquired through continuing professional development; and ensure that individuals, enterprises, and not-for-profit organizations have ready and timely access to the information they need.

CILIP is the only body in the United Kingdom to accredit university courses in library and information studies, and its Royal Charter empowers it to award Chartered professional status to Members who fulfil its professional criteria.

CILIP is governed by a Council and an Executive Board, supported by a number of special Committees, Panels, and Boards. It provides a full range of services to its Members, details of which can be found on its web site at http://www.cilip.org.uk.

MISSION

CILIP's mission is to

- Set, maintain, monitor, and promote standards of excellence in the creation, management, exploitation, and sharing of information and knowledge resources.
- Support the principle of equality of access to information, ideas, and works of the imagination, which it affirms is fundamental to a thriving economy, democracy, culture, and civilization.
- Enable its Members to achieve and maintain the highest professional standards in all aspects of delivering an information service, both for the professional and the public good.

GOVERNANCE

All aspects of CILIP's work are governed by its Council, supported by Committees, Panels, and Boards drawn from the Members of CILIP, usually through a process of annual elections. Members can also make their voice heard through the Annual General Meeting when the

Encyclopedia of Library and Information Sciences, Fourth Edition DOI: 10.1081/E-ELIS4-120030201

annual report and accounts of CILIP are presented for scrutiny by the Membership at large.

In this process of governance and accountability, the Honorary Officers have an important part to play. The President of CILIP is elected annually by the Membership at large with the President, President-Elect, and Past President forming three of the six Honorary Officers. The Honorary Treasurer is also elected by the Membership at large, while the Chairs of Council and of the Executive Board are elected by the Council at the first meeting of the year.

CILIP plays a major role in the formulation of policy and development of service delivery across the library and information domain. To assist with this, CILIP has created a range of Advisory Panels covering specific areas of policy, representing key sectoral interests, and providing a locus for consideration of particular aspects of professional activity.

CILIP is a democratically accountable Membership body, and this process of democratic governance is mirrored by CILIP's Branches and Groups, which also hold elections to their various offices and Committees.

Council, Executive Board, Committees

CILIP's governing body is its Council, composed of representatives of Branches and Groups, a number of Councillors elected nationally, and the Honorary Officers of the organization. CILIP is a registered charity and Councillors are the Trustees of the charity.

The Council meets three or four times every year to decide on major issues of policy and resource allocation, scrutinize the work of its various Committees, and review the Regulations that govern the ways in which CILIP conducts its business. As a Chartered Institute, CILIP has a Royal Charter and associated Byelaws that are subject to approval by the Privy Council. These set a broad framework within which the details of rules and procedures are determined by the Council.

In between meetings of the Council, matters of policy and resource allocation and the overall management of CILIP are dealt with by the Executive Board, which also has responsibility for the organization's equal opportunities' policy and practice. The Executive Board reports to the Council on matters affecting general policy, legal and parliamentary business, on developments proposed in the work of the Institute, and on business not assigned to other Standing Committees, and acts on behalf of the Council, in an executive capacity, in matters of urgency.

In addition, there are three broad areas of Committee work to cover in detail the various activities of CILIP:

1. First, at the heart of any professional body are processes of professional development and standards of professional practice. In this area, the Committee structure covers activities such as the accreditation of courses in librarianship and information science, the framework of qualifications awarded by CILIP, the code of professional conduct, the work of Branches and Groups, and other matters related to the profession.

2. Second, there are the areas of ethics, discipline, and professional conduct, which are also covered by the Committee structure.

3. Finally, there is CILIP's portfolio of Enterprises, which generates more than half of the income used to fund the organization. To oversee these income-generating activities, CILIP has an Enterprise Board, and also an Editorial Board to advice the Editor of CILIP's monthly professional magazine, *Update*.

CILIP's Committees and subordinate Panels include the following.

Policy Development Committee

To formulate and develop an effective program of Library and Information Services (LIS) policy at the national and international levels and to promote good practice in policy implementation. Its Panels include:

Youth and Schools' Panel: To advice Council, develop policy, and promote good practice in relation to LIS to young people.

Post 16 Learning Panel: To advice Council, develop policy, and promote good practice pertaining to LIS as they relate to Post 16 Learning.

Public Libraries' Panel: To advice Council, develop policy, and promote good practice in relation to the Public Library Service.

Workplace and Information Services' Panel: To advise Council, develop policy, and promote good practice in relation to LIS in the "workplace" sector and in relation to the work of independent information specialists.

International Panel: To oversee the international work of CILIP, including the implementation of its international policy and the conduct of international relations.

Preservation and Conservation Panel: To formulate policy and initiate action on issues of preservation, conservation, security, and heritage whether written, visual, printed, spoken, or electronic.

Freedom of Information Panel: To examine the emerging statutory and regulatory framework relating to access to information in the United Kingdom and Europe and to advice CILIP on how to promote the best interests of the public and users, and how to maximize opportunities for CILIP members and the LIS profession in this area.

Professional Development Committee

To formulate policies, initiate action, and monitor performance in matters relating to the qualifications framework and structure (including Chartered status and all aspects of the scheme for Continuing Professional Development) and to the framework of Course Accreditation. Its Boards include:

Chartership Board: To manage all matters relating to applications for admission to Chartered Membership and Fellowship of CILIP (excluding Honorary Fellowships); to establish and maintain standards for approved training programs, submissions for Chartered Membership, and submissions for Fellowships; to assess training programs designed to fulfil the requirements for admission to the Register; to assess applications for Chartered Membership and make decisions on their acceptability; to assess applications for Fellowship and make decisions on their acceptability; to advice the Professional Development Committee on any matters relating to admission to the Register of Chartered Members, including the regulations governing the award of Chartered Membership and Fellowship; to establish and maintain a program of Continuing Professional Development for Chartered Members; to establish and maintain a program of certification of Affiliate Members.

Accreditation Board: To manage all matters relating to applications for approval of courses for the purpose of admission to the Register; to apply the Procedures for the Accreditation of Courses as approved by Council; to assess courses submitted for approval and make decisions on their acceptability; to conduct such enquiry as may be necessary to determine the suitability of overseas qualifications for approval; to advice the Professional Development Committee on any matters relating to the approval of courses, including the regulations governing their acceptability.

Professional Practice Committee

To formulate policies, initiate action, and monitor performance in matters pertaining to Branches and Groups, issues of ethics and standards including the Code of Professional Conduct, membership recruitment, and in matters relating directly to personal members including membership benefits. Its subordinate panels include:

Ethics Panel: To develop the Code of Conduct and Code of Professional Practice for CILIP and to deal with any matters related to the ethics of the library and information profession.

Membership Recruitment and Retention Panel: To develop and oversee strategies for Member recruitment and retention including market research into Membership satisfaction and the development of Membership benefits.

CILIP Enterprise Board

To oversee the affairs of CILIP's Enterprises in such a way that professional concerns are supported while achieving maximum income generation. Its subordinate bodies include:

Facet Publishing Advisory Panel: Provides a sounding board and guidance for the publishing team, particularly in relation to the publishing program, ensuring that it is of a high standard and reflects the needs of the information community.

Training and Development Panel: Provides a sounding board and guidance for the development of CILIP's training and development function, ensuring that it reflects the needs of CILIP members and their employers, and the wider information community.

Update Editorial Board: Communicates the views of members to the Editor to ensure that members of CILIP receive a relevant and high-quality magazine, which is in touch with issues of concern and relevance to the profession.

Umbrella Planning Sub-Committee: Works with the Conference Department, to help plan a biennial conference that both reflects the current training needs and interests of members and provides an effective meeting and networking opportunity for all CILIP members.

BRANCHES AND GROUPS

CILIP has 12 branches, one for each of the English regions plus CILIP in Scotland, CILIP Cymru for Wales, and CILIP Ireland. All CILIP Members are automatically assigned to one of the 12 Branches and can choose whether they wish it to be based on their home or work address. All Branches receive a central grant from CILIP to allow them to produce regular newsletters and arrange meetings for their Members.

In addition, CILIP has over 20 special interest groups. Membership of two groups is included in the CILIP subscription, and Members may join others for a nominal fee. CILIP's special interest groups include:

Affiliated Members: A special category of CILIP Membership for paraprofessional and other library and information workers, whose National Committee runs special events and publishes a newsletter.

Branch and Mobile Libraries' Group: For staff working in smaller libraries in all types of public library service, and particularly those working on or with mobile libraries.

Career Development Group: Encourages Members to involve themselves in all aspects of professional activity and is committed to giving a voice to newer Members of the library and information profession.

Cataloging and Indexing Group: Unites Members engaged or interested in the organization and retrieval of information and in the planning, production, maintenance, and exploitation of library catalogs, bibliographies, and indexes.

Colleges of Further and Higher Education Group: Promotes the role of LIS, and of the profession, in further education, higher education, and sixth form colleges.

Community Services Group: Under the banner "information, equality, opportunity", the Group promotes equal access for all communities to LIS, and combats disadvantage.

Diversity Group: Newly formed in 2003, the Group promotes and celebrates diversity within the library and information profession.

Education Librarians' Group: Concerned with the provision of library and information services to all involved in education as a profession, or the study of education.

Government Libraries' Group: Represents the professional interests of library and information workers in Government Departments, Agencies, Parliamentary and National LIS.

Health Libraries' Group: Unites all those working or interested in LIS for medical, nursing, and allied health professions, for people with disabilities and health problems, the housebound and those in residential care, and for carers and patients in hospital.

Industrial and Commercial Libraries' Group: Represents library and information workers in a wide range of commercial and industrial workplaces, and those acting as independent consultants. Also includes an Aerospace and Defence Librarians' Sub-Group.

Information Services' Group: Supports Members' interests in the provision of information services by promoting activities that improve the effectiveness of information provision to all sectors of society.

International Library and Information Group: Unites Members worldwide who have a strong interest in international work, fostering good international relations, encouraging closer understanding and contributing to the development of library and information services overseas.

Library and Information History Group: Aims to raise awareness of library and information heritage within and beyond the profession, frequently through activities with an international flavour.

Library and Information Research Group: Promotes the value of information research and links research with practice.

Local Studies' Group: Improves public and professional awareness of local studies' library and information services and the valuable role they play within their community.

Multimedia Information and Technology Group: Aims to unite Members engaged or interested in multimedia information and technology developments within the profession, enabling communication and promotion of professional interests.

Patent and Trade Mark Group: Acts as a collective voice for Members involved in patent and trade mark searching and other related information matters in dealing with Government and other official bodies, both nationally and internationally.

Personnel, Training, and Education Group: Provides a focal point for study and discussion of every aspect of personnel work (including training) relating to staff in library and information services and to professional education.

Prison Libraries' Group: Unites Members concerned with the provision of library and information services to penal establishments and serves as a focus for staff who could otherwise feel isolated owing to the nature of their working environment.

Public Libraries' Group: Concerned with all aspects of public librarianship, including standards, staffing, service delivery and promotion, with Membership open to all interested in the work of public libraries.

Publicity and Public Relations Group: Demonstrates to the library and information profession that continuous and planned public relations is essential in every type of library and information service.

Rare Books' Group: Unites library and information workers responsible for collections of rare books, manuscripts, and special materials with other interested individuals.

Retired Members' Guild: Enables retired library and information workers to keep in touch with each other, participate in activities, and assist CILIP in promoting library and information services.

School Libraries' Group: Promotes school libraries and school library services as being essential to all areas of the curriculum, to enable the exploitation of a wide range of resources, develop pupils' information skills, encourage the reading habit and support equal opportunities and multicultural education.

The UK Online User Group (UKOLUG): Advancing the effective use of electronic information resources. The national user group for online, CD-ROM, and Internet searchers, aiming to act as a user forum and also as a consumer group to represent users' interests within the information industry.

University, College, and Research Group: Concerned with the interests of library and information specialists in national, research, university, and other higher-education libraries, including playing a significant part in continuing professional development.

Youth Libraries' Group: Works independently and with other professional organizations to preserve and influence the provision of quality literature, LIS for children and young people in public libraries, and school library services.

MEMBERSHIP

To make sure that every level of our profession is represented, CILIP offers a number of different categories of membership:

Chartered: Member CLIP (MCLIP)—Chartered Members who have met the standards for admission to the professional register through demonstration of professional competence. Fellow CLIP (FCLIP)—Fellowship is awarded for achievement and contribution to the profession.

Associate: For members who are eligible to Charter (i.e., have undertaken an accredited course or have met work requirements).

Honorary Fellow: For persons who, in the opinion of Council, have rendered distinguished service in promoting the objects of the Institute. Nominations may be made by members, Branches, Groups, or committees and subcommittees of Council.

Student Member: For people in full or part-time education on an accredited course in library and information science in the United Kingdom, and graduate trainees on pre-postgraduate experience.

Affiliated Member: Any person working in a post within a LIS or information service that does not require professional qualifications.

Supporting Member: For people interested in LIS.

Overseas Member: For any person in the above categories but resident overseas.

Institutional Membership: For organizations working in or interested in the library and information field.

Suppliers' Network: For members of the library and information supply industry, to develop a closer dialog and program of joint action.

PROFESSIONAL EDUCATION AND QUALIFICATIONS

CILIP currently accredits undergraduate and postgraduate library and information courses in universities throughout the United Kingdom. Courses accredited range from first degrees to postexperience courses, where candidates are expected to have previous library and information experience at a professional level. Courses come in all forms—full- and part-time, face-to-face or distance learning—and often in combination with other subjects such as business or health information, art history, or languages. All are regularly reaccredited by CILIP's experts, to ensure that they remain up-to-date, relevant to today's issues, and effectively delivered.

In addition, there are courses leading to para-professional/vocational qualifications that are designed to assess levels of competence in a current job. They are designed to improve practitioners' chances of employment and promotion by honing their skills and helping them demonstrate their commitment to the profession. They provide a combination of practical experience and theoretical knowledge and can help candidates find their first job in library and information work.

Chartered Membership

Chartered Membership is the first level of professional qualification awarded by CILIP. Most Members gain Chartered Membership 2 or 3 yr after graduating. It is open to any Member who fulfils the requirements of the Byelaws and complies with the regulations laid down by Council. These include holding academic qualifications in librarianship and information management that are approved by CILIP, having been in Membership for a minimum of 1 yr and having had a period of practical professional experience on which to base an application for Chartered Membership.

The award of Chartered Membership is based on evidence of continuing professional development in practice and on the ability to learn from experience. It is not a re-examination of the theoretical knowledge acquired on an information studies' course. Candidates seek to demonstrate how that knowledge has been applied and what has been learned as an outcome of that application. Gaining Chartered Membership provides concrete evidence of professional development and progression since the completion of academic studies.

Application for Chartered Membership is made through submission of a two-part application. The first part is a form on which candidates must provide information about the knowledge and skills they have developed since gaining their information studies qualification. The second part is a portfolio of evidence of continuing professional development. There are two routes to Chartered Membership. One requires completion of a period of supervised training, the other a period of self-directed continuing professional development.

1. Route A: One-year full-time equivalent work experience following a CILIP-approved training and development program supervised by a Chartered Member. Qualifications required: CILIP accredited degree.

2. Route B: Two-year full-time equivalent work experience without direct supervision following a Personal Development Plan. Qualifications required: CILIP accredited or other approved qualification.

The achievement carries with it the right to the designation Chartered Member of the Chartered Institute of Library and Information Professionals and the right to the use of the postnominal letters MCLIP.

Fellowship

Fellowship is the highest professional qualification available to Members of the Chartered Institute of Library and Information Professionals. It is open to any Corporate Member who has been on the Register and in professional practice for at least 5 yr. full-time or its equivalent. Professional practice includes any aspect of librarianship of information work. Fellowship signifies that a Chartered Member has developed the potential identified by that award and has applied an increasing level of professionalism both through personal professional practice and the contribution made to the profession at large.

Candidates for Fellowship have to demonstrate that they have built on the potential identified by the award of Chartered Membership, through developing the ability to carry out demanding tasks and handle complex professional issues and by making a contribution to all or part of the profession. At this level, the selection of material for submission is of considerable significance. Work presented for the award of Fellowship will almost invariably contain an element of originality, demonstrating intellectual and professional development.

Occasionally, a Member who has not become a Chartered Member may be allowed to make an application for direct admission to Fellowship. Such a candidate must demonstrate that the level required for Chartered Membership has been achieved by some other means (for example, by an equivalent qualification gained in another country).

The achievement carries with it the right to the designation Chartered Fellow of the Chartered Institute of Library and Information Professionals and the right to the use of the postnominal letters FCLIP.

Framework of Qualifications

The CILIP Corporate Plan 2002–2005 stated that CILIP must

> provide Members with the means to ensure that their expertise is recognised by the wider community, and to enable them to extend that expertise, so that they can remain abreast of new developments and compete effectively in the employment marketplace. It can do this by ensuring that CILIP's framework of academic and professional qualifications remain rigorous and credible, by

> providing new forms of access that recognise paraprofessional roles and nonconventional routes to qualification . . ..

Consequently, CILIP has been developing a new Framework of Qualifications, which it is commited to implementing by March 2005. The Framework is based on research and analysis of the skills and competences needed by staff working in LIS in the 21st century, and it will allow for multientry points and progression routes, catering for differing portfolios of experience and qualifications.

The Qualifications Framework introduces a Certification Scheme for Affiliated Members and a Revalidation Scheme for Chartered Members. The Corporate Plan also articulates the need for CILIP's current Body of Professional Knowledge to be reviewed and updated. Following discussion within both the Accreditation and Chartership Boards, and the Skills and Competencies Steering Group (now called the Framework of Qualifications Steering Group), it was agreed that this work would be undertaken in several stages.

A think tank of representatives of the sector has been meeting to undertake a preliminary investigation. This will be developed and refined through further consultation and debate among a wider stakeholder group, including representatives from outside the library and information sector. The work has been undertaken by a joint working group, under the direction of CILIP's Chartership and Accreditation Boards. The final document will provide a crucial underpinning to the work of designing and developing new Regulations for Chartered Membership, including Fellowship, and also to the review of the Accreditation procedures for assessing programs of academic study in the discipline.

Additionally, CILIP is taking forward various initiatives to support work on its Equalities agenda; this includes investigation of a bursary scheme information and library staff from minority ethnic groups to enable study for professional and paraprofessional qualifications.

Overseas Qualifications

CILIP has a reciprocal agreement with The American Library Association and The Australian Library Association, which means that academic qualifications accredited by those bodies are recognized in the United Kingdom. This allows graduates holding American or Australian bachelor's and master's degrees in library and information studies to apply for posts asking for qualified librarians and information professionals in the United Kingdom.

Qualifications from European Union member states are also recognized in the United Kingdom, provided they have been assessed as being at the degree level or its equivalent.

Other qualifications are individually checked and inquirers should contact the Qualifications section at CILIP.

All inquirers whose qualifications are accepted by CILIP are eligible to register to Charter with CILIP.

ETHICAL PRINCIPLES AND CODE OF PROFESSIONAL PRACTICE

CILIP has drawn up guidelines to provide a framework to help library and information professionals, who are Members of CILIP, to manage the responsibilities and sensitivities that figure prominently in their work. There is a statement of Ethical Principles and a more extended Code of Professional Practice, which applies these principles to the different groups and professionals to which its Members must relate. The Code also makes some additional points with regard to professional behavior. Given the diversity of the information profession, it is inevitable that not every statement in the Code of Professional Practice will be equally applicable to every Member of CILIP. However, the Ethical Principles ought to command more general support, even though some Members may not feel the force of each one of them to the same extent in their day-to-day experience. The Principles and Code assume that respect for duly enacted and duly enforced law is a fundamental responsibility for everybody. However, the Principles and Code may provide additional guidance where there appears to be a conflict of responsibilities.

By the terms of its Royal Charter, CILIP has a responsibility to "the public good." It is therefore anticipated that its Ethical Principles and Code of Professional Practice may be of interest well beyond the immediate limits of the Membership of CILIP, both to those whose work bears close comparison with that of CILIP Members and to those who may, from time to time, want a clear statement of our ethical principles and what we consider to be good professional practice.

Associated with these Principles and Code, there is a growing collection of practical examples, illustrating how information professionals and others can use the Principles and Code to help them cope with the ethical dilemmas they may face. In further support of the Principles and Code, CILIP has established an Ethics Panel of experienced members of the profession, and they and the professional staff of CILIP are available to Members who may need additional help in resolving ethical issues. In those instances where there appears to have been a significant breach of the Code of Professional Practice, this may be a matter for the CILIP Disciplinary Committee. According to the Regulations, the Disciplinary Committee is required to have regard to the Code of Professional Conduct in its work.

SERVICES TO MEMBERS AND OTHERS

CILIP provides a comprehensive range of services to its Members, with the overall aim of helping them remain both informed and employable. In addition, CILIP Enterprises, the Institute's revenue generating arm, provides services to all who require them, usually with discounts for CILIP Members. Further details of all these services can be found on CILIP's website—http://www.cilip.org.uk.

CILIP's direct services to Members include:

Qualifications and Professional Development

- Assessment and accreditation of undergraduate and postgraduate university courses in information and library studies.
- Advice on academic study and professional qualifications in library and information work.
- Chartership—full support from expert CILIP staff throughout the process of becoming professionally qualified.

Information and Advice

- Dedicated enquiry service for members' personal queries—including free searching of selected commercial databases.
- CILIP *Daily News, Weekly Information World*, and *International News Bulletin*—member-only e-mail news and current awareness services, delivered direct to CILIP Members' desktops (on-line sign-up required).
- Confidential one-to-one advice and guidance on professional issues and personal development.

News and Comment

- *Library & Information Update*—CILIP's monthly magazine, including in-depth coverage of professional and industry news and features (also available separately on subscription).
- *Library & Information Gazette*—CILIP's fortnightly tabloid newspaper with Institute-related news, views, comment, and approximately 12 pages of jobs (available to CILIP members only).

Networking and Further Support

- Free membership of the appropriate regional CILIP Branch and two special interest groups (further groups can be joined at nominal charge).
- Exclusive use of CILIP's Information Centre, which includes a library, e-mail and Internet facilities, meeting area, and Members' lounge (available to guests when accompanied by a CILIP Member).
- Libex International Library and Information Job Exchange—Clearinghouse for U.K. CILIP members interested in arranging job exchanges with library and information professionals in other countries.

- Discounts on other CILIP products and services listed below, plus a growing range of exclusive bonus benefits—details are available at http://www.cilip.org.uk.

Details of all other services available from CILIP (usually available to nonmembers for a charge and to Members at a discount) are also given on its website, http://www.cilip.org.uk. Services include:

Library and Information Update (including Buyers' Guide supplement)

- *Library and Information Update*—A monthly magazine with in-depth articles and news on current library and information issues, supplied automatically to Members and available to others on subscription.
- *Update Buyers' Guide*—Quarterly supplement to *Library and Information Update* listing library and information service suppliers' products and services. Also available on-line.

LIS Jobnet

- On-line summary of currently available jobs on offer, available through the CILIP website (details also mailed exclusively to CILIP members in *Library & Information* Gazette).

Facet Publishing

- CILIP's own publishing house, widely regarded as the best source of quality, timely, and useful books for library and information professionals worldwide. Details of available titles and sample chapters are accessible via the CILIP web site, and CILIP Members enjoy a 20% discount on all titles.

INFOmatch

- CILIP's in-house recruitment consultancy, offering services to recruiters, and jobseekers. Covers permanent, temporary, and contract employment. Infomatch services are open to all, but the consultancy also offers special job search advice services to CILIP members.

CILIP Training and Development

- Comprehensive program of training workshops and executive briefings, provided both in-house and on-site. Sessions are usually open to all, but CILIP Members enjoy discounts of up to 30% on course fees.

CILIP Conferences

- CILIP's in-house conference management service, creating tailor-made events for CILIP organizations and outside clients.

CILIP Consultancy Services

- Specialist library and information consultancy with a track record in a wide range of projects and disciplines.

CONCLUSIONS

Vesting Day on April 1, 2002 saw the birth of CILIP, but the new organization will not be fully grown for some time after this. An action plan was mapped out for the transitional period to December 2004 during which a number of important elements of the new organization were being put in place:

- A new structure of qualifications.
- New arrangements for regional Branches in England.
- A new code of conduct and ethics.
- New arrangements for Special Interest Groups.
- A new subscription framework.
- A new web site.

For some time, CILIP will continue to be a "work in progress"—in consultation with the Membership—while at the same time providing a full range of products and services for CILIP Members and the wider library and information community. For up-to-date information on CILIP and its activities, readers are adviced to revisit its website regularly—http://www.cilip.org.uk.

Chemistry Literature and Its Users *[ELIS Classic]*

Judith N. Currano
University of Pennsylvania, Philadelphia, Pennsylvania, U.S.A.

Abstract

The chemical literature is large and varied, crossing many other scientific disciplines. It includes review sources, which summarize past work done in a particular field and are excellent background reading; primary literature, such as research articles in journals; indices and abstracts, which help one to find review and primary documents; catalogs for books, chemicals, and equipment; and handbooks, which present values for physical and chemical properties and the references that report them. There are many nonkeyword access points to all of the various types of literature. Names, formulae, structures, sequences, and other unique identifiers help chemists to locate compounds, while substructure, reaction, and sequence searching are powerful tools for finding structurally similar substances and their reactivity.

INTRODUCTION TO CHEMISTRY AND THE CHEMICAL LITERATURE

Chemistry has been described as "the central science," in part because it has close links to all other sciences. Mathematics is used to describe some physical phenomena, and a basic knowledge of physics is necessary to understand how chemicals behave and why reactions occur. Chemistry takes place in biological systems, fuels transportation devices, and produces cleaning products, medicines, and personal adornments, such as cosmetics and jewelry. Anyone who has baked a cake, lit a candle, or thrown salt on a driveway to melt ice in the winter has set a chemical process in motion.

Chemistry has traditionally been broken into five subdisciplines: organic chemistry, inorganic chemistry, physical chemistry, biological chemistry, and analytical chemistry. Organic chemists are concerned with the synthesis, reactions, and properties of compounds containing carbon. Inorganic chemistry is a vast field; some of the many substances studied by inorganic chemists are elements, compounds or salts containing no carbon, alloys, glasses, ceramics, and substances that combine metals with organic molecules (coordination compounds). Physical chemists study the underlying physical processes involved in chemical behavior, while biochemists look at the chemistry that occurs in biological systems. Analytical chemistry is used, to some extent, by all of the above groups; it involves the characterization of chemical substances and the study of the structure of matter. Although undergraduate-level chemistry still tends to be divided along these lines, chemical research is becoming increasingly interdisciplinary, such that other subcategories and "overlap categories" (theoretical chemistry, medicinal chemistry, polymer chemistry, organometallic chemistry, environmental chemistry, nanochemistry, energy research, etc.) are becoming the norm, rather than exceptions.

Researchers in each subdiscipline ask different types of questions and seek different kinds of information, but all have certain things in common. They are all concerned with chemical substances or processes, whether they perform reactions using them in the lab or model them on a computer. In order to locate information successfully, chemists must understand the structure of the chemical literature, be familiar with its unique access points, and make use of specialized search techniques.

STRUCTURE OF THE CHEMICAL LITERATURE

Primary Literature

Like the literature of most disciplines, the chemical literature is divided into two basic categories, primary and secondary sources. As a general rule, primary sources contain the results of original research, as well as experimental procedures. Since chemists are constantly seeking to build on the work of others without reproducing it from scratch, they are avid readers. Bench chemists, or chemists who work with chemicals in a laboratory, rely on the primary literature to get recipes and instructions for running reactions, and all experimental and theoretical chemists read to stay up-to-date with recent advances in their fields. Commonly used primary documents include: journal articles that describe new research, monographs that consist of collections of original articles, patents, governmental and industrial technical reports, preprints, and some Web sites. Chemists also share information about their research at conferences; however, these meetings do not always result in published conference proceedings. For example, the largest chemistry meetings, the American Chemical Society National Meetings, publish abstracts for talks or posters but have no formal conference proceedings. In recent years, the American Chemical Society

Encyclopedia of Library and Information Sciences, Fourth Edition DOI: 10.1081/E-ELIS4-140000265

has begun recording and making available online a subset of the talks presented at the meetings, and individual divisions of the society might publish their papers presented at the meetings in serial publications or as *ACS Symposium Series* volumes. Researchers looking for more detailed information from a paper or poster presented at a meeting for which conference proceedings are not available can always try contacting the author directly to get a copy of the material.

Journal articles

The bulk of the primary literature in chemistry is published either as journal articles in peer-reviewed publications or as patents. Academic chemists try to publish in prominent journals with high impact factors or that are central publications in their fields. They tend to publish two different kinds of primary articles describing their research: communications, or letters, which are short pieces intended rapidly to introduce important findings, and articles, which are longer pieces that present more details than communications. Chemists turn to the journal literature for general or specific instructions for a particular reaction, programming code for a simulation, methods of preparing substances, etc. They can use a variety of secondary sources to identify research articles of interest in the journal literature, many of which are discussed later in this entry.

Patents

Not all important chemical research, however, is published in the journal literature. Chemistry is not only an academic discipline; it also has a strong industrial sector. While chemists at companies with large research and development groups do publish in the journal literature, important advances by companies are more frequently *patented*. This gives the company the right to exclude others from using the patented invention for the term of the patent, which is, for example, 20 years in the United States. Patents will only protect the invention in the countries in which they are filed; therefore, if a chemist wants her invention protected in the United States, China, and Japan, she must file her patent with the patent offices in each of these countries. There are several overarching intellectual property organizations, including the European Patent Office, a regional patent office whose patents protect inventions in most European countries, and the World Intellectual Property Organization (WIPO), which administers the Patent Cooperation Treaty (PCT). This treaty allows an inventor to file a single patent application with WIPO and use it to apply for protection within any member country.[1] Patents for the same invention filed in different countries constitute a *patent family* and contain roughly the same information. Therefore, if a scientist locates a useful patent in a language that he does not read,

it can be helpful to search for that patent's family and see if it contains an "equivalent" patent in a known language.

Chemists file utility patents that protect substances themselves (drugs, agricultural agents, polymers, etc.), methods of producing substances, and scientific instruments or equipment. Within the patent, the scientist must prove that the invention described is novel, useful, and nonobvious. He or she must also present instructions so that someone skilled in the art would be able to reproduce the results. Therefore, in addition to being legal documents, patents are very important scientific documents, presenting the same kinds of recipes and instructions that the journal articles do. It is important to note that a large percentage of the chemistry published in the patent literature is not published in any other place, and so it is wise to consider searching both patents and journal articles when performing an exhaustive search on a subject. Chemists can identify useful patents using the search features on the individual patent offices' Web sites,[2,3] or by using proprietary resources like the Derwent World Patents' Index, available through the Derwent Innovations Index, or CAS's SciFinder product.[4]

Publication of primary data

In the early 2010s, many government funding agencies began requiring grant awardees to make the products of their research freely available to any who wanted to benefit from them. Initially, their attention focused on open access journal articles, but this was quickly followed by open data. At the time of this writing, many U.S. government agencies require chemists to include in their grant proposals a *data management plan* describing how data resulting from the project will be preserved and made accessible to other researchers. Whenever possible, the chemists are being asked to make their data available through open access repositories, either at their home institutions or through external entities like FigShare.[5] Chemists may also choose to deposit data in domain data repositories, such as the Protein Databank and the Cambridge Crystallographic Data Centre, which are discussed further later in this entry. The purpose of this requirement is to allow other scientists to use and benefit from the data gathered from publicly funded projects. Many data repositories supply the data sets with digital object identifiers (DOIs), which others can use to cite the data in their work. Calrivate Analytics tracks citations to data using the Data Citation Index, and this activity may encourage chemists to take citations to data, as well as to articles, into account when evaluating academics for promotion and tenure, although it is still too early to tell.

Secondary Literature

Secondary sources do not directly report research results; instead, they serve as a "key" to the primary literature, and chemists use them to locate the original research that they require. They can be divided into four further categories. *Review sources* and *handbooks* are edited by experts in the field and aim to supply the most reliable information in their areas. Chemical information professionals occasionally refer to these two categories of literature as the "tertiary literature" to distinguish them from the other two categories, *indexing and abstracting services* and *catalogs*, which are much less judgmental. These resources allow researchers to locate primary documents on a subject of interest but offer little indication of the quality of the information retrieved.

When approaching a new project, a chemist will usually seek background information on the subject, in order to hone the idea and determine which experiments or models to use. A piece of review literature generally serves as an excellent introduction to a subject; an experienced scientist has summarized the literature written in this area and provided an extensive bibliography of primary documents and additional reviews. Once the chemist enters the lab, he or she tends to rely on the primary literature, located using appropriate indexing and abstracting sources, as well as catalogs, to find procedures, suggestions, and even substances or equipment that help to move a project from stage to stage. Handbooks can be invaluable sources of quick information and, most importantly, properties and reactions of compounds. In fact, when searching for properties, it is always best to start with a handbook, which will include both the value of the property and the primary literature reference in which it was reported. The following sections more completely describe each type of secondary or tertiary resource and introduce some of the most important sources of each type.

Review Sources

Review sources in chemistry can be divided into three basic categories: encyclopedias, treatises, and review articles in journals. All are helpful to a scientist attempting to find general or background information on a subject of interest. Of the three categories, encyclopedias tend to treat the most general subjects, while the topics of review articles can be extremely specialized. The problem with review sources, as a category of information, is that they are out-of-date as soon as they are published. Therefore, it is very important to pay attention to the publication date of the source and to supplement an older review with searches of the recent primary literature.

Encyclopedias

Encyclopedias are usually multivolume sets that deal with a fairly broad subject. Some examples of chemistry encyclopedias include the *Encyclopedia of Analytical Chemistry*,[6] the *Encyclopedia of Chemical Physics and Physical*

Chemistry,[7] the *Encyclopedia of Inorganic Chemistry*,[8] the *Encyclopedia of Inorganic and Bioinorganic Chemistry*,[9] and the *Encyclopedia of Reagents for Organic Synthesis* (EROS).[10,11] Encyclopedias serve a dual purpose; a scientist can get an overview of a very broad subject by reading large sections at a time, or he or she can pick up quick information and definitions by using the indices and tables of contents. For example, EROS has in-depth articles about various reagents used to synthesize organic molecules. However, using the online edition, a chemist can search for a particular transformation and be taken directly to the point of the article at which this transformation is discussed. Encyclopedias in the field of chemistry are published in both print and electronic formats, with parity between the two formats becoming increasingly rare. It is a monumental undertaking to publish a complete, new edition of an encyclopedia, meaning that they get updated in their entirety rather infrequently. Leveraging the speed of Web-based publishing, publishers can update articles as needed, and many have begun selling "annual updates" to customers who choose to purchase an electronic encyclopedia outright rather than licensing it through an annual subscription. Electronic editions of encyclopedias tend to be much more expensive than their print counterparts.

One of the most important encyclopedias in any area of chemistry is the *Kirk-Othmer Encyclopedia of Chemical Technology*,[12,13] which is a great starting point in a search for information on a broad or general area of chemistry or chemical engineering. Many articles are about commonly used chemicals and classes of substance and contain information about their production, physical and chemical properties, biological activity, and natural occurrence. Because of *Kirk-Othmer*'s emphasis on chemical technology, many of the articles dealing with chemicals also include information on economic aspects, industrial uses, and safety or hazards associated with the chemical, the first of which can be extremely difficult to find elsewhere.[13] In addition to pieces about chemicals, *Kirk-Othmer* also contains articles describing chemical processes and pathways, techniques, and instrumentation. It is available in two formats; the fifth print edition, consisting of 26 volumes, began publication in 2004 and was completed in 2007. It is organized alphabetically by concept, with subject and contributor indices. The electronic edition, which contains the same information as the print, can be browsed alphabetically by article title or searched by keywords in any field of the record. It has options that allow the user to search a specific field of the record or limit to articles in a specific subject area or written during a particular time period.

Treatises and review articles

Treatises can range from enormous, multivolume sets, such as *Organic Syntheses*[14] and *Methods in*

Enzymology,[15] to short monographs on a subject, like the books in the Oxford University Press *Practical Approach* series. All are written or edited by experts in the field of the volume, and all provide the reader with information that is slightly more specific than that found in an encyclopedia but is still general enough to be understood by someone new to the area. The print editions of the larger sets, including *Comprehensive Organic Functional Group Transformations 1* and *2*[16,17] and *Comprehensive Organometallic Chemistry 1, 2,* and *3*,[18–20] tend to be kept in library reference collections, although many libraries are now purchasing these types of tools in electronic format, due to the superior searchability and ease of access of that format. As with encyclopedias, the electronic editions tend to be much more expensive than print editions. Comprehensive sets are updated regularly but infrequently, with each updated edition picking up the review of the literature where the previous one stopped. The topics of the sets tend to be fairly broad, and the individual volumes frequently deal with a single subject or a set of subjects in a reasonable amount of detail.

One of the most impressive treatises is the enormous *Houben-Weyl Methoden der Organischen Chemie*, or *Houben-Weyl Methods of Organic Chemistry*, published by Georg Thieme Verag.[21] This resource aims to present a comprehensive set of methods of synthesizing compounds and classes of compounds. The first edition was created in 1909, by Theodor Weyl, and it reviews literature dating back as far as 1834.[22] The current series consists of 183 volumes. In 2000, Thieme decided to extend and update Houben-Weyl with a 48-volume series called *Science of Synthesis*,[23] released almost simultaneously in print and database format between 2000 and 2008. Mindful of the datedness of review-type publications, Thieme began releasing periodic "Knowledge Updates" to the original 48-volume set; these volumes are aimed at updating information encapsulated in the original set and adding topics not originally included. *Science of Synthesis* can be searched online via its native interface, but articles from it and from its parent series are also referenced in *Chemical Abstracts*, making it easy for chemists to be drawn to information of interest. The online edition features the ability to search by structure or reaction for molecular transformations, as well as detailed text search capabilities. The previous volumes of *Houben-Weyl* are also available online through the *Science of Synthesis* interface, although the search features are not as advanced.

For background information on a more specific subject, chemists tend to turn to books in their library collections. Chemistry books appear in both print and electronic formats, and, at the time of this writing, libraries tend to select one or the other on a case-by-case basis. Chemistry e-books are sold either as individual items or as part of e-book packages, and some publishers allow libraries to pick the purchase option that they prefer, while others use

a single option. Libraries choosing an e-book package get access to all books published that year in the chosen subject area. Some monographs have records in *Chemical Abstracts*, but most can be more efficiently located through a search of the local library catalog, a union catalog, such as OCLC's WorldCat,[24] or an e-book aggregator or publisher platform. Monographs can also be discovered by word of mouth, and scientists will frequently recommend books to one another. Many chemistry books are described as "textbooks," as opposed to "books of original articles"; some of them are actually textbooks, in the traditional sense of the word, but many are simply treatises written by a single author, which provide excellent background information.

The most specific type of review literature is the review article, found either in journals or in books of original articles. Review articles in journals are submitted and undergo the same peer review process as experimental articles. They can be submitted either to journals that publish only review articles, such as *Chemical Reviews*, or journals that publish all kinds of scholarly articles, such as *Science*. Scientists can identify review articles on a subject of interest using indexing and abstracting services, all of which include an option to limit document or treatment types to review articles. The reviews in books do not always undergo as strenuous a review process as those in journals, but they have been requested and edited by the volume editor. It can be more difficult to locate these, as book indexing in indexing and abstracting services is not always consistent or detailed. However, most recent library catalog records include table of contents information in their notes fields; so, a keyword search across all fields in a local catalog will frequently locate books containing an article of interest.

Indexing and Abstracting Services

Indexing and abstracting services in chemistry are not fundamentally different from their counterparts in other disciplines, although they frequently have access points that are unique to chemistry. The most comprehensive index to the literature of chemistry is the gargantuan *Chemical Abstracts*,[25] produced by Chemical Abstracts Service (CAS), a division of the American Chemical Society. This resource covers all areas of chemistry and currently indexes chemistry articles from thousands of scholarly journals, as well as books, book chapters, patents from 63 different patent-issuing authorities, dissertations, reports, preprints, and Web sites.[26] The *Web of Science*[27] provides access to both topical information and citation data for all areas of science and technology, including chemistry. In addition to *Chemical Abstracts* and the Web of Science, researchers in specific chemical disciplines use other indexing and abstracting services, as well. Physical chemists may use *Inspec*,[28] which indexes over 3500 journals in the areas of physics and electronics and contains information dating back to 1896.[29] Biochemists prefer information from *PubMed* or *MEDLINE*[30] and other resources from the *National Center for Biotechnology Information (NCBI)*[31]; and some inorganic and materials chemists find useful references with the electronic version of *Engineering Index*, *EI Compendex*, which dates back to 1884 and contains information on all engineering disciplines.[32]

Chemical Abstracts

No discussion of the chemical literature would be complete without a look into *Chemical Abstracts*, one of the world's largest indexing and abstracting publications. *Chemical Abstracts* began publication in 1907. Prior to its inception, several other sources, including *Comptes Rendus*, *Bulletin de la Société Chimique de France*, *Index Medicus*, *Engineering Index*, and *Chemisches Zentralblatt*, provided abstracts of American and international chemical literature; American chemistry was highlighted in the *Review of American Chemical Research*, *Chemical Abstracts'* direct precursor, which began publication in 1895 and became a part of the *Journal of the American Chemical Society* two years later.[33] For a long time, *Chemical Abstracts* relied on volunteer abstractors to write abstracts for journal articles; currently, they take author abstracts and enhance them, making them more informative and easily searchable. Like many other indexing and abstracting services, *Chemical Abstracts* uses a thesaurus of index terms, as well as supplemental, descriptive terms. Its print indices included the Author Index, General Subject Index, Formula Index, Chemical Substance Index, Patent Index, and Ring Index, as well as the Index Guide, which provides searchers with supplemental terms on which to search, and the Registry Handbook, which lists CAS Registry Numbers® of newly published substances and substance names.

Chemical Abstracts is currently accessible online via the STN or SciFinder[4] interfaces. Information professionals in companies and the government prefer the command-line driven STN interface, which allows for superior query generation and great specificity of search options. End user chemists and most academic librarians use the more "intuitive" SciFinder interface, which seamlessly links the CAS Registry database with the Chemical Abstracts and MEDLINE abstract databases, as well as a reaction database called CASREACT. Therefore, a researcher can perform a search for a compound in the Registry, click a single button to get all references that contain preparations of that compound, and then click another button to be taken to all reactions that appear in those references. In addition to these four main databases, SciFinder also incorporates a commercial availability source called CHEMCATS and a regulated chemicals listing called CHEMLIST. These are linked from the compound listings in the Registry, although they can be accessed by clicking on a chemical structure or CAS Registry Number (see pp. 37–38) from any database in the system.

Chemical Abstracts is most chemists' first stop for information since its literature coverage is so extensive and it handles compounds and reactions better than any other article database. SciFinder was one of the first of the major science and engineering resources to introduce the analyze feature, allowing users to get some "demographics" of a large answer set, such as publication years, prolific authors and institutions, or substances used in the papers; this feature is now standard in many resources, but it still offers chemists the ability to easily refine their queries.

Web of Science

The Web of Science, available from Clarivate Analytics, is a unique database. Its core collection indexes scientific journal literature from over 12,000 sources.[34] The original electronic database dates back to 1945, but the previous owners, Thompson-Reuters, expanded this coverage with a supplemental back file extending back to 1900. The Web of Science allows topic, author, and institution searching, with a wide range of refinements available. A topic search of the database searches the titles of articles, their abstracts, when available, and author- and indexer-generated keywords. Results can be analyzed according to any category in the articles' records, refined by keyword or other limits, and exported into a usable format for the scientist.

The true power of the Web of Science, however, lies in its ability to perform cited reference searches. While many databases and search systems, such as SciFinder, can link from an article to those that cited it for a limited portion of their coverage, the Web of Science lets users perform a true cited reference search across the entire breadth of the database.[35] Although each Web of Science record links directly to the articles that cite it correctly, the most comprehensive way of searching for citing references in Web of Science is to use the cited reference search interface. Authors will frequently make mistakes in their bibliographies: citing an incorrect volume number, making a typing error in the page number, inverting the issue number and page numbers, etc. A cited reference search will retrieve all of these variants and allow the user to select those that he or she thinks refer to the original document. By entering the name of the first author, the standard Web of Science abbreviation for the journal title, and the year of publication, the user retrieves a list of documents that match these three criteria. From this list, users can easily see the correct variant (it links to the Web of Science record for the article itself) and can select the other variants that they think actually cite the article of interest.

Another advantage to the Web of Science is the many options that it offers for citation analysis. A researcher can generate a citation report on any list of results generated through Web of Science searching. While the most common use of the citation report is to determine an author's h-index, one can also look at the citation metrics for a cluster of articles on a topic or published by a journal. The core collection also links to the *Journal Citation Reports (JCR)*,[36] so, researchers can immediately view basic impact metrics for any article in a result set and can link across to the full JCR in order to view more journal metrics and compare the title with others.

Chemists use citation searching in a very similar manner to other scientists. It is frequently employed by tenure and promotion committees to demonstrate the impact that the scientist has had on his or her field of science. This is frequently done by generating a citation report for that author's publications to locate his or her h-index or by examining the Impact Factors of the journals in which he or she has published. However, it can also be used in more creative ways. If a chemist is having difficulty with a literature search, it can be helpful to perform a cited reference search on one article that is highly relevant to the matter at hand. This will indicate the uses that other researchers have made of that information and can yield some results that a simple keyword search might miss. In addition, the multidisciplinary nature of the resource allows a user to see the applications of chemistry research in other areas of study.

Inspec and Compendex

Inspec's topics lie in the areas of physics, physical chemistry, and electrical and computer engineering, as well as some information science. As a result, it can be quite helpful for chemists examining the physical aspects of a project. One particular boon for chemists using this service is the chemical indexing field, which was first added to the Inspec data structure in 1987.[37] The chemical indexing claims that it does not include organic compounds, although small molecules like methane and ethane can actually be located, as can fullerenes, which are large, spherical "organic" molecules. The structure of "formulae" in the database is truly unique, and users should refer to the help files for exact formatting. However, in addition to having the chemical's formula, it also includes a list of every element that makes up the chemical or system. Formulae and elements are tagged with indicators of their roles in the paper, which include element, binary, system, adsorbate, and surface. The last two roles make the database very useful for physical chemists interested in systems in which a small molecule or atom interacts with a surface. For these reasons, Inspec is probably the most "chemical friendly" of the databases whose primary focus is not chemistry.

Compendex, which is primarily *Engineering Index* online, employs more traditional keyword searching, supplemented by author and controlled vocabulary

indices. It is strong in materials science; it has good coverage in the areas of nanochemistry and materials chemistry, both organic and inorganic; and it also contains useful information for polymer scientists, fuels chemists, and energy researchers. It does not have any specific chemical search capabilities and thus is most frequently recommended for research topic or author name queries that overlap its fields of study.

MEDLINE, the NCBI resources, and the Protein Data Bank

The information in the National Library of Medicine's (NLM) MEDLINE database currently dates back to approximately 1946 and is devoted to all areas of medicine, including clinical medicine, nursing, medicinal chemistry, biochemistry, and pharmaceuticals. The NLM provides the MEDLINE database free of charge through an interface called PubMed, and it is also available via many different vendors' platforms including CAS's SciFinder and through the Web of Science.

MEDLINE is obviously of great use to biochemists, particularly those interested in studying the chemistry of biological systems or drug development, and many such scientists will turn to PubMed before searching in any other resources. MEDLINE, like *Chemical Abstracts*, is thesaurus driven, and the Medical Subject Headings (MeSH) thesaurus can be viewed online. Many of the subject headings are accompanied by subheadings or aspects, which can be searched on their own; some of the ones that are most useful to chemists are "chemistry," "biochemistry," "isolation and purification," and other similar terms. CAS Registry Numbers were added to MEDLINE records in 1985, and a search in this field will retrieve information written since that date. However, the CAS Registry Number and substance indexing in MEDLINE is not nearly as exhaustive as that in *Chemical Abstracts*.

The other NCBI resources are mainly used by biochemists and molecular biologists. The tools are organized on the NCBI Web site[31] according to the type of information that they search, including Chemicals & Bioassays, DNA & RNA, Domains & Structures, Proteins, and Literature, and they represent an interesting mix of secondary search tools and deposition databases for experimental data. The literature database PubMed is a true indexing and abstracting service, incorporating MEDLINE records, as well as non-MEDLINE articles that come from MEDLINE-indexed journals, while the other resources are varied and include deposition and curated databases of substances, sequences, gene information, and diseases. Some examples of molecular and substance databases offered through NCBI are Nucleotide, Protein, Structure, Gene, Genome, and PubChem. These sequence data, three-dimensional structures, entire genomes, and small molecules deposited by scientists, as well as references to these entities in the literature. Additionally, some of the databases, such as Gene, contain summary information prepared by curators to supplement data deposited by submitters, as well as links to additional information resources. The NCBI resources all link seamlessly to one another and to PubMed, making it easy for a searcher to move from one to another. For example, with a few clicks, a researcher can search for articles dealing with a genetic disease, learn about the gene that controls it, link to nucleotides connected to that gene, and end with the three-dimensional structures of the proteins coded by those nucleotides.

Catalogs

Chemists use several different types of catalogs as they search for information. Library catalogs are extremely valuable for determining the holdings of a local library, as well as for locating treatises and review sources. Union catalogs, like WorldCat,[24,38] can assist chemists who want to examine a broader spectrum of books and periodicals. Most searching in catalogs parallels that done in other disciplines; researchers use title and author searches to locate known items and use keyword searches, as well as the occasional subject heading search, to find items on a topic of interest.

In addition to catalogs of books, however, chemists require other types of catalogs. Since bench chemists are performing reactions and studying substances, they need to purchase chemicals and equipment in order to do their research. There are several popular chemical catalogs, including CHEMCATS, available via links from the Registry file in SciFinder; the Aldrich, Sigma, and Fluka catalogs, which can be obtained by request from the companies or accessed online through their combined catalog[39]; *ChemSources USA*[40] and *ChemSources International*[41]; the PerkinElmer Available Chemicals Exchange (ChemACX)[42]; ChemExper[43] and e-Molecules,[44] free sources that harvest information from many different online catalogs. There are an equal number of equipment catalogs, and glassware and equipment can also frequently be obtained from the Thomas Register,[45] most conveniently searched online.

Many chemical catalogs provide, in addition to the availability, quantity, and price of the catalog, some basic physical properties. The Sigma-Aldrich online catalog is one of the best catalogs in this regard, including such properties as melting point, boiling point, density, and solubility, as well as links to pdf images of the infrared, Raman, and nuclear magnetic resonance spectra of many substances. This catalog also goes one step further, referencing the compound's location in important handbooks, such as the Beilstein Handbook of Organic Chemistry and the Merck Index.

Chemical companies also provide another useful piece of information for every substance that they sell. Called

Safety Data Sheets (SDS), formerly Materials Safety Data Sheets, these information sources are designed to inform scientists of the hazards involved in working with the compounds that they describe. To do this, they include physical and chemical properties of the substance; its chemical reactivity; information on safe storage, transportation, and disposal techniques; appropriate first aid information; and other useful information to ensure safe use and handling of the substance. The companies are required by law to disclose this information for each substance that they sell, and OSHA regulations require that chemists know the location of the SDS for each substance that they use in the lab. The Internet has become a common location for safety data sheets, and most companies link to the SDS for each substance from its catalog entry. One of the easiest methods of finding SDSs is through a simple Google search for the name of the company that supplied the substance and the term "safety data sheet." A chemist can use any SDS in order to find general safety and hazards information about a substance, but, to fulfill the regulatory requirements, they must keep a copy of the SDS from their specific supplier on file.

Handbooks

Finding physical and chemical properties of substances using indexing and abstracting sources can be like searching for a needle in a haystack. Abstracts are infrequently written to include statements like, "The following physical properties of the new compound are presented in this paper," and index terms, while they may indicate that properties of substances are included, do not always tell which properties of each compound are present. Presenting different properties in an easily read manner is the job of handbooks, a category that includes general and specific handbooks, spectral atlases, and crystallography collections and that falls into the "tertiary" classification of literature. A good handbook will be edited by someone knowledgeable in the field and should include the best possible values for each property presented. In addition to the value of the property, a reference to the primary document from which the value was obtained should be given. This allows a chemist to refer to the conditions of the original experiment and can help to explain inconsistencies in the reported values of properties. Handbooks tend to deal with a particular class or category of compounds; for example, the *The Merck Index*,[46,47] now owned by the Royal Society of Chemistry, covers only drugs, biologicals, and agricultural agents. However, some handbooks, like the *CRC Handbook of Chemistry and Physics*[48] and the *International Critical Tables*[49] include a wide variety of compound types.

It is important to note that no handbook is exhaustive. They generally contain a limited universe of compounds (the largest handbook discussed here, Reaxys,[50] presents only about 26 million of the more than 100 million compounds reported in the CAS Registry), and not every compound has all properties covered by the handbook. There are several reasons for this. In order for a property to appear in a handbook, it must first be published somewhere in the literature. The editor of the handbook must locate it and decide to include it in the book. If one of these steps does not occur, it may be necessary for the scientist to rely on his or her own experimentally determined values for a given property.

In the online environment, several companies have made an effort to compile collections of handbooks that are simultaneously searchable. One of the most comprehensive of these collections is the Knovel Engineering and Scientific Online Reference Books.[51] The Knovel collection includes many classic chemical handbooks, also available in print format, including *Yaws' Thermophysical Properties of Chemicals and Hydrocarbons*,[52] and *The International Critical Tables*,[49] as well as other information sources, such as *DIPPR Project 801 Database*,[53] which lists constant and temperature-dependent properties for chemical substances. When accessing handbooks and databases through Knovel, however, it is very important to check the edition of the handbook being presented. Publishers will occasionally make older editions available through Knovel, while keeping the newest edition for distribution in print only or on their own online platform. Also, as publishers make and leave agreements with Knovel, books may be added or removed from the platform.

Reaxys

Reaxys is an interesting, hybrid handbook/indexing and abstracting source. It has as its basis two important and historic print sources, the *Beilstein Handbuch der Organischen Chemie*[54] and the *Gmelin Handbuch der Anorganischen Chemie*,[55] as well as the Elsevier Patent Chemistry Database. The data from the three seed sources have been completely integrated and are now being updated as a seamless whole, but it is important to understand the historic antecedents of the database in order to get a sense of its strengths and weaknesses.

Beilstein. The *Beilstein Handbuch der Organischen Chemie*, or the *Beilstein Handbook of Organic Chemistry*, is an enormous work that was, for a long time, the work of one individual. Friedrich Konrad Beilstein, a Russian chemist of German descent, decided to create a comprehensive handbook of all organic chemicals, their properties, and their reactions, and he edited the first (1881), second (1885), and third (1906) editions himself, before his death in 1906.[56] The work of compiling the data then fell to the German Chemical Society, the Beilstein Institute, and, most recently, Elsevier, which incorporated the data into Reaxys. References to the literature date back to the 1770s, making it also one of the oldest secondary or tertiary sources in chemistry. Although the first through fourth editions in print are published in German, the online text available through Reaxys has mostly been translated and is accessible even to non-German speakers. The handbook volumes do have some narrative information that is not included in Reaxys; however, a savvy searcher should be able to find most desired information by referring to the many references to the primary literature found in the compounds' records.

Gmelin. The *Gmelin Handbuch der Anorganischen Chemie*, or *Gmelin Handbook of Inorganic Chemistry*,[55] is the inorganic/organometallic version of Beilstein. Named after Leopold Gmelin, who edited the first edition of the work in 1817,[57] it was published by the Gmelin Institute for some time, before the data were purchased by Elsevier Science. Gmelin reviewed the literature from 1772 to the present and is incorporated in the Reaxys database. Although the series was begun with printed, German-language books, some of which may still be available from used book dealers, the print version is no longer being updated. Unlike Beilstein, which focused on compounds and is organized by substance, Gmelin focused on elements and the substances that they form. Such substances can include the pure elements, glasses, ceramics, organometallic substances, alloys, polymers, dopants, solid solutions, and isotopes. In the print version, substances were organized by key elements within them, with a set of volumes for each element, which contained all of the information both about the element and about its compounds and alloys. The handbook included reaction information, as well as hundreds of physical and chemical properties.

Searching Reaxys. At the time of this writing, Reaxys is most effectively used to find information about substances, their properties, and their reactions, and the substance and reaction information derives from a few hundred journals. Although Elsevier has added title and abstract-level references to articles from over 16,000 journals to Reaxys' "Literature" search context, these articles are not deep indexed for substance and reaction information. Chemists can search for known substances using a substance identifier (discussed below) in order to find physical and chemical properties or reactions. However, one of Reaxys' strengths is its structure search interface, which allows users to locate reactions of interest using a partial or complete reaction search (see Reaction Searching), as well as to profile substances by substructure or by properties, entering possible values or ranges of values for a list of properties and retrieving all substances that meet these criteria. It is also fairly easy to search for structures and property values simultaneously or to limit structure search results to only those substances for which a particular property is reported. Special mention should be made of Reaxys' unique way of describing organometallic substances and "coordination compounds," both of which are frequently difficult to locate using a structure or formula. A special code, called a "ligand formula" allows a chemist to search for the metals and the types of organic structures that are bound to them. This way, a variety of coordination compounds with the same basic connections and components can be retrieved.

Spectral atlases and crystallography collections

Spectra and crystal structures are frequently desired properties of compounds that serve similar purposes. *Spectroscopy* and *spectrometry* of substances falls into the realm of analytical chemistry. Broadly stated, when taking a spectrum of a substance, a researcher exposes that chemical to particular wavelengths of radiation and records the absorbances, reflections, vibrations, or bond breaking that occurs. The results are presented in a graph that indicates characteristic peaks or absorbances, which can be interpreted by a scientist to arrive at a structure for the compound. There are several kinds of spectra that are commonly used by chemists. Mass spectra are taken when a compound is hit with radiation and decomposes into fragments in an instrument called a mass spectrometer. The mass spectrometer measures and records the molecular weights of these fragments, and a knowledgeable scientist can deduce the composition of the parent compound from the size of the fragments. To obtain a nuclear magnetic resonance (NMR) spectrum, a chemist places a sample in an instrument that generates a strong magnetic field around it. He or she then obtains a graph, indicating the vibrations of and interactions between its atoms. Infrared (IR) and ultraviolet-visible (UV-VIS) spectra both indicate the wavelengths of light absorbed by a particular substance on a sloped graph.

Many scientists desire a graphical spectrum to compare to one that they have been taken themselves, and there are a number of free and proprietary print and online spectral atlases, including BioRad's KnowItAll products,[58] the *Sadtler Handbook of Proton NMR Spectra*,[59] the Aldrich NMR and IR/Raman sets[60,61] (also available, free of charge, through the online Aldrich/Sigma/Fluka catalog), the NIST Chemistry Web Book,[62] and the SDBS: Spectral Database of Organic Compounds[63] from the National Institute of Advanced Industrial Science and Technology (AIST) in Japan. These resources have varying levels of quality and varying numbers of compounds, but all provide the user with graphical spectra. However, not all substances have spectral information available in this format. There are several handbooks that compile spectral lines, giving the wavelengths at which peaks occur, including the *CRC Atlas of Spectral Data and Physical Constants*[64] and the *Handbook of Ultraviolet and Visible Spectra of Organic Compounds*.[65] Other resources, like Reaxys, simply refer to articles in the literature that report spectra. CAS Registry

database on SciFinder (Scholar) has a mixture of spectral information; it links to graphical spectra collections from Wiley, BioRad, and AIST for many substances, provides literature references where others' spectra can be found, and, for some substances, has no spectral information at all.

A *crystal structure* of a substance uses X-rays to determine its structure unambiguously, including exact bond lengths and angles. A crystal structure of an organic, inorganic, or organometallic substance can prove the identity of a substance. However, crystal structures can also be used to determine the average bond length of a certain type of bond, as well as the differences in angle between three specific atoms in different types of substance. A crystal structure of a protein, in addition to providing bond lengths and angles, can indicate the way in which the protein folds. When searching for crystal structures, a scientist is generally looking for the exact distances and angles between all atoms in the substance. Therefore, he or she will want to download the "coordinates," the location in space of all atoms present, in the .cif file format. The Cambridge Crystallographic Data Centre,[66] a registered charity in the United Kingdom, curates a repository of small-molecule crystal structures that can be downloaded by individuals free of charge or searched through the Cambridge Structural Database (CSD).[67] Inorganic compounds and substances can be found in the Inorganic Crystal Structure Database (ICSD),[68] a proprietary database produced by FIZ Karlsruhe, while proteins are deposited in the RCSB Protein Data Bank (PDB),[69] managed by Rutgers and UCSD and based on the Rutgers campus. While individuals are welcome to deposit their crystal structures in a structural database on their own initiative, some primary journal publishers go so far as to request that authors including crystal structures in their publications deposit their data with one of the three repositories. Although these three tools have robust search and retrieval engines, it is important to note that they contain curated versions of researcher-deposited crystal structures and therefore cross the line from secondary to primary literature. All three systems will permit interested parties to download the crystal structure information files (.cif) of substances in the database, which can then be used in crystal structure visualization or manipulation programs.

IDENTIFYING SUBSTANCES FOR INFORMATION RETRIEVAL

One of the greatest challenges to a searcher unfamiliar with chemistry or chemical information is navigating the multitude of unique access points to the literature. In addition to performing successful topic searches, a researcher will be called upon to find information about chemicals, which have many different forms of identification. The following sections describe various identifiers that can be used when searching for chemicals, times at which they are particularly helpful, and general strengths and weaknesses of each type.

Ambiguous Chemical Identifiers

Of the many ways of identifying compounds, relatively few are completely unambiguous, one-to-one identifiers. Ambiguous identifiers, or those that are not one-to-one, abound and include chemical names, formulae, molecular weights, and various physical properties. This section discusses two of the most important ambiguous identifiers: chemical names and formulae.

Chemical names

Chemical nomenclature is frequently an art, rather than a science. Names are difficult identifiers to use in information retrieval because they are infrequently one-to-one identifiers for substances. There are two official systems of nomenclature that are widely used: the *IUPAC* system, which employs rules developed by the International Union of Pure and Applied Chemistry, and the *CAS* system, with rules made by the Chemical Abstract Service. One of these two systems is usually required when naming substances in a journal article; however, frequently used chemicals are generally given at least one common name, also called a *trivial name*, and substances that are commercially available often have at least one *trade name*, as well. In late 2015, the CAS Registry database showed 134 systematic, trivial, and trade names for the compound commonly known as aspirin.[70] This creates a many-to-one problem for information retrieval; there are many possible names for a single compound, and a searcher who wishes to locate chemicals by name must hope that the name variant that he or she has is the same as the one found in the index of a reference book or the electronic record in a database. A further problem arises because, in electronic information sources, the chemical name field is a "string" field, in which one must exactly match the input search string to an identical string in the chemical name field of a record. No typing errors are tolerated, and the databases do not have a "did you mean" feature since the alteration of a single character could indicate a completely different substance. For example, the substances "ethanol" and "ethanal" are two completely different molecules. For this reason, if one is having difficulty locating a substance by its chemical name, the best approach is usually to locate the name in a resource with an extensive synonym list and find the molecular formula or CAS Registry Number, which can then be used in the original resource to obtain the desired information.

Chemical formulae

A chemical formula describes the number or ratio of atoms of each type present in a substance. There are three general types of formula. The *molecular formula* is the formula most frequently used both by chemists and in information retrieval. A molecular formula lists the symbol for each atom in the substance, found by consulting the periodic table, followed by the number of that type of atom that appears in the substance. The formulae are written using a convention called *Hill Order*, which provides some degree of standardization. The first step in constructing a Hill Order formula for any substance is to group all like atoms together, ignoring functional groups or units. For organic compounds, defined as substances containing one or more carbon atoms, the atomic symbols are then ordered as follows: carbon, hydrogen, and all other atoms in alphabetical order. For example, the molecular formula for 4-aminobutanoic acid, which contains four carbon atoms, two oxygen atoms, nine hydrogen atoms, and a nitrogen atom is written $C_4H_9NO_2$. For inorganic substances, defined as substances containing no carbon atoms, all atomic symbols appear in alphabetical order. For example, the molecular formula for sodium chloride, which contains one sodium atom and one chlorine atom, would be written as ClNa, not NaCl.

The other two types of formula, empirical formula and structural formula, are used very infrequently in information retrieval. The **empirical formula** gives the ratio between the different types of atom found in a substance. The molecular formula of glucose is $C_6H_{12}O_6$; so, its empirical formula is CH_2O. The **structural formula** is written to give some inkling as to the connectivity of the atoms in the molecule. For example, 4-aminobutanoic acid, $C_4H_9NO_2$, has the following structure (Fig. 1).

The structural formula for this substance would then be either COOH–CH$_2$–CH$_2$–CH$_2$–NH$_2$ or CO$_2$H–CH$_2$–CH$_2$–CH$_2$–NH$_2$. While empirical formula information can be used in some advanced search systems, such as the Registry file on STN, to search for compounds that have a given ratio of atom types, the use of structural formula has mostly been replaced by chemical structure searching in online resources, although some biochemists will still write out a structural formula instead of drawing a structure for simple molecules.

Searching by molecular formula presents the opposite kind of problem to that experienced when searching by chemical name. Since a molecular formula gives no indication of the connectivity of the various atoms in the molecule, it is very easy to find many molecules with the

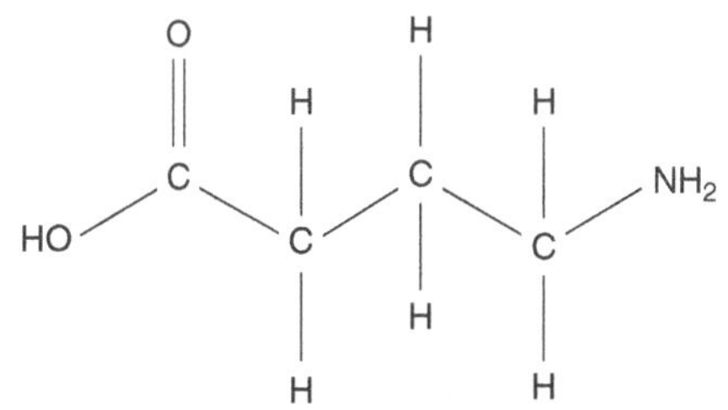

Fig. 1 Structure of 4-aminobutanoic acid.

same formula. However, most resources present the names or structures alongside the list of formulae in the book index or electronic search results, making it easier for a searcher to select the correct substance from the list. Another method of surmounting this problem is by selecting a different identifier by which to search.

Unambiguous Chemical Identifiers

It is preferable, although not always possible, to use an unambiguous identifier when searching for a substance. The three most commonly used one-to-one identifiers are chemical structure, sequence, and CAS Registry Number, although there are others. A relatively new identifier, the InChI, is a unique, text-based string that can be used with Web search engines, such as Google, but is most commonly used by database providers behind the scenes to link information sources that contain the same substances. Spectra, discussed earlier, serve as the fingerprints of chemicals, presenting a graph with characteristic peaks that enable chemists to determine the exact structure of the substance in question. Each identifier has its drawbacks in information retrieval, yet the use of each will generally retrieve a single substance.

Chemical structures

Structure is the least ambiguous identifier most commonly used for small, organic, or organometallic compounds. A substance's structure is akin to its photo ID; it shows not only the types and numbers of atoms that make up the substance, but also how they are connected. The structure of dicyclohexyl methanone ($C_{13}H_{22}O$) appears below (Fig. 2), using normal conventions for drawing organic compounds. Carbon atoms appear as line termini, and hydrogen atoms are understood.

At present, most chemistry databases and electronic resources have some form of structure search capability, generally provided through the means of a Java plug-in, a non-Java editor, or, in a few cases, specialized client software. Such resources allow a user to draw a structure of choice and then search for either exact matches or for larger molecules that contain the structural elements as drawn. The tools available vary from resource to resource; free resources tend to offer only basic search options, while resources like Reaxys, which rely heavily on structure searching, allow the user to construct extremely

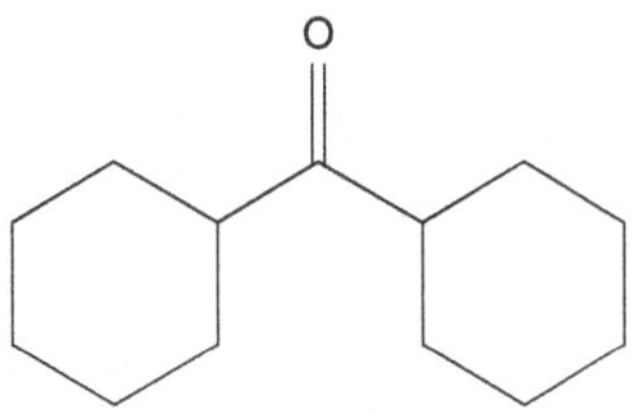

Fig. 2 Structure of dicyclohexyl methanone.

complex queries. Although it is not possible to search for structures in most print reference works, it is easy to count the atoms in a structure, generate the substance's molecular formula, and look it up in a formula index.

Sequences

Many biological chemists study very large molecules called proteins and nucleotides. These are, essentially, polymers consisting of many smaller units. The components of proteins are amino acids, while nucleotides are composed of bases. Because the sequence of the component amino acids (also called *residues*) or bases is very important to the function of the biomolecule, a molecular formula is not a good way to describe its composition. Biochemists use identifiers called sequences to describe the order of the component pieces. Each component is given a letter code. The letters are then strung together in the order in which the segments appear in the biomolecule. Resources that contain proteins or nucleotides generally allow sequence searching, and many let researchers locate sequentially similar substances using an algorithm like BLAST, described later in the article.

CAS Registry Numbers®

The Chemical Abstract Service assigns a unique, one-to-one identifier, called the *CAS Registry Number* (*CAS RN*), to each compound published in the literature. CAS RNs are formatted in the following manner, where X, Y, and Z represent any of the digits 0–9:

XXXXXXX-YY-Z

The first set of digits (X) is arbitrarily sized but has at least two digits. The second set (Y) contains two digits, and the third set (Z), or the check digit, is a single digit. CAS RNs are helpful because they aim to be completely unambiguous. They can be difficult to search because few people memorize them, and therefore, a source must be used to determine the CAS RN for each substance. In addition, since they are unique identifiers, a CAS RN search will not retrieve compounds that are structurally identical but contain one or more element with a higher or lower number of neutrons than usual, called an isotope. At times, it is important to exclude these "isotopically labeled" compounds, but, since their formation and general behavior is usually identical to their unlabeled counterparts, useful information can be missed if they are omitted. Although most resources have a CAS RN index or search function, these numbers are proprietary, and database providers must request permission from CAS to use them in their products.

InChIs™

An *InChI™*, or an *International Chemical Identifier*, can be described as IUPAC's version of the CAS Registry

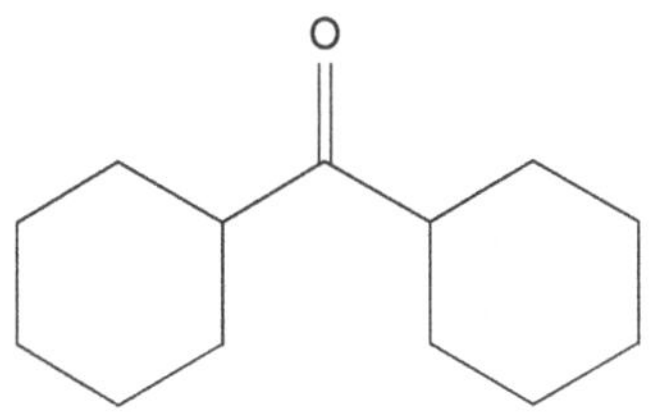

InChI = 1S/C13H22O/c14-13(11-7-3-1-4-8-11)
12-9-5-2-6-10-12/h11-12H,1-10H2

Fig. 3 Structure and InChI for dicyclohexyl methanone. The first set of characters refers to the InChI standard being used, the second set is the molecular formula, the third set tells how the molecular backbone is connected, and the fourth set indicates the locations of hydrogen atoms.

Number, only with structural information built in.[71] IUPAC defines an InChI™ as "a non-proprietary identifier for chemical substances that can be used in printed and electronic data sources thus enabling easier linking of diverse data compilations."[71] InChI strings are generated using free software provided by IUPAC, and two free drawing programs, ACD's ChemSketch and the PubChem Server Side Structure Editor, can both generate InChIs from structures. InChIs appear as a long text string and can therefore be used for searching the Web, as well as text-based databases and search engines. Below are the structure and corresponding InChI for dicyclohexyl methanone (Fig. 3):

InChI=1S/C13H22O/c14-13(11-7-3-1-4-8-11)12-9-5-2-6-10-12/h11-12H,1-10H2

InChIs carry all of the advantages of CAS RNs, as well as the added advantage that database providers do not have to request permission to use them in their records. As was previously mentioned, they are most likely to be used as linkers by information providers, but it is possible to use them within those databases that include them in the substances' records.

SEARCHING FOR SUBSTANCES IN THE CHEMICAL LITERATURE

Specialized Search Techniques

Chemical names, molecular formulae, and CAS Registry Numbers can all be used to retrieve information about chemicals. In online sources, the use of structure and sequence are also prevalent. However, there are other specialized search techniques that can be used to locate substances, their properties, and their reactions in electronic resources. Substructure searching and sequence similarity searching, using algorithms such as BLAST, can be used to locate substances that are similar in composition. Reaction search techniques can be used to find all ways of executing a particular reaction, to learn the best way to perform a reaction with a specific reactant and product,

and to find out exactly what will happen when two substances react.

Substructure searching

Frequently, chemists will want to search the literature, not for specific structures, but for structures that resemble a substance of interest. For example, assume that a scientist has discovered that some natural products have been found to have anticancer activity, which can be traced to a certain portion of their structure. He would like to figure out how to make that structural segment in the lab and is writing a grant application to fund this research; so, he wants to locate many examples of substances containing that fragment that also exhibit anticancer activity. Another example of the utility of substructure searching is a scientist who tries and fails to make a new substance. She can search for papers that report the synthesis of structurally similar substances and then apply the techniques to her own system.

Substructure searching, simply put, is a truncation search for a molecule. The searcher draws the portion of the structure that interests him or her, and the database retrieves all molecules that contain that structural fragment. In general terms, the query substructure can be thought of as a template that is superimposed over all substances in the database. A substance is retrieved as part of the hit set only if all atoms and bonds in the template exactly match atoms and bonds found in that substance.

In Fig. 4, the searcher input the boxed substructure in the center and retrieved the three structures surrounding it. Note that, when performing a substructure search, hydrogen atoms must be drawn; they are no longer understood. This substructure, therefore, contains nine "free sites," places where atoms, in this case carbon, chemically must form additional bonds. Any kind of atom or group can be attached to each of these sites. In Fig. 4, the substructure query is bold in each of the three retrieved substances, and the additional substituents appear in a lighter color. If the searcher wanted to be more specific about the type of substance retrieved, he or she would need to place additional restrictions on these free sites. For examples, the chemist could specify that atoms attached must not be part of a ring; that only nonhydrogen atom attachments are allowed; or that only carbon, nitrogen, or oxygen can attach at a particular site.

Reaction searching

Since many chemists seek to make new compounds or study the reactivity of known compounds, it is logical to assume that searching for particular reactions is a valuable tool. Reaction searching is most frequently used by chemists attempting to synthesize novel compounds or seeking new and improved methods of making known substances. For example, a chemist may wish to convert one

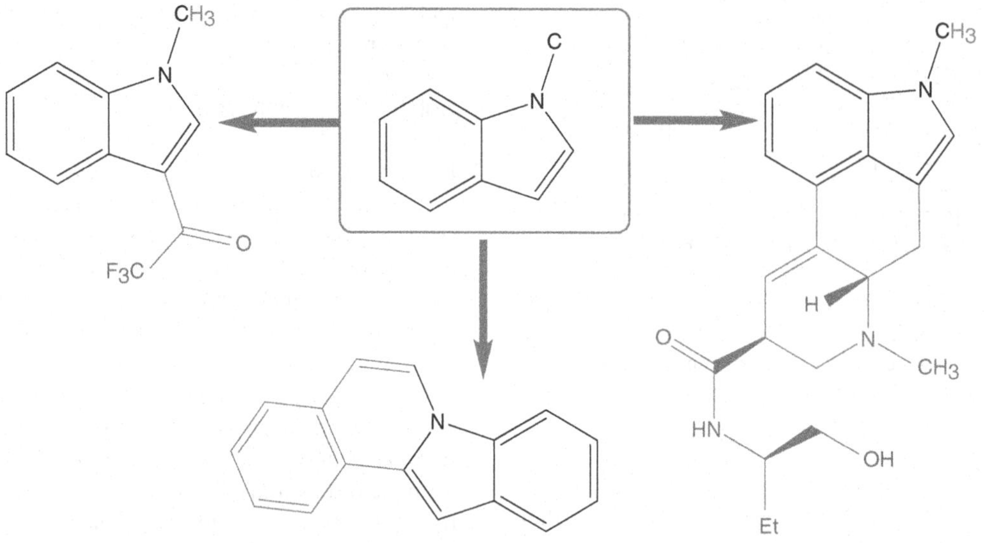

Fig. 4 A sample substructure and possible results obtained when using it to search. Note that the substructure is highlighted in black in each of the search results.

compound into another, but he may not know the proper reagents or conditions to apply to make this reaction happen. Another chemist may want to synthesize a compound without having a particular starting material in mind. Still another might be interested in all types of reactions performed by a given class, or type, of compound.

Many databases allow both partial and complete reaction searching using either exact structures or substructures. The chemist who wishes to use a particular reactant to make a product will perform a *complete reaction* search (Fig. 5A), drawing both the starting material and the product into the search engine. The chemist exploring possible methods of synthesizing a compound, who does not care which starting materials they use, will instead use a *partial reaction* search (Fig. 5B), drawing only the product, labeling it as such, and indicating by means of a hash mark the bond that is to be formed in the course of the reaction.

There are many reaction databases available, and each has different methods of search available to users. Some of the more common reaction databases are the CASREACT database from CAS and the reaction module on Reaxys.

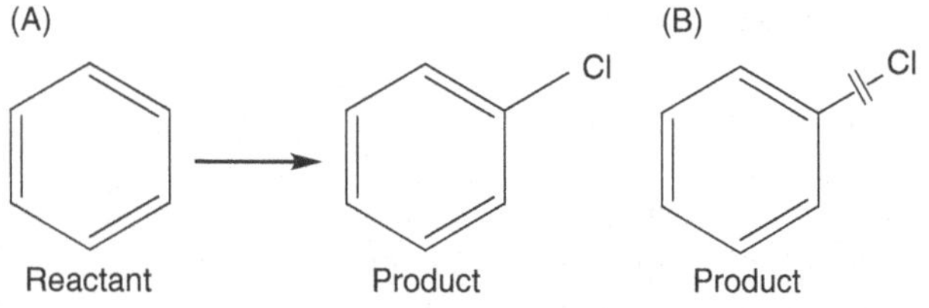

In recent years, reaction databases have begun adding synthesis planning options to their search interface. For example, from a substance search in SciFinder, one can click on the structure and select an option to "Synthesize this…." Reaxys offers a more sophisticated synthesis planner that allows you to explore various routes of making a molecule in question. Starting with the target, researchers can click on the "Synthesize" links to retrieve a list of potential reactions that result in that product, from which they can choose their desired preparation. As they work backwards, the synthesis planner constructs a tree-like reaction scheme, indicating the chosen reactants and reagents for each step, and generates a list of references in which the protocols can be located. InfoChem's IC_{SYNTH} product will also allow chemists to generate potential synthetic routes to a target molecule.[72]

Sequence searching and BLAST

Frequently, scientists will want to locate proteins or nucleic acids that have sequences similar to a sequence of interest. If a biological chemist is studying a human protein that has never been studied, it might be helpful for him to see whether there are any similar proteins in other organisms that have been more extensively researched. Searching for sequentially similar proteins or nucleic acids in different organisms can also give indications of evolutionary relationships between species. Frequently, locating intensely studied proteins or nucleic acids with similar sequence can help a researcher determine the putative identity and function of a given substance. The best method for accomplishing these goals is to perform some kind of similarity search in a database of sequences.

"**BLAST**" stands for "Basic Local Alignment Search Tool," and it is one of the most common methods of

Fig. 5 (A) A complete reaction search, in which a chlorine atom is added to a benzene molecule. (B) A partial reaction search intended to locate all possible methods of adding the chlorine to the benzene ring.

locating sequentially similar proteins or nucleic acids. The BLAST algorithm is complex, but it basically looks for sequences in a database, or **subject** sequences, that have a small sequence fragment that is identical or highly similar to one found in a query sequence. Starting at this sequence fragment, the system then works outward in both directions, comparing each nucleotide or amino acid of the query sequence to those in each subject sequence in the database. It then determines the length of the "matching" section between the query and each subject sequence and assigns each subject a score, based on the length of the similar section and the closeness of the match, and presents the results in order of score, from most to least similar. Advanced searchers can adjust the parameters of a search to be more or less sensitive, allowing retrieval of more or less disparate sequences. BLAST searching is frequently used to identify similar sequences in different organisms, often with an eye to discovering evolutionary patterns or functional similarities.[73]

CONCLUSIONS

The literature of chemistry is as varied as the types of research that chemists perform, and is likely to become more so as chemical research becomes increasingly multidisciplinary. Chemists are avid readers, partly driven by the need to experiment efficiently because their research is so expensive. As a result, the chemists frequently desire or need to do their own searches, evaluate their results, and immediately modify or refine their searches, requiring a large degree of autonomy and strong searching skills. Occasionally, particularly in industry, they will ask an information professional to perform searches for them, evaluate the results, and request modifications. However, many academic chemists have a decent familiarity with their literature and, while they will occasionally require assistance framing searches, they often wish to be taught rather than spoon fed. Many of the tools, particularly the SciFinder and SciFinder Scholar interfaces, are aimed at end user searchers. With appropriate instruction in the specialized search techniques and entry points to the resources, chemists can be efficient searchers and find most of what they need to do their research.

Chemists should be taught to use review sources, including encyclopedias, treatises, and review articles, for background research, before proceeding to the primary literature in journals, books, and patents. Indices, abstracts, and catalogs will assist them in identifying good primary research on which to build, as well as chemicals and equipment. Handbooks can supply quick values for properties and references to the literature in which they were reported. All resources can be searched with unique access points, including chemical name, formula, structure, sequence, and CAS Registry Number, and many allow specialized searching, such as substructure searches, reaction searches, and BLAST.

ACKNOWLEDGMENTS

I would like to thank the University of Pennsylvania Libraries for their support and acknowledge the assistance of Eric Shively, Thomas Krimmer, Renata Geer, Carlos Rodriguez, and Danianne Mizzy, who provided valuable input during the preparation of the previous edition of this manuscript.

REFERENCES

1. White, M.J. Chemical Patents. In *Chemical Information for Chemists: A Primer*, Judith, N.C.; Dana, L.R., Eds.; Royal Society of Chemistry: Cambridge, U.K., 2013.
2. Espacenet, http://worldwide.espacenet.com/ (accessed December 14, 2015).
3. Search for Patents: USPTO Patent Full Text and Image Database, http://www.uspto.gov/patents-application-process/search-patents (accessed December 14, 2015).
4. SciFinder, http://www.cas.org/products/scifinder (accessed December 14, 2015).
5. Figshare, https://figshare.com/ (accessed December 14, 2015).
6. Meyers, R.A. *Encyclopedia of Analytical Chemistry*; Wiley: Chichester, U.K.; New York, 2000.
7. Moore, J.H.; Spencer, N.D. *Encyclopedia of Chemical Physics and Physical Chemistry*; Institute of Physics: Bristol, U.K.; Philadelphia, PA, 2001.
8. Bruce King, R. *Encyclopedia of Inorganic Chemistry*; Wiley: Chichester, U.K.; Hoboken, NJ, 2005.
9. *Encyclopedia of Inorganic and Bioinorganic Chemistry*. John Wiley & Sons, 2015, doi: 10.1002/9781119951438.
10. Paquette, L.A. *Encyclopedia of Reagents for Organic Synthesis*; Wiley: Chichester, U.K.; New York, 1995.
11. e-EROS: Encyclopedia of Reagents for Organic Synthesis, http://onlinelibrary.wiley.com/book/10.1002/047084289X (accessed December 14, 2015).
12. *Kirk-Othmer Encyclopedia of Chemical Technology*, 5th Ed.; John Wiley: Hoboken, NJ, 2004–2007.
13. *Kirk-Othmer Encyclopedia of Chemical Technology*, http://mrw.interscience.wiley.com/emrw/9780471238966/home/ (accessed December 14, 2015).
14. *Organic Syntheses*, John Wiley & Sons: New York, 1921.
15. *Methods in Enzymology*, Academic Press: New York, 1955.
16. Katritzky, A.R.; Meth-Cohn, O.; Rees, C.W. *Comprehensive Organic Functional Group Transformation*; Pergamon Press: Oxford, U.K.; New York, 1995.
17. Katritzky, A.R.; Taylor, R.J.K. *Comprehensive Organic Functional Transformations 2*; Elsevier Pergamon: Amsterdam, the Netherlands; Boston, MA, 2005.
18. Wilkinson, G.; Stone, F.G.A.; Abe, E.W. *Comprehensive Organometallic Chemistry: The Synthesis, Reactions, and Structures of Organometallic Compounds*; Pergamon Press: Oxford, U.K.; New York, 1982.

Chemistry–China

19. Abel, E.W.; Stone, F.G.A.; Wilkinson, G. *Comprehensive Organometallic Chemistry II: A Review of the Literature, 1982–1994*; Pergamon: Oxford, U.K.; New York, 1995.

20. Crabtree, R.H.; Mingos, M. *Comprehensive Organometallic Chemistry III: From Fundamentals to Applications*; Elsevier Science: Oxford, U.K.; New York, 2006.

21. *Methoden der Organischen Chemie (Houben-Weyl)*, Georg Thieme: Stuttgart, Germany; New York, 1909.

22. Georg Thieme Verlag. *Houben-Weyl Methods of Organic Chemistry Users' Guide*; Georg Thieme Verlag: Stuttgart, Germany; New York, 2000.

23. *Science of Synthesis*, Thieme: Stuttgart, Germany; New York, 2000-.

24. WorldCat, http://www.worldcat.org/ (accessed December 14, 2015).

25. *Chemical Abstracts*, American Chemical Society: Columbus, OH, 1907.

26. Chemical Abstracts Service, http://www.cas.org/ (accessed December 14, 2015).

27. Web of Science, http://thomsonreuters.com/en/products-services/scholarly-scientific-research/scholarly-search-and-discovery/web-of-science.html (accessed December 15, 2015).

28. Inspec, http://www.engineeringvillage.com/search/quick.url (accessed December 15, 2015).

29. Engineering Village, http://help.engineeringvillage.com/Content/Inspec.htm (accessed December 15, 2015).

30. PubMed, http://www.ncbi.nlm.nih.gov/pubmed (accessed December 15, 2015).

31. Search NCBI Databases, http://www.ncbi.nlm.nih.gov/sites/gquery?itool=toolbar (accessed December 15, 2015).

32. Compendex, http://www.engineeringvillage2.org/controller/servlet/Controller?CID=quickSearch&database=COMPENDEX (accessed December 15, 2015).

33. Shively, E. CAS surveys its first 100 years. Chem. Eng. News **2007**, *85*, 41–53.

34. The Web of Science Journal Selection Process, http://wokinfo.com/essays/journal-selection-process/ (accessed December 16, 2015).

35. Stich, S. Personal communication, Baltimore, MD, 2008.

36. Journal Citation Reports, http://thomsonreuters.com/en/products-services/scholarly-scientific-research/research-management-and-evaluation/journal-citation-reports.html (accessed December 16, 2015).

37. Inspec Chemical Indexing on Engineering Village, http://www.theiet.org/resources/inspec/support/docs/eichemgd.cfm?type=pdf (accessed December 15, 2015).

38. WorldCat, http://www.oclc.org/worldcat.en.html (accessed December 16, 2015).

39. Sigma-Aldrich Online Catalog, http://www.sigmaaldrich.com/catalog/AdvancedSearchPage.do (accessed December 16, 2015).

40. In *Chem Sources U.S.A.* Directories Publishing Company: Olando Beach, FL, 2015.

41. *Chem Sources International*, Directories Publishing Company, Inc.: Clemson, SC, 2015.

42. Available Chemicals Exchange, https://www.cambridgesoft.com/Ensemble_for_Chemistry/ChemACX/ (accessed December 16, 2015).

43. ChemExper Chemical Dictionary, http://www.chemexper.com/ (accessed December 16, 2015).

44. eMolecules, https://www.emolecules.com/ (accessed December 16, 2015).

45. ThomasNet, http://www.thomasnet.com/ (accessed December 16, 2015).

46. O'Neil, M.J. *The Merck Index: An Encyclopedia of Chemicals, Drugs, and Biologicals*, 15th Ed.; Royal Society of Chemistry: Cambridge, U.K., 2013.

47. The Merck Index Online, https://www.rsc.org/merck-index (accessed December 16, 2015, 2015).

48. Haynes, W.M. *CRC Handbook of Chemistry and Physics*, 96th Ed.; CRC Press: Cleveland, OH, 2015.

49. National Research Council of the United States of America. *International Critical Tables of Numerical Data, Physics, Chemistry and Technology*; McGraw-Hill: New York, 1926–1933.

50. Reaxys, https://www.reaxys.com (accessed December 16, 2015).

51. *Knovel Engineering and Scientific Online Reference Books*, http://app.knovel.com/web/index.v (accessed December 16, 2015).

52. Yaws, C.L. *Yaws' Thermophysical Properties of Chemicals and Hydrocarbons (Electronic Edition)*; Knovel, 2010, http://app.knovel.com/hotlink/toc/id:kpYTPCHE02/yaws-thermophysical-properties/yaws-thermophysical-properties.

53. DIPPR Project 801 Database, http://www.knovel.com/web/portal/browse/display?_EXT_KNOVEL_DISPLAY_bookid=1187 (accessed December 16, 2015).

54. Beilstein, F.K. *Beilsteins Handbuch der Organischen Chemie*; J. Springer: Berlin, Germany, 1881.

55. *Gmelins Handbuch der Anorganischen Chemie*, Verlag Chemie g.m.b.h.: Leipzig-Berlin, Germany, 1924.

56. Friedrich Konrad Beilstein, 1838-1906, https://www.lib.utexas.edu/chem/info/beilsteinbio.html (accessed September 26, 2007).

57. Habashi, F. Gmelin and his *Handbuch*. Bull. Hist. Chem. **2009**, *34*, 30–31.

58. BioRad, http://www.bio-rad.com/en-us/spectroscopy (accessed December 15, 2015).

59. Sadtler Research Laboratories & Simons, W.W. *The Sadtler Handbook of Proton NMR Spectra*; Sadtler: Philadelphia, PA, 1978.

60. Pouchert, C.J. & Aldrich Chemical Company. *The Aldrich Library of FT-IR Spectra*, 2nd Ed.; Aldrich: Milwaukee, WI, 1997.

61. Pouchert, C.J.; Behnke, J. & Aldrich Chemical Company. *The Aldrich Library of C and H FT NMR Spectra*; Aldrich Chemical Co.: Milwaukee, WI, 1993.

62. *NIST Chemistry Web Book*, http://webbook.nist.gov/chemistry (accessed December 16, 2015).

63. Spectral Database of Organic Compounds, SDBS, http://sdbs.db.aist.go.jp/sdbs/cgi-bin/cre_index.cgi?lang=eng (accessed December 15, 2015).

64. Grasselli, J.G. & Chemical Rubber Company. *CRC Atlas of Spectral Data and Physical Constants for Organic Compounds*, 1st Ed.; CRC Press: Cleveland, OH, 1973.

65. Hirayama, K.O. *Handbook of Ultraviolet and Visible Absorption Spectra of Organic Compounds*; Plenum Press Data Division: New York, 1967.

66. Cambridge Crystallographic Data Centre, http://www.ccdc.cam.ac.uk/ (accessed December 16, 2015).

67. Cambridge Structural Database, http://www.ccdc.cam.ac.uk/solutions/csd-system/components/csd/ (accessed December 16, 2015).

68. Inorganic Crystal Structure Database (ICSD), https://icsd.fiz-karlsruhe.de/search/ (accessed December 15, 2015).

69. Protein Data Bank, http://www.rcsb.org/pdb/home/home.do (accessed December 16, 2015).

70. This number was obtained by counting the synonyms in the CAS Registry record for aspirin, 50–78-2, using the SciFinder interface.

71. The IUPAC International Chemical Identifier (InChI), http://www.iupac.org/inchi/ (accessed December 16, 2015).

72. Bøgevig, A.; Federsel, H.-J.; Huerta, F.; Hutchings, M.G.; Kraut, H.; Langer, T.; Low, P.; Oppawsky, C.; Rein, T.; Saller, H. Route design in the 21st Century: The IC*SYNTH* software tool as an idea generator for synthesis prediction. Org. Process Res. Dev. **2015**, *19*, 357–268. doi: 10.1021/op500373e.

73. Geer, R. Personal communication, Bethesda, MD, 2007.

ADDITIONAL READING

1. Currano, J.N.; Roth, D.L. *Chemical Information for Chemists: A Primer*; Royal Society of Chemistry: Cambridge, U.K., 2014.

2. Heller, S.R. *The Beilstein System: Strategies for Effective Searching*; American Chemical Society: Washington, DC, 1998.

3. Maizell, R.E. *How to Find Chemical Information: A Guide for Practicing Chemists, Educators, and Students*, 3rd Ed.; John Wiley & Sons: New York, 1998.

4. Ridley, D. *Information Retrieval: SciFinder*, 2nd Ed.; John Wiley & Sons: Hoboken, NJ, 2009.

Chemistry–China

Chemoinformatics

Peter Willett
Department of Information Studies, University of Sheffield, Sheffield, U.K.

Abstract
The entry summarizes the principal tools in modern chemoinformatics systems, principally in the pharmaceutical industry. These tools enable molecules to be selected for biological testing as potential drugs, and include methods for searching databases of two-dimensional and three-dimensional chemical structures, and for predicting the properties of molecules from their structures.

INTRODUCTION

Information systems in chemistry have a long history, first in printed and then in computerized form, and the great bulk of the world's chemical information is now available on the scientist's desktop.[1] Much of this information is textual (e.g., the full-text of a journal article) or numeric (e.g., a molecule's boiling point) in nature, but there is an additional data type that distinguishes chemical information systems from those designed for more general use: the structures of chemical molecules, normally in the form of a two-dimensional (2D) structure diagram but increasingly also in three-dimensional (3D) form. Molecules (and their reactions and properties) lie at the heart of chemistry and this has spurred the development of systems for the representation of structures, not just as images but in a form that will enable sophisticated processing to be carried out on them. The focus on the structure is the principal distinguishing feature of chemical information systems, in much the same way as biological and geographic information systems highlight the importance of biological sequences and of cartographic information, respectively.

Computer-based systems for the manipulation of structural information started to be developed in the early 1960s, most notably the establishment of the Chemical Abstracts Service Registry System to record all the molecules that are reported in the world's scientific literature.[2] Systems such as this focused on tools for rapid and effective database searching; at the same time, scientists, principally in the pharmaceutical industry, were developing computer systems for modeling individual molecules so that they could be displayed interactively and their properties, shapes, and reactions computed from their two-dimensional (2D) or three-dimensional (3D) structures. These two areas of research developed strongly over the next two decades,[3,4] with the establishment of chemoinformatics—"the application of informatics methods to solve chemical problems"[4]—as a distinct discipline being driven in part by the need to integrate these two approaches to the manipulation of structural

information. This need has been strengthened by technological developments (specifically, the techniques of combinatorial chemistry and high-throughput biological screening) that have brought about an increase by at least two orders of magnitude in the volumes of data that need to be processed in chemical research and development. Chemistry is by no means unique in needing to assimilate and to rationalize vast bodies of data, and informatics tools are thus being increasingly developed and applied in many subject domains. Here, we summarize the components of modern chemoinformatics systems, describing the main techniques that are used to search databases of chemical structures and to correlate the biological properties of molecules with their structures. Much of the discussion relates to the pharmaceutical industry since that is where many of the developments have taken place to support the discovery of new drugs; however, the techniques are increasingly being applied in many areas of chemistry, such as structure elucidation, reaction prediction, and synthesis design. The entry focuses on methods for searching chemical databases, with brief accounts of some of the other approaches that are used to support drug-discovery programs; more detailed accounts of chemoinformatics are provided in the textbooks by Gasteiger and Engels[4] and by Leach and Gillet,[5] and in the standard reference work edited by Gasteiger.[6]

SEARCHING DATABASES OF 2D STRUCTURES

Search lies at the heart of any type of information system, and methods for searching chemical databases have been studied now for over four decades. These methods can be divided into two broad classes: those that are used with databases of 2D structures, where molecules are represented by conventional chemical structure diagrams; and those that are used with databases of 3D structures, where molecules are represented by sets of atomic coordinates in 3D space. This entry deals with the first group of methods although, as we shall see in the following entry,

Encyclopedia of Library and Information Sciences, Fourth Edition DOI: 10.1081/E-ELIS4-120043664

many of the techniques are also applicable in the 3D context.

Representation and Structure Searching

The two most important types of representation that have been used to describe a chemical structure in machine-readable form are the *line notation* and the *connection table*. A line notation encodes the structure of a molecule in a text string, in which individual symbols encode atoms or groups of atoms, with the bonds linking these atoms normally implicit in the ordering (which is subject to strict preference rules). Line notations were widely used in the 1960s and 1970s, with the Wiswesser Line Notation in particular forming the basis for both corporate and public chemical information systems.[7] The most popular current line notation is the SMILES (Simplified Molecular Input Line Entry Specification) notation, a compact text string that can be used for the input of chemical structures and for *structure search*. Structure search is one of the principal types of database search (the others are described later in this entry)

and involves scanning a database for the record associated with a specific molecule. Such searches are typically carried out to retrieve data associated with that molecule, e.g., how it can be synthesized or its solubility. This is the chemical equivalent of a known-item search, e.g., looking for an ISBN in a library catalog to see if a copy of a book is available for loan or scanning a telephone directory to get a person's telephone number, and can be effected using conventional computer techniques such as string matching or hash coding. However, line notations are far less suitable for the other types of chemical searching, which require an explicit and detailed description of the pattern of bonds in a molecule to enable effective searches to be carried out. This information is encoded in a connection table, which can be regarded as a *chemical graph*, in which the nodes and edges of a graph represent the atoms and bonds, respectively, of a molecule. The hydrogen atoms are normally excluded from a connection table since their presence can be deduced from simple considerations of atomic valency. An example of a structure diagram and the corresponding chemical name, connection table, and SMILES are shown in Fig. 1.

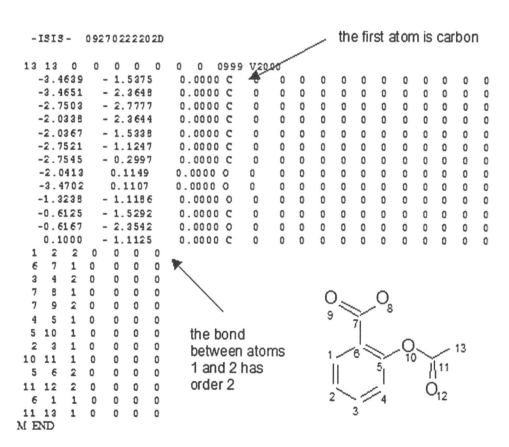

Fig. 1 Example of (A) a structure diagram, (B) systematic nomenclature, (C) connection table in MDL format (see URL http://www.mdli.com), and (D) SMILES for a molecule.

Substructure Searching

The availability of the graph-based, connection-table representation means that chemical database applications can make use of algorithms originally developed for the matching of graphs, in particular the use of a subgraph isomorphism algorithm to carry out *substructure searching*.[8] This involves scanning a database for all of those molecules that contain a user-defined partial structure, e.g., all of the molecules that contain the four linked rings that characterize a steroid. This is the chemical equivalent of a Boolean text search, e.g., looking for all documents satisfying the logical constraint (chemical AND database* AND search*), and requires rapid access not just to the entire structure of a molecule but also to all of its constituent parts. An example of a substructure search is shown in Fig. 2.

A subgraph isomorphism algorithm checks whether a query graph is contained within another graph, and such an algorithm hence provides a simple and direct way of carrying out a substructure search given a set of connection-tables. However, while this is an effective search procedure, it is a very inefficient one, since subgraph isomorphism, like many graph algorithms, has an expected time complexity that is a factorial function of the numbers of nodes in the two graphs that are being compared. The computational requirements are lessened, when compared to graphs in general, because chemical graphs are small (typical organic molecules contain 20–30 nonhydrogen atoms); are of low complexity (since each atom is bonded to only a very few other atoms, the exact number depending on its valence state); and have node and edge labels (i.e., the atom and bond types) that can be used to constrain the number of graph matches that need to be considered. Even so, substructure searching of large chemical databases using subgraph isomorphism would be totally infeasible if it had not proved possible to provide an initial, *screening* search that eliminates the great bulk of a database from the time-consuming subgraph search.

Screening is based on the idea that a database-molecule cannot possibly contain the sought query moiety unless that molecule contains all of the fragment substructures that are contained in the query. Only if each and every one of these fragments is present is it worth carrying out the subgraph search to determine whether they are joined together in exactly the same way as they are in the query. A range of types of fragment can be algorithmically generated from a molecule's connection table. One simple approach is to use common rings and functional groups so that, e.g., a molecule might characterized in chemically meaningful terms as containing a phenyl ring, an acid amide group, and a methyl group (in much the same way as a paper in an academic journal might be characterized by some number of keywords). More commonly, the fragments are small atom-, bond-, or ring-centered substructures; for example, a molecule might be characterized

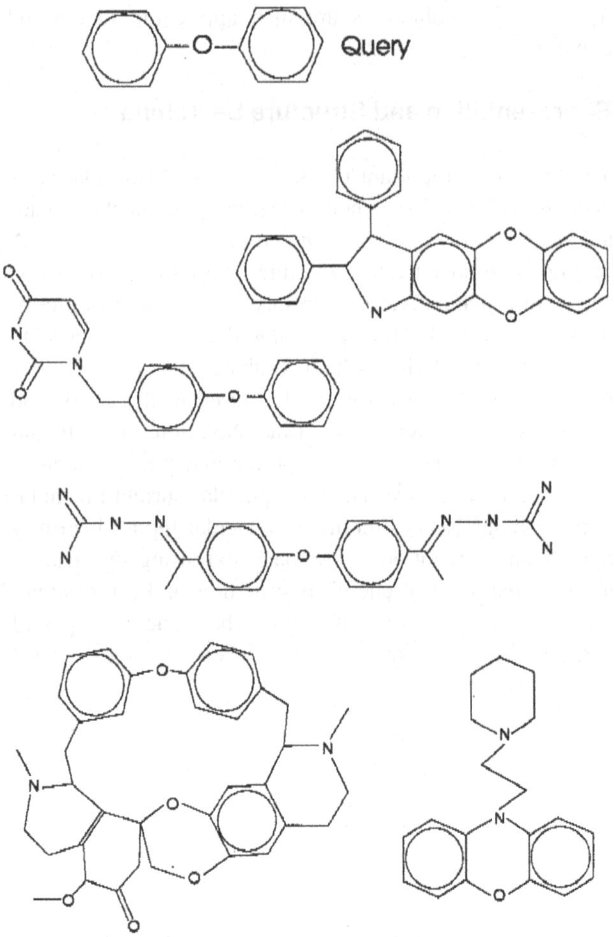

Fig. 2 Example of a 2D substructure search. The search is for the diphenyl ether query substructure at the top of the figure, below which are shown five of the hits resulting from a search of the National Cancer Institute database of molecules that have been tested in the U.S. government anticancer program (see URL http://dtp.nci.nih.gov/). This database is also used for the search outputs shown in Figs. 3 and 4.

by *augmented atoms*, where an augmented atom is an atom together with the atoms that are bonded directly to it, or by a chain of four atoms and the three bonds that link these atoms together.

The presence or absence of such fragments (either in a query or in a database molecule) is encoded in a *fingerprint* or *bit-string*. A fingerprint is a binary vector where each of the bits (or groups of bits in some cases) is set to one to indicate that a particular fragment (or fragments) is present in the connection table describing a molecule. A screen search is then carried out by comparing the bit-string describing the query with the bit-string describing a database molecule; only if a logical intersection (Boolean AND) of the two fingerprints confirms that all the specified query fragments are indeed present will the detailed and time-consuming subgraph isomorphism match be carried out for that database molecule. An effective screening system will ensure that less than 1% of the database molecules need to undergo this second-level search. Other approaches to 2D substructure searching have been described,[9] but the fragment-screening approach continues to be by far the most common; moreover, fingerprints are used not just for 2D substructure searching but also for many other applications in chemoinformatics, as discussed below.

Similarity Searching

The advent of the Web has meant that Boolean searching, although used for many years by library and information specialists, is now used far less than the alternative best-match or ranked-output approaches that characterize Web search engines. The chemical equivalent of this approach to database access is called *similarity searching*.[10] Here, a user enters a complete molecule, which is normally referred to as the *reference* or *target* structure, and the similarity is computed between this reference structure and each of the database molecules. The database molecules are then ranked in order of decreasing similarity and the most similar, the *nearest neighbors*, presented to the user as the output from the search.

The basis for similarity searching is the Similar Property Principle, which states that molecules that are structurally similar are likely to have similar properties. Thus, if a biologically active molecule is used as the reference structure then its nearest neighbors are also likely to be active (in much the same way as a Google search based on the keywords from a known relevant document is likely to identify further relevant documents). This is clearly a simple way to search a database but it will only be effective if an appropriate measure of intermolecular similarity is used. There is a large, growing literature on chemical similarity,[11] but current systems are overwhelmingly based on the use of fingerprint-based measures of structural similarity. In a substructure search, two fingerprints are compared to determine if one is contained within the other; in a similarity search, two fingerprints are compared

to determine how many bits (normally the bits that are switched on) are in common. The number of common bits represents the number of common fragments and generally after a normalization stage to give a value between zero and unity, the overall degree of resemblance of the two molecules whose fingerprints are being compared. This simple approach has proved to be very popular, enabling the identification of biologically active molecules in chemical databases at minimal computational cost and often more effectively than other, more complex types of similarity measure.[12] An example of a fingerprint-based similarity search is shown in Fig. 3.

Patent and Reaction Searching

There is another type of 2D structure that is of particular importance in industrial research and development, and this is a molecule in a chemical patent. Patents in chemistry resemble those in other fields in describing novel entities and their uses (in this case chemical molecules and some sort of useful property), but they differ in the way that the molecules are described. Specifically, whilst individual, specific molecules are generally included in a patent, either as a name or as a structure diagram, there may also be one or more *generic*, or *Markush*, structures. A generic structure is a high-level description not of a single molecule but of a whole class of molecules that possess common structural features; for example, there may be a range of different substituents possible at a single position on an invariant central ring system, or there may be limits on the numbers and types of atoms allowed in a heterocycle.[13] A single generic structure may represent many thousands, or even millions, of individual specific molecules, and is included in a patent so that the originating company can claim patent protection for all of the molecules implied by the high-level description, without the need to describe (or even, in most cases, to synthesize and test) the individual molecules. Fragment-screening and graph-matching procedures analogous to those

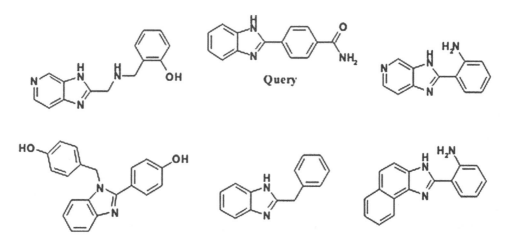

Fig. 3 Example of a fingerprint-based 2D similarity search, showing a query molecule and five of its nearest neighbors.

described above have been developed for patent databases; however, it can still be difficult to describe precisely some types of patent and to carry out searches that are as effective as those possible on databases of conventional, fully defined molecules.[14]

Finally in this entry, it is appropriate to mention search techniques for databases of chemical reactions. Here, a database record consists not of a single molecule but of two, linked sets of molecules, i.e., the sets of reactants and products; in addition, there may also be reagents or catalysts that are necessary for the reaction to proceed in high yield. Some types of query that a user might wish to pose to a reactions database, e.g., all syntheses of a specific molecule or how to convert one molecule to another, can be achieved using simple modifications of conventional structure searching procedures. However, an effective reactions database also needs to be able to represent and to search not just the molecules that are involved in a reaction but also their constituent *reaction sites*, i.e., the parts of the reactants and products where the substructural change engendered by the reaction has taken place.[15] For example, a user might wish to retrieve all reactions involving the combination of two acid groups to form a heterocycle, i.e., a form of substructure searching that will again involve simple modifications of conventional fingerprint and graph-match algorithms. In addition, however, this sort of search will require effective algorithms to recognize the substructural differences between the reactants and products, and hence the location of the reaction sites, and then the ability to link together information about both the reacting molecules and the reaction sites. For example, a user might wish to retrieve all reactions involving the combination of two acid groups to form a heterocycle (as previously) whilst also specifying that another acid group elsewhere remains unchanged during the reaction. Systems providing such comprehensive retrieval capabilities are now well established,[16] and facilities can also be provided for reaction similarity searching.

SEARCHING DATABASES OF 3D STRUCTURES

Systems for structure and 2D substructure searching were available for both corporate and public databases by the early 1980s but a decade was to pass before techniques were developed for the effective processing of 3D structures.[17] Indeed, even today, 3D searching systems are restricted to corporate environments where the file-sizes are much less than the large public databases available from Chemical Abstracts Service (at http://www.cas.org) and from Beilstein (at http://www.beilstein.com).

The principal source of experimental data on the 3D structures of small molecules is the Cambridge Structural Database (at http://www.ccdc.cam.ac.uk/), which contains atomic coordinate data for approximately 400K molecules for which an x-ray crystal structure determination has

been carried out.[18] X-ray techniques are constantly evolving but this number is less than 2% of the number of molecules for which the 2D structure is known; accordingly, if 3D searches need to be carried out, computational, rather than experimental, techniques must be used to generate the requisite atomic coordinate data. Molecular modeling provides a range of tools that can be used to generate 3D structures, using sophisticated approaches such as quantum mechanics, molecular dynamics, and molecular mechanics,[19] but these are too slow if structures need to be generated for hundreds of thousands or millions of molecules. Instead, *structure generation* programs have been developed that can rapidly generate reasonably accurate sets of atomic coordinates from a 2D connection table.[20] The set of coordinates for a molecule can then be used to compute the distances between all pairs of (nonhydrogen) atoms. These distances form the basis for a 3D chemical graph, in which the nodes and edges of the graph characterize the atoms and interatomic distances, respectively (as against the atoms and bonds in a 2D chemical graph).

Substructure Searching

A *pharmacophore*, or *pharmacophoric pattern*, is the geometric arrangement of features in a molecule that interacts with a biological receptor and that allows a molecule to exhibit the desired biological activity. Potentially bioactive molecules can hence be identified by searching a database for all those molecules containing a query pharmacophore, this typically consisting of a small numbers of atoms and associated interatomic distances. An example of a pharmacophore is shown in the upper part of Fig. 4. Such patterns are derived from analysis of sets of known bioactive molecules to identify the geometric features that they have in common.[21] The 3D graph for a molecule is more complex than the corresponding 2D graph since there are far more edges present (each atom is separated by a distance from every other atom in the molecule but is only bonded to some small number of other atoms) but the fact that a graph representation is available means that we can again apply the screening and subgraph isomorphism approaches described previously.

The condition for a subgraph match in 3D substructure searching is now not that atoms are bonded together in the correct way but that they are separated by the correct distances, normally to within some small level of tolerance such as ± 0.5 Å, and a subgraph isomorphism algorithm can be modified to handle such data. The screens that are used are based on interatomic distance ranges, e.g., a bit in a fingerprint might be set to denote the presence of an oxygen and a nitrogen atom separated by 3.5–5.0 Å. The lower portion of Fig. 4 illustrates some of the molecules retrieved in the search for the pattern in the upper portion of the figure, and demonstrates the wide range of types of molecule that contain the query

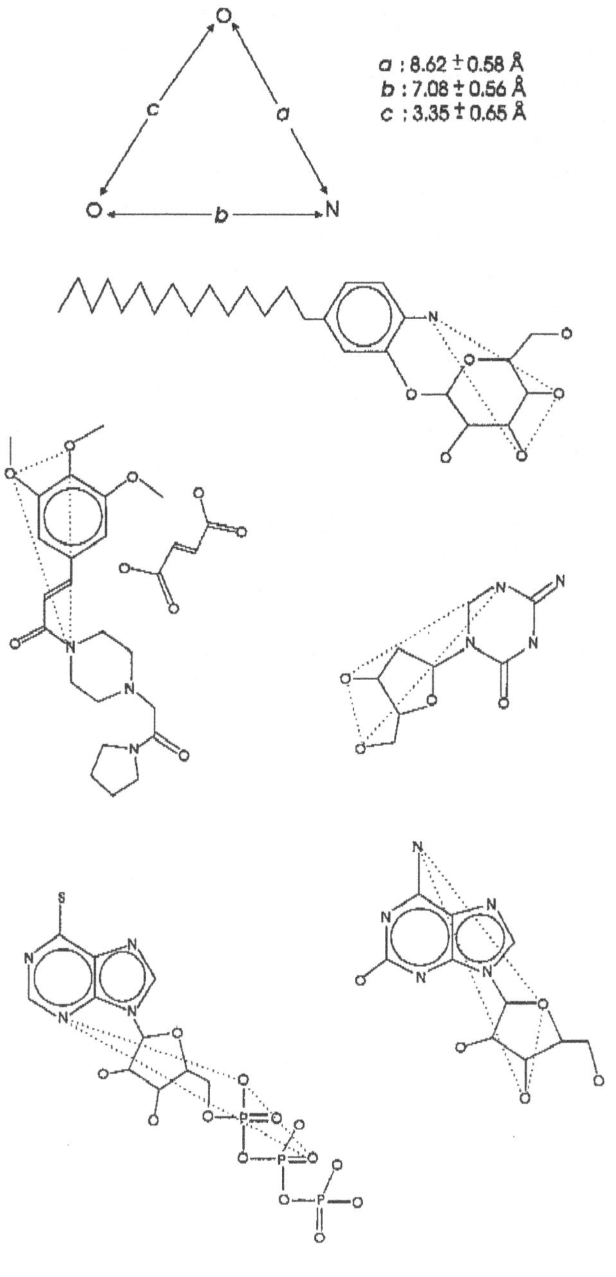

a : 8.62 ± 0.58 Å
b : 7.08 ± 0.56 Å
c : 3.35 ± 0.65 Å

Fig. 4 Typical hit structures for the antileukemic pharmacophore shown at the top of the page, with the presence of the pharmacophore in the retrieved molecules shown by dotted lines.
Source: From Zee-Cheng and Cheng.[22]

pharmacophore. Thus the structures retrieved from a 3D substructure search are typically far more diverse than those retrieved from the corresponding 2D search. The former is hence well equipped to identify novel structural classes that might not be covered by existing chemical patents, a commercially important capability that is increasingly referred to as *scaffold hopping*.[23]

The use of a graph in which the distance between a pair of atoms is fixed is not generally correct, since most molecules are *flexible*, i.e., they can adopt a large number of

different conformations, which vary both in shape and in energetic stability. Different conformations can result in different sets of interatomic distances, and a 3D substructure search of a database of rigid molecules may thus fail to retrieve many of them containing the query pharmacophore if each molecule is represented by a single, low-energy conformation. One way to overcome this problem is to store multiple conformations in the database for each molecule, with the conformations chosen to encompass the entire range of energetically feasible shapes that the molecule can adopt; there are many ways in which such a conformational analysis can be carried out.[19] The distance-based screening and subgraph isomorphism searches are then applied to all of the conformations describing each of the database-molecules. An alternative approach, more precise but also potentially much more time consuming, carries out a conformational analysis during the execution of the search, with the screening and subgraph-isomorphism stages being used to minimize the numbers of molecules and numbers of conformations that need to be explored by the conformation-analysis routine. This approach also requires the use of a different type of graph. Whereas the edges in a graph for rigid 3D searching encode interatomic distances, the edges for flexible 3D searching encode distance-ranges, the lower- and upper-bounds of which correspond to the minimum- and maximum-possible distances between each pair of atoms. The resulting graph encompasses all possible geometrically feasible shapes that the molecule can adopt; the final conformational analysis then checks whether hits that are geometrically feasible are also energetically feasible.[24]

Similarity Searching and Docking

Pharmacophore searching is now well established, although a flexible search for a broadly defined 3D pattern can be extremely time consuming unless other information can be used to constrain the search. Similarity searching in 3D is less well established. As noted previously, similarity measures based on fingerprints are used in nearly all 2D similarity searching systems, but there is still much debate as to how similarity in 3D should be quantified. Approaches based on comparing sets of interatomic distances (and more complex distance functions), the shapes of molecular surfaces, and surrounding electrostatic fields, *inter alia*, have all been discussed in the literature.[25] Thus far, however, it is not clear that any one approach is consistently superior to the others or, indeed, that the increased (in some cases massively increased) computational load results in searches that are more effective than similarity searches based on conventional 2D fingerprints.[10,11]

There is, however, one type of 3D search that is very widely used: *docking*. Similarity searching seeks database-molecules that are structurally similar to the reference structure; docking seeks database-molecules that are structurally *complementary* to the binding-site of a protein, i.e., that part of a protein that is involved in a biochemical pathway that a molecule needs to modify if it is to function as a drug. The need for complementarity arises from the so-called *lock-and-key* theory of drug action, which assumes that a molecule is likely to be able to act as a drug if it fits into a binding-site in much the same way as a key fits into a lock. A docking search hence requires that we know the 3D structure of the protein, information that is increasingly available from studies using x-ray crystallography and NMR (nuclear magnetic resonance) spectroscopy: the Protein Data Bank (at http://www.wwpdb.org/) is the principal repository of such data.[26] The first program for docking was described by Kuntz et al.,[27] whose DOCK program was based on complementarity of shape, as encoded in sphere-like descriptions of the shapes of the binding-site and the database-molecules. This basic approach has since been much extended, with enhancements including the use of chemical complementarity (e.g., areas of positive charge fit best with areas of negative charge) and the inclusion of algorithms that permit the docking of flexible molecules (although it is not generally possible, as yet, to allow for flexibility in the protein).[28]

COMPUTER-AIDED DRUG DISCOVERY

This final entry describes the use of chemoinformatics to support drug discovery since the pharmaceutical industry has been, thus far, chemoinformatics' principal application domain. However, it is also being increasingly used in related specialty areas, e.g., the agrochemical and biotechnology industries, and is applicable in principle to any area of chemistry where there is need to identify molecules with particular types of property. We focus here on three applications: *quantitative structure–activity relationships*, *molecular diversity analysis*, and *ADMET prediction*. All of these, and the searching methods described thus far, can be considered as examples of *virtual* (or *in silico*) *screening*.[29,30] Even with the significant developments that have taken place in the speed of biological screening, this is still the most time consuming and most expensive part of the discovery stage of pharmaceutical research (although the costs of this stage are far outweighed by the costs of the subsequent development and clinical stages). The cost-effectiveness of drug discovery will hence be maximized if molecules with a low probability of activity can be eliminated at as early a stage as possible from the discovery process; virtual screening is one of the most important tools available to achieve this end.

Quantitative Structure–Activity Relationships

Thus far, we have focused on the searching capabilities of modern chemoinformatics systems. Of equal importance is their ability to correlate structural information with the biological properties of molecules, which in the case of

pharmaceutical research is normally some sort of therapeutic property, e.g. lowering a person's blood pressure. Biological experiments are time consuming and expensive, even at the *in vitro* level, and hence an effective method for predicting a molecule's properties from its 2D or 3D structure can help to enhance research productivity by focusing experimental studies on those few molecules that are predicted to exhibit the desired activity. The basic methodology is to take some number of molecules for which the necessary biological data are available, and then to use this *training-set* to develop a mathematical model relating the experimental measurements to structural descriptors. If a statistically significant relationship can be derived, then it can be used to predict the property values for previously untested molecules in the *test-set*, and hence to identify those worthy of further, more detailed study. This is analogous to the use of known relevant documents to compute weights that can then be used in a relevance-feedback text search.

The development of what came to be called quantitative structure–activity relationships (QSAR) derives in large part from the pioneering work of Hansch and his collaborators.[31,32] Hansch analysis, as the approach has come to be called, involves the use of multivariate statistical methods, such as multiple regression or partial least-squares, to correlate molecular physicochemical properties (such as the octanol/water partition coefficient or the molar refractivity that are relatively easy to compute or measure) with quantitative biological data (that are much more difficult to measure). The approach is still widely used but does have two principal limitations: it can only be applied to small sets of structurally similar molecules, typically groups that have a common central ring system and that differ just by the nature of the substituents on this central scaffold; and it is based on the correlation of physicochemical properties computed from the structure, rather than the structure itself (which can be used to compute a very wide range of types of descriptor[33]). The latter limitation is addressed in the widely used CoMFA (for Comparative Molecular Field Analysis) approach to QSAR, where 3D variables describing the shape and the electrostatic charge of molecules are correlated with biological activity. CoMFA (and related approaches) is now the standard method for the analysis of small datasets but is still restricted to structurally related sets of molecules.[34] With developments in high-throughput biological testing, there are now large amounts of biological data for massive, structurally diverse sets of molecules, and this data explosion is currently driving the application of machine-learning techniques (such as support vector machines, neural networks, and naive Bayesian classifiers) to chemoinformatics datasets.[35]

Molecular Diversity Analysis

The virtual screening methods described thus far can be used if some molecules have already been tested, e.g., a similarity search if just one active is available or a docking search if the 3D structure of the biological receptor is known. If no such information is available then molecular diversity analysis is used to select molecules for testing. The Similar Property Principle means that molecules with similar structures are expected to have similar biological activities, and hence a virtual screening model is likely to have significant predictive power only if the molecules selected for inclusion in the training set are as structurally disparate as possible. The selection of such structurally disparate sets of molecules for biological testing is effected using the techniques of molecular diversity analysis.[36,37]

There are many ways in which a diverse set of molecules can be identified: we will illustrate the approach by cluster-based selection, which is perhaps the best established of the methods.[38] In the present context, cluster analysis involves partitioning a database into groups (or clusters) so that the molecules within each of the clusters are strongly similar to each other but dissimilar to the molecules in the other clusters. The similarities are normally computed using 2D fingerprints (as described for 2D similarity searching) and a clustering method then applied to the sets of intermolecular structural similarity values to derive the clusters. There are many different clustering methods that can be used, with the Jarvis-Patrick and Ward methods being the most common for chemical applications. Once the database has been clustered, one molecule (normally that closest to the centre) is drawn from each cluster in turn, with the expectation that the resulting set of selected molecules will have only a limited degree of similarity. If one of the molecules that has been selected proves to be biologically active when tested, then the other molecules in its parent cluster are also candidates for testing.

ADMET Prediction

Thus far, we have focused on the use of structural information in drug discovery. However, the fact that a molecule contains the correct substructural features is not sufficient for it to be a useful drug when administered to a patient. In particular, it is vital that it has an appropriate profile of pharmacokinetic properties and that it is not toxic: for example, molecules that are rapidly metabolized in the body will be unable to exhibit the desired therapeutic activity. Historically, ADMET (standing for absorption, distribution, metabolism, excretion, and toxicity) testing was carried out once a potential drug molecule had been identified. However, it became clear that this meant that a lot of time was spent optimizing the structures of molecules that subsequently proved to be unsuitable and ADMET testing is increasingly being carried out in parallel with chemical and biological screening. In addition, in just the same way as QSAR is used to direct a research program by predicting the biological activity of molecules that are being considered for synthesis (or acquisition) and testing, so there is much current interest in the development of ADMET methods that could predict the pharmacokinetic and toxicity behavior of molecules.

A very simple approach involves analyzing simple physical properties of successful drugs to enable an assessment to be made of the *drug-likeness* of a molecule. There is now considerable evidence that properties such as the molecular weight, the octanol/water partition coefficient, the numbers of heteroatoms, and the degree of conformational flexibility provide an effective basis for screening out large numbers of molecules that cannot possibly be effective drugs.[39] More sophisticated approaches have adopted the statistical techniques that are used in QSAR to obtain correlations between substructural descriptors or physicochemical properties and important characteristics such as intestinal permeability and absorption, oral bioavailability, aqueous solubility, interactions with cytochrome P450s, and toxic side-effects.[40,41]

CONCLUSIONS

The discovery of novel drugs is costly, time consuming, and scientifically demanding. The productivity of drug research is maximized if attention can be focused on just those few molecules that have a high a priori probability of success, and chemoinformatics provides a range of tools to support this aim. The brief introduction here has focused on the methods that are available for searching and for processing databases of 2D and 3D chemical structures, summarizing methods for structure, substructure and similarity searching, docking, quantitative structure–activity relationships, molecular diversity analysis, and the prediction of the pharmacokinetic and toxicity characteristics of molecules.

REFERENCES

1. Maizel, R.E. *How to Find Chemical Information*, 3rd Ed.; Wiley: New York, 1998.
2. Weisgerber, D.W. Chemical Abstracts Service Chemical Registry System: history, scope and impacts. J. Am. Soc. Info. Sci. **1997**, *48*, 349–360.
3. Chen, W.L. Chemoinformatics: past, present and future. J. Chem. Info. Model. **2006**, *46*, 2230–2255.
4. Gasteiger, J., Engel, T., Eds. *Chemoinformatics: A Textbook*; Wiley-VCH: Weinheim, 2003.
5. Leach, A.R.; Gillet, V.J. *An Introduction to Chemoinformatics*; Kluwer: Dordrecht, 2003.
6. Gasteiger, J., Ed. *Handbook of Chemoinformatics*; Wiley-VCH: Weinheim, 2003.
7. Ash, J.E., Hyde, E., Eds. *Chemical Information Systems*; Ellis Horwood: Chichester, U.K., 1975.

8. Weininger, D. SMILES, a chemical language and information-system.1. Introduction to methodology and encoding rules. J. Chem. Info. Comput. Sci. **1988**, *28*, 31–36.

9. Barnard, J.M. Substructure searching methods: old and new. J. Chem. Info. Comput. Sci. **1993**, *33*, 532–538.

10. Willett, P.; Barnard, J.M.; Downs, G.M. Chemical similarity searching. J. Chem. Info. Comput. Sci. **1998**, *38*, 983–996.

11. Sheridan, R.P.; Kearsley, S.K. Why do we need so many chemical similarity search methods?. Drug Discov. Today **2002**, *7*, 903–911.

12. Brown, R.D.; Martin, Y.C. Use of structure-activity data to compare structure-based clustering methods and descriptors for use in compound selection. J. Chem. Info. Comput. Sci. **1996**, *36*, 572–584.

13. Barnard, J.M., Ed. *Computer Handling of Generic Chemical Structures*; Gower: Aldershot, Hamsphire, U.K., 1984.

14. Berks, A.H. Current state of the art of Markush topological search systems. World Patent Info. **2001**, *23*, 5–13.

15. Willett, P., Ed. *Modern Approaches to Chemical Reaction Searching*; Gower: Aldershot, Hamsphire, U.K., 1986.

16. Zass, E. A user's view of chemical reaction information sources. J. Chem. Info. Comput. Sci. **1990**, *30*, 360–372.

17. Martin, Y.C., Willett, P., Eds. *Designing Bioactive Molecules: Three-Dimensional Techniques and Applications*; American Chemical Society: Washington DC, 1998.

18. Allen, F.H. The Cambridge Structural Database: a quarter of a million crystal structures and rising. Acta Crystallograph. **2002**, *B58*, 380–388.

19. Leach, A.R. *Molecular Modeling. Principles and Applications*, 2nd Ed.; Pearson: Harlow, U.K., 2001.

20. Sadowski, J.; Gasteiger, J. From atoms and bonds to three-dimensional atomic coordinates: automatic model builders. Chem. Rev. **1993**, *93*, 2567–2581.

21. Guner, O., Ed. *Pharmacophore Perception, Development and Use in Drug Design*; International University Line: La Jolla, CA, 2000.

22. Brown, N.; Jacoby, E. On scaffolds and hopping in medicinal chemistry. Mini-Rev. Med. Chem. **2006**, *6*, 1217–1229.

23. Clark, D.E.; Jones, G.; Willett, P.; Kenny, P.W.; Glen, R.C. Pharmacophoric pattern matching in files of three-dimensional chemical structures: Comparison of conformational-searching algorithms for flexible searching. J. Chem. Info. Comput. Sci. **1994**, *34*, 197–206.

24. Bender, A.; Glen, R.C. Molecular similarity: a key technique in molecular informatics. Org. Biomol. Chem. **2004**, *2*, 3204–3218.

25. Berman, H.M.; Battistuz, T.; Bhat, T.N.; Blum, W.F.; Bourne, P.E.; Burkhardt, K.; Feng, Z.; Gilliland, G.L.; Iype, L.; Jain, S.; Fagan, P.; Marvin, J.; Padilla, D.; Ravichandran, V.; Schneider, B.; Thanki, N.; Weissig, H.; Westbrook, J.D.; Zardecki, C. The Protein Data Bank. Acta Crystallograph. **2002**, *D58*, 899–907.

26. Kuntz, I.D.; Blaney, J.M.; Oatley, S.J.; Langridge, R.; Ferrin, T.E. A geometric approach to macromolecule-ligand interactions. J. Mol. Biol. **1982**, *161*, 269–288.

27. Leach, A.R.; Shoichet, B.K.; Peishoff, C.E. Prediction of protein-ligand interactions. Docking and scoring: Successes and gaps. J. Med. Chem. **2006**, *49*, 5851–5855.

28. Bohm, H.-J.; Schneider, G., Eds. *Virtual Screening for Bioactive Molecules*; Wiley-VCH: Weinheim, 2000.

29. Klebe, G., Ed. *Virtual Screening: An Alternative or Complement to High Throughput Screening*; Kluwer: Dordrecht, 2000.

30. Martin, Y.C. *Quantitative Drug Design*; Marcel Dekker: New York, 1978.

31. Hansch, C.; Leo, A. *Exploring QSAR: Fundamentals and Applications in Chemistry and Biology*; American Chemical Society: Washington DC, 1995.

32. Todeschini, R.; Consonni, V. *Handbook of Molecular Descriptors*; Wiley-VCH: Weinheim, 2000.

33. Kubinyi, H., Folkers, G., Martin, Y.C., Eds. *3D QSAR in Drug Design*; ESCOM: Leiden, 1998.

34. Goldman, B.B.; Walters, W.P. Machine learning in computational chemistry. Annu. Rep. Comput. Chem. **2006**, *2*, 127–140.

35. Dean, P.M., Lewis, R.A., Eds. *Molecular Diversity in Drug Design*; Kluwer: Amsterdam, 1999.

36. Ghose, A.K., Viswanadhan, V.N., Eds. *Combinatorial Library Design and Evaluation: Principles, Software Tools and Applications in Drug Discovery*; Marcel Dekker: New York, 2001.

37. Gorse, A.-D. Diversity in medicinal chemistry space. Curr. Top. Med. Chem. **2006**, *6*, 3–18.

38. Lipinski, C.A.; Lombardo, F.; Dominy, B.W.; Feeney, P.J. Experimental and computational approaches to estimate solubility and permeability in drug discovery and development settings. Adv. Drug Deliv. Rev. **2001**, *46*, 3–26.

39. Clark, D.E. Computational prediction of ADMET properties: Recent developments and future changes. Annu. Rep. Comput. Chem. **2005**, *1*, 133–151.

40. Dearden, J.C. *In silico* prediction of drug toxicity. J. Comput. Aided Mol. Des. **2003**, *17*, 119–127.

BIBLIOGRAPHY

For a general introduction, see Refs. 3–6 above.

Other useful texts are

1. Bajorath, J., Ed. *Chemoinformatics. Concepts, Methods and Tools for Drug Discovery*; Humana Press: Totowa, NJ, 2004.

2. Gasteiger, J. The central role of chemoinformatics. Chemometrics Intell. Lab. Syst. **2006**, *82*, 200–209.

3. Hann, M.; Green, R. Chemoinformatics—a new name for an old problem?. Curr. Opin. Chem. Biol. **1999**, *3*, 379–383.

4. Oprea, T.I., Ed. *Chemoinformatics in Drug Discovery*; Wiley-VCH: Weinheim, Germany, 2005.

5. Wild, D.J.; Wiggins, G.D. Challenges for chemoinformatics education in drug discovery. Drug Discov. Today **2006**, *11*, 436–439.

6. Willett, P. A bibliometric analysis of chemoinformatics. Aslib Proc. **2008**, *60*, 4–17.

7. Willett, P. From chemical documentation to chemoinformatics: fifty years of chemical information science. J. Info. Sci. **2008**, *34*, 477–499.

The principal research journals in the field are the *Journal of Chemical Information and Modeling*, the *Journal of Computer-Aided Molecular Design*, the *Journal of Molecular Graphics and Modeling*, and *QSAR & Combinatorial Science*.

Children and Information Technology

June Abbas
School of Library and Information Studies, University of Oklahoma, Norman, Oklahoma, U.S.A.

Abstract

This entry presents research on the complex topic of children and information technology. Covered are children aged 0–18. Information technology has changed significantly over the last few years as has the research covered by Library and Information Science. This entry includes a brief overview of research between the years 1995 and 2009 and more in-depth coverage of the years 2010–2014. Children have increased using information technologies in every aspect of their lives to play, learn, communicate, and participate in online ecologies. A multidisciplinary perspective is taken to show that children are engaged participants, connected continuously using many technologies, including mobile devices such as smartphones and tablets, and creative content developers, but who still are plagued with poor understanding of how to effectively use retrieval systems. The technological, psychosocial, ethical, security, and legal issues children encounter while online are also presented.

INTRODUCTION

Children and information technology is a very broad topic, thereby requiring broad coverage. For the ease of the reader, the term "children" will be used to indicate both children [ages 0–11] and young adults [ages 12–17]. This entry does not include discussion on young adults between the ages of 18 and 26. The term "information technology" is defined broadly as "any electronic format designed to help people access information."[1] This definition allows us to include any textual, audio, video, image, or virtual media, including the Internet and World Wide Web, as well as mobile technologies such as smartphones and tablets. The popular perception is that children are "digital natives" who are adept at using information and communication technologies.[2] This population of children represents the first group who have grown up with technologies such as computers, mobile devices, and social media interwoven into many aspects of their lives. The research, as will be outlined within this entry, is beginning to paint a picture of children as engaged, connected, creative users, not just consumers of information technologies, but who are still plagued with issues of information illiteracy and poor understanding of how to use retrieval systems effectively.

Along with technology use are the psychosocial, ethical, security, and legal issues that children face daily as they interact in the new information ecologies or "networked publics"[3] of the Web, and particularly, social media. As we learn more about how children are using, and are users of, information technology, it is important to remember that children will still go through the same experimental, explorative process of play, communication, and emotional and psychosocial development as children always have, and to them information technology is a necessity in many of their social worlds.

This entry does not seek to provide a comprehensive review of all of the literature, but rather will synthesize our understandings of children's use of information technology and to present important research areas being explored in Library and Information Science. As some of the research is multidisciplinary, guided by theories and studies within the fields of Education and Communication, this entry will include studies from those fields as relevant to understanding the complex relationship between children and information technology and to explore sociocultural issues not fully addressed in library and information science literature. Furthermore, as previous editions have provided coverage of earlier research, this entry will include only a brief summary of research conducted prior to 2010. For earlier research, refer to previous editions of this entry.[4–6]

OVERVIEW

Children globally have unprecedented levels of access to information technology, whether through the use of computers located in their homes, schools, libraries, or other locations, or through their cell and smartphones or other mobile devices. For example, China has invested significant effort to add information and communication technologies (ICTs) to schools. In 2007, 270,000 elementary and secondary schools in central and western regions added facilities with ICTs, with the majority of these facilities connected to the Internet for the first time.[7] Schools in remote rural areas, however, in 2008 remained largely unconnected.[8] The International Telecommunication

Encyclopedia of Library and Information Sciences, Fourth Edition DOI: 10.1081/E-ELIS4-120053124

Union has estimated the worldwide population of digital natives as 363 million or 5.2% of the world's population of 7 billion in 2012. They define digital native as the population of networked youth, aged 15–24, with 5 or more years of online experience. This estimate equates to 30% of the world's youth population as digital natives. Digital natives, however, still represent a minority among the world's youth due to low Internet usage rates in developing countries. The total population of digital natives varies between countries, from 0.1% in Timor-Leste to a high of 14% in Iceland; median population of digital natives in Belarus and Syria with 5.5 and 5.4, respectively. Notably, the populations with the highest proportions of digital natives are all high-income or upper-middle-income countries with very high overall levels of Internet penetration, including Iceland, New Zealand, Republic of Korea, and the United States (19).[9]

Other studies focused on the U.S. children reveal that information technology use begins at a very early age. A 2013 study conducted by the Common Sense Media group found that U.S. children aged 8 and under spend an average of 1 hour and 55 minutes a day with screen media, an increase of 21 minutes spent in 2011. Screen time measured included watching TV, playing video games, using a computer, and using mobile devices such as smartphones and tablets (15).[10] Further telling is that in 2011 only 8% of children aged 8 and under had access to and used tablets, while in 2013 this figure increased to 40%, with many of the children having access to their own tablets, not having to share it with other members of the family. Smartphone ownership within the family has also increased from 41% in 2011 to 63% in 2013. Use of mobile devices has also increased for this age group and begins at a young age, with 38% of children of age 2 and under using a mobile device for any media activity, compared with 10% in 2011. Among 2- to 4-year-olds, the rate increased from 39% in 2011 to 80% in 2013; and among 5–8-year-olds, from 52% to 83% in the past 2 years (20).[10] Older children (ages 12–17) have been the focus of multiple large-scale studies. For example, a 2012 joint Berkman Center for Internet & Society at Harvard (Berkman) and the Pew Research Center (Pew) study found that 78% of U.S. teens (ages 12–17) own a cell phone, with half of those phones being smartphones. This figure is an increase over 2011, in which only 23% owned smartphones. One in four teens or 23% own a tablet; three in four or 74% say they primarily access the Internet on cell phones, tablets, and other mobile devices. Thirty-four percent of teen girls aged 14–17 report that they mostly go online using their cell phone, compared to 24% of boys in the same age range. Fifty-five percent of teen girls who own smartphones report they access the Internet mostly from their phone (2).[11] It is also important to note that a digital access divide still exists among teens from lower-income households. Teens in lower-income and lower-education households are "still somewhat less likely to

use the Internet in any capacity"; however, the income and education level of parents does not affect the likelihood that teens in these families own cell or smartphones (7).[11] Increased access to information technologies provides children, especially older youth, with opportunities to learn, play, create, socialize, and participate in civic life at unprecedented levels than earlier populations of youth.

AREAS OF RESEARCH

Research Prior to 1995 (years of each section based on years that correspond to earlier editions of this entry).

There is a rich history of research on children's use of information technology, with the majority of the research focusing on older children (middle and high school students of ages 11–17), and much of the research employing small, nonrepresentative samples. Research prior to 1995 (when more widespread use of the Internet and World Wide Web began) focused on children's use of electronic resources, such as online public access catalogs (OPACs), databases, and CD-ROM software in libraries and school media centers. This body of research on children's use of electronic resources "reflected the pragmatic concerns of librarians and educators who saw a need to train students in the effective use of these new information resources" (2).[12] Much of the research during the 1980s and prior to the Internet use provided descriptive data on which schools provided access to electronic resources, and the effect (whether positive or negative) using these new electronic sources had on children's information retrieval abilities. It examined the role that system design, search skills such as formulating Boolean searches, and the use of synonyms, truncation, and controlled vocabularies had on children's abilities to find information in electronic resources. Research did not focus on children's information seeking behaviors and the cognitive, physical, emotional, etc. factors that might affect retrieval.[12] The reader is referred to Cool[12] and to an earlier edition of this entry[4] for further coverage of the research conducted in the 1980s and prior to 1995.

Research 1995 through 2004

Research conducted between the years 1995 and 2004 continued to explore children's use of electronic media, but it also began to examine 1) how children were using the new technologies of the Internet and World Wide Web, search engines, and digital libraries (for a comprehensive look at children and the Web during this time span, see Large[13]); 2) other information technology devices such as electronic books (e-books) and PDAs; 3) collaboration between children and technology designers; 4) use of computers in libraries and schools; 5) the impact Internet access and use had on children's use of the public library; and 6) use of new technologies to reenergize old practices (blogs, e-books, literature circles). Also investigated were older children's selection criteria of Web pages and the factors considered when librarians design Web pages for use by children. Refer to the 2003 and 2005 editions of this topic[4,5] for more in-depth descriptions of the research conducted during 1995–2004.

It is also important to note that beginning in 2001, several large-scale national surveys within the United States as well as in Canada were conducted to learn more about children's online activities while they use the Internet. The Pew Research Institute's American Life Project[14] conducted numerous surveys using both nationally sampled, random digit dialing telephone surveys as well as focus groups with children and their parents. Other groups, such as Environics Research Group, the U.S. Department of Education, Grunwald Associates with cooperation of the Public Broadcasting Service, also conducted large studies on youth's online activities in the United States and Canada. The results of these surveys served as our main source of nationally representative, generalizable findings on what activities children engaged in while online, locations of access,[15,16] attitudes of parents and children,[17] and youth's educational and recreational uses for information technologies (included teachers' perspectives as well).[18] These earlier studies helped us develop a more complete view of what children were doing online, the activities they engaged in, and their attitudes, opinions, and purposes for using the Internet. Findings indicated that 1) children viewed themselves as tech-savvy, especially more than their parents and/or teachers; 2) the Internet played a pivotal role in children's lives and they both rely on it and value its use; and 3) children used the Internet for communication with friends, to surf for fun, and for recreational and educational purposes. These studies did not, however, reveal any findings about children's information seeking processes, problems encountered while searching and using search engines, nor the effect cognitive, developmental, physical, or emotional variables can have on children's search success.

Research 2005 through 2009

Research conducted in 2005 through 2009 continued with and expanded upon the research emphases of prior years (information seeking processes and factors that affect retrieval of digital resources, the role that children can play in collaborative design of systems for children, i.e., digital libraries, search engines, Web pages, and children's online activities). Information seeking success can be influenced by many cognitive, developmental, and system factors. Previous research findings indicate that children in all age groups encounter a range of difficulties while searching for information due to 1) a lack of understanding about how the system works; 2) limited search and semantic skills; 3) the system's use of an inappropriate controlled vocabulary to describe the resources;

4) resources were not current, not age-appropriate or contained incomplete or low-quality information; and 5) systems were not designed for children and included features that distracted children and/or made navigation confusing and inefficient. During 2005 through 2009, research continued to help us understand children's search processes, the factors that impact children's success while seeking information, and their seeking within specific contexts (OPACs, databases, the Internet using search engines, and digital libraries). Beginning in 2005, two new areas of research appeared in the literature on children's information seeking. These areas included the effect of affective variables such as emotion on information seeking outcomes and the multicultural use of information technologies, mostly in the context of digital libraries. While affective variables are not new to studies conducted in the fields of psychology, computer science, education, or cognitive science, affective variables have not been emphasized as a research area in information science until recent years. Bilal[19] explains that children "need to possess not only adequate information-seeking skills but also intelligent affective strategies that will help them cope with its [information technology's] complexity" (198).

Also of importance, during the years of 2005–2009, we saw a radical shift in how children interact with information technology. Instead of just being passive users of information technologies such as library OPACs and the Internet to locate information, children, especially older children, became very active content creators, designers, teachers, and participants in social networking, gaming, and virtual environments. This "shift" opened up new areas of research, as well as presented many pragmatic, ethical, and safety-related issues for children, their parents, and practitioners and libraries. While our understanding of children's use of the Internet is informed by the areas of research outlined earlier (use of electronic and multimedia resources, their information-seeking activities, the problems they encounter when using systems, and the cognitive, affective, physical, and developmental factors that can impact their system use and retrieval activities), examining children's use of the Internet is a very complex issue that requires us to not just look at their use through a traditional information-seeking and system use lens but rather, we need to look broader at the activities and environments they engage within, the social issues that are becoming more prevalent with universal Internet access such as cyberbullying, privacy, and safety. New areas of exploration during this time period were related to 1) the use of social networking sites, such as MySpace and Facebook;[20] 2) content creation on blogs and social sharing sites such as YouTube;[21] 3) social issues of cyberbullying, identity, privacy, and safety;[22–24] and 4) information technologies used for communicative purposes, including cell phones, email, and texting.[20,25] Refer to the 2010 edition of this topic for more on the research conducted during 2005 through 2009.[6]

Research 2010 through 2014

The research emphases that had begun in earlier years became even more important in 2010 through 2014 as more researchers focused on the "digital native" or "digital youth" and understanding more about their information behaviors, information literacy, online participatory activities, and the impact the information technologies had on their intellectual and psychosocial development. Much of the research during this time period is on older children, or teens, with scant research focused on younger children. While traditional research areas of information behavior and information retrieval continue to help build understanding of the digital youth, much of the research during this time period focused on youth's use of and participation in online ecologies, such as social networking and collaborative sites. Research of youth within this context has explored their frequency and motivation of use, psychosocial issues such as identity development, privacy and safety issues, and the potential benefits and drawbacks of participating in online environments. This section will outline the research areas prevalent during this time period with examples of research that contribute to our understanding of children and information technology.

Information behavior

Research on the information behaviors (IBs) of children can help us better understand today's digital youth. Wilson defines IB as "the totality of human behavior in relation to sources and channels of information, including both active and passive information seeking, and information use."[26] Information behavior can be purposive, having a specific goal in mind, and may be engaged in as part of a person's everyday information activities. Several models have been proposed throughout the years to portray the iterative, interactive, dynamic processes humans engage in when browsing or seeking information to meet an information need. (Refer to Fisher et al.[27] for discussion on information behavior models.) The research conducted between 2010 and 2014 included various contexts and frameworks for understanding information behavior of youth, including for example, studies based on the everyday life information seeking (ELIS) framework, the creating behavior of youth as an additional aspect of IB,[28,29] health information seeking,[30–35] information behaviors of specific populations[36,37] who examined the understudied population of Latino youth in poor California communities, and studies concerned with information retrieval factors.

Everyday life information seeking

The everyday life information seeking (ELIS) framework was proposed by Savolainen and has been adapted by other researchers. The ELIS framework describes an individual's daily life information activities and the role

information plays in decision making. Furthermore, it proposes that the individual habits we form when monitoring daily events and seeking information, as well as the sources and channels we use to find information, are based on values, attitudes, and interests learned in sociocultural contexts.[38] A chapter by Abbas and Agosto,[39] in Behesti and Large's recent book on the information behavior of the digital generation,[40] outlines research in youth's ELIS and describes how ELIS is useful in understanding digital youth. Synthesis of the research to date on youth's ELIS found:

- Youth search for information for various purposes (problem solving, coping, entertainment, self-development).
- Youth prefer to use informal human channels first, such as family and friends and use various information technologies to communicate with friends and family.[41,42]
- Youth use the Internet to find information related to various everyday information needs, for entertainment, and to participate in social networks.[39]

What ELIS research has not uncovered is whether or not youth are using information technologies such as cell and smartphones and social network sites to find information. Many of the ELIS studies outlined in this entry took place prior to large-scale adoption of information technologies by youth but the research has illustrated how this framework can be very useful for understanding digital youth.

Creating behavior

The most prevalent models of information behavior include the recognition of an information need and the process an individual follows to satisfy that need. What is generally not explored is the complex creation process undertaken by youth when they use found information to develop new information or products. Online environments afford youth many opportunities to create information products such as YouTube videos, websites, social media posts, online photos posted on sharing tools (e.g., Flickr, Snapchat, Instagram). Youth creating behavior, then, would seem to be a necessary aspect of understanding their information behaviors; however, few studies to date have explored this component of information behavior. Harlan et al.[29] and Koh[28] have proposed that creating behavior be included in information behavior models. Harlan asserts that "the affordances of social media—ease of use, ubiquitous access, and communal nature—have made creating and sharing content an appealing process for teens." (p. 569) She also links creating behavior to learning and information literacy. Her research explored how teens experience using information to learn as they engage in online communities. Koh examined older children's information creating behaviors while participating in an online community using the programming tool Scratch. Her findings indicate that creating behavior includes 1) the development of content, 2) organization, and 3) presentation of information. Furthermore, the findings illustrate the complex processes youth engage in when creating content in online, collaborative environments, including 1) visualizing (using visual tools and multimedia to communicate their ideas); 2) remixing (building on or adding to the original information or projects of others and then sharing the product with others); and 3) tinkering (iterative design process youth engage in while creating). Youth also felt a sense of empowerment as they contributed to the Scratch community and took on new, more responsible roles. Koh's study also shows how youth seek and evaluate information from multiple sources to determine their accuracy and how they demonstrated an understanding of the relationships connecting the various sources they used.

Health information seeking

Health information seeking by youth has increased in recent years. Fox and Jones in 2009[43] found that 28% of older youth (12–17) have used the Internet to look for health-related information. In 2010, Purcell and Lenhart[44] reported that of the 93% of the U.S. youth (aged 12–17) who went online, 31% had searched for health information. Furthermore, a multidisciplinary literature review between the years 2000 and 2012[31] examined 82 articles on teen's health information seeking and found that 57% of teen health information behavior studies were focused on specific topics such as sexual health, mental health, nutrition and eating issues, and those related to alcohol, drugs, and tobacco; 43% covered more general health topics. The majority of the studies included online resources as the context of the study, with 47% focused only on online resources and 36.5% including both online and other types of resources. The review also found that the number of studies focused on teen health information seeking increased beginning in 2011. Health information behavior studies have examined many aspects of youth information behavior including 1) the information coping strategies and online activities of young people,[30,34,35] 2) searching for nutrition-related information,[45] 3) using text messaging and other information technologies to assess adolescents' health information needs,[32,46] 4) the issue of trust as a factor in user-centered design of systems promoting sexual health in African-American youth,[33] 5) the use of social media to find health information,[47,48] and ELIS as a way to understand the "coming-out-process" of gay youth.[49]

Information retrieval

Information retrieval studies are concerned with the seeking or retrieval process of information behavior. The studies include models of information seeking/seekers, search processes, barriers to retrieval, and factors to consider in retrieval system design. Research during 2010 through 2014 continued to explore children's web searching and technoliteracy;[50–54] roles that youth of all ages display while seeking information;[55,56] and innovative ways to increase precision and recall in systems designed for children.[57] As noted earlier, children encounter many issues when searching for information using information technologies. Today's digital youth are no exception. Research has shown this to still be an issue in children's information seeking. For example, Spink and colleagues studied web searching of 4- and 5-year-olds and discovered that young children use search engines to both search and browse for information. Young children are also capable of complex web searches, could evaluate sources for relevance to their query, and engaged in successive, collaborative search behaviors like those of adults. Their technoliteracy was measured as competent as they proficiently used the mouse, cursor, and keyboard to effectively navigate the websites. The children did, however, exhibit issues while constructing queries related to spelling and word acquisition.[50] Behesti, Large, and Tam's study of transaction search logs from a Canadian history web portal designed for children showed that children preferred to browse using the topic taxonomy feature, followed second by the alphabetical word search (combined 83%), rather than search using key words or the advanced search feature.[53] Bilal and Ellis[51] and Bilal[52] took a different approach as they compared the performance of five search engines, two being specifically designed for children, and found that the engines designed for children did not perform as high as, based on relevance of documents retrieved, the larger engines. The child-centric engines did, however, retrieve higher precision results on partially relevant results. The results of the studies illustrate that children continue to encounter many barriers when searching for information on the Internet such as using advanced features of engines that enable them to filter results, the ability to formulate effective search strategies and to interpret and evaluate the results retrieved, and possessing adequate reading skills (189).[52]

Teachers also provide a valuable perspective on children's information literacy and technological fluency. A survey of Advanced Placement (AP) and National Writing Project (NWP) teachers revealed that teens' research habits are changing in the digital age. The study findings indicate that 75% of AP and NWP teachers report that while the Internet and search tools have had a mostly positive effect on students' research habits, 87% said these technologies are creating an "easily distracted generation with short attention spans," and 64% say "today's digital technologies 'do more to distract students than to help them academically'" (2).[58] Some of the positive effects include access to a "greater depth and breadth of information on topics that interest them," engaging multimedia formats, and that many become self-reliant searchers. Teachers are, however, concerned with increasing dependence on search engines, the difficulty children have on judging reliable, quality information, increasing distractions, poor time management skills, and the general level of literacy of children (2).[58] Furthermore, the teachers report that the Internet has changed the nature of research. To children, research means "Googling," in which the student no longer engages in a slow, intellectual process of discovery, but rather is concerned with quickly finding just enough information to complete the assignment (3).[58]

Teachers also noted many barriers to incorporating information technologies into their classrooms, such as policies restricting use of cell/smartphones in school, Internet filters on school computers, and provisions in a school's acceptable use policy (5).[58] In a related report from the Berkman Center for Internet & Society at Harvard University (Berman Center), youth report similar observations. Youth reported a wide variety of school policies related to laptop use, phones, iPads, and other mobile devices and how the policies served as barriers to access. An interesting finding was that youth mentioned being frustrated with school initiatives to provide them with new tablets for academic purposes when they would have preferred laptops instead.[59]

While most information retrieval studies of children take place in schools, libraries, or in laboratory settings, Foss and colleagues[55,56] studied children of ages 7, 9, 11, and 14–17 in their homes. The goal of their study was to understand how children search the Internet in their homes and to uncover potential triggers to searching, search rules, emotional and social factors encountered, and how they handle multistep, complex search tasks. Their study developed a framework of seven search roles children can be characterized by including 1) Power (awareness of sources to use and ability to use advanced search features); 2) Developing (limited knowledge of search tools, unable to plan searches or to verbalize their search process, and use a variety of search approaches); 3) Distracted (tendency to drift easily off task, and to encounter information not related to the task); 4) Nonmotivated (compliant with directions to search but generally do not choose searching or the computer as an activity); 5) Domain-specific (use search abilities to gather information on specific topics of interest); 6) Visual (a desire to retrieve information from visual sources, like pictures or videos); and 7) Rule-bound (displayed constrained searching patterns, repeating the same steps each time).[55] Younger children (ages 7, 9, 11) displayed different roles than adolescents. For example, there was an absence of Distracted Searchers in adolescents, while an additional role emerged for adolescents, that of Social Searcher, whose main use of the computer was driven by social factors such as communicating with friends using social networking sites. The other notable difference between younger children and adolescents was that Power searchers were more advanced in their searching than younger children (178–179).[56] These studies illustrate that children do not all search the same, in fact they take on a variety of different roles when

searching. Gossen and Nurnberger[60] note that one of the current problems in IR research for children is that researchers view children as a consistent user group. Furthermore, researchers do not consider that children of different age groups may require different solutions that influence the design of information systems. The studies outlined here, as well as earlier studies by Bilal and other researchers,[5,6] illustrate how children's abilities differ from adult searchers, their ideas of research and how to find useful information are changing, and that age and cognitive abilities are factors that still require further exploration.

Internet Use: Social Networking

During 2010 through 2014 the use of the Internet increased with an estimated 95% of teens in 2012 reporting they go online. Eight in ten online teens have used some form of social media (19).[61] Online environments have changed the way that people seek information, interact with others, contribute to participatory cultures, create, learn, and play. LIS research on the Internet during this time period continued to focus on the pragmatic, ethical, legal, and literacy issues related to use of the Internet and social networking sites. Research of youth in social networking sites has explored their frequency and motivation of use, information technologies used to go online, psychosocial issues such as identity development and privacy and safety issues, and the potential benefits and drawbacks of participating in online environments. Anttiroiko and Savolainen[62] defined Social Network Sites (SNS) as "profile-based hosted services that allow people to create and maintain networks of friends and contacts based on general social interests" (p. 89). Examples of the most popular SNS currently are Facebook and Twitter, though use of SNS continues to change as new different, subject-specific, or media-specific sites appear. For example, Instagram and Snapchat are becoming favorite sites among older children. These new SNS allow teens to post images and/or short videos that can be instantly shared with friends, without requiring the content development and upkeep of a Facebook profile page. The sites allow teens to communicate quickly and easily with their friends, without the drama or time investment of Facebook.

Compared with adults, U.S. teens are heavy users of SNS. In 2012, 77% of online teens reported they have a Facebook account (81% reported using social media), and 24% of them used Twitter, while 67% of adults used social media and 16% used Twitter.[61] Research related to SNS use by children has also continued to increase. A multidisciplinary literature review conducted by Agosto and Abbas in 2012, including studies focusing on youth between the ages of 12 and 18, showed that 38 studies were published between the years 2006 and 2011. Their study concluded:

The burgeoning body of literature paints a multifaceted picture of youth people's SNS practices, and the major issues that surround their participation in social networking communities. For the most part, the kinds of activities taking place in SNS are the same kinds of activities that took place offline among previous generations of young people. The difference is not so much the kinds of activities that are occurring online, but the *amount*, *frequency*, *and semipublic nature* of these activities (pp. 123–124).[63]

This conclusion is supported by other researchers such as Boyd,[64,65] and Livingstone and Brake.[66] Agosto and Abbas outline major themes in the literature including:

- Motivation (social interaction/communication;[41,42,64,65,67–75]; relationship building and maintenance;[41,42,68–71,76–79] emotional support;[68–70,80] convenience[41,42,71,81]).
- Benefits (identity exploration and formation;[64,65,68–70,78,80,82–87] technological literacy;[67,70,77,80,86,88,89] educational support/formal learning;[73,86,85,90] positive self-esteem[41,76,91]).
- Harms (privacy risks;[67,92–95] security risks[41,67,92,94–101]).

These themes have been reflected by the large-scale studies conducted on this topic between 2010 and 2014. More recent studies are outlined briefly as follows.

Bullying in a Networked Era:[102] As part of the Kinder and Braver World Project at the Berkman Center for Internet & Society at Harvard University (Berkman Center), this report provides a multidisciplinary literature review of academic research on the topic of bullying. The review focuses on research published between 2008 and 2012 but includes some important earlier studies as well. The study captures both offline and online bullying and is guided by two questions, "What is bullying?" and "What can be done about bullying?" A companion to this report is an overview of state antibullying legislation and other related laws in the United States.[103] This report provides an overview of existing and pending antibullying state legislation, as well as specifics of how the laws define and address bullying, cyberbullying in multiple contexts, and procedures for reporting and prosecuting offenses.

Teens and Technology 2013:[11] This report, a collaborative effort by the Pew Research Center's Internet and American Life Project and the Berkman Center, describes cell and smartphone adoption among teens and how using cell or smartphones has afforded them 24/7 mobile access to the Internet. See Overview section for key findings.

Social Media, Social Life: How Teens View their Digital Lives:[104] This Common Sense Media research study gives another glimpse into teens and their use of social media. Their study complements other studies

conducted by Pew and the Berkman Center. Key findings include:

- Nine out of 10 or 90% of 13–17-year-olds have used some form of social media.
- Seventy-five percent have a profile on a social media site; 22% have a Twitter account.
- For the vast majority of teens, social media and other forms of digital communication are a daily part of life. Sixty-eight percent text every day; 51% visit social media sites daily; 34% visit their social media site several times a day; 11% receive tweets at least once a day.
- One in four (23%) are "heavy" social media users and use at least two different types of social media every day (9).
- Most teens prefer face-to-face communication. About 49% prefer in person communication with friends. Texting is their next favorite (33%), followed by social media (7%), talking on the phone (4%), and tweeting (1%). They prefer in person communication for various reasons, mostly because it is fun (38%) and they can understand what people mean better (29%) (11).
- Some teens wish they could disconnect more often and that others would too. Forty-one percent said they were "addicted" to their phones; 43% strongly or somewhat agree and wish they could unplug sometimes. The teens who reported they are most interested in unplugging are the ones who either are not using social networking or who have had a bad experience online (2).

Teens, Social Media, and Privacy:[61] This report, a collaborative effort by the Pew Research Center's Internet and American Life Project and the Berkman Center, provides up-to-date research on teen's (ages 12–17) use of social media, their sharing and privacy practices, and impressions of online privacy. Some key findings include:

- Teens are sharing more information about themselves on social media than they did in the past; 91% post photos of themselves, 71% post their school name, 71% post their city or town, 53% post their email address, and 20% post their cell phone number. These figures differ across age, with older teens (14–17) sharing more content than younger teens.
- The typical teen Facebook user has 300 friends, while the typical teen Twitter user has 79 followers. Older teens tend to be friends with a variety of people than younger teens, with most of their friends being people they know.
- Teens are losing interest in Facebook and reported a dislike of the adult presence, people sharing excessively, and the stressful drama in many of the posts as

reasons. They continue using Facebook because it is an essential part of teen socializing.

- 60% of teens keep their profiles private and say they can confidently manage their privacy online.
- Teens use multiple measures to maintain their reputations online and to manage their networks, including for example, deleting people from their friends/followers list, pruning their profile content, posting false information such as fake name, age, or location.
- Teens did not report a high level of concern about third-party access to their data, only 9% reported they were "very concerned."
- Teens reported more positive experiences than negative experiences (2–7).

Where Teens Seek Online Privacy Advice:[105] This report, a collaborative effort by the Pew Research Center's Internet and American Life Project and the Berkman Center, sought to determine the resources teens used to learn about protecting their online privacy. Some key findings include:

- Teens (ages 12–17) in the United States care about their online privacy and take steps to manage access to their online social media spaces.
- Many teens report relying on themselves for learning about online privacy measures; however, the majority of teens (70%) found themselves asking for outside advice at one point
  — 42% asked a friend or peer for advice
  — 41% asked a parent
  — 37% asked a sibling or cousin
  — 13% used a website for advice
  — 9% asked a teacher
  — 3% have gone to some other source
- Younger teens (12–13) are more likely to seek out advice than older teens.
- Girls are also more likely to seek out advice than boys.
- White teens from high-income and high-education households are more likely to turn to parents for advice.
- Teens who have sought advice take similar measures to protect their online presence as do those who have not sought advice.

It is evident from the research that social networking sites figure prominently and are an essential part of children's lives. The data show that almost all teens have used social media at some point, many use more than one site, and may visit the site more than once a day. Teens are, however, becoming less enthusiastic about using some social media, such as Facebook, and wish they could disconnect at times and that others would do so also. Children feel that they do a good job of managing their online profiles and employ various measures to keep their information private, though at the same time, they are not worried about third-party access to their personal data.

Digital Media, New Literacies, Digital Youth

A related research area which serves to help us better understand children and information technology is that of digital media use and new literacies from the fields of education and communication. While a bit out of scope for this entry, what we are learning from studies in this area is informing research and practice, specifically in public and school libraries. To study the "digital native" or "digital youth," Ito and colleagues undertook a ground breaking study to explore the social and cultural influences of new media practices on today's youth, and to determine how digital media are changing the way young people learn, play, socialize, and participate in civic life. Their 3-year multiproject study funded by the MacArthur Foundation included a comprehensive ethnographic study of 700 youth. The researchers developed a framework of "genres of participation" that helped to describe different levels of commitment of youth engagement with new media such as social networking sites, YouTube, or chatrooms.[72,106] According to Ito and colleagues, "Instead of looking to rigid categories that are defined by formal properties, genres of participation are a way of identifying, in an interpretive way, a set of social, cultural, and technological characteristics that participants recognize as defining a set of practices" (16).[72] Ito and colleagues' genres of participation include:

- *Friendship-driven* genres of participation, the dominant and mainstream practices of youth as they go about their day-to-day negotiations with friends and peers in various contexts, such as school, religious groups, school sports, and other local activity groups. Facebook is an example of an online context for friendship-driven genres of participation.
- *Interest-driven* genres of participation put specialized activities, interests, or niche and marginalized identities first. Interest-driven practices of youth are described by young people as "the domain of the geeks, freaks, musicians, artists, and dorks, who are identified as smart, different, or creative, and who generally exist at the margins of teen social worlds" (13).[72] Interest-driven genres of participation are driven by a young person's interests in hobbies, finding information on specific topics, and in their desire to be seen as an "expert" in their particular interest. Relationships are formed on this premise, rather than for social or interaction interests as seen in the friendship-driven genre.

Ito and colleagues also determined that young people engage with media at different levels of commitment: "1) they 'hang out' with friends in social spaces such as Facebook and MySpace; 2) they 'mess around' or tinker with digital media, making simple videos, playing online games, or posting pictures in Flickr; and 3) they 'geek out' in online groups that facilitate exploration of their core interests" (9).[3,72]

This typology of engagement by digital youth is called HOMAGO and is the basis for the connected learning philosophy [website], and the pedagogical framework for emerging interactive learning spaces in libraries and museums called Learning Labs and Makerspaces.

Dresang's Radical Change Theory may provide the bridge that is needed to explore the issues associated with digital youth's media use and ELIS. Dresang and Koh[107] suggest using Radical Change Theory as a framework for understanding more about how digital youth think and seek information, perceive themselves and others, and access information and seek community. They explain that Radical Change theory is "based on the digital age principles of interactivity, connectivity, and access. This theory provides a promising theoretical framework for explaining contemporary changes in information behavior and resources as well as for serving as a guide for investigative studies and professional practice." (27) The typology[108] includes three facets:

1. *Interactivity* refers to the dynamic, nonlinear, and nonsequential learning and information behavior in the digital age.
2. *Connectivity* is the sense of community and development of online social worlds that have emerged from young people's changing perspectives and expanded associations.
3. *Access* is described as breaking down the longstanding information and access barriers and giving young people access to a wider diversity of formerly largely inaccessible opinions.

Building on Dresang's earlier typology and incorporating findings from new media studies,[72,106,107,109–111] Dresang and Koh extended the theory to identify three types of information behavior of digital age youth. The three types include:

1. Type One: Changing forms of seeking information and learning (or how youth seek information and learn)
   a. obtaining information from a variety of sources
   b. multitasking
   c. preference for graphic and visual information
   d. seeking information nonlinearly and nonsequentially
   e. developing self-defined and controlled paths
2. Type Two: Changing perspectives (or how youth perceive themselves and others)
   a. expressing opinions for themselves
   b. portraying flexible and multiple identities
   c. encountering information from various perspectives
3. Type Three: Changing boundaries (or how they access information and seek community)
   a. obtaining instant access to a wide array of information

   b. seeking, sharing, and creating information collaboratively
   c. forming new types of social networks
   d. participating in community engagement (29).[107]

An outcome of the digital media, new literacies, and connected learning initiatives that is directly related to LIS and to libraries specifically is the integration of technologies into interactive learning spaces, such as Learning Labs or Makerspaces, to facilitate STEM learning. Little research has been done on the efficacy and usefulness of these spaces and while the literature itself is proliferating almost as quickly as these new spaces themselves, it focuses mainly on: 1) history and models of Makerspaces/Learning Labs;[112,113] 2) case studies or informal reports of how specific libraries or museums developed their Makerspace or Learning Lab;[114–116] 3) advice and resources for how to start a Makerspace or Learning Lab;[117,118] and 4) models and technology suggested for use and sample projects.[119] The limited research literature relates to surveying libraries in the United States and seven other countries about the presence of Makerspaces in their organization or their plans to develop one in the future; issues related to funding, programming, and the top technologies used by library Makerspaces[120] and a study by Koh and Abbas about the competencies needed by library and information professionals who work in Learning Labs or Makerspaces in U.S. libraries or museums.[121]

CONCLUSIONS

The research focused on children and information technology shows a picture of children as digital youth who are engaged, connected, creative users, not just consumers of information technologies, but who still encounter many issues when searching for information using information technologies. Information behavior and retrieval studies provide us with a better understanding of how children use information technology to search for information they need for activities and decision making within their everyday lives, to create within collaborative environments, and the roles children display while searching online. Research has also found that social networking sites have become even more essential in the daily, digital lives of children, thereby requiring more research into the sociocultural, psychosocial, ethical, legal, and pragmatic issues faced by youth as they use these information and communication technologies to engage with others. As we learn more about how children interact with information technology, and within digital ecologies, it is important to remember that children are still children who will still go through the same experimental, explorative process of play, communication, and emotional and psychosocial development as children always have, and to them information technology is a necessity in many of their social worlds.

ACKNOWLEDGMENTS

My sincere thanks to my research assistant, Anna-Rose Cozad, for her invaluable assistance in searching, sifting, and making sense of the morass of literature on children and information technology. I would also like to thank my long-time collaborator and friend, Dr. Denise Agosto, for always championing the view that children and information technology must be studied as a unique subgroup but also approached from a holistic perspective.

REFERENCES

1. Fasick, A. Children's use of information technology. In *Encyclopedia of Library and Information Science*; Marcel Dekker, Inc.: New York, 1995, Vol. 55, 51–69.

2. Prensky, M. Digital natives, digital immigrants. Horizon **2001**, *9*, 1–5.

3. Boyd, D. *It's Complicated: The Social Lives of Networked Teens*; Yale University Press: Boston, MA, 2013.

4. Abbas, J. Children and information technology. In *Encyclopedia of Library and Information Science*, 2nd Ed.; Marcel Dekker, Inc.: New York, 2003; 512–521.

5. Abbas, J. Children and information technology. In *Encyclopedia of Library and Information Science*; Taylor & Francis: New York, 2005; 1–9.

6. Abbas, J. Children and information technology. In *Encyclopedia of Library and Information Science*, 3rd Ed. 1:1; Marcel Dekker, Inc.: New York, 2010; 930–941.

7. Ministry of Education. *10th News Conference: The Situation of Chinese Rural Education Development and Reform*, October 27, 2008, http://moe.gov.cn/edoas/website18/89/info1224841874637489.htm (accessed September 30, 2014).

8. Ministry of Education. *2nd News Conference: The Utilization of Rural Distance Education Equipment*, http://www.moe.gov.cn/edoas/website18/88/info1203994285182188.htm (accessed September 30, 2014).

9. International Telecommunication Union. *Measuring the Information Society*. 2003 Executive Summary. International Telecommunication Union: Geneva, Switzerland, http://www.itu.int/go/mis2013 (accessed September 30, 2014).

10. Rideout, V. *Zero to Eight: Children's Media Use in America 2013*; Common Sense Media: San Francisco, CA, 2013, http://www.commonsense.org/research (accessed September 30, 2014).

11. Madden, M.; Lenhart, A.; Duggan, M.; Cortesi, S.; Gasser, U. *Teens and Technology*; Pew Research Center: Washington, DC, 2013, http://www.pewinternet.org/Reports/2013/Teens-and-Tech.aspx (accessed September 30, 2014).

12. Cool, C. Information-seeking behaviors of children using electronic information services during the early years: 1980–1990. In *Youth Information Seeking Behavior*; Chelton, M.K., Cool, C., Eds.; Scarecrow Press: Lanham, MD, 2004; 1–36.

13. Large, A. Children, teens and the Web. In *The Annual Review of Information Science and Technology*; Cronin, B., Ed.; Information Today: Medford, NJ, 2005; 347–392.

14. Pew Research Center's Internet and American Life Project. http://www.pewinternet.org (accessed September 30, 2014).

15. Lenhart, A.; Simon, M.; Graziano, M. *The Internet and Education: Findings of the Pew Internet & American Life Project*; Pew Research Center: Washington, DC, 2001, http://www.pewinternet.org (accessed September 30, 2014).

16. Corporation for Public Broadcasting. *Connected to the Future: A Report of Children's Internet Use from the Corporation for Public Broadcasting*, Washington, D.C., 2004, http://cpb.org/ed/resources/connected (accessed September 30, 2014).

17. Media Awareness Group. *The Young Canadians in a Wired World: The Student's View*, 2003, http://www.media-awareness.ca/english/research/ycww/index.cfm (accessed September 30, 2014); See also the companion piece, *Canada's Children in a Wired World: The Parents' View* (available online at the same URL).

18. NetDay. *Voices and Views from Today's Tech-Savvy Students: National Report on Netday Speak Up Day for Students*, 2003, http://www.tomorrow.org/index.html (accessed September 30, 2014); See also the companion piece, *Preliminary High-lights from Netday Speak Up Day for Teachers 2004* (available online at the same URL).

19. Bilal, D. Children's information seeking and the design of digital interfaces in the affective paradigm. Libr. Trends **2005**, *54* (2), 197–208.

20. Pew Research Institute. *Teens and Technology: Youth Are Leading the Transition to a Fully Wired and Mobile Nation*; Pew Research Center: Washington, DC, 2005, http://www.pewinternet.org/pdfs/PIP_Teens_Tech_July2005web.pdf (accessed September 30, 2014).

21. Pew Research Institute. *Teen Content Creators and Consumers*; Pew Research Center: Washington, DC, 2004, http://www.pewinternet.org/pdfs/PIP_Teens_Content_Creation.pdf (accessed September 30, 2014).

22. Pew Research Institute. *Cyberbullying and Online Teens*. Memo Released June 27, 2007, Pew Research Center: Washington, DC, 2007, http://www.pewinternet.org/pdfs/PIP%20Cyberbullying%20Memo.pdf (accessed September 30, 2014).

23. Pew Research Institute. *Teens, Privacy and Online Social Networks*; Pew Research Center: Washington, DC, 2006, http://www.pewinternet.org/pdfs/PIP_Teens_Privacy_SNS_Report_Final.pdf (accessed September 30, 2014).

24. Pew Research Institute. *Protecting Teens Online: More than Half of American Families with Teenagers Use Filters to Limit Access to Potentially Harmful Content Online*; Pew Research Center: Washington, DC, 2005, http://www.pewinternet.org/pdfs/PIP_Filters_Report.pdf (accessed September 30, 2014).

25. Pew Research Institute. *Teens and the Internet*; Pew Research Center: Washington, DC, 2006, http://www.pewinternet.org/ppt/Pew%20Internet%20findings%20%20

teens%20and%20the%20internet%20-%20fi (accessed September 30, 2014).

26. Wilson, T.D. Human information behavior. Inform. Sci. **2000**, *3* (2), 49–55.

27. Fisher, K.E.; Erdelez, S.; McKechnie, L. *Theories of Information Behavior*; Information Today, Inc.: Medford, NJ, 2005.

28. Koh, K. Adolescents' information-creating behavior embedded in digital media practice using Scratch. J. Am. Soc. Inf. Sci. Technol. **2013**, *64* (9), 1826–1841.

29. Harlan, M.A.; Bruce, C.; Lupton, M. Teen content creators: experiences of using information to learn. Libr. Trends **2012**, *60* (3), 569–587.

30. Hwang, J.; Cheong, P.H.; Feeley, T.H. Being young and feeling blue in Taiwan: examining adolescent depressive mood and online and offline activities. New Media Soc. **2009**, *11* (7), 1101–1121.

31. Kim, S.U.; Syn, S.Y. Research trends in teens' health information behavior: a review of the literature. Health Inf. Libr. J. **2014**, *31*, 4–19.

32. Schnall, R.; Okoniewski, A.; Tiase, V.; Low, A.; Rodriguez, M.; Kaplan, S. Using text messaging to assess adolescents' health information needs: an ecological momentary assessment. J. Med. Internet Res. **2013**, *15* (3), e54.

33. Veinot, T.C.; Campbell, T.R.; Kruger, D.J.; Grodzinski, A. A question of trust: user-centered design requirements for an informatics intervention to promote the sexual health of African-American youth. J. Am. Med. Inform. Assoc. **2013**, *20*, 758–765.

34. Sen, B.A.; Spring, H. Mapping the information-coping trajectory of young people with terminal illness. An evidence based approach. J. Doc. **2013**, *69* (5), 638–666.

35. Lu, Y.-L. Children's information seeking in coping with daily-life problems: an investigation of fifth- and sixth-grade students. Libr. Inf. Sci. Res. **2010**, *32*, 77–88.

36. Haras, C. Information behaviors of Latinos attending high school in East Los Angeles. Libr. Inf. Sci. Res. **2011**, *33*, 34–40.

37. Robinson, L. Information channel preferences and information opportunity structures. Inf. Commun. Soc. **2011**, *14* (4), 472–494.

38. Savolainen, R. Everyday life information seeking: approaching information seeking in the context of 'way of life'. Libr. Inf. Sci. Res. **1995**, *17*, 259–294.

39. Abbas, J.; Agosto, D. Everyday life information behavior of young people. In *The Information Behavior of a New Generation*; Beheshti, J., Large, A., Eds.; Scarecrow Press: Toronto, Ontario, Canada, 2013; 65–91.

40. Behesti, J.; Large, A. *The Information Behavior of a New Generation*; Scarecrow Press: Toronto, Ontario, Canada, 2013.

41. Agosto, D.E.; Abbas, J. High school seniors' social network and other ICT use preferences and concerns. Proc. Am. Soc. Inf. Sci. Technol. **2010**, *47*, 1–10.

42. Agosto, D.E.; Abbas, J.; Naughton, R. Relationships and social rules: teens' social network and other ICT selection practices. J. Am. Soc. Inf. Sci. Technol. **2012**, *63* (6), 1108–1124.

43. Fox, S.; Jones, S. *The Social Life of Health Information*; Pew Internet & American Life Project: Washington, DC, 2009, http://www.pewinternet.org/~/media//Files/Reports/2009/PIP_Health_2009.pdf (accessed September 30, 2014).

44. Lenhart, A.; Purcell, K.; Smith, A.; Zickuhr, K. *Social Media and Mobile Internet Use among Teens and Young Adults*; Pew Internet & American Life Project: Washington, DC, 2010, http://pewinternet.org/Reports/2010/Social-Media-and-Young-Adults.aspx (accessed September 30, 2014).

45. Larsen, J.N.; Martey, R.M. Adolescents seeking nutrition information: motivations, sources and the role of the internet. Int. J. Inf. Commun. Technol. Educ. **2011**, *7* (3), 74–89.

46. Gabarron, E.; Serrano, J.A.; Wynn, R.; Armayones, M. Avatars using computer/smartphone mediated communication and social networking in prevention of sexually transmitted diseases among North-Norwegian youngsters. BMC Med. Inform. Decis. Mak. **2012**, *12*, 120.

47. Rasmussen-Pennington, D.; Richardson, G.; Garinger, C.; Contursi, M.L. I could be on Facebook by now: insights from Canadian youth on online mental health information resources. Can. J. Inf. Libr. Sci. **2013**, *37* (3), 183–200.

48. Van der Velden, M.; El Emam, K. Not all my friends need to know: a qualitative study of teenage patients, privacy, and social media. J. Am. Med. Inform. Assoc. **2013**, *20*, 16–24.

49. Mehra, B.; Braquet, D. Process of information seeking during 'queer' youth coming-out experiences. In *Youth Information Seeking Behavior II: Contexts, Theories, Models, and Issues*; Chelton, M.K., Cool, C., Eds.; Scarecrow Press: Lanham, MA, 2007; 93–131.

50. Spink, A.; Danby, S.; Mallan, K.; Butler, C. Exploring young children's web searching and technoliteracy. J. Doc. **2010**, *66* (2), 191–206.

51. Bilal, D.; Ellis, R. Evaluating leading Web search engines on children's queries. In *HCII'11: Proceedings of the 14th International Conference on Human-Computer Interaction: Users and Applications*, Part IV; Jacko, J.A., Ed.; Springer: Berlin, Germany, 2011; 549–558.

52. Bilal, D. Ranking, relevance judgment, and precision of information retrieval on children's queries: evaluation of Google, Yahoo!, Bing, Yahoo! Kids, and Ask Kids. J. Am. Soc. Inf. Sci. Technol. **2012**, *63* (9), 1879–1896.

53. Behesti, J.; Large, A.; Tam, M. Transaction logs and search patterns on a children's portal. Can. J. Inf. Libr. Sci. **2010**, *34* (4), 391–402.

54. Inamullah, A.; Ansari, M.N. Internet browsing habit of school children: a comparison of Metric and Cambridge School children. Pak. Libr. Inf. Sci. J. **2012**, *43* (2), 3–10.

55. Foss, E.; Druin, A.; Yip, J.; Ford, W.; Golub, E. Children's search roles at home: implications for designers, researchers, educators, and parents. J. Am. Soc. Inf. Sci. Technol. **2012**, *63* (3), 558–573.

56. Foss, E.; Druin, A.; Yip, J.; Ford, W.; Golub, E. Adolescent search roles. J. Am. Soc. Inf. Sci. Technol. **2013**, *64* (1), 173–189.

57. Torres, S.D.; Hiemstra, D. Query recommendation in the information domain of children. J. Assoc. Inf. Sci. Technol. **2014**, *65* (7), 1368–1384.

58. Purcell, K.; Rainie, L.; Heaps, A.; Buchanan, J.; Friedrich, J.A.; Chen, C.; Zichur, K. *How Teens Do Research in the Digital World*; Pew Research Center: Washington, DC, 2012, http://www.pewinternet.org/Reports/2012/Student-Research (accessed September 30, 2014).

59. Cortesi, S.; Haduong, P.; Gasser, U.; Aricak, O.S.; Saldana, M.; Lerner, Z. *Youth Perspectives on Tech in Schools: From Mobile Devices to Restrictions and Monitoring*; The Berkman Center for Internet & Society, Harvard University: Cambridge, MA, 2014. https://cyber.law.harvard.edu/publications/2014/youth_perspectives (accessed September 30, 2014).

60. Gossen, T.; Nurnberger, A. Specifics of information retrieval for young users: a survey. Inf. Process. Manage. **2012**, *49*, 739–756.

61. Madden, M.; Lenhart, A.; Cortesi, S.; Gasser, U.; Duggan, M.; Smith, A.; Beaton, M. *Teens, Social Media, and Privacy*; Pew Research Center: Washington, DC, 2013, http://pewinternet.org/Reports/2013/Teens-Social-Media-And-Privacy.aspx (accessed September 30, 2014).

62. Anttiroiko, A.; Savolainen, R. Towards library 2.0: the adoption of web 2.0 technologies in public libraries. Libri **2011**, *61*, 87–99.

63. Agosto, D.; Abbas, J. Youth and online social networking: what do we know so far?. In *The Information Behavior of a New Generation*; Beheshti, J.; Large, A., Eds.; Scarecrow Press: Toronto, Ontario, Canada, 2013; 117–141.

64. Boyd, D. Friends, friendsters, and MySpace top 8: writing community into being on social network sites. First Monday, **2006**, 11. http://www.firstmonday.org/issues/issue11_12/boyd/index.html.

65. Boyd, D. Why youth (heart) social network sites: the role of networked publics in teenage social life. In *Youth, Identity, and Digital Media*, The John D. and Catherine T. MacArthur Foundation Series on Digital Media and Learning; Buckingham, D., Ed.; The MIT Press: Cambridge, MA, 2008; 119–142.

66. Livingstone, S.; Brake, D. On the rapid rise of social networking sites: new findings and policy implications. Child. Soc. **2010**, *24*, 75–83.

67. Agosto, D.E.; Abbas, J. Teens, social networking, and safety and privacy issues. In *Teens, Libraries, and Social Networking: What Librarians Need to Know*; Agosto, D.E., Abbas, J., Eds.; Libraries Unlimited: Santa Barbara, CA, 2011; 59–75.

68. Bonetti, L.; Campbell, M.; Gilmore, L. The relationship of loneliness and social anxiety with children's and adolescents' online communication. Cyberpsychol. Behav. Soc. Netw. **2010**, *13*, 279–283.

69. Clarke, B.H. Early adolescents' use of social networking sites to maintain friendship and explore identity: implications for policy. Policy Internet. 2009; 1. http://www.psocommons.org/policyandinternet/vol1/iss1/art3.

70. Greenhow, C.; Robelia, B. Old communication, new literacies: social network sites as social learning resources. J. Comput.-Mediat. Commun. **2009**, *14*, 1130–1161.

71. Hundlcy, H.L.; Shylcs, L. US teenagers' perceptions and awareness of digital technology: a focus group approach. New Media Soc. **2010**, *12*, 417–433.

72. Ito, M.; Judd, A. *Hanging Out, Messing Around, and Geeking Out: Kids Living and Learning with New Media*; MIT Press: Cambridge, MA, 2010.

73. Luckin, R. Do Web 2.0 tools really open the door to learning? Practices, perceptions and profiles of 11-16-year-old students. Learning, Media Technol. **2009**, *34*, 87–104.

74. Pierce, T. Social anxiety and technology: face-to-face communication versus technological communication among teens. Comput. Hum. Behav. **2009**, *25*, 1367–1372.

75. Spires, H.A.; Lee, J.K.; Turner, K.A.; Johnson, J. Having our say: middle grade student perspectives on school, technologies, and academic engagement. J. Res. Technol. Educ. **2008**, *40*, 497–515.

76. Baker, R.K.; White, K.M. Predicting adolescents' use of social networking sites from an extended theory of planned behaviour perspective. Comput. Hum. Behav. **2010**, *26*, 1591–1597.

77. Livingstone, S. Taking risky opportunities in youthful content creation: teenagers' use of social networking site for intimacy, privacy, and self-expression. New Media Soc. **2008**, *10*, 393–411.

78. Mallan, K. Look at me! Look at me! Self-representation and self-exposure through online networks. Digit. Cult. Educ. **2009**, *1*, 51–66.

79. Pfeil, U.; Arjan, R.; Zaphiris, P. Age differences in online social networking: a study of user profiles and the social capital divide among teenagers and older users in MySpace. Comput. Hum. Behav. **2009**, *5*, 643–654.

80. Williams, A.L.; Merten, M.J. Adolescents' online social networking following the death of a peer. J. Adolesc. Res. **2009**, *24*, 67–90.

81. Read, P.; Shah, C.; O-Brien, L.S.; Woolcott, J. Story of one's life and a tree of friends'—understanding Millenials' information behavior in social networks. J. Inf. Sci. **2012**, *38* (5), 489–497.

82. Ahn, J. The effect of social network sites on adolescents' social and academic development: current theories and controversies. J. Am. Soc. Inf. Sci. Technol. **2011**, *62*, 1435–1445.

83. Ahn, J. Teenagers and social network sites: do off-line inequities predict their online social networks? First Monday. **2012**, *17* (1), http://journals.uic.edu/ojs/index.php/fm/rt/printerFriendly/3752.

84. Antheunis, M.L.; Schouten, A.P. The effects of other-generated and system-generated cues on adolescents' perceived attractiveness on social network sites. J. Comput.-Mediat. Commun. **2011**, *16*, 391–406.

85. Durrant, A.; Frohlich, D.; Sellen, A.; Uzzell, D. The secret life of teens: online versus offline photographic displays at home. Vis. Stud. **2011**, *26*, 113–124.

86. Greenhow, C.; Robelia, B. Informal learning and identity formation in online social networks. Learn. Media Technol. **2009**, *34*, 119–140.

87. Williams, A.L.; Merten, M.J. A review of online social networking profiles by adolescents: implications for future research and intervention. Adolescence **2008**, *24*, 253–275.

88. Helsper, E.J.; Eynon, R. Digital natives: where is the evidence? Br. Educ. Res. J. **2010**, *36*, 503–520.

89. Livingstone, S.; Helsper, E. Balancing opportunities and risks in teenagers' use of the internet: the role of online skills and internet self-efficacy. New Media Soc. **2010**, *12*, 309–329.

90. Dike, V.; Eke, H.N.; Babarinde, E.T. Social media and reading among secondary school students in Enugu State Nigeria. Mousaion **2013**, *31* (1), 61–82.

91. Valkenburg, P.M.; Peter, J.; Schouten, J. Friend networking sites and their relationship to adolescents' well-being

and social self-esteem. Cyberpsychol. Behav. **2006**, *9*, 584–590.

92. Christofides, E.; Muise, A.; Desmarais, S. Hey Mom, what's on your facebook? Comparing facebook disclosure and privacy in adolescents and adults. Soc. Psychol. Personal. Sci. **2012**, *3* (1), 48–54.

93. De Souza, Z.; Dick, G.N. Disclosure of information by children in social networking-not just a case of 'you show me yours and I'll show you mine'. Int. J. Inf. Manage. **2009**, *29*, 255–261.

94. Hinduja, S.; Patchin, J.W. Personal information of adolescents on the internet: a qualitative content analysis of MySpace. J. Adolesc. **2008**, *31*, 125–146.

95. Patchin, J.W.; Hinduja, S. Trends in online social networking: adolescent use of MySpace over time. New Media Soc. **2010**, *12*, 197–216.

96. Fuller, H.A.; Damico, A.M. Keeping pace with teen media use: implications and strategies for educators. J. Educ. Res. **2008**, *101*, 323–330.

97. Moreno, M.A. Real use or 'real cool': adolescents speak out about displayed alcohol references on social networking websites. J. Adolesc. Health **2009**, *45*, 420–422.

98. Rosen, L.D.; Cheever, N.A.; Carrier, L.M. An association of parenting style and child age with parental limit setting and adolescent MySpace behavior. J. Appl. Dev. Psychol. **2008**, *29*, 459–471.

99. Sengupta, A.; Chaudhuri, A. Are social networking sites a source of online harassment for teens? Evidence from survey data. Child. Youth Serv. Rev. **2011**, *33*, 284–290.

100. Ybarra, M.L.; Mitchell, K.J. How risky are social networking sites? A comparison of places online where youth sexual solicitation and harassment occurs. Pediatrics **2008**, *121*, 350–357.

101. Davidson, J.; Martellozzo, E. Exploring young people's use of social networking sites and digital media in the Internet safety context. Inf. Commun. Soc. **2013**, *16* (9), 1456–1476.

102. Levy, N.; Cortesi, S.; Gasser, U.; Crowley, E.; Beaton, M.; Casey, J.; Nolan, C. *Bullying in a Networked Era: A Literature Review*; The Berkman Center for Internet & Society, Harvard University: Cambridge, MA, 2012, http://cyber.law.harvard.edu/node/7491 (accessed September 30, 2014).

103. Sacco, D.; Silbaugh, K.; Corredor, F.; Casey, J.; Doherty, D. *On Overview of State Anti-Bullying Legislation and Other Related Laws*; The Berkman Center for Internet & Society, Harvard University: Cambridge, MA, 2012, http://cyber.law.harvard.edu/State_Antibullying_Law_Overview_0.pdf (accessed September 30, 2014).

104. Rideout, V. *Social Media, Social Life: How Teens View Their Digital Lives*; Common Sense Media: San Francisco, CA. http://www.commonsense.org/research.

105. Lenhart, A.; Madden, M.; Cortesi, S.; Gasser, U.; Smith, A. *Where Teens Seek Online Privacy Advice*; Pew Research Center: Washington, DC, 2013, http://pewinternet.org/Reports/2013/Where-Teens-Seek-Privacy-Advice.aspx (accessed September 30, 2014).

106. Ito, M.; Horst, H.; Bittanti, M.; Boyd, D.; Herr-Stephenson, B.; Lange, P.G.; Pascoe, P.J.; Robinson, L. *Living and Learning with New Media: Summary of Findings from the Digital Youth Project*, The John D. and Catherine T. MacArthur Foundation Series on Digital Media and Learning. MIT Press: Cambridge, MA, 2008, http://www.macfound.org/press/publications/living-and-learning-with-new-media-summary-of-findings-from-the-digital-youth-project/ (accessed September 30, 2014).

107. Dresang, E.; Koh, K. Radical change theory, youth information behavior, and school libraries. Libr. Trends **2009**, *58* (1), 26–50.

108. Dresang, E. *Radical Change: Books for Youth in a Digital Age*; H.W. Wilson: New York, 1999.

109. Buckingham, D. Introducing identity. In *Youth, Identity, and Digital Media*; MIT Press: Cambridge, MA, 2008; 25–47.

110. Gee, J.P. *What Video Games Teach Us About Learning and Literacy*; Palgrave McMillan: New York, 2007.

111. Jenkins, H. *Convergence Culture: Where Old and New Media Collide*; New York University Press: New York, 2006.

112. Abram, S. Makerspaces in libraries, education, and beyond. Internet Schools **2013**, 18–20.

113. Mayo, J. Learning labs learning curve: The Digital Media Lab-Kansas City Project. Young Adult Library Services **Winter 2013**, 32–34.

114. Britton, L. A fabulous laboratory: the makerspace at Fayetteville Free Library. Publ. Libr. **2012**, *51* (4), 30–33.

115. Jensen, K. Tapping into teen's creativity and turning libraries into makerspaces. Voya **2013**, *36* (3), 25.

116. Haug, C. Here's how we did it: the story of the EPL makerspace. **Feliciter 2014**, *60* (1), 21–23.

117. American Library Association. *Digital Literacy, Libraries, and Public Policy*. Report of the Office for Information Technology Policy's Digital Literacy Taskforce. American Library Association: Chicago, IL, 2013, http://www.districtdispatch.org/wp-content/uploads/2013/01/2012_OITP_digilitreport_1_22_13.pdf (accessed September 30, 2014).

118. Maker Media. *MakerSpace Playbook School Edition 2013*, http://makerspace.com/wp-content/uploads/2012/04/makerspaceplaybook-201204.pdf (accessed September 30, 2014).

119. Loertscher, D.; Preddy, L.; Derry, B. Makerspaces in the school library learning commons and the Utec Maker Model. Teach. Libr. **2013**, *41* (2), 48–51.

120. Burke, J. *MakerSpaces in Libraries Survey Results*. 2013, http://www.users.miamioh.edu/burkejj/Makerspaces%20in%20Libraries%20Survey%20Results%202013.pdf (accessed September 30, 2014).

121. Koh, K.; Abbas, J. Competencies for information professionals in Learning Labs and Makerspaces. J. Educ. Libr. Inf. Sci. **2015**, *56* (2), 114–129.

Chemistry–China

Children's Literature

Judith V. Lechner
Department of Educational Foundations, Leadership, and Technology, Auburn University, Auburn, Alabama, U.S.A.

Abstract
"Children's Literature" describes literary works written for children and young adults. The entry uses a genre approach to organize the literature and focuses on historical and contemporary English language and to a lesser degree international children's literature that has been translated into English.

INTRODUCTION

The adults concerned about the books children read—parents, educators, authors, editors, critics, though not the children—define "literature" using demarcations based on quality, genre, and even format. The poet Walter de la Mare's comment that "only the rarest kind of best in anything can be good enough for the young" (cited in Silvey, p. 121),[1] exemplifies the emphasis on literary quality in books for children, as do most literary awards such as the Newbery and Caldecott Medals. Instructions for the awards committees state that popularity is not a consideration. In terms of genre, "literature" is often restricted to imaginative writing. Although occasionally the Newbery Medal has been awarded for informational books and biographies, not until 1990 and 2001 did the National Council of Teachers of English and the American Library Association (ALA), respectively, establish awards for informational books and biographies for children. Concepts of formats that can be considered literature have also changed over time. Two graphic novels, a format that was formerly labeled "subliterature," were recognized for the first time in 2007 by two ALA awards.

Childhood too is a relative concept. The age of responsibility, when childhood is considered to be at an end, has risen since the beginnings of the industrial revolution, while the age at which children are considered capable of comprehending complex issues, from sexuality to social problems, has fluctuated across both time and place. The trend since the 1960s has been to introduce complex issues to children at younger ages than in the nineteenth and early twentieth centuries, but serious social issues are more likely to be introduced in European than American children's books for elementary school age children.[2]

This entry will use Rebecca Lukens's definition of children's literature in *A Critical Handbook of Children's Literature*: "...the body of writing that exists because of inherent imaginative and artistic qualities" (p. 3).[3] Lukens emphasizes the importance of pleasure the author aspires to evoke in the implied reader, the child; the understanding the work is likely to engender through the "exploration of the human condition"; and the form literature provides for the reader to make meaning of the fragmented experiences of life (pp. 4–6). Children's literature will refer to literature written for an audience from the youngest child to age 14, the limitation set for the Newbery Medal, but each section of the entry will also discuss literature written for young adults, which refers to literature that considers the perspectives and interests of young people between ages 11 and 18. After a brief history of children's literature, the entry will discuss various genres of children's and young adult literature; international and multicultural children's literature; and nonbook media, and will list literary awards and some of the major organizations devoted to children's literature.

HISTORY OF CHILDREN'S LITERATURE

The history of children's literature in the sense the term is used today, is no more than 250 years old. Social, economic, and technological factors contributed to its development in the industrializing England of the eighteenth century. Similar developments took place elsewhere in Europe and North America in the nineteenth century and in East Asia in the late nineteenth, early twentieth centuries. Children's literature in Latin America, Africa, and much of Asia has been developing since the middle of the twentieth century. The costs of paper, printing, and distribution, as well as standard of living affect the extent to which a country or region can afford to create books for children.

For most of human history, children and adults shared the orally transmitted stories passed on within communities for the purpose of acculturating, instructing, and entertaining them in both secular and sacred matters. Some recorded fables and books of prayer, however, did become available to children and were used for their education. Manuscripts of Aesop's fables, for instance, were used throughout Western Europe in the Middle Ages to teach

Encyclopedia of Library and Information Sciences, Fourth Edition DOI: 10.1081/E-ELIS4-120043452

Greek and Latin, rhetoric and grammar, as well as ethical behavior to a small minority of children.[4,5] The majority of children, however, continued to be educated through sacred and secular oral narratives; drama; poetry and nursery rhymes; and visual representations.

The democratization of literacy and the slow evolution of material published expressly for children began with the development of the printing press by Gutenberg in the mid-1400s. One of the first English printed books, published in 1484, William Caxton's *Aesop's Fables*, however, was not meant for children alone, but rather for ordinary people of all ages, "for to shewe to all maner of folk what maner of thing they ought to ensyeew and folowe" (p. 9).[5] The books published in the following few centuries for children were didactic, meant for their spiritual and social edification, with little regard to the pleasures of reading. The hornbook (see Fig. 1), published

Fig. 1 Facsimile/replica of a Horn Book—printed by Otto Miller at Thomas Todd printing shop on Beacon Hill for the Horn Book, Inc. With permission.

between the sixteenth and mid-eighteenth centuries, consisted of the alphabet and a syllabary, as well as the Lord's Prayer. The battledore, a trifold piece of cardboard, which largely replaced the hornbook in the middle of the eighteenth century as paper became less expensive, included not only the alphabet and a syllabary, but also single words with woodcut images accompanying them and a brief verse or Biblical quotation. Grammars, books of manners, and religious tracts designed to induce children to lead virtuous, Christian lives, were the staple of seventeenth century English publishing. Much of this material was meant for the schoolroom, but some books, such as James Janeway's *A Token for Children, an Exact Account of the Conversion, Holy and Exemplary Lives of and Joyful Deaths of Several Young Children*, (1671–1672), were intended for children's leisure reading. Aesop's fables continued to be used as well, as one of the more entertaining ways of teaching, and were frequently republished with new morals. John Locke in 1703 first emphasized the importance of using Aesop with illustrations specifically meant for children to help them understand the meanings of the words and to entice them to a love of reading.[5]

During the late seventeenth and early eighteenth centuries, folk and fairy tales became popular adult literature and influenced children's literature. The 12 volume *Arabian Nights Entertainment* or *One Thousand and One Nights (Mille et une Nuits)*, known as *Alf layla wa layla* in Arabic, translated into French by Antoine Galland between 1704 and 1712, and into English between 1705 and 1716, was one of the most influential sources. This compilation of oral and written tales included philosophical, romantic, and even pornographic stories. "Aladdin," "Ali Baba and the Forty Thieves," and "Sinbad" as well as the frame story of Scheherazade have been most frequently retold for children. The stories influenced European writers, such as the German Wilhelm Hauff, to create their own "Oriental" stories. Even more influential were the artfully retold folk tales and literary fairy tales written by French upper class women, and some men such as Charles Perrault, who used them as a safe form of protest against both Louis the XIV's excessive taxation and the social conditions of marriage for women.[6,7] Charles Perrault's 1697 *Histoire ou Contes du Temps Passé* popularly known as *Contes de ma Mère l'Ois* [Tales of My Mother Goose], translated into English in 1729, and Jeanne Marie le Prince de Beaumont's "La Belle et la Bête" (1756), translated into English in 1761 as "Beauty and the Beast," have remained popular as children's literature and were the sources of Disney's film adaptations. The popular title of Perrault's fairy tales collection, "Mother Goose," however, has been attached to nursery rhymes, rather than fairy tales, ever since John Newbery published *Mother Goose's Melody or Sonnets for the Cradle* (1765).

To obtain imaginative literature, seventeenth and eighteenth century children adopted adult books as their own.

The three most influential and popular of these were John Bunyan's *The Pilgrim's Progress* (1678), a Christian allegory with an adventurous plot; Daniel Defoe's *Robinson Crusoe* (1719), a celebration of middle class self-reliance; and Jonathan Swift's *Gulliver's Travels* (1726), a political and philosophical satire with a fantasy setting.[5]

The chapbook was the main source of imaginative literature for children of the eighteenth century. Door-to-door peddlers, or chapmen, carried a variety of inexpensive wares, including these cheaply made folded paper books whose front page served as the cover and whose stories often ended where the paper had to be cut. Chapbooks, with their legends; medieval romances, including those of King Arthur; fairy tales, including stories from the Arabian Nights and Perrault; lurid true crime stories; jokes; and recipes, stimulated the imaginations of children such as the poet William Wordsworth, who had to read them surreptitiously because they were considered low class.[8,9]

Active publishing for children began with John Newbery, a book publisher whose sideline of selling patent medicines allowed him to finance his venture into publishing for the children of the newly rising middle class. Newbery's *A Little Pretty Pocketbook* (1744), a small attractive illustrated book, is often credited with having been the first book for children. It was based on John Locke's educational philosophy of enticing children to learn through entertainment.[5] (A facsimile of the first American edition of the book is available through the Library of Congress at http://lcweb2.loc.gov/cgi-bin/ampage?collId=rbc3&fileName=rbc0001_2003juv05880page.db). Newbery's books include numerous editions of Aesop; the first comprehensive book of nursery rhymes, *Mother Goose's Melody* (1765); a series of informational books for children entitled *The Circle of Sciences* (1746–1748); and a didactic fictional book designed to improve children's morals, *The History of Little Goody Two-Shoes; Otherwise called, Mrs. Margery Two-Shoes* (1765), which some have attributed to Oliver Goldsmith.[5]

It was not until the 1820s, after Jacob and Wilhelm Grimm's *Kinder-und-Hausmärchen* (1812), the first comprehensive collection of folktales, was translated from German into English as *German Popular Stories* (1823), with high quality engraved illustrations by George Cruikshank, that folk and fairy tales became accepted as literature for children in England. In Germany, these folktales became popular once the Grimms, seeing the success of their book in its illustrated English translation, had their brother Ludwig Emil Grimm add illustrations, and began to edit their collection to make the stories more readable for children. The Grimms also edited the fairy tales to suit German parents' expectations for teaching their children the virtues society considered important: obedience, hard work, orderliness, cleanliness, and piety.[10] The Grimms' collection has been translated into more than 100 languages and the stories have entered the written as well as oral tradition of numerous countries throughout the world.

Many of the English-speaking world's stories, such as the familiar versions of "Hansel and Gretel" and "Rumpelstiltskin," now considered part of our heritage, were first introduced through the Grimms' fairy tales. Even more importantly, the Grimms inspired people all over the world to collect and retell their own folktales for children. Joseph Jacobs's *English Fairy Tales* (1898) has been particularly influential for English-speaking children's literature.

Throughout the nineteenth century, the debate continued over what constitutes good literature for children. Moral purpose remained important and imaginative literature began to be an important vehicle for inculcating positive values. Much of the literature of the beginning of the nineteenth century was didactic with thin storylines and characters whose only function was to demonstrate correct behavior, but by the second half of the nineteenth century imaginative literature began to have strong plots and memorable characters.

The literary fairy tale's popularity, begun in France in the seventeenth and eighteenth centuries, was greatly enhanced in the nineteenth century by the Danish Hans Christian Andersen and German writers such as E.T.A. Hofmann, the author of "Nussknacker und Mauskönig (1816) [The *Nutcracker and the Mouse King*, 1817]. Andersen, the author of *Eventyr, fortalte for børn* (1835–1842) [translated by Mary Howitt as *Wonderful Stories for Children*, 1846] used a lively, conversational style as well as memorable imagery to develop his themes through literary fairy tales such as "The Ugly Duckling" and "The Little Mermaid." Fantasy classics, such as James Barrie's *Peter Pan* (1906), best known for its stage version, and L. Frank Baum's *The Wonderful Wizard of Oz* (1900), elaborated on the tradition of literary fairy tales.

The nineteenth century also saw the birth of modern high fantasy with heroes fighting evil powers, often of mythic proportions, in the publication of George MacDonald's *The Princess and the Goblin* (1872) and *The Princess and Curdie* (1882). Although MacDonald had a moral agenda, he allowed children to discover his themes rather than stating them explicitly.[11] By contrast, the primary purpose of Lewis Carroll's (pseudonym for Charles Dodgson) fantasy novels, *Alice's Adventures in Wonderland* (1865) and *Through the Looking Glass* (1872), was to give pleasure rather than to teach a moral. It is Carroll's playfulness, and to some extent subversive conspiracy between adult author and child reader against "the grown-ups," which marks a turning point in children's literature.[12,13] While the subversiveness is minimal—in the end, Alice turns the cards upside down and returns to the ordered world of her family and school—most children's books, since *Alice*, have been taking the child's perspective, even as the child protagonist grows and ultimately resolves inner as well as external conflicts without the author resorting to providing explicit morals.

The last quarter of the nineteenth century and the first quarter of the twentieth century also saw the beginnings of another type of modern fantasy in which personified animals and toys explore themes of concern to children. Carlo Collodi's (pseudonym of Carlo Lorenzini) Italian classic, *Le avventure di Pinocchio* (1883), translated into English as *The Adventures of Pinocchio* (1892), follows a puppet's exploration of what it means to be human. Kenneth Grahame's animal characters, Rat, Mole, and Toad, in *The Wind in the Willows* (1908), explore friendships in an idyllic setting, while Rudyard Kipling's *The Jungle Book* (1894) and its sequel transport European and American children to "exotic" settings.

Fiction for children, especially the adventure novel, with its possible if not always plausible plots, was another development of the nineteenth century. Juvenile nineteenth century fiction was largely didactic, designed to inculcate duty, honor, kindness to the less fortunate, and decent treatment of animals, as in Anna Sewell's *Black Beauty* (1877).

Although fewer of the nineteenth and early twentieth century works of fiction for children have stood the test of time compared to fantasy, several of this era's books have become classics and continue to be read or remain a part of our culture through their film adaptations. Many children, for instance, are familiar with one of *Robinson Crusoe's* numerous offshoots, *The Swiss Family Robinson* (1814) [*Der Schweizerische Robinson* (1812–1813)] by the Swiss author Johann D. Wyss, through the Disney film, and some early twentieth century books, such as *Pollyanna* (1913) by Eleanor Porter, might have been forgotten, had it not been for their film versions.

Boys' adventures and domestic novels for girls dominated the market and children's reading. Boys' adventures were produced in both England and the United States, while girls' domestic novels tended to be more popular in America.[14] Mark Twain's *The Adventures of Tom Sawyer* (1876), loosely based on the author's pre-Civil War era childhood experiences in Hannibal, MO, represents one of the most outstanding examples of the boy's adventure genre. It started a trend of adventure books about boys who get into scrapes, but are good at heart.[15]*Huckleberry Finn*, (1885), with its social satire and complex themes continued the genre but took it to much greater heights, while avoiding didacticism. By contrast, Horatio Alger's *Ragged Dick; or Street Life in New York with the Boot Blacks* (1867) exemplified the didactic rags-to-riches urban adventure story.

Among the English adventure novels, the school adventures of Thomas Hughes' *Tom Brown's School Days* (1857) started a spate of British public (i.e., private) school-life stories; Robert Louis Stevenson's books, such as *Treasure Island* (1883), captured its readers through exciting plots, colorful characters, and exotic settings; and British author G. A. Henty's historical fiction, such as *With Clive in India* (1884), introduced historical fiction

and brought the countries of the British Empire into the homes of English and American children.

Louisa May Alcott's *Little Women*, (1868), which was the first of a series of books about Meg, Jo, Amy and their offspring (Beth having died in the first book), was one of the best of the domestic novels. Alcott's independent-minded girls and their strong mother can be seen as early feminists. Other girls' domestic series which were popular in the late nineteenth and early twentieth centuries, such as Margaret Sidney's (pseudonym for Harriet Lothrop, 1844–1924) immensely popular *Five Little Peppers and How they Grew* (1881), are known today mainly by their titles.

The redeeming power of the innocence of childhood, often combined with the idea of nature's restorative power, whether in its wilder state or in the cultivated garden, was a dominant theme of many of the most popular books of the late nineteenth, early twentieth centuries. Several of the best, with their strong plots, appealing characters, and a sense of place, continue to be published, read, and adapted to film and television. Swiss author Johanna Spyri's *Heidi* (1880, translated into English in 1884), set in the Swiss Alps, and English/American author Frances Hodgson Burnett's *The Secret Garden* (1911), set in an English garden on a country estate, epitomize the above themes. Canadian author L. M. Montgomery's *Anne of Green Gables* (1908) and its sequels, too, attained their popularity from their independent-minded yet innocent and loving protagonist, as well as from their picturesque and nostalgic setting.

Finally, the turn of the twentieth century saw in Edith Nesbit's books of realistic family fiction the introduction of a strong child narrator whose concerns are those of children rather than of adults. The children respond with intelligence, wit, and shrewd insight into the world of the adults, while continuing to maintain their innocence (p. 104).[13] Nesbit's *The Railway Children* (1906) is still read and translated into other languages. The family adventure reached classic heights in Arthur Ransome's books of the Walker family's camping and sailing adventures in England's Lake District, starting with *Swallows and Amazons* (1930).

History of Illustration in Children's Books

Illustration has been used worldwide to convey information and tell stories throughout human history, from cave paintings to fourth century Chinese scrolls illustrating moral lessons of the Buddha, to medieval European stained glass windows, and Indian storytelling cloths used by village storytellers in India.

In illustrated books, although the text is dominant, the pictures capture significant moments in the narrative, often adding to characterization or setting. Book illustration in medieval Europe was primarily religious in nature and included illuminated manuscripts of The Bible as well as prayer books such as the Duc de Berry's renowned "Book of Hours," *Les très riches heures* [The Very Rich Hours, often referred to as Book of Hours], (ca. 1424 A.D.) (See http://www.ibiblio.org/wm/rh/).

Woodblock printing made it possible to illustrate early printed books. William Caxton's 1484 *Aesop's Fables*, for instance, featured a picture of Aesop. Moravian minister John Amos Comenius's 1658 *Orbis Sensualium Pictus* [The World in Pictures] (see http://www.mhs.ox.ac.uk/gatt/tower/catalog.asp?CN=40), a picture encyclopedia, is often considered the first fully illustrated book for children. Comenius used illustrations to clarify and expand upon the text. It was not until the middle of the eighteenth century, however, that high quality illustrations began to be used in children's books, when John Newbery commissioned woodcut artists to illustrate his children's books. One of the finest among the late eighteenth–early nineteenth century woodcut artists, Thomas Bewick, was in much demand by the newly developing children's publishing trade throughout England, as was his brother John.[5]

The development of metal engraving techniques in the late eighteenth and early nineteenth centuries made it possible to create more realistic images than those made with woodcuts. The mystical English poet William Blake illustrated his books using copper engraving and watercolors. George Cruikshank's illustrations for the Grimms' *German Popular Stories* (1823), translated by Edgar Taylor, provided detail and characterization unavailable in earlier illustrated books. Color began to be used in early nineteenth century alphabet books and nursery rhymes, although the colors had to be added by hand, often using child labor. By the 1860s and 1970s color printing using both woodblock and lithographic techniques, developed by the printer Edmund Evans, allowed artists such as Walter Crane, Randolph Caldecott, and Kate Greenaway to create full-color illustrated books.[5] Some of the most enduring nineteenth century illustrations for children's books were by newspaper caricaturists and illustrators, such as John Tenniel, who immortalized the look of Alice and the other characters in Lewis Carroll's *Alice's Adventures in Wonderland* (1865) and *Through the Looking Glass* (1872), and the German Wilhelm Busch, creator of *Max und Moritz* (1865).

The turn of the twentieth century is often referred to as "The Golden Age of illustration." British illustrator Ernest H. Shepard created memorable characters for the *Wind in the Willows* (1908) by Kenneth Grahame (as well as for *Winnie-the-Pooh* (1926) and *The House at Pooh Corner* (1928) by A. A. Milne). French illustrator Maurice Boutet de Monvel with his delicate designs and colors influenced American children's illustrators.[16] Arthur Rackham, a prolific illustrator from Britain, used strong lines and patches of light and shadows in his illustrations for children's books, including *The Fairy Tales of the Brothers Grimm* (1900), James Barrie's *Peter Pan in Kensington Garden* (1906), and *Mother Goose* (1913). Danish-born Kay Nielsen (*East of the Sun and West of*

the Moon, 1914 by Peter Asbjørnsen and Jorgen Moe) and French-born Edmund Dulac (*The Sleeping Beauty and Other Fairy Tales*, 1910 by Arthur Quiller-Couch) illustrated books in England for children and adults using delicate lines and romantic representations of palaces and clothes in an Art Nouveau style. American illustrator Howard Pyle retold and illustrated in black and white the legends of King Arthur and of Robin Hood at the end of the nineteenth century, while N.C. Wyeth created dramatic scenes in oil colors for adventure books such as *Treasure Island* (1911) by Robert Louis Stevenson. Although the ascendance of picture books in wealthier countries seems to have supplanted illustrated books for children, illustrators of novels have continued to memorialize incidents and characters. A few of the illustrators who have created memorable characters using line drawings and halftones include Ilona Wikland (Pippi Longstocking); Pauline Baynes (Narnia series); Garth Williams (Little House series and Wilbur); Alan Tiegreen (Ramona Quimby); and Timothy Ering (Despereaux). Both Jerry Pinkney in *Tales of Uncle Remus* (1987) by Julius Lester and Barry Moser in *Jump!* (1986) by Van Dyke Parks and Malcolm Jones have provided new images for B'rer Rabbit, and Moser has also created a new look for Alice.

PICTURE BOOKS

Definitions

The modern picture book format is a recent phenomenon, having been developed in the 1870s by British illustrators Kate Greenaway (1846–1901) and Randolph Caldecott (1845–1886). Greenaway's full-color illustrations for books such as *Under the Window* (1879), which consisted of original verse by Greenaway, depicted children playing in pastoral settings wearing light, airy clothes. Greenaway influenced both the depiction of children in picture books and children's fashions in the late nineteenth–early twentieth centuries.[14] It was Caldecott, however, who created the first genuine picture books by providing characterization and setting as well as action-filled narrative through illustrations for each event in a nursery rhyme or story. He divided the text into 32 page segments, creating a parallel narrative through illustrations. Caldecott's skilled use of line to create dynamic images as well as his humorous interpretation of characters and events such as those for *Hey Diddle Diddle* (1883) (see Fig. 2) make his books classics. Beatrix Potter brought picture books to new heights by creating total unity between text and illustrations. She used expressive anthropomorphized animals, spare, naturalistic details, and plenty of white space to allow children to give scope to their imaginations, as in *The Tale of Peter Rabbit* (1901/1902), the picture book from the era that children most often continue to ask for.[17]

Fig. 2   From *Hey Diddle Diddle and Baby Bunting* by Randolph Caldecott. London: Frederick Warne, n.d. original edition London: Routledge, 1883.

The two narratives of a picture book, textual and pictorial, encompass a wide range of interrelationships. The text may consist of one or two words or up to a long paragraph, usually written at a child's listening vocabulary level, but above his or her reading level, while the pictures may be simple, to match the single words or phrases meant for toddlers as in *Max's First Word* (1979) by Rosemary Wells, or they may be complex, adding a new dimension to the text. The parallel narratives of picture books—words and pictures—usually tell the same story, as in Tomie de Paola's *Strega Nona* (1975), with the pictures supporting every step of Big Anthony's misadventure. Frequently, however, the picture and text are even more integrated, neither being complete without the other, as in *Where the Wild Things Are* (1963) by Maurice Sendak and in *Officer Buckle and Gloria* (1995) by Peggy Rathmann, in which the pictures create dramatic irony. Sometimes the pictures are sufficient with few or no words, as in the case of *Tuesday* (1991) by David Wiesner. Generally, however, the complex relationship between image and text distinguishes picture books and creates the total reading/listening experience.

The Text of Picture Books

The traditional audience for picture books, children ages preschool through 7, is usually not expected to read the text but rather to look at the illustrations while listening to the story, responding to both the verbal narrative and the pictures. The best of children's book authors do not speak down to their audience, but, like Kevin Henkes, the author/illustrator of Caldecott Medal and Honor winning books, they choose their words for effect, not for simplicity. In *Kitten's First Full Moon* (2004) Henkes describes Kitten's fall using carefully selected words and phrases of varied lengths: "But Kitten only tumbled-/ bumping her nose and banging her ear/ and pinching her tail./ Poor Kitten!" The phrase "Poor Kitten" serves as a refrain, giving the text rhythm. There are, however, picture books that are deliberately written with the child as beginning reader in mind, most notably Dr. Seuss's *Cat in the Hat* (1957); the Theodore Geisel Award honors those writers who are able to create varied and interesting language while adhering to a limited vocabulary.

Styles of Illustration in Picture Books

The primary function of the illustrations is to heighten emotional response through the use of color, line, shape, layout, texture, scale and point of view. Throughout the twentieth century, picture book artists experimented with the picture book format, while advances in technology also influenced picture book styles. Because of the cost

Fig. 3   From *YO! YES?* by Chris Raschka. Copyright © 1993 by Chris Raschka. Reprinted by permission of Orchard Books, an imprint of Scholastic Inc.

of full-color illustration before the 1960s, artists had to be creative to achieve their effects with few colors. Artists created award-winning picture books entirely in black and white, focusing on line, shape, and layout, as did Wanda Gág in *Millions of Cats* (1928); monochrome pictures of sepia or blue, as did Robert McCloskey in *Make Way for Ducklings* (1941) and *Blueberries for Sal* (1948); or with a few flat colors, as did Jean de Brunhoff in *Histoire de Babar, le petit éléphant* [*The Story of Babar*, 1931]; and H. A. Rey in *Curious George* (1941). The development of photographic offset printing eliminated the older, more tedious method, and the 1980s and 1990s brought further sophistication in color printing through the use of computers. Since the beginning of the 1980s there has been a trend toward more painterly oil and acrylic illustrations, such as Paul Zelinsky's images for *Rumpelstiltskin* (1986) with its shimmering scenes of golden straw. Artists, however, continue to use all of the earlier styles in combination with newer techniques. Mo Willems, for instance, used a few deft lines in *Don't Let the Pigeon Drive the Bus* (2003) to create Pigeon's expressions ranging from wheedling to sly to furious, and line work combined with touches of watercolor continues to be widely used, as for instance by artists Betsy Lewin in *Click, Clack, Moo: Cows That Type* by Doreen Cronin (2000) and Chris Raschka in *Yo! Yes?* (1993) (See Fig. 3). Increasingly, artists use computers to develop complex combinations of materials. Once electronic books become more accessible to the general public, artists are likely to take advantage of the computer's

capabilities for nonlinear sequencing with multiple linkages between scenes and actions.[18]

Picture book artists use a wide range of art styles, some developing a signature style, others matching the style of a specific book to its subject, theme, or setting. Jerry Pinkney always uses an impressionistic style, as in Pat McKissack's *Goin' Someplace Special* (2001). Bryan Pinkney typically uses flowing lines and deep colors in scratchboard for subjects from folktales to biographies such as *Duke Ellington: The Piano Prince and His Orchestra* (1998) by Andrea Davis Pinkney. Cubist styles are reflected in some works of illustrators, including Christopher Myers's in *Harlem: A Poem* (1997) by Walter Dean Myers. Mixed media, combining collage and other media, such as paint in picture book illustration, pioneered by Ezra Jack Keats (*The Snowy Day*, 1962) and Leo Lionni (*Inch by Inch*, 1960), is used by many artists. Bryan Collier in *Uptown* (2000), for instance, created a tapestry of shapes and textures to depict Harlem (see Fig. 4). The influence of cartoon art is also apparent in many pictures books, as for instance Ian Falconer's *Olivia* (2000) and Eric Rohmann's *My Friend Rabbit* (2002) (see Fig. 5).

Wordless Picture Books

Wordless picture books, which used to be an exception in picture book format, are increasing in numbers. These books rely entirely on the sequence of illustrations for their narratives. Some wordless books are designed to help young children interpret the visually told story through

Fig. 4 Illustration from *Uptown* by Bryan Collier. Copyright 2000 by Bryan Collier. Reprinted by permission of Henry Holt and Company.

carefully constructed sequences showing scenes of familiar actions, as in Australian author/illustrator Jan Ormerod's *Sunshine* (1981). Alexandra Day's *Good Dog Carl* (1985), a story about a Rottweiler and the toddler he baby-sits, is more fanciful and leaves greater leeway for interpretation by young readers. More sophisticated wordless books for somewhat older audiences include Jeannie

And he is my friend.

Fig. 5 Illustration from *My Friend Rabbit* by Eric Rohmann. Copyright 2002 by Eric Rohmann. Reprinted by permission of Henry Holt and Company.

Baker's *Home* (2004), which shows the passage of time in a city neighborhood; Mitsumasa Anno's *Anno's Journey* (1978), which is replete with cultural and historical allusions; David Wiesner's *Free Fall* (1988), an explorations of the boundaries between dream and reality; and Brian Selznick's *The Invention of Hugo Cabret* (2007), a 533 page historical fiction told through several hundred pages of images interspersed with some text. Other artist-storytellers who have told complex stories in wordless picture books include Russian artist Nikolai Popov in an antiwar book *Why?* (1996), and Belgian-born artist Gabrielle Vincent in *A Day a Dog* (1999), about a dog's quest for home.

Specialized Types of Picture Books: Alphabet Books, Counting Books, Concept Books, Engineered Books, and Graphic Novels

Traditionally alphabet books have introduced preschool children to the shapes and sounds of letters. Kate Greenaway's *A Apple Pie: An Old Fashioned Alphabet Book* (1886) has one concept for each letter. Well conceived alphabet books help develop phonemic awareness as children learn to hear and associate the sounds with the letters as well as the words (usually initial sounds) in which they appear as in Helen Oxenbury's *ABC of Things* (1972). Many alphabet books, however, go beyond direct representation to introduce new words and concepts, play with language, and stimulate visual perception and imagination. *Antics!* (1992) by Cathi Hepworth plays with language—An Einstein-like chemist ant illustrates "**B**rilliant"; *Animalia* (1986) by Graeme Base and *Alphabet City* (1995) by Stephen T. Johnson, evoke close observation; and Chris Van Allsburg stimulates the imagination as readers try to guess what fate may have befallen each letter of the alphabet, in *The Z Was Zapped: A Play in Twenty-Six Acts* (1987) (see Fig. 6).

Counting books may introduce the counting sequence and show a one-to-one correspondence between the numeral and the number of objects on the page, or they may cluster the images into groupings to match numbers, as does *Anno's Counting Book* (1975). Like alphabet books, counting books can be playful and stimulating. For instance, Czech artist Kveta Pacovska shows numbers doing acrobatic contortions in *One, Five, Many* (1990), and Bruce McMillan introduces fractions through photographs of children eating in *Eating Fractions* (1991).

Concept books introduce preschoolers to single concepts: (e.g. opposites, colors or shapes). Photographer Tana Hoban focused mostly on this genre, stimulating children to discover specific concepts and to look closely at the world around them, with books such as *Is it Larger, Is it Smaller* (1985) and *Shapes, Shapes, Shapes* (1986). Other award winning artists who create concept books include Donald Crews, Lois Ehlert, and Steve Jenkins.

Fig. 6 Illustration from *The Z was Zapped* by Chris Van Allsburg. Copyright © 1987 by Chris Van Allsburg. Reprinted by permission of Houghton Mifflin Company. All rights reserved.

Engineered books, books with tactile, three-dimensional, or moveable parts, have a long history. The first lift-the-flap book designed for children was Robert Sayer's *Harlequinade* (1765). Victorian engineered books included dial-turnable scenes as well as pop-up scenes. Lothar Moggendorfer in Germany created intricate pop-ups at the end of the nineteenth century. Due to the economic hardship of WWI and the Great Depression, the market for these elaborate books disappeared.[19] Simpler engineered books, however, such as Dorothy Kunhardt's *Pat the Bunny* (1940) with fuzzy inserts and Eric Hill's *Where's Spot* (1980) with open-the-flap surprises continue to be enjoyed. Sophisticated engineered books are making a revival. Robert Sabuda's three-dimensional pop-ups and movable parts have greatly developed paper engineering, as in an adaptation of Baum's *The Wizard of Oz* (2000). Other contemporary pop-up artists of children's books include David Carter, Jan Pienkowsky, and Matthew Reinhart.[20,21]

Influenced by both Western style comic books and by Japanese manga, graphic novels are book-length, self-contained works. Despite the term "novel," graphic novels represent every genre of literature, though they are best known for fantasy hero stories. Most graphic novels are written for young adults and adults. Many of the works produced in graphic novel form are intellectually and emotionally challenging, as are Art Spiegelman's *Maus: A Survivor's Tale* (1986) and Marjane Satrapi's autobiographical *Persepolis* (2003), which captures a child's point of view about life in Iran before and during the 1979 revolution. Her theme, the use of ironic humor, and the haunting black and white images suggest a young adult and adult audience. Even when not emotionally challenging, the themes focus on young adult concerns such as romance or finding values to live by, as in *Garage Band* (2007) by Italian author/artist Gipi. Reading the text and pictures in a highly interactive way and interpreting the visual symbols are also sophisticated literacy skills.[21,22] Graphic novels for young adults also include adaptations of classics, as, for instance, Peter Kuper's version of Franz Kafka's *Metamorphosis* (2003) and Stephane Heuet's adaptation of Marcel Proust's *Remembrance of Things Past: Combray* (2001).

Graphic novels for younger children include *The Greek Myths* (1991) by Marcia Williams; popular children's series such as Raina Telgemeier's adaptation of *The Babysitters Club* (2006) by Ann Martin; original modern fantasy such as Newbery Honor-winning writer Jennifer Holm's and artist-brother Matthew Holm's *Babymouse: Queen of the World* (2005) and other titles in the series; and biographies/autobiographies such as Michael Foreman's *War Boy: A Country Childhood* (1989) and Siena Cherson Siegel's account of her days at the Juilliard School in *To Dance: A Memoir* (2006).

Trends in Picture Books

Many picture books are for an older audience than the traditional preschool through 7 year old, or they are for multiple audiences of older and younger readers, because of their complex formats and allusions to other texts and visuals with which younger readers may be unfamiliar, as well as their use of sophisticated language. David Wiesner's *The Three Pigs* (2001), for instance, can be enjoyed on different levels by various ages; the youngest would likely enjoy seeing the pigs get away from the wolf while older children might understand the idea of moving in and out of stories and would be more likely to recognize the allusions. The dual audience for English author and illustrator Anthony Browne's *Willy the Dreamer* (1998) is distinct: while the daydreams of Willy, a chimp, about what he will do when he grows up are readily accessible to a young audience, the visual allusions are meant for adults familiar with both popular culture—Elvis Presley—and modern artists—René Magritte. Other picture books with sophisticated explorations of time and space include *The Red Book* (2004) by Barbara Lehman; *Black and White* (1990) by David Macaulay; and *Flotsam* (2006) by David Wiesner. Jon Scieszka's *The Stinky Cheese Man* (1992), illustrated by Lane Smith, is a book of fractured fairy tales, playing with the conventions of story structure as well as a book's accustomed format. Australian author Margaret Wild's and illustrator Ann Spudvilas's *Woolvs in the Sitee* (2007) is a psychological exploration of fear. Frequently, picture books introduce subjects that require a sense of history or of social conditions usually considered beyond the cognitive and emotional level of preschool through first grade. Books like these include Peter Sis's *The Tree of Life: A Book Depicting the Life of Charles Darwin, Naturalist, Geologist, and Thinker* (2003); Emily Arnold McCully's *Bobbin Girl* (1996); Japanese author/illustrator Toshi Maruki's *Hiroshima No Pika* (1982); and Mary Williams's *Brothers in Hope: The Story of the Lost Boys of Sudan* (2005) illustrated by Gregory Christie.

For major English language picture book awards, see "Awards."

POETRY

Poetry for children differs from poetry for adults only in degree, not in kind—poets who write with children in mind select their words carefully, calling on the reader's/listener's emotional memory through description and imagery and creating sensory experiences through rhythm and devices of sound: rhyme, alliteration, onomatopoeia, etc. Children's poems focus on experiences and concepts of concern to children, from daily events like dealing with homework to questions about friendship, family, adult authority, and death. Delight in the immediate—the feel of mud, the taste of chocolate, the way it feels to swerve on a skateboard—are all likely themes in poems for children, as are emotions ranging from sibling rivalry to joy at a parent's return at the end of the day. Narrative poems might tell of humorous or dramatic events, or they might be biographical. Though children prefer humorous and accessible poems, they respond to a wide range of poetry if they hear or read it without being required to analyze it. Children can develop a love of poetry early in life.

> If children are lucky enough to have heard lullabies, nursery rhymes, and folk songs, to have played to the accompaniment of street and game chants, then they come to the forms of poetry with a firm grasp of its bare bones—rhyme, rhythm, meter, and the *singingness* of language (p. 89).[23]

The traditional nursery rhymes, or Mother Goose rhymes, are children's first poems. Even infants respond to the strong beat and predictable rhymes. Collections of nursery rhymes abound, their illustrations ranging from personified animals, as in Iona Opie's and Rosemary Wells's *My Very First Mother Goose* (1996) to contemporary urban settings, as in Nina Crews's *Neighborhood Mother Goose* (2004).

William Blake, the author of *Songs of Innocence* (1789) and of *Songs of Experience* (1794) whose poems "The Lamb" and "The Tyger" are frequently included in anthologies of poetry for children, was one of the first poets who wrote for children, though only his *For Children: The Gates of Paradise* (1793) explicitly stated the audience.[24] Sir Isaac Watts, however, was better known in his own lifetime and throughout the nineteenth century. His gently didactic verses in *Divine Songs for Children* (1715) were a staple in homes and schools. During the eighteenth and most of the nineteenth centuries children also heard or read poems meant for an adult audience. These included folk ballads about Robin Hood. The chief form of poetry written deliberately for children was moral verse, which used rhythm and rhyme to help them remember lessons.[5] Some of these verses, such as "Mary's Lamb" by Sarah Josepha Hale (1830) have passed into folklore. "A Visit from Saint Nicholas" by Clement Moore (1823) was one of the few poems for children that was written primarily for enjoyment during this era. Published as a book with Thomas Nast's illustrations in 1860, it influenced American images of Christmas[13] and continues to be popular in many picture book versions. Other nineteenth and early twentieth century narrative poems republished as picture books include Robert Browning's *The Pied Piper of Hamelin* (1889), illustrated by Kate Greenaway (http://www.indiana.edu/~librcsd/etext/piper/cover.html) as well as by more recent illustrators; Henry Wadsworth Longfellow's "Paul Revere's Ride" (1860), illustrated by Christopher Bing (2001); and Alfred Noyes's "The Highwayman" (1902), illustrated by Charles Keeping (1981). Contemporary poets sometimes use narrative poems for biographies and informational books. Bobbi Katz celebrated American history through poems of varied styles to fit each topic in *We the People* (2000); Marilyn Nelson wrote *Carver: A Life in Poems* (2001) as well as *A Wreath for Emmett Till* (2005); and Carmen T. Bernier-Grand portrayed Frida Kahlo in *Frida: Viva la vida! Long Live Life!* (2007).

Edward Lear's verses were perhaps first in a long line of English language nonsense poetry, designed to amuse through imaginative juxtaposition of incongruities and through language play. Many of Lear's limericks are included in children's anthologies, and his "The Owl and the Pussycat" (1870) has appeared frequently as a picture book, including one by James Marshall. Laura Richards was one of the first Americans to publish nonsense verse: her "Eletelephony" in *Tirra Lirra: Rhymes Old and New* (1932) is a classic. Poets throughout the twentieth century who have played with nonsense verse for children as well as adults include Dylan Thomas, John Ciardi, and Theodore Roethke. Some contemporary practitioners of the art include X. J. Kennedy (*Exploding Gravy: Poems to Make You Laugh*, 2002); Dennis Lee (*Alligator Pie*, 1974), J. Patrick Lewis (*July is a Mad Mosquito*, 1994), and Jack Prelutsky (*Scranimals*, 2002). Where nonsense verse ends and humorous poetry begins is hard to determine. Well known poets such as David McCord, Russell Hoban, Karla Kuskin, and Douglas Florian continue to play with the English language—"Just when you think you know the boa/ there's moa and moa, and moa, and moa." (from *Beast Feast*, 1994 by Douglas Florian). Shel Silverstein's (*Where the Sidewalk Ends*, 1974) great popularity rested on his ability to make everyday experiences, from watching TV to taking out the garbage, seem hilarious. These and other poets also look at serious topics from a humorous angle. Jane Yolen's "Homework" (from Michael Hearn's *Breakfast, Books, and Dreams*, 1981) pokes light-hearted fun at excuses, and Eve Merriam's socially ironic poems combine wordplay and social commentary on topics ranging from alienation in a technological world to war.

While children respond most readily to humorous and narrative poems in the early years, even the youngest can respond to the musicality of lyrical poetry, such as that of two early poets who wrote for children: Christina Rossetti, *Sing Song: A Nursery Rhyme Book* (1871) and Robert Louis Stevenson, *A Child's Garden of Verses* (1885). By the middle elementary grades children also appreciate lyrical poetry in which the author speaks of personal experiences without nostalgia or condescension. The reader is invited to see through the poet's eyes the familiar in a new way, as in Aileen Fisher's and Valerie Worth's nature observations and Patricia Hubbell's vision of the modern world: "Concrete mixers are urban elephants/their trunks are raising a city" from *8 A.M. Shadows* (1965). The reader might realize that the poet has put words to a familiar experience: Lillian Morrison, who has specialized in sports poetry, captures the moment of "flow" when the player becomes one with his or her activity in "The Sidewalk Racer *or On the Skateboard*" (*The Sidewalk Racer*, 1977); Myra Cohn Livingston describes a child's fear in "The Dark" (*Worlds I know and Other Poems*, 1985); and Eloise Greenfield tells about things an urban child delights in, from the gushing of a fire hydrant, a "flying pool," to cuddling in her mother's arms in "Honey, I Love" (*Honey, I Love and Other Love Poems*, 1977).

Concrete poems wittily represent the meaning of the words through the layout of the text. In *Flicker Flash* (1999), poet Joan Graham laid the words out in the form of the subject of the poem: for instance, a birthday cake. J. Patrick Lewis's *Doodle Dandies* (1998), Paul Janeczko's *A Poke in the I: A Collection of Concrete Poems* (2001), illustrated by Chris Raschka, and John Grandits' *Blue Lipstick* (2007) offer a variety of concrete poems for children and young adults.

Poetry for young adults, in keeping with their need for identity development, often uses a first person perspective to speak of love and loneliness, doubts, and dreams. Paul Janeczko writes of being a young teen in his working class neighborhood in *Brickyard Summer* (1989), and Gary Soto in *Neighborhood Odes* (1992) shares both universal

experiences of love and longing, and those more specific to his experience as a Latino teen. Mel Glenn in *Class Dismissed!* (1982) and Nikki Grimes in *Bronx Masquerade* (2002) use a first person perspective to express young people's hurts and hopes.

Sources for identifying outstanding poets for children include anthologies by Catherine Clinton, Beatrice Schenk de Reniers, Stephen Dunning, Donald Hall, Lee Bennett Hopkins, X. J. Kennedy, Paul Janeczko, Nancy Larrick, Bruce Lansky, Myra Cohn Livingston, Lilian Moore, Naomi Shihab Nye, Jack Prelutsky, and Michael Rosen, as well as the National Council of Teachers of English Award for Poetry for Children, http://www.ncte.org.

TRADITIONAL LITERATURE

Storytelling seems to be integral to the human experience. Traditional stories were used to educate and acculturate children and adults to the mores and values of their society as well as to entertain and to express a group's hopes and wishes. Charles Perrault's eight fairy tales artfully retold in *Histoire ou Contes du Temps Passé* (1697), established the popular notion that folktales are for young people. The idea was solidified with Jacob and Wilhelm Grimm's retelling of German folktales in *Kinder-und-Hausmärchen* (1812). Today children throughout the world learn the traditional stories of their culture as well as those of other cultures through books, though storytelling continues to survive.[25]

In many countries traditional literature represents the bulk of publishing for children; even in countries with a large children's publishing industry, such as Australia, Japan, the United Kingdom, the United States, and Western European countries, a large proportion of picture books are retellings of fables, folktales, myths, and legends. The influence of traditional stories in every culture goes beyond the publishing of traditional literature: original stories too, whether in picture books or in fiction and fantasy for older readers, as well as in film and even advertising, draw on the structures, themes, and characters of traditional stories.[17,26]

Traditional literature published for children tends to fall into the categories of fables, folktales, myths and legends. Fables are didactic stories. They are brief and often use animal characters to teach ethical lessons that help hold society together. In the most familiar of fables, the Aesop fables, the morals are usually stated at the end. Though less well-known in the West, the fables of India, the Panchatantra and Jataka, are becoming available through picture book versions. Because of the brevity of Aesop's fables, collections of fables are particularly enjoyable and have been reissued with different artists' interpretations, such as those of Jerry Pinkney (2000); Tom Paxton with Robert Rayevsky's illustrations (1988); and Lisbeth Zwerger (1989). Reinterpretations or humorous modern versions include Leo Lionni's *Frederick* (1967); Arnold Lobel's *Fables* (1980); and Toni and Slade Morrison's *The Ant or the Grasshopper?* (2003), illustrated by Pascal Lemaitre. Two collections of Panchatantra tales retold for children include Gloria Kamen's *Ringdoves* (1988) and Asha Upadhyay's *Tales from India* (1971). Demi in *Buddha Stories* (1997) and Jeanne M. Lee in *I Once Was a Monkey: Stories Buddha Told* (1999) have produced collections of the Jataka tales. For a collection of international fables, see *Feathers and Tails: Animal Fables from Around the World* (1992) retold by David Kherdian.

Folktales serve a variety of functions, from teaching lessons to entertainment. Folktales are about ordinary people and anthropomorphized animals, and include a range of story types. Fairy tales or wonder tales delight listeners and readers with their courageous and often kind heroes who achieve extraordinary goals through perseverance and the good sense to listen to wise advice offered by magical helpers. Fairy tale heroes who win through patience and kindness characterize the hundreds of world-wide variants of kind-and-unkind sisters and related Cinderella stories, many of which have been retold in picture book format. A few of these are *Yeh-Shen: A Cinderella Story from China* by Ai-Ling Louie (1982); the Korean *Kongi and Potgi* by Oki Han (1996); *The Irish Cinderlad* by Shirley Climo (1996); and the Russian *Baba Yaga and Vasilisa the Brave* by Marianna Mayer (1994). The equally ubiquitous questing hero, who wins the prize through courage, perseverance, and usually magical help, is featured in stories such as *Song Bird* (1999) from Africa by Tololwa Mollel; *Inch Boy* (1986) from Japan by Junko Morimoto; and *The Black Bull of Norroway* (2001) from Scotland by Charlotte Huck.

"Pourquoi" or "why" tales, which purport to explain how a custom, plant, or other observed phenomenon came to be, often used to teach children how they should behave, and cumulative or chain stories, characterized by events repeating themselves in longer and longer chains, are especially popular with children. Native American stories are rich in pourquoi tales such as Gayle Ross's *How Turtle's Back Was Cracked* (1995). Pourquoi tales are also told in Africa, as in Ashley Bryan's "How the Crab Got his Shell" in the collection *Turtle Knows Your Name* (1989). "The Gingerbread Boy," with its many picture book variants such as *The Pancake Boy* (1988) by Lorinda Cauley, is a cumulative tale, as is *Too Much Talk* from Ghana, retold by Angela Medearis (1995). Humorous tales, whether of numbskulls or of tricksters, are told for entertainment, as negative exemplars, or as a way to express a group's belief in the possibility of survival against the odds. Some popular numbskulls and tricksters include the Appalachian Jacks, most famously collected by Richard Chase in *The Jack Tales* (1943) and more recently retold by Gail Haley in *Mountain Jack* (1992); the West African and Caribbean Ananse as in *Ananse and*

the Lizard: A West African Tale* (2002) by Pat Cummings, and *First Palm Trees: An Anancy Spiderman Story* (1997) by James Berry; the Native American Coyote (or Rabbit or Iktomi or Raven, depending on the region) as in *Ma'ii and Cousin Horned Toad* by Shonto Begay (1992); the Puerto Rican Juan Bobo as in *Juan Bobo* (2000) by Marisa Montes; the Goha from Arab-speaking countries as in *Goha, the Wise Fool* (2005) by Denys Johnson-Davies; and The Hodja from Turkey as in *Watermelons, Walnuts, and the Wisdom of Allah and Other Tales of the Hoca* (1967, 1991) by Barbara Walker. Though some popular tall tales are not true folktales, they are nevertheless part of American lore. Steven Kellogg's retellings with amusing illustrations include *Paul Bunyan* (1984) and *Pecos Bill* (1986). In *Cut from the Same Cloth* (1993) Robert San Souci retells tall tales about American women, some historic, others folkloric. Illustrated collections of international folktales and collections of specific countries, regions, or ethnic groups abound. Some of the resources for identifying the best of these collections include professional textbooks listed under "Bibliography," while individual stories in collections can be found through Margaret Reade MacDonald's *The Storyteller's Sourcebook: A Subject, Title and Motif Index to Folklore Collections for Children, 1983–1999* (2001), Joseph Sprug's *Index to Fairy Tales* (1994), as well as this index's earlier editions by Norma O. Ireland and by Mary Huse Eastman.

Every culture has its myths, stories that give concrete expression to their belief systems. Best known in the West are the Greek and Roman myths. The *D'Aulaires' Book of Greek Myths* (1962) and Aliki's *The Gods and Goddesses of Olympus* (1994) introduce 8–11 year olds to the Greek pantheon, while William Russell retells the stories in a lively collection *Classic Myths to Read Aloud* (1989) with pronunciations and explanations of common words derived from the myths. Less known are the Norse myths, which have been retold by authors such as Kevin Crossley-Holland in *Axe-Age, Wolf-Age: A Selection of Norse Myths* (1985) and Mary Pope Osborne in *Favorite Norse Myths* (1996). Native American myths have been retold in several collections by Joseph Bruchac, including in a science activities book by Michael Caduto, *Keepers of the Earth: Native American Stories and Environmental Activities for Children* (1989; 1999). John Bierhorst, a folklorist, has retold North, Central, and South American myths for children in books such as *The Mythology of Mexico and Central America* (1990). Chinese-Canadian artist Song Nan Zhang has retold Chinese myths of origins in *Five Heavenly Emperors* (1994), and English-Indian author Debjani Chatterjee has retold the Hindu myths in *The Elephant-Headed God* (1989). Virginia Hamilton's *In the Beginning: Creation Stories from Around the World* (1988), and Steven Zeitlin's *The Four Corners of the Sky: Creation Stories and Cosmologies from Around the World* (2000) are two of many international collections of myths. Bible stories have been retold by outstanding authors such as Miriam Chaikin, Tomie de Paola, Peter Dickinson, Erik Kimmel, Julius Lester, Jan Mark, Geraldine McCaughrean, and Martin Waddell.

Legends are told as history, whether of the exploits of a group's hero, of important events in the history of the group itself, or of a symbolic animal, plant, landmark, or object of importance to the group.[27] Legendary heroes embody the ideals of their societies. Children's books about legendary heroes include *The Epic of Gilgamesh* (2003) by Geraldine McCaughrean; *Black Ships Before Troy: The Story of the Iliad* (1993) by Rosemary Sutcliff; *The Adventures of Odysseus* by Neil Philip (1996); *Sundiata: Lion King of Mali* (1992), as well as *Golem* (1996) by David Wisniewski; *John Henry* (1994) by Julius Lester; and *The Magical Monkey King: Mischief in Heaven: Classic Chinese Tales* (2002) by Ji-Li Jiang. Legends of places and plants in North America are retold in Joseph Bruchac's *Between Earth and Sky: Legends of Native American Sacred Places* (1996).

Traditional literature offers an introduction to cultures around the world. Whether retold by people from the tales' culture of origin or someone outside the culture, authors and artists should treat the material with respect, avoid trivializing it, research the background of the story, credit their sources, and indicate in what way they may have altered it from its traditional origins according to storytellers Betsy Hearne[28] and Joseph Bruchac.[29]

REALISTIC FICTION

Fiction, though presenting imaginary characters and situations, can be realistic. The author creates a world which is simpler than real life, but the events, characters, and settings are within the realm of the possible in the natural world, even if at times they stretch the reader's credulity. Two subcategories of realistic fiction are Contemporary Fiction and Historical Fiction.

Contemporary Fiction

Contemporary fiction deals with characters who live contemporaneously with the author and the author's initial readers. In 1868, when Louisa May Alcott's *Little Women* was published, her readers were familiar with the events, the language, and the concerns of the characters. In the same way, today's contemporary fiction has relevant themes for today's young readers, as well as realistic plots, characters, settings, and dialogue. Dialogue that includes the latest in slang may date the work; outstanding contemporary fiction, however, transcends through theme, plot, and characterization, the limitations imposed by language, while adding, over time, a historical element the author did not originally intend. By minimizing setting and avoiding the most up-to-date slang, some contemporary fiction maintains its currency for 30 or 40 years, as have

Beverly Cleary's early books which were written in the 1950s and 1960s (*Ramona the Pest*, 1968).

Two of the major changes since the nineteenth century have been the degree of social realism and the tone authors use. Themes of personal development or coming of age and relationships within the family, with peers, and within the larger society continue to dominate children's fiction, but children's problems and the perspectives presented tend to be more complex and diverse than in early twentieth century fiction. While in British author Arthur Ransome's *Swallows and Amazons* (1930) the children develop their skills and demonstrate their ingenuity and courage during a sailing adventure in the idyllic setting of the Lake District in England, the skill and courage the protagonist of *The Wanderer* (2000) by Sharon Creech demonstrates as she sails with her adoptive family across the Atlantic must be matched by her courage in search of her identity. The family that meant a safe haven for children in earlier fiction, as in Eleanor Estes's *The Moffats* (1941), today may be the source of conflict. Parents remarry and children and stepparents may not get along, as in *My War with Goggle-Eyes* (1989) by British author Anne Fine; children may be abandoned by one or both parents, as in *A Catalogue of the Universe* (1985) by New Zealander Margaret Mahy, or dumped on a frail grandparent, as in *The Same Stuff as Stars* (2002) by Katherine Paterson; or a child may have to deal with abuse, as in *What Jamie Saw* (1995) by Carolyn Coman and in *I Hadn't Meant to Tell You This* (1994) by Jacqueline Woodson. Other themes of social realism include teens struggling with drug addiction, as in *A Hero Ain't Nothin' But a Sandwich* (1973) by Alice Childress, and *Smack* (1998) by British writer Melvin Burgess; AIDS, as in *Eagle Kite* (1995) by Paula Fox; homelessness, as in *Stone Cold* (1993) by British author Robert Swindell; coming to terms with homosexuality, as in *Deliver Us from Evie* (1994) by M. E. Kerr; and illegal immigration, as in *Ask Me No Questions* (2006) by Marina Budhos—in short, the issues of concern to adults and young people at the time of writing. In spite of the serious tone and subject of many of these books, however, the underlying themes are personal growth, the redeeming power of caring for others, and hope.

Humorous treatments of families and their struggles or of children and their peers continue to play an important part in engaging children with life issues. Barbara Park's *Junie B. Jones* series and British author Hilary McKay's Casson family series, starting with *Saffy's Angel* (2002), have children consider everything from learning to fit in at school to searching for one's identity; Canadian Polly Horvath's ever-optimistic hero's misadventures make children laugh in *Everything on a Waffle* (2001); a teen whom everyone else has given up on finds self-respect and a sense of purpose as a foster child in a riotously creative family in *Surviving the Applewhites* (2002) by Stephanie Tolan; and a child's yearning for a mother is poignantly and humorously told in *The Higher Power of Lucky* (2006) by Susan Patron. Humor has also lightened the tone in books dealing with serious social issues, such as fear of homelessness in *Money Hungry* (2001) by Sharon Flake, and protecting the environment in *Hoot* (2003) by Carl Hiassen.

Adventure and survival in nature also continue as important subjects of fiction. Wilderness adventures, such as *Hatchet* (1987) by Gary Paulsen, provide children a chance to vicariously test their ingenuity and mastery of their environment, as do urban adventures, such as Cornelia Funke's magic realistic adventure *The Thief Lord* (2002) set in Venice. Urban adventures, however, can also have much more serious themes, as in *The Planet of Junior Brown* (1971) by Virginia Hamilton, in which Junior Brown is introduced to the world of squatter children in New York City.

Besides increased social realism and a more serious tone, point of view has become more complex since the 1960s. Young adult author Paul Zindel pioneered the telling of a story from multiple or unusual perspectives in *The Pigman* (1968).[30] Since then authors have frequently used the technique, especially in books for young adults, as in *Nothing But the Truth* (1991) by Avi in which an unreliable narrator tells us about his "unfair" treatment by a teacher; in *Monster* (1999) by Walter Dean Myers, in which a teen arrested for acting as an accessory to a robbery ending in murder examines himself through a pretend camera lens; and in Virginia Walter's *Making Up Megaboy* (1998), which shows the reactions of the parents, only friend, the media, classmates, the victim's widow, and, finally, the young perpetrator to a deadly shooting.

Historical Fiction

In historical fiction authors set the action in the past, usually after doing research, in order to create an authentic setting, with the characters' concerns and language fitting the era depicted. Historical fiction, like contemporary fiction, is realistic. It too sheds light not only on the era in which it is set but also on contemporary times, as the stories frequently deal with issues of concern at the time of writing. Katherine Paterson's *Lyddie* (1991), set in a textile factory town in the 1830s, for instance, explores the issue of child labor which is still relevant in some parts of the world. Besides introducing a historic era, the authors usually explore universal themes such as the quest for personal identity or questions of honor, loyalty, friendship, and death. There is almost no limit to the historic settings that authors have attempted to evoke for young people, but certain eras are particularly well represented, as for instance the European Middle Ages in the books of Karen Cushman, Eric Haugaard, and British author Rosemary Sutcliff. The American Civil War and slavery are also frequently explored as in Patricia Beatty's *Charley*

Skedaddle (1987) and *Turn Homeward, Hannahlee* (1984); Sharon Draper's *Copper Sun* (2006); Paul Fleischmann's *Bull Run* (1993); Joyce Hansen's *Which Way Freedom* (1986); and Maureen Stack Sappey's *Letters from Vinnie* (1996). World War II and its aftermath can be seen from multiple perspectives. Many of the books have been translated from other languages. Settings include: Denmark (Bjarne Reuter's *The Boys from St. Petri*, 1994); Germany (Peter Härtling's *Crutches*, 1988); Greece (Alki Zei's *Petros' War*, 1974); Japan and Korea (Yoko Kawashima Watkins's *So Far from the Bamboo Grove*, 1986); Korea (Linda Sue Park's *When my Name Was Keoko*, 2002); Netherlands (Els Pelgrom's *The Winter When Time Was Frozen*, 1980); the United Kingdom (Nina Bawden's *Carrie's War*, 1973); and the United States (Mary Downing Hahn's *Stepping on the Cracks*, 1991 and Patricia Rielly Giff's *Lily's Crossing*, 1997). The Holocaust and its context have been treated by many European and American authors including in titles such as *Daniel Half Human and the Good Nazi* by David Chotjewitz and *Friedrich* (1970) by Hans Peter Richter, both set in Germany; *Run, Boy, Run* (2003) by Uri Orlev, set in Poland; and *Upon the Head of the Goat* (1981) by Aranka Siegal (1981) as well as *Marika* (2002) by Andrea Cheng, both set in Hungary.

The Civil Rights era has been portrayed in books such as *The Watsons Go to Birmingham, 1963*, (1995) by Christopher Curtis, which begins with the humorous interactions of an African American family and their journey South, but turns serious during the trip, with sibling rivalry and teasing replaced by siblings helping each other survive emotionally. The Great Depression has been frequently depicted from various perspectives: *Esperanza Rising* (2000) by Pam Munoz Ryan, from a Mexican-American immigrant farm worker perspective; *Out of the Dust* (1997) by Karen Hesse from an Oklahoma farm girl's perspective; and *Bud, Not Buddy*, (1999) by Christopher Curtis from an African American perspective. Successful works of historical fiction have believable characters, vivid and accurate settings, and plausible plots.

MODERN FANTASY

Fantasy is one of the most enduring forms of children's literature. Only poetry and the genre's closest forebears, the traditional folk-fairy tales, legends, and myths have persisted longer, and for some of the same reasons. By transcending specific geographic settings and symbolically representing ideas, authors have been able to speak to audiences across both time and space.

Modern fantasy contrasts with its folkloric antecedents by its complexity, highly developed themes, and carefully crafted characters, many of whom are, in spite of the fantasy element, recognizable young people in search of identity, friendships, and values to live by. It was Tolkien who articulated the essential quality a fantasy writer must strive for if the reader is to achieve "willing suspension of disbelief." Tolkien called for consistency based on the "laws" set up for the imagined world and for treating the magic seriously, not as something to explain away or to smirk at.[31]

Some of the typical categories of fantasy include literary fairy tales, which are halfway between traditional folktales and modern fantasy; high fantasy or quest fantasy; animal fantasy; toy fantasy; enchanted journeys and alternative worlds; supernatural and time-shift fantasy; and science fiction.

Contemporary authors of literary fairy tales for children include the American novelists Robin McKinley (*Beauty*, 1978 and *Rose Daughter*, 1997—both a reenvisioning of Jeanne-Marie Leprince de Beaumont's 1757 classic "Beauty and the Beast"); Gail Carson Levine (*Ella Enchanted*, 1997—a psychological exploration of the Cinderella figure); Donna Napoli (*The Magic Circle*, 1993—a look at the witch's perspective in Hansel and Gretel); and Jane Yolen who is sometimes referred to as the American Hans Christian Andersen. Literary fairy tales continue to draw on traditional fairy tale characters such as elves, dragons, princesses, wizards and witches, etc. as do works of high fantasy, also referred to as quest fantasy.

The high fantasy genre whose heroes begin life inauspiciously but prove their nobility through valor, perseverance, and the willingness to fight against the forces of evil—begun by George MacDonald in the nineteenth century—continues strong in the twenty-first century. The international popularity of the Harry Potter series by J. K. Rowling, starting with *Harry Potter and the Philosopher's Stone* (1997, i.e., *The Sorcerer's Stone*) has rekindled interest in the genre, partly because though the evil is of mythic proportions, Harry is a less-than-perfect, seemingly ordinary boy who defeats the embodiment of evil by relinquishing the temptations of power, choosing through love to save his companions and ultimately the world. With a few exceptions, high fantasy with its complex plots, often strange secondary-world settings, literary allusions, and symbolism is generally more accessible and of greater interest to upper elementary students through adults than to younger readers. A few of the American award-winning writers of high fantasy include Lloyd Alexander whose Welsh mythology-inspired Prydain series (beginning with *The Book of Three*, 1964) presents adventurous male and female heroes as well as humorous secondary characters; British-born Susan Cooper (The Dark is Rising series, starting with *Oversea, Under Stone*, 1965, in which contemporary children protect the land as they communicate with Arthurian heroes); Ursula Le Guin whose *Earthsea* series (*A Wizard of Earthsea*, 1968) begins with a 12-year old boy wizard and ends six volumes later with a young adult female hero in *Tehanu* (1990); and Robin McKinley who has created strong female heroes in books such as *The Blue Sword* (1982).

A few of the many great British fantasy writers since the mid-twentieth century include C. S. Lewis (The Chronicles of Narnia series, starting with *The Lion, the Witch and the Wardrobe*, 1950, a Christian allegory in which four ordinary children must choose between Aslan, the good king of Narnia and the evil white witch); Diana Wynne Jones (The "Chrestomanci" series, 1977–2005 about a young boy magician, his sisters, and their schooling); and Philip Pullman (*Northern Lights*, 1995, i.e., *The Golden Compass* and the rest of His Dark Materials series), whose male and female protagonists explore complex issues of belief, the uses of technology, and issues of power). International writers of high fantasy whose works have been translated into English include German author Michael Ende (*Die Unendliche Geschichte*, 1979, i.e., *The Neverending Story*, 1983); Italian author Silvana De Mari (*L'Ultimo Elfo*, 2004, i.e., *The Last Dragon*, 2006); and Japanese author Miyuki Miyabe (*Bureibu sutori*, 2003, i.e., Brave *Story*, 2007).

Animal fantasy has dominated picture books since Beatrix Potter first dressed Peter Rabbit in a blue jacket and gave him a sense of adventure. Because preschoolers readily identify with the animal protagonist, authors/illustrators can focus on universal feelings and can have animals do more extreme and more dangerous activities than would be realistic for young children. This last consideration is also true for the animal fantasies written for early elementary age children, such as Beverly Cleary's *The Mouse and the Motorcycle* (1965). Most animal fantasy is for younger readers, but some, because of their complexity and literary allusions, are more likely to appeal to middle and upper elementary age students than to younger children: *Mrs. Frisby and the Rats of NIMH* by Robert O'Brien (1971); *Watership Down* (1972) by Richard Adams; *Redwall* (1987) and its series by Brian Jacques; and *The Amazing Maurice and His Educated Rodents*, (2001), by Terry Pratchett.

Since Carlo Collodi's Pinocchio first strove to become human in 1883, toys in children's books have been talking about their feelings, making friendships, and discussing philosophical questions of what it means to be loved (*The Velveteen Rabbit*, 1922 by Margery Williams Bianco); how to be a friend (*Winnie-the-Pooh*, 1926 and *The House at Pooh Corner*, 1928 by A. A. Milne); and whether it is better to take your chances with life or to be the perfect manufactured object (*Alexander and the Wind-up Mouse*, 1969 by Leo Lionni). While books about toys are usually written for younger children, books such as Russell Hoban's *The Mouse and His Child* (1967), replete with social commentary, appeal to somewhat older children.

Alice's Adventures in Wonderland (1865), with its combination of playfulness and satire, set a high mark for journeys to a parallel universe. In some books it is the children of this world who find a way to the alternative world, as in *The Phantom Tollbooth* (1961) by Norton Juster; *Coraline* (2002) by Neil Gaiman; and *Dangerous*

Spaces (1991) by Margaret Mahy. In other stories it is the inhabitants of the parallel world who slip into our world, as in *The Borrowers* (1952) by Mary Norton and in *Moorchild* (1996) by Eloise McGraw. Or, the story takes place entirely in what Tolkien called a secondary world, as in Diana Wynne Jones's *Cart and Cwidder* (1975) and the rest of the Dalemark quartet and Terry Pratchett's *Wee Free Men* (2003) and all of the books in the Discworld series.

Time slip/time travel is often a device for introducing historical eras or to help a protagonist get in touch with people in the past in order to understand their perspectives or to understand themselves better, as in *Playing Beatie Bow* (1980) by Australian author Ruth Park, who takes a modern-day girl back to her grandmother's days in late nineteenth century Sidney, and *The Ultimate Game* (2000) by Christian Lehmann, in which three boys discover that war is not a game. Other time slips include *Tom's Midnight Garden* (1958) by British author Philippa Pearce; *Building Blocks* (1984) by Cynthia Voigt; *The Devil's Arithmetic* (1988) by Jane Yolen; and *If I Should Die Before I Wake* (1994) by Han Nolan.

Many children and young adults like tales of haunting, horror, and the supernatural in both traditional literature and in modern fantasy, as the popularity of Stephen King with adolescents attests. Tales of the supernatural for elementary school age children include: *The Improbable Cat* (2004) by Allan Ahlberg; *The Children of Green Knowe* (1954) and its sequels by Lucy Boston; *The Ghost of Thomas Kempe* (1973) by Penelope Lively; *The Ghost Drum* (1987) by Susan Price; *Whispers in the Graveyard* (1994) by Theresa Breslin; as well as the humorous spoof of the genre, *Bunnicula* (1979) by Deborah and James Howe.

Some fantasy works are hard to classify. A few of these include modern classics such as Natalie Babbitt's philosophical *Tuck Everlasting* (1975) with its exploration of death and the cycle of life; Roald Dahl's *James and the Giant Peach* (1961) and *Charlie and the Chocolate Factory* (1964); Alan Garner's *The Owl Service* (1967); and Geraldine McCaughrean's *A Pack of Lies* (1988).

Science fiction, while less generally popular with children than fantasy, has its enthusiastic followers.[14] Jules Verne (*Vingt Mille Lieues sous le Mers* 1870, i.e., *20,000 Leagues Under the Sea*) and H. G. Wells (*The Time Machine*, 1895) introduced the genre. Since its inception, science fiction, though based on scientific and technological concepts, is speculative rather than accurate, dealing with technological possibilities as well as their social ramifications. Madeline L'Engle in *A Wrinkle in Time* (1962) with its contemporary settings and technological dystopia explores the concept of free will within the contexts of both a totalitarian government and Christian theology. Other works of science fiction address issues such as the meaning of civilization (*The Green Book*, 1981 by Jill Paton Walsh); the uses and abuses of cloning people

(*House of the Scorpion*, 2003 by Nancy Farmer and *Galax-Arena*, 1992 by Gillian Rubinstein); and what it would mean if we could eliminate pain, sorrow and even the memories of painful history from our lives (*The Giver*, 1993 by Lois Lowry). Other authors who have written science fiction for children and young adults include Monica Hughes, Andre Norton, Kenneth Oppel and William Sleator.

INFORMATIONAL BOOKS AND BIOGRAPHIES

Although children's informational books are not a new genre—John Newbery published many informational books, including the series *The Newtonian System of Philosophy* (1761) by "Tom Telescope," changes in attitudes toward children and changes in publishing technology have fueled a dramatic increase in engaging, quality informational books for children.

Changes in attitudes toward children involved viewing them as capable of responding to the inherent interest of factual material without the need for a thin story veneer, formerly thought essential in order to fascinate young readers. The use of a story line to introduce informational material, however, does remain common for preschoolers through first or second grade, and research suggests that the emotional involvement with the story characters helps these children remember the information.[32] One of the most successful among informational books with a story line is the *Magic School Bus* series by Joanna Cole, illustrated by Bruce Degan, in which the author and illustrator make use of fantasy by having the magic school bus explore a wide range of scientific concepts from the inner world of the circulatory system to the eye of a hurricane. Most outstanding authors of informational books, however, have chosen to eschew fictionalizing even for younger children in favor of using an engaging style. They involve readers by stimulating their thinking through demonstrating the process of research, asking provocative questions, and leaving unanswered questions for children to ponder and dream about researching in the future. Vivid photographs, diagrams, and images extend the information. Jean Fritz, in a series of biographies for 2–4th graders about American Revolutionary War figures (*And Then What Happened Paul Revere?* 1973) pioneered the use of a lively, informal style of writing while adhering to strictly documented information and presenting a balanced view of her subjects, flaws included, in order to help her readers realize that they too can strive to be great. When Fritz chose accuracy over idealized models, she broke new ground in writing biography for children. Judith St. George (*So You Want to be President*, 2000) and Kathleen Krull (*Lives of the Musicians: Good Times, Bad Times, and What the Neighbors Thought*, 1993) have continued in the same vein.

Writing informational books for children is challenging, as another outstanding writer, Russell Freedman

(*Lincoln: A Photobiography*, 1987 and numerous other award winning books) has written,

> I welcome the discipline of a book such as that [history or biography] imposes on the author. It is something like writing a sonnet: your words must fit within a certain format, and every word counts …The art lies in the selection and arrangement of documented facts, in the closely observed and painstakingly constructed narrative, and in the imposition on those facts of the author's unique sensibility. It requires a feat of imagination as well as diligent research to make the past live again for the reader. (p. 25)[33]

Imagination and diligent research are certainly the hallmarks of the best of informational books, along with the advantage of high quality photographic reproduction at affordable prices. Freedman, for instance, specializes in using reproductions of archival photographs, letters, diaries, and other primary documents to enhance readers' understanding of his subjects.

Similar to biography and history, the presentation of science for children has also undergone a major change, the field having particularly benefited from technological developments. Children's books feature photographs from the field, as well as electron microscopic, satellite, and fiber-optic images. As with biography and history, ideas about what constitute good science informational books for children have changed in the last quarter of the twentieth century. Newer children's science books focus on the processes of science as well as on science concepts and discoveries, thus involving readers in the painstaking but exciting work of scientific research. Patricia Lauber's *The News About Dinosaurs* (1989) is an example of this approach: she presents the reader with established scientific information about dinosaurs, then shows how, because of new research evidence, these beliefs had to be reevaluated. Similarly, Susan Quinlan involves the readers in both science concepts and processes as she presents 12 rain forest ecology mysteries in *The Case of the Monkeys that Fell from the Trees* (2003), and Sy Montgomery and Nic Bishop document the work of field scientists in books such as *Quest for the Tree Kangaroo: An Expedition to the Cloud Forest of New Guinea* (2006).

Even before children are ready to think formally about hypothesis testing, trade books introduce them to the scientific method, involving them in observation and classification. Following the lead of Milicent Selsam, a science teacher and writer during the 1950s and 1960s whose works stimulated preschool and early elementary school age children to observe their world and to develop hypotheses about their observations, science writers/artists such as Jim Arnosky (*Crinkleroot* nature series) and Steve Jenkins (*What Do you Do with a Tail Like This?* 2003), engage children through biological and visual puzzles. Others have young children consider factorials (Masaichiro and Mitsumasa Anno in *Anno's Mysterious*

Multiplying Jar, 1983) and very large numbers (David Schwartz in *How Much is a Million?* 1985). Informational books also deal with other topics. For instance, they play with language (Fred Gwynne, *A Chocolate Moose for Dinner*, 1976); make grammar and punctuation lessons fun (Lynne Truss's *Eats, Shoots, and Leaves: Why Commas Really Do Matter*, 2006, which is based on her book for adults, *Eats, Shoots, and Leaves: The Zero Tolerance Approach to Punctuation*); or explain to children a range of personal experiences.

It is impossible here to convey the variety of informational books and biographies available to children and young adults; however, the following recommended book lists provide a beginning for exploring the many outstanding authors and illustrators, and their works.

- "Best Science Books for Children" named annually by *Science Books and Films* a publication of the American Association for the Advancement of Science
- "Notable Trade Books for Young People" by the National Council for the Social Studies/ Children's Book Council. This extensive list is published every May in the association's journal *Social Education*, or order directly from Children's Book Council. Also at NCSS: http://www.ncss.org/resources/notable/
- "Outstanding Science Trade Books for Students K-12" by National Science Teachers Association, Children's Book Council. This extensive list is published every March in the association's journal *Science and Children*, or order directly from Children's Book Council. Also at NSTA: http://www.nsta.org/publications/ostb/

See also "Awards" for major informational book and science trade book awards.

INTERNATIONAL CHILDREN'S LITERATURE

International books are defined as having been written in another country for the readers of that country, and then imported and made available either in the original language or in translation. The nineteenth and early twentieth centuries produced classics that readers in many countries consider their own, regardless of the books' origins: The Grimms' and Hans Christian Andersen's fairy tales; *Alice's Adventures in Wonderland*; *Pinocchio*; Jules Verne's books; *Heidi*; *Tom Sawyer*; *The Wonderful Wizard of Oz*; *Winnie the Pooh*; *The Story of Babar*; and *Pippi Longstocking*. With the exception of such classics, however, relatively few children's books are truly international, the worldwide success of English author J. K. Rowling's Harry Potter (1998–2007) series being a rare exception. Furthermore, children in English-speaking countries are exposed to few translated books, with imports representing 1% of the total output of children's books per year as compared with Germany or Japan, where translated books represent around 30% of children's publishing.[2] Reading international books, however, is important as they give children a more balanced view of their world than do the news and commercial films, open a window to the lives of children whose experiences are different from theirs, and connect children to each other through shared readings.[2]

Because children's books from Australia, Great Britain, Canada, the United States and New Zealand are more readily available than translated books, this section will focus on translated books. (For awards from English-speaking countries, see "Awards" section).

In spite of the challenges, it is possible to identify books that were first published in non-English speaking countries. Awards lists highlight authors and illustrators who are known in many countries. The most important award for international literature is the Hans Christian Andersen Award given by the International Board on Books for Young People (IBBY, http://www.ibby.org/index.php?id=273). Margaret Mahy of New Zealand (2006), whose works range from picture books to young adult fiction and fantasy, represents the breadth and quality of writing of the winners. Some of the other recipients who are known worldwide include Finnish author Tove Jansson, who created the Moomintroll family, Swedish author Astrid Lindgren with her irrepressible Pippi Longstocking, and Irish author Martin Waddell, who has written many tender picture books such as Can't You Sleep Little Bear? (1988) as well as retellings of legends and contemporary fiction. The award is an excellent way to become acquainted with writers and illustrators from other countries such as Brazilian authors Lygia Bojunga Nunes and Ana Maria Machado; Japanese illustrator Suekichi Akaba; Norwegian author Tormod Haugen and French illustrator Tomi Ungerer. (Six Americans have also received the award.) The works of most of the awards recipients are available in English.

The Mildred L. Batchelder Award (http://www.ala.org) is an important resource for outstanding translated books available in the United States. While earlier winners of the Batchelder award tended to be translations from Germanic-speaking countries—Denmark, Germany, Netherlands, Norway, Sweden[34]—in more recent years awards have gone to Brazilian, French, Israeli, Italian, Japanese, Spanish, and Turkish authors as well.

The Batchelder Award books have included all genres, but they are especially rich in historical fiction. The stories have been set in Renaissance Italy in The Apprentice (1993) by Pilar Molina Llorente; Napoleonic era Germany in Innocent Soldier (2005) by Josef Holub; and 1950s Syria in Hand Full of Stars (1990) by Rafik Schami. Most frequently represented, however, has been the time period just before, during and right after World War II, including the Holocaust, making the Batchelder Award winners a good source for studying this historic era from multiple perspectives (specific titles are discussed in the section on "Fiction.").

Batchelder winners also include lighthearted books and books set in the present. Some genres and topics include works of contemporary fiction such as the serious yet also humorous exploration of friendship and its healing power in The Friends (1996) by Japanese author Kazumi Yumoto; fantasy, such as Rabbit Island (1978) by Swiss author Jörg Steiner, an allegory of freedom; and science fiction, such as Konrad (1977) by popular Austrian author Christine Nöstlinger about what it means to be human.

Some of the best ways to identify high quality children's books that were first published in another country which are available in the United States are through the three annotated bibliographies sponsored by the United States Board on Books for Youth (USBBY): Carl Tomlinson, Children's Books from Other Countries (1998); Susan Stan, The World Through Children's Books (2002); and Doris Gebel, Crossing Boundaries with Children's Books (2006). (See "Bibliography"). Other international children's book awards are also listed under "Awards."

The following are additional sources for discovering international authors/illustrators and their works:

- Books available in English in the United States: USBBY's "Outstanding International Books" annual list, posted at http://www.usbby.org.
- The "IBBY Honour List," published biennially at the IBBY Web site (under Activities) at http://www.ibby.org/, lists the best written, illustrated, and translated book of each member nation.
- IBBY's journal, Bookbird, provides insight into the national children's literatures of different countries.
- White Ravens, an annual annotated list of international books compiled at the International Youth Library (Internationale Jugend Bibliothek) in Munich available at the International Children's Digital Library (http://www.icdlbooks.org/servlet/WhiteRavens).
- The International Children's Digital Library http://www.icdlbooks.org/index.shtml, full text digitized children's books in their original languages.

LITERATURE REPRESENTING DIVERSE PERSPECTIVES

Readers need to encounter both windows showing the lives of others and mirrors reflecting themselves.[35] Literature written by and about nonmainstream groups is essential to accomplishing this. This entry will focus primarily on multicultural books, that is, books of underrepresented ethnic groups, but will also discuss children's literature that deals with disabilities and alternative sexual orientation.

Multicultural Books

For multicultural literature to be successful, authors must be able to portray the culture of the ethnic group authentically, based on familiarity with the cultural nuances, whether through intimate personal experience or through intensive research.[36] While most librarians and other educators agree that books presenting diverse perspectives are important, building a multicultural collection continues to be a challenge. The Cooperative Children's Book Center (CCBC) at the University of Wisconsin, Madison, reported in 2007 that of the approximately 5000 children's trade books published annually in the United States, five percent (5%) of the books had significant African American or African content, 2.9% having been created by African American authors or illustrators. The numbers were even smaller for other nonmainstream ethnic groups, with 1.3% of the books having Native American content and only 0.4% having been created by Native American authors or illustrators.[37]

The Coretta Scott King Award (http://www.ala.org) has been instrumental in highlighting the works of outstanding African American authors and illustrators. Themes range from the universal to the culturally specific. Recurrent themes include developing relationships and a positive self concept, as in picture books by Eloise Greenfield (*Nathaniel Talking*, 1988, illustrator Jan Spivey Gilchrist) and Angela Johnson (*When I am Old With You*, 1990, illustrator David Soman); a sense of history and pride in the accomplishments of famous and unsung African Americans, as in the books of Tonya Bolden, James Haskins, and Patricia and Frederick McKissack; and realistic portrayals of the struggles of contemporary young people, as in the works of Sharon Draper, Sharon Flake, Walter Dean Myers, and Jacqueline Woodson. The illustrators who have received the award include, among many others, artists mentioned in earlier sections, such as Gregory Christie, Bryan Collier, Floyd Cooper, Leo and Diane Dillon, Christopher Myers, Brian Pinkney, and Jerry Pinkney. For an extensive annotated bibliography, see Rand and Parker's *Black Books Galore* (in "Bibliography").

While most of the approximately 2.2% of children's books representing Asian Americans are folktales, there are many authors and illustrators who portray Asian American experiences realistically, although Chinese or Japanese Americans are best represented among both authors and subjects.[38] Striking a balance between striving for acceptance by the mainstream culture through assimilation and maintaining ethnic identity have been dominant themes in contemporary and historical fiction as in many of Laurence Yep's books, such as *Child of the Owl* (1971); Gene Luen Yang's *American-Born Chinese* (2006); Cynthia Kadohata's *Kira, Kira* (2004); An Na's *A Step from Heaven* (2001); Tanuja Hidier Desai's *Born Confused* (2002); and the picture books *Apple Pie 4th of July* (2002) by Janet Wong, and *Halmoni and the Picnic* (1993) by Sook Nyul Choi. Many books also celebrate cultural heritage, as in Kam Mak's *My Chinatown: One Year in Poems* (2002), Grace Lin's *Year of the Dog*

(2006), and Madhur Jaffrey's *Seasons of Splendor* (1985). The Asian Pacific American Award for Literature (http://www.apalaweb.org/awards/) honors authors and illustrators who portray Asian or Asian-American culture authentically.

Latino/Latina authors and illustrators portray the diversity of experiences in Latin American countries and U.S. Latino communities. George Ancona's, Monica Brown and Raul Colon's, and Carmen Lomas Garza's informational picture books document both daily lives and the lives of famous people; the narrative poetry of Carmen T. Bernier-Grand and Margarita Engle celebrate historical and contemporary figures while the lyric poems of Francis X. Alarcon, Juan Felipe Herrerra, Pat Mora, and Gary Soto give voice to children's experiences; and Francisco Jimenez, Pam Muñoz Ryan, and Victor Martinez portray through autobiography and fiction the importance of family and the challenges of being poor and an immigrant. While much of Latino/Latina, children's literature is specific to Mexican American experiences, Alma Flor Ada and Lulu Delacre are two of the authors who also portray Cuban and Puerto Rican culture and folklore. Three awards that recognize outstanding Latino books include The Pura Belpré Award (http://www.ala.org), the Americas Award (http://www.uwm.edu/Dept/CLACS/aa/index.html), and the Tómas Rivera Award (http://www.education.txstate.edu/departments/Tomas-Rivera-Book-Award-Project-Link.html)

Until recently most children's books about Native Americans were written by non-Native writers. Even when well-meant, these books' themes, characterizations, details of everyday life, and values were and often still are inauthentic.[39] Increasingly, there are children's books in all genres created by American Indian writers and illustrators. Besides retelling traditional legends and myths, Joseph Bruchac (Abenaki) for instance, has written picture books (*Fox Song*, 1993), fiction (*The Heart of a Chief*, 1998), and modern fantasy (*Skeleton Man*, 2001). Other authors, such as National Book Award winner Sherman Alexie (Spokane/Coeur d'Alene) and Cynthia Leitich Smith (Muscogee) show the lives of contemporary Native Americans through realistic fiction while Louise Erdrich (Ojibwe) and Tim Tingle (Choctaw) have provided Native American perspectives on historic eras and events through historical fiction. Sources for authentically written/illustrated books about Native American experiences include: The online catalog of Oyate, http://www.oyate.org, a nonprofit Native American organization; *A Broken Flute: The Native American Experience in Books for Children* (2005) by Doris Seale and Beverly Slapin (See "Bibliography"); and the American Indian Youth Literature Award http://aila.library.sd.gov/News/2008youthlit/index.htm.   (See "Awards").

Finding books representing Middle Eastern Americans or Muslims is a particular challenge, but children's books written by Middle Eastern Americans are beginning to appear. Naomi Shihab Nye has written about Palestinian Americans' experiences visiting family in Palestine in picture books such as *Sitti's Secret* (1994) and in contemporary fiction such as *Habibi* (1997) and has translated Arabic poetry for young people. Nye's books of poetry and anthologies express hope for a peaceful world. Other writers describe refugee experiences, as do Ibtisam Barakat in *Tasting the Sky* (2007); Deborah Ellis, a Canadian author, in *The Breadwinner* (2000) and its sequels; and Rukhsana Khan in a picture book, *The Roses in my Carpets* (1998).

For reviews of current multicultural books, see:

MultiCultural Review, the official publication of EMIERT, the Ethnic and MultiCultural Information Exchange Round Table of the ALA. http://mcreview.com/

For annotated bibliographies, see "Bibliography"

Books about Children with Special Needs

In the nineteenth century children with disabilities were presented in children's books as exemplars of virtue, often acquired by the child after developing the disability. Sentimental and unrealistic presentations continued in the twentieth century though a few children's books did present children with disabilities realistically, focusing on not only their struggles but their strengths. *Johnny Tremain* (1943) by Esther Forbes is an early example. The Schneider Family Award of the ALA (http://www.ala. org), begun in 2004, was established in order to recognize books of literary/artistic quality that present the disability experience, whether of the protagonist or of the family. Disabilities can be physical, mental, or emotional, such as Cynthia Lord's *Rules* (2006) about an autistic boy and his older sister, Pam Muñoz Ryan's *Becoming Naomi León* (2004) about a Mexican American girl and her learning disabled brother, and Pete Seeger and Paul DuBois Jacobs's *The Deaf Musicians*. Another excellent resource, especially for younger children, their families, and teachers is a 300 item bibliography compiled by Crystal and Kaiser (2007) (see "Bibliography").

Books Featuring Gay, Lesbian, or Trangendered Characters

Few picture books for children feature homosexual protagonists or same-sex parents. Of the few, Justin Richardson and Peter Parnall's *And Tango Makes Three*, a picture book account of two male penguins in a New York City Zoo raising a penguin chick, is one of the best picture books on the topic of same-sex households. There are far more well-written young adult books with gay or lesbian characters by writers like Nancy Garden, Julie Peters, Alex Sanchez, and Ellen Wittlinger. The best of the books feature characters who are not defined solely by their sexual identity. The "Stonewall Award," listed in

ALA-Awards (http://www.ala.org) recognizes children's books dealing with gay/lesbian/transgendered issues.

NONPRINT MEDIA

Children's literature has long been tied to toys, decorative objects, and other products, such as children's dishes and linens, the best known of which may be those depicting Beatrix Potter's characters. While most of these products are commercial ventures, libraries have made good use of the puppets and dolls that have been created from literary characters, such as Madeline, The Cat in the Hat, and The Wild Things, to generate interest in the books.

The new forms of media that changes in technology have made possible have added to rather than supplanted books as a source of children's literary experiences. Besides original films meant for children, children's classics, such as *Little Women*; *Heidi*; *Pinocchio*; and *The Secret Garden* have been adapted to film, most several times, in both live action and animation, and are available through videotapes/DVDs and Web-based film sources. One of the films made from a children's book that has achieved classic status in its own right is *The Wizard of Oz* (Dir: Fleming, 1939). A few of the many more recent award-winning children's books with film adaptations include *Bridge to Terabithia* by Katherine Paterson; *Charlie and the Chocolate Factory* by Roald Dahl; *Ella Enchanted* by Gail Carson Levine; the *Harry Potter* series by J. K. Rowling; *Holes* by Louis Sachar; *The Polar Express* and *Jumanji* by Chris Van Allsburg; *A Wrinkle in Time* by Madeline L'Engle; and many of Dr. Seuss's books, including his *How the Grinch Stole Christmas*. Some children's books, such as *Anne of Green Gables* by L. M. Montgomery; *Carrie's War* by Nina Bawden; *Sarah, Plain and Tall* and its Sequels by Patricia Maclachlan; and *Konrad* by Christine Nöstlinger have been made directly into television movies. The International Movie Database, http://www.imdb.com is a good source for identifying different productions of these films.

Besides commercial film and television, several producers have used film/video to recreate picture books, as close to the original as possible. These productions preserve the original text and art, adding animation or iconography, music, narration, and sound effects. These formats are available in school and public libraries and are meant primarily for preschool and elementary age children. Weston Woods Studios pioneered the format and set the standard for painstaking effort to make possible for classroom sharing the literary and visual delights of a picture book. The Andrew Carnegie Medal (http://www. ala.org) honors the producers of an outstanding children's video. Award-winning videos range from iconographic images of picture books such as Mordecai Gerstein's *The Man who Walked Between the Towers* (2005), produced by Michael Sporn and Paul Gagne, to live action such as

Jump in Free Style (2007), produced by Kevin Lafferty, directed by P. Hoen. Children's videos are reviewed in *School Library Journal* and *Booklist*.

Audiobooks have moved with the technology from vinyl records to cassette tapes to compact discs and have gained a far wider audience, as adults and young adults have begun to listen to audiobooks. High quality children's and young adult books are available in audio format. Because the quality of narration is important, audiobooks are reviewed in such professional journals as *Horn Book Magazine, School Library Journal, Booklist* and *VOYA (Voice of Youth Advocates)*. Three major awards for audiobooks are: the Audie Award (http://www.hbook.com/resources/awards/default.asp), the *Audiobook Hall of Fame* (http://www.hbook.com/resources/awards/default.asp and the Odyssey Award from Association for Library Services to Children(ALSC) and Young Adult Library Services Association (YALSA) divisions of ALA (http://www.ala.org). Award-winning audiobooks may be read by a full cast, as in *Knuffle Bunny* (2006) which was read by author Mo Willems and his family, but more often are narrated by a single narrator with occasional musical accompaniment as in 2008 Odyssey Award winning *Jazz* (2007) by Walter Dean Myers.

Electronic books, also referred to as e-books or digital books, are becoming increasingly important for reference work for high school students and adults, but children's trade books, while available in digital form since the mid-1990s, have not yet become widely popular. Nevertheless CD-ROM and online digital versions exist and are reviewed in *School Library Journal*. The best of the e-books take advantage of computer animation and use it to enhance the text and allow children to interact with the medium, as is the case with David Macaulay's *The New Way Things Work*, Version 3.2 (DK, 2007). Most electronic books, even the better ones, however, make limited use of the technology. The potential for great changes to the delivery method of picture books and novels is only beginning to be realized, but picture book artists, such as Jean Gralley, are excited about the possibilities of "lifting the book off the page" and onto portable, rollable, back-lit and searchable e-paper which will have the advantages of both the book and digital technology.[18]

Another use of electronic texts, accessibility from anywhere, is already a reality. Besides digital archives of historical children's books from university and national libraries, The International Children's Digital Library (http://www.icdlbooks.org/) is a growing collection of electronic texts which allows readers to access full-text books from a wide range of countries. Most of the books are in-copyright books that authors and publishers have made available to children worldwide, but the digital library also includes historic nineteenth and early twentieth century books.

Computer games with sophisticated graphics which allow multiple players to interact in virtual environments have become a major form of "literature" as players become creators of realistic contemporary or futuristic worlds as in *Sims 2*. The realistic visuals allow players to better immerse themselves in the worlds they are exploring, while the roles they build allow them to look at the ramifications of the decisions they make within the game.[40]

CHILDREN'S LITERATURE AWARDS, ORGANIZATIONS, AND COLLECTIONS

Children's literature research collections have burgeoned nationally and internationally since the mid-twentieth century, when an ALA survey identified 153 collections in the United States and Canada. In 1995, there were over 300 American collections, and 119 collections internationally. National libraries have comprehensive collections, and their catalogs can be accessed online. The International Federation of Library Associations (IFLA) provides links to National Library Catalogues (http://www.ifla.org/VI/2/p2/national-libraries.htm#U). Two of the oldest international research collections include the International Youth Library in Munich (http://www.ijb.de/) and the International Institute for Children's Literature, Osaka (http://www.iiclo.or.jp/english/english.htm). For other major collections and research centers identified by country, see the International Children's Literature Research Society's Web page (http://www.irscl.com/). Besides links to collections, the society's Web page also lists journals of children's literature.

The following Awards list identifies organizations and their children's book awards. Because of space limitations it is not possible to identify all national awards; the list was therefore limited to English Language and major international awards. The Database of Award Winning Children's Literature compiled by Lisa R. Bartle provides access to award winning books by author, title, and subject (http://www.dawcl.com/).

International Awards:
Swedish Arts Council

The Astrid Lindgren Memorial Award.

(http://www.alma.se/default_a.aspx?id=247&epslanguage =EN) : Given for a *body of works*, living authors, illustrators, storytellers and promoters of reading are eligible. Annual, started 2002.

International Board on Books for Young People. (http://www.ibby.org/ see Activities)

Hans Christian Andersen Award: for a *body of works* (total contribution to children's literature) by an internationally acclaimed author; total work by international illustrator (two different awards). Every 2 years, started 1956.

International Reading Association (http://www.ira.org)

Children's and Young Adult's Book Awards for author's first or second publication. Fiction and nonfiction for primary, intermediate, and young adult readers. (Annual, since 1975)

U.S. Awards:

American Institute of Physics. (http://www.aip.org/aip/writing/winchild.html)

Science Writing Award—Children (Annual since 1988) by the ALA—Association for Library Services to Children (http://www.ala.org/ala/alsc/awardsscholarships/awardsscholarships.cfm):

Andrew Carnegie Medal for Excellence in *Children's Videos*. Annual, started 1991.

Caldecott Medal: for best *illustrated picture book* by U.S. illustrator (citizen or resident). Annual, started 1938.

Laura Ingalls Wilder Award: for a *body of works* by U.S. author or illustrator. Every 3 years, started 1954.

Mildred L. Batchelder Award: Given by the ALA to the U.S. publisher of the *best-translated book* of the previous year, which had been originally published in another language. Annual, started 1968.

Newbery Medal: for best *written* children's book by U.S. author (citizen or resident). Annual, started 1922.

Odyssey Award for *audiobooks*. Annual, started 2008.

Pura Belpré Award given jointly with REFORMA for a *Latino/Latina author and illustrator*. Annual, started 1996.

Robert F. Sibert *Informational Book* Medal: Annual, started 2001.

Schneider Family Book Award for authors or illustrators of outstanding books that depict the *disability experience* for grade school, middle school, teens. Annual, started 2007.

Theodore Seuss Geisel Award for most outstanding *beginning reader trade books for authors and illustrators*. Annual, started 2004.

American Library Association Ethnic and MultiCultural Information Exchange Round Table (http://www.ala.org/ala/emiert/corettascottkingbookaward/corettascott.cfm)

Coretta Scott King Award and Honor books: best written text by an *African American writer*, best picture book by an *African American illustrator*. Annual, started 1970.

Asian/Pacific American Library Association an ALA Affiliate (http://www.apalaweb.org/awards/awards.htm)

Asian Pacific American Awards for Literature. Children's categories include authors and illustrators of an outstanding book of fiction or nonfiction that is related to *Asian/Pacific Heritage*, not necessarily by someone of that heritage. Annual, started 2004.

Boston Globe-Horn Book Awards (http://www.hbook.com/bghb/)

Picture book, Fiction, Nonfiction category by *The Boston Globe* and *Horn Book Magazine*. Annual, started 1967.

Center for Latin American and Caribbean Studies. University of Wisconsin, Madison

The Americas Award. (http://www.uwm.edu/Dept/CLACS/aa/index.html)

U.S. works of fiction, poetry, folklore, or selected nonfiction (from picture books to works for young adults) published in the previous year in English or Spanish that authentically and engagingly portray *Latin America*, the *Caribbean*, or *Latinos in the United States*. Annual, started 1993.

Jane Addams Peace Association (http://home.igc.org/~japa/index.html) and Women's International League for Peace and Freedom (WILPF).

Jane Addams Children's Book Awards

The award is given for "children's books published the preceding year that effectively *promote the cause of peace, social justice, world community and the equality of the sexes and all races* as well as meeting conventional standards for excellence." Annual, started 1953.

National Council of Teachers of English (http://www.ncte.org)

Award for Excellence in Poetry: Every 3 years, started 1977

Orbis Pictus Award: For an outstanding *informational book* (including biography) of the previous year. Annual, started 1990.

Texas State University College of Education. (http://www.education.txstate.edu/departments/Tomas-Rivera-Book-Award-Project-Link.html)

Tomas Rivera Mexican American Children's Book Award. Honors authors and illustrators who create literature that depicts the *Mexican American* experience. Annual, started 1995.

The Horn Book Magazine Web page (http://www.hbook.com/resources/awards/default.asp) lists a wide variety of national and international children's media awards, including the *National Book Award; The Golden Kite Award*; the *Audie* for Audiobooks, the *Audiobook Hall of Fame* and the *Will Eisner Award* for comic books and graphic novels.

British Awards:

Chartered Institute of Library and Information Professionals (CILIP) http://www.carnegiegreenaway.org.uk/home/index.php

Carnegie Award to the *author* of best children's book first published in the United Kingdom (or copublished within three months) the previous year. Annual, started 1937.

Kate Greenaway Award to the *illustrator* of the best children's book first published in the United Kingdom (or co-published within three months) the previous year. Annual, started 1955.

Australian Awards:

Children's Book Council of Australia, in the categories of *older readers, younger readers, early childhood, picture book* and *informational book*. Annual. http://cbca.org.au/

Canadian Awards:

Canadian Council for the Arts, Governor General's Literary Awards: in seven categories, including

Children's literature (text) and *Children's literature (illustration)*http://www.canadacouncil.ca/prizes/ggla/

Canadian Library Association http://www.cla.ca "CLA at Work"-Awards-Book Awards

Book of the Year for Children Award for *text*. Annual, started 1947

Amelia Frances Howard-Gibbon Award for *Illustrator*. Annual, started 1971

Young Adult Canadian Book Award. Annual, started 1981.

New Zealand Awards:

Library and Information Association of New Zealand http://library.christchurch.org.nz/Kids/LiteraryPrizes/EstherGlen/

Esther Glenn Award for the most distinguished contribution to *children's and young adult* literature. Annual, started 1945.

REFERENCES

1. Silvey, A. *The Essential Guide to Children's Books and Their Creators*; Houghton Mifflin: Boston, MA, 2002.
2. Tomlinson, C.M. An overview of international children's literature. In *Children's Books from Other Countries*; Tomlinson, C.M., Ed.; Scarecrow Press: Lanham, MD, 1998; 6–17.
3. Lukens, R.J. *A Critical Handbook of Children's Literature*, 8th Ed.; Allyn & Bacon: Boston, MA, 2007.
4. Bottigheimer, R. Fairy and folk-tales. In *International Encyclopedia of Children's Literature*; Hunt, P., Ed.; Routledge: London, 1996.
5. Darton, F.J.H. *Children's Books in England*, 3rd Ed.; Alderson, B., Ed.; Cambridge University Press: Cambridge, U.K., 1982.
6. Hearne, B. *Beauty and the Beast: Visions and Revisions of an Old Tale*; University of Chicago Press: Chicago, IL, 1989.
7. Zipes, J. *Beauties, Beasts, and Enchantments: Classic French Fairy Tales*; Penguin: New York, 1991.
8. Avery, G. Chapbooks. In *The Oxford Encyclopedia of Children's Literature*; Zipes, J., Ed.; Oxford University Press: New York, 2006; Vol. 1, 279–284.
9. Jackson, M.V. *Engines of Instruction, Mischief, and Magic: Children's Literature in England from Its Beginnings to 1839*, University of Nebraska Press: Lincoln, NE, 1989.
10. Zipes, J. *The Brothers Grimm: From Enchanted Forests to Modern Worlds*; Routledge: New York, 1988.
11. McGillis, R. MacDonald, George. In *The Oxford Encyclopedia of Children's Literature*; Zipes, J., Ed.; Oxford University Press: New York, 2006; Vol. 3, 11–12.
12. Lurie, A. *Don't Tell the Grown-Ups: Subversive Children's Literature*; Little, Brown: Boston, MA, 1990.
13. Hunt, P. *Children's Literature*; Blackwell: Oxford, 2001.
14. Russell, D. *Literature for Children: A Short Introduction*, 5th Ed. Allyn and Bacon: Boston, MA, 2004.
15. Jacobson, M. *Being a Boy Again: Autobiography and the American Boy Book*; University of Alabama Press: Tuscaloosa, AL, 1994.
16. Kümmerling-Meibauer, B. Illustrations. In *The Oxford Encyclopedia of Children's Literature*; Zipes, J., Ed.; Oxford University Press: New York, 2006; Vol. 3, 276–281.
17. Hearne, B. Perennial picture books seeded by oral tradition. J. Youth Ser. Libr. Fall **1998**, *12*(1), 26–33.
18. Gralley, J. Liftoff: When books leave the page. Horn Book Mag. January/February **2006**, *LXXXII*(1), 35–39.
19. University of North Texas, A brief history of early movable books. *Pop-up and Movable Books: A Tour through Their History*, http://www.library.unt.edu/rarebooks/exhibits/popup2/ (accessed November 30, 2008).
20. Dales, B. Pop-up books that make the cut. Book Links **2007**, *16*(6), 29–32.
21. Hunt, J. The trickle-up effect: An interview with David Saylor. Child. Libr. **2007**, Spring *5*(1), 8–11.
22. Schwartz, G.E. Graphic novels for multiple literacies. Reading Online. 32–36.
23. Saltman, J. *The Riverside Anthology of Children's Literature*, 6th Ed.; Houghton Mifflin: Boston, MA, 1985.
24. McGillis, R. Blake, William. In *The Oxford Encyclopedia of Children's Literature*; Zipes, J., Ed.; Oxford University Press: New York, 2006; Vol. 1, 169.
25. MacDonald, M.R. *Traditional Storytelling Today: An International Sourcebook*; Fitzroy Dearborn: Chicago, IL, 1999.
26. Dég, L. *American Folklore and the Mass Media*; Indiana University: Bloomington, IN, 1994.
27. Dorson, R. *American Folklore and the Historian*; University of Chicago Press: Chicago, IL, 1971.
28. Hearne, B. Swapping tales and stealing stories: The ethics and aesthetics of folklore in children's literature. Libr. Trends **1999**, *47*(3), 509–528.
29. Bruchac, J. The continuing circle: Native American storytelling past and present. In *Who Says: Essays on Pivotal Issues in Contemporary Storytelling*; Birch, C.L., Heckler, C.A., Eds.; August House: Little Rock, AK, 1996; 90–105.
30. Nilsen, A.P.; Donelson, K.L. *Literature for Today's Young Adult*, 8th Ed.; Allyn and Bacon: Boston, MA, 2008.
31. Tolkien, J.R.R. On fairy stories. *Tree and Leaf*; Allen and Unwin: London, U.K., 1964.
32. Brabham, E.; Boyd, P.; Edgington, W. Sorting it out: Elementary students' responses to fact and fiction informational storybooks as read-alouds for science and social studies. Read. Res. Instruct. **2000**, *39*, 265–290.
33. Freedman, R. May Hill Arbuthnot honor ;lecture: the past isn't past: How history speaks and what it says to the next generation. Child. Libr. **2006**, *4*(2), 21–28.
34. Nist, J.S. The Mildred L. Batchelder Award: Around the world with forty-two books. Lang. Arts **1979**, *56*(4), 368–374.
35. Bishop, R.S. Mirrors, windows, and sliding glass doors. Perspectives **1990**, *6*, ix–xi.
36. Temple, C.; Martinez, M.; Yokota, J. *Children's Books in Children's Hands: An Introduction to Their Literature*, 3rd Ed.; Allyn and Bacon: Boston, MA, 2006.
37. Horning, K.; Lindgren, M.; Michaelson, T.; Schliesman, M. *Publishing in 2006*, Cooperative Children's Books Center: Madison, WI, 2007; http://www.education.wisc.edu/ccbc/books/choiceintro07.asp (accessed April 12, 2008).
38. Loh, V.S. Quantity and quality: The need for culturally authentic trade books in Asian American young adult literature. ALAN Rev. **2006**, *34*(1), 36–53.

39. Seale, D.; Slapin, B. *The Broken Flute: The Native American Experience in Books for Children*; Oyate: Berkeley, CA, 2005.

40. Stoerger, S. Virtual worlds, virtual literacy: An educational exploration. Knowl. Quest **2008**, *36*(3), 50–56.

BIBLIOGRAPHY

1. East, K.; Thomas, R. *Across Cultures: A Guide to Multicultural Literature for Children*; Libraries Unlimited: Westport, CT, 2007.

2. Fox, D.L.; Short, K.G. *Stories Matter: The Complexity of Cultural Authenticity in Children's Literature*; National Council of Teachers of English: Urbana, IL, 2003.

3. Gebel, D., Ed.; *Crossing Boundaries with Children's Books*; Scarecrow Press: Lanham, MD, 2006; Sponsored by USBBY.

4. Hallett, M.; Karasek, B. *Folk & Fairy Tales*; Broadview Press: Peterborough, 2002.

5. Harris, V.J. *Teaching Multicultural Literature in Grades K-8*; Christopher-Gordon: Norwood, MA, 1992.

6. Helbig, A.K.; Perkins, A.R. *Many Peoples, One Land: A Guide to New Multicultural Literature for Children and Young Adults*; Greenwood Press: Greenwood, IN, 2001.

7. Horning, K.T. *From Cover to Cover: Evaluating and Reviewing Children's Books*; HarperCollins: New York, 1997.

8. Hunt, P. *Children's Literature*; Blackwell: Oxford, 2001.

9. Kaiser, C. Is your early childhood literature collection disability-inclusive and current?. Child. Libr. **2007**, *5*(3), 5–12.

10. Kiefer, B.Z.; Hepler, S.; Hickman, J. *Charlotte Huck's Children's Literature*, 9th Ed.; McGraw-Hill: New York, 2006.

11. Lynch-Brown, C.; Tomlinson, C.M. *Essentials of Children's Literature*, 6th Ed.; Allyn and Bacon: Boston, MA, 2007.

12. MacDonald, M.R. Sturm, B.W. *Storyteller's Sourcebook: A Subject, Title and Motif Index to Folklore Collections for Children, 1983–1999*; Gale Group: Detroit, MI, 2001.

13. Nikolajeva, M. *Children's Literature Comes of Age: Toward a New Aesthetic*; Garland: New York, 1996.

14. Nilsen, A.P.; Donelson, K.L. *Literature for Today's Young Adult*, 8th Ed.; Allyn and Bacon: Boston, MA, 2008.

15. Nodelman, P. Reimer, M. *The Pleasures of Children's Literature*, 3rd Ed.; Allyn and Bacon: Boston, MA, 2002.

16. Norton, D.E. *Through the Eyes of a Child: An Introduction to Children's Literature*, 7th Ed.; Merrill/Prentice Hall: Columbus, OH, 2007.

17. Rand, D.; Parker, T.T. *Black Books Galore: Guide to Great African American Books About Boys*; John Wiley: New York, 2001; (See also same title for girls.).

18. Russell, D. *Literature for Children*, 6th Ed.; Allyn and Bacon: Boston, MA, 2008.

19. Seale, D.; Slapin, B. *The Broken Flute: The Native American Experience in Books for Children*; Oyate: Berkeley, CA, 2005.

20. Sprug, J.W. *Index to Fairy Tales 1987–1992*, Scarecrow Press: Metuchen, NJ, 1994.

21. Stan, S., Ed. *The World through Children's Books'*; Scarecrow Press: Lanham, MD, 2002; Sponsored by USBBY.

22. Temple, C.; Martinez, M.; Yokota, J. *Children's Books in Children's Hands*, 3rd Ed.; Allyn and Bacon: Boston, MA, 2006.

23. Tomlinson, C.M., Ed. *Children's Books from Other Countries*; Scarecrow Press: Lanham, MD, 1998.

24. Tomlinson, C.M.; Lynch-Brown, C. *Essentials of Young Adult Literature*, Allyn and Bacon: Boston, MA, 2007.

25. Yokota, J., Ed. *Kaleidoscope: A Multicultural Booklist for Grades K-8*, 3rd Ed.; National Council of Teachers of English: Urbana, IL, 2001.

26. Zipes, J. *The Oxford Encyclopedia of Children's Literature*; Oxford University Press: New York, 2006.

Chemistry–China

Children's Services in Libraries

Virginia A. Walter
Department of Information Studies, University of California, Los Angeles, Venice, California, U.S.A.

Melissa Gross
School of Information, Florida State University, Tallahassee, Florida, U.S.A.

Abstract

Children's services in libraries began at the end of the nineteenth century in the United States and were well institutionalized by the 1950s. Service to children birth to age 12 or 14 is now understood to be a standard element of public library operations. This entry looks at the nature of those services, the education and work of children's librarians, and some emerging challenges and issues. The focus is on contemporary services to children in the United States. However, a brief discussion of international approaches to the field is also provided.

INTRODUCTION

On a typical day, more than a third of the people who enter an American public library are children under the age of 14. They arrive in strollers and on skateboards. They come to hear stories; find a book to read; get help with homework; play games; make things; borrow a device, such as an iPad or e-reader; or use the computers. The lucky ones find a glorious space especially designed to appeal to young people with professional librarians available to help them meet their needs that day. All of them will find a basic level of service that is an affirmation of the vision of the women who developed the concept more than 100 years ago.

This entry will outline the historical development of library service to children and describe how it is implemented today. It will look at the role of the children's librarian in providing that service and discuss some of the more urgent challenges facing them today—the increasing diversity of their clientele, rapidly changing information and communication technology, and the pressure to document the outcomes of their services. Finally, it will look briefly at some of the international dimensions of library service to children.

HISTORY

Children were not welcome in the first public libraries in the United States. The philanthropists and civic leaders who established these institutions in the early 1800s intended to provide uplifting literature to adults who were unable to purchase their own books. They also wanted to help newly arrived immigrants assimilate to the American way of life. Children, with their dirty hands and noisy behaviors, were specifically prohibited from using these early public libraries.

The situation began to change after the publication in 1876 of a study of the "history, condition, and management" of public libraries by the U.S. Bureau of Education. One of the contributors to that study, William I. Fletcher, argued that public libraries should change their policies limiting access to children. He based his argument on the need to develop a taste for refined reading early in life, writing,

> If there is any truth in the idea that the public library is not merely a storehouse for the supply of the wants of the reading public, but also and especially an educational institution which shall create wants where they do not exist, then the library ought to bring its influence to bear on the young as early as possible.[1]

Fletcher's message was consistent with other ideas beginning to circulate at that time about the need to reach children early in their lives in order to influence the kind of adults they would become. John Dewey's ideas about education and G. Stanley Hall's theories of child psychology began to influence other fields. The new specialists in library services to children, the first children's librarians, were convinced that young people who were exposed to the best in fine, uplifting literature would grow up to become fine, uplifted adults. Betsy Hearne and Christine Jenkins describe their approach as a kind of visionary quest in which the "grail was not just information or even knowledge but the enrichment of experience through whole reading, the kind of reading that engulfs the heart as well as engaging the head and ultimately shapes a lifetime."[2]

By the end of the nineteenth century, libraries across the country had begun to open their doors to children. Administrators began to recognize the need for specialist staff—children's librarians—who would provide services for this new clientele. Some remarkable women answered the call and defined those services with such passion and

Encyclopedia of Library and Information Sciences, Fourth Edition DOI: 10.1081/E-ELIS4-120053114

force that they left an indelible imprint that has lasted for more than 100 years.

Among the pioneering children's librarians were Frances Jenkins Olcott, the first head of the children's department of the Carnegie Library of Pittsburgh, Caroline Hewins at the Hartford Public Library, and Anne Carroll Moore, supervisor of children's services at the New York Public Library from 1906 until 1941. Moore deserves special mention for her role in defining and institutionalizing public library services for children.

Anne Carroll Moore believed that the library should be an inviting and gracious environment for children. To this end, she created children's rooms that were warm and welcoming with books displayed on low, open shelving. She established circulation policies that did not discriminate against young library patrons. She provided rigorous training for the young women who worked under her supervision. She searched out the best books for children at a time when few existed except for a few nineteenth century classics and then encouraged publishers to establish separate children's divisions. She encouraged authors and illustrators to create new books for children, and then she reviewed those books for some of the most influential publications of the day. Her opinions were never tepid, and not everyone in the children's literature community appreciated her hegemony over the field. However, her contributions to the early development of children's librarianship are unrivaled.[3]

The pioneering children's librarians took their message about the importance of libraries in forming children's reading interests to the annual meetings of the American Library Association (ALA). Their voices were heard; and by the end of the 1920s, even the smallest public libraries stocked books for children and provided some of the services that were becoming standard, such as summer reading and storytelling programs. Andrew Carnegie did his part by including designated space for children in his massive public library building program.[4] The events of the Great Depression of the 1930s and World War II put further development of children's services on hold. However, the post-War years proved to be boom times for American families and for public library services to children.

Many innovations in those services were institutionalized during the last half century. An explosion in children's book publishing led to a new focus on evaluating books, systematically developing collections, and promoting the books with children through techniques such as booktalking and merchandising. Preschool story hours introduced 3- and 4-year-olds to the experience of listening to stories in a group. A new awareness of poverty and racial inequities in the 1960s led to outreach efforts and nontraditional programming designed to appeal to populations who had not been library users in the past.

Taxpayer revolts in the 1980s resulted in a movement for accountability in local government operations;

children's librarians responded with the development of output measures.[5] The rise of the Internet generated apocalyptic talk about the death of the library; children's librarians responded with programs to teach children and their families how to use information and communication technology more effectively. There was national concern about children's poor reading skills; children's librarians responded with a research-based program designed to educate parents in techniques to prepare their young children to learn to read.[6]

Today's library, in response to concerns about preparing children for the future, has expanded services to support learning in science, technology, engineering, art, and math. Many libraries are incorporating Makerspaces, where a variety of tools (anything from sewing machines to 3D printers) are available for children and families to learn, share knowledge, and make things. Libraries are also sites for community gardens and summer lunch programs. In fact, the majority of programs in public libraries are geared for youth and the demand for these programs continues to grow.[7]

A Pew Internet study states that "70% of parents report their child visited a public library in the last 12 months and 55% say their child has his/her own library card."[8] The report also points out that adults who have children or grandchildren are more likely than other adults to use the library themselves. A vast majority of parents hold the opinion that access to the library is important for their children. The remainder of this entry will examine how children's services in libraries are organized and will explore current issues in the field. Finally, it will look briefly at children's services at international libraries.

CONTEMPORARY LIBRARY SERVICES TO CHILDREN

Implementing Children's Services within the Public Library

Library service to children has evolved into a distinct specialization within the profession. In most public libraries, these services are provided through a designated department or division. In large libraries, these departments are ordinarily headed by a manager or coordinator of children's services who provides training and general oversight for service to children. In smaller libraries, an individual children's librarian may be responsible for the work.

A few public library systems have moved away from specialist designations for children's and adult reference librarians in favor of a more generalist approach. In these situations, all public service librarians are presumed to be able to serve the needs of children, as well as teenagers and adults. A children's services coordinator or manager may be on staff to organize programming and train all staff in some of the skills needed to serve children well.

Service to children is almost always provided in a special space within the library. Lower shelving and child-sized furniture are the basic elements in a separate children's room or the children's wing in a library with an open floor plan. However, most of these open floor plans use other features such as color, wall decorations, toys, games, fish tanks, and puppet stages as indicators that this part of the library is meant for young patrons. Computers have become a standard feature in children's areas everywhere. Some are especially designed for the youngest patrons, loaded with educational software and games.

Two recent trends in library spaces for children are worth mentioning. One is the creation of "destination" sites, designed as exciting discovery centers for children.

These libraries use elaborate decorative elements and interactive installations to lure children and families to spend time there. One of the most striking of these new approaches is the ImaginOn, a collaborative venture of the Charlotte–Mecklenburg Public Library and the Children's Theater of Charlotte in North Carolina (Fig. 1). Opened in 2005, this 102,000 ft^2 building is filled with dynamic modules intended to "bring stories to life through extraordinary experiences that challenge, inspire, and excite young minds."[9] The Phoenix Public Library employed a designer with a background in children's museum work to create custom installations in its picture book areas. These installations encourage young children to develop small motor skills, phonemic awareness, and letter awareness in a developmentally appropriate and child-friendly environment.

The second significant trend in library facilities for children is the Family Place Movement.[10] Family Place Libraries is a joint initiative of the Middle Country Public Library in New York and Libraries for the Future. It is now a nationwide network that includes 435 librarians from 25 states. Family Place Libraries aim to help parents and caregivers become more intentional, informed, and active participants in their young children's development. A key component of their program is a specially designed space within the library where parents can gather with their young children to play, learn, and observe. These spaces have collections of toys, music, and parenting materials in addition to the usual books for preschool children.

Range of Services

The overarching goals of contemporary library services to children are to promote reading and literacy and to ensure that children have access to information in all formats. These goals are achieved through a wide range of services. Collection development is the foundation for most of those services.

With more than 5000 juvenile titles published in the United States each year, it becomes critical to select the most appropriate books for any particular library collection. Children's librarians in large library systems may have access to review copies that they can evaluate firsthand. Most, however, rely on reviews in sources such as *School Library Journal*, *Booklist*, *Kirkus Reviews*, and *The Horn Book*. They make their decisions based on budget, community needs, judgments about quality, and other standards, all codified in a collection development policy. Knowledge of the collection—and the broader field of children's literature—is a fundamental part of the children's librarian's toolkit.

After books are added to the collection, they are typically organized on the shelves according to format and genre. Picture books are housed in low shelving designed to accommodate large formats. Nonfiction and fiction

Fig. 1 Interior of the Spangler Library, ImaginOn, Charlotte, North Carolina.

are separated, and there may be special sections for easy-to-read primer, ABC and other concept books, folk and fairy tales, and parenting materials. CDs and videos (DVDs) are also standard materials in children's collections today.

Since reading promotion is the *raison d'etre* for the book collection, children's librarians promote the books in a variety of ways. They create book displays and book lists to highlight segments of the collection. They work one-on-one with patrons in the library, providing expert readers' advisory and reference services. They promote specific books to groups such as school classes—an activity known as booktalking. They mount summer reading programs designed to motivate children to read during the months when they are not in school.

Storytelling is another basic service provided in almost all public libraries. Originally, as conceived by Anne Carroll Moore at the New York Public Library in the early 1900s, this was exclusively the telling of traditional folktales to audience of school-aged boys and girls. While some librarians still practice the traditional art of storytelling, it is much less common than story hours for preschool children.

The preschool story hour was popularized in the years after World War II when the baby boom was impacting communities—and libraries—in all parts of the country. As originally conceived, it catered to 3- and 4-year-olds who were developmentally ready to participate in a brief group experience away from their parents and caregivers. In a period of about half an hour, the children's librarians would present a variety of picture books, flannel board stories, finger plays, and nursery rhymes or songs. While the traditional preschool story hour is still a staple in many public libraries, it has evolved into a broad menu of programs for young children—lapsit programs for infants, toddler storytimes for 2-year-olds, and family storytimes designed for the broadest possible age range. Increasingly, the use of technology is being incorporated into storytimes and it is now considered good practice to include parents and caregivers in library programs for young children. In fact, parent education is now an integral part of much early childhood programming in libraries.

In addition to programs in which librarians and other storytellers read or tell stories to children, there are also planned ongoing programs in which children are encouraged to read aloud, a practice that helps to develop reading fluency. Grandparents and Books is one such program. Older adults are trained in techniques for engaging children in literacy and literacy-oriented activities, including having the children read to them. The grandparents then volunteer to be available to the children after school in the library reading rooms.[11] Literacy dogs are another recent innovation in library programming. Children are invited to read aloud to specially trained dogs. Reluctant or less fluent readers apparently find the patient animals to be perfect listeners. There are programs using specially trained therapy dogs as reading partners for children at

many public libraries. One good example is R.E.A.D. (Reading Education Assistance Dogs) at the Salt Lake City Public Library.[12]

Besides storytelling, children's librarians typically provide other kinds of programming: puppet and magic shows, visits from Seeing Eye dogs and snake handlers, cooking and sign language classes, and much, much more. Makerspaces are becoming commonplace in libraries. Makerspaces provide space and tools for creativity, knowledge sharing, and collaboration. While they are often thought of as providing access to technology such as 3D printers, special software, and electronic devices, in fact they can provide a wide variety of learning and creative opportunities. Makerspaces can be a place to learn to fix a bicycle, knit, solder, code, or otherwise make things depending on the needs and interests of the community.

Community gardens are another increasingly popular library program. Community gardens serve a variety of educational and recreational needs and are being used in libraries with children of all ages. In addition to teaching gardening skills, they foster nutritional and environment literacies, and teach plant identification. The garden experience connects quite naturally to books and other information sources provided by the library.

Another recent innovation is summer meal programs in public libraries. Often partnering with the U.S. Department of Agriculture, these programs help to ensure that young people in low-income areas have access to healthy food during summer vacation from school. Summer meal programs introduce the library to often underserved populations to the resources the library offers, build community partnership, and provide opportunities for positive youth development.[13]

Many of the programs provided by the public library are not held in the building itself but are taken out into the community into a variety of venues from schools to recreation centers to parks and playgrounds. This kind of outreach is intended to extend the library's sphere of influence, to enhance the library's visibility, and to make services available to children who might not be able to physically get to the library itself. Children's librarians also work to develop strategic partnerships with other child-serving leaders and organizations in their community. Almost all children's librarians maintain some kind of relationship with the schools in their communities. They may invite school classes to visit the library or go into classrooms themselves to promote library services and reading.

In spite of this emphasis on programming, the heart of library service to children is still one-on-one readers' advisory and reference work. Children's librarians bring their specialized knowledge of their collection together with their understanding of children to advise young people as well as their parents, caregivers, and teachers about books to read for pleasure, information, and enlightenment. Queries range for a mother's request for a book to help her 3-year-old adjust to the death of a grandparent to a 12-year-old's pleas for a book as good as the last Harry Potter to a fifth-grade teacher's need for good fiction titles to supplement the American History curriculum.

Reference services for children are often related to homework needs. While school libraries are the best first resource for homework, their hours are often limited. Furthermore, not all schools provide adequate libraries. The public library fills the gap. Many public libraries allocate special resources to provide homework help during after-school hours.[14] These can be as modest as a special shelf of homework-oriented reference books or as elaborate as well-equipped Homework Centers staffed with aides or tutors especially trained to assist young people with their homework needs. These homework services are particularly appreciated by families in which parents are not fluent in English or familiar with the American school system and by working parents who have limited time to spend with their kids on school nights. Homeschool families also make extensive use of public library facilities.

As electronic resources have become increasingly useful resources for children's homework needs, librarians have also begun offering instruction in the information literacy skills needed to navigate the Internet effectively. They may offer this instruction informally, as part of their reference interview, or more formally through classes and workshops.[15]

Children's Librarians

In 1905, in a report to the ALA, Frances Jenkins Olcott described the ideal applicant to the newly established training school for children's librarians at the Carnegie Library of Pittsburgh:

> Sympathy with and respect for children, strength of character, a genial nature, a pleasing personality, an instinct for reading character, adaptability, and last but not least, a strong sense of humor. Her home training and education should have given her a love and knowledge of books, a fund of general information, a quick and accurate mind. These qualities are difficult to find combined in one person.[16]

It is no longer assumed that the ideal children's librarian is female, but many of the desirable characteristics described more than 100 years ago are relevant today, and they are still difficult to find combined in one person. However, perhaps in keeping with newer thinking in human resources management, we tend to think today in terms of competencies rather than personal traits. The Association for Library Service to Children (ALSC) has developed and maintained a comprehensive outline of the competencies that children's librarians are expected to demonstrate on the job. The most recent edition of this document was released in 2015.[17] The competencies are

grouped into seven broad categories: commitment to client group; reference and user services; programming skills; knowledge, curation, and management of materials; outreach and advocacy; administrative and management skills; and professionalism and professional development.

Outstanding Library Services to Children, a publication sponsored by ALSC, provides useful guidance for achieving and maintaining those competencies. The author makes clear that nobody is expected to have mastered all of the competencies before starting his or her first job and that most children's librarians will be more proficient in some areas than others. They acknowledge the extremely broad range of knowledge and skills required to do the job well, calling children's librarians, "the original multitaskers of the library world."[18]

A master's degree from an ALA-accredited graduate school is the standard educational requirement for children's librarians. In addition to the core curriculum that prepares all professional librarians, they typically take courses related to children's literature, collection development, and children's programming. In many master's degree programs, there is an emphasis on customer service, understanding the user group, and management. The integration of technology into LIS education has furthered the inclusion of technology tools into course content including a variety of media and applications.[19]

The Laura Bush 21st Century Librarian Program of the federal Institute of Museum and Library Services (IMLS) has provided resources to help libraries and graduate schools of library science fund the development of new information professionals, including youth librarians. Grants have provided scholarship funds for both master's and doctoral students, helping to meet the need for children's librarians and faculty to teach them.

Children's librarians are supported in their efforts to serve children and in their own professional development by various professional associations. The primary national organization is the ALSC, a division of the ALA. State library associations usually have a division or section devoted to children's services as well and often provide an entry point for professional involvement by novice children's librarians. Some children's librarians also participate in related professional associations such as the International Literacy Association or the National Association of the Education of Young Children.

Issues

IT is significant that library service to children has continued to evolve over more than 100 years since it began. Some of the core values and service that were identified by the early leaders in the field remain at the heart of the specialization today. However, society has undergone major changes in the last century, and the rate of change continues to increase. Children's librarians are struggling to redefine and reinvent the services they offer in a turbulent environment. This section will outline some of the issues that are currently driving calls for innovation in the field—specifically, changing notions of childhood; the increasing cultural, ethnic, and racial diversity of the populations served by public libraries; technological imperatives; and the demand for demonstrable outcomes of services.

The founding mothers of library services to children had few doubts about the clientele they served. Their patrons were school-age children. While some of the great early illustrators such as Randolph Caldecott and Kate Greenaway had produced picture books for young children, there was not yet a well-defined preschool market for publishing or for public library services. Adolescence had yet to be identified as a distinct developmental stage, and childhood for middle- and upper-class children extended at least into the early teens. Working-class children were usually expected to take on adult responsibilities by the age of 13 or 14.

As many historians and sociologists of childhood have demonstrated, however, childhood is a malleable social construct.[20] By the beginning of the twenty-first century, American childhood had contracted. Adolescence was occurring both physically and socially at an earlier age, and children as young as 8, 9, and 10—"tweens"—were taking on the characteristics of teens in training.[21] At the same time, discoveries in cognitive science made it clear that the earlier years of human life, from birth to age four, are enormously important developmentally. Many children's librarians have responded to this shift in our understanding of the span of childhood by shifting their priorities away from the older middle school child in favor of working with parents and caregivers of very young children. The ALSC continues to define its clientele as children from birth to age 14, while the Young Adult Library Services Association, a sister division of ALA, claims the age group from 12 to 18. Public libraries are not consistent in their classification of service population by age, and presumably, young people between the ages of 12 and 14 will gravitate to the area of the library in which they fell most comfortable.

Whatever their age, twenty-first-century children live in a world that would be almost unrecognizable to Anne Carroll Moore and her peers. Two dramatic changes in American society have a particular impact on children and on the services provided for them by public libraries. One is the ever-increasing racial and ethnic diversity in our country as well as changing attitudes toward this diversity. The other is the impact of new and emerging communications and information technologies.

The changing ethnic and racial composition of the United States has been well documented. In 2014, only 52% of children in the United States were non-Hispanic White. Non-Hispanic Black children were 14% of the population; Asians, 5%; and Hispanic, 24%. Immigration patterns and differential birth rates do much to explain the shifts, and some states—such as California—show more dramatic changes. There, the 2014 statistics show that only 26% of the children were non-Hispanic White. Non-Hispanic Black children were 5% of the population. About 52% of California children are Hispanic; 11% are Asian.[22] Understandably, library patrons are also increasingly diverse.

The increasing diversity of the children using public libraries impacts both collections and the services provided for them. Many communities now find it appropriate to stock books, videos, and recordings in languages other than English. The International Children's Digital Library has filled a gap for some libraries by seeking out and digitizing books in languages that are more difficult to find in the United States, such as Farsi, Croatian, or Maori.[23] Collections of children's books in languages other than English are particularly important resources in immigrant communities. These collections enable parents to share books with their children in their mother tongue and often serve as tangible evidence that the public library is a welcoming and relevant institution in their adopted country.

The increasing diversity of library patrons has highlighted some staffing and recruitment needs. Bilingual librarians are in great demand, as are those from diverse racial and ethnic backgrounds. Unfortunately, the library profession has traditionally attracted White females. Demographic statistics for the total library workforce are somewhat elusive, but ALA estimates that about 73% of credentialed librarians in 2010 were White.[24] There have been numerous efforts to recruit more diverse students to library school through such efforts as the ALA Spectrum Scholarships. For the academic year 2013–2014, approximately 67% of students graduating from ALA-approved master's degree programs were White and approximately 77% were female.[25]

The rapid proliferation of digital information and communication technologies has generated other kinds of challenges for the traditionally book-oriented field of children's librarianship. The children being served in public libraries today have grown up with computers and the Internet. IT has affected the way they learn and play. However, disparities caused by income gaps have created what has become known as the digital divide. Discussion about the digital divide includes concerns about access to computers as well as access to broadband (continuous high-speed connection to the Internet). The Children's Partnership reports that

Compared to their peers in households with annual incomes over $75,000, children in households with annual incomes less than $15,000 are

- 1/2 as likely to have a computer at home
- 1/3 as likely to have the Internet at home
- 1/7 as likely to have broadband at home[26]

Public libraries have responded aggressively to help bridge the digital divide. Public access to the computers and to the Internet is now a standard service in libraries across the country. Because of the provisions of the Children's Internet Protection Act, many libraries have installed filtering software on computers in their children's areas.[27] This restriction has been a source of conflict for many children's librarians who are torn between their advocacy for children's intellectual freedom rights and their desire to protect children from exposure to pornography and other harmful matters.

It is not unusual to see three or four children crowded around each computer in the children's area while the book stacks stand as empty as ghost towns. Many librarians applaud this development, citing in particular the welcome sight of boys returning to the library. Some are concerned, however, that children seem to be using the Internet primarily to access games sites rather than for informational purposes. In any case, the seamless integration of computers into the service plan and general operation of library service to children has not yet been fully accomplished. Computers still feel like add-ons in many children's libraries (Fig. 2).

There are some promising developments, however. Libraries that offer after-school homework assistance have found that computers are a natural learning tool. Some libraries have made an effort to offer tutorials in information literacy skills to parents and children. Many libraries are integrating games of all types into library programming.

The third issue of interest in contemporary library service to children is the pressure to document demonstrable outcomes. Funding sources ranging from granting agencies to local governments are asking for evidence that the services libraries provide make a difference in the lives of children and families. No longer satisfied with simple output measures such as circulation and reference counts that tell "how many" or "how much," they now want answers to the question, "so what?" The kind of research necessary for conducting good outcomes evaluation studies is rigorous and often expensive. Eliza Dresang, Melissa Gross, and Leslie Edmonds Holt have produced a good how-to-do-it manual based on their own IMLS-funded work at the St. Louis Public Library, but doing this work still requires more commitment and expertise than most public libraries can command.[28] Some library systems have contacted with academic partners to do outcomes evaluation of specific grant-funded projects, but the resulting studies have not been generalizable to other libraries.

INTERNATIONAL DIMENSIONS

Service to children has tended to be included as an element of public library services in countries around the world. In most respects, this service has followed the American model with an emphasis on books and reading. The Standing Committee on Libraries for Children and Young Adults of the International Federation of Library Associations and Institutions (IFLA) has published guidelines for children's services that advocate the kind of outreach, networking, collection development, and programming that are institutionalized in most American libraries. The IFLA document cites the United Nations' "Convention on the rights of the Child" as an underlying statement of principles that should guide library services.[29]

Of course, countries vary in their funding base, opportunities for professional education, and local community values and practices. Scandinavian libraries, for example, have a tradition of partnering with local cultural

Fig. 2 Computer stations in the children's room of the Central Library, Minneapolis, Minnesota.

institutions and of furthering what they call "children's culture," including such manifestations as children's theater and musical performances. In some cases, they have also pioneered effective technological innovations. The Interactive Children's Library of the Aarhus Public Libraries in Denmark is designed especially to attract children through applications of digital technology. The Children's Community Libraries in Singapore are also known for their integration of technology with book collection in English, Chinese, Malay, and Tamil in well-designed modern facilities. The children's library of the Bibliotheca Alexandrina on the site of the original ancient Library of Alexandria in Egypt, limited to children over the age of seven, is a beautiful section in the iconic new building offering many of the services we have come to expect in a contemporary public library. Interestingly, children are not permitted in the adult department of the library there. Websites for each of the libraries mentioned include some information in English. Public libraries in Croatia have responded to the lack of early childhood education offerings in their country by creating special playrooms for children from birth through six, the age at which they are able to enroll in school. Many libraries employ people with dual degrees in library science and early childhood education to provide formal programming in the playrooms (Fig. 3).

In some developing countries, library services to children are provided as often through nonprofit organizations and volunteer initiatives as through government-funded public libraries. An interesting example is the Banco del Libro in Caracas, Venezuela. This volunteer effort begun by a group of women more than 49 years ago was instrumental in developing the first library network and the first bookmobile service in that country. The Banco del Libro went on to form a children's literature examination center, the first children's book publisher, and the first specialized children's bookstore in Venezuela.[30]

Public libraries in African countries struggle to find funding for services to children. They are also hampered by the lack of material in local languages since there is little or no publishing or trade of children's books in sub-Saharan Africa. Almost all efforts to put books into the hands of children are supported by international nongovernmental organizations such as the British Book Aid or the Canadian CODE. These groups work with local individuals and institutions to produce children's books in local languages. The results are often didactic and fall well below the quality standards of Western publishing houses, but they do meet some important local needs.

Another interesting example is the Lubuto Project that is currently operating in Zambia. The Lubuto libraries began as an individual voluntary initiative on the part of one American librarian living in Lusaka. She began by volunteering to read to street children made homeless by the loss of parents to AIDS at Fountain of Hope, an agency providing services for that overwhelmingly needy population. This led to a temporary library housed in an abandoned shipping container. The project celebrated its 10th anniversary in 2015 and has received grant funds to build their fifth library.[31]

CONCLUSION

Library service to children has evolved from the first specialization within library services in the United States to a well-institutionalized practice. Its proponents have redefined its mission and extended its parameters while retaining the original values exemplified by the motto, "the right book for the right child." Some aspects of the service—summer reading programs, preschool story hours, and individualized reading guidance—are near universal elements of public library service. Emerging

Fig. 3 Playroom, Medvescak Public Library, Zagreb, Croatia.

services such as promotion of early childhood literacy through education of parents and caregivers, after-school homework assistance, and the provision of Internet access have achieved wide acceptance in the field. Children's librarians network actively and form partnerships with other community organizations in their efforts to advocate for children more generally.

REFERENCES

1. Fletcher, W.I. Public libraries and the young. In *Public Libraries in the United States: Their History, Condition and Management*; Department of the Interior, Bureau of Education: Washington, DC, 1876; 412–418.

2. Hearne, B.; Jenkins, C. Sacred texts: What our foremothers left us in the way of psalms, proverbs, precepts, and practices. Horn Book **1999**, *75* (5), 536–558.

3. Sayers, F.C. *Anne Carroll Moore*; Atheneum: New York, 1972.

4. Van Slyck, A.A. *Free to All: Carnegie Libraries and American Culture 1890–1920*; University of Chicago Press: Chicago, IL, 1995.

5. Walter, V.A. *Output Measures for Public Library Service to Children: A Manual of Standardized Procedures*; American Library Association: Chicago, IL, 1992.

6. Public Library Association. Every Child Ready to Read @ Your Library, 2011–2015. http://www.everychildready toread.org/ (accessed November 29, 2016).

7. Miller, C.; Zickuhr, K.; Rainie, L.; Purcell, K. *Parents, Children, Libraries, and Reading*, Washington, DC: Pew Research Center, 2013, http://libraries.pewinternet.org/2013/05/01/parents-children-libraries-and-reading/.

8. Miller, C.; Zickuhr, K.; Rainie, L.; Purcell, K. *Parents, Children, Libraries, and Reading*, 2013, http://libraries.pewinternet.org/2013/05/01/parents-children-libraries-and-reading/.

9. ImaginOn. http:imaginon.org. A good review of the facility written shortly after its opening is Kenney, B. Imagine this. School Libr. J. **December 2005**, 52–55.

10. Family Place Libraries. What Makes a Family Place Library, Friends of the Studio City Branch Library: Studio City, CA, 2009–2011, http://www.familyplacelibraries.org/whatMakes.html.

11. Friends of the Studio City Branch Library. *Grandparents and Books*, 2010, http://studiocitylibraryfriends.org/?p=71.

12. Mott, M. Canine companions may help kids learn to read. National Geographic News, October 9, 2002, http://news.nationalgeographic.com/news/2002/10/1001_021001_READ dogs.html.

13. Cole, N.; Chamberlin, P. Nourishing bodies & minds when school is out: California's public library summer meal programs. Public Libr. *54* (2), 22–28.

14. Mediavilla, C. *Creating the Full-Service Homework Center in Your Library*; American Library Association: Chicago, IL, 2001.

15. Walter, V.A. Information literacy: A new role for public libraries?. In *Proven Strategies for Building a Successful Information Literacy Program*; Curzon, S., Ed.; Neal-Schuman: New York, 2007.

16. Jenkins, F.J. In *Rational Library Work with Children and the Preparation for it*, Proceedings of the American Library Association Conference; American Library Association: Chicago, IL, 1905; 75.

17. Association for Library Services to Children (ALSC). Competencies for Librarians Serving children in Public Libraries, 2015. http://www.ala.org/alsc/edcareeers/alsc corecomps.

18. Cerny, R.; Markey, P.; Williams, A. *Outstanding Library Service to Children: Putting the Core Competencies to Work*; American Library Association: Chicago, IL, 2006.

19. Welch, C. What and how we teach now: A survey of youth services faculty. J. Edu. Libr. Informat. Sci. *54* (3), 220–234.

20. Aries, P. *Centuries of Childhood*; Random House: New York, 1962.

21. Mesa, A. Marketing and tweens. Businessweek, October 12, 2005, See for example http://www.bloomberg.com/businessweek.

22. Annie, B. Casey Foundation; Kids Count Data Center, Baltimore, MD. http://datacenter.kidscount.org/ (accessed November 29, 2016).

23. International Children's Digital Library. http://en.childrens library.org/ (accessed November 29, 2016).

24. American Library Association. Office for Research and Statistics and Office for Diversity. Diversity Counts 2009–2010 Update http://www.ala.org/offices/diversity/diversitycounts/2009-2010update.

25. Association for Library and Information Science Education (ALISE), 2015 Statistical Reports, 2015, http://www.alise.org/.

26. Kirkhart, A.; Lau, J.; Lazarus, W.; Lipper, L. Helping our children succeed: What's broadband got to do with It? http://www.childrenspartnership.org/publications/138.

27. American Library Association. Children's Internet Protection Ac. http://www.ala.org/advocacy/advleg/federal legislation/cipa.

28. Dresang, E.T.; Gross, M.; Holt, L.E. *Dynamic Youth Services through Outcome-Based Planning and Evaluation*; American Library Association: Chicago, IL, 2006.

29. International Federation of Library Services, Libraries for Children and Young adults Section. Guidelines for Children's Libraries Services, 2003. http://www.ifla.org/publications/guidelines-for-children-s-library-services.

30. Dearden, C.D. Banco del Libro: The bearable lightness of being there. The Horn Book, July/August 2007; 363–369.

31. Lubuto Library Partners, 2007–2015. http://www.lubuto.org/.

BIBLIOGRAPHY

1. Burke, J.J. *Makerspaces: A Practical Guide for Librarians*; Rowman & Littlefield: Lanham, MD, 2014.

2. Dresang, E.T.; Gross, M.; Holt, L.E. *Dynamic Youth Services through Outcome-Based Planning and Evaluation*; American Library Association: Chicago, IL, 2006.

3. International Federation of Library Services, Libraries for Children and Young adults Section. Guidelines for Children's Libraries Services, 2003, http://www.ifla.

org/publications/guidelines-for-children-s-library-services (accessed November 29, 2016).

4. Mediavilla, C. *Creating the Full-Service Homework Center in Your Library*; American Library Association: Chicago, IL, 2001.

5. Sayers, F.C. *Anne Carroll Moore*; Atheneum: New York, 1972.

6. Walter, V.A. *Children and Libraries: Getting It Right*; American Library Association: Chicago, IL, 2001.

China: Libraries, Archives, and Museums

Priscilla C. Yu
University Library, University of Illinois at Urbana-Champaign, Urbana, Illinois, U.S.A.

TzeHuey Chiou-Peng
Spurlock Museum, University of Illinois at Urbana-Champaign, Urbana, Illinois, U.S.A.

Abstract
This entry examines the challenges and the path of library development in China, with emphasis being given to the twentieth century when new library institutions and practices were first introduced. In just over 100 years Chinese libraries and librarianship have evolved from ancient royal depositories to modern information centers. This entry discusses the underlying political and social changes and examines the contributions of important leaders who have promoted China's library development. An overview of some of the important archives and repositories in the country is presented.

INTRODUCTION

The largest of all of the Asian countries, China (Zhongguo) occupies nearly the entire East Asian land area. It extends for about 3,100 miles (5,000 km) from east to west and 3,400 from north to south, covering an area of about 3,696,100 square miles (9,572,900 square km). In size China is almost as large as the entire continent of Europe. China's land frontier is approximately 12,400 miles in length and its coastline is about 8,700 miles. The country is bounded by Mongolia to the north; Russia and North Korea to the northeast; the Yellow Sea and the East China Sea to the east; the South China Sea to the southeast; Vietnam, Laos, Myanmar (Burma), India, Bhutan, and Nepal to the south; Pakistan to the southwest; and Afghanistan, Tajikistan, Kyrgyzstan, and Kazakhstan to the west. China also faces South Korea and Japan, across the Yellow Sea, and the Philippines, beyond the South China Sea (see Fig. 1, Map).

China has the largest population of any country in the world, 1,330,044,544 (July 2008 est.). Similar to other large countries, China is multiethnic. The Han people comprise 91.5% of the majority group in China, while the remaining minorities the Zhuang, Manchu, Hui, Miao, Uyghur, Tujia, Yi, Mongol, Tibetan, Buyi, Dong, Yao, Korean, and other nationalities comprise 8.5%. The Han group speaks Chinese and most of the minorities speak other languages.[1]

History

Until the mid-nineteenth century, China was the dominant power in East Asia. Chinese Confucian teachings, along with institutions and practices, were introduced into Japan, Korea, and Vietnam. The Chinese system of education, based upon the Chinese classics, was reverently followed and mastered by scholars in these countries.

In China the earliest known documents were those carved on tortoise shells and animal bones. The collection and preservation of such documents can be traced back to as early as the Shang Dynasty (1600–1100 B.C.) when royal archives or libraries were first maintained. China had an imperial library in each dynasty throughout her long history, from the Shang to the Qing (1644–1911 A.D.) dynasties. The imperial libraries served as depositories of national literature and archival documents and were for the use of the imperial family, high officials, and noted scholars. These libraries were not opened to the public. The keeper of the library was little more than protector of this private collection; there was no known formal training for librarianship.

China's traditional libraries experienced remarkable development during the Tang Dynasty (618–906 A.D.) and Song Dynasty (960–1279 A.D.) when block printing became popular and movable type printing was invented. During this time there was a much wider diffusion of printed materials and both official and private collections blossomed. From the tenth century onward, printed versions of the classics and other writings were more readily available, and the door was opened for education for greater numbers—especially those training for governmental service. China's libraries were then composed of royal collections, academic and private collections, and cloister or temple collections. Access to these volumes was mainly restricted to nobles and scholars.

Not until the nineteenth century was the importance of libraries recognized in the context of developing a modern educational system for China. Following the defeat of China in the Sino-Japanese War of 1894–1895, political

Encyclopedia of Library and Information Sciences, Fourth Edition DOI: 10.1081/E-ELIS4-120043546

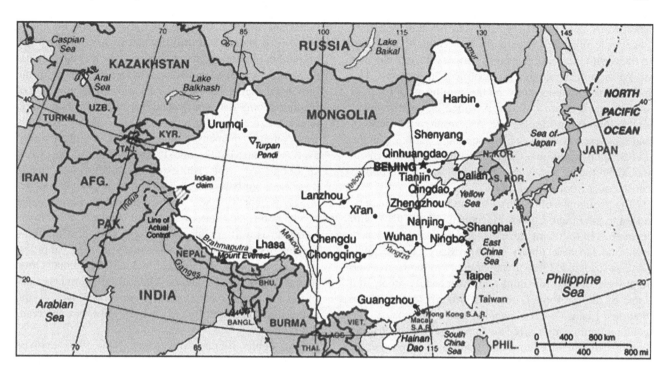

Fig. 1 Map of China.
Source: CIA World Fact Book.[1]

leaders and intellectuals realized the need to modernize and improve the educational system in order for China to prosper and be strong. The Reform Movement of 1898 was launched and part of the proposed reform plank was educational reform following Western practices. Among the Chinese intellectuals advocating a new model of librarianship was Wang Kang Nian. In 1896, he wrote that

> The key to revitalize China lies in education. Education depends on the ability to master new knowledge and the mastering of new knowledge can only be accomplished through the establishment of schools, study, societies, and libraries... Every Western library collects tens of thousands of books in all languages and herein lays the key to a prosperous China.[2]

Libraries were now linked directly to China's education and overall development.

The founding of the Republic in 1912 brought an end to the institutions and practices of the imperial system, and China began the difficult and long process of economic, intellectual, and political change. New knowledge was diffused to the population and the use of a Chinese phonetic alphabet was introduced. Following the May 4 Movement in 1919, books and periodicals in the colloquial language were published. Soon translated works of Peter Kropotkin and other foreign writers were in high demand among Chinese intellectuals. Libraries to meet the demands and needs of the new era were now faced with changing conditions and new challenges.

Beginning in the 1920s, four main types of Chinese libraries developed: public libraries, college libraries, society libraries, and special libraries. Of the four, college or academic libraries held the best collections of Chinese and foreign books. These new academic libraries began to use the latest organizational and cataloging systems; their library facilities and equipment were also of higher quality than those of the public libraries.

The Republican period on mainland China (1912–1949) witnessed the beginnings of the introduction of modern librarianship, albeit repeatedly curtailed by civil and international conflicts. Beginning with the founding of the People's Republic of China (PRC) in 1949, and especially following the initiation of the "opening and reform" policy in the early 1980s, library development greatly accelerated.

Modern Librarianship in China

By the mid-nineteenth century, Chinese sovereignty was severely compromised as a result of the "unequal treaties" following China's defeat by Britain in the first Opium War (1839–1842). The economic, cultural, and political penetration and exploitation of China by the Western and Japanese powers and the decline of the Qing (Manchu) Dynasty (1644–1911) over the next half-century contributed to the instability of the nation. Although the Manchu governing class had introduced some reforms at the end of the nineteenth century, popular uprisings from the mid century on—from the Taiping Rebellion (1850–1864) to the Boxer Rebellion (1900)—demonstrated that all was not well. The traditional Confucian order of guarding against any contact between the Chinese and foreigners (who were regarded as barbarians) eventually gave way to trade with the West, missionary endeavors, introduction of Western technologies and political institutions. The influx of foreign educators and the enrollment of Chinese students in Western colleges provided external political and cultural stimuli for change. As a result of the Western and Japanese intrusions in Chinese affairs beginning in the 1840s, many traditional Chinese institutions were shaken, including the closed-access model of Chinese libraries carried over from ancient times.

The beginnings of modern Chinese librarianship can be traced to the Public Library Movement (1840–1926), with its interest in following developments in European, American, and Japanese library systems. Many Chinese intellectuals recognized that it was essential to modernize and improve education for China to prosper and be strong, and some of these reformers recognized the potential role of libraries. Liang Qi-Chao, scholar, literary journalist, and political figure, emphasized the importance of establishing libraries to spread culture and train talented people; he introduced into China the term library, "tushuguan," from Japan.[3] This new term appeared for the first time in 1896 in *Current Affairs Newspaper*, which Liang Qi-Chao edited. Later Liang traveled to the United States and visited public, university, and national libraries in Boston, New York, and Washington, District of Columbia in the early twentieth century. He quickly discerned that public libraries were necessary for public education. What impressed him most was the open-shelf arrangement of American college libraries. He also became convinced that libraries were linked directly to America's educational and economic development.

The Public Library Movement (*Gong Gong Tushuguan Yundong*)

The Public Library Movement marked an end of Chinese feudal society and the beginnings of great changes and reform, socially and politically. European, American, and Japanese library systems played a predominant role during this period.

During 1917–1926, the Chinese public library movement was at its height. Two primary factors contributed to this: 1) the Literary Revolution and Renaissance Movement, which occurred during 1917 when "pei hua" or the colloquial language was introduced as a medium of literary expression; and 2) the May 4th Movement of 1919 which unleashed the New Culture Movement in China by challenging aspects of traditional culture that dominated the lives of the Chinese for more than 2000 years. Confucianism was repudiated, setting the stage for dramatic cultural changes.[4]

Influenced by the West, the Mass Education Movement of 1920 had the goal of teaching illiterates to read and write using 1000 characters. Such initiatives had important implications for the development of public libraries. It should be noted that at this time the majority of public libraries were maintained by the educational budget of local districts and were under the control of the provincial commissioners of education. The majority of reading rooms had noncirculating materials. Imposition of a small fee even for in-house use of library materials was common in many public libraries, mainly to keep away vagrants. By the mid-1920s the traditional idea of charging fees for admission gradually was being discarded, but borrowing books for home use was not yet widely accepted. It was in the free public libraries that newly published works on various subjects were made available as well as copies of Chinese classics. Children's reading rooms were also maintained in these libraries, though they were still in their infancy in China. Often preexisting buildings (such as old palaces, former academies, and abandoned temples) were turned over by the authorities to be used free of charge as libraries and reading rooms.

The Public Library Movement, 1840–1926, evolved into the Modern Library Movement (*Xin Tushuguan Yundong*), 1911—to the present, which not only advocated for more public libraries, but also promoted the development of college and university libraries, and special libraries. At this time special libraries were most prevalent in major cities such as Beijing, Shanghai, and Guangzhou (formerly known as Canton) and were founded mainly to provide information for government organizations and bureaus in China. The Modern Library Movement (also called the New Library Movement) sought to eradicate traditional library practices, promoted Western librarianship throughout China, introduced Western library science and technology, and raised the social standing of Chinese librarians.[5]

Library Science

At the beginning of the Chinese Republic in 1912, many reformers realized the need to replace the traditional practices of Chinese library administration. Since many Chinese intellectuals were influenced to some extent by Japanese culture and science before the Revolution of 1911, Japanese library science was the first foreign model introduced into China. In 1910 Xie Yun-Cang translated *Library Education* which was authored by a Japanese scholar and published by Fengtian Press; this was the first book about library science published in China.[6] After Shen Zhu Rong returned from the United States in 1917 (discussed in the "American Influences" entry) and launched the Modern Library Movement, the emphasis on foreign library science shifted from Japan to the United States. Between 1919 and 1949, many articles were translated into Chinese that dealt with "American Public Libraries" and "American Librarianship." Even lectures on the Library of Congress (LC) Classification, Dewey

Decimal Classification (DDC), Brown Subject Classification, and Cutter's Expansive Classification were translated and published by Chinese librarians. Thus the concept of an American-type library administration prevailed and later spread throughout China.

Prior to 1900 there were no card catalogs in China, only book catalogs. After the introduction of both Japanese and Western library science, card catalogs became popular. The Library of the North China Branch of the Royal Asiatic Society had catalog cards with Dewey classification numbers. Cutter's author numbers and index entries were in usage as early as 1908. The Boone Library (founded by Mary Elizabeth Wood in 1910, in Wuchang, now a district of the city of Wuhan, Hubei province) and Beijing libraries began using card catalogs in 1918. After the 1920s the majority of Chinese libraries adopted the card catalog system. Beijing Library as early as 1936 began to print and issue cards for the use of all libraries in China.

Sun Yu Xiu was the first person to introduce the DDC system into China. Sun said, "It is the most important and popular classification among all the classifications in English."[7] Introduction of the DDC precipitated major changes in the development of modern Chinese classification system. Soon it was found that DDC was not adequate for Chinese works; the Chinese Si Ku classification or fourfold scheme was eventually merged into the DDC system: the four Chinese schemes included the following categories of works:

1. The six classics, lexicography, philology.
2. Philosophy, military science, mathematics, and divination.
3. History, anecdotes, state documents, and miscellaneous writings.
4. Poetry, eulogies, and treaties.

Shen Zhu Rong and Hu Qing Sheng led the way to combine the class heading of both Si Ku and DDC. The Boone Library published Shen and Hu "Modified Dewey Decimal Classification" in 1927. This had a great impact on all of the succeeding Chinese classifications. At the time, DDC was classified into the following 10 categories: General Works, Philosophy, Religion, Sociology, Philology, Natural Science, Useful Arts, Fine Arts, Literature, History and its many subdivisions, together with the fourfold Chinese classification. This led to several changes in the development of modern Chinese classification: 1) supplemented DDC to suit the headings for Chinese libraries; 2) mixed the class headings of both Si Ku and DDC; and 3) used DDC as a basis for class headings with additional new class headings according to the subject of the Chinese publications.

It can be seen that Anglo-American library science indeed had a strong impact influencing Chinese librarianship. But some technical functions could be adopted and others could not. For example, China could not completely replicate America's classification system to their own library's system, since China had its own set of traditions and books that often could not coincide with those introduced from abroad. Therefore, modification and adaptation were the result of such encounters.

American influence

Let us examine the specific impact and role that America had on Chinese librarianship in modern times, exemplified by the work of Mary Elizabeth Wood and Arthur E. Bostwick. Mary Elizabeth Wood (1861–1931) came from a family of missionaries. She, herself, was later named a lay missionary of the American church. In 1899 Miss Wood visited her brother who was a missionary in Wuchang, China. At his suggestion Wood stayed on to take charge of an elementary English class in the small, missionary-run Boone College. While working as a teacher she became aware of the inadequate library facilities and collected donations (which she used along with her own funds) to open the independent Boone Library in Wuchang in 1910. The Library was opened to the public as well as students from Boone College. Here Miss Wood advocated the Western practice of open access to the stacks, which set a precedent in Chinese librarianship. In order to attract users to the library and to introduce American librarianship, Miss Wood conducted lectures in the Boone Library. Realizing that training of young professionals was essential to the development of Chinese librarianship, she financially assisted Shen Zhu Rong and Hu Qing Sheng to go to the United States and study library science. Miss Wood sowed the seeds for the rise of the Chinese Modern Library Movement by promoting professional training for Chinese librarians.

Shen Zhu Rong and Hu Qing Sheng, the two students who went abroad to study in 1914 and 1917, returned only to find that the knowledge they gained would be applicable primarily to foreign libraries and could not be completely adopted in Chinese libraries. Therefore, it became imperative that a Chinese institution of library education to train librarians be established. Shen Zhu Rong and Hu Qing Sheng worked with Miss Wood to found the Department of Library Science of Boone College in 1920. This was the first institute for modern library education in China. The institute, which became the Boone Library School was accredited as a college by the Ministry of Education in 1930, and became the premier institution for the training of librarians in China. The School was financially supported by American funding during 1920–1949; for example, American churches contributed $8,000 annually and the American government returned each year $13,500 of the Indemnities Fund of 1900 (Boxer Rebellion). It was through the determined efforts of Miss Wood that a campaign was launched to persuade the American government to return the indemnities of 1900 in order that the money could be used to advance Chinese librarianship. Through two trips to the United States Miss Wood and her supporters succeeded in persuading the American government to return all the indemnities of 1900, allowing some of the funds for Chinese libraries.

In 1924 Miss Wood prevailed upon the American Library Association (ALA) to help her Chinese colleagues establish a national library association in China. She also invited Dr. Arthur E. Bostwick, Director of the St. Louis Public Library, to visit China and lecture on the philosophy and practices of American libraries. Dr. Bostwick arrived in Shanghai in 1925 and visited more than 50 libraries in China where he lectured and also presented films on American librarianship. He was so successful in advocating American library philosophy and practices such as open-access that many librarians in China wanted to emulate the American way of operating libraries. Bostwick's visit coincided with the founding of the Library Association of China (LAC) by the Beijing Library in 1925.

With the growth of the Modern Library Movement in the early 1920s, there was a growing need for coordination. The Chinese Association for the Advancement of Education (CAAE) (*Zhonghua Jiaoyu Chujinhui*) proposed in 1923 to establish local library associations. By 1924 a number of provincial and local library associations developed, with Beijing Library Association being the primary one. These local associations paved the way for the establishment of a national library association. In April 1925, the national LAC, *Zhongguo Tushuguan Xuehui*, was founded to welcome the visit of Dr. Arthur E. Bostwick. During its existence, the accomplishments of the LAC included providing services to academic and public libraries, publishing a series of reference works and two periodicals, and encouraging library cooperation on the national and international levels. In 1927, the LAC was one of the founders of the International Federation of Library Associations (IFLA). From its inception this association of Chinese librarians became the leading force in the Modern Library Movement or New Library Movement. Its aim was to encourage research in library science, to develop Chinese librarianship, and to strive for the cooperation of the libraries. Through the efforts of LAC the development of Chinese librarianship evolved from the promotion of American librarianship to the reformulation of Chinese librarianship.

The period 1925–1937 witnessed the beginning of Chinese national political consolidation and economic and social reconstruction. In the 1930s the national government at Nanjing under Chiang Kai-shek launched a program to make the library an indispensable agency in the construction of new China. Notwithstanding insufficient funds to further the movement, Chinese libraries continued to develop. According to a survey conducted by the LAC in 1935, there were 933 public libraries and 1002 popular libraries in China, as compared to 1922 when there were only 51 public libraries and 239 free

public libraries.[8] Popular libraries were the result of the mass education movement beginning in the 1920s. They pushed these institutions to a new level and laid the foundation for further developments. Instead of just being a storehouse for the preservation of books, popular libraries began to serve the general public. Under the second Chinese library law (1915) on public libraries there were two sets of regulations: 1) regulations regarding governing popular libraries—these libraries were small, containing a few thousand books and a few reference books, including popular books, magazines, and current newspapers for everyone; and 2) regulations that libraries be established in all provinces and every administrative district—public libraries in this category would emphasize more the academic materials. These rules led to the growth and reorganization of public libraries.

Subsequent political events and discords had an adverse affect upon library development in China. For example, during the Sino-Japanese conflict of 1937–1945, the National Library of Peiping (*Guoli Peiping Tushuguan*) received very few books from foreign countries. During the years when much of Eastern China fell under Japanese occupation, limited foreign materials were collected in the cities of Chongquing and Kunming. After 1941 when the Japanese occupied major coastal ports, the importation of books and periodicals from abroad became scarce.

The founding of the People's Republic of China (PRC) and the Cold War

When the PRC was founded in 1949 the new government faced many challenges. China was in a state of chaos, economically, politically, and socially. Much of the country's industry, educational facilities, and social base were destroyed during the years of Japanese aggression (1937–1945) and during the civil war in China (1947–1949). The new government immediately set up plans for national, social, and economic reconstruction. Libraries and library service were to play a critical role in the reconstruction of China during this period. To assist in national development, China adopted Russia's experiences, theories, and principles for the construction of a socialist model of library service. The goals of the library were to be aligned with the following principle:

> The main tasks of the People's Government in its cultural and educational work are to elevate the cultural standard of the people, train personnel for national construction, eradicate all feudalist comprador-type and Fascist thinking, and foster thoughts of service.

Thus libraries were to serve as providers of ideological doctrine and work related information.

With the establishment of the new government under Mao Zedong, China turned toward the Soviet Union and

Eastern European countries for assistance in building a productive socialist state. During this time many non-Eastern bloc countries, including the United States, adopted an embargo against China. Meanwhile the National Library's acquisition of Western materials diminished greatly and its mission was realigned, following Soviet library principles which were "to serve politics, production, workers, peasants, soldiers, and scientific studies."

As early as June 1949, Mao Zedong declared,

> All Chinese without exception must lean either to the side of imperialism or to the side of socialism. Sitting on the fence will not do. Internationally, we belong to the side of the anti-imperialist front headed by the Soviet Union, and so we can turn only to this side for genuine and friendly help, not to the side of the imperialist front.[9]

This principle was implemented on February 14, 1950 with the Treaty of Friendship, Alliance, and Mutual Aid between the People's Republic of China and the USSR. Mao's "lean to one side" policy reinforced the importance of Soviet influences on librarianship in China. As the national economy was gradually restored, the Ministry of Culture took steps to restructure the libraries, and promulgated a new slogan of "serving the readers by every means." All types of libraries, especially public libraries, promoted book circulation by providing recommended book lists to readers and book exhibits.

Libraries were replenished with new revolutionary publications which were placed alongside the classical works of Marx, Engels, Lenin, Stalin, and Mao Zedong. The government also banned books that opposed the policies and ideology of the Chinese Communist Party, including works that referred to capitalism (particularly to American life), feudalism, idealism, imperialism, and individualism. Throughout the country, libraries were required to inventory their historical works and to identify and remove all "reactionary" publications, including "Fascist," pornographic, and factitious types of literature. Collection development was closely tied to the various political objectives; when a policy was declared, books, relating to the policy were purchased and those with opposing viewpoints were banned.

During the early 1950s libraries developed rapidly throughout China. Chinese officials were interested in establishing an effective library system and sought to learn the operations and practices of librarianship from the Soviet Union. At this time many works on library sciences written by Soviet specialists and librarians were translated into Chinese. These works were collected in 1957 and published as *Translations on Library Science*. The Chinese also adopted many of the technical aspects of Soviet librarianship; for example, the new classification scheme was based on the four main classes of the 1955 Soviet Classification Model: 1) Marxism-Leninism; 2) social sciences; 3) natural sciences; and 4) generalia.

During the 1950s, examples of the most successful newly created libraries were the rural and labor libraries. The slogan, "Culture going to the mountains and the countryside," was used everywhere to foster Marxist education and the popularization of socialist culture. The Government threw open the library doors to readers; no longer was there admission charged, unlike the republican period when users were charged a fee. Under the new government, the masses were the ruling class and libraries were organized to serve the workers and peasants.

During the First Five-Year Plan, 1953–1957, there was a great push for the rapid development of the national economy. This was the time of the 1956 "March toward the Sciences" movement. There was a surge in the rural areas to establish commune libraries. These commune libraries grew; they were administered by local Party committees and run by local people. The materials were acquired through municipal libraries or donations and carried directly to users at work sites. Realizing the importance of education and culture, a major literacy campaign was undertaken during the 1950s. Schools attached to reading rooms in communes and work places taught literacy skills. During these years there was seen also a surge in the growth of labor union libraries. By the end of 1956, it was reported rural reading rooms reached 182,960 and it was these reading rooms that enabled the laborers and peasants to study the current events and policies during the agricultural cooperation period, to elevate their ideological awareness and the standard of their scientific knowledge and production techniques. The libraries for the workers were established to help increase productivity by making more science materials available. After the 1960s there was progress in conducting research on users' needs and demands to further improve scientific scholarship.

Various government ministries held administrative control over libraries:

- The public library system, which included the national, provincial, municipal, county, and cultural center libraries were under the Ministry of Culture.
- College and university libraries were under the Ministry of Education.
- Elementary and secondary school libraries were under the Ministry of Education.
- Trade union libraries were under the Trade Union.
- Special libraries were under appropriate government agencies.

It should be noted that this administrative structure was also based upon the Soviet system.

Beginning in 1952, as a result of the Cold War, China secured few Western language materials, due to the strained relations between China and Western countries. It was difficult to find channels through which to purchase Western language books, except through third parties such as India, because of the strict embargo act imposed upon China by the United States and many of its allies. By the latter half of 1953 the great majority of foreign books acquired in China were from the Soviet Union and East European countries; these works were acquired not only through purchase, but also through bilateral exchange agreements. Through 1957, Soviet materials relating to science and industry were translated in great quantities; these Chinese translations of Russian works amounted to 38% of the total number of publications issued in China.[10] Other books and periodicals were acquired, by purchase, gift, or exchange, from the Soviet Union and distributed to libraries, where they contributed to the development of Russian language collections, including those in the National Library of China's (NLC) collection.

For China, the decade of the 1960s was one of domestic unrest and foreign conflicts. This was the period of waning relationship with the Soviet Union. In the early 1960s, the Soviet Union withdrew all scientific and technical assistance to China, including library development aid. The ability of China to purchase and/or acquire on exchange the necessary Soviet scientific publications was largely curtailed. In an attempt to rectify this problem, China looked toward Japan and Western Europe for materials in advanced science and technology. Meanwhile, China also began a movement toward self-reliance; the populace was discouraged from reading foreign literature, and access to new scientific and technological developments from abroad was restricted.

The Cultural Revolution and recovery

During the decade between 1966 and 1976 the leaders of the Cultural Revolution sought to eradicate old thoughts, old culture, old customs, and old habits of the bourgeois classes of China's past. Many libraries in China were closed and some destroyed. All educational and cultural activities came to a grinding halt. Meanwhile, the West continued to impose an embargo on relations with China. During this time the progress of modern librarianship was interrupted.

After the Cultural Revolution, beginning in the late 1970s, Chinese librarianship recovered and began to adapt many of the new Western ideas and practices of library science and technology. Libraries in China were rebuilt, transformed, modernized, and began to play a key role in national development. After the introduction of economic reforms and the opening up of China in the 1980s, Chinese libraries developed rapidly. Chinese students enrolled in American and other Western library schools, and some also attended special seminars for practicing Chinese librarians in China. Those seminars held in China included some sponsored by national and provincial library organizations. For example, the National Library had organized many seminars across the country to stimulate library development; the Institute of Scientific and Technological

Information of China (ISTIC) sent information specialists to lecture to library and information science students in universities and colleges; in 1978, a national conference was held in Nanjing for libraries with significant classical collections to discuss the 1982 preparation of the National Union Catalog of Ancient Classical Books project—this led to special training classes held in Sichuan province to coordinate the project.

By 1979 China reestablished interaction with the West, including diplomatic relations with the United States. To facilitate China's quest to gain access to Western knowledge, an agreement was signed between the United States and China in August 1979. The Implementing Accord for Cultural Exchanges between the governments of the United States and China provided for the LC to send a full set of U.S. government documents to China's National Library of Beijing (*Guoli Beijing Tushuguan*) beginning January 1, 1980. In return the National Library agreed to send in exchange to the LC a comparable number of Chinese publications. For the first year, LC sent 20,000 publications to Beijing and received only 800 publications from the National Library. A year later, in 1981, the National Library of Beijing raised its number to 13,000 publications. The issue of equivalent content was also raised by LC, for Chinese titles included a wide selection, from scientific treatises to children's books. In 1995 LC urgently requested only Chinese government publications. Since China owned and controlled the country's publication activities, everything it published was classified as a government publication.[11] Other exchange agreements with foreign nations provided an avenue for further acquisition of much needed scientific and technical information.

LIBRARY AND INFORMATION SYSTEMS AND SERVICES

Legislation

As early as 1909, the first library law in China was enacted by the Ministry of Education. According to this law, the aim of the library was to preserve Chinese classics, to disseminate knowledge, to provide research facilities, and to collect materials for the free use of the public. No one was permitted to check books out of the library. There were two kinds of materials in the library—rare editions for safe keeping in the library and ordinary publications for general reading. The rare items included those editions published in the Sung and Yuan dynasties and permission to use them was required by the library authority. Books classified for general reading were government and private publications. Regarding foreign publications, the library was not allowed to obtain foreign books for fear it would contain ideas distasteful to the Emperor, known as "Son-of-Heaven." The library law of 1909 applied not only to the national library, but also to libraries at provincial capitals and county and district libraries. The national library was called the Metropolitan Library. The second Chinese library law on public libraries, Regulations Governing Popular Libraries in 1915, elaborated and specified that public libraries should collect popular books for the general public. This became the turning point in Chinese library history, that is, libraries became more democratic and were expected to provide education for everyone; they not only served provincial and other administrative units, but also public and private schools.

Later in 1916, the Ministry of Education requested that all publishers deposit a copy of their publications in the Metropolitan Library. It also mandated that every library in the provinces, counties, and districts be encouraged to collect books and manuscripts pertaining to the history and culture of their respective locality. The official deposit law was revised in 1926 when it required that every publisher should submit four copies of each new publication to the provincial department of education. These publications were to be distributed to the Metropolitan Library, the National Bureau of Compilation and Translation, the provincial library, and the local county library. Through the years, many rules and regulations concerning libraries have been issued: for example, three of the most important were the National Book Coordination Act of 1957, relating to fostering library service in China; the *Summary Report of Library Work*, 1980, encouraging governments at all levels to develop libraries and expand their services as part of their national planning; and the *Report Pertaining to the Improvement and Enhancement of Library Work*, 1987, from the Ministry of Culture and other ministries, urging the coordination of libraries, reform of library management, and adoption of modern technology. Since 1987 there have been many sets of regulations for special libraries in the development of science and technology to advance economic progress. In 2008, the first standard for the construction of public libraries was issued by the Ministry of Culture. The Ministry and the Library Society of China (LSC) are striving to draft legislation on libraries for the People's Congress, China's highest legislative body. The regulations that have been approved through the years have served the administrative management and smooth operations of libraries well.

National Library of China (*Zhongguo Guojia Tushuguan*)

In 1929 the Chinese Ministry of Education recommended that the Beijing Library and the Metropolitan Library be amalgamated under one management to form a National Library. The two libraries were reorganized under the name of the National Library of Peiping (NLP). Although the National Library functioned mainly as a reference library, it was open to all classes of readers, and in 1929 loan services were offered to libraries and individuals.

At that time the NLP also expanded its services as a center of bibliographical information, both nationally and internationally, and it served as a National Information Center for China. The years 1929 to 1935 were one of growth and development in the foreign language collection. During this time 68,479 volumes of foreign language materials were acquired through purchase, gift, and exchange. A total of 39,113 volumes (representing 57% of the total acquisitions) of foreign language materials were purchased. Approximately 40% of the collection acquired was for natural and applied science materials. Political upheavals and crises had a definite impact upon China's library modernization. The affect of procuring foreign collections was an example. During the Sino-Japanese conflict of 1937–1945, the NLP received few books from foreign countries. Beijing came under Japanese occupation and the library transferred part of its resources to Chongqing and Kunming. At that time, the policy of the NLP was to maintain and manage the various reference collections in Beijing, while the Chongqing and Kunming offices were responsible for the continued collection of Chinese and foreign materials. In the early part of the war, foreign language materials could still be obtained through Hong Kong and then shipped inland. There was, however, the problem that the National Library had no permanent library facilities in Chongqing and Kunming and the two cities were subjected to Japanese bombardments, resulting in the transfer of a portion of the collection to the countryside and another portion to various universities. Later in the war, especially after 1941, with Japanese occupation of all the coastal areas, books and periodicals from abroad became scarcer and their acquisition was finally suspended. After the Japanese surrender in 1945, part of the library's collection at Chongqing and Kunming was shipped to Beijing, but the number of volumes was not large.

From 1945 until the early years following the establishment of the PRC in 1949, the NLP received a considerable number of Chinese and foreign materials which had been held by the Japanese supported puppet government of Wang Qingwei. This was especially true of Japanese language materials that numbered in the tens of thousands. During World War II, though the Japanese had burned many Chinese library collections, the Japanese collection at the National Library remained intact. In 1949, the National Library had a total holdings of 1,400,000 volumes of books and journals of which 292,162 volumes consisted of foreign language materials; this represented approximately 21% of the total collection.

In March 1950 the PRC changed the name of the National Library of Peiping to the National Library of Beijing. Beginning in 1978, when the PRC embarked on a reform policy, the national library began a major drive to modernize its facilities, equipment, functions, personnel, and organization. The goal of the government was to create one of the world's foremost national libraries. In 1988 after a new building was opened, the State Council approved a name change from National Library of Beijing to the National Library of China. (NLC—*Zhongguo Guojia Tushuguan*).

Following the establishment of relations with the United States and other foreign countries, beginning in the 1970s, the national library's collections increased rapidly. The Library found it could no longer accommodate all the incoming materials. In March 1975, after a proposal from Premier Zhou Enlai, the State Council approved the building of a completely new National Library adjacent to the Purple Bamboo Park in Beijing, in an area where many colleges and research institutes were located. The building plans were to reflect China's large population, long history, rich cultural heritage, and many nationalities. Construction of the new library building began on November 18, 1983, an undertaking involving more than 5000 workers. Completed on July 1, 1987 the new building is one of the largest libraries in the world. It has a total of 170,000 m² of floor space, which can accommodate 30 reading rooms with a seating capacity of more than 3,000 and the capability of receiving 7,000–8,000 readers per day. The old library continues to serve as a branch library for books published before 1949.

As the most noted library in China (under the Ministry of Culture) the NLC has the largest collection of Chinese books in the world; through legal deposit, it continues to comprehensively collect all books currently published in China. As of 2007, the NLC's collection consisted of the following: 6,379,096 Chinese books; 3,410,844 foreign books; 50,283 Chinese periodicals; and 43,407 foreign periodicals. It ranked fifth among national libraries in the world. The Library holds a rich collection of 270,000 volumes of rare books [rare books include the volumes of the Song (960–1279 A.D.) and Yuan Dynasties (1271–1368 A.D.) as well as volumes of rare books and manuscripts of notable authors]; 1,600,000 volumes of general ancient books [ancient books consist mainly of thread-bound books after Qianlong Emperor in the Qing Dynasty (1644–1911) and some collections in the Yuan and Ming Dynasties (1368–1644 A.D.)]; and 35,000 pieces of the scripted turtle shells and animal bones from the Yin-Shang Dynasty, ca. 1600–1046 century B.C. In addition, the NLC has the largest collection of foreign language publications in China. Similar to national libraries throughout the world, NLC serves as a depository library for UN publications; NLC also collects publications of other international organizations and foreign governments. It also acquires numerous microforms and AV materials, hundreds of CD-ROM databases, and more than 8000 titles of electronic publications. Like other national libraries, NLC represents an important cultural institution in China, for it has promoted exchanges and cooperation with libraries and cultural institutions all over the world. It has publications exchange relations with more than 1000 libraries and academic institutions in more than 120 countries and regions of the globe.

The NLC is not only a national repository of Chinese and international publications, but also a national bibliographic center, a national center of library information networks, and a library research and development center. In addition to serving the central government, research institutions, academic institutions, business, and the general public, the NLC plays a leading role in standardization, digitization, and networking efforts in China. With the use of modern technology, various kinds of bibliographical databases and subject databases were being created and improved. These include:

- The China National Bibliography Retrospective Databases (1949–1987), created by NLC and other cooperating libraries.
- The China National Bibliographical Databases (1988 to date) created by NLC.
- The China National Bibliographical Database (comprised of the two databases above).

In addition, the Online Computer Library Center (OCLC) becomes a center for creating, processing, and distributing bibliographical records, providing MARC records of Chinese books to scholars throughout the world. The NLC will add its bibliographic records to the OCLC WorldCat database, by developing software to convert the format of its records. It was expected that some 1.5 million records will be sent to OCLC by 2008. (http://www.oclc.org/news/releases/20085.htm). The Library will continue to add records beyond 2008 once the format has been converted. Through these activities, the NLC forms the center of a system covering the entire country. Administratively the NLC is under the PRC Ministry of Culture, which also supervises all public libraries—including provincial, municipal, county, and cultural center libraries.

Similar to libraries in the West, NLC divides its reference services along subject specializations: Social Sciences Reference Service, Sci-Tech Reference Service, Legal Information Reference Service, Abstracts and Indexes Reading Room, and Information Service. There is also a Newspaper Clipping Center and a Document Supply Center that provides subject research, document delivery, and photocopying service. NLC also has two main electronic reading rooms, the largest of their kind in China. These rooms were opened to the public in March 1995, which provided electronic information access services to readers—resources include CD-ROMs (as of 2005, there were 22,429 CDs) on various subjects, multimedia CD-ROMS, CD-ROM bibliographic databases, Web-databases, and over 10,000 full-text e-journals in Chinese or English. The users can phone, write, or visit in person. Service to the users includes training on the Internet, CD-ROM retrieval, and Web page design. The CD-ROM network in the electronic rooms is connected to all major information networks in China: 1) the network of exchange data of the People's Liberation Army (PLA); 2) by wireless with the network of the Ministry of Posts and Telecommunications; and Military Medicine Academy; and 3) by phone with more than 10 institutions' network such as Nankai University Library at Tianjin, Life Science Institute of Beijing University, Zhejiang University, Zhejiang Industry University, Shanghai Huadong University of Science and Engineering, Xi'an Institute of Foreign Language, Ningbo Science and Information Technology Institution, and many more. These connections provide information exchange with all major institutions in China, the Internet, and remote access services for users around the world. With the Gigabit Ethernet library-wide network and an Internet service system open 24 hr a day all year, NLC is able to provide electronic information services, such as Internet Navigation, Full-Text Books Online, and OPAC Access. The NLC has become a center of network information resources. Furthermore, with the advanced Gigabit Ethernet technology developed in February 1999 and the opening of NLC Web site, the library has become a major network resource center connecting with high speed 100 MB leased lines to the State Council, Peking University, and Tsinghua University and also connecting ChinaNet, CERNet (China Education and Research Network), CSTNet (China Science and Technology Network), Beijing Cable TV Network, the National Cable TV Network, and CNC (China Netcom).[12]

While the NLC adapted many modern library concepts and practices from the West, it also strove to utilize these practices to maintain the cultural heritage of China by preserving the great books of the past. The Library has maintained China's rich culture by preserving the books of the past, including works from the royal collection of the Southern Song Dynasty of the twelfth century as well as the Dunhuang manuscripts, the valuable Zhao Cheng Zang (the collection of Buddhist Scriptures preserved in Zhao Cheng County, Shanxi Province), the monumental Yong Le Da Dian (the Yong Le Encyclopedia), and the multivolume Si Ku Quan Shu (Complete Collection of Four Categories of Literature), all regarded as unique copies in the world. Along with the rare books and special collection, NLC maintained about 2,000,000 volumes of thread-bound books. Emphasis is placed on preservation and conservation of the library's exceptionally rich cultural heritage; staff members are engaged in restoration and conservation of rare books, applying traditional rare book conservation techniques and modern microfilming technology.

Since 1995, NLC has been keeping up with the latest development in digital libraries. In 1998, the Ministry of Culture approved a new building project "China National Digital Library." The project proposal of NLC Phase II and the National Digital Library of China Project was completed in November 2001. *The Feasibility Study Report on the National Library of China Phase II and National Digital Library of China Project* was approved by the State Planning Commission in 2003; 12.23 billion Renminbi (RMB) was distributed to NLC for the project;

in 2003, the RMB exchange rate was 8.3 to US$1. Construction was completed in June 2008 and the Library was opened to the public on September 9, 2008. The National Digital Library of China has developed newer models of services, has become a center of Internet knowledge, and a base for information service without limitations of space and time. NLC provides unlimited digital resources, such as digital television, handheld mobile electronic reader for walk-in readers, E-government network, special area and equipment for the visually impaired, satellites, CDs, etc. Architecturally, the new building represents ideas of the past, present, and future: more open reading rooms, free access to publications, spacious reading areas, quiet areas for research, and modern exhibition and instruction areas.

The new library can accommodate an average of 8000 readers per day, with a collection capacity of 12–14 million volumes. The total floor space amounts to 80,538 m^2 and 2,900 seats. The total area of the National Library including both old and new buildings is 250,000 m^2, ranking it third among the world's national libraries.[13]

Academic and Research Libraries

In the 1950s China's educational system, which had been modeled after the Western educational institutions, was reoriented toward using Soviet teaching techniques, curricula, textbooks, and materials. Beginning in the 1950s, higher education came under new directives, with its primary goal being the socialist reconstruction of China. Foreign policy, too, dictated China's educational practices and orientation; the Soviet "model" was widely adopted. Translations from Russian works on library science flourished and Soviet librarians were invited to visit China to consult and give lectures. Academic libraries were called on to engage in national development, subject to the same ideological and political constraints and requirements as other institutions. For example, purchase of Russian books exceeded those of other Western publications during the 1950s. However, a severe setback occurred during the Cultural Revolution (1966–1976) when all university libraries were isolated from the outside world. Foreign acquisitions ceased, creating a 10-year hiatus in book and periodical acquisition.

When universities and colleges finally reopened in 1978, academic libraries recovered and adapted many of the new Western ideas and practices of library science and technology. After the introduction of economic reforms and the opening of China in the 1980s, Chinese libraries developed rapidly. Academic libraries in China were rebuilt, transformed, and modernized and began to play a key role in national development. In the twenty-first century, many Chinese colleges and universities have the best-organized and finest collections. Examples of the development of academic libraries can be seen in Peking University Library (PUL) and Tsinghua University Library.

Peking University Library (PUL)

PUL was first established in 1902, under the name of Capital College Book Storage; at that time it had a core collection of 78,500 volumes. After the revolution of 1911, the present name was adopted. (Peking University kept the name Peking, because of its historic past. It was founded over 100 years ago and was the cradle of the 1919 May 4th Movement.) The reorganization of Chinese colleges and universities was initiated in the 1950s, following the founding of the PRC; PUL absorbed the Yenching University Library as well as collections from other universities. In 1998 when the construction of the new library building was completed, PUL became the largest academic library in Asia, with over 51,000 m^2, 4,000 seats in its reading rooms. By 2002, the centennial anniversary of PUL, the library contained approximately 6.5 million items and was ranked as the largest of any university collection in China. Its holdings included works in the fields of liberal arts, natural sciences, applied sciences, and social sciences. In addition to 2,700,000 volumes in Chinese, the library also holds 900,000 volumes in foreign languages as well as CD-ROMs, microforms, AV materials, and databases for many disciplines. PUL has been steadily developing its collection, with an increase of 80,000 items annually and it maintains exchange relationships with more than 500 foreign libraries, schools, and research institutes.

With a history of more than 100 years of collection development, PUL's Chinese rare book collection is ranked first among academic libraries in China. Among its treasures are 1,500,000 traditional thread-bound books. In addition, the PUL holds 56,000 copies of Chinese rubbings from inscriptions on ancient bronzes and stone tablets. These rubbings are very important for the study of ancient characters, calligraphy, and fine arts (Fig. 2).

On the cutting edge of technology, PUL operates the UNICORN-integrated automation system that includes an online public access catalog (OPAC), as well as modules for the acquisitions, circulation, reference, serials control, acquisitions, etc. In 1998, the headquarters of the China Academic Library Information System (CALIS) was established at the PUL. CALIS is a nationwide academic library consortium with members throughout 27 provinces, cities, and autonomous regions in China. Funded primarily by the Chinese government, its purpose is to digitize resources and develop an information service network in order to serve multiple resource-sharing functions among the participating libraries; these functions include online searching, interlibrary loan, document delivery, and coordinated acquisitions and cataloging.[14]

Tsinghua University Library

Tsinghua University Library was founded in 1912 in Beijing, 1 year after the university was built. In 1928 the

Fig. 2 Peking University Library, Beijing.

Tsinghua School became the National Tsinghua University. Between 1928 and 1935 the Tsinghua University Library expanded rapidly. In 1931 the collection held 300,000 volumes and the library building was 7,700 m^2, with 700 seats. During the Sino-Japanese War (1937–1945) the University moved to Kunming. In 1938 Tsinghua University merged with Peking University and Nankai University to become the Southwest Associated University. The Tsinghua Library shipped 23,000 volumes to the new university. During the move, 10,000 volumes which were temporarily stored in Chongqing were damaged by Japanese bombings, and only 3,000 volumes were saved. In Beijing, the library building became a Japanese military hospital. By 1946, the collection returned to the original campus in Beijing, but the Library had lost 175,000 volumes during the war. After the PRC was established in 1949, there was restructuring which included a reexamination of its collection development policy to support the University's mission of education and research. While there was a strong focus on engineering materials, the library also collected literary works and other subjects in the humanities. The library's collection had grown to 1.35 million volumes by 1966. During the Cultural Revolution period, 1966–1976, the budget of the Library was cut deeply. However, with the help of faculty members, students, and librarians the majority of the library collection survived that tumultuous period. The collection since 1978 grew rapidly reaching 2.5 million volumes by 1990 (Fig. 3).

When the new library was built in 1991, a new stage in library development began. Since then, Tsinghua University Library has made substantial progress in automation and networking. The new library has a floor space of 39,000 m^2 and more than 2,500 seats for patrons. The Library maintains a rich collections of 3,923,000 volumes (books and journals) which cover the humanities, social sciences, and management, but there is primary emphasis on the natural sciences, engineering, and technology. The printed collections contain: 300,000 thread-bound ancient books; over 4,000 current serials and more than 400,000 bound periodicals; over 30,000 Tsinghua University dissertations and theses; and 70,000 microforms. In addition the library has special collections of antiques and rubbings from inscriptions on ancient bronzes and stone tablets; it also contains manuscripts and videotapes donated by faculty members, staff, alumni, and others.

An advanced information infrastructure has been established. The CD-ROM network provides students and faculty with the literature and information searching services via the campus network. An increasing number of electronic resources and virtual resources have been made available in the library or online. Tsinghua University's virtual library is a network of information databases including approximately 42,000 full-text e-journals; over 350 electronic databases; more than 920,000 e-books; more than 35,000 multimedia collections (not including online databases and Internet resources). The system supports the university's goal of becoming a world-class institution.

Tsinghua University Information Network Engineering Research Center was established in June 1994 as an engineering research entity that includes Computer Science and Communication. The center has completed "Sample Project of CERNET (China Education and Research Network)" which was undertaken jointly by Tsinghua and nine other well-known Chinese universities. The first CERNET in China to adopt the TCP/IP system structure was also established here; its aim was to provide a common communication platform for information exchange, scientific computing, and international networking for China's universities and schools. The center served as an important base for the state computer and Internet technology research.

Fig. 3 Tsinghua University Library, Beijing.

Subject librarian system. Tsinghua University Library has a Reference and Information Service Desk at the main hall of the new building in order to provide assistance and advice to individual library patrons. In addition to helping the faculty and students make better use of library resources, the librarians have also attempted to strengthen ties between library and academic departments through "Subject Librarian System," which was begun in 1998. Since then, every academic department has appointed a departmental library coordinator to keep the library apprised of the needs of the department. The subject librarians have academic credentials related to the discipline of the department which they serve. The responsibilities of the subject librarians include:

- Offering training programs to new faculty and new students in March and September of each year.
- Conducting customized workshops on library utilization for their department.
- Introducing new information resources and new services to their department.
- Collecting and introducing useful Web resources for their department.
- Soliciting information in regard to the needs of their department for journals, books, electronic resources, and services of library.

Public Libraries

The public libraries of cities, counties or districts, and villages are all supervised by the Ministry of Culture. They play an important role by enabling Chinese citizens to obtain cultural and educational information as well as meeting the needs of economic construction and scientific research. Some function as research libraries. Organizationally, public libraries are under the Ministry of Culture and are not centrally controlled except for the NLC. They are mainly self-governed and self-financed through the Bureau of Culture of their respective governmental level. At the local level, this consists of provincial regulations characterized by regulations of the operations and organization of libraries in cities, counties, towns, and villages.

For the year 2005, Tables 1–3 provide an example of the number of public libraries and the size of their collections and staff. Table 1 gives the total number of libraries, staff, and collection at the national, provincial, municipal, and counties level in China. Tables 2 and 3 provide examples of major municipal and autonomous regions/

Table 1 Chinese public libraries 2005.

Categories	Number of libraries	Staff	Collection
National	1	1,372	25,050,000
Provincial	38	7,706	143,555,000
Municipal	338	12,704	120,548,000
Counties	2385	28,641	191,407,000

Source: From Ref.[49]

Table 2 Major Chinese municipal public libraries 2005.

Municipality	Number of libraries	Staff	Collection
Beijing	25	1219	11,214,000
Chongqing	43	755	7,675,000
Dalian, Liaoning	12	461	4,675,000
Ningbo, Zhejiang	12	228	2,641,000
Shenzhen	8	444	4,464,000
Tianjin	32	1057	8,694,000
Qingdao, Shandong	13	267	3,294,000
Xiamen, Fujian	8	153	1,925,000

Source: From Ref.[49]

provincial libraries with the number of libraries, staff, and collection.

Official statistics for township and village libraries (rural libraries) do not exist; however, scattered evidence seems to indicate that this particular class of libraries expanded greatly. In Hunan Province, the number of township and village libraries grew from 1,800 in 1985 to 14,000 in 1997.[15] Starting in the 1980s with the surge of economic reforms, public libraries at all levels regarded economic development as the main feature in their work. For example, in rural libraries, public libraries collected and published works on the production technology of planting to be sent out to peasants. These public libraries delivered books by bookmobile or mobile book store and set up service points for circulating books.

Shanghai Library

Established in 1952, the Shanghai Library is the second largest public library in China, next to the NLC. In 1995 the Shanghai Library merged with the Institute of Scientific and Technical Information of Shanghai (ISTIS) (*Shanghai Kexue Jishu Qingbao Yanjiusuo*). In 1996, the

Table 3 Major Chinese autonomous regions/provincial public libraries 2005.

Location	Number of libraries	Staff	Collection
Anhui	88	1217	8,474,000
Fujian	84	1110	12,735,000
Guangdong	129	3252	31,194,000
Hebei	153	1690	13,071,000
Heilongjiang	96	1669	12,910,000
Henan	136	2742	14,292,000
Hunan	120	1963	16,665,000
Inner Mongolia	110	1776	7,435,000
Jiangsu	103	2363	31,785,000
Liaoning	126	2888	23,256,000
Shaanxi	111	1691	8,870,000
Shandong	145	2690	27,464,000
Sichuan	141	1869	20,023,000
Tibet	4	62	421,000
Qinghai	43	365	3,242,000
Xinjiang	96	951	8,174,000
Yunnan	149	1661	13,709,000

Source: From Ref.[49]

new institution moved to its new quarters on Huai Hai Zhong Lu. It is now a comprehensive research library as well as a public library. The Shanghai Library together with the ISTIS has holdings of approximately 51 million items. The location covers 3.1 hectares of land, with a floor space of 83,000 m². The architectural design comprises of two towers connected by a glassed-in-walkway; the taller tower is for sci-tech holdings, the other for social sciences and humanities. Within the social sciences–humanities building is a glass-enclosed atrium crisscrossed by escalators leading to different floors (Fig. 4).

The merger of the Shanghai Library and the ISTIS has established the Library as a center of information resources, an information clearinghouse, and as a center for lifelong literacy. After reorganizations, a new three-dimensional model of services has emerged:

1. Service to the general public—The Library's public services include, reading and lending, reference service, public lectures, exhibitions, and cultural meetings. The policy is to have the Library open to everyone (people outside the city can get a temporary pass with an ID card) and open everyday. The Library maintains 21 local branch public libraries (they share the same circulation system and overall resources). The Shanghai Library has a municipal network of four-level public libraries: 33 district libraries, 215 community/township public libraries, and thousands of local/village reading rooms. In addition, the Shanghai Library serves as a coordinator among all kinds of libraries and information services in the city; there is a consortium of 60 research libraries. This is an indication of the role of the Library's mission to reach out to the people.

2. Service to the research community—Reference service for the city's social and industrial development is provided by both the Shanghai Library and ISTIS. With the Institute's over 100 specialists in various scientific and technical subjects, the Library has organized information research think tank projects for the industrial and technical community.

3. Service to the city government and legislature—Since 2001, the Library has successfully served the city government and legislature, by producing bulletins in two series: General and Technology. This enriched service has been well received because of the information on city development, comments from noted experts, and new trends in world economy and technology. Since the service was so well received, the government has assigned the Library numerous research projects.

The library's mission is to pursue excellence through service. The library has a user-centered policy and sponsors outreach activities to the public. Through their combined collections, the Shanghai Public Library and the ISTIS respond to the educational, social, and industrial needs of the city. The historical documents in the collection include 100,000 manuscripts and letters, approximately 5,400 local records dated before 1949, 18,000 titles of

Fig. 4 Shanghai Library, Shanghai.

genealogical files (342 family names), 150,000 pieces of epigraphs and rubbings, and 1.7 million ancient books (25,000 titles amounting to 170,000 volumes are rare editions). There are more than 50,000 letters, diaries, inscriptions, pictures, and rare documents from famous people of the late Qing Dynasty; and many of these items are being digitized. Materials in the collection range from ancient artifacts, such as those described above, to the latest technical reports, patent files, sound and video recordings, and digital databases. As many as 1 million books are displayed in its 25 reading rooms and open stacks.

With the twenty-first century being the information era, Shanghai Library is giving priority to the building of a digital library. Nine digital reference services have been established: Shanghai Classical Pictures, Shanghai Classical Texts, Music Station, Ancient and Rare Books, Books of the Republic of China (1911–1949), Database of Index of Papers presented at Chinese Professional Conferences, Chinese Newspapers and Periodicals, Foreign Periodicals, and Science and Technology Garden.

School Libraries

After 1949, the development of school libraries became a priority of the Chinese government. School libraries together with academic libraries were under the Ministry of Education (from 1985 to 1998 called the State Commission of Education). Between 1949 and 1965, the number of school libraries multiplied in every province, region, and municipality. In 1989, the State Commission of Education held a national conference on school libraries and a Preparatory Committee for the National Association of Primary and Secondary School Libraries was formed to oversee their development at the local level. In 1991 the Committee issued an official document, *Regulations on School Libraries*. Since then, each province has issued its own provincial rules in accordance to its specific local conditions.

In addition to libraries managed by cultural and educational departments of the central and local governments, there were libraries and reading rooms for children run by Trade Unions. It was estimated that in 1989, there were more than 200 children's libraries or reading rooms established by neighborhood service centers in Beijing, Tianjin, and Shanghai. Also book dealers had set up private libraries, reading rooms, and lending deposit stations to provide an important service to children living in rural areas, in the expectation that the Ministry of Culture and other departments would provide support to these new libraries and help train librarians. Taken as a whole, the development of the school libraries was uneven. There were great differences in areas, given the economic, cultural, and educational level of developments. Over 80% of those schools that had libraries were chiefly located in large and medium-sized cities along the coast. In the economically backward areas of the West, with a low level of education

70% of the schools had not yet established any libraries. This uneven distribution of service was one of the major problems in the growth of school libraries in China.

In China there are also primary and high schools belonging to universities. In May 2007, author visited Xibei University (Xian) Elementary School library and interviewed Headmistress Sun Shu Min. At Xibei University (Xian), there is a provincial university primary school with 1600 students whose families are members of the faculty and staff of the university; others from the province who wish to enter were tested and carefully selected. According to Sun Shu Min, the school's goal was to emphasize reading ability. Each month there was a contest to see which class read the most books, and a prize was awarded to the winning group. On each of the four floors of the school there was a reading corner where students could sit and read various children's magazines. Other incentives to encourage reading are the regular reading discussion groups and parent–teacher conferences. Since 2000, an electronic room was also being used for classes; it was there students learned to use the computers. The annual library budget was approximately 20,000–30,000 yuan in 2007, emphasizing the purchase of electronic books. There was an audiovisual room which included a television set, videos, a language lab, and other facilities. However, the library had no set hours and there was only a part-time staff member to maintain the collection.

Special Libraries

Prior to 1949, research in China was mainly conducted in universities. After the establishment of the new government, it reorganized scientific research according to the Soviet system, which meant that the sole function of universities was teaching. From then on, research was to be carried out in specialized units such as the Chinese Academy of the Sciences (*Zhongguo Kexueyuan*) and Chinese Academy of the Social Sciences (CASS) (*Zhongguo Shehui Kexueyuan*). To support research, special libraries were set up under the jurisdiction of the government agencies and institutions: libraries of the Academy of Sciences (natural sciences) and libraries in the respective research institutions under the academies. There were also libraries in the various ministries or commissions of the government such as the ministries of geology, medicine, agriculture, and industry as well as their numerous branches. As examples of such libraries, two of the research units of the Academy of Social Sciences Library will be discussed: the Institute of Law Library (ILL) and the Institute of West Asian and African Studies Library.

Chinese Academy of Social Sciences (CASS) Library Center for Documentation and Information

In May 2007, the author visited the chinese Academy of Social Sciences Library and interviewed Jiang Ying,

Deputy Director of the library. The CASS was founded in 1977; prior to that time, CASS evolved from the Research Division of Academic Information, Department of Philosophy and Social Sciences under the Chinese Academy of Sciences in the late 1950s. The Division was later named Division of Academic Materials. From the Division, the Institute of Information of the CASS was founded in 1977. In October 1985, the Center for Documentation and Information (CDI) emerged as a result of the amalgamation of the Institute of Information and the Materials Division. In 1994 the Chinese Academy of Social Sciences Library (CASS Library) *(Zhongguo Shehui Kexueyuan Tushuguan)* was founded. A new library building was constructed in 2002, covering an area of 18,000 m^2. The CDI (*Wenxian Qingbao Zhongxin*) is a part of the CASS Library.

The CASS Library has not only applied the most advanced computer and network technologies for researchers in the institutes but also for other scholars. However, the CASS Library is not open to the general public. The library collects, catalogs, shelves, and loans primary documents for researchers in the humanities and social sciences. The emphasis is on collecting in the areas of economics, sociology, and international studies. The collection is almost evenly divided between Chinese and English language materials. The CASS Library has approximately 5,000,000 items; this includes 2.4 million volumes (journals and books), covering all areas of the humanities and social sciences in more than 40 languages. Other items in the collection include:

- Thread-bound ancient books 650,000 vols.
- Paperback books 880,000 vols.
- Foreign books 410,000 vols.
- Academic degrees theses 100,000 vols.
- Bound-volumes of newspapers and periodicals 300,000 vols.

In the early 2000s, the collection consisted of 1800 Chinese and 900 foreign language periodicals, in addition to 1780 literary journals published from 1919 to 1949.

A series of CD and online databases are also available; they include: Bibliographic Database of CASS and Database of Citations of the Humanities and Social Sciences in China; Full-Text Database of the People's Daily for over 50 years; Full-Text Database of Duplicated Newspapers and Journals of the Renmin University of China; Gale's (United States) Database of Full Texts and Abstracts in the Social Sciences, and 13 other databases of OCLC. The budget has grown to accommodate the need for electronic resources. In 2007, the budget for electronic resources was 2,000,000 yuan as compared with 8,000,000 yuan for books. CASS actively engages in exchanges with institutions and academic organizations in Russia, United States, Great Britain, France, Germany, Holland, Finland, Japan, R.O. Korea, Vietnam, Israel, Taiwan, Hong Kong, and Macao. Annually foreign books acquired through exchanges account for 20% of the total acquisition of foreign books.

Institute of Law Library (ILL) of the CASS

In May 2007, the author visited the ILL of the CASS and interviewed Zhang Qun of the Institute of Law. Established in 1958, the ILL (*Faxue Yanjiusuo Tushuguan*) of the CASS is considered the preeminent law library in China. The Library's collection was mainly acquired from three sources:

1. Tsinghua University in 1958 when universities were restructured.
2. The Legal Bureau of the State Council and the Legal Press in 1959.
3. Donations of nationally and internationally famous jurists.

After 1959 the Library has grown through purchase, exchange, and donations, becoming the largest and most comprehensive legal library in China.

In 2007 the total area of the Library was approximately 1127 m^2. Eight hundred thirty-five square meters were used for Chinese books, books in western languages, Japanese books, ancient books, journals, and newspapers. The reading rooms occupied 210 m^2, including separate reading rooms for newspapers (Chinese and foreign languages), reference books, Chinese data, electronic data, and catalogs.

The law collection includes theories of law and various branches of legal sciences. The main emphasis is on legal history, laws and regulations from various countries, and international and domestic literature on every aspect of law. At the end of 2001, the library's holdings contained 385,000 titles; of the 177,000 Chinese books, there were 38,227 ancient legal books and documents, of which 2,795 were rare and solely existing copies. In addition, the library holds over 60,000 foreign language works, including books in English, Japanese, Russian, French, German, and many other languages.

In this foreign language collection there are a large number of modern Japanese legal texts and materials on human rights in English. The library also has 25,000 journals (17,000 in Chinese and 8,000 in foreign languages). The collection also includes 24,193 pages of English books on microfilm, as well as 110,000 Chinese newspaper clippings on law. In 2006, the budget was 600,000 yuan, which was mostly spent on printed books. Few foreign books were purchased because of the high inflationary rates. Even the purchase of e-journals became difficult, therefore, the CASS database network was utilized.

The library provides various services to the legislative, administrative, and judicial sections of the state, the legal practitioners and law school professors, and students, but it does not offer interlibrary lending services. There were eight professional staff in the library, five had library science degrees, and three had law degrees.

Institute of West Asian and African Studies Library of the CASS

The Institute of West Asian and African Studies Library (IWAASL) (*Xiyafeizhou Yanjiusuo Tushuguan*) of the CASS, established in 1981, is considered the best library in African collections in China. In May 2007, the author visited the IWAASL of the CASS and interviewed Chen Hong, Librarian and Chen Yulai, Deputy Director of the Center of Southern African Studies of IWAAS. There are more than 20,000 books, one-half relating to the Middle East and the other half to Africa. The library subscribes to over 100 Chinese journals, as well as more than 100 English and a few French language journals. Most of the budget is spent on foreign journals (70%), with few books purchased from overseas. The remaining 30% is for Chinese newspapers and some Chinese books. The library subscribes to no overseas newspapers, due to high costs. The budget was little more than 300,000 yuan in 2007.

Ms. Cheng Hong, librarian of the IWAASL, created several magazine and book databases for IWAASL:

- The Chinese academic journal database, which is an index for articles relating to the Middle East and African studies.
- The database for Western language magazine articles on Middle East and African studies, began in 1983, which includes indexing and some abstracts.
- Full-text databases for Chinese articles began somewhere between 1990 and 2001.
- The book database which includes abstracts of books published in China and abroad on the Middle East and African Studies.

The CASS database network contains other works not found in the IWAASL. The Institute has a separate room with compact shelving for the 20,000 plus collection. The materials are shelved in two sections, Africa and the Middle East, with half of the materials in Chinese in each area.

Digital Library Collections and Services

During the past decade, the information infrastructure of China has expanded greatly. According to the China Internet Network Information Center (CNNIC) Survey, June 30, 2007, there were 162,000,000 Internet users and 1,311,600 Web sites. A majority of the Internet users live in the capital and coastal cities, which is where the major universities and scientific research institutions and industries are located; these cities are also centers of research and development activities. With increased access to the Internet, the development of digital libraries in China has become a priority and a significant component in the national information infrastructure. Digital libraries in China are defined as

> research institutions where computer specialists and content service providers focus on technology improvements for digitizing, organizing, distributing, preserving, retrieving, and searching data, or as projects with practical applications designed to create digital collections or provide digital library services.

After the 1996 IFLA Conference held in Beijing, the first national level digital library project in China, the National Pilot Digital Library Project (NPDLP) was initiated in 1997 by the Ministry of Culture and the State Planning Commission. The NPDLP included the NLC and five large public libraries (the Shanghai Library, Liaoning Library, Nanjing Library, Zhongshan Library, and Shenzhen Library). The project's aim was to experiment a digital system of collaboration and resource sharing with participants. Since 1998 many additional research and development projects related to digital libraries have been launched by universities (under the Ministry of Education) and by the science and technology research institutes and the Chinese Academy of Sciences.[16]

Chinese National Science Digital Library (CNSDL)

The CNSDL began in 2001 and was part of the Knowledge Innovation Project of the Chinese Academy of Sciences. The primary goal of CNSDL was to build a national information resources and management system that would provide a document delivery and interlibrary loan service system accessible from every scientist's desktop in China. CNSDL has also constructed several Chinese scientific literature databases with more than 1 million records, covering major topics in chemistry, biology, physics, mechanics, optics, mathematics, astronomy, geography, and computer science. CNSDL provided more than 10,000 full-text foreign scientific magazine and other virtual reference services.[17]

China National Knowledge Infrastructure (CNKI)

Established in 1996, the CNKI is a significant national e-publishing project in China. This project was founded by Tsinghua University that developed the Tsinghua Tongfang Knowledge Network Technology Company. The CNKI full-text databases reach out not only inside China, but also globally, covering resources such as journals, newspapers, dissertations, proceedings, yearbooks, reference works, and others. CNKI has been a great encouragement for Chinese libraries to digitize as well as to aid researchers. As of 2006, the CNKI academic databases have served more than 5500 universities, public libraries, and other research institutions.[18]

World Digital Library (WDL)

Developments in digitization are progressing in China. On November 2008, the LC signed an agreement with the NLC to collaborate in developing the WDL, which included: to provide content to the WDL in such areas as the development of the Chinese-language interface; to set up international working groups to plan the project; and to establish an advisory committee of leading scholars to suggest major collections relating to the Chinese culture and history in the WDL. Signing took place between Zhan Furui, General Director, NLC and James Billington, Librarian of the Library of Congress. The goal is to digitize important primary Chinese materials, including manuscripts, maps, rare books, musical scores, recordings, films, prints, photographs, architectural drawings, and many more; to provide important resources on the Internet to scholars; and to promote international understanding.

The background to the WDL began in October, 2007, when the LC and other institutions around the world, in collaboration with the United Nations Educational, Scientific and Cultural Organization (UNESCO) presented a prototype of the future WDL. Major institutions participating in the WDL included Brazil, Egypt, Iraq, Israel, Russia, Serbia, and Sweden; also included were the U.S. National Archives and Records Administration, the John Carter Brown Library, and the libraries of Brown and Yale Universities. The project is to be launched in April 2009.[19]

Peking University Library (PUL) Providing Virtual Reference

PUL has been in the forefront of the development of a modern digital library. When the library launched its virtual reference service in 2002, it adopted OCLC's QuestionPoint, a collaborative reference system using technology that can handle the complexities of the Chinese language and easy to use. Question Point allows libraries to reach out to patrons, instead of waiting for the patrons to come to the library to ask questions. PUL has a well-trained reference staff and has developed clear guidelines and effective implementation plans. Question Point has an interface that enables libraries to offer online reference services locally and to refer questions to libraries locally, regionally, or globally.

Since 1998, PUL Library has served as the administrator of the CALIS, which includes over 60 academic libraries as members; these members collaborate within China to share cataloging information and library resources. In 2007, collaboration in digital reference service was limited, since only five CALIS members used Question Point; these libraries included Peking University, Tsinghua University, Shanghai Jiaotong University, Sun Yat-Sen University, and Beihang University. In the future CALIS would like to plan its own collaborative digital reference system for academic libraries in China.[20]

Digital library projects in China continue to be developed. The concept of a digital library was first introduced in China at the IFLA Conference in 1996, which was held in Beijing. China has made much progress, but more remains to be accomplished.

Library and Information Science Education

Formal library training in China began in 1920 when a program was set up at Boone College, jointly founded by Mary Elizabeth Wood, Shen Zhu Rong, and Hu Qing Sheng. However prior to 1949, the development of library education was limited, due in part to the turbulent political situation. With the establishment of the PRC the entire concept of library service changed. The new government sponsored a great expansion of libraries as well as reconstruction of facilities that had been destroyed during the Japanese occupation and the civil war. The number of libraries grew from 400 in 1950 to more than 33,000 in 1958. To meet the growing demand for library personnel in the 1950s a new library education system was set up following the Soviet principle of dividing libraries and information services into two separate systems where by library study was a part of *literary* study and information science was regarded as the study of *science*. This separation between library and information science later turned out to be impractical.

The Department of Library Science at Peking University was created in 1949 and 3 years later the Boone library school was absorbed by Wuhan University, where it became a department of library science. At first Wuhan and Beijing both operated junior college level programs that offered high school graduates 2 years of professional training; later the programs were extended to become 4-year college degrees. However, in the 1960s the Cultural Revolution disrupted China's educational programs and formal education was halted. Universities did not resume regular instructions until the late 1970s.

College-level library education also became an important component in the library and information education system in China. Wuhan and Peking universities both had two divisions: one specializing in the humanities and social sciences and the other in science and technology. Students could enroll in a 4-year college program with a bachelor's degree and a 2- or 3-year certificate programs. Graduates of this degree program spent equal time in professional training and in other courses, such as liberal arts, social science, law, or computer science offered by other departments.

Beginning in the early 1980s, the entire political/education ideology in China shifted to a more pragmatic and open policy. Economic reform to further modernization became the rallying cry of the 1980s, and it soon became apparent that well qualified librarians and information specialists were urgently needed. In 1979, the first 3-year master's program was created at the Departments of Library Science at Wuhan and Peking. In 2007 there were 18 institutions offering master's degree—9 were accredited to grant M.A. degrees in library science and the other 9 eligible to grant an M.S. degree in information science. Entrance exams were required for graduate education and general higher education. Students spent approximately one-third of the total course hours in internship and conducting research projects, and about the same number of hours in writing a thesis during the third year.

Since 1984, there have been other graduate programs which required only 2 years of course work and no thesis. Between the years 1978 and 1993 there have been approximately 700 graduates, primarily in the master's program. As of 1986, 18 of the government-recognized comprehensive universities had library and information programs, with more than 2000 new students enrolled annually. In 1989, there were 50 institutions that had developed departments with specialized programs for formal library and information courses.

The rapid growth of information industry has challenged educational institutions to update their curriculum and expand their teaching programs to meet new needs. In 1991, Ph.D. programs were first introduced at Wuhan and Peking universities and the following year the Department of Library Science at Peking University changed its name to Department of Information Management. The 3-year doctoral program at Peking University consists of coursework and a dissertation. In 2007, there were four institutions offering Ph.D. degrees: Peking University and the Chinese Academy of Sciences were qualified to confer the Ph.D. in library science, while Wuhan and Nanjing Universities were allowed to grant the degree in information science.

Informal education has developed rapidly and provided opportunities to deliver library and information education in remote regions such as Xinjiang and Inner Mongolia. These programs were offered to adults who had no formal degrees but worked in the library and information fields. Three types of programs were available: correspondence programs, television programs, and in-service training. The Ministry of Culture and the Ministry of Education declared that upon completion of the required courses, students could earn a college diploma or certification. The programs differed little from the formal 3-year certificate education.

Night and "Spare-time" Schools, Workshops, and Seminars organized in metropolitan areas offer library education to tens of thousands of experienced library workers who lack formal education, but wish to take advantage of the opportunity to gain the basic knowledge of the library profession. The NLC set up the Sparetime Workers' College and Nanjing Normal College set up the Night College of Library Science. Conferences, workshops, and seminars were organized within libraries and others were held jointly with the China Society of Library Science (CSLS). This has resulted in a great improvement in the quality of personnel.

Professional Associations

The LAC founded in 1925 was an important force for library reform during the 1920s and 1930s. In 1949, LAC moved with the Nationalist government to Taiwan and was inactive until November 1953 when it was reconstituted in Taipei.

In China there were no professional societies for 30 years. It was only until the "opening up" of China in the late 1970s did various professional societies reemerged. In 1979 The China Society for Library Science (CSLS), *Zhongguo Tushuguan Xuehui*, was established. Soon after international and bilaterally organized seminars were presented in China: a UNESCO-sponsored seminar was held in Beijing on the topic of automation and how to access databases. Seminars were organized by the CSLS with international agencies. International viewpoints were exchanged and discussed.

Though China was one of the founding members of IFLA (1927) it was not active in IFLA for many years due to war, political unrest, and the Taiwan issues. Slowly as China regained its membership in UNESCO, CSLS returned to IFLA in 1981.

As of 2000 the CSLS had 10,000 individual members and 47 institutional members. The CSLS is an affiliate institution of the NLC and a national association on librarianship under the joint leadership of the China Association for Science and Technology (CAST) (*Zhongguo Kexue Jishu Xuehui*) and the Ministry of Civil Affairs. It functions as a liaison between the Government and librarians; it also has the status of a national nongovernmental and nonprofit organization. CSLS is a member of the China Association for Science and Technology and a consultative body of UNESCO. The CSLS guidelines and policies as set up by the state are to promote and contribute to the development of librarianship for the purpose of modernization. Its principle responsibilities as stated in the Constitution are to promote library science research; in addition the society has conducted seminars and training classes on particular topics. General membership meetings are held every 5 years.

A core national library journal sponsored by the CSLS and the NLC is the Journal of Library Science in China, JLSC (former name was the Bulletin of the China Society for Library Science, 1979–1990). JLSC presents the theoretical and practical results of research and development by professionals, professors, and students in the field. Since the establishment of CSLS, the number of professional journals has been growing. More than 50% of library and information journals published in China originate from library societies at the national, provincial, and municipal levels.

The English name of CSLS was changed in 2005 to the LSC. Annual meetings are conducted. At the 2007 annual conference in Lanzhou, Gansu Province, China, LSC invited members from the ALA and Chinese American Librarians Association (CALA), an affiliate of ALA, to participate. The main theme of the conference was "The Library: New Environment, New Changes and New Development." Barbara Ford, former president of ALA, Director of the Mortenson Center for International Library Programs at the University of Illinois at Urbana-Champaign participated in the seminars. More than 50 presentations were conducted and over 20 discussion panels were conducted. Approximately 300 attendees from all over China came to the conference. The forums were very successful and the speakers were all well-known in their fields; it provided a learning exchange with Sino-American librarians.

After China's return to IFLA in 1981, its activity with IFLA has promoted programs beyond its national boundaries. International exchanges, cooperation, and relationships with foreign library associations have all developed. In 1996, the 62nd IFLA General Conference was held in Beijing. The theme of the conference was the Challenge of Change: Libraries and Economic Development. The IFLA Conference gave librarians all over the world an excellent chance to exchange ideas and explore librarianship in China.

Other significant organizations for information professionals include the China Society for Scientific and Technical Information (CSSTI) (*Zhongguo Kexue Jishu Qingbao Xuehui*) and the Chinese Archives Association (CAA) (*Zhongguo Dang'an Xuehui*). The CSSTI was founded in 1964 and was a part of the CAST. CSSTI was a nongovernmental organization of science and technology professionals and its mission was to promote the development of information science and its services; to serve science, technology, and economic construction in China; to edit and publish information in books and periodicals, and to strengthen international academic exchanges.

ARCHIVES AND ARCHIVAL SCIENCE

The responsibility and overall direction of archival work in China reside in the State Archives Bureau (SAB) (*Guojia Tanganju*) which was established in 1954 under the State Council, the highest executive organ of the PRC. The main principles of archival work in China are to administer national records, to protect the safety of the records, and to facilitate the work of the state by making archival documents available. In other words, the role of the archives is to serve the priorities of the state. The main emphasis in Chinese archival study is on the dissemination of select documents centered on historical themes considered by archivists and historians to be significant in Chinese history.

Legislation

In 1987, the Archives Law was adopted by the Standing Committee of the National People's Congress and enacted on January 1, 1988. It defined the establishment of archival administration and records department, the collection, utilization, and protection of archives. The Archives Law of the PRC allowed, but did not require, that records in state archives be opened to researchers 30 years after their dates of origin. Economic, scientific, technical, and cultural records may be opened earlier. Records that are highly confidential may be restricted up to 50 years or longer. The law also requires that records must first be processed, arranged, and described before they may be opened for consultation. The function of the SAB is to outline broad archival policies and principles for the entire nation, and to work in consultation with each national-level ministry to devise and institute archival management, records management, and records disposition guidelines for use by archival repositories at every level. Below the National SAB are archives bureaus at the provincial, municipal, and county levels.

Chinese Archival Classification

The Chinese Archival Classification (CAC) together with the Chinese Thesaurus for Archives and the Cataloging Guidelines for Archival Descriptions were first published in 1987 under the auspices of the SAB; a second edition appeared in 1997. Because classification schemes based primarily on subjects are not considered suitable for archives, the administrative structure of the government is used as the basis for archival classification schedules. The CAC has been adopted by archival institutions at all levels in China.

Archive Management Bureaus and Archival Repositories

It was reported in 1992 that there were more than 3400 archive management bureaus and more than 3500 archival repositories in China. What ties all these diverse entities together is the role of the SAB in Beijing and archives bureaus of the provincial and local governments. The role of the SAB is to create general archival policies and principles for the entire country, and in consultation with each national-level ministry to disseminate archives management, records management, and guidance for disposition of records for archives bureaus or archival repositories at all levels. The provincial level archives are responsible for the acquisition and preservation of local records. They function and receive guidance from the SAB. The SAB not only implements regulations and archival records management, but staff members go out to provincial archive bureaus to review, offer advice, and offer suggestions in improving local applications. Archival repositories differ from archival management: the latter is concerned with policy management and the former with care and service. There are two kinds of repositories, comprehensive archives and specialized archives. Each performs at different levels, be it national, provincial, or local. A comprehensive repository houses all kinds of records from different units in a geographic area and a specialized repository is limited to keeping records in a special medium, for example, motions pictures, photos, audio and video recordings.

National Archives

The national archives in China are The First Historical Archives (in Beijing) and Second Historical Archives (in Nanjing). They are directly under the SAB. The Central Archives (in Beijing) contains contemporary records and those relating to Communist party history, and is directly subordinate to the State Council.[21]

In May 2007, author visited the first Historical Archives of China in Beijing and interviewed Zou Ailian, Director. The First Historical Archives in Beijing was established in 1925 and was also known as the Ming-Qing Archives or the Palace Museum Archives; it was the most important historical archives in China for the pre-1912 period. The collection consists of records of the central governments of the Ming (1368–1644 A.D.) and Qing (1644–1911 A.D.) dynasties; it holds over 10,000,000 items (jian). Published reports estimate that more than 317,000 items in the First Archives collection were from the Manchu (Qing dynasty). There were at least 10 catalogs for different types of Manchu documents which have been made available to researchers. They contain valuable research materials on military affairs and relations with Mongolia, Tibet, and Xinjiang. The Archives have been used heavily by Chinese and foreign scholars. An extremely useful guide was published by the archives under the title *Collection of the First Historical Archives of China*, 1985 (*Zhongguo Diyi Lishi Dang'An Guan Guancang Dang'Angaishu*). Scanning, microfilming, and photocopying are available.[22] There were 14 Divisions, 170 full-time staff, and 100 part-time employees in 2007. The Archives, since 1975, is housed in a modern building; 10% of its records are digitized. It is under the SAB.

The Second Historical Archives of China (SHAC) in Nanjing was the first archive to be established after the founding of the PRC. It is also under the administration of the SAB. The collection consists of original records of the previous central governments and their subordinate organs (Republic of China, during the 1912–1949 period). The Second Historical Archives was formally opened to scholarly inquiry in 1980; it now has state-of-the-art storage facilities, preservation programs, cataloging systems, and retrieval capacities. SHAC has five departments: 1) Archive Processing and Cataloging Department; 2) the Conservation Department; 3) the Public Services Department; 4) the Technical Department; 5) the Computing Center; and 6) the Compilation Department. The aim of the SHAC is to collect, arrange, catalog, preserve, compile, and facilitate the use of the holdings of the Archives. The Archives are equipped with microfilming, photocopying, and computer technologies. Various types of finding aids are available. The SHAC has led the way in redefining the nature of a state archive by extending their holdings well beyond those of formal government bodies; the SHAC collection now includes papers of Republican-era institutions such as the private industrial companies, banks, and educational institutions that had been nationalized either during the Guomindang period or the early years of the PRC. By the end of 2000, the records of the Republican governments (and their subordinate organs during the 1912–1949) were estimated to comprise 1,800,000 files in more than 900 classes (Fig. 5).

The bulk of the holdings in the SHAC is made up of official documents; also included are photographs, medals, seals, currencies, postal stamps, trade marks, geographical handbooks, paintings, and calligraphy. These items are useful for historical research and verification of historical artifacts. Since SHAC was opened to the public in 1980, it has been used by approximately 300,000 researchers who have consulted more than 1 million files; these users are from China and abroad (Taiwan, Hong Kong, the United States, Japan, the United Kingdom, France, the Netherlands, and Germany). To make records more accessible to the public, the SHAC staff have published more than 50 different compilations of primary sources. The SHAC also publishes the journal *Republic Archives* relating to historical sources held at the archives.[23]

Provincial Archives

The archives of provinces, autonomous regions, and municipalities take their directions from the respective provincial, regional, or municipal governments. While the SAB offers advice, it does not manage or administer the local archives. An example is the Sichuan Provincial Archives (*Sichuan Sheng Dang'an Quan*). In May 2007, author visited Sichuan Provincial Archives in Chengdu and interviewed Feng Shaocheng, Director of Circulation. The Sichuan Provincial Archives was established in 1966, but it was dispersed during the Cultural Revolution; it resumed activities in 1979 and moved into a new building in 1988. The total collection consists of approximately 1.3 million files, making it one of the largest provincial archives in China. The emphasis is on the Qing Dynasty, the Republican and contemporary periods as it relates to Sichuan. All of the documents of the Qing Dynasty are on microfilm, but as of 2007 documents from the Republican and contemporary periods had not yet been microfilmed. The Sichuan Provincial Archives does not collect any new materials on Chongqing (in 1990, Chongqing became a separate administrative district directly under the national

Fig. 5 The Second Historical Archives of China, Nanjing.

government of China, therefore, is no longer part of Sichuan) or any separate files on warlords and military matters. The Ba-xian county archives during the Qing period (1644–1912) are the most comprehensive collection of its kind of any county in the country, and records of the Sichuan Railway Protection Movement of 1911 archives are considered especially valuable. Select official documents of the former province of Xikang during the Republican period (1930s–1940s) are also available. (Xikang was merged with Sichuan following the founding of the PRC in 1949.) Also available are a limited collection of Western language files, including 136 files of documents of the French Consulate in Chengdu from 1908 to 1949 and the 872 files of English language documents of the Chongqing office of the Chinese Maritime Customs Service, 1891–1949. Sichuan Provincial Archives has published a very comprehensive 759 page guide to its collection. The majority of visitors are professors and graduate students from Sichuan. Some of the archival documents have been locally scanned and it may take several years more to digitize all the materials. It was agreed that to preserve the archives, digitization was the answer and they were moving in that direction. The Archives hoped to integrate all the archives into a national system. There was a card catalog which was organized by topics.

Religious Archives

A special repository which should be mentioned is **The Archives on the History of Christianity in China** at the Hong Kong Baptist University Library, Hong Kong.

The Archives was established in 1996 to serve as a research center in Asia for scholars. The collection covers both primary and secondary English and Chinese language source materials concerning Chinese Christians, missionaries stationed in China, church history, and other materials pertaining to the history of Christianity in China. There are over 3,400 volumes of correspondences, diaries, manuscripts, monographs, and serials, as well as over 31,000 microform items. The extensive microform collection was a result of the generosity of a 3-year $120,000 grant from the Henry Luce Foundation. There are hundreds of biographies and memoirs in the Archives. For the period between 1950 and 1970 there were newspaper clippings on the history and development of religions in China. In addition, a digitization project on *China through the Eyes of CIM (China Inland Mission) Missionaries* database was completed. The database includes 225 lantern slide and glass plate negative images of portraits, landscapes, scenery, and architecture in China as well as photos documenting the socioeconomic activities of the Chinese from the 1900s to the 1930s.[24]

China's Archival Education

Since 1949 Chinese archival education has been regulated by the state. There are archival training programs in secondary schools, colleges, postgraduate institutions, as well as in-service training, adult education, correspondence courses, and television courses. In 1992 there were approximately three dozen Chinese institutions of higher learning offering archival education courses, with a full-time faculty of 500 and over 7000 students enrolled. Sixty secondary schools offered archival service training and in 1992 there was a total enrolment of more than 1000 students at that level. In-service training from the provincial level to the Archival Administrators' Education Centre in Beijing offers courses to thousands of mid-level and higher-level archivists. The SAB, the Ministry of Education, and the Chinese Archives Society were all involved in archival education.

China People's University

At the China People's University (Renmin Daxue), the Archives College, a teaching and research center, was established in November 1952; since then Renmin has been the leader in China's archival education. Located in the western suburbs of Beijing, the College was designed to train professionals engaged in archival work. It also trained faculty to teach archival science. The Archives College has a faculty of 54, including 30 professors and associate professors. The 4-year undergraduate curriculum offers majors in three areas: archival science, administration of scientific and technical work, and archival preservation. The 3-year graduate studies program offers concentrations in archival science and in the history of Chinese archival systems. A 2-year certificate program of specialized education is awarded to majors in archival science and in document administration. Not until 1994 did the college develop a doctoral program in historical document science, including archival science. In the 40 year period from 1952 to 1992, a total 4489 graduate students completed their archival training, and many of these alumni have become well-known scholars and leaders in the archival profession. Students from other countries have studied at People's University and professional archivists and educators from Russia, Canada, and the United States have taught there.

Professional Associations

Founded in 1981, the CAA (*Zhongguo Dang'an Xuehui*), is a professional organization of Chinese archivists, and is a member of the China Association for Science and Technology. There are branch associations at the provincial level and in local districts. The headquarters of the CAA is in the SAB; its leadership is drawn from the national archival management system and from academics of archival science in universities. The society encourages research in archival preservation, the history of archival management, and archival management education. The CAA has as its goals:

1) to encourage archival academic exchanges with foreign archive institutions, learned societies, and individual archivists; 2) to raise the academic level of members; 3) to spread archival knowledge among members; and 4) to make known Chinese developments and achievements in archive academic research at home and abroad. Examples of some of the special committees work include: records management, editing and publishing of historical documents, automation, microfilming and reproduction, and conservation. CAA also publishes two professional journals: the bimonthly *Archives Work* and the quarterly *Historic Archives*.[25]

Chinese archives have undergone major changes, especially since the PRC Archive Law in the 1980s. The Archive Law states that archives should be opened to researchers and to citizens. The range of services as well as the scope and variety of uses for archives has been slowly expanding. Researchers particularly engaged in early twentieth century history from 1900 to 1949 will find increasing opportunities to gain access to the original documents. As China's modernization accelerates, electronic comprehensive cataloging of archival holdings is being explored; it will soon be possible to use online finding aids to locate materials in any Chinese archives that are pertinent to pre-1949 Chinese history.

MUSEUMS AND MUSEOLOGY

Modern Chinese museums appear in a remarkable diversity with regard to size, function, form, and content. The majority of them are public museums administered as facilities of the state, province, municipality, or district, while private museums are operated under different rules. Their focuses frequently evolve around the following subjects: history, religion, ethnicity, cultural relics, science and technology, arts and crafts, famous people, sports, and paleontology and archaeology. They encompass most ordinary types ranging from aviation to natural history museums, in addition to unique ones such as those on modern Chinese revolutionary history, traditional Chinese medicine, historical salt /mining industry, ancient astronomical instruments, and silk and tea industries.[26]

Since the past two decades, China has been rebuilding and expanding existing museums, as well as updating exhibition facilities and constructing new ones. While only less than 30 museums were visible in major cities when PRC came into existence in 1949, 480 museums were recorded in the 1950s, and a rapid flourishing of museums concurrent with the rise of market-based economy was observed in the last decade of the twentieth century. The number reached 1357 in 1999, and a total of 1722 public museums of all varieties were operating in 2008.[27] The list is estimated to have more than 2300 when nongovernmental museums are also being included.[28] It appears that only a mere 300 are related to subjects in scientific studies, and most were established after the turn of the twenty-first century.[29]

Of all the Chinese museums, approximately 120 currently located in the capital city constitute the highest concentration in a single city. Among them are some of the most popular ones scattering along the western section of the east–west oriented Chang'an Street. The Palace Museum in the Forbidden City, now commonly known as the "former Palace," as well as its 1,000,000 pieces of artifacts in the collection, represents a complete ancient palatial complex dating back to 1420. The walled complex of 720,000 m^2 was the seat of a succession of Ming and Qing imperial houses until the last emperor Pu Yi was expelled in 1924.[30] The Palace Museum in the Forbidden City along with the Shenyang Palace Museum in Liaoning Province[31,32] are important sources for understanding the life and history of the Qing imperial house.

Near the Palace Museum of Beijing is the Chinese National Museum in a structure composed of two separate units: the Museum of the Chinese Revolution and the Museum of Chinese History. The former is designed to interpret the modern history of China with a focus on the Communist Party. The latter had been expanded from its predecessor, the Beijing History Museum originally built in 1912. The items in the collection include the fossils of Chinese *homo erectus*, Neolithic potteries, bronzes and ceramic wares from dynastic periods, in addition to a rare bronze human sculpture marked with acupuncture points.[33] Besides the Palace Museum in the Forbidden City, the Museum of Chinese History with its 300,000 items in its collection has only two rivals in terms of the size of their collections: the Tianjin Natural History Museum of Hebei Province and the Nanjing Museum (formerly National Central Museum) of Jiangsu Province.[34]

The new version of the Beijing Capital Museum farther west inaugurated in 2006 is regarded as one of China's leading museums to exemplify elements of a modernized institution. The architectural complex of outstanding design is built to accommodate a maximum of 2000 visitors for exhibitions, educational activities, and conferences requiring multilanguage interpretation services. In the galleries, special exhibitions such as "Ancient Calligraphy," "Stories of the Capital City," and "Treasures of Peking Opera" complement permanent installations to recount the history and cultural aspects of Beijing city, with topics ranging from its Paleolithic beginnings to the recent past. These are designed to reflect the goal of the museum that stresses integration of collection, exhibition, restoration, and research into education.[35]

Apart from museums dedicated mainly to China's past, the China Science & Technology Museum located near the northern section of the 3rd Ring Road is a national institution to demonstrate that China is abreast with rest of the world in an increasingly globalizing world of technology. Its programs are carried out through permanent and short-term exhibitions, onsite activities, and shows at a domed-shaped Astro-vision film theater, which is one of the largest worldwide. In the museum complex constructed in 1988 and expanded in 2000, exhibits of different fields of modern science introduce the basics of mechanics, electromagnetism, heat, acoustics, optics, air and space, energy, transportation, mechanics, material

science, environmental science, nuclear technology, and information technology. The return capsule of Shenzhou No. 1 spaceship and its parachute are also displayed to explain the science of astronautics. Others are presentations on ancient Chinese technology (astronomy, compass, gunpowder, bronze metallurgy, papermaking, and printing) to document China's scientific inventiveness and technological preeminence in the past. Prior to 1999, the museum was one of the few in the country to have encapsulated training-based education programs and experiment-based displays.[36]

The new building of the Chinese Science and Technology Museum located in the Olympic Green just north of the National Stadium (nicknamed "Bird Nest") is built with government investment. As one of the auxiliary facilities of the 2008 Olympics, this new facility has debuted with an exhibit on scientific and technical innovations of ancient China, and is anticipated to be in full operation during 2009. It will be a milestone to follow two other supersized hands-on interactive museums: Shanghai Science and Technology Museum (2001) and Guangdong Science and Technology Museum (2008). Concurrent with the opening of the Summer Olympics is the inauguration of the Beijing Jingcheng Olympic Education Museum in the northeastern section of the city, sponsored by a private educational organization in commemoration of the 2008 game.[37]

Among the 30 museums in Beijing showcasing materials associated with scientific studies, the Beijing Museum of Natural History in an area south of the Tiananmen Square is one of the old national museums founded in the 1960s. Its reputation is built upon rare specimens displayed in four specialized sections (paleontology, zoology, botany, and anthropology), domestic and foreign traveling exhibits, award-wining museum projects, and research projects collaborated with international teams, museum publications, and its museum association.

The museums in the capital city encompass the oldest and the newest aspects of human existence. The Beijing Museum of World Art at the Millennium Monument is the first in China to have focused on diverse artistic aspects known in world history and modern societies. The museum emerged onto the international art map in 2002 when an electronic display entitled "Salvador Dali: A Journey Into Fantasy" was held in its digital gallery. Its exhibitions cover a wide spectrum of subjects and media pertaining to a convergence of art and technology, including different forms of digital imageries facilitated with links to the World Wide Web.[38] Aside from having become a window through which art and technology communicate in a contemporary global setting, the Beijing World Art Museum also has pioneered in incorporating enterprise-style management into its operation system, which appears atypical at traditional Chinese museums.[39]

Less well known in the city is the Arthur M. Sackler Museum of Art and Archaeology on the campus of Peking

University in northwestern Beijing, an institution characterized by its modern concepts in artifact display and conservation. As an affiliate of the Department of the Archaeology at a university similar to its peers at the Northwest University, Sichuan University, and Shandong University, its hands-on projects in laboratories and archaeological sites are major educational resources for scholarly research and a training ground for new-generation archaeologists and museologists. The Sackler Museum of Beijing opened in 1992 and is accessible to general public.[40]

Away from the capital city are local-based museums of different nature, administered by state, provincial, municipal, regional, or private organizations. One of the prominent museums in the south is the Nanjing Museum (formerly National Central Museum) of Jiangsu Province. In 1933, it was conceived as a national institute and the prototype of modernized Chinese museums when Mr. Tsai Yuan-Pei (Cai Yuanpei), the head of the national academy, proposed to construct a public museum complex to address distinct themes pertaining to culture, technology, and natural science. The museum was eventually established as an organization to exclusively house collections of works of art and artifacts acquired through purchase, archaeological excavation, and exchange, as well as to engage in research and conservation of these materials. Incorporated into its large artifact collections are also important archaeological finds taken from sites in nearby regions, including the Neolithic jades from Liangzhu cultural area. The Nanjing museum is famous for having actively published periodicals and research materials, conducted educational programs and archaeological excavations, and hosted special exhibitions from foreign collections in addition to organizing exhibitions to travel internationally.[41] The museum also serves as the headquarter of regional cultural organizations, including the Association of Jiangsu, Institute of Archaeology of Jiangsu, and the Association of Folk Culture of Jiangsu.[42]

An additional sophisticated museum in the same province is the internationally renowned Shanghai Museum. It is the base for a collection of 120,000 pieces of ancient Chinese art works and archaeological materials. Displayed in separate exhibition halls are some of the finest and rare specimens ever created in Chinese history. Aiming to conserve, display, and promote aspects of cultural diversity,[43] the essentials of a modernized museum can be discerned in its featured exhibitions and research facilities, educational, visiting, and exchange programs, along with eleven galleries, three special temporary exhibition halls, its superb conservation department, library, gift shop, coffee shop, cafeteria, and a multimedia meeting room equipped with translation services. The innovated museum building of 1997, which symbolizes traditional Chinese understanding of the universe: the circular heaven above and the square earth beneath, attests to the changing taste from the norm of old socialistic aesthetics.[44] The museum operates with 85% government funding in conjunction with donations from private sectors.[45]

Rich collections of historical relics and archaeological materials also have become highlights at the major provincial or district museums, such as the Shaanxi Historical Museum, Hubei Provincial Museum, Zhejiang provincial Museum, Yunnan Provincial Museum, and the Ordos Museum in Inner Mongolia. Nevertheless, one of the most unique forms of museums in China are those with exhibition halls constructed at archaeological sites that have been designated as protected cultural areas. Among them, the Museum of Banpo Neolithic Site in Xi'an City, the Terracotta Warriors' Museum of the First Emperor of Qin in Shaanxi Province, Dunhuang Cave Museum in Gansu Province, the Sanxingdui and Jinsha Museums in Sichuan Province, and the Yinxu Museum in Henan province rank among the top tourist attractions. Many of these have been incorporated into the UNESCO list of World Cultural Heritage sites.

In addition to exhibitions, activities such as research projects, seminars, and conferences also are parts of the fabric of Chinese museums. The results of these works are made available to the public through museum publications. The Chinese museum literature shows a long list of research reports and monographs, along with preeminent professional journals such as "Party History Research Data (Dangshi Yenjiu Ziliao)," "Journal of National Museum of Chinese History (Zhongguo Lishi Wenwu)," and "Palace Museum Journal (Gugong Bowuyuan Yuankan)." Others are popular magazines edited by professionals at the Geological Museum of China, Beijing Planetarium, and the China Science and Technology Museum, to name a few. They enjoy equal fame with "The Great Nature (Daziran)" of the Beijing Museum of Natural History, a favorite magazine for young readers nationwide. The illustrated monthly "The Forbidden City (Zijincheng)" of the Palace Museum is also one of the popular magazines on cultural history and art.

Additional museum periodicals with sections dedicated to museum studies include the "Southeast Culture (Dongnan Wenhua)" of the Nanjing Museum and "Relics of Yunnan" (Yunnan Wenwu)" of Yunnan Provincial Museum. These in conjunctions with relevant works from non-museum publications, such as "Beijing Relics and Museology (Beijing Wenbo)," "Chinese Museums (Zhongguo Bowuguan)," "Newsletter of the Chinese Society of Museums (Zhongguo Bowuguan Tongxun)," and "News Letter of the Chinese Association of Natural Science Museum (Zhongguo Ziran Bowuguan Xiehui Tongxun) have contributed significantly to the field of museology. The last two belong to the Chinese Society of Museums (Zhongguo Bowuguan Xuehui) and the Chinese Association of Natural Science Museums (Zhongguo Ziran Kexue Bowuguan Xiehui), respectively, both of which are members of the International Council of

Museums (ICOM). The former also is the largest museum association in the country for organizations related to cultural and historical studies. As an affiliate of the State Administration of Cultural Heritage (*Guojia Wenwuju*), it has been the driving force in organizing workshops and conferences on topics pertaining to museum studies and authentication, collection, and assessment of artifacts. Besides its professional journal "Chinese Museum (*Zongguo Bowuguan*)" and other publications on the subject of museology, "The Annals of China Museum (*Zhongguo Bowuguan Zhi*)" published in 1995 is a compendium of the history of Chinese museums. Currently, the Chinese Society of Museums is collaborating with two other institutions to compile a revised edition of this book. It also will be the organizer of the 22nd General Conference of ICOM, to be held in Shanghai in 2010.

The general outlook of Chinese museums underwent obvious transformation during the past decade due to forces of globalization. The government endorses exchanges of display materials between museums and encourages exhibits of legal nongovernmental collections from domestic and international sources. Frequent blockbuster shows at major museums and corporate-operated exhibition facilities in large cities encourage competition and open-mindedness not known previously, while a free-admission policy introduced at the country's public museums in 2008 assists in promoting appreciation of China's national heritage. The negative side of an explosive rise of museums is that shortage of trained museum professionals and training programs in museum studies has become a key issue in the history of twenty-first century Chinese museums.[46]

Although the exhibition narratives in state-sponsored museums remain to serve the interest of the Party and to dutifully fulfill their roles in the realms of education and social service, changes in the exhibition practices have altered the progression course of Chinese museums. Unique concepts such as virtual museums and "ecomuseum"[47] have been introduced into the country as novelties; some of the new government funded science museums, frequently mammoth in sizes with multitheaters and being positioned in close proximity to shopping arcades, are morphed into market-based enterprises. In the meantime, private art museums have become profit-generating engines in disguise for artists, collectors, and urban-developers.

CONCLUSION

This study has documented the development of modern librarianship, archives, and museum studies in China. It was not until the nineteenth and twentieth centuries that the transformation of libraries, archives, and museums was initiated, and China began the long process of change; new institutions, values, and techniques were gradually introduced, through self development and foreign influences. Successive waves of internal and foreign conflicts and influences assisted and hindered cultural developments. Under the PRC, library reforms patterned on Soviet practices were implemented in the 1950s. Following the social upheavals of the Cultural Revolution, Chinese library development resumed, beginning in the early 1980s. In the twenty-first century era of globalization, information and digital techniques have significantly advanced and expanded the role of libraries, archives, and museum services in China. Digital libraries have become an important priority, as well as a significant component in the national information infrastructure. New museums have been built also to showcase China's ancient and recent past, together with changes in exhibition practices. Archives are opening up to researchers and citizens, and with the expansion of online finding aids, location of archival holdings will be easily found.

In November 2008, the U.S. Institute of Museum and Library Services (IMLS) and the Ministry of Culture of the PRC signed an agreement on the *Partnership for Cultural Exchange* between museum, library, archive, and information services at the LC. The agreement is to share in library and museum services, including education in museums, application of new technologies, and the availability of online information in libraries and museums. A part of the agreement is to establish cultural exchange between American and Chinese librarians. Professor Paula Kaufman, University Librarian and Dean of Libraries at the University of Illinois at Urbana-Champaign, and Dr. Zhan Furui, Director of the NLC and President of the LSC signed the *Think Globally, Act Globally* agreement. This is a 2-year IMLS project with additional support from the LSC. Chinese librarians, library educators, managers of library technology will be introduced to American public library service. U.S. librarians in turn will work with the Chinese librarians to identify Chinese information resources that could be made publicly available through an online portal developed by the team. Training will be in the United States as well as in China. CALA is included as a project partner. In addition IMLS is supporting training for the care of collections—both parties will exchange and disseminate information to promote best practices in the care of collections held in museums, libraries, and archives.[48]

With new technologies ever developing, it makes it easier to share China's cultural heritages; but that alone is not enough. It is critical that we must continually engage in dialog and exchange to further build understanding and cooperation among our global counterpart scholars, archivists, librarians, and museum professionals.

ACKNOWLEDGMENTS

I wish to thank Huang Si Ying for her able research assistance and helpful comments from the anonymous reviewers. I also am appreciative of the assistance of Zhu Qiang, Director of the Peking University Library. In the final section dealing with museum studies in China, I wish to gratefully acknowledge the assistance of Dr. TzeHuey Chiou Peng, Associate Curator of the Spurlock Museum at the University of Illinois, Urbana-Champaign; her knowledge and expertise are invaluable.

APPENDIX

Table A1 Chronology of Major Dates in Chinese History, Libraries, Archives, and Museums

16–11 B.C.	Shang Dynasty—documents carved on tortoise shells and animal bones.
221–206 B.C.	The Qin Dynasty unified China and established China's first central Government.
16 B.C.–1911A.D.	Imperial libraries served as depositories of national literature and archival documents.
105 A.D.	Cai Lun invented paper.
618–906 A.D.	Tang Dynasty—Printing was invented, beginning with wooden blocks.
960–1279 A.D.	Song Dynasty—Movable types invented; printed books became available in China.
1644–1911	Qing Dynasty (Manchus).
1839–1842	Opium War, concluded with the signing of the Treaty of Nanjing and China's forced opening to the West.
1840–1926	Public Library Movement.
1850–1864	Taiping Rebellion.
1894–1895	Sino-Japanese War.
1898	Hundred Days Reform.
1899–1900	The Boxer Rebellion.
1909	The Ministry of Education promulgated the first library law in China for public libraries: to preserve Chinese classics, to disseminate knowledge, to provide research facilities, and to collect materials for the public to use freely; also to establish the Metropolitan Library (National Library) and other provincial, county, and district libraries.
1910	Xie Yun-Cang translated from Japanese, *Library Education*, first book on library science published in China.
1910	Mary ElizabethWood founded the Boone Library, to serve as a public library, Wuchang, China.
1911	Overthrow of the Qing Dynasty.
1911 to the Present	Modern Library Movement.
1912	On January 1, the Republic of China was declared with Sun Yat-sen as provincial president. Yuan Shikai, a Manchu general, was elected President.
1916	Legal deposit was established.
1919	May 4th Movement, cultural and intellectual revolution.
1920	Mass Education Movement.

(Continued)

Table A1 Chronology of Major Dates in Chinese History, Libraries, Archives, and Museums *(Continued)*

1920	First library school, the Boone Library School in Wuchang, China, founded by Mary Elizabeth Wood, together with Shen Zhu Rong and Hu Qing Sheng.
1921	Founding of the Chinese Communist Party.
1922	Chinese National Association for the Advancement of Education founded; a division on Library Education was formed.
1924	China Foundation for the Promotion of Education and Culture was established; administered a portion of Boxer remission indemnity funds to be used for public library developments in China.
1925	The national Library Association of China (*Zhongguo Tushuguanh Xuehui*) founded.
1925	The Palace Museum, Beijing, founded. China's largest museum. Listed by UNESCO as a World Cultural Heritage Site in 1987.
1925	First Historical Archives of China (Beijing) established—Ming-Qing archives.
1933	Nanjing museum established—a national institute of historical and cultural interests; includes many cultural relics, paintings, calligraphies, and ancient books.
1937	Marco Polo Bridge incident commences Japan's invasion of China.
1945	Japan surrenders. Civil war continues between the Communists and the Nationalist government.
1949	On October 1, Mao Zedong proclaims the founding of the People's Republic of China (PRC).
1950	Treaty of Friendship, Alliance and Mutual Aid between the PRC and the Soviet Union.
1953–1957	China's First Five Year Plan.
1954	State Archives Bureau (*Guojia Tanganju*) established.
1957	The National Book Coordination Act.
1957	Russian library works translated into Chinese and published as *Translations on Library Science*.
1958	The Great Leap Forward.
1961	Beginning of the Sino-Soviet Conflict.
1964	China Society for Scientific and Technical Information (CSSTI) founded.
1966–1976	The Cultural Revolution.
1978	Deng Xiaoping launches "opening and reform" policy.
1979	The China Society for Library Science, CSLS (*Zhongguo Tushuguan Xuehui*) was established in China.
1979	United States and the PRC formally establish diplomatic relations.
1980	Summary Report of Library Work, encouraging governments at all levels to develop libraries and expand their services.
1980	Second Historical Archives (Nanjing) opened—documents relating to the 1912–1949 period.
1981	Chinese Archives Association (*Zhongguo Dang'an Xuehui*) founded.

(Continued)

Table A1 Chronology of Major Dates in Chinese History, Libraries, Archives, and Museums *(Continued)*

1987	Report Pertaining to the Improvement and Enhancement of Library Work, issued by the Ministry of Culture and other ministries, urging for the coordination of libraries, reform of library management, and adoption of modern technology.
1987	Dedication of the new library building, National Library of China, Beijing.
1991	Journal of Library Science in China (former name Bulletin of the China Society for Library Science). Core leading national journal in library and information science. Jointly sponsored by the China Society for Library Science and the National Library of China, under the auspices of the Ministry of Culture.
1996	Sixty-second International Federation of Library Associations and Institutions (IFLA) General Conference held in Beijing.
1996	China National Knowledge Infrastructure (CNKI). Founded by Tsinghua University and Tongfang Knowledge Network Technology Company; full-text database created to integrate important resources in China, to be disseminated in China and globally.
2005	China Society for Library Science (CSLS) name changed to the Library Society of China.
2008	Opening of the National Digital Library, National Library of China, Beijing.
2008	Signing of the agreement between the Library of Congress and the National Library of China to develop the World Digital Library project.
2008	Olympic Games held in Beijing.
2008	Opening of the Guangdong Science and Technology Museum, Guangzhou, world's largest science and technology museum.

REFERENCES

1. The Central Intelligence Agency (CIA), The World Factbook. China, https://www.cia.gov/library/publications/the-world-factbook/geos/ch.html (accessed October 2008).
2. Wang, K.N. The strategy of making China flourish. Shi Wu Bao. **1896**, *13*, 1–2 (English title: Curr. Aff. Newspap.).
3. Ye, B.S. Discussion on the book preservation buildings and libraries. Tushuguan **2003**, (1), 1–3 (English title: Library).
4. Hu, Y.J. Chinese books and libraries at the juncture of the 19th and 20th centuries. Changsha Jiaotong Xueyuan Xuebao. **1997**, *13*(4), 108–110 (English title: J. Changsha Commun. Univ.).
5. Wu, Y.N. Three stages of the development of Chinese modern library. Jin Tushukan. **2001**, *3*(68), 34–36 (English title: Shanxi Libr. J.).
6. Wang, X.; Peng, X. Development of modern Chinese libraries. Zhenjiang Shizhuan Xuebao **1998**, (4), 86–88 (English title: J. Zhenjiang Educ.Coll.).
7. Cheng, H.W. The impact of American librarianship in Chinese librarianship in modern times (1849–1949). Libr. Cult. **1991**, *26*(2), 372–387.
8. Yu, P.C.; Davis, D.G., Jr.; Arthur, E. Bostwick and Chinese library development. Libr. Cult. **1998**, *33*(4), 389–406.
9. Yu, P.C. Leaning to one side: The impact of the Cold War on Chinese library collections. In *Books, Libraries, Reading & Publishing in the Cold War*; Anghelescu, H.G.B., Poulain, M., Eds.; Library of Congress, The Center for the Book: Washington, DC, 2001; 253–266.
10. Nunn, R. Libraries and publishing in Mainland China. Libr. J. **1966**, *91*, 3327–3332.
11. Wang, R. Traveling uncharted waters: The exchange of government information between the United States and China. J. Gov. Inform. **1998**, *25*(4), 353–358.
12. http://www.nlc.gov.cn/old/old/newpages/english/serve/index.htm.
13. http://www.nlc.gov.cn/en/news/nlcnews_2008091102.htm.
14. Yu, P.C. *Chinese Academic and Research Libraries: Acquisitions, Collections, and Organizations*; JAI Press: Greenwich, CT, 1996; vol. 36 Foundations in Library and Information Science.
15. Yu, L. The political economy of public library development in post-1978 People's Republic of China. Libri **2006**, *56*, 117–132.
16. Liu, W.; Zhao, L.; Ma, Y. Digital library development in China. In *Knowledge without Boundaries*; Chopey, M.A., Ed.; Association for Library Collections & Technical Services: Chicago, IL, 2005; ALCTS Papers on Library Technical Services and Collections, no.12; (21) (21).
17. http://209.85.173.132/search?q=cache:Igo9JZhCRMYJ:www.kc.tsukuba.ac.jp/dlkc/e-p.
18. http://china.eastview.com/kns50/single_index.aspx.
19. http://www.worlddigitallibrary.org/project/english/index.html.
20. http://www.oclc.org/questionpoint/about/testimonials/default.htm.
21. Moss, W. Archives in the People's Republic of China revisited. Am. Archiv. **1986**, *49*(4), 481–490.
22. Wa, Y.; Esherick, J.W. *Chinese Archives: An Introductory Guide*, Center for Chinese Studies, Institute of East Asian Studies; University of California: Berkeley, CA, 1996.
23. http://www.shac.net.cn/en/Holdings/BriefIntroductionOfThe Holdings.asp.
24. http://www.hkbu.edu.hk/lib/sca/ahc.html.
25. Lin, S.C. *Libraries and Librarianship in China*; Greenwood Press: Westport, CT, 1998.
26. http://www.chinabaike.com/article/sort0525/sort0557/2007/20070803157435_4.html.
27. Xinhua News, http://english.cri.cn/2946/2008/10/06/2001s411892.htm, (accessed October 6, 2008).
28. http://www.gzcm.gov.cn/show.aspx?cid=46&id=294.
29. http://www.china.com.cn/aboutchina/zhuanti/kexue08/2008-06/04/content_15628675.htm.
30. Ru, J.; Peng, H. *Ancient Chinese Architecture*, Springer-Verlag Wien: Palace Architecture; New York, 1998; 116–139.
31. Fu, X. et al. *Chinese Architecture*; Yale University Press and New World Press: New heaven and London, 2002; 268–272.

32. Ru, J.; Peng, H. *Ancient Chinese Architecture*; Springer-Verlag Wien: Palace Architecture, New York, 1998; 140–148.
33. http://www.ibiblio.org/chineseculture/contents/arts/p-arts-c04s04.html.
34. http://www.chinabaike.com/article/sort0525/sort0557/2007/20070803157435_4.html.
35. An, Y.A. New concept: Capital, my museum. Mus. Int. **2008**, May *60*(1–2), 89–99 nos. 237–238 http://www.capitalmuseum.org.cn/en/.
36. http://www.china.org.cn/english/features/museums/128862.htm.
37. http://en.beijing2008.cn/culture/headlines/n214452016.shtml.
38. China Daily, http://www.chinadaily.com.cn/english/doc/2005-01/11/content_407755.htm, January 11, 2005.
39. Wang, L. The Beijing World Art Museum at the China Millennium Monument. Mus. Int. **2008**, May *60*(1–2), 140–147 nos 237–238.
40. Spens, M. *The Arthur M. Sackler museum of art and archaeology*, Studio Int., 1993; 201, 5–9 Special Issue, no. 1021.
41. http://www.njmuseum.com/zh/nb/nbgs.html.
42. http:www.njmuseum.com/english/zh/4nbls.htm.
43. Chen, X. The conservation of Shanghai's diverse cultural heritage. Museum Int. **2008**, May *60*(1–2), 100–107 nos 237–238.
44. Li, B. Bowuguan jianzhu mantan (Discussing museum architecture) Proceedings of the 2nd Annual Meeting of the Chinese Society of Museums Wensu Press: Beijing, China, 1986; 165–170.
45. Anonymous, N.D. *Shanghai Bowuguan (Shanghai Museum)*, Shanghai Museum: Shanghai, , China.
46. Pollack, B. Making 1,200 museum bloom. Art News **2008**, March 122–127.
47. Su, D. The Concept of the Ecomuseum and its Practice in China. Museum International **2008**, May (nos 237–238), 29–37.
48. http://www.imls.gov/news/2008/111808b.shtm.

BIBLIOGRAPHY

1. Archive Users' Experiences, http://orpheus.ucsd.edu/chinesehistory/archive_users.htm (accessed May 2007).
2. Archives Work in China; Organizing Committee XIIIth International Congress on Archives Beijing, China, 1995.
3. Banpo Museum of Xian, Ed. *Neolithic Site at Banpo Near Xian*; Wenwu Press: Beijing, People's Republic of India, 1982.
4. Barclay, J. *The Seventy-Year Ebb and Flow of Chinese Library and Information Services, May 4, 1919 to the Late 1980s*; The Scarecrow Press: Metuchen, NJ, 1995.
5. CALA Twenty-first Century Librarian Seminar Series, http://uic.edu/depts/lib/projects/resources/calamw/project/workshop.shtml (accessed Sept. 2008).
6. China National Knowledge Infrastructure (CNKI),http://www.global.cnki.net/grid20/index.htm (accessed October 2008).
7. China Society for Library Science,http//www.nlc.gov.cn/old/old/newpages/english/org/index.htm (accessed September 2008).
8. Chinese Academy of Social Sciences Library (Center for Documentation and Information, CASS); CASS: Beijing, China [n.d.].
9. Chongqinghttp://encyclopedia.farlex.com/Chungqing (accessed October 2008).
10. Denton, K. Museums memorial sites and exhibitionary culture. China Quart. **2005**, *183*(September), 565–586.
11. Dong, X. Transition of library and information science education in China: problems and perspective Conference proceedings of the 62nd IFLA General Conference Beijing, China August, 25–31, 1996 http://www.ifla.org/IV/ifla62/62-xiad.htm (accessed April 2007).
12. Foskett, D.J. Chinese libraries in the 1990s: A Western view. Asian Libr. **1999**, *9*(1), 23–31.
13. Feng, Gengwu, Ed. *Shaanxi History Museum*; Shaanxi Tourism Publishing House: Xian, China, 2001.
14. Gong, Y.; Gorman, G.E. *Libraries and Information Services in China*; The Scarecrow Press: Lanham, ML, 2000.
15. Hongkong Baptist University Library, Special Collections and Archives. http://www.hkbu.edu.hk/lib/sca/ahc.html (accessed August 2007).
16. Jia, X.; Du, Y.; Si, A.; Zhang, X. China's primary and secondary school libraries: Yesterday, today, and tomorrow Conference proceedings of the 62nd IFLA General Conference Beijing, China August, 25–31, 1996 http://www.ifla.org/IV/ifla62/62-xiaj.htm (accessed April 2007).
17. Kelly, D. At last, an arena: Current policies in Chinese social science. Aust. J. Chinese Aff. **1979**, *2*, 123–136.
18. Kirby, W., Ed.; *State and Economy in Republican China: A Handbook for Scholars*; Harvard University Asia Center: Cambridge, MA, 2000; 2 vols.
19. Libraries in China. Papers Prepared on the Occasion of the Tenth Anniversary of the Library Association of China; Library Association of China: Peiping, China, 1935.
20. Li, X. et al. *China's Museums*, China Intercontinental Press: Beijing, China, 2004.
21. Liu, X. Public libraries and economic development in China IFLANET, 62nd IFLA General Conference-Conference Proceedings Beijing, China, August, 25–31, 1996 8.
22. Moss, W. Dang'an: Contemporary archives. China. Quart. **1996**, *45*(145), 112–129.
23. Moss, W. Archives in the People's Republic of China. Am. Archiv. **1982**, *45*(4), 385–409.
24. Mueller, M.; Tan, Z. *China in the Information Age: Telecommunications and the Dilemmas of Reform*; Praeger: Westport, CT, 1997.
25. National Library of Chinahttp://www.nlc.gov.cn/en/aboutus/history.htm (accessed October 2008).
26. National Library of China to add its records to OCLC WorldCat, http://www.oclc.org/news/releases/2008.5.htm (accessed October 2008).
27. Ning, G.; Gao, X.; Du, C. Development for the undertaking of children's library in China IFLANET, 62nd IFLA General Conference-Conference Proceedings Beijing, China August, 25–31, 1996 11.
28. *Part II, Business and Economic History Archives of Republican China. In State and Economy in China: A Handbook for Scholars*; Kirby, W.C., Shih, J.C., Lin, M.H., Pietz, D.A., Eds.; Harvard University Asia Center

and distr. by Harvard University Press: Cambridge, MA, 2000; Vol. 1.

29. Peking University Library. http://162.105.138.207/enhtml/introduction.htm (accessed October 2008).

30. Proett, P.A. *A history of libraries in the people's republic of China: Including some aspects of college and university library development, 1949–1974*, University Microfilms: Ann Arbor, MI, 1974, PhD dissertation.

31. Shanghai Library, Institute of Scientific and Technical Information of Shanghai; Shanghai Library, Institute of Scientific and Technical Information of Shanghai: Shanghai [n.d.].

32. In *Sichuan Sheng Dang'an Quan Zhinan*; Sichuan Provincial Archives, Ed.; China Archival Publishing Company: Beijing, China, 2002; (English title: Guide to Sichuan Provincial Archives).

33. Sickman, L. et al. *In The Art and Architecture of China*, Penguin Book: Baltimore, MD, 1971; 468–471.

34. The technological challenges of digital reference: An overview, http://www.dlib.org/dlib/february03/penka/02penka.html (accessed July 2007).

35. Tsinghua University Library. http://www.tsinghua.edu.cn/eng/board1/boardlist.jsp?bid2=37&pageno=1 (accessed October 2008) http://www.lib.tsinghua.edu.cn/english/service.html (accessed July 2007).

36. Wu, J. Developing a borderless hybrid library: The Shanghai experience,. http://www.vala.org.au/vala2004/2004pdfs/71Wu.PDF (access October 2008).

37. Wu, J. *New Perspectives on the Library of the 21st Century*, Shanghai Scientific and Technological Literature Publishing House: Shanghai, China, 2003.

38. Yang, G. The development of the China Digital Library. Electron. J. Acad. Spec. Libr. **2002**, *3*(3), 1–5.

39. Yu, P.C. Chinese university libraries: the Nanjing scene. In Libraries in China—Past, Present and Future Proceedings of the International Association of Oriental Librarians, 9th General Meeting at the 34th ICANAS (International Congress for Asian and North African Studies) Hong Kong, China August, 24–25, 1993; Chan, J.L.Y., Lee, B.W.,

Eds.; University of Hong Kong Libraries: Hong Kong, China, 1993.

40. Yu, P.C. The development of foreign language collections at Peking University Library: Problems and prospects. Libr. Acquis. Pract. Theor. **1991**, *15*(4), 433–442.

41. Yu, P.C. Building a foreign language collection: China's National Library. In International Papers Proceedings of the Fifth National Conference of the Association of College and Research Libraries Cincinnati, Ohio April, 5–8, 1989; Fennell, J.C., Ed.; Association of College and Research Libraries, A Division of the American Library Association: Chicago, IL, 1989.

42. Yu, P.C. History of modern librarianship in East Asia. Libr. Hist. **2008**, *24*(1), 64–77.

43. Yu, P.C. International exchange and Chinese library development. In *Advances in Library Administration and Organization*; McCabe, G., Kreissman, B., Eds.; JAI Press: Greenwich, CT, 1984; Vol. 3, 1–24.

44. Yu, P.C. National Library of China: The acquisition of foreign language materials. Libr. Acquis. Pract. Theor. **1984**, *8*(1), 1–9.

45. Zhang, W. The development and the nature of the Chinese archive classification. J. Educ. Media Libr. Sci. **2002**, *39* (3), 235–250.

46. Zhang, T. Report on the state of Chinese archives. Am. Archiv. **1982**, *45*(2), 224–226.

47. Zhang, W. The development and the nature of the Chinese archive classification. J. Educ. Media Libr. Sci. **2002**, *39* (3), 235–250.

48. Zheng, L. Status quo and prospects of the children's libraries in China Conference Proceedings of the 62nd IFLA General Conference Beijing, China August, 25–31, 1996 http://www.ifla.org/IV/ifla62/62-lilz..htm (accessed April 2007).

49. *Zhongguo Tushuguan Nianjian 2006*(English title: China Library Yearbook 2006; Contemporary Publishing Company: Beijing, May 2008.) Annual reference work providing a complete conspectus of China's systems of libraries. In Chinese only.

Chemistry–China

Circulation Services

Vanessa Irvin
Library and Information Science Program, Information and Computer Sciences Department,
University of Hawaii at Mānoa, Honolulu, Hawaii, U.S.A.

Jeff E. Bullard
Free Library of Philadelphia, Philadelphia, Pennsylvania, U.S.A.

Abstract

Circulation services in public libraries are pivotal to the success of library services. The circulation desk is where library service typically begins and ends for library patrons (users). Patrons come into the library and ask for directions at the circulation desk, to apply for library membership in the form of a library card, and to learn library policy information regarding circulation of materials, computer use, programming confirmations, and more. After receiving reference services from the librarian, patrons go back to the circulation desk to check out materials, pay fines, learn of library programs, and status of requests.

Throughout the history of public libraries in America, circulation areas have been in tune with the technological trends of the day. From due date cards to keypunch operating machines to self-check-out modalities, circulation desks have always been and continue to be the focal point for library patrons to learn the value of the library.

INTRODUCTION

"Circulation services" is the term used to describe many of the most important, yet oftentimes invisible activities of today's libraries. Circulation services include all activities that are involved in the making of library books, journals, and other materials directly available to the people who need them. Public, school, special, and academic circulation services can be defined as the full cycle of a user borrowing library material and subsequently returning it within a designated time frame. This borrowing cycle has a history alongside the existence of libraries, and even with the advent of technology in library services during these contemporary times, the borrowing cycle continues to be the impetus for library circulation services today.

Circulation in American libraries has been documented since 1856.[1] Library book circulation over the decades has been relatively stable with an average of 11 books checked out per American public library borrower per year.[2] With the accessibility of books, films, recordings, videos, CDs, DVDs, software, and audiovisual products in both print and electronic formats, circulation of library materials amongst the reading public has increased (mainly due to electronic borrowing privileges), while physical library visits have decreased.[2]

It should be taken into account that what was defined as a "public library" or an "academic library" during the nineteenth century may differ from what we define as a public or academic library today. Thus circulation statistics of yesteryear may include public use from libraries that we now consider as school or special libraries. For example, subscription libraries were considered public libraries during the nineteenth century.[1] Subscription libraries are considered special libraries today. In the case of academic libraries, when a group of learned men pooled their books together to create a library upon which Yale University was founded, such collaboration attests to what was once perhaps a social library that quickly evolved into an academic library.

Another aspect of circulation services that should be taken into consideration is the circulation of juvenile materials. During the nineteenth century, juvenile materials were not as readily available in public libraries (nor in academic libraries) as they are today. During that time, adult materials counted for a large percentage of public library circulation, whereas today, juvenile borrowing typically counts for a significant proportion of circulation statistics in public libraries. Children's literature collections are frequently available in academic libraries where the institution offers majors in education, library science, and other related disciplines. Some academic libraries, like University of North Carolina at Chapel Hill and Kent State University, offer extensive specialized collections in picture books. Specialized collections such as these are circulated by adults, as opposed to high circulation rates being attributed to children in public libraries. This increase in juvenile literature circulation correlates with the increase of the publication of children's literature.

In recent years, there continues to be a rise in the circulation of young adult literature, multicultural materials, and audiovisual mediums such as DVDs, language videos, audiobooks, and electronic books (e-books). This rise in audiovisual circulation speaks of an increase of equitable access to a variety of information in popular

Encyclopedia of Library and Information Sciences, Fourth Edition DOI: 10.1081/E-ELIS4-120053483

formats, thus libraries can reach broader and more diverse audiences with different learning styles and informational needs. More and more libraries are taking this option to the next level by offering streaming video and e-book services, bypassing the need to download, a feature optimally set for the burgeoning set of smartphone-using patrons. Finally, free online classes (aka MOOCs: Massively Open Online Classes) are being "circulated" through public library catalogs through such vendors as Coursera, Input, Universal Class, Khan Academy, and others.[3]

Digital technology continues to inspire an evolution in circulation services and practices in libraries of all kinds. Self-service automated systems for users and graphical interfaces for facilitating circulation services by library staffers continue to grow and improve as technological innovations emerge. Staffers and users alike experience new learning opportunities as technology impacts circulation of library materials on-site, in remote storage facilities (physically and in the cloud), and virtually online.

Overall, with staffers continuing to learn new technologies and to employ vital customer service to diverse populations, circulation services remain an important and vital mainstay of library services for all types of libraries.

ETHICS

The privacy of patron library records reaches into the issue of intellectual freedom. As part of the first amendment's assertion for freedom of expression, libraries hold library records to be confidential because what is checked in and checked out illustrates a patron's intellectual and personal interests. A library record is like a record of one's thoughts, ideas, and curiosities. These records must be respected and protected. Staffers are held to the highest form of professional confidentiality and integrity when interacting with and maintaining library borrower records. Even in this age of the US PATRIOT ACT and the Foreign Intelligence Surveillance Act of 1978 Amendments Act of 2008 (FISA), librarians have been uncompromising stalwarts in respecting the privacy of patron records and even insisting that the U.S. Federal Government do so as well.

Librarians' enforcement of Sections 215 and 505 of the PATRIOT ACT, amendments that have been made to the law to preserve confidentiality of library borrower records echo the professional standards of the American Library Association's Code of Ethics.[4] Many academic and public library administrations have also enacted policies, guidelines, and best practices for librarians and circulation staff to follow in the event of legal requests for private patron information.

CIRCULATION DESK

The circulation and reference desks are the two focal service points in a library. At its most basic, the circulation desk is the location within the building where library users borrow (check-out) materials, renew, and return (check-in) borrowed materials. The circulation desk is mostly staffed by paraprofessionals (library assistants, library technicians, clerks, and, in some cases, volunteers) as opposed to the reference desk which is mostly staffed by librarians, assistant librarians, and library trainees.

As the initial entry and exit point for library users, the circulation desk serves three primary functions: 1) facilitating user information needs, 2) collecting and filtering library materials, and 3) facilitating user-centric information needs such as processing library card applications, library card renewals, paying fines, and handling borrowing privileges. Another set of functions involves the collections. As borrowed material is returned, or as material used in-house is gathered up, the circulation desk serves as a collection point and a filtering point. It is at the circulation desk that any damaged or mutilated returned items, or any item returned with missing parts (i.e., cases, discs, and pamphlets that make up many audiovisual items), will be first noticed. From the circulation desk, items are then sent on to the appropriate area depending on whether the items are to be re-shelved or sent to the processing room for repair or de-accessioning if the item is damaged.

A third set of functions served at the circulation desk rises from the fact that the circulation desk is usually the first point for anyone entering a library and is the last point before leaving the library. Because of this important position, the circulation desk itself should be clean, clear of clutter, and inviting. The circulation desk staff, then, is responsible for greeting people, being inviting, and having knowledge of the library's policies and procedures as well as a basic knowledge of locations of materials (sometimes known as simple reference). Upon entering the library, users, in many cases, will come to the circulation desk first and then be directed further into the library to confer with the librarian(s). In short, the circulation desk is the touchstone for user experience in most libraries.

The circulation desk is a locus of technology in many libraries. Check-in and check-out terminals, cash registers, camera equipment for library cards that carry photos; sometimes photocopying machines, faxes, and public telephones are found at or near the circulation desk and, in any case, tend to be under the purview of the circulation desk staff.

Libraries may designate various names to the circulation desk such as "Information Desk," or "Information." Libraries will typically have dominant signage that indicates the location of the circulation desk as the initial point of contact for library users.

The circulation desk may be the most important location in a library, at the very least equal in importance to the reference desk. Whereas the reference desk is where users learn and access the content of the library, the circulation desk is the contact point between the library, as a whole, and the wider community outside the library.

KINDS OF CIRCULATION

Circulation is the movement of library materials usually from within the building out into the service community of a library and back again. Library users are the prime catalysts of this movement; it is the users' information wants and needs that cause books and materials to go out of the library, and thus the user is responsible for returning the material. This output–input process is commonly known as checkout (also known as "charge" and "borrow") and check-in (also called "discharge" and "return"). This culminates the most basic understanding of what it means to circulate library materials.

Typically, not all items and materials in a library are allowed to circulate. Materials that do not circulate are typically referred to as the reference collection or non-circulating collection. Reference materials can be checked out in special circumstances based on the borrower's needs and at the librarian's discretion. Reference materials typically are borrowed overnight, two days, sometimes as long as a week, in public libraries. In academic libraries, reference materials can be checked out for an extended amount of time for faculty and/or course use.

Circulation can take many forms, depending on the kind of library, the service community, how technologically advanced the library's systems are, and the size of the library's circulating collection. Aside from charging and discharging materials, if a borrower returns material past the due date, a fine is typically incurred on a daily basis until the material is returned. In public library systems, this fining schedule will often have a capitalizing limit whereas after a certain amount of fines are accrued, the entire cost of the material is charged to the patron instead. In this situation, upon return of the late material a patron either returns the material and pays the maximum capped fine or does not return the material (the item is lost) and instead pays the cost of the material for purposes of item replacement.

If a patron's borrower record illustrates a pattern of lost and/or missing materials along with unpaid fines, his/her record can be blocked from further circulation activities until the record is expunged either by payment, return of materials, or some other arrangement coordinated with the library administration. In school and academic libraries, lost library item costs can be added to a student's financial record and can block administrative services such as the release of grades and transcripts. Similar sanctions can occur in special libraries and archives.

At a basic level, in most libraries users may borrow up to a set limit of items from the circulating collections—fiction and nonfiction books, audiovisual material including DVDs, videos and audiobooks, and magazines (in print and electronic formats), and can hold items for a set period of time (two weeks, four weeks, seven days, overnight, etc.) before returning them. These set limits and time periods, known as borrowing privileges, differ from library to library. If a library has a small collection, the maximum number of items that can be borrowed might be less than in a library with a larger collection. By the same token, the time period a person may place a request on an item (also known as putting an item "on hold") may be shorter, creating a quicker turnaround time ensuring the item will be available more often. Items that are in high demand may have shorter due dates for the same reason. Multimedia items, such as DVDs, videos, music CDs, gaming, and software discs, might have shorter due dates based on the premise that these items do not take as long to listen to, or view, or use as the time it may take to read a book. To meet the demand of largely requested titles or items, librarians may keep multiple copies of an item "on reserve" for patron use in-house. Reserves are commonly offered in academic libraries to accommodate instructors who want textbooks or other materials available for class review.

Another kind of circulation involving technology involves the use of a library's website and downloadable material. In this kind of circulation, the library user enters his/her library card number (or some other acceptable code) and downloads a digital file containing an entire book, music, or video, onto his/her computer, tablet, or handheld device. Once downloaded, the file can be read or viewed by the user. After the established due date is reached, libraries commonly enact digital rights management to cue the file to automatically disappear from the user's library account. Libraries comply with legalities associated with digital rights management (DRM) to enact the ethical return of digital data and files to the library collection. Digital rights management technologies serve to control copyright protection so that users cannot copy, sell, or inappropriately possess library materials. It is DRM technology that is in play when electronic library materials are "returned" (via disappearance in user's account) to the library's holdings.

The option to stream books, music, and video is beginning to appear on many libraries' websites. As technology improves, vendors marketing products proliferate, and the availability of platforms (smartphones, advanced e-readers, tablets, laptops, PCs) to access these features spreads, patrons are able to bypass the standard check-out/check-in paradigm.[5] The nature of streaming is immediate and temporary (while the patron is actively using the item), so it does not resemble the typical circulation transaction. Still, accessing these services requires a library card number to be entered for the transaction to occur and the patron's library card needs to be in good standing regarding the amount of overdue fines, late books, or lost item fees exactly as in traditional circulation transactions involving print items. Vendors such as Overdrive, Freegal, Hoopla, Indieflix, Zinio, and Smithsonian Global Sound for Libraries are just some examples of companies offering streaming features on library websites.

As streaming technology and accessibility improves, libraries are in a unique position to consider content creation as another service to the community. One of the strengths of libraries is the ability to collect and preserve the history and culture of a community. The library collects knowledge of local relevance to the community and, in many cases, is the only source for such information.[6] How this local content creation is circulated, and what impact it will have on circulation overall, will pose an interesting question for library administration to consider.

The kind of community the library serves can have an effect on circulation. A special library in a law firm or business or an academic library catering to a specific population might have a very different circulation policy than a public library serving a broad and diverse geographic community. A library with more funding, and thus able to buy larger collections and replace items more easily may have more generous borrowing privileges than a library with less funding.

In certain special libraries, because of the population served, circulation, if tracked at all, is considered the number of items taken from the shelves and used in-house as there is no need to take material from the library. In academic libraries, faculty are sometimes given the privilege of checking out materials for extended periods of time, and can place course textbooks and articles on reserve at the circulation desk for student reference use. Nowadays, academic libraries also circulate materials via electronic delivery methods, whereby scholarly articles can be retrieved via interlibrary loan (ILL) and with delivery notices sent by email to students and faculty alike. Such documents are typically delivered in PDF format on the library's secured website, whereupon entering one's login information, a patron can locate and download the requested materials.

The value of circulation, no matter the various kinds it can take in various locations around the world, is a symbol of a library's relevancy and connection to its community.

USER COMMUNITIES

"User community" is a term used to identify any group of library users based on a wide variety of defining terms. Defining terms of a user community can be based on demographics of any kind, whether age, gender, culture, education, profession, socioeconomic status, ethnicity, geographic/region, or nationality.

Each user group would have specific information needs that would differ from other user groups, but might not necessarily be completely exclusive or removed from the information needs of other groups. The age levels and reading levels of books; types of circulating collections, reference works, and fiction and nonfiction; the availability and diversity of multimedia; borrowing privileges; and many policies and procedures are dependent upon the user

groups that a library serves. It is the duty and responsibility of administrative librarians, reference librarians, and library staff to be knowledgeable of, sensitive to, and accommodating of the user groups within their service community.

> User groups based on age are lapsit, toddler, preschool, school age, high school, teen, home-schooled, young adult, adult, and seniors.
> User groups based on culture, nationality, or ethnicity may include immigrants, as well as communities identifying with a specific heritage, language, or history.
> User groups based on socioeconomics could be centered on income levels: urban, suburban, rural communities, home-ownership, homelessness, transience, and migrancy.
> User groups based on civic status include immigrants, travelers, court-appointed volunteers, recovery outpatients, patrons of varying mobilities, and prisoners.
> User groups based on educational criteria would be concerned with level of schooling, groups working in the field of education, people with college, and graduate degrees.

Users groups are unique and specific to their communities, often comprising an admixture of citizens cross-pollinating in multiple groups at one time. Thus all library communities are diverse and must strive to create library collections that can be inviting for users to circulate materials amongst one another with the circulation desk and staff as a friendly interface.

STAFFING

Paraprofessionals are typically the staffers of the circulation desk in public libraries. Paraprofessionals usually possess a high school diploma (or equivalent) as the minimum educational requirement for working at the circulation desk. Paraprofessional staffers go by various titles, but common titles are "Library Assistant" or "Library Technician." Competencies for library assistants include excellent organizational skills, ethical proficiency in mathematical skills, being detail-oriented and technologically savvy, being culturally competent with high-quality customer service skills, and performing entry-level reference services. Through years of experience, library assistants/technicians become very proficient with their knowledge of literature, technology, the community, and library trends. Library assistantship is a common gateway through which paraprofessionals become professional librarians, initially seeking their bachelor's degree in higher education and ultimately earning the master's degree in library science to qualify as a professional librarian.

Paraprofessionals are a vital part of the library staff as they work to control the circulation flow of the library.

Library users check out books at the circulation desk, thus good customer service skills are vital for the successful library assistant. Paraprofessionals also enforce library policy making sure that patrons pay fines as well as ensuring ethical practices with the processing of monies from collected fines and other fees.

Library assistants also work to maintain the order of the library collection. In larger public library systems, paraprofessionals may package and log in new materials for the collection, and they may frequently serve as the primary shelvers of new and circulated materials. A lead paraprofessional may, at times, serve as the librarian in the absence of one. In smaller libraries such as in rural locations, a paraprofessional may be the librarian for his/her location, often running the entire library with a few volunteers.

Paraprofessional training and skill development tends to be an internal function of the library or library system. In larger systems, there is usually a staff training office (most likely within the Human Resources Office) that schedules training sessions, workshops, and professional development opportunities such as webinars, conferences, and guest speakers. In smaller systems or libraries, training may be hands-on, at the circulation desk, during the workday as the new staff member "shadows" the experienced staff members. The efficacy of the latter and financial challenges posed by the former is an ongoing conversation in librarianship.[7,8]

In best case scenarios, paraprofessionals are encouraged and supported by librarians and library administrators to continue their education through professional development activities. Such activities may include attendance to staff meetings, conferences, technology workshops, and community seminars. Paraprofessionals may also join paraprofessional library divisions within their state library associations. For example, the Nebraska Library Association has a Paraprofessional Section, and the Georgia Library Association has a Paraprofessional Division. Across cultural lines, paraprofessionals are also welcome constituents to ethnic library groups such as REFORMA (The National Association to Promote Library and Information Services to Latinos and the Spanish-Speaking), APALA (Asian Pacific Library Association), and the Black Caucus of the ALA (BCALA).

STACK MANAGEMENT

Stack management, also known as collection maintenance, is that aspect of any library system or unit concerning the care, handling, shelving and storing, and accessibility of library materials, on-site and beyond.

There is a dearth of current discussion on issues relating to stack management in libraries today.[9] But perusing the written record going back 15 years and further reveals some basic concepts of stack management that remain relevant to this day.

There are five divisions to the process of stacks management also known as collection maintenance.[10,11] The five divisions are storage and shelving systems (to hold and protect a wide variety of unique materials), housekeeping routines (cleaning stacks and vacuuming books; knowing and reacting to specific material needs and environmental conditions), general care and handling practices (broad set of activities that protect materials that are handled, proper techniques to handling materials and how material should be shelved and stored), care and handling routines in processing (proper techniques in handling items throughout the journey of processing, borrowing, charging, and storing the item repeatedly, during its life in the library), and collection improvement activities (noting when and how to best screen and identify damaged and problematic materials within the circulation cycle and the processing stream). These divisions hold for libraries across the profession whether public, academic, or special.

The primary responsibility for maintaining a robust stacks management program and implementing collection maintenance activities rests primarily with circulation staff. In many situations, responsibility during acquisition, cataloging, shelf preparation, and binding will lie with technical processing staff. Cleaning and buildings staff might well play a role in housekeeping functions or when the literal nuts and bolts of the shelving systems to be used are discussed and established. And, as in so many systems or programs, the role of library administration is to ensure that clear, firm policies are established, disseminated, and accessible and that priorities are set, known, and supported.[12]

In recent years, stack management has evolved to include the relocation of print collections to digital format and/or to off-site locations. Print collections are becoming smaller in many libraries due to the changing focus of the library from a collection storage facility to a more inclusive space for community interaction and exchange.[13] With the shift of the foci on libraries from artifacts to community building, some libraries blend collection maintenance and stack management routines into one circulation department. Large systems such as university libraries may opt to separate the stacks management functions from the circulation department to promote better efficiencies in getting the material in question back to the shelves and made available in a more timely fashion.[14] Many large public library systems also have a separate stacks section removed from the functions of the circulation department while at the same time allowing a blending of both routines on the branch or unit level as needed (author's observation, 2014).

The digital age has also delivered new formats for books that affect the circulation and management of library stacks and collections. E-books (as well as e-magazines and e-audiobooks) can now be checked out and loaned and renewed online via in-house electronic circulation systems, mobile applications, and library websites with digital platforms such as Overdrive, OneClickdigital, and Bookshare, without library patrons needing to be physically at a library circulation desk.[15,16] Facilitating circulation of e-books and managing their circulation records often falls within the professional purview of library circulation managers and clerks.

Earlier challenges for making e-books accessible from the publisher to the reader have been progressively met. With e-book access having progressed due to the work of librarians, stakeholders, and the ALA Digital Content Working Group (DCWG), the challenge now is to make e-book lending a satisfactory user experience for library patrons by incorporating emerging trends such as e-book subscription models, self-published authors, and the online availability of e-book retailers such as Amazon and Netflix. All these trends shape reader expectations requiring the knowledge base of librarians and circulation staff to constantly change to meet user information needs.[17]

With the increased availability of print, audiovisual, and electronic resources on the Internet and through databases, and the trend toward virtual reference, the need for physical stacks and collections is changing dramatically with an increase in library collections being moved to digital records and/or remote storage locations in order to afford more physical space for human interaction within library walls. Remote services and management of customer knowledge and patron usage patterns continue to grow in importance in this online, mobile, virtual world era. The policies and procedures, the theories and applications, for the future of stack management and collection maintenance are even now being discussed, formulated, and written.[18]

TECHNOLOGY

Since the formal professionalization of librarianship in 1876, technology in libraries has continuously evolved to employ the latest technology of the times. During the nineteenth century, books were checked out using a handwritten ledger system, where librarians would write down a user's due date as a line item action for each title borrowed. Technology quickly evolved where systems for circulation services were comprised of permanent card systems and metal plate systems by the early twentieth century.

With the card system, a permanent identifying card was generated for every book acquired for the library collection. The card was kept in the book, and then removed from the book when borrowed. This system is still employed today in some rural public libraries, school libraries, and academic libraries for in-house reserve materials. The metal plate system was considered an improvement over the card system because the user's information was permanently embossed on a metal plate, allowing for a decrease in error when recording borrower information. With the plate

system library staffers were also able to automatically set due dates on library cards.

In the late 1940s, early efforts at using new data processing techniques revolved around the idea of batch processing using key punch cards. These new systems were fast and dependable, could produce overdue notices on demand, and did not require any filing. Some of the drawbacks to the batch processing system were lack of a user database, and lack of inventory control of collections. Most batching processes took hours to complete, so would occur overnight in many public and academic library systems. The batch would process information about materials checked out, but not record information about materials still on the shelves. This made the quality of expanded circulation services, such as book reserves and interlibrary loan, cumbersome and unreliable, as books were hard to locate in the library, since there was no consistent inventory record. Not offering much improvement on older circulation technologies like the ledger and metal plate systems (in terms of keeping record of whole collection management schemes), batch processing was eventually superseded by computer online systems during the later half of the twentieth century.

Subsequently by the 1970s, circulation services in both public and academic library systems were incorporating bar code readers, scanners, and laser technology, to process check-ins, checkouts, holds, reserves, and interlibrary loan requests, as well as modernizing inventory storage records into the form of digitized data. Radio-frequency identification methods (RFID) allow for library users to manage their own check-out processes with the use of wireless technology that scans a microchip embedded in a user's library card and also tagged within the library material to be borrowed. Self check-out machines read the information on the library card and connect that information with the borrowed material via a radio signal, creating a transaction record that is logged in the library catalog. RFID technology can also assist library circulation staff with the book handling process of returned items with systems that automatically read returned items from the book drop, processes the check-in procedure on a user's library record and sends the library item to the appropriate bin for re-shelving.[18] Along with ILS, RFID, and graphics-oriented interfaces for managing borrowing processes at the circulation desk, technology continues to impact circulation services by incorporating self-service automated developments for public and academic libraries.

Newer advances in technology appearing at the circulation desk include cash registers networked to the check-in and check-out terminals and RFID terminals that allow library users to check out material themselves by placing the item on a scanning plate or waving a light wand over the item's barcode. This produces a receipt with information on which items were checked out, how many items were checked out, and due dates. It is the responsibility in most libraries for the circulation desk staff to assist library users with this new technology and to come to the aid of the user when technical glitches occur.

In more recent years, innovations in web development allow library users to access their library accounts via the Internet to renew materials, manage requests, and pay fines. Users can now access their library accounts from library websites via their personal computer, laptop, tablet, or cell phone. Library users can also borrow technologies to use in the library and to check out to use at home. Some technologies that are now circulated in libraries include computer laptops, headphones, calculators, voice recorders, CDs, DVDS, gaming items, and digital cameras.

REFERENCES

1. Galbi, D.A. Book circulation per U.S. public library user since 1856. Draft—Version 1.01. July 29, 2007. http://www.galbithink.org/libraries/circulation.htm (accessed November 2014).
2. Reid, I. The 2013 public library data service statistical report: characteristics and trends. *Public Libraries Online*, May 9, 2014. http://publiclibrariesonline.org/2014/05/2013-plds/ (accessed November 2014).
3. Enis, M. NYPL partners with Coursera: pairing aims to teach both more about MOOCs. Libr. J. **June 15, 2014**, 13+.
4. Hill, J.; Delaney, J. *The USA PATRIOT Act in Libraries: What It Currently Means for Libraries*; Illinois Library Association: Chicago, IL, 2013. http://www.ila.org/the-usa-patriot-act-in-2012-what-it-currently-means-for-libraries (accessed November 2014).
5. Friedlander, A. The Internet and Harry Potter: what users want; users seek a variety of formats. Inf. Outlook **December 2003**, 18+.
6. Yelton, A. Where to go next. Library Technol. Rep. **2012**, 48.1, 25+.
7. Blakiston, R. Building knowledge, skills, and abilities: continual learning in the new information landscape. J. Libr. Admin. **October–December 2011**, 728+.
8. Evans, H.; Sweeney, G. Defining stack management. Libr. Collect. Acquis. Tech. Serv. **2005**, *29* (1), 51–60.
9. Hodnett, D.M. *Management of Circulation Functions in Health Science Libraries: Medical Library Association Courses for Continuing Education: CE 57*; Medical Library Association: Chicago, IL, 1979; 56–62.
10. Byrne, S. Collection Maintenance and Improvement. *Preservation Planning Program Series*; Association of Research Libraries: Washington, DC, 1993; 1–3.
11. Tabacaru, S.; Pickett, C. Damned if you do, damned if you don't: Texas A&M University Libraries' collection assessment for off-site storage. Collect. Build. **2013**, *32* (3), 111–115.
12. Qureshi, K. Behind the scenes: managing the piles of books returned! *Falvey Library Blogs*, http://blog.library.villanova.edu/news/2008/12/10/behind-the-scenes-managing-the-piles-of-books-returned/ (accessed November 2014).
13. Vollmer, T. *There's an App for That! Libraries and Mobile Technology: An Introduction to Public Policy Considerations*; American Library Association, Office of Information Technology Policy: Washington, DC, 2010. Policy Brief No. 3, http://www.ala.org/offices/sites/ala.org.offices/files/content/oitp/publications/policybriefs/mobiledevices.pdf (accessed November 2014).
14. Albanese, A. What's next for e-books in libraries?. Publishers Wkly. **2014**, *261* (25), 6. http://www.publishersweekly.com/pw/by-topic/industry-news/libraries/article/62991-what-s-next-for-e-books-in-libraries.html (accessed November 2014).
15. Garcia-Murillo, M.; Annabi, H. Customer knowledge management. J. Oper. Res. Soc. **August 2002**, *53* (8), 875–884.
16. Deardorff, T.C.; Aamot, G. *Remote Shelving Services*; Association of Research Libraries: Washington, DC, 2006.
17. Breeding, M. Circulation technologies from past to future. Comput. Libr. **2008**, *28* (2), 19–22.
18. Greenfield, J. What's new with libraries and ebooks? In conversation with the American Library Association. *Forbes.com*, October 2013, http://www.forbes.com/sites/jeremygreenfield/2013/10/03/whats-new-with-libraries-and-e-booke-books-in-conversation-with-the-american-library-association/ (accessed November 2014).

Citation Analysis

Howard D. White
College of Computing and Informatics, Drexel University, Philadelphia, PA, U.S.A.

Abstract

References *from* publications are at the same time citations *to* other publications. This entry introduces some of the practical uses of citation data in science and scholarship. At the individual level, citations identify and permit the retrieval of specific editions of works while also suggesting their subject matter, authority, and age. Through citation indexes, retrievals may include not only the earlier items referred to by a given work but also the later items that cite that given work in turn. Counts of citations received over time, and measures derived from them, reveal the varying impacts of works, authors, journals, organizations, and countries. This has obvious implications for the evaluation of, e.g., library collections, academics, research teams, and science policies. When treated as linkages between pairs of publications, references and citations reveal intellectual ties. Several kinds of links have been defined, such as cocitation, bibliographic coupling, and intercitation. In the aggregate, these links form networks that compactly suggest the intellectual histories of research specialties and disciplines, especially when the networks are visualized through mapping software. Citation analysis is not without critics, who have long pointed out imperfections in the data or in analytical techniques. However, the criticisms have generally been met by strong counterarguments from proponents.

INTRODUCTION

In specialties with literatures, citations link earlier and later work. They denote unique writings and connote concepts associated with those writings. They reveal the citer's intellectual sources in preparing a new text and enable readers to retrieve them. In Derek Price's useful distinction,[1] further discussed in Wouters,[2] a work's *references*, made in its footnotes or endnotes, are "outgoing mail" that it sends to older works. A work's *citations*, in contrast, are "incoming mail" that it receives from newer works. It is common, however, to refer to both as "citations" and let the context indicate whether they are incoming or outgoing.

Such linkages may be interesting even at the level of individual documents. In general, however, more interesting patterns emerge when citations from many sources are analyzed in the aggregate. Then one can learn such things as a field's most highly cited authors or works (intellectual bestsellers, so to speak), the primary influences on a particular author's body of writings, and authors or works that are repeatedly cited together over time, indicating that in the eyes of citers they are highly related. Researchers use the latter sort of information to investigate the intellectual structure of learned specialties and disciplines. Citation analysis along these lines is a major part of bibliometrics, the subdiscipline of library and information science (L&IS) devoted to the quantitative study of literatures.[3] It is also the form of L&IS research most widely adopted by other fields—in part because citation analysts have long used visualization techniques to make relationships in their data easier to grasp.[4–6]

Entries complementing the present one are McVeigh's "Citation Indexing and the Web of Science" (p. XXXX), Bar-Ilan's "Informetrics" (p. XXXX), and Brooks' "Citer Motivations" (p. XXXX). This entry focuses on research in which citation counts come into play as raw data. It draws examples from the Web of Science (WoS), because of that system's historical importance in revealing the possibilities and problems of citation-based bibliometrics, especially in the journal-oriented sciences. Examples are also drawn from the WoS citation databases on the Dialog Classic retrieval system, because its software could quickly retrieve and display bibliometric data in useful formats not seen elsewhere. Dialog was retired by ProQuest, its parent company, in 2013.

The WoS continues to be a major resource, but after decades of being the only widely regarded source of citation data, it now has formidable competition from Elsevier's Scopus, Google Scholar (GS), and Microsoft Academic. WoS and Scopus can themselves generate reports for subscribers with routine bibliometric questions, while a free system called Publish or Perish[7] does the same for GS and Microsoft Academic. Nevertheless, many studies can be carried out only by downloading records from these services and analyzing or visualizing them with external software, such as the Sci2 toolset,[8] CiteSpace,[9] or VOSviewer.[10]

Specific citation analyses are matters of practical concern, since they are often published as evidence for knowledge claims and are sometimes used in making consequential decisions. They have been brought to bear on national scientific and technical policies, evaluations of

Encyclopedia of Library and Information Sciences, Fourth Edition DOI: 10.1081/E-ELIS4-120053692

organizations to determine funding, and academic tenure and promotion cases. They are used to map literatures, reveal networks of citers and citees, and assess the impacts of organizations, authors, journals, and individual works. They also have uses in library collection evaluation. Historically, citation data have come largely from journal articles, but other document types, such as books, conference papers, dissertations, and patents, are increasingly mined as well.

Bibliometrically speaking, however, publications are no longer judged solely by the citations they have received. Shared document repositories (e.g., arXiv), reference managers (e.g., Mendeley), and social media (e.g., Twitter) have led to alternative measures, which are called "altmetrics," to differentiate them from citation-based measures. Altmetrics include counts of the times that publications have been viewed in or downloaded from repositories, bookmarked or shared in reference managers, mentioned or discussed in social media, and, in the case of books, formally reviewed. Another altmetric for books is the number of libraries that hold them in union catalogs such as WorldCat.[11] Yet none of these measures is likely to replace citation measures; instead, the best of them complement citations as indicators of reader interest in publications and perhaps as raw data for measures of greater complexity.

Many citation analyses require readers to know statistics or mathematics. This entry points to reviews of that research but presents ideas, resources, and analytic techniques at a basic qualitative level. Zhao and Strotmann[12] covers some of the same topics in greater technical detail.

CITATIONS AS VERBAL OBJECTS

Both citers and bibliographers briefly describe written works, but they have different aims. Citers adduce other writings in the context of a new work of some creativity—a work for which authorship and a byline are claimed (or claimable). More particularly, they adduce works to support a line of discourse—e.g., as evidence, background, example, or proof. By contrast, when bibliographers make entries in a catalog, bibliography, or abstracting service, they merely register or subject-index works without developing new lines of thought; they are not arguing and documenting a point. Typically, they are not considered authors and do not get bylines.

The distinction between citers and bibliographers bears on collection evaluation. Librarians often evaluate their holdings by checking them against bibliographers' products, such as *Resources for College Libraries*. However, some librarians draw samples of citers' products—that is, the works cited in books, articles, and dissertations.[13] Every item in these checklists has already proved useful in real research, and the librarian can ask, "Could my library have supported that research by providing this title?" Alternatively, if the sample consists of citations by local authors, the librarian can ask, "Which of the titles in my collection does the home team most heavily use?"

Citations show the *editions* of the works the citer referred to—the copies of a text made from a particular master. The routine fields of conventional citations (e.g., author, title, journal, date, and pagination) function jointly to identify editions. The author and title by themselves name a work but not the specific version of the work's text—the edition—that was consulted. While many published works exist in only one edition, there is a permanent possibility of more than one, and since they may vary in quality (to the point of having different evidentiary or aesthetic value), we want a means of telling different texts of the same work apart, even if we never actually retrieve more than one. Conventional citations have just enough data to disambiguate in this fashion. They lead to "known item" retrievals in bibliographic databases and library catalogs, which typically use editions as their units of analysis.

More abstractly, citations represent written works as to *authority, age, subject matter,* and *form of knowledge.* The last is the author's orientation toward the subject matter—e.g., scientific, technical, historical, or personal.[14] *Authority* is rendered, first, by naming whoever is responsible for the content of the work, and, second, by naming whoever released that particular version of it to the world—respectively, the author(s) and the publisher, both of whom exercise editorial quality control over content. *Age* is implied by publication date. *Subject* and *form of knowledge* are rendered through the content and style of the title (and possibly subtitle). They may also be rendered by a name connected with the publisher—e.g., the title of the journal or monographic series in which the work appears.

The four kinds of information are not always present. This may result from citers' carelessness or from defects in the works themselves, as when they lack a publication date or have unrevealing titles. Less often, it results from convention, such as the journal *Science*'s policy of omitting titles from citations to save space. Ideally, however, citations communicate all four, and the ideal is frequently realized in practice.

At the level of a self-contained citation, the four are simply qualitative variables whose values have both explicit and implicit meanings. Explicit meanings are those that any educated reader might receive without special knowledge of the field in which the citation is made. Implicit meanings are those accessible to a field's insiders through their knowledge of reputations, technical vocabulary, rhetorical styles, and the like. To insiders, a citation can connote subject matter not explicit in the title of the work. Such connotations are part of a field's intellectual history, as doctoral students come to know it. In information science, for example, one might happen on this citation:

Bradford, S. C. (1934). Sources of information on specific subjects. *Engineering* 137 (3550): 85–86.

From the opaque title, outsiders could not guess that this paper is the origin of Bradford's law of scattering, a pillar of modern bibliometrics. Bibliometricians, on the other hand, might be surprised that the paper is cited at all, since the findings it announced have long been a staple of their thought. As a result, Bradford now goes relatively uncited—a phenomenon the sociologist of science Robert K. Merton termed "obliteration by incorporation."[15]

CITATION COUNTS

Talk of relative citedness leads to the notion of citation counts, by which individual citations enter into larger structures of meaning. These structures are the main subject of this entry.

Many published writings are never cited. But many others are drawn into citation networks that preserve information about the history of learned specialties and disciplines. A natural metric in these networks is how frequently authors have cited specific earlier publications. This measure resembles figures on book sales, journal subscriptions, and visits or links to web pages. Like them, it is not a gauge of absolute worth; quality and popularity are not identical.[16] But when properly used, citation counts are a reasonably valid indicator of reputation in any field, granting that reputations may be increased by controversy.

The counts are metadata that emerge as citations to works accumulate in files. Until 1960, when Eugene Garfield founded the Institute for Scientific Information (ISI) in Philadelphia, there were no such files. *Shepard's Citation Index*, one of Garfield's influences, had enabled the legal profession to trace precedent decisions in court cases since 1873, but *Shepard's* was not regarded as a bibliometric tool. It was only when ISI created the *Science Citation Index*, the *Social Sciences Citation Index*, and the *Arts and Humanities Citation Index* for purposes of document retrieval that analysts could exploit them further as large-scale databases from which to mine statistics on learned literatures.[17,18] The three previously mentioned ISI tools, which started as printed publications, were moved online as, respectively, Scisearch, Social Scisearch, and Arts and Humanities Search. In 1992, ISI was taken over by a new owner, Thomson Reuters, but the same databases remained available on the Internet, in time marketed jointly as the WoS. At this writing, WoS is offered by a Thomson Reuters spin-off called Clarivate Analytics.

The WoS indexes, described in McVeigh (p. XXX), are designed for "forward citation retrieval"—that is, they allow searchers to look up an earlier work and find the later documents that cite it. (When a later work is used to find an earlier one, it is called "backward citation retrieval" or "footnote chasing.") For example, a forward retrieval on Arthur C. Danto's 1964 article *The Artworld* in Arts and Humanities Search leads to (among other things) *Farewell to Danto and Goodman*, a 1998 article by Joseph Margolis in the *British Journal of Aesthetics*. All such later articles add up to the earlier work's citation count, or rather to its WoS count—a qualification necessary for two reasons.

First, while the citations in WoS may be *to* works of any sort, they are primarily drawn *from* articles and other types of publications that appear in journals. (Some WoS journal files date from as early as 1900.) WoS now also offers an index to citations from scholarly books (from 2005 on) and another to citations from conference proceedings (from 1990 on), but these require separate subscriptions, and many millions of older works are not covered. Second, WoS bases its coverage of contemporary journals, books, and proceedings in part on their international citedness: publications with citation counts below a threshold are not indexed and cannot contribute to the counts. This citedness policy also tends to favor inclusion of publications in English, the international language of science, and publications from countries dominant in scientific research, e.g., the United States and the United Kingdom.

The most widely used alternatives to WoS are Scopus and GS, both dating from 2004. Scopus, another high-quality subscription service, indexes current materials, especially scientific journals, even more broadly than WoS, but its retrospective coverage at this writing goes back only to 1996. Like WoS, its editorial selection policies determine what it will cover. Also like WoS, it has sought in recent years to improve its indexing of citations from books and proceedings, but again with the same careful selectivity. GS is different: it simply crawls the web, extracts citations from accessible documents regardless of their origin or language, and makes them and their counts available everywhere without charge. GS is increasingly used in serious bibliometrics—for example, in Bensman et al.[19] Its counts for all sorts of works frequently exceed those in WoS and Scopus,[20] although in some fields and periods, the latter two have better coverage of the literatures. The policies behind GS data gathering are opaque, and it has been faulted for unreliable data.[21] But data from the other two major services may require cleaning as well.[22] Ideally, researchers would combine vetted citations from all of the services (omitting duplicates) to arrive at counts.

MICROLEVEL DATA

The counts of a publication's outgoing references and incoming citations are not the same. For example, Stephen P. Harter's 1992 article "Psychological Relevance and

Information Science" makes *references* to 49 older works (a fixed count). At this writing, it has *citations* from more than 200 newer works in WoS (a changing count). Disciplines vary in the average number of references in their articles and in the average number of citations those articles receive in the years after publication. The latter sets a standard for what a *high* citation rate would be within a discipline, which can be compared in turn with rates in other disciplines. Harter's article is highly cited in the relatively small field of L&IS, but not in science as a whole.

Table 1 displays what is actually counted. It is a lightly edited bibliographic record from *Arts and Humanities Citation Index* in WoS (in an old-fashioned, space-saving format). It identifies both a 1993 article by Russ Pottle and the publications he cites. His work is thus a "source" article in WoS—that is, a source of the "cited references" in the CR field.

These highly abbreviated CR strings are sufficient to identify works. In Pottle's case, there are 14, as shown in the NR (number of references) field. Among them are an article by Nina Baym and a book by Ann Douglas, two older works to which Pottle's is now related. (Either could retrieve Pottle if entered into a Cited Reference search in

Table 1 Source article record from Web of Science with tagged fields

AU	Pottle, R
TI	The Monkey before the Whale, Signifyin(g) and Melville's 'Mardi'
SO	Journal of Narrative Technique
LA	English
DT	Article
RP	Pottle, R (Reprint Author), Louisiana State Univ, Baton Rouge, LA 70803, USA
CR	Baym N, 1979, PMLA, V94, P909, DOI 10.2307/461973
	Beaver H, 1984, H Melville Reassessm
	Davis Merrell, 1960, Lett H Melville
	Davis Merrell R., 1952, Melvilles Mardi Char
	Douglas Ann, 1977, Feminization Am Cult
	Durer CS, 1986, Romanticism Past Pre, V10, P45
	Gates HJ, Signifying Monkey Th
	Giltrow J, 1980, Am Lit, V52, P18, DOI 10.2307/2925185
	Jubak J, 1979, Genre, V9, P121
	Melville H, Moby Dick
	Melville H, Typee
	Melville H, Mardi
	Samson John, 1989, White Lies Melvilles
	Saussure FD, 1989, Course General Lingu
NR	14
PY	1993
VL	23
IS	3
BP	36
EP	53
PG	18
SC	Literature

WoS.) The citation frequency for any work is obtained by counting the CR strings that identify it in source (SO) publications. For example, occurrences of "Baym N, 1979, PMLA, V94, P909" are counted to get a total for the Baym article, and occurrences of "Douglas A, 1977, Feminization Am Cult" are counted to get a total for the Douglas book.

Baym and Douglas are sole authors, but who gets credit for a citation when coauthors are involved? In WoS databases, citations formerly accrued only to the first author, because CR strings identify no one else. Now, coauthors receive credit along with first authors in WoS, just as they do in Scopus. But in downloaded WoS data, one still sees only the CR strings. If one nevertheless identifies all the coauthors, there are two major ways of crediting them: either all get full credit for the citation (their counts all go up by one) or all share equal fractions of credit (e.g., three coauthors get a third of a credit each). Besides affecting authors' citation records, this choice determines who appears in author maps.[23–25]

The CR strings themselves can be split into additional variables that are countable across the database. For instance, a count for Herman Melville as a cited author can be obtained from occurrences of "Melville H"; a count for *Publications of the Modern Language Association* as a cited journal by occurrences of "PMLA." A count for items published in a cited year—say, 1979—is obtained from occurrences of "1979," as seen in the Baym and Jubak articles in Table 1. Counts of items published in a cited year are used in half-life statistics, described later.

For entities above the level of individual works, such as authors and journals, citation counts may be incremented by how frequently their names occur in the CR strings, or by how many source publications cite them. For example, Melville's count could go up by *three* because three of his works appear in Pottle's references, or by *one* because one more source publication—Pottle's article—cites him. Scopus and WoS display counts of both kinds. GS simply counts citations to individual works and then totals them for authors.

What the citation databases do *not* count are the times a later work refers to an earlier one in its body text—instances of *op., cit.,* and *ibid.,* as it were. Systems do not yet exist for routine analysis of that kind. For example, no matter how many references Margolis may make to "The Artworld" within his text, it is his "Farewell" article that is counted, and so the citation count for "The Artworld" increases only by one. But with greater computer power, frequencies of internal references may in time be captured as an indicator of the importance of works to the citer.[26]

Fields other than the CR field can be analyzed in WoS records. Given data like those in Table 1, analysts can learn the number of items published by particular authors (AU) and source journals (SO). Institutional affiliations and geographic data for authors can be mined from the "reprint author" (RP) field. (Records for newer articles give affiliations and geographic data separately in a field tagged C1.) While these data may need extensive cleaning, they are obviously useful in evaluating institutions and countries. One can also get totals of items by language (LA), publication year (PY), and document type (DT). The subject category (SC) field characterizes not individual articles but the journals in which they appear. The SC assigned to the belletristic *Journal of Narrative Technique* in Table 1, for instance, is "Literature." (Some journals are assigned to more than one subject category.) The full SC scheme in WoS covers most of the sciences, social sciences, and humanities and allows literatures to be broken out by disciplines and subdisciplines.

HOMONYMS AND ALLONYMS

An introduction to citation analysis must warn about the errors caused by homonyms and allonyms. These occur in the strings of text that designate articles, books, journals, authors, organizations, and other entities.[27] They must be dealt with if the citation counts for any entity are to be accurate. No current software solves the problems entirely; checking is always necessary, and data cleaning may well be.

A *homonym* is a name that is the same for two or more *different* cited entities. In L&IS, for instance, the string "Wilson P" denotes at least two authors (Patrick Wilson and Pauline Wilson). Homonyms require disambiguation. If the right disambiguator does it—someone who can interpret contextual clues correctly—this may be simple enough. For others, it may be difficult or even impossible. The homonym problem is made worse by the abbreviations in citation databases that nullify disambiguations inherent in natural language. At this writing, WoS has a module for disambiguating abbreviated authors' names, while Scopus, a newer system, permits retrievals on full names. However, full names, too, can be homonymic.

An *allonym* is one of two or more different names for *the same* cited entity, such as "Jones KS" and "Sparck Jones K" when both denote the information scientist Karen Sparck Jones, or "Am Lit" and "AL" when both denote the journal *American Literature*.[27] Allonyms require conflation. This may require as much insider's knowledge as disambiguating homonyms. To assign accurate counts to certain information scientists, for example, one must know that the name Derek de Solla Price takes many forms in citations, or that Karen Markey is also cited as Karen Drabenstott. If serials have appeared under more than one title, or books in more than one edition, one must decide whether their allonymic citation counts should be conflated or kept separate.

Citers often inadvertently create allonyms by getting names wrong or by misnumbering journal volumes, pages, and years of publication. (These are called "citation variants" in WoS; the broader "allonym" includes both

erroneous and nonerroneous variants.) While such errors may be too singular to affect counts much, inconsistent data entry in all the citation databases can affect counts greatly. WoS has reconciled different versions of the same journal name in the SO field of its records for source articles, but it has not done so in the abbreviated journal names or book titles that appear in the CR strings. Clean sets of older *Journal Citation Reports* (*JCR*) data are available for comparison studies.[28,29]

Both homonymic and allonymic problems can beset the same name. For example, the American founder of cocitation analysis, Henry Small, has published under bylines both with and without his middle initial. He is thus cited as both "Small H" and "Small HG." Since both counts are sizable, these allonyms should be conflated. But other Smalls with the same initials also contribute to the counts, and their homonymic names need to be disambiguated from "the right Small's." In the case of Chinese, Japanese, and Korean researchers, name problems are severe.

MEASURES DERIVED FROM COUNTS

Citation counts are the basis of some important summary statistics, such as impact factors for journals and the h-index for authors (see also McVeigh, p. xxxx; Bar-Ilan, p. xxxx). Handbooks from Sweden's Karolinska Institute[30,31] describe in detail many of the indexes that can be derived from counts. Further introductions will be found in books by Harzing[7] and Moed[32] and in reviews by Mingers and Leydesdorff[33] and Waltman.[34] Several indexes are quite controversial; critics challenge their validity for evaluating authors, organizations, and journals.

Journal statistics. As part of WoS, *JCR* provides statistical data like those in Table 2. Such reports are available for journals in the natural and social sciences (not the arts and humanities). They are pegged to individual *JCR* years, e.g., 2013. The "Total Cites" column tells how many citations went in the *JCR* year to all articles published in that journal in a specific year. These numbers have obvious interest for journal editors and also for library serials managers as they decide how to allocate subscription money.

Table 2 ranks by "Journal Impact Factor" some well-known journals in the subject category "Information Science and Library Science" in *JCR* year 2013. The impact factor, which varies from year to year, adjusts journal citation counts by the number of items published, so as to counteract the effects of journal size and age. To compute it, all citations to a journal's articles in the two years before the *JCR* year are divided by the number of articles the journal published in the same two years. A factor of 1 means that the articles of those two years averaged one citation each. In Table 2, the impact factors for *JCR* year 2013 are based on citations to articles published during 2011 and 2012. At the

Table 2 Ten L&IS journals ranked by impact factors in *JCR* year 2013

Full journal title	Total cites	Journal impact factor	Immediacy index	Cited half-life	Citing half-life
Journal of Informetrics	1152	3.58	0.6	3.2	6.4
Scientometrics	5129	2.274	0.329	6.5	8.1
Journal of the American Society for Information Science and Technology	5125	2.23	0.29	6.6	8.1
Online Information Review	558	1.443	0.042	4.8	8.2
Library & Information Science Research	562	1.384	0.056	7	8.7
College & Research Libraries	528	1.333	0.182	9	7.7
Journal of Information Science	937	1.087	0.117	7.2	8.2
Information Processing & Management	1836	1.069	0.236	8.3	7.8
Journal of Documentation	1046	1.035	0.195	>10.0	9.4
Library Quarterly	291	0.861	0.143	>10.0	>10.0

top, the *Journal of Informetrics* articles averaged almost 3.6 citations each; at the bottom, the *Library Quarterly* articles averaged less than 1 each. (In the hard sciences, one sees much larger impact factors than those of Table 2.)

Researchers know that it is important to publish in good journals, and impact factors are one measure of this. However, such factors do not necessarily indicate the quality of *individual papers* in the journals.[35] Much of a journal's citation impact depends on a relatively small number of highly cited contributions that the "average" paper may scarcely resemble. Thus, a paper being evaluated (e.g., in a tenure case) should also be judged on other grounds, such as its own citation count and comments from peers.

The "Immediacy Index" is an indicator of how fast-moving a field is—how quickly articles in a journal are cited. To obtain the index, all citations to a journal's articles in the *JCR* year are divided by the number of the articles the journal published in that year. In Table 2, the 2013 immediacy index for *Scientometrics* reflects a faster-moving research field than the one represented by, say, the *Journal of Documentation*.

The "Cited Half-life" of a journal is the median age of the articles in it that are cited in a *JCR* year. Article age is measured from year of publication. In Table 2, half of the articles in the *Journal of Informetrics* that were cited in 2013 were no more than 3.2 yr old. The half-lives of the other journals indicate that citers were drawing on somewhat older materials. Bibliometricians have done considerable work on how publications age (or "obsolesce") in terms of citedness[36]—a process relatively fast in many sciences and relatively slow in the humanities and the softer social sciences.

Whereas cited half-life pertains to the citations a journal receives, *JCR* also provides data on the references the journal sends out. This is called its "Citing Half-life," and it is the median age of publications that appear in the bibliographies of its articles. Again, contributors to the *Journal of Informetrics* tend to cite newer materials than do contributors to comparable journals.

JCR creates a web page for each journal it covers. The page displays graphs of the journal's half-life trends over

time, its citing and cited relationships with other journals, and the raw counts from which the Table 2 statistics were calculated.

The WoS subject categories define fields in which journals can be compared. One can rank journals by any of the indexes in Table 2 (plus several others) and also alphabetize them by title. It is possible as well to obtain those indexes for aggregates of journals representing entire WoS subject areas. For example, by clicking on the "Categories by Rank" button, one can compare "International Relations" with "Law" in terms of the median impact factors of journals in the two disciplines.

Since 2007, *JCR* has made available two other measures of impact called eigenfactor metrics.[37] A journal's "Eigenfactor Score" starts with a count of all citations it has received from other journals in the five years preceding the *JCR* year. Then the other journals are weighted by how many citations *they themselves* have received, so that citations from highly cited journals raise the eigenfactor score more than do those from less-cited journals. The second measure, derived from a journal's eigenfactor score, is the "Article Influence Score." It summarizes, in a single value, the influence of all the articles in a journal over the five years since their publication. A score of 1 indicates that the articles have had average influence. Scores above 1 indicate influence above average, as is desirable; scores below 1, the reverse.

Scopus has its own "CiteScore" metrics of journal quality, including the "SCImago Journal Rank" and the "Source Normalized Impact for Paper," as noted in its downloadable guide. GS has also instituted some quality measures for journals under a "Metrics" link and explained how publications qualify for GS indexing under an "Inclusion" link.

Author statistics. Within appropriate domains, authors' raw citation counts always have human interest. They range in order of magnitude from 1 to 10 for obscure scribblers to more than 10,000 for world eminences such as Noam Chomsky and Michel Foucault.

A summary measure for authors that caught on quickly is the "H-Index."[38] When an author's publications are ranked high to low by their citedness, h is the lowest number of publications that have received at least that many citations. For example, an h-index of 20 means that a scientist has published 20 papers that have been cited at least 20 times each. The index is intended to capture career achievement by balancing the productivity of authors (their publication counts) with the reception of their work (their citation counts). It should be used to compare authors only within their fields, since disciplines vary in size and citing norms. Errors in counts attributable to homonyms and allonyms must be corrected; otherwise, the h-index can be very inaccurate.

The h-index is now automatically calculated by Scopus, WoS, and (for GS and Microsoft Academic data) Publish or Perish. As with impact factors, the strengths and weaknesses of this index have received critical scrutiny, and alternative measures have been devised to supplement it.[39] One is the "G-Index,"[40] which is the last rank at which the author's *cumulative* citation count is at least the square of the rank. For example, moving down the ranks, the g-index = 10 when the total citations to an author's top 10 papers equal or exceed 10^2 (i.e., 100), but not 11^2 (i.e., 121). The g-index takes into account the actual number of citations received at the top end, thus complementing the h-index, which is blind to this.

Organizational and national statistics. Increasingly, policy-makers consider bibliometric data as evidence in deciding how to allocate funds to scientific and scholarly organizations. Given past funding as input, organizational outputs can be assessed qualitatively by experts. They can also be assessed quantitatively through indicators such as counts of research publications and patents, and of their citations over time. In the hurly-burly of politics, where money and prestige are at stake, opinions on bibliometric indicators run from enthusiastic acceptance to litigious rejection.

The unit of analysis here is not individual authors but the organizations themselves. The Centre for Science and Technology Studies at Leiden University in the Netherlands is a world leader in research of this kind. The Centre's former director, Anthony van Raan, notes that disciplines and specialties can be compared at the national level and across universities, faculties, and institutes. In his view, the studies most relevant for policy-makers are those that examine "the real 'workfloor' of research practice: departments, research groups and programs within universities and large institutes" (p. 21).[41]

To learn a research unit's international scientific influence, several ratios from WoS data are brought to bear. For example, to determine the impact of a German institute in medical research, van Raan's team obtained 1) its mean citation rate per publication over a multiyear period (with self-citations removed) and for the same period 2) the mean citation rate of all papers published in all journals in the subject fields relevant to the institute. Dividing 1) by 2) gives the original "Crown Indicator," a

measure of the institute's internationally standardized citation impact in the Western world. If the ratio is around 1 (0.8 to 1.2), the program is average. A ratio of 0.5–0.8 indicates the program is below standard (less than 0.5 would be far below). Conversely, a ratio above 1.2 suggests distinction; above 1.5, high distinction. The German institute scored above 1.5, and the analysts could apply the same ratio to other programs in the institute to learn which contributed most to the excellence of its output. The Centre is engaged in ongoing improvement of the crown indicator, and a new one has been proposed.[42]

Bibliometrics may yield insights for academics and policy-makers even when data are at the highest levels of aggregation. For example, Sylvan Katz[43] compares nations within the world science system and finds that the number of papers they publish ("production") and the citations those papers receive ("recognition") have a very strong power-law relationship that is constant over time and independent of system size and nationality. This means that both production and recognition in science are inherently nonlinear or skewed, with small minorities of researchers producing disproportionately high numbers of papers and receiving disproportionately high numbers of citations. Science evolves this way naturally; its systems at all levels—regional, sectoral, national, and international—are "self-organizing" and "self-similar." A major policy implication of this finding is that governmental attempts to change a nation's science system through reallocations of funding are not likely to be simple or quick.

Other introductions to policy-related citation research in this vein are Leydesdorff[44] and Lundberg.[45]

INTERDOCUMENTARY RELATIONS

Citation analysts are not limited to counting attributes of documents taken singly. They can analyze counts of attributes taken jointly—for example, attributes of both citing and cited documents. It is in pairwise relations that analysis of citations may attain its greatest interest (see also Bar-Ilan, p XXXX). A nonexhaustive view of possibilities may be gained by looking at the two records in Table 3. (The Dialog Classic tags in them—CS, GL, and JN—are a bit clearer for present purposes than their analogs in WoS.) Table 3 shows the simplest pairwise link—direct citation, in which one document cites another. From that link, more complex structures can be created, such as the following.

The titles (TI) of citing and cited documents can be searched for coinciding vocabulary that suggests thematic connections. (No title words coincide in the records in Table 3, but the relations sketched here presume large pools of such records.) Data from the author (AU) field can reveal citer–citee patterns, including those of self-citation. The organizations that other organizations cite can be learned through corporate source (CS) data, which name

Table 3 Pairwise relations can be computed from raw data such as these

Cited document	Citing document
TI- The Artworld	TI- Farewell to Danto and Goodman
AU- Danto AC	AU- Margolis J
CS- Columbia Univ, New York NY	CS- Temple Univ, Philadelphia PA
GL- USA	GL- USA
JN- Journal of Philosophy, V62, N19, P571-84	JN- British Journal of Aesthetics, V38, N4, P353-74
PY- 1964	PY- 1998
DT- Article	DT- Article
SC- Philosophy	SC- Philosophy
LA- English	LA- English

authors' employers. The global locations (GL) of those employers permit similar analyses to be performed country to country. Journal names (JN) that a particular journal cites or is cited by—again including self-citations—are a standard bibliometric measure of influence. Publication year (PY) data, which are separable into cited and citing years, have multiple uses—for example, in WoS and Scopus statistics on authors and journals and in studies of document obsolescence. The PY variable can be combined with other variables in Table 3 to demonstrate chronological trends.

The last three fields suggest analyses parallel to those already described. In what proportion does each document type (DT) cite itself and other document types? What is the corresponding breakdown for languages (LA)? And finally, from what subject categories (SC) does a given research area receive citations, and to what SCs does it send them? SC data resemble those in import–export tables that quantify international flows of trade. They show the disciplines from which a field is importing ideas and the disciplines to which it is exporting them.

Intercitation. In studying intellectual connections, one can look at how members of a closed set cite each other. For example, among a set of aestheticians, how frequently does Margolis cite Danto or Danto cite Margolis over time? This is a rough measure of influence in the broadest sense. At this writing, Margolis has cited Danto in 11 articles, and Danto has cited Margolis in one. The citer–citee relation is asymmetric: A's citations to B need not be the same as B's to A.

Analysis of pairwise counts for a closed set of citers and citees—say, 20 philosophers in aesthetics—is a form of network analysis,[46] and the methods available for studying social networks are perfectly adapted to it. With network software such as UCINET, identical techniques can be used to analyze the social ties, interpersonal communications, and citation ties of Danto, Margolis, and other aestheticians. If the nodes representing papers in citation networks are numerous, the researcher needs

software capable of analyzing and visualizing very large matrices. Pajek, which may be downloaded free, is one solution.

Intercitation is also of interest at the level of journals. Over some time period, for example, how many articles in the *Journal of Documentation* cite those in the *Journal of Information Science*, and vice versa? (This may bear on subscription decisions by serials managers in libraries.) Studies of intercitation among journals include Leydesdorff[28,29] and Morris and McCain.[47]

Bibliographic coupling. Originally proposed by M. M. Kessler,[48] this measure is a count of the references that two publications make in common. ("Co-references" some call them.) Thus, if Paper A and Paper B cite two of the same other works, they are said to have a bibliographic coupling strength of 2. (Margolis's "Farewell" article and Danto's "Indiscernibility and perception: A reply to Joseph Margolis" have a strength of 2 because both refer to the same two books by Danto.) The fact that papers share one or two references may mean little substantively, but as their bibliographic coupling strength increases, so does the probability that they have similar content.

Bibliographic coupling is used in the Related Records module of WoS (see McVeigh, p. XXX). If one retrieves a publication of interest and wants to retrieve others like it, the "Related Records" button on its individual web page will call up other writings whose bibliographic coupling strength with the seed is at least 1. Unfortunately, such a low threshold retrieves many publications with no obvious ties to the seed. Moreover, the retrievals are based on only one seed at a time. To study *networks* of papers that are bibliographically coupled at a respectable strength, one must download records and use other software.

Cocitation. Whereas bibliographic coupling links *citing* documents, cocitation links *cited* documents. Bibliographic coupling is a static measure, because the references shared by two citing documents will not change. Cocitation, in contrast, is dynamic. It occurs whenever a later work cites any two earlier works in its footnotes or endnotes. Clearly, repetitions of the same pairing can occur in other later works indefinitely. Rousseau[49] has a useful discussion of cocitation counts, bibliographic coupling counts, and their elaborations.

Cocitation is a symmetric relation; A's count with B is the same as B's with A. As with bibliographic coupling, a cocitation strength of 1 or 2 may mean little, but repeated cocitation of the same two works (especially if done by different citers) predicts high relatedness. In expository writings, the connection will usually be on grounds of subject matter, method (e.g., quantitative vs. qualitative), and form of knowledge. When dissimilar imaginative works such as *Moby Dick* and *Huckleberry Finn* are frequently cocited, the connections will be on deeper levels of inferred themes and meanings.

Even so, two works cocited in the same publication may have nothing to do with each other. This problem has recently been addressed by weighting the tie between any two cocited works by the width of the narrowest text window in which the tie occurs—the narrower the window, the higher the weight. In other words, the more closely two works are cocited in body text, the likelier they are to be intelligibly connected. Text windows of course require access to digital documents in full, not just their reference lists. In Liu and Chen,[50] which builds on Gipp and Beel[51] and Callahan et al.,[52] four degrees of cocitation proximity are weighted high to low: within the same sentence > within the same paragraph > within the same section > within the same article. The conclusion is that cocitations at *sentence* level preserve "the most important structural components in the traditional co-citation network" while reducing the size of the data set 20-fold (pp. 509–510). They are thus a more efficient unit of analysis than the far commoner but looser cocitation ties at article level.

Cocitation as a measure was independently introduced by Henry Small[53] in America and Irina Marshakova[54] in Russia. Both focused principally on pairs of scientific *papers* as their unit of analysis. Small soon collaborated with Belver C. Griffith et al.[55] to develop algorithmic maps of science based on papers cocited above specific thresholds. Much subsequent work has continued to use papers to define scientific specialties. The early results are described in Garfield;[17] more contemporary results, in the four reviews mentioned earlier.[3–6]

With Griffith, Howard D. White[56] introduced maps based on cocited *authors*. The data here are counts of the times any two authors are cited together in later publications, regardless of which of their works are involved. Put differently, they are counts of the times authors' oeuvres have been cocited. Karl Erik Rosengren[57] anticipated this line of thought in Sweden by studying how frequently famous literary authors (e.g., Ibsen and Tolstoy) were "co-mentioned" in book reviews.

Cocited authors should not be confused with coauthors. Danto and Margolis, for example, have never coauthored anything, yet Arts and Humanities Search on Dialog Classic showed various items from their oeuvres cocited in 64 articles. Like papers, highly connected oeuvres tend to share subject matter or research methods or both. Once authors as oeuvres are connected, the analyst can also explore possible ties between the same authors as persons—for example, as mentor and student, coworkers, or intellectual opponents. Social facts like these often help to explain the groupings in author maps and heighten the interest of the maps to a field's insiders.

Katherine McCain began the cocitation analysis of *journals*.[58,59] Her maps at this higher level of aggregation are based on how frequently any two journals are cited together, regardless of what in them is cited. Cocitation groups journals not on the basis of the superficial similarities perceived by indexers, but on conjoined use by researchers. Analysis can be limited to a specific field or expanded to uncover supporting disciplines and related topic areas. It is therefore relevant to serials management and information retrieval.

Illustrating several of the possibilities, McCain has used journal cocitation mapping to study interrelationships in the literatures of genetics, economics, and aquatic sciences/fisheries. In the genetics and fisheries studies, visualization of the cocitation data demonstrated the existence of a basic-to-applied continuum of journals representing major themes in research and development. The genetics and economics studies combined cocitation data with intercitation data to identify, map, and cluster journals central to fields.[13]

Cocitation analysis can be broadened to include *organizations* and even *countries*. Whatever the unit of analysis, algorithmically produced cocitation maps are usually quite intelligible. The same is true of maps based on bibliographic coupling. Zhao and Strotmann,[60] for example, mapped a set of information scientists using their cocitation counts and their bibliographic coupling counts from 1996 to 2005 as separate indicators of relatedness. Both metrics proved informative and complemented each other. In another study involving many thousands of biomedical articles from 2004 to 2008, Boyack and Klavans[61] found that an enhanced form of bibliographic coupling outperformed cocitation and direct citation in identifying clusters of documents at research fronts.

A cocitation map. Fig. 1 is a map of cocited information scientists. It was generated in 2004 by entering the name of a seed author, here Marcia J. Bates, into a web-based system called AuthorMap. This system was developed by a Drexel University team to visualize cocitation data instantly on the fly. At the time, AuthorMap was connected to Social Scisearch on Dialog Classic, and in the first step it retrieved the 24 other authors most highly cocited with the seed. In the second, it put these authors into a 25 × 25 matrix and retrieved the cocitation count of every unique pair. In the third, it used the Pathfinder Network (PFNET) algorithm to draw links reflecting only the *highest* cocitation counts among the 25 authors.

PFNETs are fully connected networks that simplify intellectual structure to its most salient aspects. The numbers above the links in Fig. 1 are cocitation counts. While Bates (lower center) is cocited with everyone in the map, her *highest* cocitation count is with Nicholas Belkin. Similarly, the highest counts for Carol Fenichel, Christine Borgman, Raya Fidel, and Karen Markey are with Bates. The same principle holds throughout the map—for example, the highest count for Amanda Spink (upper right) is not with Bates but with Tefko Saracevic. In this manner, the PFNET algorithm creates groupings that anyone familiar with information science can interpret.

Briefly, the central group around Belkin, which includes Bates and Saracevic, consists of authors associated with "the cognitive turn" in information science, which dates from the late 1970s. This group's goal has

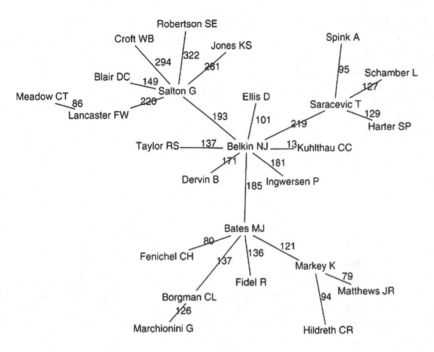

Fig. 1 PFNET of top 25 names in Marcia J. Bates' citation image, with cocitation counts.

been to redirect research emphasis from systems to users, construed both psychologically and sociologically. Belkin, for instance, has explored the effects of ignorance (under the name "anomalous state of knowledge") on attempts to specify information needs to a retrieval system. Saracevic and the authors around him are keen on elucidating the notion of relevance in judging documents. Bates' group often study particular classes of persons (e.g., children, college students, humanities scholars) who seek answers from library catalogs or bibliographic databases in natural settings. The focus is on how users actually behave as they search online and what in system design helps or hinders their progress.

The cognitivists were reacting against the relatively impersonal tradition typified by the authors around Gerard Salton (upper left). Whether experimenting with retrieval from small testbeds of documents or appraising systems such as Medline, the latter group tends to stress algorithms, indexing vocabularies, and quantitative evaluations with formal measures like recall and precision. In their research, people function mainly as judges of system output and remain invisible otherwise.

Note, however, that the relationships of these cocitees are not so much adversarial as complementary. All seek to fill gaps in information retrieval theory and practice. Salton (symbolizing systems) and Belkin (symbolizing users) are here directly linked, and the entire field as mapped is ultimately generated from Bates' name. The cocitation metric and PFNET algorithm pack a great deal of historical information into a comprehensible whole.

Images, identities, and recitation. Fig. 1 is based on the top 25 names in Bates' "citation image." This term is defined in White[27,62] as a rank-ordered list of the authors with whom a seed author is cocited. Citation images are

created by citers in general and give "the field's-eye view" of the seed author as it has developed across multiple publications.

The citers who create a seed's image can themselves be ranked by the number of publications in which they have cocited anything by the seed with anything by others. Given this fact, White[27,62] calls them "citation image-makers."

Just as works and authors can be characterized by the number of citations they have received, they can be characterized by the number of *unique authors* who have cited them. The result is a new way of looking at impact. In the case of a work, do its citations come from many different authors or from relatively few authors who cite it again and again? A work with many different citers would seem to have had greater impact, in the sense that it has attracted more people's attention. Citer counts can thus reveal the intellectual *reach* of a seed author, which mere counts of citations obscure. In studies of American and British L&IS[63] and then of nine fields in the natural and social sciences,[64] Ajiferuke and colleagues used cited authors (rather than works) as seeds and counts of their unique citers as an impact measure. Although citation counts and citer counts were significantly correlated, the rankings of seeds they produce were not identical, and the differences were greater in the social sciences than in the natural sciences.

Another way to study a seed author is to obtain the author's "citation identity." As defined in White,[27] this is not the field's-eye view, but that of the seed author. It is a list of the author's own citees, rank-ordered by frequency of citation over time. As the seed author's publications grow, some names will be cited more than once, and a fraction of these will be cited many times. These

Table 4 Names cited at least 10 times in Margolis's citation identity

Rank No.	Items	Term
1	48	MARGOLIS J
2	28	PUTNAM H
3	28	QUINE WV
4	25	GADAMER HG
5	22	RORTY R
6	20	DAVIDSON D
7	19	KUHN TS
8	18	GOODMAN N
9	16	DERRIDA J
10	15	CHOMSKY N
11	14	FOUCAULT M
12	13	DENNETT DC
13	13	HABERMAS J
14	12	DUMMETT M
15	12	WITTGENSTEIN L
16	11	DANTO AC
17	10	BEARDSLEY MC
18	10	POPPER KR
19	10	STRAWSON PF

```
Rank: S1/1-85  Field: CA=  File(s): 439.(Rank
fields found in 77 records—510 unique terms).
```

heavily *recited* names are compact clues to an author's intellectual history. Almost always, the top name on the list will be the seed author's own: self-citation is ubiquitous in science and scholarship. Self-citation is no more egotistical than bylines are; it is the way in which authors bind their oeuvres into wholes, a task for which they are uniquely qualified.

We have seen that citations connect the philosophers A. C. Danto and Joseph Margolis. Danto's citation identity shows that he cites quite sparsely in his many journal publications. His single citation to Margolis came in response to the "Farewell" article in Table 3. Margolis, whose identity appears in Table 4, is much more prolific in his recitations. Names he cites 10 or more times reveal him to be a generalist of modern philosophy; aesthetics (represented in the identity by, e.g., Goodman, Danto, and Beardsley) is only one of his interests.

Until late 2013, citation images, image-makers, and identities were readily obtainable with the Rank command on the Dialog Classic system.[62] Table 4 was made by forming the set of Margolis's 77 publications in Arts and Humanities Search (File 439) on Dialog and then entering a command that ranked his citees high to low. WoS has some useful modules for analyzing citations, but, unlike Dialog, not for obtaining images, identities, or cocitation counts of any sort. Nor do Scopus, GS, or Microsoft Academic. (The tools named in[8–10] enable bibliometric mappers to extract cocitation counts from downloaded data.)

Historiographs. Eugene Garfield and a programming team have patented a free, web-based tool called HistCite that makes "historiographs" possible.[65] These show networks of citing and cited papers that define a specialty or

that descend from the influential work of a predecessor. Analysts choose the specialty (e.g., Digital Libraries) or the predecessor (e.g., M. M. Kessler) to investigate. The term "historiograph" indicates that the data, drawn from the WoS, can be graphed as a time-ordered cascade of papers whose linkages are pertinent to the history of a line of research. Certain papers stand out in historiographs because they have numerous links to or from other papers, suggesting a high degree of intellectual interest.

Although HistCite has its own graphics module, Fig. 2 is a diagram of HistCite data made with Pajek software. It shows a subset of the network of papers that descend from the original paper on bibliographic coupling.[48] The downward-pointing arrows mean "cited by"—that is, the foundational work, labeled Kessler-MM-1963b, was cited by Garfield-E-1963, which in turn was cited by Garfield-E-1964 and so on. The chain Weinberg-BH-1974, Smith-LC-1981, and Liu-MX-1993 are literature reviews.

HistCite diagrams reveal not only direct citation links between papers but also indirect links—that is, connections through intermediary papers. In Fig. 2, the link between Brooks-TA-1985 and Chakrabarti-S-1999 (lower left) is not direct but runs through Lui-MX-1993 and Savoy-J-1997. Were this a chain of influence in the development of an idea, it might interest intellectual historians. Serious large-scale investigation of such chains will require computerized analysis of the full texts in which citations are embedded, but that is increasingly a possibility.

Long before HistCite, an important early historiograph appeared in a study that Garfield and two ISI colleagues made in 1964 on classic research in genetics. As reproduced in Garfield,[66] the hand-drawn historiograph shows 40 interlinked papers keyed to major events in the development of DNA theory from 1820 to 1962. The baseline for the ISI study was a narrative history of this development, Isaac Asimov's 1963 book *The Genetic Code*. The ISI citation analysis independently corroborated Asimov's conclusions at many points. It also turned up intellectual connections he had missed but that enriched his history.

Through HistCite, existing data on many networks of papers are also freely available on the web. The linked HistCite Guide explains the pertinent variables and the algorithmic mode of visualization. New analyses may be conducted on data downloaded from WoS.

Recently, van Eck and Waltman[67] have introduced another free tool for analyzing and visualizing citation-linked chains of WoS documents. Called CitNetExplorer, it can interrelate papers historically, cluster them by topic, and reveal papers new to the user for retrieval.

Documents by the millions. Klavans and Boyack[68] is a succinct history of attempts to make citation-based subject classifications more accurate. At the same time, it captures the gradual transition to "big data" in the visualization of scientific and scholarly knowledge. Researchers today can map data sets involving millions of documents (e.g.,

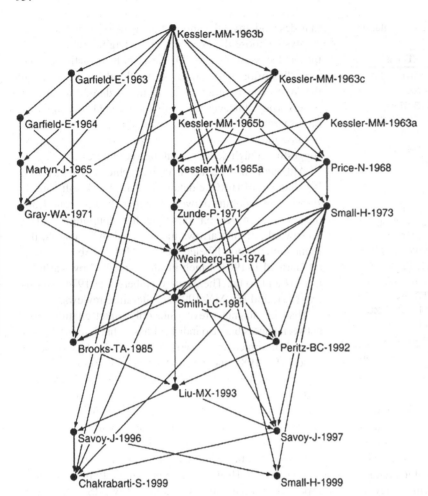

Fig. 2 Histograph of papers descending from Kessler's paper on bibliographic coupling.

Waltman & van Eck[69]). Some of their achievements are on colorful display in two large, handsome atlases by Katy Börner.[70,71] The best-known visualization at present is perhaps Klavans and Boyack's beautiful map of the interconnectivity of all science.[72] Originally drawn from 7.2 million papers in more than 16,000 journals covered by WoS and Scopus during 2001–2005, it has since been extensively updated.[73] It depicts a network in which the nodes represent *groups of journals,* and the links represent intercitation among the groups. Strong intercitation connotes highly shared literatures and thus defines disciplines (e.g., physics) or specialties (e.g., brain research) for color-coding. Weaker intercitation connotes literatures shared *across* fields; fields with considerable sharing (e.g., physics and mathematics) are adjacent in the network, while fields with little or no sharing (e.g., brain research and earth sciences) are apart. The network also serves as a base map against which aspects of particular disciplines or specialties (e.g., funding) may be highlighted and compared.

CONTENT, CONTEXT, AND IMPACT

Can we finally say what citation counts mean? This question has long been debated—especially whether citation

counts can be taken as indicators of quality. That is what the persistent calls for "a theory of citing" are all about.

The root of the problem is that counts treat citations as identical units, when clearly they are not. First, as pointed out in Cronin,[74] counts hide the fact that citations refer to writings at different levels of granularity, from entire oeuvres down through individual works, passages, and sentences to single words and numbers. Second, counts mask the disciplinary provenance, subject matter, and genre of citing works. Third, they also mask the varying functions of citations in context. There are differences between identifying one's theoretical tradition, adopting a method, suggesting background readings, acknowledging a mistake, nailing down a quote, and so on. Fourth, counts may be increased by negative citations that reflect adversely on what is cited. Fifth, counts often merge self-citations with citations to other authors. Sixth, counts fail to discriminate between citations that are essential to a new text and citations that could be dropped from it without loss. Seventh, counts may include citations to works the citers have not even read. Eighth, works that citers typically leave uncited—reference books, popularizations, technical manuals, and the like—cannot accumulate counts and so be recognized. Worse, omissions of this sort may occur with important substantive works—works that *should* be cited. Ninth, counts are unrevealing as to citers' deeper intentions: Are they simply crediting intellectual predecessors? Symbolizing concepts? Marshaling everything relevant to their topic? Showing off their erudition? Summoning authorities to persuade readers of their own credibility? Inflating the citation counts of cronies from whom they expect the same?

This multipronged critique requires that citations be analyzed as to their contexts and content—their implicit as well as explicit meanings. It requires that citations be categorized in various ways and then recounted. In what is called "citation content analysis," researchers extract *explicit* phrases from the text surrounding citations in multiple documents. They are looking for stable meanings that emerge as the phrases pile up.[75] Ding et al.[76] describes techniques that are emerging in this long-standing area of interest, since, in some fields at least, citations mark passages whose rhetorical significance is algorithmically detectable.[77] One possible goal is simply to improve citation indexing, such as giving text-based clues as to *why* writings were cited and at what level of granularity. A more immediate goal is to discover linked knowledge claims in citing documents by extracting phrases from the sentences in which citations are made. Information scientists have begun to use such micro data to automatically summarize individual texts and to produce literature reviews across texts (Small–Elkiss et al.[78–80]).

In another line of inquiry called "citation context analysis," researchers must discover the *implicit* relations between citing and cited texts, such as what citations accomplish and the motives behind them.[77,81] Studies of this sort traditionally require extensive reading and inference by human judges. Two examples: Garfield[17] reproduces an early set of 15 inferred citer motives; among them are crediting related work, identifying methods and equipment, providing background information, and substantiating claims. Another influential work, by Moravcsik and Murugesan,[82] calls for decisions such as whether the cited work is essential to the citer's new argument and whether the citer's attitude toward the cited work is positive or negative. Despite the growth of automated analyses, findings from older, labor-intensive studies like these have not lost their relevance (see, e.g., Baird,[18] White,[77] and Small–Nicolaisen[83–87]). Some conclusions to be drawn from reviews of citation analysis are as follows:

- Relatively few citations are negative, and negation is also judged inconsistently across studies; it comes in many degrees of severity. ("Smith is wrong" is clearly a negative citation, but what about "Smith only partially covers my topic"?) Moreover, the negative citers may themselves be wrong. Even if they are not, to criticize something is by no means necessarily to destroy it. Controversies are frequently worthwhile; indeed they are a major driver of science and scholarship.

- While relatively many citations are indeed "perfunctory,"[82] this does not mean they are useless. They do things like ritualistically invoking a pioneer, providing background reading, or mentioning distantly related work. Their opposites, which Moravcsik and Murugesan[82] call "organic," identify writings to which the new writing is directly indebted. These, too, are numerous. A possible predictor of organically related writings is multiple references to them in the same text.[26,88] Another is an author's relatively heavy recitation of them over time.[27]

- Works may be repeatedly cited because they symbolize concepts.[75] For example, chemists can allude either to "hydrogen scattering factors" or to "Stewart et al." and mean the same thing. Occasionally, a paper comes to stand for more than one concept,[89,90] and full-length books may stand for many.[91] When citations are inconsistent in what they connote—an unpublished study has shown this to be the case for citations to Wittgenstein's *Philosophical Investigations*—citers are referring to different passages or interpreting the same passages differently.

- Self-citations are no less legitimate in function than other kinds.[27,92] If evaluators see self-citations as a problem, existing software can remove them from counts. For some measures (e.g., eigenfactor scores), removal is automatic.

- Authors may sometimes cite items without checking or even reading them. Clerical errors can be traced to the blind copying of flawed secondary sources.[87] More seriously, cited works may be misrepresented as to content.[93] But imperfections like these should not detract from the many millions of citations that function properly.

- The supposed norm in science and scholarship that "all relevant materials should be cited" means that authors should pay known intellectual debts and not suppress contrary evidence. In practice, authors do not take "all relevant materials" literally. If they did, lists of references would be too long for journals to accommodate. For example, no foundational work could ever be, in Merton's sense, incorporated and obliterated. To discredit citation counts, MacRoberts and MacRoberts[94] claim that relevant materials are grossly undercounted, arguing that authors cite only about 30% of them. But this percentage depends wholly on the MacRobertses' own relevance judgments, for which they offer no supporting data. By second-guessing what authors *should* have cited, one can arrive at any percentage whatever.

- Social constructivists, for example, the MacRobertses,[95] assert that the true motive of citers is to borrow prestige for their own texts from big-name authorities and to ingratiate themselves with editors, referees, and colleagues who can return favors. This is a bald form of the "persuasion hypothesis,"[96,97] which holds that authors cite to persuade others to accept their works. Undoubtedly, authors want to be persuasive—how could they not?—and cite others to achieve that goal. But are they trying to manipulate readers underhandedly, or are they simply giving proper credit? The latter view—called "the reward hypothesis"—is associated with Merton and his school of sociologists of science. Where statistical evidence has been gathered, it supports the Mertonians rather than the constructivists.[87,98] In fact, the constructivists rarely present hard evidence; their case is closer to satirical folklore. The most trustworthy critics of citation analysis are those who have actually done it.

The issue, once again, is how seriously to take citation counts as indicators of quality.[99] Cautionary examples include Gregor Mendel, whose now-famous work in genetics was relatively little cited until years after his death, and Arthur Jensen, who is highly cited but whose writings on race and IQ many academics deplore because of their implications for American education. With regard to Mendel, there are indeed cases of delayed recognition in science—van Raan has called them "Sleeping Beauties"[100]—but they are rare. According to Glänzel and Garfield (p. 8),[101] "Nearly all significant research is well cited within the first three to five years of publication." Jensen is a somewhat ironic case in point: his foes quickly and repeatedly attacked his research to keep it from influencing policy-makers. But no one has been swayed simply by his citation rate. As Garfield (p. 652)[102] puts it, with Jensen in mind, "Not all high impact science is great science."

The word *impact*, in both the cognitive and social sense, is the best name for what citation counts measure. Work deemed bad for one reason or another may still have high impact. Conversely, good or even excellent work may have little or no impact, at least for a while. However, cases like Mendel's and Jensen's are exceptional. The trick for interpreters of citation counts is not to lose sight of the norm: high citation impact is frequently correlated with high marks on other scales, such as a favorable peer review[103,104] and receipt of prizes and awards.[99] As citationists themselves point out, counts should be compared only within disciplines and checked against other measures, but they are no less informative for that.

They are in some ways like election results. Delving below vote totals, one finds that voters differ in their affiliations and demographics, that different issues motivate them, that not all are equally well-informed, that ballots contain mistakes, that ballots may be fraudulent, and so on. Nevertheless, vote totals by themselves determine the central fact in all political battles—who wins and who loses. Citation counts, too, can be broken down in many interesting ways, but none is more interesting than what they reveal as aggregates—the current standing of works, authors, journals, and organizations in the battle for attention.

REFERENCES

1. Price, D. de S. Citation measures of hard science, soft science, technology and nonscience. In *Communication among Scientists and Engineers*; Nelson, C.E., Pollock, D. K., Eds.; Heath Lexington Books: Lexington, MA, 1970; 3–22.
2. Wouters, P. The citation culture; PhD dissertation, University of Amsterdam: Amsterdam, the Netherlands, 1999.
3. White, H.D.; McCain, K.W. Bibliometrics. Annu. Rev. Inform. Sci. Technol. **1989**, *24*, 119–186. [Web of Science ®].
4. Börner, K.; Chen, C.; Boyack, K. Visualizing knowledge domains. Annu. Rev. Inform. Sci. Technol. **2003**, *37*, 179–255. [CrossRef], [Web of Science ®].
5. Morris, S.A.; Martens, B.V. Mapping research specialties. Annu. Rev. Inform. Sci. Technol. **2008**, *42*, 213–295. [CrossRef], [Web of Science ®].
6. van Eck, N.J.; Waltman, L. Visualizing bibliometric networks. In *Measuring Scholarly Impact: Methods and Practice*; Ding, Y., Rousseau, R., Wolfram, D., Eds.; Springer: Cham, Switzerland, 2014; 285–320.
7. Harzing, A.W.K. *The Publish or Perish Book: Your Guide to Effective and Responsible Citation Analysis*; Tarma Software Research: Melbourne, Victoria, Australia, 2010.
8. Science of Science (Sci2) Tool Manual; University of Indiana: Bloomington, IN, 2013, http://sci2.wiki.cns.iu.edu/display/SCI2TUTORIAL/Science+of+Science+(Sci2)+Tool+Manual (accessed February 2015).
9. Chen, C. *The CiteSpace Manual*; Drexel University: Philadelphia, PA, 2014. http://cluster.ischool.drexel.edu/~cchen/citespace/CiteSpaceManual.pdf (accessed February 2015).
10. van Eck, J.N.; Waltman, L. *VOSviewer Manual*; University of Leiden: Leiden, the Netherlands, 2013, http://www.vosviewer.com/documentation/Manual_VOSviewer_1.5.4.pdf (accessed February 2015).
11. White, H.D.; Boell, S.K.; Yu, H.; Davis, M.; Wilson, C.S.; Cole, F.T.H. Libcitations: A measure for comparative assessment of book publications in the humanities and social sciences. J. Am. Soc. Inform. Sci. Technol. **2009**, *60* (6), 1083–1096.
12. Zhao, D.; Strotmann, A. *Analysis and Visualization of Citation Networks (Synthesis Lectures on Information Concepts, Retrieval and Services)*; Morgan & Claypool: San Rafael, CA, 2015.
13. McCain, K.W. Bibliometric tools for serials collection management in academic libraries. Adv. Ser. Manag. **1997**, *6*, 105–146.
14. Langridge, D.W. *Subject Analysis: Principles and Procedures*; Bowker-Saur: London, U.K., 1989.
15. McCain, K.W. Obliteration by incorporation. In *Beyond Bibliometrics: Metrics-Based Evaluation of Research*; Cronin, B., Sugimoto, C.R., Eds.; MIT Press: Cambridge, MA, 2014; 129–149.
16. Ioannidis, J.P.A.; Boyack, K.W.; Small, H.; Sorensen, A. A.; Klavans, R. Is your most cited work your best? Nature **2014**, *514* (7524), 561–562, http://www.nature.com/news/bibliometrics-is-your-most-cited-work-your-best-1.16217 (accessed February 2015).

17. Garfield, E. *Citation Indexing: Its Theory and Application in Science, Technology, and Humanities*; Wiley: New York, 1979.

18. Baird, L.M.; Oppenheim, C. Do citations matter? J. Inform. Sci. **1994**, *20* (1), 2–15.

19. Bensman, S.J.; Daughtery, A.; Smolinsky, L.J.; Sage, D.S.; Katz, J.S. Power-law distributions, the h-index, and Google Scholar (GS) citations: A test of their relationship with economics Nobelists, Preprint 2015, http://arxiv.org/ftp/arxiv/papers/1411/1411.0928.pdf (accessed February 2015).

20. Amara, N.; Landry, R. Counting citations in the field of business and management: Why use Google Scholar rather than the Web of Science. Scientometrics **2012**, *93* (3), 553–581.

21. Jacsó, P. Metadata mega mess in Google Scholar. Online Inf. Rev. **2010**, *34* (1), 175–191.

22. Bar-Ilan, J. Which h-index? A comparison of WoS, Scopus and Google Scholar. Scientometrics **2008**, *74* (2), 257–271.

23. Persson, O. All author citations versus first author citations. Scientometrics **2001**, *50* (2), 339–344.

24. Rousseau, R.; Zuccala, A. A classification of author co-citations: Definitions and search strategies. J. Am. Soc. Inform. Sci. Technol. **2004**, *55* (6), 513–529.

25. Zhao, D. Towards all-author co-citation analysis. Inform. Process. Manag. **2006**, *42* (6), 1578–1591.

26. Zhao, D.; Strotmann, A. In-text author citation analysis: Feasibility, benefits, and limitations. J. Am. Soc. Inform. Sci. Technol. **2014**, *65* (11), 2348–2358.

27. White, H.D. Authors as citers over time. J. Am. Soc. Inform. Sci. Technol. **2001**, *52* (2), 87–108. [CrossRef].

28. Leydesdorff, L. Visualization of the citation impact environments of scientific journals: An online mapping exercise. J. Am. Soc. Inform. Sci. Technol. **2007**, *58* (1), 25–38. [CrossRef], [Web of Science ®].

29. Leydesdorff, L. Journal mapping. http://www.leydesdorff.net/software.htm (accessed February 2015).

30. Rehn, C.; Gornitzki, C.; Larsson, A.; Wadsk, D. *Bibliometric Handbook for Karolinska Institutet*; Karolinska Institutet: Stockholm, Sweden, 2014, http://kib.ki.se/sites/default/files/bibliometric_handbook_2014.pdf (accessed February 2015).

31. Rehn, C.; Gornitzki, C.; Wadsk, D.; Larsson, A. *Bibliometric Indicators: Definitions and Usage at Karolinska Institutet*; Karolinska Institutet: Stockholm, Sweden, 2014, http://kib.ki.se/sites/default/files/bildarkiv/Dokument/bibliometric_indicators_2014.pdf (accessed February 2015).

32. Moed, H.F. *Citation Analysis in Research Evaluation*; Springer: Dordrecht, the Netherlands, 2005.

33. Mingers, J.; Leydesdorff, L. A review of theory and practice in scientometrics. Eur. J. Operation. Res. **2015**, *246* (1), 1–19.

34. Waltman, L. A review of the literature on citation impact factors. J. Informet. **2016**, *10* (2), 365–391.

35. Seglen, P.O. Why the impact factor of journals should not be used for evaluating research. BMJ **1997**, *314* (7079), 497, http://www.bmj.com/cgi/content/full/314/7079/497 (accessed February 2015). [CrossRef].

36. McCain, K.W.; Turner, K. Citation context analysis and aging patterns of journal articles in molecular genetics. Scientometrics **1989**, *17* (1–2), 127–163.

37. Jascó, P. Eigenfactor and article influence scores in the Journal Citation Reports. Online Inf. Rev. **2010**, *34* (2), 339–348.

38. Hirsch, J.E. An index to quantify an individual's scientific research output. Proc. Natl. Acad. Sci. **2005**, *102* (46), 16569–16572. [CrossRef], [PubMed], [Web of Science ®].

39. Wildgard, L.; Schneider, J.W.; Larsen, B. A review of the characteristics of 108 author-level bibliometric indicators. Scientometrics **2014**, *101* (1), 125–158.

40. Egghe, L. Theory and practice of the g-index. Scientometrics **2006**, *69* (1), 131–152.

41. van Raan, A.F.J. The use of bibliometric analysis in research performance assessment and monitoring of interdisciplinary scientific developments. Technikfolgen-abschätzung-Theorie und Praxis [Technology assessment-theory and practice] **2003**, *1* (12), 20–29, http://www.tatup-journal.de/english/tatup031_raan03a.php (accessed February 2015).

42. Waltman, L.; van Eck, N.J.; van Leeuwen, T.N.; Visser, M. S.; van Raan, A.F.J. Towards a new crown indicator: An empirical analysis. Scientometrics **2011**, *87* (3), 467–481.

43. Katz, S. The self-similar science system. Res. Policy **1999**, *28* (5), 501–517.

44. Leydesdorff, L. Caveats for the use of citation indicators in research and journal evaluations. J. Am. Soc. Inform. Sci. Technol. **2008**, *59* (2), 278–287.

45. Lundberg, J. Lifting the crown—citation z-score. J. Informet. **2007**, *1* (2), 145–154. [CrossRef], [Web of Science ®].

46. Börner, K.; Sanyal, S.; Vespignani, A. Network science. Annu. Rev. Inform. Sci. Technol. **2007**, *41*, 537–607. [CrossRef], [Web of Science ®].

47. Morris, T.A.; McCain, K.W. The structure of medical informatics journal literature. J. Am. Med. Inform. Assoc. **1998**, *5* (5), 448–466.

48. Kessler, M.M. Bibliographic coupling between scientific papers. Am. Doc. **1963**, *14* (1), 10–25. [CrossRef], [Web of Science ®].

49. Rousseau, R. Bibliographic coupling and co-citation as dual notions. The Janus Faced Scholar: A Festschrift in Honour of Peter, Special volume of the e-zine of the ISSI, 2010, vol. 06-S, 173–183, http://issi-society.org/peteringwersen/pif_online.pdf (accessed February 2015.

50. Liu, S.; Chen, C. The proximity of co-citation. Scientometrics **2012**, *91*, 495–511.

51. Gipp, B.; Beel, J. Citation proximity analysis (CPA): A new approach for identifying related work based on co-citation analysis. Proceedings of the 12th International Conference on Scientometrics and Informetrics, Rio de Janeiro, Brazil, 2009, *2*, 571–575.

52. Callahan, A.; Hockema, S.; Eysenbach, G. Contextual cocitation : Augmenting cocitation analysis and its applications. J. Am. Soc. Inform. Sci. Technol. **2010**, *61* (6), 1130–1143.

53. Small, H. Co-citation in the scientific literature: A new measure of the relationship between two documents. J. Am. Soc. Inform. Sci. **1973**, *24* (4), 265–269. [CrossRef], [Web of Science ®], [CSA].

54. Marshakova, I.V. Document coupling system based on references taken from Science Citation Index [in Russian]. Nauchno-Teknicheskaya Informatsiya **1973**, *2* (6), 3–8.

55. Griffith, B.C.; Small, H.G.; Stonehill, J.A.; Dey, S. The structure of scientific literature, II: Toward a macro- and micro-structure for science. Sci. Stud. **1974**, *4* (4), 339–365.

56. White, H.D.; Griffith, B.C. Author cocitation: A literature measure of intellectual structure. J. Am. Soc. Inform. Sci. **1981**, *32* (3), 163–171. [CrossRef], [Web of Science ®], [CSA].

57. Rosengren, K.E. *Sociological Aspects of the Literary System*; Natur och Kultur: Stockholm, Sweden, 1968.

58. McCain, K.W. Mapping economics through the journal literature—An experiment in journal cocitation analysis. J. Am. Soc. Inform. Sci. **1991**, *42* (4), 290–296. [CrossRef], [Web of Science ®], [CSA].

59. McCain, K.W. Core journal networks and cocitation maps: New bibliometric tools for serials research and management. Libr. Quart. **1991**, *61* (3), 311–336.

60. Zhao, D.; Strotmann, A. Evolution of research activities and intellectual influences in information science 1996–2005: Introducing author bibliographic-coupling analysis. J. Am. Soc. Inform. Sci. **2008**, *59* (13), 2070–2086.

61. Boyack, K.W.; Klavans, R. Co-citation analysis, bibliographic coupling, and direct citation: Which citation approach represents the research front most accurately? J. Am. Soc. Inform. Sci. Technol. **2010**, *61* (12), 2389–2404.

62. White, H.D. Toward ego-centered citation analysis. In *The Web of Knowledge: A Festschrift in Honor of Eugene Garfield*; Cronin, B.; Atkins, H.B., Eds.; Information Today: Medford, NJ, 2000; 475–496.

63. Ajiferuke, I.; Wolfram, D. Citer analysis as a measure of research impact: Library and information science as a case study. Scientometrics **2010**, *83* (3), 623–638.

64. Ajiferuke, I.; Lu, K.; Wolfram, D. A comparison of citer and citation-based measure outcomes for multiple disciplines. J. Am. Soc. Inform. Sci. Technol. **2010**, *61* (10), 2086–2096.

65. Garfield, E.; Pudovkin, A.I.; Istomin, V.S. Why do we need algorithmic historiography? J. Am. Soc. Inform. Sci. Technol. **2003**, *54* (5), 400–412.

66. Garfield, E.; Sher, I.H.; Torpie, R.J. *The Use of Citation Data in Writing the History of Science*; Institute for Scientific Information: Philadelphia, PA, 1964.

67. van Eck, N.J.; Waltman, L. CitNetExplorer: A new software tool for analyzing and visualizing citation networks. J. Informet. **2014**, *8* (4), 802–823.

68. Klavans, R.; Boyack, K. Which type of citation analysis generates the most accurate taxonomy of scientific and technical knowledge? J. Am. Soc. Inform. Sci. Technol. **2017**, *68* (4), 984–998.

69. Waltman, L.; van Eck, N.J. A new methodology for constructing a publication-level classification system of science. J. Am. Soc. Inform. Sci. **2012**, *63* (12), 2378–2392.

70. Börner, K. *Atlas of Science: Visualizing What We Know*; MIT Press: Cambridge, MA; London, England, 2010.

71. Börner, K. *Atlas of Knowledge: Anyone Can Map*; MIT Press: Cambridge, MA; London, England, 2015.

72. Klavans, R.; Boyack, K.W. Maps of science: Forecasting large trends in science. Places & Spaces: Mapping Science 2007, http://scimaps.org/maps/map/maps_of_science_fore_50/detail (accessed February 2015) (Also in [70] p. 171.).

73. Börner, K.; Klavans, R.; Patek, M.; Zoss, A.M.; Biberstine, J.R.; Light, R.P.; Larivière, V.; Boyack, K.W. Design and update of a classification system: The UCSD map of science. PLoS ONE **2012**, *7* (7), e39464 (accessed February 2015).

74. Cronin, B. Tiered citation and measures of document similarity. J. Am. Soc. Inform. Sci. **1994**, *45* (7), 537–538.

75. Small, H. Cited documents as concept symbols. Soc. Stud. Sci. **1978**, *8* (3), 327–340. [Web of Science ®], [CSA].

76. Ding, Y.; Zhang, G.; Chambers, T.; Song, M.; Wang, X.; Zhai, C. Content-based citation analysis: The next generation of citation analysis. J. Am. Soc. Inform. Sci. Technol. **2014**, *65* (9), 1820–1833.

77. White, H.D. Citation analysis and discourse analysis revisited. Appl. Linguist. **2004**, *25* (1), 89–116. [Web of Science ®], [CSA].

78. Small, H. The synthesis of specialty narratives from cocitation clusters. J. Am. Soc. Inform. Sci. **1986**, *37* (3), 97–110.

79. Teufel, S.; Moens, M. Summarizing scientific articles: Experiments with relevance and rhetorical status. Comput. Linguist. **2002**, *28* (4), 409–445.

80. Elkiss, A.; Shen, S.; Fader, A.; Erkan, G.; States, D.; Radev, D. Blind men and elephants: What do citation summaries tell us about a research article? J. Am. Soc. Inform. Sci. Technol. **2008**, *59* (1), 51–62.

81. Case, D.O.; Higgins, G.M. How can I investigate citation behavior? A study of reasons for citing literature in communication. J. Am. Soc. Inform. Sci. **2000**, *51* (7), 635–645.

82. Moravcsik, M.J.; Murugesan, P. Some results on the function and quality of citations. Soc. Stud. Sci. **1975**, *5* (1), 86–92.

83. Small, H. Citation context analysis. Progress in Communication Sciences; Dervin, B.J., Voigt, M.J., Eds.; Ablex: Norwood, NJ, 1982; Vol. 3, 287–310.

84. Liu, M.X. The complexities of citation practice: A review of citation studies. J. Doc. **1993**, *49* (4), 370–408.

85. Wilson, C.S. Informetrics. Annu. Rev. Inform. Sci. Technol. **1999**, *34*, 107–247. [Web of Science ®].

86. Borgman, C.L.; Furner, J. Scholarly communication and bibliometrics. Annu. Rev. Inform. Sci. Technol. **2002**, *36*, 3–72. [Web of Science ®].

87. Nicolaisen, J. Citation analysis. Annu. Rev. Inform. Sci. Technol. **2007**, *41*, 609–641. [CrossRef], [Web of Science ®].

88. Herlach, G. Can retrieval of information from citation indexes be simplified? Multiple mention of a reference as a characteristic of the link between cited and citing article. J. Am. Soc. Inform. Sci. **1978**, *29* (6), 308–310.

89. Cozzens, S.E. Split citation identity: A case study from economics. J. Am. Soc. Inform. Sci. **1982**, *33* (4), 233–236.

90. Small, H. The lives of a scientific paper. In *Selectivity in Information Systems*; Warren, K.S., Ed.; Praeger: New York, 1984; 83–97.

91. McCain, K.W.; Salvucci, L.J. How influential is Brooks' Law? A longitudinal citation context analysis of Frederick Brooks' *The Mythical Man-Month*. J. Inform. Sci **2006**, *32* (3), 277–295.

92. Hyland, K Self-citation and self-reference: Credibility and promotion in academic publication. J. Am. Soc. Inform. Sci. Technol. **2003**, *54* (3), 251–259. [CrossRef].

93. Wright, M.; Armstrong, J.S. Verification of citations: Fawlty towers of knowledge? Interfaces **2008**, *38* (2), 125–139. [CrossRef], [Web of Science ®].

Circulation–College

94. MacRoberts, M.H.; MacRoberts, B.R. Problems of citation analysis: A critical review. J. Am. Soc. Inform. Sci. **1989**, *40* (5), 342–349. [CrossRef], [Web of Science ®].

95. MacRoberts, M.H.; MacRoberts, B.R. Problems of citation analysis. Scientometrics **1996**, *36* (5), 435–444.

96. Gilbert, G.N. Referencing as persuasion. Soc. Stud. Sci. **1977**, *7* (1), 113–122.

97. Cozzens, S.E. What do citations count? The rhetoric-first model. Scientometrics **1989**, *15* (5–6), 437–447. [CrossRef], [Web of Science ®], [CSA].

98. White, H.D. Reward, persuasion, and the Sokal Hoax: A study in citation identities. Scientometrics **2004**, *60* (1), 93–120. [CrossRef], [Web of Science ®].

99. Bornmann, L.; Daniel, H.-D. What do citation counts measure? A review of studies on citing behavior. J. Doc. **2008**, *64* (1), 45–80.

100. van Raan, A.F.J. Sleeping Beauties in science. Scientometrics **2004**, *59* (3), 467–472.

101. Glänzel, W.; Garfield, E. The myth of delayed recognition. The Scientist **2004**, *18* (11), 8–9.

102. Garfield, E. High impact science and the case of Arthur Jensen. Essays of an Information Scientist. In *Essays of an Information Scientist*; ISI Press: Philadelphia, PA, 1978; Vol. 3, 652–662.

103. Rinia, E.J.; van Leeuwen, T.N.; van Vuren, H.G.; van Raan, A.F.J. Comparative analysis of a set of bibliometric indicators and central peer review criteria: Evaluation of condensed matter physics in the Netherlands. Res. Policy **2000**, *27* (1), 95–107.

104. Meho, L.I.; Sonnenwald, D.H. Citation ranking versus peer evaluation of senior faculty research performance: A case study of Kurdish scholarship. J. Am. Soc. Inform. Sci. **2000**, *51* (2), 123–138.

Circulation-College

Citation Indexes and the *Web of Science*

Marie E. McVeigh
JCR and Bibliographic Policy, Thomson Reuters - Scientific, Philadelphia, Pennsylvania, U.S.A.

Abstract
The *Web of Science*, an online database of bibliographic information produced by Thomson Reuters—draws its real value from the scholarly citation index at its core. By indexing the cited references from each paper as a separate part of the bibliographic data, a citation index creates a pathway by which a paper can be linked backward in time to the body of work that preceded it, as well as linked forward in time to its scholarly descendants. This entry provides a brief history of the development of the citation index, its core functionalities, and the way these unique data are provided to users through the *Web of Science*.

INTRODUCTION

In 1997, the Institute for Scientific Information (ISI®, now part of Thomson Reuters) released the *Web of Science*, an online database of bibliographic information. It currently contains records from more than 13,000 journal titles spanning nearly 110 years of published information in the physical, chemical, natural, and applied sciences, all aspects of the social sciences, as well as the leading scholarly publications in arts and humanities. The library and scholarly communities immediately recognized that the hyperlink and search capabilities of the Internet could simplify the retrieval and navigation of scholarly information. The origin of the *Web of Science* and its real power, however, lay in an older and more radical innovation in information—the scholarly citation index. A citation index is a specific type of bibliographic and bibliometric database that has a specific structure and functionality. In this entry, I will outline the fundamental concepts of the citation index as well as describe how the *Web of Science* uses the key insights of citation indexing to offer both simple and powerful tools for the retrieval, navigation, management, and analysis of scholarly literature.

The primary uses of the *Web of Science* center on its structure as a citation index, containing an extensive, selective index of source materials, and an index of cited references. A simple topic or author search will present a user with a set of articles. The record for each article contains a list of the works referenced by the author, giving a look backward in time to important, relevant materials. It also contains a link to works published subsequently that reference the earlier article, giving a look forward in time to how the earlier article was interpreted by the scholarly community. Because citation searching retrieves articles based on relationships created by scholarly authors, it does not require subject vocabulary. It is possible to research an area that has emerging and complex terminology, without having to search on all that vocabulary. Citation searching can also bypass ambiguous terms that are shared among several fields. Finally, the cited reference index, which allows a user to search all references in the database, enables a thorough analysis of citations, even if the cited materials are not part of the source database.

THE REVOLUTIONARY IDEA OF CITATION INDEXING

Among the most fundamental activities in research are collecting and comprehending the current knowledge. Thus the practice of citing prior literature is closely bound to the practice of scholarship itself. For the author, the list of cited references assembles a body of prior works within which the context of the current report can be considered. It is a way to acknowledge the shoulders of the giants on which you stand, either to climb higher, or to identify the point from which you depart. For the reader, pursuing the cited materials is a way to begin a guided exploration of the literature, to deepen understanding of the current work, and to inform the process of intellectual critique that allows the creation of the next scholarly work.

Eugene Garfield realized that the references created in the process of scholarship could construct a unique bridge between the creator of information, the author, and the consumer of information, the reader.[1] Cited references were highly informed connections between scholarly works created by the scholars themselves, that could provide an authoritative statement of relevance. These connections were already available in each article, but could only point backward in time. The key insight underlying the citation index is that, when collected across many papers, cited references can connect an earlier work to many subsequent works, reframing the paper in terms, not of its origin, but of its consequences. If the cited references in a paper are descriptors added by the author, the citations to a

Encyclopedia of Library and Information Sciences, Fourth Edition DOI: 10.1081/E-ELIS4-120044569

paper are descriptors added by later scholars that can indicate the developed meaning of the work.[1,2]

At the time of writing a paper, there is no way for the author to anticipate fully the later development of the ideas or methods contained in his/her current description. By codifying the retrospective sweep of each work, and by linking many later works to the original work they all cite, a citation index creates a pathway by which a paper can be linked forward in time to its descendants. Through this, the community of publishing authors became what Garfield called "an army of indexers" providing information about their own and others' works, and far exceeding the productivity, capacity, and expertise of any group of subject indexers. In a more modern parlance, citing authors are tagging each prior work by relating it to their own paper. Garfield's goal was to create a new method of document collection and indexing that would harness this highly informed tagging to improve information retrieval. His solution was to create a citation index.

WHAT IS A CITATION INDEX?

In its simplest sense, a citation index is a structured list of all the cited references from a defined collection of original source materials[3,4] and organized so that each cited reference can be associated with the article(s) that cite it. A citation index for a single article would thus be a list of cited references and the information about the article in which they appeared. A citation index for a journal would then be a list of all the substantive texts (exclusive of marginalia, advertisement, and similar content), along with the cited references that appeared in these texts.

Immediately, the complexity becomes apparent, as several articles in a journal could cite the important prior work. This shared citation, indicative of a topical relationship among the works, would be visible in the citation index in a way that is difficult to capture by reviewing the reference lists of each article individually.

A true citation index has two aspects—a defined source index and a standardized/unified cited reference index (Fig. 1).

The defined source index is a fully described set of materials from which cited references will be compiled. It can be a list of articles that is collected by subject and timespan, or a list of journals or other materials from which articles are drawn. In all cases, the content must be clearly defined bibliographically and temporally. Without clear definition of the source materials, the meaning of the citations themselves becomes unclear and they are of limited use. Selecting a random set of articles across subjects and across time results in a collection having no clear meaning and very limited utility.

The standardized cited reference index is the set of cited references that appear in the source material. The cited references are not harvested as they are presented in the journal, as journals will vary in the information and format they require for each cited reference. Rather, in the construction of the index, data elements from the references are standardized to allow like citations to be collected, or unified.[5] Citation unification allows all articles that cite the same reference to be collected, thus visualizing the relationship among them that is implied by the reference. The functionality of a true citation index depends on these two interconnected databases and will be discussed in detail below.

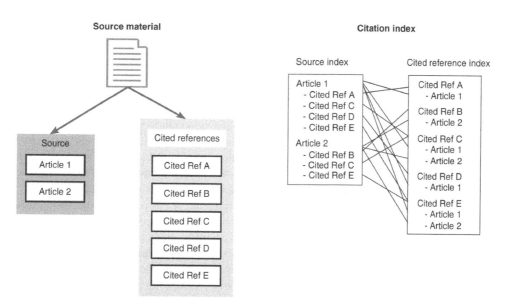

Fig. 1 Creation and structure of a citation index. A citation index is derived from a two-part indexing of source materials. Bibliographic entries are created for each source item; cited references are captured into a separate index where identical references are unified. The resulting two-part structure is the basic architecture of a citation index.

In 1963, the first robust, multidisciplinary implementation of a citation index was published commercially as the *Science Citation Index* (SCI). The first printing used a source index created from 613 scientific, technical, and medical journals and all substantive materials published in those journals in the year 1961. The cited reference index contained more than 1.4 million cited references. The intricate methodology needed to navigate the several print indexes[3] did not prevent information scientists' recognizing the unique utility and great potential of the SCI, not only for retrieving an exhaustive (if exhausting) list of articles relevant to a subject, but also for navigating, mapping, and evaluating the research literature.[2,4,6–9]

THE FUNCTIONS OF CITED REFERENCES IN CITATION INDEXES

The conceptual and practical applications of the scholarly citation index as envisioned by Garfield in the 1950s waited more than 40 years for a technological advance that would radically transform their use. When the maturing Internet met the "hyperlinked, relational database" that underlay the ISI citation indexes, the potential of Garfield's novel concept was finally realized. In 1997, ISI® (now a part of Thomson Reuters) released the first version of the *Web of Science*, containing the *Science Citation Index-Expanded*, the *Social Science Citation Index*, and the *Arts & Humanities Citation Index* in a single interface. When the citation indexes were mounted as a fully searchable, hyperlinked, relational database, the real power of the citation indexes was suddenly very simple to use.

Before describing the *Web of Science* product, it is necessary to describe the key functions of a citation index. A true citation index attaches three functions to cited references as an aspect of the scholarly literature: cited reference capture, cited reference linking, and cited reference searching, each being dependent on the effective implementation of the one prior to it.

Cited Reference Capture

Cited reference capture is the inclusion of the cited references as an aspect of the bibliographic data for each source article in the source index. An increasing number of bibliographic resources, such as databases, aggregators, and institutional or subject-specific archives, provide cited references as part of the data associated with each article. In addition, many publishers, in moving to electronic access to journals, freely provide not only table of contents of issues, but also the abstracts and cited references of articles, making much of this information readily available. The cited references provide additional information about the content of the indexed item in that they sketch the context in which the author is placing his/her work.

Besides this subtlety of indexing or cataloging, the presence of cited references allows a citation index to echo a critical aspect of how researchers interact with the literature when they review the full text: author, title, abstract, and a perusal of the cited references allow a more informed decision about the importance of obtaining the full text for close reading.

Cited Reference Linking

The most basic and most important function of a cited reference is allowing the reader to locate the particular works cited and to expand his/her knowledge of the subject area, as well as, in some sense, to retrace the intellectual or methodological path taken by the author. Cited reference linking was a natural extension of capturing and providing access to cited reference lists. A cited reference is, by its nature, a link to the prior literature, even in a print journal or in the print SCI. In electronic resources, this link can be made literal, functional, and immediately navigable, thereby expanding the role of cited reference capture in online information resources, both bibliographic and full text. The creation of a navigable link to the citing works allows a scholar to view not just the antecedents of a work, but its descendants. Citation linking allows each article to collect a continuously evolving set of user-generated commentary in the form of citation acknowledgment.

Cited reference linking is limited by three things: availability of content, correctness of cited references, and effectiveness of linking methodology.

Cited reference linking is first limited by the content of the resource in which the link exists. If the material being cited is not resident in, or is not available to, the resource, no functional link can be created. Publishers will often provide links to/from only those materials that are also resident on their sites. Bibliographic databases can link from an article record to another article record in their holdings, or suggest a link to an external source. However, the number of links to an article (the citation count) that can be assembled and navigated will be determined by the publication sources from which these citations were captured. If the cited reference was not captured, or the source item is not available, no link can be made. For example, if a specific book is not indexed as a source item, and its cited references are not captured, the book will not appear as a citing item for any record in the database, nor will there be a bibliographic record for the book that can collect all the citations to the book. Because the importance and volume of books in scholarly communication will vary somewhat by subject area, the absence of these links will affect scholarship and bibliometrics in some fields more than others. Scholarly books are less prominent in the physical, biomedical, and applied sciences than in the social sciences or the humanities, but their role in the latter fields can be critical to fully understanding the current research.

Secondly, cited reference linking is limited by the correctness of the bibliographic data in the cited reference itself. Many studies have examined the occurrence of citation errors in the primary literature as well as in citation indexes and speculated about their source.[10–13] The advent of online journals both enabled and, in some ways, complicated cited reference linking. While the online form of a journal can support a live link to cited works, the relatively new and still-evolving bibliographic metadata associated with electronic materials create some confusion among authors as to the correct citation. The familiar data elements of author, source title, volume, page, and year (and possibly other elements) have given way to article numbers, electronic pagination, summary-versus-complete versions of a text, preprint versus published versions, HTML, PDF or print versions, and so on. Some electronic journals eschew volume or issue numbers, pagination or article numbers, leaving authors with a host of numbers they can attach to a reference in an effort to link their reader to a prior work. This leads to an increasing diversity of ways a given work is cited and hinders the creation of links. The Digital Object Identifier (DOI) foundation (http://www.doi.org) offered a solution that seemed simple and powerful, given that it originated in an online publishing environment for the use of online publications. The DOI is a unique and permanent identification of a document. It is associated with the document itself, not its electronic location, so it can be used to create a links to any and all places where the document might reside, such as a journal Web site, an online repository, an author Web site, etc.[14] The advantage of the DOI is that it is machine-readable and designed for an electronic, Web-based navigation. This is also something of a disadvantage in that the DOI is not human-readable. A single character error in a DOI is both fatal and undetectable in the way a similar error in a journal title is not. It is not often that a citation to the *Brutish Medical Journal* would go unnoticed and uncorrected, nor would it usually prevent a reader from seeking out the article in the *British Medical Journal*.

The third and most problematic limitation on cited reference linking has to do with the linking methodology. How robust is the system in overcoming citation errors and in its ability to locate the correct material even when the cited reference provided is incorrect? A reference to an incorrect author, or some error in source, or page, or DOI results in a citation that is not linked to the source item, and so is not visible in the Cited By links on that source item. When cited reference linking is the only way to retrieve citing articles, an incorrect reference is a lost reference.

Cited Reference Searching

Direct search within the cited references is the most powerful (and possibly the least utilized) function of cited references, as it requires a true citation index to be most effective. Often it is assumed that cited reference indexing and cited reference linking are all that is required for a citation index, but there are important differences. A cited reference search operates on the structured, standardized data in the cited reference index, independently of the source index. The separate index of cited references is the critical distinction between a citation index and a bibliographic resource with linked cited references, but lacking a searchable cited reference index. Cited reference searching allows the feature of cited reference capture to break through the limitations of cited reference linking. To find materials that have cited an item in a bibliographic resource that lacks a cited reference index, you can locate the source item and navigate to the linked cited references, but you will have no way to find the items when citation or linking was imperfect. An incorrect citation to this article can only be found if you happen across the misciting article and peruse its reference list and recognize the unlinked, but familiar cited work. This is, ironically, no different from the problem of finding such citing works prior to the creation of the SCI, when even the most rigorous literature review could not identify all citing works.

Further, cited reference searching is a way to overcome the inevitable incompleteness of any individual source index. A citation index, through cited reference search, can collect all materials in the source index that cite a work, even if the work itself is outside the source coverage. For a bibliographic database without cited reference searching, comprehensive coverage is indispensable for citation analysis, as effective analysis is limited to those works that are in the source index. However, no matter how monumental the coverage, it will be insufficient if the item of importance to the searcher is not a source item. No matter how large the source index, cited references can only be collected to other items in the source index. With cited reference searching, the boundary around the coverage is less fixed. The searchable cited references provide pointers to external sources, which are then available to collect and to quantify.

Cited reference searching becomes more critical for scholarship in fields where the complete source materials cannot possibly be covered. In the natural sciences, citations to GenBank or the arXiv preprint server form an important part of the literature. In the social sciences, cited materials can include not just journal articles, books, and conference proceedings, but additionally demographic and census data, government reports, newspapers, and other ephemera, and a complex array of grey literature source materials. Even more problematic is scholarship in the arts and humanities, where materials cited can include original works of art, specific performances, primary and historical works, and a host of multimedia online resources. These works are critical for scholars, and so are critical for scholarly communication, but they usually defy indexing as source materials.

The enabling reach of cited reference searching reveals a logic to the selective development of a source index. Although Garfield meditated on the possibility of achieving H.G. Wells' vision of a "World Brain" of all knowledge,[4] and despite the incomprehensible enormity of the Internet, no perfect, comprehensive, all-inclusive resource is on the immediate horizon. However, repeated works have confirmed Bradford's law that 80% of scholarly references are to 20% of source journals. This logic underlies the selection of source materials for the earliest productions of the *Science Citation Index*, as well as the current expansion of the Thomson Reuters indexes to include journals that publish more nationally and regionally relevant scholarship.[15,16] Knowing that the source literature providing the citations has been studied and selected for both quality and representational breadth provides the user confidence in the value of the citations.

THE *WEB OF SCIENCE* AS A CITATION INDEX

Content

The *Web of Science* has, as its backbone, a suite of citation indexes spanning more than 100 years of published literature in a wide array of subject areas. The *Science Citation Index-Expanded* contains the *Century of Science* back file, and so indexes both source materials and cited references back to the year 1900. The *Social Science Citation Index* currently begins in 1956, but a *Century of Social Science* file back to 1900 is in preparation. The *Arts & Humanities Citation Index* includes materials back to 1975. The source index for these databases includes nearly 41 million items from more than 13,000 titles. The citation index includes 600 million indexed cited references, which resolve to approximately 155 million unified cited references. In the years since its first release, the *Web of Science* has added other data sources to expand the citation index. These include *Index Chemicus* (from 1993 to the present), *Current Chemical Reactions* (with an expanded file back to 1850), and, in fall 2008, the *Conference Proceedings Citation Index* with 10 years of published papers from scientific and scholarly meetings. The content of the *Web of Science* is updated weekly with between 20,000 and 60,000 new source records and up to 1 million cited references.

Source Records and Searching

The *Web of Science* was redesigned in 2007 to allow a deeper integration with the other databases in the *ISI Web of Knowledge* platform. The enhancement retained all the key functionality of the *Web of Science* interface, with improved navigation to the most-used features, additional functionality, and a more streamlined search process. The source index can be searched by topic (a combined search field that includes article title, author keywords, *KeyWords Plus*®, and complete author abstract), article title, author (individual author or collective, corporate, or group author), publication name, year published, address word, language, or indexed document type. The interface allows a simple text string entry, but more experienced searchers can use Boolean logic either within a search field or to combine multiple fields to create intricate and precise searches. The Advanced Search option supports command-line searching that is familiar to many information professionals. Specialized searches for specific chemical structures are enabled using a plug-in. Both General Search and Advanced Search allow the user to limit searches to specific databases and/or time intervals (such as latest week, or 2 weeks, year to date, or just the past 5 years).

Several features in the search page provide assistance and information for users who may be unfamiliar with searching structured data. Search Aids are activated by a link located to the right of the search box when an appropriate field is selected. The Search Aid will provide access to the index terms in that field, collected across the entire database, and will allow users to add precise, specific terms to their search with a click. The Author Finder tool guides the user through a series of search steps to facilitate locating the works of an individual author. Author searching was further enhanced by the addition of the Distinct Author Sets feature, which uses advanced bibliographic analyses across the entire *Web of Science* citation indexes to cluster source items that are likely written by the same author.

Cited Reference Searching

Cited reference searching is a two-step process. Because the very strength of cited reference searching lies in the ability to surface unlinked, imperfect citations or citations to materials not included in the source index, some flexibility in the search terms is important. First, the user enters one or a combination of the following elements: cited author, cited work, and cited year. Understanding that cited references can be presented in various ways (for example, author names with or without a first initial, variations in the abbreviation of the title of the cited work, etc.) suggests the use of truncation and wildcards to retrieve the errant cited references. The user is then presented with a list of records from the cited reference index that match the criteria. Selecting items from that list according to one's understanding of the variations in citation allows a more complete retrieval of citing articles. Finishing the search will then display a list of the citing articles.

For example, R.J. Charlson wrote an influential paper on global warming, published in the journal *Science*.[17] Searching for Cited Author = Charlson and Cited Work = Science retrieves a large number of variants for this search, some of which clearly show errors in cited author, cited volume, or cited page (Fig. 2). To date, 1242 citing articles are linked to this record, but an additional 42 citing articles can only be retrieved using cited reference searching. This is a simple cited reference search, where the goal is to retrieve all items citing a known article. Cited reference searches using author only can be used (with care) to collect all articles citing any of the author's papers. Using Advanced Search (or the Search History page), one can combine that cited reference search with an author search using the Boolean operator NOT. This will give a list of articles citing Charlson's work but for which Charlson was NOT an author, i.e., a count of citing articles that excludes the author's citations to his own work.

Cited reference searching in the print SCI was meticulous work, cycling from the source indexes to the cited reference indexes and back, pulling multiple volumes off the shelf of imposing orange volumes. Although moving this activity into an online environment made it easy, cited reference searching still requires some effort on the part of the user. Clicking a link in the *Web of Science* or in other electronic resources is so easy that it distracts most users from any other method of locating citing articles. Even the most powerful linking methodologies and the most extensive coverage of source materials will have missing links and lost references, blind spots, and gaps. Thorough scholarship still requires a thorough search.

Search Results and Results Navigation

The results list from any search is not a flat list of records, the end point of a search, but a functional list of items that can be a starting point for a greater understanding of the network of literature available. Lists of results may be sorted by latest date (most current records presented first),

Cited Author	Cited work	Cited Year	Cited Volume	Cited Page	# of citing papers	Link to source record
CHARLSON	SCIENCE		255	423	1	
CHARLSON	SCIENCE	1992	255	423	2	
CHARLSON R	SCIENCE	1992	255	6423	1	
CHARLSON RJ	SCIENCE	1992	255		1	
CHARLSON RJ	SCIENCE	1992	255	254	3	
CHARLSON RJ	SCIENCE	1992	255	422	23	
CHARLSON RJ	**SCIENCE**	**1992**	**255**	**423**	**1242**	**View Record**
CHARLSON RJ	SCIENCE	1992	255	424	1	
CHARLSON RJ	SCIENCE	1992	255	425	1	
CHARLSON RJ	SCIENCE	1992	255	2423	1	
CHARLSON RJ	SCIENCE	1992	225	423	2	
CHARLSON RJ	SCIENCE	1992	43	152	3	
CHARLSON RJ	SCIENCE	1992	25	423	1	
CHARLSON RJ	SCIENCE	1992	25	426	3	

Fig. 2 Cited Reference variants. Citation variants for the search Cited Author = Charlson and Cited Work = SCIENCE. A total of 43 cited references for this author and work were retrieved. The 14 references above represent those that are likely to be citations to the same article. The cited reference in bold represents the item where cited reference linking was successful. In these results, 1242 citing articles are linked to this source, representing 96% of the citing articles.

times cited, relevance, first author, source title, or publication year. The sort options facilitate the navigation of large and small results lists, rather like shaking a box of cereal to get the prize to float to the top.

The Refine feature allows the user to manipulate the set of results to eliminate or to focus on records that contain some item of particular interest. Refine will display the count of records within the set of results according to subject area (the index categories, or *Journal Citation Reports* categories), document type, author (from all authors, not just the first author), source title, publication year, institution, language, or country/territory. The various Refine options can be used singly or in combination. For example, using Refine by document type = Review and by publication year = 2007 or 2008 will winnow your results set to display only review articles from the past 2 years.

The Analyze feature uses the same data elements as Refine, but allows the user to characterize the set of retrieved records as a whole entity. While also supporting the same kind of filtering as Refine, this view of the data allows bibliographic analysis of a search set, by displaying not just numbers of records according to the selected field, but the percentage of records in the results set that contain this element (Fig. 3). For example, a search on Topic = "global warming" retrieves 8037 records (as of this writing); analyzing this group by publication year shows the emergence of the specific term in 1975. No other papers using the term appeared until 1981, but fewer than 10 papers per year were published through the remainder of the 1980s. The number increased to 40 papers in 1989, then jumped to 151 in 1990. The term, and presumably, the more general field of the study of climate change had a steady increase in publication activity through the 1990s, and early part of the new millennium. In the year 2007, more than 940 papers using the term were published, a number likely to be equaled or exceeded in the year 2008.

Users can also highlight the institutions, journals, and authors that have made the greatest contribution to the literature. Result sets of up to 100,000 records can be navigated using Refine and Analyze.

The Citation Report creates a rapid overview of several bibliographic analyses for any results set (up to 10,000 records). It includes graphical display of the number of items in each publication year, as well as the number of citations in each year. Basic bibliometric data are created for the set, such as the sum of all times cited, a link to all the citing items (with or without citing articles that are, themselves, part of the results set), the average number of citations per item, as well as the emerging metric, the h-index.[18] It displays the list of results, as well as the citations per year for each (Fig. 4). The analyses in the Citation Report can be printed or e-mailed or the data can be exported as a delimited file.

The Bibliographic Full Record

Although the manipulation and review of large sets of results is an important aspect of information retrieval, the *Web of Science* is first and foremost a database of bibliographic records, connected and navigable by citations. Each record in the *Web of Science* contains all basic bibliographic and Thomson Reuters' indexing metadata, but the record has evolved from its early form as a flat bibliographic entry in the *Science Citation Index* to an information node that is linked to a wide array of internal and external resources (Fig. 5). A simple and powerful use of the Internet enables a user to link directly from the *Web of Science* bibliographic record to the full-text record in journals for which the library holds an electronic subscription. However powerful the bibliographic data, scholars require the full text to fully comprehend and use an article.

Full records also include a link to the captured cited references as well as to the citing articles—through the Times Cited (and Cited By) links. This allows the immediate collection of the citing articles as a results list. There is a deceptiveness to this simple retrieval. The citing articles are obviously related to the work at hand, but they will also be subtly related to one another. For example, an article describing a specific method or technique in biochemistry can be cited by other works in various experimental systems. The citing articles may share no keywords or title words, but their common use of the original technique means that each is likely to add some incremental insight to the method, including caveats or modifications that may be of great use to other, later scientists seeking to replicate or apply the method.

Cited Reference and Cited By links can be enabled even in resources that are not citation indexes. However, *Related Records*®—another feature available on each bibliographic full record—is a higher order function built on the cited reference index itself. *Related Records*® uses a method called bibliographic coupling,[19,20] in which the cited references in the starting document are used to retrieve all other materials that share at least one of those cited references. A citation index is derived from the insight that the list of cited references in each article functions as a set of bibliographic descriptors provided by the author; therefore, if two authors cite several identical references, it suggests that the source items are related. These relationships might not be revealed from standard topic searching, nor are the articles necessarily directly connected by citation linking. Because the cited references are available at the time of indexing, *Related Records*® can be linked long before any later citing papers appear. This allows a record to expand into a broader literature immediately upon indexing while the development of a citing article context is still evolving. Enabling the retrieval of relevant articles through these more subtle relationships was one of the first goals in creating the citation index.[1]

View Records / Exclude Records	Field: Publication Year	Record Count	% of 8037	Bar Chart
□	1975	1	0.0124 %	ı
□	1981	2	0.0249 %	ı
□	1983	2	0.0249 %	ı
□	1984	2	0.0249 %	ı
□	1985	2	0.0249 %	ı
□	1986	5	0.0622 %	ı
□	1987	3	0.0373 %	ı
□	1988	9	0.1120 %	ı
□	1989	40	0.4977 %	ı
□	1990	151	1.8788 %	▮
□	1991	245	3.0484 %	▮
□	1992	264	3.2848 %	▮
□	1993	241	2.9986 %	▮
□	1994	226	2.8120 %	▮
□	1995	258	3.2102 %	▮
□	1996	278	3.4590 %	▮
□	1997	312	3.8820 %	▮
□	1998	332	4.1309 %	▮
□	1999	385	4.7903 %	▮
□	2000	378	4.7032 %	▮
□	2001	449	5.5867 %	▮
□	2002	431	5.3627 %	▮
□	2003	492	6.1217 %	▮
□	2004	550	6.8433 %	▮
□	2005	657	8.1747 %	▮
□	2006	696	8.6599 %	▮
□	2007	948	11.7954 %	▮
□	2008	678	8.4360 %	▮
View Records / Exclude Records	Field: Publication Year	Record Count	% of 8037	Bar Chart

Circulation–College

Fig. 3 Section of the Analyze Results screen. The search Topic = "global warming" retrieved 8037 records; the figure shows the results analyzed by publication year. Selecting a publication year and using View Records filters the results.

In 2008, a long-awaited feature was added—in a beta version—to the full records in *Web of Science*. The Citation Map creates a visual representation of the cited references and/or the citing articles that are connected to the starting record. The feature was recently reviewed by Simboli[21] and will not be discussed in detail here. Visual display of citation relationships is complicated when the number of citation links is very large, and of limited use when the number of citations links is very small. The *Web of Science* dataset is rich, deep and densely linked, and presents challenges to visualization methods that are as large as the potential benefits. Robust visualization can reveal elusive connections among sets of articles, such as many articles in a set of results citing a single item that is, itself, not in the results set. It might also be desirable for some users to navigate through a visual map of the citation space in a field or arrayed around the works

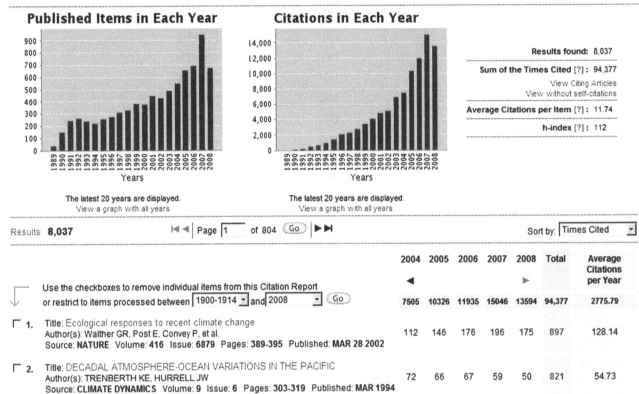

Fig. 4 Section of the Citation Report. Citation Report on the 8037 records retrieved using a topic search for "global warming." The default ranking is in descending order by times cited to allow identification of the h-index core, i.e., the set of articles with a citation count greater than or equal to the value of the h-index. Data from Citation Report can be saved to a delimited file to allow customized analyses.

of an individual author. The irregular density and complexity of the citation network underlying the *Web of Science* makes this an ambitious goal. The Citation Map feature is an initial step, allowing references to be organized, color-coded, and in other ways, made to reveal patterns and trends.

Additional Features and Services

Additional features of the *Web of Science*, while enhancing the access to and manipulation of bibliographic records and data, are less directly related to the fundamental concept of a citation index and will be mentioned only briefly here. Record exporting has been made more accessible through a quick export. This allows users to bypass the Marked List to export records with a minimum, standard set of data elements or with a complete set of tagged data. Users also have access to the Web version of the popular bibliographic management tool, *EndNote* as part of the *ISI Web of Knowledge* platform, allowing them to store a library of references that is accessible via any computer. *ResearcherID* offers a new

way to develop, view, and manage the record of one's own publications, and uses the analytical tools from *Web of Science* to reveal patterns within the collection of articles that cite one's own work. An ever-improving set of customizations, alerts, saved searches, and personal journal lists in the *ISI Web of Knowledge* platform embed the information in the *Web of Science* within the ways scholars use information.

CONCLUSION

The 11 years since the first release of the *Web of Science* have seen sweeping changes in almost every aspect of scientific communication and publishing, as well as in the interrelated fields of library and information sciences, information management, retrieval, and use. As the needs and practices of researchers change, the functionality, content, and interface of the *Web of Science* continue to evolve, but the critical insight and immense usefulness of citation indexing and cited reference searching remain at the very heart of the product.

Ecological responses to recent climate change

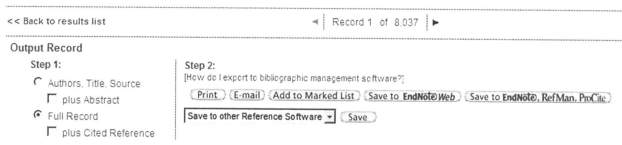

(Full Text)   (Print) (E-mail) (Add to Marked List) (Save to **EndNote Web**) more options

Author(s): Walther GR, Post E, Convey P, Menzel A, Parmesan C, Beebee TJC, Fromentin JM, Hoegh-Guldberg O, Bairlein F

Source: NATURE   **Volume:** 416   **Issue:** 6879   **Pages:** 389-395   **Published:** MAR 28 2002

Times Cited: 897   **References:** 97   [::] Citation Map *beta*

Abstract: There is now ample evidence of the ecological impacts of recent climate change, from polar terrestrial to tropical marine environments. The responses of both flora and fauna span an array of ecosystems and organizational hierarchies, from the species to the community levels. Despite continued uncertainty as to community and ecosystem trajectories under global change, our review exposes a coherent pattern of ecological change across systems. Although we are only at an early stage in the projected trends of global warming, ecological responses to recent climate change are already clearly visible.

Document Type: Review
Language: English

KeyWords Plus: ECOSYSTEM RESPONSE; SOUTHERN-OCEAN; SEA; VARIABILITY; PHENOLOGY; MIGRATION; RED; CONSEQUENCES; DETERMINISM; TEMPERATURE

Reprint Address: Walther, GR (reprint author), Univ Hannover, Inst Geobot, Nienburger Str 17, D-30167 Hannover, Germany
Addresses:
1. Univ Hannover, Inst Geobot, D-30167 Hannover, Germany
2. Penn State Univ, Dept Biol, Mueller Lab 208, University Pk, PA 16802 USA
3. British Antarctic Survey, NERC, Cambridge CB3 0ET, England
4. Tech Univ Munich, Dept Ecol, D-85354 Freising Weihenstephan, Germany
5. Univ Texas, Patterson Labs 141, Austin, TX 78712 USA
6. Univ Sussex, Sch Biol Sci, Brighton BN1 9QG, E Sussex England
7. IFREMER, Ctr Halieut Mediterraneen & Trop, F-34203 Sete, France
8. Univ Queensland, Ctr Marine Studies, St Lucia, Qld 4072 Australia
9. Inst Vogelforsch Vogelwarte Helgoland, D-26386 Wilhelmshaven, Germany

Publisher: NATURE PUBLISHING GROUP, MACMILLAN BUILDING, 4 CRINAN ST, LONDON N1 9XW, ENGLAND

Subject Category: Multidisciplinary Sciences

IDS Number: 534UX

ISSN: 0028-0836

<< Back to results list   ◄ | Record 1 of 8,037 | ►

Output Record

Step 1:
  ○ Authors, Title, Source
    □ plus Abstract
  ● Full Record
    □ plus Cited Reference

Step 2:
[How do I export to bibliographic management software?]

(Print) (E-mail) (Add to Marked List) (Save to **EndNote Web**) (Save to **EndNote**, RefMan, ProCite)

[Save to other Reference Software ▾] (Save)

Fig. 5 Section of a bibliographic full record. An example article full record from the *Web of Science* shows the bibliographic metadata, link to publisher full text, cited references and times cited links, *Related Records*®, and Citation Map features. Quick export and *EndNote Web* export are also visible.

ACKNOWLEDGMENTS

I would like to thank Angela Martello, Maureen Handel, and Lauren Gala for their careful review and helpful comments on the manuscript, and James Pringle and Eugene Garfield for many instructive discussions of citation indexing and bibliometrics. Also I would like to extend my thanks to Marie Cafone-Moss, for her help with preparing graphics.

REFERENCES

1. Garfield, E. Citation indexes for science: A new dimension in documentation through association of ideas. Science **1955**, *122*, 108–111.
2. Margolis, J. Citation indexing and evaluation of scientific papers. Science **1967**, *155*, 1213–1219.
3. Weinstock, M. Citation indexes. In *Encyclopedia of Library and Information Science*; Kent, A., Ed.; Marcel Dekker: New York, 1971; Vol. 5, 16–40.

4. Garfield, E. Science citation index—A new dimension in indexing. Science **1984**, *144*, 649–654.

5. Atkins, H. The ISI® Web of Science—Links and electronic journals. D-Lib Mag. **1999**, *5*(9), doi: 10.1045/september99-atkins.

6. de Solla Price, D.J. Networks of scientific papers. Science **1965**, *149*, 510–515.

7. Garfield, E. Citation indexing for studying science. Nature **1970**, *227*, 669–671.

8. Garfield, E. The concept of citation indexing: A unique and innovative tool for navigating the research literature. **1997**. Available at http://www.garfield.library.upenn.edu/papers/vladivostok.html.

9. Scharnhorst, A.; Thelwall, M. Citation and hyperlink networks. Curr. Sci. **2005**, *89*, 1518–1524.

10. Steel, C.M. Read before you cite. Lancet **1996**, *348*, 144–144.

11. Moed, H.F.; Vriens, M. Possible inaccuracies occurring in citation analysis. J. Inform. Sci. **1989**, *15*, 95–107. doi: 10.1177/016555158901500205.

12. Garfield, E. Journal editors awaken to the impact of citation errors. How we control them at ISI. *Essays of an Information Scientist: Journalology, KeyWords Plus, and Other Essays.* ISI Press: Philadelphia, PA, 1991; 13, 367–375.

13. Simkin, M.V.; Roychowdhury, V.P. Stochastic modeling of citation slips. Scientometrics **2005**, *62*, 367–384.

14. Rosenblatt, B. Enterprise content integration with the digital object identifier: A business case for information publishers. June 2002. doi: 10.1220/whitepaper5. Available at http://dx.doi.org/10.1220/whitepaper5 (accessed August 10, 2008).

15. Testa, J. The Thomson scientific journal selection process. Available at http://scientific.thomsonreuters.com/free/essays/selectionofmaterial/journalselection/ (accessed August 14, 2008).

16. Testa, J. Regional content expansion in web of science: Opening borders to exploration. Available at http://scientific.thomsonreuters.com/free/essays/selectionofmaterial/regionalcontent/ (accessed August 14, 2008).

17. Charlson, R.J. Climate forcing by anthropogenic aerosols. Science **1992**, *255*, 423–430.

18. Hirsch, J.E. An index to quantify an individual's scientific research output. Proc. Natl. Acad. Sci. USA **2005**, *102*, 16569–16572.

19. Kessler, M.M. Bibliographic coupling between scientific papers. Am. Doc. **1963**, *14*, 10–25.

20. Cawkell, T. Web of Science. *Encyclopedia of Library and Information Science*, 2nd Ed.; Drake, M., Ed.; Taylor & Francis: New York, 2003; 2133–3125. doi: 10.1081/E-ELIS-120008892.

21. Simboli, B.D. Web of science's "Citation Mapping" tool. Issues Sci. Technol. Librar. *54.* Available at http://www.istl.org/08-summer/electronic-1.html (accessed August 20, 2008).

Citer Motivations [ELIS Classic]

Terrence Brooks
iSchool, University of Washington, Seattle, Washington, U.S.A.

Abstract
Much informetric research is based on the analysis of the citations that authors make to the publications of other scholars and researchers, whose work they have used in their own articles and books. If such measures are to be useful for understanding scientific recognition and the ways in which scientific results build on earlier work, then an understanding of the motivations of the people doing the citing can be helpful in evaluating the validity of the research based on the citation analysis.

—*ELIS Classic, from 1988*

INTRODUCTION

Citations are one of the hallmarks of scholarly writing. They reside in one text, and point to other texts that the author wants to bring to the attention of his reader. Why would an author want to do that? The study of citer motives begins with this question.

Citations are examples of unobtrusive or nonreactive social science measures.[1] Unobtrusive measures are physical evidences of activity that exist independently of their source: the private act of authorship produces citations that are public objects available for scrutiny and analysis. As with many of these unobtrusive measures, it is difficult to ascertain in any given application what social or psychological construct the citation counts are measuring.

Many people consider citations as positive evidences of scholarly opinions. In this view, heavily cited works enjoy the attention of scholars while uncited works suffer their neglect. This is a naive correlation of citation activity and scholarly opinion. It assumes that there are identifiable citer motives that govern the behavior of scholars. This article surveys attempts to catalog what those citer motives might be.

Citations have prima facie validity because it is plausible to consider them as measures of scholarly eminence, intellectual worth, or subject value. Many of the univariate models of citer motivations surveyed below portray a citation as a signal that the writer was influenced by the material cited. The prima facie validity of citation analysis is reinforced by several credible studies that report correlations among highly cited individuals and other measures of scientific achievement. Both Narin[2] and Myers[3] report strong correlations among frequently cited authors and other independent measures of eminence. Virgo found citation analysis to be a consistent and accurate predictor of important scientific papers; better on the average than the individual scientist's judgment which "is a reasonable conclusion if one considers that citations actually reflect a consensus of a large group of readers as compared to the evaluation of a single individual" (p. 423).[4]

When citations are considered as artifacts of the psychological state of an individual writer, they are less credible. There are many possible motives driving citation behavior that have nothing to do with scholarliness, intellectual worth, or subject value. Self-citation, collusive arrangements among researchers, and even universal condemnation among peers are examples. As Ravetz succinctly put it, "by appropriate nuance of mention, one can under-cite without actually stealing results, or overcite with the effect of inflating the value of the property of a colleague" (p. 257).[5]

There have been two lines of attack on the validity of citation analysis; both involve citer motives. The first is that citer motives have not been studied empirically, and therefore exist only as objects of speculation. Thorne[6] and Bavelas[7] are vociferous critics of citation analysis who follow this tack. Advocates of citation analysis have responded to such criticisms by developing citer motivation models, each with a certain prima facie validity or special application. Many citer motives have been suggested from simple univariate models to complex multivariate taxonomies. These models are reviewed below.

The second line of attack on citation analysis was suggested by Martyn.[8] He speculated that two or more citers may not be targeting the same informational unit in a mutually cited paper. Martyn broadly defined informational units as simple propositions, computer bits, or any other feasible unit. Consequently, linking two authors together based on shared citations may be spurious: each was targeting different informational units in the cited paper. While Martyn intended this caveat to pertain only to bibliographic coupling, he nevertheless added another dimension to the citer motivation problem. It appears to be quite possible that authors perceive cited papers as harboring several information units, and at the same time, they may employ complex motives in targeting those informational units. About a decade later, Small[9] made

Encyclopedia of Library and Information Sciences, Fourth Edition DOI: 10.1081/E-ELIS4-120044756

the contradictory observation that scholars regard cited papers as representing a single concept, which would be only one information unit as defined by Martyn. Furthermore, Small suggested that authors are uniformly motivated when they cite such a paper. He used content analysis to examine the text surrounding individual citations, and found textual regularities suggesting that certain works act as shared symbols. In his view, citations act as symbols of single concepts. This implies that many scholars share the same motives when they cite works that stand for shared symbols in their fields. Both lines of attack on citation analysis are unresolved at this time. As can be seen below, there are many candidate citer motivation taxonomies and the one, or several, most appropriate models have yet to be articulated. The Martyn/Small confrontation is similarly unresolved.

Content analysis[10] has been the major tool used in deducing citer motivations. This approach quantitatively analyzes texts for signs, symbols, or messages. The validity of this approach, and therefore the validity of the resultant citer motivation taxonomies based on content analysis, is premised on a consistent classification procedure: different people should code the text in the same way. Consistent text coding is not easy, and few researchers who categorize citations are as candid as Stigler and Friedland about the pitfalls of using a content analytic approach:

> Usually a citation is easy to classify. . ... Often, however, the classification taxes one's casuistical skill. Consider Hicks's review article on Patinkin, which begins by stating: "The main things I have learned from [the book] are not what the author meant to teach me. ..." It is not complimentary to be told that one did not understand his own message; it is complimentary for an economist to be able to teach Sir John anything–so the passage is classified as neutral. Although these is no ambiguously correct classification, we believe the classification has been fairly consistent. (p. 489)[11]

These comments illustrate several liabilities of the content analytic approach. Stigler and Friedland[11] used a simple univariate citer motivation model with categories of "favorable," "unfavorable," and "neutral." The citation under examination did not easily fit into either "favorable" or "unfavorable," so they compromised and called it "neutral." This suggests that their results may be method bound. Several of the following models used in content analytic experiments also find a disconcertingly high percentage of neutral or perfunctory references. These results probably illustrate the limitations of the citation taxonomies employed. Stigler and Friedland[11] were also struggling with an apparently mixed citation motive since they considered Hicks to be both complimentary and critical simultaneously. Many of the following models fail to recognize that authors may be motivated by a complex psychological state when they cite other works. Finally, it is worth speculating that much enlightenment about these matters might be gained by interviewing authors

themselves about their citation behavior. Historically, however, the approach of content analysis has been favored over any other. Given the problems inherent in a content analytic approach described above, future researchers may be prompted to try other, more fruitful approaches.

UNIVARIATE MODELS OF CITER MOTIVATIONS

A univariate model of citer motivations attempts to represent the psychological state of a citer along one dimension such as favorable-neutral-unfavorable. Many early citer motivation models are of such a simple nature. They can be roughly grouped into categories such as:

SCIENTISTS ALL ACT THE SAME

Price[12] postulated an average conscientiousness, and Martino[13] a scholarly custom of citer motivations. Many people agree with Whitley[14] that scientists cite anything and everything they consider important.

RULES OF BIBLIOGRAPHY

Creager and Harmon[15] suggested that the arduous task of compiling a list of references will tend to inhibit authors from including irrelevant citations. Kaplan[16] felt that some rules of bibliography were passed informally from teacher to student.

NEED FOR CURRENCY

Both Bavelas[7] and Line and Sandison[17] suggested that scholars cite to show an awareness of the important work in their field, or to show up-to-dateness.

In the last decade, a new discipline, the social studies of science, has also produced several citer motivation models. These motives relate to a scientist's need to claim new intellectual territory,[12] to recognize intellectual property rights,[16] or to provide a form of "income" in terms of status.[5] Gilbert[18] considered citations as elements of the rhetoric of argumentation. He portrayed an author as struggling to present his best case to his reader, and as using references as tools of persuasion.

Citations have also aided sociologists and historians of science in tracing the development of intellectual models or paradigms. Fleck[19] described the establishment and transmission of ideas within a scientific community, and categorized the active use of cited material as forming part of the "thought collective" of a group of scientists. The passive use of cited material denoted information less useful in a paradigm. Dolman and Bodewitz[20] used

Fleck's active/passive categories to calibrate how papers have become accepted, or in their jargon, "sedimented." With the passage of time, the increasing number of active-type citations shows that an idea has become sedimented.

MULTIVARIATE MODELS OF CITER MOTIVATIONS

A number of researchers have offered complex multivariate taxonomies of citer motivations. Several have specific subject application.

GARFIELD'S TAXONOMY

Eugene Garfield[21] commented on the difficulty of automatic indexing for several reasons including the many citer motives authors may use. He offered the following list of citer motives.

1. Paying homage to pioneers
2. Giving credit for related work (homage to peers)
3. Identifying methodology, equipment, etc.
4. Providing background reading
5. Correcting one's own work
6. Correcting the work of others
7. Criticizing previous work
8. Substantiating claims
9. Alerting readers to forthcoming work
10. Providing leads to poorly disseminated, poorly indexed, or uncited work
11. Authenticating data and classes of fact–physical constants, etc.
12. Identifying original publications in which an idea or concept was discussed
13. Identifying original publication or other work describing an eponymic concept or term (e.g., Hodgkin's disease, Pareto's law, Friedel-Crafts reaction, etc.)
14. Disclaiming work or ideas of others (negative claims)
15. Disputing priority claims of others (negative homage)

LIPETZ'S CITATION RELATIONSHIPS IN SCIENCE LITERATURE

Ben-Ami Lipetz[22] sought to improve citation indexing by using codes to indicate the precise relationship of the citing work to the cited reference. His model was the legal citation indexes that provide information that a later case affirms, refutes, and so on, an earlier case. The following taxonomy was developed by examining articles in physics.

Group One. Original scientific contribution or intent of citing paper.

1. Description of observed phenomena
2. Data transformation
3. Explanation
4. Hypothesis or theory
5. Calculation from theory
6. Prediction
7. Definition or notation
8. Statement of experimental technique

Group Two. Contribution of citing paper other than original scientific contribution.

9. Review article
10. Bibliography
11. Data cumulation

Group Three. Identity or continuity relationship of citing paper to cited paper.

12. One or more authors in common
13. Same text
14. Abstract or condensation
15. Erratum
16. Continuation
17. Precursor
18. Inclusion

Group Four. Disposition of the scientific contribution of the cited paper in the citing paper.

19. Noted only
20. Distinguished
21. Reviewed or compared
22. Applied
23. Improved or modified
24. Replaced
25. Changed the precision (plus or minus)
26. Changed the scope of applicability (plus or minus)
27. Questioned
28. Affirmed
29. Refuted

HODGES'S TAXONOMY

Theodora Hodges[23] evaluated the potential of citations indexing for bibliographical control, and produced the following elaborate taxonomy. The entries have been abbreviated here; her dissertation provides extensive discussion of each category.

Evidential references: Writings which are cited later in other writings as providing evidence for what those later writings are themselves contending. . ..

Corroborative references: . . . A corroborative reference is to parallel rather than to sequentially related work.

General informational references: References made for the purpose of providing general information cast a very wide net. . . . The apparently dissimilar writings juxtaposed by having referred to the same work or works as general background information may contain a common element. . . .

Specific information references: . . . The class of writings they lead to is neither so wide nor so heterogeneous [as general informational references].

Historical references: . . . From a subset of either general or specific background references. . . .

Documentary references: . . . Those in which the documents referred to are of such specific content in themselves that works citing them are likely to have something in common. . . .

Sibling references: . . . The term "sibling" is attached to references which are to other pieces of the same series of experiments, experiments which should be of interest as a set simply because they were so planned.

Methodological references: Forward links from writing cited in explanation of the methods used are undoubtedly of interest to those working directly on whatever method is cited. . . .

Oppositional references: References which mention opposing explanations for the same observed phenomena as are explained in the citing paper are probably very important links to helpful writings.

Corrective references: There can be no doubt at all that references which point out work which is corrected are important as forward links.

Clarificational references: A clarificational reference helps an author delineate his position: he does not usually in the course of making such a reference, add anything to the exposition of the work he is using.

Logical references: The relationship of a paper to that or those which it cites as logically antecedent to itself is thus very close, so close that a man interested in a paper cannot afford not to know how its implications are further developed. . . .

Expositional references: Most people interested in a given work are concerned with understanding it, and can be expected to find works devoted to furthering the general understanding of that work helpful.

Illustrative references: Illustrative references are seldom of any more than rhetorical importance in the development of the ideas in any one: they serve the same function, though at a more superficial level, as clarificational references.

PERITZ'S SOCIAL SCIENCE TAXONOMY

Bluma Peritz[24] streamlined Hodge's unwieldy taxonomy down to eight categories, and applied it to five social science journals. Peritz also noted how her categories related to those of Hodges's.

Setting the stage for the present study. . .Citations to previous work which leads up to the research questions asked in the present investigation. Hodges calls this group "evidential."

Background information. . .Citations which document basic data. . .or support factual information. . . . Hodges distinguishes between general and specific information but this distinction did not seem to be workable, or relevant, in practice.

Methodological. . .Citations describing some aspect of the methods used. . . .

Comparative. . . Citations to other studies with which the present one is being compared. (Hodges speaks about "corroborative" citations; some of her "oppositional" and "corrective" citations, would also fit into this category.)

Argumental, speculative, hypothetical. . .Citations made in supporting the formulation of new hypotheses and conjectures. . .No such category appears in Hodges's classification.

Documentary. . .Citations which refer to the sources of raw data. . . . This category includes also most of what Hodges calls "sibling" citations. . . .

Historical. . .citations made while retracing the history of the subject. . . .

Casual. . .Citations not directly tied to the issue at hand. . . .

Peritz reported enthusiasm for the content analytic approach. Her comments reflected unintentionally on the Martyn/Small controversy (p. 308).[24]

> The classifying procedure itself is easy to carry out, even without in-depth knowledge of the field; a general understanding of the paper's main message is sufficient. In most cases the text surrounding the citation provides unequivocal clues for its classification.

FROST'S CITATION CLASSIFICATION FOR LITERARY RESEARCH

Carolyn Frost[25] proposed the following taxonomy for literary research. She applied it to a small sample of works in German literature.

A. Documentation of primary sources–references to literary texts, letters, etc.
   1. To support an opinion or factual statement on the specific literary author(s) discussed in the citing work;
   2. To support an opinion outside the central topic of the citing work; or
   3. To support a factual statement outside the central topic of the citing work.

B. Documentation of secondary sources–references to previous scholarship.
1. Independent of approval or disapproval of the citing author.
   a. To acknowledge the pioneering work of other scholars;
   b. To indicate the state of present research, a range of opinions, or prevailing views on a topic; or
   c. To discuss the meaning of a term or refer to a work in which a given term or symbol first appears.
2. Representing the approval of the cited scholar.
   a. To support an opinion of the citing author;
   b. To support a factual statement of the citing author;
   c. To take an idea a step further; or
   d. To acknowledge intellectual indebtedness.
3. Representing the disapproval of the citing author.
   a. To disagree with an opinion of the cited author;
   b. To disagree with a factual statement of the cited scholar; or
   c. By expressing a mixed opinion.
C. Documentation of sources either primary or secondary.
1. To refer to further reading; or
2. To provide bibliographic information on a specific edition.

CITATION CATEGORIES OF MORAVCSIK AND MURUGESAN

This multivariate citer motivation taxonomy was refined by Moravcsik and Murugesan[26] in a series of papers, and represents a model from the social studies of science field.

Conceptual references: If a concept or theory of the cited paper is used directly or indirectly in the citing paper in order to lay foundations to build on it or to contribute to the citing paper, then the citation is a conceptual one.

Operational references: When a concept or theory is referred to as a tool...[or] when it borrows mathematical or physical techniques, results, references, or conclusions from the cited paper.

Organic references:... Those [papers] from which concepts or theories are taken to lay the foundations of the citing paper, or papers from which certain results (including numerical ones) are taken to develop the ideas in the citing paper, or papers which help to better understand certain concepts in the citing paper.

Perfunctory references:...Those [papers] which describe alternative approaches are not utilized in the citing paper...references which are used to indicate the fact that a certain method employed is routine in the literature, and references which merely contribute to the chronological context of the citing paper.

Evolutionary references:... [The paper] provides a concept or theory to build on, or a mathematical technique to use, or results of an analysis which is used in the development of the citing paper, or notation used in the citing paper.

Juxtapositional references: ...[The paper] refers to alternative approaches...[and] refers to other analysis used in the citing paper only to make comparisons, refers to other works which may help to clarify some ideas but do not contribute to the development of the citing paper, or refers to a paper only for references given in the latter.

Confirmative references: A reference is confirmative if the author of the citing paper considers the paper referred to as correct.

Negational references:... The author of the citing paper is not certain about the correctness of the cited paper.

This has been an influential taxonomy. Dolman and Bodewitz[20] compared their active and passive categories to the conceptual and operational categories listed above, and Ruff[27] used the perfunctory and organic categories to analyze papers citing the life work of Istvan Kovacs, a theoretical molecular spectroscopist. It also directly influenced the work of Chubin and Moitra.

CITATION CATEGORIES OF CHUBIN AND MOITRA

This taxonomy also originates in the social studies of science. Chubin and Moitra[28] were unhappy with the high percentage of perfunctory references reported by Moravcsik and Murugesan, and wished to redefine their taxonomy into mutually exclusive categories.

Affirmative Citations

Essential Citations

Basic citations. If the referenced paper is declared central to the reported research....

Subsidiary citations. If a specific method, tool, or mathematical result is not directly connected to the subject of the paper....

Supplementary Citations

Additional citations. When the referenced paper contains an independent supportive observation (idea or finding)....

Perfunctory...Papers referred to as related to the reported research without additional comment.

Negational Citations

Partial...This paper is erroneous in part....

Total...The paper is completely wrong....

VALIDATION OF CITER MOTIVATION MODELS

Little work has been done toward validating the citer motivation taxonomies enumerated above. One reason has been the lack of rationalization of the numerous categories that overlap, or leave gaps, in the multivariate taxonomies. A second reason is that certain taxonomies may be more appropriately applied in certain subject fields than others. Both of these problems present large challenges to future researchers.

Brooks[29] attempted a general rationalization of the citer motivation models presented above with the following categories: currency, negative credit, operational information, persuasiveness, positive credit, reader alert, and social consensus. He interviewed 26 authors who assessed each reference they gave in a recently published paper, and described their motives by using one or more of these scales. Persuasiveness was one of the most popular motives.

In a follow-up study, Brooks[30] explored complex interactions among these seven motives, and found they could be reduced to five: (1) persuasiveness; (2) negative credit; (3) currency, positive credit, and social consensus; (4) reader alert; and (5) operational information. A finer analysis of positive and negative citations showed they were often correlated. In other words, when an author gave a negative reference, he often associated it with a countervailing positive credit, currency, or social consensus reference. Brooks considered this to be empirical evidence of the hypothesis of MacRoberts and MacRoberts[31] that scholars dissemble when giving negative references.

CITATION CONTEXT ANALYSIS

Small's contention that citations are concept symbols is an area of active research interest. There is the possibility that advances in related fields such as rhetoric and semiotics will contribute tools to analyze the conceptual use of citations. Concept analysis has firm philosophical support from the study of science:

> Cognition is the most socially conditioned activity of man, and knowledge is the paramount social creation. The very structure of language presents a compelling philosophy characteristic of that community, and even a single word can represent a complex theory. . .. This social character inherent in the very nature of scientific activity is not without its substantive consequences. Words which formerly were simple terms become slogans; sentences which once were simple statements become calls to battle. This completely alters their socio-cognitive value. They no longer influence the mind through their logical meaning–indeed, they often act against it–but rather they acquire a magical power and exert a mental influence simply by being used. . . . Whenever such a term is found in a scientific text, it is not examined logically, but immediately makes either enemies or friends. (p. 42)[19]

Small[9] found that all of the mostly highly cited papers in chemistry were used uniformly, as based on his content analysis of their textual settings. For example, one of these, the most highly cited paper in all of science:

Lowry, O.H.; Rosebrough, N.J.; Farr, A.L.; and Randall, R.J. Protein Measurement with the Folin phenol reagent, *J. Biol. Chem.* 193: 265, 1951.

was used in all cases to refer to a certain protein determination method. Small concluded that scholars who cite Lowry et al. in their text were placing a commonly understood symbol that other scholars would immediately recognize as the concept of protein determination. In this way scholars share concepts, and use citations to represent those concepts.

Two recent developments have complicated the relationship between a citation and its conceptual use. For example, a citation's conceptual meaning may change with time. Small[32] found a paper that in its early history was symbolic of a unique collagen type. Later, after contradictory evidence emerged, its symbolic function changed to that of a controversial hypothesis. This implies that the conceptual use of a citation may evolve throughout its lifetime. Cozzens[33] introduced a further complication that the same citation can have more than one conceptual meaning at any given time. She found that two different groups of scholars were referring to the same paper–in each case treating the paper as the symbol of one concept–but the groups did not agree as to which symbol the paper represented. She called this phenomenon a split citation identity.

CONCLUSION

This survey has illustrated that to inquire why authors give citations is to pose a complex question that cannot be answered satisfactorily at this time. Univariate models of citer motivations lack credibility, and multivariate models suffer a lack of coordination in scope and purpose. Major future challenges to researchers in this field are to rationalize the multivariate citer motivations taxonomies, and to develop the study of the conceptual use of citations. Advances in both of these areas will probably require the application of social science methodologies other than content analysis.

REFERENCES

1. Webb, E.J.; Campbell, D.T.; Schwartz, R.D. *Nonreactive Measures in the Social Sciences*, Houghton, Mifflin: Boston, MA, 1981.
2. Narin, F. *Evaluative Bibliometrics: The Use of Publication and Citation Analysis in the Evaluation of Scientific Activity*, Computer Horizons: Cherry Hill, NJ, 1976.
3. Myers, C.R. Journal citations and scientific eminence in contemporary psychology. Am. Psychol. **1970**, *25*(11), 1041–1048.
4. Virgo, J.A. A statistical procedure of evaluating the importance of scientific papers. Libr. Quart. **1977**, *47*(4), 415–430.

5. Ravetz, J.R. *Scientific Knowledge and Its Social Problems*, Clarendon Press: London, U.K., 1971.

6. Thorne, F.C. The citation index: Another case of spurious validity. J. Clin. Psychol. **1977**, *23*(4), 1157–1161.

7. Bavelas, J.B. The social psychology of citations. Can. Psychol. Rev. April **1978**, *19*(2), 158–163.

8. Martyn, J. Bibliographic coupling. J. Doc. **1964**, *20*(4), 236.

9. Small, H.G. Cited documents as concept symbols. Soc. Stud. Sci **1978**, *8*(3), 327–340.

10. Weber, R.P. *Basic Content Analysis*, Sage Publications: Beverly Hills, CA, 1985.

11. Stigler, G.J.; Friedland, C. The citation practices of doctorates in economics. J. Polit. Econ. **1975**, *83*(3), 477–507.

12. De Solla Price, D.J. *Little Science, Big Science*, Columbia University Press: New York, 1963.

13. Martino, J.P. Citation indexing for research and development management. IEEE Trans. Eng. Mgt. **1971**, *EM-18* (4), 146–151.

14. Whitley, R.D. Communication nets in science: Status and citation patterns in animal physiology. Sociol. Rev. **1969**, *17*(2), 219–231.

15. Creager, J.A.; Harmon, L. R. *On-the-Job Validating of Selection Variables*, National Academy of Sciences, National Research Council: Washington, DC, 1966.

16. Kaplan, W. The norms of citation behavior: Prolegomena to the footnote. Am. Doc. **1965**, *16*(3), 179–184.

17. Line, M.B.; Sandison, A. 'Obsolescene' and changes in the use of literature with time. J. Doc. **1974**, *30*(3), 283–350.

18. Gilbert, G.N. Referencing as persuasion. Soc. Stud. Sci. **1977**, *7*(1), 113–122.

19. Fleck, L. *Genesis and Development of a Scientific Fact*, University of Chicago Press: Chicago, IL, 1979.

20. Dolman, H.; Bodewitz, H. Sedimentation of a scientific concept: The use of citation data. Soc. Stud. Sci. **1985**, *15*(3), 507–523.

21. Garfield, E. Can, citation indexing be automated?. *Essays of an Information Scientist*; ISI Press: Philadelphia, PA, 1977; vol. 1.

22. Lipetz, B.-A. Improvement of the selectivity of citation indexes to science literature through inclusion of citation relationship indicators. Am. Doc. April **1965**, *16*(2), 81–90.

23. Hodges, T.L. Citation indexing: Its potential for bibiographical control. University of California-Berkeley, Berkeley, CA, 1972, PhD dissertation.

24. Peritz, B.C. A classification of citation roles for the social sciences and related fields. Scientometrics **1983**, *5*(5), 303–312.

25. Frost, C.O. The use of citations in literary research: A preliminary classification of citation functions. Libr. Quart. **1979**, *49*(4), 399–414.

26. Moravcsik, M.J.; Murugesan, P. Citation patterns in scientific revolutions. Scientometrics **1979**, *1*(2), 161–169.

27. Ruff, I. Citation analysis of a scientific career: A case study. Soc. Stud. Sci. **1979**, *9*(1), 81–90.

28. Chubin, D.E.; Moitra, S. D. Content analysis of references: Adjunct or alternative to citation counting?. Soc. Stud. Sci. **1975**, *5*(4), 423–441.

29. Brooks, T.A. Public acts and private objects: An investigation of citer motivation. J. Am. Soc. Inform. Sci. **1985**, *36*(4), 223–229.

30. Brooks, T.A. Evidence of complex citer motivations. J. Am. Soc. Inform. Sci. **1986**, *37* (1), 34–36.

31. MacRoberts, M.H.; MacRoberts, B.R. The negational reference: On the art of dissembling. Soc. Stud. Sci. **1984**, *14*(1), 91–94.

32. Small, H.G. The lives of a scientific paper. In *Selectivity in Information Systems, Survival of the Fittest*; Warren, Kenneth S., Ed.; Praeger: New York, 1985.

33. Cozzens, S.E. Split citation identity: A case study from economics. J. Am. Soc. Inform. Sci. **1982**, *33*(4), 233–236.

Classification Theory

Clare Beghtol
Faculty of Information Studies, University of Toronto, Toronto, Ontario, Canada

Abstract

In the library and information sciences, classification theories are used primarily for knowledge organization, either in a manual or in a machine environment. In this context, classification theories have usually been developed initially as a support for specific knowledge organization classification systems, although the theories and the systems have influenced and re-influenced each other in particular ways throughout their lives. This entry discusses theories for knowledge organization classifications using examples from a number of classification systems, but no one system is discussed at length. Instead, the entry is organized into sections that deal first with classificatory issues in general and then with theories of content, theories of structure, and theories of notation for knowledge organization classifications.

INTRODUCTION

Theories of how knowledge organization classifications should be created, developed, structured, used, and communicated to others underlie the systems themselves. To classify means to put things into meaningful groups. Things can be physical objects, ideas, events, or anything else that human beings can perceive or imagine, and a meaningful group can be formed using any characteristic or combination of characteristics of the things. Groups can be considered to be permanent or they can be considered temporary responses to a need of the moment. These groups of things can then be combined and arranged to make a knowledge organization classification system. A knowledge organization classification is a structured plan that ideally shows all the groups that have been created and their relationship(s) to each other.

GENERAL ISSUES IN CLASSIFICATION

Knowledge organization classification theories and the systems they give rise to are cultural artifacts that directly reflect the cultural concerns and contexts in which they are developed. This cultural dependence means that no knowledge organization theory or system can be useful for every time and in every place because knowledge organization theories and systems for one time and place will be unsuitable or irrelevant for another. For example, different countries have different educational systems, and a knowledge organization classification for education in one country is not helpful for education in another country. The same constraint applies to different times in the same place—education in the nineteenth century was very different from education in the twenty-first century. This cultural component in classifications of all kinds also means that each knowledge organization classification will need adjustments in order to accommodate both new content and also the diverse ways human beings have devised to record and to communicate information and knowledge. For example, the modern phenomenon of electronic information technology has meant, among other things, that the existence of the new tools, the characteristics of electronic retrieval, and the kinds of electronic information objects computers can make available have had to be accommodated by knowledge organization classification theories and systems.

It follows, too, that the study of knowledge organization classification theories and systems is transdisciplinary. Classificatory issues are important intellectual components of every field, and classification literatures can be found in databases and other finding aids for every topic or field of study. For example, classification is an important activity in biology and other scientific fields, statistics and other mathematical areas, sociology and other social science areas, and music and other arts and humanities areas. Numerous publications exist on classificatory issues in every field. For example, Vickery[1] provided Appendix A, "Historical Aspects of the Classification of Science" (pp. 147–180), which includes some representative classifications of science (pp. 174–180). Veltman[2] examined knowledge organization in the visual arts. Douglas and Hull[3] and Ellen and Reason[4] provide essays on a wide variety of classification topics in the social sciences. Classificatory activities in all fields are driven by the theories that are appropriate for that purpose, topic, time, and/or place.

Groups of things can have many different purposes, and a knowledge organization classification may contain groups of things that may not seem intuitively related to each other. For example, suppose we grouped together a painter's easel, a cow, a lunar landing pod, and the map of a journey we plan to take. All those things have "legs," either literally or figuratively. This group could belong in

Encyclopedia of Library and Information Sciences, Fourth Edition DOI: 10.1081/E-ELIS4-120043230

a knowledge organization system the purpose of which was to gather and organize the literal and figurative meanings of words relating to the human body. It would not, however, belong in a knowledge organization classification the purpose of which was to group objects that have been created by human beings because a cow is not a human creation. It follows that creating a group or class for one purpose entails omitting things that do not fit into that class. Classifying thus simultaneously creates two major groups: 1) a group of things that all belong to a particular larger group and 2) another group of things that do not belong to that larger group. Normally, the group of things that are omitted is larger than the group of things that are included because the omitted group includes everything in the world that does not belong in the included group (e.g., the group of all things that do not have legs).

For human beings, classifying is a cognitive imperative; infants begin to group things as soon as they are born. Perhaps the most basic tool we use for grouping is natural language, either spoken or written. A natural language is a language that has evolved over time and that people use in their daily lives. If we say something is a "chair," that word gathers all the things that could be called chairs and omits from that group all the things that could not be called chairs. A number of complications arise from natural language, however. One complication is that words can be used both literally and figuratively as in the example of things with legs given above, and another complication is that each group needs to have a name or a label that describes what belongs in the group. Thus, the problems of language recur throughout all the levels of every classification system.

This discussion implies that one result of creating a knowledge organization classification system is to provide a context in which to understand the intended meaning of a particular word. By saying that a cow belongs to a group of things that have legs helps us to understand which of the possible meanings of the words cow and leg is intended. Other implications are that the relationship(s) of all the things in the knowledge organization classification needs to be shown in some way in the groups and in their names, that the relationship(s) among the groups themselves will need a name, and that the knowledge organization classification itself will need to have an appropriate inclusive name. Knowledge organization systems for the whole world of knowledge are called general or universal knowledge organization systems, and knowledge organization systems for a smaller part of the world of knowledge (e.g., astrophysics) are usually called special classifications.

Traditionally, the groups in a classification system should be "mutually exclusive" and "jointly exhaustive." The criterion of mutual exclusivity applies throughout the classification system. It means: 1) that a certain named thing should occur in only one class and 2) that the class in which the thing occurs should have no overlapping content within itself. The criterion of joint exhaustivity means that each class in the classification system and the entire classification itself should contain all and only those things that are appropriate to the classes and to the entire system. Nothing relevant should be omitted, and nothing irrelevant should be included. Taken together, mutual exclusivity and joint exhaustivity mean that the classification system should contain all and only the appropriate things for each class and for the classification as a whole, and that there should be no overlap of content among the various classes.

These criteria create a number of problems, especially when they are considered in relation to the problems of natural languages. It is probable that no knowledge organization classification system completely meets both criteria. Suppose we have a knowledge organization classification for "physical objects that people have created." One major class in this system might be called Furniture and another major class might be called Vehicles. One of the requirements of the criterion of mutual exclusivity is that only kinds of furniture should be in Furniture and only kinds of vehicles should be in Vehicles. The problem then arises of things people have created that could legitimately belong to either major class. Where should a wheelchair or a baby's stroller be placed? These objects belong in the classification system because they have been created by human beings, but both of them function both as furniture and as vehicles. On the criterion of joint exhaustivity we can also anticipate problems. What will happen when a new kind of furniture or a new kind of vehicle is invented? Before airplanes were invented, we had no name for this kind of vehicle, and it could not have been included in a knowledge organization classification for objects people have created. Yet, as soon as machines that could fly were invented, a knowledge organization classification for things that people have created that did not include these flying machines was immediately out of date. For this reason, knowledge organization classifications need to be updated regularly. The ability to include new things in the appropriate place in a knowledge organization classification is called hospitality.

Organizations

The International Society of Knowledge Organization (ISKO) (http://www.isko.org/) has active chapters in Asia (China and India), Europe (France, Germany, Austria and Switzerland, Italy, Poland, Spain, and the United Kingdom), and North America and South America. International conferences are held every two years, and these conference proceedings are published. ISKO's official quarterly journal is *Knowledge Organization*. The Special Interest Group for Classification Research (SIG/CR) of the American Society for Information Science and Technology (ASIST) holds a yearly workshop during the annual conference of its parent organization (http://www.asis.org/SIG/cr.html). Regional chapters have been formed in the continental United States and Taipei. The proceedings of the yearly workshops are published as *Advances in Classification Research*. These two organizations deal with classificatory activities and debates in all fields and are two of the major sources of information about classificatory issues.

Terminology

In this field, the same term can be used in different ways. For example, the person who creates a classification system is a "classificationist" or a "classifier," but "classifier" can also be used for the person who applies an existing knowledge organization classification. "Classed" or "classified" can be used interchangeably, as in "classed catalog" or "classified catalog." These differences mirror preferences in the culture or discipline of the writer.

"Theory" as used in this field is not testable or replicable in the strict scientific sense. These theories are not subject, for example, to double blind experiments or similar kinds of empirical validation. The theories presented here are not susceptible to statements of truth or falsity. Instead, writers on classification consider a certain theory better or worse, more useful or less useful, than other theories for various reasons. Theories necessarily contain assumptions and discussions about what would be better or worse in a particular situation, and they attempt to establish classificatory principles that will achieve better results than other possible principles would achieve. These issues in relation to classificatory cognition and behavior are discussed in Lange.[5] Often, classification theorists combine their own theories and principles with those of others, either consciously or unconsciously.

"Document" is a generic term for a container of information objects. The container can be in any form or format, for example, in a book, on a Web page, in an architectural drawing, from a piece of music, or in any other way in which people record information and knowledge in order to remember it and to communicate it to others. This inclusive perspective on recorded knowledge allows us to reveal the pervasiveness of classification in human life, language, and culture. It generalizes discussions of theories and issues in knowledge organization classification and other kinds of information work in order to emphasize they are not restricted to one medium of information exchange.

"Warrant" is a term that in this field means the justification and rationale for important types of decisions about a knowledge organization classification theory and the systems to which it gives rise. For example, the cultural dependence of a knowledge organization classification is called its cultural warrant. In the knowledge organization literature, a number of kinds of warrant have been identified, such as literary warrant, user warrant, institutional warrant, and ethical warrant. The different kinds of warrant

individually or in combination seek to provide a consistent theoretical foundation for decision-making about the various elements of a knowledge organization classification.

Scope and Perspective

Given the ubiquity and importance of classificatory activities in human language and interaction, it is important to set out the scope of any discussion of classification theory. This entry deals primarily with bibliographic library knowledge organization classification theories and their assumptions, principles, and elements. Bibliographic library knowledge organization classification theories and systems have been developed for whole documents, not for parts of documents. Historically, these kinds of classifications were developed as knowledge organization classifications for collections of books in libraries and were primarily used for shelving and in some cases for catalog arrangement in specific library catalogs, union catalogs, or bibliographies. The knowledge organization classification theories developed for these purposes were often used as the basis for particular classification systems and were adapted and modified by other theorists for their own purposes. At the same time, other accessing methods, such as indexing (see also Indexing), addressed the content of parts of documents. In cases of both whole and partial document accessing methods, the original theories assumed manual, nonelectronic accessing capabilities. More recently, both bibliographic library knowledge organization classifications and indexing theories and methods are being adapted for electronic purposes in information retrieval applications, both for whole documents and for parts of documents, and other theories are being developed solely for electronic media. Thus, to obtain a complete view of issues of document analysis and access over time, this entry should be read in conjunction with related entries in *ELIS*, including those on specific classificationists and on specific systems (see also the Table of Contents).

Structure of This Entry

After this introduction, the entry is organized in six parts. First, three theoretical planes of work for knowledge organization classification are identified. Next, background and foundations for current knowledge organization theories and systems in the library and information sciences are briefly described. Using the three planes of work previously identified, theories of: 1) how to decide on the appropriate sources for the content of a knowledge organization classification system; 2) how to structure knowledge organization systems; and 3) how and what kind of notations to provide for the systems are discussed. Like all systems of organization, the one adopted for this entry is artificial, the boundaries between the concepts are not rigid, and the issues that arise are not mutually exclusive.

For that reason, a final section bringing together all the theories is provided.

BIBLIOGRAPHIC LIBRARY KNOWLEDGE ORGANIZATION CLASSIFICATION

Three Theoretical Planes of Work

S.R. Ranganathan suggested that classificatory work could be divided into three planes: the idea plane, the verbal plane, and the notational plane. Each of these elements has been theoretically examined and developed extensively in the literature. The idea plane is the conceptual basis for a knowledge organization classification system, including appropriate considerations of its purpose, its warrant, its content and its structure. The idea plane deals with the foundations of knowledge organization and theoretically governs all the decisions that go into the development of a knowledge organization classification.

The verbal plane comprises the words that are used to describe concepts in the schedules of a knowledge organization classification. The verbal plane instantiates the principles of the idea plane and helps to express and demonstrate the relationship(s) between and among concepts in the knowledge organization classification. If the system has an alphabetic index, the verbal plane provides complementary access to the schedules using terms from the schedules and synonyms for them that might be looked up by a user trying to find the place for a topic in the schedules. Two kinds of indexes for this purpose are the relative index, invented by Melvil Dewey, and the chain index, invented by S.R. Ranganathan.

The notational plane requires decisions to be made about the coding that stands for the place of the concepts in the system. Once the sources of content and the structural principles have been chosen for a classification system, a notation is usually provided for helping to identify the order in which documents have been organized by the knowledge organization classification. Notation is a code that stands in place of the name of a class and ideally facilitates use of the classification: 1) by demonstrating the position of the class in the system and 2) by showing the relationship(s) of the class to other classes. A notation is assigned to each class and subclass in the system, and the documents in these classes are then uniquely identified by their separate notations. Notation can be visible to the information seeker, as in a library where users can browse open stacks using the notation to find materials that have the same general topic and that are physically located near each other. Alternatively, notation can be invisible to the information seeker, but still used to organize information for display in an electronic environment (e.g., on a Web page or in an electronic library catalog). A number of different kinds of notation have been developed based on different principles (e.g., expressive, faceted, retroactive),

and the characteristics of each kind are considered when choosing one for a particular classification system.

Background and Foundations

In the library and information sciences, knowledge organization classification theories and the systems that have been based on them have a long history. Usually, Aristotle (384–322 BCE) and Sir Francis Bacon (1561–1626) are credited with being among the historically important figures who have influenced knowledge organization classification theory in library and information sciences fields, but modern authors have more directly shaped the theories and systems we use today. For example, Melvil Dewey (1851–1931), Henry Evelyn Bliss (1870–1955), James Duff Brown (1862–1914), Paul Otlet (1868–1944), Henri La Fontaine (1854–1943), Charles Martel (1869–1945), and Shiyali Ramamrita Ranganathan (1892–1972) have all been influential. In this field, classification is also known as taxonomy or ontology, although with somewhat different meanings (see also Taxonomy and Ontology). In general, the purpose of library and information sciences knowledge organization classification systems is to organize recorded knowledge so that it can be accessed and acquired for use. Two kinds of these knowledge organization systems are usually recognized: general systems for organizing and accessing documents for the whole world of recorded knowledge and special systems for organizing and accessing documents for a particular area of recorded knowledge (e.g., biology or information studies). Knowledge organization classification systems, then, are tools initially for organizing and subsequently for retrieving information and knowledge for any kind of purpose in any kind of information container. Knowledge organization classification theories provide the conceptual bases of the systems and help govern which concepts are included and what principles of organization manifest themselves in the systems.

The foundations of most current knowledge organization classification theories and systems were established in the late nineteenth century. The *Dewey Decimal Classification* (DDC), the *Subject Classification* (SC), the *Universal Decimal Classification* (UDC), and the *Library of Congress Classification* (LCC) as well as less influential systems (e.g., the *Expansive Classification* (EC)) were all initiated before the beginning of the twentieth century. Further, two of the most influential classificationists, Henry Evelyn Bliss, who created the *Bibliographic Classification* (BC), and S.R. Ranganathan, who created the *Colon Classification* (CC), were born and began their education during the nineteenth century. Dates for the first editions of these systems were: DDC, 1876, Melvil Dewey; SC, James Duff Brown, 1908; UDC, Paul Otlet and Henri La Fontaine, 1899; LCC, Charles Martel, 1898; EC, Charles Ammi Cutter, 1891. Later, BC, Henry Evelyn Bliss 1940; CC, S.R. Ranganathan, 1933.

Except for UDC and LCC, each of these systems began as a library classification for open stack libraries where library users were able to browse the shelves, and each, including UDC and LCC, added to the store of knowledge organization classification theories, classificatory devices, and common practices for bibliographic classification systems. The foundation of these systems in nineteenth century thought has greatly influenced their development, but the evolution of these knowledge organization theories and systems has been neither entirely cumulative nor entirely linear. Instead, each has tried to address various theoretical and practical issues that arise in creating, maintaining, and using knowledge organization classification systems, initially in libraries that collected physical objects and now also including venues that collect virtual objects.

Originally, knowledge organization classifications were enumerative and precoordinated. An enumerative classification is one in which all the classes are decided upon in advance and are then arranged in an appropriate overall order. In an enumerative knowledge organization classification, all of the classes and subclasses of the system were enumerated in the printed schedules that ideally showed both the classes themselves and their relationship(s) to other classes. An enumerative knowledge organization classification is difficult to keep up to date because the pace of knowledge creation and change means they must be continually expanded to accommodate new concepts and ideas. At the same time, however, a knowledge organization classification must in addition continue to accommodate concepts that are of historical interest, although not currently considered valid. For example, chemists no longer study alchemy, but the literatures of alchemy from earlier times must still be enumerated in the schedules because scholars continue to study them. Similarly, many of the early knowledge organization classifications have now expanded their frames of reference and are applying their theories and principles to the wider realm of knowledge organization classification as retrieval devices for electronic information objects.

These kinds of systems are also precoordinated. That is, the document is analyzed to determine its "aboutness," the result of that analysis is translated into the notation of the classification system, and document retrieval takes place using the notation for the document. The overall purpose of these systems is to help people find information that they can use for whatever purpose they had in seeking it. In a precoordinated knowledge organization classification, searching must be carried out in the order of the classes in the classification. For example, if we enumerate four classes for cats and give these classes a notation

  Acats
  ABcats—kinds
  ABC cats—kinds—domestic
  ABD cats—kinds—wild

we must then search for wild cats using the notational sequence ABD for cats—kinds—wild, and not a notational sequence AD for cats—wild because the notation AD will have a different meaning. Currently, we have replaced the theory of enumerative classifications with the theory of faceted classifications in which all the classes do not have to be enumerated in detail at the time of the creation of the classification. Similarly, the theory of precoordinated searching has been replaced with post-coordinated searching in which notational elements can be combined at will at the time of the search electronically. Discussions of these evolutionary changes appear throughout this entry.

Theories for the Basis of Knowledge Organization Classification Systems

Three major theories have emerged to describe the best place to start in creating a knowledge organization system: 1) the theory of literary warrant; 2) the theory of scientific and educational consensus; and 3) the theory of phenomenon based knowledge organization classifications. These theories deal with issues of where the sources for the content of a knowledge organization classification should be found. The theories themselves are not mutually exclusive, and elements from more than one theory can be seen in different knowledge organization systems. In addition, it is necessary to remember that the various theories were used to create knowledge organization systems. It is not useful or appropriate to divorce the theories from the knowledge organization classifications they were used to create.

The theory of literary warrant

The theory of literary warrant was developed by English librarian E.W. Hulme in his 1911–1912 essay "Principles of Book Classification." He wrote that the name of a class should rest upon a

> purely literary warrant…. A class heading is warranted only when a literature in book form has been shown to exist, and the test of the validity of a heading is the degree of accuracy with which it describes the area of subject-matter common to the class.[6]

Here, Hulme implied that we need to classify existing books, not the more numerous potential books that could be written. In this, he relied on his view that putting things (books) in groups (classes) does not imply anything about how these groups should be arranged. He rejected the idea that the arrangement of the groups should be based on philosophical theories about the order of nature or the order of science. Instead, for Hulme, the purpose of book arrangements was to expedite locating the literature of interest, and the arrangement of groups of books should be based on the contemporaneous common understanding of where books could be found. Classification in Hulme's view was not designed to educate library users, but to help them find books that they wanted to read.

Two conclusions followed from these views. First, Hulme suggested that each library would probably need its own classification system, just as each library had its own collection of holdings. The holdings in a particular library reflected the needs and interests of its users, who presumably supported the collection policies of the library, and their needs and interests should, therefore, drive the arrangement of the groups of books, both on the shelf and in the catalog. To Hulme, then, debates about classification did not entail debates about whether or not a classified arrangement was better or worse than an alphabetical one. By divorcing ideas about which groups to form from ideas about which arrangement of the groups to use, Hulme rejected theories of knowledge organization classification that relied upon philosophical or scientific theories about how knowledge should be arranged. Instead, Hulme espoused basing the knowledge organization classification upon the actual books the library had acquired or was likely to acquire in the future.

Second, Hulme demonstrated that, by examining the actual number of documents that were produced during different eras, we would be able to follow changes that had taken place in the development of what he called "civilization." The number of documents in each group would, Hulme believed, show the extent of the literature that existed in that knowledge area in that time and in that place, and, in consequence, show what people in that era were interested in. For example, using statistics of patented inventions and their applications in England between 1449 and 1921, he charted the course of the Industrial Revolution.[7] This kind of statistical method of using bibliographic output as a way to understanding an age was the beginning of the development of what is now called bibliometrics.[8]

Hulme's ideas were confined to classification of books in libraries because at the time he wrote books were the most prevalent library collections. Subsequently, a number of different kinds of warrant have been identified (e.g., terminological warrant, institutional warrant, user warrant, cultural warrant), and the theory of literary warrant has been extended to include these different warrants as foundations for grouping documents by means of knowledge organization classification systems. Similarly, during the twentieth century, libraries collected many kinds of documents other than books, and the theory of literary warrant was expanded to include those other kinds of documents (e.g., video recordings, music recordings, journals, research reports).

It is usually thought that development of LCC was based on the idea of literary warrant, even though Hulme did not publish his "Principles" until after the beginning of LCC in 1898. Nevertheless, the idea that the rationale for a knowledge organization classification system resides chiefly in the content of the materials it seeks to describe is still an influential and useful theory. Regardless of any other rationale that is put forward, a warrant in what is being classified is fundamental. Clearly, if the purpose of the knowledge organization classification is to organize architectural drawings, the characteristics of the architectural drawings to be classified must be taken into account. In that case, the system would be based on "architectural drawing warrant." Further, it is clear that any system can have more than one warrant. All classification systems are embedded in cultural warrant and they can each have other kinds of warrants too.[9,10]

The theory of scientific and educational consensus

The theory of scientific and educational consensus was put forward by H.E. Bliss initially in a 1910 essay "A Modern Classification for Libraries with Simple Notation, Mnemonics and Alternatives" and later in *The Organization of Knowledge and The System of the Sciences* (1929) and in *The Organization of Knowledge and the Subject-Approach to Books* (1933). He also summarized his ideas briefly in an essay "The System of the Sciences and the Organization of Knowledge" (1935).[11–14] Bliss' idea was that a classification system should be based primarily on what he called the "scientific and educational consensus." He maintained that bibliographic knowledge organization classifications

> should be organized in consistency with the *scientific and educational consensus*, which is *relatively stable* and tends to become more so as theory and system become more definitely established in general and increasingly in detail[15]

To Bliss, the term "science," which is derived from the Latin "scientia," meant "knowledge in general." He believed that, over time, human beings would grow toward increasing agreement about the answers to fundamental questions that were asked not only in science but also in every other area of human enquiry (e.g., religion, aesthetics, and sociology). Further, he believed that this increasing consensus was mirrored in the way educational institutions organized themselves to pass recorded knowledge to future generations efficiently and effectively. The implication of the consensus idea was that classification systems for knowledge organization should be based on the consensual foundations that knowledgeable people used to organize their own studies and those of the educational institutions they established. Bliss gleaned and justified his ideas through his extensive and widely admired scholarly and theoretical studies of the philosophy of science,[16] and he summarized his conclusions in five synoptic tables that showed the correspondences between The Order of Nature, The Developmental Order of Knowledge, The Pedagogic Order, Logical Order, and [Order] by Speciality.[17]

According to Bliss, only this consensual kind of knowledge organization classification would be appropriate for libraries because they collected materials that people would require for their studies in every area. He believed that expert advice on this consensus would assist the classificationist in developing an appropriate way of classifying every area of recorded knowledge, but he also understood that consensus was not yet complete. For that reason, he believed that a knowledge organization classification should provide alternative placements for topics about which there was still some level of disagreement or for libraries that needed to collect a particular group of documents in one place rather than scattering them throughout the classification. Bliss believed that alternative locations of topics within a knowledge organization classification were necessary in order to provide for the variety of purposes and interests that library patrons brought to their researches The correlation of these views with the theory of scientific and educational consensus required that another principle, that of maximal efficiency, be added to the theory of consensus. Maximal efficiency meant that a knowledge organization classification should be designed so that both those who agreed with the common consensus and those who did not would find their views and/or purposes reflected in the schedules of the classification, depending on the library that was using the system. In turn, the search for maximal efficiency required two other principles to be established, those of subordination and collocation.[18] These two structural principles are discussed below in the section on theories of structure for knowledge organization classification.

Bliss' contribution to theories of knowledge organization classification was highly influential for later theorists, but the first edition of his BC was not widely used or particularly well-regarded in the United States. Nevertheless, BC was the basis for the second edition (BC2) which is now considered the most theoretically advanced knowledge organization classification. Bliss' work has been related to the later work of Ranganathan on facet theory and facet analysis,[19] and his various principles can also be usefully compared and contrasted with Ranganathan's Five Laws of Library Science (see also S.R. Ranganathan).

The theory of phenomenon-based knowledge organization

The theories of literary warrant and consensus were recognized as important and potentially influential when they were first enunciated, but phenomenon-based knowledge organization classification was little known when it was first developed and is only now gaining some prominence. Literary warrant and consensus both implied that the world

of recorded knowledge should be initially subdivided roughly on the prevailing academic disciplines, which are also sometimes called "forms" of knowledge (e.g., science, humanities, and social sciences). DDC, UDC, LCC, and BC first subdivided the world of knowledge along those lines, but the theory of phenomenon-based classification did not require an initial subdivision by academic disciplines or by the forms of knowledge.

The theory of phenomenon-based knowledge organization classification was enunciated and attempted by James Duff Brown, who developed what he called a "one-place" classification system in SC. Brown initially subdivided SC into five main groups: generalia, matter and force, life, mind, and record. The subdivisions of these main classes correspond somewhat to the forms of knowledge as instantiated in the academic disciplines, but Brown believed

> there is not the slightest difficulty in working out a complete scheme from any basis, nor does it matter much into what main divisions specific subjects are put, provided always they are kept together on the shelves.[20]

He did not, then, subscribe whole-heartedly to either the theory of literary warrant or to the theory of consensus. Instead, Brown believed that literature on "concrete" subjects (which he did not define) should be kept together on the shelves so that library patrons could find materials of interest at the same place. Using the example of the Rose, he wrote that the Rose could be treated from many different standpoints such as

> Biological, Botanical, Horticultural, Historical, Geographic, Ethical, Decorative, Legal, Emblematical, Bibliographical, Poetical, Musical, Sociological, and so on to any extent.[21]

In SC, Rose would be at one place in the classification, qualified by these various standpoints from which the subject Rose could be viewed. In that way, people interested in all aspects of the Rose would find all the literature on the Rose together because, using the special devices of SC's notation, all the books on the Rose would be gathered together on the shelves. Brown thus provided the theoretical rationale and a practical example for discussion of phenomenon-based knowledge organization classification. SC was used in the Clerkenwell Public Library in North London where Brown was chief librarian and was regarded as particularly suitable for public libraries in Great Britain.

The phenomenon basis for classification has not been widely accepted, and no completely phenomenon-based scheme has been tried. Special "phenomenon classes," however, have been included in two modern classification systems, the Broad System of Ordering (BSO) and BC2. In these two knowledge organization classifications, the phenomenon class acts as a place where grouping on the basis of some phenomenon can occur if desired. That is, all the materials that can be said to focus on one phenomenon can be gathered together, even though these materials would normally be scattered throughout the classification. All materials on "logic," for example, can be brought together in one place in the classification instead of being scattered in various disciplines such as philosophy, computer science, and mathematics. If desired, more than one phenomenon class can be established for any particular collection of documents.

The idea of basing knowledge organization classifications on phenomena is considered to be particularly useful in developing systems that can deal effectively with multidisciplinary and/or multi-format documents because the phenomenon idea corresponds to a similar trend in educational institutions, where departments are now often organized on the basis of a phenomenon (e.g., information studies, women's studies, Canadian studies). Langridge believes, however, that "primary division by phenomena is not possible throughout a general scheme,"[22] even though it has not been tried. One problem is that no accepted definition of "phenomenon" exists for use in knowledge organization classification. Clearly, if one intends the word to be taken in a sense broad enough to be useful, then academic disciplines, forms, and formats must also be considered to be phenomena. If only material phenomena (e.g., the Rose) are considered, however, the Langridge's assertion seems correct. Nevertheless, the phenomenon idea may take its place in classification theory along with literary warrant and consensus as one possible basis for the content of a classification system. Phenomenon-based groupings within classification systems founded on literary warrant and/or consensus demonstrate that a single classification system can effectively use more than one principle of grouping in the same system.

The relationships among these three theories for the sources of content for a knowledge organization classification are relatively complex. Literary warrant uses the topic of documents as the basis for developing a knowledge organization classification. Consensus, likewise, considers the topics of documents, but then extends the idea of literary warrant to include the position the authors take about these topics. It posits that authors will increasingly adopt the same point of view toward the topics. Clearly, too, the idea of consensus implies that many documents will be created based on consensual ideas. It follows that more and more documents will presumably be published validating this consensus. The idea of basing at least part of a system on a phenomenon of particular interest in a particular library includes not only the content of the documents themselves, their authors, and their topics, but also extends these other two theories to include the needs of the users of libraries that may have important special collections that should be kept together.

Three Types of Structure for Knowledge Organization Classification Systems

We have concentrated on theories relating to the content of a knowledge organization classification. Like natural language, however, knowledge organization classifications have a structure by which the content is organized. The most common structure for classification systems is a hierarchical arrangement with classes and their various levels of subclasses. Another structural principle for classification systems is faceted subdivision, which was introduced into library classification by S.R. Ranganathan in the first edition of CC in 1933. More recently, the biological theory of integrative levels was investigated by the British Classification Research Group (CRG) for structuring a knowledge organization classification. The CRG's work was not successful, but the Italian Chapter of ISKO has begun investigating the theory of integrative levels more fully.

Hierarchical structure

No one definition of hierarchy is commonly accepted, but all definitions include the notion of different levels of a thing.[23] That is, one level in a hierarchy is subdivided to create lower levels, and different kinds of levels are given names to distinguish them from each other and to show their relationships. For example, in the hierarchical downward sequence

Mammals

Mammals—Cats

Mammals—Cats—Domestic cats

Cats is subordinate to Mammals and superordinate to Domestic cats. These hierarchical vertically linked concepts are called chains. If Cats were subdivided into Domestic cats and Wild cats, those two subordinate classes of cats are considered to be coordinate with each other.

Such horizontally related coordinate classes are called arrays.

These technical terms apply to the same concepts in different relationships to each other. In the chain

Mammals

  Cats

    Domestic cats

      Angora cats

Domestic cats is subordinate to Cats and superordinate to Angora cats. In addition, subdivision of hierarchies can be based on equally valid but conceptually quite different principles. For example,

Mammals

  Cats

    Domestic cats

is subdivided by kind, that is, cats are a kind of mammal, and domestic cats are a kind of cat. Equally, however, mammals could be subdivided by preferred foods, for example,

Mammals
    Carnivores
        Cats
or
  Mammals
     Herbivores
       Cows

Similarly, things can be subdivided by function, by materials, by time, by place, or by a multitude of other characteristics of division. A characteristic of division is the concept used to create the subdivisions of a group. Clearly, the first subdivision of the whole class will have an influential effect on subsequent choices. In our example of subdivisions of mammals, the first subdivision (whether by kind or by choice of food) governs the kinds of subdivisions that can appropriately come lower in the hierarchy. The choice of subdivision principles depends on the overall purpose of the knowledge organization classification system and on the content appropriate to each class.

The idea of hierarchical levels is apparently present in all cultures,[24] and until the work of S.R. Ranganathan beginning in the 1920s, classification systems for knowledge organization were all hierarchically structured. That kind of structure was not questioned. For example, Melvil Dewey assumed a hierarchical structure and developed his classification system in such a way that the structure was more important than the content. He wrote

> In all the work, philosophical theory and accuracy have been made to yield to practical usefulness. The impossibility of making a satisfactory classification of all knowledge…has been appreciated from the beginning, and nothing of the kind attempted. Theoretical harmony and exactness has been repeatedly sacrificed to the practical requirements of the library… Theoretically, the division of every subject into just [ten] heads is absurd.[25]

In this passage, Dewey asserts that the structure of DDC is absurd because subdivision of every class and subclass into tens cannot be justified on any theoretical basis, but the structure is nevertheless more important than its content because it improved library practice. He advocated and adopted this kind of decimal subdivision because it was practical and he ignored issues of theoretical elegance or accuracy. Dewey's position on this issue is very strong—not even inaccurate names for content should stand in the way of the practicality of the structure of his classification system for arranging books on shelves and surrogate records for these books in catalogs.

Various criteria have been developed for the hierarchies of knowledge organization classification systems. In the principle of maximal efficiency, Bliss, for example, provided two similar criteria, "gradation in speciality" and "subordination." Gradation in speciality meant that basic classes, particularly in the sciences, should lead to their derivatives. For example, chemistry should lead to chemical technology. Subordination meant that special subjects should be subordinate to general subjects. For example, Platonic philosophy should be subordinate to philosophy in general. In addition, writers usually mention that subdivision in a hierarchy should be well-modulated and big leaps in subordination should be avoided. For example, mammals should not jump down suddenly from mammals in general to Angora kittens with no intervening hierarchical steps. In general, these criteria are applied to knowledge organization classifications in which the schedules of the system were printed and established in the hierarchical order required by the creator of the system. These kinds of systems are enumerative and precoordinated knowledge organization classification systems, as discussed above.

Facet structure

A facet is a group formed by the consistent application of only one characteristic of division at a time. Ideally, a facet contains all the terms that could reasonably be used when we want to subdivide by a certain characteristic. Each element in a facet is called a focus (plural foci). For example, in subdividing furniture by the materials facet, we might include wood, plastic, and metal, but not cobwebs, which cannot be a focus of the materials facet for Furniture because cobwebs are not used to make furniture. Similarly, in subdividing Furniture by kinds, we might include tables, chairs, lamps, and beds, but not automobiles because automobiles are not a kind of furniture. If we want to subdivide more deeply to another hierarchical level, we can use a subfacet of the original facet. For example, if Furniture is subdivided by kind to produce Chairs, Chairs can also be subdivided by kind to produce a list of kinds of chairs (e.g., dining room chair, kitchen chair, rocking chair, armchair, and lounge chair) or by material to produce a list of all the materials chairs are commonly made of (e.g., metal, plastic, wood). In contrast, we would not subdivide furniture into such groups as "metal chairs" or "plastic lamps" because more than one characteristic of division is operating at each level.

S.R. Ranganathan, who began his career as a mathematician, became university librarian at the University of Madras in India, and was subsequently sent to England to study library science in 1924. While he was in London, he began to develop the idea of faceted structures for knowledge organization classification. He postulated that there were five fundamental categories that could be used to state notationally the content of documents, both books, and other kinds of texts like journal entries. The five fundamental categories were assumed to be personality, matter, energy, space, and time. These five facets were established in his famous "facet formula" PMEST. The

Personality facet was the basic idea, entity, or concept of the document. The Matter facet dealt with the substances, properties, or materials involved. The Energy facet was the processes, operations, or activities involved. The Space facet included nations, geographic features, etc., as appropriate. The Time facet included periods, dates, seasons, etc., as appropriate. The issues raised by these five facets have generated considerable discussion in the literatures of the library and information sciences. It is important to note that the five fundamental categories were postulated, that is, not proven.

Ranganathan's principles of analytico-synthetic classification were supported by these five fundamental categories. In analytico-synthetic classification, unlike enumerative classification, the content of a document was to be analyzed into separate concepts that each was assumed to belong to one of the five fundamental categories. These individual concepts would then be given the appropriate notational element, and these notational elements were then synthesized into a notational statement that expressed the subject of the document. In general, the schedules of an analytico-synthetic knowledge organization classification are much shorter than the schedules of an enumerative classification because all possible combinations of notation do not have to be enumerated and listed in the schedules. On the journey back to India in 1925, Ranganathan began work on the CC, which was first published in 1933.

The theory of facet analysis was primarily a theory of structure for creating a notational statement by combining separate notational elements that, when joined together, would express the subjects of documents. The facet structure is often discussed, however, as if it were the opposite of hierarchical structure. Faceted knowledge organization classification can include hierarchical structures such as hierarchical levels of sub-facets, and the two kinds of structure are not mutually exclusive. A faceted knowledge organization classification is, however, fundamentally unlike an enumerative structure because a faceted structure does not require all possible combinations to be established in the classification schedules. Instead, a faceted classification establishes facets and their foci and then allows notational combinations from the facets and foci to be formed in order to state the subject of a document. It is also sometimes stated that faceted classification shows the relationships between the elements present in a document and stated in a notation. This assertion is invalid because the five fundamental categories do not stand in a constant relationship with each other within different documents. For example, if we have two documents about "the influence of the moon on the tides," one may emphasize the phenomenon of gravitational force (Energy facet) and the other may emphasize the tidal response (Materials facet) to gravitational force. In this case, the notation for both documents will be the same, but the content of the documents is quite different.

Ranganathan's contribution was to apply the principles of mathematical set theory to concepts as a way of making a classificatory structure predictable, rational, and economical. Like the other knowledge organization classifications we have discussed, CC had main classes based on academic disciplines as the forms of knowledge. In CC, these were called basic classes. Each basic class had a standard facet formula for its own content that was a variation on the PMEST formula. In addition, it became clear that documents often contained more than five conceptual elements that corresponded exactly to the five fundamental facets. For this reason, Ranganathan extended the facet formula in practice in such a way that more than one occurrence of various facets could be used in what were called rounds and levels of notation.

Ranganathan's basic ideas were brought to Great Britain in 1951 in a textbook called *The Fundamentals of Library Classification* by B.I. Palmer and A.J. Wells.[26] Before that publication, Ranganathan's ideas were known in Great Britain, but his explanations of technical terms were considered obscure. For example, Ranganathan did not use the term "facet" in the present meaning of the term until the third edition of CC in 1950. Before that, Ranganathan used the terms "standard unit," "sequence," or "train of characteristics" for what he later called a "facet." In his *Prolegomena to Library Classification*, for example, he wrote

Complete Division of a universe is the process of extending division of that universe on the basis of a sequence of characteristics until no multiple group is left.[27]

Further, his mathematical background suggested terms such as postulates, rules, laws, and formulae to him, and he brought those terms into knowledge organization classification theory. These kinds of terms added to the difficulty others sometimes encountered in understanding his ideas and how they could be applied in knowledge organization theories and systems for the library and information sciences. Palmer and Wells' textbook clarified Ranganathan's vocabulary and concepts for English classificationists, classifiers, and students.

In consequence, Ranganathan's ideas rapidly caught on, and in 1955 the CRG in England published a manifesto called "The Need for a Faceted Classification as the Basis of All Methods of Information Retrieval."[28] The members of the CRG had analyzed the theory, principles, and practices of existing knowledge organization classifications and found that they were inadequate for the tasks for which they had been designed. The CRG extolled the theory of facet analysis and the analytico-synthetic facet method as the only method that would be adequate for the increasing number of documents that were being published, many of them on highly detailed, multidisciplinary, and specialized topics. The members of the CRG created a number of special knowledge organization classifications using Ranganathan's principles, and a manual on how to make faceted systems was published.[29]

Circulation-College

Despite the group's admiration for Ranganathan's work, however, they disagreed with his postulation of only five fundamental categories. The CRG extended the idea of fundamental categories to include other categories that seemed necessary for the particular classificatory domain they were considering. For example, Vickery's classification for soil science had nine facets, and D.J. Foskett's classification for container manufacture had four facets and one set of common subdivisions (both classifications are in Vickery[30]). These differences may have arisen from the work of CRG's members in special libraries and bibliographic venues.

Ranganathan himself disagreed with the CRG's emphasis on special knowledge organization systems for domains smaller than the whole universe of knowledge because he saw the world of knowledge as a unitary circular structure, as expressed in the acronym APUPA. The center of the world of knowledge was the Umbra, surrounded by concentric circles of Penumbra and Alien areas that were increasingly farther away from the center. The CRG, too, realized that special domains could not entirely be separated from the rest of the world of knowledge. They saw their special knowledge organization classifications as consisting of a core area of knowledge surrounded by fringe topics that were related to the core in some particular way. For example, a knowledge organization for a special area of knowledge would also need to accommodate educational, legal, and ethical issues for that area, and the CRG also recognized that these fringe areas were actually complete core fields of study in themselves.

The CRG's research during this period was highly fruitful. After their work on the North Atlantic Treaty Organization (NATO) grant was over, as discussed below, the Group produced LISA (Library and Information Science Abstracts) knowledge organization classification, their most successful scheme. In addition, Derek Austin began work on Preserved Context Indexing System (PRECIS), and Jack Mills began work on BC2. Although BC2 is not yet finished, it is generally considered to be the most theoretically sophisticated modern knowledge organization classification. It is based on the research the CRG conducted under the NATO grant and it uses the analytico-synthetic theory of facet analysis and retroactive notation, which was developed as in part as a result of the CRG's work on a general scheme. BC2 is regarded as a fully-faceted scheme in the sense that each main class uses facet theories and principles exclusively in its development. The Introduction to BC2 is probably the most comprehensive discussion of facet theory, principles, and methods outside Ranganathan's own writings,[31] and an exposition of BC2's principles appears in Mills.[32]

Facet analysis and faceted classification theories have been highly influential in the revision of the major general classification schemes such as DDC, UDC, and LCC. Currently, research is being conducted on revising UDC on the basis of work carried out for BC2.[33] Further, facet theories, principles, and methods are considered particularly effective for Web-based classification and information retrieval, and interest in elements of facet theories and principles are increasing in computer science, in other technical areas, and for relatively untrained computer users (discussion and examples can be found at Denton).[34] Ranganathan's theoretical work on structural issues in knowledge organization is generally seen as the most fruitful and highly-regarded knowledge organization work in the twentieth century. The influence of facet theory and the CRG's work has been brought up to date in a current entry with the same title as the CRG's original paper on faceted classification and in a special issue of the journal *Axiomathes*.[35]

Theory of integrative levels

In 1962, NATO gave the Library Association £5000 (about $14,000) to develop a new general classification system for scientific documents. The Library Association approached the CRG for this work, and the group began to create this new system. For the new system, the CRG planned to use facet analysis as the basic structural principle and method, and they decided to use the theory of integrative levels to design how the classes would be formed. The theory of integrative levels is a biological theory about how individual cells combine into different organisms.[36,37] This theory meshed neatly with facet theory because it appeared to be a special case of an analytico-synthetic method worked out for the biological sciences. The CRG was unable, however, to create a knowledge organization classification system based on the theory of integrative levels, and the NATO grant was not renewed when the Group reapplied in 1969.

The theory of integrative levels was based on a series of Laws of the Levels and Rules of Explanation. As described by the CRG, the theory of integrative levels maintains

> that the world of things evolves from the simple towards the complex by an accumulation of properties, and that, at a succession of levels, these aggregations reach new degrees of complexity and become new wholes, with individual and unique identities. Each whole is greater than the sum of its parts, and ceases to possess its identity if broken down again. It acts as a unit, and the units at each level can engage in processes characteristic of that level; an influence acting on one part of the unit affects the whole unit, even though other parts may continue to function as before.[38]

The description of the CRG's examination of integrative levels and the conclusions it reached are presented in their report *Classification and Information Control*.[39] A number of problems arose, among which were their efforts to find appropriate levels with which to analyze the ideas that human beings created and worked with (which the CRG termed "mentefacts") and also the physical creations of human beings (e.g., works of art). Further, the group realized that a general knowledge organization classification for documents would need to classify documents about certain things, not the things themselves. This situation became known as "the Chinese plate syndrome," which the CRG used to draw the distinction between classifying books about Chinese plates and classifying the Chinese plates themselves.[40]

The CRG was not able to resolve the problems they faced, and they abandoned the theory of integrative levels when the NATO grant ran out was not renewed. Nevertheless, the theory of integrative levels remained intriguing and became the basis for Dahlberg's Information Coding Classification (ICC).[41] More recently, the Italian chapter of ISKO (http://www.iskoi.org/) has embarked on a series of investigations into the theory of integrative levels and has begun developing the Integrative Levels Classification (ILC).[42] These investigations appear to be fruitful new directions in research on the structure(s) of knowledge organization classification.

Notation for a Knowledge Organization Classification System

Notation is used in many fields as a way of coding and communicating complex ideas, such as music, dance, and mathematics.[43] All the knowledge organization classification issues we have discussed have implications for notational systems. There is general agreement that the notation is the final step in creating a knowledge organization classification. Once a notation is in place, the system is considered to be frozen. At that point, it is more difficult (but not impossible) to make a system hospitable by adding new concepts at the right places. Notational development is important for knowledge organization classification because the notation shows the position of the concept in the schedules and that concept's relationship(s) to other concepts. Notation thus allows individual documents and related groups of documents to be retrieved. In theory, notation is a device that describes the structure and content of a knowledge organization system without using words. Ranganathan aspired to create an "artificial classificatory language"[44] that would systematize and regularize notation.

Discussions of desiderata for notation have included a number of characteristics, for example, it should be pure (use only numbers or only letters); it should be mixed (letters, numbers and/or other symbols); it should be expressive (show the hierarchical level of the concept in the system); it should be mnemonic (suggest its own meaning in some way); it should be short (for memorability); and it should be pronounceable. Clearly, all of these characteristics cannot occur together. For example, an expressive notation that shows a hierarchical depth of 15 levels of subdivision cannot also be short and will probably not also be memorable or pronounceable. A useful chart showing how various kinds of notations work and how they compare with each other in length appears in A. C. Foskett's *The Subject Approach to Information*.[45] Detail about the CRG's research into notation appears in Vickery.[46]

Although Dewey probably did not invent the decimal notation that DDC uses, he popularized it and demonstrated its usefulness in bringing books on like topics together on the shelves. Before DDC, books were usually arranged on shelves in broad classes with an ordinal call number that was based on the book's accession number. That practice was called a fixed place notation and meant that books on the same topic would not be shelved in proximity to one another unless they had been acquired at the same time. One argument in favor of fixed place notations was that a library patron could learn where a favorite book was placed and find it immediately because it was always shelved in the same place. That characteristic was helpful at a time when much indoor lighting used candlelight, or, at most, oil or gas lights. The idea that decimal notation was superior to fixed place notation spread quickly at least in part because of Dewey's charismatic personality and tireless promotion of DDC. As interest in Ranganathan's ideas became established, faceted classification structures created a renewed interest in notation because an analytico-synthetic faceted system depended on being able to notate separate content elements to express the subject of a document. This development meant that two new issues had to be addressed concurrently when creating a notational system for a faceted classification: citation order and facet indicators.

Citation order

A citation order for the separate elements of a faceted notation needed to be established. Citation order is the sequence in which notational elements are set down in a complete notation. The analytico-synthetic method meant that the subject of the document was analyzed into its parts, each of which was given its own notation. Once these notational elements were identified for the document, they had to be synthesized in a standard predictable order. The requirements of information retrieval meant that these stand-alone notational elements could not be combined randomly. If random order were used, it would not be possible to predict what each notational element meant in the notation as a whole and accurate retrieval could not occur. For this reason, a standard notational sequence had to be established.

Ranganathan's PMEST facet formula specified the citation order in which notational elements needed to be combined for CC. Other faceted classifications, for example, those developed by the CRG, have different citation orders based on the requirements of knowledge organization classifications. The group did, however, develop what they called a "standard" citation order that could be established for each class. The CRG's standard citation order was class, thing (purpose), kind, part, property, process, operation, agent, space and time. This standard citation order added detail and flexibility to Ranganathan's PMEST facet formula. In the CRG's version, thing (purpose) corresponded to personality; kind, part and property were included in material; and process, operation and agent were included in energy. Space and time always stand at the end of a notation and are included in every faceted classification system and in most enumerative ones. Time is usually the last element because it is considered to be a more abstract concept than space and has no universal referent.

Citation order did not pose a similarly difficult problem for non-faceted enumerative notations because the schedules of that kind of system did not allow the flexibility of combining notational elements at will. The device of combining notational elements was not entirely new with faceted systems, however. For example, the second edition of DDC (1885) allowed one to subdivide certain topics geographically by adding numbers from the 900 class to the notation for the topic. The topics that could be subdivided in this way were shown in Table 1 of the second edition. Similarly, UDC, which was based on the fifth edition of DDC, provided from the beginning seven auxiliary tables for this kind of notational synthesis, six of which are still included in the UDC schedules today. Individual schedules in LCC also have tables for combining notations. SC had an auxiliary table, the categorical table, which provided about 900 "standpoints" by which any topic in the schedules could be modified. In addition, SC allowed both intra- and inter-facet notational synthesis, that is, synthesis within one facet and between different facets. The rationale for this kind of notational synthesis in enumerative systems is that the use of auxiliary tables meant that every possible combination does not have to be printed in the schedules. Further, there is usually some choice about when to use the auxiliary tables (except in LCC). Thus, in enumerative knowledge organization systems notational synthesis is seen as device to provide economy in the schedules and a citation order is built into the schedules, but in faceted systems notational synthesis is a fundamental principle that is driven by the theory of analytico-synthetic classification. In this case, citation order must be explicitly decided and rationalized by the classificationist.

Facet indicators

As we have seen, at the advent of Ranganathan's analytico-synthetic method in classification, the level of analysis of an information object changed from notation summarizing the whole information object to notation expressing different elements that would, when combined, describe the intellectual characteristics of the document. Thus, in addition to requiring a citation order, analytico-synthetic theory, principles, and practices required facet indicators. Facet indicators are punctuation marks or other symbols that show where the synthesized notation is divided into its separate facets. Facet indicators are required so that separate notational elements may be used in information retrieval. Without an indication of where a new facet begins: 1) one cannot search for an instance of a notational element and 2) one cannot add digits to the notation for that facet when required by the demands of hospitality. In the first edition of CC, Ranganathan used the colon as a facet indicator between the notation for each of the facets. Later, different punctuation marks were inserted at the beginning of each facet. For example, the topic "Classification of theses by the LCC classification system in Canadian university libraries in 1978" would be notated 234;494:51;M98.72'N78 where 2 was the basic class for library science; 34 was the personality facet for university libraries ; ;494 was the matter facet for theses ; :51M98 was the energy facet for classification by LCC ;.72 was the space facet for Canada; and 'N78 was the time facet for 1978.

Like citation order, facet indicators had been used before Ranganathan's views were known, but in a somewhat different way and without a theoretical basis. UDC used what were essentially facet indicators from the beginning, although they were called "signs of association." UDC has, however, no prescribed citation order, and it is thus possible to arrange notational elements in the way that is most useful for a particular situation. It should be remembered, too, that the UDC was not created as a knowledge organization classification for books on shelves, so that the problems created by differing citation orders are not as prominent as they are for a knowledge organization system for shelving. For example, notation for the topic "A thesis in French on the classification of books on education in Canada in 1979, written from the economics point of view" would be notated 025.4:37.003.1(71)"1979"(043) = 40 but could be written in a different order if required. 025.4 stands for BC; :37 means in relation to education; .003.1 means from the economic point of view; "1979" means the date; (043) means thesis; and = 40 means in French. UDC has undergone many revisions since its beginning, and the meanings of these signs of association have changed periodically. Nevertheless, the influence of UDC on other classificationists and classification systems has been strong. The most comprehensive work on the origins and development of UDC is Rayward.[47] A shorter treatment appears in McIlwaine.[48]

As we can see from these examples, facet indicators create lengthy and complex notations. Although they were necessary to implement the theory of faceted classification, these indicators produced notations that were considered too complex to be easily understood and too long to be given to documents, especially for the spines of books. These issues were particularly important in an era when library classifications were used primarily to organize books on shelves (except for UDC).

The CRG undertook a number of experiments on notation, and probably the most successful was retroactive notation. Retroactive notation has been used in a number of schemes, principally in BC2. Retroactive notation does not need facet indicators, and it can be either numerical (0–9) or alphabetical. It mechanizes notational synthesis because the citation order is built into the classification schedules. In a retroactive notation, the order of the schedules is from general to specific (moving from the beginning of the schedules to the end), but the notation is applied from the specific to the general (moving from the end of the schedules to the beginning). When devising a retroactive notation, only letters in the alphabet that come after the initial letter of the notation are used. For example, the topic "a program of training for the advertising of public utilities" might have the notation ttvstwrw or ttv stw rw. We can see that the first notational element (ttv), which comes at the end of the schedules, is followed by the notational element (stw). In this example, s is closer to the beginning of the alphabet than its immediately preceding letter (v). Therefore, s begins a new facet. Similarly, in the next notational element (rw), r is closer to the beginning of the alphabet than its immediately preceding letter (w). Therefore, r begins a new facet. Retroactive notation can thus be checked by referring to alphabetical order and this kind of checking is a quick and easy procedure for computers to do. It creates a shorter notation because no facet indicators are needed, but devising the schedules is difficult. This example was developed from Barbara Kyle's classification for the social sciences in Kyle.[49] Retroactive notation has, however, been suggested as appropriate for computer applications because of the power of computers to analyze long strings text and a suggested system that uses some of the characteristics of retroactive notation has been developed.[50]

CONCLUSION: THE THEORIES BROUGHT TOGETHER

Ranganathan believed that knowledge organization classification had three planes: the idea plane (the overall conception of the system); the verbal plane (the schedules and index of the system); and the notational plane (the way the concepts in the schedules were expressed in notation). The separation of topics in this entry into content, structure, and notation is roughly analogous to Ranganathan's three planes of work. As we have seen, from their beginnings in the late nineteenth century to the present, knowledge organization classification systems have undergone major shifts in all three planes. The

initial enumerative classifications (e.g., DDC, LCC, UDC, SC) can be thought of as "universe of knowledge" classifications. That is, they began with the whole universe of knowledge and subdivided it from the top down in successive steps to create classes and subclasses at various levels of hierarchical depth. Once the schedules were arranged in the desired order, a notation was applied. As theoretical development proceeded through Ranganathan and the CRG, this top-down universe of knowledge classification systems was partially transformed into bottom-up "universe of concepts" classification systems. Wilson distinguished between universe of knowledge classifications and universe of concepts classifications in Wilson.[51] That is, within each class and subclass, the most important concepts were identified first and their facets and subfacets were then established. On the basis of Ranganathan's theory of analytico-synthetic classification theories, principles and methods, concepts were identified in documents, and notation was assigned to each concept. These notational elements were then synthesized in the correct citation order that had been established for the knowledge organization classification. The development of BC2 is described in Mills.[52]

BC2 is the best example of this kind of classificatory thought, but all the major classification theories and systems have been revised to a greater or lesser extent on the basis of facet theory and its extensions. Library and information knowledge organization classification theories and systems have influenced and re-influenced each other throughout their evolutionary histories. In a rough chronological sequence, DDC was the basis for UDC, which was influential in the development of CC. Facet theory and method moved through all the systems and came to their highest point of development in BC2. Facet theory and method have then retroactively influenced DDC, UDC, and CC. CC has influenced all the others in both theoretical and practical ways, and they have all influenced the various revisions of CC. This analysis is based on Cockshutt.[53] Thus, despite the differences in concept, application, and history of the various knowledge organization classifications, they share with each other important theoretical developments that have occurred throughout their lives. In addition, it must be remembered that all the theories and systems that have been discussed are constrained by the cultural warrants of their times and places because "classification systems are intellectual, and fundamentally also political, constructs: they represent, and impose, a view of the world at a certain time and in a certain environment."[54]

ACKNOWLEDGMENTS

Support for this entry came from the Social Sciences and Humanities Research Council of Canada (SSHRCC) grant no. 410-2005-0337.

REFERENCES

1. Vickery, B.C. *Classification and Indexing in Science*, 3rd Ed. Butterworths: London, 1975.
2. Veltman, K. Knowl. Organ **1993**, *20*(1), 2–54.
3. Douglas, M. Hull, D. *Nelson Goodman: How Classification Works*, Edinburgh University Press: Edinburgh, 1992.
4. Ellen, R.F. Reason, D. *Classifications in Their Social Context*, Academic Press: London, 1979.
5. Lange, J. *The Cognitivity Paradox: An Inquiry Concerning the Claims of Philosophy*, Princeton University Press: Princeton, NJ, 1970; 40–45.
6. Hulme, E.W. Principles of book classification. Libr. Assoc. Rec. **1911**, *13*, 354–358 389–394 444–440 **1912**, *14*, 39–46, 174–181, 447.
7. Hulme, W.E. *Statistical Bibliography in Relation to the Growth of Modern Civilization*, Butler & Tanner: London, 1923.
8. Pritchard, A. Statistical bibliography or bibliometrics. J. Doc. **1969**, *25*(4), 348–349.
9. Beghtol, C. Semantic validity: Concepts of warrant in bibliographic classification systems. Libr. Resour. Tech. Ser. **1986**, *30*(2), 109–125.
10. Lee, J.M.E. Wyndham Hulme: A reconsideration. In *The Variety of Librarianship*; Rayward, W.B., Ed.; Library Association of Australia: Sydney, 1976.
11. Bliss, H.E. A modern classification for libraries with simple notation, mnemonics and alternatives. Libr. J. **1910**, *35*, 351–358.
12. Bliss, H.E. *The Organization of Knowledge and the System of the Sciences*, Holt: New York, 1929.
13. Bliss, H.E. *The Organization of Knowledge and the Subject-Approach to Books*, Wilson: New York, 1933.
14. Bliss, H.E. The system of the sciences and the organization of knowledge. Phil. Sci. **1935**, *2*, 86–103.
15. Bliss, H.E. *The Organization of Knowledge and the Subject-Approach to Books*, 2nd revised Ed. Wilson: New York, 1939; 42–43 Original emphasis.
16. Fiering, N.S. President Samuel Johnson and the circle of knowledge. William Mary Quart. **1971**, *28*, 199.
17. Bliss, H.E. *The Organization of Knowledge and the System of the Sciences*, Holt: New York, 1929; 229–235.
18. Bliss, H.E. *A Bibliographic Classification, Extended by Systematic Auxiliary Schedules for Composite Specification and Notation*, 2nd Ed. Wilson: New York, 1952.
19. Broughton, V. Henry Evelyn Bliss—The other immortal, or a prophet without honour. J. Libr. Inform. Sci. **2008**, *40*(1), 45–58.
20. Brown, J.D. Classification and cataloguing. Library **1897**, *9*, 142–156.
21. Brown, J.D. *Subject Classification, with Tables, Indexes, etc., for the Subdivision of Subjects*, 2nd revised Ed. Grafton: London, 1914; 8.
22. Langridge, D.W. Alternative starting points in classification. Catalog. Classif. Quart. **1995**, *19*(3/4), 7–15.
23. Arras, R.J. *A Critical Evaluation of the Concept of Hierarchy*, Temple University, 1991. Ph.D. thesis.
24. Goddard, C. Wierzbicka, A. Introducing lexical primitives. In *Semantic and Lexical Universals: Theory and Empirical Findings*; Goddard, C., Wierzbicka, A., Eds.; John Benjamins: Amsterdam, 1994; 31–54.
25. Dewey, M. *A Classification and Subject Index for Cataloguing and Arranging the Books and Pamphlets of a Library*, Case, Lockwood & Brainard: Amherst, MA, 1876; 4–6 Passim.
26. Palmer, B.I. Wells, A.J. *The Fundamentals of Library Classification*, George Allen & Unwin: London, 1951.
27. Ranganathan, S.R. *Prolegomena to Library Classification*, Madras Library Association: Madras, 1937; 11. Original capitalization.
28. Classification Research Group. The need for a faceted classification as the basis of all methods of information retrieval. Libr. Assoc. Rec. **1955**, *57*(7), 262–268.
29. Vickery, B.C. *Faceted Classification: A Guide to the Construction and Use of Special Schemes*, Aslib: London, 1960.
30. Vickery, B.C. *Classification and Indexing in Science*, 3rd Ed. Butterworths: London, 1975; 181–192 Appendix B.
31. Mills, J. Broughton, V. *Bliss Bibliographic Classification. [v. 1] Introduction and Auxiliary Schedules*, Butterworths: London, 1977; 11–114.
32. Mills, J. Faceted classification and logical division in information retrieval. Libr. Trends **2004**, *52*(3), 541–570.
33. McIlwaine, I.C. Williamson, N.J.W. Medicine and the UDC: The process of restructuring. In *Culture and Identity in Knowledge Organization*; *Advances in Knowledge Organization* Arsenault, C., Tennis, J., Eds.; 2008; Vol. 11.
34. Denton, W. How to make a faceted classification and put it on the web. Available at http://www.google.com/search?ie=UTF-8&oe=UTF-8&sourceid=navclient&gfns=1&q=denton+and+facet (accessed May 30, 2007).
35. Broughton, V. The need for a faceted classification as the basis for all methods of information retrieval. Aslib Proc. **2006**, *58*(1–2), 49–72 See also the Special Issue on facets, 2008, *Axiomathes* 18.
36. Needham, J. Integrative levels: A reevaluation of the idea of progress. *Time, the Refreshing River*; Allen & Unwin: London, 1943.
37. Feibleman, J.K. Theory of integrative levels. Brit. J. Philos. Sci. **1954**, *5*, 59–66.
38. Foskett, D.J. Classification and integrative levels. In *The Sayers Memorial Volume*; Foskett, D.J., Palmer, B.I., Eds.; Library Association: London, 1961; 136–250.
39. The Classification Research Group, Ed. *Classification and Information Control*; The Library Association: London, 1969.
40. Classification Research Group. Bulletin No. 11. J. Doc. **1978**, *34*(1), 21–50.
41. Dahlberg, I. The information coding classification (ICC): A modern, theory-based fully-faceted, universal system of knowledge fields. Axiomathes **2008**, *18*, 161–176.
42. Gnoli, C. Categories and facets in integrative levels. Axiomathes **2008**, *18*, 177–192.
43. Daniels, P.T. Bright, W. *The World's Writing Systems*, Oxford University Press: New York, 1996 contains chapters on a number of notational systems, e.g., Phonetic notation, Movement notation systems, and Numerical notation.
44. Sayers, W.C.B. *A Manual of Classification for Librarians and Bibliographers*, 3rd revised Ed. Grafton: London, 1955; 206.
45. Foskett, A.C. *The Subject Approach to Information*, 4th Ed. Library Association Publishing: London, 1982; 204–205.

46. Vickery, B.C. Part 1: Notational symbols in classification. J. Doc. **1952**, *58*, 15–32 Part II: Notation as an ordering device. J. Doc. **1956**, *12*(2), 73–87. Part III: Further comparisons of brevity. J. Doc. **1957**, *13*, 72–77. Part IV: Ordinal value of symbols. J. Doc. **1958**, *14*(1), 1–11. Part V: Signposted and retroactive notation; Part VI: Pronounceable retroactive ordinal notation. J. Doc. **1959**, *15*, 12–16.

47. Rayward, W.B. *The Universe of Information: The Work of Paul Otlet for Documentation and International Organisation*, Moscow, 1978. FID 520. VINITI.

48. McIlwaine, I.C. The universal decimal classification: Some factors concerning its origins, development, and influence. J. Am. Soc. Inform. Sci. **1997**, *48*(4), 331–339.

49. Kyle, B. Towards a classification for social science literature. Am. Doc. **1958**, *9*(3), 168–183.

50. Lin, S. Online classification notation: Proposal for a flexible faceted notation system (FNNS). Int. Classif. **1990**, *17* (1), 14–20.

51. Wilson, T.D. The work of the British Classification Research Group. In *Subject Retrieval in the Seventies: New Directions*; Wellisch, H., Wilson, T.D., Eds.; Greenwood Publishing in conjunction with the School of Library and Information Services, University of Maryland: Westport, CT, 1972; 62–71.

52. Mills, J. Faceted classification and logical division in information retrieval. Libr. Trends **2004**, *52*(3), 541–570.

53. Cockshutt, M.E. Dewey today: An analysis of recent editions. In *Major Classification Systems: The Dewey Centennial*; Henderson, K.L., Ed.; Graduate School of Library Science: Urbana-Champagne, IL, 1976; 22–46 Papers Presented at the Allerton Park Institute, November 9–12, 1975.

54. Dudbridge, G. *Lost Books of Medieval China*, The British Library: London, 2000; 12.

BIBLIOGRAPHY

1. Bowker, G.C. Star, S.L. *Sorting Things Out: Classification and Its Consequences*, MIT Press: Cambridge, MA, 1999.

2. Kipfer, B.A. *The Order of Things: How Everything in the World Is Organized—Into Hierarchies, Structures and Pecking Orders*, Random House: New York, 1998.

Circulation–College

Clinical Decision-Support Systems

Kai Zheng
Department of Health Management and Policy, University of Michigan, Ann Arbor, Michigan, U.S.A.

Abstract
Clinical decision-support systems (CDSS) apply best-known medical knowledge to patient data for the purpose of generating case-specific decision-support advice. CDSS forms the cornerstone of health informatics research and practice. It is an embedded concept in almost all major clinical information systems and plays an instrumental role in helping health care achieve its ultimate goal: providing high-quality patient care while, at the same time, assuring patient safety and reducing costs. This entry introduces the concept of clinical decision support from early generation artificial intelligence-based systems to the evolution of modern systems based on evidence-based clinical guidelines. The discussion also includes the key technological considerations of CDSS and the barriers inhibiting its widespread adoption and effective use.

INTRODUCTION

The notion that artificial intelligence (AI) might one day rival the decision-making capability of human brain sparked the first generation of computerized clinical decision-support systems (CDSS) developed from the 1960s into the 1980s.[1,2] However, years of trials and frustrations convinced AI enthusiasts that the enormous variations in patient care cannot be reduced to systematic decision making to render qualitative medical treatments.[3] These limitations became even more apparent with the increasing awareness that patient care outcomes are also subject to other factors including quality- and value-of-life judgments, economic and psychosocial considerations, and social well-being of the patient as a whole. This brought a disappointing close to the first chapter in the use of computers to aid in medical decision-making.[4]

The story did not end there. Computerized clinical information systems proliferate throughout health care organizations today, significantly reducing the costs to acquire and store patient data. These changes, however, have invited new challenges, including an explosion of patient information that far exceeds any practitioner's capability of processing such data.[5] This situation is further compounded by a wellspring of medical knowledge resulting from the "evidence-based medicine" (EBM) movement over the past 20 years that has revolutionized the way medicine is practiced. EBM requires physicians to rely less on their own experience and more on the current best evidence in making decisions about the care of individual patients.[6] Unfortunately, "current best evidence" is a temporal concept that may become outdated rapidly as medical research advances or the mechanisms causing diseases change (e.g., new varieties of flu virus).

Further, the U.S. health care system has been criticized for its high costs, low efficiency, poor quality, and unacceptable rates of preventable medical errors. In 2007, $2.2 trillion or 16.3% of national gross domestic product (GDP) was spent on health care in the United States,[7] while this number was only 8.7% on average in other industrialized countries, based on 2006 data.[8] Despite the twofold higher health care expenditure, the quality of care provided in the United States ranks last among major industrialized countries.[9] As a result, 31% of Americans rated the U.S. health care system as "poor" in 2008.[10] Further, the landmark 2001 report published by the Institute of Medicine, *To Err is Human: Building a Safer Health System*, showed that preventable medical errors in the U.S. health care system cost a total of 44,000–98,000 patient lives and $17–29 billion a year.[11] In response to these challenges, regulatory bodies and payer systems are actively establishing new regulations and incentive policies to assure health care institutions operate optimally. Joint Commission on the Accreditation of Healthcare Organizations (JCAHO, http://www.jointcommission. org/), for example, publishes *Comprehensive Accreditation Manual for Hospitals* every year articulating a wide range of accreditation criteria on facility operation, care provision, and patient safety. Similarly, the National Committee for Quality Assurance (http://www.ncqa.org) specifies a comprehensive set of measures for monitoring patient care performance through its annual publication *The Healthcare Effectiveness Data and Information Set (HEDIS)*. While these may help to address the problems in U.S. health care, they also add a new layer of complexity to the already chaotic clinical workspace. This is the reason the medical community is embracing more than ever the idea of using computer systems to aid in medical decision making.

Encyclopedia of Library and Information Sciences, Fourth Edition DOI: 10.1081/E-ELIS4-120044944

CLINICAL DECISION-SUPPORT SYSTEMS

Broadly speaking, a decision-support system is an interactive, flexible, and adaptable computer-based information system developed specifically for supporting the solution of a nonstructured management problem for improved decision making. It utilizes data, provides an easy-to-use interface, and allows for the decision maker's own insights.[12] Google Maps™ (http://maps.google.com) provides a good example. The site applies intelligent algorithms to geographic data to provide "optimal" routes for traveling from location A to location B while, at the same time, allowing the travel planner to manually intervene in the process, such as creating a more preferred route with click-and-drag options.

Likewise, in the health care arena, clinical decision-support systems provide clinicians, staff, patients, and other individuals with knowledge and specific, individualized information, intelligently filtered and presented at appropriate times, to enhance clinical performance and patient outcomes. It encompasses a variety of tools and interventions such as computerized alerts and reminders, clinical guidelines, order sets, patient data reports and dashboards, documentation templates, and diagnostic support.[13] The essential component of CDSS is *inference engine*, which applies the knowledge stored in a knowledge base to patient data to derive case-specific recommendations. CDSS is usually interfaced with, or as a part of, other clinical information systems such as electronic health records (EHR) or computerized provider order entry (CPOE) systems. For example, every full-fledged commercial EHR system provides certain types of electronic templates for managing chronic disease conditions. These templates offer individualized treatment and lifestyle change advice based on clinical guidelines and patient data.

With its capability of generating decision-support alerts warning against drug–drug interactions and drug–allergy interactions, CDSS is being increasingly mandated by regulatory bodies and advocacy groups such as JACHO, the Leapfrog Group for Patient Safety (Leapfrog, http://www.leapfroggroup.org/), and the Certification Commission for Healthcare Information Technology (CCHIT, http://www.cchit.org/). The JACHO accreditation manual has a dedicated Management of Information section clearly specifying the data requirements for enabling clinical decision support. Leapfrog, a voluntary group of large employers that ranks hospitals based on their quality and safety performance, has specific requirements to evaluate whether a hospital is equipped with CPOE decision-support systems capable of warning against drug interaction, allergy, and overdose. CCHIT, a recognized certification body (RCB), incorporates the clinical decision-support provision as a key component of its clinical information system certification process.

History of Clinical Decision Support

Started in the 1960s, the initial objective of introducing computers into medical practice was very clear: to provide doctors with decision aids using AI-based medical diagnostic reasoning. The enthusiasm was primarily spurred by the capability of computers to solve complex decision models in real time. This stream of research eventually developed into a dedicated discipline, Artificial Intelligence in Medicine (AIM), with wide appeal and broad consensus for optimism. In 1970, Schwartz announced in the New England Journal of Medicine that clinical computing would likely be commonplace in the "not too distant future."[14] *DXplain*, shown in Fig. 1, is a representative example of the early generation diagnostic tool. Developed at the Massachusetts General Hospital, *DXplain* uses a modified form of Bayesian logic to produce a ranked list of possible diagnoses based on symptom manifestations. Table 1 lists several other influential systems developed during this time period. For a comprehensive bibliography of these early generation CDSS systems, readers can refer to Miller 1994.[15]

Unfortunately, the plethora of clinical computing, as predicted by many, never occurred. A large number of AI-based diagnostic reasoning systems were developed and tested, but most was not adopted in practice. A plausible reason accounting for this failure is that the AI-based diagnostic reasoning "functioned more like the 'Greek Oracle' rather than permitting a more flexible, interactive approach" (p. 4).[2] A "decision-making," rather than a "decision-supporting" structure, was perceived by physicians as a threat to clinician autonomy.[2] Moreover, most of these early generation systems were stand-alone, self-contained applications. They were not integrated with other computerized systems supporting hospital operation and patient data management, which were not readily available at the time. As a result, the decision-support advice generated by these early generation CDSS was often inaccurate or irrelevant. For example, Berner et al. (1994) tested four diagnostic systems and found that the proportion of correct diagnoses ranged from 0.52 to 0.71, and the mean proportion of relevant diagnoses ranged from 0.19 to 0.37.[16] This level of performance made the adoption of such systems for treating real patients unrealistic. Another major reason accounting for the failure of early generation CDSS was the lack of financial returns. The dominant pay-for-service model—reimbursement was determined based on what was done rather than how well it was done—provided little incentives for medical practices to invest in expensive computer-based decision-support technology.

New Generation of Guideline-Based CDSS

The use of computerized clinical information systems to support hospital operation as well as clinical activities

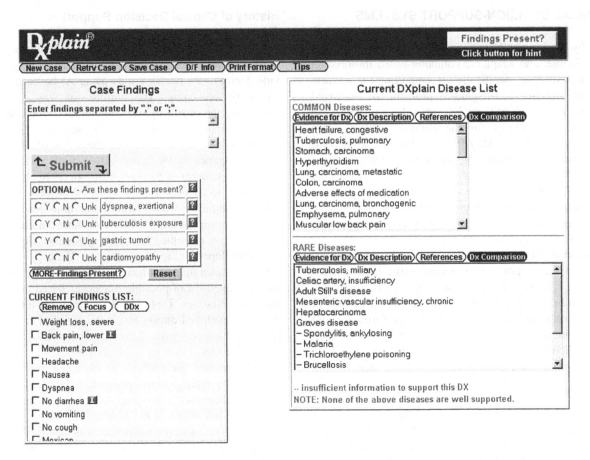

Fig. 1 *DXplain*: A representative early generation clinical decision-support system.
Source: MGH Laboratory of Computer Science, http://dxplain.org.

Table 1 Examples of early generation clinical decision-support systems.

De Dombal	1972	Developed at the Leeds University, United Kingdom, De Dombal is a clinical decision-support tool that uses naive Bayesian approach to provide automated reasoning under uncertainty for diagnosing acute abdominal pain and recommending the need for surgery.
INTERNIST I	1974	INTERNIST I is a rule-based expert system for solving complex diagnostic problems in general internal medicine. It was developed at the University of Pittsburgh and later commercialized under the brand name Quick Medical Reference (QMR).
MYCIN	1976	MYCIN is a rule-based expert system developed at Stanford University. It was used to diagnose and recommend treatments for certain blood infections and other infectious diseases.
DXplain	1984	Developed at Massachusetts General Hospital, DXplain uses a modified form of Bayesian logic to produce a ranked list of diagnoses that might explain or be associated with the clinical manifestations.

started to flourish in the early 1990s. Besides the significant technological breakthroughs, including the availability of enterprise-level database management systems (DBMS) and health data standards such as ICD and HL7, new legislation and advocacy by federal funding agencies also played a key role. International Statistical Classification of Diseases: Standard diagnostic classification developed by the World Health Organization (WHO) for its member states to report mortality and morbidity statistics. In the United States, ICD-9-CM (ICD 9th Revision, Clinical Modification) is widely used to codify diagnostic data for administrative (such as billing) purposes. http://www.cdc.gov/nchs/datawh/ftpserv/ftpICD9/ftpICD9.htm. Health Level Seven (HL7) is an all-volunteer, not-for-profit organization. It oversees the development of international health data exchange standards. http://www.hl7.org. Financial investments to implement large-scale health IT systems were made by the Agency for Healthcare Research and Quality (AHRQ, http://healthit.ahrq.gov), Health Resources and Services Administration (HRSA, http://www.hrsa.gov/healthit/), and many other foundations and private funding sources. Insurance companies have also been actively engaged. They either funded health IT directly, or provided financial incentives to medical practices for adopting information technology. The purpose was to reduce administrative costs in processing paper-based claims, thereby improving the quality and timeliness of health data submitted by medical facilities.

This provides a platform warranting the rise of a new generation of CDSS. Fewer of these new generation systems remain as stand-alones because of the need to provide clinicians with a unified interface to access all patient data and all clinical functionalities. Instead, CDSS often appears as modules embedded in other computerized systems, such as EHR and CPOE. Compared with their AI-based ancestors, these new generation systems represent a new class of CDSS—evidence-adaptive decision support—that provides decision aids with a knowledge base constructed from, and continually adapting to, new evidence based on research and practice, i.e., EBM. EBM is the conscientious, explicit, and judicious use of current best evidence in making decisions about the care of individual patients (6). It distills scientific evidence from the systematic analysis of medical literature using statistical or data mining approaches.[17] These systems are primarily used to help improve the coherence of preventive care and chronic disease management guidelines. A significant portion of clinical decision support is also provided using rather primitive database look-up rules. For example, dosage levels may be suggested based on patient age and body mass index (BMI), or prompts may appear for medication interactions based on commercially available medication lexicons, or reminders for vaccines based on well-specified childhood or adulthood vaccination schedules. The rationale behind these CDSS systems is simple: the majority of quality care problems and patient safety issues are due to human omissions, rather than lack of medical knowledge. Hence, CDSS should focus on "reminding" clinicians to avoid potential omissions instead of providing direct diagnostic aids by assuming clinicians are unable to solve a problem. As shown by Garg et al. 2005, such passive reminding systems are far more effective than proactive diagnostic systems.[18]

In 2006, the American Medical Informatics Association (AMIA) published *Roadmap for National Action on Clinical Decision Support*, which identifies three key objectives for CDSS research and practice: 1) Best Knowledge Available When Needed; 2) High Adoption and Effective Use; and 3) Continuous Improvement of Knowledge and CDS Methods.[19] Objective 1 of the AMIA CDS Roadmap suggests that providing clinical decision support should be based on up-to-date medical knowledge and should occur "as part of clinician workflow" and "at the time and location of decision-making" (p. 765).[20] Objectives 2 and 3 are related to medical knowledge engineering and the implementation and user resistance barriers of CDSS, which is discussed in detail in the following two sections.

Guideline Ontologies for Effective Medical Knowledge Engineering

The up-to-date medical knowledge implemented in CDSS is primarily derived from evidence-based clinical guidelines. AHRQ's National Guideline Clearinghouse (http://www.guideline.gov) is the principal resource for the latest guidelines spanning a wide variety of disease areas. However, these clinical guidelines are usually disseminated as unstructured, narrative documents that often lack sufficient detail for computing. For example, a very simple guideline for breast cancer screening recommends "screening mammography, with or without clinical breast examination, every 1–2 years for women aged 40 and older." U.S. Preventive Services Task Force, Screening for breast cancer, Recommendations and rationale. http://www.ahrq.gov/clinic/3rduspstf/breastCancer/brcanrr.htm. To convert this guideline into a computable form, "screening mammography," "women," and "age" all need to be rigorously defined with standard medical terminology, shown in Fig. 2. The location of the corresponding patient data elements and how to retrieve them must also be specified. Oftentimes, this task is not trivial. For example, "mammography" may be stored in a laboratory information system (LIS) that does not communicate with the CDSS, or the terminology representing "mammography" in the LIS may not conform to the terminology used in the CDSS.

Arden Syntax, a procedural language for representing medical logics, was introduced in 1989 to enable effective and standard-based computation of medical knowledge. It soon became a standard of the American Society for Testing and Materials (ASTM) and was later adopted by HL7. Arden Syntax provides a specification for encoding medical logic as individual rule-based procedures, also known as Medical Logic Modules (MLMs). Each MLM contains sufficient computational detail and data requirements to make a single medical decision. For example, the following MLM code determines when to issue the alert, "Consider impaired kidney function" based on the most recent creatinine level and blood urea nitrogen (BUN) test results:

```
data:
  last_creat  := read last { "Creatinine
level"} ;
  last_BUN := read last { "BUN level"} ;
;;
logic:
  if last_creat < 1.5 or last_BUN > 30
  then alert_text := "Consider impaired
kidney function.";
  conclude true;
  end if;
;;
```

Arden Syntax, however, is not suitable for representing comprehensive guidelines. Each MLM represents a discrete

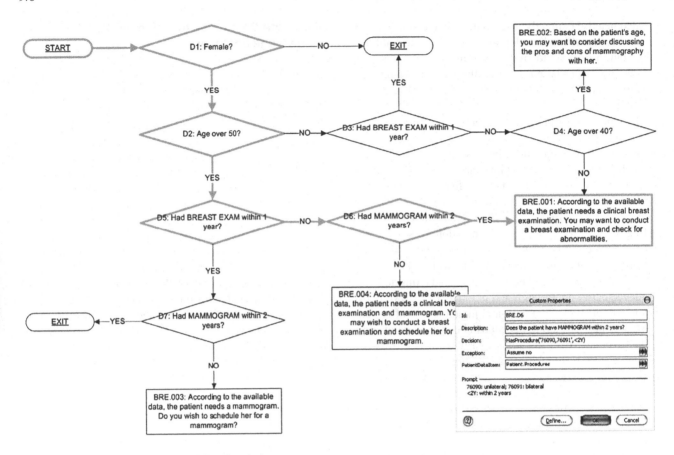

Fig. 2 A computerized clinical guideline flowchart.

decision-making logic, like the example above, and could easily become unmanageable as guidelines become more complex. This limitation has led to the development of several ontology-based guideline representation models.

A guideline representation ontology is a specification of elements that constitute evidence-based guidelines. It represents the elements by specifying their attributes and defining the relationships that hold them together. For example, a guideline may represent a set of medical decisions and actions (attributes) and a set of rules (relationships) that link the evaluation of a decision criterion to a set of further steps to be taken. A rigorously defined computational ontology provides considerable promise of producing computable representations that can be visualized, edited, executed, and shared using CDSS. Several ontology-based guideline representation models have been developed over the past 20 years. The influential ones include Asbru (http://www.asgaard.tuwien.ac.at), EON (http://www.smi.stanford.edu/projects/eon/), GLIF (Guideline Interchange Format, http://www.glif.org), and SAGE (Sharable Active Guideline Environment, http://sage.wherever.org), developed in the United States; and GUIDE (http://www.labmedinfo.org/research/dsg/decision_support.htm), PRODIGY (http://www.prodigy.nhs.uk) and PRO*forma* (http://www.acl.icnet.uk/lab/proforma.html), developed in Europe. Some models, such as GLIF and SAGE, aim to achieve a general, interchangeable

format.[21] Others, such as PRODIGY, focus on representing guidelines in specific disease areas.[22]

Barriers to Implementing and Using Clinical Decision Support

Clinician time is the most precious resource in a medical practice. Average time for seeing each outpatient visit is less than 20 min.[23,24] Considering other administrative time loss, the amount of time for accomplishing the actual work—examining patients, reviewing historical data, making judgments, and documenting new findings and performing treatments—is extremely limited. Any innovations that slow things down are bound to fail.

Unfortunately, very few CDSS systems benefit time efficiency. In fact, most require extra clinician time to enter patient data and review and act upon decision-support prompts. Managing complex chronic disease conditions such as diabetes, for example, is very time-consuming and often distracts clinicians from the main focus of a patient visit.[25] As a result, the actual efficacy and effectiveness achieved by new generation CDSS are still mixed.[17,26,27] Overriding or ignoring computer-generated decision-support advice is common,[28] and many CDSS systems are abandoned altogether.[29]

Patient data codification

A fundamental barrier in CDSS adoption is the need for patient data codification. All patient data must be properly codified, according to certain standard taxonomies, in order to be computed in the inference engine of a CDSS. However, picking a right code is a mechanical, time-consuming process that generally keeps clinicians away from focusing on the content of clinical documentation. The codified patient data also risks losing the narrative, story-telling nature that used to be conveyed in free-text patient notes. Moreover, numerous competing and conflicting taxonomies exist for historical reasons. ICD-9-CM, for example, is widely used in the United States to prepare diagnosis-based billing claims. Nevertheless, many clinical observations and findings are intermediate disease stages that are not necessarily "diagnoses," and hence cannot be meaningfully represented using ICD-9-CM.[30,31] To address this issue, new observation-oriented clinical data taxonomies, such as SNOMED-CT, have been proposed. Systematized Nomenclature of Medicine-Clinical Terms (SNOMED-CT): A clinical terminology that provides unique meanings and formal logic-based definitions for diseases, clinical findings, and procedures. http://www.ihtsdo.org/snomed-ct/. The National Library of Medicine also maintains the Unified Medical Language System (UMLS, http://www.nlm.nih.gov/research/umls/), a meta-thesaurus for translating terminologies across different medical vocabularies whenever compatible.

System interoperability

Another significant barrier inhibiting CDSS adoption is the system interoperability issue. In order to generate case-specific advice, CDSS must have access to complete and up-to-date patient data. While computerized clinical systems are now commonly used to manage a variety of patient information, many of these systems do not readily talk to each other. Creating one-to-one data exchange interfaces is possible, but can be very costly and difficult to maintain as systems constantly upgrade. Enabling patient data sharing across health care settings is further challenged by the lack of regional health data exchange networks. Personal Health Records (PHR), that allows all care providers to upload patient data to a common repository, have shown some promise as a solution to the issue. Google Health™ (http://www.google.com/health/) and Microsoft HealthVault™ (http://www.healthvault.com) are examples of PHRs that are currently being tested in the field.

Other contextual factors

Lastly, there are many other concerns in using CDSS beyond technological considerations. CDSS introduces a radical impact on patient care delivery and, in particular,

can be detrimental to the quality of point-of-care physician communication if not used properly. Using computers in front of patients and the resulting loss of eye contact is considered rude and often listed among common reasons causing user resistance.[32] The threat to clinical autonomy is also an enduring issue for physicians. Many new-generation CDSS systems are now associated with certain evaluative mechanisms to "score" clinician performance. This unpleasant characteristic could further erode user acceptance. As Anderson et al. 1994 commented, "despite the fact that they are technologically sound, more than half of medical information systems fail because of user and staff resistance" (p. 1).[33] These contextual human factors must be taken into account when implementing CDSS in real practice.

Case Study: The Clinical Reminder System

The clinical reminder system (CRS) was jointly developed by the H. John Heinz III School of Public Policy and Management at Carnegie Mellon University and the Western Pennsylvania Hospital (WPH). Since February 2002, CRS has been deployed in two WPH medical practices treating real patients.

CRS uses evidence-based clinical guidelines to support the management of four chronic health conditions (asthma, diabetes, hypertension, and hyperlipidemia), and five preventive care procedures (breast cancer, cervical cancer, influenza, pneumonia, and steroid-induced osteoporosis). A guideline representation model built upon existing ontologies (e.g., GLIF) was implemented in CRS for enabling structured acquisition and automated execution of evidence-based guidelines. Fig. 2 shows a sample visual representation encoded in this model. These visual representations, with embedded medical decision-making logic (shown at the bottom right corner in Fig. 2), are stored in XML files that theoretically can be shared with other CDSS systems if they implement the same underlying guideline representation model.

In order to generate case-specific reminders, CRS stores and manages comprehensive patient information, such as patient descriptors, symptoms, and orders. Standard medical vocabularies are used whenever possible. For example, ICD-9-CM is used in CRS for encoding diagnoses, CPT4 for procedural treatments, and the National Drug Code (NDC) for medication prescriptions. Current Procedural Terminology: A directory of descriptive terms and identifying codes for reporting medical services and procedures under public and private health insurance programs. CPT4, its 4th edition, is the most widely adopted version in the United States. http://www.ama-assn.org/ama/pub/category/3113.html. National Drug Code Directory: A directory that lists universal product identifier for human drugs. Its current edition is limited to prescription drugs and insulin products. http://www.fda.gov/cder/ndc/. CRS also retrieves patient data from many

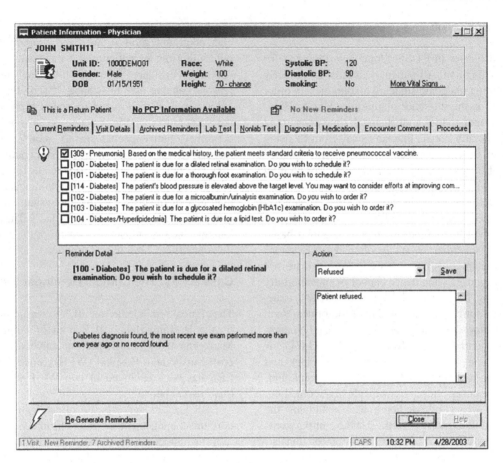

Fig. 3   The main workspace of the clinical reminder system.

other hospital information systems, most in real time. The clinic staff use CRS to manage appointments, patient check-in and check-out, and record vital signs. The residents and attending physicians use CRS to document clinical observations, prescribe medication and laboratory test orders, and generate reminders to aid in their decision making. The reminders usually take the form of recommended actions to have certain tests performed, to receive vaccinations, or to discuss the pros and cons of alternative treatments. The main workspace of CRS is shown in Fig. 3, where residents and attending physicians can act upon the reminders by selecting "Performed," "Deferred," "Not Compliant," among several other possible responses.

A series of research studies were conducted to examine the user adoption and acceptance of CRS. Periodical user satisfaction surveys showed that while CRS was rated "satisfactory" on all interface-related items, it received very poor user evaluation on system-related items as indicated by the survey comment, "the system is ineffective in helping me complete my work quickly." Follow-up semi-structure interviews were conducted to investigate the issue. The results revealed several challenges to overcome, including iterative advisories ("the same reminder was generated time and time again"), cumbersome data entry ("it is too difficult and takes too

long to enter data"), workflow disruption ("slowed down my work"), solicitation for one single system ("we should have only one system to access all information needed"), disrupted physician–patient communication ("my patient felt upset when I used my computer"), and lack of guidance in the application workflow ("I don't know where to start"). These problems are primarily associated with the sociotechnical integration issues when clinicians try to incorporate CRS into their routine clinical practice.[34]

CONCLUSION

This entry introduces the concept, history, and key considerations and barriers to providing computerized decision support to clinicians, with a particular focus on systems that provide prompts based on evidence-based clinical guidelines. This stream of CDSS has become increasingly popular and viewed as a key solution to addressing the quality and safety problems of the U.S. health care system. Cutting-edge research is also being conducted to explore the efficacy and applicability of more sophisticated decision models particularly those accommodating decision making under uncertainty. Readers who wish to develop a full spectrum of knowledge of CDSS may refer to the OpenClinical

Project (http://www.openclinical.org/dss.html) or Berner's textbook *Clinical Decision Support Systems: Theory and Practice*.[35] Practitioners interested in the design, development, and implementation of CDSS may refer to the CDSS Implementer's Guide developed by the Healthcare Information and Management Systems Society.[36]

REFERENCES

1. Ledley, L.L.B. Reasoning foundations of medical diagnosis; symbolic logic, probability, and value theory aid our understanding of how physicians reason. Science **1959**, *130* (3366), 9–21.

2. Ledley, L.L.B. Computers in medical data processing. Oper. Res. **1960**, *8*(3), 299–310.

3. Engle, R.L., Jr. Attempts to use computers as diagnostic aids in medical decision making: A thirty-year experience. Perspect. Biol. Med. **1992**, *35*(2), 207–219.

4. Berner, E.S.; Detmer, D.E.; Simborg, D. Will the wave finally break? A brief view of the adoption of electronic medical records in the United States. J. Am. Med. Inform. Assoc. **2005**, *12*(1), 3–7.

5. Berner, E.S.; Moss, J. Informatics challenges for the impending patient information explosion. J. Am. Med. Inform. Assoc. **2005**, *12*(6), 614–617.

6. Sackett, D.L.; Rosenberg, W.M.; Gray, J.A.; Haynes, R.B.; Richardson, W.S. Evidence based medicine: What it is and what it isn't. BMJ **1996**, *312*, 71–72.

7. Keehan, S.; Sisko, A.; Truffer, C.; Smith, S.; Cowan, C.; Poisal, J.; Clemens, M.K. National Health Expenditure Accounts Projections Team. Health spending projections through 2017: The baby-boom generation is coming to medicare. Health Aff. (Millwood) **2008**, *27*, w145–w155.

8. Organisation for Economic Co-operation and Development. *OECD Health Data 2008*. Available at http://www.oecd.org/document/30/0,3343,en_2649_34631_12968734_1_1_1_1,00.html.

9. American College of Physicians. Achieving a high-performance health care system with universal access: What the United States can learn from other countries. Ann. Intern. Med. **2008**, *148*, 55–75.

10. Employee Benefit Research Institute. *The Health Confidence Survey*. Available at http://www.ebri.org/pdf/notespdf/EBRI_Notes_10–2008.pdf.

11. Institute of Medicine. *To Err Is Human: Building a Safer Health System*, National Academies Press: Washington, DC, 2000.

12. Turban, E. *Decision Support and Expert Systems: Management Support Systems*, 4th Ed. Prentice-Hall: Upper Saddle River, NJ, 1995.

13. Payne, T.H. Computer decision support systems. Chest **2000**, *118*(2), 47S–52S.

14. Schwartz, W.B. Medicine and the computer. The promise and problems of change. N. Engl. J. Med. **1970**, *283*(23), 1257–1264.

15. Miller, R.A. Medical diagnostic decision support systems—Past, present, and future: A threaded bibliography and brief commentary. J. Am. Med. Inform. Assoc. **1994**, *1*(1), 8–27.

16. Berner, E.S.; Webster, G.D.; Shugerman, A.A.; Jackson, J. R.; Algina, J.; Baker, A.L.; Ball, E.V.; Cobbs, C.G.; Dennis, V.W.; Frenkel, E.P.; Hudson, L.D.; Mancall, E.L.; Rackley, C.E.; Taunton, O.D. Performance of four computer-based diagnostic systems. N. Engl. J. Med. **1994**, *330*(25), 1792–1796.

17. Sim, I.; Gorman, P.; Greenes, R.A.; Haynes, R.B.; Kaplan, B.; Lehmann, H.; Tang, P.C. Clinical decision support systems for the practice of evidence-based medicine. J. Am. Med. Inform. Assoc. **2001**, *8*(6), 527–534.

18. Garg, A.X.; Adhikari, N.K.; McDonald, H.; Rosas-Arellano, M.P.; Devereaux, P.J.; Beyene, J.; Sam, J.; Haynes, R.B. Effects of computerized clinical decision support systems on practitioner performance and patient outcomes: A systematic review. JAMA **2005**, *293*(10), 1223–1238.

19. The American Medical Informatics Association. *A Roadmap for National Action on Clinical Decision Support*. Available at http://www.amia.org/files/cdsroadmap.pdf.

20. Kawamoto, K.; Houlihan, C.A.; Balas, E.A.; Lobach, D.F. Improving clinical practice using clinical decision support systems: A systematic review of trials to identify features critical to success. BMJ **2005**, *330*(7494), 765.

21. Peleg, M.; Tu, S.; Bury, J.; Ciccarese, P.; Fox, J.; Greenes, R.A.; Hall, R.; Johnson, P.D.; Jones, N.; Kumar, A.; Miksch, S.; Quaglini, S.; Seyfang, A.; Shortliffe, E.H.; Stefanelli, M. Comparing computer-interpretable guideline models: A case-study approach. J. Am. Med. Inform. Assoc. **2003**, *10*(1), 52–68.

22. Ohno-Machado, L.; Gennari, J.H.; Murphy, S.N.; Jain, N.L.; Tu, S.W.; Oliver, D.E.; Pattison-Gordon, E.; Greenes, R.A.; Shortliffe, E.H.; Barnett, G.O. The guideline interchange format: A model for representing guidelines. J. Am. Med. Inform. Assoc. **1998**, *5*(4), 357–372.

23. Cherry, D.K.; Burt, C.W.; Woodwell, D.A. *National Ambulatory Medical Care Survey: 2001 Summary. Advance Data from Vital and Health Statistics*, National Center for Health Statistics: Hyattsville, MD, 2003.

24. Mechanic, D.; McAlpine, D.D.; Rosenthal, M. Are patients' office visits with physicians getting shorter?. N. Engl. J. Med. **2001**, *344*, 198–204.

25. Østbye, T.; Yarnall, K.S.; Krause, K.M.; Pollak, K.I.; Gradison, M.; Michener, J.L. Is there time for management of patients with chronic diseases in primary care?. Ann. Fam. Med. **2005**, *3*(3), 209–214.

26. Hunt, D.L.; Haynes, R.B.; Hanna, S.E.; Smith, K. Effects of computer-based clinical decision support systems on physician performance and patient outcomes: A systematic review. JAMA **1998**, *280*, 1339–1346.

27. Kaushal, R.; Shojania, K.G.; Bates, D.W. Effects of computerized physician order entry and clinical decision support systems on medication safety: A systematic review. Arch. Intern. Med. **2003**, *163*(12), 1409–1416.

28. Van der Sijs, H.; Aarts, J.; Vulto, A.; Berg, M. Overriding drug safety alerts in CPOE. J. Am. Med. Inform. Assoc. **2006**, *13*, 138–147.

29. Roukema, J.; Steyerberg, E.W.; van der Lei, J.; Moll, H.A. Randomized trial of a clinical decision support system: Impact on the management of children with fever without apparent source. J. Am. Med. Inform. Assoc. **2008**, *15*(1), 107–113.

30. Rhodes, E.T.; Laffel, L.M.; Gonzalez, T.V.; Ludwig, D.S. Accuracy of administrative coding for type 2 diabetes in children, adolescents, and young adults. Diabetes Care **2007**, *30*(1), 141–143.

31. Tang, P.C.; Ralston, M.; Arrigotti, M.F.; Qureshi, L.; Graham, J. Comparison of methodologies for calculating quality measures based on administrative data versus clinical data from an electronic health record system: Implications for performance measures. J. Am. Med. Inform. Assoc. **2007**, *14*(1), 10–15.

32. Linder, J.A.; Schnipper, J.L.; Tsurikova, R.; Melnikas, A.J.; Volk, L.A.; Middleton, B. Barriers to electronic health record use during patient visits. AMIA Annu. Symp. Proc. **2006**, 499–503.

33. Anderson, J.G.; Aydin, C.E.; Jay, S.J. *Evaluating Health Care Information Systems*, SAGE Publications: Thousand Oaks, CA, 1994.

34. Zheng, K.; Padman, R.; Johnson, M.P.; Diamond, H.S. Understanding technology adoption in clinical care: Clinician adoption behavior of a point-of-care reminder system. Int. J. Med Inform. **2005**, *74*(7–8), 535–543.

35. Berner, E.S. *Clinical Decision Support Systems: Theory and Practice*, 2nd Ed.; Springer: New York, 2007.

36. Osheroff, J.A.; Pifer, E.A.; Teich, J.M.; Sittig, D.F.; Jenders, R.A. *Improving Outcomes with Clinical Decision Support: An Implementer's Guide*, Productivity Press: New York, 2005.

Circulation–College

College Libraries

Thomas G. Kirk, Jr.
Earlham College Libraries, Earlham College, Richmond, Indiana, U.S.A.

Abstract

College libraries, through a combination of forces have made unprecedented strides in the development of access to information resources and in offering services to help students and faculty make greater use of these resources. In so doing, college libraries have become more critical to the success of the host institution. They are now poised to build on the advancements of the past 30 years to respond to the environmental changes and user expectations and to meet the challenges of being even more integral to the academic program.

INTRODUCTION

For this entry, "college libraries" includes the libraries in the 527 institutions classified as either Baccalaureate Colleges-Liberal Arts or Baccalaureate Colleges-General in the 2000 Carnegie Classification.[1] A sampling of the 527 institutions using data from the 2000 edition of *Peterson's Guide*[2] indicates that the average enrollment of this group is 1239 students. The libraries of these institutions average about 182,000 volumes. The averages are deceiving because the collection sizes range from 50,000 volumes to well over a million, and enrollment ranges between 98 to more than 4000 students. Therefore, neither size of collections, and thus probably neither facilities nor staff size, nor size of student body can neatly define the group. The definition of the category as having primarily or exclusively 4-year undergraduate programs is the one characteristic that the institutions share.

BACKGROUND

The history of college libraries is documented through the early 1960s in Richard Harwell's article in the earlier edition of this encyclopedia.[3] Harwell focused largely on the development of college library buildings and collections with particular attention to special collections. However, stimulated by such publications as Daniel Gore's "zero growth,"[4] Evan Farber's "university-library syndrome,"[5–7] A.P. Marshall's "librarians as educators,"[8] and William Moffett's "life and redemption this side of ARL,"[9] in the 1970s and early 1980s, college librarians began to broaden their activities. Although the specifics of each article are important, and in fact could be the subject on a separate essay, what is especially important here is that, together, they signal the recognition of college libraries' potential to play an important role in the education of undergraduates. Since their writing, the messages of these entries have been given substance and texture in the development of library programs.

It is important to understand the changing nature of higher education over these 30 years. As Edward Holley has indicated, the early 1970s were a time of great pessimism in higher education. Support for higher education had declined in the federal and state governments since the 1950s and 1960s, and high inflation in the economy and a sharply declining birth rate all made the future of higher education look bleak.[10] In contrast, by the end of the millennium, inflation had declined, enrollment had increased, and a broadened social role had very much changed the ethos of higher education.[11] As a result, the challenges faced by undergraduate libraries changed over the 30-year period. Libraries that had to make do with fewer resources in the 1960s, by the 1990s had increasing resources but faced increasing user expectations for access to information resources.

To reflect the shifting challenges in college libraries, the rest of this entry addresses six areas: the use of information technology; collection development; interlibrary loan; bibliographic instruction/information literacy; changes in assessment and accreditation standards; and library management, structure, and staffing. There are a number of other topics that might have been treated, but it is the author's judgment that these six are not only the most critical and most central to the recent developments in college libraries, but will likely be the central and critical issues in the near future.

DEVELOPMENT OF INFORMATION TECHNOLOGY

Despite the beginnings of the application of data processing in business and in large academic libraries, none of the four articles by Farber, Gore, Marshall, and Moffett mentions the potential of computer technology in

Encyclopedia of Library and Information Sciences, Fourth Edition DOI: 10.1081/E-ELIS4-120008641

college libraries, nor is there much written on computers in college libraries in the early to mid-1960s. Although some visionaries may have seen the coming importance of computer technology in college libraries, in practice computers were of little concern for college librarians. For example, the 1974 edition of the venerable *The Administration of the College Library* by Guy Lyle, almost a textbook for college librarians, although it does discuss the potential use of computers in acquisitions, cataloging, and circulation in college libraries, it is very tentative about its role.[12] Typical of Lyle's attitude is the conclusion to the section on circulation, where he writes:

> It must be said, of course, that few college libraries, and then only the very large ones have fully automated their circulation services. . . At what stage it is practical to make the conversion from manual or semi-automated circulation systems to a fully automated system. . .has not yet been clearly settled.[12]

If Farber and others had written their articles in the 1990s, they would have been compelled to discuss computer technology's impact on their topics. In fact, Farber later did so in an article discussed below.[13] The absence of discussion of computers in college libraries in the 1960s is not a reflection on college librarian's lack of foresight but rather indicates the rapidity of change in the status of computer technology over the next 30 years. Some would say technology has been *the* critical issue and will continue to be in the future.

College libraries have generally not been leaders in the implementation of new technologies because of the equipment and labor costs of implementation and the rapid obsolescence of experimental technologies. On the other hand, college libraries have rapidly embraced technologies when standardized and relatively easy-to-implement services and products became available. Perhaps the best example is the implementation of OCLC, originally the Ohio College Library Center, and now the Online Computer Library Center. It began operations in Ohio in 1971 and spread nationally beginning a year later.[14,15] The impetus for OCLC's development came from the large academic libraries in Ohio that funded its early development.[16] Once the service was well established and began to spread beyond Ohio, college libraries were quick to embrace it. In recognition of the difficulty colleges had in paying for the implementation of OCLC, the W.K. Kellogg Foundation provided 302 college libraries grants to support the purchase of equipment, training, and a portion of the operational costs for a few years. OCLC is central to library operations, and almost all college libraries are members of OCLC, usually through a regional or state network.

The implementation of OCLC in college libraries had a profound and almost immediate impact on technical operations of the library (e.g., cataloging, acquisitions,

and interlibrary loan). OCLC's services replaced many manual processes within libraries' technical operations. As a result, there were changes in work assignments and the organization of technical operations within college libraries.[17,18] However, the implementation of OCLC in college libraries was almost totally invisible to library users and had very limited impact on other parts of the library (e.g., circulation, reference).

A similar pattern of development occurred in the next major stages of technology's use in college libraries: electronic databases and library automation systems. University libraries typically began their library automation efforts by building their own systems, whereas most college libraries waited until commercial systems that could be installed and operated with modest technical support became available. Although many colleges did use CD-ROM databases and a few even networked the databases, it was not until services such as Silver Platter and First Search became available over the Internet that use of electronic databases became common and have now almost entirely replaced the use of print indexes.

Unlike the implementation of OCLC, which largely affected only technical operations of the library, online library systems or, later, the provision of online databases had a profound impact throughout the college library.[19] The combination of integrated systems and the provision of patron access to the technology both united the organization and fundamentally expanded the role of the library. The use of the integrated system by all departments created an entity in which the entire staff had a vested interest. Because the system is the working tool for all activities, the quality of the system and information it provides is of paramount interest to all members of the library staff. Furthermore, the library staff must now work more closely with a variety of external groups to make the system work effectively. Most obvious are the technical staff who operate the system such as computer center staff, vendor, and/or consortia support staff. The other major external group is library users. The uniqueness of local system configurations, the rapidity of change and the inherent difficulties in understanding how the systems operate have increased the instructional and reference support role of librarians.

Computer technology, including OCLC, local systems, on-line bibliographic databases, and online full texts, has had a significant impact on college library budgets. First and foremost has been building and maintaining the computer infrastructure. Although some of the costs may have been absorbed by the computing services budget, these new expenses have doubtless had an impact on the library's budget through competition with computing services for campus funding. Beyond the infrastructure support, college libraries have also had to absorb the costs of purchasing the content of indexes, online journals or electronic books. Although the annual costs of purchasing the content may replace or at least reduce the costs of building new space and maintaining print collections, budgeting for electronic resources will continue to be a challenge to college libraries.

Technology has extended its replacement of print resources well beyond indexes and now is on an accelerating pace to replace print periodicals and is making significant inroads in providing electronic books. That electronic texts will replace many print books is not debatable any more; the question now is how quickly and to what degree.

College libraries now face competition from commercial enterprises that offer "libraries" of electronic resources, for a fee, directly to students. Carol Ann Hughes of Questia, one of these commercial enterprises, talks about the "new competitive space,"[20] pointing out that academic libraries no longer have the exclusive role as the gatherer and supplier of information. If college librarians are to be effective in supporting students' information needs, they must go well beyond providing space and collections. College libraries must provide, to use the business language of the day, added value to their collections and facilities. Such added value includes reference and instructional services both within the library's facilities and over the network, which are tailored to the unique needs of course assignments. Convincing the college community of the value of such activities remains the single most important challenge to college libraries. This is not new; it is the perennial challenge of college librarianship now made imperative by the real competition of commercial enterprises such as Questia. [The Questia service is a commercial activity, begun in 1999, which plans to sell access to "libraries of full-text of books and periodicals directly to students at an annual or monthly rate." More details are available at Questia[SM]—The Revolutionary Online Research Service. Questia Media: n.p.; http:// www.questia.com/what.html (accessed January 20, 2001).] In so doing, college librarians will demonstrate to administrators their unique contributions to the academic program through curriculum-related collection building, development of enhanced methods for accessing information resources, teaching the use of information resources, and providing personal assistance. The impact of such activities is to enhance the teaching and learning process.

COLLECTION DEVELOPMENT

Collection development in college libraries had long been ignored in the overall collection development literature.[21] In 1991, Joanne Schneider Hill and her coauthors produced the first book devoted to collection development in college libraries. In their introduction, they noted the strong belief that collection development activity was the same regardless of the size of the library.[22] Therefore, it was assumed that articles and books about university collection development were applicable to smaller libraries

as well. However, beginning in the late 1970s, perceptions began to change. In her essay, "Collection Development in College and University Libraries: A Comparison,"[23] Mary Casserly thoroughly vitiates that notion. Her point that college and university libraries are different is consistent with Farber's university library syndrome concept. The differences fall into two main categories: purpose and organization. The development of college library collections is highly focused on meeting the immediate needs of undergraduates and only secondarily are other audiences and the long-term future taken into account. This focus is illustrated in a sample collection development policy included in ACRL's CLIP Note #11 on this topic:

> …the major responsibility and top priority of the library lies with the teaching programs at the undergraduate level. The library endeavors to serve the needs of the faculty either by purchasing (if the materials can also be used by the student body) or by securing through interlibrary loan those resources needed for faculty study and research. Although at a much lower priority, the library services the entire college community through the purchase of recreational, cultural and general information materials.[24]

The second difference is in the organizational structure that supports collection development. University libraries often have a separate unit that is responsible for collection development even when there is a broad based liaison relationship of librarians with faculty. The separate unit is seen as critical in managing large budgets and in proactively seeking out material to develop the collection to meet the current and future research needs of faculty and graduate students. In college libraries, there may be one staff member such as the director or an acquisitions or collection development librarian who is responsible for authorizing purchases. However, other librarians, particularly those who work in reference or public services, share responsibilities for developing the collection.

Although the idea that collection development in college libraries should focus on supporting the needs of undergraduates is a broadly shared one, there has been controversy over how the idea might be interpreted and implemented. William Miller and Stephen Rockwood, in a 1979 article, proposed that collection development should be carefully tied to the level of bibliographic instruction activity because that activity is an excellent indicator of library use.[25] However, Evan Farber, an active supporter of bibliographic instruction, claimed that such a narrow basis for collection development was inappropriate on several counts. It is politically problematic because it makes bibliographic instruction an arbiter of budget allocations and thus appears punitive. More importantly, it focuses "support of the curriculum" too narrowly.[26] Farber pointed out that bibliographic instruction is not an end in itself. Rather, like all aspects of the library's program, including collection development, bibliographic instruction is just one way, albeit a critical way, for the library to support the academic program. There are ways in which the library's collection can support the curriculum without the presence of instruction within a department or major program. Farber pointed to the need to support the curriculum as the basic focus of collection development in college libraries.

Throughout much of the twentieth century, college librarians have explored the notion of a core collection. Hardesty and Mark in "searching for the Holy Grail," reviewed the history of the various attempts to create core lists of titles that were considered to be the most important for or best suited to an undergraduate library. However, their review of overlap studies revealed that college library collections have not developed as though there were such a thing as a core collection. Rather, the overlap studies of consortial groups of libraries found that large portions of college library collections, even in the smallest libraries, were unique.[27]

As electronic resources developed, college librarians looked to them as a boon for college libraries: they would greatly enhance the availability of resources and "level the playing field" for college libraries relative to university libraries.[28] However, as the availability of electronic resources has developed, the playing field has not been as level as was hoped because of the high costs, even when there are small library pricing plans. Although there is no doubt that electronic resources have improved access across campus, they are not cheap. In fact, electronic versions of periodical indexes and journals are likely to be more expensive than the print versions or may be an added cost to a required print subscription. Despite that expense, college libraries have acquired electronic resources to improve services and access. To mitigate the high costs of electronic resources, college libraries have either joined state networks (e.g., Galileo, ILLINET),[29] OhioLink, or formed their own consortia (e.g., PALNI[30]) to make joint purchases. Although there is no doubt these joint purchases reduce the out-of-pocket costs to individual libraries, such joint purchases add administrative overhead costs such as participation in consortial governance, the group selection processes for databases, and the management of group license agreements and budgeting.[31]

The development of electronic journal collections has created new entities—block purchases—for college libraries to consider in their collection development. Although many journal titles in electronic format are available individually, publishers have often packaged their periodicals in bundles that require purchase of the entire bundle. These discounted packages greatly benefit large academic and public libraries, but for most college libraries, they are often beyond their financial means, unless purchased consortially. Furthermore, all parts of the package are not items needed to support an undergraduate curriculum.

INTERLIBRARY LOAN

Interlibrary loan may seem a minor service of college libraries and, therefore, undeserving of a separate section. However, those who work in college libraries know that, as a result of a changed view of collection management, as well as economic and technological developments, interlibrary loan is now a central service in college libraries.

Daniel Gore and others foreshadowed the changed view in a 1975 collection of papers entitled *Farewell to Alexandria: Solutions to Space, Growth, and Performance Problems of Libraries*.[32] Throughout the essays, but particularly in Gore's essay of the same title,[33] the idea is presented that if libraries would continue to grow exponentially as they had in the previous three decades, costs of major space and building needs and their attendant costs would be prohibitive. Instead, libraries and their users needed to develop a new view of the role of libraries. That new view was of college library collections as working collections designed to meet the immediate needs of the curriculum,[34] with the complimentary development of services that provide access to those materials, which are occasionally needed. Therefore, the role of interlibrary loan became more important in college libraries. College libraries, whether they subscribed to Gore's "zero-growth" concept or not, were forced to curtail their purchasing because of the inflation in the cost of library materials in the 1970s and 1980s, especially periodicals,[35] and the cost of construction. Concurrently, college librarians came to realize that their libraries could better serve patrons with a smaller carefully selected collection.[36] Also, as Karen Liston Newsome pointed out, improved bibliographic access and the automated request systems through such services as OCLC greatly facilitated increased use of interlibrary loan.[37] In the early 1990s, the availability of electronic databases led to an increase in the use of interlibrary loan.[38] Together, the change in the focus of collection development, the growing costs of library materials, and the application of technology to interlibrary loan, increased the use of interlibrary loan in college libraries.

This increase in the use of interlibrary loan is dramatically illustrated in data from a group of Midwest liberal arts colleges.[39] Over a 20-year period, 1977–1997, lending increased 980%, and borrowing increased 703% (Table 1).

Table 1 Interlibrary loan activity in a selected group of Midwest liberal artscolleges.

	1977–1978	1982–1983	1987–1988	1992–1993	1997–1998
Lent	557	840	1798	2696	6025
Borrowed	852	1001	2101	2622	6844

Although the volume of interlibrary loans borrowed by this group grew dramatically, the number of items lent increased more rapidly. Other reports[40] also showed that college libraries were lending at least as many items as they borrowed and in many cases more. College libraries had become full partners in the national interlibrary loan system, and not as some had predicted, raiders of the collections of larger libraries.

User-initiated interlibrary loan has moved from a possibility to a reality. OCLC's FirstSearch now provides users of their databases with the capacity to initiate an interlibrary loan through the OCLC system.[41] Furthermore, in consortia such as OhioLink, the users can request items directly from member libraries without making the request personally to a local library staff member. This practice has significantly increased the volume of interlibrary borrowing while reducing the volume of material processed through the traditional OCLC system.[42] User-initiated interlibrary loan request are another example of how technology can increase access while reducing unit costs. At the same time, by making requests for loans so easy, the volume of requests may increase and intensifies the need for library users to be more effective and thoughtful users. Some, if not many, college reference librarians have regarded their interactions with students about interlibrary loan requests as "teachable moments" (i.e., occasions to talk over with students their requests). Although such encounters obviate the rapid access and lower cost that technology can provide, the elimination of individual consultation increases the importance of teaching students to evaluate resources and effectively use the local collection before the self-initiated interlibrary loan events occur.[43]

BIBLIOGRAPHIC INSTRUCTION/INFORMATION LITERACY

Perhaps the most significant programmatic change in college libraries has been the development and main streaming of instructional programs. Such programs take many forms, but they all share a common focus: providing students with skills that both help them complete assignments in their courses more effectively and help prepare them for a life of self-directed learning. Such goals serve both the practical short-term needs of students and the long-term goals of an undergraduate education.

Mark Tucker has provided a history of instruction in academic libraries prior to the early 1960s.[44] In that history, Tucker focuses primarily on developments in university libraries. The one exception was the Library-College movement, which began in 1928 and continued into the late 1960s. The history of the concept was told in 1966 in the last major publication on the idea.[45] The Library-College idea was to integrate the library into the curriculum so that the library becomes the college,

melding classroom teachers and librarianship.[46] The concept questions the traditional structure of college personnel by requiring staffing with individuals who do not have the background and training of traditional graduate and professional education. Because of this incongruity, the concept only gained a temporary foothold in a few institutions where the administration could mold the structure of the faculty and the library to approximate what is needed to realize the concept. The idea never survived beyond the few initial implementation efforts.

Despite the failure of the Library-College movement to change the relationships of teaching faculty and librarians, the movement did introduce a new idea to the library profession. Patricia B. Knapp, without mentioning the Library-College concept or the name Louis Shores, the movement's foremost promoter, used the exploration of "methods of developing more vital relationships between the library and college teaching"[47] in her Monteith College project in the early 1960s. Knapp's contributions were cut short by her untimely death in 1972.[48] Nevertheless, her work had a significant impact on the development of bibliographic instruction in college libraries by demonstrating the effectiveness of course-related and course-integrated approaches.

At about the time of the Monteith College experiment, another institution, Earlham College, was beginning to experiment with the concept of course-related instruction. Evan Ira Farber was appointed college librarian at Earlham in 1962 and almost immediately recognized the need for instruction to help students with their course assignments.[49] As Thomas Cottle described the institution in the early 1970s, Earlham gave unusual attention to a range of general education goals, which included preparation for a life of self-directed learning.[50] In this fertile ground, Farber developed a program that would became a model[51–53] that continues to this day.[54] Patricia Breivik writing about the Earlham program says:

> Basic to this entire program—to its integration, its structure and its extensiveness—is a close working relationship between librarians and teaching faculty in planning and implementing library instruction.[55]

This model of close working relationships between librarians and teaching faculty was recognized by librarians such as Breivik as key to the successful incorporation of the library into the academic program, and many sought to explore means to overcome the inherent barriers that the Library-College concept had not overcome. In response, Earlham conducted a number of workshops from the early 1970s to 1995—workshops that gave librarians and faculty an opportunity to examine the Earlham model and to explore how they might build these critical working relationships in their own institutions.[56]

The decade of the 1970s was the golden age of bibliographic instruction in college libraries. In addition to

Earlham's developing program, the Council on Library Resources (CLR) funded 51 projects (36 of them with assistance from the National Endowment for the Humanities) in an effort to support "experimental endeavors to improve the relationship between libraries and faculty."[57] The 51 institutions were predominantly undergraduate institutions, and 35 of those were small liberal arts colleges. This infusion of funding into experiments in library programming designed to enhance the role of libraries in academic programs generated a smorgasbord of examples on which college librarians feasted over the next decade. A bibliography of the publications describing the outcomes of these projects is available in Nancy Gwinn's 1980 review of the CLR programs.[57]

With the increased availability of electronic resources and on-line tools for massaging information, new ideas changed the scope of instruction. Lori Arp[58] and Loanne Snavely and Natasha Cooper[59] have reviewed the semantics, the conceptual dimensions, and the politics of the shift. Over the course of the twentieth century, the terms orientation, library instruction, bibliographic instruction, and information literacy have been used. In succession, the proponents of each new term have claimed the new term is more encompassing and better frames the concept of teaching the use of information resources in relation to the other aspects of the liberal arts. In each case, the new concept is seen as encompassing all previous concepts. For example, bibliographic instruction was seen as including the former content of library instruction, while adding the notion that the instruction should be focused on a broader set of ideas than just how to use a particular library. The scope of the enterprise has been conceptualized in still broader terms, and the responsibilities of librarians have expanded. Jeremy J. Shapiro and Shelley K. Hughes define this expanded scope when they wrote that:

> ... information literacy should in fact be conceived more broadly as a new liberal art that extends from knowing how to use computers and access information to critical reflection on the nature of information itself, its technical infrastructure, and its social, cultural and even philosophical context and impact—as essential to the mental framework of the educated information-age citizen as the trivium of basic liberal arts (grammar, logic and rhetoric) was to the educated person in medieval society.[60]

The implication is that information literacy is not just the responsibility of librarians; it is the responsibility of the entire faculty and the institution.

In response to this change in the concept in the 1990s, the Andrew Mellon Foundation began awarding grants to colleges that, as the CLR grants of the 1970s did, bring librarians, faculty, and the new partner, instructional technologists—those who focus on the application of technology to educational activities—together to develop model programs.[61]

Despite the changing terminology and the expanded scope driven by technology, the critical dynamic remains the working relationship of librarians and classroom faculty. Evan Farber points to this similarity in "Plus Ça Change...."[13]

COLLEGE LIBRARY STANDARDS AND CHANGES IN ASSESSMENT AND ACCREDITATION PROCESSES

College library standards were first promulgated in 1959 by the Association of College and Research Libraries for the purpose of providing "...a guide for the evaluation of libraries in American colleges and universities which emphasize four-year undergraduate instruction...."[62] During the 41 years since then, there have been four revisions, in 1975, 1986, 1995, and 2000. The standards have continued to provide a guide for evaluation despite the changes in the assumptions on which they were founded and the resultant changes in content. The changes in standards can help one understand the changing assumptions about what is most important in assessing a library's quality.

The 1959 standards are in the form of a series of prescriptive statements on the appropriate characteristics of a college library. These are grouped in seven categories: functions, structure and government, budget, staff, collections, building, quality of service and its evaluation, and interlibrary cooperation. The statements of characteristics were written in general terms; for example, in the statement on collections: "The collections should meet the full curricular needs of undergraduate students and should be easily accessible to them."[62] There were only a few quantitative measures such as staff work space (125 square feet per person) and collection size (minimum of 50,000 volumes and 10,000 volumes for each 200 additional students over 600).[62]

Not until 1975 did a new set of standards appear.[63] Although "should" was changed to "shall" and there were other minor changes in language, the major changes were the addition of "commentary" and quantitative standards. Organized under eight categories (objectives, collections, organization of materials, staff, delivery of service, facilities, administration and budget) each standard has appended "a brief explanatory exegesis...citing the reasons for its inclusion and providing suggestions and comments upon its implementation."[63] This "commentary" appears to be a reaction to the vagueness of the 1959 standards. The intention of the authors seemed to be to provide some guidance about implementation through specific suggestions.

The second major change was the addition of quantitative measures for collection, staff, building, and budget size. In each case, a formulaic approach was developed that took into account the size of the institution and the scope of the curriculum. By using these formulas, it was deemed possible to provide some objective evidence of library quality and minimum. It was further hoped that by providing a basis for comparison among college libraries, poorly supported libraries would have the data to argue for enhanced resources. In fact, the writers went so far as to assign grades (A, B, C, D, and unacceptable) to various levels of achievement for each quantitative standard.[63]

The 1986 and 1995 revisions of the standards[64,65] resulted in little substantial change, despite serious questions raised by RayCarpenter[67] who analyzed how well—actually how poorly—libraries performed relative to the standards, and despite a growing body of literature that pointed to performance measures as a more appropriate mechanism for assessing the quality of libraries. Nevertheless, the formulas for collections, staffing, building, and budget were left the same. Revisions in the language of the standards and the commentaries were updated in the 1986 edition to better account for nonprint collections and services and networking and cooperative activities, but the overall structure was left intact.[64]

The introduction to the 1995 standards noted the rapid changes in technology and acknowledged that although more technological developments would have significant impact on library operations, it "will take about thirty years" for libraries to really respond to advances in technology.[65] Thus, they left it to the next generation of revisors to incorporate technology into the standards.

Even before the 1995 standards were written, Ronald Leach had called for academic librarians to focus more on outcomes as an indicator of quality in academic libraries.[67] The increasing recognition of outcomes as an indicator of quality led the Association of College and Research Libraries to establish a Task Force on Academic Library Outcomes Assessment in 1998. In its report, the task force went to some length to distinguish among inputs, outputs, and outcomes. With these three different ways of looking at library performance in mind, the task force concluded:

> ...that standards should be based on evidence of normative practice or...programmatic success as determined by the measurement of outcomes. ...Wherever possible, inputs should be related to and support desired outcomes, rather than vice-versa.[68]

One recommendation of that report was that ACRL should revise its library standards; as a result, the College Library Section's Standards Committee took the initiative to write the first ACRL set of standards that used the tripartite concepts of inputs, outputs, and outcomes as the paradigm. The 2000 edition of the Standards for College Libraries[69] has sections not unlike the earlier editions, but it also has newly titled sections that reflect a focus on services and activities (e.g., instruction, and access). The 2000 edition includes a series of "should" statements, not

unlike those of the 1959 standards, but each of these statements is followed by a series of questions that give definition and specificity to the "should." In the 2000 standards, the quantitative standards were removed, and a new section was added on "Planning, Assessment and Outcomes Assessment." The new standards do not reject input measurements as part of the assessment process. Rather, they suggest a combination of measures, One measure is based on ratios that take into account an institution's size (e.g., acquisitions expenditures per student). A second measure examines outputs and outcomes.

The ACRL Standards are the principal means by which librarians have measured quality in college libraries, but for the regional accrediting agencies, the quality of college libraries is measured through a set of standards that are less specific and placed in the context of the larger institution. Despite the differences, according to Paul Coleman and Ada D. Jarred's analysis, the assessment criteria for libraries in five regional accrediting associations' standard focused on issues similar to those in the 1986 Standards for College Libraries, although the ACRL Standards are more quantitative.[70]

As Coleman and Jarred acknowledge, the accreditation standards go beyond the measurement of inputs to focus on output measures. It appears that in the 2000 revision of the Standards, ACRL was trying to catch up with the regional accrediting associations' emphasis on output and outcome assessment.

As this entry was being written, some accrediting agencies were in the process of revising their criteria for accreditation. The changes continued to move further in the direction of outcomes by framing the criteria in student learning, As Jane Wellmen, senior associate of the Institute for Higher Education Policy, pointed out, "Learning outcomes assessments have been a long time coming and are, in many ways, a welcome and necessary change."[71] However in over emphasizing them at the expense of basic measures of resources available (e.g., size of faculty, size of library collection, and amount of time spent in class), Wellmen fears that assessment of learning outcomes that best serves the internal development of the institution is too narrow a gauge of quality for the external world of the larger society. Through input measures an institution is better able to demonstrate the resources that are needed to strengthen the institution. Furthermore, not everything in an institution should be viewed through the lens of student outcomes. For example, it would be futile to try to assess the quality of a library facility through the level of student learning because of the indirectness of the connection between student performance and quality of facilities and the number of mitigating factors such as number of library assignments and the quality of information literacy program.

In the fall of 2000, the Accreditation Review Project of the Commission on Colleges, an arm of the Southern Association of Colleges and Schools (SACS) illustrates another problematic trend in library assessment. In an effort to create a performance assessment statement that encompass all types of service deployment—traditional building based library and virtual electronic collections—the standards statement is written in the most general terms. In the draft "Principles and Requirements for Accreditation" issued in September 2000 for membership comment, the criteria for library services are stated as follows:

Core Requirement Related to Learning Resources

The institution provides and supports student and faculty access and user privileges to adequate learning and information resources which are consistent with the degrees offered and are sufficient to support all educational, research and public service programs (Core Requirement#9).[72]

This statement is not only vague but begs the question of what is a quality library. Furthermore, the statement lacks any interest in the college library's educational role beyond supplying sufficient resources. The efforts to measure effectiveness in outcomes and to describe adequacy in the most general terms—sufficiency to meet program needs—tend to confuse those interested in understanding the characteristics of a quality college library.

LIBRARY MANAGEMENT, STRUCTURE, AND STAFF CHANGES

A number of factors have had and will continue to have a profound impact on the staffing of college libraries: the changing nature of assessment and accreditation, economics, the increased use of technology, the declining supply of librarians, and the expanding mission of libraries. This impact is evident at every level of the college library staff—student employees, paraprofessionals, librarians, and library managers—as well as the organization as a whole.

A series of articles have appeared on the roles, responsibilities, and management of student employees[73–75] and paraprofessionals.[76] The increased sophistication in their work is the result of the increased use of technology and the shift in work tasks of librarians to instructional programming and management of technology. These articles identify the increasing complexity of their work and the resultant need for more training.

Although many aspects of college library organization have gotten considerable attention, the relationship between computing and the library has probably gotten more attention than any other. In an early article, Guskin et al. concluded the library is the appropriate part of the academic institution to take on the responsibility for helping institutions use microcomputers and their applications software effectively in their educational programs.[77]

That was a prescient comment, and a number of libraries followed that advice. But most did not, and the relationships between the two units varied greatly. In 1997, Larry Hardesty studied the variety of organizational relationships between computing and the library which developed in the absence of any consensus about the college library's role vis-a-vis computing. He concluded:

Libraries and computer centers face similar challenges. ...Nevertheless, no organizational structure will solve all, or even most, of these challenges. ...We must define carefully the problems we seek to solve and consider individual and group differences before hastening to solutions that may prove to be only temporarily fashionable.[78]

Hardesty's conclusion that situational factors should dictate organizational structure is a wise one. It suggests that the preferred structure should not be some imposed ideal but rather the one that best addresses the library's needs.

The challenges of adequately preparing leaders for college libraries has been a concern of the profession,[79] and in response, under the leadership of Larry Hardesty, the Association of College & Research Libraries' College Library Section has conducted the College Library Directors Mentor Program since 1992.[80] This program provides each newly appointed novice director with a mentor, an experienced college library director, with whom she or he could consult; after a few months all first-year directors—15 or so a year—attend a workshop that explores commonly faced issues and approaches to addressing them. This program has become increasingly important as young and less experienced librarians become directors to fill the increasing number of open leadership positions caused by retirements.

CONCLUSION

College libraries, through a combination of forces have made unprecedented strides in the development of access to information resources and in offering services to help students and faculty make greater use of these resources. In so doing, college libraries have become more critical to the success of the host institution. They are now poised to build on the advancements of the past 30 years to respond to the environmental changes and user expectations and to meet the challenges of being even more integral to the academic program.

The authors of the 1995 Standards for College Libraries, beginning to feel the impact of technology, indicated that it would be 30 years before the full impact of technology would be realized in the operation and use of college libraries. What was more likely is that in the 1990s college libraries entered a new world in which change is permanent. College libraries will be constantly adapting to changes in technology, curriculum, economic health of the host institutions, and to the nature of the profession. One doesn't even know if "library" as we know it today will still exist on college campuses. The new forms of competition developed by commercial interests and delivered over the internet could supplant the concept of the library as a physical space and a source of expert advice in using information resources. The ultimate challenge for college libraries is to deliver, at a high level of quality, those services and facilities that are unique and cannot be provided by others. To do that, the following is needed:

1. An adequately trained staff who not only know the traditional technical skills of librarianship but are also effective teachers and collaborators with classroom faculty and other academic professionals.
2. An effective alliance of computing services and the library so that adequate technology can be deployed.
3. A strong program of information literacy/bibliographic instruction that assists students in effectively using information resources for course work and provides them with the skills and attitudes to be effective life-long learners.
4. A balanced approach to collection development and programs of access that maximize the availability of needed information resources within a constrained budget.
5. An active program that both markets the library's services to the community and listens and responds to community needs.

REFERENCES

1. Lively, K. Changes planned for carnegie classifications. Chron. High. Educ. **1999**, *46*(11), A46.
2. *Peterson's 4 Year Colleges*, 30th Ed. Peterson's: Princeton, NJ, 2000.
3. Harwell, R. College libraries. In *Encyclopedia of Library and Information Science*; Kent, A., Ed.; Marcel Dekker: New York, 1970; Vol. 4, 269–281.
4. Gore, D. Zero growth: when is not-enough? A symposium. J. Acad. Librariansh. **1975**, *1*(5), 4–11.
5. Farber, E. College librarians and the university-library syndrome. In *Academic Library: Essays in Honor of Guy Lyle*; Farber, E.I., Walling, R., Eds.; Scarecrow: Metuchen, NJ, 1974; 12–23.
6. Farber, E. College librarians and the university-library syndrome. In *User Instruction in Academic Libraries*; Hardesty, L.L., Ed.; Scarecrow: Metuchen, NJ, 1986; 243–253.
7. Farber, E. College librarians and the university-library syndrome. Coll. Undergraduate Libr. **2000**, *7*(1), 61–69.
8. Marshall, A.P. This teaching/learning thing: librarians as educators. In *Academic Libraries by the Year 2000: Essays Honoring Jerrold Orne*, Herbert, P., Ed.; Bowker: New York, 1977; 50–63.
9. Moffett, W.A. Reflections of a college librarian: looking for life and redemption this side of ARL. Coll. Res. Libr. **1984**, *45*(5), 338–349.
10. Holley, E.G. What lies ahead for academic libraries?. In *Academic Libraries by the Year 2000: Essays Honoring Jerrold Orne*, Herbert, P., Ed.; Bowker: New York, 1977; 7–33.
11. Lazerson, M.; Wagener, U.; Shumanis, N. What makes a revolution? Teaching and learning in higher education, 1980–2000. Change Mag. High. Learn. **2000**, *32*(3), 12–19.
12. Lyle, G. *The Administration of the College Library*, 4th Ed. H.W. Wilson: New York, 1974; 80.
13. Farber, E.I. Plus Ça change.... Libr. Trends **1995**, *44*(2), 430–438.
14. Wayne, S.K. OCLC: yesterday, today and tomorrow. In *OCLC, 1967–1997: Thirty Years of Furthering Access to the World's Information*, Wayne, S.K., Ed.; Haworth Press: New York, 1998; 251–270.
15. Wayne, S.K. Yesterday, today and tomorrow. Libr. Adm. **1998**, *25*(2/3), 251–270.
16. Wayne, S.K. *OCLC, 1967–1997: Thirty Years of Furthering Access to the World's Information*, Haworth Press: New York, 1998.
17. Johnson, P. *Automation and Organizational Change in Libraries*, G.K. Hall: Boston, MA, 1991.
18. Hong, X. The impact of automation on job requirements and qualifications for catalogers and reference librarians in academic libraries. Libr. Resour. Tech. Serv. **1996**, *40*(1), 9–31.
19. Morris, D.E. Electronic information and technology: impact and potential for academic libraries. Coll. Res. Libr. **1989**, *50*(1), 56–64.
20. Hughes, C.A. Information services for higher education: a new competitive space. D-Lib. Mag. **2000**, *6*(12). http://www.dlib.org/dlib/december00/hughes/12hughes.html (accessed December 20, 2000).
21. Hill, J.S. Hannaford, W. E., Jr. In *Collection Development in College Libraries*; Epp, R.H., Ed.; American Library Association: Chicago, IL, 1991.
22. Hill, J.S. Hannaford, W. E., Jr. Epp, R. H. Introduction. In *Collection Development in College Libraries*; Hill, J.S., Hannaford, W.E., Jr., Epp, R.H., Eds.; American Library Association: Chicago, IL, 1991; v–vii.
23. Casserly, M.F. Collection development in college and university libraries: a comparison. In *Collection Development in College Libraries*; Hill, J.S., Hannaford, W. E., Jr., Epp, R.H., Eds.; American Library Association: Chicago, IL, 1991; 3–14.
24. Taborsky, T. Lenkowski, P. Webb, A. Lewis, L. *Collection Development Policies for College Libraries*, Association of College and Research Libraries: Chicago, IL, 1989; 19.
25. Miller, W.; Stephen, R.D. Collection development from a college perspective. Coll. Res. Libr. **1979**, *40*(4), 318–324.
26. Farber, E.I. A collection development from a college perspective: a comment and a response. Coll. Res. Libr. **1979**, *40*(4), 325–326.
27. Hardesty, L.; Mak, C. Searching for the holy grail: a core collection for undergraduate libraries. J. Acad. Librariansh. **1994**, *19*(6), 362–371.
28. Cain, M. Leveling the playing field: college libraries in an electronic age. Coll. Undergrad. Libr. **1996**, *3*(1), 25–29.

29. Potter, W.G. Recent trends in statewide academic library consortia. Libr. Trends **1997**, *45*(3), 416–434.

30. Frye, L.; Lucas, V.; Miller, L. Technology partnerships: the PALNI success story. Indiana Libraries **1999**, *18*(Supplement 1), 41–45.

31. Shoaf, E. The effects of consortia membership on library planning and budgeting. Libr. Admin. Manage. **1999**, *13*(4), 196–201.

32. Gore, D. *Farewell to Alexandria: Solutions to Space, Growth, and Performance Problems of Libraries*, Greenwood Press: Westport, CT, 1975.

33. Gore, D. *Farewell to Alexandria: Solutions to Space, Growth, and Performance Problems of Libraries*; Gore, D., Ed.; Greenwood Press: Westport, CT, 1975; 164–180.

34. Farber, E.I. Limiting college library growth: bane or boon?. In *Farewell to Alexandria: Solutions to Space, Growth, and Performance Problems of Libraries*; Gore, D., Ed.; Greenwood Press: Westport, CT, 1975; 34–43.

35. Frazer, S.L. Impact of periodical cost escalation on small and medium-sized academic libraries: a survey. J. Acad. Librariansh. **1992**, *18*(3), 159–162.

36. Worley, J.H. The importance of being small: collection development in the college library. In *Collection Development in College Libraries*; Hill, J.S., Hannaford, W.E., Jr., Epp, R.H., Eds.; American Library Association: Chicago, IL, 1991; 15–23.

37. Newsome, K.L. Changing strategies: interlibrary loan in the 1990s. Illinois Libraries **1990**, *72*(8), 636–639.

38. Crawford, G.A. The effects of instruction in the use of psyclit on interlibrary loan. RQ **1992**, *31*(3), 370–376.

39. Associated Colleges of the Midwest/Great Lakes Colleges Association. *Annual Library Statistics*, Compiled from data submitted voluntarily by individual institutions by various compilers: Dennis Ribbens, Lawrence University, 1975–1991; Sara McGowan, Ripon College, 1991–1995; Patty Terveer, 1995–1996; Larry Frye, Wabash College, 1996–1998. All available from author of this entry.

40. Some small Illinois libraries are really net lenders. Libr. J. **1986**, *111*(17), 20.

41. OCLC ILL Direct request allows user- initiated, library controlled interlibrary loan. OCLC Syst. Serv. **1998**, *14*(1), 4.

42. Sessions, J.A.; Pettitt, R.N. OhioLINK inter-institutional lending online: the Miami university experience. Libr. Hi Tech. **1995**, *13*(3), 11–25.

43. Walters, S.A. End-user document delivery services: to mediate or not to mediate. Colorado Libraries **1996**, *22* (Fall), 11–13.

44. Tucker, J.M. User education in academic libraries: a century in retrospect. Libr. Trends **1980**, *29*(1), 9–37.

45. Shores, L. Jordan, R. Harvey, J. *The Library-College: Contributions for American Higher Education at the Jamestown College Workshop, 1965*, Drexel Press: Philadelphia, PA, 1966.

46. Shores, L. The college becomes a library. In *User Instruction in Academic Libraries: A Century of Selected Readings*; Hardesty, L. L., Schmitt, J. P., Tucker, J.M., Eds.; Scarecrow Press: Metuchen, NJ, 1986; 204–224. (Reprinted from Drexel Library Quarterly January 1968).

47. Knapp, P.B. *The Monteith College Library Experiment*, Scarecrow Press: New York, 1966; 11.

48. Obituary. Wilson Libr. Bull. **1973**, *47*(1), 407.

49. Farber, E.I. Library instruction throughout the curriculum: Earlham college program. In *Educating Library Users*; Lubans, J., Ed.; R.R. Bowker: New York, 1974; 145–162.

50. Cottle, T.J. A learning place called Earlham. Change Mag. High. Learn. **1971**, *3*(1), 52–59.

51. Rader, H.B. Bibliographic instruction programs in academic libraries. In *Increasing the Teaching Role of Academic Libraries*; Kirk, T.G., Ed.; New Directions for Teaching and Learning Jossey-Bass: San Francisco, CA, 1984; Vol. 18, 63–78.

52. Taylor, S.K. *An Examination of Course-Related Library Instruction Programs at Three Small Private Liberal Arts Colleges*. Ph.D. dissertation, Kansas State University, 1991.

53. Wilkinson, B.R. *Reference Services for Undergraduate Students: Four Case Studies*, Scarecrow Press: Metuchen, NJ, 1972.

54. Kirk, T. G., Jr. Programs that work: Earlham college. In *Programs That Work*; Shirato, L., Ed.; Library Orientation Series Pierian Press: Ann Arbor, MI, 1996; Vol. 24, 35–40.

55. Breivik, P.S. Making the most of libraries; in search for academic excellence. Change Mag. High. Learn. **1987**, *19*(3), 44–53.

56. Hardesty, L. Hastreiter, J. Henderson, D. *Bibliographic Instruction in Practice: A Tribute to the Legacy of Evan Ira Farber*, Pierian Press: Ann Arbor, MI, 1993.

57. Gwinn, N.E. Academic libraries and undergraduate education: the CLR experience. Coll. Res. Libr. **1980**, *41*(1), 5–16.

58. Arp, L. Information literacy or bibliographic instruction: semantics or philosophy? RQ **1990**, *30*(1), 46–49.

59. Snavely, L.; Cooper, N. The information literacy debate. J. Acad. Librariansh. **1997**, *23*(1), 9–14.

60. Shapiro, J.J.; Hughes, S.K. Information literacy as a liberal art. Educom Rev. **1996**, *31*(2). Available at http://www.educause.edu/pub/er/review/reviewarticles/31231.html (accessed December 16, 2000).

61. Boyd, A. *Five Colleges of Ohio Information Literacy/Bibliographic Instruction*, Oberlin College: Oberlin, OH, 2000. Available at http://www.oberlin.edu/library/services/reference/infolit/Ohio5/ (accessed November 18, 2000).

62. Association of College and Research Libraries. Standards for college libraries. Coll. Res. Libr. **1959**, *20*(4), 274–280.

63. Association of College and Research Libraries. Standards for college libraries. Coll. Res. Libr. News **1975**, *36*(9), 277–279, 290–295, 298–301.

64. Association of College and Research Libraries. Standards for college libraries. Coll. Res. Libr. News **1986**, *47*(3), 189–200.

65. Association of College and Research Libraries. Standards for college libraries. Coll. Res. Libr. News **1995**, *56*(4), 245–257.

66. Carpenter, R.L. College libraries: a comparative analysis in terms of the ACRL standards. Coll. Res. Libr. **1981**, *42*(1), 7–18.

67. Leach, R.G. Academic library change: the role of regional accreditation. J. Acad. Librariansh. **1992**, *18*(5), 288–291.

68. Association of College and Research Libraries. Task Force on Academic Library. *Outcomes Assessment Report*, Association of College and Research Libraries: Chicago, IL,

1998. Available at http://www.ala.org/acrl/outcome.html (accessed November 25, 2000).

69. Association of College and Research Libraries. *Standards for College Libraries*, Association of College and Research Libraries: Chicago, IL, 2000. Available at http://www.ala.org/acrl/guides/college.html (accessed November 25, 2000).

70. Coleman, P. Regional association criteria and the standards for college libraries: the informal role of quantitative input measures for libraries in accreditation. J. Acad. Librariansh. **1994**, *20*, 273–284.

71. Wellman, J.V. Accreditors have to see past 'learning objectives'. Chron. High. Educ. **2000**, *47*(4), B20.

72. Southern Association of Colleges and Schools, Commission on Colleges. *Accreditation Review Project. A Proposal: Principles and Requirements for Accreditation*, Southern Association of Colleges and Schools: Decatur, GA, 2000. Available at http://www.sacscoc.org/COC/AccrProposal.htm (accessed December 22, 2000).

73. Kathman, J. McG.; Kathman, M.D. Training student employees for quality service. J. Acad. Librariansh. **2000**, *26*(3), 176–182.

74. Kathman, M.D. Kathman, J. McG. *Managing Student Workers in College Libraries*, Association of College and Research Libraries: Chicago, IL, 1986.

75. White, E.C. Student assistants in academic libraries: from reluctance to reliance. J. Acad. Librariansh. **1985**, *11*(2), 93–97.

76. Oberg, L.R. Paraprofessionals: time to celebrate or time to move the agenda?. Coll. Undergraduate Libr. **1999**, *6*(1), 17–22.

77. Guskin, A.E.; Stoffle, C.J.; Baruth, B.E. Library future shock: the microcomputer revolution and the new role of the library. Coll. Res. Libr. **1984**, *45*(3), 177–1183.

78. Hardesty, L. Computer center-library relations at smaller institutions: a look from both sides. Cause/eff. **1998**, *21*(1), 35–41. Available at http://www.educause.edu/ir/library/html/cem9817.html (accessed November 11, 2000).

79. O'Keeffe, J. Small college library directors: getting in the door and surviving on the job. Coll. Res. Libr. **1998**, *59*(2), 140–153.

80. Hardesty, L. College library directors mentor program: passing it on: a personal reflection. J. Acad. Librariansh. **1997**, *23*(4), 281–290.

Circulation-College

Communication and Communication Studies

Brenda Dervin
School of Communication, Ohio State University, Columbus, Ohio, U.S.A.

CarrieLynn D. Reinhard
Department of Communication, Business, and Information Technologies, Roskilde University, Roskilde, Denmark

Abstract

The focal purpose of this entry is to lay out the contours, within historical contexts, of the structural arrangements and intellectual foci of the various areas of study and emphases in institutions of higher education generally clustered under the much used and abused term "communication." Because communication studies has been a presence in the academy for less than 60 years, and because it has evolved in the midst of an exploding and rapidly changing communication environment, there are necessarily multiple and competing stories to be told. This entry attempts to focus both on convergences and divergences. The entry reviews in turn: different meanings for the word "communication" and how and when the term came into popular usage; the two primary historical lineages out of which communication studies has emerged— speech communication and mass communication; the forces leading to institutionalization, including the exploding emergence of mass media. The entry examines the phases in which communication studies became institutionalized and how supporting structures of organizations and journals have handled seemingly overwhelming diversity. The entry concludes with a discussion of how communication studies necessarily holds within its core a series of contradictions that are in essence symptom and cause of both centralities and dispersions, struggles and successes.

INTRODUCTION

Communication is a much used and abused term. In everyday parlance, it most often refers to humans sharing experiences, ideas, and feelings with each other via some kind of verbal or nonverbal symbolic language, including words, gestures, body language, tonality, and nonverbal expressions. Sometimes this sharing is done in person; sometimes over an increasingly wide variety of mediated means, across stretches of time and space. Sometimes the sharing is one person to one; sometimes one to many; sometimes many to many.[1–3]

Much emphasis is placed in our society on improving communication. At one and the same time it is felt that improved communication will make each of us more successful at persuading others; and simultaneously help us get along better with each other within and between families, groups, organizations, and nations. Good communication is expected to help us to be better informed and more knowledgeable, increase both human happiness and effectiveness, and facilitate justice, democracy, and peace. Communication is assumed to be a fundamental and essential social process.[2,4] Much is asked of a phenomenon about which there are, when one digs below the surfaces, an extraordinary number of differing and competing definitions, theories and expectations of what role communication does, could, or should play in human affairs.[2,5–14]

It is not known who first used the word "communication." The term itself is visibly identifiable in a variety of forms in biblical and philosophic writings in the fourteenth century. But, before that in the first century B.C., the ancient Greeks focused on concerns for effective communication with their emphases on rhetoric and oratory. Throughout the ages, tales focusing in some way on communication have appeared in literature, folklore, poetry, and religious treatises. One famous example is Persian Omar Khayyam's Rubaiyat in which concerns for communication between leaders and the people are a frequent focus. Another is the Anansi myth, a generative base for numerous tales that originated in West Africa and spread via imposed slavery and diasporic immigration of African communities throughout the globe.[15–19]

It is fair to say that communication has been a fundamental concern for the human species since antiquity.[16,19] Yet, the appearance of institutionalized emphases labeled communication via academic courses and programs did not begin to appear until the late 1930s and 1940s. The appearance of these emphases emerged from a convergence of long journeys from disparate origins with sometimes incommensurate understandings. Major players in the story have journeyed from such diverse fields as anthropology, education, engineering, literature, family life, linguistics, literature, government, philosophy, political science, psychology, rhetoric, semantics, semiotics, sociology, and written and oral

Encyclopedia of Library and Information Sciences, Fourth Edition DOI: 10.1081/E-ELIS4-120043528

composition.[5,15–17,20–25] The result has become an array of institutional arrangements that still, despite some 70-plus years of development, appears chaotic both to outside and inside observers.

The story of communication must be told in a way that allows this chaos to remain apparent while making some sense of what must be called an extraordinary revolution in scholarly attention—a revolution that moved us from a time when no academic unit admitted to focusing on communication to a time when communication has become virtually everyone's concern with emphases on communication spread throughout virtually every academic institution. At the same time, the story must be told in a way that allows not only the divergences and differences to show but centralities as well. Particularly important is the centrality of what for many in communication studies, including most of the notable founders, is more than merely an intellectual focus but a passion for and a vision of what difference it would make to look at humans and their institutions, cultures, communities, nations, and societies through a new kind of lens. This lens, a communication lens, focuses not on separate habit-driven entities, as the common conception of human beings and their collectivities comes to us from psychology, sociology, and anthropology, but on how these entities use communication to forge the human experience in the constantly changing and often chaotic conditions that constitute the contexts within which humans live.[8,14,27–29]

Finally, because communication studies, as a relatively recent arrival on the academic scene, has struggled with self-definition and with self-defense in often rigid academic hierarchies, there has been an extraordinary self-consciousness in the field resulting in a plethora of self-examining articles.[5,7,9,11,12,14,27,30] The literature is large, disparate, and incomplete.[5,20] References in this entry must be understood as illustrative rather than comprehensive. This entry limits specific details to the U.S. context although the available histories suggest that the impelling forces and consequences have been much the same worldwide except for how specific cultural environments have changed qualitative emphases in each national, regional, and cultural context.[5,15,17,22–24] Brief examples will be given of these differences but the story as told here applies primarily to the United States.

The presentation of the varying stories of communication and communication studies is presented below in six sections: 1) meanings for the word "communication" and how these anchor on a common core but also vary markedly; 2) two primary institutions that became the sites of communication studies—speech and mass communication; 3) the exploding emergence of media; 4) the phases of the institutionalization; 5) structures for handling the diversity; 6) communication studies and its productive tensions.

The narrative is organized around a presentation that examines: 1) how emerging societal attentions to something called communication, particularly as sparked by the exploding diffusion of mass media, led to two streams of communication studies, one based in ancient humanistic studies of rhetoric; the other focusing on the scientific study of media; 2) how these different streams have moved toward each other while retaining their historical characters; and 3) how communication studies in general manages the necessary diversities of attention imposed by the fact that communication—the phenomena of interest—always occurs in particular contexts with distinctive attributes.

Meanings for the Word "Communication"

Purpose in this section is to examine the emergence of the term "communication" and how it was put on policy and popular agendas, and ultimately, academic agendas. The second purpose is to survey the various definitions applied to the term, focusing on both a common core while exhibiting the many divergences.

While the species has addressed concerns about communication since ancient times, early systematic attentions were limited to the study and practice of rhetoric as artful oratory in public and institutional settings.[5,15–17,26] Below the surfaces of these systematic attentions there were the ruminations of poets, storytellers, and religious leaders capturing what they saw as wisdoms for understanding essential struggles of human existence—the problems of getting along even within relatively homogenous enclaves and temporally and geographically confined boundaries.[18,19] The varying uses of the term communication as we know them today did not begin to emerge until advances in technology permitted mass production of messages and the transmission of these messages across time and space The term first drew large-scale attention in policy debates and in popular imagination. These attentions were impelled by the exploding diffusion of mass media in the first half of the twentieth century as well as by the increased struggles to gain public space in which to be heard by diverse populations worldwide. It was these attentions and events that made the institutionalization of academic studies in communication possible.[5,16,17,20,26,31]

Most definitions of communication have a common core although this common core goes beyond the "sharing" focus that dominates popular usage. Definitions focus on sharing but also relaying, transmitting, imparting, or exchanging in some way a message or messages of some kind via some means from one or more entities to one or more other entities in some context. The entities to which this core definition of communication has been applied have included not only human beings and their various collectivities and symbolic artifacts, but also other living animals as well as nonliving entities such as radio systems and railroads.[1–3,5,20,23]

The last point deserves special emphasis because, in fact, the emergence of communication as a term in the

English language between the late 1700s and the late 1970s was as likely to focus on communication as linkages between humans as to refer to connecting passages, sea channels, railroads, electrical transmissions, and other technological and natural avenues that permitted movement across space and time.[5,20] When the term referred to human communication, it was as likely to imply a view of humans as transmitting senders and receivers as it was to focus on humans relating, sharing, or exchanging with each other. Further, it was as likely to refer to communication as instrumental manipulation and persuasion as it was to engendering mutual understandings. It was rarely used to refer to something now called intrapersonal communication—self communicating with oneself across time and space.[8,14],28]

Some observers suggest that the tensions between these branches of emphasis still mark communication studies today.[5,11,12,20] Some have argued that the U.S. emphasis on instrumental communication that dominated communication studies from the 1950s through 1980s was an unconsciously adopted preference for meanings that reflected the instrumental ideologies that had dominated the very character of U.S. expansion.[10,13,20,23] Some have charged that this hidden hegemony is one cause of why histories of communication study and its emphases vary sometimes quite markedly between portraits emphasizing instrumental values and those emphasizing humanistic values. These issues remain among the many enduring debates in communication studies. In particular, there remain concerns about whether or not conceptualizing human beings as if they are transmitters and receivers is useful for understanding the role communication plays in the human condition.

When the core definitions above are applied specifically to human communication, on the surface at least the definitions seem to have much in common. One simple and common definition of communication is "how people use messages to exchange meaning."[1] From this simple core, one finds a large variety of definitions that bring in more and more aspects of the phenomena as the definers see it. Two typical more complex definitions might read as follows: how people use messages to generate meaning within and across contexts, cultures, channels, and media; or, the processes by which people inform, persuade, manage, relate to, and influence via channels and media through contexts and culture.[2,3]

As will be shown below, within these seemingly congruent definitions, those doing communication studies have launched upon a dizzying array of topics, theories, models, and approaches. Most of the differences are accountable in terms of how different researchers have chosen to focus on different goals, contexts, levels of analysis, and so on. We find, for example, different scholars defining communication in ways useful to the study of communication: 1) at different levels of social analysis, e.g., interpersonally, intergenerationally,

cross-culturally, internationally; 2) in different content or knowledge domain applications, e.g., health, politics, democracy, marriage; 3) in terms of the goals they see communication serving, e.g., persuasion, negotiation, dialogue; or, 4) in terms of how communication serves and impacts different socially defined groups, for example, women, minorities, disabled, gays, and lesbians. These are but examples for the differences are many.[3,5,32–34] The differences can be seen as details on which the study of communication must be based. Yet, communication studies must also bracket the differences in order to look at communicative essences.

It is important to note, however, there are more subtle variations that mark attempts to define communication. Various authors have identified these in different ways and many different words are used for the relaying, transmitting, imparting, sharing, or exchanging that seems central to all definitions. To illustrate these variations, consider the word relaying. Cutting across the differences, it can be said that definitions of communication and implementations of these definitions focus on communication as: 1) behavior: the act of relaying; 2) codes: the languages and symbolic systems used in the relaying; 3) information: the contents that are being relayed; 4) message: the package in which the contents are wrapped so they can be relayed; 5) means: the channel, media, or system through which the message is relayed; 6) skills and techniques: the relaying practices and procedures; 7) process: the steps involved in the relaying across time-space; 8) meanings: interpretations of the message as understood by those involved in the relaying; and 9) outcomes: impacts of the relaying, often an assessment of whether the relaying was successful.[5]

These subtle differences in definitional emphasis make a great deal of difference when it comes to understanding what is being addressed. Take, for example, the difference between a definition that focuses on communication as process versus one focusing on it as outcome. For the latter, communication is an end point, it comes after the relaying. For the former, it is the very process of relaying itself. As another example, compare a definition focusing on information with an external authoritative representation of message content versus one focusing on meanings where interpretation occurs within a person or cultural context. The mischief caused by these differences is, understandably, the subject of enduring debates in communication studies.

Two Primary Institutions—Speech and Mass Communication

As will be shown below, communication as a focus of study eventually spread into every nook and cranny of the academy. However, the history of the institutionalization of communication studies has been essentially the story of two major emerging structural arrangements. One focus has become today's emphases on mass communication, broadcasting, and journalism; media studies; advertising and public relations; communication and information technology; and communication law, policy, and economics. The other focus has become emphases on speech, rhetoric, debate, argumentation, and oral interpretation; communication codes; interpersonal and intercultural communication; group, organizational, network communication, and, sometimes, speech and hearing science. These basic categories of attention in the two root structures can be found in varying combinations across academic units. The two root structures are themselves most often referred to as mass communication and speech communication.[9,16,17,21,23,25,31,35]

In today's academia, many units still reflect these historical divisions, although rarely as cleanly as suggested above. Further, when one sees a unit named simply communication, that unit will usually be reflective of one or the other of these lineages. Sometimes one finds a comprehensive or unified unit that cuts across the lineages. In the United States, these are more likely to be found at second tier and teaching-oriented institutions. In top tier universities, the lineages often remain divided even to the extent that sometimes the media-oriented unit will be located in a social sciences college while the speech-oriented unit will be in a college of humanities. When one looks at the two major journeys that constituted the advance of communication studies—that of mass and speech communication—it becomes possible to understand why to this date the histories of the field and descriptions of its emphases show great diversity and competing narratives.

The mass communication journey involved the introduction of new, modern emphases on artifacts with relatively recent introductions—newspapers, radio, film, telephones, television, digital games, and the Internet. In a relatively short span of time, new media units were introduced from one end of the country to the other in academia first with a focus on skills trainings and not long after in order to understand the rise and role of media in people's lives and society at large.[5,17,23,26]

In contrast, the speech communication journey arose from its ancient legacy focusing on rhetoric, dialogue, discussion, argumentation, and oratory. It involved absorbing into traditionally anchored and agreed upon discourses entirely new emphases, focusing, for example on: fostering long distance romantic partnerships, improving intercultural communication for transnational corporations, managing organizational knowledge production and memory. The rise of newer media such as e-mail, videoconferencing, and virtual worlds began to blur the lines between what was traditionally seen as in person versus mediated communication. Speech-oriented units quickly turned their attentions to these developments.[5,16,20,21]

Today, as the media landscape of society still rapidly changes, communication-labeled units in the academy

continue to evolve. Some disappear. Some reappear. Some combine, voluntarily or by administrative mandate. Most find ways to collaborate and share resources. Most acknowledge that despite their different origins, today they have common interests.

Other important polarities have stood as barriers between the two root structures. These are reviewed below. For purposes here, the important point is that during the first 30 years of the formal emergence of institutionalized academic units carrying the communication label, the two emergent institutional forms—mass and speech communication—evolved in relative isolation and sometimes mutual ignorance, even though many of the same forces were impacting both.

Given these divergent paths, it is small wonder that these isolated journeys resulted in competing narratives of communication studies—what it is, where it came from, and why. Amid rapidly changing conditions, there has been little time for building historical consciousness.[5,16,20] Historical descriptions are still sparse and incomplete. Even on fundamentals such as the identification of the presumed founding heroes, the histories tell different stories. In the arena of studies now identified as mass communication, an often named founder is Wilbur Schramm;[5,17,25] in studies now identified as speech communication, Kenneth Burke.[5,16] When one adds to the mix founding heroes in communication studies in other parts of the world, different heroes are eulogized.[5,22–25] In Canadian communication studies, for example, they point to Harold Innis and Marshall McLuhan; in Europe, again as examples, Raymond Williams or Jurgen Habermas. Each arena within communication studies has developed its own isolated history, often presented as "the" history. Founding fathers have only recently been identified as shared across these terrains.

Comprehensive histories only began to emerge in the late 1990s and early 2000s.[5,20] Communication studies must still realistically, then, be seen as a meeting place where diverse roads have converged out of a plethora of different and rapidly changing labels, sponsorships, leadership goals, and resistances.[5] There are agreements on central visions and important debates. Even now, however, these can be hard to see through a sea of competing, sometimes contesting details.

Unlike many older traditional fields—e.g., library science, mathematics, philosophy—communication as a field of study exploded onto the scene in our recent modern era, an era characterized by rapidly diffusing media technologies; the uses and abuses of these media for propaganda, publicity, and play; two devastating world wars; the fall of colonial powers; the rise of populist movements; and increasing global connectivity. Simultaneously, there occurred a rising interest in using the emerging social sciences as scholarly approaches to understanding humans and their societies. Part of this surge of interest involved a concern for using the increasing body of social science knowledge to create better individuals, citizens, and societies. Better was variously defined in terms of values within specific cultural and political-economic contexts. The confluence of these forces meant that governmental agencies and educators worldwide were increasingly concerned about both the potentials of media for what they defined as positive change (e.g., education, literacy, modernization) as well as negative (e.g., injurious propaganda, the spreading of base values, the potentials of mob rule). They turned to the academy for help.[5,15–17,26,31]

At the same time, an intellectual ferment was brewing that did not fully erupt to impact communication studies in the United States until the 1980s but accounts for some of the differences in how communication is defined, studied, and historicized. This ferment involved collisions between scientific and humanistic ways of conducting scholarship focused on humans and their societies. There were two important trajectories here. One was that studies of media were being introduced in the United States primarily as scientific study while studies of speech had been traditionally anchored in the humanities. During the institutionalizing process, speech-oriented units had no choice but to absorb the social sciences.[5,16] But, speech communication units were more likely to retain the humanistic traditions as well. This proved over the years another source of debates as the emerging institutional streams were forced to pay attention to each other.

Simultaneously, philosophic thinking about humans and their societies was burgeoning, riding on the surge of interest in the writings of such thinkers as Cooley, Darwin, Dewey, Freud, Marx, Mead, Simmel, Park, and Weber.[523,25] Most of these writings directly addressed communication-pertinent topics and were fertile sources of ideas about communicating drawn on heavily, but quite differently, in the writings of the various founders of the emerging communication units. These philosophic writings are seen by some as part of a worldwide thrust of attention away from focusing only on individual humans and human collectivities as static entities toward focusing on communication as a lens for examining and understanding human conditions and the communicative forces that constrain or enable human life. In this framework, communication is seen as explanatory of how humans and their collectivities become, rigidify, and/or change.[8,14,27–29]

Uses of these writers' works were sometimes anchored in stereotypical positivistic or instrumental orientations, focused especially on using scholarship to change people and societies for the better. Others focused on stereotypical humanistic or romanticist orientations, focusing on understanding and nurturing creativity, expressiveness, and human fulfillment. Numerous debates emerged within and between the social sciences and the humanities. In general, because of their differing lineages, United States, speech-oriented communication studies was more open to these debates while media-oriented studies were less so.

In contrast, in Europe and Canada, as examples of regional differences, there was earlier and far more robust attention to these differences.[22–24] Ultimately by the mid-1980s, these debates became a top agenda item in both mass and speech communication units for at least the next decade—a period sometimes labeled as a time of "ferment in the field."[5,9] The debates still continue today, albeit in a more quiescent form.

The Exploding Emergence of Media

There is essential agreement about the importance in the histories of communication studies of the spread of the media and the impacts of this spread on personal, political, economic, and other societal arrangements. Media made it possible to communicate faster across time and space and reach geographically disparate populations. Further, messages came to have a more durable presence in material form. This explosion of changes led to governmental and policy attentions and, hence, academic attention. In the context of the current speed of the diffusion of the Internet, it is difficult to remember that each of the mass media diffused at speeds considered astonishing in their times. This was as true for books, newspapers, telephones, and radios as it has been for televisions, videotape recorders, personal computers, and Internet use.

Gutenberg's invention of the printing press around 1440 is seen by many as the first small step in the rise of mass media. The period between its invention and the 1800s was marked primarily by small scale uses serving the needs of religious and educated elite. By 1800, further technological advances introduced by the industrial revolution made large and inexpensive runs possible both for religious and secular works. In the early 1800s, one found massive runs of Bibles both in the United States and Europe. In 1836, Dicken's *Pickwick Papers* became the first wildly popular novel, a business enterprise unto itself with attached theatrical performances, bootleg copies, and merchandizing.[5,17,19,26,31,36]

As the book became a tool of mass communication, newspapers were moving forward on their own fast-moving course, showing the same movement from elitist defined contents and formats to more popularized approaches incorporating illustrations, games, comics, and news of popular culture and celebrities. The first newspapers are said to have been circulated in both the United States and Europe in the late 1600s and early 1700s. By the early 1850s, there were some 2500; by the late 1800s, some 11,000. A downward trend in newspaper circulation is attributed to the impact of electronic media. Newspapers have been responding, however, with increases in their online presences.[5,17,19,22,23,31,37]

The same story of rapid diffusion is documented for radio and television. Licensed commercial radio began in the early 1900s with the first radio stations being introduced in the 1920s in the United States and Europe.

Today, there are some 12,000 radio stations—commercial and noncommercial in the United States alone. Television broadcasting with a regular schedule was introduced by a station in New York City in 1931. By 1960, roughly 9 of 10 households in the United States owned at least one television, and as of the late 1990s, there were some 219 million television sets in U.S. homes. Riding on these developments was the spread of advertising and public relations as massive enterprises. The first advertising agency as such opened in 1850. U.S. Census figures reported more than 11,000 advertising agencies in the United States and at least half that number of firms specializing in public relations.[5,17,19,38–40]

The speed of the spread of Internet use is even more startling. The worldwide infrastructure as we know it today first became available for public use in the early 1990s with the development of graphic interfaces and the World Wide Web. Current penetration to the U.S. population is more than 70%; Europe 48%; Oceania/Australia 59%; globally 22% (more than 1.5 billion users).[41]

The astounding growth and diffusion of all media technologies has had extraordinary impacts on the social fabrics of societies already changing rapidly because of the impacts of the industrial revolution. The growth in the entrepreneurial working class meant, for example, more leisure time for many, leading to clamoring for more diversions to fill that time. The rise of mass production of products and services coupled with the use of advertising and public relations as dissemination tools spread in rapid succession of all manner of changes in the distribution of goods and services, and impacts on lifestyles. Those with more flexible incomes clamored for products. Those with reading literacy reached for newspapers, books, and magazines, and, of course, eventually all media. The projection that some media would disappear during these evolving conditions is only in part true. Particular technologies have disappeared but the differential needs they serve varied audiences remain. If anything, the brunt of evidence suggests complementarities between media technologies rather than competitions.[18,19,28]

One major phenomena that must be emphasized as characteristic of the growth of mass media is that for first time media did not demand reading literacy as defined by elites. In general, media formerly controlled by and serving elites became mass-based. Citizens worldwide began to get access to pictures of their worlds formerly hidden from their views. They learned, for example, of misdeeds of their own leaders not reported locally; or how ordinary citizens lived in other parts of the world. Some media observers worried about an era of rising expectations that could not be met in a realistic (in one framing of the critique) or brutal (in another) reality. Others foretold how ordinary citizens would seize media for their own purposes as, for example, Bolivian miners' unions did as early as the 1950s. Others were deeply worried about the impact of media, such as film and radio on ordinary

citizens, particularly children. Others were concerned with the need to educate populations with a new kind of literacy—media literacy.[5,15–17,20–22,31,35,42]

These polarizing concerns between potentially positive and negative communication impacts got entangled in growing arguments about who gets to decide what is positive and what is negative. Lack of consensus mirrors the now documented truism that media developments as envisioned by those controlling media technology rarely turn out as expected. This has been particularly so as the media have evolved from elites communicating with elites, to elites communicating to the masses, to masses communicating with each other, to masses organizing and communicating back at elites.

As we look broadly at historical media developments, the same expectations of communication and its potential impacts in society have been repeated for each successive media development. But the debate is not new. Even in the very early years of rhetoric in ancient Greece, there were discussions on the ethics of using persuasive manipulation. The debate centered on whether these approaches to communicating were necessary as an antidote to ignorance and mob rule, or abuses of power and intrusions upon the sanctity of human consciousnesses.[5,16]

The Phases of Institutionalization

Most histories of the rise of communication studies have essential agreement on the phases of events. In the very earliest period—prior to the institutionalizing of communication-named units—the teaching of rhetoric was fairly well established. Rhetoric was part of the first curriculum at Harvard in 1636. By the end of the 1700s, it was well established in most of the Ivy League. An emphasis on rhetoric spread throughout the country. However, as more institutions were established, this emphasis slowly evolved to focusing primarily on the practical skills of discussion, speaking, and oratory. Increasingly these courses were usually located in departments focusing on English. By 1910, the academics focused on teaching speech and were large enough in numbers that they founded their own association.

While attention to media studies does not have this long history, the same practice emphasis characterized early developments. As the media were introduced and began to diffuse to mass circulations, it was not long before academic courses focusing on media skills began to appear. The earliest known course in journalism was introduced at the University of Leipzig in 1671. In the United States, in the 1860s, Southern Civil War leader Robert E. Lee introduced journalism training to assist postwar reconstruction at what is now the University of Washington and Lee. The University of Missouri introduced journalism training in 1878. The Wharton School started a business journalism school in the early 1900s.[5,17,22,23]

The same growth patterns ensued for each media development in turn. The first instruction in advertising was offered at New York University in 1905. Less than 30 years after Edison's invention, cinema studies courses followed in both Europe and the United States by 1920. Courses in radio broadcasting also began to appear in the 1920s and early 1930s. The first master's degree in radio broadcasting was offered in the United States in 1931 at the University of Wisconsin.[5,17,31]

These early attentions to communication education did not include the term "communication" in their names and almost all focused on practical training. While in general, speech training was located in departments of English and journalism training was either located there or in new separate units, it is really impossible to generalize where these units were placed in academic structures. Until attention to media began to coalesce in a consciousness of media as part of a communication revolution, the spread had a capricious character.[5]

It was when the mass media exhibited widespread diffusion and potentially negative impacts on society that attentions were directed to studying these impacts in the hopes of understanding and abating them. In the 1930s and 1940s, most of these attentions were manifested in the development of temporary centers, institutes, and programs. Columbia University, for example, established an office of radio research, launched a readability laboratory, and subsequently established a bureau of applied social research which specialized for a period in studying communication problems. Princeton University, with Rockefeller funding, established a center for monitoring shortwave broadcasting during WWII. The Chicago School introduced an interdisciplinary course focusing on communication and propoganda that eventually led to an interdisciplinary center. Ohio State University's Bureau of Educational Research launched the Payne Fund studies on the impacts of film on children with funding from the Motion Picture Research Council.[5,17,31]

From the 1940s on, new programs, centers, and projects began to emerge at what has been estimated as at least one per year.[5] Audience research was introduced into already established journalism units, for example, at the University of Minnesota in 1944 and University of Iowa in 1946. Speech focused units began to add social scientists to their faculties and introduce social science focused courses.[5,16,21]

In the 1940s, units with the communication label began to appear. The first unit to specifically use the communication label was a communication research center at the University of North Carolina, emerging out of speech and theater. The Institute of Communication Research with a media focus was established at the University of Illinois as was the University of Iowa's communication research center, also with a media focus.[5,17]

By the 1950s, the label communication was popular both in academic and governmental circles as well as public imagination. The first mention of communication studies as an academic enterprise in *Webster's Dictionary* was in 1951. The first college identified as such was established at Michigan State University in 1955. The first doctorate was awarded under the communication label in 1956. Courses and institutes in higher education that focused on something they specifically called communication increased from the early entrees in the 1950s to explosive developments of the 1960s and 1970s. Most of the early developments occurred at the Big 10 universities of the Midwest. Exceptions to this were the robust communication-labeled units at the University of Pennsylvania, the University of Washington, and Stanford. Later, communication-labeled units diffused virtually everywhere except, notably, in the Ivy League. Despite the fact that Ivy League institutions were among the first to promote communication research initiatives, they have not incorporated communication studies into their formalized curricular hierarchies.[5,17]

As the growth of communication studies marched on, the various media focused units—journalism, radio, advertising, film, and television—began to change their names to incorporate the "communication" word. Programs merged and coalesced into schools and colleges of mass communication. Likewise, units coming from the speech communication trajectory began to change their names.

The growth statistics on the introduction of departments, schools, and colleges were remarkable. In less than 50 years, by 2006, some 1300 colleges and universities in the United States had communication focused programs or departments. In 2005–2006, according to the Chronicle for Higher Education, 81,661 degrees were awarded in communication at the bachelor's, master's, or doctoral level—about 5.2% of all degrees conferred. This number rose from 14,794 in 1967–1968 (1.8% of all degrees).[43]

With continued growth, there were challenges. Primary among these were the impacts of academic cutbacks in the 1980s and resulting pressures on the different communication-focused programs for retrenchment. This involved mandates for mergers and elimination of duplications. This also led to many attempts by communication scholars to show internal coherencies in communication studies with its emphasis on communication as fundamental process. These efforts continue today.

Further, communication suffered and continues to do so in many locales from being seen as academically inferior, in many minds tarnished by its legacies in practical training. Some have seen this as a result of academic elitism and erroneous stereotyping of communication studies as merely a field that focuses on practice and not a discipline that focuses on basic research and theory development.[5] Yet, at the same time, communication skills and understandings have increasingly been documented as among the skills and understandings college educated graduates need.[4] Further, students continue to seek out higher education courses in communication, both for media or speech emphases. Popular sentiment has supported this trajectory. One sample indicator of the place of communication in public consciousness is that as of November 11, 2008, there were more than 649 million Google hits to Web pages dated 2008 with the word "communication" in them and more than 140,000 titles dated 2008 with the "communication" word in them in Google scholar.

Structures for Handling the Diversity

Space prevents any attempt to show the numerous ways in which those involved in the study of communication have partitioned and organized their topics of interest. There are some basic large categories of attention most easily discerned by examining texts developed for introductory courses. These are listed in the first paragraph of the section "Two Primary Institutions—Speech and Mass Communication." However, from textbook to textbook these can markedly disagree, not so much in the specific details but in the ways in which the categories are organized.

For the most part the categories for organizing curricula and attentions in communication studies capture some basic enduring nouns into which the communication terrain has been divided. What is missing are the many ways in which different researchers, academic units, organizations, and journals have parlayed their interests into specialized contexts, cultures, and domains. Looking across category schemes, we find divisions emphasizing, for example: societally important foci of attention (e.g., health, political communication, marriage, peace); communication processes (e.g., sense-making, dialogue, leadership); goals (e.g., persuading, informing, educating); audiences (e.g., women, men, children, parents, minorities). The list goes on.

The diversity shows most clearly by examining Tables 1–3, profiles of the three largest comprehensive organizations that have emerged over the years to support communication studies with annual conferences and journal production. These three organizations, as well as a number of equally robust but more specialized organizations, have grown from relative isolation over a 50-plus year period to their current formations. Each has a distinctive character arising from its own historical lineage. Each has exploded in growth in short periods of time and has robust conferences and supports a roster of journals. Each over the years has converged more and more onto common interests while retaining their distinctions, providing room for the diversities of interests of their members, and simultaneously setting aside a significant portion of attentions to communication in the broadest and most widely applicable sense.[1,2,5,32–34]

Today, the three most comprehensive organizations that attract members from the United States are, in order of historical emergence: the National Communication

Association (NCA), the International Communication Association (ICA), and the International Association of Media and Communication Research (IAMCR).[32–34] There are important organizations with more specialized foci that are not being highlighted here. In the U.S. context, examples include the Association for Education in Journalism and Mass Communication, the Broadcast Educators Association, and the American Association for Public Opinion Research. Each has robust membership and conference attendance. Each supports one or more journals. There are as well numerous communication studies associations in virtually every country and region of the world, each exhibiting the same essential core foci on communication as fundamental process and each exhibiting differences arising from their unique historical lineages and current cultural and political-economic interests.[5,17,22,23]

The importance of focusing only on the three most comprehensive organizations which today attract substantial U.S. membership is to examine them as exemplars of how the structures that support communication studies focus on core interests in communication while simultaneously handling the diversity in contexts, cultures, domains, and environments that are the locales where essential communication processes play out their roles and impacts. Tables 1–3 profile each organization's history, current membership composition, and current emphases as displayed in subgroup category names and journal titles. It is in these lists that one gets a glimpse of both the core of communication studies and its parts.

In 2008, ICA (Table 2), for example, had a special interest group focusing on game studies, a recent emergence, while at the same time its journals covered a broad spectrum of communication interests. One special interest group in ICA focuses on communication and history, a reflection of how ICA, strongly anchored in emphases on social scientific studies, is admitting more and more humanities based interests into its roster. For NCA (Table 1), one of the most recent divisions to be added focuses on spiritual communication, a reflection of a general societal turn to interests not usually covered by normative studies of how people use media and messages. National Communication Association's journals also reflect a broad spectrum of interests—both humanistic and scientific—and retain as well the organization's focal origins on communication education. International Association of Media and Communication Research's (Table 3) subgroups reflect its historical lineage and cover a number of special foci more likely to be catapulted into membership attentions by the historically international character of the organization. In 2008, working groups were listed, for example, for diaspora and communication, Islam and media, as well as for emerging media foci common to all three organizations—e.g., the digital divide, comic art, and popular culture.

Table 1 Profile of the National Communication Association.

Main organization	Subgroup structures as of 2008
National Communication Association	*Divisions*
http://www.natcom.org	African American Communication and Culture
	American Studies
Founded 1914	Applied Communication
	Argumentation and Forensics
Former names	Communication and Aging
Speech Communication Association	Communication and the Future
National Association of Academic Teachers of Public Speaking	Communication and Law
	Communication Apprehension and Competence
Current mission statement	Communication Assessment
. . .a scholarly society that works to enhance the research, teaching,	Communication Ethics
and service provided by its members on topics of both intellectual	Communication and Social Cognition
and social significance	Communication as Social Construction
. . .the oldest and largest national association	Critical and Cultural Studies
promoting communication scholarship and education	Environmental Communication
. . .promotes study, criticism, research, teaching, and	Ethnography Division
application of the artistic, humanistic, and scientific	Experiential Learning in Communication
principles of communication	Family Communication
	Feminist and Women's Studies
2008 statistics	Freedom of Expression
7700+ members	Gay, Lesbian, Bisexual, Transgender and Queer Communication
Home locations of members	Group Communication
20+ countries, mostly United States	Health Communication
	Human Communication and Technology
Conference attendance	Instructional Development
4000+ attendees at typical annual conference	International and Intercultural Communication
an estimated 4000+ presentations	Interpersonal Communication
in 1000+ programs	Language and Social Interaction
	Latino/Latina Communication Studies
Conference sites	Mass Communication
2008, San Diego	Nonverbal
2007, Chicago	Organizational Communication
2006, San Antonio	Peace and Conflict
2005, Boston	Performance Studies
2004, Chicago	Political Communication
*4 regional U.S. associations—eastern, southern,	Public Address
western, central, sponsor own annual meetings and journals	Public Relations
	Rhetorical and Communication Theory
Journals available to members	Semiotics and Communication
Communication & Critical/Cultural Studies	Spiritual Communication
Communication Education	Theater
Communication Monographs	Training and Development
Communication Teacher	Visual Communication
Critical Studies in Media Communication	*Sections*
Journal of Applied Communication	Communication Centers
Journal of International & Intercultural	Community College
Communication	Elementary and Secondary Education
Quarterly Journal of Speech	Emeritus/Retired Members
The Review of Communication	Master's Education
Text & Performance Quarterly	Student
	Undergraduate College and University

In each of these organizations, the subgroups and journals represent the presence of discourse communities substantial enough in size that they have parlayed for themselves a share of convention and journal resources. Each is, as well, a trace of the many different topics and emphases brought to bear on teaching and research foci. Throughout academic units focusing on communication studies in the United States and throughout the world, the same play between the past and the present, the center and the peripheries can be observed.

Table 2 Profile of the International Communication Association

Main organization	Subgroup structures as of 2008
International Communication Association	*Divisions*
http://www.icahdq.org	Communication and Technology
	Communication, Law, and Policy
Founded 1950	Ethnicity and Race in Communication
	Feminist Scholarship
Former names	Global Communication and Social Change
National Society for the Study of Communication	Health Communication
	Information Systems
Mission statement	Instructional/Development Communication
. . .aims to advance the scholarly study of human	Intercultural Communication
communication by encouraging and facilitating	Interpersonal Communication
excellence in academic research worldwide. The purposes of the Association	Journalism Studies
are: (1) to provide an international forum to enable the development,	Language and Social Interaction
conduct, and critical evaluation of communication research; (2) to sustain	Mass Communication
a program of high quality scholarly publication and knowledge exchange;	Organizational Communication
(3) to facilitate inclusiveness and debate among	Philosophy of Communication
scholars from diverse national and cultural	Political Communication
backgrounds and from multidisciplinary	Popular Communication
perspectives on communication-related issues; and	Public Relations
(4) to promote a wider public interest in, and	Visual Communication Studies
visibility of, the theories, methods, findings and	*Interest groups*
applications generated by research in	Children, Adolescents and the Media
communication and allied fields.	Communication and History
	Game Studies
2008 statistics	Gay, Lesbian, Bisexual and Transgender Studies
*4000þ members	Intergroup Communication
Home locations of members (estimates for 2008)	
*66% from the United States; 34% from other countries	
Conference attendance	
*2100þ attendees at 2008 annual conference	
representing 51 nations	
an estimated 1800þ presentations	
464 different sessions	
Conference sites	
2008, Montreal	
2007, San Francisco	
2006, Dresden	
2005, New York City	
2004, New Orleans	
Journals available to members	
Communication Theory	
Communication, Culture … Critique	
Journal of Computer-Mediated Communication	
Human Communication Research	
Journal of Communication	

In essence, across the many diversities can be found a core concern for researching, theory building, and applying through practice understandings of communication as a fundamental and universal process by which humans somehow transmit, exchange, or share meanings. While, for example, in the big three organizations each subgroup may have its own emphasis, the boundaries between them have not been impermeable. Subgroups within and between the organizations regularly come together in journals and conventions to intermingle and produce collaborative work that recognizes core interests in communication. As a bottom line, it is fair to describe communication studies as an academic force that has continuously encouraged unity amid its essential diversity.

Table 3 Profile of the International Association of Media and Communication Research.

Main organization	Subgroup structures as of 2008
International Association of Media & Communication Research	*Sections*
http://www.iamcr.org	Audience Communication Policy and Technology
Founded 1957 with UNESCO support	Community Communication
	Emerging Scholars Network
Former names	Gender and Communication
International Association of Mass	History
Communication Research	International Communication
	Journalism Research and Education
Mission statement	Law
...worldwide professional organization in the	Media and Sport
field of media and communication research	Media Education Research
...promotes global inclusiveness and	Mediated Communication, Public Opinion and Society
excellence within the best traditions of critical	Participatory Communication Research
research in the field	Political Communication Research
....supports the public presence of the field of	Political Economy
communication research	*Working groups*
*promotes and supports the input of media	Comic Art
and communication researchers in local,	Communication and HIV/AIDS
national, and global agendas	Diaspora and Media
	Digital Divide
2008 statistics	Environment, Science, and Risk Communication
1601 individual and institutional members	Ethics of Society and Ethics of Communication
	European Public Broadcasting Policies
Home locations of members (*estimates for 2008*)	Global Media Policy
Africa, 18.4%	Islam and Media
Asia, 15.6%	Media Production Analysis
Europe, 35.6%	Media, Religion and Culture
Latin American and Caribbean, 9.7%	Popular Culture
Middle East, 3.7%	Post-Socialist and Post-Authoritarian
North America, 23.3%	
Oceania, 4.8%	
South East Asia, 2.3%	
Conferences attendance	
950+ attendees at 2008 annual conference,	
representing 82+ nations	
presenting an estimated 1100+ papers, in	
some 300+ sessions	
Conference sites	
2008, Stockholm	
2007, Paris	
2006, Cairo	
2005, Taipei	
2004, Porto Alegre	
Journals available to members	
International Communication Gazette	
New Media & Society	
Global Media & Communication	

Communication Studies and Its Productive Tensions

Communication studies as a terrain of academic focus was welcomed into the academy on the tail of the explosive

spread of mass media and the interest, particularly by government and policy makers, to apply the tools of social sciences to studying, understanding, and curbing negative effects from the media as well as promoting positive ones. Yet, from the beginning the forces that put the "communication" word on the map harbored contradictions within them.

These contradictions are many. In terms of historical lineages, communication studies attached itself to two established teaching missions: one focused on training media practitioners; the other focused on training citizens and leaders for oratory and discussion in public forums. This introduced immediate contradictions between practice and scholarship, one that remains today. As science was emphasized more and more as an appropriate form for study, the humanities way of knowing the world collided with the scientific way.

These two historical polarizations in many ways were simply surface symptoms of a host of other contradictions that have beset communication studies. Those studying communication disagree about: how to know the world, what to do with the knowledge, how to handle differences, and what to call deviance and what not; whether the role of leadership is to control, correct, and persuade, or facilitate and engender opportunity; how best to understand others and even whether the understanding is worth the effort; whether communication and, in particular, media damages us and our societies, or helps; whether communication is something that might be used to make the world a better place; whether this very idea can be considered ethical or impositional.[5,10–15]

These tensions and many more can be seen galloping through discourses in more traditional fields of study, both in the humanities and the social sciences. They can also be seen galloping through media news reports on our TV screens and in our newspapers.[28,34] Yet, it can be argued that communication studies is more impacted because these tensions, if resolvable, must be resolved in communication.[8,28] Add to this the fact that increasingly our lives are structured and patterned within landscapes of electronic communication that now seem to be making the old distinctions between mediated versus non-mediated irrelevant. These converging forces put communication studies in the center of a hurricane. The subjects of communication studies are what make the hurricane whirl. But, communication studies, like all other centers of academic attention, is whirling along as well.

Both insiders and outsiders look at communication studies and what appears to be a chaotic jumble of incoherent interests and emphases and ask: How can this be a discipline or it is merely a field? Is this even a field, or merely a meeting place? Is this a specialty requiring a discipline or a phenomenon that is now everyone's business? Debates on these issues continue and are expected to do so for some time.

Yet, despite these disagreements, an examination of communication studies shows that it keeps trying to hold onto the vision of many of its founding fathers—that there is a communicative way of looking at the world and that worldview provides special strengths. Some see this strength as growing out of communication studies as the practical discipline where one studies how humans use communication to make and unmake and remake their worlds. Others see this as a distinction between the nouns that are the specialized foci of most of the social sciences and humanities, and the verbs of communicating that forge the linkages between peoples across time and space. Some see communication studies' continuing efforts to retain this core and vision as its special strength and potential greatest contribution. In this sense, the contradictions and chaos that seem to give communication studies an incoherent face can be seen as symptom and cause of both its centralities and its dispersions, its weaknesses and its strengths.

CONCLUSION

The goal of this entry has been to describe the historical emergence and current states of attentions to communication as a phenomenon of academic study; and, to describe the various academic formations today nested under the term communication studies. Because communication studies has been a presence in the academy for less than 60 years, and because it has evolved in the midst of an exploding and rapidly changing communication environment, there are necessarily multiple and competing stories to be told. This entry has attempted to focus both on convergences and divergences across these stories. The entry has reviewed in turn: different meanings for the word "communication" and how and when the term came into popular usage; the two primary historical lineages out of which communication studies has emerged—speech and mass communication; the forces leading to institutionalization and the exploding emergence of the media. The entry has examined the phases in which communication studies became institutionalized and how it has handled its diversity with supporting structures of organizations and journals. The entry concluded with a discussion of how communication studies necessarily holds within its core a series of contradiction that are in essence both symptom and cause of its centralities and its dispersions, strengths, and weaknesses.

ACKNOWLEDGMENTS

The authors wish to acknowledge the extraordinary help provided by the most recent attempts of Arcenas,[5] Craig and Carlone[20] to address communication studies and its lineages comprehensively and evenhandedly. The Arcenas dissertation was, in particular, invaluable. The authors also thank Jordan D. Bennett, undergraduate research assistant at Ohio State University for his help with library research.

REFERENCES

1. National Communication Association. *Behavior Matters: Communication Research on Human Connections*, National Communication Association: Washington, DC, 2007.

2. National Communication Association. *Communication: Ubiquitous, Complex, Consequential*, National Communication Association: Washington, DC, 2007.

3. Reinhard, J. *Introduction to Communication Research*, McGraw Hill: Boston, MA, 1998.

4. Morreale, S.P.; Pearson, J.C. Why communication education is important: The centrality of the discipline in the 21st century. Commun. Educ. **2007**, *2* (April), 224–240.

5. Arcenas, E.M. *"Communication" in the Making of Academic Communication*, Doctoral dissertation, University of Pennsylvania: Ann Arbor, MI, 1995.

6. Beniger, J.R. Communication—Embrace the subject, not the field. J. Commun. **1993**, *43* (3, Summer), 18–25.

7. Berger, C.R. Chautauqua: Why are there so few communication theories? Communication theories and other curios. Commun. Monogr. **1991**, *58* (1, March), 110–113.

8. Carter, R.F. Communication, a harder science. In *Communication, a Different Kind of Horserace*; Dervin, B., Foreman-Wernet, L., Eds.; Hampton Press: Cresskill, NJ, 2003; 369–376.

9. Craig, R.T. Why are there so many communication theories?. J. Commun. **1993**, *43*(3), 26–33.

10. Hardt, H. *Critical Communication Studies: Communication History and Theory in America*, Routledge: London, 1992.

11. Kivikuru, U. Communication research: Is there such a thing?. Nordicom Rev. **1998**, *1*, 7–11.

12. Nordenstreng, K. Discipline or field. Nordicom Rev. **2007**, (Jubilee Issue), 213–222.

13. Simpson, C. *Science of Coercion: Communication Research and Psychological Warfare 1945–1960*, Oxford University Press: New York, 1994.

14. Thayer, L. What would a theory of communication be for?. J. Appl. Commun. **1982**, *10*, 21–28.

15. Barnouw, E.; Gerbner, G.; Schramm, W. *International Encyclopedia of Communication*, Oxford University Press: Cambridge, U.K., 1989.

16. Cohen, H. *The History of Speech Communication: The Emergence of a Discipline, 1914–1945*, National Communication Association: Washington, DC, 1994.

17. Gerbner, G.; Schramm, W. Communication, study of. In *International Encyclopedia of Communication*; Barnouw, E., Gerbner, G., Schramm, W., Eds.; Oxford University Press: Cambridge, U.K., 1989; 358–368.

18. Peters, J.D. *Speaking into Air: A History of the Idea of Communication*, University of Chicago Press: Chicago, IL, 1999.

19. Schramm, W. *The Story of Human Communication: Cave Painting to Microchip*, Harper & Row: New York, 1988.

20. Craig, R.T.; Carlone, D.A. Growth and transformation of communication studies in U.S. higher education: Towards reinterpretation. Commun. Educ. **1998**, *47*, 67–80 (January).

21. Delia, J.G. Communication research: A history. In *Handbook of Communication Studies*; Berger, C.R., Chaffee, S.H., Eds.; Sage: Newbury Park, CA, 1987; 20–98.

22. McQuail, D. Communications research past present and future: American roots and European branches. In *Public Communication: The New Imperatives*; Ferguson, M., Ed.; Sage: London, 1991; 135–151.

23. Pietila, V. *On the Highway of Mass Communication Studies*, Hampton Press: Cresskill, NJ, 2004.

24. Robinson, G.J. Remembering our past: Reconstructing the field of Canadian communication studies. Can. J. Commun. **2000**, *25*(1), 195–225.

25. Rogers, E.M. *A History of Communication: A Biographical Approach*, The Free Press: New York, 1994.

26. Schramm, W. *The Beginnings of Communication Study in America*, Sage: Thousand Oaks, CA, 1997.

27. Craig, R.T. Communication as a practical discipline. In *Rethinking Communication: Volume 1: Paradigm Issues*; Dervin, B., Grossberg, L., O'Keefe, B.J., Wartella, E., Eds.; Sage: Newbury Park, CA, 1989; 97–124.

28. Dervin, B.; Foreman-Wernet, L. *Sense-Making Methodology Reader*, Hampton Press: Cresskill, NJ, 2003.

29. Stephenson, W. *The Play Theory of Mass Communication*, University of Chicago Press: Chicago, IL, 1967.

30. Katz, E.; Peters, J.D.; Liebes, T.; Orloff, A. Canonic texts in media research: Are there any? Should there be? How about these?. J. Commun. **2005**, March 199–203.

31. Lang, K. Communication research, origins and development. In *International Encyclopedia of Communication*; Barnouw, E., Gerbner, G., Schramm, W., Eds.; Oxford University Press: Cambridge, U.K., 1989; 368–369.

32. International Association of Mass Communication Research, Homepage. Available at http://www.iamcr.org (accessed November 10, 2008).

33. International Communication Association Homepage. Available at http:// www.icahdq.org (accessed November 10, 2008).

34. National Communication Association Homepage. Available at http://www.natcom.org (accessed November 10, 2008).

35. Katz, E. Communications research since Lazarsfeld. Public Opin. Quart. **1987**, *51*, S25–S45.

36. Finkelstein, D. *An Introduction to Book History*, Routledge: New York, 2005.

37. Project for Excellence in Journalism. State of the news media 2007. Available at http://www.stateofthenewsmedia .org/2007/execsummary.pdf

38. Radio-Locator, Homepage. Available at http://www.radio-locator.com/ (accessed November 11, 2008).

39. Fletcher, J.E. Mapping a discipline—Broadcasting in America. J. Broadcast. Electron. Media **1996**, *40*(4, Fall), 570–573.

40. U.S. Bureau of the Census Homepage. Available at http:// www.census.gov/ (accessed November 11, 2008).

41. Internet World Stats, Homepage. http://www.internet-worldstats.com/stats.htm (accessed November 11, 2008).

42. Lerner, D.; Nelson, L.M. *Communication Research: A Half-Century Appraisal*, University of Hawaii Press: Honolulu, HI, 1977.

43. Chronicle for Higher Education. *2008–9 Almanac*, Available at http://chronicle.com/weekly/almanac/2008/nation/0102001.htm (accessed November 11, 2008).

Communication Policy: United States

D. Linda Garcia
Communication Culture and Technology, Georgetown University, Washington, District of Columbia, U.S.A.

Abstract

This piece examines the impact that competition will have in determining communication policies and goals. It makes the case that, in a regulated environment in which communication technologies were regulated according to a different basis—common carriage, first amendment rights, and public interest standards—it was possible to meet a variety of communication goals. Each technology fostered a different goal. Given convergence, and the deregulation of the communication policy environment, such flexibility is no longer viable. One approach serves all. The result has been that, more than ever before, policy goals must be traded off, one against the other.

INTRODUCTION

The U.S. communication regime reflects the pattern of economic relationships that exist among and between key players as well as the public policy goals and corresponding rules that govern them. For years, the goals and rules of the system and the balance among interested parties were generally accepted and relatively stable. Typically, industry leaders have been the driving forces in developing and promoting communication technologies, competing among themselves for primacy. At certain periods, however, the government has intervened, crafting a new set of communication policies to bring private sector players more in line with public sector needs.

Today the existing set of arrangements is once again being called into question, as technological and socioeconomic developments give rise to new possibilities, new players, and new types of problems. In particular, deregulatory communication policies have shifted more decisions to the market at the same time that technological advances have generated new opportunities in all realms of life. Some applaud these developments, seeing in them new possibilities for innovation and growth. Others fear that if decisions about new technologies are made solely in the marketplace, important social, cultural, and political opportunities might be lost. The contest will continue to be played out in Congress and the courts over issues ranging from telecommunications reform to those having to do with intellectual property rights, privacy, and networking security.

Information-based networks will serve to coordinate economic and political activities in a knowledge-based global economy. The market choices, institutions, and policies that govern them will determine not only the nature of society and the performance of the economy, but also how wealth and power are distributed. For a discussion of the role of institutions in determining economic outcomes, see North.[1]

Whatever the institutional choices made, they will have far-reaching consequences, for in an increasingly networked society, what is at stake in crafting communication policy is the system of property rights itself. The outcome is not predetermined, nor will it necessarily be efficient. Instead, these new institutional arrangements will evolve over time in response to pressures from economic and political actors who want to restructure the rules of the game in their favor.[2] Policy outcomes will also be irreversible, at least in the short and medium terms, for once a decision is made, technology tends to become firmly fixed on a given trajectory. This pattern is especially evident with networked information technologies, which require vast amounts of capital and social investment.

Periods of rapid technological advances such as we are witnessing today therefore provide a rare opportunity to reassess the nature of communication policy goals and the mechanisms designed to achieve them. With this opportunity in mind, this entry examines the extent to which today's deregulatory, competitive policy can be expected to meet the wide range of goals that have traditionally been associated with U.S. communication policy and/or new goals that might be required in an increasingly networked environment. First, it lays out the challenges entailed in establishing communication policy goals. Second, it examines the historical goals that have driven U.S. communication policy to date. Next, the entry considers the technological advances and associated social and economic changes that have led to efforts to restructure the telecommunications infrastructure along more competitive lines. Finally, it considers the goals that will be favored in a more market-oriented environment and identifies some new tensions among goals that are likely to emerge as a result.

The entry contends that communication policy based on a strategy of competition alone will not suffice in a networked information society. Given the enhanced role

Encyclopedia of Library and Information Sciences, Fourth Edition DOI: 10.1081/E-ELIS4-120044381

Communication–
Corporate Art

of communication and information in all realms of life, even greater trade-offs among policy goals are likely. Far from reconciling competing communication goals, the shift in decision making from the political arena to the marketplace will serve to obscure these trade-offs, leading to the emergence of new and perhaps more thorny issues over the long run. To resolve these issues, the government must play a delicate balancing act, employing as it has so successfully done in the past a variety of roles and policy mechanisms.

CRAFTING COMMUNICATION POLICY

Goal setting provides a unique opportunity for policy makers to change course in response to technological advances and changing social and economic circumstances. Rarely, however, do politicians seize such an opportunity, given the dangers and difficulties involved. More often than not, policy goals are instead established and implemented in the context and course of "politics as usual." When goal setting does take place formally, it usually occurs within the context of major organizational and structural changes.

In the case of communication policy, the effects are likely to be especially far-reaching, because communication is the basis for all interactions and one of the means for organizing society. Given the central role of communications, policy making in this area is generally coupled to other important policy areas. Thus, for example, political concerns about freedom of speech and the free flow of information may easily come into conflict with defense-related concerns, as has recently happened with respect to encryption policy. Similarly, in cases involving pornography or violent media content, concerns about cultural norms and values must be balanced against First Amendment rights.

In crafting communication policy, decision makers must also be sensitive to the importance of three interrelated sectors of the economy—transportation, communications, and information. Mirroring the role of communications in society, these industries are significant, and not just because of their contribution to trade and gross national product. Communication- and information-based goods and services are both intermediary goods and end products, so the impact of policies that affect their costs, availability, and use reverberate across all industry sectors as well as throughout the economy as a whole.

Consideration needs to be given not only to the impact of policy on these key industry sectors, but also on the competitive relationships among communication- and information-related industries. When industry players are able to translate their economic power into political leverage, as is often the case, the problem of sorting out these relationships is greatly compounded. Because political leverage is often distributed unevenly, some industry players

are likely to be favored over others, with little regard for broader public policy goals.

Technology also complicates matters greatly. Because communication is both dependent on as well as mediated by a technology-based infrastructure, decision makers have to craft communication policies with technologies and their distinct characteristics and capabilities in mind. Technologies, however, are very difficult to fathom. Not only are technologies highly complex; they are constantly changing. Crafting sound communication policies therefore requires considerable vision as well as technical expertise.

Even when communication policies are well designed to take technologies into account, they are highly subject to unintended consequences and events. Technology advances, for example, can easily undermine the assumptions on which policy is based. One need only consider, for instance, what can happen to policies designed to affect market structure. Technology advances can alter the rules of the game by affecting economies of scale and scope, the availability of product substitutes, and the costs of production. By providing new opportunities and challenging conventional ways of thinking, technology advances place new demands on the system, creating the need to reassess and reconsider basic communication-related goals.

The U.S. experience in setting communication policy goals reflects the magnitude of the challenges involved. Legislative mandates laying out specific goals have been rare. Once the major guidelines have been established, U.S. communication policy strategies have been derived incrementally over time through a process of administrative and judicial interpretation. This incremental approach only succeeded, however, as long as social and economic conditions were relatively stable and there was a broad consensus on related goals. As described below, in periods of major crisis or upheaval, such as the shift from an agrarian to an industrial society or from a peacetime to a wartime economy, new sets of rules designed to solve new challenges and accommodate new players became imperative.

COMMUNICATION GOALS: AN HISTORICAL PERSPECTIVE

Examining the U.S. communication policy regime from an historical perspective, a number of major communication policy goals can be identified. Established in the context of major social and economic changes—oftentimes brought about by technological advances—these goals were broadly conceived. Recognizing the link between communication and the social and economic orders, policy makers viewed communication as a means and not just as an end in and of itself. In pursuit of these goals, the government adopted a variety of roles and a broad range of policy mechanisms

Table 1 Goals, roles, and policy mechanisms.

| Goals | Government Roles | | | | |
	Broker	Regulator	Educator	Promoter	Market maker
Achieving democracy	Newspaper exchange	First Amendment		Postal roads; mail subsidies	Intellectual property
National integration	Public school movement	Rate regulator	Extension service; libraries	RFD; land grants; Express Mail	
Efficient interconnection	REA	Common carriage rate regulator		Rate averaging	Antitrust legislation
Cultural concerns	Voluntary constraints	Spectrum licensing must-carry	Educational TV	Public Broadcasting	Ownership rules
Defense and security	Standards industry broker	Censorship; wiretapping		R&D; roads; ARPANET	Procurement policies

that were designed not only to take advantage of new technologies, but also to serve the needs as they were perceived by both key stakeholders and the nation as a whole. These goals, government roles, and policy mechanisms are depicted in Table 1, and they are briefly described and discussed below.

Securing Democracy by Promoting Information Access

Some of the most far-reaching and enduring communication policy goals were established at the time of the nation's birth in the context of a political revolution and a total revision of governmental affairs. These goals reflected the Founding Fathers' preoccupation with establishing a democracy and the importance they attributed to communication and information in securing it.

Occurring at the height of the Enlightenment, the American Revolution was a battleground of ideas. The dissemination of these ideas, and the revolutionary fervor accompanying them, was linked to print technology and the emergence of new channels of communication, such as the religious and merchant networks associated with the growth of discursive literacy. In nineteenth century England, for example, not only did the number of newspapers and periodicals grow by a factor of 10; equally important, journals were distributed more widely—beyond cities to small towns and villages in which a single copy might be read and discussed by a number of persons.[3]

In the U.S. colonies, for example, newspapers and pamphlets served as the primary vehicle for public protest and revolt, providing a network of political communication that was crucial to revolutionary activities. Thus it was that with the onset of the revolution, printers—functioning as editors and publishers—generated and controlled the flow of public information. In fact, it was in their shops that many political accounts and ideas were exchanged, and although they had strongly opposed British control of the press, they were equally prepared—during the Revolution—to suppress dissenting opinions.[4,5]

No one appreciated the power of the pen more fully than the Founding Fathers—the architects and ideologists

of the revolution. Fearful of misinterpretation, they excluded journalists from the Constitutional Convention. Seeking to build support for the Constitution, Alexander Hamilton and James Madison disguised themselves as the columnist Publius, and wrote *The Federalist Papers*, a series of newspaper articles, on its behalf. In the new nation, however, in which competing interests were institutionalized and balanced against one another, open communication was to be the rule.

Distrusting government as much as they valued information, the Founding Fathers looked to the federal government to play a minimalist role. To promote the free and independent flow of communication, they relied for the most part on prohibitions against government interference in content, as well as on subsidies and targeted economic incentives. At the same time, however, the government was authorized to use its postal authority to promote information. For these purposes, the Founding Fathers incorporated three clauses into the Constitution. These provisions guaranteed freedom of speech, assembly, and the press, and authorized the federal government to protect intellectual property and to establish a system of postal roads. Designed with print technologies in mind, this approach provided adequate for an agrarian society, in which people who had dealings with one another were in close proximity and the costs of producing and distributing information were well within individual reach.

The first amendment

The First Amendment to the Constitution, covering freedom of speech, religion, assembly, petition, and the press, forbade Congress from any actions abridging those freedoms. The amendment gave American newspapers a degree of liberty unknown elsewhere. Applied most fully to print media, it has consistently meant private ownership, freedom from prior restraints, virtually no content controls, and relatively limited liability for the consequences of a message. Except during times of war and social stress, this value included the right to criticize government vigorously. Viewed as a centerpiece of American government, major cases involving its applicability did not arise until after World War I with the introduction of the "clear and present danger" standard. Subsequent Court interpretations have ranged from a strict absolutionist view, which interprets the First Amendment literally, to a more restrictive view, which allows for exceptions in cases such as obscenity, libel, and national security. The Court has generally adopted an intermediary stance between these two positions; however, while consistently holding that freedom of speech is not absolute, it has defined exceptions very narrowly.

The protection of intellectual property

Article 1, section 8 of the Constitution authorizes the federal government to grant intellectual property protection. Its express purpose was "To Promote the progress of the Exclusive Right to their respective Writings and Discoveries." Generally speaking, there are four different forms of intellectual property protection—copyright, patents, trademarks, and trade secrets—each with its own set of rights and obligations. Of these, the copyright regime is the one that has until recently been most closely associated with communications policy.

Like the free flow of information, the promotion of sciences and the useful arts was closely linked to democracy; a democratic polity was viewed as a prerequisite for advancement in applied science, while technological achievements were expected to provide the physical means of achieving the democratic objectives of political, social, and economic equality.[6,7] To assure that intellectual property protection would play this dual role, the Founding Fathers made it a statutory right granted not as a reward per se but rather as an incentive to achieve a specific public policy goal. James Madison—the principal author of the intellectual property clause—was aware of the monopolistic connotations of such a governmentally granted, exclusive right. He distinguished the American system of intellectual property rights from previous ones that he believed were more pernicious. To avoid the evil of monopoly, Madison intended that the exclusive right afforded by copyright be narrowly circumscribed; owned by "many" and "granted for only" limited period of time (p. 84).[7]

Although the rights grated under the first Copyright Act of 1790 corresponded to the capabilities of the printing press, the law has been extended over time to incorporate new technologies.

Establishing postal roads

Like its constitutional counterparts, Article 1, section 8, paragraph 7, which authorizes Congress to establish a system of postal roads, was intended to assure that all citizens in the burgeoning democracy had access to a broad range of information. The writers of the Constitution were acutely aware that building a nation would require a national communication infrastructure, and the development and evolution of the postal system was designed to serve this end. Setting aside factional differences, Federalists and Republicans rallied behind a postal policy to encourage newspaper circulation. Favoring the exchange of political and business information over interpersonal transactions, Congress set postal rates several times higher for letters than for newspapers. The distribution of news was also encouraged through postage-free exchanges among newspaper editors. In 1936, the Post Office also inaugurated postal express services to speed the flow of market information.[8]

PROMOTING NATIONAL INTEGRATION BY SUPPORTING MASS MEDIA AND EDUCATION

The situation facing policy makers in the post-Civil War period was radically different from that which had confronted the Founding Fathers a century before. No longer unified around a set of revolutionary goals, the nation was coming apart at the seams. Pressing problems included the reconciliation of the North and South, the integration of the western territories, urbanization, the absorption of new immigrants, and the shift from agriculture to industrialization.

Like the Founding Fathers, post-Civil War decision makers turned to communications policies for answers. Instead of focusing on ways for people to exercise their individual differences and choices, however, they began to view communication from a more organic perspective—as a means of socializing individuals and integrating them into specialized roles within a larger community. Such a radical change in approach is understandable, given the prevailing intellectual and political thinking of the day. Support came from the Progressive movement as well as from the burgeoning field of sociology, which stressed the role of communication.[9] These groups looked to the media not only to enhance public understanding but also to improve society. As the philosopher John Dewey described, "The duty of the present is the socializing of intelligence—the realizing of its bearing upon the social practice."[10]

Support for the mass media

In keeping with this perspective, in the late 1800s the federal government extended its postal subsidies to the newly emerging mass media. Taking advantage of technology advance and advertiser financing, publishers launched a new media genre—low-cost magazines that were geared to a mass, middle-class audience. Magazines such as *The Saturday Evening Post* and *The Ladies' Home Journal* provided a mechanism, by which mass retailers—advertising brand name consumer goods—could reach out to the public.[11]

Given the country's expansion westward, the mass media were considered essential to the development of a national market. Moreover, because the mass media could breech the social and economic cleavages that beset the nation, many hoped it would foster a sense of national identity as well as the peaceful resolution of differences.[12] Members of the influential Progressive Movement were especially hopeful in this regard. To assure widespread access to magazines, the government—in 1890—inaugurated the Rural Free Delivery (RFD) Program. The targets of the RFD subsidies were the underserved, remote, high-cost rural areas. Although costly, rural free delivery helped to improve access. Over the next four decades, the distribution of periodicals increased 20 times faster than the population at large.[13]

The public school movement

Nowhere was the new communication philosophy embraced more enthusiastically than in the realm of public education. Whereas in the early years of the republic education was regarded as a private affair—provided for the benefit of the well-to-do and the professional classes—in the post-Civil War era it was considered a matter of national survival.[14] Looking to education to unite the nation and preserve its social and economic integrity, politicians and educators joined together in a public school crusade. By educating American youth in public schools, they hoped to inculcate a common set of patriotic, Protestant, and republican values.[15,16] Moreover, they believed such schools would socialize the growing number of people from so many different backgrounds for increasingly differentiated economic roles.

To perform this function, public schools were structured in accordance with business principles. Vocational education and guidance were introduced as part of the educational curriculum. Assuming that the majority of Americans would be working at industrial jobs, educators believed that vocational education would serve not only the best interests of individuals, but also society.[17,18]

Public libraries were likewise targeted for support. In rural areas, book deposit stations were set up in grange halls, neighborhood stores, fire stations, and women's clubs. In cities, libraries and adult education programs were set up to provide a haven for working class immigrants.[19]

Agricultural extension

In its educational efforts, the government also reached out to farmers, who bore much of the brunt of the socioeconomic changes taking place. Describing this situation, Wayne Rasmussen notes,

> The revolution generated by the Civil War catapulted the nation's farmers not only into a world of complex social and economic forces that were too volatile and powerful

for individual farmers to confront by themselves. It seemed that the appearance of more complex and productive tools intended to guarantee the farmer's survival had made that survival more complex.[20]

To help them adjust to changes in the economy, the government began to develop and transfer modern technology to agriculture. It thus initiated the Agricultural Extension Service in 1914. As provided under the Smith-Lever Act, the U.S. Department of Agriculture and the land grant agricultural colleges were charged with establishing partnerships between university extension and experiment stations, and between country extension agencies and country farm bureaus. Within a few decades, an elaborate network of public and private partners had achieved its goal of farm modernization.[20]

Land grant colleges and industrial education

Universities were also overhauled to keep pace with social and economic changes. The land grant colleges, provided for under the Morrill Act of 1762, played a critical role in this regard. Under this law, land was provided to the states, the proceeds of which were to be used to teach agronomy and mechanical arts. Subsequent legislation provided federal support for research and the operation of land-grant colleges. Designed to meet the role of an industrial economy, these universities were called on to expand beyond the traditional role of training gentlemen as preachers, lawyers, and doctors. Democratic and populist in origin, they were open to children of all backgrounds. Moreover, unlike traditional colleges, they were not isolated in their communities. Through their agricultural experiment stations and their service bureaus, their activities were designed to foster economic development in the states.[21]

The impact of the Morrill Act was clearly evident in the field of engineering. Before its passage, state legislatures had been reluctant to invest in technical education. By 1886, there were 110 schools of engineering.[22]

Promoting Universal Efficient Interconnection via Regulation

To meet the needs of a rapidly expanding and increasingly complex industrial economy, large-scale, integrated networks, as well as a more activist federal policy, were called for. Although new technologies—such as the railroads, the telegraph, and the telephone—emerged to accommodate the needs of an industrial economy, acting on its own, the market could neither generate the financing nor promote the economic coordination necessary for their ubiquitous deployment and diffusion.

The public was also much less inclined to provide unquestioned support for business. Middle class reformers describing themselves as "progressives" opposed the concentration of economic power. They called on government to control corporate abuses and reduce the negative impacts of rapid industrialization and urbanization. Farmers and others living in the West accused big business, especially the oil companies and railroads, of price gouging. In addition, labor—emerging as a movement in its own right—became increasingly critical of business.

This decline in the support of business reflected the economic uncertainty of the time. The exceptional growth that had characterized the period from the end of the Civil War to the turn of the century was accompanied by fierce competition. Growth in economic activity gave rise to overproduction, which led in turn to three severe economic downturns (from 1873 to 1877, 1885 to 1887, and 1893 to 1897). In this economic climate, the rate of business failure was exceedingly high. To survive, businesses employed whatever measures they could, including cartels and other pooling arrangements, predatory pricing, or direct control through horizontal mergers.[23]

Seeking a more stable economic environment, business and political reformers alike called for a new transportation and communication policy regime. In developing a new strategy, the federal government drew on the concept of a public service company, which in England dated back to the fourteenth century.[24] As the term was applied in the United States, public service companies were those whose products or services were considered essential to a community's well-being and way of life. Given their importance, these companies were required to provide services to everyone on a nondiscriminatory basis, while government was called on to assure compliance.

United States policy makers adopted this model for regulating the rapidly growing and increasingly powerful transportation and communication industries, which fit neatly into its framework. Embedded first in the Interstate Commerce Act of 1887 and later in the Communications Act of 1934, this regulatory solution allowed businesses to operate in the private sector while providing some social control over the single-mindedness of the market. Facilitating inter- and intraindustry coordination—even, when necessary, at the expense of monopoly—it promoted network interoperability, economic viability, and universal service at the time in which the communication infrastructure was becoming ever more important to the American way of life.

The railroads and the interstate commerce commission

Because of its high fixed costs, fluctuating demand, scale of operations, and need for coordination and specialized engineering skills, the railroad industry was from its inception prone to exceptionally high transaction costs. After numerous failed efforts by companies to jointly develop standards, coordinate operations, stabilize prices, and rationalize the industry, railroad industry magnates

began to merge their operations, frenetically buying up their customers and competitors. In their efforts to establish greater market stability, the railroad companies alternated their strategies between two extremes—cutthroat competition or pooling and price fixing. Because the economic stakes and uncertainties were so high, neither strategy proved successful. Cutthroat competition was ruinous for all, but cooperative agreements were untenable without some mechanism for enforcement.[25]

Railroad companies' competitive machinations quickly spilled over into the political arena, giving rise to demands for reform. Most vocal in calling for reform were small business owners and farmers in the West who had been forced by the railroad companies to subsidize the discounted rates offered to the large eastern industrialists. An increasingly disgruntled and activist labor force soon joined these voices.

Under mounting pressure, the government established the Interstate Commerce Commission in 1987 to regulate the railroads to assure just and reasonable rates.

Regulating the telegraph

Requiring large-scale technologies and national interconnection, the telegraph—like the railroads—posed questions about the industry's structure and its relationship to government. Although the federal government had provided $30,000 for the construction of the first telegraph lines in the United States, it was reluctant to play a more active role. The post office, already burdened by deficits, was disinclined to assume responsibility for the Washington D.C./Baltimore line, which appeared to have only limited commercial value.

Absent government involvement, telegraph firms strung wires between towns of any commercial consequence. With dozens of companies competing, however, customers were wont to secure rapid, reliable transmission. Under these circumstances, businesses preferred dealing with a few reliable national firms. Happy to oblige, Western Union absorbed its competitors, obtaining a near monopoly.[26] Concerned lest a single national telegraph abuse its power, the government opted once again for a common carrier system. In 1866, Congress granted monopoly privileges to Western Union in return for its promise to provide "services like a common carrier, namely to all comers without discrimination." In 1893, the U.S. Supreme Court ratified the telegraph's status as a common carrier, and Congress legislated it in the Communications Act of 1934.

Regulating the telephone

The history of the telephone industry followed a similar pattern. By 1902, 451 out of 1,200 cities had two or more phone companies. As with the telegraph, business users found competition burdensome. At the same time, cities and states increasingly expected telephone providers to operate for the public's convenience. Responding to a serious movement for government ownership, AT&T mounted a public campaign, arguing that telephony was a natural monopoly and regulation was the only way to reduce "wasteful competition" and assure universal service. As Theodore Vail, AT&T's chief operating officer, described his vision of the telephone industry in the annual report of 1910,

> The position of the Bell system is well known.... The telephone system should be universal, interdependent, and interconnected, affording opportunity for any other subscriber of any other exchange...annihilating time or distance by use of electrical transmission.

Congress was amenable. It gave the Interstate Commerce Commission regulatory authority over the Bell system in 1910 and shifted jurisdiction to the Federal Communications Commission (FCC) in 1934 with the passage of the Communications Act.

Managing Cultural Concerns

Electronically based media presented government with a novel dilemma, which threatened to pit public concerns about media impacts against the constitutional guarantee of First Amendment rights. Early in American history, political thinkers and policy makers had looked to the newspapers to enlighten and empower the public. With the advent of popular electronic media such as film and broadcasting, however, concerns about cultural values and negative impacts came to the fore.

Electronic media were considered different in a number of respects. Capable of reaching a mass audience on a simultaneous basis, film, radio, and television broadcasting appeared inordinately influential. At the same time, their commercial nature and dependence on advertising raised concerns lest these media demean culture and stifle political discussion by appealing to humanity's lowest common denominator. Because these media transmitted content directly into the home, listeners and viewers seemed powerless in defending against unsolicited messages.

As Secretary of Commerce Herbert Hoover described the situation with respect to radio:

> Radio has passed from the field of an adventure to that of a public utility. Nor among the utilities is there one whose activities may yet come more closely to the life of each and every one of our citizens, nor which holds out greater possibilities of future influence, nor which is of more potential public concern. Here is an agency that has reached deep into family life. We can protect the home by preventing the entry of printed matter destructive to its ideals but we must double guard the radio.[27]

The fear that mass media would unduly influence the public was fueled by their use of propaganda during the Second World War. Although propaganda had proved critical to the military effort, it appeared more sinister in the postwar period. People were concerned lest the media's manipulative techniques be used against them. In fact, in his best-selling book *The Hidden Persuaders*, Vance Packard had accused advertisers of cynically using propaganda to manipulate American consumers.[28]

Postwar scholars and social critics reinforced these worries. Bemoaning the public's reaction to the media's "pseudo-environments," Walter Lippman called for the replacement of journalists by social scientists who, he claimed, would organize and interpret events more objectively.[29] At the same time, social psychologists—such as David Riesman in his book *The Lonely Crowd*—began to link the mass media and mass opinion to negative social and political outcomes.[9]

In addressing these concerns about content, the government was limited by the First Amendment. By leveraging its ownership of the public airways and allocating them according to "public interest criteria," however, the government was able to pursue a number of content-related policy goals within the bounds of the Constitution.

Voluntary censorship

Voluntary private censorship was the preferred means of influencing media content. With voluntary censorship, not only could the government achieve its public interest goals; industrywide standards also allowed media providers to appease the public without being competitively disadvantaged. Responding to its critics and the threat of government intervention, the motion picture industry was the first media provider to set voluntary content standards through the National Board of Censorship of Motion Pictures. Movie critics were concerned lest films lead to the vulgarization of daily life. As Michael M. Davis of the Russell Sage Foundation argued in 1912, "recreation within the modern city has become a matter of public concern; laissez faire, in recreation as in industry, can no longer be the policy of the state." Responding, local governments began to employ ordinances, such as those pertaining to Sunday blue laws, safety, and community morals, to censor content and when deemed necessary to shut theaters down (p. 44).[9]

When faced with the prospect of regulation, broadcasters followed suit. Thus, as soon as the Federal Radio Commission made its intention known to scrutinize broadcast content in allocating renewal license, the National Association of Broadcasters (NAB) wasted no time in developing an industry code of standards. Similarly, the first NAB television code was adopted in 1951 shortly after Senator William Benton threatened to establish a national citizen's advisory board that would oversee programming and submit an annual report to Congress assessing the extent to which broadcasting served the public interest.[30]

Communication–
Corporate Art

Although voluntary in nature private sector content standards have proved problematic. Indeed, over the years broadcasters have often been chastised for "self-censorship." Critics claim that because broadcasters must appeal to a broad advertising base, they avoid controversy by diluting their programming. Voluntary content standards have also been challenged on both antitrust and First Amendment grounds. In 1979, for example, the court—in *Writers Guild of America, West, v. ABC*—questioned whether the government had unduly pressed the NAB to voluntarily agree to a one-hour evening segment of programming for "family viewing." When the Justice Department challenged the code on antitrust grounds, the NAB abandoned its standards altogether.[31]

Spectrum licensing

When voluntary standards have not sufficed, the government has leveraged its ownership of the public airwaves to force broadcasters to operate stations in accordance with "the public interest, convenience, and necessity," as provided for in the Communications Act of 1934. Such a proactive regulatory structure was considered justified, given the chaotic situation in the early days of broadcasting and the industry's reliance on a limited public spectrum. Policy makers and industry representatives alike believed that without some means of allocating the public spectrum the airwaves would become so overcrowded and interference so rife broadcasting would be precluded. Thus it was, for example, that broadcasters aligned in 1922 to form the NAB, with the express purpose of promoting radio regulation. Commenting on the public mood of the time, Secretary of Commerce Herbert Hoover described the situation as "one of the few instances that I know of when the whole country is earnestly praying for more regulation."[32]

Accordingly, broadcasters have been required to provide among other things local content, news and public affairs programming (with adequate and unbiased coverage given to controversial issues), and educational fare for children, as well as equal time for the use of stations by political candidates. While restraining the FCC from actions considered excessive, the courts have generally sanctioned the broadcast regulatory regime on the grounds that spectrum—being scarce—needed to be rationed.

Setting the tone for the future in the landmark case *Red Lion Broadcasting Co. v. FCC*, the Supreme Court considered the constitutionality of the Fairness Doctrine:

> Broadcast frequencies constitute a scarce resource whose use could be regulated and rationalized only by Government. Without Government control, the medium would be of little use because of the cacophony of competing voices, none of which could be clearly and predictably heard. [Thus] Every licensee who is fortunate in obtaining

a license is assumed to operate in the public interest and has assumed the obligation of presenting important public questions fairly and without bias.[48]

Must carry rules

The availability of spectrum was not an issue, however, when the FCC issued the *Cable Television Report and Order* in 1972, laying out comprehensive rules for the cable industry. In the late 1960s, small cable operators were joined by larger systems that aimed to greatly expand their markets. In response, broadcasters pressured Congress to restrict cable. The FCC reluctantly issued a series of rulings that had the cumulative effect of restricting cable development.

Under the *Cable Television Report and Order* in 1972, cable systems were freed to expand to the top 100 markets, but as a quid pro quo they were subject to "must carry rules" requiring operators to provide channels for educational institutions, municipal governments, and public access. Moreover, to assure the viability of free television and the availability of community programming, cable operators had to carry local broadcasting companies' signals.

Cable posed a potential threat to the FCC's vision of a localized television system, because if cable operators began to import distant signals into local markets, they might drive local stations out of business. This danger only became apparent as cable began to grow and expand into major markets.

Public broadcasting

Although public interest regulation helped to limit some of the negative aspects of broadcasting, it did little to foster high-quality content. For such purposes, a more direct and concerted effort was required. In the United States, in which government ownership of the media was not an option, a hybrid system of public broadcasting was devised. To preserve the system's integrity, Congress devised a decentralized structure, which placed the individual stations at its center.[34] In addition, it set up the Corporation for Public Broadcasting (CPB) with the dual purpose of developing a nationwide broadcasting system and acting as a buffer between broadcasters and government. The corporation itself was prohibited from owning and operating any broadcast or cable organization, interconnection system or facility, program production house, or public telecom organization; nor could CPB produce, schedule, or distribute programs to the public.[35] At the same time, however, Congress maintained tight reigns on funding through the annual appropriations process.

Communications for National Security and Defense

Communication goals have evolved not only in response to changing social and economic needs. At times, they have been radically reoriented to meet the exigencies of war. In most countries, reordering priorities for defense purposes was relatively easy. Owned and operated by the government, these companies were designed to serve the state's needs. In contrast, in the United States, in which the First Amendment precludes government interference, establishing a communication system to support national defense has been more problematic. To minimize the tension between defense and other communication-related goals, the government has involved itself in communications-related activities only on a sporadic and/or indirect basis.

This pattern was set at the time of the U.S. involvement in the First World War. In the autumn of 1918, for example, Congress directed the postmaster general to assume operation of the nation's telephone and telegraph companies. Under the post office's management, the telegraph and telephone systems worked smoothly, although rates increased. Shortly after the government took control, however, the war ended and Congress restored the wires to the private sector.[36]

World War II and the Cold War that followed led to a much more compelling and pervasive preoccupation about national security. Although the government consistently turned to the private sector to promote its defense-related goals, an increased emphasis on national defense and security sometimes collided with those of free speech and a free market.

Limits on speech

Speech first became an issue during wartime with the passage of state and federal sedition laws, which were premised on the notion that speech could undermine the war effort. Early on, convictions were common because courts applied a "reasonable tendency" test. Later, justices began to fashion a standard that was more protective of free speech—the "clear and present danger" test, which cut off speech only if it posed an imminent and substantial danger to some vital interest.[37] On rare occasions during peacetime, the government sought to enjoin the press from publishing information whose disclosure might undermine national security.

The government's attempt to invoke national security to stop publication of the *Pentagon Papers* failed when the Supreme Court, acknowledging that national security was sufficient reason to impose prior restraint on publication, ruled that in this instance the government had failed to show that anything more than embarrassment would result. In effect, the door was left ajar. Where atomic secrets have been involved, the government has been better positioned to justify a prior restraint. In 1970, for example, the government obtained a district court injunction that stopped publication of an article by *The Progressive* magazine, which depicted the making of a hydrogen bomb.

Promoting defense technology

Communication and information technologies have generally been high on the list of technologies meriting government promotion. Recognizing the defense potential of radio, for example, the government played a critical role in its development. The U.S. Navy, in cooperation with AT&T, not only helped to develop the emerging technology, it also spearheaded the corporate–government alliance to consolidate and centralize radio during and after World War II. The Wilson administration's goal was to challenge British domination of international communication and to protect U.S. military and commercial interests. After failing to get Congress to pass legislation that would make wartime government control of wireless permanent, the administration pursued a different strategy. In 1919, British Marconi was the only company negotiating with General Electric to buy exclusive right to the Alexanderson alternator, a high-powered radio transmitter used for transoceanic work during the war. Through a series of delicate negotiations, the government stepped in and served as the midwife to the birth of the Radio Corporation of America. RCA, with GE as the major stockholder, bought out Marconi (which had been controlled by the British), thus assuring America a powerful position in world communication (p. 70).[9]

The military's role in developing the computer and other advanced communication technologies was also critical, even if indirect and behind the scenes. The government not only subsidized the early research and development of satellites, computers, and semiconductor chips, it also used its procurement powers to assure that these industries had stable, guaranteed markets.[38,39]

Securing the infrastructure

The government's ability to balance government and free market interests was greatly aided by the existence of a government-regulated telephone monopoly, which was renowned for quality and research in all communications fields. As the only company supplying end-to-end telecommunications service to the Defense Communication Agency, AT&T was directly involved in formulating national security telecommunications specifications and requirements and in making adequate provisions governing robustness, ubiquity, and restorability. Nonetheless, believing AT&T's centralized, hierarchical structure to be vulnerable to attack, government researchers at the Advanced Research Project Agency developed a packet-switched network based on a decentralized architecture. By 1971, the ARPAnet—precursor to the Internet—linked defense scientists and engineers at 16 university-based nodes. To ensure their seamless and transparent interconnection, the Defense Department also sponsored two key networking standards: the transmission control protocol (TCP) and the Internet protocol (IP).

TRANSITION TO A COMPETITIVE ENVIRONMENT

As this short history illustrates, despite periods of upheaval and change, the U.S. communication policy regime—like the Constitution in which it is grounded—has proven to be quite flexible and stable over time. Old rules survived even as new ones were added. Multiple goals coexisted—even when they competed with one another—because each goal was associated with a particular communication technology having unique technical characteristics and imperatives as well as its own set of industry players. Thus, for example, First Amendment goals have generally been associated with print technologies, whereas universal service goals have been more closely linked to telephony and the transportation infrastructure. If—as was sometimes the case—the boundaries among technologies began to blur, policy makers intervened to reinforce the lines of demarcation.

Today, however, achieving flexibility in this way is increasingly problematic. Not only have new technologies been developed that do not fit neatly into old categories; with the convergence of print, carrier, and broadcasting technologies, old categories themselves no longer apply.

In light of such convergence, pressures have mounted to create a more level playing field and to establish a uniform regulatory regime based on market competition. As early as 1962, for example, a number of regulatory economists began to question the public utility concept. Together their work—if it did not give rise to the new deregulatory climate—served at least to legitimate it. As Roger Noll has described:

> Economists generally entered the study of regulation with the naïve view that regulatory institutions were set up for the purpose of rectifying market failures. Unfortunately, and almost without exception, the early empirical studies—those commencing in the late 1950s and continuing into the 1970s—found the effects of regulation correlated poorly with the stated goals of regulation. By the early 1970s, the overwhelming majority of economists had reached consensus on two points. First, economic regulation did not succeed in protecting consumers against monopolies and indeed often served to create monopolies out of workable competitive industries or to protect monopolies against new firms seeking to challenge their position. Second in circumstances where market failures were of enduring importance (such as environmental protection) traditional standard-setting regulation was usually a far less effective remedy than the use of markets and incentives.[40]

At the same time regulators, impressed by the potential of new technology to reduce costs and increase capacity, were also willing to experiment with competition. As former FCC Commissioner Nicholas Johnson commented on the occasion of the FCC's decision to approve MCI's application to establish long-distance service:

> On this occasion three Commissioners are urging a perpetuation of more Government regulation of business, and four want to experiment with the market forces of American free private enterprise as an alternative to regulation. No one has ever suggested that Government regulation is a panacea for men's ills. It is a last resort: a patchwork remedy for the failings and special cases of the marketplace….I am not satisfied with the job the FCC has been doing. And I am still looking, at this juncture, for ways to add a little salt and pepper of competition to the rather tasteless stew of regulatory protection that this commission and Bell have cooked up.[41]

Equally important, the growing importance of telecommunications and media-related industries within the economy changed the way communications came to be conceived. Instead of being perceived as a means to an end, communication was viewed increasingly as a commodity much like any other, to be bought and sold in the marketplace. In the process, the public interest came to be measured not by the quality of social and economic life, but rather by the state of the media industry and consumer demand.[42]

Tensions and discrepancies within the old system first manifested themselves in the case of cable—a hybrid technology —but it was not long before they emerged in more traditional arenas such as telephony and broadcasting. Early attempts to address these tensions within the old regulatory framework were short-lived.

Fitting Cable into the Regulatory Regime

The inherent tension in broadcast regulation—between First Amendment rights and the public interest standard—became increasingly apparent with the advent of cable television, which did not fit well in either category. With its multiplicity of channels, cable was, moreover, the first technology to defy the long-held belief in scarcity.

Cable was originally intended to enhance television signals in communities located in areas outside good broadcasting reception. At first, the FCC ignored CATV, viewing it as an auxiliary to broadcasting. Seeking to avoid the administrative burden of regulating another industry, the FCC pointed out that CATV was neither a common carrier (because the subscriber did not determine the nature of the signal being carried) nor a form of broadcasting (because signal transmission was completely by wire). Thus, what attention the FCC did pay to CATV in the early years was centered on possible interference or problems for the broadcast sector. For a history of the FCC and the regulation of cable see.[43]

The situation changed in the late 1960s, however, when cable operators sought to expand their markets by importing broadcast signals. Under pressure from broadcasters, the FCC issued rulings curtailing cable growth. Then in 1972 the FCC reversed itself, allowing cable to expand on the condition that it provided community programming and adhere to must carry rules. Two factors served to stimulate industry's growth. First, the rise of pay-cable services such as Home Box Office revealed an extensive latent demand for alternative programming. Second and more important in the long run, cable programming became linked to satellite. Communication satellites created reliable and economically feasible distribution networks, while the availability of new and specialized programming stimulated nationwide demand.

As cable's fortunes improved and programming became available, operators characterized the industry as analogous to newspapers rather than broadcasting.[44] On this basis, they called for deregulation and full First Amendment rights (See, e.g., Shapiro).[45] Because spectrum scarcity had been used to justify broadcast regulation, cable's multichannel capacity lent credibility to its demands. As characterized by Laurence Tribe:[46]

> The clear failure of the 'technological scarcity argument' as applied to cable television amounts to an invitation to reconsider the tension between the Supreme Court's radically divergent approaches to the print and electronic media. Indeed, since the scarcity argument makes little sense as a basis for distinguishing newspapers from television even in the late 1960s and early 1970s, such reconsideration seems long overdue.

Seeking to rectify the situation, Congress passed the Cable Communications Policy Act of 1984, deregulating the cable industry. Nevertheless, considerable confusion about the nature of cable was embodied in the act itself. Cities lost the authority to regulate subscribers' rates and much of their discretion over franchise renewal. The act also prohibited the regulation of cable as a common carrier or public utility. At the same time, however, cities were allowed to charge franchise fees and require public access channels and other kinds of programming. The outcome represented as a compromise between the cities, which wanted to continue to charge franchise fees, and the cable operators, who wanted to facilitate the franchise-renewal process, but the compromise sidestepped the issue of the First Amendment.

Thus, the issue of cable regulation, and its relationship to the First Amendment, did not disappear. In fact, given rising cable prices and increased concentration, Congress reregulated the industry in 1992 under the Cable Television Consumer Protection and Competition Act. The new law reinstated rules for common carriage and rate of return regulation. In addition, it prohibited exclusive franchise agreements between cable and municipalities as well as affiliations between cable programmers and cable operators.

Subsequent court cases also failed to resolve the question of how cable should be handled from a regulatory perspective. In fact, while acknowledging that scarcity was no longer a problem, the courts—in the cases of

Turner I, Turner II, and Denver Area—upheld the must carry rules.[47] Looking at the cable industry's structure and noting Congress' concerns about over-the-air broadcasting, the Court departed from a traditional doctrinaire interpretation of the First Amendment. As one critic of the decision characterized it:

> In Denver *Area Educational Telecommunications Inc. v. FCC*, the plurality assiduously managed not only to avoid defining the First Amendment status of cable within fairly well-established boundaries, but seemed to grope at a new ad hoc constitutional approach somewhere between intermediate and strict scrutiny.[48]

Instead it argued that First Amendment cases must be decided on a case-by-case basis and with reference to the context involved. Only by looking at the context, said the Court, is it possible to balance the vendor's First Amendment rights to provide information against the user's First Amendment right to access it.[49]

Tensions in the Telecom Regime

As in the case of cable, technology advances helped to undermine the long-standing common carrier regime. Given the convergence of information and communication technologies, there was no longer a clear distinction between what constituted a monopoly (and hence regulated) service and what constituted a competitive service to be provided in the market. Convergence also gave rise to a new network architecture, in which intelligence was dispersed. As a result, the network could more easily be unbundled, allowing users to purchase, and new providers to offer, separate portions of it. Barriers to entry were also reduced, given technology advances that increased performance but greatly reduced costs.

Economic developments also generated incentives for new entrants. As information came to play a greater and more strategic role in business, large users sought alternative ways to meet their telecommunication needs. In some cases they set up their own internal networks. In others, they simply bypassed the Bell system, purchasing services in lower-priced, unregulated markets. Equally important from a political perspective, business users joined forces with burgeoning new service providers to press for greater competition.

In light of these developments, policy makers were more receptive to the idea of competition. In 1959, the FCC took a first step toward breaking up the Bell system with its "above 890" decision. This decision liberalized the licensing of private microwave systems, allowing the newly created Microwave Communications, Inc. (MCI) to offer a new product—discount private line service. With the subsequent Carterphone decision in 1969, the FCC opened the customer-premises market. Finally, with its Execunet decisions in 1976 and 1978 requiring AT&T to connect to MCI, the FCC struck a final blow to the 100-year-old AT&T monopoly.

In 1982, AT&T entered into a consent decree with the Justice Department, following a decade-long antitrust suit. A modified final judgement (MFJ) went into effect in 1984, clarifying and expanding the terms of the 1982 consent decree. The basic premise of this divestiture was that the Bell system's competitive markets should be separated from their noncompetitive markets to prevent unfair monopoly abuses. Accordingly, AT&T was broken into eight companies, the reorganized AT&T and several regional holding companies. The Bell system's 22 local telephone companies were separated from the parent company, and grouped into seven regional Bell holding companies (RBOCs), which were prohibited from the three lines of businesses deemed competitive and therefore assigned to AT&T. These were designing and manufacturing telecommunications networks and customer premises equipment, providing information services (such as electronic yellow pages), and providing long-distance service.

While the MFJ settled the Department of Justice's antitrust suit, it could not resolve the tension between the goals of efficiency and competition that are inherent in any telecom regulatory policy. As Noll has emphasized,

> Pending regulatory issues reflect an enduring characteristic of telecommunications policy; neither the pricing nor the structural issue has even been or is likely to be resolved. The telecommunications system is not, and never was, broken. Rather, its underlying technical and economic characteristics create an enduring policy dilemma. One can regulate prices and structure to encourage maximum feasible competition, or to promote an integrated monopoly. What is infeasible is a 'neutral' formulaic policy regarding prices and structure that will assure the right mix of monopoly and competition. The current policy agenda continues the futile search for better regulatory instruments, and also includes rear guard actions by the people who lost the last time around—who are not, and probably cannot be convinced that deregulated competition is the best policy (p. 233).[39]

No sooner had the parties agreed to the MFJ when these issues re-emerged in the waiver process, the triennial review, and in public policy debates about how open the telephone network should be.

In this context, the FCC—eager to promote competition in the local exchange—devised a plan allowing RBOCs to enter new markets in exchange for opening their networks. To assure compliance, the local telephone companies had to make their basic network services (referred to as basic service elements) available in a uniform and nondiscriminatory fashion. Subsequently, in 1987 the ban against providing information services was amended, and then in 1991—following continued challenges by the RBOCs in court—all information service restrictions were eliminated. In an effort to promote innovation and greater competition in the cable market, the FCC also established video dial tone rules that allowed local exchange companies to provide video services on a common carrier platform. None of the telephone companies saw it in their interest to pursue this option, however. Like cable companies, they wanted to be released from the yoke of regulation and to be brought within the First Amendment regime.

Efforts to Deregulate Broadcasting

Broadcasting had long been a target for deregulation. Challenges to the broadcast regulatory framework first got underway during President Carter's administration, when FCC chairman Charles Ferris initiated a deregulatory policy much in keeping with the administration's overall policy on deregulation. These efforts only achieved their full momentum, however, during the Reagan years, when Chairmen Mark Fowler and Dennis Patrick set out to revamp the entire regulatory structure, substituting marketplace constraints in place of regulatory controls.[50]

Citing past FCC failures, opponents claimed that regulation was inappropriate for achieving broadcast policy goals, and at times counterproductive, as in the case of the FCC's efforts to constrain cable TV. Regulatory critics argued, moreover, that with the development of high-capacity cable scarcity no longer justified government intervention. Deregulation, they argued, was also more in keeping with First Amendment principles. Industry players echoed this claim, although they were much more pragmatic than principled in their enthusiasm, generally favoring only those measures that were economically advantageous.

To bring about a more competitive media market, the FCC began to undo the elaborate structure of rules and regulations that had been set up over the years.[51] Thus the FCC eliminated most advertising constraints as well as rules requiring broadcasters to devote a given amount of time to different classes of nonentertainment programming—even fair use. At the same time, the agency relaxed a number of ownership rules.

Despite these changes, tensions persisted in broadcasting. Although broadcasters favored deregulation, they wanted to maintain the benefits, particularly access to free spectrum and the congressional favor that the public interest regime had afforded. Moreover, broadcasters could anticipate an even greater need for congressional support in the future, given the emergence of new technologies competing for spectrum. Relying heavily on broadcasters for financial and political advantages, members of Congress were also unwilling to unravel the public interest regime, thus there occurred the anomalous situation in which the FCC refused to enforce the Fairness Doctrine while key members of Congress championed it and promised to codify it at the first opportunity. As described by Le Duc, "At the moment, then, the broadcast deregulation has reached an impasse, Congress refuses to release the

Communication–
Corporate Art

commission from its obligation to regulate American broadcast service, while the agency refuses to discharge this obligation with any more diligence or dedication than absolutely required by law."[52]

THE TELECOMMUNICATIONS ACT OF 1996

Despite these tensions and mounting pressure for reform, efforts to fundamentally restructure the regulatory regime lacked an overriding vision and a set of guiding principles. Without such vision, reformers were unable to generate a broad political consensus in support of their efforts.[53] As a result, reform proposals typically fell victim to the hassling and squabbles of the legislative process and to Congress' reluctance to offend powerful interests. In the absence of legislative guidelines and in the face of rapid technology advance, decisions about communication policy were often regulated to the courts. It was only when Vice-President Gore successfully captured the unique potential of the Internet in his vision of a national information infrastructure (NII) that a groundswell for reform emerged.

The Internet Vision

The rapid rise of the Internet provided a unique opportunity as well as the necessary momentum to generate a new vision of communication policy for the future. Providing a digital platform for all forms of electronic communication, the Internet defied the technology and industry boundaries that had sustained three distinct regulatory regimes.

From a regulatory perspective, the most promising feature of the Internet was its open architecture and decentralized organizational structure. Viewed in these terms, the Internet could be best be described as a very loosely coupled "network of networks." Given common interfaces, networks on the Internet can be interconnected while they are at the same time operated and managed independently of one another, thus control is decentralized and horizontally structured. Given a common suite of protocols, interconnection is seamless, allowing traffic to flow easily and to be exchanged across disparate networks and applications. As described by the Computer Science and Telecommunications Board:

> Most users of the Internet see it through experiencing its applications, most obviously the World Wide Web, but also the ubiquitous electronic mail, remote login, file transfer, and other applications. But from the perspective of Internet designers, the essence of the Internet is not the applications, but rather the more basic functionality that makes the Internet a suitable place for those applications to operate. The structure of the Internet reflects two major design objectives: first, to support as many sorts of applications as possible, and second, to operate over as many sorts of network infrastructures as possible.[54]

According to this vision, in an Internet environment public policy goals could be achieved with minimal government interference (for this perspective, see McKnight).[55] For example, with nonpropriety, widely available interfaces, interconnection and access would not be a problem, thus fostering competition and innovation. Moreover, diffusion would be rapid and widespread, given low costs and positive externalities resulting from shared provisioning and usage. Consumers also would be empowered. Because interoperability allows applications and intelligence to be unbundled and extended outward, individuals could control the provisioning and use of networks and applications.

When the Democrats came to power, Vice-President Gore incorporated this vision in the administration's NII initiative, which was launched in September 1993. The initiative emphasized the hope of achieving broad-based social, economic, and political goals in the context of a competitive environment. The key principles included the need to: (1) encourage private investment, (2) promote and protect competition, (3) provide for open access to networks, (4) avoid the creation of a society of haves and have-nots, and (5) encourage network flexibility.[56]

The NII initiative was intended not only to foster an open network architecture but also to provide a more open communication policy-making process. To support this process, the president established the Advisory Council on the National Information Infrastructure, which compromised 37 members—two-thirds from business and the remainder from the nonprofit sector, organized labor, and state and local government.[57] Even more unprecedented, the government took advantage of the Internet itself to include the broader public in the debate.

The NII initiative served as a catalyst to bring together public interest groups and citizens who shared a common vision of a public-oriented infrastructure. In October 1993, they created the Telecommunications Round Table, a peak organization to lobby on behalf of their goals. Inspired by the Internet and the range of possibilities that it allowed, they called for a NII that would provide support for universal access, two-way communication, active and participatory public debate, competition and diversity of information, an equitable workplace, privacy protection, network security, and democratic policy making. While favoring market solutions, the coalition wanted proof of competition and consumer choice, as well as assurances that there would be no redlining, before government took steps to deregulate the industry. Equally important, they advocated that 20% of the bandwidth of the NII be reserved for public use as a public "right of way"(p. 328).[57]

The national debate on the NII engendered enough momentum to break the congressional logjam, which had dashed all previous efforts at reform. Once the center of action shifted to Congress, however, the public interest groups generating this momentum had very little impact on the final legislative outcome.

Communication–
Corporate Art

The Missed Opportunity

Although the Communications Act of 1996 was generally welcomed as being long overdue, none of the parties to it was totally satisfied with the results. Arrived at through intense congressional lobbying, the law that was eventually adopted represented a carefully crafted compromise rather than a blueprint for the future. Concerned primarily that technology advance deprive them of some strategic competitive advantage, most key players ultimately preferred retrenchment to reform. A major opportunity was lost as a result.

Defeat in the 103rd Congress

In 1993, three bills relating to industry restructuring were introduced in Congress: the Brooks–Dingell bill (H.R. 3626), the Markey–Fields bill (H.R. 3636), and a companion bill in the Senate, the Hollings–Danforth bill (S 1822). Focusing primarily on industry deregulation, the Brooks–Dingell bill was the most narrow and permissive. As originally written, the bill called for a three-stage process of entry by which the local telephone companies could enter into long-distance services. Under pressure from the RBOCs, however the bill was modified to allow local telephone companies to seek authorization to enter long-distance from the Justice Department and the FCC on the same day the law took effect.

Strongly influenced by both the administration and increasingly vocal public interest coalition, the Markey–Fields bill went much further. Stressing the importance of an open network, the bill had much more stringent conditions for telephone company entry into other markets. According to the bill, local exchange carriers could enter other markets, but only after they had sufficiently opened up the local loop to competition. Telephone companies were also authorized to provide video services, but on a common carrier basis. In addition, the bill required the FCC to study the costs and benefits of the telephone companies providing an open network platform. At the same time, the Markey bill mandated open interfaces for set-top boxes and outlined steps to achieve social and economic goals, such as the provision of services to schools, health care centers, and libraries. In the summer of 1994, the House passed a somewhat watered-down version of H.R. 3636 by an overwhelming vote of 420 to 4, while the Senate moved to take up the companion bill, S 1822.

As fate would have it, a number of events intervened to bring Senate passage to an abrupt halt. The coalition supporting the legislation began to disintegrate in committee when Senator Daniel Inouye amended it, attaching S. 2195, which required carriers to allocate up to 20% of their capacity to noncommercial information suppliers in exchange for using public rights of way. This amendment was strongly opposed by industry players, who successfully lobbied to reduce reserved bandwidth to 5%. The public interest coalition was similarly riled when Senator James Exxon introduced an amendment requiring the FCC to monitor and censor the Internet for pornographic materials. The final blow to the legislation, however, came when the RBOCs withdrew their support, protesting a provision that denied them access to competitive markets absent "actual and demonstrable" facilities-based competition. Unwilling to compromise on this point and faced with increasing Republican opposition, Senator Hollings, chairman of the Senate Commerce Committee and sponsor of the bill, allowed it to die in committee.[57]

Retreat in the 104th Congress

In the November 1994 elections, Republicans returned to Congress with a mandate calling for deregulation. In keeping with the mood of the country, the leadership wanted to take immediate steps to deregulate the cable industry and greatly relax the limits on broadcast station ownership. Disagreements among industry players and concerns about a presidential veto made them more cautious,[58] however. Although most members of industry were staunch supporters of deregulation and greater competition, they strongly disagreed about how best to achieve these goals. Long-distance carriers and cable operators, for example, called for more stringent prohibitions on local phone companies, while the RBOCs argued that competition was being impeded by MFJ restrictions. Broadcasters in turn contended that for competition to survive they needed free spectrum.

Faced with such difficult choices, the Republicans looked to industry to help them write reform legislation. With this objective in mind, they invited top industry CEOs to Washington to find out precisely what they wanted to incorporate in a bill.[58] Hustling and jockeying for advantage continued right up to the end of the congressional debate. In the last six months before passage, for example, the top three long-distance companies contributed $2.1 million in political campaign funds to member of Congress, while the seven regional Bells gave $2.3 million.[59] Not surprisingly in light of the outcome, the RBOCs favored the Republicans with their contributions, the long-distance carriers the Democrats. As reported in *Business Week*, changes in political fortunes had a significant impact on the flow of campaign funds. When the Democrats controlled the Congress, the money from political action committees was evenly divided between parties. In contrast, after the elections, the Republicans received $1,267,122 while the Democrats received only $473,289. Similarly, Congressmen who had the greatest political leverage in the telecom debate—such as Senator Larry Pressler, chairman of the Senate Commerce Committee—received the larger shares."[60]

The Legislative Outcome: Winners and Losers

Despite congressional gridlock over the budget, Republicans and Democrats joined together to pass the telecommunications reform legislation in early February 1996 by a vote of 414 to 16 in the House, and 91 to 5 in the Senate. On February 8, President Clinton, having originally threatened to veto the bill for being too lax, signed it into law. The stated purpose of the new legislation was to promote deregulation and competition. Hailed as a major step forward, the reform bill was essentially a well-honed bipartisan political compromise, providing some concessions to just about all. Sorely missing from the law, however, was an overriding vision of the role of communications in society and a clear set of principles linking deregulation and competition to a larger set of social and economic goals.

The stakeholder group that could perhaps be most pleased with the outcome was the RBOCs. Eager to enter the competitive fray, the RBOCs boycotted the previous Democratic-sponsored legislation on the grounds that it was too restrictive. The Republic legislation went much further in meeting their needs. According to the law, local telephone companies no longer had to prove the actual existence of facilities-based competition before entering competitive markets. Instead, they only need to gain approval of the FCC and state regulators based on a somewhat vague set of criteria outlined in the legislation.

For cable companies, there was also much to boast about. Four years previously, the FCC had ordered them to cut their rates by up to 17%. Under the 1996 act, all cable rates were to be deregulated after 3 years. In small communities, regulation ended immediately. With greater cash flow, cable companies could compete more easily in telephone company markets, and some companies were already upgrading their systems to provide phone service as well as consolidating their businesses to establish a better geographic fit with the telephone company markets.[60]

The fate of the broadcasters under the new law was less certain. On the positive side, the law relaxed the previous cross-ownership rules, allowing broadcasters to own as many stations as they wanted as long as they did not exceed 35% of the U.S. market. Broadcasters failed, however, to eliminate a legislative provision requiring them to equip television sets with devices to block violent or sexual programs. Nor did broadcaster receive a clear mandate for free spectrum, as they had wished. Last-minute opposition from Senator Dole led to the postponement of this decision.

Nor did the long-distance companies fare as well as they had hoped. From their point of view, the longer RBOCs could be restrained from providing long-distance services the better. Given the status quo, long-distance carriers could gradually gain access to local exchange markets while local operating companies would still be precluded from entering long-distance markets. The new legislation, which provided less stringent criteria for determining competition in the local loop, was thus generally viewed as a major setback.[61] On the other hand, with the opening of the local loop to competition, long-distance carriers gained an opportunity not only to enter this lucrative market but also to bypass local exchange carriers by providing end-to-end services.

Society at large was perhaps the real loser in telecom reform. The primary focus of the bill was limited to deregulation and competition. Even when measured solely in terms of this narrow set of goals, however, the new legislation was sorely lacking. In contrast to the Markey bill, which had sought to promote open, two-way access, the Telecommunications Act eliminated most of the explicit requirements for interconnection and open interfaces. Instead of addressing the issue of competition head-on, it postponed the debate, delegating the thorny problems entailed in determining what constitutes "competition" to the FCC and the Department of Justice.[62] Thus, for example, the law required the FCC to write no fewer than 80 rules determining how the transition to competition would take place and how the costs and benefits among industry players would be distributed.[63,64]

Social considerations were not totally absent from the new legislation. For example, the act mandated the delivery of advanced telecommunications services to rural schools, libraries, and health care facilities at rates that are discounted to assure affordable access and use of such services. While reiterating the goal of universal service, however, the act charted a new course for achieving it. In contrast to earlier efforts, which relied almost exclusively on price averaging and other subsidies, the new legislation sought to achieve the goal of universal service—"to the extent technically feasible and economically reasonable"—in the context of a competitive market environment. The act also called for restrictions on content. It required television equipment providers to embed technological filtering devices—V-chips—into all new television sets, and Internet providers to monitor and censor content on the Web in order to prevent juveniles from accessing pornography.

The passage of telecom reform legislation in the United States was heralded as a major step forward in bringing communication policy into line with technology advances. Amidst the high-minded congratulatory statements and general sighs of relief, a few dissident voices could be heard. Focusing on the lack of competitive safeguards, these skeptics were concerned lest the law provide the means and incentives for the communications industry to reintegrate itself along vertical lines. Perhaps the most disturbing and prescient in this regard was the assessment of Judge Harold H. Green, who had overseen the 1984 consent degree governing the breakup of AT&T. As he confided

I'm a little concerned [whether] there are sufficient safeguards against the kinds of mergers and acquisitions that
might give some small group of companies or individuals
a strong hold over U.S. markets. . . .I'd hate to see the
AT&T monopoly be reconstituted in some form. It would
be like I'd wasted the past 18 years.[65]

Recent events and speculations about the future suggest
that Judge Green's concerns were not without foundation.

COMPETITION IN RETROSPECT

The 1996 Telecom Act aimed to achieve a level playing
field among industry players so that the market rather than
government might effectively set the basis for interconnection among competing providers. The law, however,
has proven much easier to write than to implement.
Instead of promoting competition among communication
services as was intended, it has led instead to a rash of
mergers and the industry's reintegration. Equally discour-
aging, the promise of new, interindustry competition has
dwindled as providers have begun to fully comprehend the
costs and risks entailed in invading each other's markets.[66] Not surprisingly under the circumstances, many
consumers are now paying more for their phone and cable
services than they did prior to the Act.[67,68]

Nor has the Communications Act led to the deregulation of the communications industry or the demise of the
FCC as so many of its proponents had hoped. To the
contrary, in its effort to establish competition, the FCC
had found it necessary to "reregulate," thus it had become
more embroiled than ever in creating an elaborate set of
detailed prescriptions to govern competition among the
converging communication industries.[69]

The problems entailed in implementing the 1996
act have been exacerbated not only by the high stakes
involved and the complex and controversial nature of the
issues, but also by the fact that the act itself left so much
unresolved. To fulfill its mission, for example, the FCC
was charged with carrying out three interrelated tasks:
setting access charges, establishing the rule for interconnection, and establishing a mechanism for meeting
universal service requirements. To meet the legislative
requirement for nondiscriminatory access and pricing, in
each case the FCC had to establish a means of determining
real costs. The bane of all past regulatory proceedings,
determining costs is anything but an exact science, and
thus it has always been done in a somewhat arbitrary
fashion. The problem of pricing is especially challenging
in the case of universal service, given both the historical
ties between pricing and universal service and the inherent
tension between competition and universal service goals.

Given the uncertainties entailed in working out these
issues, the FCC encountered political maneuverings and
judicial litigation at every turn.[70] No sooner had the Act

been passed, for example, when AT&T petitioned the
FCC to bar the Bell companies from sharing market data
with their out-of-region long-distance companies.
Ameritech complained that Time-Warner's Home Box
Office had refused voice and video on the Internet, competitive access providers complained that the RBOCs were
holding up negotiations on access charges, and the Bell
Companies contended that their competitors were using
the regulatory process to block their entry into the long-
distance market.[63]

Disappointed by the FCC's performance, many have
chastised the agency for overstepping its authority. Challenging the FCC's carrier interconnection order in court,
for example, the states have clamed that the FCC lacks the
authority to establish interim proxy prices or to prescribe
the pricing methodologies that they might use. Politicians
have similarly gotten involved, threatening to pass legislation constraining the FCC's future actions. By far the most
outspoken legislator has been Senator John McCain, chairman of the Senate Commerce Committee. Proposing legislation to limit the FCC's role in determining antitrust
cases, McCain has criticized the FCC in the following
terms:

a majority of this Commission places too little confidence
in competition and way too much in regulation. It tends to
ignore the demands of making orderly, efficient, and fair
decisions on the matters before it, preferring to pursue
issues that are within neither their expertise nor their jurisdiction. It has shown a distressing tendency toward inconsistent and ad hoc decision-making, and toward picking
and choosing which parts of the law it will choose to
follow.[71]

Market realities have also served to undermine the basic
assumptions underlying the telecom act. Thus, for example, the act was based on the premise that the local loop
was the only remaining network bottleneck. Today, however, with convergence and the development of Internet-
based e-commerce, new bottlenecks have appeared. By
integrating infrastructure services and applications, providers can benefit not only from economies of scale and
scope, but also from the many positive externalities associated with networked technologies. Equally important,
integrated networks command higher service prices
because businesses need a seamless networking platform
to link their operations. In addition, by offering an integrated platform, providers can gain a first-mover advantage using the network as a barrier to entry. Offering a
wide range of business services, they can also position
themselves best to collect and make optimal use of transactional data. Perhaps the best example continues to be
Microsoft. Building upon the Internet, Microsoft has
pieced together an entire suite of business applications,
ranging from accounting to procurement.[72]

Not surprisingly, network providers are scurrying to
take advantage of these opportunities. Mergers and

acquisitions in information technology, communication, and media industries jumped 97% in 1997, to $488 billion.[73] Nor are Internet companies immune to these developments. In fact, given the lack of barriers to market entry, they are far more inclined to engage in mergers and acquisitions than established lower tech companies. As noted by one consulting firm, for the top 25 Internet companies, the average number of years before significant merger and acquisition activity take place is 6 years, as compared to 72 years for the top 50 U.S. companies.[74]

This kind of integration will not be limited to large-scale infrastructure industries. As described by Hof

> That could prove all the more true thanks to a rapidly emerging new class of net middlemen in a wide range of consumer and industrial markets. Online, with few limitations of time and geography, these new market makers can quickly generate a virtuous loop of buyers and sellers whose very presence attracts yet more buyers and sellers. For this reason, they're expected to dominate many industries from chemical suppliers to rolled steel.[75]

Equally disturbing, where competition among providers has been rampant, it has had major unintended consequences. Thus, for example, network providers competing to be the first to fiber the country have generated a major glut in capacity. According to one source, these companies spent $90 billion to lay approximately 39 million miles of fiber optic cable, of which only 2.6% is in use. Not surprisingly, many of these companies are verging on bankruptcy.[76] The failure of these companies has taken a major toll on related industries, such as equipment manufacturers, venture capital, and the stock market.[77] As the author notes:

> Nearly every technology sector is linked with telecom: phone companies buy networking equipment to route Internet traffic, computer servers to offer Web hosting, software to dish up services, and fiber-optic gear to transport bits of information. Last year, spending on communications gear in the U.S. totaled $124 billion, or 12% of business spending on equipment and software, according to the Commerce Department. Moreover, it accounted for one-quarter of the rise in business spending (p. 102).[77]

The impact on the economy as a whole has yet to be measured. Estimates are that the recession generated by the collapse of the high-tech sector may not show signs of recovery till late 2002.

THE MARKET AS MEDIATOR

Much of the criticism of the Telecom Act of 1996 has been directed at the problems and side effects associated with its implementation. Over the long term, however, even more serious problems are likely to emerge, which cannot be mediated within the framework of a competitive marketplace. The market works best to allocate resources when such resources are fungible; that is to say, when their values can be reduced to an equivalency or common denominator. Notwithstanding recent efforts by policy makers and industry stakeholders to characterize communication as a commodity, communication resources are highly problematic in this regard. For example, harking back to former Chairman Fowler's comparison of televisions and toasters, the present chairman of the FCC—William Powell—recently analogized the "digital divide" to the inequities associated with car buying.

One need only consider, for instance, the multifaceted nature of communication. Communication resources serve not only to meet consumer needs but also social and economic goals, which are much more difficult to measure adequately. Often the prices consumers are willing to pay for communication as a commodity diverge significantly from its social and economic value. Declining public support for the First Amendment provides a case in point. Notwithstanding the First Amendment's central role in the U.S. political system, a growing number of Americans now believe that the media has "too much freedom." A recent survey conducted by the First Amendment Center found, for example, that 39% of the respondents believed the First Amendment "goes too far in guaranteeing rights, compared with slightly more than 22% last year."[79] Imagine how much less support there would be if consumers were called upon to pay for this freedom directly!

Compounding the problem of measurement is the fact that the value of communication is not constant. To the contrary, it is highly dependent on time and circumstances. As the survey of U.S. communication goals clearly illustrates, the priorities that policy makers give to certain communication goals and the way in which they seek to implement them are highly contingent on historical conditions and the social and economic problems that loom large at the time. Thus just as the Founding Fathers' reluctance to involve government in media affairs is traceable to their experiences during the Revolutionary War, so too the government's willingness to take a more proactive approach in the latter half of the 1800s can be attributed in part to the perceived need to heal the wounds left by the Civil War.

We should expect no less today. As our social and economic circumstances change, new tensions and problems that call for communication-related policy responses are likely to emerge. Certainly, for example, the rise of Web-based networked commerce will provide a major stimulus in this respect. With the convergence of networks, markets, and firms, issues that were at one time clearly situated in the realm of economic policy will become enmeshed with those in the realm of communications.[79] Already a number of privacy issues are emerging that span these two realms. According to one recent industry-sponsored study, new privacy rules will cost industry between \$9 billion to \$36 billion.[80] Other likely candidates include issues related to taxation, licensing, property rights, and antitrust. Crosscutting issues in the area of defense and security are also likely, given the decentralized nature of the Internet and the ability to circumvent traditional lines of authority.

Globalization will also present new policy problems and choices. As the World Trade Organization conflict over audiovisual content makes clear, the task of valuing communication resources and making trade-offs among communication-related goals is greatly exacerbated by cross-cultural differences. Whereas U.S. policy makers consider audiovisual materials to be commodities that should be freely traded, Canadians and French policy makers view them as a cultural heritage to be protected and supported by government. Even when there is general agreement among countries with respect to goals, policy makers may interpret goals differently and/or choose alternative ways of implementing them. Whereas in the United States, for example, antitrust decisions are typically determined based on the potential harm to consumers, in Europe they are decided based on the potential harm to competitors.

In a capitalist society, the market mechanism will always play an important role in sorting out communication policy issues. As the history of U.S. communication policy makes clear, however, the market is only one among several policy tools that government can call upon to implement its goals. In fact, by employing different policy mechanisms in the past, the government was able to avoid making difficult trade-offs among competing goals; freedom of expression, ubiquitous infrastructure deployment, and education could all be accommodated. Conflicts among policy goals are likely to be even greater in the future, given the enhanced role of communications and information in all respects of life. To resolve emergent communication issues while taking full responsibility for our choices, we cannot simply defer to the marketplace. In addition to its role as "market maker," government must—depending on the circumstances—continue to play the supporting roles of broker, educator, regulatory, and promoter.

REFERENCES

1. North, D. *Institutions, Institutional Change and Economic Performance*; Cambridge University Press: Cambridge, U.K., 1990.
2. Lindberg, L. N., Campbell, J. L., Jr., Hollingsworth, R., Eds. *Governance of the American Economy*; Cambridge University Press: New York, 1991; 10.
3. Mann, M. *The Rise of Classes and Nation States; 1760-1914*, Cambridge, University Press: Cambridge, 1993; Vol. 3 The Sources of Social Power.
4. Buel, R., Jr. Freedom of the press in revolutionary america: the evolution of libertarianism, 1760-1820. In *The Press and the American Revolution*; Bailyn, B., Hench, J. B., Eds.; American Antiquarian Society: Worcester, MA, 1980.
5. Emery, E. *The Press in America*; Prentice Hall: Englewood Cliffs, NJ, 1962.
6. Patterson, L. R. *Copyright in Historical Perspective*; Vanderbilt University Press: Nashville, NY, 1968.
7. Bugbee, B. W. *Genesis of American Patent and Copyright Law*; Public Affairs Press: Washington, DC, 1967.
8. Kielbowicz, R. B. *News in the Mail: The Press, Post Office and Public Information*; Greenwood: Westport, CT, 1991.
9. Czitrom, D. *Media and the American Mind: From Morse to McLuhan*; University of North Carolina Press: Chapel Hill, NC, 1984; Chap. 4.
10. Dewey, J. *Outlines of a Critical Theory of Ethics*; 1871; 106 as cited in Ref. 9.
11. Peterson, T. *Magazines in the Twentieth Century*, 2nd Ed. University of Illinois Press: Urbana, IL, 1967.
12. Carey, J. W. The communications revolution and the professional communicator. Sociol. Rev. Monogr. **1969**, *13*. (January), 23–38.
13. Fuller, W. E. *RFD: The Changing Face of Rural America*; Indiana University Press: Bloomington, IN, 1964.
14. Welter, R. *Popular Education and Democratic Thought in America*; Columbia University Press: New York, 1962.
15. Tack, D.; Hansot, E. Conflict and consensus in American public education. *American Schools: Public and Private, Daedalus, Summer;* **1981**.
16. Carlson, R. A. *The Quest for Conformity: Americanization through Education*; Wiley: New York, 1975.
17. Conen, S. A. The industrial education movement 1906–1917. Am. Q. **1969**, *Spring*.
18. Trow, M. The second transformation of american secondary education. Int. J. Compar. Soc. **1961**, 7.
19. Matthews, W. H. *Libraries for Today and Tomorrow*, Hippocrene: Garden City, NY, 1976.
20. Rasmussen, W. D. Stone, P. Toward a third agricultural revolution. In *Food Policy and Farm Programs, Proceedings of the Academy of Political Science*; Hadwiger, F., Talbot, R., Eds.; Academy of Political Science: New York, 1982; 179.
21. Kerr, C. *The Uses of the University*, Harvard University Press: Cambridge, MA, 1972.
22. Layton, E. T., Jr. *The Revolt of the Engineers: Social Responsibility and the American Engineering Profession*, The Press of Case Western Reserve University: Cleveland, OH, 1971.
23. Galambos, L. Pratt, J. *The Rise of the Corporate Commonwealth: U.S. Business and Public Policy in the Twentieth Century*, Basic Books: New York, 1989.
24. Stone, A. *Public Service Liberalism: Telecommunications and Transitions in Public Policy*, Princeton University Press: Princeton, NJ, 1991.
25. Kennedy, R. D., Jr. The statist evolution of rail governance in the United States, 1830-1986. In *Governance of the American Economy*; Lindberg, L. N., Campbell, J. L., Jr., Hollingsworth, R., Eds.; Cambridge University Press: New York, 1991; 10.
26. Duboff, R. B. Business demand and the development of the telegraph in the United States. Bus. Hist. Rev.; **1980**, *54*(Winter), 459–479.

27. Proceedings of the National Radio Conference. *New York Times,* October 9, **1924**; 2–3 25 as cited in.

28. Packard, V. *The Hidden Persuaders*, David McKay: New York, 1957.

29. Carey, J. The 'mass' in mass communication. In *Communication and Culture*; Care, J., Ed.; Routledge: London, U.K., 1998.

30. MacCarthy, M. M. Broadcast self-regulation: the NAB codes, family viewing hour, and television violence. Cardozo Arts Entertain. Law J. **1995**, *15*(3).

31. Chisman, F. P. Achieving the public interest in an era of abundance. In *Digital Broadcasting and the Public Interest: Reports and Papers of the Aspen Institute Communication and Society Program*; Firestone, C. M., Garner, A. Korzick, Eds.; Aspen Institute: Washington, DC, 1998; 135.

32. Baughman, J. L. *Television's Guardians: The FCC and the Politics of Programming, 1858-1967*, University of Tennessee Press: Knoxville, TN, 1967; 5.

33. da Sola Poole, I. *Technologies of Freedom*, Belknap Press: Cambridge, MA, 1984; 130.

34. Rowland, W. D., Jr. The Institution of U.S. Public Broadcasting. In *Public Television in America*; Noam, E., Walterman, J., Eds.; Bertelsmann Foundation Publishers, Gutersloh, Germany, 1998.

35. Price, M. E. Public Broadcasting and the Crisis of Corporate Governance. Cardozo Arts Entertain. J. **1999**, *17*(417).

36. Fuller, W. *The American Mail*; University of Chicago Press: Chicago, IL, 1972; 187–188.

37. Murphy, P. L. *The Meaning of Freedom of Speech: First Amendment Freedoms from Wilson to FDR*; Greenwood: Westport, CT, 1972.

38. Flamm, K. *Creating the Computer: Government, Industry and High Technology*; Brookings Institute: Washington, DC, 1988.

39. Mowery, D. Rosenberg, N. *Technology and the Pursuit of Economic Growth*, Cambridge University Press: Cambridge, MA, 1989.

40. Noll, R. G. Regulation after reagan. AEI J. Gov. Soc. **1988**, (*3*), 12–22.

41. *Microwave Communications, Inc.*, 971–972 18 FCC 2d 953.

42. Aufderheide, P. *Communications Policy and the Public Interest: The Telecommunications Act of 1996*, Guildford: New York, 1999.

43. LeDuc, D. *Cable Television and the FCC: A Crisis in Media Control*; Temple University Press: Philadelphia, PA, 1973.

44. Reuben-Cooke, W. M. Rethinking legal and policy paradigms. In *Television for the Next Century: The Next Wave*; Firestone, C. M., Ed.; Aspen Institute: Washington, DC, 1993.

45. Shapiro, G. Kurland, P. Mecurio, J. *Cablespeech: The Case for First Amendment Protection*; Harcourt Brace Jovanovich: New York, 1983.

46. Tribe, L. *American Constitutional Law*; Foundation Press: Mineola, NY, 1988; 699.

47. *Turner Broadcasting System Inc. v. FCC*, No. 95-992, WL 141375 at 19-20 U.S.

48. Winder, L. H. The red lion of cable, and beyond?—Turner broadcasting v. FCC. Cardozo Law J. **1997**, *15*.

49. Price, M.; Duffy, J. F. Technological changes and doctrinal persistence, telecommunications reform in congress and the court. Symposium: Unscrambling the Signals, Unbundling the Law, Columbia Law Review May 1997; 976 .

50. Derthick, M. Quick, P. J. *The Politics of Deregulation*; Brookings Institute: Washington, DC, 1985.

51. Tunstall, J. *Communications Deregulation: The Unleashing of America's Communication Industry*; Basil Blackwell: Oxford, U.K., 1986.

52. Le Duc, D. *Beyond Broadcasting: Patterns in Policy and Law*, Longman: New York, 1987.

53. Geller, H. Reforming the U.S. telecommunications policymaking process. In *The New Information Infrastructure: Strategies for U.S. Policy*; Jrake, W. J., Ed.; Twentieth Century Fund: New York, 1995; Chap. 4.

54. Computer Science Telecommunications Board, National Research Council. *The Unpredictable Certainty: Information Infrastructure through 2000*, National Academy Press: Washington, DC, 1996; 124.

55. McKnight, L. Newman, R. Solomon, R. *The Gordian Knot*, MIT Press: Cambridge, MA, 1996.

56. Gore, A. Our vision of telecommunications. Aspen Inst. Q. **1994**, *6*(2), 18.

57. Drake, W. J. The national information infrastructure debate. In *The New Information Infrastructure: Strategies for U.S. Policy*; Drake, W. J., Ed.; Twentieth Century Fund: New York, 1995; Chap. 12.

58. Lynch, D. J. Strategic errors offset contributions. *USA Today/Internat. Ed.*, October 17,**1995**, *7B*.

59. Jaik, G. Landmark telecom bill becomes law. Wash. Post February 4, **1996**, H8.

60. Telephone vote signals competitive free-for-all: likely mergers herald an era of megacarriers. Wall St. J. February 5, **1996**, B4.

61. Telecom's new age: the giants aren't sleeping. Bus. Wk. April 7, **1996**.

62. Naik, G. Bell companies ready to charge into long distance. Wall St. J. February 5, **1996**, B4.

63. Gruley, B. The FCC is besieged as it rewrites rules in telecommunications. Wall St. J. March 29, **1996**, A1.

64. Telecom's new age: show/time for the watchdog. Bus. Wk. April 8, **1996**.

65. Cauley, L. Telecom Czar Frets over new industry Rules. Wall St. J. February 12, **1996**, B1.

66. Solomon, D. AT&T trims plan to offer interactive TV. Wall St. J. June 8, **2001**.

67. Blumenstein, R. Reform act hasn't delivered promises to customers. Wall St. J. May 3, **2001**, B1.

68. Young, S. Complaints rise as phone service problems mount. Wall St. J. May 3, **2001**, B1.

69. Klinger, R. *The New Information Industry: Regulatory Challenges and the First Amendment*, Brookings Institute: Washington, DC, 1996.

70. Solomon, D. Everyone's got a solution for industry's woes. Wall St. J. May 3, **2001**, B1 .

71. McCain Canes FCC, proposes merger limitation bill. CNN Finan. News May 26, **1999**.

72. Greene, J. Microsoft: How it became stronger than ever. Bus. Wk. June 4, **2001**.

73. Reinhardt, A. The main event: Bernie vs. Mike. Bus. Wk. October 18, **1999**, 44.

74. Internet companies: Merging young. Bus. Wk. December 6, **1999**, 8.

75. Hof, R. D. A new race of giants?. Bus. Wk. July 26, **1999**, EB 72.

76. Blumenstein, R. How the fiber barons plunged the nation into a telecom glut. Wall St. J. June 18, **2001,** A1-A8.

77. Zuckerman, G. Telecom debt debacle could lead to loses of historic proportions. Wall St. J. May 11, **2001,** A1.

78. Timmons, H. Telecom meltdown. Bus. Wk. April 23, **2001**.

79. Strupp, J. Americans less supportive of 1st amendment poll: many think press has too much freedom. Ed. Pub. Mag Available at http://www.mediainfo.com/ephome/news/newshtm/stories/070301n1.htm.

80. Internet privacy rules cost business as much as $36 billion. Wall St. J. May 8, **2001**, B1.

BIBLIOGRAPHY

1. Garcia, D. L. Networks and the evolution of property rights. Paper presented to the International Studies Association: Chicago, IL, March 2001.

2. Influence peddlers reach out and touch some POL. Bus. Wk. March 4, **1996**.

3. King, C. W. *Social Movements in the United States*, Random House: New York, 1956; 24.

Community Informatics

Kate Williams
University of Illinois at Urbana-Champaign, Champaign, Illinois, U.S.A.

Joan C. Durrance
School of Information, University of Michigan, Ann Arbor, Michigan, U.S.A.

Abstract

Community informatics is an emerging field focusing primarily on the interaction between local communities and information technologies and a more particular focus within social informatics. It is rooted in library practice, most notably the outreach that led to information and referral (I&R) services, as well as other innovative practices, for example the community technology center and the community network, aimed at strengthening communities faced with the digital era and its attendant disruptions and opportunities. Community informatics research and teaching is carried out at a growing number of library/information schools and elsewhere, as appropriate to this interdisciplinary endeavor.

Community informatics is an emerging field that encompasses both study and practice, although the focus here is on the former. Loader (2000, cited in Keeble)[1] has described it as navigating the interaction between *transformation* as expressed in information technology and *continuity* as expressed in a local, historical community. This is a specification of Kling's definition of the field of social informatics, of which community informatics is a part: "the interdisciplinary study of the design, uses and consequences of information technologies that takes into account their interaction with institutional and cultural contexts."[2] While social informatics historically most often concerned itself with business and government settings, community informatics looks at a third realm of social activity, the community. The concept of community and the tensions within that concept, set in the context of the nascent information society, are the basis for the core ideas of community informatics. Community informatics practitioners can be found in public libraries, community technology centers, community networks, and in an increasing range of community and economic development activities, employed in the private, public, or nonprofit sectors. Researchers come from the disciplines of library and information science, communications, community development, computer science, informatics, sociology, urban and regional planning, and other fields. Fortunately, the discussion in this encyclopedia entry is informed by the fact that one author (Durrance) comes to community informatics through library practice and scholarship, and the other through community practice and study of the digitization of society, or social informatics (for example, see Williams).[3] This allows the entry to trace multiple paths that have led to a single, if fuzzy-bounded, interdisciplinary field. By all accounts, however, the starting point is very much the local, historical community.

COMMUNITY AS THE BASIS FOR COMMUNITY INFORMATICS

Most scholars have defined information technology very concretely as a particular, if evolving, set of digital tools and applications. But defining and understanding community is a challenge that has productively engaged more than a century of scholars. With the last major wave of U. S. migration from country to city, the fate of community within the metropolis occupied a generation of scholars, who themselves referenced the scholarship of those who had earlier grappled with the meaning of the European migration to the cities. The earlier discourse was very much driven by the ideas of Marx, Tönnies, and Durkheim, while the Chicago School (including among others Frazier, Mead, Park, and Wirth) was the most influential in the United States.

Community is variously defined in the social sciences and has been examined in many of its guises in community informatics literature. Most often, it refers to a population living within certain geographic boundaries (geographic community), and this gives rise to a local history and culture which is the context for whatever else happens. This definition is bolstered by the fact that planning and funds flows are channeled according to those boundaries and political battles are often fought within these jurisdictions. This can be seen during the 1980s when various cities implemented community technology projects. (For a comparison of four cities, see Guthrie).[4]

Encyclopedia of Library and Information Sciences, Fourth Edition DOI: 10.1081/E-ELIS4-120043669

But there can be communities within these geographic communities, as for instance the communities of interest that contended—homeless and their allies, and local business and real estate interests—within Santa Monica's Public Electronic Network.[5] Or Bishop et al.'s[6] work on a Web tool for local African-American women working on health issues. And there are communities with a particular geographic, historical origin that are now spread across large or small distances. Diasporic communities have taken to the Internet to maintain close ties with people far away, for example Trinidadians.[7] And one's community may be spread across a single metropolis, as in Wellman.[8] Wellman, in fact, later proposed[9] and then tempered his assessment[10] that every individual with their ties now represents a distinct personal community, more or less place-based.

Benjamin[11] used a recursive definition of community—"people living in a geospatial area who define themselves as part of a community"—in order to analyze why some telecenters succeed and others fail to attract local involvement. This definition has a history in ethnography and acknowledges that communities are quite often self-identified or socially identified.

Human activity itself has been theorized as taking place in communities.[12] Rheingold documented the arrival of the virtual community[13] and the cell phone based social network.[14] Rheingold's online or phone based communities interact in particular ways with the local, the historical community. Online discussion lists, games, and other social computing phenomena have generated interesting work that enriches and is enriched by community informatics per se.

There are tensions and overlaps between these various communities. The field of community informatics, by studying the interaction between transformation and continuity, between information technology and local community, is building up a picture of how the social, historical places we live in are evolving as we move from the industrial age to the information age, with particular attention to social and digital inequalities. Moreover, it has done this very much based on practice, both inside and beyond libraries.

ROOTS OF THE FIELD OUTSIDE THE LIBRARY: THE SOCIAL INFORMATICS PERSPECTIVE

Setting aside for the moment the important role of libraries and library scholars in community informatics, several other interrelated but distinct social trends have also given rise to and continue to shape the field. These can be summed up as the network society, the hacker ethic, and the digital divide.

For some time now the network society has been unfolding on and in local communities. What does this term mean? It means that today society is characterized by networks rather than organizations; flexible production with a flexible workforce; an economy that is globally coordinated in real (or chosen, as with e-mail) time. A new space has been identified that contrasts with the space of place, that is, the geographic communities where we live and breathe. This new space is the space of flows that is based on digital tools and systems; in other words, the sum total of all the communications and transportation flows that link the global, mobile, network of human networks.[15] The world's economies, east and west, adopted digital technologies even as they experienced the economic crises of the 1960s and 1970s; what has resulted is spaces of place that are threatened, because they are mostly bypassed, by the space of flows. In the industrialized countries, one can think for example of Rust Belt, United States or vast stretches of the North of England as thus threatened. Other spaces of place, Silicon Valley, for example, have certainly not been bypassed, and yet even there the space of flows has left toxic dumps for the space of place to cope with.

Faced with this, local governments responded with digital initiatives of their own. Among many: In 1989, Santa Monica, California, offered its residents free online discussion lists, accessible in public libraries or from home, and access to city officials, as mentioned above.[16] In 2000, Lagrange, Georgia, offered its entire population free cable Internet.[17]

An interesting reflection in academia of this space of place-space of flows or network-communities tension was the 1996 colloquium that became the edited volume *High Technology and Low Income Communities*.[18] This arose from a dialogue between two mutually exclusive groups in urban planning at MIT, one focused on opportunities for Information and Communication Technology (ICT) and the other on low-income communities. They recruited Manuel Castells to the event and produced a proceedings volume that discussed, but did not name, community informatics.

On the heels of early experimentation, the second social trend that has given rise to community informatics is the discourse and the activity around the concept of the digital divide. This emerged in the mid 1990s as a popular phrase for the gap between people who access and use information technology and those who do not.[19] In the United States, the Department of Commerce was an early implementer of both research and policy on this. The department launched a (continuing) series of survey reports on individuals' access to and use of computers and later the Internet and other particular tools such as cell phones.

In the realm of practice, the same agency within the Department of Commerce began more than a decade of annual rounds of grantmaking (Telecommunications and Information Infrasture Assistance Program (TIIAP), later the Technology Opportunities Program, or TOP) to organizations in local communities to support their community technology projects. The Department of Commerce initiative was rooted in the economic imperative to develop a market for computers and for e-business and to develop a skilled workforce via education and public provision of information technology. Such experiments as TOP were echoed by private and other public funders, including technology companies and even the National Science Foundation, which helped Playing to Win launch the nationwide Community Technology Centers Network. One could certainly say that the dot-com technology bubble fueled the digital divide discourse in the United States, with corporations supporting local and national projects.

A third social trend giving rise to community informatics can be summed up as the hacker ethic, which took hold as computers and software became a hobby and a profession. In contrast to the media's definition of hacker as thief, the hacker ethic is the practice of building computers and writing code for the fun of it, for the creativity of it, and for the community-building. This is what[20] calls "the spirit of the information age." The hacker ethic expressed itself in the origins of the personal computer out of the milieu of the Homebrew Computer Club and in the production of Linux and other such software. It also expressed itself in projects where hackers joined up with others to produce tools such as:

- PLATO, where by 1972 hackers and teachers were writing online courses for all levels of students.[21]
- Berkeley Community Memory, the public terminals established in 1973 that provided an online bulletin board for all passers by.[22]
- Community technology centers such as Playing to Win, opened in 1983 by math teacher Antonia Stone in a Harlem housing project,[58] and
- Freenets or community networks such as the Cleveland Free-net, which began life in 1984 as St. Silicon's Hospital and Information Dispensary, an online communications tool for doctors and patients.[23]

The community network and community technology center phenomena each grew into international movements, with associations, publications, and annual conferences for practitioners. Community technology projects emerged out of the grassroots—as in Toledo, Ohio[24–27] and inner-city Wilmington, North Carolina[28]—and blossomed in both virtual and actual space. Community network developers soon connected with librarians and library scholars, for reasons given below.

ROOTS OF THE FIELD WITHIN LIBRARIES

Urban social unrest provided the backdrop for librarians developing new approaches to service that resulted in the creation of early community information services. The riots of the late 1960s marked the beginning of change in the nation's urban libraries. The decay of the inner city had resulted in a mismatch between the services that agencies such as public libraries offered in the mid-1960s and the needs of a changing population. Librarians had traditionally used library circulation figures to measure their effectiveness in the community. As the middle class left the nation's major cities, urban libraries suffered a drastic drop in circulation. At the same time researchers found that, "citizens are uninformed about public and private resources, facilities, rights, and programs. . . and frustrated in their attempts to get information required for everyday problem solving" (p. 20).[29]

By the early 1970s, the federal government had provided funding for both the development of information and referral (I&R) services and a series of educational programs and guides aimed at helping professionals gain skills in developing I&R services.[30–32] The federal government's active fostering of the development of I&R services by various institutions drew in both practitioners and academics, including a group of pioneering urban libraries and a small cadre of LIS (library and information science) researchers.[29,33,34]

Academics who focused on community information in the 1970s worked with practitioners through associations and consultancies, analyzed practice, contributed articles and reports, made public presentations and developed academic curricula in the established LIS programs at Syracuse University, the University of Maryland, Drexel University, and the Community Specialist Program at the University of Toledo.

Clara Jones, then Director of the Detroit Public Library and its first African-American leader, argued at the time that:

> The welfare of the public library is inextricably interwoven with the destiny of the city, the financial dilemma of libraries being one manifestation of characteristic urban ills. Although we are a predominantly urban nation, there is widespread indifference or resignation to the desperate plight of cities. . . It seems increasingly evident that we can no longer depend solely on the traditional cornerstone of public library service to adults-reference work, reading guidance, and programming–to stimulate sufficient interest and satisfy a broad enough range of needs (pp. 85–86).[35]

The purpose of I&R was to provide a link between a person with a need and the resources in the community that would meet that need. To accomplish this, pioneering I&R staff created community information files, provided information about community services, and engaged in active question negotiation. Information and referral services, considered essential to avoid fruitless agency ping-pong—people seeking services bouncing from one office to the next in an environment where social services by hundreds of agencies and nonprofit organizations were delivering social services. Information and referral work was considered by many to be a radical departure from standard public library services.

At their outset, I&R services were also confusing and lacked definition.[33] The Alliance for Information & Referral Services in 1973 defined I&R and outlined a set of activities including: file development, simple and complex information giving, actively helping clients make contact with a resource (referral), working with the client to overcome obstacles (advocacy), and assuring that clients actually reached the appropriate resources (follow-up); some of these were divergent from traditional library practice. In the late 1970s, Childers conducted a benchmark study of I&R in public libraries and found that while public libraries in his study embraced the information role, for the most part they did not engage in referral and follow-up.[33]

In spite of the limitations in adopting the I&R model in the 1970s, library engagement in the community-focused information services discussed above laid the groundwork for the public library's community-focused roles in the digital age and the beginnings of academic response to community problems.

By the 1990s, librarians and library scholars were ready to join forces with the grassroots activists, local government staffers, foundations and other nonprofits, and businesses who were experimenting with technology in communities. A particular series of three conferences helped to catalyze the community networking movement. The Ties that Bind conferences (1994, 1995, 1996) were sponsored by Apple Computer's Library of Tomorrow Project and the Morino Foundation. They brought together a wide range of individuals and groups to foster community networking.[36] The encompassing goals of these conferences were:

> to provide information and case studies on the types of community networks that have proven viable, including economic, collaborative, and technical models; to help individuals representing schools, non-profits, foundations, businesses, media, and government agencies realize how community networking can be used as a tool to help advance the goals and needs of the community; to understand the importance of community networking in the formation and effective use of the National Information Infrastructure; to understand the emerging context – the social, economic, technical political, and sustainability issues which characterize the challenges and potentials for Community Networking.[37]

These conferences, led by Steve Cisler of the Apple Library of Tomorrow, resulted in the creation of the Association for Community Networking and strongly influenced the encompassing thought processes that resulted in the development of the community informatics framework.

A major study funded by Institute of Museum and Library Services (IMLS) and conducted in 1999–2000 by Durrance & Pettigrew found that community information provision had undergone major change as a result of Internet adoption by libraries. They found increased use of networked community information, a variety of digitization projects, a strong Internet presence, adoption of digital reference, increased collaboration between libraries and other community organizations, and, as a result of these innovations, increased visibility and community support.[38,39]

One noteworthy example of library-community information projects is the Tallahassee FreeNet (TFN), Florida's oldest community network. It was started in 1993 by faculty from the Florida State University supercomputer center. Quickly the LeRoy Collins Leon County Public Library became an operating partner and the TFN became one of the nation's first library-university community networking projects. Tallahassee FreeNet's mission statement reflected the aims of all the early collaborative community networks:

> TFN is more than an operator of an information system. It is the agent guiding Tallahassee and to some extent Florida, into the Information Age. Therefore, it is further the mission of TFN to precipitate community cooperation that is the basis for having community-wide electronic communication.[40]

University Contributions

During the 1990s, a number of universities, armed with excess computing power and aware of the digital disparities between the universities and communities, worked with local agencies to form community networks. Several of the long-lived projects among these are worth noting:

1. The Community Networking Initiative (later joined with the Alliance for Community Technology) at the University of Michigan School of Information and Library Studies, now School of Information. The University of Michigan Community Networking Initiative (UM-CNI) began with support from the W. K. Kellogg Foundation in 1994. This project enabled faculty and students to take a leadership role in Internet-based community networking (see, for example, Durrance).[41] A collaborative venture involving the UM-CNI, the Flint Public Library, the Mideastern Michigan Library Cooperative, the Library of Michigan, and the Apple Library of Tomorrow Program created in 1995 the Flint Community Networking Initiative, a model public library Internet training laboratory featuring an extensive training program first for staff and later for community members—especially teens—and an ongoing community-focused Internet presence in Flint. Today the Alliance for Community Technology carries out a variety of teaching, research, and service projects.

2. Prairienet and the Community Informatics Initiative at the University of Illinois at Urbana-Champaign Graduate School of Library and Information Science. Prairienet, a partnership between the university and

local community members and nonprofit organizations, was founded in 1993. It seeks to:

promote equity of access to computer resources for everyone in the community; facilitate information and resource sharing in support of community development efforts; empower individuals by teaching computer skills and providing access to the Internet; and strengthen community organizations by assisting them with access and the sharing of information.[42]

The Community Informatics Institute focuses on research and teaching, especially through Prairienet and its other community partnerships, among them the East St. Louis Action Research Project and the Puerto Rican Cultural Center in Chicago.[43,44]

3. Blacksburg Electronic Village at the Virginia Polytechnic Institute and State University. This program is connected to researchers in architecture and design (and later information architecture) as well as human-computer interaction. This collaboration included the Town of Blacksburg and a major communication company in order to bring high-speed Internet and social computing to the community. Planning began in 1991; the Blacksburg Electronic Village became operational in 1993. It has been an international model for networked community through its innovative collaboration and citizen involvement.[45]

EMERGENCE OF COMMUNITY INFORMATICS AS A UNIFYING CONCEPT

Allowing for the caveats summed up by Stoecker,[46] a loose network of scholars can today be seen to comprise a core of community informatics research. The scaffolding of the field features two processes that have contributed to drawing together scholars via conferences, proceedings volumes, and at least one journal. The first of these two processes is the series of seven Dimensions in Advanced Computing (DIAC) conferences sponsored by Computer Programmers (later Professionals) for Social Responsibility since 1987; this has generated both proceedings volumes and edited books (most recently Day and Schuler[47] and Schuler and Day).[48] Dimensions in Advanced Computing's organizer Doug Schuler, a cofounder of Seattle Community Network, launched an undergraduate program in community informatics and authored *New Community Networks: Wired for Change.*[49]

The second process has been anchored in the north of England, where Brian Loader and others have generated a flow of edited and authored volumes,[1,50–55] several conferences, and the quarterly journal *Information, Communication and Society* (since 1998), all while guiding several community technology projects.

Other integrative processes are: 1) the work of[56] defining community informatics and bringing particular

attention to work in Australia, Canada, and elsewhere; 2) the annual Community Informatics Research Network meetings; 3) the broader biennial Conference on Communities and Technologies; 4) the also more broad but still highly useful conferences of the Association for Internet Research (annual since 2000) and 5) the journals *First Monday* (launched 1996), *The Information Society* (1981), *Journal of Computer Mediated Communication* (1995), *New Media and Society* (1999), and the *Journal of Community Informatics* (2004).

NEW DIRECTIONS

As technology has evolved, converged, and diffused, the binary concept of the digital divide has revealed itself as containing multiple digital *inequalities* bearing deeper analysis. (For a recent example see Mossberger).[57] Four trends are worth noting: datasets, globalization, a turn towards theory, and a recent expansion of community informatics curriculum in library information science schools.

First, academic and policy researchers have produced hundreds of case studies, and the color and texture of these continue to be highly valuable. The multitude of studied and not-yet-studied community informatics projects and practices and the need for research to guide policy present scholars with an opportunity to standardize our approach to case studies and to collect and analyze larger datasets. This will allow us to generalize and confirm trends in communities. Second, related to this, is the imperative to study community technology as a global phenomenon rather than a national one. The search for community development through technology, for community sustainability in the digital age, is turning up lessons in one part of the world that others cannot afford to ignore.

Third, as researchers turn increasingly to theorizing as well as describing, our work on communities can be usefully placed alongside the work of others on the informatics of our government, education, and business sectors. A number of theoretical concepts and frameworks are already proving powerful in this regard: information use, community inquiry, civic intelligence, social networks and social capital,[59] and the public sphere among them. These summations will help community informatics and others scholars to revisit and update our conceptions of the Information Society, which first took shape with very little actual data from the localities where we all live.

A fourth trend is not within the research but relies on it: the expansion of community informatics and community information in the curricula of the library and information science schools. The iSchools conferences are playing a role here; offering sessions focusing on community informatics. Today courses in this area are taught at the graduate level at 7 of the 57 library and information science programs in the United States and Canada. It is expected that Gurstein such efforts will grow, in and beyond the LIS programs.

REFERENCES

1. Keeble, L.; Loader, B.D., Eds. *Community Informatics: Shaping Computer-Mediated Social Relations*; Routledge: London, U.K., 2001.

2. Kling, R. What is social informatics and why does it matter? D-Lib Mag. **1999**, *5*(1), http://www.dlib.org/dlib/january99/kling/01kling.html.

3. Williams, K. Social networks, social capital, and the use of information and communications technology in socially excluded communities: A study of community groups in Manchester, England. Unpublished Ph.D. dissertation, University of Michigan, Ann Arbor, MI, 2005.

4. Guthrie, K.K.; Dutton, W.H. The politics of citizen access technology: The development of public information utilities in four cities. Policy Stud. J. **1992**, *20* (4), 574.

5. Rogers, E.M.; Collins-Jarvis, L. Schmitz, J. The pen project in Santa Monica: Interactive communication, equality, and political action. J. Am. Soc. Inf. Sci. **1994**, *45* (6), 401–410.

6. Bishop, A.; Bazzell, I.; Mehra, B.; Smith, C. Afya: Social and digital technologies that reach across the digital divide. First Monday April **2001**, *6*(4), http://www.firstmonday.org/issues/issue6_4/bishop/.

7. Miller, D.; Slater, D. *The Internet: An Ethnographic Approach*; Berg: Oxford, U.K., 2000.

8. Wellman, B.; Leighton, B. Networks, neighborhoods, and communities: Approaches to the study of the community question. Urban Affairs Q. **1979**, *14* (3), 363–390. http://www.chass.utoronto.ca/~wellman/publications/index.html.

9. Wellman, B. Physical place and cyberplace: the rise of networked individualism. In *Community Informatics: Shaping Computer Mediated Social Relations*; Keeble, L., Loader, B., Eds.; Routledge: London, U.K., 2001.

10. Wellman, B. The rise (and possible fall) of networked individualism. Connections **2002**, *24* (3), 30–32.

11. Benjamin, P. Telecentres and universal capability: A study of the telecentre programmes of the universal service agency, 1996–2000. Ph.D. dissertation, Aalborg University, Aalborg, Denmark, 2001.

12. Lave, J.; Wenger, E. *Situated Learning: Legitimate Peripheral Participation*; Cambridge University Press: Cambridge, U.K., 1991.

13. Rheingold, H. *The Virtual Community: Homesteading on the Electronic Frontier*; Addison-Wesley Publishing Company: Reading, MA, 1993.

14. Rheingold, H. *Smart Mobs: The Next Social Revolution*; Perseus Publishing: Cambridge, MA, 2002.

15. Castells, M. *The Rise of the Network Society. Vol. I, The Information Age: Economy, Society and Culture*; Blackwell Publishers: Oxford, U.K., 1996.

16. Rogers, E.M.; Collins-Jarvis, L.; Schmitz, J. The pen project in Santa Monica: Interactive communication, equality, and political action. J. Am. Soc. Inf. Sci. **1994**, *45* (6), 401–410.

17. Youtie, J.; Shapira, P.; Laudeman, G. *Transitioning to the Knowledge Economy: The Lagrange Internet Access Initiative*; Impacts of Public Infrastructure Access Working Paper 3; Georgia Institute of Technology: Atlanta, GA, 2002.

18. Schön, D.A.; Sanyal, B.; Mitchell, W.J. *High Technology and Low-Income Communities: Prospects for the Positive Use of Advanced Information Technology*; MIT Press: Cambridge, MA, 1999.

19. Williams, K. What is the digital divide?. In *d3: Proceedings of the Digital Divide Doctoral Students Workshop*; University of Michigan School of Information: Ann Arbor, MI, August 2001.

20. Himanen, P. *The Hacker Ethic and the Spirit of the Information Age*; Random House: New York, 2001.

21. Woolley, D.R. *Plato: The Emergence of On-Line Community*; University of Illinois at Urbana-Champaign Computer-Based Education Research Laboratory: Urbana, IL, 1994.

22. Felsenstein, L.; Aboba, B. How community memory came to be, Part 1: The origins of community memory. Internaut **1994**, *1*, http://madhaus.utcs.utoronto.ca/local/internaut/comm.html (accessed August 24, 2005).

23. Bluming, A. *History of the Los Angeles Free-Net;*. Los Angeles Free Net: Los Angeles, CA, n.d.

24. Stoecker, R.; Stuber, A.C.S. Limited access: The information superhighway and Ohio's neighborhood-based organizations. Comput. Hum. Serv. **1997**, *14*, 39–57.

25. Stoecker, R.; Stuber, A. Building an information superhighway of one's own: A comparison of two approaches. Res. Politics Soc. **1999**, *7*, 291–309.

26. Alkalimat, A.; Williams, K. Social capital and cyberpower in the African American community: A case study of a community technology center in the dual city. In *Community Informatics: Shaping Computer Mediated Social Relations*; Keeble, L., Loader, B., Eds.; Routledge: London, U.K., 2001.

27. Williams, K.; Alkalimat, A. A census of public computing in Toledo, Ohio. In *Shaping the Network Society: The New Role of Civic Society in Cyberspace*; Schuler, D., Day, P., Eds.; MIT Press: Cambridge, MA, 2004.

28. Mele, C. Cyberspace and disadvantaged communities: The Internet as a tool for collective action. In *Communities in Cyberspace*; Smith, M.A., Kollock, P., Eds.; Routledge: London, U.K., 1999; 290–310.

29. Kochen, M.; Donohue, J. *Information for the Community*; American Library Association: Chicago, IL, 1976.

30. Cronus, C.L.; Crowe, L., Eds. *Libraries and neighborhood information centers*, Allerton Park Institute Proceedings 17, University of Illinois at Urbana-Champaign Graduate School of Library and Information Science, Champaign, IL, 1971, http://www.ideals.uiuc.edu/handle/2142/1552 (accessed online October 3, 2007).

31. Long, N. *Information & Referral Services: Research Findings. Volume One of the Interstudy Information and Referral Center Study*; U.S. Administration on Aging, Department of Health, Education, and Welfare: Washington, DC, 1975.

32. Croneberger, R.; Luck, C. Analyzing community human information needs: A case study. Libr. Trends January **1976**, *24* (3), 515–525.

33. Childers, T. *Information and Referral: Public Libraries*; Ablex: New York, 1984.

34. Durrance, J.C. Community information services: An innovation at the beginning of its second decade. Adv. Libr. **1984**, *13*, 100–128.

35. Jones, C.S. The urban library: Proving utility. Libr. J. **1976**, 101, 81–86.

36. Hallman, J. Community networking [hyperlinked timeline] 2006, http://www.ibiblio.org/rtpnet/community-net.html (accessed October 10, 2007).

37. Cisler, S. Ties that bind: Community networking (conf. announcement); March 2, 1995. http://scout.wisc.edu/Projects/PastProjects/NH/95-03/95-03-14/0014.html (accessed October 10, 2007).

38. Durrance, J.C.; Pettigrew, K.E. Community information: The technological touch. Libr. J. **2000**, *125* (2), 44–46.

39. Durrance, J.C.; Pettigrew, K.E. *Online Community Information: Creating a Nexus at Your Library*; American Library Association: Chicago, IL, 2002.

40. TFN (Tallahassee FreeNet), About us, n.d. http://www.tfn.net/TFN/ (accessed October 10, 2007).

41. Durrance, J.C. Community connector. University of Michigan School of Information Community Networking Initiative, 1994, http://www.si.umich.edu/Community/ (accessed October 15, 2007).

42. PrairieNet Community Network, 2005, http://www.cii.uiuc.edu/prairienet (accessed October 10, 2007).

43. Bishop, A.P.; Bruce, B. Community informatics: Integrating action, research, and learning. B. Am. Soc. Inform. Sci. Tech. August/September **2005**, *31* (6), 6–10.

44. Bruce, B.C.; Bishop, A.P. New literacies and community inquiry. In *The Handbook of Research in New Literacies*; Coiro, J., Knobel, M., Lankshear, C., Leu, D., Eds.; Erlbaum: Hillsdale, NJ, 2007; 703–746.

45. Cohill, A.M.; Kavanaugh, A.L., Eds. *Community Networks: Lessons from Blacksburg, Virginia*; Artech House: Norwood, MA, 1999.

46. Stoecker, R. Is community informatics good for communities? Questions confronting an emerging field. J. Commun. Inform. **2005**, *1* (3), 13–26.

47. Day, P.; Schuler, D., Eds. *Community Practice in the Network Society: Local Action/Global Interaction*; Routledge: London, U.K., 2003.

48. Schuler, D.; Day, P. *Shaping the Network Society: The New Role of Civil Society in Cyberspace*; MIT Press: Cambridge, MA, 2004.

49. Schuler, D. *New Community Networks: Wired for Change*; ACM Press: New York, 1996.

50. Loader, B. *The Governance of Cyberspace: Politics, Technology and Global Restructuring*; Routledge: London, U.K., 1997.

51. Loader, B.; Hague, B. *Digital Democracy: Discourse and Decision-Making in the Information Age*; Routledge: London, U.K., 1999.

52. Loader, B.; Thomas, D. *Cybercrime: Law Enforcement, Security & Surveillance in the Information Age*; Routledge: London, U.K., 2000.

53. Loader, B.; Dutton, W.H. *Digital Academe: The New Media and Institutions of Higher Education and Learning*; Routledge: London, U.K., 2002.

54. Loader, B.; van de Donk, W.; Nixon, P.; Rucht, D. *Cyberprotest: New Media, Citizens and Social Movements*; Routledge: London, U.K., 2003.

55. Loader, B.; Keeble, L. *Challenging the Digital Divide? A Literature Review of Community Informatics Initiatives*; Joseph Rowntree Foundation: York, U.K., 2004.

56. Gurstein, M., Eds. *Community Informatics: Enabling Communities with Information and Communications Technologies*; Idea Group Publishing: Hershey, PA, 2000.

57. Mossberger, K.; Tolbert, C.J.; McNeal, R.S. *Digital Citizenship: The Internet, Society, and Participation*; MIT Press: Cambridge, MA, 2007.

58. Stone, A. *CTCNET: History, Organization and Future*; CTCNET: Newton, MA, 1996.

59. Williams, K.; Durrance, J.C. Social networks and social capital: Rethinking theory in community informatics. J. Commun. Inf. **2008**, *4*(3).

Communication–
Corporate Art

Complexity and Self-Organization

Francis Heylighen
Free University of Brussels, Brussels, Belgium

Abstract

This entry introduces some of the main concepts and methods of the science studying complex, self-organizing systems, and networks, in a nontechnical manner. Complexity cannot be strictly defined, only situated in between order and disorder. A complex system is typically modeled as a collection of interacting agents, representing components as diverse as people, cells, or molecules. Because of the nonlinearity of the interactions, the overall system evolution is to an important degree unpredictable and uncontrollable. However, the system tends to self-organize, in the sense that local interactions eventually produce global coordination and synergy. The resulting structure can in many cases be modeled as a network, with stabilized interactions functioning as links connecting the agents. Such complex, self-organized networks typically exhibit the properties of clustering, being scale-free, and forming a small world. These ideas have obvious applications in information science when studying networks of authors and their publications.

INTRODUCTION

A new paradigm for scientific inquiry has been emerging: complexity. Classical science, as exemplified by Newtonian mechanics, is essentially reductionist: it reduces all complex phenomena to their simplest components, and then tries to describe these components in a complete, objective, and deterministic manner.[1,2] The philosophy of complexity is that this is in general impossible: complex systems, such as organisms, societies, or the Internet, have properties—emergent properties—that cannot be reduced to the mere properties of their parts. Moreover, the behavior of these systems has aspects that are intrinsically unpredictable and uncontrollable, and cannot be described in any complete manner. At best, we can find certain statistical regularities in their quantitative features, or understand their qualitative behavior through metaphors, models, and computer simulations.

While these observations are mostly negative, emphasizing the traditional qualities that complex systems lack, these systems also have a number of surprisingly positive features, such as flexibility, autonomy, and robustness, that traditional mechanistic systems lack. These qualities can all be seen as aspects of the process of self-organization that typifies complex systems: these systems spontaneously organize themselves so as to better cope with various internal and external perturbations and conflicts. This allows them to evolve and adapt to a constantly changing environment.

Processes of self-organization literally create order out of disorder.[1] They are responsible for most of the patterns, structures, and orderly arrangements that we find in the natural world, and many of those in the realms of mind, society, and culture. The aim of information science can be seen as finding or creating such patterns in the immense amount of data that we are confronted with. Initially, patterns used to organize information were simple and orderly, such as "flat" databases in which items were ordered alphabetically by author's name or title, or hierarchically organized subject indices where each item was assigned to a fixed category. Present-day information systems, such as the World Wide Web, are much less orderly, and may appear chaotic in comparison. Yet, being a result of self-organization, the Web possesses a nontrivial structure that potentially makes information retrieval much more efficient. This structure and others have recently been investigated in the science of networks, which can be seen as part of the sciences of complexity and self-organization.

The concept of self-organization was first proposed by the cyberneticist W. Ross Ashby[3] in the 1940s and developed among others by his colleague Heinz von Foerster.[4] During the 1960s and 1970s, the idea was picked up by physicists and chemists studying phase transitions and other phenomena of spontaneous ordering of molecules and particles. These include Ilya Prigogine,[1] who received a Nobel Prize for his investigation of self-organizing "dissipative structures," and Hermann Haken,[5] who dubbed his approach "synergetics." In the 1980s, this tradition cross-fertilized with the emerging mathematics of nonlinear dynamics and chaos, producing an investigation of complex systems that is mostly quantitative, mathematical, and practiced by physicists. However, the same period saw the appearance of a parallel tradition of "complex adaptive systems,"[6] associated with the newly founded Santa Fe Institute for the sciences of complexity, that is closer in spirit to the cybernetic roots of the field. Building on the work of John Holland, Stuart Kauffman,

Encyclopedia of Library and Information Sciences, Fourth Edition DOI: 10.1081/E-ELIS4-120043869

Robert Axelrod, Brian Arthur, and other SFI associates, this approach is more qualitative and rooted in computer simulation. It took its inspiration more from biology and the social sciences than from physics and chemistry, thus helping to create the new disciplines of *artificial life* and *social simulation*. The remainder of this entry will mostly focus on this second, simulation-based tradition, because it is most applicable to the intrinsically social and cognitive processes that produce the systems studied by information science. Although the other, mathematical tradition sometimes uses the term "complex systems" to characterize itself, the labels of "nonlinear systems" or "chaos theory" seem more appropriate, given that this tradition is still rooted in the Newtonian assumption that apparently complex behavior can be reduced to simple, deterministic dynamics—an assumption which may be applicable to the weather, but not to the evolution of a real-world social system. Extending both traditions, the turn of the century witnessed a surging popularity of research into complex networks. This was inspired mostly by the growth of the World Wide Web and the models proposed by Watts and Strogatz,[7] and Barabasi and Albert.[8]

At present, the "science of complexity" taken as whole is still little more than a collection of exemplars, methods, and metaphors for modeling complex, self-organizing systems. However, while it still lacks integrated theoretical foundations, it has developed a number of widely applicable, fundamental concepts and paradigms that help us to better understand both the challenges and opportunities of complex systems. This entry will try to introduce the most important of these concepts in a simple and coherent manner, with an emphasis on the ones that may help us to understand the organization of networks of information sources.

COMPLEX SYSTEMS

There is no generally accepted definition of complexity:[9] different authors have proposed dozens of measures or conceptions, none of which captures all the intuitive aspects of the concept, while they are applicable only to a very limited type of phenomena, such as binary strings or genomes. For example, the best-known measure, "Kolmogorov complexity," which is the basis of algorithmic information theory, defines the complexity of a string of characters as the length of the shortest program that can generate that string. However, this implies that random strings are maximally complex, since they allow no description shorter than the string itself. This contradicts our intuition that random systems are not truly complex. A number of more complex variations on this definition have been proposed to tackle this issue, but they still suffer from the fact that they are only applicable to strings, not to real-world systems. Moreover, it has been proven that

the "shortest possible" description is in general uncomputable, implying that we can never be sure that we really have determined the true complexity of a string.

In spite of these fundamental problems in formalizing the notion of complexity, there are a number of more intuitive features of complex systems that appear again and again in the different attempts to characterize the domain.[2] One that is more or less universally accepted is that complexity must be situated *in between order and disorder*: complex systems are neither regular and predictable (like the rigid, "frozen" arrangement of molecules in a crystal), nor random and chaotic (like the ever-changing configuration of molecules in a gas). They exhibit a mixture of both dimensions, being roughly predictable in some aspects, surprising and unpredictable in others. This intermediate position, balancing between rigidity and turbulence, is sometimes called the "edge of chaos." A number of theorists have proposed that this precarious balance is precisely what is necessary for adaptation, self-organization, and life to occur, and that complex systems tend to spontaneously evolve toward this "edge."[6]

Another fundamental feature is that complex systems consist of many (or at least several) parts that are connected via their interactions. Their components are both *distinct* and *connected*, both autonomous and to some degree mutually dependent. Complete dependence would imply order, like in a crystal where the state of one molecule determines the state of all the others. Complete independence would imply disorder, like in a gas where the state of one molecule gives you no information whatsoever about the state of the other molecules.

The components of a complex system are most commonly modeled as *agents*, i.e., individual systems that act upon their environment in response to the events they experience. Examples of agents are people, firms, animals, cells, and molecules. The number of agents in the system is in general not fixed as agents can multiply or "die." Usually, agents are implicitly assumed to be goal-directed: their actions aim to maximize their individual "fitness," "utility," or "preference." When no specific goal can be distinguished, their activity still follows a simple cause-and-effect or condition–action logic: an agent will react to a specific condition perceived in the environment by producing an appropriate action. The causal relation or rule connecting condition and action, while initially fixed for a given type of agent, can in some cases change, by learning or evolutionary variation.

The environmental conditions to which an agent reacts are normally affected by other agents' activity. Therefore, an action by one agent will in general trigger further actions by one or more other agents, possibly setting in motion an extended chain of activity that propagates from agent to agent across the system. Such interactions are initially *local*: they start out affecting only the agents in the immediate neighborhood of the initial actor. However, their consequences are often *global*, affecting the system of agents as a whole, like a ripple produced by a pebble that locally disturbs the surface of the water, but then widens to encompass the whole pond.

Nonlinearity

The spreading of a wave is not a complex phenomenon, though, because its propagation is perfectly regular and predictable, and its strength diminishes as its reach widens. Processes in complex systems, on the other hand, are often *nonlinear*: their effects are not proportional to their causes. When the effects are larger than the causes, we may say that there is an amplification or *positive feedback*: initially small perturbations reinforce themselves so as to become ever more intense. An example is the spread of a disease, where a single infection may eventually turn into a global pandemic. Another example is the chain reaction that leads to a nuclear explosion. When the effects are smaller than the causes, there is a dampening or *negative feedback*: perturbations are gradually suppressed, until the system returns to its equilibrium state.

Interactions with positive feedback are very *sensitive to their initial conditions*: a change in that condition may be so small that it is intrinsically undetectable, yet result in a drastically altered outcome. This is called the *butterfly effect* after the observation that, because of the nonlinearity of the system of equations governing the weather, the flapping of the wings of a butterfly in Tokyo may cause a hurricane in New York. The nonobservability of the initial perturbations means that the outcome is *in principle* unpredictable, even if the dynamics of the system were perfectly deterministic: no weather monitoring system can be so accurate that it senses all the movements of butterfly wings. This explains why weather forecasts cannot be truly reliable, especially for the longer term. Positive feedback will amplify small, random fluctuations into wild, unpredictable swings, making the overall behavior of the system chaotic. An illustration can be found in the erratic up-and-down movements of quotations on the stock exchange.

In spite of the omnipresence of fluctuations, most systems around us appear relatively stable and predictable. This is due to the presence of negative feedback, which suppresses the effects of such fluctuations. However, while negative feedback makes a system more predictable, it also makes it less controllable: if we try to change the state of such a system, we may find that our changes are counteracted, and that whatever we do the system always returns to its own "preferred" equilibrium state. Examples can be found in social systems where attempts from leaders or governments to change the behavior often are actively resisted so that they eventually come to nothing.

The dynamics of complex systems typically exhibits a combination of positive and negative feedbacks, so that certain changes are amplified and others dampened. This makes the system's overall behavior both unpredictable and uncontrollable. Moreover, such systems are normally open, which means that they exchange matter, energy and/ or information with their wider environment. For example, an economy or ecosystem is dependent on the climate, and the amount of sunlight, rain, and heat that it produces. These in-going and out-going flows make the dynamics even more complicated, since we cannot know every external event that may affect the system. For example, a thriving economy or ecosystem may suddenly collapse because of the invasion by a foreign pest. Furthermore, the input of energy (such as sunlight) tends to feed amplification processes, so that they never reach the equilibrium that would otherwise follow the exhaustion of resources.

Modeling Complex Systems

For the above reasons, traditional deterministic models (such as systems of partial differential equations) of truly complex systems are in general impracticable,[10] if not in principle uncomputable.[11] In nonlinear systems, simplifying the model by using approximations is dangerous as well. The common way to approximate the effect of complex interactions by reducing it to the "mean field" (i.e., the average effect of many discrete actions performed by independent agents) can actually lead to fundamental errors. For example, a differential equation representing the "mean field" effect may predict that a certain perturbation will die out because it is too small, while a computer simulation of the individual agents finds that its effect is amplified by positive feedback until it dominates the system.[12]

Because of these intrinsic difficulties with mathematical models, complexity researchers typically prefer computer simulations, which, while of course being approximations as well, are easier to manipulate, so that more different factors and variations of the model can be explored. Here, the system's evolution is traced step-by-step by iteratively applying the rules that govern the agents' interactions, thus generating the subsequent states of the system. Such simulations typically include a generator of random variations, to represent the effect of unpredictable perturbations. A typical setting is inspired by the Darwinian mechanism of natural selection, in which the rules that determine an agent's behavior are randomly "mutated" and sometimes recombined with the rules of another agent, after which the "fittest" or best performing agents or rules are selected to carry on, while the others are eliminated. To explore the possible behaviors of the system, many different "runs"—with different initial conditions or random variations during the process—of the simulation are performed. The main variable values for each run are collected. These results are then analyzed statistically to discover recurring trends.

This sometimes produces very robust results, in the sense that all runs, however different in their initial behavior, eventually appear to converge to the same type of stable pattern. In the majority of cases, the outcomes can be classified into a relatively small number of distinct categories. This provides the researchers with a qualitative picture of the most likely results—and hopefully an insight into the factors that promote one outcome rather than another one. It is only exceptionally that no clear pattern can be discerned in the outcomes of the different simulation runs. The reason that complex systems in spite of their intrinsic unpredictability tend to settle into a relatively small set of recognizable behaviors is their inherent tendency to *self-organize*.

SELF-ORGANIZATION

Self-organization can be defined as the spontaneous emergence of global structure out of local interactions. "Spontaneous" means that no internal or external agent is in control of the process: for a large enough system, any individual agent can be eliminated or replaced without damaging the resulting structure. The process is truly *collective*, i.e., *parallel* and *distributed* over all the agents. This makes the resulting organization intrinsically *robust* and resistant to damage and perturbations.

As noted, the components or agents of a complex system initially interact only locally, i.e., with their immediate neighbors. The actions of remote agents are initially independent of each other: there is no correlation between the activity in one region and the activity in another one. However, because all components are directly or indirectly connected, changes propagate so that faraway regions eventually are influenced by what happens here and now. Because of the complex interplay of positive and negative feedbacks, this remote influence is very difficult to predict and may initially appear chaotic.

To explain the appearance of organization, we need to make one further assumption, namely that the outcome of interactions is not arbitrary, but exhibits a "preference" for certain situations over others. The principle is analogous to *natural selection*: certain configurations are intrinsically "fitter" than others, and therefore will be preferentially retained and/or multiplied during the system's evolution. When the agents are goal-directed, the origin of this preference is obvious: an agent will prefer an outcome that brings it closer to its goals. For example, in a market a firm will prefer the outcome that brings it more profit. In an ecosystem, an animal will prefer an outcome that brings it more food or that reduces its risk of being attacked by a predator. But even inanimate, physical objects, such as molecules or stones, have an in-built "preference," namely for the state that minimizes their potential energy. Thus, a stone "prefers" the stable state at the foot of a hill to an unstable state on the top. Here, "preference" simply means that the unstable state will sooner or later be abandoned, while the stable one will be retained.

Coevolution and Synergy

Given such a preference, it is clear why an individual agent tends to "organize" itself so as to settle down in its preferred situation. The problem is that what is best for one agent is in general not best for the other agents. For example, more profit for a firm generally means less profit for its competitors, and an animal safe from attack by a predator means a predator that goes hungry. However, interaction is in general not a *zero-sum game*: a gain by one party does not necessarily imply an equivalent loss by the other party. In most cases, an outcome is possible in which both parties to some degree gain. For example, a firm may increase its profits by developing a more efficient technology, which it then licenses to its competitors, so that they too become more productive. In that case, we may say that the interaction exhibits *synergy*: the outcome is positive for all parties; all involved agents "prefer" the outcome to the situation without the interaction.

In general, such a collective solution is still a compromise, in the sense that not all agents can maximally realize their preferences. Not all the stones can end up in the same, lowest spot at the bottom of the hill, but they can all end up much lower than they were, by reducing the irregular hill to an even plain. Such a compromise reduces the tension or "conflict" between competing agents. (Such conflict would otherwise lead to instability as every action of the one triggers a counteraction by the other.) In that sense, we may say that the agents have *mutually adapted*; they have *coordinated* their actions so as to minimize friction and maximize synergy.

The achievement of this stable, synergetic state is in general a process of trial-and-error or variation-and-selection. Because agents are independent and interact locally, and because the dynamics of the system is unpredictable, they in general do not know what the effect of their actions on the other agents will be. They can only try out actions because they appear plausible, or even choose them at random, and note which ones bring them closer to their goals. Those actions can then be maintained or repeated, while the others are abandoned. This is the fundamental dynamics of natural selection. The main difference with traditional Darwinian evolution is that trial-and-error happens simultaneously on different sides: the agents *coevolve*, the one adapting to the other, until they mutually "fit."

From Local to Global Organization

To shift from local coordination to global organization, we just need to note that all interactions between all agents in the complex system will tend toward such a coherent, stable state, until they are all mutually adapted. This process generally accelerates because of a positive feedback. The reason is that if two or more agents have reached a mutually fit state, this defines a stable assembly to which other agents can now adapt, by trying to "fit" into the assembly as well. The larger the assembly, the more "niches" it has in which other agents can fit. The more agents join the assembly, the larger it becomes, and the more niches it provides for even more agents to join. Thus, the assembly may grow exponentially until it encompasses the global system.

This growth is typically faster when the agents are identical (e.g., molecules of the same substance) or similar (e.g., individuals from the same species), because the solution found by one agent will then suit the other agents as well, so that minimal further trial-and-error is needed once a good arrangement is locally found. This typically happens in processes of physical self-organization, such as crystallization, magnetization, or the emergence of coherent light in a laser.[5] When the agents are all different (e.g., species in an ecosystem), each in turn needs to explore in order to find its unique niche in an environment that continues to evolve, resulting in a much less explosive development.

In the case of identical agents, the global structure that emerges is typically uniform or regular, because the arrangement that is optimal for one agent is also the one optimal for the other agents. As a result, they all tend to settle into the same configuration. An example is a crystal, where all molecules are arranged at regular intervals and in the same orientation. In this case, self-organization produces a perfectly ordered pattern. In cases where the agents are diverse, like in an ecosystem or a market, the resulting structure is much more complex and unpredictable.

Global Dynamics

If we now consider the system as a whole—rather than the agents individually—we may note that the system too undergoes a process of variation. This can be seen as an exploration by the system of different regions of its state space, thus following an intricate trajectory. (The state space of the system is merely the Cartesian product of the state spaces of all its components.) Self-organization then means that the system reaches an *attractor*, i.e., a part of the state space that it can enter but not leave. In that sense, an attractor is a region "preferred" by the global dynamics: states surrounding the attractor (the attractor *basin*) are unstable and will eventually be left and replaced by states inside the attractor.

A nonlinear system has in general a multitude of attractors, each corresponding to a particular self-organized configuration. If the system starts out in a basin state, it will necessarily end up in the corresponding attractor, so that the long-term behavior can in principle be predicted (assuming we know what the attractor is, which is generally not the case). However, if it starts out in a state in between basins, it still has a "choice" about which basin and therefore which attractor it ends up in,

and this will depend on unpredictable fluctuations. An attractor generally does not consist of a single state, but of a subspace of states in between which the system continues to move. The self-organized configuration, while more stable than the configuration before self-organization, is therefore in general not static but full of ongoing activity.

Self-organization can be accelerated by augmenting the initial variation that makes the system explore its state space: the more different states it visits, the sooner it will reach a state that belongs to an attractor. The simplest way to increase such variation is to subject the system to random perturbations, i.e., "noise." For example, if you shake a pot filled with beans, the beans will explore a variety of configurations, while tending to settle into the one that is most stable, i.e., where the beans are packed most densely near the bottom of the pot. Thus, shaking will normally reduce the volume taken in by the beans. This principle was called "order from noise" by the cyberneticist von Foerster[4] and "order through fluctuations" by the thermodynamicist Prigogine.[1]

Emergence

The pattern formed by the stabilized interactions, mutual "fittings," or "bonds" between the agents determines a purposeful or functional structure. Its function is to minimize friction between the agents, and thus maximize their collective "fitness," "preference," or "utility." Therefore, we may call the resulting pattern "organization": the agents are organized or coordinated in their actions so as to maximize their synergy.[5] However, such organization by definition imposes a *constraint* on the agents: they have lost the freedom to visit states outside the attractor, i.e., states with a lower fitness or higher friction. They have to obey new "rules," determining which actions are allowed, and which are not. They have lost some of their autonomy. The resulting mutual dependency has turned the collection of initially independent agents into an organization, i.e., a cohesive whole that is more than the sum of its parts. The goal of this "superagent" is to maximize overall synergy rather than individual utility. In a sense, the agents have turned from selfish individualists into conscientious cooperators. They have become subordinated (or "enslaved" in the terminology of Haken)[5] to the regulations of the collective.

This whole has *emergent* properties, i.e., properties that cannot be reduced to the properties of its parts. For example, a cell has the property of being alive, while the molecules that constitute it lack that property; gold has the properties of being shiny, malleable, and yellow, but these properties do not exist for individual gold atoms.[2] Rather than the parts individually, emergent properties characterize the pattern of interactions or relations between them. They typically include global or "holistic" aspects, such as robustness, synergy, coherence, symmetry, and function.

Different attractor regimes imply different properties for the system obeying that regime. For example, a circulating convection current may rotate clockwise or counterclockwise. Since it cannot be a priori predicted which attractor the system will end up in, the emergent properties of the whole cannot be derived from the properties of its parts alone. Once the attractor regime has stabilized, the behavior of the parts is rather regulated or constrained by the properties of the higher-level whole. This is called *downward causation*. For example, the correspondence between DNA triplets and amino acids in the genetic code is not determined by the chemical properties of the molecules that constitute DNA, but by evolutionary history producing a particular mechanism for "reading" DNA triplets in living cells. A random variation of that history might well have produced a different mechanism and therefore a different code. The languages that different people speak are not determined by the neurophysiology of their brain, but by the self-organization of shared lexicons and grammatical rules within a community of communicating individuals.

While the self-organized whole is intrinsically stable, it is still flexible enough to cope with outside perturbations. These perturbations may push the system out of its attractor, but as long as the deviation is not too large, the system will automatically return to the same attractor. In the worst case, the system is pushed into a different basin but that will merely make it end up in a different attractor. In that sense, a self-organizing system is intrinsically *adaptive*: it maintains its basic organization in spite of continuing changes in its environment. As noted, perturbations may even make the system more robust, by helping it to discover a more stable organization.

COMPLEX NETWORKS

The structure emerging from self-organization can often be represented as a network. Initially, agents interact more or less randomly with whatever other agents happen to pass in their neighborhood. Because of natural selection, however, some of these interactions will be preferentially retained, because they are synergetic. Such a preferentially stabilized interaction may be called a bond, relationship, or *link*. A link couples or connects two agents, in the sense that linked agents preferentially interact with each other. The different links turn the assembly of agents into a *network*. Within the network, the agents can now be seen as *nodes* where different links come together. Perhaps the most intuitive example is a social network, which links people on the basis of friendship, trust, or collaboration. Other well-known examples are the Internet, which connects computers via communication links, and the Web, which connects documents via hyperlinks. A more abstract example is the biochemical network that connects

the molecules that react with each other within a cell in order to produce further molecules.

It is easy to define an abstract mathematical network. You just need a set N consisting of nodes n_i, and then select any subset L of links from the set of all possible connections between two nodes:

$$L = \{(n_i, n_j)\} \subset N \times N$$

However, complexity researchers have observed that "natural" (i.e., self-organized rather than artificially designed) or "complex" networks tend to exhibit a number of specific features: they are *scale-free*, *small-world*, and *clustering*. These features are defined statistically: certain configurations of links appear with a much higher probability than chance. We will here try to explain these particular link distributions from the dynamics of self-organization of a network.

Random Networks

Let us assume that we start with a collection N of independent agents (future nodes of the network) that initially interact randomly, thus creating random links. This produces a *random network*, i.e., a network where the links have been selected by chance from the set $N \times N$ of all possible connections. Random networks have been extensively studied in mathematics. They exhibit the phenomenon of *percolation*: when links between randomly chosen nodes are added one by one, larger and larger subsets of N become connected into cohesive subnetworks. When more links are added, subnetworks will become connected to each other, defining a larger connected subset. When a certain threshold is passed, all subsets become connected so that there is now just a single connected network. It is said that the network *percolates*: imagine the links as tubes and a liquid being injected into one of the nodes; when the network percolates, the liquid will spread throughout the whole system, because any node is now directly or indirectly connected to any other node by an uninterrupted path or chain of links. Whatever happens in one node of the network can now in principle propagate to every other node in the network.

Small-World Networks

The maximum length of the shortest path connecting two nodes in a connected network is called the *diameter* of the network. If the diameter is small relative to the number of nodes, the network is said to be a *small-world network*. The notion derives from the "it's a small world" phenomenon in social networks: two people encountering each other will often find that they have one or more acquaintances in common. Studies of social networks have indicated that it is in general possible to find a short sequence of friend-of-a-friend links connecting two people. It has been estimated that on the scale of the world as a whole, two randomly chosen individuals are unlikely to be more than six such links removed from each other ("six degrees of separation").

Whereas random networks have the small-world property, the opposite applies to regular networks. An example of such a network is a two-dimensional lattice or grid, where each node is connected to its four direct neighbors (left-right-up-down), each of which is connected to its four neighbors, and so on. In a square grid of 100,000 × 100,000 = 10 billion nodes, the nodes at the opposite ends of a diagonal are 200,000 links apart. This is the diameter of the network. Compare this to the distance of a mere six links that apparently characterizes the world social network with its nearly 10 billion nodes! Regular networks, where nodes are linked according to strict, repetitive rules rather than random connections, are typically large-world networks. This means that a change in one node will normally take a very long time to propagate to the rest of the network. As a result, the network will be slow to react to perturbations or innovations.

We may conclude that complex networks are not regular. But they are not random either: their linking patterns do obey certain regularities, albeit not strictly. In fact, it has been shown that a regular network can easily be turned into a small-world network by adding a small number of randomly chosen links to the otherwise strictly constrained links.[7] These random links by definition do not care about the "distances" within the regular grid: e.g., they may directly connect nodes that are otherwise 100,000 links apart. Such random links create "wormholes" or "shortcuts" between otherwise remote regions, thus bringing them suddenly within easy reach. As a result, a small number of random links added to a regular network spectacularly decreases the shortest path length between nodes.

Clustering

One of the nonrandom features that characterize complex networks is *clustering*. Clustering means that when A is linked to B, and B to C, then the probability is high (or at least much higher than could be expected in a random network) that A is also linked to C. In other words, two randomly chosen connections of B have a much higher than chance probability of being connected themselves.

The origin of this can best be explained by considering social networks. Here, the clustering property can be formulated as "the friends of my friends are (likely to be) my friends." In other words, friends tend to form a cluster or community in which everyone knows everyone. The reason is simple: when you regularly encounter your friends, you are likely to encounter their friends as well. More generally, if an agent A frequently interacts with an agent B, and B interacts with C, then the probability is high that

A will sooner or later interact with C as well. If A and B have some similarity in aims that helps them to find synergy, and the same applies to B and C, then A and C are likely to discover a synergetic relationship as well.

Scale-Free Networks

A less intuitive feature of complex networks is that their distribution of links tends to follow a *power law*:[8] there are many nodes with few links, and few nodes with many links. More precisely, the number of nodes N with a given degree (i.e., number of links) K is proportional to a (negative) power of that degree:

$$N(K) \sim K - a$$

(The values of the exponent a tend to vary between 1 and 3.) A network that obeys a power law is called *scale-free*. When $a = 1$, N is inversely proportional to K: in other words, as the number of links goes up, the number of nodes with that number of links goes down proportionally.

This property has been established empirically, by counting the number of links in various networks, such as the Web or social networks. It turns out that a few nodes have an inordinate amount of links. They function as the *hubs* of the network, the central "cross-roads" where many different connections come together. The most common nodes, on the other hand, have just a few links. This means that nodes are strongly differentiated: something that happens to a hub will have a disproportionately large influence on the rest of the network, while something that happens to an ordinary node may have little or no consequences. This has great practical implications: an innovation or perturbation that appears in a hub (e.g., a central network server, a high-visibility Web page, or a person who is known by many) may change the whole network in a short time, because it is immediately propagated far and wide. By identifying the hubs in a network, it becomes easier to manipulate its dynamics, for good or for bad. Obvious applications are the spread of computer viruses, contagious diseases, new ideas, or fashions.

Whereas clustering tends to increase distances in a network, by creating locally connected clusters that have few links outside the cluster, the presence of hubs has the opposite effect. Because hubs have a very large number of links they are likely to link into many different clusters, thus acting as shortcuts that reduce the distance between the clusters. But this also means that removing a hub may break the connections between otherwise remote regions of the network. This is a danger especially in communication networks such as the Internet, where the failure of a small number of hubs may split up the network into separate "islands" that no longer communicate with each other. Similar dangers exist in ecosystems where the disappearance of one or more key species—i.e., "hubs" on which many other species depend—may lead to a complete breakdown of the system.

Barabasi and Albert[8] have proposed a theoretical explanation for power-law distributions based on the mechanism of *preferential attachment*: new nodes joining the network preferentially establish links with nodes that already have a large number of links. They have shown that when the probability of linking to a node is exactly proportional to the number of links of that node the resulting network obeys a power law with $a = 3$.

For a more general scenario for the self-organization of a complex network, consider a collection of agents that initially only interact locally with those that happen to pass in their neighborhood. Some of these interactions will be stabilized into enduring links. Once they have some links, the locality principle entails that agents are more likely to forge links with the "friends of their friends" than with randomly chosen others, thus promoting clustering. But agents that already have a high number of links also have many "friends of friends" (i.e., nodes two links away) and therefore they will be more likely to develop additional links within this two-step neighborhood or cluster. The more links an agent has, the larger its neighborhood, and therefore the larger the probability that it will receive even more links from within this neighborhood. Similarly, the larger the cluster, the more likely it is to receive random links from outside, thus extending the neighborhood outwards and linking it into other clusters. This determines a positive feedback, which leads to an explosive growth in the number of links. The agents that happen to be in the center of such a quickly growing cluster will become the hubs of the network.

APPLICATION TO KNOWLEDGE NETWORKS

Having reviewed key concepts typifying complex, self-organizing systems, and networks, we will sketch some possible applications of these ideas in the area of information science. Information science focuses on the knowledge that is available in the documents that are available in libraries and databases across the world. These documents are typically produced by authors or researchers who investigate a domain, building further on the results of other authors, and publishing their results in new papers or books that refer to these used sources. This knowledge producing system can be viewed as a very complex network, formed by the researchers, the concepts they use and the publications they produce. All the "nodes" of the network are linked directly or indirectly, by relations such as citation, collaboration, or information exchange. This complex system is intrinsically self-organizing: no individual or organization is in charge, or can decide in which direction knowledge should develop. Novel, globally available knowledge emerges out of the spontaneous, local interactions between the individual agents.

By applying the concepts and methods from the domain of complexity, we may hope to better understand the development and structure of this network. We can view it as a complex, adaptive system that generates new patterns (knowledge) through the complex, nonlinear interactions between multitudes of autonomous agents (individual scientists and organizations). This system has the structure of a heterogeneous network (Fig. 1), consisting of three basic types of nodes:[13] agents, i.e., the individuals or organizations who actively process and produce knowledge, containers, i.e., the documents, databases, or journals in which the produced knowledge is stored and made available to other agents, and concepts, i.e., the abstract elements of knowledge itself, which are typically represented as keywords.

There already exists some preliminary work on subnetworks of this encompassing network, such as collaboration networks between authors[14] or citation networks between documents. This research has found that they possess typical features of complex networks, such as being scale-free and small-world. For example, citation

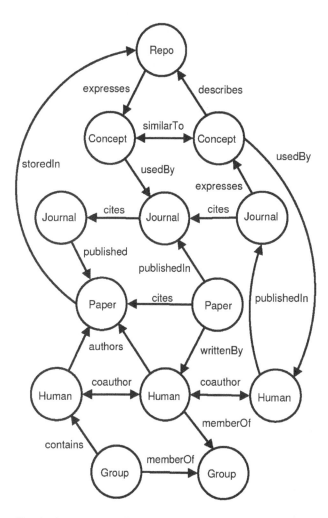

Fig. 1 heterogeneous knowledge network, containing authors, concepts, and documents.

networks typically contain a small number of hubs ("citation classics") with very many links, while most publications only gather a few citations. Some of the most successful recent methods for information retrieval, such as the PageRank algorithm underlying the Google search engine, or the HITS method developed by Kleinberg,[15] implicitly use this network structure to identify the "hubs" of a hypertext network.

More interesting even than the static analysis of existing networks is the modeling of their evolution. We may assume that an information network will self-organize through the propagation of information between nodes across links, creating new links and nodes in the process. For example, assume that information is transferred from paper A to researcher B. After reading the paper, B may decide to get some more information linked to paper A, e.g., by contacting A's author, or reading some of A's references. These in turn may refer B to other authors or papers relevant for B's interests, and so on. Some of these additional sources may turn out to be particularly important for B's research, inspiring B to develop a new concept, published in the form of one or more papers. This process will create links (e.g., B may start collaborating with another author, or refer in new papers to papers discovered in this way) and nodes (e.g., new papers, new concepts, new journals). Such links and nodes will tend to cluster around a small number of "hubs"— thus defining a new "community" of related authors, documents, and ideas.

The emergence of a new scientific domain is a good example of the self-organization of such a community of knowledge,[16] where people from initially diverse backgrounds find each other around a common interest, which gradually coalesces into a new paradigm. This process could be observed by mapping the network of authors, publications and keywords in a particular domain at regular intervals (e.g., every 2–5 years), and analyzing it in terms of clustering, hubs, average distances, etc. The change of these features over time may show processes of self-organization taking place. A good theory of the self-organization of knowledge communities would propose a number of processes and parameters that allow us to predict where, when, and how such self-organization is most likely to take place. Such a theory would help us to find not only the presently most authoritative concepts, publications, or authors (hubs), but those that are likely to become so in the future. This would provide a very powerful instrument to uncover emerging trends and to direct attention and investment toward the most promising people, ideas, and information sources.

CONCLUSION

The science studying complex, self-organizing systems and networks is still in its infancy. Yet, it already provides us with a powerful new perspective and a number of promising conceptual and modeling tools for understanding the complex phenomena that surround us, including organisms, the Internet, ecosystems, markets, and communities.

On the one hand, the complexity perspective reminds us to be modest in our aims: many phenomena in nature and society are simply too complex to be analyzed in the traditional scientific manner. Openness and nonlinearity make a complex system in principle unpredictable and uncontrollable: the tiniest internal or external perturbations can be amplified into global changes. Therefore, we will never be able to capture it in a complete and deterministic model. Still, agent-based computer simulations can help us to get an insight into the qualitative dynamics of the system, and to classify and delimit the likely scenarios for its further evolution.

On the other hand, the complexity perspective gives us new reasons for optimism: while we cannot truly control a complex system, it tends to self-organize to a state where it regulates itself. This state tends to increase the utility or fitness of the system's active components or agents, by coordinating their interactions so as to maximize synergy. The resulting organization is distributed over all the agents and their interactions, and thus much more robust and flexible than any centralized design. Moreover, it determines a number of emergent, global properties that cannot be reduced to the properties of the individual components. By understanding the underlying mechanisms, we may be able to facilitate and stimulate such self-organization, or to drive it in one direction rather than another.

One of the most recent applications of the complexity perspective is the analysis of complex networks, such as the World Wide Web, and the nonlinear processes that generate them. This has led to the identification of common statistical features of such networks: small-world, clustering, and scale-free link distributions. These notions promise a wealth of applications in the analysis of information networks, potentially helping us with the organization, management, retrieval, and discovery of relevant knowledge within masses of ill-structured and continuously changing data.

REFERENCES

1. Prigogine, I. Stengers, I. *Order Out of Chaos;* Bantam Books: New York, 1984.
2. Gershenson, C.; Heylighen, F. How can we think the complex?. In *Managing the Complex. Vol. 1: Philosophy, Theory and Application*; Richardson, K., Ed.; Institute for the Study of Coherence and Emergence/Information Age Publishing: Charlotte, NC, 2005; 47–62.
3. Ashby, W.R. Principles of the self-organizing system. In *Principles of Self-organization*; von Foerster, H., Zopf, G. W., Jr., Eds.; Pergamon Press: New York, 1962; 255–278.

4. von Foerster, H. On self-organising systems and their environments. In *Self-organising Systems*; Yovits, M.C., Cameron, S., Eds.; Pergamon Press: London, 1960; 30–50.

5. Haken, H. *Information and Self-organization: A Macroscopic Approach to Complex Systems;* Springer-Verlag: New York, 2000.

6. Waldrop, M.M. *Complexity: The Emerging Science at the Edge of Order and Chaos;* Viking: London, 1992.

7. Watts, D.J.; Strogatz, S.H. Collective dynamics of small-world networks. Nature **1998**, *393*, 440–442.

8. Albert, R.; Barabasi, A.-L. Statistical mechanics of complex networks. Rev. Modern Phys. **2002**, *74*, 47–97.

9. Edmonds, B. What is complexity? The philosophy of complexity per se with application to some examples in evolution. In *The Evolution of Complexity*; Heylighen, F., Bollen, J., Riegler, A., Eds.; Kluwer: Dordrecht, 1999; 1–18.

10. Holland, J.H. Studying complex adaptive systems. J. Syst. Sci. Complex. **2006**, *19*(1), 1–8.

11. Levin, S.A. Complex adaptive systems: Exploring the known, the unknown and the unknowable. Bull. Am. Math. Soc. **2002**, *40*(1), 3–19.

12. Louzoun, Y.; Solomon, S.; Atlan, H.; Cohen, I.R. Modeling complexity in biology. Phy. A: Sta. Mech. *297*(1–2), 242–252.

13. Rodriguez, M.A. A multi-relational network to support the scholarly communication process. Int. J. Public Inform. Syst. **2007**, *1*, 13–29.

14. Newman, M. The structure of scientific collaboration networks. Proc. Natl. Acad. Sci. USA **2001**, *98*, 404–409.

15. Kleinberg, J. Authoritative sources in a hyperlinked environment. J. ACM **1999**, *46*(5), 604–632.

16. Wagner, C.S.; Leydesdorff, L. Network structure, self-organization, and the growth of international collaboration in science. Res. Policy **2005**, *34*(10), 1608–1618.

BIBLIOGRAPHY

1. Axelrod, R. Cohen, M.D. *Harnessing Complexity: Organizational Implications of a Scientific Frontier;* Simon and Schuster: New York, 2000.

2. Bar-Yam, Y. *Dynamics of Complex Systems;* Westview Press: Boulder, CO, 2003. Available at http://necsi.org/publications/dcs.

3. Haken, H. *Information and Self-organization: A Macroscopic Approach to Complex Systems;* Springer-Verlag: New York, 2000.

4. Heylighen, F. The science of self-organization and adaptivity. In *Knowledge Management, Organizational Intelligence and Learning, and Complexity*; Kiel, L.D., Ed.; Eolss Publishers: Oxford, 2002. Available at http://www.eolss.net In: The Encyclopedia of Life Support Systems (EOLSS).

5. Holland, J.H. *Hidden Order: How Adaptation Builds Complexity*; Addison-Wesley: Reading, MA, 1996.

6. Kelly, K. *Out of Control;* Addison-Wesley: New York, 1994.

7. Miller, J.H.; Page, S.E. *Complex Adaptive Systems: An Introduction to Computational Models of Social Life;* Princeton University Press: Princeton, NJ, 2007.

8. Newman, M.E.J. The structure and function of complex networks. SIAM Rev. **2003**, *45*, 167–256. Available at http://arxiv.org/abs/cond-mat/0303516.

9. Prigogine, I.; Stengers, I. *Order Out of Chaos;* Bantam Books: New York, 1984.

10. Waldrop, M.M. *Complexity: The Emerging Science at the Edge of Order and Chaos;* Viking: London, 1992.

Communication–
Corporate Art

Computer-Mediated Communication (CMC)

Michael A. Chilton
Roger McHaney
Department of Management, Kansas State University, Manhattan, Kansas, U.S.A.

Abstract

Computer-mediated communication (CMC) is a field that studies the use of computers and related technologies as a means of facilitating human communication. With the decrease in cost of computer-based systems, use as a communication and collaboration medium has increased dramatically. Applications have been developed for businesses, educational institutions, and governmental agencies to meet the demand of emerging environments, and to enhance personal use of social networks. Scholarly research in the area of CMC has mirrored this growth. This entry first provides a description of CMCs, including areas in which computers have been used to facilitate collaboration, automation, and management. The second section categorizes both synchronous and asynchronous applications of CMC conferencing and communication technology by breaking applications down between task-specific and non-task specific areas of application within interpersonal, group, and mass communication venues. The remainder of this entry explores academic research in the area of CMC.

INTRODUCTION

The term *computer-mediated communication* or CMC was developed to represent the use of computers as a means of facilitating human communication. Computer-based systems have gained momentum as a communication and collaboration medium. Computer-assisted communications takes on a greater role in society as the cost of technology declines, as the communications infrastructure grows (e.g., the World Wide Web), as the cost of face-to-face meetings increases, and as social pressure to communicate and network with others more efficiently increases. Applications have been developed for businesses, educational institutions, and governmental agencies to meet their increasing demand for networked communication capability and for personal use to enhance social networks. Scholarly research in the area of CMC has mirrored this growth. The study of the impact of computers on human communications and information flow has resulted in a large collection of practical and theoretical papers. This growth has also fueled newer research streams as the number of uses for computers as an instrument of human communications continues to increase. A scholarly journal devoted to CMC (the *Journal of Computer-Mediated Communication*) has been created.

This entry will first provide a description of CMCs, including areas in which computers have been used to facilitate collaboration, automation, and management. Next it provides a framework for classifying various types of CMC and discusses each portion of the framework in terms of both example applications and research topics.

DESCRIPTION OF CMC

CMC has been described in various ways by academics and practitioners. Although some would describe CMC as virtually all computer uses that employ a user interface or involve the manipulation of data, this description may not include data or information flow between two or more people. Thus, computer applications such as statistical analysis programs, remote-sensing systems, and financial modeling programs would fit within this concept.[1] A narrower view holds that CMC only encompasses those applications that directly assist human communication. That the term includes the word, "mediate," implies reliance upon a third party or entity to enhance the information flow between two or more people. This entity adds something to the communication that helps improve (or at least provides the opportunity to do so) the efficiency and/or effectiveness of information flow. The addition of elements to aid information flow is what distinguishes CMC from ordinary telephone conversations, FAX communications, and electronic broadcasts (such as "webinars," which are unidirectional). An example of an element that a computer might provide to enhance communications is the storage and presentation of large amounts of data, which is beyond the capability of human short-term memory to store. From this perspective, CMC encompasses not just the communication itself, but the entire process by which people create and exchange information using electronic systems and the extent to which computers assist the communications by adding some element of facilitation.

Encyclopedia of Library and Information Sciences, Fourth Edition DOI: 10.1081/E-ELIS4-120044411

CMC can further be described according to its function. CMC is utilized in such diverse areas as teaching and learning, in social networking (for both personal and professional reasons), for dissemination and/or control of information, and for entertainment of various kinds. The methods by which each of these functions are accomplished provide additional ways of classifying a particular CMC system. Systems may require synchronous communications or allow sharing of information asynchronously; systems may provide for unidirectional communications or they may allow interactive participation; systems may provide for either small or large numbers of simultaneous participants; and systems may provide elaborate interfaces in very controlled circumstances or they may allow very informal settings that utilize simple interfaces.

This entry will discuss CMC first in terms of function as described above; next, it will provide some descriptions of systems currently in use and discuss how these systems achieve these functions; finally, we will present the various categories of research both by discipline and by topical area and journal publication. This entry is not meant to be all inclusive of every system that might be classified as a CMC, but to provide a broad taxonomy of current systems such that future systems might be understood and classified using these criteria.

There are several characteristics of CMC that can be used for classification. If communications between people occurs in real time (i.e., if one person must hear what another is saying at the time it is said), this is called synchronous communications. Conversely, if the speaker leaves a message for the receiver, which can be retrieved at a later time, this is termed asynchronous communications. Whether a message is unidirectional or bidirectional also provides us with a classificatory characteristic. Directionality can be further subdivided into active and passive components depending upon whether the receiver is expected to interact with the speaker with more than just a verbal response, as by engaging in a business transaction, for example. The complexity of the system from both the designer's point of view and the user's point of view (so-called user friendliness) is another feature used to classify systems. Finally, the degree of control exercised when the system is used can also be used to classify systems. As we discuss each example, we will use these categories to describe them.

CMC scholarship covers a wide range of applications. This is due in part to the number of potential applications for this technology and in part to the number of fields it spans. The term CMC has been used to describe research in diverse areas such as from electronic messaging,[2] office automation,[3] distributed decision-making,[4] electronic boardrooms,[5] teleconferencing, informatics,[1] computer-supported cooperative work or CSCW, decision support systems and group support systems or GDSS,[6] and computer-assisted instruction or CAI.[1,7]

In general, CMC systems can be broken into three distinct areas based on application. These areas are conferencing, informatics, and CAI. While each area has unique characteristics, elements common to all CMC include communication, computers, and information exchange. Rather than attempt to describe each individual area fitting within CMC, this entry concentrates on the commonalities shared by CMC applications. The first section develops a general understanding of the primary divisions within CMC by discussing conferencing and communication, informatics, and CAI.[8] The second section categorizes both synchronous and asynchronous applications of CMC conferencing and communication technology by breaking applications down between task-specific and non-task specific areas of application in interpersonal, group, and mass communication venues. The remainder of this entry explores academic research in the area of CMC.

PRIMARY FUNCTIONS OF CMC

Teaching and Learning

CMCs are used in several distance education scenarios. Lectures can be prerecorded and broadcast to students all at once or provided on a file server to allow asynchronous use. Lectures can also be broadcast live and can allow for either active or passive audience participation. Technology is available that allows for storage of recorded lectures and for notifying students when new lecture content is available using RSS (Really Simple Syndication) feeds. Live lectures can be uni- or bidirectional so that students can either sit passively and listen, or they can respond with questions and/or supplemental content while the lecture is broadcast. Lectures such as these are not limited to a single instructor or class, but might include several instructors located in various places broadcasting to several classrooms also located in various places. For example, a class on human resources might be enriched if some or all of the lectures were broadcast from several locations throughout the world so that students can get a better taste of the international climate and cross-cultural issues. A lecturer in Chicago might teach a local class and be piped into classrooms in New York, Los Angeles, London, Capetown, and Singapore, and be joined by lecturers in each of these locations.

Classroom-assistance programs have been developed to facilitate communications between instructors and students. Initially designed to replace the teacher's grade book, systems such as Axio, Blackboard, and others have evolved into a system that allows not just (near) real-time delivery of grades, but also for content storage and delivery to enhance learning and improve efficiency. Students can electronically complete assignments and upload them to the class repository (usually hosted by a Web server), download and view assignments and other information pertinent to the class, and communicate with each other either synchronously or asynchronously. The idea behind these systems us to free time for both students and instructors that might otherwise be devoted to administrative tasks so that the time can be used more effectively for learning.

Classroom participation programs have also been developed and are currently being studied for their effectiveness. These systems were developed to provide real-time feedback to the instructor so that changes and assessment of learning can be made while class is conducted. Students are provided with electronic devices with which they can interact with a central recording unit when prompted by the instructor. An instructor can present a question regarding material covered in the class and allow the students to enter their answer using these electronic devices. Answers can be recorded and assessed immediately so that both the instructor and the students may become aware of learning progress. The instructor can then decide whether to repeat information not well understood or continue on to additional topics for information that has been assimilated.

Computer labs and computer simulation is another method by which teachers can transfer information to students. Prewritten lab exercises can be performed by students either in a live lab or asynchronously outside of class time so that students can see and learn the topics by performing exercises designed to provide new information to the students. This type of instruction is especially suitable for software training. Computer simulations are similar to see-and-perform lab exercises, except that the student is now required to prepare a simulation environment and then let the computer perform the actual steps. Simulations are beneficial when large amounts of data must be created and analyzed in a short period of time.

Conferencing and Collaboration

A primary use of CMC has been to facilitate direct human communication through conferencing and collaboration applications. To understand the differences in these two types of applications, we can divide them into task-related and non-task related scenarios. When people meet to accomplish specific tasks, we can categorize this as collaboration. Task-related communication systems therefore imply that such systems are designed to help participants concentrate on specific goal completion with human communication as a necessary link in the process. On the other hand, when people meet to discuss agenda items for which there is no immediate result (except perhaps plans to act in the future), we can categorize this as conferencing.

Several types of computer applications have been designed to support group conferencing and collaboration. These include instant messaging, chat rooms, text messaging, blogging, wikis, GDSS systems, groupware, and audio

and video teleconferencing. Table 1 provides a framework to categorize these systems based on whether they are primarily used for conferencing or collaboration and whether they are used synchronously or asynchronously.

Many of these systems have gained widespread acceptance and use in both personal and business settings. Instant messaging, blogging, and wikis are all examples. On the other hand, systems such as GDSS have received an enormous amount of attention in the scientific literature (e.g., Nunamaker),[9] but have largely been used in business settings.

The term group decision support systems or GDSS has been used to describe a particular area within CMC, specifically developed from the need to support organizational decision-making processes which are being implemented by more than an individual. Unlike the non-task specific CMC applications, GDSS are generally used to facilitate a particular task. As such, GDSS can be described as an interactive computer-based system used to support collective decision making. The term *group support systems* is often associated with GDSS, but focuses specifically on processes within the group. However, a GDSS may also include provisions for collaboration from outside the group and for information management.

Generally, decision makers utilize data and models within a GDSS to communicate and solve problems. However, researchers have classified a variety of applications as GDSS ranging from systems to facilitate electronic meetings to systems to support complex decision processes.[10]

The simplistic GDSS may consist of no more than a personal computer and voting pads combination. In this arrangement questions are answered with a simple yes and no. The results are tabulated real time and the results are displayed graphically. In more complex GDSS implementations, anonymously entered data can be displayed and options such as data consolidation, statistical analysis, voting tabulation, ranking, and agenda planning exist.

Other GDSS systems have been developed to support an organizational paradigm of computing. In this view, the GDSS integrates data from corporate transaction processing systems and decision support systems and uses this information to demonstrate various outcomes.

GDSSs have been developed for use in several different environments. Among these are decision rooms, local networks, and remote networks. In the decision room scenario, a traditional conference center is equipped with computerized aids. This allows both the advantages of face-to-face communication and electronic interaction to

Table 1 Group application classifications.

	Synchronous	Asynchronous
Conferencing	Instant messaging, chat rooms, audio and video teleconferencing	Text messaging, blogging, and wikis
Collaboration	GDSS	Groupware

be enjoyed. A networked GDSS is designed to allow participants to interact remotely. Using their own computers, communication and access to data and decision support tools is enabled. Such systems allow collaborators to be located within the same building or to be geographically dispersed.

GDSS applications enjoy several benefits, among these are anonymity, extension of group memory, parallel task completion, and democratization of decision making.

Researchers report anonymity enhances group member participation by reducing inhibition.[10] Groups working anonymously produce greater numbers of solution clarifications, critical comments, questions about solutions, and total comments. In addition, members were more likely to be critical of ideas, to ask questions about new ideas, and to clarify or add to ideas. Anonymity acts as a buffer between people, disassociating them from their comments. This reduces behavioral constraints on group members and allows them to contribute more freely to the group discussion.[11]

The efficiency of group work is also improved by a GDSS through the structuring of team member interactions. Resulting time savings allows a greater focus on its task performance and problem solving activities.[12] Parallel entry also provides an increase in group efficiency. Members do not need to wait for someone to finish speaking before beginning the entry of additional information.[13]

GDSS tools can also enhance group memory. Retaining group memory has been a traditional barrier in face-to-face interaction and often results in information loss. Features of GDSSs such as electronic information capturing and display have been specifically designed to reduce information loss. A single garrulous person cannot raise his or her voice to dominate a meeting when GDSS is used. GDSS tends to democratize the process giving members the same opportunity to express their ideas through their terminal.

GDSS applications are not without shortcomings. The use of GDSS tends to reduce face-to-face interpersonal communication and increase social distances between members. In addition, the technology used to implement a GDSS can make meetings more complicated, particularly to the facilitator.

A variety of commercial products have been developed in the area of GDSS. Among these are *VisionQuest*, an electronic meeting support software supporting anonymous brainstorming, voting, allocation, and meeting documentation. Like most GDSS products, it runs in a variety of environments and requires that network software already be in place. Other tools include Autotel Information System's *Clarity* which provides a permanent record of the group's interactions; *CM*/1 by Corporate Memory Systems—a graphical meeting map combining a hypertext interface with an object-oriented database to allow groups to collaborate and organize ideas during brainstorming sessions; *Group Systems V* by Ventana, an electronic meeting software that captures anonymous text-based ideas and displays the results in a shared screen environment; and *OptionFinder* from Option Technologies, an interactive GDSS that allows each meeting participant to vote using a numeric keypad attached to a PC then collects, calculates, and graphically displays results in real time.

Newer products that can be classified as GDSS systems include IBM's Sametime, Microsoft NetMeeting, and Citrix's GoToMyPC. These systems allow users to interact via a public or private computer network using audio, video, file sharing, Web page sharing, voting, and other functions depending on the setup at each individual computer. A server is used to run the software and host the meeting. Each participant can then log into the meeting using a Web browser. Users can share their desktops and even allow another group participant to take control. This is especially helpful in which technical support is needed or in which users can utilize a common screen to share ideas, yet are geographically dispersed.

Dissemination and Control of Information

Two aspects of information sharing among people that can have separate meanings but are many times interactive because of social agendas are the dissemination of information and the control of information. Dissemination can range from *freely available* as one would find in a public library to *strictly controlled*, as might be the case for government classified documents. Information control is easier when less information is available for dissemination, but as the volume of information grows, one technique used to protect it is through selective release. To accomplish this, an organization can simply filter the available information so that only those topics considered public by the organization are disseminated. This is especially prevalent when persuasion of the information receiver is the goal, such as in marketing/sales situations, politics, and fund raising activities. It is also prevalent when protecting confidential or proprietary information, or when misleading the information receiver is the goal (e.g., Gup).[14]

While these concepts are not new, the use of computers to store and disseminate data and information has brought with it an increased ability to disseminate voluminous amounts of data and to control what is disseminated. The Internet and the World Wide Web have proven to be a nearly universally available conduit for information sharing for which search engines have been developed so that interested researchers can find answers to just about any question that has an answer. The other half of this complex maze of information is the information providers who make both old and new information available in electronic form and post it in Web sites on the Internet. Users can easily formulate a simple query regarding an item of interest and submit it to a search engine that will return a myriad of related Web sites that are relevant to the query. These search engines are free to the user, but for this access, the user is subjected to advertising, which is not free, thus turning the search engine into a (hugely) profitable business.

Additional methods for dissemination of information are Web logs (blogs), wikis, and other commercial Web sites, especially those devoted to news and weather and to special interest groups such as professional organizations and political action committees. Commercial Web sites are usually devoted to advertising by providing company, product, and service information, but may be transaction-enabled so that consumers can make purchases directly online. Other forms of information disseminated electronically via the World Wide Web include legal (e.g., Legal-Zoom.com) and medical information (e.g., WebMD.com), government information such as governmental activities and welfare benefits, and information disseminated from professional societies, religious groups, lobbyists, and political organizers and terrorist organizations.

The mediating effect of the computer is seen first in the ability to store massive amounts of information in diverse places, as in blogs, wikis, and Web sites and second in the ability to quickly search through this information and retrieve only that which is relevant to the question.

Informatics

Informatics dates back to 1957 when Karl Steinbuch published a paper that dealt with automatic information processing. Since that time it has been defined and redefined so that it is now often confused with other disciplines such as computer science and cognitive science. For the purpose of this discourse, we focus solely on the automation of information processing as it deals with CMCs. In that sense informatics can be described as the treatment of data and information by computers to present it in such a way as to be understood and used by humans. It works like this: humans determine that certain raw facts must be stored for later use and so these facts are entered into an electronic database for storage onto electronic, magnetic, or optical media. When later retrieved, the data is processed by the computer (according to preprogrammed human instructions) and is presented in usable format as information. As the science of data storage and treatment grows, so does the ability for computers to do more of the work by picking the details that must be stored, organizing them in certain ways to eliminate repetition, and to search through available data banks to obtain only that which is necessary to solve a particular problem or perform a task.

As an example, consider a patient's medical record. The care providers can enter patient data into an electronic medical record so that it can be reviewed at a later date by a doctor who might diagnose or treat a condition, but must be cognizant of a previous history, which might add to or in some way affect the outcome of current treatment. As

more information is programmed into the computer, some decisions can be made by the computer itself, such as warning the doctor of possible drug interactions. Providing just-in-time information to the care giver is a highly desirable goal because it can improve the efficiency of medical care—improve its effectiveness and reduce its cost.[15,16] As knowledge workers extract information on the factors that lead a physician to a certain diagnosis and a course of treatment, and program this knowledge into a computer, expert systems are created that allow the less knowledgeable care giver to analyze and perform actions that were previously left to the more educated ones. The effects of this are to push more and more of care and treatment responsibilities to the lower end of the care giver spectrum such that nurses, physician's assistants, and midwives are now relied upon for care that has become "routine" but which used to require in-patient care.[17]

Computer-Supported Cooperative Work

The study of people working together using computerized technology is the focus of computer supported cooperative (or collaborative) work or CSCW. While this area can be classified under the umbrella of CMC, the goal of researchers in this area is to develop better ways to use computer technology to further enhance the group work process. Key concerns include trying to better understand the role time and location play in the process. The focus of CSCW is the social interaction of people, not technology. Typical topics in CSCW research include e-mail, shared applications, databases, hypertext, and other technical developments that improve a participants' awareness of other users and their activities. Like CMC in general, CSCW can be divided into synchronous and asynchronous domains. The term *Groupware* is used to refer to the technology used by individuals wishing to collaborate on a project. CSCW on the other hand refers to the field that studies human use of that technology.

APPLICATION VENUES

A second way of classifying CMC is to view how applications are used in various communication venues. In general these venues are: interpersonal, group, and mass communication.

Interpersonal

CMC systems developed specifically for communication support between two individuals or within a very small group are classified as interpersonal. Interpersonal communication systems can be synchronous or asynchronous with text, audio, and video based-communication being passed between system users. Synchronous communications operate in a real-time or near real-time atmosphere.

Text-based chat, video chat, and voice communication have all been implemented using computer technologies to facilitate synchronous interpersonal communication. Asynchronous systems generally are based on stored text, audio, or video files. One of the most common asynchronous interpersonal communication systems is e-mail, but other applications are gaining popularity with video, text, and audio implementations. These applications involve digitally storing information then transmitting them to the receiver who can listen to or view the message at his/her leisure.

Text-based chat and messaging

Chat and messaging systems provide a synchronous, text-based way to communicate with people all over the world. Most real-time chat systems rely on the Internet as a transmission medium. In general terms, Internet relay chat (IRC) systems consist of various separate networks of chat servers or machines that allow users to connect. Once connected to a server, text-based communication can begin. Besides providing a means for interpersonal communication, chat systems are often used to enable communication between larger groups of people. The largest chat networks at this time are EFnet, IRCnet, QuakeNet, and Undernet. In most applications, the user will run a program called the client and connect to a server on one of the nets. The server relays information to and from other servers on the same net. Some of the best-known client programs include mIRC which runs in a windows environment, X-chat runs under Mac's OS X, and ircII which runs on Linux systems. A client connected to a chat network has the option of joining one or more channels. These channels are used to categorize and separate conversations by topics. Chat networks may have several thousand channels available at any time and the user can generally initiate a new channel. Conversations may be public (everyone in the channel will see the typed messages) or they may be private (communication is between only invited people) depending on the way in which the channel was created.

IRC chat is currently declining in use largely due to the popularity of instant messenger software systems. Providers such as Yahoo, Microsoft, and AOL all have provided software focused on allowing users connected to the Internet via computer or mobile device to send and receive text messages in real time. Additionally, other features such as webcam use, file transfers, and message storage have added to the sophistication and desirability of these applications.

Video conferencing

Interpersonal video conferencing facilitates synchronous communication using video and audio. Like many CMC tools, this communication method can save time and reduce travel costs. Video conferencing software currently offers everything from compressed low-bandwidth images on desktop PCs with messenger software to full-motion, broadcast quality video. Frequent users may utilize private line video conferencing and less frequent users may opt for standard Internet access. Video conferencing can be either one-way or two-way interactive and provide a multimedia mix of voice and graphics in addition to video. Personal video conferencing is focused on one-on-one, person-to-person interaction. Other applications of video conferencing might be directed toward larger groups of people. One of the best-known video conferencing software packages is Polycom. Instant messenger softwares such as Yahoo!Messenger also allow video conferencing.

Voice communication

Audio conferencing programs digitize speech as the user speaks and sends the digital data over the Internet or other transmission media. Often this is called voice over IP or VOIP. In order to match sound quality comparable to regular telephone service, most audio communication applications compress sound information before transmitting. In full duplex conversations, sender and receiver can speak and hear the other person simultaneously. In half duplex applications, only one person can speak at a time.

Various commercial products have been developed to support audio CMC applications. Currently, cable television companies market Internet phones and applications such as Skype provide VOIP services for users via their computers. Messenger software also incorporates VOIP services.

The main disadvantage with VOIP communication applications is that most offer proprietary compression schemes, which make compatibility across applications difficult. Internet bottlenecks and transmission interruptions can also slow the natural cadence of communication as well.

E-mail

Electronic mail or e-mail provides a means of sending text-based messages over a communications channel. E-mail is similar to regular mail with an added advantage—speed. E-mail allows both the sender and receiver to asynchronously communicate at convenient times.

Asynchronous voice and video

Developed as an extension to e-mail software, asynchronous voice and video applications have become more popular. Digitized voice and video files are transmitted as attachments to email and viewed or heard at a time convenient to the receiver. Some messenger software allows asynchronous messages to be sent to off-line users.

Communication–
Corporate Art

Groups

CMC systems have also been developed specifically to support communication within groups. Like the interpersonal systems, group CMC has been developed to support both synchronous and asynchronous modes of communication. Text, audio, and video formats can be used to facilitate the exchange of information between system users. In terms of synchronous communication, chat systems, real-time video systems, networked meeting systems, multiple user dialog systems, and group collaboration systems have all been implemented. Asynchronous applications such as discussion boards, blogs, and electronic mailing list software have also been developed.

Chat systems

Most text-based chat systems were designed to support synchronous communication within groups. The same applications used to support interpersonal communication are also used to support groups over the Internet or other computer networks.

Real-time video

Several real-time video conferencing software packages are currently available. Some of these have been developed for use in educational settings. Of these, Polycom is one of the best known and most widely used. Polycom allows users to hold desktop video conferences using the Internet as a transmission channel.

Networked meeting software

Networked meeting software generally refers to a package which supports synchronous collaboration tools like group chats, shared whiteboards, multiuser editors, Web slide shows, or and shared applications running simultaneously on the Internet or other network. A number of these platforms have emerged in both the business and education arenas.

Multiple user dialog

A variety of multiuser environments have become available to support real-time group communication and collaboration over computer networks. Multiple User Dialogs or MUDs and related systems such as Object-Oriented MUDs or MOOs were derived from systems developed by the gaming community in the 1970s and 1980s. Many of the original MUDs have been extended to provide real-time conferencing and collaborative environments. Sometimes called text-based virtual realities, these multiuser environments can be used to facilitate group interaction. MUDs are generally text-based sites that allow people to connect to the same place at the same time. Unlike conventional chat rooms, they allow program manipulation and interaction through supporting software. In other words, the decision of one user can impact the perceived environment of another user. Synchronous communication is usually a component of the system.

When logged onto a MUD, an individual types rather than talks, reads rather than listens, and manipulates programs to describe themselves and the current state of the virtual environment. Resulting descriptions are generally text-based and in real time.

Recent advances in Internet bandwidth and software sophistication have enabled these same concepts to be enhanced with 3-D graphics and additional features such as voice. Gaming and social software systems such as World of Warcraft (WOW) and Second Life have added avatar capability to give users an appearance and facilitate communication more closely emulating real-world interpersonal communication.

Groupware and collaboration

Groupware encompasses a wide set of technologies used to support interpersonal and group collaboration. Groupware ranges from e-mail to Electronic Meeting Systems (EMS) to workflow collaboration tools. Generally speaking, groupware provides tools to solve *collaboration-oriented* business problems. The general concept driving groupware is the intent to foster collaboration and interpersonal productivity. This is accomplished through the technical automation and enhancement of a variety of tasks. Some groupware applications seek to integrate the functionality of e-mail with other technologies such as calendar/scheduling software. Others integrate group work processes, workflows, and meetings.[18]

Newsgroups and blogs

Unlike the related asynchronous interpersonal CMC technology, e-mail, newsgroups facilitate group asynchronous communication. Rather than receiving messages directly, newsgroup messages are posted to groups. These groups are organized into topic headings. The user can decide which topics are of interest and choose which messages to view or download. An early newsgroup system was called the Usenet. Usenet was an international forum where asynchronous discussions on myriad topics are constantly taking place. Usenet discussion was been described as liberating because of its anonymous nature. As in many applications of CMC, participants are judged on their words, rather than on outward appearance, age, or gender.

Newsgroups have declined in popularity over time until they have almost become a relic of early Internet use. Their functionality has largely been replaced with Blogs and discussion boards which provide much of the same functionality.

Electronic mailing lists

Like newsgroups, electronic mailing lists are an asynchronous group communication technology. Mailing lists use e-mail technology to disseminate information and facilitate discussion. In many mailing list systems, a user subscribes to a list. After acceptance, copies of every message sent to the group will be routed to each member on the list. If the list is moderated each message will be reviewed by a moderator prior to being disseminated to each member. Most mailing lists will have three email addresses. These are:

- The Subscription e-mail: To subscribe to the list.
- The List e-mail: To send messages to the list.
- The Administrator/Moderator e-mail: To contact the administrator or moderator of the list.

Mailing lists fall into two categories, manual and automatic. Manual lists are generally moderated or controlled by a particular person. This person accepts, rejects, or edits message contents. Automatic lists are not generally moderated. Instead computer programs called robots are used for administration. Two common robots are LISTSERV and Majordomo. Other types of mailing lists allow readers to read messages but not send new messages.

Social networking software

Like groupware, social networking software provides communication capabilities suited to group communication situations. However, beyond group communication, social networking also allows participants to engage in individual discussions and mass communication within a shared environment. In general, social networking focuses on the construction and development of like-minded online communities and provides a variety of Web-enabled ways for users to interact. Social networking is currently used by millions of people in both work settings and in their personal lives. Some of the most common social networking sites are MySpace, Facebook, Bebo, Orkut, Second Life (a virtual 3-D social network), and Cyworld (also 3-D).

Mass

CMC systems have also been developed specifically for mass communication. This means computer systems facilitate one-to-many communication in either a synchronous or asynchronous mode.

Text

Technologies such as mailing lists, newsgroups, and Web sites have been implemented to effectively allow one-to-many communication. This is particularly true of mediated newsgroups, Blogs, and mailing lists where a single individual is able to communicate to an audience which cannot be limited.

Audio

Systems have been developed to present real-time audio over the Internet and other networks. Users with conventional multimedia personal computers, a network connection, and the appropriate software are able to listen to real-time sound broadcasts. The term podcasts has been used as a descriptor.

Video

One-to-many video applications operate over the Internet and other networks. Multicast provides one-to-many and many-to-many network delivery services. Sometimes called video casting, vidcasts, video podcasts, video streaming has become a very important Internet application. Web sites such as YouTube and iTunes have provided infrastructure that has allowed video casting to become commonplace.

CMC RESEARCH

CMC research has been found in a multitude of disciplines including communications and journalism, library science, engineering and computer science, business, criminology and forensics, knowledge and operations management, education, psychology, including cognitive science, sociology and anthropology, law and ethics, and both human and veterinary medicine. Research is not limited to each single discipline, however, and the norm is more multidisciplinary. As examples, engineering teams with medicine to discover new ways of treating and detecting disease and communicating these techniques to both engineers and physicians; computer science may team with anthropology to discover new ways to analyze ancient texts.

The range of research is also quite broad. Research may be focused entirely on hardware improvement so that data and information can be shared much more quickly than before. (As an example, consider that a 10 GB connection that stretches across the United States is fast enough to transmit an entire 24-volume encyclopedia from Los Angeles before the first bit is received in New York.) Research is also focused on software improvements to allow organizations to do more with the hardware that they have. (In fact software development often creates a need for further hardware improvement because newer software usually requires more powerful processing than was previously available.)

As research helps humankind to improve the sharing of information and to solve intractable problems, much of the problem solving is turned over to the computer because of its ability to store massive amounts of data and recall it quickly and to process massive numbers of calculations in a short period of time. Thus, this type of research is *auto-catalytic* in nature—bigger and more powerful machines allow us to solve more problems, and this in turn provides even more problems to solve. This germinates the need for bigger and better machines, and the cycle is repeated.

The other end of the research spectrum focuses on the user. Such questions as the perceived value of an information system, the perceived success of an installed information system, and how well a user is able to interact with a system (so-called human–computer interaction) are some of areas which have received a lot of attention.

Additional topical areas fall in between the devices and the programs and the users, and include group work and interactions, individual work, performance and productivity enhancement, software that supports social networking, religion and cross cultural issues, security, cyber and information warfare, comparisons of different communications techniques, and entertainment.

Techniques used to accomplish CMC are also studied. Most people are familiar with instant messaging, chat rooms, electronic mail, blogging, and wikis and these areas have received attention in the literature. Newer techniques include VoIP, which provides telephone service over the Internet instead of the legacy telephone circuits, text messaging and other forms of communications using cellular and satellite technology, and audio and video conferencing using tools suitable for Internet transmission. One reason that the move from the legacy telephone circuit to the Internet infrastructure gets so much attention from both researchers and practitioners is that the older telephone systems utilize a method known as circuit switching, while the Internet uses a different technique born of data communications technologies called packet switching. With circuit switching, a physical line is held during the course of a phone call; with packet switching, a communications message is divided into chucks called packets and each is sent autonomously to the receiver. The need to tie up a single physical line is eliminated with packet switching and alternate routes may be used when sending the packets. This technology brings both advantages and disadvantages and so much effort is devoted to analyzing and improving upon the technique.

REFERENCES

1. Santoro, G.M. What is computer-mediated communication?. In *Computer Mediated Communication and the Online Classroom. Overview and Perspectives*; Berge, Z. L., Collins, M.P., Eds.; Hampton: Cresskill, NJ, 1995; Vol. 1.
2. Johansen, R. Vallee, J. Spangler, K. *Electronic Meetings: Technical Alternatives and Social Choices*, Addison-Wesley: Reading, MA, 1979.
3. Rice, R.E.; Case, D. Electronic message systems in the university: A description of use and utility. J. Commun. **1983**, 33 (1) –152.
4. Wellens, A.R. Group situation awareness and distributed decision making. In *Individual and Group Decision Making*; Castellan, N.J., Jr., Ed.; Lawrence Erlbaum: Hillsdale, NJ, 1993; 267–293.
5. Pinsonneault, A.; Kraemer, K.L. The effects of electronic meetings on group processes and outcomes: An assessment of the empirical research. Eur. J. Operat. Res. **1989**, 46 (2), 143–161.
6. Jessup, L.M. Valacich, J.S. On the study of group support systems: An introduction to group support system research and development. In *Group Support Systems*; Jessup, L.M., Valacich, J.S., Eds.; Macmillan: New York, 1993; 3–7.
7. Ferris, P. What is CMC? An overview of scholarly definitions. Available at http://www.december.com/cmc/mag/1997/jan/ferapp.html (February 22, 1997).
8. Berge, Z.L.; Collins, M. Computer-mediated scholarly discussion groups. Comput. Educ. **1995**, 24 (3), 183–189.
9. Nunamaker, J.F., Jr.; Briggs, R.O.; Mittleman, D.D.; Vogel, D.R.; Balthazard, P.A. Lessons from a dozen years of group support system research: A discussion of lab and field findings. J. Manag. Inform. Syst. Winter **1996–1997**, 163–207.
10. DeSanctis, G.; Gallupe, R.B. A foundation for the study of group decision support systems. Manag. Sci. **1987**, 33 (5), 589–609.
11. Jessup, L.M.; Connoly, T.; Galegher, J. The effects of anonymity on GDSS group process with an idea-generating task. MIS Quart. September **1990**, 14 (3), 312–321.
12. Alavi, M. Group decision support systems. J. Inform. Syst. Manag. Summer **1991**, 36–41.
13. Thornton, C.; Lockhart, E. Groupware of electronic brainstorming. J. Manag. Syst. October **1994**, 10–12.
14. Gup, T. The short distance between secrets and lies. Columb. J. Rev. May/June **2002**, 74–75.
15. Peters, D.H.; Kohli, M.; Mascarenhas, M.; Rao, K. Can computers improve patient care by primary health care workers in India?. Intl. J. Qual. Health Care. **2006**, 18 (6), 437–447.
16. Mitchell, C.C.; Ashley, S.W.; Zimmer, M.J.; Moore, F.D., Jr. Predicting future staffing needs at teaching hospitals. Archiv. Surg. April **2007**, (142), 329–331.
17. Alper, P.R. The decline of the family doctor. Pol. Rev. May **1995**, (124), 41–62.
18. Coleman, D. *Groupware: Technology and Applications*, Prentice Hall: Englewood Cliffs, NJ, 1995.

Computer-Supported Cooperative Work (CSCW)

Kevin L. Mills
National Institute of Standards and Technology, Gaithersburg, Maryland, U.S.A.

Abstract

In this entry, we consider various definitions for computer-supported cooperative work (CSCW) and related terms, and we draw outlines around the large scope covered by CSCW. Subsequently, we consider the main challenges that have impeded us from realizing the great promise of CSCW and we identify some factors that could help CSCW succeed. We review the current state of practice for CSCW, along with some promising technologies. We close with our outlook for CSCW.

Few contest the claim that modern information technology, supported by computers and communications, contributes to a dramatic improvement in productivity and effectiveness among individuals engaged in a wide range of tasks. Computer-supported cooperative work (CSCW) aims to provide similar improvements for "multiple individuals working together in a conscious way in the same production process or in different but related production processes."[1] If achieved, this aim, which has proven elusive during the relatively few years since the term CSCW was coined in 1984, promises to multiply our productivity, perhaps by more than the square of the number of users, as compared against the productivity improvements that personal computers provide to each of us as individuals.

In this entry, we consider various definitions for CSCW and related terms, and we draw outlines around the large scope covered by CSCW. Subsequently, we consider the main challenges that have impeded us from realizing the great promise of CSCW and we identify some factors that could help CSCW succeed. We review the current state of practice for CSCW, along with some promising technologies. We close with our outlook for CSCW.

DEFINITIONS

The term CSCW first appeared in 1984 to identify an interdisciplinary workshop organized by Irene Greif and Paul Cashman at MIT in August of that year for invited researchers to consider how computers might be used more effectively to support people in their various work arrangements. A second, open workshop on CSCW followed in December 1986, attracting 300 people. Since then, an international CSCW workshop[2] has been held every 2 years starting in 1988. Because CSCW is such a new area of investigation, one might expect significant controversy and fluidity regarding its definition and focus. Surveys of the CSCW literature support this expectation.

Most observers seem to agree that CSCW, an emerging interdisciplinary field, entails some combination of computing and social science. For example, Greif[3] suggests that CSCW is an interdisciplinary endeavor encompassing artificial intelligence, computer science, psychology, sociology, organizational theory, and anthropology. Similarly, Paul Dourish[4] sees CSCW as a highly diverse discipline involving psychology, sociology, anthropology, network communication, distributed systems, user-interface design, and usability. Beyond agreement on the interdisciplinary nature of CSCW, opinions vary widely about a detailed definition and an exact focus for the field.

CSCW researchers seem to adopt one of two main viewpoints. One viewpoint is technology-centric, placing an emphasis on devising ways to design computer technology to better support people working together. For example, Greif[1] defines CSCW as a distinct and identifiable research field focused on the role of the computer in support of group work. A second viewpoint is work-centric, placing an emphasis on understanding work processes with an aim to better design computer systems so as to support group work. For example, Suchman[5] defines CSCW as "the design of computer-based technologies with explicit concern for the socially organized practices of their intended users." Similarly, Bannon and Schmidt[6] believe that "CSCW should be conceived as an endeavor to understand the nature of cooperative work as a foundation to designing information systems to support the work." In a subsequent article, Schmidt and Bannon[7] restate their position, and identify several important questions, listed below, which they believe CSCW researchers must answer.

1. What characteristics distinguish cooperative work from individual work, and what support requirements derive from those characteristics?
2. Why do people work together, and how can computers by applied to address the requirements arising from the specific reasons?

Encyclopedia of Library and Information Sciences, Fourth Edition DOI: 10.1081/E-ELIS4-120043882

3. How can coordination requirements arising during cooperative work be accomplished more easily using computer technology?

4. What do the identified requirements imply for the development of system architectures and services?

The main emphasis of researchers holding the work-centric viewpoint is to understand cooperative work so as to design computer systems to better support cooperative work. The main emphasis of researchers holding the technology-centric viewpoint is to design computer systems to better support the requirements of cooperative work. Further, as Mahling[8] observes, some social scientists also work in the field of CSCW.

Typically, social scientists working in the field of CSCW aim to describe and analyze the behavior that they see as people work together: focusing purely on description, not prescription. On the other hand, work-centric and technology-centric CSCW researchers aim to create computer systems that address the requirements of cooperative work groups. As such, these researchers hope that the social scientists, through their studies, will prescribe the requirements for successful CSCW systems. To date, this expectation remains unrealized, but much energy has been expended as CSCW researchers work to understand and reconcile these different views. The outlooks suggested by Suchman and by Bannon and Schmidt indicate that some researchers are attempting to work across the gap between description and prescription. In fact, some consensus appears to be building among researchers that CSCW is fundamentally a design-oriented research area. Under this view, the main focus of CSCW should be toward the design of systems that embody a deep understanding of the nature of cooperative work, and its forms and practices. As we will outline in a bit, the current scope of cooperative work, in terms of forms and practices, proves so large that the challenge for CSCW researchers may be overwhelming. First, though, we need to provide some explanation about the many confusing terms and concepts surrounding the field of CSCW.

SELECTED TERMS

Due to its broad scope and relative youth, the field of CSCW encompasses a wide array of specific and sometimes confusing terms. In this section, we introduce and attempt to distinguish among some of the more common terms. People often use *groupware*[9] as a catchy term to refer to CSCW. More specifically, we can think of groupware as computer software and related computer networks that enable collections of people to work cooperatively. Groupware might include application-sharing programs, videoconferencing software, software for tracking document changes, electronic-mail software, and software to support the collaborative viewing of Web pages. *Workflow*[10] is another term

often used to refer to CSCW. Workflow deals with the specific issues surrounding movement of transactions through a set of people who must act together to complete some required work. In this sense, workflow is a more specific term than groupware; however, workflow software typically supports formal work processes, and so is often excluded from the scope of groupware, which is usually considered to be software that supports less formal forms of collaboration. *Team computing*, a term coined at Xerox PARC,[11] refers to collaborative systems to support group meetings. In general, such meetings are envisioned to occur in face-to-face settings. More recently and more conventionally, another term, *electronic meetings*,[12] has been used to describe group meetings enhanced through the use of computers, networks, and software. A less common term, *media spaces*,[13] occasionally appears in discussions of CSCW. The intent of media spaces is to provide a virtual meeting space where distributed collaborators can congregate electronically, meet informally, and gain all the advantages of collaborators who work together within the same physical location.

KEY DIMENSIONS OF CSCW

As indicated in the brief discussion of definitions and selected terms, CSCW involves a broad, multidimensional scope. Here we aim to distinguish some of the important dimensions inherent in CSCW, and to clarify the essential features that must be supported by CSCW systems. Table 1 lists 10 key dimensions of the complex design space for CSCW; for each dimension the table indicates two extreme design points. One important dichotomy facing designers of CSCW technology occurs along the *time* dimension: is there a requirement to support cooperative work that occurs simultaneously (synchronously) or separately (asynchronously) or both? Another decision relates

Table 1 Ten key dimensions in the CSCW design space.

Dimension	Extreme design points
Time	Fully simultaneous vs. fully disjoint
Space	All collocated vs. fully distributed participants
Group size	Small team vs. mass audience
Interaction style	Assigned workflow vs. ad hoc
Context	Single vs. unlimited collaborations per participant
Infrastructure	Fully homogeneous vs. fully heterogeneous
Collaborator mobility	All in fixed locations vs. all mobile
Privacy	Assigned by authority vs. controlled by participant
Participant selection	Assigned by authority vs. free for all
Extensibility	None vs. all functionality defined by participants

to *space*: must the individual collaborators be physically located at the same site, such as a room or an auditorium? Of course, a more complicated requirement might also exist for multiple, physically distant, sites of collocated collaborators to be brought together virtually. A third important dimension is *group size*: must the system support a small team, a department, an enterprise, or a mass audience? A fourth dimension must consider *interaction style*: does the group require support for planned or impromptu interactions or both? A fifth dimension covers *context*: do group members participate in many distinct collaborations or do they tend to participate in only one or few? A sixth dimension relates to *infrastructure*: will the group permit the deployment of homogeneous computing platforms tailored to collaboration or must the CSCW system operate across already deployed, heterogeneous computing systems? A seventh dimension defines *collaborator mobility*: will the collaborators remain at fixed locations or will some or all of the collaborators move among locations? An eighth dimension considers the degree of *privacy*: how much information can be made available about the collaborators and who should control the release of information? A ninth dimension considers *participant selection*: must the group's participants be assigned by existing group members or by some external authority or can participants self-select or search for additional participants from a larger population? A tenth dimension covers *extensibility*: does the CSCW system define the complete functionality available to collaborators or can the collaborators extend the functionality to support changing needs? These 10 dimensions provide a rich design space through which the developers of CSCW technology must navigate. Despite such richness, CSCW researchers have been able to focus on some essential features that CSCW systems must provide.

Essential Features in CSCW Systems

Much of the CSCW research literature focuses on providing collaborators with tools to support *articulation work*:[7] establishing and evolving organizational structure, plans and schedules, standard operating procedures, and conceptual schemes for classifying and indexing information objects. In other words, CSCW aims to support the overhead that arises when work is conducted among distributed, independent agents. Articulation work includes two important threads: construction and management of a common, shared information space and workflow management. In the past, designers of workflow systems automated written procedures as maintained by each target organization, which in all cases turned out to be a fictional, idealized version of the real work process. Now, CSCW researchers understand that most work situations entail a continuous renegotiation of task descriptions and allocations. Further, researchers understand that collaborative communication must allow for ambiguity in

the negotiation processes surrounding articulation work. To support articulation work, CSCW researchers investigate essential design features in five main areas: communication, configuration, coordination, information access, and interaction. Table 2 indicates some of the specific features encompassed by each of these areas. We discuss these features further below.

Communication

Successful negotiation on issues related to organization, planning, and control requires provision of an effective system for communication among the individuals involved. For this reason, human-to-human communication is one of the key features needed for CSCW. Previous research[14] suggests that audio is the most important channel for successful communication. Some CSCW researchers[15,16] have investigated the effectiveness of conference calls, or open-loop multiparty audio channels. Other researchers[17] have shown the value of shared audio channels even when a group of workers is physically collocated. The importance of collaborating around data or documents is also well established. For this reason, a group audio channel is sometimes augmented with a separate distribution channel for sharing views of a document and for highlighting on the document. More sophisticated communication systems integrate audio and data distribution channels together with video channels to compose a form of multimedia conferencing. Whether communicating live (synchronously) or in playback mode (asynchronously), humans can benefit from such multimedia channels.

For live communication, multimedia transmissions often stream data among multiple points in some form of videoconferencing arrangement so that all parties can simultaneously see and hear each other, along with any relevant documents. Satisfactory video viewing usually requires a rate of at least 15 frames/sec. Typically, multimedia communication includes an associated audio channel that requires reasonably tight synchronization with the video, within at least 200 msec. These factors place a

Table 2 Five CSCW design areas and some key design features in each.

Design area	Key features
Communication	Asynchronous, audio, data, private, shared, structured, synchronous, text, unstructured, video
Configuration	Adaptation, composition, evolution, extension
Coordination	Access control, concurrency, consistency, delegation, scheduling, versioning
Information access	Distribution, filtering, retrieval, structure
Interaction	Attention management, awareness, context management, relationship establishment and maintenance

Communication–
Corporate Art

premium on the quality of service (QoS) provided by the underlying data transmission channels. For this reason, much of the research[18] related to networking for CSCW has investigated techniques to provide the necessary QoS transmission characteristics. Currently, the required QoS can usually be arranged by configuring a conference topology to support multiparty communications at transmission bandwidths (typically ranging up to 2.0 Mbps) provided by H.320-compliant products. Bandwidth requirements for satisfactory multimedia conferencing vary depending upon the configuration of the devices at conference endpoints—a minimal conferencing arrangement typically requires around 300 Kbps. Unfortunately, most collaborators must use the more ubiquitous Internet, which does not provide built-in mechanisms to request and achieve specific targets for QoS. For this reason, much network research[19] related to CSCW has focused on establishing QoS for multiparty transmissions on the Internet.

In the absence of either multimedia conferencing support or audio communication channels, successful collaboration can still be conducted through the use of text-based interaction systems, known variously as chat (instant-messaging) applications or chat rooms. Text-based chat applications can also provide private channels for a subset of collaborators to hold side conversations outside the purview of the main proceedings. As chat applications become more sophisticated, they can also provide a convenient means to distribute documents, data, and images related to a collaborative session. Beyond free-flowing text-based chat applications, CSCW researchers have developed and assessed a number of techniques for enforcing structure on the dialog and interactions associated with a collaborative session. Such systems, which include newsgroups, dialog-threading applications, and indexed electronic-mail lists, have proven useful in limited ways. Studies[20,21] have shown that the rather fixed capabilities provided by most of these systems can sometimes impede their effectiveness as a collaboration tool.

Due to the growing role of globalization in the workplace, CSCW researchers have begun to investigate how to facilitate cross-cultural communications, which must bridge differences in natural languages and social norms. Setlock and colleagues[22] investigated the influence of cultural differences among teams, comprising American and Chinese members who work synchronously, either face-to-face or through computers, to solve two tasks. The teams worked in English. The study compares teams, consisting of all Americans, all Chinese, and a mix of Americans and Chinese, with respect to several factors (e.g., communication style, quality of interaction, persuasion, and task performance). Yamashita and Ishida[23] considered effects of machine translation on teams, consisting of Chinese, Japanese, and Korea members, who worked through instant-messaging software to agree on an ordering of 10 figures. The study compared working with the aid of machine-translation software against collaborating

in a common second language (English). The area of cross-cultural and cross-lingual collaboration is due for increased study.

Configuration

Whether supporting small or large groups, CSCW systems have proven difficult to setup and configure. The scope of such systems is large, covering several layers of system and application software and many points in a distributed topology, both within the network and at network end points. Though relatively few CSCW researchers[24] have chosen to investigate these issues, we suspect that the viability of CSCW systems depends in some large measure on the ease with which collaborative sessions can be established. A number of researchers[25–29] have investigated the difficult problems associated with: (1) extending the capabilities of CSCW systems after deployment; (2) automating adaptation to changes in available resources for transmission and display of data; (3) composing CSCW systems from a range of supporting components; and (4) evolving system components to suit the changing needs of collaborators. Research surrounding the configuration of CSCW systems has not yet received the attention it warrants. Successful adoption of CSCW technology will certainly require an ease of configuration that at least equals and tracks the ease with which desktop computer software can be configured.

Coordination

Much of the communication associated with CSCW is used to coordinate work among the disparate, independent parties engaged in a collaborative endeavor. For this reason, CSCW researchers investigate features and mechanisms to help groups coordinate their activities. A major aspect of group coordination involves scheduling, whether of people, processes, or resources. While some CSCW researchers[30] have investigated techniques to more tightly integrate calendaring software with other aspects of collaboration, such as document distribution, situation awareness, and personnel location tracking, more of the research to date has focused on process or workflow scheduling and coordination. For example, Glance et al.[31] investigated process-structure grammars as a means to introduce flexibility into workflow languages. Such grammars describe the relationships among documents and tasks, and use constraints to express soft dependencies, rather than the hard dependencies more often introduced with process-flow languages. Similar goals motivate related research[32] by Paul Dourish and colleagues. Other researchers[33] focus on mechanisms that permit coordination policies to be established and changed as collaboration unfolds. CSCW researchers should also be interested in techniques for expressing, catching, and handling exceptions during the processing of workflows.

The need for such techniques arises because to date implementing workflow procedures has proven brittle. Researchers must also take interest in the issues surrounding delegation of authority and work within a workflow. Such techniques are often used by people in day-to-day work but are usually not supported well in automated workflow systems.

Aside from coordinating direct activities among people, CSCW requires mechanisms to coordinate indirect activities as individuals asynchronously access and update shared documents, files, objects, and other resources. The needed mechanisms include: control of access and concurrency and maintenance of versioning and consistency. A number of researchers have investigated concurrency control techniques. For example, Prakash[34] has uncovered a range of concerns that arise when providing concurrency control for concurrent editing applications. These concerns include: (1) ensuring adequate response time for shared edit operations; (2) maintaining consistency of results under simultaneous updates; (3) providing adequate capabilities for a per-user "Undo" feature; and (4) ensuring effective awareness of the activities of others engaged in editing the same files. Adopting a formal approach, Ressel and colleagues[35] use a transformation-oriented scheme to represent and reason about concurrency and "Undo" operators, as used within group editors. In a more general look at the relevant issues, Munson[36] and Dewan[37] discuss the larger design space, encompassing a framework for consistency control in synchronous, shared-access applications.

Achieving effective concurrency and consistency control in information sharing applications requires two underlying foundations: access-control policies and versioning policies. Access-control policies establish the ground rules under which various users may access shared information objects. Versioning policies define the ground rules under which different versions of the same object may be combined into a single, consistent copy. In a typical desktop computer, a small set of standard access-control policies is applied to each directory and file that a user creates. Should the user need to extend access to various groups for particular objects, the access-control policies can become quite difficult to establish, understand, and verify. This is one aspect of the problem that faces designers of access-control policies for CSCW. As discussed by Keith Edwards[38] another aspect of this difficult problem is that access-control policies must be changeable during run-time as the requirements of a collaboration change.

While most access-control policies seek to enforce consistency by limiting access to a single user at once, many collaborative activities, such as joint authoring of documents, proceed more efficiently when multiple users can access the same information simultaneously. In such cases, consistency among independent, concurrent updates becomes a key concern. In an attempt to provide an effective system for coauthoring of documents, Rees and colleagues[39] describe a mechanism that separates proposed changes to a shared document space from the orthogonal issues of concurrency control and repository management. Specifically, as a collaborator updates a copy of a shared document, the updates are recorded in change proposals that track information the collaborator expects to revise and that record consistency relationships that must be maintained. Once recorded, change proposals can themselves be treated as shared documents. At an appropriate point, multiple versions of shared documents can be combined and residual inconsistencies can be raised for case-by-case consideration. The area of concurrency and consistency control within multiuser distributed systems remains fertile territory for research, whether applied to CSCW or other relevant applications.

Information Access

All collaborations require access to information in two classes: subject-matter information and collaboration-support information. Subject-matter information includes the data, images, video clips, spreadsheets, and Web pages that contain content related to the subject being discussed in a collaborative session. Collaboration-support information encompasses overhead data, such as session transcripts (which can include all media types: audio, video, text, images, and interaction events) of previous discussions and agreements about plans, procedures, and schedules for the work. CSCW requires the ability to structure, retrieve, distribute, filter, and index information in both classes, whatever the media type. CSCW researchers, as well as researchers in the related fields of information management and digital libraries, work on all of these techniques.

Vannevar Bush[40] provided one of the earliest discussions of automated structuring and retrieval of information when he outlined the possibility of the *memex*, an associative memory enabling the retrieval of information encoded on microfilm, and permitting people to construct an associative web of trails through the information. The ideas behind Bush's memex foreshadowed several later developments, such as the World Wide Web, publish-subscribe tuple spaces,[41] and globally accessible persistent storage. These later developments (discussed in subsequent sections of this entry) seem poised to provide CSCW with a tremendous increase in capabilities to structure and access information. For example, hypertext, a direct descendant of Bush's memex, possesses some significant strengths exploited early on by researchers of Web-based systems for collaboration[42–45] and later adopted in several commercial products, such as Netscape Collabra™, WebMeeting™, and eAuditorium™. Unfortunately, as discussed by Jeff Conklin,[46] hypertext has two significant drawbacks as an information access technique. First, users often experience disorientation while navigating through hypertext, finding it difficult to identify their current place in the information, such as their route to the current page and routes to return to previous pages. Second, users who structure information as hypertext often report a significant cognitive burden associated with creating, naming, and tracking a large number of hyperlinks. For these reasons, information structuring and access remain important research topics.

Information distribution provides one possible alternative to information retrieval. Information distribution aims to automatically promulgate relevant information to people who might be interested. Such capabilities can be very handy for disseminating information in collaborative sessions. In general, information dissemination systems require some means of description, coupled with mechanisms for matching and delivery. Information subscribers must be able to indicate the characteristics of information they would find interesting and producers must be able to indicate the essential characteristics intrinsic to the information that they create. With these characteristics properly expressed, a computer program can identify matches between subscriber needs and producer data. Once matches are made, distribution can be carried out through a messaging system.

The key issues in information distribution surround description techniques. As discussed by Thomas Malone and colleagues,[47] semistructured messages enable computers to process automatically a much wider range of information than would be possible with free-form text messages alone. In addition, semistructured messages enable people to communicate nonroutine information, which would be impossible within the confines of rigidly structured messages. Malone points out that much of the processing that people already undertake reflects a set of semistructured messages, so even if no automated processing is anticipated, people can benefit from having an available set of semistructured message templates to help them formulate messages that contain all relevant information for particular tasks. Further, by adopting a set of semistructured message templates, automated systems could be adopted and incrementally enhanced more easily over time. Malone and colleagues also illustrate that semistructured message templates can be arranged in a type hierarchy that can then be supported with a consistent set of display-oriented editors to help people construct messages. Semistructured messages seem particularly appropriate for collaborative systems because both computers and people can create, read, interpret, and act on the same messages. Semistructured messages foreshadow the later development of the eXtensible Markup Language (XML), a means to specify computer-interpretable messages that can also be read by people.

While semistructured messages work well for text data, much of the information associated with collaborative systems exists in the form of image, video, and audio information. Such rich, but unstructured, information presents significant problems with respect to access. The key problems revolve around indexing multimedia information so that people can access it through filters and queries. Some researchers[48] investigate techniques that employ speech-recognition technology to create text transcripts from audio streams. Once an unstructured text database exists, additional technologies can be applied to create multiple indices that identify people, places, dates, and topics included within the data. Using this approach, an audio stream, or repository of audio streams, can be indexed for retrieval or filtering. Some researchers[49] consider audio and video together. Video presents new challenges associated with automatically dividing video clips into scenes or segments. While the audio indexing techniques can help in this process, other techniques can also be applied. For example, if an audio–video stream comes with an associated closed-caption text stream, then information can be extracted directly using topic and subject identification techniques. Other techniques can be applied directly to the video frames in an attempt to identify scene changes. Further, some researchers[50,51] attempt to look inside video frames to identify objects and to extract text, for example on trucks, buildings, and street signs. While analysis and indexing of multimedia streams is typically tackled off-line, some researchers[52] are attempting to perform a rough level of filtering in real-time. The challenging problems surrounding automated indexing of multimedia data continue as targets for active research; however, progress along these lines promises to boost substantially the capabilities of CSCW systems that include video and audio conferencing.

Interaction

CSCW must include support for people-to-people interaction at a distance: maintaining awareness of the state and activities of others, managing attention and context when a collaborator becomes involved simultaneously in multiple distinct collaborative sessions, and building and maintaining relationships among people who meet infrequently, if ever. These problems might be among the most difficult that CSCW researchers must address. Still, some progress can be discerned.

An important focus of interaction research deals with awareness at a distance. In order to stimulate ad hoc discussions or to coordinate work, collaborators working in distinct locations must maintain some awareness about the availability and progress of others. This can also extend to awareness about the state of collaborators in multiple, distinct collaborative sessions. The issue is further complicated by the fact that people seem averse to allowing others to peak into their personal space or activities. In a sense, there appears to be a fine line between maintaining awareness and allowing unwanted intrusions. Hudson and Smith[53] have considered associated tradeoffs. Several researchers[54,55] investigate video-based techniques that can reduce the problem of intrusiveness, while simultaneously facilitating ad hoc interactions among distributed groups. Nomura and colleagues[56] experiment with techniques to provide peripheral awareness through shared workspaces. Others[57–59] propose mechanisms to provide awareness within the context of application sharing and groupware systems. Some researchers[60] even imagine that desktop computers can be used successfully for impromptu interactions. Taking a less constrained view, Tollmar and colleagues[61] have designed and experimented with several techniques intended to enhance social awareness within the work place. Awareness in CSCW systems remains an important and fertile area for research.

Another difficult challenge for CSCW researchers involves development of techniques to effectively manage the attention of collaborators, especially when individuals may become involved in multiple, but separate, collaborative sessions at the same time. Belotti and Bly[62] examined the problem of context management in an environment where people move among physical locations to engage in various collaborations. Fitzpatrick and her colleagues[63] studied the problem for virtual collaborations; specifically, they investigated the issues that arose as a group of system administrators collaborated remotely with each other and with system users to identify and solve problems with the configuration of computer systems. Results from the study influenced the design of Orbit,[64] a research system to support desktop collaboration where the user engages simultaneously in multiple collaborative contexts. Other researchers attempt to solve the problem of context management through the use of various metaphors, such as "virtual places" and "virtual spaces"[65] and "team rooms."[66] Even in a physical workspace, many people find it difficult to manage multiple working contexts, as well as to manage their own time and attention. Computer systems bring the possibility for people to engage in many more activities at once. Aiding people to effectively manage these more numerous contexts remains a challenging research issue.

CSCW researchers must also address a subtler problem: how can people find appropriate collaborators and then build and maintain effective relationships without much physical contact? These issues will become increasingly important as business interactions move more and more to the digital realm, which can reduce the inconvenience, cost, and other inefficiencies associated with physical travel to face-to-face meetings. One typical problem confronting people, even within the same organization, is to find appropriate experts to answer a specific question or problem, or to apply a particular body of knowledge. For this reason, several researchers[67–69] have investigated systems to facilitate finding knowledge and expertise through a social network. Other researchers[70–72] have explored the use of collaborative filtering systems, which do not necessarily include information about the expertise of the participants but which can be applied on a large

scale, such as the World Wide Web (the Web). Since the Web encompasses millions of users, some researchers attempt to leverage typical behaviors among Web users to help connect them to possible collaborators without incurring additional cognitive overhead. For example, Payton and colleagues[73] devised a novel way for people to discover potential collaborators based on comparisons among individual patterns of Web browsing, which are typically logged by a computer. After converting logs of Web accesses into graphs associated with each user, a matching program can measure similarities and differences and then bring people into contact through electronic mail. Included within this research are several mechanisms intended to protect individual privacy, a concern that might be raised by potential users when a computer system is applied to passively monitor their activities. Even in some face-to-face situations, such as large conferences or meetings, electronic systems can be used to help stimulate new collaborations. For example, Borovoy and colleagues[74] developed "Meme Tags," wearable devices with displays that enable conference attendees to electronically share succinct ideas or opinions. Based on the shared information, conference attendees could form into groups with similar interests. Behind the scenes, a server system monitors and collects information about tag exchanges and then reflects the information back to conference attendees in "Community Mirrors," which are publicly visible displays that present real-time views of the unfolding dynamics within a community. Similar ideas have been used within cyberspace to permit groups of individuals with related interests to form and interact from among millions of undifferentiated participants. Usenet[75] pioneered in 1979 by Jim Ellis, provides one of the earliest examples. Usenet enables the creation of newsgroups focused on particular topics. Individual users can discover the existence of such groups, subscribe to those of interest, and then participate in asynchronous conversations through threaded, text postings. The more popular newsgroups sustain interactions among hundreds or thousands of users. Newsgroups continued in popularity as tens of millions of users moved onto the Internet during the 1990s. In fact, newsgroups have helped to form the ocean of Internet users into smaller collections of folks with similar interests. From these smaller collections, some individuals form and sustain deeper connections, a human art which can require additional assistance in the digital domain.

Establishing, developing, and maintaining human relationships typically relies on:[13] (1) informal social contact; (2) chance encounters in hallways; (3) chats before and after formal meetings; (4) discovery of shared interests; (5) feelings of community; and (6) implicit knowledge of the state of others. While many of these factors occur naturally among collocated people, some researchers[76] have observed that social responsibility and commitment appear to diminish when people do not meet face-to-face.

Communication–
Corporate Art

For this reason, CSCW researchers often attempt to recreate these relationship-building factors when people must interact at a distance. We have surveyed much of the relevant research already. A few CSCW researchers[77,78] have focused specifically on building relationships with significant depth and trust while working at a distance. Research surrounding these topics will increase in importance as work becomes more reliant on digital interaction at a distance.

CSCW CHALLENGES

To derive the greatest benefit from CSCW, the supporting technology must infiltrate as widely as possible throughout the populace. CSCW researchers have conducted studies that support this assertion. For example, Steve Whittaker,[79] in a study of users of Lotus Notes, a technology intended to support asynchronous collaboration, found that both conversations and the creation of group archives proved more successful with large numbers of diverse participants, as compared against small, more homogeneous, project teams. Similarly, Whittaker reports that a large database of material was more likely to be used and extended than a small database. Further, the presence of a moderator was found to inhibit rather than enhance discussions. In other words, Whittaker's study suggests that the larger and more diverse the population of participants and the more free-flowing the conversations, the more effective the results.

What factors inhibit the widespread adoption of CSCW technology? First, CSCW technology generally relies on a big stack of computer and network technology, operating systems and protocols, data formats and user-interface devices. The dissemination of such capabilities, while growing at a rapid pace, is far from ubiquitous, and even where these technologies have penetrated, the systems, protocols, formats, and software is far from homogeneous. We can safely observe that the telephone handset appears to be ubiquitous, while the networked desktop computer is far less so. Some progress can be discerned regarding de facto standardization of desktop computer systems and software, as well as the adoption of standards associated with the World Wide Web. Even so, these technical underpinnings on which CSCW depends continue to evolve. Further, there exists little penetration of the systems, and associated networking QoS required, to support effective videoconferencing. These facts suggest that to some large degree the pace of progress in CSCW depends upon, and must be tied directly to, those supporting technologies that achieve near ubiquitous adoption. On the other hand, as selected technologies evolve over time to become ubiquitous, the degrees of freedom available to CSCW researchers and designers also diminish.

Even assuming that the necessary networking and computing technologies achieve complete penetration throughout society, the deployment of CSCW may still be retarded by various administrative and policy decisions, which paradoxically may in part be taken in reaction to the depth of penetration of the technologies themselves. For example, as more people gain access to the Internet the potential increases for various unwanted intrusions, eavesdropping, information theft, and denial-of-service attacks. To limit the effects of such incursions, network managers have deployed security firewalls. Such firewalls are typically configured to impede the free flow of communication among nodes on the Internet. These restrictions attempt to turn a physically ubiquitous system of nodes into logically partitioned and protected enclaves of nodes, and thus interfere with the ability of people to collaborate—especially when the potential collaborators exist within separate administrative domains.

Beyond the need for widespread adoption of the necessary underlying technology, CSCW can suffer from Grudin's inequality,[20] which states: those who devote the time and effort to capture and record the articulation work associated with collaboration, may not be the ones who benefit most from the results. This same issue appears again, but on a larger scale associated with knowledge management, in a panel discussion held at the 1998 conference on CSCW, where participants considered the question: "can an organization shape its culture so that people will network and share expertise, making knowledge explicit whenever possible, rather than just whenever convenient?" In this case, an entire organization stands to benefit from the time invested by its individual members, while the members themselves might not gain directly from the time they invest.

Another impediment to progress in CSCW concerns a general inability to measure progress within the field. In hardware-related fields progress can be measured easily along many relevant dimensions, such as component density, execution speed, power consumption, and heat dissipation. To date progress in software-related fields has proven less amenable to quantification. A compounding factor, identified by Whittaker,[79] is that user perceptions about the effectiveness of CSCW technology often do not match the effectiveness as measured by an unbiased, outside observer. This finding implies that measuring progress in the field of CSCW cannot rely solely on surveying the experiences of users. For this reason, large companies often spend substantial resources to set up human-factors laboratories where users can be observed and recorded while using specific technologies and where the observations and recordings can be studied to glean information about the effectiveness and efficiency of various software features. Understandably, because CSCW encompasses a complex and multifaceted research domain, measuring progress will remain difficult. Some researchers[80] have proposed a framework intended to encompass the important dimensions along which progress can be measured, and have provided some examples[81,82] showing how to apply the framework.

While conducting research and measuring progress in CSCW appears challenging enough, we must also consider the fact that the underlying technology on which CSCW builds continues to change at an alarming rate. Because CSCW builds on a wide range of software and networking technologies, significant advances in those fields can challenge the assumptions on which CSCW applications are constructed. In fact, CSCW applications live at the end of a long food chain of technologies, and so must adapt to any changes that arise. Further, several technologies within the food chain can change simultaneously, making it difficult for CSCW researchers and developers to track and understand the significance of the changes, let alone adapt to them. Even if CSCW researchers could adapt fast enough to technological changes, there still remains the problem of understanding and evaluating the effectiveness of the adaptations. By the time researchers gain an understanding, the underlying technologies have typically moved on again. This cycle poses quite a challenge to CSCW. Even worse, the adoption of new technologies and CSCW applications by people and organizations inevitably leads to changes in the way people work, as well as in the assumptions that people make about what should be possible or expected from CSCW in any given circumstance. For example, Olson and Teasley[76] discuss how working arrangements among a team changed to become more loosely coupled when the team was forced to work virtually at a distance. Similarly, Malone[83] predicts a shift in the organizational structure of corporations as they come to depend on computer-mediated coordination technologies. This coevolution between CSCW technology and the reaction of people and organizations to the technology appears even more challenging when we consider the fact that evolution along each dimension operates on different timescales. While technology evolves quickly, people and organizations tend to resist change, or to change fairly slowly, perhaps even at a generational pace. This mismatch in the pace of change adds to the difficulty CSCW researchers face when they attempt to assess progress in the field.

CSCW SUCCESS FACTORS

Given the challenges facing the field of CSCW, can we identify some keys to success? First, success depends on the degree to which CSCW technology becomes ubiquitously deployed throughout society. This implies that CSCW researchers must target their innovations and developments to ride on underlying technologies that appear poised for widespread adoption by a substantial portion of the population. Past examples of such technologies include telephones (in 1999 the Federal Communications Commission estimated that about 94% of Americans had telephones) and televisions (Nielsen Media Research-NTI reported that sometime between 1980 and 1985, televisions penetrated 98% of U.S. households). Potential future examples include the World Wide Web, which connects millions of desktop computers together, and to information and communication services. To date, World Wide Web technology has penetrated to between 50% and 70% of the population in industrialized nations, depending on the specific country, as reported in a study, "Truly a World Wide Web: Globe Going Digital," conducted by the Pew Global Attitudes project, released in May 2006. That study reported that the percentage of Americans with online access increased from about 64% in 2002 to 70% in 2005, while Internet usage by the world's two most populous countries lags: only 38% of Chinese and 14% of Indians used the Internet in 2005. While not certain, desktop computers and the Web seem likely candidates for near ubiquitous deployment.

Second, CSCW researchers must focus their efforts to understand and account for the characteristics of cooperative work. Some researchers have already contributed in this way. For example, Ehrlich[9] reports themes from research about group work. Communication among groups is generally ad hoc, informal, and unplanned, which implies that CSCW researchers should develop techniques that can support such interactions in the digital world. Group members also need to maintain awareness about the availability of others to communicate, and about the state of joint work, which implies that CSCW researchers should seek to improve our ability to accomplish these tasks when working through computers and across networks. Further, issues related to sharing information often hinge on subtle notions of anonymity, which suggests the CSCW researchers should continue to experiment with mechanisms to manage the release of personal information in cooperative settings. In another contribution, Schmidt and Bannon[7] suggest some guidelines to consider when designing systems to support cooperative ensembles. Cooperative ensembles: (1) exist as large assemblies or as groups embedded within larger assemblies (which implies that CSCW researchers should focus on techniques that scale); (2) often emerge to handle a particular situation, then dissolve (which implies that CSCW researchers should explore techniques that ease the burden of establishing collaborative sessions); (3) exhibit continuously changing membership, or membership that cannot be determined (which implies the CSCW researchers should investigate techniques for finding and forming effective subsets from larger populations); and (4) often intersect (which implies that CSCW researchers should develop techniques to manage multiple collaborative contexts, including mechanisms to control the dissemination of information in accordance with policies that might conflict). MacKay[13] highlights another key to success when she identifies the importance of mechanisms that enable people to control who can see or hear them at any time, and to know when someone is seeing or hearing them. MacKay also discusses a critical issue surrounding interaction and interruption. Specifically, individuals desire to determine the intention of any proposed connection or interaction, and to avoid communications that might disturb their work. These observations imply that CSCW researchers could focus productively on mechanisms to automate the initiation and management of interactions.

A third key to success for CSCW relates to automated support for coordinating group activities. While CSCW researchers are now convinced that most workflow and coordination processes demand continuous negotiation among participants and entail liberal application of techniques to handle unanticipated exceptions, the work of coordination remains largely a domain where only people add value. While selected CSCW researchers investigate automated, language-based support for flexible workflow processes and for negotiation and coordination, this territory remains wide open. Will agent-based coordination systems really work effectively? Can constraint-based languages be applied to achieve flexible information and transaction flow? Can automated methods support coordination among people, or are the problems too hard? Finding the right balance between automated support and human responsibility could improve the prospects for CSCW technology to go beyond communication to include coordination.

CURRENT PRACTICE OF CSCW

While some technologies appear promising as foundations for advances in CSCW, it should prove instructive to consider the current state of the practice. The typical collaborative session today consists of a telephone conference where collaborators discuss content, which might include faxed documents or perhaps some shared electronic documents, such as presentation slides or word-processing files that might be supported by change tracking capabilities. In some advanced situations, a collaborative activity that extends beyond particular real-time sessions might also be supported by a Web site, with one person elected as the editor. Usually, files to be added to the Web site would be sent by electronic mail to the editor. This typical collaborative session leverages a ubiquitous technology, the telephone network, which also happens to provide one of the most important channels, audio, for quickly conveying information among people and for conducting the real-time interactive dialog that helps to coordinate understanding and consensus building among participants. Typical collaborative sessions might also exploit the telephone network to distribute paper documents through facsimile machines. This permits discussions to center around shared documents, but relies on the use of the audio channel to ensure that all participants focus their attention on the same locations within a document. Increasingly, electronic mail is replacing the facsimile as

a mechanism to distribute documents, and the documents usually adopt a widely available format, such as Adobe portable document format or Microsoft Word™ format, which also provides change-tracking capability, along with PowerPoint™ format for shared viewgraphs. These techniques help, particularly the change-tracking capability, which can be useful when several people wish to propose amendments to shared documents. Even in this case, either the document must be distributed serially to ensure all changes are recorded, or the collaborators are left to ponder changes independently proposed on various copies of the document. No clear advantage exists for either approach because it can be somewhat difficult to follow documents marked up with proposed changes. Notice that the use of electronic mail to distribute electronic documents still relies on the audio channel to coordinate the focus and attention of all participants during a collaborative session.

Some technologies aimed at improving the state of the practice have failed as yet to provide much help. For example, application-sharing systems exist (e.g., Microsoft's NetMeeting™) that provide a means to visually indicate focus on electronic documents, that support simultaneous markup of electronic documents among a group of users, and that also include audio and video conferencing capabilities. Yet, these systems are not in widespread use. Why? Few widely agreed standards exist. The systems prove difficult to configure and use. They require support for a level of network QoS that is not widely available. Videoconferencing systems, such as the roll-around stations and room-based systems available from PictureTel and Polycom, have failed to achieve ubiquity as well. Why? Such systems tend to be expensive; thus, they are deployed selectively and must be scheduled and shared. This limits their applicability for spontaneous collaboration. Further, such systems require specialized support for network QoS, usually provided through H.320-compliant dial-up lines. The Internet, while more widely deployed, does not provide the necessary support for guaranteed QoS. Systems (such as Lotus Notes) that support asynchronous collaboration can be used to disseminate documents and discussions and to trigger alerts when various events occur. Such systems have not achieved wide usage. Why? The litany of reasons should be familiar by now: lack of widely agreed standards; difficult to configure, deploy, and use; expensive to buy and maintain. A similar story can be told for collaboration servers, such as Collabra and TeamWare, another form of collaboration technology available today, but not widely used.

While the current state of the practice in CSCW appears rather primitive and the landscape of more advanced technical solutions appears strewn with failures, some technologies promise to better support CSCW in practice. For example, the Web, with a growing infiltration in society and an increasing base of widely agreed technical standards, looms as a mass medium that can likely be exploited for collaborative purposes. In fact, as the Web's inventor, Tim Berners-Lee, has often observed,[84] collaborative software development provided the original motivation behind the Web. Of course, Mr. Berners-Lee has also rued the fact that at its current state of development the Web appears to be a mass medium more suited for TV-like distribution of multimedia. Despite its current state, Mr. Berners-Lee and many other researchers[85] and developers continue to seek mechanisms to improve the Web's support for collaboration. Great potential exists for CSCW on the Web because ubiquitous availability provides a crucial key to success.

Another significant development for CSCW appears to be the growing role of distributed, collaborative software development, as fostered by the "Open Source" movement.[86] Of particular interest is SourceForge (http://www.sourceforge.net), a Web site that provides services to open-source software development projects distributed around the globe. SourceForge provides hosted projects with Web-based tools for collaborative software development, a project Web server, tools for software maintenance and bug tracking, mailing lists and discussion forums, databases and compile farms, software release services, and advertising. SourceForge users have the option to mix-and-match these tools, and are free to design and contribute tools that might enhance collaboration. As of May 2007, SourceForge hosted over 150,000 open-source development projects and more than 1.6 million registered users. These figures represent a fivefold increase over 5 years. We might conclude that SourceForge employs Web technology in a form intended to realize the original motivation cited by Mr. Berners-Lee: collaborative software development.

What can we conclude from our examination of the current state of the practice in CSCW? The successful CSCW technologies appear to share some traits: ubiquitously available, easy to understand, easy to set up and use, few administrative constraints, reasonable technical requirements, and affordable prices. The unsuccessful CSCW technologies fail with respect to one or more of these traits. The expansion of users on the Web seems likely to continue, perhaps achieving near ubiquity at some future date. Such ubiquity would provide a key foundation to improve computer-mediated collaboration at a distance. SourceForge provides an early glimpse of what might become possible. While current practice appears quite limited, growth in Internet-based communication suggests that we are living near the dawn of effective CSCW. A number of technologies seem particularly promising.

PROMISING CSCW TECHNOLOGIES

If we look a bit beyond the horizon of today's widely deployed systems, we can identify a few technologies that exhibit significant promise with regard to CSCW. One suite of technologies might enable us to divide the general Internet up into virtual communities inside which we can securely conduct collaborative sessions, both in real-time and across time. Such technologies can replace the current firewalls, which divide the Internet up along administrative boundaries, with virtual enclaves, which might divide the Internet up, on demand, along the lines of function or context. Already elements of such technologies are commercially available. For example, Microsoft Windows ships with networking technology that enables users to form virtual private networks, which use encryption to establish confidential, virtual Internets on top of the physical Internet. Other commercial products, such as VMware and the XenServer, permit a single desktop computer to be divided into virtual operating systems, which provide multiple, separate contexts for users or to divide Web servers into segregated enclaves so that a single physical Web server can appear as multiple, logically distinct Web servers. Desktop, network, Web server—these assets form the ingredients needed to support collaborative sessions among distributed users across organizations, and the ability to "virtualize" each of these assets in order to support multiple but separate contexts already exists in the commercial market. What remains to be developed are: (1) techniques for connecting these distinct virtual assets into unified virtual enclaves, each consisting of virtual desktops, a virtual network, and virtual servers; and (2) mechanisms to quickly establish virtual enclaves and to support mobility among the virtual desktops and virtual servers. Some networking researchers[87] have already investigated techniques for composing virtual enclaves, while other networking researchers[88] have refined technology that can allow virtual networks to be established simply and on demand. Recent research[89] promises to deliver on-demand allocation of optical communications paths, which should support virtual networks and provide sufficient QoS to support a wide-range of multimedia channels to support collaboration. At the forefront of current research, grid software available as part of the Globus software distribution[90] is being developed to allow collaborators from multiple administrative domains to contribute resources into a virtual organization hidden from unauthorized members.

Above the networking and operating system layers, technologies for the Web are evolving in interesting ways that also promise to support improved CSCW. We previously mentioned the advantage of the XML for describing the syntax and content of information in a form both readable by people and interpretable by computers. XML[91] seems likely to become the standard language for defining information objects exchanged among computers. Future evolutions of XML[85] promise to annotate information objects with semantic tags that can enable intelligent interpretation on the part of supporting software applications. CSCW researchers and developers should be able to build safely on this base. Early examples of what might be possible exist in the form of community-based Web sites, such as MySpace (with its 182 million users) and Facebook (which has 23 million members), and Web sites aimed at establishing and extending business networks, such as LinkedIn (11 million users).

XML does not include a means to describe the behavior associated with various objects, except in the form of references to programs that can implement services associated with the object. The ability to express behavior directly in a form that can be transferred between computers seems to have an important place in future automated systems. At present, candidates for this role include portable scripting languages, such as Python, RubyScript, TclScript, and network programming languages, such as C# and Java. Some researchers[27] have used Java to implement Habanero, a combined synchronous–asynchronous collaborative system that shows how the power of mobile programs can be applied to bring unprecedented interoperability, function, and performance to CSCW.

While XML and Java suggest how metadata and behavior can be described for dissemination among a network of computers, other technologies promise to provide new mechanisms to accomplish the distribution. Already, industry is busy working on notification services and publish-subscribe (pub-sub) technology that will facilitate the distribution of events and notifications to all people who have an interest. These pub-sub technologies, such as Web-Services Notification and JXTA, build on research conducted by David Gelertner,[41] who investigated the applicability of "tuple spaces" as a means for efficient, large-scale coordination among many distributed processes.

Gelertner, a creative and visionary computer scientist, also investigates[92] techniques for organizing multimedia experiences, so-called lifestreams, into a readily accessible form. Such technology would serve admirably to enhance the ability of collaborators to locate relevant information. Earlier, we discussed other research along these lines, such as Rough'n'Ready[48] and Informedia,[49] when we considered the importance of access to raw multimedia recordings of collaborative sessions. While this class of research has not yet matured to the point of widespread commercial availability, CSCW developers should be poised to make effective use of the technology.

As outlined earlier, existing technology for videoconferencing has failed to achieve widespread acceptance, probably due to expense, configuration complexity, and requirements for guaranteed QoS from the network. Despite the seeming failure of this technology, some researchers continue to investigate the possibility for radical advancements in multimedia conferencing. For example, Jaron Lanier[93] advocates tele-immersion, a technology that aims to facilitate live multimedia interaction. The goal of Lanier and colleagues is to exploit computers, sensors, display technology, and networks to enable remotely distributed collaborators to hold virtual meetings with the same degree of quality as if they were collocated. Similarly, Rick Stephens and colleagues[94] have developed software to integrate large numbers of multimedia devices with high-speed networking channels to provide various sizes of Access Grid, aimed at enhancing remote collaboration across administrative domains. Success along these lines would prove invaluable to enhance the power and effectiveness of CSCW.

Not to be overlooked is research intended to exploit and enhance familiar modes of interaction as a basis to support human collaboration. For example, Paul Luff and colleagues[95] are devising techniques that enable paper to become an input device for selecting functions, and fulfilling roles now played by computer mouse devices and graphics tablets. As another example, technology for creating digital paper[96] and thin, flexible displays[97] promises to enable the use of paper-like devices to load and exhibit information, which could provide significant improvements over current forms of visualization, freeing mobile collaborators from reliance on bulky, expensive, power-hungry displays. Companies (such as E Ink and Universal Display Corporation) are already developing some products along these lines. More work will be required to integrate paper-based input modalities along with digital paper or flexible displays in order to provide mobile collaborators with the ability to interact conveniently while consuming little power. CSCW developers and researchers would be well advised to increase their investigation of techniques that can exploit familiar human interaction devices, such as whiteboards, walls, tape, paper pads, markers, and pens, while simultaneously crossing the boundary between the physical and digital worlds. Examples of promising lines of research include the Easy Living[98] and Sentient Computing[99] projects, the Mixed Reality Architecture,[100] and Microsoft's "Surface"[101] interactive table. Finding effective methods to bridge the gap between people and computers promises to yield great improvement in the interaction of groups.

OUTLOOK FOR CSCW

CSCW has become a hot technology and seems likely to remain so for the foreseeable future. The information age, and related exigencies associated with increasing globalization and specialization in our modern society, impels an ongoing transformation in the organization of work. Work is becoming more information-based, relying on computers and communications, and increasingly involves the activities of teams, often across organizational boundaries and time zones. Usually, people work on multiple teams, where the team composition changes depending upon the context, subject, and business arrangements. In this demanding environment, organizations and people naturally seek to employ any technology that can help get the job done better, faster, and cheaper. These factors presage difficult, long-term problems whose solutions hold immense potential to benefit companies, individuals, nations, and society. Today we stand only 25 years into what might be a 50-year endeavor to research, develop, deploy, and refine effective, efficient and affordable technology for CSCW. CSCW might encompass the greatest challenges facing information technology researchers and developers, but CSCW also promises to deliver the greatest benefits that computer, network, and software technologies have to offer mankind. The central question guiding the CSCW field can be stated simply. How can computing systems enhance cooperative work without unduly constraining human collaborative processes? The question has no simple answer.

REFERENCES

1. Marx, K. Das Kaptial. Zur Kritik der Politischen Okonomie. (Hamburg 1867). In *Gesantausgabe (MEGA)*; Marx, K.; Engels, F., Eds.; Dietz Verlag: Berlin, Germany 1983; Vol. II/5.
2. Jacovi, M.; Soroka, V.; Gilboa-Freedman, G.; Ur, S.; Shahar, E.; Marmasse, N. The Chasms of CSCW: A Citation Graph Analysis of the CSCW Conference Proceedings of CSCW'06 2006 289–298 Interested readers might consult a paper () by Michal Jacovi and colleagues, who propose the core and most prominent clusters in CSCW research from a structural analysis of the citation graph covering the proceedings of the first 20 CSCW conferences and related publications.
3. Greif, I. Overview. In *CSCW A Book of Readings*; Greif, I., Ed.; Morgan Kaufmann: San Mateo, CA, 1988.
4. Dourish, P. Software Infrastructures. In *Computer-Supported Cooperative Work*; Beaudouin-Lafon, M., Ed.; Wiley: Chichester, U.K., 1999.
5. Suchman, L. *Notes on Computer Support for Cooperative Work;* WP-12, Department of Computer Science, University of Jyväskylä, Jyväskylä, Finland Finland, 1989.
6. Bannon, L.; Schmidt, L. CSCW: Four Characters in Search of a Context Proceedings of the 1st European Conference on Computer Supported Cooperative Work; Bowers, J.M., Ed.; North-Holland: Amsterdam, the Netherlands 1991.
7. Schmidt, L.; Bannon, L. Taking CSCW seriously supporting articulation work. J. Comput. Support. Cooper. Work **1992**, *1*(1–2), 7–40.
8. Mahling, D. Computer-Supported Cooperative Work. *Encyclopedia of Library and Information Science*, 1st Ed; Kent, A., Ed.; Marcel Dekker: New York, 2000; Vol. 67, 91–108.
9. Ehrlich, K. Designing groupware applications: a work-centered design approach. In *Computer-Supported Cooperative Work*; Beaudouin-Lafon, M., Ed.; Wiley: Chichester, U.K., 1999.
10. Ellis, C. Workflow Technology. In *Computer-Supported Cooperative Work*; Beaudouin-Lafon, M., Ed.; Wiley: Chichester, U.K., 1999.
11. Stefik, M.; Foster, G.; Bobrow, D.; Kahn, K.; Lanning, S.; Suchman, L. Beyond the chalkboard: Computer support for collaboration and problem solving in meetings. Comm. ACM **1987**, *30*(1), 32–47.
12. Weatherall, A.; Nunamaker, J. *Introduction to Electronic Meetings;* Electronic Meeting Services, Ltd.: Hampshire, UK, 1996.
13. MacKay, W. Media spaces: Environments for informal multimedia interaction. In *Computer-Supported Cooperative Work*; Beaudouin-Lafor, M., Ed.; Wiley, Chichester, U.K., 1999.
14. Chapanis, A. Interactive human communication. Sci. Am. **1975**, *232*, 36–42.
15. Watts, J. Voice Loops as Cooperative Aides in Space Shuttle Mission Control, Proceedings of CSCW '96 Boston, MA, 1996.
16. Hindus, D.; Ackerman, M.; Mainwaring, S.; Starr, B.; Thunderwire: A Field Study of an Audio-Only Media Space, Proceedings of CSCW '96; Boston, MA, 1996; 238–247.
17. Heath, C.; Luff, P. Collaboration and control: Crisis management and multimedia technology in London underground line control rooms. J. Comput. Support. Cooper. Work **1992**, *1*(1–2), 69–94.
18. Karr, D.; Rodrigues, C.; Loyall, J.; Schantz, R. Controlling Quality-of-Service in a Distributed Video Application by an Adaptive Middleware Framework, Proceedings of ACM Multimedia; Ottawa,Ontario, Canada, 2001; 15–18.
19. Yamamoto, L.; Leduc, G. An Active Layered Multicast Adaptation Protocol, Proceedings of the 2nd International Working Conference on Active Networks; Tokyo, Japan, 2000.
20. Grudin, J. Why groupware applications fail: problems in design and evaluation. Off. Technol. Peop. **19**, *4*(3), 85–93.
21. Ellis, C.; Gibbs, S.; Rein, G. Groupware: some issues and experiences. Commun. ACM **1991**, *34*(1), 38–58.
22. Setlock, L.D.; Fussell, S.R.; Neuwirth, C. Taking it out of context: Collaborating within and across cultures in faceto-face settings and via instant messaging, Proceedings of CSCW'04; Chicago, IL, 2004; 604–613.
23. Yamashita, N.; Ishida, T. Effects of Machine Translation on Collaborative Work, Proceedings of CSCW'06; Banff, Alberta Canada, 2006; 515–523.
24. Banavar, G.; Doddapaneni, S.; Miller, K.; Mukherjee, B. Rapidly Building Synchronous Collaborative Applications by Direct Manipulation, Proceedings of the CSCW '98 Seattle, WA,DC, 1998; 139–148.
25. Moran, T.; van Melle, W.; Chiu, P. Tailorable Domain Objects as Meeting Tools for an Electronic Whiteboard, Proceedings of the CSCW '98 Seattle, WA,DC, 1998; 295–304.
26. Amir, E.; McCanne, S.; Katz, R. An Active Service Framework and its Application to Real-time Multimedia Transcoding, Proceedings of SIGCOMM '98 Vancouver, British of Columbia, Canada, 1998.
27. Jackson, L.; Grossman, E. Integration of synchronous and asynchronous collaboration activities. ACM Comput. Surv. **1999**, *31*(2es).
28. Neuwirth, C.; Morris, J.; Regli, S.; Chandhok, G. Envisioning Communication: Task-Tailorable Representations of Communication in Asynchronous Work, Proceedings of CSCW '98 Seattle, WA,DC, 1998; 265–274.

29. Lee, J.H.; Prakash, A.; Jaeger, T.; Wu, G. Supporting Multi-User, Multi-Applet Workspaces in CBE, Proceedings of CSCW '96 Boston, MA, 1996; 344–353.

30. Marx, M.; Schmandt, C. CLUES: Dynamic Personalize Message Filtering, Proceedings of CSCW '96 Boston, MA, 1996.

31. Glance, N.; Pagani, D.; Pareschi, R. Generalized Process Structure Grammars (GPSG) for Flexible Representations of Work, Proceedings of CSCW '96 Boston, MA, 1996.

32. Dourish, P.; Holmes, J.; MacLean, A.; Marqvardsen, P.; Zbyslaw, A. Freeflow: Mediating Between Representation and Action in Workflow Systems, Proceedings of CSCW'96 Boston, MA, 1996; 190–198.

33. Li, D.; Muntz, R. COCA: Collaborative Objects Coordination Architecture, Proceedings of CSCW '98 Seattle, WA, 1998.

34. Prakash, A. et al.In *Computer-Supported Cooperative Work*; Beaudouin-Lafon, M., Ed.; Wiley: Chichester, U.K., 1999.

35. Ressel, M.; Nitsche-Ruhland, D.; Gunzenhauser, R. An Integrating, Transformation-Oriented Approach to Concurrency Control and Undo in Group Editors, Proceedings of CSCW '96 Boston, MA, 1996.

36. Munson, J.; Dewan, P.A. Concurrency Control Framework for Collaborative Systems, Proceedings of CSCW '96 Boston, MA, 1996.

37. Dewan, P. Architectures for Collaborative Applications. In *Computer-Supported Cooperative Work*; Beaudouin-Lafon, M., Ed.; Wiley: Chichester, U.K., 1999.

38. Edwards, K. Policies and Roles in Collaborative Applications, Proceedings of CSCW '96 Boston, MA, 1996.

39. Rees, J.; Ferguson, S.; Virdhagriswaran, S. Consistency management for distributed collaboration. ACM Comput. Surv. **1999**, *31*(2es).

40. Bush, V. As We May Think [reprint]. In *CSCW A Book of Readings*; Greif, I., Ed.; Morgan Kaufmann: San Mateo, CA, 1988.

41. Gelernter, D. Multiple tuple spaces in Linda. PARLE '89, Proceedings of the Parallel Architectures and Languages Europe; Vol. 2, 20–27.

42. Bentley, R.; Horstmann, K.; Sikkel, K.; Trevor, J. Supporting Collaborative Information Sharing with the World-Wide Web: The BSCW Shared Workspace System, Proceedings of the 4th International World Wide Web Conference Boston, MA, 1995.

43. Fuchs, M. Let's Talk: Extending the Web to Support Collaboration, Proceedings of the 5th Workshop on Enabling Technologies: Infrastructure for Collaborative Enterprises Stanford, CAalifornia, 1996.

44. Haake, A.; Haake, J. Take CoVer: Exploiting Version Support in Collaborative Systems, Proceedings of CHI '93 Amsterdam: the Netherlands, 1993.

45. Haake, J.; Wilson, B. Supporting Collaborative Writing of Hyperdocuments in SEPIA, Proceedings of CSCW '92 Toronto,Ontario, Canada, 1992.

46. Conklin, J. Hypertext: An Introduction and Survey. In *CSCW a Book of Readings*; Greif, I., Ed.; Morgan Kaufmann: San Mateo, CA, 1988.

47. Malone, T.; Grant, K.; Kumuew, L.; Rao, R.; Rosenblitt, D. Semistructured Messages are Surprisingly Useful for Computer-Supported Coordination. In *CSCW A Book of Readings*; Greif, I., Ed.; Morgan Kaufmann: San Mateo, CA, 1988.

48. Kubala, F.; Colbath, S.; Liu, D.; Makhoul, J. Rough'n'-Ready: A meeting recorder and browser. ACM Comput. Surv. **1999**, *31*(2es).

49. Wactlar, H.; Christel, M.; Hauptmann, A.; Gong, Y. Informedia experience-on-demand: Capturing, integrating and communicating experiences across people, time and space. ACM Comput. Surv. **1999**, *31*(2es).

50. Hori, O. A Video Text Extraction Method for Character Recognition, Proceedings of the 5th International Conference on Document Analysis and Recognition Bangalore, India, 1998.

51. Sato, T.; Kanade, T.; Hughes, E.; Smith, M.; Satoh, S. Video OCR: Indexing digital news libraries by recognition of superimposed caption. ACM Multimed. Syst.: Video Libr. **1998**, *7*(3), 385–395.

52. Dao, S.; Shek, E.; Vellaikal, A.; Muntz, R.; Zhang, M.; Potkonjak, M.; Wolfson, O. Semantic multicast: intelligently sharing collaborative sessions. ACM Comput. Surv. **1999**, *31*(2es).

53. Hudson, S.; Smith, I. Techniques for Addressing Fundamental Privacy and Disruption Tradeoffs in Awareness Support Systems, Proceedings of CSCW '96 Boston, MA, 1996.

54. Obata, A.; Sasaki, K. OfficeWalker: A Virtual Visiting System Based on Proxemics, Proceedings of CSCW '98 Seattle, WA, 1998.

55. Zhao, Q.; Stasko, J. Evaluating Image Filtering Based Techniques in Media Space Applications, Proceedings of CSCW '98 Seattle, WA, 1998.

56. Nomura, T.; Hayashi, K.; Hazama, T.; Gudmundsom, S. Interlocus: Workspace Configuration Mechanisms for Activity Awareness, Proceedings of CSCW '98 Seattle, WA, 1998.

57. Rodden, T. Populating the Application: A Model of Awareness for Cooperative Applications, Proceedings of CSCW '96 Boston, MA, 1996.

58. Palfreyman, K.; Rodden, T. A Protocol for User Awareness on the World Wide Web, Proceedings of CSCW'96 Boston, MA, 1996.

59. Gutwin, C.; Roseman, M.; Greenberg, S. A Usability Study of Awareness Widgets in a Shared Workspace Groupware System, Proceedings CSCW '96 Boston, MAassachusetts, 1996.

60. Isaacs, E.; Tang, J.; Morris, T.; Piazza: A Desktop Environment Supporting Impromptu and Planned Interactions, Proceedings of CSCW '96 Boston, MAassachusetts, 1996.

61. Tollmar, K.; Sandor, O.; Schomer, A. Supporting Social Awareness @ Work, Design and Experience, Proceedings of CSCW '96 Boston, MA, 1996.

62. Belotti, V. Bly, S. Walking Away from the Desktop Computer: Distributed Collaboration and Mobility in a Product Design Team, Proceedings of CSCW'96 Boston, MA, 1996.

63. Fitzpatrick, G.; Kaplan, S.; Mansfield, T. Physical Spaces, Virtual Places and Social Worlds: A Study of Work in the Virtual, Proceedings of CSCW '96 Boston, MA, 1996.

64. Reed, D.; Kaplan, S. Orbit/virtue: Collaboration and visualization toolkits. ACM Comput. Surv. **1999**, *31*(2es).

65. Harrison, S.; Dourish, P. Re-Place-ing Space: The Roles of Place and Space in Collaborative Systems, Proceedings of CSCW '96, 1996.

66. Roseman, M.; Greenberg, S. Team Rooms: Network Places for Collaboration, Proceedings of CSCW '96, 1996.

67. Ackerman, M. Augmenting Organizational Memory: A Field Study of Answer Garden, Proceedings of CSCW '94, 1994.

68. Kautz, H.; Selman, B.; Shah, M. Referral Web: combining social networks and collaborative filtering. Commun. ACM **1997**, *40*(3), 63–65.

69. Foner, L.; Yenta: A Multi-Agent, Referral-Based Matchmaking System, Proceedings of Agents'97 Marina Del Rey, CA, 1997.

70. Goldberg, D. Using collaborative filtering to weave an information tapestry. Commun. ACM **1992**, *35*(12), 61–70.

71. Hill, W.; Terveen, L. Using Frequency-of-Mention in Public Conversations for Social Filtering, Proceedings of CSCW'96 Boston, MA, 1996.

72. Konstan, J. GroupLens: Applying collaborative filtering to Usenet news. Commun. ACM **1997**, *40*(3), 77–87.

73. Payton, D.; Daily, M.; Martin, K. Dynamic collaborator discovery in information-intensive environments. ACM Comput. Surv. **1999**, *31*(2es).

74. Borovoy, R.; Martin, F.; Vemuri, S.; Resnick, M.; Silverman, B.; Hancock, C. Meme Tags and Community Mirrors: Moving from, Conferences to Collaboration Proceedings of CSCW '98, 1998.

75. Daniel, S.; Ellis, J.; Truscott, T. *USENET, a General Access Unix Network*, Durham, NC, 1980; Summer Unpublished leaflet.

76. Olson, J.; Teasley, S. Groupware in the Wild: Lessons Learned from a Year of Virtual Collocation, Proceedings of CSCW '96 Boston, MA, 1998.

77. O'Neill, D.; Gomez, L. Sustaining Mentoring Relationships On-line, Proceedings CSCW'98 Seattle, WA, 1998.

78. Van House, N.; Butler, M.; Schiff, L. Cooperative Knowledge Work and Practices of Trust: Sharing Environmental Planning Data Sets, Proceedings of CSCW '98 Seattle, WA, 1998.

79. Whittaker, S.; Terveen, L.; Hill, W.; Cherny, L. The Dynamics of Mass Interaction, Proceedings of CSCW '98 Seattle, WA, 1998.

80. Damianos, L.; Hirschman, L.; Kozierok, R.; Kurtz, J.; Greenberg, A.; Walls, K.; Laskowski, S.; Scholtz, J. Evaluation for collaborative systems. ACM Comput. Surv. **1999**, *31*(2es).

81. Kurtz, J.; Damianos, L.; Kozierok, R.; Hirschman, L. The MITRE map navigation experiment. ACM Comput. Surv. **1999**, *31*(2es).

82. Bayer, S.; Damianos, L.; Kozierok, R.; Mokwa, J. The MITRE multi-modal logger: Its use in evaluation of collaborative systems. ACM Comput. Surv. **1999**, *31*(2es).

83. Malone, T.; Yates, J.; Benjamin, R. Electronic Markets and Electronic Hierarchies. In *CSCW A Book of Readings*; Greif, I., Ed.; Morgan Kaufmann: San Mateo, CA, 1988.

84. Festa, P. Charting the Web's next transformation. An Interview with Tim Berners-Lee in CNET News.com. December 12, 2001.

85. Fensel, D.; Wahlster, W.; Lieberman, H.; Hendler, J. *Spinning the Semantic Web: Bringing the World Wide Web to Its Full Potential*, MIT Press: Cambridge, MA, 2002.

86. Newman, N. The origins and future of open source software. A NetAction Whitepaper **1999**.

87. Meushaw, R.; Simard, D. NctTop: Commercial technology in high assurance applications. Tech. Trend Notes. **2000**, *9*(4).

88. Touch, J. Dynamic Internet Overlay Deployment and Management Using the X-Bone, Proceedings of the 8th International Conference on Network Protocols Osaka, Japan, 2000.

89. van Oudenaarde, S.; Hendrikse, Z.; Dijkstra, F.; Gommans, L.; de Laat, C.; Meijer, R. Dynamic paths in multi-domain optical networks for grids. Fut. Gener. Comput. Syst. **2005**, *21*(4), 539–548.

90. Foster, I. Globus toolkit version 4: Software for service-oriented systems. Intl. Conf. Netw. Par. Comput. **2005**, *3779*, 2–13.

91. Berners-Lee, T.; Hendler, J.; Lassila, O. The semantic web. Sci. Am **2001**, *284*(5), 34–43.

92. Freeman, E. *The lifestreams software architecture*, Yale University: New Haven, Connecticut, 1997, Ph.D. dissertation.

93. Lanier, J. Virtually there. Sci. Am **2001**, *284*(4), 66–75.

94. Childers, L.; Disz, T.; Olson, R.; Papka, M.; Stevens, R.; Udeshi, T. Access Grid: Immersive Group-to-Group Collaborative Visualization, Proceedings of the 4th International Immersive Technology Workshop Ames, IA, 2000.

95. Luff, P.; Heath, C.; Norrie, M.; Signer, B.; Herdman, P. Only touching the surface: Creating affinities between digital content and paper, Proceedings of CSCW '04 Chicago: IL, 2004; 523–532.

96. Ditlea, S. The electronic paper chase. Sci. Am **2001**, *285* (5), 50–55.

97. Sugimoto, A.; Ochi, H.; Fujimura, S.; Yoshida, A.; Miyadera, T.; Tsuchida, M. Flexible OLED displays using plastic substrates. J. Sel. Top. Quant. Electron **2004**, *10*(1), 107–114.

98. Brumitt, B.; Krumm, J.; Meyers, B.; Shafer, S. Ubiquitous computing and the role of geometry. IEEE Pers. Commun **2000**, *7*(5), 41–43.

99. Hopper, A. The Clifford Paterson lecture 1999 sentient computing. Phil. Trans. R. Soc. Lond. A **2000**, *358*, 2349–2358.

100. Schnadelbach, H.; Penn, A. Steadman, P.; Benford, S.; Koleva, B.; Rodden, T. Moving Office: Inhabiting a Dynamic Building, Proceedings of CSCW'06 Banff, Canada, 2006; 313–322.

101. Wilson, A. TouchLight: An Imaging Touch Screen and Display for Gesture-Based Interaction, Proceedings of the 6th International Conference on Multimodal Interfaces State College: PA, 2004; 69–76.

BIBLIOGRAPHY

1. *Readings in Groupware and Computer-Supported Cooperative Work: Assisting Human-Human Collaboration*; Baecker, R.M., Ed.; Morgan Kaufmann: San Francisco, CA, 1993.

2. Beale, R. *Remote Cooperation: CSCW Issues for Mobile and Teleworkers;* Springer: Santa Clara, CA, 1996.

3. *Computer-Supported Cooperative Work: A Book of Readings*; Grief, I., Ed.; Morgan Kaufmann: San Mateo, CA, 1988.

4. Rosenberg, D.; Hutchison, C. *Design Issues in CSCW;* Springer-Verlag: New York, 1994.

Conservation and Preservation of Museum Objects

Ellen Pearlstein
Information Studies and UCLA / Getty Program in the Conservation of Ethnographic and Archaeological Materials, University of California, Los Angeles, Los Angeles, California, U.S.A.

Abstract

This entry describes the history and evolution of the field of conservation of culturally valued materials found in museum collections. Significant steps in the evolution of museum conservation in the twentieth century include the introduction of chemists to a field previously dominated by artists and craftsmen, and a redefinition to include the prevention of damage through environmental management rather than only through activities designed to restore already damaged works. Professionalization of the field coincides with the introduction of standards and codes of practice, membership organizations, and scholarly publications. A description is included of the historical development of these standards and codes, which are generally referred to as conservation ethics. A final section examines the professional emphasis on textual, graphic, and photographic documentation used to monitor conditions and practices, and the way in which conservation activities and records have moved from behind the scenes to become part of the museum information accessible to the public.

INTRODUCTION

Conservation professionals are those whose activities are devoted to the preservation of cultural heritage for the future. Since conservation is also a term applied to the protection of biodiversity, cultural heritage specialists often distinguish their field by applying the limiting phrase of "art conservation," perhaps more accurately termed cultural conservation as the field encompasses a broad range of specialties including natural history specimens, archives, and books. This larger purview is often described using the term preservation, notably when referring to the activities used to conserve and protect archives and books. While museums are not the only employers of conservators, who may work for universities, libraries, government agencies, research institutes, and in the private sector, museums constitute an important employer because of the significance of the collections they hold. As social institutions of cultural memory and transmission, museums are involved in the interpretation, presentation, and preservation of cultural materials (or of culturally valued natural science materials and living collections), and museum conservators contribute to all of these efforts. The evolution of museum conservation is always tied to the practice of restoration, the act of returning damaged objects to an apparently unimpaired or even improved state. Restoration has a narrower focus than conservation and one that is tied to presentation value. The complete emphasis on presentation without regard for preservation or accurate interpretation has been emphatically rejected in the modern definition of conservation.

(See "Conservation and Preservation of Library and Archival Materials," p. 1250.)

The role of the museum conservator began at the very end of the nineteenth century, however restoration practices were always conducted on valued objects. Since museums are not static and their role continues to evolve, the museum conservator has shifted emphasis by contributing to presentation, then to research and preservation, and finally to both technical and contextual interpretation of museum objects, while continuing to work in all of these areas.

It will be illustrated how museum conservators are currently contributing to public engagement with collections; however, the development of museum conservation and its access by the public were not synchronous. The period when museums hired their first conservators occurred between 1900 and 1940, with an emphasis in those early years on either ancient collections whose condition was challenged by the transfer from an archaeological to a museum climate, or paintings, which had a high monetary value and were the focus of considerable art historical investigation. Publications by this early generation did provide some access by nonspecialists to information about the field of museum conservation. However the field was more successfully promoted by world-changing events such as the emergency transport of paintings from British museums into underground railroad stations and quarry caves during World War I and II,[1,2] and the international recovery efforts of museum and library collections following flooding of the Arno River in Florence in the 1960s. Both events, reported in the popular press,

Encyclopedia of Library and Information Sciences, Fourth Edition DOI: 10.1081/E-ELIS4-120043701

captured public sentiment about the significance of these collections and the importance of their preservation.[3–5]

Conservation has joined all museum functions that are witnessing a shift in public access and interpretation resulting from the use of information technology. Until recently, conservators examined and documented museum objects, and carried out procedures designed to enhance their stability and appearance, and this documentation was shared with professional colleagues. The nature of this documentation, which has been standardized and codified through professional consensus, has been revised to include didactic and even entertaining components for pubic access. As museums increasingly recognize the fascination with technical clues and transformative treatments and seek content for Web sites, blogs, and online community platforms, museum conservators have sought to use these tools to engage the public about the value and interpretation of objects.

HISTORY OF THE MUSEUM CONSERVATION FIELD

The terms restoration and conservation have a long and richly debated history, with philosophical underpinnings that are the subject of numerous books and articles.[6–8]

Restoration is recognized as a longstanding undertaking encompassing repairs made to extend the serviceable life of objects and buildings and the aesthetic life of sculptures and paintings. In terms of museum objects, the origins of restoration are frequently cited as when Italian Renaissance sculptors recarved and augmented Classical stone statuary,[9,10] and artists retouched and revarnished earlier important paintings, all to permit display.[11] It is important to point out that artists' materials had historically been applied to significant collections of all types with a goal toward an acceptable display appearance, without a prior understanding about how such materials might behave upon aging or interaction with collections. Once the term conservation was adapted in the late nineteenth century, it was held in opposition to restoration. Paul Coremans, an analytical chemist whose early pioneering work in conservation included founding Brussels' Institute Royal du Patrimoine Artistique, considered it "essential to differentiate between conservation and restoration."[12,13] It was recognized in the late twentieth century that these terms cannot be easily separated: "[conservation] revolves around research, the understanding and long term preservation of the materials of which the object is made, and [restoration] relates to their enhancement."[14] As decisions are made about the steps necessary for the preservation and public access of museum objects, all of these activities are considered under the modern rubric of conservation.[15]

The nineteenth century was something of a florescence in the founding of museums, each with workshops and studios dedicated to the preparation and maintenance of collections for display. It was not until the beginning of the twentieth century that conservation facilities were founded. Conservation facilities in museums were distinguished by the hiring of chemists who worked alongside existing staff including craftsmen skilled in areas such as sculpture, painting, cabinetry, model making, and taxidermy.[16,17] Even museums founded in the seventeenth century such as the Ashmolean in Oxford, England employed sculptors, watchmakers, and portrait painters to care for the collections until the 1950s, when the first conservators were hired.[18] Activities carried out by "repairers" in 1856 at the Victoria and Albert Museum, and preparators at American museums as recently as 1976, included "duties involving the handling of museum specimens or art objects for a variety of purposes including exhibitions, research and teaching; [and to] assist the Curators in the maintenance of collections." Preparators were supervised by Senior Museum Preparators, who

perform preservation and restoration, including the cleaning of specimens for exhibition; sort, arrange, and integrate specimens or art objects into classification or storage systems; condition and install works of art; and assemble and re-file specimens or art objects, including checking material returned from loan for possible damage.[16,19]

Museum Conservation Laboratories

The world's oldest scientific museum laboratory, no longer called a workshop or studio, is the Chemical Laboratories of the Royal Museums of Berlin, founded on April 1, 1888, and renamed in 1975 the Friedrich Rathgen Laboratory after its founder.[20]

Rathgen's primary contributions to conservation were in the area of archaeological materials, including a publication in 1898 of *Die Konservierung von Altertumsfunden*, translated into *Preservation of Antiquities* in 1905.[20,21] Archaeological materials were also the focus of Gustav Rosenberg (1878–1941) the first conservator at the National Museum of Denmark whose tenure extended from 1895 to 1940.[22] An even broader emphasis on research and preservation was pursued in the Department for Scientific and Industrial Research, founded in 1919 at the British Museum, with chemist Dr. Alexander Scott at the lead.[21,23] Dr. Scott was succeeded at the British Museum by Harold Plenderleith in 1924. Plenderleith is well known for his book *The Conservation of Antiquities and Works of Art, Treatment, Repair, and Restoration*, which was published in 1956, and represents what many consider to be the first attempt to codify a conservation approach to a broad range of museum materials. It is lauded for its emphasis on object examination, scientific methods, and the inclusion of case studies.[24] Another conservation pioneer is Alfred Lucas, a British analytical chemist with a strong background in forensic science, who in 1923 became a consultant to the Egyptian Department of Antiquities in Cairo, working both with excavations and with collections at the Egyptian Museum.[25]

In the United States, the appointment of Edward W. Forbes as director of the Fogg Art Museum at Harvard in 1909 initiated an emphasis on technical examination of artists' materials that is a mainstay of modern museum conservation. Forbes also believed that the diagnosis and treatment of artworks should rely on the same rigorous academic training afforded to other fields at Harvard.[26] Forbes' assembly of a set of over 1400 western and oriental pigments for use as reference materials remains familiar to most contemporary conservators as a model for approaching comparative analysis.[27] Forbes' tenure at the Fogg Art Museum culminated in the creation in 1928 of the Technical Department, with George Leslie Stout as its first conservator.[26] While Stout was an art historian by training, he hired chemistry student John Rutherford Gettens and radiography expert John Burroughs in what was in 1931 to become the Department for Conservation and Technical Research.[26] These men are lauded with playing a "crucial role in the early professionalization of the discipline through the introduction of innovative conservation techniques and through the development of systematized methods for examination, analysis, and documentation."[28]

The 1930s and 1940s saw the foundation of conservation laboratories in many museums, including the Louvre Museum, the Walters Art Museum, the Boston Museum of Fine Arts, and the Metropolitan Museum of Art.[29] The emphases on thorough examination and investigation of both collections, and materials used in conservation processes, along with careful documentation of observations and activities, are critical components of a modern museum conservation approach.

While chemistry and craft persist as important aspects of responsible conservation, there is a debate between scientific and humanistic approaches to cultural preservation that continues to rage. Art historians specializing in paintings have been the most outspoken about the potential of scientific methods to overshadow aesthetic judgments necessary for the conservation process.[30,31] This controversy extended to sculpture when the cleaning methods for Michelangelo's *David* were debated in the American press.[33] The concerns pit the value of scientific methods against the value of changes wrought by time, function, and cultural use, overlooking the nuanced decision making that actually occurs between these positions.

A humanistic approach persists alongside science and requires that conservators consider culturally varied standards and intentions for what it means to preserve, and that they work collaboratively with artists, community members, and other stakeholders to foster communication on these issues. For example, a revised approach to the

conservation of indigenous cultural objects and human remains involves a negotiation of context and values, since conducting research and performing treatments may alter the object or its cultural meanings.[33–36] A committee of American conservators proposed a commentary to the Guidelines for Practice, accepted in 1997, which revised decision making for the preventive care of certain cultural objects. This commentary recognizes that deterioration may be the culturally appropriate intention for some objects:

> Special cultural or contextual considerations may influence preventive conservation measures taken for a specific cultural property (e.g., sacred, contemporary, conceptual). In some cases a decision to allow deterioration to occur by avoiding certain preservation practices may be appropriate. Such decisions should be made only in collaboration with appropriate individuals connected with the cultural property.[37]

This concept has since been accepted into national and international charters governing museum work.

CONSERVATION ETHICS

The evolution of conservation from a field of artisanal skills toward a profession that integrates technical studies and scientific research resulted in the acknowledged need for standards, responsibility, and transparency. The first such standard developed in 1931 is the Charter of Athens, devoted to "the Restoration of Historic Monuments." This code of behavior was adopted by international participants to the First International Congress of Architects and Technicians of Historic Monuments, meeting in Athens. The Charter of Athens advocated for the open critical review of restoration procedures, reliance on scientific methods, and legislative measures for the prevention of damage as a first step rather than interventions to address damage. It also stressed respect for the original materials of the monument, and collaboration with relevant experts.[38] Like the Charter of Athens, the 1964 Charter of Venice also focused on monuments and not museum collections, and this document extends preservation beyond the monument to include the site. The Venice Charter values the physical changes wrought by all periods of use, further endorses use of scientific materials and methods, and argues against falsification by promoting restorations which are harmonious but distinguishable. This charter advocates publication of conservation work.[39]

The first set of ethical principles applicable to conservation work in the museum was drafted in 1960 by a Committee of Ethical Standards and Procedures of the International Institute for Conservation–American Group. The resulting document adopted in 1963 is known as the "Report of the Murray Pease Committee: I.I.C. American

Group Standards of Practice and Professional Relations for Conservators," known thereafter as the Murray Pease Report. Pease, the committee chairman and a conservator at the Metropolitan Museum of Art, considered the report to outline "...objective procedural requirements for the proper conduct of professional work by members of I.I. C.-A.G."[40] By outlining sound business practices, client confidentiality, and avoidance of conflict of interest for monetary rewards, the Pease report acknowledges the role of conservators working for private clients as well as museums. Important principles introduced in the Venice Charter are incorporated into the Pease report, including not working beyond your knowledge, not modifying known qualities of the original work to be conserved, clearly documenting sample sites and condition before carrying out any sampling or treatment, and full documentation of treatment.[40] In 1967 the I.I.C.-A.G. membership adopted a Code of Ethics proposed by the Committee of Ethical Standards, and this document along with the Murray Pease Report are the foundation documents for the Code of Ethics and Guidelines for Practice followed by professional members of the American Institute for Conservation today.[41]

Core concepts of ethics and guidelines continue to be reviewed and updated by committee members of the American Institute for Conservation (née I.I.C.-A.G.).[42]

Roughly every 10 years since the adoption of the Murray Pease report, the contents and language of these documents have been revisited by the American conservation community. Increased professional specialization and the founding of graduate education for conservation in the United States prompted a review of the core documents in 1977. In 1986, the concept of reversibility was challenged. The obligation to render reversible all interventions applied as part of a conservation treatment had developed as an ethical standard in opposition to past treatments, where intractable and damaging methods and materials had been used routinely in restoration. In the 1990s a more nuanced approach to reversibility was adopted, stressing the selection of materials and methods which will not themselves age poorly or result in deterioration, compromise research potential or cultural viability, or inhibit future treatment steps. So critical is this concept that it took another 10 years of debate and discussion before the AIC membership would revise their ethics and guidelines to reflect this principle.[42]

A second fundamental change in the professional practice of conservation, also reflected in ethical codes of conduct, has been a shift from physical interventions carried out on cultural property to management of the environment surrounding the property in order to reduce risk. These two approaches are referred to as interventive conservation versus preventive (or preventative) conservation, the latter drawn from medical terminology of preventive care. The maturation of preventive conservation as an approach has been supported by the increased

emphasis on doing no harm and respecting cultural norms, as well as on a considerable body of research conducted from the 1960s to present, which proves the benefits to collections of environmental control. This significant shift in assessment and practice was incorporated into the language of the Code of Ethics and Guidelines for Practice in the 1990s. In 1994, based on the recognition that the application of ethical conduct is varied and evolutionary for different specialties within the conservation field, Commentaries to the Guidelines for Practice were proposed by an Ethics and Standard Committee of the American Institute for Conservation and were adopted by the membership.[43]

The European Confederation of Conservator-Restorers' Organization (ECCO) was founded in Belgium in 1991 with the aim to "...develop and promote, on a practical, scientific and cultural level, the profession of Conservator-Restorer of Cultural Property."[44] The organization adopted Professional Guidelines in 2002, in which the Conservator-Restorer's role is described as contributing "...to the perception, appreciation and understanding of cultural heritage in respect of its environmental context and its significance and physical properties." These Guidelines reflect current shifts in the profession by defining the Conservator-Restorer, diagnostic examination of cultural heritage, preventive conservation, conservation (direct action on cultural heritage), restoration (direct action carried out with the "...aim of facilitating its perception, appreciation and understanding."), and documentation.[45] As is the case with the American document, the ECCO Guidelines outline ethical conduct in compliance with legal and environmental principles and collegial behavior.

DOCUMENTATION AND PUBLIC ACCESS

Increasingly professional practices in the twentieth century include museum conservators sharing their work with each other and with the public. Before this stage, museum staff often kept diaries or logs about collections care activities. In chronicling conservation history at one of the earliest museums in North America, the Smithsonian Institution, the authors indicate that

> archival evidence for collections care is scant until the curatorial annual reports begin in 1881. Records from the next three decades are replete with references to care of collections and exhibition including annual reports with summaries of daily activities, diaries, letters, and other documents (p. 185).[16]

The first publicly accessible venue for routine museum conservation reporting is the museum annual report. Evidence for collections care can be found in Annual Reports authored by the Ashmolean Museum's Keeper Arthur

Communication–Corporate Art

Evans beginning in 1896.[18] In many other institutions including the Metropolitan Museum of Art, the Philadelphia Museum of Art, and the Brooklyn Museum, conservation staff begins reporting activities involving analysis, equipment purchases, and treatments in annual reports in the 1950s.[46–48]

In addition to annual reports, many early museum conservation laboratories are rich repositories of correspondence from the first quarter of the twentieth century documenting exchanges about conservation challenges, methods and materials.[49,50] This trend toward outreach and exchange provides a marked contrast to what was previously a field with jealously guarded workshop practices, undocumented, and designed to result in invisible and transformative reconstructions completed in restoration studios.[9]

The increased professionalization of conservation has also included the development of written, graphic, and photographic documentation as standard components of museum work, as well as the development of peer reviewed journals for the publication of conservation research and practice, and organizations dedicated to professional conservation standards. Conservation documentation in the 1930s continued to take the form of diary entries, index cards, and written reports, where remarks and treatment steps were recorded, sometimes accompanied by drawing and photographs. The first professional publication in English, *Technical Studies in the Field of Fine Arts*, was published by the Fogg Art Museum at Harvard beginning in 1932.[28] The year 1950 saw the founding in London of the International Institute for the Conservation of Museum Objects, now called the International Institute for the Conservation of Historic and Artistic Works (IIC), and this organization began publishing the journal *Studies in Conservation* in 1952.[51,52] Beginning in 1958, countries began to form regional groups that abided by the aims and objectives of the IIC, which include excellence in professional practice in the preservation of cultural heritage and the promotion of knowledge, practice, and standards. The United Kingdom and the United States were two of the earliest regional groups of IIC, and seven other countries and regions currently maintain chapters.[53]

The IIC-American Group had its first meeting in 1960, and this group, now known as the American Institute for Conservation of Historic and Artistic Works, meets annually and publishes the peer reviewed quarterly *Journal of the American Institute for Conservation*. In 1946, the International Council of Museums (ICOM) was founded in agreement with UNESCO, and 20 years later a Committee for Conservation was created that actively participates in triennial meetings and publications.[54] The International Centre for the Study of the Preservation and Restoration of Cultural Property was established in Rome in 1959, and it is known by the acronym ICCROM. Focusing on both museums and monuments, it offers publications, research meetings, seminars, and training based on

interdisciplinary collaboration involving scientists, conservators, restorers, archaeologists, art historians, curators, architects, engineers, and city planners.[55]

Perhaps the most dramatic change to the practice of conservation documentation occurred when typed, handwritten, or printed documents and film based images were superseded in the 1970s by digital technology which became the infrastructure of all museum operations.[56,57] Many museum conservation laboratories are believed to have switched to a digital format for their text documents by the 1980s, and digital imaging followed later with best practices documents created only this year.[58,59] The incorporation of conservation records into a museum's digital collections management database is the subject of a major initiative by the Andrew W. Mellon Foundation which in 2008 launched the Mellon Conservation Documentation Survey, encouraging participation by "all who document objects, analysis, treatments and other processes in museum, library, or archive conservation and science departments, or who use such documentation in their work."[60] The survey results, which will be available at the end of 2008, will establish priorities for preservation through digitization of museum conservation archives, as well as explore how to take advantage of broadening access to these records by scholars and the museum public.[61] This could result in 100 years of diaries, logs, papers, and photographs being digitized and made Web accessible to varied audiences.

While conservation documentation has not heretofore been produced for public access, and is in fact considered confidential when it refers to privately held collections, the museum-going public has had a sustained interest in conservation, evidenced by exhibitions dedicated to the exposure of fakes *The Art of the Fake: Egyptian Forgeries from the Kelsey Museum of Archaeology*, An Internet Public Library exhibition of selected Egyptian artifacts—both real and fake, *Unearthing The Truth: Egypt's Pagan And Coptic Sculpture*, Brooklyn Museum, opening February 2009, *Fake?, The Art of Deception*, British Museum, September 30, 1990, *Fakes and Forgeries*, Minneapolis Institute of Arts, July 11–September 29, 1973, to the study of technology *Gian Lorenzo Bernini: Sketches in Clay*, Fogg Art Museum, February 28, 1998, *Gifts for the Gods: Images from Egyptian Temples*, The Metropolitan Museum of Art, October 16, 2007–February 18, 2008, *Rembrandt/Not Rembrandt in the Metropolitan Museum of Art. Aspects of Connoisseurship*, October 10, 1996, and to the process of conserving works in a museum collection. *Star-Spangled banner, The Preservation Project*, National Museum of American History, 1998–present. Conservation in public institutions has experienced a shift from activities conducted behind the scenes, with records intended only for museum staff, to an activity designed for public exploration. The Smithsonian National Museum of American History created a visible laboratory behind glass walls in 1998 to permit visitors to observe the ongoing examination and conservation of the Star Spangled Banner, the flag that inspired America's national anthem. Additional staff for this project included educational and interpretive specialists and an exhibitions curator, unusual staffing for a conservation project, and one which won awards for public relations and exhibition.[62]

Another pioneer in this effort to make conservation public is the Lunder Conservation Center at the Smithsonian American Art Museum and National Portrait Gallery, which includes multiple laboratories with different specialties separated from the public by glass viewing walls. Elaborate didactics in front of each laboratory include videos and text panels about completed and ongoing projects. In June 2008, conservators at the Lunder Center began posting details of conservation treatments on Twitter,[63] a free Web-based short messaging service designed for use with mobile devices.[64]

Though no survey exists to provide a precise number, dozens of museum Web sites now feature videos, daily diaries, and blogs about conservation. A search on the Brooklyn Museum Web site produced 2020 locations with the term conservation. The Museum has a blog under the heading of "Community," to which conservators contribute along with other museum staff, and where the public is encouraged to comment and inquire about activities. Postings describe reattaching paint on a delicate nineteenth century watercolor by Frances Flora Palmer, inviting the pubic to look through the microscope to compare the condition of paint before and after treatment. Another set of postings show the reuniting of the portrait and mummy of a first century A.D. Roman citizen of Egypt, separated by museum conservators in 1939.[65]

This public aspect of conservation has culminated in a Wikipedia article entitled Conservation–Restoration, with a majority of its postings added in 2008. The use of the term Restoration aligns the site with cultural heritage preservation rather than wildlife management, the subject of another Wikipedia entry entitled Conservation. The Conservation–Restoration article received minor editorial attention until 2006, since when it has been edited 445 times, with 307 of these edits occurring between October 2007 and October 2008.[66] In April 2008, the Publications Committee of the American Institute for Conservation recognized the audience impact and outreach potential of an article in Wikipedia, and took on the project to expand the site and increase accuracy. This expansion has included the addition of sections on ethics, the history of the profession, professional specializations, training, and links to organizations and journals, bringing the field of conservation more fully into the public domain.

CONCLUSION

Conservation is a field whose professional activities are devoted to the preservation of cultural heritage for the future. An understanding of the foci on ethical practice, documentation, balancing humanism and science, and public outreach in the field of museum conservation make sense when viewed in the context of the profession's beginnings and its historical achievements. The evolution of the field to include the introduction of science to a craft-based activity explains the need to develop standards and formalized ethical practices. As a profession that contributes to both the interpretation and preservation of tangible and intangible values in cultural objects, conservators are intimately tied to the museum function of memory transmission. Conservation records grew from an informal form of note-keeping, to an internally valuable report on museum accomplishment, to part of the story that assists the public in appreciating and understanding collections.

REFERENCES

1. Saunders, D. The national gallery at war. In *Materials Issues in Art and Archaeology III*; Vandiver, P.B.; Druzik, J.; Wheeler, G.S.; Freestone, I., Eds.; Materials Research Society: Pittsburgh, PA, 1992; Vol. 267, 101–110. Materials Research Society Symposium Proceedings;.
2. http://www.nationalgallery.org.uk/about/history/war/month.htm.
3. Hamblin, D.J. Science finds way to restore the art damage in Florence. Smithsonian **1974**, *2*, 26–35.
4. Klein, R.M. The Florence floods. Nat. Hist. **1969**, *77* (7), 46–55.
5. Judge, J. Florence rises from the flood. Natl. Geogr. **1967**, *132* (1), 1–43.
6. Brandi, C. Theory of restoration, I. In *Historical and Philosophical Issues in the Conservation of Cultural Heritage*; Price, N.S.; Talley, M.K. Jr.; Vaccaro, A.M., Eds.; Getty Conservation Institute: Los Angeles, CA, 1996; 230–235.
7. Philippot, P. Restoration from the perspective of the humanities. In *Historical and Philosophical Issues in the Conservation of Cultural Heritage*; Price, N.S.; Talley, M.K. Jr.; Vaccaro, A.M., Eds.; Getty Conservation Institute: Los Angeles, CA, 1996; 216–229.
8. In *Historical and Philosophical Issues in the Conservation of Cultural Heritage*; Price, N.S., Talley, M.K., Jr., Vaccaro, A.M., Eds.; Getty Conservation Institute: Los Angeles, CA, 1996.
9. Marijnissen, R.H. Degradation, conservation, and restoration of works of art: Historical overview. In *Historical and Philosophical Issues in the Conservation of Cultural Heritage*; Price, N.S.; Talley, M.K. Jr.; Vaccaro, A.M., Eds.; Getty Conservation Institute: Los Angeles, CA, 1996; 275–280.
10. Pinelli, O.R. The surgery of memory: Ancient sculpture and historical restorations. In *Historical and Philosophical Issues in the Conservation of Cultural Heritage*; Price, N.S.; Talley, M.K. Jr.; Vaccaro, A.M., Eds.; Getty Conservation Institute: Los Angeles, CA, 1996; 288–306.
11. Brommelle, N.S. Material for a history of conservation; The 1850 and 1853 reports on the National Gallery. Stud. Conserv. *2* (4), 176–188.

12. Keck, C. Salute to Paul Coremans. J. Am. Inst. Conserv. **1991**, *30* (1), 1–2.

13. Coremans, P. The training of restorers. *Problems of Conservation in Museums*; Travaux et Publications de l'ICOM 8: Paris, 1969.

14. Di Matteo, C. Restauration des oeuvres d'art. Encyclopedia Universalis **1985**, *15*, 11035–11043.

15. Berducou, M. Introduction to archaeological conservation. In *Historical and Philosophical Issues in the Conservation of Cultural Heritage*; Price, N.S.; Talley, M.K. Jr.; Vaccaro, A.M., Eds.; Getty Conservation Institute: Los Angeles, CA, 1996; 248–259.

16. Austin, M.; Firnhaber, N.; Goldberg, L.; Hansen, G.; Magee, C. The legacy of anthropology collections care at the National Museum of Natural History. J. Am. Inst. Conserv. **2005**, *44* (3), 185–202.

17. Webber, P. Rising damp, a history of the Conservation Department at the Victoria and Albert Museum. Conserv. J. **2005**, Summer 50 http://www.vam.ac.uk/res_cons/conservation/journal/number_50/ (accessed October 2008).

18. Norman, M. It is surprising that things can be preserved as well as they are: Conservation and the Ashmolean since before 1683. In *Past Practice, Future Prospects. Occasional Papers*; Oddy, W.A., Smith, S., Eds.; British Museum: London,U.K., 2001; 159–166 (British Museum) 145.

19. http://www.chr.ucla.edu/chr/cmp/webdocs/ClassSpecAlpha_files/pdfclassspecs/museumprep.pdf.

20. Riederer, J. The Rathgen Research Laboratory at Berlin. Stud. Conserv. **1976**, *21* (2), 67–73.

21. Plenderleith, H.J. A history of conservation. Stud. Conserv. **1998**, *43* (3), 129–143.

22. http://www.natmus.dk/cons/x/ww/rosenbrg.htm.

23. http://www.britishmuseum.org/the_museum/departments/conservation_and_science/history.aspx.

24. Pease, M. Book review of the conservators of antiquities and works of art, treatment, repair, and restoration by J. H. Plenderleith. Am. J. Archaeol. **1957**, April *61* (2), 191–2.

25. Gilberg, M. Alfred Lucas: Egypt's Sherlock Holmes. J. Am. Inst. Conserv. **1997**, *36* (1), 31–48.

26. Bewer, F.G. Technical research and the care of works of art at the Fogg Art Museum (1900 to 1950). In *Past Practice, Future Prospects. Occasional Papers*; Oddy, W.A., Smith, S., Eds.; British Museum: London, 2001; 13–18 (British Museum) 145.

27. Keyser, B.W. Technical studies and visual values: Conservation and connoisseurship at the Fogg Museum 1900–1950 12th Triennial Meeting, Lyon, France, 29 August–3 September 1999: Preprints; Bridgland, J., Ed.; Earthscan/James & James: London, U.K 1999, 172–176 (ICOM Committee for Conservation).

28. Spronk, R. Standing on the shoulders of giants: The early years of conservation and technical examination of Netherlandish paintings at the Fogg Art Museum. In *Recent Developments in the Technical Examination of Early Netherlandish Painting: Methodology, Limitations and Perspectives*; Faries, M.; Spronk, R., Eds.; Harvard University Art Museums: Boston, MA, 2003; 39–56.

29. http://en.wikipedia.org/wiki/List_of_dates_in_the_history_of_art_conservation.

30. Beck, J.H. Daley, M. *Art Restoration: The Culture, the Business and the Scandal*; John Murray Publishers Ltd.: London, 1993.

31. Talley, M.K. Jr. Connoisseurship and the methodology of the rembrandt research project. Intl. J. Mus. Manag. Curator. **1989**, (2), 175–214.

32. King, R. Dirt on David. N. Y. Times **2003**, July 15. Available at http://query.nytimes.com/gst/fullpage.html?res=980DE6DD173CF936A25754C0A9659C8B63&scp=1&sq=dirt%20on%20david&st=cse (accessed September 2008).

33. Clavir, M. *Preserving What Is Valued: Museums, Conservation, and First Nations*; University of British Columbia Press: Vancouver, BC, 2002.

34. Drumheller, A.; Kaminitz, M. Traditional care and conservation, the merging of two disciplines at the National Museum of the American Indian Preventive Conservation: Practice, Theory and Research. Preprints of the Contributions to the Ottawa Congress, 12–16 September 1994; Roy, A.; Smith, P., Eds.; International Institute for Conservation of Historic and Artistic Works: London, U.K., 1994; 58–60.

35. Kaminitz, M. Kentta, R. Bridges, D.M. First person voice: Native communities and conservation consultations at the National Museum of the American Indian ICOM Triennial meeting (14th), The Hague, 12–16 September 2005: Preprints James & James: London, U.K., 2005; 96–102.

36. Odegaaard, N. Changing the way professionals work: Collaboration in the preservation of ethnographic and archaeological objects. *Newsletter*, Getty Conservation Institute, 2005, Spring 20.1.

37. Guideline 20D, Preventive conservation, special practices, commentaries to the guidelines for practice, American Institute for Conservation. *Directory of the American Institute for Conservation of Historic and Artistic Works*, 2008, AIC-31.

38. *The Athens Charter for the Restoration of Historic Monuments*, http://www.icomos.org/athens_charter.html (accessed October 2008).

39. http://www.icomos.org/venice_charter.html The Venice Charter, International charter for the conservation and restoration of monuments and sites.

40. Anonymous, The Murray Pease report. Stud. Conserv. August **1964**, *9* (3), 116–121.

41. Code of Ethics and Guidelines for Practice. American Institute for Conservation. *Directory of the American Institute for Conservation of Historic and Artistic Works*, 2008; AIC-20.

42. http://aic.stanford.edu/pubs/coe/history/ethsup1a.html Evolution of the AIC Code of Ethics. Guidelines for Practice, Ethics and Standards Committee, Supplement Number 1.

43. Commentaries to the Guidelines for Practice. American Institute for Conservation. *Directory of the American Institute for Conservation of Historic and Artistic Works*, 2008; AIC-27.

44. http://www.ecco-eu.org/about-ecco/aims-and-objectives.html.

45. http://www.ecco-eu.org/about-e.c.c.o./professional-guidelines.html.

46. Pease, M. Technical laboratory. The Metropolitan Museum of Art Bulletin New Series. Incorporating the Eightieth

Annual Report of the Trustees for the Year 1949, **1950**, Summer *9* (1), 31–32.

47. Siegl, T. Conservation. Phil. Mus. Art Bull. **1966**, Autumn *62* (291), 127–156.

48. Keck, S. Keck, C. Conservation laboratory. *The Brooklyn Museum Annual II-III, 1960–1962*; The Brooklyn Museum: Brooklyn, NY, 1963.

49. Drayman-Weisser, T. A Perspective on the history of the conservation of archaeological copper alloys in the United States. J. Am. Inst. Conserv. **1994**, *33* (2), 141–152.

50. Gänsicke, S.; Hatchfield, P.; Hykin, A.; Svoboda, M.; Tsu, M. The ancient Egyptian collection at the Museum of Fine Arts, Part 1. Review of treatments in the field and their consequences. J. Am. Inst. Conserv. **2003**, *42* (2), 167–192.

51. Anon, International Institute for the Conservation of Museum Objects. Nature **1950**,*195* (4206), 903–904.

52. http://www.iiconservation.org/about/.

53. http://www.iiconservation.org/about/history2.php.

54. http://cool-palimpsest.stanford.edu/icom/chronology.html.

55. http://www.iccrom.org/eng/00about_en/00_03history_en.shtml.

56. http://www.getty.edu/conservation/publications/newsletters/21_2/news_in_cons.html.

57. Thomas, S. Introduction. In *The Digital Museum: A Think Guide*; Din, H.; Hecht, P., Eds.; American Association of Museums: Washington, DC, 2007; 1–8.

58. Warda, J., Ed.; *The AIC Guide to Digital Photography and Conservation Documentation*; American Institute for Conservation of Historic and Artistic Works: Washington, DC, 2007.

59. Pozeilov, Y. *Digital Photography for Conservators*, 2008; Available at http://www.lulu.com/content/4002004.

60. http://mac.mellon.org/issues-in-conservation-documentation/mellon-conservation-documentation-survey.

61. Roy, A.; Foister, S.; Rudenstine, A. Conservation documentation in digital form, a continuing dialogue about the issues. Stud. Conserv. **2007**, *52* (4), 315–17.

62. http://americanhistory.si.edu/about/dept-detail.cfm?deptkey=179.

63. http://twitter.com/lunder.

64. http://twitter.com/help/aboutus.

65. http://www.brooklynmuseum.org/community/blogosphere/bloggers/category/conservation/.

66. http://vs.aka-online.de/cgi-bin/wppagehiststat.pl?lang= en.wikipedia&page=Conservation-restoration.

BIBLIOGRAPHY

1. American Institute for Conservation, *How to select a conservator*, Available at http://aic.stanford.edu/public/index.html.

2. Conservation OnLine, *Resources for conservation professionals*, Available at http://palimpsest.stanford.edu/.

3. Conservation–Restoration, Wikipedia. Available at http://en.wikipedia.org/wiki/Conservation-restoration.

4. Getty Conservation Institute: Research resources. Available at http://www.getty.edu/conservation/research_resources/.

5. International Council for Museum–Committee for Conservation. Available at http://icom-cc.icom.museum/Start/.

6. International Institute for Conservation of Historic and Artistic Works. Available at http://www.iiconservation.org/.

7. Stoner, J.H. Changing approaches in art conservation: 1925 to the present*Scientific Examination of Art: Modern Techniques in Conservation and Analysis*, Proceedings of the National Academy of Sciences 2005. Available at http://books.nap.edu/openbook.php?record_id=11413&page=41.

Controlled Vocabularies for Art, Architecture, and Material Culture

Murtha Baca
Getty Research Institute, Los Angeles, California, U.S.A.

Abstract

There are a number of controlled vocabularies that can be used for describing and enhancing access to information resources relating to art, architecture, and material culture. These data value standards are essential for the description of movable art works, built works, and objects of material culture, as well as their visual and digital surrogates. Local, collection-specific authority files for museum and visual resource collections also play a key role in describing collection materials and providing access points for a wide range of users, both internal and external to the particular organization. So-called *folksonomies*, which are the result of *social tagging*, are not true controlled vocabularies but can be useful in providing additional access points.

INTRODUCTION

The simplest way to define vocabularies is to say that they are groupings of terms or names; vocabularies are said to be *controlled* if they are limited to a particular domain or set of concepts, and to designate a preferred form for each concept, person, or entity represented. Controlled vocabularies are organized collections of words, phrases, and/or names structured to show the relationships between terms and concepts. Authority files and thesauri are types of controlled vocabularies, but a simple *picklist* (a feature that allows users to select terms from a preset list) can also be controlled. An *authority file* is a type of controlled vocabulary that serves as a source of standardized forms of names, terms, or titles. Authority files normally include references or links from variant forms (terms or names that are equivalent to the preferred term or name) to preferred forms or "headings." For example, in the Library of Congress Name Authority File, the name form "Ovile Master" links to the preferred form "Bulgarini, Bartolomeo" for the fourteenth-century Italian artist whose hand has been variously identified with the "Master of the Ovile Madonna," "Ugolino Lorenzetti," and "Bartolommeo Bulgarini," which are all considered to be variants or synonyms for the preferred name form. Authority files, originally designed to regulate usage in library catalogs, also provide additional access points, thus potentially increasing both the precision and recall of many searches. A *thesaurus* is a type of controlled vocabulary in which each entry or record is restricted to a single meaning (unlike a dictionary). It is further characterized by relationships explicitly expressed in the structure of the vocabulary. Relationships include equivalence relationships (between synonyms in a single record), hierarchical relationships (whole/part, genus/species, and instance between records), and associative relationships (other types of relationships between records, not hierarchical). Hierarchical and associative relationships are semantic; equivalence relationships are lexical. For example, in the *Art & Architecture Thesaurus* (AAT), a "gisant" is a type of funerary sculpture (genus/species relationship); a "predella" is the decorated base of a large altarpiece (whole/part); "firedogs," "andirons," and "chenets" all refer to the same type of device used to support logs in a fireplace (equivalence relationship); and "arriccio" (a type of plaster used in the creation of frescoes) is conceptually rather than hierarchically related to "fresco," a specific type of painting (associative relationship). Associative relationships can also be used to distinguish terms from one another; for example, "rhyta" are drinking vessels held over the head. In the AAT, the record for "rhyta" is linked (conceptually and electronically) to the records for "Sturzbechers" and "stirrup cups," which are different types of vessels but, like rhyta, rest on their side when not in use. "National Gallery of Art" and "Tate Modern" as narrower terms of "art museums" are an example of an instance relationship in a thesaurus (in this case, dealing with corporate bodies such as museums and other cultural institutions).

Controlled vocabularies can be powerful tools for describing and enhancing access to collections of any kind. They can range from a simple alphabetical list of approved terms to a complex, carefully structured thesaurus, including broader and narrower concepts, related concepts, and any number of equivalent or near-equivalent terms or names denoting the same concept, as shown in the examples discussed. In information science, controlled vocabularies are often referred to as *data value standards*,

Encyclopedia of Library and Information Sciences, Fourth Edition DOI: 10.1081/E-ELIS4-120053291

since they provide the specific terms, names, and other data values that are used to populate *data structures* or metadata schemas such as MARC (Machine-Readable Cataloging), MODS (Metadata Object Description Schema), Dublin Core, LIDO (Lightweight Information Describing Objects), EAD (Encoded Archival Description), and others.

The cataloging rules that are used to guide the way that data values are entered into data structures are often (and, for many people, confusingly) referred to as *data content standards—Resource Description and Access* (RDA), *Describing Objects: A Content Standard* (DACS), and *Cataloging Cultural Objects* (CCO) are examples of data content standards for bibliographic materials, archival collections, and unique cultural objects, respectively. For a chart that clearly outlines the types of data standards, with examples, see Gilliland.[1]

CONTROLLED VOCABULARIES FOR ART AND ARCHITECTURE

In the areas of art, architecture, and material culture, there are several vocabulary tools that have been specifically designed for describing these types of collections, such as the AAT. Other vocabularies have been developed for other types of materials but can also be applied to art and architecture, such as the *Library of Congress Subject Headings* (LCSH) and the *Thesaurus for Geographic Materials* (TGM), also maintained by the Library of Congress.

Controlled vocabularies have three main uses. They can be used as sources of standard terminology for descriptive cataloging and other forms of documentation; as knowledge bases or lookup tools for discovering the meaning of a particular term or a term for a particular concept or object, or a description of a particular individual or corporate body in the case of a name authority file; and as online searching assistants that can enhance both precision and recall in querying databases that can have multiple data values representing the same concepts, objects, or persons.

EXAMPLES OF USES OF CONTROLLED VOCABULARIES

As sources of terminology for catalog records and other forms of documentation: In a catalog record for a painting in a museum's collection or an image in a photographic archive, the following database fields or metadata elements should be populated with values from appropriate controlled vocabularies: object type, creator name, materials/techniques, creation location, subject matter, and so on. See the cataloging examples provided on the

Categories for the Description of Works of Art (CDWA) website: http://www.getty.edu/research/publications/ electronic_publications/cdwa/examples.html, which indicate which fields in a database record should be populated with values from a controlled vocabulary.

As knowledge bases or lookup tools: A user wishes to know what "trompe-l'oeil" means; he or she does a search in the AAT on that term (or on a right-truncated version of the term, in the event of being unsure of the exact spelling) and retrieves a record with the scope note that begins "French term meaning 'deceive the eye,' applied to images so realistic that they may fool the viewer into thinking that the represented objects, scenes, textures, or points of view are real rather than images." If a controlled vocabulary has carefully constructed hierarchical relationships and scope notes, users can even find terms for concepts for which they do not know the word. In her article "Indexing and Access for Digital Libraries and the Internet: Human, Database, and Domain Factors," Marcia J. Bates[2] discusses the issues associated with the fact that many users are essentially trying to describe something they do not know or for which they have knowledge gaps, while indexers know what they are describing and use specific terminology in the process of purportedly providing access points for specific materials. The use of carefully structured thesauri and other vocabularies that link both specific and more generic terms, and even "right" and "wrong" (but frequently used) terms, can go a long way toward bridging the gap between indexers and end-users. For example, in the AAT, users can navigate down the Visual Works hierarchy from "sculpture" to "funerary sculpture" to "ushabti," or they can enter a key word search for "Egyptian and tombs" on the scope notes and also find the record for "ushabti" (with eight variant spellings), the small sculptures that the ancient Egyptians buried with their dead to accompany them in the afterlife. Or a user may have come across the name "Beggarstaff Brothers" and wants to know who these artists were. A search in the *Union List of Artist Names* (ULAN) reveals that this was the pseudonym adopted by brothers-in-law William Nicholson and James Pryde (each a well-known artist in his own right) while they were collaborating in the 1890s as poster artists. The ULAN record also has links to the individual records for each artist.

As online searching assistants: An Italian searcher wishes to know if the Getty Museum has any works by the artist designated in the scholarly literature and exhibition catalogs in the Italian language as "Gherardo delle Notti." He enters this name in the Getty search engine and retrieves works by "Gerrit van Honthorst," the name used in non-Italian-language publications and institutions to designate this Dutch artist who was active in Italy during the first half of the seventeenth century. This is because the ULAN, with all the variant names for this artist clustered together in a single record, is being used as an intermediary between the searcher and the resources being searched. Similarly, a user can search on "desk" and retrieve a "cartonnier" in the Getty's collection, even though the word "desk" does not appear on the web page for that object. This is because the power of the AAT hierarchy is being used to assist the searcher who is using a more generic, nonexpert term for a very specific object. Bates[3] discusses the power of faceted searching (made possible by faceted thesauri like the AAT) in "Speculations on Browsing, Directed Searching, and Linking in Relation to the Bradford Distribution."

Vocabularies in the realm of art, architecture, and material culture may contain personal names (e.g., *Leonardo da Vinci*), corporate names (*Richard Meier & Partners*), object names (*squat lekythoi*), iconographic subjects (*Hercules and the Nemean Lion*), geographic names (*Luxor, Qina governorate, Upper Egypt*), proper names of built works (*Hagia Sophia*), and so on. They can take a variety of forms. *Alphabetical lists* of approved terms or names are often used in local applications to ensure consistency and accuracy. In a controlled list, all terms should be equal in specificity and should not have overlapping meanings. *Subject headings* are terms and phrases, usually arranged in an alphabetical order, that can be combined to express compound concepts (e.g., *Triptychs—Italy—Florence—Congresses*). A *taxonomy* is an orderly classification system for a defined domain, with hierarchical relationships (e.g., *Flagellation of Christ, Passion of Christ, New Testament, Bible*, in an ascending hierarchical order). A *thesaurus* is a structured vocabulary that explicitly includes the semantic relationships between and among terms and concepts. As indicated earlier, the types of relationships in a thesaurus are "equivalence" (*still life = natura morta*), "hierarchical" (a *gisant* is a type of *effigy*, which is a type of *funerary sculpture*), and "associative" (a *charterhouse* or *chartreuse* is a type of building associated with the *Carthusian* monastic order). Any one of these types of controlled vocabularies can be used as an *authority file*—that is, a vocabulary that is used to enforce consistency by providing standardized forms of names, terms, titles, and so on. Authority files not only regulate usage, but also provide additional access points for users who may be searching on nonpreferred forms of names or terms. For example, in the *Union List of Artist Names* (ULAN), "Schiavone, Andrea" is the preferred name form for a Dalmatian artist active in Italy during the sixteenth century, but searchers can also enter queries on variant forms as diverse as "Medulić, Andrija" and "Andrea Meldolla."

"UNCONTROLLED" VOCABULARIES AND FOLKSONOMIES FOR VISUAL WORKS

The phenomenon known as *social tagging* (also referred to as *collaborative tagging, social classification, social indexing, mob indexing,* and *folk categorization*) that is prevalent on image websites such as Flickr (https://www.flickr.com/) and museum websites such as the Brooklyn Museum (http://www.brooklynmuseum.org/opencollection/collections/) is the decentralized method by which individuals and groups create, manage, and share terms, names, and so on (called "tags") to annotate and categorize digital resources in an online "social" environment. Another example of social tagging for artworks is the Public Catalog Foundation's "Your Paintings" tagging application (http://tagger.thepcf.org.uk/).

A folksonomy, which is simply an assemblage of concepts represented by tags, is the result of social tagging. It should be noted that in spite of the "onomy" at the end of the word, a folksonomy is not a taxonomy, which is an orderly, structured classification that explicitly expresses the relationships, usually hierarchical, between and among the things being classified.

Social tagging and other forms of user-generated metadata such as "crowdsourcing" are a trend in online resources that is garnering considerable attention and interest. If unstructured, nonstandardized terminology created by social tagging and other forms of user-generated metadata is linked to more highly structured, standard thesauri and vocabulary tools, the potential for enhanced end-user access is significantly increased.

COLLECTION-SPECIFIC LOCAL VOCABULARIES

Many museums and other collecting institutions have learned that merely taking terms from a published controlled vocabulary such as the Library of Congress authorities, the AAT, or ICONCLASS and using them to populate descriptive records for objects in their collections is not enough. They may find that they need to supplement these sources with scholarly or other specialized terms that are out of scope for discipline-specific vocabularies, or too specific for the level of indexing supported by more general vocabularies. Or they may use nonexpert, generic, or even erroneous terms or misspellings that cannot be found in a published, standard vocabulary tool to enhance access to collections for a wide range of users. The National Gallery of Art in Washington, DC allows users to browse its collections by using controlled lists of object types and artists' nationalities. The Getty Museum uses collection-specific thesauri of both object types and subject matter to enable users to familiarize themselves with the works in its collections, both on the Web and in the touchscreen kiosk system in its galleries. In a collection-specific thesaurus aimed at enhancing access to nonexpert users and museum visitors, a term as unscientific as "bottles and pots" can be used to lead users to more specific types of vessels with names that would be known only to experts. While this type of "folk classification" is not legitimate for a published, standard authority such as the AAT or LCSH, it is extremely useful in a local thesaurus, where it can be linked to the more accurate expert terminology as well.

CONTROLLED VOCABULARIES EXPRESSED AS LINKED OPEN DATA

Linked Open Data (LOD) are data created according to the best practices for publishing and interlinking structured data using the Resource Description Framework (RDF) syntaxes and made publically available on the Web; see http://linkeddata.org/. The Virtual International Authority File (VIAF), the Getty vocabularies, and the Library of Congress Thesaurus for Graphic Materials (TGM) are examples of controlled vocabularies that are made available as Linked Open Data in addition to their familiar formats as web lookup tools. Controlled vocabularies expressed as LOD can enable meaningful machine-generated linking, thus greatly enhancing the research potential of the online environment and enabling users to easily access related resources that they otherwise might never have found. Formats for expressing vocabulary data as LOD include RDF and JavaScript Object Notation (JSON). As of this writing, Bibliographic Framework (BIBFRAME) is the emerging data model for expressing bibliographic records using Linked Open Data.

CONCLUSION

The three main ways by which users attempt to find information online are browsing, directed searching, and following links.

For online collections of art, architecture, and material culture, all three of these methods can be extremely powerful. Museums can use their collection-specific thesauri and descriptive cataloging records to enable users who are unfamiliar with their collections to browse by object type, creation place, chronological period, subject matter, and so on. As shown in the examples discussed, directed searching can be significantly enhanced via both the terms and the hierarchical relationships in controlled vocabularies. Likewise, controlled vocabularies can be used to lead users to other materials of interest via links from one specific term or name to another. Many of the debates that are currently taking place among information professionals about how the library profession can modernize itself, compete with commercial search engines like Google, and ultimately not only survive but re-create itself center on authority control rather than on item-level description. The 2008 final report of the Library of Congress Working Group on the Future of Bibliographic Control (http://www.loc.gov/bibliographic-future/news/lcwg-ontherecord-jan08-final.pdf) also stresses the need

for increased focus on authority files and controlled vocabularies in a collaborative model among different institutions and communities, and the potential value of mapping values from different controlled vocabularies.

Controlled vocabularies, combined with less structured data values such as those generated by social tagging, may very well be one of the key elements in the future of access to the constantly growing body of online resources. Since the mission of museums, archives, and other collecting and memory institutions is not merely to collect and preserve, but also to provide access to what they collect, the use of controlled vocabularies to describe and lead users to their collections should be as essential as the use of security systems and climate control to protect and preserve those collections.

SPECIFIC VOCABULARY TOOLS

Following is a list of published vocabulary tools that can be used to describe and provide access to materials relating to the visual arts, architecture, and material culture:

Art & Architecture Thesaurus® (AAT)

http://www.getty.edu/research/tools/vocabularies/aat/

A structured vocabulary that contains terminology and other information related to art, architecture, and related disciplines. Updated monthly.

Cultural Objects Name Authority® (CONA)

http://www.getty.edu/research/tools/vocabularies/cona/

A structured vocabulary comprising unique numeric identifiers and brief records for works of art, architecture, and material culture. As of this writing, CONA is in pilot release phase.

Getty Thesaurus of Geographic Names® (TGN)

http://www.getty.edu/research/tools/vocabularies/tgn/

A structured vocabulary containing names and other information about geographic places, focusing on but not limited to places important to art, architecture, and related disciplines. Web version updated twice monthly.

ICONCLASS

http://www.iconclass.nl

A classification system for iconographic research and documentation of images. *ICONCLASS* is a collection of definitions of objects, persons, events, situations, and abstract ideas that can be the represented in the visual arts. The system is organized in 10 broad divisions within which subjects are ordered hierarchically. Although

ICONCLASS is primarily a classification system, the textual correlates of the alphanumeric classification codes can be used to describe and/or index visual materials, as can the associated key words be.

Also available in print:

> van de Waal, H. *ICONCLASS*: *An Iconographic Classification System*, 9 Vols., completed and edited by L.D. Couprie with E. Tholen, G. Vellekoop. Amsterdam, the Netherlands/New York: North-Holland Pub. Co., 1973–1983.

Library of Congress Name Authority

http://authorities.loc.gov/

A controlled vocabulary consisting of records for names and titles of works established by the Library of Congress and cooperating libraries. Updated daily.

Library of Congress Subject Headings

http://authorities.loc.gov/

A structured vocabulary designed to represent the subject and form of the books, serials, and other materials in the Library of Congress collections, with the purpose of providing subject access points to the bibliographic records contained in the Library of Congress catalogs. More broadly, LCSH is used as a tool for subject indexing of library catalogs and other materials (including visual materials). Updated daily.

English Heritage Thesauri

http://thesaurus.english-heritage.org.uk/

A set of thesauri developed by the National Monuments Record Center, English Heritage Project (officially known as Historic Buildings and Monuments Commission for England). The thesauri include Monument Types, Archaeological Objects, Building Materials, Defence of Britain, Components, Maritime Place Names, Maritime Craft Type, Maritime Cargo, Evidence Thesaurus, Archaeological Sciences, and a Historic Aircraft Types thesaurus.

Subject Index for the Visual Arts

Glass, E., comp. *A Subject Index for the Visual Arts*. London: H. M. Stationery Office, 1969.

A structured vocabulary used for subject access to materials in the Print Room of the Victoria & Albert Museum, London.

Thesaurus for Graphic Materials (TGM)

http://id.loc.gov/vocabulary/graphicMaterials.html

A thesaurus of terms that describe the subjects and the work types of graphic materials.

Union List of Artist Names® (ULAN)

www.getty.edu/research/conducting_research/vocabularies/ulan/

A structured vocabulary containing names and other information on artists, architects, and other creators of art and architecture. Web version updated twice monthly.

REFERENCES

1. Gilliland, A.J. Setting the stage (Chapter 1). In *Introduction to Metadata*; Baca, M., Ed.; Revised Edition; Getty Research Institute: Los Angeles, CA, **2016**.
2. Bates, M.J. Indexing and access for digital libraries and the Internet: human, database, and domain factors. J. Am. Soc. Inf. Sci. **1998**, *49*, 1185–1205.
3. Bates, M.J. Speculations on browsing, directed searching, and linking in relation to the Bradford distribution. In *Emerging Frameworks and Methods: Proceedings of the Fourth International Conference on Conceptions in Library and Information Science* (CoLIS 4); Libraries Unlimited: Greenwood Village, CO, 2002. 137–150.

BIBLIOGRAPHY

1. Harpring, P. *Introduction to Controlled Vocabularies: Terminology for Art, Architecture, and Other Cultural Works*, Updated Ed.; Getty Research Institute: Los Angeles, CA, 2013.

Corporate Archives

Philip Mooney
Heritage Communications, Coca-Cola Company, Atlanta, Georgia, U.S.A.

Abstract

Over 300 North American businesses support archival programs as part of their corporate structure. This entry provides an overview regarding the rationale for these archival programs, their organizational structure, the services they provide to the business, a sampling of internal marketing initiatives, and a description of the records contained in these collections. The entry also explores the differences between the work of corporate archivists and others in the profession.

While academic libraries, historical, and cultural agencies have collected voluminous records relating to the political, literary, and social history of North America, few repositories have included business collections as focal points of their acquisitions strategy. Certainly, institutions like the Baker Library and Eleutherian Mills at Harvard University, the Eleuthesian Mill Historical Society, the Minnesota Historical Society, and the Hartman Advertising Collection at Duke University have acquired very significant collections that partly fill the void, but the vast majority of American business records have been ignored by the major academic research centers. Consequently, the prime responsibility for preserving business records has fallen to the businesses themselves.

Corporations supporting internal archival programs tend to fall into three major groups: financial services companies including banks and insurance firms; consumer goods and services units; and technology-driven enterprises like. Representing the first group are companies like Aetna, Nationwide, State Farm, AIG, and Allstate from the insurance sector while Wells Fargo, American Express, Scotiabank, J.P. Morgan Chase, Royal Bank of Canada, and the New York Stock Exchange provide a wide range of financial services. Well-known consumer product companies include Ford Motor Company, Procter and Gamble, McDonald's, Walt Disney, Kraft, Coca-Cola, Eli Lilly, NBC, Williams Sonoma, Levi Strauss, UPS, and Gap. Technology-driven firms like IBM, Microsoft, and Hewlett-Packard also maintain their own collections.

Less than 10% of the Society of American Archivists 5000+ institutional and individual members manage business records, but business archivists have been an important component of the profession from the beginning. The Firestone Tire and Rubber Company formed one of the earliest corporate archives in 1943,[1] just 7 years after the formation of SAA itself, and Firestone's archivist, William Overman, later became president of the society in 1957–1958. Since that time, there has been a steady increase in the number of companies supporting an archival program growing from 133 business archives in 1969[2] to nearly 350 in early 2008.[3]

The single-most compelling reason for companies to create an archives is an anniversary of some note. As businesses reach significant milestones, documentation is required to provide historical context and to define those qualities and characteristics that separate one firm from another. Regardless of size or scope, anniversaries generate interest in creating a book, pamphlet, audiovisual production, exhibit, or some combination of those programs. The anniversary creates a unique opportunity for the organization to focus on its history and to allocate resources for the collection, organization, and utilization of its historical resources.

As these historic dates approach, many corporations realize that the records required to support commemorative programming are not easily found. Most likely, they are scattered throughout the business, disorganized, and stored in less than optimal conditions. The anniversary provides the catalyst to begin segregating these records and determining whether they offer a longer value proposition than the celebration of the anniversary itself.

A second driver for corporate archives, frequently connected to the first, is the CEO initiative. While corporations are normally forward-looking and disinclined to consider history as a relevant element in strategic thinking, senior managers want their legacy to be preserved and to become imbedded in the corporate culture. As leaders approach the end of their term in office, they become much more reflective on their accomplishments and much more inclined to take positive steps to see that those achievements are institutionalized. The CEO archival mandate is more common in family run enterprises but such initiatives can occur in businesses of any size. An archives stands as a visible reminder to both internal and external audiences of the legacy that has been established.

Litigation support and the recognition of an information gap are the other factors that can influence the foundation of an archives. In order to protect trademarks and

Encyclopedia of Library and Information Sciences, Fourth Edition DOI: 10.1081/E-ELIS4-120044471

other forms of intellectual property, corporations must have detailed files that document the creation and utilization of their advertising concepts and campaigns, packaging, technology, and marketing initiatives. In many instances, an archives charged with the collection and management of these materials offers the best low-cost option for protecting these assets.

Similarly, an archives provides a unique resource for the business that other information management specialists do not provide. The archivist looks across the entire spectrum of records being generated by the parent body and determines which materials have long-term value to the ongoing work of the business. In most cases the total volume of retained records is no more than 2–3% of all records generated, but the retention of those materials will define what future generations know about the organization and can help to educate new managers, agencies, and suppliers about the core principles that define the brands and programs they direct.

Once a decision has been made to create an archives, the placement of that function within the business becomes the next critical decision. Most corporate archives reside within one of four areas: the public relations or communications function; the office of the general counsel, the corporate secretary's office or some administrative placement such as the president's office. All of those scenarios can work well as long as the decision-making ladder is relatively short. If the archives has easy access to senior management for resources, allocation, a specific organizational structure is less relevant.

Still, there are some positives and negatives to be considered in any of these arrangements. The communications placement may be the most symbiotic as both archivists and public relations professionals respect and appreciate the power of information. The communications function has a broad view of the organization and provides enhanced visibility for an archival program. The principal drawback to this linkage is that the public relations activities are often ranked lower than other functional areas and frequently receive lesser funding. Ties to the General Counsel or to the Corporate Secretary's office place the archives in areas that are well regarded and operate from positions of strength. Funding for programs is easier to obtain and access to senior management is streamlined. The potential negative in this placement is that the archives can be easily neglected because of critical business priorities facing the functional leadership. The most dangerous positioning is the administrative one. This situation usually occurs if a President or Chairman has made a unilateral decision to create an archives to preserve the history of a specific administration or when the archives is dumped into a general administrative area that handles nonessential business activities. In this scenario, the archives is the likely victim in a change of executive leadership or a financial slowdown that necessitates a prioritization of resource allocation.

Corporate archivists will often create a wide array of tools to help them attain greater visibility in the corporation and to better define their role. One of the most important documents for a corporate archives is a mission or policy statement, distributed company-wide, that defines the responsibilities of the department and provides the authorization for the archives to collect records from individual business units. Such documents may detail the specific functions of the archives, may identify records considered to be archival, and may even outline the specific processes for transferring records to the archives.

The creation of a broad-based, cross-functional advisory board to help the archivist define the institution's collecting canons can broaden the client base of the archives and develop an in-house support system for its mission. By holding regular meetings of this group, the archivist ensures that the collection represents the company's key functions while creating a group of auxiliary archivists with a vested interest in securing important records from their respective functions.

Many archivists place a high priority on outreach programming to extend the influence of their institutions to external audiences, attracting new researchers to their collections and generating a broader support base for their activities. In the corporate world, outreach is also critically important, and the overall objectives are similar, but the tactics and execution are internally directed. Unlike academic programs where the value of preserving historical documentation is clearly understood or government repositories where retention is mandated, corporate archives exist in an environment that focuses on the future and pays little more than lip service to the past. To succeed over the long term, the corporate archives must be relevant to the business and be able to justify the costs of the program.

One of the most natural alliances is with the public relations team as the archives is a tremendous resource for the generation of media coverage of the business. The archives can provide the historic background data, photographs, film, and video that add depth and color to the new releases and media stories that shape the image of the business to the outside world. The archives provides content to in-house magazines, newsletters, annual reports, social responsibility, and citizenship publications that communications groups produce and distribute. Additionally, the archivist can become an adjunct member of the public relations department by authoring features on heritage and serving as a company spokesperson on historical issues.

During an anniversary celebration, the archives becomes even more critical as it serves as the primary resource for the publications that will inevitably mark the event. Books, magazines, case studies, timelines, brochures, and pamphlets signal important milestones in organizational growth and development and create special opportunities for the archives to shine in the corporate spotlight. During these moments of historical focus, the relevance of the archival program is obvious. It is in the nonanniversary years that a program must have a broader organizational impact to sustain itself.

Technology offers new possibilities to make archival materials more accessible to broader audiences. The emergence of digital technology allows users access to thousands of images, documents, and audiovisual materials via intranet sites. With a few clicks of a keyboard, materials that had been held in a single geography can be shared with associates in hundreds of locations in high-resolution formats, resulting in cost-savings that can be calculated and communicated to the management. Similar techniques are used throughout the archival profession, but the business archives application has a robust revenue stream that establishes a clear return on investment (ROI), a calculation that every business recognizes and appreciates. Many business operations rely on a network of agencies and suppliers to provide them with high-resolution photography files for commercial applications at costs that frequently exceed $100 per unit. The existence of the archives removes these middlemen and concentrates the collection and preservation of images at a single contact point, supplying materials through the organization in a cost-efficient manner. In addition to the information sharing, many corporate archives license their images to third parties for commercial application. These licensing programs generate thousands of dollars that can reduce, if not totally offset, the costs of maintaining an archives.

The Internet also provides business with an interactive communications tools to reach out to important constituencies: consumers, stakeholders, students, the media, regulators, and nongovernmental organizations. A section of the site devoted to Heritage can provide a large volume of useful information to individuals and groups interested in the historical and cultural impact of the firm. By placing this data in one convenient location, the business connects with key audiences while gaining some cost-savings through the reduction of personnel handling consumer inquiries.

The use of blogs as a social media tool offers new opportunities for corporate archivists to engage proactively, using rich content from their collections on the Web. Rather than relying on traditional media outlets to publish positive stories on the history of the business, archival bloggers can post stories and commentary on a schedule of their choice and can interact with groups and organizations that would not normally receive information directly from the business. With over 100 million blogs in existence, an archival blog may be one of the easiest methods of delivering historical information through nontraditional outlets.

Exhibitions are excellent tools to enhance the archival presence, signal the importance of history to the organization, and create an experience that helps shape the corporate culture. Most corporate archives use them, in one

form or another, to create an atmosphere that encourages the study of the past to inform the future. The size and scope of these exhibits can vary from small window and case displays near the archives entrance, to more robust lobby displays greeting visitors to the business, to freestanding museums open to the general public, but the archivist administering these share one strategic objective. The exhibit makes history and the archives come alive for the people reviewing it, providing an overt rationale for the larger program.

Within the marketing arena, the archives can play a pivotal role in helping managers understand business and brand basics. By securing a representative collection of advertising, promotional, packaging, and product files, the archives can document the strategies, positioning, and philosophies that have marked both successful and unsuccessful programs. Management can then repurpose the best practices into contemporary executions that will resonate with consumers. Conversely, by understanding why projects failed, there is a stronger likelihood that a new generation of management will not make the same mistakes.

As noted earlier, one of the reasons businesses choose to establish archives is their critical role in litigation. Trademarks, patents, designs, copyrights, and other forms of intellectual property uniquely define the corporation and represent its most valuable assets. By maintaining records of the development, implementation, and continued use of those elements, the corporation secures its unique standing in the marketplace and ensures its long-term viability.

The archives serves as a powerful resource in this arena. The scope of the collection itself can frequently discourage frivolous lawsuits from ever being filed, but the more quantitative value is established when records maintained by the firm form the basis for a successful legal action. All of the costs associated with the creation and maintenance of the archival program could be recovered with a single piece of litigation.

The human resources function represents yet another client for archival services. Employee orientation presentations, training programs, department briefings, and retiree organization all benefit from an in-house historical department that can supply materials that underscore the company's mission statement and reinforce those values that shape the corporate culture. Frequently, the archivists play a pivotal role in such activities, while the films, photos, music, videos, and artifacts from the archives add depth and color to the presentations.

The types of records collected by corporate archivists are similar to those collected by any other repository that collects institutional documentation, but the volume of records generated by business and the sensitivity of certain categories of records (personnel, financial, research, and development) requires rigorous appraisal criteria. The nature of the business itself and the frequency of use are the two primary criteria that determine the volume of materials collected and the hierarchy assigned to them. A financial services company will tend to collect records with fiscal content more heavily than a consumer goods company that will focus more energy against identifying and securing marketing and advertising files. Not only are those records more indicative of the functions of the respective businesses, they also are the records used most frequently by business units.

Conversely, corporations generally will not retain certain record types as part of the archives if they have high litigation potential. Federal and state regulations mandate the retention of specific personnel, technical, and financial data, but at the expiration of the required life cycle, these materials will be destroyed unless there is a more compelling historical reason to retain them. In an era when class action lawsuits can yield millions of dollars in settlements, corporations will not run the risk of preserving records of tangential research value.

Most corporate collections will include records from the senior executives of the organization. The papers and working files of the Chairman of the Board of Directors, the President, the Chief Financial Officer, and the Corporate Secretary's office will provide a strong overview of the events and issues that characterized each administration. Functional records from Finance, Legal, Human Resources, Technical, Public Relations, Community Affairs, and Administration provide the detailed documentation of the operations of the enterprise that will comprise the historical record and allow for interpretation and repurposing in the future.

In developing an organizational scheme for the records, corporate archivists look at the work product from each group and establish record groups that document their activities. For instance, a record group titled Marketing would contain data relating to the advertising, promotion, and packaging of goods and services. A Human Resources record group would contain data on the workforce, policies and procedures, training information, and employee benefits. The record groups will vary in size and importance depending on the focus of the business, but they should reveal the essential activities of the parent body.

The collections will also hold extensive audiovisual collections, clippings files, small library collections, and reference files, as well as the records of predecessor or merged companies that may have their own unique records structure. Many archives will also function as the corporate museum and will preserve extensive collections of artifacts encompassing packaging, awards, promotional items, premiums, and a host of advertising and marketing samples, ranging from small signs and posters to large pieces of equipment.

The biggest differences between the work of corporate archivists and others in the professional falls into three areas: descriptive practices, access policies, and the institutional approach to reference and research. While most

archives are interested in fully describing their collections and making them available as broadly as possible, corporate programs have a very different vision. Their clients and users are the employees, suppliers, and business partners of their host institution. Their mandate does not extend to any third parties beyond that limited definition.

Many corporate archives have sophisticated information management and digital asset management systems that allow them to share detailed information about their holdings internally and externally, but they seldom report or contribute to national databases that make similar information available to researchers around the world. The corporate archivist does not seek or encourage the external researcher who would certainly materialize if holdings were more widely reported. Similarly, the descriptive tools used by the archivists are designed for internal use and frequently are based on proprietary software developed by the business itself.

Most business archives limit access to the collections to employees and designated partners. They do not solicit or cultivate scholarly research nor do they feel obligated to share their resources with the general public. The corporation provides all of the funding for the program and determines how the collection will be used. Equal access is not a concept utilized in the corporate environment.

The archives receives funding because it provides a unique set of services that the business could not secure from any other source. It is intellectual capital that is as important as trade secrets or patents. Consequently, there is a reluctance to share this collateral with others by opening the doors of their historical vaults to the outside world. From the corporate perspective, there is little to be gained and a very serious downside to releasing materials to third parties who do not have a vested interest in the business.

Reference and research also look considerably different from academic models. In academic settings, researchers travel to the host institution, request the desired records, study the documents, and formulate their conclusions. Reference specialists respond to written and oral inquiries in a structured fashion that normally requires the researcher to wait several days, if not weeks, before receiving a formal reply.

In business, the archivist processes the records, prepares finding aids for them, and then assumes all of the research and reference responsibilities. As to the subject matter expert, there is an expectation that the archivist will search through the records to expeditiously retrieve the requested information and deliver it to the client. Researchers seldom visit the archives and even less often volunteer to go through the materials themselves. There is the further expectation that the requested information will be provided in a time-sensitive fashion measured in minutes and hours rather than days and weeks. Businesses operate on cycles that require speed and efficiency to produce financial results that benefit their shareowners.

Archivists operating in that environment must mimic those qualities if they are to be successful.

Salaries for business archivists tend to be higher than those of other archival practitioners. The mean salary for academic archivists hovers around $50,000, while government archivists earn about $3000 more. The mean salary in the business arena exceeds $61,000, with manager salaries approaching $70,000.[4] Additionally, compensation packages in corporations frequently include annual bonuses and stock options not reflected in the salary figures. Total compensation in the corporate sector can easily exceed $100,000 per year.

While the compensation levels for the corporate archivist are appealing, this segment of the profession is the most unstable. The continued existence of the program totally depends on the financial health of the parent organization. In years of strong earnings and profitability, the archives will prosper and enjoy management support, but in an economic downturn, the first targets of downsizing are those functions considered overhead. Unfortunately, archival programs can be consigned into this category, resulting in reduced, outsourced, or discontinued programs. Some of the major business archives programs in the United States including those at Firestone, United Technologies, Arco, Bank of America, and Polaroid disappeared in retrenchment initiatives.

The number of business archives in North America will probably continue to grow though not as rapidly as programs in the nonprofit sector. For current information about business archives, the best resource is the Web site of the Business Archives Section of the Society of American Archivists (http://www.archivists.org/saagroups/bas). This site includes member's profiles, news and announcements, information on section initiatives, and technical guidance on issues of concern to the group. Dr. Gregory Hunter, a professor at Long Island University, maintains the "Directory of Corporate Archives in the United States and Canada" at his Web site (hunterinformation.com), and Dr. Hunter also posts the notes of the Corporate Archives Forum there. The CAF is an informal group of about a dozen business archivists from large companies who have met annually since 1998 to discuss issues of mutual interest and to share best practices. Additionally, the Society of American Archivists sponsors a workshop on Establishing and Managing a Business Archives on an annual basis.

REFERENCES

1. Bakken, D.A. Corporate archives today. Am. Arch. **1982**, 45(3), 284.
2. Smith, D.R. A historical look at business archives. Am. Arch. **1982**, 45(3), 275–276.
3. http://www.archivists.org/saagroups/bas/welcome.asp (accessed January 2008).
4. Walch, V.I. A*census: A closer look. Am. Arch. **2006**, 69(2), 336–340.

Corporate Art Collections

Laura Matzer
Arizona Museum for Youth, Mesa, Arizona, U.S.A.

Abstract

What propels a for-profit corporation to collect and invest in the collection management of an art collection, to buy original works of art to display, care for, and store? What are the benefits of placing art in the workplace? What does the future hold for corporate art collecting? The term "corporate art collection" has become a generic, catchall phrase that often encompasses the art collecting activities of law and accounting firms, small companies, government, cities, port authority, transit, and other types of organizations. The purpose of this entry, however, is to discuss art collecting activity conducted within corporate business workplaces specifically. Does a corporate art collection reveal a corporation's viewpoints, long-term goals and aspirations, and culture? And what are the philosophical concerns of mingling art and commerce in the presentation of art in a corporate setting? This entry seeks to address such questions and provide a cursory history of corporate art collecting in the United States and abroad.

INTRODUCTION

The notion that to place art in the workplace is simply *decorative* is to take a simplistic viewpoint. Corporations buy artworks to fill many needs: to fill blank walls, to improve a *workplace* environment, to enhance their *image* (internally, externally, or both), to support the local art community, to make a social statement, and to demonstrate their company values.[1] While most companies do not purchase art for financial gain, some track the current market value of their collections for insurance and other purposes. For many corporations, *accessibility* and image are key elements in the contemporary world of corporate art collecting.

An emphasis on contemporary art seems to be a trend in corporate art collecting, the currently high-paced—and priced—art marketplace notwithstanding. Popular amongst companies with a *global* presence, is to collect art with an international focus, reflecting their workforce, or reflect a *regional* art focus in specific locations. Corporations today are particularly savvy in finding new ways of utilizing their art collection for *marketing*, advertising, and *commissioning* artwork to promote their company's image and products.

Every corporate art collection, from its origins, to its objects, to its operations, is unique. There currently remain very few books and articles written on the subject of corporate art collecting. While the *Directory of Corporate Art Collections* profiles over 1000 collections, and some companies promote their art collections and attendant activities online and in print, much remains hidden and private in regard to how corporate art collections are formed, managed, and maintained. This entry aims to illuminate the world of corporate art collecting.

HISTORY

The collaboration between art and business dates back to Renaissance Italy and in more recent years has become a common partnership.[2] In earliest examples, financial institutions were leaders in terms of corporations collecting art; presenting art in the workplace demonstrated to their clients the sophistication and wealth of their institution, as well as the path of portfolio investment. Deutsche Bank, one of the largest corporate art collections in the world at present, has over 50,000 objects in their collection, housed in over 1000 locations. Regardless of institution type, the history of each corporate art collection can provide a fascinating glimpse into the history and culture of a company. Many corporate art collections were willed into being by notable CEOs with personal interest in art and art collections of their own, and a vision for wanting to bring art—and the appreciation of culture that comes with art—into their corporate culture. Others begin their art collecting activity by forming grassroots committees of interested executives and employees.

In the United States, in late nineteenth and early part of the twentieth century, art was explicitly used for marketing: railroads such as Union Pacific and Santa Fe would use art as a publicity medium to encourage travel and to publicize themselves.[3] Abbott Laboratories began their collection in 1930, the Anheuser-Busch collection dates back to the late 1890s, and what is generally regarded as the first modern-day corporate art collection is the International Business Machines (IBM) collection of contemporary American art, begun in 1939.[4] Image making continued to drive art collections that began in the 1960s and the 1970s, with a large number of collection facilities being created in Japan. The 1980s witnessed a significant

Encyclopedia of Library and Information Sciences, Fourth Edition DOI: 10.1081/E-ELIS4-120044063

rise in corporate art collection activity, particularly in the United States and Britain. By the 1990s, as a result of an economic recession, some corporate art collections disbanded or were sold, leading many to consider corporate art collecting as a mere phenomenon of the times. In fact, the sheer number of corporations collecting art on an ongoing basis far outweighed the few collections that were dismantled. Today, corporate art collecting is now an "established segment of the art world, with its own corps of professionals and specialists, its own philosophies and standards of ethics, and its own professional organizations" (Fig. 1).[3]

In Europe, with more general, broad-based government support to museums and artists, culture is more widely considered a part of life. With this intrinsic way of thinking, European corporate art collections have been innovators in terms of collecting activity, commissions, and corporate-supported artist projects. The Deutsche Bank art collection was essentially founded on a friendship. Herbert Zapp, a former bank board member, lent his chauffeured limousine to the artist Joseph Beuys while Zapp drove an accompanying security car, en route to a Beuys exhibition, and they became friends. Another board member, Hermann J. Abs, years previously, had introduced Beuys to the bank. Together Abs and Zapp shaped the bank's art policy in the 1970s, and jointly initiated a significant acquisition of a comprehensive series of Beuys drawings for the Deutsche Bank art collection.[5]

In addition to placing art in the workplace, some corporations have designated spaces solely dedicated to displaying their collections in corporate art museums, galleries, and sculpture gardens. The first corporate art museum was founded by Josiah Wedgwood & Sons Ltd. in 1906 in Barlaston, Stoke-on-Trent, and other corporate art museums and galleries began to proliferate in the 1920s.[6] By the 1990s the corporate art museum model was challenged. Occidental Petroleum Corporation's Armand Hammer Museum of Art and Cultural Center in Los Angeles was created in the late 1990s, which brought about lawsuit from dissident stockholders challenging the right of Chairman Armand Hammer and the Occidental Petroleum Corporation to finance a museum housing the chairman's private collection of artworks. The lawsuit further charged that the museum had no tangential connection to the company and offered no stockholder benefit. While a settlement was reached, the ruling was in line "with long-time corporate beliefs and practices in the United States and other countries" that spaces can be created if the facilities are in the best interest of the company, "on the grounds that it is in the company's best interests— meaning good for business and public relations."[6]

PROMOTING CULTURE

Although internal and external publicity varies amongst them, corporate art collections typically exhort the role they play in promoting arts and culture in their respective workplaces. They have many reasons to do so: In addition to directly supporting artists through tangible object acquisitions, their collections also can be considered a valued intangible asset for the public relations of a corporation that supports a professional and inspiring environment for employees and the public. Regardless of intent, a corporate art collection serves as an ongoing visual reminder of the value of inspiration, creativity, and innovation, and the corporation's support of such values. That said, there are numerous philosophical issues surrounding the intermingling of art and commerce, as companies that delve into art collecting, art sponsorship, and other modes of engagement, can "convert cultural capital into economic capital, in sometimes politically pernicious forms."[7]

Responses in a 2001 survey of 32 companies by the Business Committee for the Arts (BCA) and the International Association for Professional Art Advisors (IAPAA) assert that art in the work environment fosters elements essential to a company's success. The survey found that 78% of respondents believe that art in the workplace

Fig. 1 Microsoft Redmond Campus installation view of Bean Finneran, Orange Cone, 2006, fired ceramic and glazes, 20 × 20 × 14 in.
Source: Photo copyright of Adam L. Weintraub.

Communication–
Corporate Art

reduces stress, while 64% believe it increases creativity and productivity. Another 67% believe it enhances morale, while 77% agree that it "broadens employee appreciation of diversity and encourages discussions, and expression of opinions."[8]

ACQUIRING ART

Corporations acquire artwork for their collections in a number of ways. In fact, there is a constellation of entities that can be involved in any one corporate art program. Some companies employ in-house curators, who work with decision-makers in their company and outside resources—such as art galleries, artists, auction houses, and print publishers—to select works of art. Other companies outsource art advisors to recommend artworks to a decision-making committee or individual within the company. Depending on the project, an in-house art curator or an outsourced art advisor can work with architects, landscape architects, contractors, lighting designers, and building occupants to determine an art installation plan, proper lighting, and architectural opportunities for special art placement.

The type of art purchased on behalf of a corporation is as varied as the companies amassing them. Some corporate art collections purchase and commission art tied to their products or marketing campaigns, while others collect and commission artworks intended as visual counterpoints to the workplace environment. Most corporate art collections have a mission or vision statement to guide their collecting activity and programming. Ultimately, corporations that collect and display art in their facilities are stating, either overtly or subtly, that they support culture within and without the workplace walls.

For artwork acquisitions, regardless of purchase decisions made by committee or by those considered subject-matter expert(s), such decisions require research, timing, and negotiation. In most cases a rigorous initial selection process in undertaken. Corporate art curators and art advisors can consult numerous sources: art fairs, museum exhibitions, art journals, newspapers, magazines, artist monographs, art galleries, exhibition catalogs, juried exhibitions, and artist studio visits. When a work of art is purchased, items such as shipping, framing, digital image, accession number, provenance, artist and exhibition articles, artist curriculum vitae, gallery announcements, and condition reporting are just a few of the items that go into the typical processing of an artwork as an asset into a corporate art collection.

Those that purchase the artwork, in addition to keeping in mind the project's budget, building installation plan, hanging or placement requirements, have many other variables to consider when deciding upon what to buy. The famous dictum to "buy what you love" is a good rule of thumb. However, the purchaser's (or decision-maker(s)) taste and aesthetic is a factor, as well as, content of the

piece, media, style, artist, size, installation requirements, price, and expected maintenance. Further, it is the job of the procurer to examine the strengths and weaknesses of an existing art collection and how a new acquisition would fit within that collection. Other items that a purchaser will likely weigh are authenticity, historical significance, provenance, practicality, region, and ethnicity of artist.

When a project's scope is assessed, the individual(s) determining artwork purchases can look to the primary art marketplace: art galleries, artist studios, rental/sales galleries, and to the trade commercial art procurers, or, to the secondary art marketplace: auction houses and consignment art galleries. In addition to filling their buildings with artworks, many companies also commission artists to create site-specific works in designated locations within their facilities. Commissioned work gives the company an opportunity to have an iconic, unique piece of art to both support artists and to enhance their image. In a recent example, BMW commissioned Icelandic artist Olafur Eliasson, an artist concerned with tangible topics such as civilization, technology, and nature, as well as renewable energies, and ephemeral works, to design the 16th BMW Art Car, to be added to the BMW Art Car Collection.[9] Eliasson's work, an H2R BMW metal car frame covered in 2 tons of frozen water and lit from within, is a sharp visual commentary intended to raise awareness to automotive industry practices and their effects on global warming. His work, which initially may seem an indictment of the automotive industry, ultimately aligns with BMW's values for their product, which is to provide sustained mobility based a regenerative fuel source.

While modern day media may obsess upon corporate art collections that have been disbanded or sold, corporate art collecting comprises a large segment of the art marketplace—some attribute up to 30% of sales worldwide toward this specific market—however it is difficult to fully assess as many dealings are kept secret.[7] For artists interested in their work being added to a corporate art collection, F. David Fowler, managing partner for KPMG Peat Marwick, who works with the art advisors for their corporate art collection, states:

> The key to being included in a corporate collection is no different from being in an outstanding private collection: you have to be known, have a good gallery. A typical corporate art curator or art advisor gets invitations to every gallery opening in town, every exhibition and show, but it is tough...I wish we could do more with local artists but budgetary constraints limit us.[4]

ART AS INVESTMENT

While there have been certain art collections that have applied an art as investment philosophy to their collecting

Communication–
Corporate Art

activity, by and large, most corporations do not buy art for investment. While artwork typically appreciates in value rather than depreciates, and corporate executives may find satisfaction in that fact, corporations that are in the position to begin or support a corporate art program typically have a product or products that bring in significant profit, so looking to an art collection as a potential money-making investment is not typical. One challenge to a corporate art program is to demonstrate, particularly in a tenuous situation, such as a company merger, executive shuffle, bankruptcy, or buyout, that the collection's value is equally high, if not higher in intangible value to employees, customers, and visitors that interact with the art collection on a daily basis.

For a publicly held company, another concern is how a corporation's art collection is viewed amongst its stockholders. While it has been demonstrated in studies such as BCAs aforementioned survey in 2001, and in other sources, that art in a workplace environment improves productivity and employee satisfaction, stockholders may question putting company profits toward such a program. Conversely, stockholders may appreciate that artworks are a part of a company they have invested their hard-earned money in: The company invests in benefiting employee quality of life and the art community.

COLLECTION MANAGEMENT

As we have by now well established, every corporate art collection is different. So is how they are managed: One particularly large corporate art collection can have 10 different curators with various content specialties, and a smaller art collection could be overseen by a director in lieu of a curator. Corporate art collection management has been humorously described as a cross between being air traffic controller and the director of an art museum. When corporate art collections begin, collection management can sometimes be an afterthought. However, when a corporate art collection grows to a certain size, it becomes abundantly clear that professional collection management is required. Benchmarking survey data from similar-size art museums and corporate art collections can demonstrate strengths and weaknesses in a corporate art collection program assessment.

Important items in collection management that a corporate art collection typically requires are collection management database to store and track data; climate-controlled art storage facility; de-accessioning (*to sell or otherwise dispose of an item in a collection*) of objects; conservation; image library; art research and reference library; appraisal and inventory survey of collection; and maintenance schedule for cleaning select works, such as outdoor sculpture. Unlike a museum collection, which may house up to 90–95% of its holdings in storage at any given time, a corporate art collection is usually the

Fig. 2 View of Microsoft Art Collection storage vault. **Source**: Photo courtesy of Microsoft Art Collection.

opposite ratio, and the works are typically rotated within buildings owned by the company (Fig. 2).

A corporate art collection might be housed within any number of teams or departments. These can range from Human Resources, to Real Estate, to Legal, to the Executive Office, depending on how a particular company's divisional structure is arranged. Furthermore, every corporate art collection budget is unique. For a growing company, an artwork budget might be set by a metric, or measurement, involving square footage. For others, it may depend on the desire of the CEO.

ALTERNATIVE MODES OF COLLECTING

Corporations also instigate other types of involvement with artists beyond the corporate art collecting model. For art collections that become a valued and invaluable part of a stable company, many companies utilize their collections in targeted marketing campaigns, advertisements for products, and commissioning artists to literally make a mark on their products. Examples of this are seen in commissioned works for Illy Espresso company and wine labels for Baron Rothschild wineries. New forms of corporate sponsorship will continue to emerge and set trends, as the worlds of marketing and advertising, art and commerce converge.

Corporate Mentality, a book by Swedish artist Aleksandra Mir, documents the myriad ways in which artists interact with corporations and how they consider them rich subject matter in producing object-based and performative artworks. In one example of art meeting commerce, Mir interviews Martina Westin, Manager of Communications of The Absolut Company in Stockholm. Remarks Westin:

> The artists that collaborate with us are given complete artistic freedom...we don't buy art, but look for a relationship in which we ask artists to interpret our (vodka) bottle. In that, they are free to do whatever they like but ... since many of the art works are advertised, some policies and laws apply, such as no cars, no children and no pornography. That way freedom of expression may be limited, but our parameters are clearly stipulated from the very beginning when we brief the artist and he/she accepts or enters the collaboration....Maurizio Cattelan's rat in the bottle...I tell you, I have worked in the food industry for many years, and rats in conjunction with food is the ultimate no-no. But here we felt that the artistic freedom and the integrity of the artist is important, so we approved it.[10]

Created in 1984, Fondacion Cartier Pour l'art Contemporain, in Jouy-en-Josas, France, has a unique program that is a separate division of Cartier International Paris. Their foundation, historically the first corporate foundation in France, provides studio, living, and exhibition space for artists-in-residence, as well as a conference and meeting center, library, restaurants, sculpture garden, and an exhibition hall. Other corporate art collections innovate through programs training employees to lead art tours, inviting artists to speak, presenting films, offering art-related book discussions, and developing partnerships with community organizations and more.

Umeå Energi, located in northern Sweden, produces, distributes, and sells electricity, heating, and cooling. Collaborating with Umeå's College of Art, they work with students to create various art projects that are featured in differing formats for company use. Mir's interview with Anette Mångsén discusses their "Power Flower" project. States Mångsén:

> Power Flower is a sponsorship arrangement that ... is an example of how art can be used for more than just adornment. The agreement... also gave us the right to use the Power Flower theme in our advertising, in our information activities for schools, on our Web site...on T-shirts, and as a screensaver, etc. This is how sponsoring works. It should involve mutual giving and taking, in which both parties are winners...a sponsorship agreement is just like any other business arrangement. By means of artistic expressions...we can demonstrate that Umeå Energi is more than electrons and incinerators, and that we are people with warmth, feelings, and a sense of humour. Employees also benefit from seeing art in their everyday lives. We spend a large proportion of our working hours at work, and it is important to have various forms of stimulation. Art is enriching, and it liberates the senses.[10]

Another interesting model is the collaboration of BMW KulturKommunikation unit and the BMW Art Car Collection. Christiane Zentgraf, head of, Corporate Affairs, in Munich, Germany, states:

> The BMW Group has been actively engaged in the field of culture for over a quarter of a century, both regionally and internationally. Over the course of time, BMW's experience with art led to the realization that a discursive engagement with art and culture, if it is used in the right way, can be employed as an outstanding medium of communication. Art and culture are highly sensitive fields. Our primary focus is not on financial transactions or the cash value of goods, but rather the long-term interaction of partners who are interested in getting to know and understand each other and each other's worlds, exchanging ideas, and realizing joint projections that will, of course, need to be financed. The widely quoted motto, "Do good and talk about it," is not BMW's policy. BMW believes in "doing good and letting others talk about it."

The BMW Art Car Collection began in 1975 as a result of the spontaneous request of French auctioneer and racing driver Hervé Poulain to his friend Alexander Calder to design a BMW racing car. The idea "sparked enthusiasm in both Calder and BMW," and started the impetus for additional art cars by artists such as Roy Lichtenstein, Frank Stella, Andy Warhol, Jenny Holzer, and Robert Rauschenberg. Zentgraf further states: "The artists find themselves in the world of automobiles; BMW is critically received in the world of art."[10]

CHALLENGES AND CONCERNS

Some corporate art collections strategically aim through their artwork acquisitions to challenge the viewer. Others are tied to the initial vision of a CEO, such as Lloyd Cotsen's textile and folk art collection at Neutrogena (today housed in a wing of the International Museum of Folk Art in Santa Fe). Regardless of acquisition focus, by and large, those purchasing works for corporate art collections do consider sensitivity to subject matter, in light of the fact that employees are paid to be at a workplace vs. an individual willingly experiencing a boundary-breaking art exhibition. Many corporate art collections, such as Microsoft's, while pushing certain envelopes, often, do avoid artworks with overt nudity, political and religious content. Works of art with challenging media, such as materials that are highly light-sensitive, hazardous, or sculptural works with dangerous shapes must also be considered prior to being placed in a workplace setting.

As a corporate art collection grows, the overall value of the art collection can appreciate to the point that a specialized fine art insurance policy is required. In larger businesses with offices worldwide, it can be a challenge, however, to demonstrate the level of risk a company is exposing itself to if the company is large enough to deem such a specialized policy irrelevant. Many corporate art collections are difficult to formally survey and appraise, as artworks can be installed far and wide depending on the corporation's size and their art collection's overall program and scope. Finally, there are a number of legal concerns that a properly managed corporate art collection must consider, such as loaning objects to art museums and institutions; rights to reproduce images of works in the collection in various formats (print, online) and for various uses (education, commercial/advertising, product packaging); and bill of sale for purchasing artworks from primary and secondary art marketplace sources.

CORPORATE SPONSORSHIP AND PATRONAGE

With the seemingly gradual reduction of governmental funding, particularly in the United States, arts institutions increasingly turn to corporations and other sources for short- and long-term support. Through arts sponsorships, corporations gain new audiences and new platforms to market themselves, which has "become a well-known and beneficial marketing tool."[11] Deutsche Bank is a major sponsor of the Frieze Art Fair in London, and also operates a space—the Deutsche Guggenheim—an outpost in the Guggenheim Museum's global network on the ground floor of the Deutsche Bank building in Berlin. Corporations can also make an impact in rural areas or small- to medium-sized cities, such as Microsoft's campus in Fargo, North Dakota, if they are acquiring and placing art and can directly impact a regional art market, from individual artists to art galleries and collaborations with local art museums.

Corporations that support the arts, not just in corporate art collecting, but through sponsorship and other innovative programs, have often been compared to the Medicis:

> Why don't more people buy art? The benefits are considerable: offices have to be decorated anyway; it pleases and motivates the workforce; it enables a company to project a positive image and to act like a Medici, sponsoring artists; and not least, careful buying can prove a profitable investment.[11]

See Fig. 3 for an illustration. With some companies their art collection is an integral part of the culture of the company, yet for others, there is also the drive to affiliate themselves with artists to market their products in new ways. Takashi Murakami's collaboration with Louis Vuitton on their monogram handbags demonstrates that boundaries between art and the commercial sphere can easily blur. Aforementioned Olafur Eliasson also created a light piece for Louis Vuitton stores, and, almost defensively, states:

> It is about a principle that art should not be exclusive. Art doesn't have to polarize itself into a critical, quite

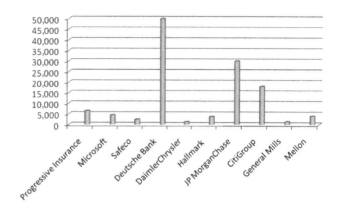

Fig. 3 Select corporate art collection sizes in object totals, August 2007.

predictable role of being oppositional. To think that a museum is a free space and a Louis Vuitton window is not is problematic.[12]

When LACMA opened its 60,000 ft annex, the Broad Contemporary Art Museum, in February 2008, real estate financier Eli Broad gave the museum $50 million for construction, and limited access to his foundation's art collection as well as his personal one. This hybrid arrangement, of which there are a few other examples, presents the viewer with a potentially confusing presentation of a museum within a museum. Finally, corporate executives with a passion for art have long held posts on museum boards and advisory committees, not only for their ability to donate to the institution, but also for their access to others with similar interests and pocketbooks.

EVOLUTION OF THE WORKPLACE

The corporate workplace is rapidly evolving, as evidenced at Microsoft, with more employees working remotely and the proliferation of open plan workstations, which decrease the overall amount of available wall space to hang artworks. For those that maintain an office, many employees no longer adhere to a 9 A.M. to 5 P.M. work schedule; some utilize their office spaces 24/7. In addition to these developments, many companies choose to "brand" their interiors with company logos, products, awards, and advertising campaigns. As a result, placing art in the dynamic setting that is today's workplace requires nimbleness and open attitude to change.

In a workplace environment, artworks are subject to a variety of variables not found in a more controlled art museum setting. Fluctuations in light, temperature, and humidity, which vary depending on the heating and cooling system activity in an office building (on weekends such systems are typically powered down) must be considered regarding art installations. Other elements, such as mail carts, construction projects to retrofit interiors, painting crews, furniture moves, all must be considered and planned for prior to art placement. Furthermore, most corporations do not have the level of security one might find in a museum setting. Corporations with art collections can counterbalance security concerns by security-mounting artworks and educating employees through programs and signage about appropriate behavior with regard to looking at art.

Due to the proliferation of technology in the workplace, placing art within such a context can strike a powerful visual counterpoint against a field of varying devices. In such a setting, art can humanize the environment, make a statement, and enhance a company's overall image. In the United States, one way corporations evaluate themselves and each other and how employees evaluate them, is through the Fortune Magazine's "Best Places to Work" survey. A company-sanctioned art program can attract future employees and retain existing work force, as a corporate art program can overtly or subtly demonstrate the environment of the corporation and how the company treats its employees.

CONCLUSION AND LOOKING FORWARD

There have been gradual and significant changes to the world of corporate art collecting. Many companies that are expanding are expanding their art programs as well, and new companies continue to start their own art collections. The often more conservative art collecting programs in the 1960s and 1970s, leading up to the extravagant purchasing in the 1980s—and wholesale selling of certain art collections during economic downturns—led to today's cautious, yet carefully optimistic and predominant viewpoint of corporate art collecting reflecting the values of a company. Corporate art collecting is now an established entity in the art world, with a variety of professional organizations to support specialists in the field.

As corporate art collections grow, some companies will consider establishing a nonprofit foundation to protect their collections from oftentimes tumultuous business cycles and executive turnover in a company.

One interesting model has emerged from Hallmark Cards, Inc.: After having built a museum-worthy photography collection, the company donated it in 2006 to the Nelson–Atkins Museum of Art for posterity and to enhance the museum's photography collection holdings. At the same time, the Hallmark Art Collection continues its collecting activity in other media.

While corporate art collecting remains an often secretive activity, employees, customers, and guests at a company have the rewarding opportunity to see and be surrounded by original art. A company's art collection is a reflection of the company and can provide an outsider with a different viewpoint and perception of a corporation. Ultimately, a well-managed and well-cared for corporate art collection not only enhances a workplace setting, it also supports the art community as a whole.

REFERENCES

1. Abbott, S. *Corporate Art Consulting;* Allworth Press: New York, 1994; 35–37.
2. Jacobsen, M. *Art for Work: The New Renaissance in Corporate Collecting*; Harvard Business School Press: Boston, MA, 1993; 10.
3. http://home.earthlink.net/~corporate.directory/id20.html.
4. Dougherty, B.L. *Making a Living as an Artist;* The Lyons Press: New York, 1998; 102–105.
5. http://www.deutsche-bank-kunst.com/collection/.
6. Danilov, V.J. *A Planning Guide for Corporate Museums, Galleries, and Visitor Centers;* Greenwood Press: Westport, CT, 1992.
7. Wu, C. *Privatising Culture: Corporate Art Intervention since the 1980s, Verso*, London, U.K., 2002; 9.
8. http://www.bcainc.org/includes/news_articles.asp.479.html.
9. http://www.theartnewspaper.com/whatson/list.asp?fm_listid= US73442.
10. Mir, A. *Corporate Mentality: An Archive Documenting the Emergence of Recent Practices within a Cultural Sphere Occupied by Both Business and Art;* Lukas & Sternberg: New York, 2003; 104484–104489.
11. Harris, P.; Flowers, J. *Art Collecting: The Benefits for Your Business;* Art & Business: London, U.K., 2001; 1–12.
12. Modern Painters: The International Contemporary Art Magazine. **2007**, *14*(7), 32, Editors, Provision.

BIBLIOGRAPHY

1. Bamberger, A. *The Art of Buying Art*; Gordon's Art Reference, Inc.: Phoenix, AZ, 2002.
2. Bielstein, S.M. *Permissions, A Survival Guide;* The University of Chicago Press: Chicago, IL, 2006.
3. Birnie, A.; Ruiz, C.F.; de Peuter, P.; Waller, J.; Wróblewska, H. *Art in the Office*; Waanders Uitgeverij: Zwolle, LA, 2006.
4. Fahy, A., Ed. *Collections Management*; Routledge: London, U.K., 1995.
5. Gingold, D.J. *Business and the Arts, How They Meet the Challenge*, National Endowment for the Arts Press: Washington, DC, 1984.
6. Hadden, P. *The Artist's Guide to New Markets*; Allworth Press: New York, 1998.
7. Lee, M., Ed. *Art at Work, The Chase Manhattan Collection*; E. P. Dutton, Inc.: New York, 1984.
8. Lerner, R.E.; Bresler, J. *Art Law: The Guide for Collectors, Artists, Investors, and Dealers;* Practicing Law Institute Press: New York, 2005.
9. Rectanus, M.W. *Culture Incorporated: Museums, Artists, and Corporate Sponsorships;* University of Minnesota Press: Minneapolis, MU, 2002.
10. Stallabrass, J. *Art Incorporated: The Story of Contemporary Art;* Oxford University Press: London, U.K., 2004; 127–149.

PROFESSIONAL ORGANIZATIONS AND DIRECTORIES

1. American Law Institute/American Bar Association (ALI-ABA). Available at http://www.ali-aba.org/.
2. Business Committee for the Arts (BCA). Available at http://www.bcainc.org/company.asp?pg=3.
3. International Association for Corporate Collections of Contemporary Art (IACCCA), c/o Groupe LHoist, 168, Rue de Rivoli, F-75044 Paris Cedex 01, T: +33 (0) 1 53 45 53 81.
4. International Association for Professional Art Advisors (IAPPA). Available at http://www.iapaa.org/mission.htm.
5. International Directory of Corporate Art Collections. Available at http://www.humanities-exchange.org/corporateart/.
6. The Society for American Archivists (SAA). Available at http://www.archivists.org/conference/index.asp.

Corporate Information Centers

Barbara M. Spiegelman
Churchill Associates, Pittsburgh, Pennsylvania, U.S.A.

Nancy Flury Carlson
Westinghouse Electric Corporation, Pittsburgh, Pennsylvania, U.S.A.

Abstract

Information has become the lifeblood of the global economy. Corporate information centers (CICs), often called special libraries, leverage this force as they provide services to meet the specialized needs of a company, organization, or group. The CICs are typically staffed by library and information professionals, "...information resource experts dedicated to putting knowledge to work to attain the goals of their organizations." They provide information support to decision makers, researchers, and administrative and technical personnel.

INTRODUCTION

Information has become the lifeblood of the global economy. Corporate information centers (CICs), often called special libraries, leverage this force as they provide services to meet the specialized needs of a company, organization, or group. The CICs are typically staffed by library and information professionals, "...information resource experts dedicated to putting knowledge to work to attain the goals of their organizations."[1] They provide information support to decision makers, researchers, and administrative and technical personnel.

A CIC provides both specialized services and a targeted collection of the information resources most needed by the organization's personnel. Since these people are generally inundated with information, do they really need the CIC? As Leigh Buchanan notes, "...the kudzulike spread of information—information that's readily accessible yet often inaccurate, confusing, and more than slightly irrelevant—has actually increased the need for librarians."[2] The staff of the CIC helps to solve this problem. They review the world of resources available, and then identify those that are accurate and applicable to their organization.

SUBJECT AND SERVICE SPECIALIZATION

Subject Specialization

Because the corporate information center serves a unique clientele, the staff is able to build both subject and service specialties. Obviously, the subject specialty reflects the goals of the parent organization. For example, the library in a textile company will have information resources— both print and electronic—that relate to aspects of the textile industry. They will have resources that cover the hard sciences, like chemistry as well as those on color, durability, and manufacturing processes.

How can we consider this textile company a specialized subject area, when it includes so many disciplines? The answer is that the information resources selected from these many disciplines all relate to textiles. Another way to look at it is to consider the disciplines that are not covered in this library. Do they have print materials related to music or resources in psychiatric medicine? Does the collection cover history and philosophy? Do they include general dictionaries or only dictionaries pertinent to the textile industry? Only resources related to the industry are included. The smaller world inside a larger universe is characteristic of a corporate information center. Fig. 1 pictures some of the areas in the Nike Design Library.

Service Specialization

Public libraries, which are funded by tax dollars, often assess their value by the size of their collections. These libraries are serving every citizen, providing content for every interest, and covering every subject imaginable. In this arena, collection is king.

The goal of the corporate information center, however, is to provide pinpoint access to exact information in the shortest time possible. In the language of corporations, the corporate information center is a key player in building competitive edge. The corporate information center client values its collection, but values its services more. Figs. 2 and 3 show work areas next to information areas at Deutsche Bank.

The focus on the organization's subject area enables the staff of the corporate information center to provide services that are unique, or at least tailored, to their customer base. A company's information center, for example, may provide an alerting (current awareness) service in a very narrow area for a small number of employees in a small department.

Encyclopedia of Library and Information Sciences, Fourth Edition DOI: 10.1081/E-ELIS4-120008625

Fig. 1 Areas of the Nike Design Library.

Imagine the library in an information technology company that specializes in enterprise-wide networking. The end users have the skills and knowledge to manipulate any database in existence, but they do not have the time or training to identify which commercial databases are the best for their specific information needs. As the information landscape of their industry changes, their corporate information center may identify new or different state of

Fig. 2 Book cabinets in a work area at Deutsche Bank allow easy access to information.

the art resources on a daily basis, and provide that information to the end users in the same tight time frame. In a large law firm, the corporate information center may provide an indexing service for depositions. In cases that include hundreds of thousands of documents, this service is worth its weight in gold to associate and partner alike. In these examples, the library provides a service that frees the end users to do what they do best. Figs. 4–10 show parts of the CIC at Deutsche Bank.

Are There Also More General CIC Services?

The CIC general services include reference, document delivery, research, electronic resource management, and internal information consulting. The collections of information include both external and internal materials. They may be traditional print collections such as books, journals and reports, or other specialized media; and objects such as images, material samples, or microscope slides. Collections may also be virtual, such as networked resources or databases. The corporate information center staff works with executives and managers to support decision making, strategic planning, and market research initiatives. They

Fig. 4 A computer work area at Deutsche Bank.

work with technical personnel to support scientific research and development, engineering, and manufacturing. The CICs also provide industry data, benchmarking, statistics, and other information to support administrative personnel in the areas of human resources, financial planning, quality assurance, and public relations.

How Many Special Libraries Are There?

Statistics provided in The Bowker Annual, Library Trade and Book Almanac, 2000, indicate that there are 9691 special libraries in the United States. This figure includes corporate, medical, law, religious libraries, but not special libraries in public, academic, armed forces, or government libraries.

QUALIFICATIONS AND ONGOING PROFESSIONAL DEVELOPMENT

How Is the CIC Staffed? What Are the Staff Qualifications?

The range of staffing for a corporate information center can vary widely based on the role of the center, the demand for

Fig. 3 Employees share an alerting area at Deutsche Bank.

Fig. 5 Storage units.

Fig. 6   Information storage.

Fig. 7   A storage wall in the Information Center.

its services, and the budget allocated to the function. The professional degree for this field is a master's degree, offered in the area of library or information science, and requiring one or two years of postgraduate education. Ongoing professional development is essential to ensure that the staff remains conversant with developing products and technology. The company itself, information vendors, and professional associations provide advanced training in the field. Depending on their needs, most experienced information professionals belong to the Special Libraries Association (SLA), American Society for Information Science (ASIS), the Medical Library Association (MLA), the American Association of Law Librarians (AALL), or other professional societies.

USERS AND SERVICES

Who Uses a CIC?

The intended user base of a corporate information center is typically defined by the CIC's mission statement or by its functional position in the organization. The CIC may serve a narrow or broad constituency. In some cases, the CIC may be intended to serve only a subset of a company. For example, it may be a technical resource used only by research scientists within a larger corporation, or a business library serving only management and executive personnel. Alternatively, the CIC may serve an entire division, business unit, department, or other organizational segment. It may be chartered to serve the entire organization, or even to serve the external customers of an organization. As an example, a pharmaceutical company's CIC may support scientists, marketing, and administrative personnel, and may also provide some information services directly to consumers of the company's products.

What Services Are Provided by the CIC?

Because a corporate information center's service offerings vary widely according to its purpose within the organization, there is no set suite of services provided by all CICs. Major areas of service may include reference, research, current awareness, collection management, information resource management, document delivery, and information consulting.

Fig. 8 An employee at work.

Fig. 9 A specially designed information cabinet.

Reference

Reference service, in a nutshell, means answering questions. The questions answered through reference services may be simple lookups of facts, dates, names, addresses, or definitions. Many libraries define reference service to include primarily quick-turnaround, limited-scope, and relatively easy-to-answer questions. But sometimes reference questions may be complex, open-ended, and even unanswerable, and the staff's response can include a range of options for further pursuit of the question. In a corporate information center the reference service can be viewed as the cornerstone for all other services, because it measures the pulse of the organization's ongoing information needs. In the course of meeting these changing needs, the staff continues to develop its complement of internal and external resources. Needs identified through the reference process subsequently influence the CIC's planning and priority setting in collection development, service offerings, planning, and staffing.

Research

Research services include literature searching, primary research, and synthesis of information. A literature search is a comprehensive review of electronic and print information resources. The goal of the search is to compile a focused set of references or documents pertinent to a specific topic. Primary research extends beyond a review of written or published data, and involves the gathering, interpretation, and synthesis of

Fig. 10 A work area at Deutsche Bank.

information directly from people such as industry experts, researchers, or authors. Primary research is especially significant for supporting functions such as competitive intelligence or market research, which are unique to each company. Information synthesis and reporting are the refined end products of literature searches and primary research. Benchmarking of products or companies is an example of this process, in which literature searches and primary interviews are used to compile data and information. This information is studied, organized, and presented with comparisons, conclusions, or recommendations for action.

Current Awareness

The information center's current awareness services provide ongoing updates of targeted information to users interested in following a specific topic, company, or technology. Current awareness may be topic-specific, such as a monthly update of new developments in the telecommunications industry, or it may be resource-specific, such as a monthly table of contents from a specific journal title. Current awareness services may be compiled and distributed directly by the corporate information center staff or set up through external vendors.

Collection Management

Corporate information centers may manage collections of internal or external documents or information. The collections may be physical, as in a print book or journal collection, or virtual as in an electronic document management or intranet system. Examples of internal collections include patents, technical reports, policies and procedures, scientific data, or organizational records. External collections can include externally published books, journals, reports, conference proceedings, audiovisuals, and standards. A formal collection development policy or statement of scope often drives collection management. These tools define the types of materials and topical areas collected, and they are useful in making decisions about how to allocate acquisitions resources to collect and organize the most important materials for the organization. Collection management includes acquisitions, cataloging, indexing, development of finding tools, and circulation. In addition to providing tools for users to locate collection materials, the corporate information center staff interacts directly with users to help them locate the specific materials or information they need.

Information Resource Management

An extension of collection management, information resource management includes the planning, purchase, implementation, and administration of intranets; content licensing, intranet subscription services; or other electronic or networked resources. Management of content licensing and intranet subscription services, in particular, enables the CIC to help control the cost of information access across the organization. Successful implementation of these services requires effective teaming between the CIC, information technology, communications, and purchasing. A teamwork approach ensures that there is less duplication of effort within the company, and less duplication of purchased resources.

Document Delivery

While a collection management effort strives to maintain key materials and frequently used documents in-house, there is always a need to quickly and cost effectively obtain materials from outside the organization. Document delivery services are designed to purchase or borrow books, photocopies, journal articles, and other resources from publishers, vendors, and other libraries. These services can be very effective in obtaining both print and electronic materials and provide good backup to the information center.

Information Consulting

Consulting services offered by the CIC may include information audits, information mapping, and project information support. Information audits can be used to identify an organization's information needs, gaps, and processes; they also serve as a basis for better information resource allocation, process improvement, and communication. Information mapping can be used to identify, document, and provide pointers to an organization's internal data and information resources, which would otherwise be underused or hidden. Project information support makes an information professional available to support new initiatives or task teams, and in many CICs it is standard practice to assign an information specialist to these teams as they begin their work. This staff member can provide topical background information, ongoing current awareness, and research specific questions that come up in the course of the initiative.

IMPACT AND STRATEGIC POSITIONING

How Does the Corporate Information Center Impact the Organization?

In addition to its primary role of access to information, the CIC can introduce new technologies to the organization; research and highlight industry measures of total quality; perform needs assessments and information audits, facilitate focus groups and design surveys, and map information in the organization to identify critical resources. All of these roles rely on the CIC's strategic positioning within the organization.

A CIC must be flexible, responsive to change, and able to extend and tailor services to provide what the organization needs before the need actually arises. These organizational needs must continually be identified and verified through frequent communication and feedback with users and organizational leaders. If the information center has the best collection in the world on large widgets, but the company has changed its strategic direction to small widgets, that collection is of little use to the company.

What Are the Corporate Information Center's Costs and Benefits to an Organization?

In addition to providing the information needed to support organizational functions, CIC services can save both money and productive time. King Research, Inc., funded by a research grant from the Special Libraries Association, compiled data from 23 studies of special library users and services, and four national surveys of scientists, engineers, and other professionals. This study reported, "it would cost these parent organizations about 2.9 times more for their professionals to obtain information from other sources than it now costs to run the library."[3] Savings of this kind are obviously important to all organizations that watch their bottom line.

Productive time is a "soft savings," that is, one that does not usually register on the company's balance sheet. One channel for loss of productive time is the inclination of a company's professional and technical employees to "surf the Net" for the information they need to do their jobs. "Most professionals with internet access on their desktop computers don't know the most efficient way to conduct a search. Further, employees are too often satisfied with finding any information on a subject—not necessarily the best data or most significant source. Top-notch librarians, however, know how to find primary sources and judge information...."[4]

Where Does a Corporate Information Center Fit Within Its Organization?

The CIC may report to information systems, human resources, records management, facilities, business planning, or a general corporate services function. The organizational placement of a corporate information center may define or reflect its overall purpose. Placement within information systems is appropriate for an organization in which the most valuable information resources are available chiefly through electronic means such as Internet, intranet, internal databases, or networking. This type of corporate information center is effective in an organization with an employee population skilled in using computer-based resources, and in an industry that relies chiefly on current rather than historical information.

A corporate information center placed within the human resources department is likely to be found in organizations that strongly associate access to information with employee development and organizational learning. A library in this setting may be expected to provide information resources to meet both the business and personal needs of employees. To support organizational learning, this library may be involved with knowledge management initiatives or other organization-wide projects to capture and redeploy employee expertise.

A CIC placed within an organization's records management setting may be more closely identified with the organization's internal information. This type of library can add value to the management of records and document management systems, especially by contributing its expertise in understanding the interface between people and information systems, and by putting into place tools to help people locate information more easily.

An information center placed within the business-planning segment indicates that the organization recognizes the value of information to the business and strategic planning function. A library in this setting is likely to provide services to management and executives, sometimes to the exclusion of the general employee population.

Finally, placement within the general services organization of a company indicates recognition that library services are needed by the organization as a whole, just as accounting and procurement may reside in this general services structure. This placement may free a library to design a wider range of services based on varied needs across the organization, but may also limit it by keeping it perennially in the crosshairs of ongoing hunts to control costs.

Is there an ideal setting for the corporate library or information center? Probably not, since placement depends on the needs of the organization, the perceptions of the company's decision makers, and the abilities of the CIC to prove that the resources and services it can provide are valuable. In reality, most corporate information centers exhibit characteristics related to all of these settings. CICs continue to change and recreate themselves, including moving from one organizational reporting structure to another, as their companies themselves continue to restructure and reorganize to meet the changing business environments.

Budget

Budgets for corporate information centers typically include line items for personnel, information resources, and general costs. Personnel costs include the cost of employee benefits and training. Information resource costs include the costs of materials purchased centrally for any library collections or directly for the company employees, commercial database fees, and annual fees for internet subscriptions or networked electronic resources. General costs included in a library's budget may include internal services such as information technology support, reproduction, phone, workstation, and facilities costs. In general, corporate libraries must justify costs on an annual basis, at budget planning, and at approval time. They must gain the approval and support of the management of the library's primary user bases, who often share in the cost to retain the corporate information center.

Many libraries are funded through chargeback or assessment to these user groups each year, often on an overall basis linked to user and service statistics, or on a transactional basis throughout the year. It is easier for special libraries to justify their budgets if they consistently assess user needs, design services to meet these needs, and communicate their value.

One challenge to a library's budget activities is the rising cost of information resources. Journal subscription costs in particular, whether print or electronic, provide a good example of the difficulty of controlling costs. Journals that focus on a specific industry segment or scientific field often rise most dramatically in cost, but are also those most needed by companies that work in these specific industries or scientific areas. It is prudent for the manager of the information center to clearly delineate the cost of these expensive resources and the customers who use them the most often.

COMMUNICATIONS

Good communication is central to the success of a corporate information center. In a business setting, information is primarily used to make decisions and, therefore, must be shared, rather than added to a collection on a shelf. A variety of communication skills are used many times every day, and it is expected that professional staff will have these skills when they begin the job.

Advanced listening skills are an absolute requirement in this setting, since the staff will be required to interpret the actual needs of the customer, rather than relying on the customer's knowledge. Customers from human resources (HR), for example, can be expected to know a great deal about HR, but may not be up to date about marketing. They may have heard a marketing information resource mentioned, and assume that since they are interested in marketing job positions, that same resource will work for them. The staff uses the reference interview process, including active listening, to identify the actual information that is needed.

The staff of the CIC is also required to be able to communicate effectively, in speech and in writing, to customers from the lowest to highest position in the organization. Communications with the manager of a technical department, for example, may include a quick précis of research techniques and technical jargon, which demonstrate that the librarian speaks his language. Communication with the chief executive officer (CEO), on the other hand, must be brief and well focused, as the CEO will probably have less time, and be more interested in bottom-line issues. In communications like this, the information specialist must take into consideration two points: what is the listener's past knowledge of the subject (are they familiar with the topic? are their perceptions based on misinformation?); and what information does the audience actually need to make a decision (statistics? anecdotal evidence? trends over time?) Keeping these ideas in the forefront will ensure that the communication is on point.

Does the prevalence of electronic messaging and e-mail indicate that written communication skills are no longer important in a corporate setting? The use of these vehicles actually makes clear and effective written communication more difficult. It is quite easy to take a wrong tone in an e-mail. Once that e-mail is delivered, the tone speaks for itself, with no in-person speaker to clarify the intent or modify the message. It is easy to eliminate the use of all capitals, which is effectively screaming at the customer, but not as easy to detect when a comment might be interpreted as sarcastic rather than as humorous. Careful editing is required for good writing, and is especially important for electronic communication.

The need for excellent communication skills becomes even more important with the growth of a global economy. Professional staff can no longer assume that every customer will speak American English. Requests for research or other services may come from foreign subsidiaries, customers from abroad, or from people who work in the same building who are not native speakers.

In a diversified corporate setting, it is easy to find yourself with a customer who is exceedingly difficult to understand, and who has trouble understanding in return. How can this problem be handled without insulting the customer? The first rule, of course, is not to speak louder, under the assumption that the problem is one of intelligence rather than of translation. In instances where the customer is providing data, it is imperative that the staff ask the customer to write the information; in this way, numbers will not be misunderstood, which can lead to disastrous results!

STRATEGIC PLANNING

The corporate information center must align its goals and objectives with those of the parent organization and reflect these goals in its own strategic plan.

The term strategic plan sounds ominously complex, but it simply means outlining where the special library is going, and how it will get there. The plan identifies the goals and objectives of the library, and the actual steps required to reach them.

As an example, a company's five-year strategic plan calls for entering a new market, which will require that the whole company shift its focus toward a new material or process. To help the company achieve this goal, the CIC must allocate a portion of its budget to cover more resources to support this initiative, and to add or develop staff to specialize in those areas. In theory this is not difficult; it simply requires moving funds from one pot to another.

In practice, however, the company has many goals, and some seem to be in conflict with others. Imagine that in the example above, the director of Marketing requests the CIC to increase support to his department next year. How can library funds and staff be allocated in this situation? The answer can be found in the company's strategic plan, which prioritizes its various initiatives. If the company's strategic plan calls for increasing allocations to product development by 10%, over the previous year's allocation of 5%, the library must shift its focus to increase resources and services related to product development. The CIC's strategic plan is, therefore, based on the organization's upper tier plan. Each request for services or resources should be considered and balanced in light of the CIC's strategic plan. In this case, the additional 5% allocated to product development cannot be allocated to other needs. When other groups request library services to support their initiatives, the strategic plan provides the basis for the allocation decision, and the explanation to the unhappy marketing director, who may not see more research into customer attitudes.

BUILDING COMPETITIVE EDGE

Understanding Competitive Edge

In the for-profit sector, time to market is everything. Time to market is the difference between a profitable product and an unprofitable one. Time to market is money.

A good example of this concept lies in over-the-counter pharmaceuticals. Name an over-the-counter product that reduces fever quickly. Most of us will name the same one, because it was the first on the market to make that unique

or specific claim. Once a product has worked for them, the average consumer is likely to buy it again. Voila! This way lies profit.

How can the corporate information center help to improve time to market and, therefore, help the organization be increase profitability? One of the best ways to understand the corporate information center's role in building competitive edge is to imagine a Slinky, the creeping toy loved by children far and wide. The rings of the toy can be pulled apart, leaving wide spaces between the coiled wires, or they can be pushed together, so that the coils are all touching. The extended Slinky, with wide open spaces, represents the infinite amount of information that can be found on almost any topic. The contracted Slinky, with every ring tightly closed, represents the goal of the CIC—targeted information located in the shortest amount of time possible.

But in a real time-to-market scenario, the end user may not even have time to ask the library for help. Outstanding corporate information centers are successful because they proactively provide the right information before anyone thinks of asking for it. They understand the organization's goals, they know their subject matter, and they deliver unique service with a smile.

Customer Intimacy

Customer intimacy is increasingly important to companies doing business in the global economy. Ongoing globalization of industries causes upheaval, realignment, and repositioning of industry players. In many industries, a company may be competing fiercely with its competitors in some arenas, yet partnering with them in others. With lines between competitors blurring, the company–customer relationship becomes even more critical. Companies must not only be responsive to their customers in a reactive way, but also proactively anticipate customer needs and provide solutions to their problems. Communication and information are foundations of this relationship. Corporate information centers must create this same relationship with their customers through expertise, effective information services, participation in knowledge management and competitive intelligence initiatives, and effective teaming with key organizational functions.

Challenges for the Future

Corporations will continue to fight the battle of information overload. For every decision that is made, there is a need for information. Sometimes not too much information is needed, since the CEO is not writing a journal article. At other times, lots of information is needed for the people in the research department, who are. And most times, there is a need for every possible choice of volume or specificity in between. Information overload will remain a challenge for the CIC. How can it continue to identify the absolutely relevant and accurate information, as the marketplace is continually flooded with everything else?

As the information industry continues to refine a pricing model, the CIC will be more strategic than ever, since it is the first line of defense against models that are too extreme. As pricing models change, CICs may need to change the way they budget and charge for services. Since budgets follow costs, that is, the next year's budget is based on this year's costs, considerable strategic planning skills will be needed to anticipate these changes. Those who are not able to anticipate accurately will find themselves lagging behind an entire budget cycle, which can affect the information center's ability to function.

Some corporations may see a centralized information center as an anachronism, since they view it as a place rather than a service. These organizations may want to employ information professionals in other venues, for example, in knowledge management, competitive intelligence, or market research functions. This change in the information professional's role will be both a challenge and an opportunity.

CONCLUSION

Finally, information vendors, including established publishers and brand-new entrants to the information markets, are grappling amongst themselves for market share and role definition. As part of their response to this instability, some vendors are attempting to subsume the role of the corporate information center. In an attempt to maintain market share, they are trying to be all things to all organizations by providing outsourced services. Maintaining the role definition of the CIC will be crucial in meeting this challenge.

Not withstanding these challenges, corporate information centers remain exciting and dynamic organizations. They are positioned to make a difference to their company and to the future of the profession.

REFERENCES

1. http://www.sla.org/content/Help/industopics/Genfaq.cfm.
2. Buchanan, L. *The Smartest Little Company in America*, Inc., 1999; January Vol. 21 (1), 43–54.
3. Griffiths, J.-M.; King, D.W. Increasing the information edge: the role of special libraries. *Special Libraries: Increasing the Information Edge*, SLA Research Series Special Libraries Association: Washington, DC, 1993; Vol. 9, 27.
4. Rurak, M. Demand explodes for librarians with high-tech research skills. Career J. Wall Street J. http://www.wsj.com (accessed Dec 2000).

Corporate Records Management

Barbara M. Cross
*Records and Information Management, Sony Pictures Entertainment, Culver City,
California, U.S.A.*

Barbara E. Nye
Ictus Consulting, LLC, Pasadena, California, U.S.A.

Abstract

Records management is the discipline used by corporations to ensure management principles are systematically applied to the recorded information created, received, and used in the normal course of business operations. The corporate records management program uses established records management methods and practices to reduce costs associated with recordkeeping, provide efficient access to and retrieval of business information, help to protect information critical to the business, and overall bring recognized value to the corporation. Corporations deal with increasingly complex recordkeeping requirements due to the continued growth of electronic records as well as legal and compliance issues. Corporations face records management issues that government entities may not as they comply with international laws and regulations, civil litigation and the impact of electronic discovery, and mergers and acquisitions.

INTRODUCTION

Corporations are legal entities established to provide goods or services in order to make a profit. In addition to managing the core operations that make the goods or provide the services, corporations also employ various management techniques (disciplines) to more efficiently manage the business and to control the costs associated with doing business. Using financial management, human resources management and other related disciplines serve to make operations more effective and efficient, thus adding to profits, the so-called "bottom line."

One of these management disciplines is records management—the systematic analysis and control of the creation, receipt, maintenance, use, and disposition of recorded information. Corporations establish records management programs (RMP) to manage all records (considered to be "information assets") in all stored formats—paper-based, photographic, or digital storage. Employing records management techniques helps to lower the cost of doing business by controlling the growth of records maintained and by facilitating efficient access to recorded information needed for business decisions.

Corporations create, receive, and maintain a considerable amount of recorded information as they document what they intend to do (writing policies and plans) and how they intend to do it (developing procedures). As work activities are completed, corporations document the results of work activities, in the form of reports, meeting minutes, training presentations, photographs, charts, tabulated data, etc. The resulting recorded information must be properly managed to be of any benefit to the corporation.

The corporate RMP is responsible for managing the recorded information.

Records management activities help to make corporate operations more efficient by supporting both internal operations and by helping to meet external recordkeeping requirements and expectations.

Internal requirements include being accountable to an executive function or to a governing board, and if publicly traded, to shareholders. This is done in part by providing proof, in the form of records, that work activities were completed and completed correctly.

External requirements (in the form of laws or statutes) are those imposed by government legislative bodies or by government agencies (in the form of rules and regulations). Conducting business is a privilege, rather than a right.[1] This privilege is conferred and controlled by one or more government agencies, and thus businesses often must comply with multiple requirements. These regulations often impose recordkeeping requirements on many business activities to make sure that there will be proof that the corporation complied with the appropriate requirement.

Corporations also operate within a larger social environment and the corporation may wish to present a positive image of the corporation to the public, establish good relations, or meet societal expectations as a "good corporate citizen."[2]

Records management supports the goals of cost savings and compliance by managing recorded information, regardless of the storage medium (paper, photographic, or electronic), from the time the records are created or received, until they are dispositioned. This concept of

Encyclopedia of Library and Information Sciences, Fourth Edition DOI: 10.1081/E-ELIS4-120043548

"cradle-to-grave" management is called the records "life cycle" and is a fundamental tenet of the discipline.

Records management is also practiced in other types of organizations in addition to public and private enterprises. Government agencies at the local, state and national level, nonprofit organizations, universities and cultural institutions, all create and maintain records as one result of their operations.

The same principles of the record management discipline apply and many of the same methods are used. Records management in government agencies differs most significantly in the granting of access to many of the records maintained. The government agencies presume that outside parties (generally speaking, the public) have some rights to access government records, as the government conducts activities on behalf of its citizenry.

At the U.S. federal level the Freedom of Information Act (FOIA) codifies this right to access.[3] States also grant similar rights to access records maintained by state and local agencies. In California, for example, the California Public Records Act, states that most records maintained are accessible by the public, delineates which records are not, and provides requirements for producing public records when requested.[4]

Private and publicly traded companies do not have to comply with FOIA, and therefore, do not need to provide the public access to their records. Indeed, as records are considered a corporate asset, and often of a proprietary nature, corporations spend considerable effort protecting records and information from unauthorized access.

A comprehensive corporate RMP has five broad elements.[5] These include:

- Records retention: determining how long to keep records.
- Compliance: ensuring that the corporation is aware of external recordkeeping requirements and complies with them.
- Active records management: arranging, organizing, and storing current or frequently referenced records to promote efficient retrieval and use.
- Inactive records management: identifying records that are no longer frequently used and transferring them out of an expensive office or work environment to low-cost warehouse storage or transferring them offline to tape or other cost-effective electronic storage.
- Vital records management: protecting records critical to support ongoing operations to ensure that they are available to respond to an emergency or disaster.

RECORDS RETENTION

As mentioned earlier, records retention is the activity of determining the value of a record to the corporation and assigning a timeframe (retention period) for maintaining it.

Records retention has been called ". . .the defining responsibility of records management as a business discipline."[5]

A key part of the corporate RMP is the "records retention schedule"—a list of each grouping or collection of records (called a "records series"), the time period the records series must be maintained (the retention period), and the assignment of business unit (e.g., department, division, section) responsible for the records series.

Records retention schedules can be developed using one of several methods and can be presented in several formats. The important point for purposes of this discussion is that the retention schedule is a policy document that states the corporation's intent to maintain its records for certain time periods.

Determining the appropriate timeframe for keeping a records series involves analysis of the business (or "operating") need to maintain the record and any pertinent legal requirements. These two considerations are applied to each record series in establishing the retention period. Once the records series meets the retention period, the records are either destroyed, or retained in an archive, if they have been identified as having historical significance.

This process of deciding how long to keep a record series is called "appraisal" as it involves determining the "value" of the records to the organization, and at what point the records no longer have value.

There is a risk management component to this decision-making process. There is a risk to both keeping the record indefinitely and to not keeping it. As records are created and maintained by organizations in order to support their position or to defend against allegations, deciding how long to keep records is very important.

The risk to maintain the record involves determining the cost of maintenance (physical storage space, equipment and supplies, as well as computer disk storage), personnel (to maintain files and ensure digital records are protected), and if the organization is involved in litigation or a government investigation or audit, the cost to find and retrieve relevant information.

The amount of risk in not maintaining a set of records indefinitely (in other words, putting a finite retention period in place) involves determining the costs that might be incurred if the organization decides after destroying the records that it now requires the information and has to recreate it, or if the records have been destroyed in error and are relevant to litigation or investigation, and therefore, should have been maintained.

Another aspect of risk management as a part of records management is the identification and protection of "vital records." Vital records are those that contain information that is critical to ensuring the continued important operations of a corporation, and protecting its rights and assets, in the event of an emergency or a disaster. Frequently, the vital records are identified as such on the records retention schedule so that the business unit assigned responsibility

Corporate Information–Custody

can ensure that they are protected and available to respond to the emergency or disaster. The records management function within the corporation works with the business recovery or disaster response function in planning for, and responding to, emergencies.

Records retention schedules must be customized specifically for a corporation. There are no "generic" records retention schedules that can be used as is. Although companies may produce many similar-type records, especially for those functions such as accounting or human resources management that all organizations have, the differences in industries, geographic locations, legal jurisdictions, and especially the corporate culture are all factors in determining how long the individual corporation is prepared to maintain records, or conversely at what point in time they are comfortable with the decision to destroy records deemed obsolete.

Legal Environment and Compliance

The legal environment in which a corporation does business influences all aspects of record keeping within the corporation. Laws and regulations can dictate the types of records an organization creates, the format in which records are kept, what access is permitted, how long the organization is obligated to retain records or how an organization may dispose of their records. Compliance with record keeping requirements helps companies avoid fines and penalties as well as reduces risks and liability during litigation, audits, or government investigations.

Corporations are governed by multiple and various jurisdictions. In the United States, companies are regulated by the states in which they incorporate, the federal government, and, if public, by the SEC. Local or regional jurisdictions may also regulate company actions. Multinational corporations have to abide by the laws and regulations of not only their "home" country but each country or territory in which they conduct business.

Key laws driving corporate compliance include antitrust and competition laws, insider trading and securities laws, privacy and data protection laws, environmental and occupational health regulations, labor laws, and tax and revenue laws.

In addition, many industries have specific laws regulating their activities. For example, financial institutions are governed by legal controls regulating money laundering (Bank Secrecy Act) and the sharing and use of customer credit information (Fair Credit Reporting Act). Other highly regulated industries include health, energy, food, securities, and telecommunications.

Publicly traded companies follow rules and regulations laid out by the U.S. Securities & Exchange Commission (SEC). In response to the corporate finance and reporting scandals of the 1990s, the U.S. federal government passed the Sarbanes–Oxley Act of 2002 which applies to all publicly traded companies and which is regulated by the SEC. The purpose of the Sarbanes–Oxley Act is to ensure the boards of directors of publicly held companies take responsibility for both receiving accurate information about the company's finances and reporting accurately on those finances to the public.[6] To demonstrate compliance, organizations develop internal guidelines, processes, reports, and other sorts of documentation that require appropriate management, retention and disposition.

U.S. laws cover not only business activities that take place within the country but also business conducted outside of the country. The U.S. Department of Justice oversees the Foreign Corrupt Practices Act (FCPA). The FCPA makes it unlawful to bribe foreign government officials to obtain or retain business. Signed into law in 1977, the FCPA requires publicly traded companies "...to maintain records that accurately and fairly represent the company's transactions......requires these companies to have adequate systems of internal accounting controls."[7] Anti-bribery provisions of the FCPA make it unlawful for a U.S. person to make a payment to a foreign official for the purpose of obtaining or retaining business for or with, or directing business to, any person.

Multinational corporations must take into consideration the laws and regulations of each country in which they conduct business. A U.S.-based records retention schedule cannot simply be applied to international offices as other country's laws may contradict U.S. law. Efforts to apply a single retention period to common business records across countries may result in keeping records longer than necessary or not long enough, both costly to the organization in terms of legal risk and operational efficiencies.

For example, privacy regulations vary across countries and every company doing business that crosses borders must be aware of the regulations and laws pertaining to information privacy. The European Union (EU) has stringent rules governing how corporations can use, retain, and store personal data. The European Directive on Data Privacy of October, 1998, governs both how information is collected and retained within the European community as well as how that information may be transferred from the EU to other countries. Data can be transferred to countries outside of the EU if there is a guarantee of "adequate" protection. The U.S. Department of Commerce, with the European Commission, developed a "safe harbor" framework for U.S. companies to comply with the EU directive. Companies certified to the safe harbor are recognized by EU organizations as providing "adequate" privacy protection, as defined by the Directive.[8]

How an organization meets its compliance obligations varies and usually multiple parties, including legal, finance, information technology, and records management are involved in corporate governance. Detailed knowledge of the organizations' records as provided by the RMP plays a key role in corporate compliance programs.

Litigation, legal holds, and discovery

Business conflicts and disputes are part of the cost of doing business for corporations. Regardless of the type of products or services provided, every company is at risk of being involved in a legal action. Antitrust actions, workers compensation claims, breach of contract, product liability, and other claims and lawsuits share in common the importance and necessity of business information as material evidence to prove or disprove their case. Company records may support or be harmful to the company's position. The corporate RMP is a component of the company's larger preventive law strategy.[9]

The RMP helps to reduce the legal risks facing an organization through the systematic retention and disposition of records. Retaining information that may be needed in defense of potential legal actions protects the organization while disposing of information no longer required by the company can reduce the risks and costs of legal discovery. Doing so systematically, in the normal course of business, protects the organization from accusations of deliberate destruction or arbitrary decision-making. Effective information management practices also protect the corporation during litigation. Well-organized physical, photographic, and digital records facilitate the identification, access, and retrieval of information that may be needed for a legal action.

In the event of, or in anticipation of, litigation, corporations have a duty to preserve relevant information. A legal hold or preservation notice is a common communication method used by corporations to ensure that records are not inadvertently or deliberately destroyed. The duty to preserve supersedes the records retention policies that mandate the destruction of records that have reached the assigned retention period. Depending upon the legal action, the duty to preserve information can be limited to specific records, individuals, and departments, or can cover all records across the entire enterprise. "The duty to preserve includes an obligation to identify, locate, and maintain information that is relevant to specific, predictable, and identifiable litigation."[10]

RMP procedures describe the process for suspending normal records and information destruction (i.e., enforcing a "legal hold" on the destruction of obsolete records). Because legal holds are an exception to the records retention policy, when the need for the hold no longer exists, the legal hold is lifted. At that time, the corporation can return to "business as usual" in terms of records disposition, and process for destruction any records which have met the assigned retention periods.

Discovery is the fact-finding process that takes place after a lawsuit is filed and before the trial, in order to allow the parties in a case to prepare for settlement or trial.[11] With the explosion in the amount of electronic information stored, the cost of electronic discovery, or "e-discovery," is significant.

In December 2006, amendments to the U.S. Federal Rules of Civil Procedure (FRCP) went into effect, which have a direct impact on how organizations respond to litigation and discovery requests. The amendments address the growing burden to organizations in terms of time, effort, and cost to respond to e-discovery requests during litigation. The FRCP amendments provide guidance for the handling of electronically stored information (ESI) during litigation. How organizations will address the impact of the guidelines remains to be seen as the risk of litigation and e-discovery is different for every organization.

ACTIVE RECORDS MANAGEMENT

Active records management involves the organization and retrieval of records that are referenced frequently within the organization to support specific business activities. Components include the methods used to organize active records, the documentation and processes supporting the methods, and the selection of appropriate housing or storage for the records. The purpose is to ensure that records are safe, available, and accessible when needed.

A filing system is the primary method used to organize active records. An organization can have both paper-based and computer-based filing systems. Filing system elements include file plans, procedures, and access controls. The file plan outlines the way the records are organized and is often closely linked to the records retention schedule. There are different types of filing arrangements which can be employed by the organization, both simple and complex, all of which are a variation on an alphabetic or numeric arrangement. Classification schemes are used within the file plan to group related materials together. Indexing techniques are employed to provide additional access points to the records. The corporate RMP brings standardization and uniformity to the methods used so that filing systems are consistent across the corporation yet flexible enough to accommodate different types of records, can provide the security and confidentiality required, and are maintained and updated regularly.

The housing of active records is important to the corporation for several reasons. One is to ensure ready access to, and quick retrieval of, the records most needed to conduct daily business. Second is to manage equipment costs and use office space in the most efficient manner available. A third reason is to make sure that vital and confidential records are safe and secure, protecting the organization from loss or unauthorized access.

Corporations select equipment that facilitates retrieval at the most efficient cost. Office space is expensive; minimizing the records equipment footprint is one way to keep costs down. This is done by selecting specialized equipment for the type of physical records being organized, such as using shelving designed to fit tapes rather than shelving for standard file folders.

Corporate Information–Custody

The format of the record influences where it is housed and how it is accessed. Employing imaging systems to digitize paper records to make the records more readily available to employees is a common corporate practice. Records that are frequently accessed by multiple people across the organization are good candidates for imaging. Records management will play a role in the imaging program to help ensure that the imaging process is documented and meets standards, to determine if or for how long the paper records shall be kept after digitization, the levels of indexing required to aid in retrieval, appropriate security controls, and that retention rules are applied to the digitized records.

Document management systems are deployed to store and help manage digitized and electronic active records. Features such as check in/check out capabilities, version control, and flexible security models, provide greater control over electronic documents than simply housing the documents on a shared drive or an employee's computer drive.

Enterprise content management (ECM) systems provide the organization with the ability to manage all digital content, whether Web sites, images, documents, video files, audio files, photographs, or multimedia in one repository. ECM systems are attractive to corporations because they offer "one stop shopping" to solve a number of requirements for the management of digital content.

Electronic Records Management

The amount of information created and maintained in electronic format increases each year in volume and importance. Records management concepts and methodologies apply to all record formats, but there are special challenges in the management and control of machine readable or electronic records. A component of the overall RMP, electronic records management requires close partnership between the information technology and records management groups to ensure the rules are applied effectively to the data within the systems and applications.

One issue with managing electronic information is the sheer volume of records of which only a small portion may be official business records. Contributing to the volume is the ease with which duplicate information can proliferate. Although duplication occurs with physical (hardcopy) records, the issue is greatly magnified in electronic form. The same electronic record can reside on numerous employee hard drives, in shared drives, in e-mail systems, content and document management systems, stored on optical disk, be backed up to tape or other storage medium, and then be printed and eventually stored. The challenge is in managing all these copies, consistently applying retention, controlling access, and facilitating retrieval.

Just as with physical records, file arrangements, standard naming conventions, metadata, classification, and taxonomy schemes improve access by providing systematic organization to the electronic information. For large stores of electronic information, the manual application of classification—human beings assigning records to categories—is labor-intensive and not economically feasible for organizations. Organizations may invest in search engines or automated classification tools to facilitate information retrieval.

The electronic record is dependent upon the hardware and software upon which it is created and therefore is vulnerable to factors such as system obsolescence, storage media instability, data migration, and potential data loss. The obsolescence of systems and applications may make long-term retention of electronic records impractical due to costs associated with the continued need to migrate data from one generation of software or system to the next.

Electronic Messaging

Electronic communication is the favored method of communication for corporate employees. The physical interoffice memorandum and carefully crafted letters to and from outside parties are a small percentage of corporate mail.

Electronic mail (e-mail) is an important method of communication and information transfer for corporations. The use of e-mail continues to grow each year. In 2005, the average user produced 75 e-mails per day; in 2008 that figure rose to 156 e-mails per day, according to the Radicati Group, a computer and technology market research firm.[12] Using the figures provided by the Radicati Group, an organization with 5,000 employees is processing 780,000 e-mails per day. Managing all of this e-mail presents a major challenge to organizations.

Initially, corporations and professional records and information management organizations viewed e-mail messages as casual, transitory means of communication and not as records. Managing e-mail focused on limiting the volume of e-mail message stored due to the high cost of storage and hardware limitations associated with storing e-mails. However, it is now standard practice for corporations to treat any e-mail message as a potential record. As a record, the e-mail message needs to be managed systematically similar to other corporate records, according to business, regulatory and litigation requirements.

Corporations employ a variety of methods to manage e-mail. Methods include the imposition of quotas or mailbox size limitations; automatic deletion of user mailbox contents after a specified period of time; archiving systems that store e-mails declared a record by users; storage systems that store all e-mails created or received by an organization, removing the employee from the decision-making; and personal archives where the employee determines what e-mails should be archived and when, storing the archives on designated drives.

Instant messaging, voice over IP, and unified messaging are other electronic communication methods used by corporations. Unified messaging combines voice mail, faxes, and e-mails into one mailbox. This is attractive to organizations as it allows employees to access voice mail from the e-mail system and e-mail from the telephone. From a records management perspective, it represents more records to be managed and protected.

Electronic communications ultimately are managed depending on the regulatory climate, business needs, and organizational culture of the corporation. For example, financial industries are regulated by the SEC and the National Association of Securities Dealers and therefore may have stricter controls than a nonregulated business.

Electronic Records Management Systems

The technology of records management has evolved from systems supporting the organization and retrieval of paper-based records to focusing on the management of electronic records. The value of electronic records management systems (ERM) is in their ability to manage retention and disposition of physical and electronic records. As discussed earlier, the volume of electronic records makes a manual application of retention schedules much too labor-intensive and time-consuming to be economically viable. Automated means to track electronic records, apply disposition rules, and apply legal holds during litigation are important to the overall management of corporate records.

The electronic records management systems themselves must be accurate and trustworthy. Trustworthiness means that an information system, whether computer- or paper-based, is accountable and can produce reliable and authentic information and records.

According to the Gartner group, records management systems have become key components of content management systems.[13] The records management software market has consolidated as large technology companies acquired smaller companies with stand-alone records management products. Now, many records management products are integrated into electronic content management systems (ECM) as part of an overall suite of products that may include Web content management, document management, and workflow. This integration can be beneficial to the corporation as they look for strong return on investment when purchasing technology solutions.

Since the late 1990s, the U.S. Department of Defense (DoD) records management standard, *DoD 5015.2-STD Design Criteria for Electronic Records Management Software Applications* (DoD 5015.2), has served as the industry benchmark for records management software standards.[14] Although developed specifically for software vendors who want to sell their products to federal agencies, it is used by government and private companies alike. Compliance with the standard or obtaining DoD

5015.2 certification is a prerequisite for many companies when selecting records management software products.

The *Model Requirements for Management of Electronic Records* (MoReq) is a European standard for electronic records management systems developed for the European community. It is also used as a benchmarking tool for corporations looking to implement ERM systems.[15]

INACTIVE RECORDS MANAGEMENT

Inactive records management involves the storage and protection of records that are no longer accessed on a frequent basis but are still necessary to the organization due to legal, audit, or other retention requirements. Ensuring the reliable retrieval of records when needed or to ensure appropriate disposal when obsolete is a key element of inactive records management strategy.

An inactive records storage program can achieve considerable cost savings per year by moving physical records out of expensive office space and into lower cost storage warehouses, achieving economies of space and equipment.

An element of inactive records management is to determine the most effective long-term storage mechanism. Determining whether to convert physical records to a micrographic or digital format for storage purposes will depend on the retention period, level of access expected, and cost-effectiveness. If the costs to store the records to the end of their life cycle are less than the cost to convert the paper to another format, then there is no reason to convert. Paper records that are stored due to space limitations with frequent access may be candidates for digitization. While the cost to store a container of records (usually a cubic-foot box) is low, the costs to retrieve, deliver, and refile boxes increase the overall cost of storage significantly. In this case, it may be cost-effective to digitize the records for access and retrieval purposes. Microfilm is a good technology for records that must be retained for a long time and are infrequently accessed. The small format requires less space than the paper records and so cost savings may be gained.

Organizations may elect to store and manage inactive records themselves or outsource the activities to vendors specializing in records storage (commercial records centers). If the latter, the role of the records management department is to manage the vendor relationship and ensure quality of service to the organization.

Corporations interested in preserving the history of their business may establish a corporate archive to provide evidence and information of their organization's functions, policies, procedures, origins, operations, products, and services. Corporate archives can incorporate documents, photographs, films, publications, and ephemera as well as objects that capture the history and development of

Corporate Information– Custody

an organization. Preserving the records of company presidents and other policy-making offices can offer valuable insight into the reasons for corporate actions. Records management and archives may be fully integrated or separate functions that work closely together. The business archive complements records management by assuring the preservation of documents of long-term management, legal, fiscal, communications, and marketing value.

VITAL RECORDS

A vital record is any recorded information that is identified as essential for the continuation or survival of the organization if a disaster strikes.[16] A vital records protection program is a key component of a corporate RMP with the purpose of ensuring the organization identifies and protects those records critical to the organization in the event of disaster. Vital records protection is often integrated into the corporation's overall business continuity or disaster recovery program. This ensures the information critical to the business is identified, protected, and available when disaster strikes.

Determining whether a record is vital is done through an appraisal process, typically as part of the development of the record retention schedule. The cost of protecting the records must always be weighed against the cost of reconstructing them and to other direct monetary losses, such as revenue, assets, and productivity if the records are destroyed prematurely. The point is to protect the information contained in the records rather than the records themselves, although the evidential value of the record is also considered and should be protected if necessary.[17]

In addition to identifying the vital records, the program determines the method of protection. Disasters can come in many forms and with varying degrees of severity. There are natural hazards such as fire, water, mildew, light, dust, insects, rodents, and acids; human hazards such as theft, loss, unauthorized access; and disasters such as earthquakes, hurricanes, and explosions. Likewise, the methods of protection can vary. An assessment to identify the types of disaster an organization might incur must be considered when determining protection needs.

The vital records program is a form of insurance for the corporation, making certain that the information needed to respond to an emergency is available. It is therefore important that the type of disaster be weighed against the likelihood of these disasters, and the consequences to the organization if they occur. Methods of protection are dependent upon the type of disaster and level of severity. Three accepted methods of protection are

- Duplication and dispersal.
- On-site storage and vaulting.
- Remote storage and vaulting.

Operating procedures cover the use of records in daily activities, in emergencies, and after disasters. A vital records master list provides the organization with a complete list of all vital records, the business group responsible for protecting the records, the method of protection, the importance of the record, and frequency of taking protective measures.

MERGERS, ACQUISITIONS, AND DIVESTITURES

When a corporation decides to merge with or acquire another company, the motivation may be to reduce competition, diversify, or revive a business. Merging companies face enormous challenges as the successful integration of information, technology, equipment, and corporate culture is critical to meeting the business objectives driving the consolidation.

The role of records management in a merger or acquisition is multifaceted. Records management will provide support and assist in the overall integration of information assets, including records and data collections (physical and electronic) and systems. For certain industries, such as healthcare and finance, there are state and federal regulations to be considered regarding the management of information during a merger.

If both entities have established RMPs, then the integration of records management functions requires review and analysis. Issues to consider include whether to change record retention periods (a potentially huge and costly undertaking for large mergers), whether to incorporate the acquired organization's retention schedule or leave separate schedules, whether to integrate records management databases and systems, identifying staffing requirements, services offered, and whether to consolidate inactive records storage.

A third facet involves managing the records created during the merger itself. This includes due diligence records, contracts, and financial records among others. The due diligence phase of an acquisition is when the organization is still determining whether the deal is beneficial to both parties. Due diligence is information-intensive and very dependent upon data, documents and evidentiary records. It is also highly confidential and in many cases the records management group will not be involved until this phase is over and the records are no longer restricted.

When a company sells off a part of the business or a joint venture between organizations ends, there are very similar records management considerations. Instead of dealing with how information assets and systems will be integrated, now the questions involve how to deal with the records of, and related to, the departing organization. The legal obligations and liabilities of the organization will help to determine the proper division or sharing of information assets. The fact that a business unit or business asset is transferred to a new owner does not exempt the original owner from responsibility nor from the need to retain the records associated with the unit or asset as required by law.

Dissolution of a company does not end its obligations to retain records. Statutes of limitations apply and the corporation can still be exposed to lawsuits. The Corporate Secretary is usually responsible for the books and records including following legal requirements for the retention of information after the dissolution.

Most relevant to the records management discussion is that ownership of the records and recordkeeping responsibilities are clearly defined and documented.

RECORDS MANAGEMENT PLACEMENT WITHIN THE CORPORATION

The records management function provides services across the corporation, supporting all departments, and working closely with other corporate support departments such as audit, finance, information technology, human resources, legal, risk management, security, and tax. Its placement in the corporation varies and depends on many different factors, including size and type of organization, management structure, organizational culture, and regulatory environment. The one constant is that there is no single place in the corporation where records management always lives.

Traditionally, it was common to find records management placed within the administrative services or operations area of the organization. The records management function was considered a "back office" operation and the perception of records managers as clerical staff (file clerks) rather than information professionals persisted for many years. More recently, due to the proliferation of electronic information and increased regulatory environment, the records management function may be placed within the information technology, audit or legal/compliance departments.

The challenge is that regardless of the placement within the corporation, records management is a non-revenue generating function. Records personnel must build collaborative relationships with key corporate support departments as well as direct relationships with the lines of business in order to implement, maintain, and grow the corporate RMP.

STANDARDS

Standards provide a means for which corporations can measure a service or a product against a set of guidelines. There are many standards incorporated into the workplace, several of which relate to records and information management. Not all corporations follow all standards; rather corporations follow standards that best support their business activities.

The International Standards Organization (ISO), issues standards covering a wide variety of subjects; standards issued by this body carry an authority that comes with obtaining consensus from many countries. ISO 15489:2001 is the international standard on records management.[18] Praised by the records management profession upon its release, it has the potential to serve as the model for RMP regardless of industries or geographic location. The U.S. National Archives and Records Administration based its approach to records management on the standard. ISO 15489 is a voluntary standard, so compliance is a business decision each organization makes depending upon their needs. This makes it difficult to measure the impact of the standard on corporate RMP.

The ISO 9000 Quality Assurance series of standards cover quality management systems in the manufacturing and service industries. Being compliant with the standards is important for certain industries—certification is required in order to do business in Europe for the manufacturers of telecommunications equipment and medical equipment. Other corporations may use the standards as a benchmarking tool without going through the accreditation process, which can be costly. Although not a "records management" standard per se, there are many records requirements in the standards. The activities that comprise the field of records management form the foundation for successful compliance with the records requirements of the standards.[19]

RECORDS MANAGEMENT AUDIT

By law, publicly traded corporations must submit to external audits for verification that their financial records and statements are accurate and the company has fairly reported its financial condition. Corporations also conduct internal audits, carried out by employees of the corporation, to evaluate financial and operational controls over processes, records, and systems. The internal audit group usually reports back to a corporate audit committee or governance board with authority to enforce change. Information audits can be conducted against the RMP or be used to gauge employee and organizational compliance with the RMP.

Audits may be conducted by an internal audit group or outside consultants. Regardless, the audit should be an independent and objective review of the RMP with clearly defined standards so that the purpose, scope and measures of success are agreed to by all parties. Factors such as company size, geographic location(s), and workloads may impact the scope of the audit, dictating whether the audit covers the entire organization, focuses on a single business unit, or covers only a sample of records created since the last audit.

The RMP audit may be used to measure how well the records management function is serving the corporation; assess whether the corporation is in compliance with the RMP policies, procedures and processes; or identify gaps and areas of improvement with the organization and the RMP. It may be used as a method of benchmarking the RMP so that future reviews of the program are measured against the initial audit. The audit findings can serve as a roadmap for the RMP and provide a link back to the overall strategic goals of the corporation.

CONCLUSION

The purpose of a corporate RMP is to support the overall goals and objectives of the corporation. The program achieves this by bringing recordkeeping efficiencies into the organization, controlling costs associated with recordkeeping, and ensuring that information is readily available to support business functions. While the specifics of a program vary depending on a number of factors discussed in this entry, a comprehensive RMP includes the core elements of record retention, compliance, active records management, inactive records management, and vital records management.

By retaining only those records required for legal, regulatory, and business need, the company can reduce storage costs, improve access and retrieval, and reduce time and effort to reconstruct information in the event of disaster. Compliance with the laws and regulations governing records helps companies avoid fines and penalties as well as reduces risks and liability during litigation and audits.

Although records management practices were initially developed to better manage records within the U.S. federal government, businesses long ago recognized the value of these practices and began adapting them to the corporate environment.[20] Corporate records management practices continue to evolve to better support the corporation by adopting appropriate technologies, by monitoring and responding to new and changing legal and regulatory requirements, and by evaluating the impact of these changes on information management.

REFERENCES

1. Skupsky, D.S. *Recordkeeping Requirements*, Information Requirements Clearinghouse: Denver, CO, 1991; 11.
2. Shepherd, E.; Yeo, G. *Managing Records—A Handbook of Principles and Practice*, Facet Publishing: London, U.K., 2003; 35.
3. Freedom of Information Act, codified in the United States Code, Title 5 Section 552.
4. California Public Records Act, codified in the California Government Code, Section 6250.
5. Saffady, W. *Records and Information Management: Fundamentals of Professional Practice*, ARMA International: Lenexa, KS, 2004; 9.
6. http://sarbanes-oxley-guidelines.com/.
7. http://www.usdoj.gov/criminal/fraud/docs/dojdocb.html.
8. http://www.export.gov/safeharbor/SH_Overview.asp.
9. Robek, M.; Brown, G.; Maedke, W. *Information and Records Management*, 3rd Ed. Glencoe Publishing Co.: Encino, CA, 1987; 110.
10. The Sedona Conference The Sedona Conference Commentary on Legal Holds: The Trigger and the Process August, 2007 3.
11. http://definitions.uslegal.com/d/discovery/.
12. http://www.radicati.com/?p=1934.
13. Chin, K.; Logan, D. *MarketScope for Records Management*, Gartner Inc., December 15, 2005 (http://www.gartner.com).
14. http://jitc.fhu.disa.mil/recmgt/standards.html.
15. http://www.moreq2.eu/.
16. ARMA International. *Vital Records: Identifying, Managing, and Recovering Business-Critical Records (ANSI/ARMA 5-2003)*, ARMA International: Lenexa, KS, 2003.
17. Robek, M.; Brown, G.; Maedke, W. *Information and Records Management*, 3rd Ed. Glencoe Publishing Co.: Encino, CA, 1987; 130–131.
18. Brumm, E.K. *Managing Records for ISO Compliance*, ASQC Quality Press: Milwaukee, WI, 1995; 2.
19. http://www.iso.org/iso_catalogue_detail?csnumber=31908.
20. Benedon, W. *Records Management*, Prentice Hall: Englewood Cliffs, NJ, 1969; vii.

BIBLIOGRAPHY

1. ARMA International. *Vital Records: Identifying, Managing, and Recovering Business-Critical Records (ANSI/ARMA 5-2003)*, ARMA International: Lenexa, KS, 2003.
2. European Commission website: http://ec.europa.eu/justice_home/fsj/privacy/index_en.htm (accessed March 30, 2008).
3. Phillips, John T. *RIM Checklist for Mergers, Acquisitions, Divestitures, and Closures*, ARMA International Educational Foundation: Pittsburgh, PA, 2005.
4. Saffady, W. *Managing Electronic Records*, 3rd Ed. ARMA International: Lenexa, KS, 2002.
5. Saffady, W. *Records and Information Management: Fundamentals of Professional Practice*, ARMA International: Lenexa, KS, 2004.
6. Schellenberg, T.R. *Modern Archives: Principles and Techniques*, University of Chicago Press: Chicago, IL, 1975.
7. Society of American Archivists (SAA), website: http://www.archivists.org/saagroups/bas (accessed March 30, 2008).
8. The Sedona Conference Working Group Series, The Sedona Guidelines: Best Practices Guidelines & Commentary for Managing Information & Records in the Electronic Age The Sedona Conference Phoenix, AZ 2004.

Credibility and Cognitive Authority of Information

Soo Young Rieh
School of Information, University of Michigan, Ann Arbor, Michigan, U.S.A.

Abstract

This entry defines the concepts of information credibility and cognitive authority, introduces the key terms and dimensions of each, and discusses major theoretical frameworks tested and proposed in library and information science (LIS) and related fields. It also lays out the fundamental notions of credibility and cognitive authority in historical contexts to trace the evolution of the understanding and enhancement of the two concepts. This entry contends that the assessment of information credibility and cognitive authority is a ubiquitous human activity given that people constantly make decisions and selections based on values of information in a variety of information seeking and use contexts. It further contends that information credibility and cognitive authority assessment can be seen as an ongoing and iterative process rather than a discrete information evaluation event. The judgments made in assessment processes are highly subjective given their dependence on individuals' accumulated beliefs, existing knowledge, and prior experiences. The conclusion of this entry suggests the need for more research by emphasizing the contributions that credibility and cognitive authority research can make to the field of LIS.

INTRODUCTION

This entry traces the evolution of the concepts of credibility and cognitive authority in library and information science (LIS) and other related fields including communication, human-computer interaction, and psychology. It provides definitions for information credibility and cognitive authority. It also introduces multiple dimensions as well as theoretical frameworks explaining the process of assessing credibility and cognitive authority, concluding by discussing the significance of the two concepts and calling for further research in the area.

Historically, credibility and cognitive authority of information were considered as criteria for making relevance judgments in LIS. Due to the recent growth of the Internet and concomitant evolution of information, communication, and publishing mechanisms, LIS researchers and practitioners have increasingly recognized the importance of understanding credibility and cognitive authority as a research agenda in its own right. Today people have access to a wider range of information resources than ever before, and as a result, face greater challenges in evaluating the usefulness of information with which they interact. Given the popularity of various self-published resources in which the source of information is vague and uncertain, the assessment of information credibility and cognitive authority has become a ubiquitous human activity.

In this entry, credibility and cognitive authority are considered as closely related yet different concepts. Most definitions of credibility revolve around the concept of believability of information.[1] This entry uses the term *cognitive authority*, coined by Patrick Wilson to differentiate it from administrative authority.[2] Unlike a person in administrative authority, the world's leading authority in a domain area has no power to command. Experts perceived as not only credible or worthy of belief but also influential in other people's thinking are termed cognitive authorities. Those people or information sources considered to be credible serve as the potential pool of cognitive authorities. That is, cognitive authority is one of the principal aspects of information credibility.

CREDIBILITY DEFINITIONS AND ORIGINS

Definitions

Credibility is an intuitive and complex concept.[3] Rather than having one clear definition, credibility has been defined along with dozens of other related concepts such as believability, trustworthiness, fairness, accuracy, trustfulness, factuality, completeness, precision, freedom from bias, objectivity, depth, and informativeness. Most credibility researchers agree that credibility assessment results from simultaneously evaluating multiple dimensions. Among these, two key dimensions are identified: trustworthiness and expertise.[4] Trustworthiness is a core dimension in credibility assessment that captures the perceived goodness and morality of the source.[5] The perception that a source is fair, unbiased, and truthful contributes to the trustworthiness of information. Trustworthiness is, however, not a synonym for credibility because people also must recognize expertise in order to deem information credible. Expertise reflects perceived knowledge, skill, and experience of the source.[5] Expertise is likewise an important factor given its close relationship to people's

Corporate Information– Custody

perceptions of a source's ability to provide information that is both accurate and valid.

Trustworthiness and expertise are not always perceived together. An expert with the title of doctor or professor might have a reputation of being knowledgeable in a certain area but still might not be considered trustworthy for the tendency to unreliability or bias. A person may think of a friend as being honest and trustworthy in general, but the advice that the friend gives is not necessarily considered credible for the friend's lack of expertise. The most credible information is found in those perceived to have high levels of trustworthiness and expertise.

Credibility does not reside in an information object, source, or person, although the characteristics of the foregoing can serve as the bases for people's assessment. It is people who ultimately make judgments of information credibility. People who have their own experience, knowledge, and beliefs are likely to make their own credibility judgments. Many studies show, in fact, that judgments of credibility are highly subjective assessment processes. In this entry, credibility is defined as people's assessment of whether information is trustworthy based on their own expertise and knowledge.

Historical Development

The fields of communication and LIS are both concerned with the credibility assessment of information and sources. Credibility research, however, has evolved in fundamentally different ways, with each field having its own origins, approaches, and goals for the study of credibility over the past five decades. Some researchers believe that scholarly interest in credibility dates back to Aristotle's examination of ethos (appeal based on character), pathos (appeal based on emotion), and logos (appeal based on logic or reason).[6] Aristotle's notion of credibility focused mainly on the characteristics of ethos, which is "the communicator's ability to inspire confidence and belief in what was being said" (pp. 422–423).[3]

Scholarly examination of credibility began in the twentieth century when psychologists investigated persuasion as a part of the propaganda efforts during the World Wars. A series of landmark studies were conducted by the Yale Group which defined credibility as a receiver-based construct and suggested that credibility is determined by an audience's acceptance of a speaker.[4] In the 1950s, mass media professionals took an interest in the notion of credibility when television became popular and subscription rates for newspapers began to decline. Professional news organizations' examination of perceived credibility of newspapers versus television then grew into the study of *media credibility* which to this day remains an established research area in the field of communication.

Credibility research began much more recently in LIS as compared to the communication field. This does not mean that LIS researchers and practitioners had no concerns

about credibility assessment in the past. Rather, LIS research into human judgments of information centered on the notion of relevance. Relevance is often seen as playing a significant, underlying, and yet elusive role for various information activities such as acquiring, organizing, storing, preserving, searching, communicating, interacting with, and using information.[7] The history of relevance started with the first libraries as library users were concerned about the problem of finding information *relevant* to them.[7] However, the notion of relevance remained hidden and implicit until Vickery's presentations at the 1958 International Conference on Scientific Information.[8] Since then, relevance has been studied extensively in terms of frameworks for defining relevance dimensions, forms of document representation affecting relevance judgment, subjectivity of relevance judgment, and identification of criteria adopted by users in judging relevance.

While the majority of relevance research has discussed relevance in terms of its topical aspect, which concerns itself with whether or not the topic of a search query matches the topic of a document, alternative notions have been suggested. For instance, utility, which is entirely subjective and based on personal judgment, is proposed as a measure of information retrieval effectiveness.[9] Relevance and utility are not the same concepts. Until the 1980s, relevance was viewed as judgments concerned with aboutness, pertinence, or topical-relatedness. Utility was considered a broad concept involving not only topic-relatedness but also quality, novelty, importance, credibility, and other evaluations. In the 1990s, a substantial body of empirical studies on relevance criteria was conducted, producing studies which consistently revealed that people use much more diverse criteria than mere topicality in making relevance judgments. The criteria identified in these user-centered relevance studies include credibility, authority, completeness, depth, currency, accuracy, quality, effectiveness, belief, and clarity.[10]

In LIS, as in other related fields, the emergence and proliferation of information technology, the Internet in particular, provided the impetus for improved and more formal understanding of the notion of credibility. Empirical studies showed that people became more concerned about quality, credibility, and authority of information as they gain awareness of the fact that the Web lacks quality control mechanisms in contrast to traditional information retrieval systems.[11] Further, when looking for information, people rely on multiple information resources and may even seek to verify across different resources given the availability and accessibility of various types of digital media and forms of information.[12] The two fields—LIS and communication—that have studied credibility from different perspectives and presumptions because of historical origins have drawn closer together than ever before as both fields have paid more attention to the significance of studying credibility and authority assessment in the contemporary digital information landscape.

TYPOLOGY OF CREDIBILITY

Communication researchers have traditionally drawn distinctions between source credibility, message credibility, and media credibility. *Source credibility* usually refers to "judgments made by a perceiver concerning the believability of a communicator" (pp. 130–131).[13] Numerous empirical studies have investigated the dimensions of source credibility from the perspectives of message recipients and identified those factors that might influence audience perceptions of trustworthiness and expertise. These factors include dynamism, composure, sociability, qualification, reliability, animation, poise, and good-naturedness.[14] A meta-analysis of 114 credibility studies revealed that source expertise is a stronger influence on persuasion than other source characteristics given that the expertise dimension of source credibility is more objective than other dimensions and consequently easier to assess.[15]

Message credibility examines how message characteristics such as content, structure, language, and presentation can impact perceptions of the believability of information. But the distinction between message credibility and source credibility is not always clear. Credible sources are likely to produce credible messages, and credible messages are likely to be seen as originating from credible sources. When people have strong interest and involvement, message characteristics become more influential than source characteristics because they are motivated to scrutinize message content. In some situations in which little information is available about the source of a message, people tend to turn to message cues in making credibility judgments.[16] Researchers have examined the influence of various factors such as message comprehensibility, number of arguments, incentives, fear appeals, one-sided versus two-sided messages, repetition, and presentation style on people's message credibility assessments.[14]

Media credibility focuses on the relative credibility of various media channels through which a message is sent. Media credibility studies typically ask which medium people would believe if they received conflicting reports on the same news story from different media such as radio, television, magazines, and newspapers.[17] This question aimed to discover people's perceptions of the relative credibility of different news media. Previous studies suggest that media credibility is strongly related to the frequency with which people use a particular medium. In them, people judge their preferred medium as being the most credible.

In recent years, media credibility studies have attempted to compare people's perceptions of traditionally-delivered information sources (newspapers, magazines, brochures, etc.) and their online counterparts (online newspapers, online news magazines, online political Web sites, etc.). The popularity and unique characteristics of the Web as a medium led to studying *Web credibility* as a distinct notion. Credibility researchers

have proceeded to note the following characteristics of the Web: lack of filtering mechanisms, form inclusive of interaction techniques and interface attributes, source ambiguity, and infancy as a medium.[18]

Computer credibility impacts the field of human-computer interaction (HCI) when computers act as knowledge repositories, instruct users, report measures, report on work performance, report on their own state, run simulations, and help in the rendering of virtual environments. Computer credibility assessment relies on simultaneous evaluation of four types of credibility: presumed credibility, reputed credibility, surface credibility, and experienced credibility.[1] *Presumed credibility* refers to the extent to which people believe information because of general assumptions in their mind. Sometimes people make assumptions based on stereotypes rather than on truth, and these assumptions and stereotypes all contribute to credibility perceptions. *Reputed credibility* describes the extent to which people believe information because of what third parties—other people, media, or institutions—have reported. These reports may come in the form of endorsements, awards, or referrals. *Surface credibility* derives from simple inspection. People make credibility judgments based on first impressions of surface traits such as of book covers, the visual designs of software, interface designs, and the information architecture of Web sites. *Experienced credibility* refers to the extent to which people believe information based on their first-hand experience. It may prove to be the most powerful form of credibility because it derives from people's interaction with others or with systems over an extended period of time.

Some credibility researchers who consider the processes of social endorsement to be crucial in credibility construction have proposed several variants of credibility including conferred credibility, tabulated credibility, and emergent credibility.[6] *Conferred credibility* indicates that people sometimes recognize credibility not based on a real source of information but on other sources' positive reputation, all of which helps alleviate skepticism. For instance, Google might confer its credibility on sponsored links in the search results page because most people are unaware of the sponsorship model and consider such links equivalent to Google's results. *Tabulated credibility* refers to the assessments people make based on peer ratings of an individual, organization, or product. The availability of aggregated ratings from other people may widen the range of social input on which people can rely in judging credibility. *Emergent credibility* arises from a pool of resources, such as Wikipedia, wikis, social networking sites, and other applications created by individuals. These forms of credibility suggest that people are not isolated evaluators of credibility as well as that social engagements and interactions must be considered in understanding credibility construction and assessment.

AUTHORITY

Authority has been defined and discussed in many different forms across numerous disciplines, including philosophy, education, psychology, political science, law, religion, and LIS. Authority is related to those areas of competence or applicability over which it is exercised. Having authority is different from being an expert because authority is a relationship involving at least two people. A person can be an expert even though others may not realize or recognize the fact. No individual by himself or herself can be an authority. All authority is "a relation among a bearer, a subject, a field, in virtue of a particular quality, attribute, and context" [[19], p. 77]. In other words, authority is limited to spheres. A person can speak with authority within one sphere, but with no authority on questions outside that sphere.

Many researchers agree on the two broad categories of authority: epistemic authority and deontic authority. The former corresponds to being an authority and the latter to being in authority.[19] As an example of epistemic authority, when people say, "He is an authority on Hegel," they mean that he is superior to others within a field in light of knowledge about Hegel. Deontic authority takes the forms of imperial authority as exercised by a state through its government and its various organs, paternalistic authority as exercised by parents over their children, and operative authority as vested in any designated leader or office. In place of epistemic authority and deontic authority, cognitive authority and administrative authority can be used as alternative terms in distinguishing more clearly these two different types of authority.[2]

COGNITIVE AUTHORITY

Definitions

Cognitive authority is a kind of influence.[2] Those who are cognitive authorities profoundly influence others' thoughts. People who are not cognitive authorities may still exert an influence in the world. What distinguishes people who are cognitive authorities from those who are not is that the formers' influence is recognized in some official manner. Cognitive authority is a matter of degree; thus the weight that a cognitive authority's words carry for others might vary. Even though it is possible for an absolute cognitive authority in a given sphere to have an answer to virtually all of the questions within the area, people in general tend to take the opinions and advice of others with different degrees of seriousness. Cognitive authorities are those people whose opinions and advice are taken more seriously with more weight being placed on their words than on the words of others.[2]

Two bases for cognitive authority need to be recognized: being an expert and being reputable.[2] To qualify as an expert, a person should show evidence of knowledge, skill, experience, training, and education. Because knowledge and skill are difficult to test directly, evidence in terms of occupational roles or advanced degrees often must provide support for claims to expert status. However, not all experts necessarily possess outstanding competence. Experience and education may provide evidence of basic qualifications but still be insufficient in providing a high degree of expertise. To be an outstanding expert, a person must have a reputation for that expertise. In addition, established cognitive authorities can transfer authority to other people. When reputation among peers is unknown, special groups of people already considered to be knowledgeable can be turned to. For instance, individual A believes individual B because individual A believes group C, and group C says that individual B can be believed. This rule—that one can trust those who are trusted by those one trusts[2]—constitutes a central feature of cognitive authority.

Bases for Assessing Cognitive Authority

When people acquire influence from cognitive authorities, there should be an answer for the question "What makes you think so?" Whatever the reasons for thinking that certain others deserve cognitive authority, it is not for the reason that people always directly test the authorities' knowledge. Rather, people often cite indirect tests that serve as the bases of cognitive authority judgments. Not only individuals are recognized as cognitive authorities: books, journals, newspapers, manuscripts, and films are all possible sources of knowledge and opinion though they give rise to the same kind of questions about cognitive authority: which works can be taken seriously?; how much weight can be given to what the texts say? When people have sufficient knowledge of certain topics, they can claim directly against what they already know. However, most texts discuss topics people do not know enough about to apply the direct test. This is because people look for information and consult texts to find what they do not know.[20] Therefore, people apply various indirect tests for recognizing the cognitive authority of a text, including personal authority, institutional authority, textual type authority, and intrinsic plausibility.[2]

The first apparent basis for recognizing a text's cognitive authority is the cognitive authority of its author. People will trust a text written by an individual or group of individuals whom they trust. The tests of personal cognitive authority are based on present reputation and accomplishments. Recognition of personal authority does not automatically transfer to past or future work. An established reputation is insufficient to establish the current authority of old texts.

Another kind of test is associated with the publisher and publication history. A publishing house can acquire a kind of cognitive authority if it is considered to be good at publishing high-quality work. Thus, publications by a publishing house people respect constitute a kind of personal recommendation. A journal can exert authority, too, which transfers to the articles it publishes. Other institutional endorsements are also used as tests of authority. For instance, sponsorship by a learned society or a professional organization serve as the basis of institutional authority, as could publication by a government agency. Then again, published reviews furnish a special indirect test. If a reviewer has cognitive authority then his or her review itself constitutes a personal recommendation.

The third kind of test, that of text type, is based on the text itself separate from its author or publisher. For instance, reference works such as dictionaries and encyclopedias do not draw attention to their compilers as people often do not know who the authors or editors are. Standard reference works tend to be revised frequently and may be considered as institutions in their own right.

Finally, the test of intrinsic plausibility is always available. Reading a few words or sentences of the text may be sufficient for people to decide whether or not to continue reading the entire text. Such rapid assessment is not entirely based on intrinsic plausibility, but does constitute a major part. If people find that a work represents a school of thought they reject or has a style of research they think worthless, they become discouraged from continuing to read the work. Although people do not always reject what they see as being in conflict with their prior beliefs and cognitive positions, they cannot avoid assessing the text's contents as plausible or implausible and accordingly bestowing or withholding cognitive authority.

THE PROCESS OF ASSESSING CREDIBILITY AND COGNITIVE AUTHORITY

Several theoretical frameworks suggest that the assessment of credibility and cognitive authority needs to be understood as a process rather than a discrete evaluative event. Most of these frameworks and models are developed in the context of Internet use and Web searching. Rieh's Model of Judgment of Information Quality and Cognitive Authority was proposed based on an empirical study conducted in the context of Web searching.[11] Her model captures the point at which people make predictive judgments about which Web site contains credible information and then follows through to include evaluative judgments by which they express preferences for information encountered. When people open a Web browser, they take the first action based on a predictive judgment that must be made before a new page is introduced. The selection of a certain Web site is based on people's knowledge and experience, recommendations from others, or other characteristics of information objects or sources. Once people open a new Web page, they make an evaluative judgment in terms of how good the information is, how useful the information is, how

trustworthy the information is, how accurate the information is, and so on. The reasons underlying such judgments are based on certain characteristics of information objects and sources. If people find that evaluative judgments of the information do not match the expectations of the earlier predictive judgments, they might return to a previous page or decide to start with a new page. By iterating the process, people can reach a point at which their predictive judgments and evaluative judgments match and they will proceed to use that information.[21]

Wathen and Burkell's model of credibility assessment, developed by synthesizing the literature in the field, also proposes that the assessment of credibility of online information is iterative.[22] Upon entering a Web site on the first level of evaluation, people rate the credibility of the medium in question based on surface characteristics such as appearance, interface design, download speed, interactivity, and organization of information. Once the site passes people's credibility criteria in the initial evaluation, they then move to the next level of evaluation. Should the site fail the first evaluation, people are likely to leave the site to seek others. On the second level of evaluation, people consider the credibility of the source and the message, evaluating source expertise, competence, trustworthiness, and credentials. The message is evaluated in terms of content, relevance, currency, accuracy, and tailoring. On the third level of the evaluative process, the interaction of message presentation and content can be assessed with respect to people's cognitive states. Wathen and Burkell point out that, given the limitless number of possible interactions among contextual and intervening variables, credibility assessment becomes quite complex and difficult to predict.

Fogg's Prominence-Interpretation Theory grew out of a series of research projects conducted at the Stanford Web Credibility Research Lab.[23] Fogg's theory describes the credibility assessment process from the point at which people notice something of interest in a Web site to the point at which they make their judgment. This theory states that two events need to occur for people to make credibility assessments on the Web: they notice element(s) in a Web site (prominence), and make judgments about what has been noticed (interpretation). If people do not notice the element, it would not have any impact on their credibility assessment of the site. Fogg's theory proposed five factors affecting prominence: involvement (motivation and ability to scrutinize Web site content), topic of the Web site, task of the user, experience of the user, and individual differences in users. Interpretation, the theory's second component, involves people's judgments about a Web site element in terms of being good or bad. Various factors relate to interpretation, including assumptions (culture, past experiences, heuristics, etc.), skills/knowledge (level of competency in the site's subject matter), and context (environment, expectations, situational norms, etc.). This process of prominence and interpretation can occur more than once because new aspects of the site can be continually noted and interpreted in the process of making credibility assessments on the Web.

A number of credibility researchers have observed that people do not always engage fully in the cognitive effort of making analytical judgments of content messages and sources. Rather, people often rely on mental shortcuts to judgmental rules (or heuristics), which have evolved as generalizations in their knowledge base and have thus been refined through the course of their experience.[24] People are often unaware of the role of heuristics in influencing their judgments, which can result in their accepting a message as credible without first attributing the specific reasons for their acceptance. Cues that trigger heuristics can either be embedded in a message or internally located within people's cognition.[25]

Sundar's research team at the Media Effects Research Laboratory at Pennsylvania State University identified four broad affordances in digital media capable of cueing cognitive heuristics pertinent to making credibility assessments: modality (M), agency (A), interactivity (I), and navigability (N).[26] The modality affordance, which often appears in the multimedia in digital devices, is the most structural (that is, tied to structure rather than to content) and apparent on an interface and accordingly triggers heuristics related to realism, novelty, and coolness, among factors. The agency affordance relates to identification of the source. Depending on who or what is perceived as a source, cognitive heuristics are triggered and in turn affect the information's perceived credibility. The interactivity affordance of digital media provides cues related to interaction, activity, choice, control, and responsiveness. Finally, the navigability affordance has dual abilities: hyperlinks on a Web site may trigger heuristics given that easily navigable sites have perceived credibility, and words on the hyperlink trigger different heuristics more closely related to the nature of the content. These four affordances are all structural features that help explain the perceived credibility of digital media beyond content characteristics. The affordances are associated with first impressions of surface-level characteristics of Web sites, which are capable of amplifying or diminishing content effects on credibility. The core idea of Sundar's model is that, while cues and heuristics do not guarantee success, they likely appeal to many individuals striving to cope with the deluge of information.

Hilligoss and Rieh's credibility framework also considers heuristics as an important component of credibility assessment.[27] The results of an empirical study about people's credibility assessment in a variety of everyday life information-seeking contexts identified three distinct levels of credibility judgments: construct, heuristics, and interaction. The construct level involves defining the notion of credibility that influences people's judgments. The heuristics level pertains to general rules of thumb for credibility assessment, applicable to a variety of general information seeking situations. The interaction level refers to credibility judgments in which particular sources or content cues are characterized. These three levels of credibility assessment are interlinked; for instance, people's constructions of credibility influence the kind of heuristics used in selecting a Web site in which people begin a search. Credibility heuristics can influence the ways in which people pay attention to certain characteristics of information and sources. As people gain more experience with a certain source of information, credibility heuristics can be changed or extended. Should a heuristic prove consistent over time, then it becomes a construct of credibility in people's minds. Their model additionally demonstrates that context is a factor importantly influencing all three levels of credibility assessment. The context is the social, relational, and dynamic frames surrounding people's information-seeking processes, creating boundaries around the information-seeking activity or the credibility judgment itself. The context of credibility judgments can either guide the selection of resources or limit judgment applicability.

CONCLUSION

This entry intends to raise awareness about notions of information credibility and cognitive authority in the field of LIS as well as to encourage additional research work in this area. The entry defines two concepts, introduces key terms and dimensions, and discusses major theories and models proposed and tested in LIS and related fields. It also lays out the foundations of credibility and cognitive authority in historical contexts in order to illustrate the importance of understanding and enhancing these concepts as foci of research and practice.

Assessment of credibility and cognitive authority is a ubiquitous human activity, given that people constantly make decisions and selections based on the value of information in a variety of school, work, and everyday life contexts. Further, credibility and cognitive authority assessment can be seen as an ongoing and iterative process rather than a discrete evaluation event. The judgments made in assessment processes are highly dependent upon people's accumulated beliefs, existing knowledge, and prior experiences. While information objects, sources, and media often provide clues and bases for assessment, it is eventually people who make assessment with respect to their information seeking goals and motivations.

Credibility and cognitive authority have long been significant concepts for both researchers and practitioners in LIS and communication fields. Theoretical developments and applications are still emerging and evolving given changing information and communication technology environments. Previous credibility research has looked at people as information consumers while holding rather narrow views of information activities, for example, by focusing on seeking, reading, receiving, and watching. Today, more people are engaging in a broad range of information activities, such as creating and mediating content while actively utilizing new and diverse information technology tools and applications. Further empirical studies need to be conducted to investigate new kinds of research problems that reflect dynamic and complex information seeking and use contexts. Additional broad and multidisciplinary theoretical frameworks need to be constructed to represent a variety of human information behaviors beyond information seeking and retrieving. Creative and insightful inquiries from researchers and practitioners into credibility and cognitive authority in the LIS field would lead to efficient systems and programs that will eventually help people become more effective information users.

REFERENCES

1. Tseng, S.; Fogg, B.J. Credibility and computing technology. Commun. ACM. **1999**, *42*(5), 39–44.
2. Wilson, P. *Second-Hand Knowledge: An Inquiry into Cognitive Authority;* Greenwood Press: Westport, CT, 1983.
3. Self, C.C. Credibility. In *An Integrated Approach to Communication Theory and Research*; Salwen, M.B., Stacks, D.W., Eds.; Lawrence Erlbaum Associates, Inc.: Mahwah, NJ, 1996; 421–441.
4. Hovland, C.I.; Janis, I.L.; Kelley, H.H. *Communication and Persuasion*; Yale University Press: New Haven, CT, 1953.
5. Fogg, B.J. *Persuasive Technology: Using Computers to Change What We Think and Do;* Morgan Kaufmann: San Francisco, CA, 2003.
6. Flanagin, A.J.; Metzger, M.J. Digital media and youth: Unparalleled opportunity and unprecedented responsibility. In *Digital Media, Youth, and Credibility*; Metzger, M.J., Flanagin, A.J., Eds.; MIT Press: Cambridge, MA, 2008; 5–28.
7. Saracevic, T. Relevance: A review of the literature and a framework for thinking on the notion in information science. Part II. Adv. Lib. **2006**, *30*, 3–71.
8. Vickery, B.C. Subject analysis for information retrieval. *Proceedings of the International Conference on Scientific Information;* National Academy of Sciences: Washington, DC, 1959; Vol. 2, 855–865.
9. Cooper, W.S. On selecting a measure of retrieval effectiveness. Part 1: The "subjective" philosophy of evaluation. J. Am. Soc. Inform. Sci. **1973**, *24*(2), 87–100.
10. Maglaughlin, K.L.; Sonnenwald, D.H. User perspectives on relevance criteria: a comparison among relevant, partially relevant, and not-relevant judgments. J. Am. Soc. Inform. Sci. Technol. **2002**, *53*(5), 327–342.
11. Rieh, S.Y. Judgment of information quality and cognitive authority in the Web. J. Am. Soc. Inform. Sci. Technol. **2002**, *53*(2), 145–161.
12. Rieh, S.Y.; Hilligoss, B. College students' credibility judgments in the information seeking process. In *Digital Media, Youth, and Credibility*; Metzger, M.J., Flanagin, A.J., Eds.; MIT Press: Cambridge, MA, 2008; 49–72.
13. O'Keefe, D.J. *Persuasion: Theory and Research*; Sage Publications: Newbury Park, CA, 1990.
14. Metzger, M.J;. Flanagin, A.J.; Eyal, K.; Lemus, D.R.; McCann, R.M. Credibility for the 21st century: Integrating perspectives on source, message, and media credibility in the contemporary media environment. In *Communication Yearbook*; Kalbfleisch, P.J., Ed.; Lawrence Erlbaum Associates, Inc.: Mahwah, NJ, 2003; Vol. 27, 293–335.
15. Wilson, E.J.; Sherrell, D.L. Source effects in communication and persuasion research: A meta-analysis of effect size. J. Acad. Market. Sci. **1993**, *21*(2), 101–112.
16. Petty, R.E.; Cacioppo, J.T. The Elaboration Likelihood Model of persuasion. In *Advances in Experimental Social Psychology*; Berkowitz, L., Ed.; Academic Press: New York, 1986; Vol. 19, 123–205.
17. Roper, B. *Public Attitudes Toward Television and Other Media in a Time of Change;* Television Information Office: New York, 1985.
18. Danielson, D.R. Web credibility. In *Encyclopedia of Human-Computer Interaction*; Ghaoui, C., Ed.; Idea Group, Inc.: Hershey, PA, 2005; 713–721.
19. De George, R.T. *The Nature and Limits of Authority;* University Press of Kansas: Lawrence, KS, 1985.
20. Taylor, R.S. Question negotiation and information seeking in libraries. Coll. Res. Libr. **1968**, *29*, 178–194.
21. Rieh, S.Y.; Belkin, N.J. Interaction on the Web: Scholars' judgment of information quality and cognitive authority, *Proceedings of the 63rd Annual Meeting of the American Society for Information Science* Chicago, IL November, 13–16, 2000; Kraft, D.H., Ed.; Information Today: Medford, NJ, 2000; Vol. 37, 25–38.
22. Wathen, C.N.; Burkell, J. Believe it or not: Factors influencing credibility on the Web. J. Am. Soc. Inform. Sci. Technol. **2002**, *53*(2), 134–144.
23. Fogg, B.J. Prominence-interpretation theory: Explaining how people assess credibility online, *Proceedings of the SIGCHI Conference on Human Factors in Computing Systems* Fort Lauderdale, FL April, 5–10, 2003; Cockton, G., Korhonen, P., Eds.; ACM: New York, 2003; 722–723.
24. Chaiken, S. Heuristic versus systematic information processing and the use of source versus message cues in persuasion. J. Pers. Soc. Psychol. **1980**, *39*(5), 752–766.
25. Chen, S.; Chaiken, S. The heuristic-systematic model in its broader context. In *Dual-Process Theories in Social Psychology*; Chaiken, S., Trope, Y., Eds.; Guilford Press: New York, 1999; 73–96.
26. Sundar, S.S. The MAIN Model: A heuristic approach to understanding technology effects on credibility. In *Digital Media, Youth, and Credibility*; Metzger, M.J.; Flanagin, A.J., Eds.; MIT Press: Cambridge, MA, 2008; 73–100.
27. Hilligoss, B.; Rieh, S.Y. Developing a unifying framework of credibility assessment: concept, heuristics, and interaction in context. Inform. Process. Manag. **2008**, *44*(4), 1467–1484.

BIBLIOGRAPHY

1. Fogg, B.J. *Persuasive technology: Using Computers to Change What We Think and Do,* Morgan Kaufmann: San Francisco, CA, 2003.
2. *Digital Media, Youth, and Credibility*; Metzger, M.J.; Flanagin, A.J., Eds.; MIT Press: Cambridge, MA, 2008.

Corporate Information–Custody

3. Metzger, M.J.; Flanagin, A.J.; Eyal, K. Lemus, D.R. McCann, R.M. Credibility for the 21st century: Integrating perspectives on source, message, and media credibility in the contemporary media environment. In *Communication Yearbook*; Kalbfleisch, P.J., Ed.; Lawrence Erlbaum Associates, Inc.: Mahwah, NJ, 2003; Vol. 27, 293–335.

4. Rieh, S.Y.; Danielson, D.R.; Credibility: A multidisciplinary framework. In *Annual Review of Information Science and Technology*; Cronin, B., Ed.; Information Today: Medford, NJ, 2007; Vol. 41, 307–364.

5. Wilson, P. *Second-Hand Knowledge: An Inquiry into Cognitive Authority;* Greenwood Press: Westport, CT, 1983.

Croatia: Libraries, Archives, and Museums

Aleksandra Horvat
Faculty of Philosophy, University of Zagreb, Zagreb, Croatia,

Josip Kolanović
Croatian State Archives, Zagreb, Croatia,

Višnja Zgaga
Museum Documentation Center, Zagreb, Croatia,

Abstract

This entry provides a short historical overview of the oldest writing systems, manuscripts, and books in Croatia. It describes the emergence of the first libraries, archives, and museums from the ninth to the twentieth centuries followed by a description of the present-day situation in the information professions, including legislation regulating the field, the most important libraries, archives and museums, professional associations, professional education, and continuing professional training. The conclusion discusses examples of present-day cooperation between information institutions.

INTRODUCTION

The Republic of Croatia is located in the south-east of Europe. It shares borders with Slovenia to the west, Hungary to the north, and Serbia, Bosnia, and Herzegovina and Montenegro to the east and south-east. The Adriatic Sea forms its southern border with Italy (see Fig. 1). Croatia covers an area of 56,538 km^2 and has a population of 4,491,543 (July 2008 est.).

According to its geographical position Croatia is a southeastern and Mediterranean country. Its location has had a significant impact on its historical development. From the ninth to the end of the eleventh century it was an independent princedom and kingdom. In 1102 it formed a union with Hungary. Starting in 1527, rulers from the House of Habsburg also became kings of Croatia. As the result of Turkish invasions in the fifteenth century, its geographic holdings were diminished both in the south and in the west. From 1409 until 1797, the coastal area along the Adriatic Sea fell under the administration of the Republic of Venice. Dubrovnik enjoyed a special status, first as an independent commune, and as the Republic of Ragusa from the fifteenth century onward. Despite attempts to unify Croatian lands after the fall of the Republic of Venice in 1797, Northern Croatia still remained in a state union with Hungary, while Dalmatia became a province to the Emperor of Austria, except for the short period between 1806 and 1814, when along with Istria it fell under the French administration, first as part of the Kingdom of Italy and after 1809 as part of the Provinces of Illyria. A stronger movement toward unification arose in the 1830s during the national revival movement. In 1918, Croatian lands were partly unified when Croatia entered the union of the Kingdom of Serbs, Croats, and Slovenes (as of 1929 the Kingdom of Yugoslavia), and were finally fully unified only after World War II when Istria joined in as part of the Federal People's Republic of Yugoslavia (FPRY). Following the dissolution of Yugoslavia in 1991, Croatia became an independent internationally recognized state in 1992.

LITERACY, BOOKS, AND LIBRARIES

Historical Overview

The political division of Croatian lands determined their affiliation to different cultures. The coastal part of Croatia was under the strong influence of the Mediterranean cultural heritage, while northern Croatia was characterized by central European culture. Croats arrived to their present homeland as illiterate in the seventh century. In the ninth century they converted to Christianity and first wrote in the Latin language and in the Latin script. This language and script appears both on stone monuments and in the correspondence between princes, kings, and bishops with popes and other rulers of that time.[1] From the eleventh century in the southwestern regions of Croatia two other indigenous scripts were used along with Latin: the Glagolitic alphabet and the Croatian Cyrillic alphabet (bosančica). These were used to record texts in the Old Slavic and the national Croatian languages. The oldest preserved Glagolitic texts written on stone monuments date from the eleventh century. One of the most famous is the Valun Tablet named after the place on the island of Cres where it was found, containing bilingual inscriptions in Croatian and Latin. The Croatian text is written in Glagolitic script and the Latin in Carolingian script. The

Encyclopedia of Library and Information Sciences, Fourth Edition DOI: 10.1081/E-ELIS4-120043675

Corporate Information–Custody

Fig. 1 Map of Croatia.
Source: *CIA World Factbook*. http://www.cia.gov/library/
publications/the-world-factbook/geos/hr.html.

Baška Tablet dating from 1100 also carries great significance for Croatian cultural history. It is a stone monument
inscribed in the Glagolitic script which was discovered in
Baška on the island of Krk and in it, a Croatian name is
mentioned for the very first time. From the river Una in the
north to Boka Kotorska in the south, the Croatian Cyrillic
alphabet was used, a variant of the Cyrillic alphabet originating from tenth century Bulgaria. The parallel use of
the Glagolitic and Cyrillic alphabets is evidenced by stone
epigraphs dating from the twelfth century and Glagolitic
manuscripts in which dates, names of authors and tran-
scribers, prayers and similar addenda which scribes or the
owners of the manuscripts entered in the Cyrillic alphabet
are found.[2]

Numerous legal and private documents were written in
Glagolitic such as laws, town statutes, minutes of town
councils, monastery rules and registers, and liturgical
books such as the richly illustrated Missal of Prince Novak
from 1368 and the Missal of Hrvoje Vukčić Hrvatinić
dating from the beginning of the fifteenth century. Many
handwritten books in the Glagolitic were translations or
adaptations of Italian and French works (theological manuals, sermons, etc.). Translated from Czech and adapted to
Croatian language was the famous Lucidarius, a type of
medieval encyclopaedia in which all the knowledge of the
time was gathered.[3]

Croatian incunabula were also printed in Glagolitic.
The first Croatian printed book is the Missal from 1483.
Since the place of printing is not indicated in the colo-
phon, it is supposed that the Missal was printed in Venice

even though some experts attempted to prove that it was
created in a domestic printing house of which no direct
information has been preserved. The first known printing
house in Croatia was established in Senj at the end of the
fifteenth century. It is known that at least seven books
were printed there in Glagolitic in the period from 1494
to 1508. The Glagolitic script was used for recording the
Croatian language until the sixteenth century when the
Latin script prevailed, yet in some parts of the country
Glagolitic remained in the liturgy until the beginning of
the twentieth century.

Literacy, education, book production, and the establishment of libraries were closely connected to monasteries
with scriptoria and libraries founded by members of individual church orders from the ninth century onward.
Benedictine monks came to Croatia at the invitation of
the Prince Trpimir. Their monasteries were the most
important cultural centers from the ninth to the thirteenth
centuries. Beautifully illustrated medieval manuscripts
were created in Benedictine scriptoria, such as the
Evangeliarium Vekenegae dating to approximately 1075
(today kept in the Bodleian Library in Oxford) and the
Evangeliarium Traguriense from the first half of the thirteenth century (today kept in the treasury of the Trogir
Cathedral). Monastery library collections were modest—
at the end of the eleventh century they had between 10 and
50 codices. These codices were purchased or acquired as
donations from distinguished and wealthy individuals.[4]

In the thirteenth century new monastic orders arrived in
the country. The first Franciscan monasteries were
established in the first half of the thirteenth century in
Zagreb, Varaždin, Zadar, Šibenik, and Dubrovnik. In the
thirteenth and fourteenth centuries Dominican monasteries became important centers of culture. Books and
schools were especially important to the Dominicans as a
means of fighting against heresy and educating young
members of their order. Schools were organized in several
Dominican monasteries, and in 1553 in Zadar the Dominicans founded "general studies." Laymen and members of
the order alike were awarded the baccalaureate after completion of the program.

In addition to monastery libraries, diocese libraries also
existed in the Middle Ages. The diocese library in Split
is considered to be the oldest library in Croatia. In the
Middle Ages there was also a scriptorium along with the
library. Some of the manuscripts from the oldest period of
the library have been preserved to this day in the treasury
of the Split Cathedral of which the most famous is the
Greek–Latin Evangeliarium known under the name
Evangeliarium Spalatense. Historically it was believed
that this manuscript originated in the seventh or eighth
century, probably from the scriptorium of the diocese, but
recent paleographic analysis confirms that it dates from
the fifth or sixth century.[5] The inventories of the Zagreb
Diocese Metropolitan Library founded at the end of the
eleventh century have been preserved through to the

present, and confirm that the library was well managed. The oldest inventory dates from 1394 and contained several codices from the eleventh century. In the preserved inventories of a later date, books were organized according to a systematic order. Care of the library was usually entrusted to a member of the monastery or chapter community. The Episcopal provision from 1348 established that funds gathered from monetary fines collected in disputes between priests were to be used for renewing library materials.[6]

The private libraries of writers and scholars of the fifteenth and sixteenth centuries were largely created in Split, Dubrovnik, Zadar, and Hvar—the literary centers of the time. The manuscript catalog of the library of the humanist and poet Marko Marulić (1450–1524), which he himself assembled, has been preserved. The catalog contains 148 volumes of religious works, works of humanists and classical writers.[7]

In the seventeenth century Jesuits arrived in Croatia and founded ecclesiastical schools (gymnasia) in larger towns: Dubrovnik, Rijeka, Varaždin, Požega, and Zagreb. According to the rules of the order each school had to also have a library. From the library of the Zagreb Jesuit Collegium, founded in 1607, the future Library of the University of Zagreb would develop, known today as the National and University Library. Besides religious orders, noblemen and scholars also possessed libraries. After the execution of the Croatian poet and nobleman Nikola Šubić Zrinski (1620–1664), his library, containing works of classical and contemporary authors, was taken to Austria, but was repurchased in 1892 for the University Library in Zagreb. The systematic catalog of that library dating from 1662 has been preserved.[8] Partially preserved is the library of the poet, scholar, and librarian of the seminary library in Split, Jerolim Kavanjin (1643–1714).[9] One of the richest and most valuable private libraries is the library of the Garanjin-Fanfogna family in Trogir, founded at the end of the eighteenth century, which besides manuscripts and books also contains family and other archival records some of which date from as far back as the twelfth century. The first manuscript catalog of the library was composed in 1796.[10]

At the end of the eighteenth and beginning of the nineteenth century, so-called reading rooms appeared in various towns. These were establishments primarily intended not only for entertainment, dances, and social gatherings, but also reading. Often they were called casinos. So from 1775 in Šibenik there was the Società del Casino, and from 1806 a casino in Rijeka. The first reading room which actually contained the word "reading" in its name was the Gabinetto di lettura, or Druxba od sctenja, founded in Zadar in 1807.[11] Those reading rooms, as well as numerous others newly established in various towns and villages during the period of the National Revival (1835–1849), were called Illyrian. After the ban of the name Illyrian in 1843, they were called public

reading rooms, and were focal points for the spread of ideas of revival. The National Revival strived toward the unification of South Slavs and thought to accomplish that goal by developing a common popular language as a strong tool for raising national awareness. The leader of the movement was Ljudevit Gaj (1809–1872), the reformer of the Croatian orthography (1830), and publisher of Novine Horvatske (Croatian Newspapers) (1835). Public reading rooms appeared to be political organizations participating in the fight for language, national identity, and freedom. Yet the majority of them also had a library which, at least partly, performed some of the present-day library functions. Public reading rooms operated until 1849 when their work was banned.[12]

Twentieth Century Library Development

Public libraries in today's sense of the word were established only at the beginning of the twentieth century, when the idea of the need for popular education appeared. Students of the Zagreb University played an important role in transmitting that idea and encouraged the opening of libraries. In 1903, as part of the Croatian Writers Society, the main administration for the establishment of public libraries was founded. In 1906 the Croatian Society for Popular Education in Zagreb, founded for the purpose of performing tasks of establishing, supporting, and monitoring public libraries, joined in those efforts. Because there was still no special legislation which would ensure the continuous financing of libraries, and thus enable them to operate unhindered, libraries were established through donations gathered from individuals. Consequently, they often occupied modest spaces, in community houses, parish houses, town halls, schools, houses or even inns, without anyone looking after them on a regular basis. For that reason they were often short-term efforts and quickly disappeared.[13]

The situation was similar in libraries in the Kingdom of Yugoslavia. In 1937 Josip Badalić (1888–1985), the librarian of the University Library in Zagreb, wrote the following:

> In the field of our public education, public librarianship [in Yugoslavia] seems to have the role of Cinderella. This is entirely true not only in the case of public librarianship, but unfortunately also in the case of state librarianship and all the way to the highest positioned university librarianship. The main reason for this is the inexistence of legislation in the field of our national librarianship...[14]

Despite efforts to promote public library development, the first Library Act would not be passed until 1960.

In World War II many libraries were destroyed. Especially devastating was the loss of the library of the Gymnasium in Zadar, destroyed by bombarding in 1943, because that library used to receive legal deposits from

Dalmatia. Many libraries were also destroyed in the 1991–1995 war. Data confirms that around 200 libraries of all types, including those containing valuable heritage material, were damaged or destroyed.[15]

Legislation

The current Library Act was adopted in 1997 and amended in 2000. The Act established within the Ministry of Culture an expert advisory body known as the Croatian Library Council. The council is charged with issuing recommendations on all important matters in the field of librarianship. The Library Act also regulates the establishment and maintenance of libraries, the organization and functioning of the library system, the delivery of legal deposits, and the conservation of book heritage.

A special chapter of the Library Act regulates the operation of the National and University Library as the center of the Croatian library system. In addition the Act prescribes that each municipality in the country must establish a public library, or contract a library in another municipality, to perform library services for its citizens. The general operation of libraries is financed by local authorities, but the Ministry of Culture assists in acquiring material, and in securing and equipping adequate library facilities. Libraries must meet the standards stipulating minimum requirements for library operation. Besides standards there are also ordinances which provide detailed descriptions of individual methods and procedures which libraries have a duty to perform.

National and University Library

The National and University Library in Zagreb (Fig. 2) is the largest library in the country, and at the same time performs the function of the national library and the central library of the University of Zagreb. This library was established in 1607 as the library of the Jesuit Gymnasium (Collegium), later the Academy. After the dissolution of the Jesuit order in 1776, it became the library of the Academy of Science (the School of Law, Philosophy and Theology). It enriched its collection primarily through donations. One of the most significant was the personal library of Adam Baltazar Krčelić, a clergyman and historian from Zagreb, who in 1777 left in his last will and testament 757 volumes of books and 50 manuscripts, under the conditions that they be open to the public, which was realized only in 1818. When the University of Zagreb was founded in 1874, it became the University Library.

In the beginning of the nineteenth century, the university library had already begun to perform the function of the national library. In 1837 it acquired the right to legal deposits from northern Croatia. In 1856 it received a permanent donation for the acquisition of books. First located in the building of the university, it moved to a building specially constructed for that purpose in 1913 which it shared with the State Archives. In 1919 it acquired the right to legal deposits from the whole territory of Yugoslavia. In 1943 it was administratively separated from the University and changed its official name to the Croatian National and University Library. After World War II it

Fig. 2 The National and University Library in Zagreb. Photograph: Damir Fabijanić.

was once again named the University Library, although it also performs the function of a national library. By virtue of a federal regulation in 1947, it became the central library of the Republic of Croatia, and after 1945 it again received legal deposits from the whole territory of Yugoslavia. Pursuant to the Library Act from 1960, it changed its name to the National and University Library and began performing the task of coordinating the acquisition of foreign literature for libraries in the country, providing expert assistance to other libraries and creating union catalogs.

In 1995 the library moved in a new building covering an area of 45,000 m². Besides its general collection containing 2.5 million volumes, it also has special collections: a collection of manuscripts and old books, a collection of prints (founded in 1919), a collection of geographical maps and atlases (founded in 1945), and a collection of music and audio materials (founded in 1943). It has 1100 seats for reading and approximately 18,000 users benefit from its services each year. It receives legal deposits, develops and organizes the national collection, develops the national current and retrospective bibliography, and cares for the protection of book heritage. In cooperation with the University Computing Centre SRCE, it harvests national digital publications which it deposits in the Digital Archives of Croatian Web Publications. It also includes the Librarianship Institute whose task is to develop the Croatian library system and librarianship in general. In the year 2001, it initiated a project under the name Digitised Heritage. So far 555 items of various formats (books, music sheets, drawings, graphics, and maps) have been digitized and may be accessed via the Web site of the Library (http://www.nsk/hr).

Academic, Research, and Special Libraries

Until the 1970s the University of Zagreb was the only university in Croatia. Today, with its 50,000 students, it is the largest. It was only in 1973 that the University in Rijeka was founded, followed in 1974 by the University in Split and in 1975 the University in Osijek. The newest universities were established in Zadar (2002), Dubrovnik (2003), and Pula (2006).

The universities were for the most part decentralized and consisted of several faculties and schools of higher education in different locations. These circumstances contributed to the emergence of numerous faculty, departmental, seminary, and other libraries at certain faculties; some of them having a very long tradition. The library of the Zagreb Faculty of Law was established back in 1906, the library at the Faculty of Engineering in 1926, at the Faculty of Economics in 1920, and at the Faculty of Veterinary Medicine in 1922. At the Faculty of Philosophy, the largest constituent part of the University of Zagreb, the oldest library is that of the Slavic seminary founded in 1906. The oldest medical library is the library of the School of Public Health and the Institute of Public Health

in Zagreb, established in 1927. That library served the students and professors of the Medical School as the only expert medical library until the Central Medical Library was established in 1947.

In the second half of the twentieth century academic libraries faced many problems: the lack of funds for acquisition of foreign titles (especially journals), inadequate and sparsely equipped facilities, the absence of union catalogs, lack of or informal cooperation between libraries, and the lack of understanding of the need and importance of libraries on the part of the administration. The collection of the National and University Library was mostly oriented toward humanities and could not meet the needs of the university community. In the 1960s a university professor of chemistry, Božo Težak (1907–1980), used the International Permanent Exhibition of Publications ISIP, an exhibiting institution founded in 1951, and developed the Referral Centre of the University as a center for dissemination of scientific and technical information.

At that time the number of special libraries belonging to companies, factories, industrial centers, and scientific institutes also grew. In the 1970s there was a tendency to transform special libraries into information documentation centers that could provide scientific information to assist in the development of the economy. At the level of the Yugoslavian state the System of Scientific and Technical Information project was initiated with the purpose of enabling libraries to provide relevant information. As part of the project, technical equipping of libraries also began. In the 1980s first the National and University Library was automated and gradually other libraries followed suit.

In 1991 the Ministry of Science and Technology initiated CARNet (Croatian Academic and Research Network), first as a project, and as of 1995, as an institution whose purpose is to assist institutions in the field of science and higher education, in adopting and applying information and communication technologies and disseminating knowledge. Today CARNet gathers 238 university institutions and scientific institutes in 37 Croatian cities. In 1994 the Ministry initiated a project intended for academic libraries, called Scientific Information System, whose purpose was to enable access to information sources to users of academic libraries. As part of that project, academic libraries were equipped with computers and connected to the Internet, and training for librarians was organized.

Public and School Libraries

Between 1945 and 1990 numerous public libraries were opened. In 1950 the first children's library with a reading room was opened as a department of the City Library in Zagreb. There, for the first time, open access to collections was introduced. In 1963 the first record collection in the country was opened in that library. In the 1970s the first network of public libraries was established in Zagreb.

Only a few new purpose built facilities were constructed for libraries, for example the City Library in Karlovac got its own building in 1976. It was only after the 1990s that a more significant number of existing buildings and facilities were adapted for city libraries such as the city libraries in Zadar (1999), Šibenik (2005), and Virovitica (2007). Today there are 256 libraries operating.[16] The majority of public libraries are connected to the Internet and have their own Web pages.

Primary and secondary schools are obligated to establish libraries by law. The adoption of the Library Act in 1997, requiring school librarians to acquire professional qualifications, constituted a significant step toward professionalizing librarianship. There are 1347 libraries of primary and secondary schools in Croatia which are members of CARNet and have Internet access (http://www.carnet.hr).

Church Libraries

Monasteries, parishes, and churches possess very valuable collections of heritage material, of which very little is known because many of them are not organized. Consequently, they are not available to the public. The Regulation of the Croatian Conference of Bishops on church libraries from 2000 prescribes that older and more valuable books are to be deposited in the central diocese library or religious province library, which should facilitate the cataloging of heritage material and its final inclusion in the national registry of cultural heritage.

Professional Associations

The Croatian Library Association was founded in 1940 by a small group of librarians from the University Library in Zagreb. Today the association is organized as an umbrella organization of 16 regional library associations with a total of 1400 members. The goals of the Association are described in the Statute adopted in 2002 and include publication of professional literature, organization of conferences and other forms of continuing professional training, proposal of relevant legislation, representation of interests of library service users, promotion of literacy, and care for cultural and book heritage (http://www.hkdrustvo.hr/hr/statut/).

The Association is the most important publisher of library science literature in the country. Between 1966, when it published its first title, and 2006, the Association published 95 titles. It is also the publisher of the oldest professional journal *Vjesnik bibliotekara Hrvatske* (1950–). As of 1999, it organizes Days of Special Libraries, an annual meeting of librarians of special and academic libraries. Beginning in 2001 it has organized the annual Round Table on Free Access to Information; these sessions are primarily intended for public librarians. Together with 17 NGOs, the Association participated in the drafting of the Act on the Right to Information Access, which was adopted in 2003. The association has awarded the Kukuljević Charter, the highest professional acknowledgment, since 1968 and the Eva Verona Award for the best young librarian since 1998.

Library and Information Science Education

Until the 1960s there was no formal schooling available for librarians and professional knowledge was acquired by passing a librarianship examination. Regulations issued in 1928 required that librarians of the University Library must pass the librarianship examination. In 1931 the same requirements were extended to include all librarians in state libraries.[17] The acquisition of professional knowledge through taking professional examinations would continue, even after the introduction of university librarianship studies. The examinations were no longer required after the Library Act of 1997.

The first university program for librarians started in 1961 as postgraduate studies in librarianship, documentation, and information sciences under the Faculty of Science. As of 1970 the studies were connected directly to the University of Zagreb. The opening of that study program significantly contributed to professionalizing librarianship and helped create a core group of formally educated librarians for all types of libraries but with an emphasis on university libraries. The program finally closed down at the beginning of the 1990s. In 1977 a graduate program in library studies was opened at the Faculty of Philosophy in Zagreb. At first this was a 2-year supplementary study program, but from 1986 onward it was constituted as a 4-year program in Information Science for librarians, archivists, and museology experts. Beginning in 1998 library science could be studied at the University of Osijek, and as of 2003 also at the University of Zadar. Postgraduate studies in information sciences for archivists, librarians, museology experts, and IT experts were started in 1994 at the Faculty of Philosophy in Zagreb. Following the Bologna educational reform the program was revised in 2005, and is now held as a 3-year doctoral study program.

In 2002 the National and University Library, the Libraries of the City of Zagreb, the Department of Information Sciences of the Faculty of Philosophy in Zagreb, and the Croatian Library Association founded the Centre for Continuing Training of Librarians. Annually it organizes an average of 60 one-day courses for more than 1000 librarians (http://www.nsk.hr/CSSU/).

ARCHIVES

Historical Overview

The tradition of keeping documents, both in monasteries' and municipal archives, is most pronounced in the

Corporate Information– Custody

Fig. 3 The chest of privileges of the Kingdom of Croatia, Dalmatia, and Slavonia (Privilegia regni) 1643.

coastal region of Croatia (Dubrovnik, Dalmatia, and Istria). The statutes of coastal communes provide numerous stipulations on keeping documents. The Split Statute, from 1312, obligates the municipality of Split to keep records about documents, indicating their quantity and the year of origin; it also specifies the location where they are to be kept and the criteria for access. In northern Croatia, an old tradition of keeping archival records is evident in the chapters which, as "loca credibilia", played a role equal to public notaries in the coastal region. Even though *Archivum Regni* was mentioned in documents as early as in the sixteenth century, it was not until 1643 that the Croatian Parliament passed a stipulation on making a chest (*Cista— Archivum privilegiorum Regni*) for keeping the most important state documents (Fig. 3).

Besides the Kingdom Archives, every county and every free royal town had their own archives where this material was kept. In the times of the Empress Maria Theresa, a reform of archives management was undertaken, and the archival material was processed and the first lists of material compiled. Nikola Škrlec (1729–1799), a royal protonotary, played an important role in these activities. In the first half of the nineteenth century, in the times of the National Revival, the most important cultural institutions were established including the National Museum (1846) and the State Archives (1849).[18]

A modern archive service was established after 1945: it establishes practices for the care for current records, the creation of a network of archives and drafting modern legislation on archives. Bernard Stulli (1915–1985), director of the Central State Archives, initiated the making of modern information retrieval tools, started a project on keeping records of material located outside the archive, and supported systematic education of archivists, thus playing a particularly important role in the modernization of archive service.

Legislation

Archive services are regulated by the 1997 Act on Archival Material and Archives and amendments to this Act from the year 2000. The Act covers public and private archival material, and records located in records governmental departments before being forwarded to archives. Public archival material is imprescriptible. The Act stipulates the obligations of the creator and the records owner in regard to the process of appraisal, transfer to archives, and the use of archival material. Since all archival material is a part of cultural heritage, the Act stipulates the obligations of all creators and also regulates the circulation of archival material of private origin. Besides legal acts, subordinate legislation, i.e., ordinances, also regulate particular procedures, e.g., the use of archival material, keeping registers in archives, etc.[19]

The archive service consists of the network of state archives and the statutory possibility of establishing specialized (university, party, church, etc.), city and municipal archives. It falls under the purview of the Department of Archival Activities, Directorate for the Protection of Cultural Heritage, in the Ministry of Culture. Advisory and professional tasks are performed by the Croatian Archival Council as an advisory body to the Minister of Culture. There are 12,680 archival fonds and collections, kept in 14 state archives and 11 collecting centers. In addition, there are 187 other institutions (libraries, museums, religious communities, institutes) where archival material is kept.[20]

Croatian State Archives

The *Croatian State Archives* originates from the *Archivum Regni*, which dates from 1643. After 1849 it is known by the name of the Royal Regional Archives, acting as an auxiliary office of the Royal Government of Croatia, Slavonia, and Dalmatia. Then in 1870 the Parliament adopted the Legal Article on the Organisation of the State Archives and the Instruction on the use of documents of the State Archives; these two measures established the status of the archive, regulated the use of documents, and stipulated the concentration of archival collections in one location. In 1923 it separated from the state administration, and in 1945 it officially became the Central State Archives. Following the independence of the Republic of Croatia, it became the *Croatian State Archives* (http://www.arhiv.hr).

The Croatian State Archives includes

- The Department for Protection and Processing of the Archival Records.
- The Croatian Film Archives.
- The Department for Information and Communication.
- The Central Laboratory for Photography, Micrography and Reprography.

Corporate Information– Custody

- The Laboratory for Conservation and Restoration.
- The Deposit of the Archbishopric of Zagreb.

The Croatian State Archives keep archival material that originated from the region of northern Croatia (Banska Croatia or the Kingdom of Croatia, Dalmatia, and Slavonia) in the period prior to 1918, and the material resulting from the work of regional and central state bodies of Croatia, covering the period after 1918. Due to specific historical circumstances, material for some parts of Croatia, which is also of importance for the entire county, is kept in the State Archives in Zadar, the State Archives in Rijeka and the State Archives in Dubrovnik.

The *State Archives in Zadar*, dating to the thirteenth century, holds the records of the Municipality of Zadar. In the course of the nineteenth century this archive collected also material from the municipal archives of Dalmatia. The Zadar Archives also keeps material important for the history of the Republic of Venice and for the history of Dalmatia as an Austrian crown province in the period from 1797 until 1918, as well as the material of the Napoleon Administration in the period from 1806 until 1814.[21]

The *State Archives in Dubrovnik* (http://www.dad.hr) contains material originating from the activities of the Dubrovnik municipality since the thirteenth century, and material of the Republic of Ragusa from the beginning of the fifteenth century to the dissolution of the Republic in 1808. The Archives in Dubrovnik has a wider significance for the historical study of the Balkans and the Mediterranean, from the fourteenth century until the fall of the Republic of Ragusa in 1808.[22]

The *State Archives in Rijeka* (http://www.riarhiv.hr) and *in Pazin* (http://dapa.hr) contain material for the wider area of Istria and the Croatian Primorje, starting from the Middle Ages with particular strength in materials from the nineteenth and first decades of the twentieth century.[23]

Other State Archives in Croatia have been established in Bjelovar, Gospić, Karlovac, Križevci, Štrigova, Osijek, Sisak, Slavonski Brod, Split, Šibenik, Varaždin, Vukovar, and Zagreb with the task of collecting and keeping local archival material.

Digital records are received by the archives only rarely. The Croatian State Archives systematically digitizes material of particular archive holdings and collections. Registers of births, marriages, and deaths are digitized, and so is the Croatian Glagolitic heritage located in Croatia and abroad; the collection of cartography and the Cadastre are currently being digitized as well. In 2007 the National Archival Information System (ARHiNET), a Web-based system for description and management of archives was introduced. Digital archival records, digital images of archives, and finding aids have been made available online (http://arhinet.arhiv.hr). The system has also been used by the members of the government and public administration, as well as by other organizations, for providing records schedules to archival institutions.

National Film Archives

The Croatian National Film Archives (*Hrvatska kinoteka*) was established pursuant to the *Cinematography Act* of 1976, operating within the Croatian State Archives since 1979. The film collection includes preserved films produced by Croatian cinematography in the period from 1904 until 2009, and foreign films distributed in Croatia in the period from 1895 until 2009. In addition to films, the Archives also keeps scripts, film photographs, posters, books and magazines, clippings, and video and audio recordings. The Film Archives has a total of 9296 titles of Croatian and foreign films.[24]

Specialized Archives

The *Croatian Academy of Sciences and Arts* Archives keeps the Glagolitic and Cyrillic manuscripts, a collection of Oriental manuscripts and the manuscript heritage of writers, playwrights, and musicians, as well as archival fonds and collections significant to the history of theatre.[25]*Religious communities* have rich archival material in episcopal, chapter and monastery archives. Some church archives are located in the state archives deposit (as for example, the Archives of the Zagreb Arch/Bishopric and the Archives of the Zadar Archbishopric).[26]*Archives of political parties* for the period prior to the Croatian independence (1991) are kept in state archives. After the period of socialism, political parties establish and maintain their own archives.

Publishing and Professional Associations

Archival periodical *Vjestnik Kraljevskog Zemaljskoga arkiva* has been published since 1898, and since 1953 under the name of *Arhivski vjesnik*. Archival journals are published also in Rijeka, Pazin, Osijek, and Split. The first textbooks on archivistics were published after 1945, while foreign professional literature used in education of archivists has been systematically translated since 1991. Professional education of archivists was introduced in the second half of the twentieth century, when persons employed in the archives were first required to pass professional examination. Archivists could enroll in a postgraduate university program in Zadar (1971–1975), or at the University of Zagreb (1961–1992), where a program for graduate students was also established in 1986.

The Croatian Archivist Association was founded in 1954, with the aim to stimulate and promote education and professional training, organize professional and scientific conferences, issue professional publications, and establish professional standards.[27]

MUSEUMS

History

Prior to the establishment of the first public museum in 1820, collections were established by patricians, intellectuals, and clergy. These were collections of curiosities, encyclopedic museums, or collections of natural history specimens or man-made objects, armory, paintings, treasury, sculptures, etc.[28] The Archaeological Museum in Split which was established in 1820 moved the following year to the first purpose built museum in Croatia. In the course of the nineteenth century, the general Central-European movement for preservation and promotion of national cultural heritage national museums had a strong influence in Croatia, and the cities Zadar, Osijek, Dubrovnik, and Zagreb established museums open to the public. The efforts of many learned and other societies led to a series of initiatives aimed at founding regional and municipal museums specializing mainly in history, natural science, and art. By the end of the century, fine arts museums (galleries) and museums of arts and crafts were established, and at the beginning of the twentieth century ethnographic museums were opened.[29]

Many specialized museums were founded in the first half of the twentieth century; examples include a museum of the history of education and pedagogy, museums and collections of medical and agricultural studies, as well as museums devoted to important persons.[30]

In the second half of the twentieth century, an effort was made to enlarge the museum network by establishing many regional, local and town museums, enacting new legislation, setting up professional associations, and expanding museums' exhibiting and publishing activities. The growth of specialized museums/permanent exhibitions devoted to the World War II and the Partisan movement was evident. In the 1970s the Museum of Medieval Croatian Culture in Split and the Museum of the Ecclesiastical Art in Zadar were opened as the tangible national investments in culture.

Following the war (1991–1995), the museums and their holdings had to be restored.[31] Great efforts were made to erect new museum buildings, to reorganize museum management and curatorship, to modernize and improve permanent exhibits, to strengthen international exhibiting program, and to implement IC technology.

Legislation and Organization

Museum activity is governed by the Museum Act (1998) and by several ordinances.[32] As cultural assets, museum holdings and documentation are covered under those ordinances which address the protection of cultural assets. The ordinances provide guidelines on museum documentation, access to museum collections and records, the maintenance of the museum register, requirements for joining the museum network, professional and technical standards, and the qualifications required for museum staff. The Museum Network was created on the principle of professional competence and flexibility. As a result, it has established unique standards and norms and supported partnerships between museums and other local regional and national heritage and cultural institutions with the aim of pursuing joint projects. The Network also strengthens intermuseum cooperation by encouraging the exchange of services and activities. It is based on two main criteria: the type of a museum and the level of regional responsibility.[33]

Information and documentation concerning Croatian museums is collected by the Museum Documentation Centre (MDC) established in 1955. The MDC (http://www.mdc.hr) is the central information, documentation, and communication point for the Croatian museum network; it keeps the Register of museums, galleries, and collections. The Register is a record of "musealized heritage" and contains information about all museum institutions in Croatia, regardless of their legal or administrative status. In 2006, according to the Register, there were 219 museums with 1428 collections and 617 documentation holdings,[34] and about 6 million objects; in addition, about 130 church collections and a large number of private collections throughout the country.

General museums are classified as national or regional, local, and town (municipal). The number of national museums is small, and the predominance of national archaeological museums is evident with one third of all museums are archaeological museums. The best known are the Museum of Croatian Archaeological Monuments and the Archaeological Museum in Split, and archaeological museums in Zadar, Pula, Narona, and Osijek. The state makes efforts to support various types of museums, such as a sports museum, a museum of ecclesiastical art, the Croatian history museum, the Croatian naïve art museum, the Old Village in Kumrovec (the birth-place of Josip Broz Tito). Technical (science) and natural history museums are funded by local authorities such as the City of Zagreb.

The famous fine arts museums are the Strossmayer Gallery of Old Masters (Italian Renaissance and Baroque paintings, along with the works of German, Dutch, Flemish, and French artists), the Mimara Museum encompassing three millennia of arts and crafts from various cultures and civilizations, and the Ivan Meštrović Foundation in Split, Zagreb, and Otavice housed in the Meštrović family houses and studios containing sculptures, drawings, and the sculptor's personal archive. The national gallery of art, known as the Modern Gallery in Zagreb, contains works of nineteenth and twentieth centuries' artists.

New museum buildings in Croatia include the Museum of Contemporary Art, the Museum of Evolution and the

Corporate Information—Custody

Site of Pre-historic Man "Hušnjakovo", and the Archaeological Museum on the Narona Site. Other buildings and sites have been modernized, such as the Science and Technology Site of Nikola Tesla and the Memorial Site in Jasenovac. The computerization of the Croatian museum network started in 2004.[35] The locally produced *M++ system* has been used by all museums and up to the beginning of 2009 around 1,000,000 museum objects have been recorded and processed. For the time being they are accessible at the local site, but the network will be implemented in the near future. Today 60% of Croatian museums have their own Web site, and a great number of CD-ROMs promoting their holdings were produced. Museum Web site addresses are available at http://www.mdc.hr.

Publishing, Staff, and Professional Association

Museum publishing of catalogs, guides, annual reports, monographs, journals and books, and professional journals is an important way of communicating museum knowledge to a wide range of audiences in Croatia. These include *Muzeologija* (1953–) and *Informatica Museologica* (1970–), and *Vijesti muzealaca i konzervatora* (1952–). The total number of museum professional staff is 907. The structure of museum employees is extremely traditional; there is a great lack of PR and marketing experts, and ICT experts. Museum professional associations are organized at the regional and national levels. The national association is the Croatian Museum Association.

CONCLUSION

Apart from the university education organized as a common study program for all three professions, there are also other examples of professional cooperation. Since 1997 the archival, librarianship, and museology professions organize regular AKM annual seminars (Archives, Libraries, Museums) whose goal is to develop cooperation among professions and exchange expertise.

In 2006 the National Programme for the Digitisation of Archival, Library and Museum Records was developed and adopted. This program provides for the development of a referral center or service for assistance. It also monitors digitization projects and supports the creation of a Web reference portal with information and data on digitization projects in progress.

REFERENCES

1. Stipčević, A. *Socijalna povijest knjige u Hrvata; Knj.1: Srednji vijek*; Školska knjiga: Zagreb, 2004.
2. Nazor, A. Cyrillic script *Three Scripts, Three Languages: Croatian Written Monuments, Manuscripts and Publications through Centuries*; Exhibition. The Royal Library Brussels January, 23, 2004 Nacionalna i sveučilišna knjižnica: Zagreb, 2004; 54–63 –February 28.
3. Nazor, A. Glagolitic script *Three Scripts, Three Languages: Croatian Written Monuments, Manuscripts and Publications through Centuries*; Exhibition. The Royal Library Brussels January, 23, 2004 Nacionalna i sveučilišna knjižnica: Zagreb, 2004; 27–53 –February 28.
4. Rojnić, M. Biblioteke, Hrvatska *Enciklopedija Jugoslavije*, 2nd Ed.; Jugoslavenski leksikografski zavod: Zagreb, 1980; Vol. 1, 655–664.
5. Stipčević, A. *Socijalna povijest knjige u Hrvata; Knj.1: Srednji vijek*; Školska knjiga: Zagreb, 2004.
6. Rojnić, M. Biblioteke, Hrvatska *Enciklopedija Jugoslavije*, 2nd Ed.; Jugoslavenski leksikografski zavod: Zagreb, 1980; Vol. 1, 655.
7. Morović, H. *Povijest biblioteka u gradu Splitu*, Društvo bibliotekara Hrvatske: Zagreb, 1971.
8. Kosić, I. Bibliotheca Zriniana. *Plava krv, crna tinta: knjižnice velikaških obitelji od 1500 do 1700*, Nacionalna i sveučilišna knjižnica: Zagreb, 2005; 17–24 Međunarodna putujuća izložba, Zagreb, Bratislava, Martin, Budapest, Burg Forchtenstein, Jesen 2005, Jesen 2007.
9. Morović, H. *Povijest biblioteka u gradu Splitu*; Društvo bibliotekara Hrvatske: Zagreb, 1971; 137–143.
10. Stipčević, A., Ed. *Libraries in Croatia*; Croatian Library Association: Zagreb, 1975.
11. Radauš, T. *Biblioteke i čitaonička društva na teritoriju SR Hrvatske od srednjeg vijeka do 1945*; Sveučilište u Zagrebu, 1980; M.Sc. thesis.
12. Mesić, Đ. *Narodne biblioteke u Jugoslaviji*; University of Belgrade: Belgrade, 1990; Ph.D. dissertation.
13. Rojnić, M. Bibliotekarstvo i nauka. Vjesnik bibliotekara Hrvatske **1955/57**, *4*, 37–74.
14. Badalić, J. *Javne knjižnice u Savskoj banovini: Njihovo stanje i potrebe*; Izdanja Društva jugoslavenskih bibliotekara, Sekcija Zagreb: Zagreb, 1937; 5.
15. Aparac-Gazivoda, T., Katalenac, D., Eds. *Wounded Libraries in Croatia*; Croatian Library Association: Zagreb, 1993.
16. *Statistički ljetopis*, Državni zavod za statistiku: Zagreb, 2006.
17. Cveljo, K. Yugoslavia, education for librarianship. In *Encyclopedia of Library and Information Science*; Kent, A., Daily, J.A., Eds.; Marcel Dekker, Inc.: New York, 1982; Vol. 33, 384–404.
18. Kolanović, J. L'institutionnalisation des archives et la quête de l'identité nationale en Croatie dans la seconde moitié du XIX-e siècle. *Archives et Nations dans l'Europe du XIX-e siècle*, L'École des chartes: Paris, 2004; 59–80.
19. Rastić, M., Ed. *Arhivi i arhivsko gradivo: zbirka pravnih propisa 1828–1997*; Hrvatski državni arhiv: Zagreb, 1998.
20. *Pregled arhivskih fondova i zbirki Republike Hrvatske*, Hrvatski državni arhiv: Zagreb, 2007; Vol. 1, 1–166.
21. Državni arhiv u Zadru (DAZD). *Pregled arhivskih fondova i zbirki Republike Hrvatske*, Hrvatski državni arhiv: Zagreb, 2007; Vol. 1, 877–914.
22. Državni arhiv u Dubrovniku (DADU). *Pregled arhivskih fondova i zbirki Republike Hrvatske*; Hrvatski državni arhiv: Zagreb, 2007; Vol. 1, 245–288.
23. Državni arhiv u Pazinu (DAPA) i Rijeci (DARI). *Pregled arhivskih fondova i zbirki Republike Hrvatske*, Hrvatski državni arhiv: Zagreb, 2007; Vol. 1, 453–584.

24. Hrvatski filmski arhivi. *Pregled arhivskih fondova i zbirki Republike Hrvatske*, Hrvatski državni arhiv: Zagreb, 2007; Vol. 1, 167–170.

25. Arhiv HAZU. *Pregled arhivskih fondova i zbirki Republike Hrvatske*; Hrvatski državni arhiv: Zagreb, 2007; Vol. 1, 167–170.

26. Arhivi vjerskih zajednica. *Pregled arhivskih fondova i zbirki Republike Hrvatske*; Hrvatski državni arhiv: Zagreb, 2007; Vol. 1, 1218–1300.

27. Heđbeli, Ž. Hrvatsko arhivističko društvo 1954–1999. Arhivski vjesnik **1999**, *42*, 289–352.

28. Zgaga, V. Počeci muzeja u Hrvatskoj. Muzeologija **1990**, *28*, 7–13.

29. Šulc, B. The beginnings of Croatian museums. *Museums and Galleries of Croatia*; Ministry of Culture and Education: Zagreb, 1993; 7–12.

30. Humski, V. Pregled povijesti muzeja u Hrvatskoj: 19. i 20. stoljeće (do 1945). Muzeologija **1986**, *24*, 5–62.

31. Pavić, V., Ed. *War Damages to Museums and Galleries in Croatia*; Museum Documentation Centre: Zagreb, 1997; 5.

32. http://www.mdc.hr/main.aspx?id=137.

33. http://www.mdc.hr/main.aspx?id=320.

34. http://www.mdc.hr/muzeji_en.aspx.

35. http://www.mdc.hr/main.aspx?id=303.

BIBLIOGRAPHY

Works in English

1. Aparac-Gazivoda, T., Katalenac, D., Eds. *Wounded Libraries in Croatia*; Croatian Library Association: Zagreb, Croatia, 1993.

2. Banac, I. *The National Question in Yugoslavia: Origins, History, Politics*, Cornell University Press: Ithaca, NY, 1984.

3. Bosnjak, M. *(Slavenska inkunabulistika engl.) A Study of Slavic Incunabula: Engl. version by Ferdinand Dobrowolsky*, Mladost: Zagreb, Croatia, 1968.

4. CIA World Factbook. http://www.cia.gov/library/publications/the-worldfactbook/geos/hr.html.

5. Croatian State Archives. *Authors of texts Jozo Ivanović and Melina Lučić*; Croatian State Archives: Zagreb, Croatia, 2006.

6. Dalbello, M. National and University Library of Croatia. In *International Dictionary of Library Histories*; David Stam, D., Ed.; Fitzroy Dearborn: Chicago, IL, 2002; 455–458.

7. Eterovich, F.H. Spalatin, C. *Croatia: Land, People, Culture*, University of Toronto Press: Toronto, Canada, 1964.

8. Katicic, R. Novak, S.P. *Two Thousand Years of Writing in Croatia*, SNL: Zagreb, Croatia, 1989.

9. Magaš, B. *Croatia through History*, 2007; the making of a European state. SAQ1: London, U.K.

10. Stipčević, A., Ed.; In *Libraries in Croatia*; Croatian Library Association: Zagreb, Croatia, 1975.

11. Tanner, M. *Croatia, A Nation Forged in War*, Yale University Press: New Haven, CT, 2001.

12. The role and importance of natural history museums and natural history collections for sustainable development. Muzeologija **2002**, *39*, 7–105.

13. *Three scripts, three languages: Croatian written monuments, manuscripts and publications through centuries*, Nacionalna i sveučilišna knjižnica: Zagreb, 2004; Exhibition. The Royal Library, Brussels, January 23–February 28.

14. Zvizdić, E. Franulić, M. *Croatian Museum*, Museum Documentation Centre: Zagreb, Croatia, 1999; 1 CD.

Works in Croatian

1. Badalić, J. *Javne knjižnice u Savskoj banovini: njihovo stanje i potrebe*; Izdanja Društva jugoslavenskih bibliotekara, Sekcija Zagreb: Zagreb, Croatia, 1937.

2. Cvjetičanin, B., Katunarić, V., Eds. *Hrvatska u 21. stoljeću: Strategija kulturnog razvitka*; Ministarstvo kulture Republike Hrvatske: Zagreb, Croatia, 2003.

3. Dobrić, B. *Kultura čitanja i nacionalni pokreti : čitalačka društva i knjižnice u Puli u drugoj polovici 19. i prvoj polovici 20. Stoljeća*; C.A.S.H.: Pula, Croatia, 2003.

4. Galić, P. *Povijest zadarskih knjižnica*; Društvo bibliotekara Hrvatske: Zagreb, Croatia, 1969.

5. Majcen, V. *Filmovi u Hrvatskoj kinoteci pri Hrvatskom državnom arhivu: (1904–1940)*; Hrvatski državni arhiv: Zagreb, Croatia, 2003.

6. Majcen, V. *Obrazovni film: pregled povijesti obrazovnog filma*; Hrvatski državni arhiv: Zagreb, Croatia, 2001.

7. Morović, H. *Povijest biblioteka u gradu Splitu*; Društvo bibliotekara Hrvatske: Zagreb, Croatia, 1971.

8. Rojnić, M. *Nacionalna i sveučilišna biblioteka*, Hrvatsko bibliotekarsko društvo: Zagreb, Croatia, 1974.

9. Stipčević, A., Ed. *Nacionalna i sveučilišna knjižnica u Zagreb 1607–2007: u povodu 400. obljetnice*; Nacionalna i sveučilišna knjižnica: Zagreb, Croatia, 2007.

10. Stipčević, A. *Socijalna povijest knjige u Hrvata*; Školska knjiga: Zagreb, Croatia, 2004–2008; Vols. 1–3.

11. Vujić, Ž. Postanak i razvoj umjetničkih muzeja i galerija u Zagrebu. Muzeologija **1991/1992**, *29–30*, 9–140.

12. Živković, D., Ed. *Hrvatsko knjižničarsko društvo: 14. III. 1940–14. III. 2000: spomenica*; Hrvatsko knjižničarsko društvo: Zagreb, Croatia, 2000.

CrossRef Publisher Linking Network

Amy E. Brand
CrossRef, Lynnfield, Massachusetts, U.S.A.

Abstract

CrossRef, the cross-publisher linking network and platform for other collaborative technologies and its services will be outlined in this entry. The impact it has had to date on various segments of the information industry and how it has progressed from a small DOI Registration Agency to a robust platform for publisher collaboration with tens of millions DOIs deposited in its system. CrossRef developments and new services will also be discussed, as will placing CrossRef as part of a larger trend in resource discovery toward virtual integration of distributed resources.

INTRODUCTION

This entry provides an overview of CrossRef, a cross-publisher linking network and platform for other collaborative technologies. It discusses CrossRef's mission and history, as well as how the system works, and the impact it has had to date on various segments of the information industry. A final section looks at recent CrossRef developments. The entry concludes by situating CrossRef as part of a larger trend in resource discovery toward virtual integration of distributed resources.

CROSSREF'S MISSION

CrossRef is a nonprofit membership association, founded and directed by publishers. Its mission is to enable easy identification and use of trustworthy electronic content by promoting the cooperative development and application of a sustainable infrastructure for online content. CrossRef operates a cross-publisher citation linking system, and is an official Digital Object Identifier (DOI) registration agency, appointed by the International DOI Foundation (or IDF).[1] A look at the history of CrossRef helps explain these core functions of the organization.

CROSSREF'S HISTORY

CrossRef was incorporated in January of 2000 as a cooperative venture among 12 of the world's leading scholarly publishers, both commercial and not-for-profit, with a mandate to provide cross-publisher reference linking throughout the online journal literature. The founding members were Academic Press, the American Association for the Advancement of Science (publisher of *Science*), the American Institute of Physics, the Association for Computing Machinery, Blackwell Science, Elsevier Science, the Institute of Electrical and Electronics Engineers, Kluwer Academic Publishers, Nature Publishing Group, Oxford University Press, Springer-Verlag, and John Wiley & Sons. Start-up funds for CrossRef were provided as loans from eight of the original publishers, all of which were paid off in full in 2007.

When the CrossRef service went live in June of 2000, it supported reference links in roughly 1100 journals from a member base of 33 publishers, using a beta system called the "DOI-X prototype."[2] CrossRef became an official DOI registration agency in September 2000 and was the first such agency, authorized by the IDF to allocate DOI prefixes and register DOIs. To date, CrossRef is the most robust implementation of the DOI model.

Although CrossRef got underway with a specific focus on linking electronic journal articles in the scientific, technical, and medical (STM) arena, it has since branched out to cover DOI-based linking of all authoritative scholarly and professional literature online, regardless of genre or discipline, with a broader mission of improving resource discovery through collective initiatives.

The Importance of Cross-Publisher Linking

Among the visitors to the Frankfurt Book Fair in October of 1999 who witnessed a demonstration of the DOI-X project were several representatives from STM publishing. Recognizing that a DOI-based lookup system for citations could enable a cross-publisher article-level linking system for serials, they took the unprecedented step of joining together in an independent association.

Linking at the article-level benefits both scholars and publishers. References are how authors make explicit the links between their work and previously published scholarship. Making a citation immediately actionable, so that it links to the cited document in a matter of a click or two, is a powerful enhancement to efficiency and functionality in online research, but not if it is bounded by digital

Encyclopedia of Library and Information Sciences, Fourth Edition DOI: 10.1081/E-ELIS4-120043885

collections defined by publisher. From the researcher perspective, neither the publisher's identity, nor even that of the journal in many instances, is considered a significant identifying feature of the published work, as opposed to who wrote it and when.

Hence, automated linking is mainly useful from a research perspective if it works across publications, across publishers, and is truly comprehensive. The usefulness of the system is directly proportional to the robustness of its coverage, and CrossRef paves the way for a truly robust, comprehensive network of connected publications.

Citation linking of this kind also offers advantages to serials publishers, because it drives readers to their publications and their Web sites. By allowing readers to connect to their content from outside resources and locations, they not only serve their subscribed user-base better, but at the same time they create opportunities for article- or chapter-based sales, whether through document delivery services, hosting intermediaries, or their own pay-per-view mechanisms.

CROSSREF TODAY

Let us look at how far the CrossRef initiative has progressed. As of October 2008, the network includes 619 publishers, 21,212 journals, and over 33 million DOIs, including 3 million DOIs for non-journal content such as books and conference proceedings, at varying levels of granularity. The CrossRef system is adding about 14,000 new DOIs every day. Many of these DOIs point to backfile, historical content, as publishers digitize archival material; roughly 400,000 CrossRef DOIs point to seventeenth, eighteenth, and nineteenth century publications. Another source for the steep growth is the addition of new content types. Publishers who have been registering journal content for some time now register DOIs for other resources, and new members who may not publish journals at all are joining to register books, proceedings, datasets, dissertations, grey literature, standards, and other scholarly materials.

The state of the CrossRef endeavor can also be measured by its impact on the research experience. Researchers are currently using the system at a rate of about 19 million DOI clicks per month. Roughly 5 million DOIs per month are retrieved from the system, which gives some indication of the number of DOI-based links being created. In addition to the 619 publishers who participate as members, there are roughly 3500 other participating organizations, including libraries, database publishers, full-text aggregators, software vendors, and journal hosting/linking platforms. These "affiliates" access the CrossRef database of DOIs and metadata on a regular basis to facilitate linking through their own products.

THE DOI[3]

The DOI syntax is a National Information Standard Organization (NISO) standard.[4] A DOI is an alphanumeric name for a digital content entity, such as a book, journal article, chapter, image, etc. The DOI is paired with the object's electronic address, or URL, in a central directory that can be readily updated, and is published in place of the URL to prevent links from breaking, while allowing the content to move as needed. The CrossRef system makes updating the URL in the central DOI directory very easy. Since CrossRef publishers have been updating their records reliably so far, reports of nonworking DOIs are rare, even with millions of DOIs being resolved each month.

Let us take a closer look at a DOI, in Fig. 1. The DOI is made up of two components, a prefix and a suffix, separated by a forward slash. The prefix is assigned to the content owner by a DOI registration agency like CrossRef. All DOI prefixes begin with "10" (to distinguish the DOI from other implementations of the Handle System®),[5] followed by a four-digit string. The prefix in this example is "10.1006." The suffix has a very flexible syntax and is composed by the publisher according to their internal content management needs, with the main restriction being that the suffix must be unique within a prefix.

Once a DOI is assigned to a digital entity, it continues to identify that entity regardless of ownership. While publishers assign DOIs using their own prefix(es), control of individual DOIs can be readily transferred. For example, if ownership of a journal passes from Publisher X to Publisher Y, control over the DOIs for articles in that journal will be given to Publisher Y, who can then update the metadata and URLs for those DOIs. Publisher X will continue to assign DOIs using their existing prefix. Therefore, the prefix of a DOI does not reliably identify the publisher. At the same time, because the DOI never changes in these cases, it means that all the links to that content that have already been published still function. Hence, one key insight of the DOI system is persistence; the other is "actionability." Like the URL itself, one click on a properly implemented DOI gets the user to the location of the content they want.

The DOI remains unique and persistent throughout changes in ownership and location of the content, but it need not be transparently meaningful or descriptive. Rather, descriptive information belongs in the metadata

Fig. 1   Sample DOI, illustrating prefix and suffix.

associated with each DOI when it is registered in the CrossRef system. Actionable, persistent identifiers like the DOI add value to publications because they enable new functionality and work reliably in the Web environment. The identifier strings themselves can be opaque if they are associated with descriptive metadata in the registration process, and, in any event, mainly being interpreted and processed by computers. At the same time, registering an identifier along with descriptive metadata lays the groundwork for constructing other automated services around the content being identified.

HOW CROSSREF WORKS

Publishers use automated (i.e., batch) processes to deposit metadata records into the CrossRef metadata database (MDDB). Each deposited record must include minimal bibliographic information, a DOI, and a current URL. The descriptive metadata includes journal title, ISSN, first author, year, volume, issue, and page number. Depositing metadata with CrossRef involves creating an XML file formatted according to a schema. A sample CrossRef metadata record with both journal-level and article-level metadata and identifiers is shown in Fig. 2.

When publishers deposit records, they automatically enable others to link to their content, because other publishers, librarians, and intermediaries can then retrieve from CrossRef the DOIs that link to that content. After a metadata record is deposited, CrossRef registers each DOI-URL pair in the central DOI directory, an implementation of the Handle System. Thus, when a user clicks on the DOI, it is resolved through the Handle System and not the CrossRef system.

In a separate process, the publisher submits the citations contained in each registered work as queries to the MDDB in order to retrieve any matching DOIs. This way, the publisher can, as part of its electronic production process, add outbound hyperlinks to any of an article's citations that point to entities already registered in the CrossRef system. CrossRef can also accept DOIs as input and return metadata as output. Fig. 3 provides an overview of the workflow for reference linking.

Non-XML interfaces for depositing and querying are now also available. A manual Web deposit form allows publishers to type in requested metadata on a record-by-record basis, and a simple text query form allows publishers and other users to cut and paste groups of references in order to retrieve matching DOIs. These services have helped make the CrossRef system readily accessible

```
<journal>
<full_title>Applied Physics Letters</full_title>
<abbrev_title>Appl. Phys. Lett.</abbrev_title>
<issn media_type="print">00036951</issn>
<issn media_type="electronic">10773118</issn>
<doi_data>
<doi>10.1063/aplo</doi>
<resource> http://ojps.aip.org/aplo/ </resource>
</doi_data>
</journal_metadata>
<journal_issue>
<publication_date media_type="print">
<year>1999</year>
</publication_date>
<journal_volume>
<volume>74</volume>
</journal_volume>
<issue>16</issue>
</journal_issue>
<journal_article publication_type="full_text">
<contributors>
<person_name sequence="first" contributor_role="author">
<given_name>Ann P.</given_name>
<surname>Shirakawa</surname>
</person_name>
</contributors>
<publication_date media_type="print">
<year>1999</year>
</publication_date>
<pages>
<first_page>2268</first_page>
</pages>
<doi_data>
<doi>10.1063/1.123820</doi>
<timestamp>19990628123304</timestamp>
<resource>http://ojps.aip.org/link/?apl/74/2268/ab</resource>
</doi_data>
</journal_article>
```

Fig. 2 Abbreviated example of journal-level and article-level metadata record in CrossRef.

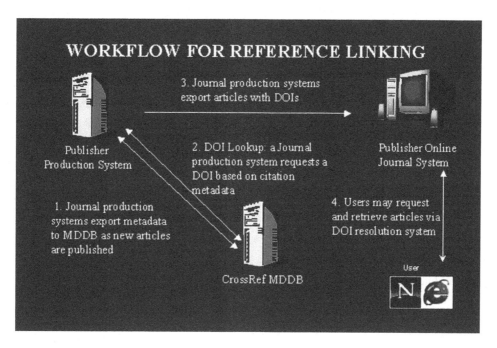

Fig. 3 Workflow for reference linking.

to smaller content providers, including those with limited resources and technical expertise.

When metadata and DOIs are deposited with CrossRef, publishers must have active response pages in place so that they can accept incoming links. As soon as a given deposit goes through, other users of the system will be able to retrieve the DOI in question and create links using that DOI. A minimal response page consists of a full bibliographic citation and some mechanism via which the user can gain access to the full text. Access to proprietary content is controlled by the publisher; most publishers take users to an abstract page and permit authenticated users to go directly to the full text. If the full text is available at no charge, all users can view it immediately. Many publishers also present unauthenticated users with pay-per-view options.

Fig. 4 shows a user clicking on a CrossRef DOI in Journal 1 and connecting to a response page at the Web site of Journal 2.

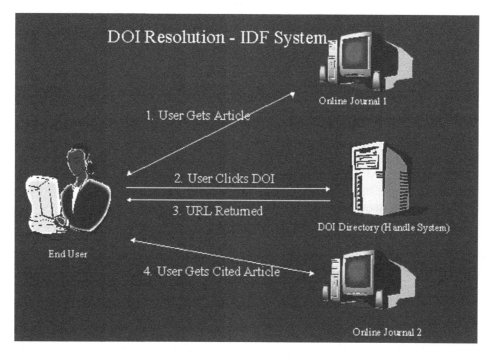

Fig. 4 DOI resolution from the end-user perspective.

In sum, CrossRef provides a database of DOIs and metadata that supports DOI lookup. If you know the DOI for a piece of content, that is all you need to know in order to locate it persistently, not unlike a homing device. If a publisher changes the location of the content, it need only update the URL in one place.

CROSSREF'S IMPACT

Let us look now to how CrossRef impacts the various communities in the information arena.

Impact on Publishers

The current system of Internet addressing made widespread linking possible several years ago. Yet cross-publisher linking remained a largely onerous and error-prone endeavor for scholarly publishers until CrossRef was formed. Before CrossRef, in order to link with one another, publishers had to enter into numerous bilateral agreements and stay on top of several publisher-specific, algorithmic linking schemes. Any change in the online location of a piece of linked content meant that previously published links to that content became obsolete.

With CrossRef, publishers have both a technology and a business infrastructure for persistent linking. On the business side, the publisher (or other interested party) signs one agreement with CrossRef and gains the right to link to all other participating publishers. With 619 dues-paying members, nearly 200,000 bilateral agreements $(1/2N(N - 1))$ would have otherwise been needed to enable the same network of connections. Hence, a linking network on this scale could never have arisen without an organizational infrastructure like CrossRef. Publishers also benefit from being part of a collaborative platform for ongoing development of shared technologies, while maintaining control over their own business practices and how their content is accessed.

On the technology side, CrossRef addresses the error-proneness of links by use of the DOI, as described above. CrossRef is the only DOI registration agency with a DOI lookup and retrieval service. For a publisher with content registered in the CrossRef database, this means that over 3500 participating organizations—other publishers, A&I databases, aggregators, and libraries—will be able to link automatically to their response pages. For electronic books such as reference works, CrossRef facilitates internal linking of components and references, as well as providing durable hyperlinks from citations to any other participating publishers' material. Assigning DOIs to book chapters gives publishers a head start in repurposing content for course-packs, for derivative works requiring a subset or reordering of the original components, and for e-commerce at the chapter level.

Impact on Libraries

With CrossRef functioning as intended, DOIs are now widely distributed by publishers as a standard part of bibliographic metadata. Libraries and their patrons regularly encounter DOIs in the primary and secondary publications that they access. DOIs are good for libraries in the same way that they are good for the research process. Namely, they make linking reliable at any level of granularity possible. In the same way that links drive readers to publisher content, libraries may also see increased usage of acquired electronic resources as an additional benefit.

Most researchers access content through the institutions with which they are affiliated. For the user working in an institutional context, it is not always appropriate to be directed to publisher's online version of a research article. For instance, the institution may not subscribe directly to the e-journal but may still be able to offer the user access to the desired article through an aggregated database or through print holdings. In addition, the library may wish to provide a range of navigational options beyond what is available at the publisher's Web site.

The OpenURL is a mechanism for transporting metadata and identifiers describing a publication, for the purpose of context-sensitive linking. The OpenURL standard has been NISO accredited (ANSI/NISO Z39.88) since 2004.[6] A "link resolver" is a system for linking within an institutional context that can interpret incoming OpenURLs, take the local holdings and access privileges of that institution into account, and display links to appropriate resources. A link resolver allows the library to provide a range of library-configured links and services, including links to the full text, a local catalog to check print holdings, document delivery or ILL services, databases, search engines, etc.

The DOI and the OpenURL work together in several ways. First, the DOI directory itself, where link resolution occurs in the CrossRef platform, is OpenURL-enabled. This means that it can recognize a user with access to a local resolver. When such a user clicks on a DOI, the CrossRef system redirects that DOI back to the user's local resolver, and it allows the DOI to be used as a key to pull metadata out of the CrossRef database, metadata that is needed to create the OpenURL targeting the local resolver. As a result, the institutional user clicking on a DOI is directed to appropriate resources.

By using the CrossRef DOI system to identify their content, publishers in effect make their products OpenURL aware. Since DOIs facilitate linking and data management processes for publishers, many publishers are beginning to require that the DOI be used as the primary linking mechanism to full text. Link resolvers can use the CrossRef system to retrieve the DOI, if the DOI is not already available from the source (i.e., citing) document.

As we have seen, static URLs are not a persistent linking mechanism. If a URL is published as a link and the content it points to is moved, then that link will no longer function. DOIs address this problem. An OpenURL link that contains a DOI is similarly persistent. OpenURLs without DOIs can function persistently only if the relevant metadata is updated within the institution's link resolver. This process is greatly streamlined via access to the CrossRef system, because CrossRef provides a single source for linking reliably to a multitude of publishers without the need to track varied metadata-based linking schemes. In short, link resolvers benefit from using the DOI when linking to publisher-designated resources is appropriate, and as a way to obtain needed metadata.

Impact on Intermediaries

CrossRef encourages its publisher members to distribute DOIs as part of the standard bibliographic metadata that they provide to database publishers, aggregators, vendors, and other intermediaries. These intermediaries can also come directly to CrossRef for a way to identify, acquire, and capture DOIs for records that do not currently contain DOIs as provided directly by the primary publisher.

Like primary publishers, intermediaries join CrossRef to create links to all CrossRef member publishers without signing bilateral linking agreements or having to track publishers' individual linking schemes. They can then also offer their customers links to the full-text content of some primary publishers who do not authorize any other type of linking relationship. In addition to the efficiencies of centralized linking agreements and the enhanced utility of indexes that link reliably to full-text resources, some intermediaries offer CrossRef implementation as part of their journal hosting services, and others integrate their own software into the CrossRef system.

Impact on Researchers

Clearly, researchers want the content that they read online to be linked. It is much more efficient to navigate a body of research at the citation level. When the researcher takes on the author role, linking can be viewed as a way of garnering additional exposure. Including outbound hyperlinks adds valuable functionality to online publications, and inbound linking increases readership and citations. Although the CrossRef linking infrastructure has not been actively promoted to the end user, researchers are increasingly aware of DOIs, and CrossRef now offers several free points of access for researchers to retrieve DOIs. Many scholars and scientists now add DOI links to their own authored works, whether journal articles or newer communication formats such as blogs.

BEYOND CITATION LINKING

The CrossRef network is currently expanding not only in terms of content coverage—to different genres and levels

of granularity—but also in terms of functionality. Some of the latest key developments are described here.

Cited-by Linking formerly Forward Linking is a way of tracking citations to a given publication as they occur. In addition to using CrossRef to create outbound links from their references, CrossRef member publishers can now retrieve "cited-by" links—links to other articles that cite their content. An optional tool is offered to CrossRef members, enabling them to display "cited-by" links in the primary content that they publish. This is a natural extension of the CrossRef linking network, and helps provide a better online reading environment for researchers and scholars. As part of the same functionality, CrossRef also offers a "match-alert" feature that saves users from having to query CrossRef repeatedly to find DOIs for citations that do not initially return a match. If the publisher chooses to enable this, then the system automatically sends an e-mail containing the matched results when the relevant content is registered in CrossRef.

CrossCheck powered by iThenticate[7] is a new initiative from CrossRef to help the scholarly publishers verify the originality of submitted manuscripts. The need of a plagiarism tool was identified as a top priority by CrossRef members in 2006 and as a result CrossRef researched the best plagiarism tools on the market to provide a solution for the CrossRef members. CrossCheck is really two products, a database of scholarly publications and a Web-based tool to check an authored work against that database. The Web-based tool can be used in the editorial process to identify matching text but it cannot, on its own, identify plagiarism. A human has to look at the matching text and use their best judgment to identify if plagiarism has occurred or not.

CrossRef Metadata Services formerly CrossRef Web Services is an optional service for publishers who would like CrossRef to disseminate metadata on their behalf. This can be useful to streamline the Web crawling carried out by search engines and others, in order to optimize the functionality of their indexes. It consists of a suite of tools to enable authorized partners to collect metadata from multiple publishers, using a variety of metadata gathering implementations such as Open Archives Initiative Protocol for Metadata Harvesting (OAI-PMH). Standard terms of use are provided for search engines, libraries, and other partners to use the metadata available from CrossRef Metadata Services.

CONCLUSION

CrossRef is about reducing friction in the means of discovering and accessing scholarly content online. Perhaps the key insight of the CrossRef initiative is that it allows publishers to create collectively the experience of integrated electronic resources for the scholarly community, without in fact requiring aggregation of anything but the most minimal metadata.

CrossRef is representative of a trend toward "distributed integration"[8] of information resources that will continue to progress as publishers take advantage of yet other ways, such as the Open Archives Initiative,[9] to expose metadata about their information products on the Web for harvesting, search, and e-commerce applications. From the end-user perspective, the outcome is a more highly integrated body of research literature, even if such integration is merely virtual. As the automated tools for exposing and harvesting metadata, classifying content, and performing intelligent search continue to be refined/improved, this trend will no doubt advance.

Interlinking of resources across publisher platforms, as in CrossRef, is a prime example of distributed integration in electronic publishing. Both content providers and content consumers benefit from initiatives that use metadata and identifier registration to enable virtual integration of scholarly literature online.

REFERENCES

1. For more information on the International DOI Foundation: http://www.doi.org

2. Atkins, H.; Lyons, C.; Ratner, H.; Risher, C.; Shillum, C.; Sidman, D.; Stevens, A. Reference linking with DOIs. D-Lib Magazine **2000**, *6*(2), http://www.dlib.org/dlib/february00/02risher.html

3. Detailed information about DOIs can be found in the DOI Handbook: http://www.doi.org/hb.html

4. Syntax for the Digital Object Identifier, Z39.84. NISO **2000**, http://www.niso.org/

5. The Handle System is a distributed computer system for naming digital objects and storing the names and the information needed to locate and access the objects via the Internet. It is managed by the Corporation of National Research Initiatives on behalf of the IDF. For more information on the Handle System: http://www.handle.net

6. For more information on the OpenURL: http://library.caltech.edu/openurl

7. For more information on CrossCheck: http://www.crossref.org/crosscheck.html

8. Schottlaender, B. Portals for integration and collaboration. In *Paper Presented at the AAP/PSP Annual Conference*, Washington, DC, February 2003.

9. For more information about the Open Archives Initiatives and it protocol for harvesting metadata: http://www.openarchives.org/

Cultural Memory

Robert DeHart
Department of History, Middle Tennessee State University, Murfreesboro, Tennessee, U.S.A.

Abstract

Cultural memory is a term used to describe interpretations of the past created by a group to address contemporary concerns. Cultural memory is transmitted to other individuals in forms such as commemorations, rituals, monuments, oral traditions, museum exhibits, books, and films. Groups or nations create and transmit cultural memory primarily to promote unity, identity, or some other political or cultural ideal. The term traces its origins to anthropology, but sociologists developed its theoretical framework. Since the 1980s, a number of academic disciplines have embraced cultural memory studies as a valuable tool of inquiry. Although it is a popular field of research, critics contend that a number of methodological issues need to be resolved. The term has entered the popular lexicon to describe how the works of a contemporary generation utilizes the traditions of a previous generation.

INTRODUCTION

Cultural memory is a term used to describe interpretations of the past shared by a group of individuals. The need to address contemporary concerns, such as preserving group identity or sustaining support for a political ideal, influences the creation and content of cultural memory. Thus cultural memory represents a reconstructed past that serves the present needs of a group. Individuals that construct, support, or preserve cultural memory usually share nationality, religion, ethnicity, politics, or some other cultural identifier, and many times these individuals did not live through the event being remembered. A group's cultural memory is reinforced and transmitted to other individuals in forms such as commemorations, rituals, monuments, oral traditions, museum exhibits, books, and films.

Scholars in fields as diverse as history, religious studies, literature, folklore, art, anthropology, sociology, and mass communications have devoted considerable research and texts to the significance of cultural memory to their respective fields. The term cultural memory has also entered the popular lexicon. It is sometimes used to describe how activities such as cooking, composing popular music, and graffiti reflect aspects of a culture's past traditions.

HISTORICAL CONTEXT AND TERMINOLOGY

Although the term "cultural memory" was not coined until the 1980s, its theoretical framework came to light during the upheaval that occurred in the humanities following the devastation caused by World War I. In an attempt to understand the ethnic, social, and political dynamics that led to the conflict, scholars sought new methods for analyzing the inner ethnic relationships and international relations of nations. From this scholarship emerged new ideas about memory distinct from its Freudian conception as created and existing purely in the minds of individuals. The scholar most frequently cited as forming these ideas into a usable theory is French sociologist Maurice Halbwachs (1877–1945). His book *Les cadres sociaux de la memoire* (The Social Frameworks of Memory), published in 1925, theorized that individuals reconstruct memories of the past only within a social context. Through day-to-day communication individuals possessing shared concerns for the present form memories of the past "collectively" that supports the needs of the group. He labeled this type of memory "collective memory." To support his theory, he demonstrated how different classes of French society (working, old wealth, new wealth, etc.) collectively possessed contrasting interpretations of French history.[1,2]

Halbwachs' ideas influenced scholars in the ensuing decades, but none had quite the impact on the development of cultural memory theory as French historian Pierre Nora. His *Lieux de Memoire* series (Realms of Memory), first volume published in 1984, solicited essays from a number of French historians that identified and examined historic and cultural sites that represented collective memories. For example, contributor Edouard Pommier demonstrated how during the late 1600s King Louis XIV employed decorative arts in the Palace of Versailles to link his reign with heroic legends of antiquity. In the process, the King hoped to fuse French history with myth to create an idealized vision of the French past that would support his administration.[3] This essay and others in the volumes for the first time placed collective memory into a broad historical context, thus establishing it as a characteristic of modernity (the era beginning in Western Europe in the 1600s that embraced science and reason as the tools to

Encyclopedia of Library and Information Sciences, Fourth Edition DOI: 10.1081/E-ELIS4-120044333

Corporate Information–Custody

propel civilization toward an ever-evolving state of progress). Nora contended that modernity and its emphasis on nation-building and industrialization had created a divide between peoples' personal experiences and their relationships to the past, especially when it came to identifying with a national or cultural ideal. Thus, a need arose for producing "external sites of memory" such as monuments and museums to preserve links between individuals and tradition. According to Nora, this "memory crisis" was further exasperated in the twentieth century with the ascendancy of popular culture and emergence of postmodernity (generally referring to the era following World War II; proponents of the term rejected the notion that civilization was in a state of continuous progress). Popular culture, such as television shows, popular music, and films, increasingly defined the shared traditions of groups, thus creating an even greater need to locate ways to preserve national and cultural traditions.[1] Nora's work had enormous influence on the potential applications of collective memory theory, leading a new generation of scholars into the field of cultural memory studies the following decade.

However, the term "collective memory" did not sit well in all disciplines. While sociologists naturally gravitated to the term in their work, scholars in other disciplines, especially historians, developed alternative terminology that better reflected their methodological framework. They employed terms like public memory, social memory, popular memory, heritage phenomenon, patriotic culture, cultural amnesia, and myth to describe what are at their core Halbwachs' original conception of collective memory. This different vocabulary had more to do with the type of research being conducted and enhancements of definition rather than a major break with the sociological foundation of collective memory.

Perhaps the most widely used memory term in academia and popular culture is "cultural memory." A frequently cited definition of the term emerged from the field of anthropology by German Egyptologists Jan and Aleida Assmann. In Jan Assmann's book *Kultur and Gedachtnis* (Culture and Memory), published in 1988, he expanded on Halbwachs' work by locating two primary modes of collective memory. Assmann defined "communicative memory" as the day-to-day communication of individuals that expresses shared viewpoints about the past. This memory has no fixed place in time and thus lasts only a few generations. "Cultural memory" is when these "communicative memories" are turned into "objectified culture," such as monuments, texts, and museums. Only then do the memories become fixed in time, become distanced from everyday communication, and achieve power.[4] To illustrate the differences between these two types of memory, imagine an American family who shares and discusses its memories of President Franklin Roosevelt's New Deal programs of the 1930s. Aspects of these memories may shift over time as some details gain or fade in importance

and the generation who lived through the era dies off. At this point, these memories would be defined as communicative. But if the family creates a text or commemoration that reconstructs its memories of the New Deal, and if this text or commemoration becomes accessible to the public, it becomes a cultural memory that can be shared with other Americans.

CHARACTERISTICS OF CULTURAL MEMORY

Defining the Group

An interesting aspect of cultural memory is that there is no formula for determining the makeup of a group who shares or creates a cultural memory. This is not to say that cultural memories do not frequently form along cultural indicators such as ethnicity and class. But it would be an oversimplification to point to this as one of its defining characteristics. Cultural memories can exist and be produced in units as small as ethnic minorities, created by the bureaucracy of a nation, or shared across lines of class and nationality. In fact, in the late 1990s the Getty Institute initiated a "Global Cultural Memory" project to "create a collective archive of digital information (text, images, and, in future, sound and video) that documents both everyday and singular events, lifestyles, and achievements that have influenced the most recent 50 years of cultural memory."[5] It is hard to imagine an application of cultural memory that could have a farther reach.

Age is one important indicator for understanding why one group may find an aspect of the past important for commemoration while another group may choose a different past. Psychologists Schuman, Rieger, and Scott conducted studies in 1989 and 1992 that sampled 1410 Americans over 18 years old. Participants were asked to name past public events that they deemed as important to their lives. The study found that events that occurred when participants were in their late teens or early twenties appeared to receive the largest positive response. Thus, for an event like the assassination of President John F. Kennedy, people who were in their twenties when the event occurred found it to be more significant to their lives than people who were in their fifties (Fig. 1). This suggested that people of the most affected generation would likely support commemorations, museums, movies, etc. that showcase the event more than earlier or later generations. The study is also significant for the number of people who recalled significant events that occurred well before they were born. In the case of the Depression of the 1930s, 10% of participants deemed the event as important to their lives even though they were not born until 29 years after the event occurred (Fig. 2). For these respondents, such is the strength of the cultural memory of the Depression that had been transmitted to them by family, texts, the media, and other sources.

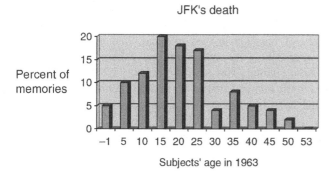

Fig. 1 John F. Kennedy's death.
Source: From Schuman and Rieger, C.[21]

Table 1 Significant U.S. historical events: Black and white Americans.

Event	Black	White
Civil rights	30 (22.4%)	9 (5.4%)
Slavery	15 (11.2)	2 (1.2)
World War II	9 (6.7)	21 (12.5)
Martin Luther King's assassination	6 (4.5)	0
Assassinations of 1960s	6 (4.5)	1 (.6)
Vietnam	6 (4.5)	19 (11.3)
John F. Kennedy's assassination	2 (1.5)	14 (8.3)
Gulf War	2 (1.5)	9 (5.4)

Source: From Rosenzweig and Thelen.[20]

Considering that many cultural memories form out of a need to establish group identity and unity, ethnicity is an important indicator. A study by Roy Rozenzweig and David Thelen, published in 1998, revealed how black and white Americans possessed very different views of U.S. history. When asked to list past events that had been important to their lives, a majority of black participants listed the Civil Rights Movement first and slavery as second. In contrast, white participants listed World War II first and the Vietnam War second (Table 1). This survey helped explain why the cultural memory of nations is so often contested. Various interest groups possess strong opinions as to what aspects of a nation's past are worth commemorating. When the preservation of that past is in jeopardy or not supported by the nation's leaders or other groups, conflict almost certainly ensues.

While interest groups form their own cultural memories of the past, nations often use cultural memory to promote particular policies. The majority of scholarly texts that focus on this aspect of cultural memory deal with contemporary issues, but scholars have been successful in demonstrating that manipulations of cultural memory by nations existed already in antiquity. Jan Assmann argued that the leaders of the ancient Egyptian Middle Kingdom (2040–1650 B.C.E.) used cultural memories of the leaders of the preceding First Intermediate Period (2150–2040 B.C.E.) to help establish their authority over the Egyptian people. The First Intermediate Period was a time of extreme chaos and uncertainty in Egypt. With its enemies defeated by the time of the Middle Kingdom, the new rulers needed to preserve the memories of the earlier period to demonstrate that "only the [current] pharaoh could restore order and balance in a world out of joint and threatening to fly apart."[6] Assmann used surviving texts from the Middle Kingdom that evoked these disturbing memories to support his theory that cultural memory is not unique to modernity.

To cite a contemporary example, American historian John Bodnar employed the rubric of public memory to examine how the battles surrounding the monuments and museums commemorating the social and political upheaval of Vietnam War/Civil Rights era America paralleled the turmoil of the 1960s itself. He viewed public memory as an "intersection of official and vernacular cultural expressions." Official culture represented the goals and beliefs of national leaders seeking unity, while vernacular culture represented the localized beliefs of various specialized interests.[7] Together they competed to form a public memory of the past that could be widely accepted yet serve the interests of each group. The tendency of a nation to manipulate the past as propaganda to support its agenda and the efforts of minority groups to contest this reconstruction of the past by asserting its positions is a recurring theme in the literature produced by historians exploring cultural memory.

Impressively, some cultural memories have the ability to reach across generational and ethnic lines with little contestation within a nation. A good example is the American cultural memory of the Holocaust. Although a minority of Americans was personally affected by the atrocities against Jews carried out in Adolf Hitler's Germany during the 1930s and 1940s, America possesses a number of museums devoted to the genocide, and dramatic portrayals in film and television have persisted in popularity. As historians Peter Novick and Michael Morgan have observed, the rise of a Holocaust consciousness in Jewish Americans, which occurred decades after the event actually happened, stemmed from a need to provide unity in the Jewish American community in light of declining religiosity and increasing assimilation. The Holocaust also provided

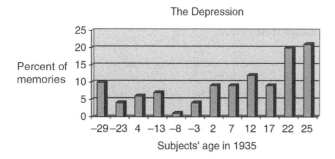

Fig. 2 The depression.
Source: From Schuman and Rieger, C.[21]

Jewish Americans a link with Israel. But in America, the story of the Holocaust was created somewhat uniquely from stories generated in Israel. American museums embraced a "universalist definition" of the Holocaust that linked Jewish victims with those of other ethnicities and nationalities killed by German sponsored pogroms during World War II. Some even went as far to link the genocide with other atrocities such as the "killing fields" of Cambodia during the 1970s or the slaughter of Armenians by Turkish soldiers during World War I, thereby removing anti-Semitism from its central place in the narrative (a fact that incensed many Jewish scholars). Scholars opine that America embraced this definition because it would better resonate with the nation's diverse population, address the societal need for tolerance, and perhaps even deflect attention from America's own history of racism.[8,9] The embedment of the Holocaust into the American consciousness has been very successful. Regardless of class, ethnicity, or religion, many Americans possess a shared knowledge of the event through museums like the National Holocaust Museum and Museum of Tolerance, films such as *Schindler's List*, and popular books like the *Diary of Anne Frank*.

Representations

As described above, representations of cultural memory may be found in museums, archives, monuments, commemorations, film, and books, and historians have made good use of this primary source material to explore how groups reconstruct the past. But representations of cultural memory can take many forms and many other disciplines have used cultural memory theory to good effect. Anthropologists found cultural memory theory to be an effective way to investigate non-Western cultures. Rejecting the use of nineteenth century colonial records to understand such cultures, anthropologists turned to observations of indigenous people "in the field" and recognized how cultural memory was deeply embedded in contemporary traditions. Utilizing this approach revealed that historical interpretations of the past existed in these cultures in a non-linear fashion, distinct from the linear properties of history in the West. For example, Levi-Strauss observed Australian aborigines performing historical or commemorative rites that recreated the sacred and beneficial atmosphere of mythical times to recall the traditions of their ancestors.[10] Rather than a simple reenactment of the past, the aborigines viewed these rites as allowing the past and the present to coexist simultaneously. These rites, which can be interpreted as cultural memories, served to reinforce identity and support social needs.

In literary criticism, scholars have used cultural memory theory to locate meaning in fictional characters. A critique of Paule Marshall's novel *Praisesong for the Widow* by Susan Rogers invokes cultural memory theory to analyze the book's protagonist Avey Johnson. A woman of African

American and Caribbean heritage, Johnson becomes obsessed with reconnecting with her African ancestors' history of bondage in the Americas. In her essay, Rogers explored how the author portrays Johnson's body as "a site of cultural expression and memory." Feeling detached from life and in denial of her heritage, Johnson struggles to find her true identity during an ocean cruise eventually rediscovering a sense of heritage in one of the oldest forms of cultural memory—the dance.[11]

Art historians have long recognized that artworks transmit the culture of the past to contemporary societies. Before Halbwachs developed his theory of collective memory, German art historian Aby Warburg (1866–1929) used anthropological methods to deconstruct art works and reveal connections between an artist's work and its social and historical contexts. Unlike many of his contemporaries, he rejected the analysis of art based purely on aesthetic principles. But he also warned against expecting too many insights into the artist's world by just looking at his or her artwork. For Warburg, all culture transmitted through art was mediated in some respect and "artistic style is a most treacherous key for ascertaining political and social developments."[12]

The interdisciplinary fields of American Studies and Cultural Studies have embraced cultural memory theory as a method of investigation. Popular culture provides much of the source material for these fields to explore the lives of ordinary citizens. Hip Hop music, Tom Cruise movies, graffiti at the Beatles' Abbey Road recording studio, and the *X-Files* science fiction TV show have all been used as source material for uncovering cultural memories.

In journalism, cultural memory as a term is sometimes used in articles and reviews. A kind of jazz may invoke a cultural memory of the big band era of the 1930s. A particular dish may produce the cultural memory of an ethnic cooking tradition. Even commemorative journalism that reports on observations of historic events draws on cultural memory theory. The meaning of cultural memory as originally defined by Assmann has likely been misused by some in the media. Nonetheless it has found wide-spread acceptance as a descriptor of the ethereal mnemonic qualities of things that pass from generation to generation.

Social Relevance

As these examples illustrate, the need to address contemporary concerns influences the creation and transmission of cultural memory. Thus, scholarly investigation of cultural memory possesses significant implications for the present. According to one critique, it appeals to scholars because it "turns academics into concerned citizens who share the burdens of contemporary memory crises."[13] Or as historian John Gillis explained, it locates "usable pasts capable of serving the heterogeneity of new groups that

[have] become active on the national and international stage: racial and sexual minorities, women, youth, and dozens of new nations and ethnic groups aspiring to sovereign status."[14] Through an examination of how groups reconstruct the past, the core issues that divide and unite people can be revealed.

The preservation of the Lorraine Motel in Memphis, Tennessee, site of the 1968 assassination of Civil Rights leader Martin Luther King, Jr., shows how cultural memories expose divisions in society and influences the urban landscape. The assassination was so shameful to the city of Memphis that it took 20 years before major efforts went forward to turn the Lorraine into a museum. But even then, city residents possessed strong opinions about whether this cultural memory deserved recognition, and opinions were divided along mostly racial lines. Most blacks felt that a museum at the Lorraine would help heal societal wounds caused by the city's history of racial discrimination and uplift the black community by recalling its role in the national Civil Rights movement. In contrast, most whites felt that the museum would only reignite the racial unrest of the 1960s. Some also felt that King's legacy was not worth remembering because of his opposition to the Vietnam War and his stances on economic equality (seen by some as an obvious reference to Communism).[15] In sharp contrast to the ease at which Holocaust museums found a foothold in America, Civil Rights museums have met resistance. The National Civil Rights Museum at the Lorraine eventually opened in the early 1990s and helped revitalize a section of downtown Memphis. An examination of the cultural memory conflict that occurred in the city during the museum's development proved to be an effective way for understanding the city's unresolved racial issues.

The social relevance of cultural memory is not a uniquely Western phenomenon. According to historian Gyanendra Pandey, beginning in the 1980s in India, a right-wing Hindu movement waged an effort to establish a national Hindu culture in the nation. Naturally, the movement focused on reconstructing history and memory to achieve its goals. The movement reclaimed national sites by tearing down historic mosques, built monuments to its leaders, and produced a widely distributed pamphlet that featured a "new" history of India that highlighted the heroic contributions of Hindus to the nation.[16] In modern China, Ban Wang sees the occurrence of a "dialectic tension between memory and history" to form a contemporary national memory. On one hand, the traumatic memories of imperialism that were used to justify the creation of an authoritarian state in China are being subdued to accommodate the economic benefits of the nation's movement into the global marketplace. But on the other, nostalgia combined with a critique of modernization attempts to hold enthusiasm for a Chinese global economy in check. Thus, according to Wang, history and cultural memory in China are in transition as current discussions about the direction of the nation create a need to reform cultural memories of the past.[17] Both of these examples underscore how present political or societal needs influence the reconstruction of the past in nations around the globe.

CRITICISMS OF CULTURAL MEMORY STUDIES

Since the 1980s, cultural memory studies have produced a flood of academic manuscripts and popular cultural references. However, a number of scholars have raised their voices to express concern about the inherent problems with drawing precise conclusions from cultural memory studies. One such concern is that too little attention is paid to how cultural or collective memory is different from individual memory and that scholars sometimes misapply psychoanalytical tools developed for understanding individual memory to the shared memories of groups. Terms familiar to discourse on individual memory such as "trauma" and "amnesia" are frequently used in conjunction with cultural memory theory, but questions persist if these same terms can be properly applied collectively rather than individually (p. 186).[2] Take for example the memories created by natural disaster such as Hurricane Katrina, which hit the United States in 2005. An individual who lived through the event may experience mental trauma. This individual might repress memories or manipulate them to deal with the trauma. These memories may even change over time as the temporal distance increases from the event. At the same time, other population samples of the United States, who are concerned by the disaster's implications for national image, may be said to have also experienced trauma from the event. But is the trauma experienced by the individual and the population sample the same? Can we accurately interpret the trauma experienced by the United States as a whole? To some scholars, cultural memory studies too frequently fail to make this distinction and treat the shared memories of groups the same as the memory of an individual. They believe that more work needs to be done on how collectives truly manage to remember and forget.

The lack of understanding of how groups receive and internalize specific representations of cultural memory is another major concern for critics of cultural memory theory. Cultural memories, as represented by monuments, museums, etc., tell us much about the people who created them, but little is known about how these memories move from monument to individuals and eventually groups. Individuals invariably bring their own interpretations of the past with them as they encounter a museum exhibit or historical film. The effect of this interplay on cultural memory is rarely addressed. Receivers of cultural memories do express opinions in newspaper editorials and other sources that provide access to the thoughts of these receptors, but even these sources are mediated by editors and do not present an unmediated representation. Wulf Kansteiner suggests that one solution to this problem would be to look at why some memories never succeed in becoming a part of a public consciousness. An example he cites is the commemoration of America's involvement in the Korean War. "The Forgotten War," as it is sometimes called, finally received some attention during the 2000s with street names and memorials in cities across the nation paying respect to the soldiers who participated. But this was after memorials for veterans of the Vietnam War, which ended two decades after the conclusion of the Korean War, had already appeared. For Kansteiner, examining why some events fail to become part of cultural memory may be as illuminating as looking at the ones that succeed.[2]

According to some critics, the similarities and distinctions between the reconstruction of the past that occurs during the formation and transmission of cultural memory and the scholarly process of producing historical texts and media needs to be explored further. Groups create cultural memory by manipulating viewpoints about the past to address contemporary concerns. The biases and current interests of historians naturally influence the subject matter and interpretation of historic persons and events found in their work. Indeed historiography is full of examples of multiple changing perspectives on historical events. This leads to the question as to what are the true distinctions between cultural memory and history. Is it simply the academic status of history that distinguishes it from the building of museums and monuments? Are not the public historians who build the collections in museums or develop historic sites deemed as professionals?[1] The cultural memory versus history debate remains unresolved.

Some scholars have also noted how the majority of cultural memory studies focus on controversial historical events and contestation. Volumes have been produced on memory conflicts regarding the Holocaust, American Civil War, French Revolution, and post-World War II Germany. The more divisive a history, the more reconstruction of cultural memory appears to come into play. However, in cases where remembrance has provoked little controversy, memory studies are typically silent. The Lorraine Motel represents a site of contentious memory, thus its preservation has been analyzed. But most likely a nineteenth century Victorian house in Memphis preserved for its architectural beauty will receive little attention in regards to the cultural memory that it represents. Psychologist Barry Schwartz argued that cultural memory studies begin to ring hollow unless

> . . .there is something to be mystified, some injustice or atrocity to be concealed. . . . In every culture and in every age we see exclusion and bias, but as the work of civil rights, multiculturalism, and inclusion continues, it becomes more difficult to squeeze out insights from [cultural memory] analysis.[18]

According to Schwartz, cultural memory studies could conceivably reach a point where it runs out of source material for study.

CONCLUSION

Despite criticisms of cultural memory theory, the use of the term cultural memory in academia and popular culture shows no sign of abating. The term persists as a way to identify reconstructions of the past created by groups or nations. Cultural memory is transmitted to other individuals in forms such as commemorations, rituals, monuments, oral traditions, museum exhibits, books, and films. Thus these forms supply the primary source material for scholars to investigate the implications and significance of cultural memory creation and transmission. The term traces its origins to anthropology, but sociologists developed its theoretical framework. Since the 1980s, a number of diverse academic disciplines have embraced cultural memory studies as a valuable tool of inquiry.

There are three main characteristics of cultural memory. First, diverse groups create and share cultural memories. There is no formula for defining the size, age ranges, ethnicity, or nationality of groups that may create or possess a cultural memory. Cultural memories frequently form along such cultural indicators, but there are examples of cultural memories that transcend this pattern. Scholars have located examples of cultural memory creation in cultures across the globe in both antiquity and modern times.

Second, representations of cultural memory occur in many forms allowing many academic disciplines to apply cultural memory theory. Historians, in their work, emphasize cultural memories transmitted through commemorations, monuments, and museums. Cultural memory may also be located in forms such as religious practices, visual arts, literature, dance, and music. Although the term is used by the popular media in a slightly different context than it is in academia, it is sometimes used by journalists to describe how a generation utilizes the traditions of a previous generation.

Third, cultural memory is created to address contemporary concerns. Thus, cultural memory studies possess social relevance because it contributes to an interpretation of national culture and reveals the core issues that divide and unite contemporary populations. Cultural memory influences preservation initiatives that affect the built environment and underscores the challenges faced by nations as they strive for continuity during times of change. As a result, contestations between groups and nations over representations and manipulations of cultural memory are a core aspect of cultural memory literature.

Critics contend that a number of methodological issues need to be addressed before cultural memory theory can emerge as a reliable tool of inquiry. Scholars sometimes misapply psychoanalytical tools developed for understanding individual memory to the collective memories of groups. How groups process and receive reconstructions of cultural memories has not been fully explored. Some scholars are troubled by the relationship between cultural memory studies and historical research. And, the study of cultural memory tends to focus primarily on contentious events.

The number of articles discussing cultural memory has declined since the 1990s. However, commemorations, monuments, and other interpretations of the terrorist attacks of September 11, 2001 will undoubtedly provide fertile ground for cultural memory studies for decades to come. Also, the continued development of Africa, Asia, and the Middle East will likely involve reassessing the past and the creation and transmission of cultural memory. The wide-spread use of the internet potentially provides a new platform representing cultural memory. E-mails, blogs, and videos posted by various groups on YouTube could prove to be key representations of cultural memories for scholars in the future.

REFERENCES

1. Crane, S. Writing the individual back into collective memory. Am. Hist. Rev. **1997**, *102*(5), 1372–1385.
2. Kansteiner, W. Finding meaning in memory: A methodological critique of collective memory studies. Hist. Theory. **2002**, *41*(2), 181–193.
3. Pommier, E. Versailles: The image of the sovereign. In *Realms of Memory*; Nora, P., Ed.; Columbia University Press: New York, 1992; Vol. 3, 293–323.
4. Assmann, J. Collective memory and cultural identity. New Ger. Crit. **1995**, *65*(Spring, Summer), 125–133.
5. http://images.library.uiuc.edu/projects/gcm/aboutproject. html.
6. Assmann, J. Memories. *The Mind of Egypt*; Metropolitan Books: New York, 1996; 107.
7. Bodnar, J. The memory debate: An introduction. *Remaking America: Public Memory, Commemoration, and Patriotism in the Twentieth Century*; Princeton University Press: Princeton, NJ, 1992; 12–15.
8. Novick, P. *The Holocaust in American Life*; Houghton Mifflin: Boston, MA, 1999; Vol. 7.
9. Morgan, M. To seize memory: History and identity in post-holocaust Jewish thought. In *Thinking about the Holocaust: After Half a Century*; Rosenfeld, A., Ed.; Indiana University Press: Bloomington, IN, 1997; 161.
10. Levi-Strauss, C. *The Savage Mind*; University of Chicago Press: Chicago, IL, 1966.
11. Rogers, S. Embodying cultural memory in Paule Marshall's Praisesong for the Widow. Afr. Am. Rev. **2000**, *34*(1), 77–93.
12. Confino, A. Collective memory and cultural history: Problems of method. Am. Hist. Rev. **1997**, *102*(5), 1387.
13. Kansteiner, W. Finding meaning in memory: A methodological critique of collective memory studies. Hist. Theory. **2002**, *41*(2), 179.
14. Gillis, J. Introduction. *Commemorations: The Politics of National Identity*; Princeton University Press: Princeton, NJ, 1994; 19.
15. DeHart, R. The National Civil Rights Museum. *Confronting Intolerance in America and The Politics of Collective Memory: The Museum of Tolerance and The National Civil Rights Museum*; Middle Tennessee State University: Murfreesboro, TN, 2001; 65–95 Master's Thesis.
16. Pandey, G. Monumental history. *Routine Violence: Nations, Fragments, Histories*; Stanford University Press: Stanford, CA, 2006; 68–92.
17. Wang, B. Memory and history in globalization. *Illuminations from the Past: Trauma, Memory, and History in Modern China*; Stanford University Press: Stanford, CA, 2004; 8–9.
18. http://www.blackwellreference.com/public/beos_collective.

BIBLIOGRAPHY

1. Assmann, J. Collective memory and cultural identity. New Ger. Crit. **1995**, *65*(Spring, Summer), 125–133.
2. Assmann, J. *The Mind of Egypt*; Metropolitan Books: New York, 1996.
3. Bodnar, J. *Remaking America: Public Memory, Commemoration, and Patriotism in the Twentieth Century*; Princeton University Press: Princeton, NJ, 1992.
4. Confino, A. Collective memory and cultural history: Problems of method. Am. Hist. Rev. **1997**, *102*(5), 1386–1403.
5. Crane, S. Writing the individual back into collective memory. Am. Hist. Rev. **1997**, *102*(5), 1372–1385.
6. Daynes, G. *Making Villains, Making Heros: Joseph R. McCarthy, Martin Luther King Jr., and the Politics of American Memory*; University of California Press: Los Angeles, CA, 1997.
7. DeHart, R. The National Civil Rights Museum. *Confronting Intolerance in America and The Politics of Collective Memory: The Museum of Tolerance and The National Civil Rights Museum*; Middle Tennessee State University: Murfreesboro, TN, 2001; 65–95 Masters Thesis.
8. Edy, J. Journalistic uses of collective memory. J. Commun. **1999**, *49*(2), 71–85.
9. Gillis, J. *Commemorations: The Politics of National Identity*; Princeton University Press: Princeton, NJ, 1994.
10. Halbwachs, M. *On Collective Memory*; University of Chicago Press: Chicago, IL, 1992.
11. Huyssen, A. *Twilight Memories: Marking Time in a Culture of Amnesia*; Routledge: London, U.K., 1995.
12. Kammen, M. *In the Past Lane: Historical Perspectives on American Culture*; Oxford University Press: New York, 1997.
13. Kansteiner, W. Finding meaning in memory: A methodological critique of collective memory studies. Hist. Theory. **2002**, *41*(2), 179–197.
14. Nora, P., Ed.; *Realms of Memory*; Columbia University Press: New York, 1992.
15. Novick, P. *The Holocaust in American Life*; Houghton Mifflin: Boston, MA, 1999.

16. Transformations. June 3, 2002. Available at http://www. transformationsjournal.org/journal/issue_03/editorial.shtml (Entire issue devoted to cultural memory).

17. Pandey, G. Monumental history. *Routine Violence: Nations; Fragments, Histories*, Stanford University Press: Stanford, CA, 2006.

18. Rogers, S. Embodying cultural memory in Paule Marshall's Praisesong for the Widow. Afr. Am. Rev. **2000**, *34*(1), 77–93.

19. Rosenfeld, A. *Thinking about the Holocaust: After Half a Century*; Indiana University Press: Bloomington, IN, 1997.

20. History in black and red. In *The Presence of the Past: Popular Uses of History in American Life*; Rosenzweig, R., Thelen, D., Eds.; Columbia University Press: New York, 1998.

21. Schuman, H. Rieger, C. Collective memory and collective memories. In *Theoretical Perspectives on Autobiographical Memory*; Conway, M., Rubin, D., Spinnler, H., Wagenaar, W., Eds.; Kluwer Academic Publishers: Dordrecht, the Netherlands, 1992; 326.

22. Wang, B. Memory and history in globalization. *Illuminations from the Past: Trauma, Memory, and History in Modern China*; Stanford University Press: Stanford, CA, 2004.

Corporate Information–Custody

Curating Archaeological Artifacts

Alex W. Barker
Museum of Art and Archaeology, University of Missouri, Columbia, Missouri, U.S.A.

Abstract

Archaeological artifacts, collections, and associated records represent arguably the most important resource for documenting the entirety of the human career. Their integrity and value, however, depend on appropriate management and curation. This entry provides a brief survey of standards and generally accepted practices for the documentation, acquisition, cataloging, care, use, and interpretation of curated archaeological collections as well as a summary of metadata standards and current ethical issues confronting archaeological curators.

INTRODUCTION

Archaeological collections represent a primary form of cultural heritage and one of the major sources of evidence regarding the human career. The value and integrity of these collections depends on appropriate curation, management, and care; this entry briefly summarizes key curatorial concerns, and addresses current trends and ethical issues relating to curatorial practice in archaeology.

Various definitions have been offered, but for our purposes, archaeology (the spelling with "ae" is generally preferred, but some U.S. federal sources prefer the spelling "archeology," and some scholars in classical archaeology continue to use the diphthong "æ") may be defined as the study of human behavior from its material correlates and physical residues. This definition places material objects—and information relating to these objects—at the center of archaeology as a scholarly enterprise. This emphasis on materiality need not limit the kinds of questions archaeologists address, but does frame the nature of the evidence on which archaeological research is based. Technically, at least, archaeologists do not actually study the past. Instead they study evidence of all kinds that has survived from the past into the present or from the present that may be more broadly applicable, in order to make inferences about the past. More than a fine distinction, this fact informs most guidelines regarding the proper management and curation of archaeological collections.

Archaeological sites are fragile, finite, and non-renewable resources. Rates of site loss and looting are alarming. The trade in antiquities is difficult to quantify, with estimates ranging from $300 million to more than $6 billion annually.[1] While rates of site loss and destruction are equally difficult to quantify, Heritage Action in the United Kingdom has estimated that between 1975 and 2015 more than 12,268,252 artifacts have been removed from sites in England and Wales alone by metal detectorists,[2] and Elizabeth Stone, a specialist in the archaeology of southern Iraq, has documented looting activities in southern Iraq between 2003 and 2007, larger in areal extent than all archaeological excavations ever conducted in the region combined. More recent research by Brodie and Contreras used Google Earth to identify looted areas at a single site in Jordan totaling more than 74,000 m^2.[3]

While new archaeological sites are being created constantly by living societies, those from any past period or society are both limited in number and subject to destruction or damage from a wide range of natural and human-induced processes. Even the act of archaeological excavation is inherently destructive, and hence archaeologists focus much attention on preserving, in situ, undisturbed archaeological material and in maximizing the information that may be gained from artifacts, collections, or samples already excavated. Most professional archaeological organizations have explicit, and all have implicit, ethical frameworks requiring that archaeologists work to minimize damage to the archaeological record.[4] Most archaeologists view that obligation as relating primarily to the preservation of intact sites or cultural resources, but equally important is the preservation of collections resulting from past research, and the maintenance of information relating to those collections that gives them meaning and significance. Properly curated, older collections can continually address new questions and be examined using new instrumentation and methods.[5]

CURATING ARCHAEOLOGICAL ARTIFACTS

The number of archaeological objects held in the world's museums and repositories is unknown, but the scale is enormous. Individual sites may produce tens of thousands of discrete, uniquely cataloged artifacts or objects, and the number of already-recorded sites is considerable, with an unknown number yet to be discovered. Japan has already

Encyclopedia of Library and Information Sciences, Fourth Edition DOI: 10.1081/E-ELIS4-120053293

Corporate Information–
Custody

recorded more than 440,000 archaeological sites within its borders, Denmark's *Kulturhistoriske Centralregister* has recorded more than 150,000 archaeological sites, with a schedule of 55,000 monuments (not including buildings), and New Mexico, USA, currently lists more than 100,000 recorded sites in its automated ARMS site registration system.[6] The U.S. Department of the Interior estimates its 2014 holdings at more than 44.9 million objects,[7] and this includes neither associated archival records (more than 122 million items relating to all scholarly disciplines, with the proportion dedicated to archaeology as yet unknown) nor major holdings administered by other arms of the federal government (e.g., the Department of Defense through, among others, the U.S. Army Corps of Engineers, or the Department of Agriculture through the U.S. Forest Service).

STANDARDS

Currently there are few standards for the curation of archaeological collections, and no generally recognized standard for the recording or interchange of information regarding archaeological collections. The irony of this situation is that archaeology has been concerned since its inception with creating order and meaning from the complex and often jumbled remains of the past that survive to the present day. In order to do so, archaeology depends upon *context*, the spatial, cultural, environmental, and temporal associations between objects. Probably the most important form of context is *provenience*, or the physical context in which an object was found. Objects without provenience have limited archaeological value, and many archaeological journals prohibit the first publication of such materials. These prohibitions reflect two concerns: (1) that validating objects recovered from looted or unknown contexts may lead to further site destruction and (2) that the inclusion of objects from unknown contexts may introduce either fakes or misattributed items into the scholarly literature in ways difficult to later remedy, biasing interpretations and creating false foundations on which later scholarship relies. Provenance, etymologically from the same root, generally refers to the chain of custody and goodness of title for objects or collections. The terms are sometimes confused, particularly by scholars in different disciplines that emphasize one concept at the expense of the other: Art historians privileging provenance will sometimes treat provenience as a subset of provenance; archaeologists privileging provenience will sometimes treat provenance as a special, postexcavation case of provenience. Both concepts are crucial for managing archaeological collections, with provenience being central to the utility of objects in making archaeological inferences and provenance being central to assessing claims for restitution, repatriation, and return of objects.

Probably the most broadly applied standard for managing archaeological collections in the United States is a set of federal regulations that govern the management of federally owned or administered archaeological materials, 36CFR79,[8] promulgated in 1990. They mandate levels of intellectual, environmental, and physical control over collections and related documentation, but for the most part these levels of control aren't clearly specified but instead must minimally correspond to changing professional standards within museums. In the United Kingdom the equivalent, and in most respects more detailed, set of guidelines is *Standards in the Museum Care of Collections: Archaeological Collections* originally prepared by the Museums & Galleries Commission.[9]

PROJECT DESIGN AND RECORDS

Management and curation of archaeological collections actually begins prior to fieldwork. The design of field projects plays a major role in determining the long-term research value of archaeological collections. Since archaeological collections include not only artifacts and other cultural material but also a range of environmental and lithostratigraphic materials, potentially including the soils, sediments, or matrix within which objects were recovered, all collections ultimately reflect sampling. Sampling in this sense assumes at least two forms: (1) sampling strategies determining which areas are surveyed, studied, or excavated and (2) recovery strategies determining what kinds of materials and samples are retained from those areas sampled. Since the absence of certain categories of material in a curated collection may represent either their absence from in situ deposits or a field decision not to collect those classes of material, documentation of the research design and data recovery plan is critical for understanding the material record.[10]

All archaeological projects generate collections, although in some cases the collections comprise only documents, photographs and records. Different kinds of survey or excavation projects employ a variety of techniques for recording the horizontal and vertical locations as well as the associations of objects, samples or measurements; this information is linked to objects by recording contextual information on the artifact, on the bag or other container housing the object or objects, or by assigning objects or groups of objects from the same context a lot number keyed to contextual information in project records, as well as by paper or electronic field notes and forms. Records also document how objects were consolidated or cleaned in the field, if applicable. Often, objects are assigned field numbers that link the object to its context and associated records; this represents a preliminary labeling system separate from identifiers used by the museum or repository.

ACQUISITIONS AND ACCESSIONS

Objects being considered for acquisition by an institution are generally examined relative to formal acquisition policies defining the kinds of material held by that institution. In some cases this is framed by the interests of the staff or stakeholders, in others by formal collecting plans or acquisition policies, and in others by the institution's mission statement or by legal mandate (e.g., governmental repositories). These policies also specify who within an organization has the authority to accept objects and who has authority or responsibility for different aspects of the acquisition process and subsequent management of the collection, and specify the conditions under which objects are accepted.[11] Usually, institutions will not acquire objects for which they cannot receive good title, which they do not expect to retain, or for which they cannot provide adequate care (although in some cases institutions may accession objects for which nominal title is retained by the government). For museums and repositories, at least, ultimate authority for acquisitions rests with the governing authority, as it is legally responsible for the institution's actions.

If objects are determined to be appropriate for acquisition, the next step is *accessioning*, which establishes legal custody and ownership of objects or collections, and documents the means by which an institution acquired the material. Depending on what kinds of information accompany the collection, it may also be the first step in establishing intellectual control over the material. While procedures vary widely, each accession generally represents one or more objects, including a whole collection from an archaeological project, from a single source, acquired by a single means of acquisition or transfer of title, and accepted on a single date. Accessioning establishes custody and title for one or more objects and is usually distinct from *cataloging*, which identifies each individual object and provides descriptive detail based on curatorial expertise. In larger institutions, at least, the registrar records accessions while the curators catalog objects. Some recording systems treat the accession and catalog number as identical, others use separate catalog and accession numbers, and some employ a hybrid system in which parts of the same numeric sequence convey accession and catalog information. Usually accession and/or catalog numbers are written on or affixed to the object. In some large museums the accession and catalog numbers are affixed to objects as barcodes or electronic tags, changing the mechanics of the registration process but not its underlying logic.

CATALOGING

Cataloging requires the identification and classification of an object and reflects the professional expertise and background of the curator. A variety of descriptive schemes and terminologies may be employed, and different archaeologists may employ differing cultural–historical frameworks, functional typologies, or nomenclatural standards.

Multiple standards for collections documentation have been proposed, and even institutions adopting one or another standard often modify the standard to better suit their individual needs. Probably the most widespread is the CIDOC International Core Standard for Archaeological Objects, developed by the Archaeological Sites Working group of the International Committee for Documentation (CIDOC) through the International Council of Museums.[12] For the most part, such standards define the kinds of information to be recorded, but not the terminology or classificatory frameworks to be employed. For the United Kingdom, Collections Trust UK provides an excellent outline of the registration and documentation process, along with links to resources for terminologies or lexicons for archaeological objects.[13] While useful for a given region, such resources are not for the most part transportable to other regions without substantial modification. Commonly employed terminologies include the Nomenclature for Museum Cataloguing (a revision of the Chenhall system)[14] and the Getty's Art and Architecture Thesaurus,[15] although neither is considered fully satisfactory by most archaeological curators. As there is no accepted standard within the discipline, the choice of terminology or lexicon is in some respects less critical than the consistent application of whatever set of terms is adopted, particularly now that most collections cataloging involves the creation of electronic records that facilitate synonymies and the cross-indexing of terms. Consistency benefits search and retrieval within an institution, and supports emerging efforts to allow searches across the collections data of multiple institutions.

Cataloging also involves identifying whence objects come. In addition to intrasite provenience information, it is also necessary to uniquely identify the site and geographic location from which objects originate. Unique site designations are normally provided by governmental agencies or ministries (in the United States by the state historic preservation officer or state archaeologist), but geographic names require some external authority or lexicon. Commonly used geographic authorities include the Geographic Names Information System for the United States and the Getty Thesaurus of Geographic Names for global place names.

METADATA STANDARDS

Metadata, or data about data, documenting the structure, format, and content of data fields or information, represents a crucial concern in establishing accessible and meaningful intellectual control over collections. Metadata standards in archaeology have not yet achieved their initial promise of allowing relatively source-transparent searches across multiple datasets. In part, this reflects the proliferation of metadata standards, and in part, a paucity of systematic application of existing standards. Most archaeological metadata is built on the Dublin Core, an ANSI (Z39.85-2001) and ISO (15836) approved standard widely used for resource recovery, with extensions to handle data of particular concern to archaeologists (see also ISO 21127, the ISO implementation of the CIDOC Conceptual Reference Model (CRM), which relates specifically to cultural heritage information).[16] In theory the Dublin Core represents the basal data used by a variety of disciplines, with discipline-specific extensions developed to meet the needs of specific communities of users. In practice the Dublin Core is generally mapped on to a subset of existing datasets that correspond to the Dublin Core elements. CIDOC, for example, provides mapping of the Dublin Core elements to the CIDOC CRM. The Darwin Core, a metadata standard paralleling the Dublin Core but aimed primarily at natural history and systematics or biological taxonomic collections, emphasizes georeferencing of objects rather than standardized place names.[17] In theory such metadata allow collaborations, gateways, and interoperable search platforms, but this promise has yet to be realized. For the most part, such searches remain limited to within either individual data archives such as The Digital Archaeological Record tDAR or the Chaco Research Archive[18] or within archaeological data publishing initiatives such as Open Context or the Comparative Archaeology Database (CADB).[19]

STORAGE AND CARE

Once cataloged, the curator and/or collections manager becomes responsible for the storage and care of the object. The logic by which storage areas are organized varies by institution, and may be based on catalog number, geographical area, or type of object. Certain classes of objects may be stored together because they share a need for specific environmental profiles (e.g., low relative humidity) or to reflect sensitivities of key stakeholders (e.g., human remains being stored separately from other collections). The creation and maintenance of appropriate storage conditions is a complex process of monitoring and controlling (or ameliorating) a variety of environmental parameters, while providing appropriate levels of physical security and access to the collections.[20]

There is, unfortunately, no ideal temperature or humidity for all objects; each kind of material has separate ideal environmental conditions, and in the case of compound or complex artifacts there may be contradictory ideal conditions for the constituent materials making up a single object. A hafted axe comprising a wooden handle, sinew lashings, organic glues or mastics, and a metal bit might be stored at low humidity to protect the metal from corrosion, but at the expense of the wood. Conversely, higher

humidity might maintain the dimensional stability of more hygroscopic materials like wood, but at the expense of the metal. And the ultimate goal is not merely preserving the constituent materials but the integrity of the artifact as a whole, and the ways they are combined to form that complex artifact.

For the most part, however, constancy in environments is crucial, and shorter-term variations in environment are more damaging than longer-term changes.[21] For museum collections absolute humidity is less relevant than relative humidity, since hygroscopic materials are affected by whether their ambient environments have little moisture relative to their capacity to hold moisture, in which case they absorb moisture from objects, or are nearer their maximum capacity for moisture, in which case they tend to release moisture into objects. This capacity is, in part, a function of temperature. From the standpoint of dimensional stability and direct damage, most objects are less sensitive to temperature changes than to humidity, although temperature and humidity are generally linked, and both natural processes of decay and the likelihood of pest infestations are accelerated at higher temperatures. Temperature and humidity levels are generally monitored using either analog thermohygrographs or multichannel digital data loggers. Other sources of environmental damage are airborne particulates and light, especially in the high-energy ultraviolet wavelengths. Light damage is cumulative, and bright lights for shorter durations do not generally cause greater damage than longer exposure to dim lights. Light levels are generally controlled by limiting the foot-candles of light to which objects are exposed, both by moderating lighting in display areas and by storing collections in closed cabinets, by sealing windows and by using ultraviolet filters on all light sources. Light levels are normally measured with a direct-reading UV light meter or less accurately with a visible light meter that estimates UV levels.

Pests are another threat to the integrity of collections and associated documentation; one (probably apocryphal) story from the American midcontinent describes rodents eating the labels off every bag from an entire archaeological field season, leaving the bags intact but with no record of their source or contents. Insects, particularly dermestid beetles, are also a significant and persistent threat to organic materials. Prevention is the preferred approach; most chemical treatments generally cause as many problems as they solve.[22] For insects, thermal treatment (freezing either at very low temperature or for a period longer than the life cycle of the pest) is a commonly employed treatment strategy, and anoxic environments can be used in some cases. In the past, a variety of hazardous materials including arsenic, strychnine, and mercury were used to treat for pests and to prevent mold or mildew; these treatments have resulted in some older collections now being classed as biohazards requiring special storage, handling, and disposal protocols. Treatments of any kind, whether to control for pests or to conserve and stabilize objects should be documented as part of the permanent record as they may inform subsequent management decisions or influence analytical testing.

Objects are also subject to physical damage, and a series of protocols on handling objects are available, varying in detail but similar in general form and practice.[23] Padding and supports for objects may be needed and can be constructed from nonacidic closed-cell foam or similar conservation-grade materials; all materials, containers, and cabinets should be inert and nonacidic.

In recent years, many institutions have adopted care policies that incorporate the concerns of descendant communities. The Museum of Indian Arts and Culture in Santa Fe, New Mexico, does not fully seal cases containing kachina dolls to allow them to "breathe," the Milwaukee Public Museum allows certain objects to be wrapped and bundled with tobacco or other ritually potent plants, and the storage facilities for the National Museum of the American Indian, part of the Smithsonian Institution, include a smoking room for the blessing of material objects by native groups. Such policies often require a compromise between museological and traditional approaches to care, and if adopted should be developed in close consultation with appropriate communities.

The physical security of collections should generally be provided by an overlapping combination of physical security (e.g., locks), electronic security (e.g., alarms or cameras), and human security (e.g., either guards or supervision by collections staff), although the degree of physical security is often contingent on both the available resources and the perceived level of threat.

ACCESS AND USE

Along with stewardship, one of the primary obligations of curators is to provide access to the collections for scholars and interested individuals or groups.[24] Stewardship and access require a balance, however, as increasing levels of access put objects at increasing levels of risk of all kinds. The movement and handling of objects increases the risk of physical damage, theft, variation in microenvironments, accumulated light damage, infestation, and generally increased wear and tear on objects. But at the same time, increased use adds to the value and intellectual potential of objects; since archaeological collections include both objects and their associated information, research adds to the collection by increasing the information associated with objects, and by clarifying the relations between objects. Access to collections is also crucial for consultation with descendant communities or other stakeholders with specific links to collections, as well as allowing opportunities for traditional forms of care including purification rites. Collections may also be loaned for study or other appropriate purposes. Past practice allowed a wide

range of loan conditions, but more recent practice generally requires that loans be for a period of 1 year or less (although loans may be annually renewable) and that the borrower be an institution rather than an individual comply with all conditions set by the lending institution, and provide a standard facility report to ensure that appropriate storage conditions can be provided. For research loans, most institutions require a copy of resulting publications or studies, and most museums and repositories loan only to institutions. Policies governing appropriate access, use, and loans should be listed in collections management policies or other documents approved by the institution's governing authority. As both usage of the web and acceptance of applicable metadata standards increases, access policies will need to address web-based access and attendant issues of fair use and copyright.

INTERPRETATION

One of the primary differences between museums and repositories is that museums have an explicit educational and interpretive mandate. As a result, curators may be involved in a range of exhibitions and interpretive programs. Exhibition or program design and museum-based informal science education are separate fields, each with their own journals, infrastructure, training, and guidelines for professional practice. Curators generally serve as content experts as part of design teams, although in smaller institutions curators may be asked to simultaneously serve in all of these roles. Programmatic use of collections must balance the preservation and protection of the objects and documents against the mission-defined value of public understanding and instruction. While allowing visitors to confront and be engaged by authentic objects is an important role of museums, in many programmatic contexts replicas may be equally effective as ancient artifacts and constitute a more appropriate option.

Museums play an important role in influencing how the public perceives cultures both extant and extinct, and potentially in reifying or rectifying stereotypical or naïve assumptions about past lifeways.[25] Interpreting the past is a complex enterprise, however, in which perceptions are an amalgam formed from at least three complex constellations of elements: (1) the past itself; (2) the viewpoints, attitudes, and assumptions of the curator selecting and interpreting the representations of the past; and (3) the viewpoints, attitudes, and assumptions of the visitor.[26] The ways in which these elements relate to one another is better documented than understood, and because the curator occupies a privileged position in influencing the ways in which the past is represented—and thus the ways in which the past intrudes into and influences the present— he or she must be particularly sensitive to the ways that their own biases and agendas influence the selection of objects, topics, and the narratives through which the past is presented and represented. Curators influence representations both by the objects or topics they select and by those they do not, as well as by how effectively they communicate concepts and information to visitors with different backgrounds, interests, and preferred learning modalities. Archaeological objects may be easier to present and interpret for visual learners, for example, whereas auditory and kinetic/tactile learners may face additional challenges in apprehending the core messages a given exhibition seeks to communicate.

In the past, exhibitions or programs were often designed as vehicles for curators to showcase artifacts and refine public sensibilities. Current best practices in museums call for program design beginning with a clearly defined set of take-home messages and with the didactic, pedagogical, and aesthetic design of the subsequent exhibition or program crafted specifically to communicate and reinforce these messages. Evaluation of the effectiveness of selected strategies is often necessary and usually results in both an iterative process of correcting weaknesses in the initial program design and ultimately in more robust and effective programs. Exhibit design thus includes not only aesthetic and pedagogical dimensions, but significant logistical, political, social, and ethical dimensions as well.

ETHICAL ISSUES

Curators of archaeological collections face a number of other ethical dilemmas. Some are common to all disciplines—making hard choices between competing needs or priorities in the face of limited resources, or choosing among optimal environments for storing complex artifacts made of multiple materials, each with a different optimal environment. Others are unique to archaeology, with five being worthy of mention here: (1) the so-called curation crisis; (2) orphaned collections; (3) deaccessioning and disposition of archaeological objects; (4) looting and the acceptance of unprovenienced antiquities; and (5) repatriation and restitution of objects or collections.

The enormous scale of archaeological collections worldwide is not mirrored in the availability of resources to maintain and properly curate them, nor to protect and document unrecorded or unexcavated sites. This has resulted in a "curation crisis," in which an increasing number of museums and repositories lack adequate space or staff to care for new collections irrespective of their importance or value, while others process new collections at the expense of bringing older collections up to acceptable standards of care and curation.[27] As stewards of cultural heritage, archaeological curators must assess whether they and the institution they represent can afford collections the necessary levels of care to ensure their integrity and security for years to come, and to meet new standards over time.

Not all archaeological collections are housed in institutions providing permanent care and support of objects. Many academic institutions generate significant archaeological collections over the professional lives of individual faculty members, but in many instances there is no mechanism in place to ensure adequate curation after the retirement or death of an individual. In other cases, institutions holding collections, but not viewing curation as central to their mission, decide at some point that that the costs of curation are unacceptably high, or the unit caring for collections is disbanded due to the vagaries of institutional funding or vision. All result in "orphaned" collections carrying with them not only the logistical and facility costs to institutions willing to offer them a permanent home, but also significant curatorial staff time to bring them to acceptable standards.[28] Recognizing this problem, some granting agencies and academic departments are requiring that curation arrangements be included in cultural resource project and academic research designs alike, and that necessary costs be included in project budgets.

All artifacts are not equally valuable in documenting the human past, and many scholars feel that only a portion of certain kinds of mass-produced or commonly encountered objects need to be preserved. Bricks from a historic site may reveal significant manufacturing and architectural information, but it is questionable whether every brick needs to be curated in perpetuity. Similarly, fire-cracked rock from prehistoric sites, or certain categories of undecorated body sherds from sites producing millions of such sherds in large-scale excavations, may reveal information that can be preserved from subsets of the mass of material encountered within a site. In some instances these issues are addressed through the project data recovery plan, which determines what kinds and quantities of objects are transferred to the museum or repository. In other cases, the issues must be addressed by the collecting institution, either by initially accepting only parts of a larger collection—in which case the status and future of the remaining parts of the collection are at best uncertain—or by selectively removing objects later in time. The pitfall of such removal is that innovative scholarship and future technical capabilities may transform categories of objects currently of little analytical or scholarly value into crucial pieces of evidence and accurately scrying the future is difficult for most students of the past.

Deaccessioning is the formal process by which an institution removes an object or objects from its collection. Most institutions have formal processes for deaccessioning requiring review and approval from multiple levels of authority—often more rigorous than those required to accession an object—and specific restrictions on the disposition of objects once deaccessioned. Many museums have policies allowing the sale of deaccessioned objects if the proceeds are used exclusively to acquire other objects for the collection (both as an ethical practice and because within the United States, museums are able to treat collections as nonfinancial assets excluded from capitalization if such practices are followed),[29] but the sale of antiquities is viewed as problematic by many within the discipline. In most cases, transfers to or exchanges with another peer institution are preferred methods of disposition. British museums have traditionally resisted deaccessioning of material, and in many parts of the world deaccessioning requires approval from appropriate governmental agencies or ministries. Within the United States, there are currently (July 2015) no guidelines under 36 CFR Part 79 to allow federal agencies or museums to deaccession and dispose of collections deemed of insufficient archaeological significance to warrant the continuation of permanent curation, although draft deaccessioning rules have been proposed by the National Park Service on multiple occasions.

Objects from looted contexts or otherwise lacking provenience generally have limited value for systematic research, but may nevertheless be works of considerable aesthetic or cultural merit. And in some instances, inherent qualities of the object may confer considerable scholarly importance on objects despite their uncertain pedigree. Site destruction in Iraq from 2003 to 2008 uncovered large numbers of cuneiform tablets whose contents have remarkable epigraphic and historical significance even if their original context cannot be reliably determined. Most archaeological organizations counsel against work with unprovenienced objects and forbid the first publication either of such objects or of research based on them, but this means that much information may be lost first through the loss of archaeological provenience, then again from loss of what information the resulting artifacts might offer. Some scholars find it difficult to reconcile that loss of information with their ethical obligations of stewardship, and question whether the validation of such finds by scholarly study will really increase rates of site destruction and looting, or further commercialize antiquities.[30] Such questions admit to no easy answers, although most professional organizations eschew unprovenienced objects for another reason as well—in the absence of detailed provenience data, it is easy for fakes or misattributed objects to mislead the unwary and jeopardize the integrity of future work based upon the shaky foundations offered by unprovenienced antiquities. Some institutions—primarily a few larger art museums—have expressed little concern for whether or not an object is from looted contexts or even whether their purchase of such objects may spur further looting. In their view, the aesthetic merit of the object outweighs both its questionable pedigree and the consequences resulting from its acquisition. Such approaches are generally condemned by scholarly and professional organizations as unethical and inappropriate.

While accessioning of collections involves an assertion of title by the museum, title actually represents a bundle of rights that have increasingly unraveled in past decades. Under the provisions of the Native American Graves

Protection and Repatriation Act of 1990 (NAGPRA), recognized tribes and native corporations may claim objects from museums if they fall within one of four defined categories: (1) human remains; (2) associated and unassociated funerary objects; (3) sacred objects; and (4) objects of cultural patrimony.[31] While museums may have held custody of these objects for a century or more, NAGPRA specified that museums did not receive good title to these objects because they were either inalienable or communally owned, and hence not subject to transfer of title by any individual. While NAGPRA has led to the return of many items from museums and repositories, it has also increased communication between repositories and native tribes, and spurred cooperative agreements between museums and descendant communities.

Claims by nation-states for objects looted from sites within their statutory boundaries have also increased in recent years, in part due to more aggressive cultural patrimony policies in source countries and the increased role of antiquities in nationalist ideologies and in part due to evolving legal standards for the applicability of the National Stolen Property Act (NSPA) of 1934 (as amended) to looted antiquities.[32] Under the so-called McClain doctrine (based on the 1979 case United States v McClain), foreign governments may invoke the NSPA if the objects were looted after the passage of an unambiguous and generally enforced cultural patrimony law in the country of origin vesting ownership of all antiquities in the state. Prior to this, the legal standing of either individuals or governments relative to unprovenienced artifacts was unclear, as in the absence of provenience information the harmed party having standing to bring suit was difficult or impossible to establish. While these details are specific to the United States, similar problems can be cited from most other developed nations; Britain continues to wrestle with Greece's demand for the return of the Elgin marbles, France with the return of a range of ethnographic objects to Native peoples, and Germany with claims for the return of the Amarna bust of Nefertiti to Egypt.

CONCLUSION

One reason that archaeological collections are the object of such contention is that they are building blocks for national and community identities, constructs that are themselves used to construct charters for present beliefs and legitimation of ideologies through the authority that rooting them in long-standing tradition confers. "The past is full of life, eager to irritate us, provoke and insult us, tempt us to destroy or repaint it," the Czech novelist Milan Kundera once wrote, adding "the only reason people want to be masters of the future is to change the past. They are fighting for access to the laboratories where photographs are retouched and biographies and histories rewritten."[33] Archaeological collections remain the clearest and most immediate record of worldwide cultural achievement and social change over the broad sweep of the human career. The legal, ethical, and procedural outlook of curators of archaeological collections has changed significantly over the last decade, and there is little reason to believe that the decades to come will be any less dynamic and demanding for the stewards of the past.

ACKNOWLEDGMENTS

I am grateful to Lana Coggeshall and Terry Childs for reading drafts of this entry and for their constructive criticisms. I am also indebted to members of the Museums, Collections and Curation Committee of the Society for American Archaeology (SAA), the SAA Ethics Committee, the Ethics Committee of the American Anthropological Association, and the AAM Ethics Task Force on Cultural Property for many productive discussions of the topics included here and to the *ELIS* editors and anonymous reviewers for their helpful comments.

REFERENCES

1. Atwood, R. *Stealing History: Tomb Raiders, Smugglers, and the Looting of the Ancient World*; St. Martin Press: New York, 2004; 221.
2. http://www.heritageaction.org.uk/erosioncounter/ (accessed July 2015).
3. Stone, E.C. Patterns of site looting in southern Iraq. Antiquity **2007**, *82* (315), 125–138; Brodie, N.; Contreras, D. The economics of the looted archaeological site of Bab edh-Dhra: A view from Google Earth. In *All the King's Horses: Essays on the Impact of Looting and the Illicit Antiquities Trade on Our Knowledge of the Past*; Lazrus, P.K., Barker, A.W., Eds.; Society for American Archaeology Press: Washington, DC, 2012; 9–24.
4. http://www.archaeological.org/pdfs/AIA_Code_of_Ethics A5S.pdf (accessed July 2015); http://www.sha.org/index. php/view/page/ethics (accessed July 2015); http://www. saa.org/AbouttheSociety/PrinciplesofArchaeologicalEthics/ tabid/203/Default.aspx (accessed July 2015); http://e-a-a. org/codes.htm (accessed July 2015).
5. Barker, A.W. Stewardship, collections integrity and long-term research value. In *Our Collective Responsibility: The Ethics and Practice of Archaeological Collections Stewardship*; Childs, S.T., Ed.; Society for American Archaeology Press: Washington, DC, 2004; 25–42.
6. Barker, A.W. Core databases: Anthropology. In *Museums: International Encyclopedia of the Social and Behavioral Sciences*; Smelser, N.J., Baltes, P.B., Eds.; Elsevier Science, Ltd.: Oxford, U.K., 2001; 5, 3240–3243.
7. Wilson, R. Chief Curator, National Park Service, personal communication July 2015.
8. Full text of the regulations is available at http://www.nps. gov/archeology/tools/36cfr79.htm (accessed July 2015); and a general discussion of its scope and role is at http:// www.nps.gov/nagpra/TRAINING/36-CFR-79_Overview.

pdf (accessed July 2015); see also http://www.nps.gov/ archeology/collections/laws_04.htm (accessed July 2015).
9. http://www.collectionstrust.org.uk/standards-toolkit/collec tions-care-standards (accessed July 2015). For Canada see http://www.historicplaces.ca/media/18072/81468-parks-s+g-eng-web2.pdf (accessed December 29, 2016).
10. The Council for the Preservation of Anthropological Records (CoPAR) has prepared guides for the preparation and preservation of various kinds of field and research records, including instructions for appointing a literary executor see http://copar.org/bulletins.htm (accessed July 2015).
11. As one example, see https://www.lsa.umich.edu/UMICH/ umma/Home/About/UMMA%20Policies/UMMA%20Poli cies%20and%20Procedures%20June%202011.pdf (accessed July 2015); http://www.nps.gov/museum/publications/hand book.html (accessed July 2015); In addition, museums accredited by the American Alliance of Museums must meet collections stewardship standards set by the AAM Accreditation Commission, http://aam-us.org/docs/ continuum/developing-a-cmp-final.pdf?sfvrsn=2pdf (accessed July 2015).
12. http://www.cidoc-crm.org/ (accessed July 2015).
13. http://www.collectionstrust.org.uk/standards-toolkit (accessed July 2015).
14. Blackaby, J.R.; Greeno, P. The Nomenclature Committee. *The Revised Nomenclature for Museum Cataloging: A Revised and Expanded Version of Robert G. Chenhall's System for Classifying Man-Made Objects*; Altamira Press: Walnut Creek, CA, 1995.
15. http://www.getty.edu/research/conducting_research/vocab ularies/aat/ (accessed July 2015).
16. http://dublincore.org/ (accessed July 2015); ISO 21127, http://www.iso.org/iso/catalogue_detail?csnumber=34424 (accessed July 2015).
17. For a summary of Darwin Core concepts, see http://www. gbif.es/ficheros/DarwinCoreV2.pdf (accessed July 2015).
18. https://www.tdar.org/about/ (accessed July 2015); http:// www.chacoarchive.org/cra/ (accessed July 2015).
19. http://opencontext.org/ (accessed July 2015); http://www. cadb.pitt.edu/ (accessed July 2015).
20. Cassar, M. *Environmental Management: Guidelines for Museums and Galleries*; Routledge: London, U.K., 1995.
21. Appelbaum, B. *Guide to Environmental Protection of Collections*; Sound View Press: Madison, CT, 1991.
22. Alpert, G.D.; Alpert, I.M. Integrated pest management: A program for museum environments. In *A Guide to Museum Pest Control*; Zychermna, L.A., Schrock, J.R, Eds.; Foundation for the American Institute for the Conservation of Historic and Artistic Works and the Association of Systematics Collections: Washington, DC, 1988; 169–173.
23. http://www.gov.mb.ca/chc/hrb/pdf/handling_museum_ objects.pdf; http://www.museumoflondon.org.uk/Resources/ e-learning/handling-museum-objects/ (accessed July 2015); see also Odegaard, N. *A Guide to Handling Anthropological Museum Collections*; Western Association of Art Conservators: Los Angeles, CA, 1991; see also Shelley, M. *The Care and Handling of Art Objects: Practices in the Metropolitan Museum of Art*; Metropolitan Museum of Art: New York, 1987.
24. Sullivan, L.P.; Childs, T.S. *Curating Archaeological Collections: From the Field to the Repository*; Altamira Press:

Walnut Creek, CA, 2003; Childs, S.T.; Corcoran, E. *Managing Archeological Collections: Technical Assistance.* Archeology and Ethnography Program; National Park Service: Washington, DC, 2000; available online atwww.nps.gov/archeology/collections/ (accessed July 2015).

25. see collected essays in Pearce, S.M. Ed., *Interpreting Objects and Collections*; Routledge: London, U.K., 1994; Barker, A.W. Exhibiting archaeology: Archaeology in museums. Ann. Rev. Anthropol. **2010**, *39*, 293–308.

26. Pearce, S.M. *Archaeological Curatorship*; Smithsonian Institution Press: Washington, DC, 1990.

27. Childs, S.T. Ed., *Our Collective Responsibility: The Ethics and Practice of Archaeological Collections Stewardship*; Society for American Archaeology: Washington, DC, 2004.

28. Bawaya, M. Archaeology: Curation in crisis. Science **2007**, *317* (5841), 1025–1026.

29. For private museums these limitations are specified in Statement of Financial Accounting Standards No. 116, http://www.fasb.org/pdf/fas116.pdf (accessed May 2008), and the governmental museum the equivalent statement is GASB-34. http://www.gasb.org/jsp/GASB/Document_C/GASBDocumentPage?cid=1176160029121&accepted Disclaimer=true (accessed December 29, 2016).

30. Owen, D. An archaeological dilemma. Science **2005**, *309* (5742), 1816.

31. http://www.nps.gov/nagpra/MANDATES/INDEX.HTM (accessed July 2015).

32. http://www2.mcdonald.cam.ac.uk/projects/iarc/culturewithoutcontext/issue%2013/gerstenblith.htm (accessed July 2015); see also http://www.archaeology.org/online/features/schultz/criminal.html (accessed July 2015).

33. Kundera, M. *The Book of Laughter and Forgetting*; Penguin: New York, 1981; 22.

Curating Natural History Collections

Kimberly S. Bostwick
Ecology and Evolutionary Biology, Cornell University Museum of Vertebrates, Ithaca, New York, U.S.A.

Abstract

Natural history collections are composed of objects of natural origin, most often of biological or mineral nature. These collections include organismal collections (like plant, insect, and animal collections) as well as anthropological and geological collections. Curating such collections requires establishing the longevity of the objects while maintaining their scientific utility. Maximum scientific utility is ensured by preserving with as little modification as possible the object, protecting the object against degradative processes, and managing the object information in an unambiguous and easy-to-retrieve way. While many specialists may be involved in curating larger, more active natural history collections, smaller collections are often managed by only one or two people. The goal of most natural history collections is to create and maintain a scientifically-useful research resource. The uses to which collections are put include educational, artistic, and scientific purposes. Several specific examples are given of how specimens have been used as unique informational resources for scientific research.

INTRODUCTION

The term "Natural History" refers to the study of all things natural, especially as it relates to the history of our planet and the lifestyles, features, and habits of animals and other organisms living on it. Natural history collections are those containing objects meant to assist natural historians, geologists, anthropologists, and biologists determine patterns through time. For the biologist this includes determining what species exist, where they existed, what their form is, and to the extent indicated by their form, what their habits are. For the geologist this might include describing the material composition of naturally-produced mineralized or earthen bodies, such as rocks or continents, and how these have been formed and changed through time.

Natural history collections include collections of natural, as opposed to manmade, objects. Typical objects in organismal collections include the bodies, body parts, or natural products thereof, of once living individuals. These individuals may be of literally any living species of plant or animal and are more often referred to as "specimens" (Fig. 1). Most natural history collections specialize in one natural, evolutionary group of organisms, or another, called taxa. Thus, we have herbaria, specializing in plant taxa, entomological collections specializing in insect taxa, vertebrate collections specializing in vertebrate taxa (such as birds, mammals, reptiles, fish), etc. Different taxa lend themselves to different subjects of study and different methods of research, and this, coupled with the shear numbers of species, necessitates professional specialization on some subset of living creatures, and explains the reason for natural history collection specialization.

Anthropological collections are a special type of organismal collection because the objects contained in these collections are often only from one or relatively few species (humans, or recent prehuman primate species), and often include significant holdings of nonbody objects (such as tools, clothes, or pottery).

Another common deviation from the rule of taxonomic specialization are paleontological collections, which tend to include diverse groups of organisms from many different taxa (i.e., plants, insects, invertebrates, and vertebrates), but which are united by their fossilized form. The mineralized form determines the kind of research that can be done on fossils, and the preservational needs of the objects in the collection. Thus, paleontology's departure from other natural history collections is caused by practical considerations—fossilized objects have shared physical features, and therefore break off naturally as objects with similar management needs.

Despite primarily being defined by the kinds of their objects, natural history collections also tend to have shared missions, goals, management needs, professionals, and activities. The mission in particular is somewhat distinctive from that of other types of collections. The mission of natural history collections is to ensure the long-term persistence of data-rich specimens specifically to facilitate future scientific studies. Given that the ultimate goal of natural history collections is to support the "current and anticipated needs of biological and/or geological science," the standard activities, and practices conducted in these collections may change through time as different technologies become available, and different scientific questions become of interest.

The orientation toward repeatable science also leads to the critical importance of data associated with natural

Encyclopedia of Library and Information Sciences, Fourth Edition DOI: 10.1081/E-ELIS4-120044101

Fig. 1 Sample natural history collection objects. A series of European stag beetles, *Lucanus cervus*, illustrates how animal specimens are often housed dry in unit trays with labels affixed. **Source:** Photo courtesy of James Liebherr, Cornell University Insect Collection.

history specimens. Since most natural history research involves fine-scaled measurement and placement of objects geographically or temporally, when and where an object was collected is critical contextual information, and is critical for the utility of a given specimen for most scientific studies. In the end, nearly as much time can be spent gathering and managing the data associated with physical specimens as is spent acquiring and managing the specimens themselves.

The following discussion is broken into three sections, each designed to add complementary perspective on what natural history collection are and how they function. The first part describes natural history collections from the perspective of bringing a new object into the collection and following it through the various activities involved in formally incorporating it into the collection. Part II views collections from a more human, managerial point of view, considering who works in collections and what their respective roles are. Finally, Part III reviews a small series of published scientific studies that together demonstrate how natural history collections are used to contribute to our understanding of the natural world. These examples hopefully serve to emphasize how science guides the fundamental principles behind the development and maintenance of natural history collections.

These discussions are structured around my experience curating organismal, specifically vertebrate, collections. However, it is important to acknowledge that different types of collection have their own specific traditions, needs, and practices.

CURATING COLLECTIONS I: THE SPECIMEN POINT OF VIEW

Below we explore the multifaceted activities that comprise curating a natural history collection. One of the most

tangible ways to understand what is involved in curating natural history collections is to follow a specimen through the process of collection, identification, preparation (the preliminary act of preservation), accession, cataloging, installation, long-term conservation, monitoring, and preservation, as well as administration of a specimen for use.

Collecting and Preparing

The "specimen" to which natural history curators constantly refer is typically the body, or body part, of an individual (Fig. 2). Occasionally, it may be a product of an individual (such as a bird's nest), the product of a group of individuals (such as a bees' nest), or be multi-individual (such as a clutch of eggs or a colonial organism), or any of a number of other, nonorganic, natural objects (crystals and rocks, for instance). For the purposes of this discussion we will imagine the body of a single individual organism.

The methods used to collect individuals depend on the type of organism. Collecting may involve simply picking or digging the individual up (as in fossils, plants, or some insects), or trapping (insects, fish, reptiles), netting (fish, birds, and bats), shooting (birds and mammals), or

Fig. 2 A natural history collection's type specimen. These three images are from one individual alcohol-preserved *Synodontis acanthoperca*, CU 89005 (this new species of catfish has no common name). **Source:** Photo courtesy of Thomas Vigliotta, Cornell University Museum of Vertebrates.

salvaging (finding dead) the specimen. Collecting is done to minimize damage to the specimen, and to maximize data collected with the specimen. Data can include: (1) minimally, when and where the specimen was collected; (2) the immediate habitat and social environment the specimen was collected in; and (3) any potentially relevant information that is present at the time of collection that will not be ascertainable from the specimen directly later on. The color of living tissues is a good example of a feature that often changes shortly after death, and is often impractical or impossible to preserve. Audio or video recordings, photographs, or notes can capture this associated specimen data.

For some organisms, preparation can happen at the time of collection (plants, insects, fish), in other organisms preparation may be labor intensive, in which case it is more efficient to separate the process of collection from the process of preparation.

For any given taxa, several "preparation types" are possible. Dry-preserved and fluid-preserved preparations are the most common. The basic principle behind dry preservation techniques is facilitating dehydration of the internal parts of the organism to retain the appearance of the external features. Thus, plant specimens can be dried to preserve vegetative patterns. Animal specimens may need to have their internal parts removed before being dried to preserve the exoskeleton, skin, and fur or feathers. Drying prevents bacteria-driven rot or decay, and hinders molding, which allows the external features—often already dry—to remain unmodified and available for study (Fig. 3).

Alternatively, specimens can be preserved in fluid. Fluid preparations prevent decay either by "fixing" or chemically altering, the tissue so that it is un-degradable by bacteria (i.e., formalin fixation), or, again, by dehydrating the specimen by removing the water while still keeping it in fluid (alcohol preservation, usually ethanol or isopropanol). These preparations are ideal for organisms with moist or thin skins (fish, reptiles and amphibians, and many aquatic invertebrates) and have the added benefit of keeping the internal organs, tissues, and structures intact. Fluid preservations often compromise the external appearance by wetting structures (feathers and fur) and colors of integument are often lost or modified.

The primary goal of all preparation techniques is to establish the longevity of the specimen and specific targeted features (determined by the method of preservation). Further efforts are made to standardize as much as possible the posture or shape of the individual to maximize information retrieval and ease of storage, and minimize likelihood of handling damage. Care is taken to minimize physical and chemical manipulation of the specimen with the goal of reducing the risk of removing or destroying potentially useful information.

Accessioning, Cataloging, and Installing

Once a specimen has been prepared, the next phase of curation is the management and long-term preservation of the collection objects and their data. Accessioning is the first step in the formal admittance of the specimen to the collection. Accessioning is a paper or computer-based process whereby a group of specimens entering the collection are recognized as a group united by their origin. The origin of the specimens may be as official as a collecting event or expedition in which a group of people travel to a specific place to collect a set of specimens, or as informal as the contents of a wildlife rehabilitator's freezer. Each accession is given a unique identifier, and correspondences, contact information, any associated specimen data, any applicable permits, etc. are held in a folder for each accession.

Determination, or identification and characterization, of a specimen is attempted before cataloging. In some cases this is a trivially easy task, as specimens coming into collections are often representatives of common and/or

Corporate Information–Custody

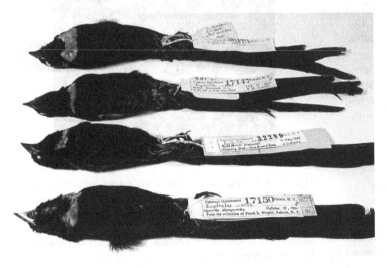

Fig. 3 Dry specimens with external features preserved. Here four *Euplectes ardens* specimens from the Cornell University Museum of Vertebrates are seen as they are in the collection, with plumage and external morphology available for study.
Source: Photo courtesy of Kim Bostwick, Cornell University Museum of Vertebrates.

easy to identify species. However, in some cases, especially in non-vertebrate groups of animals, determining the species identity of a specimen can be difficult, time consuming, and/or impossible. In these cases, the collectors and/or collection staff do their best to make as exact an identification as possible. Redeterminations can be done later when more information is available, or when an expert in a given group is available to examine the specimens.

Cataloging each of the individual specimens in an accession is the next step and achieves multiple critical functions. It results in the assignment of a unique, institution and collection-specific identifier (often a number) that will be used to identify the specimen for the rest of its term in the collection. Cataloging also results in the capture and standardization of the specimen data in a way that allows rapid and efficient generation of labels, reports, loan forms, etc. for any future activity related to that specimen. Once cataloged, a specimen may finally be considered a "curated" specimen of the collection.

Once cataloged, the specimen is ready to be installed into the collection itself. Collections are organized by species, with more closely related species being located near one another, or alternatively, alphabetically by species names according to major taxonomic groups. Within species, specimens are usually organized according to subspecies, and/or geographic locality of the specimen, and/or date information (Fig. 3). The practical reason for arrangement by species is size/preparation uniformity, and the nature of human inquiry that often seeks direct comparison of closely related things.

Long-Term Care: Housing and Monitoring

Once installed into the collection, specimen curation involves protecting the specimens from the degradative effects of their environments. Long-term care starts with the housing circumstances of the specimens. The building and rooms where the specimens are housed are literally and figuratively the building blocks upon which good curation rests. Ideally, the building will be designed or chosen as the first line of defense to protect the collections from light, water, excessive humidity and temperature fluctuations, and pests (usually insect, fungal, or rodent). This usually amounts to a tightly enclosed space with few windows, physically barricaded from any noncollection spaces (such as offices or hallways), with environmental controls.

Of perhaps equal or greater concern than the rooms in which specimens are housed, is the museum cabinetry or furniture into which specimens are placed. This furniture is chosen to further mitigate the same destructive forces the room is; light, humidity fluctuation, and pests, and to additionally protect from airborne dust particles and physical damage from exposure. Thus, in the case of dry specimens, cabinetry is sealed tightly against dermestid beetles

(a family of carpet beetles). In the case of fluid specimens, the specimens are housed in jars filled to their sealed tops with alcohol.

Inside cases, the materials directly surrounding the specimens are also critically important: buffered papers, archival ink, and inert building materials are used to minimize specimen deterioration. Acidic and basic materials can chemically alter the sensitive organic compounds of most organisms and are generally avoided.

Once a stable environment is established, from the materials touching the specimen most immediately, through to the rooms housing the collection, the last curatorial task is monitoring. Routine examination of specimens is required to ensure that the protective measures have not been compromised and to keep chaotic forces from reducing the high level of order that a specimen collection represents into disarray and deterioration.

Administering the Use of Specimens

Natural history collections exist to be used, and often use is the single greatest source of damage to collections. Thus, the goal of longevity and the mission of supporting research and education must be balanced.

Use has become more and more about using the data associated with the collections. Information requests use the data gathered in the database, and are strengthened by having specimens to "voucher," or verify by proxy, their legitimacy.

Other uses involve the direct examination of specimens for research. Some research aspires to describe patterns of diversity, and simply involves examining specimens visually, or with simple measuring devises such as calipers, spectrophotometers, etc. Other research requires "destructive sampling." In these cases use of the specimen involves a procedure that will irreversibly alter the specimen. This may be dissection of a fluid-preserved specimen, or a subsampling of tissues, such as skin or feathers. For destructive sampling, the value of the specimen as determined by its uniqueness or commonness, or overall physical or data quality, is weighted against the value or significance of the use (research vs. teaching), and against how destructive the procedure will be. Severely destructive sampling of a valuable specimen requires a more stringent justification then minor sampling of a common or data-less specimen. Whether or not to allow destructive sampling is a judgment usually made on a case-by-case basis by the collection's curator.

Data and Database Management

Increasingly, database management has become an important part of specimen curation. Individual collections manage their own data using either off-the-shelf generic database software or software customized for use by natural history collections. These databases allow the creation of electronic collection management tools for creating reports, labels, and for answering specimen queries quickly and efficiently. Collections can also make their specimen data, or some subset of it, available over the internet for general queries regarding collection holdings or data associated with specimens. Several initiatives are allowing the federation of collections data from numerous institutions. This allows the specimen data from multiple institutions to be searchable from a single portal, and mapping tools are increasingly being used to visualize geographic ranges using data from the collective natural history collection's holdings.

CURATING COLLECTIONS II: THE ADMINISTRATIVE POINT OF VIEW

Another useful way to break down these and other activities related to curating natural history collections is to consider each of the professionals, amateurs, and students who complete the tasks described above. The discussion that follows describes one commonly conceived division of the titles and divisions of responsibilities used in natural history collections (that most familiar to me), but it is important to be aware that other institutions may have different titles for the same roles, or a different breakdown of how duties are divided and shared. Nonetheless, natural history collections may have any of a number of the following people associated with them: curators, collection managers, collectors, preparators, archivists, conservators, student assistants, and volunteers. Alternatively, curation may be done by one or very few people. Either way, between them, these people strive ensure the above described curatorial activities are being done, and being done well.

Curator

Given that natural history collections are developed as a resource for scientists, the highest administrative role within a natural history collection is held by the curator. The curator is most often a scientist who uses specimens in his or her own research, has experience in scientific collections, and also has a broad and deep knowledge about the diversity and biology of the taxa held in the collection he or she is responsible for. Because the practice of science changes so rapidly, a curator must be in touch with how specimens are likely to be used, and a practicing scientist is in the best position for maintaining the appropriate perspective for guiding curatorial decisions and practices.

Like all professionals in natural history collections, the curator typically performs many activities. These can be organized into several sets of tasks. I here consider these as fulfilling each of 4 roles, that of: (1) a professional "taxologist"; (2) a practicing scientist; (3) an educator; and (4) an administrator.

In the role of the taxologist, the curator acts as the knowledgeable specialist about the various biological features and diversity of the group of plants or animals in the collection curated. As such, he or she is best equipped to strategize about collections growth, selecting the species and specimens of greatest interest for addition to the collection. The curator's active place in the larger scientific community allows him or her the social and opportunity-driven resources to "acquire" such specimens. Once acquired, judgment for "identifying" and "organizing" the specimens using the most up to date information is critical.

As a practicing scientist the curator has a unique perspective on what specimen features are important to preserve to maintain a specimen's scientific usefulness. For instance, in Ornithology, the depth of the bill is a common measure oftentimes used to distinguish among species or populations of birds. Thus, the curator will make sure newly trained preparators pay special attention to make the correct alignment of the mandibles and ensure complete closure of the mouth during specimen preparation.

The educational and administrative roles of a curator involve less direct interaction with the collections themselves. In their educational roles, curators often give talks or seminars, guide tours, or otherwise host activities meant to promote not only knowledge in different biological areas but also the value of collections themselves. This may or may not involve the production of exhibits.

In addition to overseeing the other members of the curatorial team, one of the primarily administrative ways in which a curator curates his or her natural history collection may be through grant writing and planning to enhance the environment the specimens are housed in, or expand the collections themselves. This can include everything from reorganization of the collection according to modern ideas about organismal relationships, to the purchase of new specimen cabinetry, to planning new collection building solutions, or the funding and arrangement of a major collecting expedition.

Finally, the last major administrative contribution of the curator is the negotiation of the terms of use of specimens. Keeping in mind that the mission of the collection is to serve science, and use always entails the risk of specimen damage, immediate and future use needs must be balanced by judging potential specimen damage or consumption against scientific merit of a given project, and the rarity or uniqueness of the specimen in question.

Collection Manager

The Collection Manager is the central figure in the day-to-day and hands-on aspects of the collections. His or her duties include technical, for lack of a better word "custodial," managerial, and educational roles.

On a daily basis a collection manager will be accessioning specimens, preparing them, cataloging them for installation into the collection, and/or overseeing student or volunteer assistants completing these activities. He or she will also be monitoring and ordering curatorial materials necessary for running the collection.

The collection manager has a suite of more irregular duties as well. For instance, collecting tends to occur in sporadic bouts, since it must be conducted outside the office and usually requires some planning. There are meta-specimen responsibilities as well such as making sure the collection labels are accurate, and also verifying the long-term protective measures being taken, in the collection are effective. The collection manager usually removes specimens from the collections to display for visiting classes, or to fill out and mail the loans approved by the curator.

Finally, one major and increasingly complex role assumed by the collection manager is the management of the various permits needed to maintain a functional collection and to allow legal collection and transport of the plants and/or animals of interest. Depending on the types of organisms held in the collection, this may indeed be a significant sink of time and energy.

Specialists: Collectors, Preparators, Archivists, and Conservators

Occasionally individuals are associated with natural history collections whose sole role is to collect and prepare new specimens for addition to the collection. These are often loose arrangements or affiliations of mutual benefit to the collecting/preparing individuals and the institution in which they deposit their materials. The donating individuals get an institutional affiliation, and the recipient collection gets new specimens for little cost. This arrangement was more common historically when large-scale collecting was more commonplace and full-time collecting was a viable profession.

Additionally, some larger museums, when they house many individual natural history collections, hire professional archivists or conservators whose job it is to research the practices and materials used within collections. Their goal is to make knowledge-based recommendations that will increase the longevity of the collection's specimens.

Assistants: Students, Interns, and Volunteers

Much of the work involved with curating collections is interesting and, with a little training, entirely doable by novices. This means that student trainees, interns, and volunteers can and do contribute significantly to the hands-on work done to curate natural history collections. From typing and printing labels, to preparing, installing, and even cataloging specimens, these collections assistants often account for a significant proportion of the curatorial man-hours required to maintain a well-curated natural history collection.

CURATING COLLECTIONS III: USES, SIGNIFICANCE, AND VALUE

As time has passed the primary uses, significance, and value of natural history collections has expanded. In some cases, collections are still working tirelessly on the original goals of natural history collections; documenting the diversity of species on the planet, where they live, and what they look like. For instance, Fig. 2 shows the "holotype," or the original species-name-bearing individual of *Synodontis acanthoperca* on which the species' original description was wholly or partially based. Botanical and invertebrate collections in particular still occupy this unique, critical role in the foundation-building tasks of alpha taxonomic descriptions and inventories.

In all organismal natural history collections now— including the relatively more well-known vertebrate groups, like birds and mammals—data and specimens are being used in new ways for ecological and evolutionary studies asking new kinds of questions. Below is a small set of published scientific studies using, in this case, bird skins, in nontraditional ways. These examples illustrate new uses of natural history collection specimens.

Using Specimens for Research: Documenting Changes in…Reproductive Physiology

When Peregrine Falcons' numbers were crashing in the 1950s, there were anecdotal observations of crushed eggs being found in nests, but it was difficult to know the significance of these observations. In 1968, a paper was published in *Science* describing the results of a study comparing the eggshell widths of 1729 birds' eggs.[1] The eggs, held in 39 different natural history collections, were collected across nearly 80 years of time, from six different species from all over the United States. For 57 years, the average weight and shell width of Peregrine Falcons in California were constant, then, between 1947 and 1952, eggshell weights dropped precipitously by 18.9%. Similar patterns were found in Osprey eggs, Bald Eagle eggs, and Peregrines from other parts of the United States. Where Peregrines had already been extirpated in the East, egg shells "had become" up to 26% thinner. Documentation of this dramatic change, and being able to pin it down to a very specific time period, was critical in pinning down the cause of the problem; the use of chlorinated hydrocarbons like DDT became widespread in the United States in 1946. This study became a classic example of how natural history specimens could contribute to our understanding of how animals were changing, and why.

Population Structure

A recent study of the federally endangered Marbled Murrelet used a method called age-ratio analysis to determine how the proportion of juvenile to adult birds varied from year to year.[2] Juveniles have different plumages from adults, and analysis of 170 Marbled Murrelet specimens collected off the coast of California between 1892 and 1922 indicated proportionally more young birds then adults. This information allowed inference of what the rates of reproduction and adult survivorship were around the turn of the century. The researchers discovered that the rates of adult survivorship are the same now as they were then. However, the rates of reproduction have dropped eight to nine fold; the relative number of young individuals have decreased dramatically in these birds, and this is likely responsible for the declining populations of Marbled Murrelets.

Trophic Level of a Predator

The relative proportion of Carbon and Nitrogen isotopes in feathers can tell us about what a bird was eating at the time it was growing its feathers, and therefore how "high" it feeds on the food chain. Another study on Marbled Murrelets using isotopes extracted from the feathers of museum specimens has shown that historically, young Murrelets where able to exist as higher-level predators in their environments then they can now.[3] Now they appear to be subsisting more on smaller prey items then on the sardine fishes they used to flourish on, before overfishing caused dramatic declines in sardine and other small fishes.

Symmetry and Ecological Stress

In animals where the right and left sides are mirror images of each other, like ourselves, high levels of symmetry are achieved and maintained throughout development. However, in more stressful developmental circumstances, we are more likely to have small deviations from perfect symmetry. In this way, one might determine if a group of animals is "stressed" by carefully measuring the degree of symmetry of its individuals. One study compared the lengths of the right and left leg bones in 133 specimens of six species of birds collected in an unbroken, undisturbed forest in Kenya between 1934 and 1948, with the same species netted and measured in the same forest plots in 1996–1998, after the forest had become highly fragmented and degraded. The contemporary birds in the most degraded plots of forest were four to seven times less symmetrical then their 1940s counterparts from museums, indicating although the species were still surviving in these forests, they may well be living life on "the edge."[4]

Genetic Diversity

A suite of studies have been published using DNA extracted from the toes of natural history specimens to determine the genetic diversity of bird populations decades ago and compare them with populations today.[5,6] Prairie Chickens in particular have been the subjects of studies that have shown allelic diversity is dropping in these populations, approaching levels reached by Heath Hens prior to their extinction.[7] These studies have further shown that genetic studies of modern populations alone cannot always accurately infer historical levels of diversity.[8]

Ecological Niche during Speciation

Not all studies of natural history specimens focus on changes being wrought by man and occurring in the last century. Insight to far more general processes, such as speciation, can be obtained from specimens as well. This is highlighted in a study where museum specimen data for mammals, birds, and butterflies was used to examine sister-species pairs for patterns of similarity.[9] "Sister species" are species who are each other's closest relatives. As each other's closest relatives, sister species tell us something about what changed when speciation happened. One model of speciation suggests that species become adapted to different environments and that is what causes or drives speciation. If this is true, we would expect the habitats of sister species to be demonstrably different in some ecological factor. Using sophisticated artificial intelligence algorithms, with detailed mapping of environmental parameters and massive amounts of specimen data drawn from multiple natural history collections, scientist were able to show that most often, sister species lived in environments that were completely co-habitable to one another, with no sign of ecological separation. Using this result they concluded in many circumstances it is simply vicariance—or being physically separated by a barrier for some period of time—and nonadaptive forces that drive speciation in many species.

CONCLUSIONS

Natural history collections are as diverse as the natural objects curated in them, but share the function and goal of advancing scientific research. The curatorial traditions and practices within any given collection are determined by the nature of the objects curated, and guided by the research questions likely to be asked. A diversity of professionals can share the various curatorial duties, or in the case of small or less-active collections, a single person may aspire to manage the collections. In any case, the value of collections' object tend to increase with time as they become increasingly rare vouchers of individuals from places and times that have changed or ceased to exist.

The examples discussed in Part III serve to highlight the diversity of ways in which even one type of collection (bird dry skins) are being used for science. Any type of natural history collection could generate an equal list of diverse and important scientific uses. It is worth noting that for most of these studies, the specimens used were collected decades before DNA, or stable isotopes, fluctuating asymmetry, etc., were discovered as research tools, and decades before pesticides or habitat changes like overfishing existed to have their effects studied. Thus, no framework for asking the questions answered in these studies existed at the time the specimens were collected. This highlights the unique value of natural history collections as archives of information, and this in turn guides the principles and practices therein.

REFERENCES

1. Hickey, J.J.; Anderson, D.W. Chlorinated hydrocarbons and eggshell changes in raptorial and fish-eating birds. Science. **1968**, *162*(3850), 271–273.

2. Beissinger, S.R.; Peery, M.Z. Reconstructing the historic demography of an endangered seabird. Ecology. **2007**, *88*(2), 296–305.

3. Becker, B.H.; Beissinger, S.R. Centennial decline in the trophic level of an endangered seabird after fisheries decline. Conserv. Biol. **2006**, *20*(2), 470–479.

4. Lens, L.; van Dongen, S.; Wilder, C.M.; Brooks, M.T.; Matthysen, E. Fluctuating asymmetry increases with habitat disturbance in seven bird species of a fragmented afrotropical forest. Proc. Roy. Soc. London. B. **1999**, *266*, 1241–1246.

5. Johnson, J.A.; Dunn, P.O.; Bouzat, J.L. Effects of recent population bottlenecks on reconstructing the demographic history of prairie-chickens. Mol. Ecol. **2007**, *16*(11), 2203–2222.

6. Bouzat, J.L.; Lewin, H.A.; Paige, K.N. The ghost of genetic diversity past: Historical DNA analysis of the Greater Prairie Chicken. Am. Nat. **2006**, *152*(1), 1–6.

7. Johnson, J.A.; Dunn, P.O. Low genetic variation in the Heath Hen prior to extinction and implications for the conservation of prairie-chicken populations. Cons. Gen. **2006**, *7*(1), 37–48.

8. Larsson, J.K.; Jansman, H.A.; Segelbacher, G.; Höglund, J.; Koelewijn, H.P. Genetic impoverishment of the last Black Grouse (*Tetrao tetrix*) population in the Netherlands: Detectable only with a reference from the past. Mol. Ecol. **2008**, *17*(8), 1897–1904.

9. Peterson, A.T.; Soberon, J.; Sanchez-Cordero, V. Conservatism of ecological niches in evolutionary time. Science. **1999**, *285*, 1265–1267.

Custody and Chain of Custody

Bernadette G. Callery
School of Information Sciences, University of Pittsburgh, Pittsburgh, Pennsylvania, U.S.A.

Abstract

Custody, the holding of records and objects in archives and museums for security and preservation reasons, has been a fundamental principle of collections management in those institutions. Having an unbroken chain of custody, that is, being able to accurately identify all the individuals and organizations that have owned these items since they were created, has been considered as an essential evidence of the authenticity of the object and supports the legality of its transfer from one owner to the next. However, legal custody does not necessarily imply legal ownership. In the late twentieth century, the usefulness of custody as a management principle has been challenged in museums by repatriation claims and in archival collections by replevin and the need to both preserve the authenticity and integrity of electronic records and to guarantee access to both paper and electronic records over time.

INTRODUCTION

Custody, the act of holding archival records and museum artifacts for purposes of preservation and security, has long been an important principle in the collection management practices of both archives and museums. Traditional definitions of custody combine physical possession with the assumption of appropriate care of those collections. Having custody of an object also implies controlling access to it. Public museums and archives typically operate under the mandate that their collections are held in trust for the public good. The rationale for maintaining such public collections of objects and documents is to preserve the authentic evidence of the cultural and artistic diversity of human endeavor and to protect those materials from damage or loss. Access to these collections is considered a public benefit, an attitude that museum historians trace to the Enlightenment. However, in some collections, preservation and access can be seen as mutually incompatible goals, as even careful handling can place fragile materials at risk. Such tensions can result in restricted access, although such restrictions can also be based on other considerations, such as the terms of the donor agreement or institutional policy on access to intellectually rather than physically sensitive materials.

With the increasing professionalism of museums and archives, codes of ethics have been developed that support standard practices of collection, acquisition, preservation, and interpretation. Awareness of these codes of ethics and their application in collections holding cultural heritage materials is critical to a consideration of custody as they reflect changing attitudes toward their validity of claims to cultural property, particularly that owned by indigenous, colonized, or conquered peoples. Writing on this change of focus, Brown notes that prior to the late 1980s "museum curators, archivists, and anthropologists had rarely worried about whether the information they collected and managed should be treated as someone else's property."[1]

One widely cited ethics code that deals with the acquisition and care of collections is that of the International Council of Museums (ICOM), which notes that "Museums that maintain collections hold them in trust for the benefit of society and its development." The commentary on this ethical standard specifically states that collections should not be acquired without an assurance of valid title or otherwise illegally acquired. Section 2.3 additionally establishes the value of securing and maintaining provenance information, noting that "Due diligence in this regard should establish the full history of the item from discovery or production."[2]

The ICOM Code of Ethics additionally identifies international legislation designed to protect cultural heritage materials, including the 1970 United Nations Educational, Scientific and Cultural Organization (UNESCO) Convention on the Means of Prohibiting and Preventing the Illicit Import, Export, and Transfer of Ownership of Cultural Property. With over 100 signatories, this legislation and its associated national implementations, such as the U.S. Convention on Cultural Property Implementation Act of 1983, form the basis for the international control of import restrictions of cultural objects. While much of the international legislation related to establishing ownership and custody of collections brought into museums and archives deals with art objects, natural history collections are also covered by the Convention on International Trade in Endangered Species of Wild Fauna and Flora (CITES), passed in 1973 and implemented in the United States through the U.S. Endangered Species Act. CITES protects species threatened by international trade by requiring permits issued by the source country for the export of CITES-listed species.

Encyclopedia of Library and Information Sciences, Fourth Edition DOI: 10.1081/E-ELIS4-120044657

Within the museum community, provenance research documents an object's chain of custody, accounting for the complete history of ownership of the object prior to its arrival at the museum. Anthropological collections use the term provenience to define the object's specific geographic location of origin; natural history collections use the term locality to identify the specific geographic location where the organism was collected. Documentation can take the form of field notes, photographs, site plans, collection permits, correspondence with donors and dealers, bills of sale or deeds of gift or conservation notes, all of which may be housed separately from the objects, often in the institution's archives or registrar's files. Within the archival community, the term provenance, or the respect des fonds, refers to the principle that records of different origins are to be kept separate in order to preserve their different contexts.

Once in the custody of the museum, it was assumed that the object would be protected against any further undocumented alteration or damage. The goal of museum provenance research was to identify those previous owners and confirm the circumstances of the transfer of ownership.

In many cases, identification of that sequence of owners substantiates the identity of the object itself, by locating it in specific historical times and places. A study of an object's provenance can also be used to invalidate the claims of a museum's ownership of the item, if sufficient evidence can be found to indicate that the object was obtained illegally. Since the 1998 report of the Association of Art Museum Directors Task Force on the Spoliation of Art during the Nazi Era, modern art museum provenance research has been primarily focused on the restitution of artworks confiscated during the Nazi Era (1933–1945).[3] This interest in provenance research, with its emphasis on identifying gaps in the chain of custody or items that have passed through the hands of "red-flag" dealers, those who were known to have been in collusion with the Nazis, has resulted in an increase of publicly available information about the provenance of artworks. Many museums have contributed extensive provenance information to the collaborative Nazi-Era Provenance Internet Portal Project sponsored by the American Association of Museums.[4]

The validity of American museums' stewardship of objects of cultural patrimony of Native Americans was addressed by the 1990 U.S. law, the Native American Graves Protection and Repatriation Act (NAGPRA). The purpose of this act was to protect Indian burial sites from further looting and provides a legal mechanism by which descendants of culturally affiliated tribes could request the return of human remains and sacred objects from the collections of federally funded U.S. museums. The ongoing debate has focused on the potential loss of access to these objects for scientific study versus the return of illegally obtained objects, many considered sacred or communal property and therefore not transferable outside the tribe. However, the number of objects actually repatriated has been less than what critics of the law feared, with many tribes choosing to leave these objects in the custody of the museums, although sometimes imposing more specific requirements on their storage, limiting public access to these objects, and restricting their use in exhibitions.[5]

CUSTODIAL HISTORY AND POST-CUSTODIAL APPROACHES

Donors to both archives and museums often believe that their contributions will be maintained in perpetuity under controlled circumstances, reinforcing the assumption that such custody confers lasting value on the object or collection of documents. The term "museum quality" implies that these specific items are recognized as highly representative, particularly fine examples, or otherwise worthy of special distinction and care because of their association with notable individuals or organizations. In the archives community, the term custodial history is used to describe the record of the list of successive organizations or individuals who have held these materials since their creation and can refer to both physical and intellectual possession. Institutional archives, including governmental records, are those records identified as having lasting value to provide accountability for the organization's actions toward the community it serves or for evidence of the business process or transactions, but are not in active use by the creators of the records. The practice of moving these records from the creating offices into the archives frees space for the records documenting current activities, and assures the safety and continuing availability of those materials designated as archival by protecting them against damage and unconsidered dispersal. Historical theories of custody in archives are based on the writings of European and British archivists responsible for limited numbers of decentralized governmental records dealing with land ownership and taxation based on property rights. However, with an increasing quantity of the business processes of organizations created and maintained electronically, a post-custodial theory of archives has emerged.

Recognizing the ephemeral nature of electronic records, post-custodial archivists believe that they cannot wait for the deposit of the records as delivered by the creating agency, but must be proactive, becoming involved with the agency from the earliest stages of records creation, ideally even before the record is created, in order to advise on which records are to be maintained permanently and to determine how best to capture the context in which the records were created and used. Solutions posed by the post-custodialists include leaving the records identified as having archival value in the offices and computer systems of the creating agencies rather than transferring them into the separate physical custody of the archives. The significant difference of post-custodial theory is that the responsibility of the archivist is imbedded in the ongoing management of the records of the organization rather than being an external custodian of records housed in a centralized repository to which they are delivered by the creator. Opponents to this distributed custody approach argue that this practice is counter to the traditional responsibilities of archivists and could lead to unauthorized removal or alteration of the records. Supporters of this approach state that it is impossible to maintain electronic records outside of the social and software context of the creating business practice. Post-custodial theories of archives management require a more proactive involvement of archivists in the design of information systems and their deployment and maintenance through institutional retention policies.

In these professions in which the term custody is employed, there is an expectation that objects held in custody will be protected and preserved for the common good, but not necessarily owned by the museum or archives. The lack of physicality of electronic records presents additional preservation concerns as well as the ongoing management of intellectual property.

CUSTODY AS APPLIED TO MUSEUMS

Museums often refer to their responsibility for objects in their collection as stewardship, which implies the preventative care of custody as well as the responsibility for holding the materials in trust for the public good. The American Association of Museum's 2000 Code of Ethics contains the following statement on the acquisition and retention of collections.

> The distinctive character of museum ethics derives from the ownership, care, and use of objects, specimens, and living collections representing the world's natural and cultural common wealth. This stewardship of collections entails the highest public trust and carries with it the presumption of rightful ownership, permanence, care, documentation, accessibility, and responsible disposal.[6]

The apparent permanence of the museum's custody contributes significantly to the public trust in museums. This trust can be undermined by a lack of public understanding of the process of deaccessioning, when a museum chooses to reverse its original decision to accept an object into its permanent collection. While refinements are made in a museum's collecting policy, as well as the inability of individual museums to adequately care for certain types of collections do present legitimate reasons to deaccession items, the process of deaccessioning often provokes negative public comment, which can damage the museum's position as an organization deserving of the public trust. Removal of an object from the museum's custody is seen

as devaluing that object and, by association, the donor.[7] Some commentators identify the increase in media and public concern about museum deaccessioning practices, beginning with the highly publicized deaccessions from the Metropolitan Museum in New York in the 1970s, with an increased demand for "access to records documenting the history of ownership of museum collections [which] also grew as the right of museums to continue to have custody over certain objects was challenged."[8]

Ideally, the legal status of the transfer of ownership and its implications for the legality of ownership are documented in carefully written and retained donor agreements and accession records. While museum curators, directors, and boards may be involved in the acquisition of museum objects and subsequently generate records pertaining to that transaction, those records are typically maintained by the museum's registrar.[9] As these records may be added to, and amended over, the lifetime of the object in the museum and may even outlast the object itself, these collection records are considered continuously current and often remain in curatorial or departmental offices rather than being removed to the separate custody and control of the museum's archives.

CHALLENGES TO CUSTODY IN MUSEUMS: REPATRIATION REQUESTS

In the United States in the late twentieth century, a growing number of Native Americans had been approaching museums, requesting the removal of objects of cultural significance and human remains from museum exhibitions and research collections and petitioning for the return of these materials to the custody of the associated tribes. Many of these materials were collected a century earlier in the belief that these tribal communities were in decline and would require an accelerated mode of collecting similar to that of salvage archaeology in which extreme measures are taken to collect in bulk when a cultural landscape is in immediate danger of destruction. The apparent need for speed, the market value of these objects of material culture, and the lingering belief that these indigenous peoples were uncivilized and primitive led to abuses that further threatened the continuation of these communities. Passed in 1990, the NAGPRA covers all U.S. museums receiving federal funds, with the Smithsonian Institution's United States National Museum of the American Indian covered under an equivalent legislation, the 1989 National Museum of the American Indian Act. The highly structured process of repatriation mandated by NAGPRA, which puts the burden of discovering documentation on the holding museum rather than the claimants, recognizes that legal custody does not necessarily imply legal ownership. While the law was intended to provide for the repatriation of material acquired by museums in the recent past, the most contested application of the law was the disposition of the skeleton discovered in Kennewick, Washington, in 1996, now dated to be over 9000 years old. A number of local tribes claimed the skeleton for reburial, stating that they were descendants of tribes that had occupied the area in the past, and were countered by a group of anthropologists and archaeologists who wished to maintain the skeleton's availability for continued scientific study.[10,11]

While there is a formal process of U.S. law governing the return of human remains and sacred objects to the tribal descendants, there are not similarly clear or well-defined laws addressing the return of antiquities, even when there is strong evidence that they had been illegally acquired. Arguments that the preservation of cultural treasures taken as the spoils of war was better handled by the conquering nation date back to the Napoleonic campaigns, although many of the objects exhibited in the Louvre were returned to the countries from which they were despoiled under the terms of the 1815 Congress of Vienna. The international agreement that forms the basis for modern repatriation requests of objects of cultural patrimony is the 1970 UNESCO Convention on the Means of Prohibiting and Preventing the Illicit Import, Export, and Transfer of Ownership of Cultural Property.[12]

Demands for the return of the "Elgin Marbles," marble sculptures removed from the Parthenon in Athens, Greece, between 1799 and 1803 by Thomas Bruce, seventh earl of Elgin while he was the British ambassador to Constantinople and then sold to the British Museum in 1816, are the most highly publicized of these international museum custody battles. Preservation was one of the justifications for the removal of these artifacts from their original locations and Elgin's removal of these sculptural elements can be seen as an early example of salvage archaeology. Although Elgin had paid for the privilege of removing the sculpture through negotiations with the local Ottoman occupying force, popular outcry addressing the cultural dislocation began almost immediately with their arrival in London with satirical references in several poems by English poet Lord Byron.

While the number of claims for the return of cultural property is increasing, particularly in the area of antiquities, some have been resolved to the satisfaction of the claimants, such as the return of such objects as the Euphronios Krater. Negotiations were concluded in 2006 for the Metropolitan Museum's return of this sixth century BC bowl signed by the Greek painter Euphronios to the Republic of Italy in 2008 as part of its cultural heritage. As noted in a recent overview of cultural property laws, "The debate is over not only who owns the past, but in whose hands the stewardship of cultural heritage should lie."[13] Some archaeologists claim that more restrictive import and export laws will make the black market less profitable and stem the tide of cultural heritage items from artifact-rich but resource-poor nations.

CUSTODY AS APPLIED TO ARCHIVES

Historical theories of custody in archives are based on the writings of European and British archivists responsible for decentralized governmental records dealing with land ownership and taxation based on property rights. Both the 1898 publication of a practical manual on the care of archives by three Dutch archivists and the 1922 *Manual of Archive Administration* by British archivist Hilary Jenkinson address the difficulties of maintaining the authenticity of archival collections accumulated in a number of locations without a formally documented transfer of custody. Jenkinson worked his entire professional career in the Public Records Office in London, the repository for governmental records extending back into the medieval period, and established for the purpose of centralizing British governmental records. Jenkinson "connected authenticity with continuous custody of archives by their creator and its legitimate successors. The argument is that the creating body has an interest in preserving its records free from any tampering that would affect their authenticity, of being what they seem to be."[14]

In his 1954 *Modern Archives*: *Principles and Techniques*, based on his experience in the United States National Archives, American archivist Theodore Schellenberg rejected the concept of continuous custody required by Jenkinson on the basis of the complexity of the process of the production of modern records and the impracticability of guaranteeing an unbroken line of continuous custody when records were produced by a number of different divisions of an organization in different locations. Nonetheless, Schellenberg believed that once records had crossed the threshold of the archives, they needed to stay in the custody of the archives in order to guarantee their integrity following their arrival.

With the proliferation of paper records and the technological complexity of electronic records, American archivist F. Gerald Ham recommended a post-custodial approach in his 1981 "Archival Strategies for the Post-Custodial Era," in which the archivist's role was less than that of a keeper concerned with the physical custody of records and more a proactive manager of records, taking on advisory responsibilities toward the creators of records. Both Canadian and Australian archivists have explored various aspects of post-custodial theories as applied to the records of business and government, wanting to assure both access and accountability for local records of government and business.

Physical custody of electronic records is a meaningless concept without the maintenance of the supporting environment of software and business practice, hence the development of a theory of distributed custody, in which records may remain with the creating agency, but with guidance provided by archivists as to their disposition and long-term maintenance. Various post-custodial

Corporate Information–
Custody

theories providing solutions to the problems of custody of archival records in electronic form include distributed custody, or leaving those records in the hands of their creators, with the archives providing guidance on their management and serving as a last resort.[15] (For an extended discussion of how the inter-relation of custody and access was applied to the archival records of the Virgin Islands.)[16] New skills for the archivists now include digital curation, which requires that archivists take responsibility for maintaining both the context and content of digital information, focusing "not just on preserving digital entities but on keeping them functional, supporting their continuous annotation and maintaining their fitness for purpose."[17]

Control of records, regardless of their form, is a means of protecting them and the basis for assurances of continuing authenticity. Post-custodial approaches do not mean a noncustodial approach. Archivists administering records held in distributed custody would continue to "guarantee the long-term preservation of ongoing social, cultural, historical, or symbolic value."[18]

CHALLENGES TO CUSTODY IN ARCHIVES: REPLEVIN REQUESTS

Although issues of contested custody in museums are more immediately newsworthy, particularly when they involve looted art or antiquities of dubious provenance, there are equivalent cases in archives that are no less significant. Two cases can be used to illustrate the use of replevin as a technique to challenge an archive's custody of documents. Replevin is defined in the Society of American Archivists' online *Glossary of Archival and Records Terminology* as "an action to recover property that has been improperly or illegally taken" and notes that it is a technique frequently employed to describe efforts to recover public records that are in private hands.

In December of 1955, a suit was brought against the Minnesota Historical Society contesting the ownership of a previously unknown collection of field notes compiled by William Clark substantiating details of the events of the Lewis and Clark Expedition between December 1803 and April 1805. In addition to the family in whose possession the documents had been discovered, the claimants in the suit included the United States, based on the notion that Thomas Jefferson, who had initiated the expedition, had requested that the records of the expedition be submitted to the government. However, historically, the federal government had not previously claimed any of the other Lewis and Clark expedition papers, many of which were held in private and public collections, or indeed any records of government-sponsored expeditions. There was considerable opposition to this, particularly from those collections, who were concerned that "the government's claim to Clark's 'Field Notes' posed a threat to any

privately owned historical documents."[19] The court ruled in October 1955 that the government could not sustain the burden of proof in establishing its claim; therefore, the field notes were private papers rather than public documents. Following the ruling, the family sold them to a private collector, who in turn donated them to Yale University. A scholarly edition of the papers, *The Field Notes of Captain William Clark, 1803–1805*, edited with an introduction and notes by E.S. Osgood, was published in 1964. This edition includes facsimiles of the original pages, allaying the fears that the information in the papers would become unavailable, if the papers had gone into a private collection.

A replevin case in which the reverse ruling was made in an appeal was the 1975–1977 case of the legal briefs dated 1767 and 1768 signed by William Hooper of North Carolina, considered to be one of the rarest of the 56 signers of the Declaration of Independence. Shortly after these items had been offered for sale by autograph collector B.C. West, he was informed that "the state of North Carolina claimed his two Hoopers on the grounds that title to any paper that had once been a public record remains with the state."[20] A 1977 ruling on the ownership of the Hooper documents granted custody of those documents to the state of North Carolina. While much discussed at the time, particularly by manuscript collectors, this case did not set a precedent for replevin and similar state documents were offered at subsequent public auctions and not requested by the state. Nonetheless, organizations such as the Manuscript Society have issued policies on the custody of abandoned or discarded government documents which support the rights of individual rights of ownership when the person can demonstrate legal title. This debate continues in the United States over the ownership and accessibility of presidential papers.

Another case of contested custody in archival collections deals with the acquisition of the Stanton Glantz Research Files of the Brown and Williamson Tobacco Corporation, established at the University of California, San Francisco, Library and Center for Knowledge Management in 1994, which provided public access to copies of internal documents from the tobacco company's files which had been given anonymously to Glantz, a cardiologist and tobacco-control activist at the University of California, San Francisco (UCSF). This collection, the basis for the research in the 1996 publication, *The Cigarette Papers*, was the subject of a lawsuit in which the Brown and Williamson Tobacco Corporation sought to remove the material from the University of California library that indicated that the tobacco industry had suppressed research on tobacco addiction and its health risks. The ruling of the San Francisco Superior Court allowed the release of the documents on the Internet, stating, "the public has the right to know".[21,22]

That government offices, particularly at times of political unrest, are not the most reliable of stewards has been proven so again and again, in such cases as the South African Truth and Reconciliation Commission, established in 1995, to investigate the destruction of records created during the period of apartheid.[23] Similar efforts in Argentina, Brazil, Chile, El Salvador and Guatemala have attempted to gain access to public records dealing with the rights of individuals under previous regimes. The release of previously secret files such as those maintained by the Stasi, the Ministerium für Staatssicherheit, the official secret police of East Germany raises questions as to the potential for social and personal harm caused by the availability of these records.

CONCLUSION

Museums and archives have traditionally taken custody of cultural objects and records of lasting value as a means of fulfilling their obligation to preserve the past for the future. In both types of institutions, contextual information is required in order to give meaning to the objects, including maintaining and enhancing information on the identity and use of the items as well as information on the circumstances of their acquisition through ongoing scholarship and exhibitions. Modern theories of cultural property have challenged the retention of some cultural items by these institutions, most notably NAGPRA, the U.S. law passed in 1990. The application of this legislation has resulted in the repatriation of many objects of cultural patrimony to those identified as lineal descendants. Additional legislation such as the CITES controls the transportation of animals and plants across international borders in order to help protect endangered species and their often equally endangered habitats. Provenance research applied to the return of works of art looted during the Nazi Era heightened social responsibility as chronicled in Lynn Nicholas, *The Rape of Europa*: *The Fate of Europe's Treasures in the Third Reich and the Second World War*, New York: A.A. Knopf, 1994. Although successful claims have been made for the return of antiquities from museums to the current governments of the original creators, these repatriations have not gone uncontested. Some critics argue that such actions will diminish the research collections held in modern museums, which exist to provide a critical mass of cultural material for valid comparative scholarship.

Parallel to the reasoning that museums give value to objects selected for their collections, some archival theorists argue that records held in the custody of archives retain their authenticity which would not be the case if they were left in the hands of their creators. Critics of this approach argue that the records may well have been tampered with prior to their deposit in the archives and therefore may not represent the full truth of business transactions. Post-custodial theories of archival management have been developed to deal with the custody of governmental and business electronic records which require maintaining a surrounding environment of software and business practice.

Determining the custody of an object or document is an essential responsibility of museums and archives. Responsible stewards of collections should begin by determining the deceptively simple fact of ownership of collections under their care.

REFERENCES

1. Brown, M.F. *Who Owns Native Culture?;* Harvard University Press: Cambridge, MA, 2003; ix.
2. International Council of Museums (ICOM). Code of Ethics, 2006. Available at http://icom.museum/ethics.html (accessed August 11, 2008).
3. Yeide, N.H.; Akinsha, K.; Walsh, A.L.; Nancy, H. *The AAM Guide to Provenance Research*; American Association of Museums: Washington, DC, 2001.
4. Nazi-Era Provenance Internet Portal Project. Available at http://www.nepip.org/ (accessed August 16, 2008). For the 1998 report of the Association of Art Museum Directors Task Force on Spoliation of Art During the Nazi/World War II Era (1933–1945), see http://www.aamd.org/papers/guideln.php (accessed August 16, 2008). See also the 2008 AAMD report on Acquisition of Archaeological Materials and Ancient Art, http://www.aamd.org/newsroom/documents/2008 Report And Release.pdf (accessed August 16, 2008).
5. National Museum of the American Indian, Repatriation. Available at http://www.nmai.si.edu/subpage.cfm?subpage=collaboration&second=repatriation (accessed August 16, 2008).
6. American Association of Museums. *Code of Ethics for Museums*; 2000; http://www.aam-us.org/museumresources/ethics/coe.cfm (accessed August 16, 2008).
7. Weil, S. *A Deaccession Reader*; American Association of Museums: Washington, DC, 1997.
8. Spiess, K.; Spiess, P. Museum collections. In *The Museum: A Reference Guide*; Shapiro, M.S., Ed.; Greenwood Press: New York, 1990; 141–166.
9. Longstreth-Brown, K. Documentation. In *The New Museum Registration Methods*; Buck, R.A., Gilmore, J.A., Eds.; American Association of Museums: Washington, DC, 1998; 1–40.
10. Gerstenblith, P. Cultural significance and the Kennewick Skeleton: Some thoughts in the resolution of cultural heritage disputes. In *Claiming the Stones, Naming the Bones: Cultural Property and the Negotiation of National and Ethnic Identity*; Barkan, E., Bush, R., Eds.; Getty Research Institute: Los Angeles, CA, 2002; 162–197.
11. Owsley, D.W.; Jantz, R.L. Kennewick Man—A kin? Too distant. In *Claiming the Stones, Naming the Bones: Cultural Property and the Negotiation of National and Ethnic Identity*; Barkan, E., Bush, R., Eds.; Getty Research Institute: Los Angeles, CA, 2002; 141–161.
12. Cuno, J. Museums, antiquities, cultural property and the U.S. legal framework for making acquisitions. In *Who Owns the Past? Cultural Policy, Cultural Property and*

the Law; Fitzgibbon, K., Ed.; Rutgers University Press: New Brunswick, NJ, 2005; 143–158.

13. FitzGibbon, K. Introduction. In *Who Owns the Past? Cultural Policy, Cultural Property, and the Law*; FitzGibbon, K., Ed.; Rutgers University Press: New Brunswick, NJ, 2005; xiii–xx.

14. Eastwood, T.M. Introduction. In *Selected Writings of Hilary Jenkinson*; Ellis, R.H., Walne, P., Eds.; Society of American Archivists: Chicago, IL, 2003; vii–xx.

15. Bastian, J.A. Taking custody, giving access: A postcustodial role for a new century. Archivaria **2002**, *53*, 76–93.

16. Bastian, J.A. *Owning Memory: How a Caribbean Community Lost Its Archives and Found Its History*; Libraries Unlimited: Westport, CT, 2003.

17. Ross, S. Approaching digital preservation holistically. In *Recordkeeping in a Hybrid Environment: Managing the Creation, Use, Preservation and Disposal of Unpublished Information Objects in Context*; Tough, A., Moss, M., Eds.; Chandos Publishing: Oxford, 2006; 115–153.

18. Cunningham, A. Journey to the edge of the night: Custody and the dawning of a new era on the archival threshold. Arch. Manuscr. **1996**, *24* (2), 312–321.

19. Cutright, P.R. *A History of the Lewis and Clark Journals*; University of Oklahoma Press: Norman, OK, 1976; 154.

20. Taylor, J.M. *History in Your Hand: Fifty Years of the Manuscript Society*; Praeger: Westport: CT, 1997; 71. See this publication for accounts of other replevin cases.

21. Chandler, R.L; Storch, S. Lighting up the internet: The Brown and Williamson collection. In *Archives and the Public Good: Accountability and Records in Modern Society*; Cox, R.J., Wallace, D.A., Eds.; Quorum Books: Westport, CT, 2002; 135.

22. Glantz, S.A.; Slade, J.; Bero, L.A.; Hanauer, P.; Barnes, D.E., Eds. *The Cigarette Papers*; University of California Press: Berkeley, CA, 1996. Available at http://ark.cdlib.org/ark:/13030/ft8489p25j/ (accessed August 16, 2008).

23. Harris, V. They should have destroyed more: The destruction of public records by the South African State in the Final Years of Apartheid, 1990–1994. In *Archives and the Public Good: Accountability and Records in Modern Society*; Cox, R.J., Wallace, D.A., Eds.; Quorum Books: Westport, CT, 2002; 205–228.

BIBLIOGRAPHY

1. Barkan, E.; Bush, R., Eds. *Claiming the Stones, Naming the Bones: Cultural Property and the Negotiation of National and Ethnic Identity*; Getty Research Institute: Los Angeles, CA, 2002.

2. Feldman, F.; Weil, S.E. *Art Law: Rights and Liabilities of Creators and Collaborators*; Little, Brown: Boston, MA, 1986.

3. Nicholas, L.H. *The Rape of Europa: The Fate of Europe's Treasures in the Third Reich and the Second World War*; A.A. Knopf: New York, 1994.

4. Pearce Moses, R. *A Glossary of Archival and Records Terminology*; Society of American Archivists: Chicago, IL, 2005. Available at http://www.archivists.org/glossary/index.asp (accessed August 16, 2008).

5. Renfrew, C. *Loot, Legitimacy, and Ownership: The Ethical Crisis in Archaeology*; Duckworth: London, 2000.

Data and Data Quality

Thomas C. Redman
Navesink Consulting Group, Little Silver, New Jersey, U.S.A.

Christopher Fox
Department of Computer Science, James Madison University, Harrisonburg, Virginia, U.S.A.

Anany Levitin
Department of Computing Sciences, Villanova University, Villanova, Pennsylvania, U.S.A.

Abstract

This entry presents a definition of data and their quality dimensions as the basis for a survey of data quality management and improvement techniques, with special attention to data published on the Internet. Several factors have contributed to making improved data quality an urgent priority. These factors include "data quality disasters" such as the Year 2000 Presidential Election, corporate reporting, and homeland security, and the stunning growth in data volumes, and recognition of the importance of data to the modern organization. This entry does not treat issues of database system quality, such as system reliability, accessibility, and usability, or related issues such as data security.

THE NATURE OF DATA

Of the triumvirate of concepts *data, information,* and *knowledge* at the conceptual foundations of the information age, data is by consensus regarded as the most basic. Like the other two, however, the concept of data is not well understood. Although it is basic, the notion of data is surprisingly multifaceted and complex. One reason for this is that the word is used in so many different ways in conversation. For example, one hears comments such as the following:

1. The data on this graph prove my point.
2. The data point is six.
3. See, here are the data we need.
4. I cannot get the data out of the database.
5. When you get some data like that, you know it is time to do something drastic.
6. The data misled us because they were wrong.

Some of these uses of the word treat data as tangible measurements, as in comments 1 and 2. In other uses, the term seems less tangible, but is a motivator for action, as in comments 3 and 5. Some uses seem to treat data as something abstract or conceptual, as in comment 2, and others seem to deal more with physical representations for data, as in comments 1 and 4. In some cases data are treated as factual, and in others, like comment 6, the data may not be correct. This variety of uses of the word data raises many questions about what data are, and how we should understand the term.

A thorough treatment of data quality must be based on a clear understanding of the meaning of the term data. In developing this understanding in this section, we first explore the data life-cycle, the sequence of phases through which data pass as they progress from creation to storage and use. Data's life-cycle model is, in effect, a formal way of looking at "the social life of information."[1] The life-cycle model helps account for the different uses of the term data because, at different stages in their life, data change in subtle ways. Based on the lifecycle, we consider definitions of data and select the definition that encompasses the most critical features and advances our objective of quality assessment, control, and improvement.

The Data Life Cycle

As noted, the data life cycle is the sequence of activities that create and populate a *data bank* in which data are stored, find and extract data from a data bank, and manipulate and use extracted data (Fig. 1).[2] The data life cycle includes the following activities:

1. *Defining a model*—The portion of the real world to be described by the data is defined, and the detailed mechanism of description is specified. This involves defining entity types, their attributes, and attribute domains, all discussed further below.
2. *Implementing the model*—An empty data bank, or physical data repository, is created. In a small organization, the data bank may be a sheet of paper, and implementing the model may involve laying out columns for recording data. For electronic databases, the model must be described in the language of the database management system.

Encyclopedia of Library and Information Sciences, Fourth Edition DOI: 10.1081/E-ELIS4-120008897

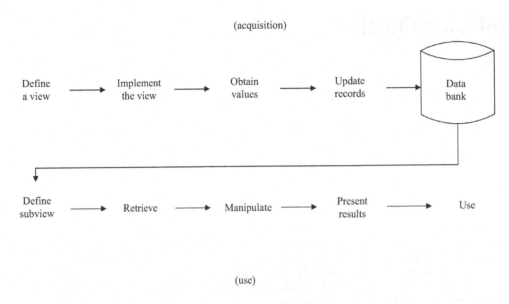

Fig. 1 The data life cycle. (© Navesink Consulting Group.)

3. *Obtaining values*—Data values are collected for the part of the world modeled in the data bank. Common ways of obtaining data values are measuring, surveying, observing, and copying another source. Poor data values are a principal issue in data quality and are discussed throughout this entry.

4. *Storing values*—Data values are recorded in the data bank according to the conventions established in the data model.

   The result of these *data acquisition* activities is data stored in a data bank. Subsequent *data usage* activities put the data to use in the following ways.

5. *Define a view*—Typically a data customer or application requires only a subset of the data available in a database. A *view* describes the portion of the data to be used. By convention, in quality management, we call those who use data, products, or services *customers*. Technologists often refer to the same people as *users*.

6. *Retrieve*—Data (values) of interest are retrieved from the data bank.

7. *Manipulate*—Data are processed in one or more of four principal ways: classification, analysis, manipulation, and synthesis. This step is sometimes bypassed when the sole intention is to present data to a customer.

8. *Present results*—The data are formatted (graphed, listed, etc.) and given to the customer. The appropriate form of presentation depends on many factors, including the results of retrieval and presentation, the presentation medium, and the customer. (People need one form of presentation, application software, another.)

9. *Use*—Data may be used on presentation to the customer.

This simplified version of the model does not include activities to access the quality of data and make adjustments. (The reader interested in such details should see Levitin).[2]

Criteria for a Definition of Data

The data life cycle suggests that data must be defined in a way that will account for the fundamental operations of defining models and views, collecting and updating values, storing, retrieving, and manipulating data, and presenting data and using them for a variety of purposes. The following criteria are also important in a good definition of data.[3]

- *Clarity and simplicity*—This criterion holds for any good definition.
- *Nonreliance on the term information*—This criterion avoids circular definitions.
- *Agreement with common usage*—We want to understand the term data, not to create a new meaning for a common term.
- *Inclusion of conceptual and representational aspects of data*—Both are too important to leave out.
- *Wide applicability*—The definition should include data as diverse as meter readings and the contents of databases and document information systems.
- *Suggestive of quality dimensions*—The definition should lead to practical data quality improvements.

Data Defined

Many definitions of data have been suggested in the literature; the one that best meets the criteria discussed in the previous section is based on the classic definition of the term accepted in the database community. (For an in-depth discussion see Whtimore).[4] This definition is really a collection of definitions of several related terms.

A *conceptual model* or a *data model* is an abstract description of some part of the world, called the *universe* or *enterprise*, that associates, or maps, objects in the world to abstract objects in the model, called *entities*. The portion of the world modeled may include both physical and abstract objects. Characteristics of the modeled real-world objects and relationships between them are captured in the model as attributes. An *attribute* is a property of an object that can assume values from a set called the *domain* of the attribute. There are no restrictions on the elements of a domain; they may be numbers, strings, entities, sets of entities and so forth. An entity is said to have an attribute when the attribute applies to the entity. Entities in a conceptual model that share a set of attributes are grouped together as an entity type.

To illustrate these definitions, consider two conceptual models used to define the reader. Consider first the conceptual model employed by his/her employer. The entities in this conceptual model consist of all past or present employees. The attributes of interest include name, employee ID, status, department, and so forth. Each attribute has well-defined domains of permissible values, for example, the domain for the attribute department includes all departments (Human Resource, Finance, Operations, etc.) of the employer's organization (note that the domain may change as the organization changes). Besides indicating the properties of entities, attributes may be used as entity identifiers. For example, this conceptual model might use the Employee ID attribute as an entity identifier.

Within this framework, we define a *datum* or *data item*, as a triple $< e, a, v >$, where e is an entity in a conceptual model, a is an attribute of entity e, and v is a value from the domain of attribute a. A datum asserts that entity e has value v for attribute a. *Data* are the members of any collection of data items. Returning to the example, a datum in the collection is $<$ John Doe, Department, "Legal" $>$, indicating that the department assigned to the employee John Doe is "Legal."

Note that the Internal Revenue Service (IRS) may also take an interest in the reader. The conceptual model it uses may overlap the employer's. For example, both include Name. But the employer's model may not include Year 2000 dividend income. Likewise the IRS's model need not include Department.

To complete this characterization of data, the mechanism of data representation must be included. A *data representation* is a set of rules for recording data triples on some medium. A *data recording* is a physical object interpretable (via a data representation) as a listing of data items. Representation of data values is accomplished via a *format*, or convention for recording data values using *symbols*, or representational elements. Publications data might be recorded in a paper index, a card catalog, or a computer database. A typical mechanism places all data values for a particular entity together in a *record* consisting of a *field* for every attribute in which the value for the attribute is stored. In many cases, the representations for values in fields will follow traditional formats. For example, author attribute values are typically recorded in a "last-name-first" format using the Roman alphabet.

This definition of data satisfies the criteria discussed in the section above in the following ways:

- The definition is set in the context of conceptual modeling, so it accounts for the data life-cycle activities of defining models and views. It also matches the standard conceptual foundations in the database literature.[5]
- The definition distinguishes data values, attributes, and entities, which are necessary to make sense of the data life-cycle operations of defining a model, of collecting and updating values, and of storing, retrieving, manipulating, and presenting data.
- The definition is simple; if necessary, it can be stated in precise mathematical terms so it is clear.
- The definition does not mention information, so information can be defined in terms of data without circularity.
- This definition of data accords with everyday uses of the word. For example, a water meter reading can be understood as a recording, using a certain data representation, of the value of an attribute (WaterConsumption) of an entity (the CUSTOMER).
- This definition accounts for both the conceptual and representational aspects of data.
- This approach is applicable in all studies of data in systems, including database systems, document information systems, and manual data systems.
- This definition of data lends itself to the study of all salient quality dimensions of data, as we will discuss below.

In summary, the ordered triple view of data meets all requirements for an adequate definition of data, and provides the necessary basis for a thorough consideration of data quality.

QUALITY AND QUALITY CONTROL

The most basic idea in quality is to "create and keep a customer."[6] One collection of data that satisfies customer needs better than a second collection is of higher quality. It follows that the most important measure of quality is customer satisfaction and that a key component of any good approach to quality is determining who the customers are and understanding their needs. Although this is simple in principle, it is complicated enormously by a

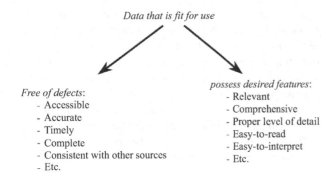

Fig. 2 Data quality defined. Data are of high quality if they are fit for their intended uses (by customers) in operations, decision making, and planning (after Juran). (© Navesink Consulting Group.)

dynamic world: customer needs change continuously, new competitors enter the market, new offerings appear, and so forth. And data customers can have a stunning array of needs. A simplifying notion is that of "fitness for use," as illustrated in Fig. 2, below.

Although data quality must ultimately be defined by the data's customers, several characteristics stand out as important to most customers. These characteristics are called *data quality dimensions*. Given the definition of data above, quality dimensions can be classified according to three major quality concerns: quality of a conceptual model, quality of data values, and quality of data representation;[7] alternative approaches developed by Massachusetts Institute of Technology's (MIT) Total Data Quality Management Research Program can be found in.[8–10] Finally, one can also take the point of view that customers should not be required to separate their requirements of data from those of database systems and that data quality dimensions should be viewed as a subset of all requirements. (See Redman[7] for a comprehensive list of dimensions).

Quality of a Conceptual Model

A *conceptual model* provides a framework for a data set by specifying entity classes, their attributes, and attribute domains. In addition, various constraints, often called *business rules*, can be included in the model. Quality dimensions of a conceptual model can be grouped into six categories: content, scope, level of detail, composition, consistency, and reaction to change. (This grouping follows Levitin and Redman;[11] see Flavin[12] and Fidel[13] for alternative views. See also Brackett[14] for an in-depth discussion of a good data modeling practice).

Content

This category includes characteristics of the facts represented by the data. The most important of them is

relevance: the degree to which a model's components are pertinent for the intended applications. Although the importance of data relevance seems obvious, lack of relevance has been singled out by several authors as among the most important issues in data quality.[15,16] Another concern is that all model components have *unambiguous definitions*. The necessity and difficulty of achieving clear definitions is discussed by Brackett,[14] Kent,[17] and Thompson.[18] The lack of clear definitions continues to plague many important databases (see Sy[16] and Gardner[19]) Finally, the *obtainability of values* for entities and attributes must be considered. Obtainability of values can meet various obstacles. For example, including gender information in a database may be illegal because it may lead to job discrimination. Obtaining blood types for all employees or citizens may not be affordable.

Scope

This characteristic involves the breadth of coverage of a model. A model should be both *comprehensive* and *essential*. In other words, a model must be broad enough to satisfy all the needs of its intended customers but not include unnecessary information. In practice, identifying the needs of even a single customer poses serious challenges for a data modeler. Integrating different sets of requirements to allow data sharing by several customers or applications as required for modern database management systems adds additional issues and difficulties.

There are several reasons for choosing a model broader than the one minimally necessary. First, the designer must usually create a model to accommodate both current and future applications. Second, redundancy can be introduced as a way to check data values. For example, a census form may ask for both the number of children in a household and a list of their names. Third redundancy speeds up some queries. For example, even though the number of employees in a DEPARTMENT can be calculated by checking the department attribute of all EMPLOYEEs, it will be available more quickly as the value of the (redundant) attribute Number Of Employees. Unless justified for one of these reasons, the expense of obtaining, storing, and maintaining unnecessary data should be avoided.

Level of Detail

Choosing the proper level of detail for a conceptual model has two aspects. The first is exemplified by the choice of size of geographic regions for recording sales. Data might be recorded for a city, a county, a state, and so forth. This characteristic is called *attribute granularity*. Lower levels of granularity provide more detail and the opportunity of keeping more data (e.g., subtotals) for finding and correcting errors. On the other hand, a lower level of granularity leads to a larger volume of data. Detailed data may be harder to obtain and usually increase costs.

Customers may also be annoyed when presented with data more detailed than needed.[20]

The other aspect of level of detail is called *domain precision*, the measurement or classification detail used in defining an attribute's domain. For example, measurements in inches are more precise than measurements in feet. Similarly, having 20 distinct values in a color attribute's domain is more precise than having 7. (See a realistic example in Sy and Robbin's[16] discussion of the Standard Industrial Classification).

Composition

This characteristic concerns the structuring or grouping of facts represented by data. Each entity type of data model should be *natural*; that is, it should be a natural grouping of natural attributes with natural domains. This requirement can be met if each entity type has a sensible counterpart in the part of the world being modeled, and each attribute captures a single fact about entities and their relationships. Such an attribute typically represents some property (e.g., the gender of an employee) or it used for identification (e.g., the Social Security number of an employee). Unnatural "multifact" attributes are often introduced to satisfy outdated implementation constraints. For example, an attribute may be defined to hold a code for both age bracket and gender in an effort to save storage space. Date[21] discusses other examples and their consequences. Although multifact attributes should be avoided, some well-established classification schemes incorporate secondary information. For example, room numbering schemes often code the floor into the number. It is hard to call this familiar scheme unnatural. (Things have a tendency to become natural when we get used to them.) Secondary facts may also be incorporated into values for redundancy and security.

In a well-composed conceptual model, each type must have a mechanism for distinguishing individual entities. This requirement, called *occurrence identifiability*, is often incorporated into the definition of an entity type. Usually, occurrence identification is accomplished with a *primary key*, one or more attributes whose value(s) uniquely identify individuals. For example, Social Security Number can serve as a primary key for an EMPLOYEE entity type.

A good model should also promote *homogeneous* types. This means that each attribute should apply to all individuals of the type. This does not preclude using values for "none," "exists but unknown," or even "existence is unknown" (each of these may apply, e.g., to Telephone Number).

Consistency

There are two aspects of this quality dimension. The first is *semantic consistency*, which requires consistency of definitions among related components of a model. Problems often arise with definitions from different databases. For example, Whitmore[22] cites a serious discrepancy in oil import figures reported by the U.S. Bureau of the Census and the Department of Energy caused by the differing definitions of "petroleum," "U.S.," and "month." Sy and Robbin[16] discuss many examples of problems with U.S. government data. The second aspect of consistency is *structural consistency*, which requires consistency in combining a model's components. For examples, such commonly used attributes as Person Name, Address, Date, and Time Of Day should have the same structure across all entity types. Tasker[23] has suggested standard structures for such attributes.

Reaction to Change

A conceptual model provides a framework for representing information about a part of the world, but both the world and customers' requirements change over time. A good model *must accommodate change*. We classify changes into four categories: addition or deletion of an entity (e.g., hiring or firing an employee), changing a value (e.g., changing a salary), changing a domain (e.g., introducing a new car model), and introducing a new attribute or entity type. The first two kinds of changes, called *updates*, are routinely performed in any computer-based database management or document information system without any change in the underlying model; the other two require changes in the model.

Most authors mention "flexibility" as the only design characteristic for accommodating change. In practice, changing a model is usually a serious and expensive task and the ability to accommodate change without redesign is an important practical need. We define a model's *robustness* as its ability to reflect changes in the world and its customer's requirement without design changes. The first step toward design robustness is to select attributes that will not change or whose changes can be easily accommodated. For example, Social Security Number is a more robust identifier of people in the United States than a Name (even if a name's uniqueness could be guaranteed) because it is easier for a person to change names than social security numbers. Another avenue to robustness is to anticipate changes and provide for them in the original design. For example, a company that currently produces sweaters with sizes "small," "medium," and "large" may produce other sizes in the future. No matter how robust a model may be, some design changes will have to be made eventually. A model's *flexibility* is its capacity to change to meet unanticipated demands. A good model is flexible as well as robust.

Quality Dimensions of Data Values

We group dimensions of data quality involving data *values* into four categories: accuracy, currency, completeness, and consistency.

Accuracy

The *accuracy* of a datum $< e, a, v >$ is the degree of closeness of v to some value $v\prime$ in the domain of attribute a considered correct for the entity e. Sometimes $v\prime$ is referred to as the *standard*. If the value v is identical to the correct value $v\prime$, the datum is said to be *accurate* or *correct*. To illustrate, consider an EMPLOYEE entity identified by the Employee Number 314159, and the attribute Year Of Birth. If the value of Year Of Birth for employee 314159 is the year the employee was born, the datum is correct.

Accuracy is most easily measured in terms of inaccuracy. Inaccuracy for a single datum may be computed as the absolute difference between the correct value $v\prime$ and datum's value v. For the example above, inaccuracy may be quantified as the absolute difference between the year of birth $v\prime$ and the value v for the attribute Year Of Birth. The (in)accuracy of a database can be measured in two ways. *Field (in)accuracy* is the fraction of triples in the database with (in)correct data values. *Record (in)accuracy* is the fraction of entities in the database whose records are error-free; that is, the fraction of all entities in the database all of whose attributes have correct data values. Records are usually composed of several fields, so record accuracy is much lower than field accuracy. Furthermore, errors in different fields may be unimportant or disastrous. These last two observations suggest caution when judging database quality on the basis of error rate.[24]

Accuracy and correctness are not as simple as they seem, especially when it comes to evaluation. It is often difficult to determine the standard. Sometimes there is not an obvious single correct value for an attribute, as is often the case in spelling, especially names. Sometimes the correct value is undefined, as when an entity identifier is wrong. In the example above, there may be no correct value for Year Of Birth if there is no employee 314159. It may also be difficult to quantify inaccuracy, even if the correct value is known, because the attribute in question may resist quantification, as do label, category, and description data. In summary, measuring data inaccuracy is often not easy when it is possible, and it is not always possible.

Currency

The ordered triple definition of data treats data as snapshots of part of the world. Most objects change with time, introducing opportunities for data to become incorrect or inaccurate. A datum is *current* or *up-to-date* at time t if it is correct at time t, and *out-of-date* at time t if it is incorrect at t but was correct at some time before t. Currency may be quantified by measuring how far out-of-date a value is. Database currency can be measured as the fraction of out-of-date triples in the database. As an example, suppose the annual salary of an EMPLOYEE can only change at the start of a calendar year, and that some employee's salary was $36,000 in 1992, $39,000 in 1993, and $43,000 in 1994. If during 1994 a datum shows the salary as $43,000, it is up-to-date; if it shows $36,000, it is two years out-of-date; if it shows $42,000, it is simply incorrect.

Completeness and Duplication

The degree to which a data collection has values for all attributes of all entities that are supposed to have values is its *completeness*. A data collection may be incomplete because of missing values in the triples present or because some triples are missing entirely. In the case of missing values, the completeness of a single datum may be measured by whether or not it has a required value; a completeness measure for an entire data collection is then the fraction of triples in the collection with missing values. When a triple is missing a value, a special "null" value may be assigned for it. The meaning of null is different, depending on whether the attribute is mandatory, optional, or inapplicable. For mandatory attributes, the null value means value unknown. For optional attributes, the null value may mean that the attribute applies but we lack its value, or that the attribute does not apply, or that we do not know whether the attribute applies. For an inapplicable attribute, like Name Of Spouse for an unmarried person, the null value signifies that the attribute does not apply. In theory, these cases could be distinguished with different kinds of null values; in practice, having even one kind of null value causes problems for database systems.[25,26]

A data collection may also be incomplete because some triples that should be included are missing. Missing record incompleteness can be measured by finding the fraction of records missing from the data collection.

Consistency and Integrity

Data are said to be *consistent* with respect to a set of conceptual model constraints if they satisfy all the constraints in the set.[27] One measure of the consistency of a datum is a binary indication (Yes or No) of whether the datum satisfies all constraints. A measure for an entire data collection is then the fraction of inconsistent triples in the collection. Correct data must be consistent. The converse statement (consistent data are correct) need not be true. Said differently, consistency is necessary but not sufficient for correctness. Nevertheless, it is important to distinguish consistency as a special dimension because checking consistency is usually much easier and cheaper than checking corrections. Data integrity is sometimes used as a synonym for consistency, but sometimes it means data accuracy or correctness and, sometimes, security and concurrency control in database management systems.[28–30]

Quality Dimensions of Data Representation

From a customer's perspective, the most important data representation issue is the means chosen to represent data values by symbols on a recording medium, called the *format*. The following are the four major formats:[31]

- *String formats* represent values by character strings over some alphabet, including alphanumeric strings, and bitstrings. This category includes numeric coding schemes, most computer storage mechanisms, and most textual representations of data.
- *Positional/marking formats* specify values by marking a particular spot on a recording medium. This category includes coding sheets used in questionnaires and graphical methods.[32–35]
- *Icon formats* use pictorial symbols to represent values.
- *Color formats* represent data values by colors.

The first two formats are the most widely used, but there are several applications in which the last two appear as well.[36]

The most important quality dimension of a format is its *appropriateness*, both for meeting customer needs and using the recording medium effectively. Customers deal with representations of data, not data triples themselves, and their needs are of primary importance. They depend on two factors: the type of customer (human, mechanical, optical, etc.), and the task the customer is to perform (communication, analysis, storage, etc.). Reliable and convenient use of recording media is obviously of practical importance.

A format should result in a correct interpretation of values represented; that is, the format should be unambiguous. For example, a format representing three ratings with the digits 1, 2, and 3 is more ambiguous (to a human) than the one using the strings "worst," "average," and "best." Ambiguity may also arise when a format does not specify a unit of measurement for quantitative data. Special care is needed with icon and color formats because there is not wide agreement about their meaning.

A third quality dimension of formats is *universality* or *portability*, which is the degree to which a format can be used by a wide range of customers. In this respect, specifying numbers with words of a natural language is inferior to using Arabic digits. Similarly, representing telephone numbers without area codes is inferior to including area codes. When using a color format, colors must be chosen bearing in mind that color-blind people can distinguish some colors but not others.

A good format must also be sufficiently *precise*, which means that there must be distinct representations for any two values in an attribute's domain. For example, formats for quantitative data must provide means for specifying numbers as precisely as required. A fifth quality dimension is *flexibility*, which is the ability of a format to accommodate changes in the domain of values represented. This issue has arisen in many information systems struggling to adapt to real-world change.[36,37] A sixth quality of a good format is its *ability to represent null values*. A good format should represent null values in a way clearly understood by customers; Celko[36] retells the tale of the motorist who got thousands of traffic tickets because his license plate read "none." Finally, a format should *make efficient use of the recording medium*.

DATA QUALITY MANAGEMENT

Over the last several decades, any number of quality techniques have been developed and applied. The greatest penetration has occurred in the manufacturing sector, where any number of industries now produce far better products at far lower cost. The service sector has begun to apply quality techniques, also with good success. And some organizations have begun to extend quality techniques to data.

Perhaps the most important lesson learned is that, more than anything else, an organization's leadership dictates the quality of its products, services, and data. While technical excellence is important, consistent, sustained management effort is essential.

Quality Systems

The totality of an organization's efforts that bear on quality define its quality system. Thus, the quality system includes leadership, management, and the application of tools to understand customer needs, measure quality, find and fix defects, and so forth. And while literally thousands of techniques have been tried, all support one of three basic quality management philosophies:

- So-called *first-generation* philosophy and techniques provide quality through inspection and rework of final products, hopefully, before they are passed on to customers.
- So-called second-generation philosophy and techniques provide quality by minimizing root causes of defects in the processes that produce final products. Here the term *process* means the sequence of work activities that produce and deliver products or services to customers.
- So-called third-generation philosophy and techniques aim to design processes so that defects cannot be produced.

Each of these approaches is discussed briefly in the following sections.

First Generation: Inspection and Rework

In this approach to quality, a product or service is inspected for conformance to needs before delivery to a customer. Products or services that fail inspection are either reworked or discarded. In the simplest case, everything is inspected, but more sophisticated acceptance sampling procedures can reduce inspection costs.[38]

The strength of this approach is that it usually improves outgoing quality. Its major drawbacks are that inspections are often difficult and expensive, and reworking or discarding products or services is always expensive. Further, process quality levels tend not to improve beyond a limiting level. Inspection and rework is the first step that an organization takes to achieve quality.

Second Generation: Process Quality Management

The fundamental tenet of process quality management is that process performance can be made predictable within limits. A process operating within expected limits is in a state of *statistical control*. For such processes, statistical and other methods can identify process weaknesses and then changes can be made to improve process performance. For example, suppose a process for collecting and filling service orders is measured and found to be out of control. After study, several problems with ill-defined procedures are identified and eliminated. The process then operates in a state of statistical control with an average error rate of 0.1%. Further study of the process then reveals error-prone activities that can be improved, thereby reducing its average error rate to 0.05%. The net results of these activities are that: 1) they make the output of the process predictable and known and 2) they produce measurable improvements in process performance. (For a fuller account of this approach see Ishikawa,[39] Wadsworth).[40,41]

Process quality management requires some investment, but as processes are brought under control and improved, total costs go down (inspecting and reworking defects is simply much more expensive than preventing them). Furthermore, process quality management can produce sustainable quality improvements as necessary to satisfy customer needs.

Third Generation: Process Design

This approach attempts to make large improvements quickly by designing or redesigning a process from scratch rather than letting it evolve through process quality management. This goal can be reached by making the process simpler and less error-prone, often by incorporating higher technology in both the process and its design.[42] A third-generation philosophy and supporting techniques are required to meet 6σ (six-sigma) quality levels; today, symbolic of world-class quality (6σ equates to 3.4 defects per million).

Combining Quality Management Approaches

All three approaches to quality management discussed above have proven effective in countless instances, especially in manufacturing settings. The two process-based approaches are more advanced and more effective than inspection and rework for the following reasons:

- Defects are expensive to find and fix; detecting and removing a defect can cost up to 10 times as much as preventing it.
- Defects that customers find have a direct impact on customer satisfaction, the ultimate measure of quality.
- Experience has shown that world-class quality levels cannot be achieved solely through inspection and rework.

Despite their weaknesses, inspection and rework have their place alongside process quality management and process design, and mature quality systems combine all three approaches. For example, an organization may have carefully designed a process to minimize errors and may be managing it actively to steadily improve and optimize its performance. Nevertheless, a bad product or service may still find its way to a customer, where it must be replaced or fixed. A mechanism for inspection and rework may thus need to be present in even the most sophisticated environments.

Although quality approaches have been pioneered in manufacturing enterprises, they have also been effective in service industries.[43] And experience confirms that they work for data as well. More specifically, experience confirms that the first two approaches work well. (See English,[44] Loshin[45] and Redman[46] for examples). The next subsection reviews specific methods for applying these three general approaches to data quality.

QUALITY CONTROL APPROACHES APPLIED TO DATA

While all dimensions of data quality are important (at least to some customers), in this section, we focus only on data accuracy. It is important to all customers and is a good vehicle for illustrating the application of quality approaches to data.

First-Generation: Error Detection and Correction

The most prevalent method for controlling and improving data accuracy is to detect and correct inaccurate values. The simplest procedure is to compare data values to the world and fix those that are wrong. For example, consider an employee database containing data on work and home addresses. It is common for the administrators of such databases to survey employees regularly to verify and correct their addresses. Depending on how cooperative employees are (and whether or not the address verification and correction form reaches them), this procedure can work very well. It is costly, however, and yields no sustained improvement in data quality over time; after a survey, the accuracy of data will deteriorate steadily until the next survey is done.

A second technique, called *database bashing*, is also used frequently when data values are stored in two or more databases. Corresponding values in the databases are compared, and when a disagreement is detected, an investigation finds the correct value, and the databases are fixed. This technique has several advantages over comparing all values to the real world. It is easier to manage and tends to cost less, especially when the databases can be compared using a computer, but, like all techniques based on inspection and rework, it does not yield sustained quality improvement.

A third technique, called *data editing*, involves computerized checking of data values against constraints. These constraints may be simple or sophisticated and typically involve the following:

- *Checks of a single field.* For example, a field whose domain is {0, 1, 2, …, 10} may have its values checked against this set.
- *Checks of several fields.* The checked fields could be in a single record or in several records. For example, a field recording the Number Of Employees of a DEPARTMENT might be checked by examining the department field of all EMPLOYEE records and counting the EMPLOYEEs in the DEPARTMENT.
- *Probabilistic field checks.* For example, a record with a gender field value of female and a height field value of 78 in. is unlikely.

Such constraints are often called business rules. See Ross[47] for further details. Once a record is found to be in error, further investigation locates and corrects the offending field(s). This technique may be used in the data life cycle during the activities of storing data values, retrieving data values, and manipulating data values, or as part of special data cleanup activities.

Data editing is popular because it is (apparently) computationally cheap. It is often difficult to generate an effective and complete list of edits, however.[14,48] Once errors are found, it is still expensive to investigate and correct them. Finally, data editing provides no lasting quality improvements.

In summary, inspection and rework methods are not very effective for improving data quality because they are conducted downstream of data-value creation, usually either during a storage activity or during usage activities

of the data life cycle. Although these methods result in short-term data quality improvements to specific data values, they cannot provide lasting improvements because they do not attack the sources of errors.

Second-Generation: Prevent Errors at Their Sources

An alternative to error detection and correction is to focus on processes that create data values. Conceptually, this is simple. As in manufacturing, one must first achieve a state of statistical control. Errors are then reduced by identifying where and how they occur and changing the process to prevent them. Improvements made this way require more effort than inspection and rework but are sustainable and, therefore, cheaper in the long run.

But there are many practical problems. One problem stems from the fact that data move around the organization so quickly. Data created to satisfy a customer's order one day are used to manage inventory, to track sales, to plan next year's marketing campaign, and so forth, the next day. Data customers are harried in doing their current jobs, be it managing inventory, tracking sales, or planning next year's marketing campaign. When confronted with inaccurate data, they are simply more inclined to correct them or compensate for poor quality in some other way, than they are to seek out the sources of incorrect data.

That said, many organizations have made substantial improvements. And they have lowered costs and sped up their business processes and decision-making (error detection and correction takes time and costs money) as a result. Ten "best practices" have been observed.[7] These are summarized as follows.

1. Senior management recognizes the importance of high-quality data and has mobilized the organization to improve. And they have focused data quality efforts on the most important data.
2. The organization holds those who create data responsible for the quality of data they create. This includes both internal and external data sources.
3. The organization identifies and actively manages its most important data suppliers.
4. The organization identifies and actively manages its most important internal business processes.
5. The organization recognizes "social issues" around data (such as that noted above) and actively manages data. It attaches value (often monetary) to data.
6. The organization understands "the most important needs of the most important customers." Data quality efforts are thus focused on the most important data.
7. The organization measures data quality levels. Measurement can be difficult. After all, data do not have physical properties such as size, weight, and impedance. Fortunately, good measurement information

can often be obtained cheaply. One simple method piggybacks process measurement on data-editing activities: failed edits can be classified and counted, and these measurements used for quality control and improvement. AT&T has developed a useful technique called *data tracking*[49] for better process measurement and error detection and localization. Data tracking follows data through a process to determine where data are corrupted. Subsequent investigation identifies the root cause(s) of errors and removes them.

8. Statistical control of data sources is achieved. Control implies that data quality levels will be predictable into the future. And controlled processes are more easily improved.

9. Organizations with the best data are good at defining and conducting improvement projects that get to the root causes of error and eliminate (or at least mitigate) them.

10. Organizations with the best data set and meet aggressive targets for improvement. Indeed, they focus less on actual quality levels than on the rate of improvement.

Third Generation: Process Design for Data Quality

The third data quality improvement approach is to design or redesign processes to minimize errors. This approach is usually initially more expensive than either inspection and rework or process quality management, but, when successful, it yields large gains in a short time and may be cheaper than either one in the long run. Typically, process design introduces new information technologies. For example, an automatic bar-code reader may be introduced into a process because it reads product codes faster and more accurately than a person can.

Limited experience in designing processes confirms that the following ideas[7] can work well:

1. Replace humans with automation in repetitive tasks in which people are likely to make errors, such as data input, data transcription or reformatting, and data searching. More generally, automating well-defined tasks and processes yields gains in speed, productivity, and quality. Conversely, automating poorly defined tasks and processes rarely works.

2. Design processes to optimize end-to-end performance, not the performance of subprocesses.

3. Capture data as close as possible to its original source. Minimize duplication, data transcription, data transformation, and redundant data storage.

4. Employ a "just-in-time" philosophy to data creation.

5. Design data editing and handling of exceptions into the process.

6. Employ simple data codes and extensive, easy-to-access data dictionaries.

7. Data quality measurement should be designed into processes that create data from the beginning. This provides nonintrusive mechanisms that can be used for quality improvement and control, especially when measurement can be built into the software that supports a process.

Process design for data quality is a promising area for further work in the future.

DATA QUALITY AND THE INTERNET

Even a casual glance confirms that the importance of data, and, hence, data quality, has grown enormously over the past decades. Many factors are involved, including the transition to the information economy, the tremendous gains in all sorts of information technologies, and the thirst for ever-more detail to support decision makers. As the importance of data has grown, so too has the need for data quality. And there is no end in sight.

The Internet, thus, is the latest in this series of technological advances and social changes. As this is written (summer 2001) the Internet is just beginning to change the data quality landscape. While the impact will evolve as the Internet evolves, a few points about data quality and the Internet are pertinent.

The first observation is that the Internet creates new data customers. Organizations are publishing data on the Internet that they had previously held as proprietary. Those who view these data almost certainly have different needs than internal customers. They have not been trained on how to interpret data, making clear definition and ease of interpretation more important. They are not familiar with the nuances inherent in the data and could be more easily misled, making accuracy more important. Their native language may be different, making dimensions associated with data presentation more important. Perhaps most importantly, they have different needs and they themselves are different. Some, such as those seeking medical advice relevant to a particular condition, may be focused and discerning but not technically sophisticated. Some, such as college students desiring to complete a report, may be technically advanced but in a hurry and not too careful about what they accept as fact, and so forth.

The second change involves the use of the Internet to conduct business operations. Supply chain management is a good but, by no means, only example. Supply chain management involves using the Internet to order goods and services, arrange and make payment, coordinate deliveries, and so forth. Without the Internet, organizations spend an enormous amount of time and money on supply chain management. Supply chain management works reasonably well, and the Internet offers the opportunity to do so at far lower cost. But only if the data are of high quality.

Third, the Internet makes things possible that are currently not. We do not wish to enter the debate about whether or not "the Internet changes everything." See Porter[50] for a compelling, though not proven, viewpoint that it does not. But it does appear that opportunities to replace standard or commodity products and services with products and services tailored specifically to the individual may indeed become realities. Certainly health care providers are beginning to talk about drugs formulated specifically for individual patients. "Markets of size one" form part of the hope of customer resource management, and so forth. All share the following characteristics:

- They require vast quantities of individual-specific data.
- The impact of poor data is much greater.

CONCLUSION

To summarize, data quality is a subject of primary importance in the twenty-first century. Many factors, including the Internet appear to be making high-quality data more important than ever. Improvement must be based on preventing errors at their sources.

REFERENCES

1. Brown, J.S.; Duguid, P. *The Social Life of Information*, Harvard Business School Press: Boston MA, 2000.
2. Levitin, A.V.; Redman, T.C. A model of the data (life) cycle with application to quality. Inf. Softw. Technol. **1993**, *35*(4), 217–223.
3. Fox, C.; Levitin, A.V.; Redman, T.C. The notion of data and its quality dimensions. Inf. Process. Manag. **1994**, *30*(1), 9–19.
4. Fry, J.P.; Sibley, E.H. Evolution of data-base management systems. ACM Comput. Surv. **1976**, *8*(1), 7–42.
5. Fleming, C.; von Halle, B. *Handbook of Relational Database Design*, Addison-Wesley: New York, 1989.
6. Levitt, T. *The Marketing Imagination*, The Free Press: New York, 1986.
7. Redman, T.C. *Data Quality: The Field Guide*, Butterworth-Heinemann: Boston MA, 2001.
8. Wang, R.Y.; Strong, D.M.; Guarascio, L.M. Data consumers' perspectives of data quality. *Technical Report TDQM-94-01, Total Data Quality Management (TDQM) Research Program*, Sloan School of Management; MIT: Cambridge, MA, 1994.
9. Wand, Y.; Wang, R.Y. Anchoring data quality dimensions in ontological foundations. *Technical Report TDQM-94-03, Total Data Quality Management (TDQM) Research Program*, Sloan School of Management; MIT: Cambridge, MA, 1994.
10. Wang, R.Y.; Ziad, M.; Lee, Y.W. *Data Quality*, Kluwer Academic Publishers: Boston MA, 2001.
11. Levitin, A.V.; Redman, T.C. Quality dimensions of a conceptual view. Inf. Process. Manag. **1995**, *31*(1), 81–88.
12. Flavin, M. *Fundamental Concepts of Information Modeling*, Yourdon Press: New York, 1981.
13. Fidel, R. *Database Design for Information Retrieval*, John Wiley: New York, 1987.
14. Brackett, M.H. *Data Resource Quality*, Addison Wesley: New York, 2000.
15. Loebl, A.S. Accuracy and relevance and the quality of Data. In *data Quality Control: Theory and Pragmatics*; Liepins, G., Uppuluri, V.R.R., Eds.; Marcel Dekker: New York, 1990; 105–143.
16. Sy, K.J.; Robbin, A. Federal statistical policies and programs: How good are the numbers? In *Annual Review of Information Science and Technology*; Williams, M. E., Ed.; Elsevier Science Publishers: Amsterdam, 1990; Vol. 25, 3–54.
17. Kent, W. *Data and Reality*, Elsevier Science Publishers: Amsterdam, 1978.
18. Thompson, J.P. *Data with Semantics: Data Models and Data Management*, Van Nostrand Reinhold: New York, 1989.
19. Gardner, E. UB-82 forms offer wealth of information, misinformation. Mod. Healthc. September 24, **1990**, 18–29.
20. Rockart, J.F. Chief executives define their own data needs. Harv. Bus. Rev. **1979**, *57*(2), 81–93.
21. Date, C.J. Don't encode information into primary keys! In *Relational Database Writings 1989–1991*; Date, C. J., Ed.; Addison-Wesley: Reading, MA, 1992; 461–466.
22. Whtimore, T. Computers take rap for bad data. Computer world August 29, **1988**, *21*.
23. Tasker, D. *Fourth Generation Data*, Prentice-Hall: Englewood Cliffs, NJ, 1989.
24. Intner, S.S. Much ado about nothing: OCLC and RLIN cataloging quality. Libr. J. February 1, **1989**, 38–40.
25. Date, C.J. *An Introduction to Database Systems*, 4th Ed. Addison-Wesley: Reading, MA, 1987; Vol. 1.
26. Imielinski, T.; Lipski, W. Incomplete information in relational databases. JACM **1984**, *31*(4), 761–791.
27. Elmassri, R.; Navathe, S.B. *Fundamentals of Database Systems*, Benjamin/Cummings: Redwood City, CA, 1989.
28. Brodie, M.L. Specification and Verfication of Data Base Semantic Integrity. *Doctoral Dissertation*; University of Toronto: Canada, 1978.
29. Tsichritzis, D.C.; Lochovsky, F.H. *Data Models*, Prentice-Hall: Englewood Cliffs, NJ, 1982.
30. Date, C.J. *An Introduction to Database Systems*, 4th Ed. Addison-Wesley: Reading, MA, 1983; Vol. 2.
31. Levitin, A.V. *Formats for Data Representation: A Taxonomy and Quality Dimensions*, Working Paper, AT&T Bell Laboratories: Holmdel, NJ, 1992.
32. Bertin, J. *Semiologie Graphique*, 2nd Ed. Mouton-Gautier: The Hague, 1973; (English translation by W. Berg & H. Wainer, published as Semiology of Graphics, University of Wisconsin Press, Madison, 1983).
33. Cleveland, B. *The Elements of Graphing Data*, Wadsworth: Monterey, CA, 1985.

34. Tufte, E.R. *The Visual Display of Quantitative Information*, Graphics Press: Cheshire, CT, 1983.

35. Tufte, E.R. *Envisioning Information*, Graphics Press: Cheshire, CT, 1990.

36. Celko, J. Make or brake your system. Database Program. Des. **1989**, *2*(3), 19–20.

37. Newmann, P.G. The clock grows at midnight. Commun. ACM **1991**, *34*(1), 170.

38. Schilling, E.G. Acceptance sampling. *Juran's Quality Control Handbook*, 5th Ed.; Juran, J. M., Ed.; McGraw-Hill: New York, 1999.

39. Ishikawa, K. *Introduction to Quality Control*, 3A Corporation: Tokyo, 1990.

40. Wadsworth, H.; Stephens, K.S.; Godfrey, A. *Modern Methods for Quality Control and Improvement*, John Wiley: New York, 1986.

41. AT&T, *Process Quality Management and Improvement Guidelines*. AT&T: Indianapolis, IN, 1988; Issue 1.1.

42. Phadke, M.S. *Quality Engineering Using Robust Design*, Prentice-Hall: Englewood Cliffs, NJ, 1989.

43. Rosander, A.C. *Applications of Quality Control in the Service Industries*, Marcel Dekker: New York, 1985.

44. English, L.P. *Improving Data Warehouse and Business Information Quality*, John Wiley & Sons: New York, 1999.

45. Loshin, D. *Enterprise Knowledge Management: The Data Quality Approach*, Academic Press: Boston, MA, 2001.

46. Redman, T.C. *Data Quality for the Information Age*, Artech House: Boston, 1996.

47. Ross, R.G. *The Business Rule Book*, The Database Research Group, Inc.: Boston, 1997.

48. Svanks, M.I. Integrity analysis: Methods for automating data quality assurance. Inf. Softw. Technol. **1988**, *30*(10), 595–605.

49. Huh, Y.U.; Keller, F.R.; Redman, T.C.; Watkins, A. R. Data quality. Inf. Softw. Technol. **1990**, *32*(8), 550–565.

50. Porter, M.E. Strategy and the internet. Harv. Bus. Rev. **2001**, *79*(3), 62–78.

Data–Dewey

Deaf and Hearing Impaired: Communication in Service Contexts [ELIS Classic]

Warren R. Goldmann
National Technical Institute for the Deaf, Rochester Institute of Technology, Rochester, New York, U.S.A.

Abstract

From the author's text: "This article provides insights on deafness, deaf and hearing-impaired people, the varied means of communication they use, and basic communications skills useful in communicating with deaf patrons. Suggestions for further reading and study are given, as are sources of in-depth information about deafness and related subjects. Minor modifications to the manner in which one converses can facilitate communication with people with various degrees of hearing impairment, enhance the level of mutual comfort of library personnel and deaf patrons alike, and lead to more productive interaction. Such accommodations can and do represent a significant step toward making libraries accessible to hearing-impaired and deaf people."

—*ELIS Classic, from 1995*

INTRODUCTION

Ideally, libraries should be accessible to all potential users without regard to any disabling condition. As depositories of information, libraries constitute a key institution of democratic societies, yet people with hearing impairments often discover that communication difficulties can be a serious barrier to their using the library to its full potential.

Librarians typically communicate with people of diverse backgrounds and characteristics. Inevitably, some of these people will be deaf or hearing impaired. According to a 1974 study at the Deafness Research and Training Center at New York University, approximately 7 percent of the population is hearing impaired, and slightly under 1% is profoundly deaf.[1] Another writer estimates that approximately 14% of the population is affected to some degree by hearing loss, including that caused by aging.[2] Hearing impairment is the single most prevalent chronic disability in the United States.[1]

The Americans with Disabilities Act of 1990 mandates that public accommodations, including libraries, must strive to provide auxiliary aids and services to clients and consumers without charge. Such aids and services appropriate for deaf and hearing-impaired clients include qualified interpreters, notetakers, written materials, telephone communication devices for the deaf (TDDs), assistive listening devices, and closed or open captioning.[3]

Unusually large numbers of deaf and hearing-impaired people live and attend colleges and universities in Rochester, New York, and Washington, D.C. A number of libraries in these areas, particularly the collegiate libraries of Rochester Institute of Technology (RIT), (which is the host institution to the National Technical Institute for the Deaf) (NTID) and Gallaudet University (in Washington), have addressed the communication needs of hearing-impaired people in various ways.

For example, at RIT there is a reference librarian specializing in services to deaf and hearing-impaired students and offering specialized training to other librarians in meeting the needs of these patrons. The coordinator of the staff resource center of the NTID serves all NTID faculty and staff, including those who happen to be deaf or hearing impaired. Both have developed sign language proficiency. The former offers instruction in the use of the RIT library for deaf students, provides library orientation tours in sign language, writes and distributes informational and public relations flyers about library services available to deaf patrons, and teaches weekly sign language classes for other RIT reference librarians. Three TDDs are available in this library, including one available for student use, thus making the library accessible by telephone for deaf patrons. An extensive collection of books and information about deafness is maintained.[4] In the greater Rochester community, several public libraries have also made themselves accessible to deaf patrons through the provision of TDDs.

Aside from the offerings of these few libraries, however, relatively little is available in the way of skilled personnel or adapted facilities to meet the needs of deaf and hearing-impaired patrons. Librarians in general still tend to be unprepared to cope with the special and varied communication needs of these patrons or to promote action toward making their facilities accessible to them. In spite of the prevalence of hearing loss in this country

Encyclopedia of Library and Information Sciences, Fourth Edition DOI: 10.1081/E-ELIS4-120044758

Data–Dewey

that disability still remains a serious barrier to communication in the use of libraries. [Generally speaking, that] barrier is a 2-way obstacle–people in the hearing world do not communicate with those in the non-hearing world, and vice versa.[2]

This article provides insights on deafness, deaf and hearing-impaired people, the varied means of communication they use, and basic communications skills useful in communicating with deaf patrons. Suggestions for further reading and study are given, as are sources of in-depth information about deafness and related subjects.

Minor modifications to the manner in which one converses can facilitate communication with people with various degrees of hearing impairment, enhance the level of mutual comfort of library personnel and deaf patrons alike, and lead to more productive interaction. Such accommodations can and do represent a significant step toward making libraries accessible to hearing-impaired and deaf people.

BACKGROUND

Terminology

Hearing impairment is the most general term used to describe all types and degrees of hearing defects, ranging from slight loss to profound deafness.

"Deaf" individuals can discern no meaning in perceivable sounds. Additionally, the capitalized word *Deaf* is used by some authors to refer to profoundly deaf people whose community and culture are based on both common experiences (such as attending institutions or programs for deaf students) and a common language, American Sign Language (ASL).

"Hard-of-hearing" describes individuals whose sense of hearing, while deficient, is still somewhat functional. They can comprehend speech to some extent with or without a hearing aid, and generally depend on speechreading, facial expression, and gestures (sometimes including sign language) to supplement what they do hear.

Additional communication and cultural characteristics of both groups are discussed later in this entry.

Deafness and Deaf People

Over the course of their lifetimes, millions of Americans live with some degree of hearing loss. *Congenitally deaf* people (those who are born with profound deafness) are in the minority, but still comprise many thousands of individuals. Significantly larger numbers are *adventitiously deaf*, having lost part or all of their hearing later in life, at any time from infancy onward. *Prelingual deafness* describes the loss of hearing before the acquisition of language, usually before 3 years of age. *Postlingual deafness* describes hearing loss occurring after (often long after) language acquisition.

A number of different factors determine the impact of deafness or hearing loss on the individual. These include the type and severity of the loss, the age of onset of hearing loss, and whether the loss is sudden or gradual. Schooling, life experiences, personality, and communication preferences are other determinants of an individual's adjustment to deafness and the communication style and skills developed.

Causes of hearing loss are diverse. Common etiologies include genetics, illness, trauma, exposure to excessively loud sounds over a period of time, and gradual deterioration due to aging.

Severity of hearing loss may range from a slight and correctable loss to profound deafness, in which case the individual literally cannot hear any sound. Moreover, there are different types of hearing loss, such as middle ear problems, or nerve deterioration or damage. Hearing impairment will usually entail greater difficulty in detecting certain frequencies than others within the spectrum of audible sound. For example, if someone has difficulty hearing high frequencies (as opposed to low or midrange frequencies), the sound of the final "s" that forms the plural of many words is often entirely missed.

Modern hearing aids can be adjusted to some extent to compensate for uneven hearing loss over the range of audible frequencies, particularly when the severity of loss is minimal. In such cases, hearing with an aid may be close to normal. However, when the hearing loss is severe, even a powerful aid may not be able to compensate evenly for losses that are distributed across the entire audible frequency spectrum. The result is that sounds are distorted and therefore harder to recognize and distinguish. The greater the severity of loss, the less effective a hearing aid is in helping an individual receive and understand information through sound alone, and the more the individual must rely on alternative strategies. Speechreading, manual communication, gestures, writing, or combinations of these methods are examples of such strategies used in communication between deaf and hearing people.

The age at which an individual experiences hearing loss or becomes deaf has a great impact on language acquisition and intellectual development. Language is ordinarily acquired through the frequent and repeated exposure to speech, usually beginning in infancy. An individual who learns speech and language patterns through such early exposure will normally retain and continue to use them even if his or her hearing deteriorates later in life. On the other hand, developing speaking skills is infinitely harder and slower for someone born deaf. Without intervention, the deaf child

must grow up not only unable to speak but denied even a concept of language, that indispensable instrument of thinking and reasoning. . .not only unable to communicate with others, he cannot even communicate with himself.[5]

It is extremely difficult to learn to produce sounds that one has never heard and that may also be difficult or impossible to read from a speaker's lips. An individual who is born with moderate hearing loss or who experiences such loss early in life will hear imperfectly, which often results in corresponding difficulties with English because of the lack of a language-based frame of reference.

In contrast to blindness, deafness is most commonly an invisible handicap. However, there are common signs and symptoms indicating that a person may have a hearing loss.

Look for these signals when the person

- Asks to have things repeated often
- Does not react to loud noise
- Does not always respond when spoken to, or responds inappropriately
- Misunderstands conversation
- Has trouble hearing in group settings
- Complains that people are mumbling
- Has difficulty hearing women's or children's voice, but can hear deeper tones, such as men's voices
- Must be close to the person speaking
- Speaks too loudly or softly in conversation
- Strains to hear
- Ignores sounds coming from behind
- Has nasal speech or less distinct articulation
- Turns head towards the person when speaking[6]

Communication Modes

Adding to the diversity previously described are disparate communication modes, strategies, and preferences. In the United States and elsewhere, communication methodology has been hotly debated among both deaf and hearing people for over a century. Even today, educators, doctors, and other professionals; parents; and deaf people themselves still argue over whether deaf children should be encouraged and taught to communicate orally (i.e., through speech and speechreading only), in ASL, in signed English, or through a combination of methods.

In describing the disparate communication strategies used by Deaf and hard-of-hearing people, respectively, certain generalizations may be made.

Deaf people, particularly those who are prelingually deaf and/or are born to deaf parents, rely primarily on vision, although some may use residual hearing to supplement their communication. Members of this group:

- Communicate through sign language and/or speechreading
- Use sign language interpreters
- Use Telecommunication Devices for the Deaf (TDDs) and Telephone Relay Services
- Use visual signaling devices for doorbell, telephone, sounds of baby crying, etc.

- Sometimes use specially trained "hearing dogs"
- Use closed-caption decoders for television viewing
- Generally are members of the Deaf culture.

Hearing impaired people rely primarily on hearing supplemented by amplification, and use their vision to supplement their communication. Members of this group:

- Generally do not use sign language
- Generally do not use interpreters
- Generally do not use TDDs or Telephone Relay Services
- Communicate using amplification and through speechreading
- Use hearing aids
- Use Assistive Listening Devices, such as induction loops. FM and infrared systems, and telephone speech and hearing amplifiers
- Use visual signaling devices
- Generally are not members of the Deaf culture.

There are some areas of overlap in the communication strategies used by these two groups.[3] Obviously, there is no typical deaf person; there is tremendous diversity among people with any degree of hearing loss.

Misconceptions about Deafness and Deaf People

Misconceptions about deaf people are common among hearing people who have little or no direct contact with deaf individuals. The same is true about the various means used by deaf people to communicate among themselves and with their hearing counterparts.

For example, good speech is not necessarily an indication that a hearing-impaired speaker can also hear well. People who lose their hearing later in life may speak almost perfectly, in spite of profound deafness. Late-deafened adults lose the ability to monitor their own speech, which usually results in deterioration of speech quality. Sometimes this deterioration leads others to suspect a speech impairment rather than the deafness that actually causes it.

A common first question asked of deaf people is, "Can you lipread?" Although most deaf people do get information through observing lip movements, skill, experience, and comfort in speechreading vary tremendously. Very few deaf people develop sufficient speechreading skill for it to become their primary means of understanding others; often they will depend more or less exclusively on other means of communication because of great difficulty with speechreading. Some deaf individuals do learn to speechread so well that hearing people may be unaware of, or forget, their deafness.

Wearing a hearing aid does not necessarily imply that the wearer can "hear" in the sense of understanding speech as a hearing counterpart would. In cases of severe impairment, wearing a hearing aid may be of little value beyond alerting the wearer to environmental sounds that are in themselves unintelligible.

COMMUNICATION WITH DEAF PEOPLE

Speaking and Facial Expression

Although speaking louder to a deaf or hard-of-hearing person is a natural inclination, this rarely, if ever, enhances comprehension. A profoundly deaf person will still hear nothing, no matter how loudly a message is spoken. Additionally, a hearing aid wearer may experience both distortion and pain when shouting or abnormally loud speech is amplified.

Leaning forward or speaking into a deaf person's ear are also counterproductive, if natural, responses to the person's deafness. When this occurs, speechreading becomes harder or impossible for the deaf person, because of the difficulty experienced in focusing on the speaker's mouth. As Wright points out, the speechreader must at all costs keep his or her line of vision to the other's face.[5]

The use of facial expression appropriate to the tone and content of the message is of considerable help in communicating with deaf people. Speakers whose facial expression, gestures, and animation supplement spoken messages appropriately will generally be much more readily understood than those who do not provide these additional message clues.

Facial expressions are also crucial in conveying the intensity of a message. Particularly for deaf people who rely heavily on sign language, they modify both signed and spoken messages in a manner analogous to the way adjectives and adverbs modify spoken English for hearing people. Whether the speaker is mildly amused, delighted, perplexed, or angry, his or her thoughts might be expressed in essentially the same signs (with some variations in pace and intensity), but facial expressions are what convey the mood being expressed.

Overcoming any personal or cultural biases that inhibit the expression of feeling through facial expression and body language will convey the intended weight and meaning of a message to deaf patrons much more effectively.

Speechreading

Lipreading entails deciphering verbal messages through watching lip movements. Speechreading, on the other hand, not only encompasses lipreading, its most important component, but also incorporates many other visual clues that assist in understanding the spoken message. Such clues include facial expression, gestures, pantomime, rate of delivery, and eye contact. Even hearing people develop and use some speechreading ability, often unconsciously, especially when background noise interferes with hearing.

People with hearing impairments vary greatly in their ability to speechread, even when other factors, including educational level attained, are essentially equal. Words and concepts must obviously be part of an individual's vocabulary and experience to be recognized through speechreading. Thus, a deaf individual who has never heard the patterns of spoken English will most likely find it difficult or impossible to speechread.

David Wright, a deaf Oxford University graduate, explains how complex lipreading is, even under ideal conditions

> Lipreading is not simply a physical operation in which the eye has learned to interpret for the ear; it is also an intellectual exercise. Lipreading is ninety percent guesswork, because while most vowels are easily distinguished, many consonants are not, since those are often produced by nearly identical lip movements. This means that in effect a great number of words and syllables which are distinct in sound appear to the eye as like as peas. The alternatives can be so many that it may take a lipreader a few seconds to make the choice while he runs the various possibilities through his mind.[5]

A missed key word can make an entire sentence incomprehensible to a speechreader. Words used out of context, as when a speaker changes the topic of his communication suddenly, are usually difficult to recognize. Stuttering and accents interfere with speechreading, as do poor lighting and visual interferences and distractions, including but not limited to bushy moustaches, objects in the mouth, or people or objects moving in the background.

Fortunately, the typical library, characterized by good lighting (i.e., bright, indirect, and uniform) and relatively few visual, tactile, or auditory distractions, is conducive to speechreading.

Although some deaf people speechread remarkably well in spite of the difficulties mentioned, it is important not to assume that every hearing-impaired person can speechread well enough so as not to require other supplemental means of communication.

Sign Language

The use of gestures is a natural communication channel for many people, particularly within and across certain cultures, and is as old as humankind. Deaf people have long communicated with one another through gestures and signs of their own invention. In various countries, some of these sign systems have become formalized into languages.

> The | French | Abbé Charles Michel de l'Epeé convinced himself that gestures and signs were the natural language or "mother tongue" of the deaf-born, and therefore set out

to construct and codify a sign language based on the natural signs' that he had learned from his own pupils.[5]

American Sign Language stems from this French sign language, as well as from a native American sign language. As is true in the cases of other modern languages, ASL continues to evolve.

Particularly over the past thirty years, linguistic studies have shown that ASL has a complex, systematic syntax of its own that differs dramatically from that of English. Moreover, the order in which concepts are signed and the ways in which they are modified are considerably different.

> Just as the tone of voice in articulate speech modifies the sense of a word, the meaning of a particular sign can be modified by an expressive variation of gesture while making it.[5]

In recent years, ASL has been recognized as a language in its own right. Many deaf people, as well as organizations such as the National Association of the Deaf, have become increasingly assertive in advocating ASL as both their language of choice and of instruction.

American Sign Language is a purely visual/gestural language, and thus has no written form. However, in the 1950s and 1960, William Stokoe, a Cornell University researcher, originated a system of symbols that accurately describe the finger, hand, face, and body movements that constitute ASL. His efforts, combined with the general recognition of ASL as a distinct language, have resulted in the publication of various dictionaries and instructional material on ASL. This in turn has led to greater standardization of ASL throughout the United States.

Many Deaf people and their advocates, notably organizations such as the National Association of the Deaf, have become increasingly assertive in advocating ASL as their language of choice in both social and instructional settings.

Fingerspelling

Simple, distinct handshapes are used in fingerspelling to represent the letters of the alphabet, as well as the digits 0 through 9. Letters are formed one after another to spell out words; slight pauses separate words from each other. Many of the letters of the alphabet are obvious in their manual representations.

Fingerspelling is most frequently used to supplement sign language, as when no sign for a particular concept exists, or when greater clarity or emphasis is desired in conveying a word or name. Because the number of letters and digits is tiny compared to the number of distinct signs, fingerspelling can be learned much more rapidly than sign language.

Simultaneous Communication and Total Communication

The use of *manual communication* (including both ASL components and fingerspelling) along with *oral communication* (speech and speechreading) is called *simultaneous communication*. This approach to communication (both to and among deaf people) tends to follow more closely the syntax and word order of English.

Total communication involves using everything at one's disposal to communicate, including simultaneous communication as just described, plus gestures and mime. Deaf people who normally use only ASL when communicating among themselves sometimes attempt to use speech as well as a word order more closely resembling that of English when communicating with hearing people.

Learning Sign Language

For those interested in developing or enhancing sign language skills, sign classes are offered by many schools, colleges, and universities, as well as by organizations serving the deaf community. The Monroe County Association for Hearing Impaired People in Rochester, New York, is one such organization. Many bookstores offer books on sign language (including fingerspelling), pictorial dictionaries, manuals that explain sign usage and word order, and collections of specialized signs.

As is true in learning any other new language, extensive practice is necessary to develop proficiency in manual communication. Interaction with a knowledgeable instructor and with deaf people is far preferable to self-instruction, because motion, mime, facial expression, intensity, and other visual clues, such important components of sign language communication, are best learned from this interaction.

However, even the use of fingerspelling alone can make a tremendous, positive difference in communicating basic information to a deaf person. So can learning and using a few signs relevant to the messages most often conveyed. This is all the more true if one is careful to verify the correctness of the signs used before using them routinely. Any appropriate communication adaptions, such as fingerspelling, the use of basic signs, or writing, help convey to a deaf person one's willingness and desire to communicate.

If asked, many deaf people will gladly provide helpful feedback to someone who is learning sign language. In communities with large concentrations of deaf people, it may be possible to find a professional (for example, a certified interpreter or teacher of sign language) who could evaluate one's skills more formally and provide feedback on appropriate or inappropriate communication strategies.

Data–Dewey

Writing to Communicate

Writing is one of the best ways to get a message across to a deaf person, especially when speech does not seem to be conveying the desired message. Writing information is particularly helpful when the message is detailed or when accuracy is essential. Brevity and simplicity often facilitate this means of communication, particularly in communicating with an individual whose proficiency in English is not well developed. Writing only the essential words of one's message may prove to be entirely sufficient.

Because ASL word order is so different from that of English, individuals whose primary language is ASL encounter some of the same difficulties with English as do others for whom English is a second language. Since qualifiers other than tenses, adjectives, and adverbs (e.g., facial expression, and rate of delivery) are used to modify ASL messages, the writing of deaf individuals sometimes exhibits errors somewhat comparable to writing errors of other nonnative users of English.

Questioning and paraphrasing by both the hearing and deaf persons can help clarify the intent and meaning of a written message when necessary.

OPTIMIZING CONDITIONS FOR GOOD COMMUNICATION

Managing the Communication Environment

Good lighting, appropriate position, unobstructed vision, and minimal distractions are essential to optimal speechreading. Although a resourceful and assertive hearing-impaired individual will try to position himself so as to optimize his own understanding, a speaker can also do much to optimize that communication. Many of the suggestions that follow are effective regardless of the hearing-impaired person's preferred communication mode.

Whenever possible, the speaker should

- Position herself so that the main source of light shines directly on her own face. Backlighting, which silhouettes the speaker's face, makes speechreading difficult or impossible.
- Position himself so that his face is at the same or a slightly higher level than that of the hearing-impaired person, rather than the other way around. This facilitates speechreading.
- Maintain eye contact. As difficult as this may be in some cultures, eye contact is of great importance in communicating with hearing impaired people. As Wright puts it:

The divining of people's moods and intentions from their eyes is so much easier (since it makes less intellectual demand) than the reading of their actual words.[5]

Avoid noisy backgrounds or locations where there is a lot of motion that can be distracting. Move to a quieter spot if necessary.[6]

General Suggestions for Interactive Communication

An individual's deafness, communication skills, and preferences remain invisible until he begins to communicate. The manner in which a deaf person initiates communication with a hearing person provides clues as to how he or she prefers to communicate in that situation. This might, for example, be through speech, a written note, gestures, or a signed message. Communication occurs through many channels other than just speech or sign language. Gestures, mime, facial expression, writing, and even drawing can be used to communicate. The less a person hears, the more important visual aids become in facilitating understanding.

It is best to respond using whatever communication techniques seem most appropriate at the moment and are within the speaker's current repertoire. Through experience and practice, and with background information of the kind presented here, hearing people may develop the ability to recognize and adapt skillfully to the diverse communication needs and preferences of hearing-impaired people.

The following tips will help in communicating with these patrons.

Initiating Communication

- Always get the hearing-impaired person's attention before starting any communication. This may be accomplished by moving into the other's line of sight, by touching him or her gently on the arm or shoulder, or by using other means that seem appropriate under the circumstances. Try not to startle the person.
- Establish and maintain eye contact.
- "Face the person directly. Stand still to communicate from a reasonably close, yet comfortable, distance."[6]
- "Ask how you can facilitate communication. People appreciate being asked. You may be doing everything just fine, or your listener may need for you to talk slower, slightly louder, or make some other adjustment. By asking how to help, you show your desire to communicate clearly."[6]

Adapting Your Communication to the Needs of the Hearing-Impaired Person

- Speak in a normal tone of voice. Don't speak loudly; doing so may embarrass the other person by drawing attention to his or her disability, and it usually does not enhance comprehension.

- Enunciate words distinctly, but without exaggeration. Exaggeration changes the appearance of speech on the lips to the point where words may actually become harder to recognize. Try not to mumble.
  "Articulate: move your lips as well as the best new seaster on television."[6]
- Speak at a moderate, uniform rate, and with normal rhythm. Slow down delivery only enough to be able to enunciate clearly. Extremely slow or excessively rapid speech may be harder to speechread.
- Paraphrase messages when appropriate. If one or tworepetitions of a word, phrase, or sentence do not seem to be conveying the message, try synonyms. Emphasize the key words in the message, as through repetition or by fingerspelling or writing these words.
- Use any gestures (or mime) that seem appropriate in helping to convey the desired message or meaning. If necessary, demonstrate an action or outline the shape of an object being discussed. For example, opening one's hands as one would open a book both conveys a clear meaning and is actually the sign for "book."
  "Give other clues to clarify miscommunication."[6]
- Minimize behaviors that make speechreading more difficult, such as gum chewing, eating, or covering the mouth in any way while speaking. Also minimize head or body movements, unless they reinforce a spoken message.
- "Ask for feedback to know [whether or not] the person is understanding the conversation. Do [whatever else] you can to further enhance communication."[6]

Demonstrating Empathy with the Listener

- "Be patient if your listener seems slow to respond. The person may just need a little time to piece together what was heard or seen. This is the processing time needed to use two senses (sight and hearing) to receive communication. Impatience may show on your face and could create tension for your listener, which only makes further communication more difficult."[6]
- "Stay positive and relaxed. If you appear frustrated or anxious, the person with a hearing loss will find it more difficult to continue the conversation or (to) give you the feedback you need to make sure you are communicating effectively."[6]
- If using an interpreter, talk *to* the hearing impaired person, not about him or her. Remember that the communication is with the hearing impaired person, not with the interpreter. Again, maintain eye contact with the former.

Facilitating Group Communication

- Aid deaf and hearing impaired persons, when applicable, with an outline, summary, script or printout, prior to a meeting.

- In a session where many new terms are being used, provide the new vocabulary in written form prior to the session.
- Make use of visual aids as much as possible. Be sure they can be seen clearly from all points in the room.
- Repeat questions or statements from the audience before answering or commenting.
- Depending on the format of the program, provide special seating for persons with hearing loss, so that they can see the speaker's face and read captions.[2]

Because of the diverse nature of hearing loss and that of the social, language, and educational experiences of people with hearing impairments, there are marked differences in communication preferences from one deaf person to another. Even though any proficiency in sign language on the part of a hearing person demonstrates caring and commitment to communicating, not every deaf person necessarily knows sign language or appreciates its use. Some deaf people still prefer to rely on speech and speechreading, especially if they themselves are not proficient in the use of sign communication.

Particularly after one has developed a repertoire of communication skills, asking deaf patrons which communication mode or modes they prefer is appropriate and will be appreciated.

CONCLUSION

As this article demonstrates, there are many straightforward, common sense things one can do to facilitate communication with hearing-impaired people. The desire to communicate and the willingness to adapt one's communication to the needs of the individual deaf person, combined with patience and empathy, are more important than extensive sign language training. Positive experiences in communicating with deaf individuals will more often than not quickly enhance one's comfort level in such situations, as well as that of one's listeners.

All the topics in this article are discussed extensively in published works, including books and journals. The bibliography lists recent works, as well as several classics, under several headings: Services for Deaf and Hearing Impaired Library Patrons, Deafness, Communication, and Sign Language. Organizational sources of further information and of relevant services are listed.

NOTE

This article is an adaptation of.[7]

REFERENCES

1. Schein, J.; Delk, M. T. *The Deaf Population of the United States*; National Association of the Deaf: Silver Spring, MD, 1974; 1, 15.
2. Dalton, P. I. *Library Service to the Deaf and Hearing Impaired*; the Oryx Press: Phoenix, AZ, 1985; 24–25. 29, 30.
3. Monroe County Association of Hearing Impaired People. *Directly of Organizations and Services for Deaf and Hard of Hearing People*; 4th Ed.; Monroe County Association of Hearing Impaired People: Rochester, NY, 1993; 66 77 113 114.
4. Norton, M. *Wallace Memorial Library*; Rochester Institute of Technology: Rochester, NY, 1994; unpublished memorandum.
5. Wright, D. *Deafness*; Stein and Day Publishers: Briarcliff Manor, NY, 1969; 63, 114, 116–117, 135, 156, 158–159.
6. Self Help for Hard of Hearing People, Inc., *People with Hearing Loss and the Workplace: A Guide for Employers to Comply with the Americans with Disabilities Act*; Self Help for Hard of Hearing People. Inc.: Bethesda, MD, 1993; 11, 23.
7. Goldmann, W.R.; Mallory, J.R. Overcoming communication barriers: Communicating with deaf people. Libr. Trends, summer **1992**, *41*(1), 21–30.

BIBLIOGRAPHY

Services for Deaf and Hearing-Impaired Library Patrons

1. Association of Specialized and Cooperative Library Agencies, Library Services to the Deaf Section, *Basic Sources of Serving Deaf Library Users*; Association of Specialized and Cooperative LibraryAgencies: Chicago, IL, 1983.
2. Dalton, P. I. *Library Service to the Deaf and Hearing Impaired*; the Oryx Press: Phoenix, AZ, 1985.
3. Dalton, P. I. Library services *Life and Work in the 21st Century: The Deaf Person of Tomorrow*; proceeding of the 1986 National Association of the Deaf forum 1986 National Association of the Deaf: Silver Spring, MD, 1986; 165–172.
4. Hagemeyer, A. *Communicating with Hearing People: The Red Notebook*; National Association of the Deaf: Silver Spring, MD, 1980.
5. In *Deafness: An Annotated Bibliography and Guide to Basic Materials*; Kovalik, G., Norton, M., Meek, S., Eds.; American Library Association. Association of Specialized and Cooperative Library Agencies Division: Chicago, IL, 1992.
6. Norton, M. J.; Kovalik, G. I. Libraries serving an underserved population: Deaf and hearing-impaired patrons. Libr. Trends. **1992**, *41* (1), Issue Eds., (entire issue focuses on this one theme).
7. White House Conference on Library and Information Services. Update National Commission on Libraries and Information Science: Washington, DC, 1973.

Deafness and Deafness-Related Topics

1. Benderly, B. L. *Dancing Without Music: Deafness in America*; Anchor Press Doubleday: Garden City, NY, 1980.
2. Brinson, W. *Deafness in the Adult: What Hearing Loss Means and What Can Be Done to Help*; Thorsons Publishing Group: Wellingborough, U.K., 1986.
3. Carmen, R. *Positive Solutions to Hearing Loss*; Prentice-Hall: Englewood Cliffs, NJ, 1983.
4. Combs, A. *Hearing Loss Help*; Alpenglow Press: Santa Maria, CA, 1986.
5. Flexer, C.; Wray, D.; Leavitt, R. *How the Student with Hearing Loss Can Succeed in College: A Handbook for Students, Families and Professionals*; Alexander Graham Bell Association for the Deaf. Inc.: Washington, DC, 1990.
6. Jones, L.; Kyle, J.; Wood, P. L. *Words Apart: Losing Your Hearing as an Adult*; Tavistock Publishers: London, U.K., 1978.
7. Lawrence, E.D. *Focus on Deafness: Selected Readings on Deafness for Paraprofessionals*; University Press of America: Washington, DC, 1978; comp.
8. Lysons, K. *Hearing Impairment: A Guide for People With Auditory Handicaps and Those Concerned with Their Care and Rehabilitation*; Woodhead-Faulkner: Cambridge, U.K., 1984.
9. Moores, D. *Educating the Deaf: Psychology, Principles and Practices*; 3rd Ed. Houghton Mifflin: Boston, 1987.
10. National Association of the Deaf, *Life and Work in the 21st Century: The Deaf Person of Tomorrow*, proceedings of the 1986 National Association of the Deaf forum, Silver Spring: MD, 1986.
11. Neissner, A. *The Other Side of Silence: Sign Language and the Deaf Community in America*; Knopf: New York, 1983.
12. Norton, M. J. Kovalik, G. L. *Perspectives on Deafness: A Selected Bibliography Prepared for Public Libraries Establishing a Deafness Collection*; National Technical Institute for the Deaf. Rochester Institute of Technology: Rochester, NY, 1989.
13. Ogden, P. W. Lipsett, S. *The Silent Garden*; St. Martin's Press: New York, 1982.
14. Rezen, S. V.; Hausman, C. *Coping with Hearing Loss: A Guide for Adults and Their Families*; Dembner Books: New York, 1985.
15. Sacks, O. *Seeing Voices: A Journey into the World of the Deaf*; University of California Press: Berkeley, CA, 1989.
16. Schein, J.; Delk, M. T. *The Deaf Population of the United States*; the National Association of the Deaf: Silver Spring, MD, 1974.
17. Self Help for Hard of Hearing People, Inc., *People with Hearing Loss and the Workplace: A Guide for Employers to Comply with the Americans with Disabilities Act*; Self Help for Hard of Hearing People. Inc.: Bethesda, MD, 1993.
18. Suteliffe, T. H. *Conversation with the Deaf*; The Royal National Institute for the Deaf: London, U.K., 1971.
19. In *Readings on Deafness*; Watson, D.; Hodge, D.; Eds.; Readings on Deafness; Deafness Research and Training Center: New York, 1973.
20. Wright, D. *Deafness*; Stein and Day Publishers: Briarcliff Manor, NY, 1969.

Communication (Especially Between Deaf, Hard-of-Hearing, and Hearing People)

1. Castle, D. L. *Telephone Strategies: A Technical and Practical Guide for Hard-of-Hearing People*; Self Help for Hard of Hearing People: Bethesda, MD, 1988.
2. Crammatte, A. B. Communication. In *Meeting the Challenge: Hearing-Impaired Professionals in the Workplace*;

Crammatte, A. B., Ed.; Gallaudet University Press: Washington, DC, 1987, 25–34.

3. DeFilippo, C. L.; Sims, D. G. New reflections on speechreading. Volta Rev. **1988**, *90* (5), (entire issue focuses on this one theme).

4. Eisenberg, A. M. *Living Communication*; University Press of America: Lanham, MD, 1983.

5. Furth, H. G. *Thinking Without Language*; Free Press: New York, 1966.

6. Garretson, M. D. Eyes, hands, voices: Communication issues among deaf people. Deaf Am. **1990**, *40* (1–4).

7. Kelly, R. R. Meeting the communication needs of deaf people. In *A world apart? Deafness and Social Policy*; Etherington, S., Ed.; Reed Business Publishing Group/Community Care and the Royal National Institute for the Deaf, 1990.

8. National Technical Institute for the Deaf, *Tips for Communicating with Deaf People (Pamphlet)*; National Technical Institute for the Deaf. Division of Public Affairs: Rochester. NY, 1992.

9. Self Help for Hard of Hearing People. *A Good Investment: Meeting the Needs of Your Hard of Hearing Employees (videotape)*; Self Help for Hard of Hearing People: Bethesda, MD, 1988.

10. Suss, E. *When the Hearing Gets Hard: Winning the Battle Against Hearing Impairment*; Insight Books: New York, 1993.

Sign Language

1. Caccamise, F. et al. *Technical Signs 1, Manual One: Project Overview*; Registry of Interpreters for the Deaf: Silver Spring, MD, 1982.

2. Carter, S. M.; Lentz, E. M. Foreword. In *American Sign Language: A Teacher's Resource Text on Grammar and Culture*; Baker, C.; Cokely, D., Eds.; TJ Publishers: Silver Spring, MD, 1980.

3. Costello, E. *Signing: How to Speak With Your Hands*; Bantam: New York, 1983.

4. Fant, L. J. *Say It with Hands*; U. S. Department of Health, Education and Welfare: Washington, DC, 1964.

5. Federlin, T. *A Comprehensive Bibliography on American Sign Language: A Resource Manual*; Federlin: New York, 1979.

6. Hoemann, H. W. *Communicating with Deaf People: A Resource Manual for Teachers and Students of American Sign Language*; University Park Press: Baltimore, MD, 1978.

7. Humphries, T.; Padden, C.; O'Rourke, T. J. *A Basic Course in American Sign Language*; TJ Publishers: Silver Spring, MD, 1980.

8. Marcowicz, H. *American Sign Language: Fact and Fancy*; Gallaudet College. Public Service Programs: Washington, DC, 1972.

9. Newell, W. *Basic Sign Communication: Vocabulary, National Association of the Deaf*; Silver Spring, MD, 1983.

10. Sternberg, M. L. *American Sign Language: A Comprehensive Dictionary*; Harper & Row: New York, 1981.

11. In *Sign and Culture: A Reader for Students of American Sign Language*; Stokoe, W. C., Ed.; Linstok Press: Silver Spring, MD, 1980.

12. *Deafness: An Annotated Bibliography and Guide to Basic Materials.* was the source of many of the bibliographical references listed above. The author gratefully acknowledges Gail Kovalik, Melanie Norton, and Susan Meck, editors of this work, as well as their contributors.

INFORMATIONAL CONTACTS

1. *Monroe County Association for Hearing Impaired People.* One Mt. Hope Avenue, Rochester, NY 14620-1088. Community clearing house on deafness. Informational and referral services. American Sign Language classes, Phone: (716) 423–9490 (voice); (716) 423–9845 (TDD).[4]

2. *National Information Center on Deafness, Gallaudet University*, 800 Florida Avenue. NE. Washington. DC 2002-3625. Can make referrals to the National Captioning Institute, the National Council of Agencies on Deafness, the Registry of Interpreters for the Deaf. Inc., as well as other centers on deafness. Phone: (202) 651–5051 (voice): (202) 651–5052 (TDD).[4]

3. *National Technical Institute for the Deaf.* One Lomb Memorial Drive, Rochester, NY 14623–0889. Has librarians specializing in services to deaf students, faculty, and staff. Interpreter training program leading to the AAS degree (Center for Sign Language and Interpreter Education). Extensive AAS degree programs for deaf students: supports deaf students matriculated in the other eight colleges of Rochester Institute of Technology. Center for Research. Teaching and Learning, Phone: (716) 475–6400 (voice): (716) 475–2181 (TDD).

4. *Registry of Interpreters for the Deaf.* 51 Monroe Street, Rockville, MD 20850, National registry of certified interpreters, Phone: (301) 279–0555.

5. *Telecommunications for the Deaf, Inc.* 814 Thayer Avenue, Silver Spring, MD 20910. Fosters telephone communication by deaf and hearing-impaired people, publishes a TDD directly, and promotes the closed captioning of television programming.

Decision Sciences

Sven Axsäter
Johan Marklund
Department of Industrial Management and Logistics, Lund University, Lund, Sweden

Abstract

This entry provides a description of the vast area of decision sciences from an operations research/ management science (OR/MS) perspective. This means that the focus is on how quantitative models can be used for improving the quality of decisions. After describing and explaining a general conceptual approach to quantitative decision modeling, some important, commonly used decision models and methods are considered in more detail. The list includes both deterministic models such as linear programming (LP), integer programming (IP), and economic lot sizing, as well as stochastic models for safety stock decisions in inventory management. Various generalizations are also discussed together with brief comments and references to other important decision modeling approaches such as game theory, multiple criteria decision making (MCDM), queuing, and simulation.

INTRODUCTION

"Decision sciences" represents a broad area of research with a common focus on advancing the understanding of decision making processes and improving the quality of decisions, organizational as well as individual. Essentially all types of decisions fall within the realms of the field, but an emphasis is placed on various types of business-related decisions or decisions with an economic dimension. From a methodological perspective, the field contains both behavioral and quantitative modeling research. The former is often closely related to organization theory and psychology, while the latter to a large extent is synonymous with operations research/management sciences (OR/ MS), and closely relates to economics, applied mathematics, and statistics. In this entry we restrict our attention to the quantitative modeling (OR/MS) area of decision sciences. The motivation is twofold: first of all, it is arguably the largest area; second, this is where our own backgrounds lie as authors.

Decision sciences research from an OR/MS perspective is usually concerned with improving the quality of decisions. This is done by describing the decision problem in a quantitative model of the real system, then use this model to generate decision alternatives and choose the best among these candidate solutions. The challenges are to model the dynamics and constraints of the underlying system with an appropriate level of detail, and to determine what criteria should be used in assessing what is the best decision. After some reflection most people find this structure intuitively appealing because it fits well with how they make their own decisions (if they are forced to dissect the situation). A set of constraints limits the choices you have and defines the possible alternatives. You then choose between these feasible alternatives according to some objective function that reflects what your goal is with the decision. In the entry on "Examples of Common Decision Models and Applications," we will look at several classical models and methods that illustrate variations of this basic model structure. For the remainder of this entry we will take a closer look at the general approach for quantitative decision modeling sketched above. We will then reflect on the past development, and the future opportunities and challenges of the field.

The general approach when using quantitative models is illustrated in Fig. 1. The goal is to find good decisions for some real system. This is very difficult in many situations. Therefore we can choose to replace the real system by a quantitative model. The model seldom provides a complete description of reality, instead it serves as an approximate, simplified version of the real system. However, an advantage is that the quantitative model quite often can be optimized, that is, we can find the best decisions for the simplified version of the real system. In some cases we cannot find the optimal decisions but still some good ones, for example, by using simulation to evaluate some reasonable alternatives. Because the quantitative model does not take all aspects of the real system into account, decisions that are optimal for the model may not be optimal for the real system. However, presuming the model is a valid description of reality, it should capture the essence of the real system at an appropriate level of detail. Decisions obtained from a validated model can be expected to work well also for the real system. Thus if the model is valid, the model decisions can be implemented in the real system with good results. It is often quite difficult to design the quantitative model at the right level of detail. If the model is too simple, it may provide a poor approximation of the real system (i.e., the model has poor validity), and it may be dangerous to use the model as a basis

Encyclopedia of Library and Information Sciences, Fourth Edition DOI: 10.1081/E-ELIS4-120043712

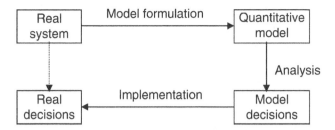

Fig. 1 Using quantitative models to improve the decision quality.

for generating decisions to be implemented in the real system. On the other hand, if the quantitative model is too complex it may be too difficult to analyze. Thus, it becomes quite useless as a tool for helping the decision maker to make better decisions.

The approach to use quantitative models to analyze and describe reality is a cornerstone in modern science and dates back to the dawn of our civilization. However, the birth of the OR/MS field, with its focus on modeling complex decisions, is often attributed to military activities during World War II. The war effort induced an urgent need to make vital decisions about allocation of scarce resources at a scale never seen before. The U.S. and British military services turned to a large number of mathematicians and other scientists to do research on these decision problems, and to develop scientific methods to help solve them. After the war, the success of these efforts spurred an interest to apply the same approaches to decisions in industry and business. The dissemination was fueled by the fast industrial development following the war, and the fact that many consultants and industry people had come in contact with OR/MS methods during their military service. The fast growth of the OR/MS research field after World War II can also be attributed to the groundbreaking research achievements in OR/MS techniques that attracted talented people into the new field. A stellar example is the Simplex method for solving linear programming (LP) problems, originating with George B. Dantzig in 1947, see Dantzig.[1] Other important areas where much progress was done early on were dynamic programming, queuing theory, and inventory theory.

Since the early days in the 1940s, the progress of the OR/MS field of decision sciences has been closely connected to the development of the computer and information technology. The revolution in computational power due to the emergence of the digital computer, and later on the emergence of the personal computer, has made it possible to model and solve increasingly complex decision problems. Another important enabler for the development of the field is the tremendous advances in information technology, not least in recent years. Access to an almost infinite amount of information at the press of a button, propels the opportunities for quantitative models to help decision makers evaluate information and decision

alternatives. Hence, the need for quantitative decision models, embedded in user-friendly decision support systems, continues to increase as the tideway of information keeps overwhelming the decision makers. From a research perspective, easy access to new and more detailed information in combination with increased computational power creates new interesting challenges and promises an interesting future for the OR/MS area of decision sciences.

Important professional associations, which among other things host some of the most influential conferences and journals in the field, include INFORMS (http://www.informs.org), Decision Sciences Institute (http://www.decisionsciences.org), and EURO (http://www.euro-online.org).

EXAMPLES OF COMMON DECISION MODELS AND APPLICATIONS

In this entry we will look closer at some commonly used quantitative decision models. The ambition is to illustrate how the general model building approach discussed above can be applied in different contexts. The models chosen are classical examples but represent a small sample of the entire field, and should not be construed as an exhaustive representation. For specific examples of OR/MS decision models applied in the library and information sciences area we refer to Kraft.[2]

Deterministic Models

A deterministic model is characterized by the absence of randomness, meaning that all input values are known with certainty (i.e., correspond to a single outcome with probability 1). A model that incorporates randomness belongs to the class of stochastic models (see the entry on "Stochastic Models"). To exemplify, consider a decision where the customer demand during next week is an important input parameter. If the demand is known to be 50 units it is deterministic. If there is a probability of 0.5 that the demand will be 25 and a probability of 0.5 that it will be 75, the demand is stochastic (or random) with a mean of 50. The advantage of deterministic models over stochastic ones is that they are generally easier to solve, thus, larger problems may be dealt with. Clearly, in most real systems there is some uncertainty present. However, in many situations this uncertainty may be low enough for a deterministic model to be an appropriate approximation. In other situations, the inherent uncertainty may be critical for the decision and must be incorporated into the model, the choice should then fall on a stochastic model.

In this entry we will consider three types of deterministic models: LP models, integer programming (IP) models, and the economic lot sizing model. Examples of stochastic models are found in the "Stochastic Models" entry.

LP models

Linear programming is perhaps the most well known and most widely used decision sciences method to date. It was originally developed by George Dantzig in late 1940s, who proposed the so-called Simplex method for solving large-scale general linear programs. As the name suggests, an LP model is restricted to linear relationships between the decision variables. Programming is, in this case, synonymous with planning, thus LP can be thought of as linear planning.

Generally speaking, an LP model consists of a linear objective function to be maximized or minimized, and a set of linear constraints that limit the decision alternatives. The objective function is a linear equation of the involved decision variables and should reflect how the decision variables impact the overall decision objective. The constraints are also linear equations of the decision variables, describing logical relationships between these variables and how they consume various types of limited resources. Because of its flexibility, the LP approach has been applied to almost any decision situation conceivable, including production planning, scheduling of personnel, investment planning, marketing, logistics, supply chain management, military strategy and tactics, agricultural planning, etc. The most common type of LP application concerns decision problems of allocating limited resources to a number of competing activities in the best possible way (as defined by the objective function). To make the discussion more concrete consider the following example of a classic product mix decision problem.

A production manager who wants to maximize profits is faced with the decision problem of how much to produce of two products A and B during the upcoming planning period. The production process involves three different machines (resources). The times (resource units) to produce a batch of product A and B, respectively, in each of the machines are specified in Table 1. One can also find the available capacity for each of the machines there, and the profit associated with each batch of product A and B sold. Demand is high so we can assume that everything that is produced can also be sold. A restriction is that previous order commitments require that at least 20 batches of product B are produced.

To formulate this decision problem as an LP, the first step is to define the decision variables, which in this case are the amounts of products A and B to be produced.

Table 1 Input data for the product mix example.

Resource	Production time per batch		Available capacity
	Product A	Product B	
1	3 hr	—	150 hr
2	1 hr	2 hr	140 hr
3	2 hr	2 hr	160 hr
Profit per batch	$1500	$2000	

X_A = number of batches to produce of product A
X_B = number of batches to produce of product B

Given these decision variables, the goal to maximize total profits (Z) translates into the objective function: Max $Z = 1500X_A + 2000X_B$.

Turning to the constraints that limit the amount of product A and B that can be produced, the capacity constraints for resource 1, 2, and 3 can be expressed mathematically as:

(1) $3X_A \qquad \leq 150$ (limited capacity in resource 1)
(2) $1X_A + 2X_B \leq 140$ (limited capacity in resource 2)
(3) $2X_A + 2X_B \leq 160$ (limited capacity in resource 3)

Similarly, the constraint that at least 20 batches of product B must be produced can be expressed as:

(4) $X_B \geq 20$ (produce at least 20 batches of product B)

Adding the non-negativity constraints, $X_A \geq 0$ and $X_B \geq 0$ (assuring that the model solution does not suggest negative production) renders the complete LP model of the product mix problem

Max $Z = 1500X_A + 2000X_B$ (objective funtion : maximize

total profits)

Subject to

(1) $3X_A + \qquad \leq 150$ (limited capacity in resource 1)

(2) $1X_A + 2X_B \leq 140$ (limited capacity in resource 2)

(3) $2X_A + 2X_B \leq 160$ (limited capacity in resource 3)

(4) $\qquad X_B \geq 20$ (produce at least 20 batches of

product B)

(5) $X_A, X_B \geq 0$ (non − negativity constraint)

Note that due to constraint[4], the constraint $X_B \geq 0$ is redundant in this formulation and it is included solely for reasons of completeness.

After formulating the decision model, the challenge is to solve it and determine the optimal decisions. For the current example with only two decision variables the problem can be solved graphically as illustrated in Fig. 2.

Scrutinizing the graphical representation in Fig. 2, the bold lines labeled (1)–(4) correspond to constraints (1)–(4) above when satisfied to equality. The gray shaded area corresponds to the feasible region, where all the constraints are satisfied (including the non-negativity constraint $X_A \geq 0$). The optimal decision must satisfy all the constraints, hence the feasible region defines all decision alternatives of interest. The optimal solution is the feasible solution that maximizes the objective function. The dashed line in Fig. 2 represents the slope (or level) of the objective function, $Z = 1500X_A + 2000X_B$. To maximize Z, we increase X_A and X_B, which corresponds to parallel-shifting

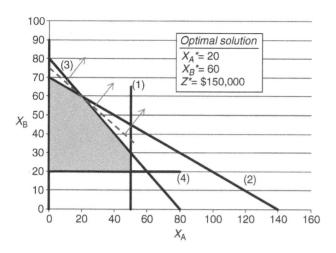

Fig. 2 Graphical solution of the product mix decision problem.

the dashed line in the directions of the arrows depicted in Fig. 2 (mathematically the arrows represent the gradient to the objective function). The optimal solution is the last point on the dashed line which belongs to the feasible region. From Fig. 2 we can see that this corresponds to the corner point of the feasible region where constraint (2) and (3) intersect. Solving the linear equation system defined by constraints (2) and (3) (or by inspecting the graph), the optimal solution $X_A^* = 20$, $X_B^* = 60$ is found. The corresponding objective function value is $Z^* = 150,000$. Hence, the optimal decision obtained from the LP model is to produce 20 batches of product A and 60 batches of product B, which renders a total profit of $150,000.

Clearly, LP problems of practical interest are considerably larger than the small example studied here (often including thousands or even millions of variables and constraints), which prohibits a graphical solution technique. Instead, these large-scale problems can be solved using, for example, an efficient algebraic technique called the Simplex method. This method utilizes the fact that an optimal solution to an LP problem is always found in a corner point to the feasible region (a consequence of the linearity of all equations). In principle, the method searches through the set of feasible corner point solutions in a structured fashion until a set of optimality conditions are fulfilled, and the optimal solution is found. More details about the Simplex method and other aspects of LP, such as duality and sensitivity analysis can be found in basic OR/MS textbooks such as Hillier.[3] For more theoretical treatment of the subject one can turn to books like Dantzig[4–6] and Vanderbei.[7]

IP models

One limitation with LP models is that the decision variables must be continuous. Hence, it is just a coincidence that the optimal solution to the product mix example above turned out to be in full batches ($X_A^* = 20$, $X_B^* =$

60) rather than fractional. If integer restrictions of the decision variables are added to an LP model, it transforms into an Integer Programming (IP) model. If some variables are allowed to be continuous while others are integer, the model is often referred to as a Mixed Integer Programming (MIP) model.

Solving a problem which contains integer variables is much more difficult than solving a LP model. The reason is that there is no longer a guarantee that an optimal solution is found in a feasible corner point solution. As a result, the number of candidate solutions to investigate increases tremendously. To avoid complete enumeration, which would severely restrict the size of the problems worth considering, much research has gone into finding good solution methods for various kinds of IP problems. One common solution approach is the family of Branch and Bound algorithms. The underlying principle with Branch and Bound is to divide a difficult problem into subproblems that are easier to solve, and then use these subproblems to bound the optimal solution. The subproblems may, for example, be linear programs. For more details about Branch and Bound techniques and other solution approaches for IP models one can turn to, for example, Wolsey.[8] For a more general introduction to IP models, including examples of formulated problems[3] is an excellent starting point.

A special case of integer-valued decision variables are binary variables, which are restricted to be either 0 or 1. The binary variables are important in decision modeling because they can be used to describe Yes/No decisions, either or alternatives, fixed charges and stepwise changes. They can also be used for representing general integer variables.

To exemplify the use of binary variables, we return to the product mix example in the "LP Models" entry. After further analysis it turns out that there is a fixed charge of $1000 associated with starting up production of product A. This start up cost is due to necessary configuration of machinery and special material handling equipment that needs to be acquired in case product A is produced. To incorporate this feature into the decision model, an additional decision variable is needed together with new constraints and a modified objective function.

Definition of the additional (auxiliary) decision variable:

$$y_A = \begin{cases} 1 & \text{if product A is produced} \\ 0 & \text{if product A is not produced} \end{cases}$$

The modified objective function (maximize total profits) that includes the fixed charge associated with producing product A becomes

$$\text{Max } Z = 1500X_A + 2000X_B - 1000y_A$$

The new constraints must assure that y_A is binary and that the contingent decision to produce A or not (modeled by y_A), is aligned with the original decision of how much to produce of A (modeled by X_A). For the formulation, we define the parameter M to be a very large number, larger than the highest possible production of product A.

(6) $X_A - My_A \leq 0$ (X_A positive only if $y_A = 1$)
(7) y_A is binary

The complete formulation of the fixed charge product mix decision problem now amounts to the following MIP model.

Max Z = $1500X_A + 2000X_B - 1000y_A$ (maximize total profits)

Subject to
(1) $3X_A + \qquad \leq 150$ (limited capacity in resource 1)
(2) $1X_A + 2X_B \leq 140$ (limited capacity in resource 2)
(3) $2X_A + 2X_B \leq 160$ (limited capacity in resource 3)
(4) $\qquad X_B \geq 20$ (produce at least 20 batches of product B)
(5) $\quad X_A, X_B \geq 0$ (non − negativity constraint)
(6) $X_A - My_A \leq 0$ (X_A positive only if $y_A = 1$)
(7) y_A is binary

The versatility of IP models means that they can be used to describe almost any kind of deterministic decision situation with a single objective. Their usefulness in practical applications may however be limited by the computational effort involved in solving large size problems. Still, the situation is continuously improving thanks to increased computer capacity and better solution algorithms. One of the most widely used software packages for solution of large-scale IP (and LP) models is CPLEX, a product sold and developed by the company ILOG.

It may be worth noting that when dealing with reasonably large integer variables it is usually an acceptable approximation to use an LP model and then round the solution to integers (although there is no guarantee that the rounded solution is feasible). However, in case of binary variables this approach is generally not feasible.

Economic lot sizing

Let us now consider a simple nonlinear decision model that has been around for a long time but still is very important in production and inventory management, the so-called classical economic order quantity (EOQ) model.

Consider an inventory location that replenishes its stock of an item from an external supplier. The problem is to determine a suitable batch quantity, that is, to decide on the size of a replenishment order. This decision is mainly affected by two costs. First there is usually a fixed "ordering cost" associated with each replenishment (independent of the batch size). This cost can be due to administrative costs associated with the handling of orders and to costs for transportation and materials handling. The other important cost that needs to be considered is a "holding cost" per unit and time unit. The holding cost includes an opportunity cost for capital tied up in inventory, but may also include other costs that increase with the inventory on hand.

Our simple model assumes that the known demand is constant and continuous. Furthermore, the batch quantity is not changed over time, the whole batch quantity is delivered at the same time, and no shortages are allowed. We shall use the following notation:

h = holding cost per unit and time unit,
A = ordering or setup cost,
d = demand per time unit,
Q = batch quantity,
C = costs per time unit.

Clearly, a batch should arrive and be placed in stock just as the previous batch is depleted. The development of the inventory level can therefore be illustrated as in Fig. 3.

We wish to determine the optimal batch quantity Q^*. The relevant costs to consider in the decision model are therefore the costs that vary with the batch quantity Q. We get

$$C = \frac{Q}{2}h + \frac{d}{Q}A$$

The first term represents the holding costs, which we obtain as the average stock, $Q/2$, multiplied by the holding cost h. The average number of orders per unit of time is d/Q, and multiplying by the ordering cost A, renders the ordering costs per unit time in the second term.

It is easy to optimize the cost function. We just set the derivative with respect to Q equal to zero (as one can show that C is a convex function).

$$\frac{dC}{dQ} = \frac{h}{2} - \frac{d}{Q^2}A = 0$$

Solving for Q we get the EOQ:

$$Q^* = \sqrt{\frac{2Ad}{h}}$$

This result was first derived by Harris in Harris[9] There is also a well-known early paper by Wilson, Wilson,[10] providing the same result.

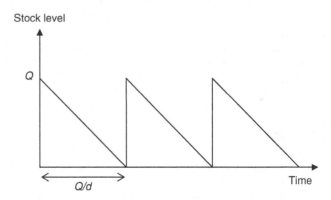

Fig. 3   Development of inventory level over time.

As we have discussed in the introduction, it is common to use decision rules that are based on certain simplified assumptions also in settings where these assumptions are not really satisfied. For example, in practice it is common to use the classical lot size formula also in case of stationary stochastic demand. The constant demand d is then usually replaced by the demand forecast. It can be shown that this approximation, in general, works quite well. The considered simple lot size formula has been implemented in an enormous number of inventory control systems. There are also many related models, see, for example, Axsäter.[11]

Stochastic Models

In many situations, the inherent uncertainty or randomness of decision input information is the main obstacle for making good decisions. Intuitively understanding the consequences of random behavior on the system performance is difficult for most people, including decision makers. This emphasizes the need for quantitative decision models that explicitly incorporate randomness and evaluates its consequences. Describing uncertainty and randomness mathematically involves the use of probability theory and stochastic variables. To make the discussion more concrete and to illustrate the usefulness of stochastic decision models, we will in this entry look closer at the classical newsvendor model, which is the foundation on which many stochastic inventory models are built.

Before turning to the newsvendor model, it is worth emphasizing that the complexity associated with stochastic behavior often prohibits the use of detailed analytical models. In these situations computer-based simulation models may be very useful for evaluating different decision alternatives and analyzing the dynamics of complicated stochastic systems. Particularly, modern discrete event simulation software packages with graphical interface represent a flexible and easy to use decision support tool. For further details on simulation modeling and the use of modern discrete event simulation software, one can turn to Law[12] and Laguna.[13] The latter also provides an introduction to analytical modeling of simple queuing systems (see also Hillier),[3] which represents another important area in stochastic decision modeling.

The newsvendor model

In this entry we consider the classical newsvendor model. In its original form, the problem deals with a newsvendor who can buy copies of a newspaper in the morning for a certain price, and sell them during the day for a higher price. The stochastic demand during the day is known through its probability distribution. The newsvendor is not paid anything for unsold copies of the newspaper.

We shall deal with a slightly more general formulation of the problem and introduce the following notation:

X = stochastic period demand,

$f(x)$ = density of the stochastic period demand,

$F(x)$ = cumulative distribution function of the stochastic period demand, that is, the probability that the demand X is less than or equal to x,

S = ordered amount,

c_o = overage cost, that is, the cost per unit for inventory remaining at the end of the period,

c_u = underage cost, that is, the cost per unit for unmet period demand.

Let us for a moment go back to the newsvendor interpretation of the problem. The period length is then one day. Assume that the newsvendor pays 25 cents for a copy of the newspaper and sells them for 75 cents during the day. We then have $c_o = 25$, and $c_u = 75 - 25 = 50$. Note that c_u in this case corresponds to the opportunity costs for lost sales.

For a certain demand X the costs are:

$$C(X) = (S - X)c_o \quad \text{if} \quad X \leq S$$

$$C(X) = (X - S)c_u \quad \text{if} \quad X > S$$

Using this we can express the expected costs $C = E\{C(X)\}$ as

$$C = c_o \int_0^S (S - x)f(x)dx + c_u \int_S^\infty (x - S)f(x)dx$$

It is relatively easy to show that the expected costs are minimized when S is chosen so that

$$F(S) = \frac{c_u}{c_o + c_u}$$

This means that the optimal S can be obtained from a very simple decision rule,

$$S = F^{-1}\left(\frac{c_u}{c_o + c_u}\right)$$

The newsvendor model has many important applications, especially when considering ordering and capacity decisions regarding products with a short selling season or product life cycle, for example, in the fashion industry. The model is also closely related to many multiperiod inventory models dealing with an infinite horizon. Assume that there are many periods and associated replenishment opportunities. The overage cost in a period is then the cost to carry a unit in stock to the next period, that is, a holding cost. Similarly, the underage cost can be interpreted as the cost for letting a customer wait to the next period, that is, a backorder cost. For overviews of different types of stochastic inventory models see, for example, Axsäter[11] and Silver.[14]

Other Types of Decision Models

So far we have considered two types of decision models, deterministic and stochastic models. For both types of models we have assumed a single decision maker who wants to find the best decision for a considered system as a whole. However, there may also be situations where there are several decision makers interacting (competing or cooperating). If the behavior and responses of these different decision makers are important to understand in order to make good quality decisions, the dynamics need to be incorporated into the quantitative decision model. To analyze game situations where there are several decision makers with different goals, different types of game theoretic models can be used. Such situations are very common in practice.

Let us return to the newsvendor model in "The Newsvendor Model" entry. In this model we only studied a single decision maker. However, it is quite natural to extend the model to include two decision makers. We let the newsvendor have the same role as in "The Newsvendor Model" section. But the newsvendor now buys the newspapers from a supplier with a certain production cost per unit. The supplier can choose the price he wants to charge the newsvendor. In this setting both the supplier and the newsvendor want to maximize their individual profits. What decisions should be taken by the two players? Will the resulting entry be optimal for the system as a whole? It turns out that the answer to the latter question is no. However, if we change the considered "wholesale-price contract" to a "buyback contract" where the supplier pays the newsvendor for left over inventory a coordinated solution may be reached. This means that it is possible to instigate a pricing and contract mechanism so that we can let the supplier and the newsvendor optimize their individual profits and still get a solution that is optimal for the system as a whole.

We refer to Cachon[15] and Chen[16] for recent overviews of the literature on coordination and contracts in such systems.

An underlying assumption for all the models we have considered in this entry is that there is a single, well-defined objective for each decision maker, for example, maximizing profits, minimizing costs, etc. However, in many situations the decision maker can be faced with several different objectives that may not be aligned, or may even be in direct conflict. For example, the objective to retain the current workforce may not be aligned with maximizing profits, the objective to maximize environmental friendliness may conflict with an objective to minimize costs, etc. Modeling and analysis of decision problems with multiple (conflicting) objectives is the focus of the multiple criteria decision making (MCDM) area. A basic question when approaching these problems is whether there is a clear order of priority between different objectives or not. An associated question is how to translate different objectives into a common scale. Monetary terms may not always be the best choice. For more about MCDM one can turn to, for example, Bouyssou.[17]

CONCLUSIONS

In this entry we have provided a description of the broad area of decision sciences from a quantitative modeling (OR/MS) perspective. An overarching objective with most research in this field is to use quantitative models to improve the quality of decisions. This means that the model is viewed as a tool for helping decision makers to generate, evaluate, and choose good decision alternatives. With this as a starting point, we have explained the conceptual approach underlying the use of quantitative decision modeling. We have also illustrated this general approach by considering some commonly used deterministic and stochastic decision models in more detail. The model types we have discussed include LP, IP, economic lot sizing, and the newsvendor model. We have also briefly commented on extensions and other modeling approaches such as game theory, MCDM, queuing, and simulation.

Looking at the development of the field in recent years, one can conclude that it is in many ways linked to the development and wide spread use of information technology and computers. With the increasing access to vast amounts of information, there is a growing potential for making better decisions that capture the value hidden in the information flow. This accentuates the need for quantitative decision models and decision support systems to help the decision makers sort, evaluate, and process input information into concrete decision alternatives. The increasing amounts of information also suggests more complex and large size models to evaluate, which can be done thanks to the fast development in computer technology, and more efficient solution methods. Altogether one can conclude that this paints a bright and interesting future for the field. However, an important challenge, in order for quantitative decision modeling to reach its full potential, is to bridge the gap between the complex quantitative model and the decision maker. The foundations for those bridges are carefully designed software packages, and easy to use decision support tools.

REFERENCES

1. Dantzig, G.B. Reminiscences about the origins of linear programming. Oper. Res. Lett. **1981/1982**, *1*(2), 43–48.

2. Kraft, D.H.; Boyce, B.R. *Operations Research for Libraries and Information Agencies: Techniques for the Evaluation of Management Decision Alternatives*, Academic Press: San Diego, CA, 1991.

3. Hillier, F.S.; Lieberman, G.J. *Introduction to Operations Research*, 8th Ed. McGraw-Hill: Singapore, 2005.

4. Dantzig, G.B. *Linear Programming and Extensions*, Princeton University Press: Princeton, NJ, 1963; 68.

5. Dantzig, G.B.; Thapa, M.N. *Linear Programming 1: Introduction*, Springer: New York, 1997.

6. Dantzig, G.B.; Thapa, M.N. *Linear Programming 2: Theory and Extensions*, Springer: New York, 1997.

7. Vanderbei, R.J. *Linear Programming: Foundations and Extensions*, 2nd Ed. Kluwer Academic Publishers: Boston, MA, 2001.

8. Wolsey, L.A. *Integer Programming*, Wiley: New York, 1998.

9. Harris, F.W. How many parts to make at once. Factory, The Mag. Manage. **1913**, *10*, 135–136, 152.

10. Wilson, R.H. A scientific routine for stock control. Harvard Bus. Rev. **1934**, *13*, 116–128.

11. Axsäter, S. *Inventory Control*, 2nd Ed. Springer: New York, 2006.

12. Law, A.M.; Kelton, W.D. *Simulation Modeling and Analysis*, 3rd Ed. McGraw-Hill: Boston, MA, 2000.

13. Laguna, M.; Marklund, J. *Business Process Modeling, Simulation and Design*, Prentice Hall: Upper Saddle River, NJ, 2005.

14. Silver, E.A.; Pyke, D.F.; Peterson, R. *Inventory Management and Production Planning and Scheduling*, 3rd Ed. Wiley: New York, 1998.

15. Cachon, G.P. Supply chain coordination with contracts. In *Handbooks in OR & MS Vol. 11*; de Kok, A.G., Graves, S.C., Eds.; North Holland: Amsterdam, the Netherlands, 2003; 229–339.

16. Chen, F. Information sharing and supply chain coordination. In *Handbooks in OR & MS Vol. 11*; de Kok, A.G., Graves, S.C., Eds.; North Holland: Amsterdam, the Netherlands, 2003; 341–421.

17. Bouyssou, D.; Marchant, T.; Pirlot, M.; Tsoukiàs, A.; Vincke, P. *Evaluation and Decision Models with Multiple Criteria: Stepping Stones for the Analyst*, Springer: New York, 2006.

Decision Support Systems

Marek J. Druzdzel
*School of Information Sciences and Intelligent Systems Program, University of Pittsburgh,
Pittsburgh, Pennsylvania, U.S.A., and Faculty of Computer Science, Bialystok Technical
University, Bialystok, Poland*

Roger R. Flynn
*School of Information Sciences and Intelligent Systems Program, University of Pittsburgh,
Pittsburgh, Pennsylvania, U.S.A.*

Abstract

Decision support systems (DSSs) are defined as interactive computer-based systems that aid users in
judgment and choice activities. The entry focuses on the core module of DSSs, notably one that directly
supports modeling decision problems and identifies best alternatives. It introduces three components of
decisions: decision alternatives, preferences, and uncertainty. It presents fundamental components of a
DSS: the database management system, the model-base management system, and the dialog generation
and management system. It discusses an emergent class of decision-analytic DSSs, based on the sound
foundations of probability theory and decision theory. Finally, it reviews issues related to user interfaces to
DSSs.

INTRODUCTION

Making decisions concerning complex systems (e.g., the management of organizational operations, industrial processes, or investment portfolios; the command and control of military units; the control of nuclear power plants) often strains our cognitive capabilities. Even though individual interactions among a system's variables may be well understood, predicting how the system will react to an external manipulation such as a policy decision is often difficult. What will be, for example the effect of introducing the third shift on a factory floor? One might expect that this will increase the plant's output by roughly 50%. Factors such as additional wages, machine weardown, maintenance breaks, raw material usage, supply logistics, and future demand also need to be considered, however, because they will all affect the total financial outcome of this decision. Many variables are involved in complex and often subtle interdependencies, and predicting the total outcome may be daunting.

There is a substantial amount of empirical evidence that human intuitive judgment and decision making can be far from optimal, and it deteriorates even further with complexity and stress. In many situations, the quality of decisions is important; therefore, aiding the deficiencies of human judgment and decision making has been a major focus of science throughout history. Disciplines such as statistics, economics, and operations research developed various methods for making rational choices. More recently, these methods, often enhanced by various techniques originating from information science, cognitive psychology, and artificial intelligence, have been

implemented in the form of computer programs, either as stand-alone tools or as integrated computing environments for complex decision making. Such environments are often given the common name of *decision support systems* (DSSs). The concept of DSS is extremely broad, and its definitions vary, depending on the author's point of view. To avoid exclusion of any of the existing types of DSSs, we define them roughly as interactive computer-based systems that aid users in judgment and choice activities. Another name sometimes used as a synonym for DSS is *knowledge-based systems*, which refers to their attempt to formalize domain knowledge so that it is amenable to mechanized reasoning.

Decision support systems are gaining an increased popularity in various domains, including business, engineering, the military, and medicine. They are especially valuable in situations in which the amount of available information is prohibitive for the intuition of an unaided human decision maker, and in which precision and optimality are of importance. Decision support systems can aid human cognitive deficiencies by integrating various sources of information, providing intelligent access to relevant knowledge, and aiding the process of structuring decisions. They can also support choice among well-defined alternatives and build on formal approaches, such as the methods of engineering economics, operations research, statistics, and decision theory. They can also employ artificial intelligence methods to heuristically address problems that are intractable by formal techniques. Proper application of decision-making tools increases productivity, efficiency, and effectiveness, and gives many businesses a comparative advantage over their

Encyclopedia of Library and Information Sciences, Fourth Edition DOI: 10.1081/E-ELIS4-120043887

Data–Dewey

competitors, allowing them to make optimal choices for technological processes and their parameters, planning business operations, logistics, or investments.

Although it is difficult to overestimate the importance of various computer-based tools that are relevant to decision making (e.g., databases, planning software, spreadsheets), this entry focuses primarily on the core of a DSS, the part that directly supports modeling decision problems and identifies best alternatives. We briefly discuss the characteristics of decision problems and how decision making can be supported by computer programs. We then cover various components of DSSs and the role that they play in decision support. We also introduce an emergent class of *normative systems* (i.e., DSSs based on sound theoretical principles), and in particular, decision-analytic DSSs. Finally, we review issues related to user interfaces to DSSs and stress the importance of user interfaces to the ultimate quality of decisions aided by computer programs.

DECISIONS AND DECISION MODELING

Types of Decisions

A simple view of decision making is that it is a problem of choice among several alternatives. A somewhat more sophisticated view includes the process of constructing the alternatives (i.e., given a problem statement, developing a list of choice options). A complete picture includes a search for opportunities for decisions (i.e., discovering that there is a decision to be made). A manager of a company may face a choice in which the options are clear (e.g., the choice of a supplier from among all existing suppliers). She may also face a well-defined problem for which she designs creative decision options (e.g., how to market a new product so that the profits are maximized). Finally, she may work in a less reactive fashion, and view decision problems as opportunities that have to be discovered by studying the operations of her company and its surrounding environment (e.g., how can she make the production process more efficient). There is much anecdotal and some empirical evidence that structuring decision problems and identifying creative decision alternatives determine the ultimate quality of decisions. Decision support systems aim mainly at this broadest type of decision making, and in addition to supporting choice, they aid in modeling and analyzing systems (e.g., as complex organizations), identifying decision opportunities, and structuring decision problems.

Human Judgment and Decision Making

Theoretical studies on rational decision making, notably that in the context of probability theory and decision theory, have been accompanied by empirical research on whether human behavior complies with the theory. It has been rather convincingly demonstrated in numerous empirical studies that human judgment and decision making are based on intuitive strategies, as opposed to theoretically sound reasoning rules. These intuitive strategies, referred to as *judgmental heuristics* in the context of decision making, help us in reducing the cognitive load, but alas at the expense of optimal decision making. Effectively, our unaided judgment and choice exhibit systematic violations of probability axioms (referred to as *biases*). Formal discussion of the most important research results, along with experimental data, can be found in an anthology edited by Kahneman et al.[1] Dawes[2] provided an accessible introduction to what is known about people's decision-making performance.

One might hope that people who have achieved expertise in a domain will not be subject to judgmental biases and will approach optimality in decision making. Although empirical evidence shows that experts indeed are more accurate than novices, within their area of expertise, it also shows that they also are liable to the same judgmental biases as novices, and demonstrate apparent errors and inconsistencies in their judgment. Professionals such as practicing physicians use essentially the same judgmental heuristics and are prone to the same biases, although the degree of departure from the normatively prescribed judgment seems to decrease with experience. In addition to laboratory evidence, there are several studies of expert performance in realistic settings, showing that it is inferior even to simple linear models (an informal review of the available evidence and pointers to literature can be found in the book by Dawes).[2] For example, predictions of future violent behavior of psychiatric patients made by a panel of psychiatrists who had access to patient records and interviewed the patients were found to be inferior to a simple model that included only the past incidence of violent behavior. Predictions of marriage counselors concerning marital happiness were shown to be inferior to a simple model that just subtracted the rate of fighting from the rate of sexual intercourse (again, the marriage counselors had access to all data, including interviews with the couples). Studies yielding similar results were conducted with bank loan officers, physicians, university admission committees, and so on.

Modeling Decisions

The superiority of even simple linear models over human intuitive judgment suggests that one way to improve the quality of decisions is to decompose a decision problem into simpler components that are well defined and well understood. Studying a complex system built out of such components can be subsequently aided by a formal, theoretically sound technique. The process of decomposing and formalizing a problem is often called modeling. Modeling amounts to finding an abstract representation of a real-world system that simplifies and assumes as much as possible about the system, and while retaining the system's essential relationships, omits unnecessary detail. Building a model of a decision problem, as opposed to reasoning about a problem in a holistic way, allows for applying scientific knowledge that can be transferred across problems and often across domains. It allows for analyzing, explaining, and arguing about a decision problem.

The desire to improve human decision making provided motivation for the development of various modeling tools in disciplines of economics, operations research, decision theory, decision analysis, and statistics. In each modeling tool, knowledge about a system is represented by means of algebraic, logical, or statistical variables. Interactions among these variables are expressed by equations or logical rules, possibly enhanced with an explicit representation of uncertainty. When the functional form of an interaction is unknown, it is sometimes described in purely probabilistic terms (e.g., by a conditional probability distribution). Once a model has been formulated, various mathematical methods can be used to analyze it. Decision making under certainty has been addressed by economic and operations research methods, such as cash flow analysis, break-even analysis, scenario analysis, mathematical programming, inventory techniques, and various optimization algorithms for scheduling and logistics. Decision making under uncertainty enhances the above methods with statistical approaches, such as reliability analysis, simulation, and statistical decision making. Most of these methods have made it into college curricula and can be found in management textbooks. Due to space constraints, we do not discuss their details further.

Components of Decision Models

Although a model mathematically consists of variables and a specification of interactions among them, from the point of view of decision making, a model and its variables represent the following three components: (1) a measure of preferences over decision objectives; (2) available decision options; and (3) a measure of uncertainty over variables influencing the decision and the outcomes.

Preference is widely viewed as the most important concept in decision making. Outcomes of a decision process are not all equally attractive, and it is crucial for a decision maker to examine these outcomes in terms of their desirability. Preferences can be ordinal (e.g., more income is preferred to less income), but it is convenient and often necessary to represent them as numerical quantities, especially if the outcome of the decision process consists of multiple attributes that need to be compared on a common scale. Even when they consist of just a single attribute but the choice is made under uncertainty, expressing preferences numerically allows for trade-offs between desirability and risk.

The second component of decision problems is available decision options. Often these options can be enumerated (e.g., a list of possible suppliers), but sometimes they are continuous values of specified policy variables (e.g., the amount of raw material to be kept in stock). Listing the available decision options is an important element of model structuring.

The third element of decision models is uncertainty. Uncertainty is one of the most inherent and most prevalent properties of knowledge, originating from incompleteness of information, imprecision, and model approximations made for the sake of simplicity. It would not be an exaggeration to state that real-world decisions not involving uncertainty either do not exist or belong to a truly limited class. As Benjamin Franklin expressed it in 1789 in a letter to his friend M. Le Roy, "in this world nothing can said to be certain, except death and taxes" (Bigelow.[3]).

Decision making under uncertainty can be viewed as a deliberation—determining what action should be taken that will maximize the expected gain. Due to uncertainty, there is no guarantee that the result of the action will be the one intended, and the best one can hope for is to maximize the chance of a desirable outcome. The process rests on the assumption that a good decision is one that results from a good decision-making process that considers all important factors and is explicit about decision alternatives, preferences, and uncertainty.

It is important to distinguish between good decisions and good outcomes. By a stroke of good luck, a poor decision can lead to a very good outcome. Similarly, a very good decision can be followed by a bad outcome. Supporting decisions means supporting the decision-making process so that better decisions are made. Better decisions can be expected to lead to better outcomes.

DECISION SUPPORT SYSTEMS

Decision support systems are interactive, computer-based systems that aid users in judgment and choice activities. They provide data storage and retrieval, but enhance the traditional information access and retrieval functions with support for model building and model-based reasoning. They support framing, modeling, and problem solving.

Typical application areas of DSSs are management and planning in business, health care, the military, and any area in which management will encounter complex decision situations. Decision support systems are typically used for strategic and tactical decisions faced by upper-level management—decisions with a reasonably low frequency and high potential consequences—in which the time taken for thinking through and modeling the problem pays off generously in the long run.

There are three fundamental components of DSSs:[3]

- *Database management system (DBMS)*. A DBMS serves as a data bank for the DSS. It stores large quantities of data that are relevant to the class of problems for which the DSS has been designed and provides logical data structures (as opposed to the physical data structures) with which the users interact. A DBMS separates the users from the physical aspects of the database structure and processing. It should also be capable of informing the user of the types of data that are available and how to gain access to them.
- *Model-base management system (MBMS)*. The role of MBMS is analogous to that of a DBMS. Its primary function is providing independence between specific models that are used in a DSS from the applications that use them. The purpose of an MBMS is to transform data from the DBMS into information that is useful in decision making. Because many problems that the user of a DSS will cope with may be unstructured, the MBMS should also be capable of assisting the user in model building.
- *Dialog generation and management system (DGMS)*. The main product of an interaction with a DSS is insight. Because their users are often managers who are not computer trained, DSSs need to be equipped with intuitive and easy-to-use interfaces. These interfaces aid in model building, but also in interaction with the model, such as gaining insight and recommendations from it. The primary responsibility of a DGMS is to enhance the ability of the system user to use and benefit from the DSS. In the remainder of this entry, we use the broader term user interface rather than DGMS.

Although various DSSs exists, the above three components can be found in many DSS architectures and play a prominent role in their structure. Interaction among them is shown in Fig. 1.

Essentially, the user interacts with the DSS through the DGMS. This communicates with the DBMS and MBMS, which screen the user and the user interface from the physical details of the model base and database implementation.

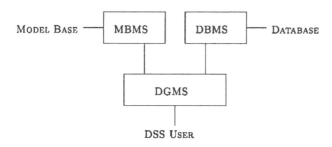

Fig. 1 The architecture of a DSS.
Source: From Sage.[4]

NORMATIVE SYSTEMS

Normative and Descriptive Approaches

Whether one trusts the quality of human intuitive reasoning strategies has a profound impact on one's view of the philosophical and technical foundations of DSSs. There are two distinct approaches to supporting decision making. The first aims at building support procedures or systems that imitate human experts. The most prominent member of this class of DSSs are *expert systems*, computer programs based on rules elicited from human domain experts that imitate reasoning of a human expert in a given domain. Expert systems are often capable of supporting decision making in that domain at a level comparable to human experts. Although they are flexible and often able to address complex decision problems, they are based on intuitive human reasoning and lack soundness and formal guarantees with respect to the theoretical reliability of their results. The danger of the expert system approach, increasingly appreciated by DSS builders, is that along with imitating human thinking and its efficient heuristic principles, we may also imitate its undesirable flaws.[5]

The second approach is based on the assumption that the most reliable method of dealing with complex decisions is through a small set of normatively sound principles of how decisions should be made. Although heuristic methods and ad hoc reasoning schemes that imitate human cognition may in many domains perform well, most decision makers will be reluctant to rely on them whenever the cost of making an error is high. To give an extreme example, few people would choose to fly airplanes built using heuristic principles over airplanes built using the laws of aerodynamics enhanced with probabilistic reliability analysis. Application of formal methods in DSSs makes these systems philosophically distinct from those based on ad hoc heuristic artificial intelligence methods, such as rule-based systems. The goal of a DSS, according to this view, is to support unaided human intuition, just as the goal of using a calculator is to aid human's limited capacity for mental arithmetic.

Decision-Analytic DSSs

An emergent class of DSSs known as *decision-analytic DSSs* applies the principles of decision theory, probability theory, and decision analysis to their decision models. Decision theory is an axiomatic theory of decision making that is built on a small set of axioms of rational decision making. It expresses uncertainty in terms of probabilities and preferences in terms of utilities. These are combined using the operation of mathematical expectation. The attractiveness of probability theory, as a formalism for handling uncertainty in DSSs, lies in its soundness and its guarantees concerning long-term performance. Probability theory is often viewed as the gold standard for rationality in reasoning under uncertainty. Following its axioms offers protection from some elementary inconsistencies. Their violation, however, can be demonstrated to lead to sure losses.[6] Decision analysis is the art and science of applying decision theory to real-world problems. It includes a wealth of techniques for model construction, such as methods for elicitation of model structure and probability distributions that allow minimization of human bias, methods for checking the sensitivity of a model to imprecision in the data, computing the value of obtaining additional information, and presentation of results (see, e.g., von Winterfeldt[7] for a basic review of the available techniques). These methods have been under continuous scrutiny by psychologists working in the domain of behavioral decision theory and have proven to cope reasonably well with the dangers related to human judgmental biases.

Normative systems are usually based on graphical probabilistic models, which are representations of the joint probability distribution over a model's variables in terms of directed graphs. Directed graphs, such as the one in Fig. 2, are known as Bayesian networks (BNs) or causal networks.[8] Bayesian networks offer a compact representation of joint probability distributions and are capable of

practical representation of large models, consisting of tens or hundreds of variables. Bayesian networks can be easily extended with decision and value variables for modeling decision problems. The former denote variables that are under the decision maker's control and can be directly manipulated, and the latter encode users' preferences over various outcomes of the decision process. Such amended graphs are known as *influence diagrams*.[9] Both the structure and the numerical probability distributions in a BN can be elicited from a human expert and are a reflection of the expert's subjective view of a real-world system. If available, scientific knowledge about the system, both in terms of the structure and frequency data, can be easily incorporated in the model. Once a model has been created, it is optimized using formal decision-theoretic algorithms. Decision analysis is based on the empirically tested paradigm that people are able to reliably store and retrieve their personal beliefs about uncertainty and preferences for different outcomes, but are much less reliable in aggregating these fragments into a global inference. Although human experts are excellent in structuring a problem, determining the components that are relevant to it and providing local estimates of probabilities and preferences, they are not reliable in combining many simple factors into an optimal decision. The role of a decision-analytic

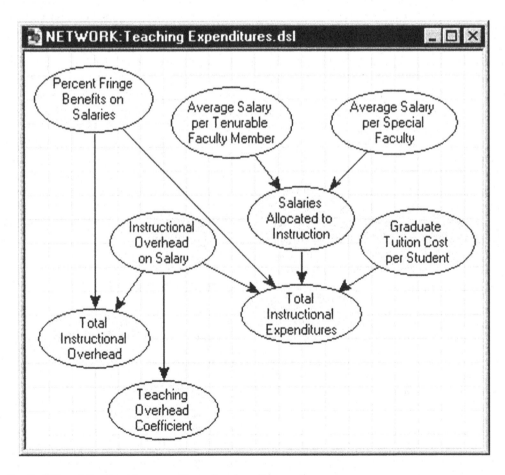

Fig. 2 Example of a BN modeling teaching expenditures in university operations.

DSS is to support them in their weaknesses using the formal and theoretically sound principles of statistics.

The approach taken by decision analysis is compatible with that of DSSs. The goal of decision analysis is to provide insight into a decision. This insight, consisting of the analysis of all relevant factors, their uncertainty, and the critical nature of some assumptions, is even more important than the actual recommendation.

Decision-analytic DSSs have been successfully applied to practical systems in medicine, business, and engineering. Some examples of applications are described in a special issue of *Communications of the ACM* on practical applications of decision-theoretic methods (Vol. 38, No. 3, March 1995). We encourage the readers to experiment with GeNIe,[10] a development system for decision-analytic DSSs developed at the Decision Systems Laboratory, University of Pittsburgh, available at http://genie.sis.pitt.edu/. As these systems tend to naturally evolve into three not necessarily distinct classes, it may be interesting to compare their structure and architectural organization.

- *Systems with static domain models.* In this class of systems, a probabilistic domain is represented by a typically large network encoding the domain's structure and its numerical parameters. The network comprising the domain model is normally built by decision analysts and domain experts. An example might be a medical diagnostic system covering a certain class of disorders. Queries in such a system are answered by assigning values to those nodes of the network that constitute the observations for a particular case and propagating the impact of the observation through the network to find the probability distribution of some selected nodes of interest (e.g., nodes that represent diseases). Such a network can, on a case-by-case basis, be extended with decision nodes and value nodes to support decisions. Systems with static domain models are conceptually similar to rule-based expert systems covering an area of expertise.
- *Systems with customized decision models.* The main idea behind this approach is automatic generation of a graphical decision model on a per-case basis in an interactive effort between the DSS and the decision maker. The DSS has domain expertise in a certain area and plays the role of a decision analyst. During this interaction, the program creates a customized influence diagram, which is later used for generating advice. The main motivation for this approach is the premise that every decision is unique and needs to be looked at individually; an influence diagram needs to be tailored to individual needs.[11]
- *Systems capable of learning a model from data.* The third class of systems employs computer-intensive statistical methods for learning models from data.[12–16] Whenever there are sufficient data available, the

systems can literally learn a graphical model from these data. This model can be subsequently used to support decisions within the same domain.

The first two approaches are suited for slightly different applications. The customized model generation approach is an attempt to automate the most laborious part of decision making, structuring a problem, so far done with significant assistance from trained decision analysts. A session with the program that assists the decision maker in building an influence diagram is laborious. This makes the customized model generation approach particularly suitable for decision problems that are infrequent and serious enough to be treated individually. Because in the static domain model approach, an existing domain model needs to be customized by the case data only, the decision-making cycle is rather short. This makes it particularly suitable for those decisions that are highly repetitive and need to be made under time constraints.

A practical system can combine the three approaches. A static domain model can be slightly customized for a case that needs individual treatment. Once completed, a customized model can be blended into the large static model. Learning systems can support both the static and the customized model approach. However, the learning process can be greatly enhanced by prior knowledge from domain experts or by a prior model.

Equation-Based and Mixed Systems

In many business and engineering problems, interactions among model variables can be described by equations that, when solved simultaneously, can be used to predict the effect of decisions on the system, and hence support decision making. One special type of simultaneous equation model is known as the structural equation model (SEM), which has been a popular method of representing systems in econometrics. An equation is structural if it describes a unique, independent causal mechanism acting in the system. Structural equations are based on expert knowledge of the system combined with theoretical considerations. Structural equations allow for a natural, modular description of a system—each equation represents its individual component, a separable and independent mechanism acting in the system—yet, the main advantage of having a structural model is, as explicated by Simon,[17] that it includes causal information and aids predictions of the effects of external interventions. In addition, the causal structure of a SEM can be represented graphically,[17] which allows for combining them with decision-analytic graphical models in practical systems.[17,18]

Structural equation models offer significant advantages for policy making. Often a decision maker confronted with a complex system needs to decide not only the values of policy variables, but also which variables should be manipulated. A change in the set of policy variables has a profound impact on the structure of the problem and on how their values will propagate through the system. The user chooses which variables are policy variables and which are determined within the model. A change in the SEMs or the set of policy variables can be reflected by a rapid restructuring of the model and predictions involving this new structure.[19]

Our long-term project, the Environment for Strategic Planning (ESP),[20] is based on a hybrid graphical modeling tool that combines SEMs with decision-analytic principles. The ESP is capable of representing both discrete and continuous variables involved in deterministic and probabilistic relationships. The powerful features of SEMs allow the ESP to act as a graphical spreadsheet integrating numerical and symbolic methods, and allowing the independent variables to be selected at will without having to reformulate the model each time. This provides an immense flexibility that is not afforded by ordinary spreadsheets in evaluating alternate policy options.

USER INTERFACES TO DSSs

Although the quality and reliability of modeling tools and the internal architectures of DSSs are important, the most crucial aspect of DSSs is, by far, their user interface. Systems with user interfaces that are cumbersome or unclear or that require unusual skills are rarely useful and accepted in practice. The most important result of a session with a DSS is insight into the decision problem. In addition, when the system is based on normative principles, it can play a tutoring role; one might hope that users will learn the domain model and how to reason with it over time, and improve their own thinking.

A good user interface to DSSs should support model construction and model analysis, reasoning about the problem structure in addition to numerical calculations, and both choice and optimization of decision variables. We discuss these in the following sections.

Support for Model Construction and Model Analysis

User interface is the vehicle for both model construction (or model choice) and for investigating the results. Even if a system is based on a theoretically sound reasoning scheme, its recommendations will only be as good as the model on which they are based. Furthermore, even if the model is a very good approximation of reality and its recommendations are correct, they will not be followed if they are not understood. Without understanding, the users may accept or reject a system's advice for the wrong reasons and the combined decision-making performance may deteriorate even below unaided performance.[21]

A good user interface should make the model on which the system's reasoning is based transparent to the user.

Modeling is rarely a one-shot process, and good models are usually refined and enhanced as their users gather practical experiences with the system recommendations. It is important to strike a careful balance between precision and modeling efforts; some parts of a model need to be very precise, whereas others do not. A good user interface should include tools for examining the model and identifying its most sensitive parts, which can be subsequently elaborated on. Systems employed in practice will need their models refined, and a good user interface should make it easy to access, examine, and refine its models. Some pointers to work on support for building decision-analytic systems can be found in.[22–25]

Support for Reasoning About the Problem Structure in Addition to Numerical Calculations

Although numerical calculations are important in decision support, reasoning about the problem structure is even more important. Often when the system and its model are complex, it is insightful for the decision maker to realize how the system variables are interrelated. This is helpful not only in designing creative decision options, but also in understanding how a policy decision will affect the objective.

Graphical models, such as those used in decision analysis or in equation-based and hybrid systems, are particularly suitable for reasoning about structure. Under certain assumptions, a directed graphical model can be given a causal interpretation. This is especially convenient in situations where the DSS autonomically suggests decision options; given a causal interpretation of its model, it is capable of predicting effects of interventions. A causal graph facilitates building an effective user interface. The system can refer to causal interactions during its dialogue with the user, which is known to enhance user insight.[26]

Support for Both Choice and Optimization of Decision Variables

Many DSSs have an inflexible structure in the sense that the variables that will be manipulated are determined at the model-building stage. This is not very suitable for planning of the strategic type when the object of the decision-making process is identifying both the objectives and the methods of achieving them. For example, changing policy variables in a spreadsheet-based model often requires that the entire spreadsheet be rebuilt. If there is no support for that, few users will consider it as an option. This closes the world of possibilities for flexible reframing of a decision problem in the exploratory process of searching for opportunities. Support for both choice and optimization of decision variables should be an inherent part of DSSs.

Graphical Interface

Insight into a model can be increased greatly at the user interface level by a diagram representing the interactions among its components (e.g., a drawing of a graph on which a model is based, such as in Fig. 2). This graph is a qualitative, structural explanation of how information flows from the independent variables to the dependent variables of interest. Because models may become very large, it is convenient to structure them into submodels, groups of variables that form a subsystem of the modeled system.[2,7] Such submodels can be again shown graphically with interactions among them, increasing simplicity and clarity of the interface. Fig. 3 shows a submodel-level view of a model developed in our ESP project. Note that the graph in Fig. 2 is an expanded version of the *Teaching Expenditures* submodel in Fig. 3. The user can navigate through the hierarchy of the entire model in her quest for insight, opening and closing submodels on demand. Some pointers to work on user interfaces of decision-analytic systems can be found in Wang,[25] Druzdzel[27,28] and Wiecha.[29]

CONCLUSION

Decision support systems are powerful tools integrating scientific methods for supporting complex decisions with techniques developed in information science and are gaining an increased popularity in many domains. They are especially valuable in situations in which the amount of available information is prohibitive for the intuition of an unaided human decision maker, and in which precision and optimality are of importance. Decision support systems aid human cognitive deficiencies by integrating various sources of information, providing intelligent access to relevant knowledge, aiding the process of structuring, and optimizing decisions.

Normative DSSs offer a theoretically correct and appealing way of handling uncertainty and preferences in decision problems. They are based on carefully studied empirical principles underlying the discipline of decision analysis, and they have been successfully applied in many practical systems. We believe that they offer several attractive features that are likely to prevail in the long run as far as the technical developments are concerned.

Because DSSs do not replace humans but rather augment their limited capacity to deal with complex problems, their user interfaces are critical. The user interface determines whether a DSS will be used at all and, if so, whether the ultimate quality of decisions will be higher than that of an unaided decision maker.

ACKNOWLEDGMENTS

Work on this entry was supported by the National Science Foundation under Faculty Early Career Development (CAREER) Program, grant IRI-9624629, by the Air Force Office of Scientific Research under grants F49620-97-1-0225, F49620-00-1-0112, and FA9550-06-1-0243 and by the University of Pittsburgh Central Research Development Fund. Figs. 2 and 3 are snapshots of GeNIe, a general purpose development environment for graphical DSSs developed by the Decision Systems Laboratory, University of Pittsburgh, and available at http://genie.sis.pitt.edu/. We want to thank Ms. Nanette Yurcik for her assistance with technical editing.

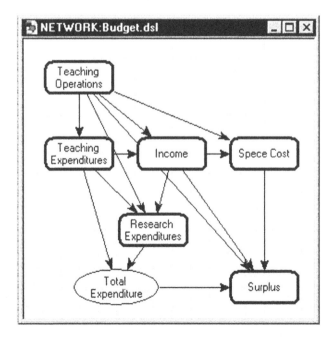

Fig. 3 A submodel-level view of a decision model.

REFERENCES

1. Kahneman, D., Slovic, P., Tversky, A. (Eds.) In *Judgment Under Uncertainty: Heuristics and Biases*; Cambridge University Press: Cambridge, U.K., 1982.
2. Dawes, R.M. *Rational Choice in an Uncertain World*, Hartcourt Brace Jovanovich: San Diego, CA, 1988.
3. Bigelow, J. (Ed.) *The Complete Works of Benjamin Franklin*; G.P. Putnam's Sons: New York and London, U.K., 1887; Vol. 10, 1700.
4. Sage, A.P. *Decision Support Systems Engineering*, John Wiley & Sons, Inc.: New York, 1991.
5. Henrion, M.; Breese, J.S.; Horvitz, E.J. Decision analysis and expert systems. AI Mag. **1991**, Winter *12*(4), 64–91.
6. Savage, L.J. *The Foundations of Statistics*, 2nd revised Ed.; Dover Publications: New York, 1972.
7. von Winterfeldt, D. Edwards, W. *Decision Analysis and Behavioral Research*, Cambridge University Press: Cambridge, U.K., 1988.

8. Pearl, J. *Probabilistic Reasoning in Intelligent Systems: Networks of Plausible Inference*, Morgan Kaufmann Publishers, Inc.: San Mateo, CA, 1988.

9. Howard, R.A. Matheson, J.E. Influence diagrams. In *The Principles and Applications of Decision Analysis*; Howard, R.A., Matheson, J.E., Eds.; Strategic Decisions Group: Menlo Park, CA, 1984; 719–762.

10. Druzdzel, M.J. SMILE: Structural Modeling, Inference, and Learning Engine and GeNIe: A development environment for graphical decision-theoretic models Proceedings of the Sixteenth National Conference on Artificial Intelligence (AAAI-99) Orlando, FL, 1999; 902–903.

11. Holtzman, S. *Intelligent Decision Systems*, Addison-Wesley: Reading, MA, 1989.

12. Spirtes, P. Glymour, C. Scheines, R. *Causation, Prediction, and Search*, Springer Verlag: New York, 1993.

13. Pearl, J. Verma, T.S. A theory of inferred causation*KR-91, Principles of Knowledge Representation and Reasoning*, Proceedings of the Second International Conference Cambridge, MA; Allen, J.A., Fikes, R., Sandewall, E., Eds.; Morgan Kaufmann Publishers, Inc.: San Mateo, CA, 1991; 441–452.

14. Cooper, G.F.; Herskovits, E. A Bayesian method for the induction of probabilistic networks from data. Mach. Learn. **1992**, *9*(4), 309–347.

15. Glymour, C., Cooper, G.F. (Eds.) In *Computation, Causation, and Discovery*; AAAI Press: Menlo Park, CA, 1999.

16. Heckerman, D.E.; Geiger, D.; Chickering, D.M. Learning Bayesian networks: The combination of knowledge and statistical data. Mach. Learn. **1995**, *20*(3), 197–243.

17. Simon, H.A. Causal ordering and identifiability. In *Studies in Econometric Method. Cowles Commission for Research in Economics*; Hood, W.C., Koopmans, T.C., Eds.; John Wiley & Sons, Inc.: New York, 1953; 49–74 Monograph No. 14; Chapter III.

18. Druzdzel, M.J. Simon, H.A. Causality in Bayesian belief networks Proceedings of the Ninth Annual Conference on Uncertainty in Artificial Intelligence (UAI-93) Morgan Kaufmann Publishers, Inc.: San Francisco, CA, 1993; 3–11.

19. Simon, H.A. Kalagnanam, J.R. Druzdzel, M.J. *Performance budget planning: The case of a research university*, 2000, Unpublished manuscript.

20. Druzdzel, M.J. ESP: A mixed initiative decision-theoretic decision modeling system. *Working Notes of the AAAI-99 Workshop on Mixed-Initiative Intelligence*, Orlando, FL, 1999; 99–106.

21. Lehner, P.E. Mullin, T.M. Cohen, M.S. A probability analysis of the usefulness of decision aids. In *Uncertainty in Artificial Intelligence 5*; Henrion, M., Shachter, R.D., Kanal, L.N., Lemmer, J.F., Eds.; Elsevier Science Publishers: B.V.: North Holland, the Netherlands, 1990; 427–436.

22. Druzdzel, M.J.; Díez, F.J. Criteria for combining knowledge from different sources in probabilistic models. J. Mach. Learn. Res. **2003**, *4*(July), 295–316.

23. Druzdzel, M.J.; van der Gaag, L.C. Building probabilistic networks: "Where do the numbers come from?" guest editors' introduction. IEEE Trans. Knowl. Data Eng. **2000**, *12*(4), 481–486.

24. Lu, T.-C. Druzdzel, M.J. Causal mechanism-based model construction Proceedings of the Sixteenth Annual Conference on Uncertainty in Artificial Intelligence (UAI-2000) Morgan Kaufmann Publishers, Inc.: San Francisco, CA, 2000; 353–362.

25. Wang, H. Druzdzel, M.J. User interface tools for navigation in conditional probability tables and elicitation of probabilities in Bayesian networks Proceedings of the Sixteenth Annual Conference on Uncertainty in Artificial Intelligence (UAI-2000) Morgan Kaufmann Publishers, Inc.: San Francisco, CA, 2000; 617–625.

26. Druzdzel, M.J. Probabilistic reasoning in decision support systems: From computation to common sense. Department of Engineering and Public Policy, Carnegie Mellon University: Pittsburgh, PA, 1992, PhD thesis.

27. Druzdzel, M.J. Five useful properties of probabilistic knowledge representations from the point of view of intelligent systems. Fund. Inform. **1997**, *30*(3/4), 241–254 (special issue on knowledge representation and machine learning).

28. Druzdzel, M.J. Explanation in probabilistic systems: Is it feasible? Will it work? Proceedings of the Fifth International Workshop on Intelligent Information Systems (WIS-96) Deblin, Poland, 1996; 12–24.

29. Wiecha, C.F. An empirical study of how visual programming aids in comprehending quantitative policy models (Volumes I and II). Department of Engineering and Public Policy, Carnegie Mellon University: Pittsburgh, PA, 1986, PhD thesis.

Demand-Driven Acquisition/Patron-Driven Acquisition

Michael Levine-Clark
Penrose Library, University of Denver, Denver, Colorado, U.S.A.

Abstract
Demand-driven acquisition (DDA), also commonly referred to as patron-driven acquisition (PDA), is a process used by libraries to provide a large pool of content to their users while only paying for portions of that content at the point of use. Typically, records for that content are displayed in the library's catalog or discovery system, and when patrons find those records and access that content, a purchase or temporary lease of that particular title is triggered. DDA has most commonly been used for e-books, but it has been used for other formats as well.

INTRODUCTION

Demand-driven acquisition (DDA) is an overarching term for a number of different models that libraries can use to provide content to their users and pay for that content at the point of use. Patron-driven acquisition (PDA) is often used synonymously with DDA but, for the purposes of this article, is considered to be a broader term. PDA in this broader sense refers to something that libraries have always done—respond to the suggestions of their users. In this sense, a librarian purchasing a book because of a patron request or adjusting an approval plan because of an analysis of usage is practicing PDA. DDA is a subset of PDA in which those patron-driven decisions are pushed to the point of demand; when a patron needs a book (or some other type of resource), the library acquires that content for her, ideally in an unmediated way.[1]

There are a number of different models for DDA, which are described in the following sections, but all allow libraries to provide a larger pool of content to their users than would be possible under traditional models. Instead of acquiring books that may or may not ever be used, a library can provide access to a broader "consideration pool" of titles and pay for only those that get used.

RATIONALE FOR DDA

DDA solves a supply and demand issue for libraries: there are far more books published than even the best funded libraries can purchase, and of the books purchased by libraries, many get little or no use. The *Library and Book Trade Almanac* reports that in 2014, 200,768 titles were published in the United States alone.[2] The International Publishers Association (IPA) has an even higher figure for 2013, with 304,912 titles (including new editions of previously published works) published in the United States. The IPA reports a figure of 444,000 for China and 184,000 for the United Kingdom. Many other countries

publish more than 50,000 titles a year, and even relatively small countries such as Slovenia publish more than 3,000 volumes.[3] Even the biggest libraries can afford to purchase only a fraction of this annual publishing output. Librarians traditionally have done the best they could to build collections that made sense for local curricular and research needs but have always needed to make choices about which books to purchase. Meanwhile, numerous studies have shown that large portions of academic library monograph collections do not get used.[4] DDA allows libraries to provide access to a wider range of this massive publishing output by reallocating some of the funds that would traditionally be spent on these unused titles.

DDA can be used to broaden the collection by providing access to more titles, from more publishers, across a wider range of subjects. If libraries do not need to make a decision about what book to buy until the point of use, they can give their users a larger choice of titles. In theory, a library could provide access to many more titles, while spending the same amount of money as in the past, thus creating a broader and deeper collection.

DDA can also be used to save money. A library could decide to select the same number of titles as it used to under traditional acquisition models, but instead of buying them, make them available for potential use and purchase. Assuming similar usage patterns, not all of these titles would be used and the library would spend less overall on monographs.

In reality, libraries have used DDA both to save money and to broaden the collection. They have provided access to more titles than they would have purchased in the past but have spent less overall.[5]

DEVELOPMENT OF DDA

An early version of DDA was developed by the Colorado Alliance of Research Libraries, which ran a consortial-level DDA program for netLibrary e-books from 1999 to

Encyclopedia of Library and Information Sciences, Fourth Edition DOI: 10.1081/E-ELIS4-120049488

Data–Dewey

2005. Participating libraries loaded records for e-books into their catalogs, and the consortium agreed with netLibrary to allow one free use of any book in the consideration pool, with purchase on the second use. The consortium paid 155% of list price to share purchased titles across the entire group. In theory, having a purchase happen only on a second use meant that titles with limited demand would not be acquired, but in practice, the consortium found that many books with just two very brief uses were purchased. Ultimately, because of the low threshold for purchase, this model proved unsustainable.[6]

A more enduring model of DDA was developed by Ebooks Corporation, which eventually became known as Ebooks Library (EBL), based on conversations with Alison Sutherland, a librarian at Curtin University in Australia, in 2001 and Jens Vigen, from CERN, in 2002. Sutherland approached Ebooks Corporation with the idea of purchasing e-books on demand. Vigen followed up a year later with the concept of pay-per-view rental access for e-books as an alternative to interlibrary loan (ILL). Out of these conversations, EBL launched in 2004 with a model that paired a 5-min free browsing period in the e-book, with paid short-term loans (STLs), and purchasing after multiple paid uses.[7] With this model, libraries did not buy books with very little use, because these uses either triggered a relatively cheap STL or if they were short enough, led only to a free browse of the book. Ultimately, this model proved successful, and e-book aggregators such as ebrary and EBSCO (which subsumed the netLibrary brand) adopted it as well.

DDA was used by a relatively small number of libraries in its early years, with a big uptake around 2010–2012. Ingram, through the MyiLibrary e-books aggregator and Coutts approval vendor, set up its four initial DDA programs in 2008. By the end of 2009, Ingram managed 17 programs. In 2010, 17 more were added, including their first consortial DDA program. DDA expanded dramatically in 2011, with 31 new programs, including the first program to include DDA for print. In 2012, Ingram added 39 programs.[8] Meanwhile, YBP Library Services, the other major academic library approval vendor, began the development of DDA services with aggregator partners in 2010. Many of these customers had already worked with aggregators directly and approached YBP for assistance in integrating this new method of collection development into their existing acquisitions workflow. In 2011, YBP implemented 63 DDA programs for customers with either EBL or ebrary. In 2012, YBP expanded to include EBSCO and added 63 more DDA programs, some of which used all three e-book aggregators.[9]

COMMON THEMES OF DDA

There are many different models of DDA, but all of them allow purchase of content at the point of use. Most programs have some aspect of free discovery, which allows users to discover whether content is worthwhile before triggering a purchase. In some programs, there is an option to pay for temporary access, allowing payment based on a brief usage of the material. And all programs have an ultimate option to purchase content, generally after passing through the free discovery and temporary paid access stages.

Free discovery works in different ways but is intended to prevent unintended purchase of content that might not actually be relevant to the user. In some cases, this free discovery period is time based, with usage under 5 or 10 min being free. In others, it is based on usage of some portion of the book, with the front or back matter free, for example. Another model allows for the first or second usage to be entirely free but triggers a purchase after the second or third usage. With this last option, there could still be multiple "accidental" uses of material that is not truly relevant to the user.

Temporary access, most commonly offered in the form of an STL, allows the library to pay for access for a day, a week, or some other brief period, based on the assumption that in many cases a patron will use a book once or twice and that then the library will never have demand for that particular title again. Rather than paying list price for a book that may never be used again, a library can provide immediate and temporary access for a fraction of list price. Libraries can generally choose how many STLs to offer, with the understanding that a higher number of STLs will mean a greater emphasis on access to content and less on ownership.

In all cases, there is an option to purchase content through DDA, though in relatively few cases a library can implement DDA with only STLs. For some libraries, the goal of the program is to use patron input to build a permanent collection. For others, the goal is to provide as wide a range of content to the user as possible, and ownership is less important. Libraries that wish to emphasize collection building will likely want to trigger purchase sooner in the process (and some do away entirely with STLs, purchasing on the first use).

DDA MODELS

Broadly speaking, there are four basic models for DDA, with wide variation within them. None of these are perfect, and there are risks and rewards for each. *Demand-Driven Acquisition of Monographs: A Recommended Practice of the National Information Standards Organization* provides a detailed overview of these models, with some exploration of how they might fit into the goals of a particular library choosing to implement DDA.[10]

The oldest model, used originally by netLibrary with the Colorado Alliance of Research Libraries, is relatively simple in concept. The first several uses of an item are free and then the next use triggers a purchase. For the Colorado Alliance, this was one free use with a purchase on the second. Ebrary and MyiLibrary both used this netLibrary model when they first adopted DDA. Though easier to implement, this model can lead to purchase of content that may not be needed, since presumably a patron could spend one second looking at a book and that would count toward purchase.

There are several examples of the risks involved with the netLibrary model, one of which occurred with the Colorado Alliance program. In this example, there was an assignment related to bananas in a geography class at the University of Colorado Boulder. Students searched within netLibrary and found e-books, whether relevant or not, that mentioned the word "banana." Because the program committed the Colorado Alliance to purchase books on the second use, regardless of length, the Alliance quickly purchased all of the books in netLibrary's collection with the word "banana."[11] It is worth noting that a free discovery period would have prevented this from happening. The University of Iowa, one of the early adopters of DDA with ebrary in 2009–2010, reported rapidly overspending their budget when using a similar model but with ten uses of any length before a purchase was triggered. After just a few months, Iowa had to cut back the number of titles in their consideration pool dramatically.[12]

A more complex model is the one developed by EBL and eventually adopted by ebrary and others. This model involves the free discovery period of 5 min (10 min for ebrary), STLs, and a purchase. Libraries can configure these as they wish, using more or fewer STLs before purchase. A library wishing to emphasize access can have more STLs, while one wishing to emphasize purchase can have fewer. The book will be purchased after that number of STLs has been surpassed. Doug Way and Julie Garrison showed that in early implementations of this model, it was cheaper overall to have more STLs prior to purchase.[13]

After wide adoption of the EBL model by libraries, publishers became concerned about the impact of STLs on their revenue. With multiple STLs before purchase, many libraries were paying for a small number of STLs of e-books but never purchasing these titles. Overall, publishers saw declining sales and responded in 2014 and 2015 with increases in the prices charged for STLs. A few publishers also pulled front list titles from STL programs.[14] It is likely that other publishers quietly pulled content from DDA programs entirely. At this point, it is unclear what the full impact of this change will be.

ProQuest Ebooks (which includes EBL, ebrary, and MyiLibrary) has recently introduced a rent-to-own model, called "Access-to-Own," in which STLs count toward purchase. The model was developed to address the concerns about STL costs and provides a trade-off of sorts: in return for accepting higher STL rates, libraries benefit by being able to apply those STL fees toward the purchase cost. Publishers benefit by having higher STL costs for

titles with low use and an easier path to a sale of the book for higher-use titles.[15]

A different model, used by several publishers on their own platforms, is evidence-based acquisition (EBA), also known as evidence-based selection (EBS). Under EBA, a library commits a certain amount of money to a publisher and agrees to buy content from that publisher at the end of the year based on an evaluation of usage data. The publisher then makes available some agreed-upon amount of content for the library's patrons to choose from throughout the year. EBA allows a publisher to offer DDA without having to develop the infrastructure that the more complex aggregator-based models require.[16]

There are risks and rewards for both publishers and libraries under EBA. Because EBA relies on a library to guarantee a certain amount of money to a publisher up front, a library runs the risk of having to purchase unused or little used content at the end of the year. On the other hand, publishers run the risk of libraries gaining access to a large amount of heavily used material for a relatively low price. Negotiating a reasonable price and mix of content up front is important for both partners in such a program.[16]

DDA FOR VIDEO

Most DDA programs thus far have involved e-books, but an increasing number of vendors are offering DDA for streaming video. Alexander Street offers both an EBA version and one in which purchases are triggered at the point of use.[17] Kanopy also has a DDA model and reports that more than 1500 institutions have adopted it globally.[18] DDA has allowed libraries to expand their video collections dramatically.

DDA FOR PRINT MONOGRAPHS

Some libraries have developed DDA programs for print monographs, often in conjunction with an e-book DDA program. The University of Vermont developed a print-only DDA program in 2007 in which they loaded records from three major publishers into their catalog, allowing patrons to identify unowned books and then request a purchase. They expanded this program to include e-books in 2011.[19] Though DDA for print is less common than it is for e-books, other libraries, such as the University of Arizona, have implemented DDA programs that combine e-books and print books.[20]

DDA for print monographs (or any other tangible formats) is complicated by the fact that the materials selected will not be immediately available to the user. Print DDA programs require clear messaging to the user that the content is not available for immediate use and may take some time to be delivered. Further, because it has to be delivered to the user, it is crucial to gather accurate data about the patron. DDA for print also requires development of forms that can be populated with bibliographic data about the item being ordered. Once data about the patron and item have been gathered, the library must order the book, determine a reasonable shipping time and process, and then deliver the item to the patron. While it is not as easy to implement, print DDA has been successful in the relatively small number of libraries with it in place.

CONSORTIAL DDA

Libraries often use consortia to negotiate substantial discounts for bulk purchasing, and based on that success, many have tried to build consortial DDA plans. The earliest, as noted previously, was the netLibrary plan for the Colorado Alliance of Research Libraries. A more recent success has been a program with EBL for the Orbis Cascade Alliance. Developed in 2010, this program uses a multiplier model to provide shared access to e-books across the consortium. While STLs are charged at the same rate as they would be for a single institution, the cost of purchasing the e-book is calculated at five times the list price and the consortium then shares perpetual access rights.[21] The multiplier model has become common across many consortia. One of the consortia using this model, the Colorado Alliance of Research Libraries, has questioned whether shared ownership makes sense for DDA. Early data from the Colorado Alliance project suggest that by some measures it would have been cheaper for libraries to do DDA on their own.[6] The Colorado Alliance experience points to an essential contradiction in consortial DDA programs: while consortial purchasing relies on a group purchase of shared content to lower overall pricing and is thus geared toward ownership of the same content across the group, DDA is predicated upon purchase based on use, and use of a given title is often not the same across institutions.

Novanet, a consortium in Nova Scotia, developed a DDA program in 2011 that uses a different model in which the consortium purchases shared access to the e-book for list price but pays for another copy of the e-book after reaching a certain threshold of usage.[22] This model solves the problem that the Colorado Alliance faced, in which the consortium paid a multiplier for e-books that ultimately had very little subsequent use. In the Novanet model, only higher-use books trigger a multiplier on the list price.

THE CONSIDERATION POOL

In all DDA programs, there must be a consideration pool, a set of titles available for potential discovery and purchase. Libraries can choose to carefully curate the titles

available in the consideration pool or can open it very broadly. Decisions about the size and scope of the consideration pool are linked both to financial pressures and the vision of the library about the type of collection DDA is intended to support.

With a smaller consideration pool, a library has less risk of overspending a budget. Some libraries have opted to limit the pool by publisher, by publication year, or by subject. The pool can be limited on the front end, as titles are published, or later on as libraries choose to remove them from view.

Similarly, libraries might choose to limit the scope of a consideration pool out of concerns for quality or curricular match. In this case, some of the same criteria might be employed but for a different purpose. Libraries opting to limit the size of the pool for quality reasons might leave older books in the pool but would be careful to include only books that match other predetermined needs. Some libraries using YBP or Coutts to manage DDA do so because of the capabilities those companies have to profile for academically relevant books.

Other libraries have taken a much broader approach to profiling and have embraced a philosophy that users know best what they need. At the extreme end of this viewpoint, a library might make all titles available in a consideration pool, whether academically relevant or not, with the assumption that in some cases popular material can serve a scholarly purpose. More likely, libraries with a broad approach to the consideration pool will consider a wider range of subjects than they would have under a traditional speculative purchasing program. For example, a library at a university without an architecture program would typically buy a handful of architecture books to support art history but would ignore most books on this topic. With DDA, this same library might choose to make available a wide range of architecture books for the same purpose.

In reality, most libraries have needs to both limit and expand the consideration pool. They will want to expand it to include subjects that were not traditionally purchased at their institutions but will need to consistently or periodically reshape the pool to exclude content for budgetary purposes.

RISKS

There are some significant risks for both libraries and publishers with DDA. With traditional purchasing, libraries knew that books that they acquired would be there in perpetuity for their patrons. They did not have to worry about titles going out of print because they were securely on their shelves. With DDA, while libraries do not have to expend scarce resources on purchasing titles that may not be in use and overall have more titles available to their users than would have been possible traditionally, they run the risk of those titles no longer being available at the point of need. Publishers occasionally either pull content in whole or in part from e-book aggregators or change prices enough that libraries need to remove some titles from the consideration pool, making them unavailable to users at the point of need.

The risk of DDA for publishers has already become clear and resulted in the rising costs of STLs. Concurrent with the rise of DDA and STLs, publishers have seen sales of books to academic libraries decrease, making it possible that some types of books may be too risky to publish.[23] While this decline in monograph sales to academic libraries has been linked to increasing adoption of DDA and STLs, it has also been coincidental to general declines in purchasing power for libraries. Nonetheless, the predictability that library sales traditionally gave to publishers is gone, and DDA is at least partially responsible.

PRESERVATION

While there is risk inherent in DDA, there is opportunity as well. Traditionally, academic libraries have concentrated purchasing at the point of publication, with only moderate addition of older titles to the collection. Because of the relatively small print runs of scholarly monographs, once these copies sold to libraries and then the title went out of print, it was hard to find older books for purchase. DDA allows libraries to extend the point of purchase well past the point of publication, but to do so requires that those titles still be available for purchase.

As consideration pools grow and become ever more important means of providing access to content, it is essential that libraries be confident that the not-yet-purchased content will still be there at some point in the future. Tools such as Portico and CLOCKSS preserve content but are geared toward providing libraries with access to the material that they have already paid for, not the content they might someday wish to pay for. A long-term preservation solution might help mitigate risk for libraries and publishers. Libraries would have the confidence that content would be available whenever their users needed it and publishers might be able to rely on sales far into the future.

INTERLIBRARY LOAN

Libraries have traditionally used ILL to provide patrons with temporary access to materials not in the collection. ILL was cheaper for libraries than purchasing a book or was the only way of supplying a book that was out of print. ILL allows libraries to share resources widely and means that low-use titles do not need to be acquired by every library. Some of the earliest examples of DDA occurred when libraries began purchasing titles requested

through ILL, either because purchasing those titles was cheaper than ILL or because they met some criteria to be added to the collection.[24] This function is largely for print monographs or other tangible materials.

On the e-book side, STLs can serve much the same function as ILL, providing temporary access to materials not in a library's collection. Publishers were willing to experiment with STLs at least in part because of this potential to serve an ILL-like function while providing some additional revenue.[23] Unlike ILL, which is staff intensive and does not provide a user with instant access to requested material, STLs could provide a better patron experience than ILL of an e-book.[25]

CONCLUSION

DDA is a means of providing access to content that libraries purchase at the point of use. By linking purchase to demand, DDA allows libraries to provide access to far more content than was possible traditionally. While mostly used for e-books, DDA has been used for print monographs and for streaming video as well. It is closely linked to ILL purchasing and could replace some aspects of ILL.

DDA has been around since 1999 but was first widely adopted around 2010. Since then, the models have been evolving as publishers and libraries get used to the cost structures and the risks. Though the models will likely continue to shift, DDA as a concept appears to be here to stay. Libraries and publishers need to work together to make sure that it is sustainable for both parties.

REFERENCES

1. National Information Standards Organization. Demand-Driven Acquisition of Monographs: A Recommended Practice of the National Information Standards Organization. June 24, 2014; 3. http://www.niso.org/apps/group_public/download.php/13373/rp-20-2014_DDA.pdf (accessed February 28, 2015).

2. Catherine, B.; Constance, H. Book title output and average prices: 2010–2014. In *Library and Book Trade Almanac*; Bogart, D., Ed.; Information Today: Medford, NJ, 2015; 455.

3. International Publishers Association. Annual Report October 2013/October 2014, p.16. http://www.internationalpublishers.org/images/reports/2014/IPA-annual-report-2014.pdf (Accessed December 16, 2015).

4. Allen, K. et al. Use of library materials: The University of Pittsburgh Study. Marcel Dekker: New York, 1979; Michael, L.C., Jobe, M.M. Do reviews matter? An analysis of usage and holdings of choice-reviewed titles within a consortium. J. Acad. Lib. **2007**, *33* (6), 639–646; Tyler, D.C. et al. Just how right are the customers? An analysis of the relative performance of patron-initiated

interlibrary loan monograph purchases. Collect. Manage. **2010**, *35* (3), 162–179; Cornell University Library, Report of the Collection Development Executive Committee Task Force on Print Collection Usage, November 22, 2010. http://staffweb.library.cornell.edu/system/files/Collection UsageTF_ReportFinal11-22-10.pdf (Accessed December 16, 2015).

5. Doug, W.; Julie, G. Financial implications of demand-driven acquisitions: A case study of the value of short-term loans. In *Patron-Driven Acquisitions: History and Best Practices*; Swords, D., Ed.; De Gruyter Saur: Berlin, Germany, 2011; 136–156; Swords, D.; Elements of a demand-driven model; In *Patron-Driven Acquisitions: History and Best Practices*; Swords, D., Ed.; De Gruyter Saur: Berlin, Germany, 2011; 169–187.

6. Michael, L.C.; Dawn, H. Mile high cooperation: Demand-driven acquisition in the Colorado alliance of research libraries. In *Shared Collections: Collaborative Stewardship*; ALA Editions: Chicago, IL, 2016.

7. Kari, P. The story of patron-driven acquisition. In *Patron-Driven Acquisitions: History and Best Practices*; Swords, D., Ed.; De Gruyter Saur: Berlin, Germany, 2011; 63–78.

8. Bob, N. Vice President for Library Services, Coutts. Email to author, July 21, 2015.

9. Barbara, K. Director of Sales, Western United States and Canada, YBP Library Services. Email to author, July 13, 2015.

10. National Information Standards Organization. Demand-Driven Acquisition of Monographs: A Recommended Practice of the National Information Standards Organization. June 24, 2014. http://www.niso.org/apps/group_public/download.php/13373/rp-20-2014_DDA.pdf (accessed February 28, 2015).

11. Wiersma, G.; Fong, Y. In *Patron-Driven E-Book Solutions: Moving Beyond the Banana Books Incident*, Proceedings of the Charleston Library Conference, 2011; http://dx.doi.org/10.5703/1288284314973 (accessed December 18, 2015).

12. Karen, F.S.; Give 'Em what they want: A one-year study of unmediated patron-driven acquisition of e-books. Coll. Res. Lib. **September 2012**, *73* (5), 469–492.

13. Doug, W.; Julie, G. Financial implications of demand-driven acquisitions: A case study of the value of short-term loans. In *Patron-Driven Acquisitions: History and Best Practices*; Swords, D., Ed.; De Gruyter Saur: Berlin, Germany, 2011; 136–156.

14. Avi, W.A. College libraries push back as publishers raise some E-Book prices. Chronicle of Higher Education, June 16, 2014. http://chronicle.com/article/College-Libraries-Push-Back-as/147085/ (accessed December 16, 2015).

15. ProQuest, ProQuest Introduces "Access-to-Own" Demand-Driven EBook Acquisition Model, November 4, 2015. http://www.proquest.com/about/news/2015/ProQuest-Access-to-Own-Demand-Driven-Ebook-Acquisition-Model.html (accessed December 16, 2015).

16. Michael, L.C. Evidence-based selection at the University of Denver. Against Grain **2015**, *27* (5) 18, 20.

17. Alexander Street, EBA vs. PDA: Examining Demand-Driven Models for Acquiring Streaming Video. Webinar. http://alexanderstreet.com/eba-vs-pda-examining-demand-driven-models-acquiring-streaming-video (accessed December 18, 2015).

18. Kanopy, About Us. https://www.kanopystreaming.com/about-us (accessed December 18, 2015).

19. YBP Library Services, The university of vermont: Demand-driven acquisitions project. http://www.ybp.com/GobiProfile_files/vermontprofile.htm (accessed December 18, 2015).

20. Hazen, T.C. In *Creating a Richer Patron-Driven Acquisitions Experience for Your Users: How the University of Arizona Forced Three PDA Programs to Play Nicely Together*, Proceedings of the Charleston Library Conference, Charleston, SC, 2013; http://dx.doi.org/10.5703/1288284315299 (accessed December 18, 2015).

21. Greg, D.; Cory, T. Patron-driven acquisition: Working collaboratively in a consortial environment: An interview with Greg Doyle. Collab. Lib. **October 2011**, *3* (4), 212–216; Hinken, S.; McElroy, E.J. Chapter 2: Consortial purchasing of E-books. Lib. Technol. Rep. **November 2011**, *47* (8), 8–13; Emery, J.; Parks, B. The demand driven acquisitions pilot project by the orbis cascade alliance: An interview with members of the demand driven acquisitions implementation team. Ser. Rev. **June 2012**, *38* (2), 132–136; Kathleen Carlisle Fountain. The evolving DDA project at the orbis cascade alliance. Against Grain **November 2015**, *27* (5), 10, 12.

22. Novanet eBook DDA Pilot Project. http://www.novanet.ns.ca/novanet-ebook-dda-pilot-project/ (accessed December 21, 2015).

23. Rebecca, S.; Lenny, A. STL: A Publisher's Perspective. Against Grain **November 2015**, *27* (5), 28, 30; Zeoli, M. Academic libraries and the scholarly book marketplace: Death by 1,000 [Paper] cuts? Against Grain **November 2015**, *27* (5), 14, 16.

24. Judith, N.M.; Saunders, S.E. A study of circulation statistics of books on demand: A decade of patron-driven collection development, part 3. Collect. Manage. **2010**, *35* (3–4), 151–161.

25. Michael, L.C. Whither ILL? Wither ILL?: The changing nature of resource sharing for E-Books. Collab. Lib. **2011**, *3* (2), 71–72.

Denmark: Libraries, Archives, and Museums

Jens Thorhauge
Jakob Heide Petersen
Danish Agency for Libraries and Media, Copenhagen, Denmark

Ole Magnus Mølbak Andersen
Danish State Archives, Copenhagen, Denmark

Abstract

The authors provide an overview of the modern development of libraries, archives, and museums in Denmark. Topics covered include: National, public, academic, special and school libraries as well as the Danish Agency for Libraries and Media, the State Archives, regional archives, university archives, the Heritage Agency of Denmark, and three major types museums: natural history, art, and cultural heritage. The legal framework for these institutions is detailed. The authors also describe the role of professional associations and the development and professional education in these three fields. Finally, recent trends and issues are discussed with a focus on digital projects.

INTRODUCTION—FACTS ABOUT DENMARK

Denmark (Fig. 1) is a northern European state and part of the Scandinavian cultural community. The country has been an independent kingdom for more than 1000 years with variable frontiers. Since 1920, the frontiers have been permanent with an area of 43,094 km^2. The population in 2006 was 5,427,459. The capital is Copenhagen.

Denmark is a fertile low-lying country, which for the most part is cultivated. Agriculture was the dominant trade until about 1850 when industrialization began. Today, the majority of the population live in towns and are employed in industry, commerce, and service. Denmark's gross national product is one of the highest per capita in the world, as is its rate of taxation. Its social and healthcare system is publicly funded, and education is free all the way to the highest university level.

The Danish constitution is based on the Constitution of the Kingdom of Denmark, most recently revised in 1953. It goes back to the Constitution of 1849, which ended a constitution of absolute monarchy introduced in 1660. In 1849, a parliament with two chambers was introduced. Today, Denmark has a one-chamber parliament and a multiparty system. Since 1972, it has been a member of the European Community, and since 1992, of the European Union.

LIBRARY AND INFORMATION SYSTEMS AND SERVICES

The First Libraries and Absolute Monarchy

As in other European countries, the earliest libraries were established in monasteries in the Middle Ages. Later, libraries were set up at the cathedral schools which from about 1100 were established in connection with a number of cathedrals, where priests were also educated till the University of Copenhagen was founded in 1479 and with it the first Danish university library. The first Danish book had been printed in 1482.

Ten years before the absolute monarchy was introduced in Denmark, King Frederic the Third had started building up a library and cabinet of curiosities. These collections formed the basis of those in The Royal Library, The National Museum, and the Danish National Gallery. In 1697, legal deposit of all printed material was introduced. The Enlightenment in the 1700s left distinct traces in Denmark. In 1775, P.F. Suhm, professor at the University of Copenhagen, opened his library of 100,000 volumes to the public. Twenty years later, the Royal Library opened its collections to the public. Government archives suggest definite moves toward systematic registration as the country became more centralized under the absolute monarchy. The Royal Cabinet of Curiosities became the Royal Art Museum in 1842 and included art as well as other museum objects.

General compulsory education was introduced in 1814 where the country, following the national bankruptcy of the previously year, started to expand in relation to education and culture. Today, the Folkeskole's (municipal primary and lower-secondary school) educational program runs for 9 years.

Democracy and public libraries

The absolute monarchy was abolished peacefully in 1849, and the royal collections went to the state. Art was separated and the Danish National Gallery established. Several

Data-Dewey

Fig. 1 Map of Denmark.
Source: CIA World Factbook (https://www.cia.gov/library/publications/the-world-factbook/geos/da.html).

art-historical collections were gathered together in what is today The National Museum. One of these collections was the collection of antiquities, which was made publicly available in 1819. Around this time, the first public libraries were established on the initiative of enlightened citizens, often organized in associations.

With the emergence of the labor movement in 1870 came a movement in favor of public enlightenment. This resulted in reading societies in the towns that built up libraries. In 1882, the State began awarding grants to chapbook collections. In 1900, A.S. Steenberg published a book on the organization and design of libraries. The book was based on his studies of English and American free public libraries. This book became the basis for the subsequent structure of a modern library system. In 1909, the State established an office for the support of library initiatives with Steenberg as its leader, and in the same year, the Royal Library's chief librarian, H.O. Lange, published his ideas of a coherent library system based on regional libraries. In 1920, the first act on public libraries was passed, based on these thoughts, and in that same year, the Book Collection Office became the State Inspectorate of Public Libraries with Thomas Døssing as director and driving force of the systematic development of public libraries all over the country.

A librarian training course was established in 1918 as a mixture of practice and theory. The Royal Library School was established in 1956. In 1999, the school gained university status and the previous education programs were replaced by bachelor's and master's programs and the possibility of Ph.D. studies.

The Royal Library (Fig. 2), the University Library and the libraries at the Technical College of Denmark and the Royal Veterinary and Agricultural University were the only academic libraries until 1902 when the State and University Library in Aarhus was founded to serve the public outside the capital. In 1928, Aarhus University was founded, and the State and University Library (Fig. 3) became its library. During the last third of the twentieth century, a number of universities and university colleges were established, and the national museum collections were supplemented by professionally run art and cultural-historical-museums in many towns.

The welfare state and the expansion of public libraries

During the interwar and postwar periods, public libraries followed the classical model with the loan of books and the administration of reading rooms as central activities. The task was to establish libraries wherever the need arose and make sure that they were run professionally. In this period, many public libraries became a driving force in study circle activities. With the 1964 amendment to the law, public libraries were made mandatory in all municipalities; cultural activity was included in the legislation, and libraries geared up to meet the educational boom that arrived with prosperity and the baby boom. In 1970, a municipal reform resulted in merging the small rural districts. This provided the basis for a sustained professionalization of the public libraries. In 1983, the responsibility for local public library service was entrusted to the municipalities. At the same time, the financing of public libraries changed from government subsidy to block grants with the municipalities' free right of disposal as a basic principle.

The last major wave of change arrived with IT development. The first initiatives within cataloging came around 1970 with OPAC (Online Public Access Catalog) as their goal. The breakthrough of the Internet in the mid-1990s brought with it a challenge to change all libraries into hybrid libraries. Home pages and Internet access for the public appeared in the latter half of the 1990s. It became obligatory with the Act regarding library services in 2000 that established free access to a Web-based National Union Catalog and mandated broad media access through public libraries.

Throughout the twentieth century, the public library system was consolidated with regional libraries in the counties, libraries in all municipalities, and more branches in larger towns. But many libraries were still owned by associations, and only with the revision of the library act in 1964 was municipal library service made obligatory. In 1983, full responsibility for the local public library was

Fig. 2   The Royal Library in Copenhagen.
Source: Photo by Mette Udesen.

Fig. 3   State and University Library in Aarhus.
Source: Photo by Martin Lund.

transferred to the municipality. But from the beginning of the century the State maintained a firm involvement in the development of the libraries.

Legislation

Library activities have been regulated by legislation since 1920; the law is changed at regular intervals. The latest act dates from the 2000, Act regarding library services (I 78, 2000) (English version: http://www.bs.dk/publikationer/english/act/index.htm). The Act addresses public libraries, regional libraries, government libraries, and government obligations. The stated objective of library service is to "promote information, education, and cultural activity." The means are making books and other relevant media available, including Internet access. The public library is open and available to everyone for the loan of materials. All services are free. Public libraries must cooperate with school libraries, which are obligatory in municipal schools and are run as part of the school activity. All municipalities are obliged to provide library service for both children and adults. The State is responsible for the national bibliography and for the union catalog, which is made available via the Internet. The State also pays for regional library service. Together with the State and University Library, the regional libraries are a "superstructure" for the public libraries and handle a number of tasks in relation to procurement of materials, advice, and competency development in the libraries.

The law provides a legal framework that deals with the way libraries should perform their tasks in the information society. It emphasizes that there are media other than print and defines the conditions for giving access to the Internet. For state libraries, including university libraries, a condition for receiving subsidies is that they must participate in interlibrary loan cooperation free of charge.

Legal deposit was introduced in 1697. In 1998, the act on legal deposit was changed so that the deposit obligation included not only printed material but also other media, such as e-publications, videograms, databases, film, and radio and TV broadcasts. The 2005 revision of the law includes harvesting the Danish part of the Internet. Legal deposit of printed material is shared between the two national libraries, the Royal Library and the State and University Library. The latter is responsible for the National Newspaper Collection, radio and TV programs, and film produced with a right to public viewing.

Public Lending Right Remuneration is distributed as a culture subsidy to Danish authors whose works are available at public and school libraries. Public Lending Right Remuneration has been paid out since 1946; Denmark was the first country in the world to introduce this subsidy scheme. The principles are stated in the Act on Public Lending Right Remuneration.

The legal framework for the school library can be seen in The Folkeskole (2) where it is determined that a school library must be established in every Folkeskole and that these must function as pedagogical service centers.

National Library and Information Services

The Danish Agency for Libraries and Media, which operates under the Ministry of Culture, is the central government organ for libraries and media. The Agency handles a number of administrative tasks related to the libraries, including administration of the Act regarding library services. Likewise, it deals with development tasks in association with the libraries' activities and administers a number of subsidies within the library area.

The Agency was founded in 1920 as the State Inspectorate of Public Libraries with tasks related to the public libraries. In 1986, it merged with The Office of the National Librarian, thereby being allocated coordinating tasks regarding the research libraries. In 1997 this office gained status as an agency entitled Danish National Library Authority. In 2008 the Agency merged with The Danish Agency for Media and gained its present name.

The Danish Agency for Libraries and Media, performs tasks that in other countries might belong to the national library. It is responsible for

- The national bibliography.
- Standards, including cataloging rules etc.
- National bibliographic databases, DanBib and Bibliotek.dk (library.dk).
- The national distribution scheme for interlibrary lending.
- Financing the regional library service.
- Handling performance contracts with 16 regional libraries, which in 2010 will be reduced to six.

The regional libraries act as central repositories for materials, advise smaller libraries and are responsible for professional development.

The Danish Agency for Libraries and Media, is secretariat for Denmark's Electronic Research Library, which is a collaboration between more than 200 special and academic libraries and handles licenses for e-resources to Danish educational and university libraries. The division of work between the Agency and the libraries means that the agency is responsible for the infrastructure, while the municipalities and research and education institutions are responsible for the actual running of the libraries. Central to the infrastructure is the union database, DanBib, which started in 1994 and registers all Danish library records. DanBib forms the basis of bibliotek.dk, the libraries' common public portal that opened in 2000. There one can search for and request any titles in a Danish library. Projects are in progress concerning the establishment of a common data well with bibliotek.dk and databases with e-resources for the purpose of establishing integrated search.

The Agency is responsible for coordinating library collaboration and ensuring national development of the libraries. This happens via subsidies for development projects and professional development. The Danish Agency for Libraries and Media has entered into a contract with Danish Bibliographic Center, a limited company owned mainly by the Danish state and municipalities, for the preparation of the national bibliography and the running of DanBib and bibliotek.dk. The Royal Library in Copenhagen and The Danish State and University Library in Aarhus both have status as national libraries, the State and University Library also being part of the infrastructure for the public libraries. As such, they are responsible for legal deposit and Netarkivet.dk that contains the Danish part of the Internet, harvested by Web crawlers. So far the Net Archive can only be used for research.

ACADEMIC AND RESEARCH LIBRARIES

Universities

Following a recent reform of Danish universities which also included the merger of some independent research institutions there are today eight Danish universities. The largest universities by far are

- Copenhagen University (est. 1479) with an academic staff of about 3500.
- Aarhus University (est. 1928) with an academic staff of about 2000.
- The Technical University of Denmark (est. 1829) is the third largest.

These three universities have stronger research profiles, than the smaller schools. The University of Southern Denmark (est. 1966), the University of Aalborg (est. 1974), the Roskilde University (est. 1972), and The Copenhagen Business School (est. 1917) are medium-sized universities while the eighth university, IT University of Copenhagen (est. 2003), is a very small university (Fig. 3).

Universities are the primary institutions for higher education in Denmark, and all of them, except IT University, have an independent research library, which the school funds and manages. In the case of Aarhus and Copenhagen universities, the libraries have an independent role, since the two national libraries also function as university libraries.

In the recent reforms of the Danish educational sector, also included the vocational educations at college/high school level. A large number of schools for engineers, nurses, teachers, and pedagogues were merged into eight university colleges. The largest of these have close to 10,000 students. The largest of these colleges have roughly the same number of students as the medium-sized universities. The students and teachers at the university colleges were originally supported by small libraries connected to the particular education but following the mergers new and larger library organizations are being established at the different university colleges.

Special Libraries

A number of academic libraries are regulated by the Act regarding Library Services. The act specifies that the libraries participate in the general interlibrary loan cooperation and are freely accessible to the public; doing so is a prerequisite to receiving a grant for the library. The Danish Agency for Libraries and Media each year publishes a list of those libraries regulated by the Act.

There are a large number of small academic libraries. The Danish library statistic collects data from 169 academic libraries; 42 of these participate in general interlibrary loan cooperation. Of these 42 libraries, 16 are large academic libraries that provide more detailed statistics. The universities have a total of 122 departmental libraries, e.g., libraries in law and medicine.

The loan of printed materials continues to play a central role in library activities. The library.dk service and the underlying interlibrary loan cooperation are important in that regard. Downloads from subscription-based electronic journals have replaced printed materials as the most important activity for the larger research libraries. In 2006, the 16 largest libraries had 2.8 million loans of books and other printed materials and 8.2 million downloads from electronic journals. That means that two out of every three loans are now electronic.

Library roles and tasks

Academic libraries are expanding the traditional role of information provision to include new services to support activities at the parent institution. In its strategy for library development, The Danish Agency for Libraries and Media identifies five major functions of academic libraries.

The most important task is still providing information through building print collections and purchasing subscriptions to electronic journals and databases. A second activity is the creation of new interfaces to the global Web of knowledge for both students and researchers. At present, efforts are focused on integrated search, i.e., creating seamless access to the many different information resources and delivering accurate search results.

The 2003 act on universities emphasized the export and mediation of knowledge from universities. Subsequently, this has become a third major task for academic libraries. An important activity is the registration of research and the operation of current research information systems (CRIS). This role is expanding into the fourth major activity—the support for a coherent e-framework for education and research at the parent institution. There is increased focus on IT systems for supporting learning and research. This can include systems for e-learning and handling of scientific primary data. The fifth and final task is development of information literacy skills.

Digital Library Collections and Services

Denmark's Electronic Research Library (DEFF) plays an important role in regard to the build-up of the libraries' digital collections. Among other things, it functions as a national framework for consortia buying electronic journals and databases. The DEFF-secretariat handles negotiations with vendors and administers practical aspects of the subscriptions. Denmark's Electronic Research Library supported the development of the national access system that allows all students and researchers to have remote access to electronic journals.

Denmark's Electronic Research Library provides the infrastructure for both consolidation and development of library services, and it supports the increasing consolidation of library systems and the joint development of common CRIS systems. It also support more specific projects, e.g., in information literacy. The SWIM tutorial at Aalborg University Library (http://www.aub.aau.dk/swim2/1024/start.html) and the library test (http://www.librarytest.dk/) developed by The Royal library are examples of such projects.

In addition to its own Web site http://www.deff.dk, DEFF has supported the development of the national science portal http://www.videnskab.dk and the national research database http://www.forskningsdatabasen.dk/.

PUBLIC LIBRARIES

The Danish public library system is regulated by the Act regarding library services, which is a framework law that obligates all municipalities to run a public library that offers both children and adults free and equal access to Danish libraries' materials. Public libraries must cooperate with school libraries. All major research and special libraries participate in the interlibrary loan cooperation free of charge.

The common database, bibliotek.dk, and a transport scheme financed by the State form the basis of extensive ILL (interlibrary loans) activity. All public libraries are to be run by professionally qualified staff. The law obliges the libraries to provide free access to all types of media, including the Internet. Public libraries together produce a number of national, Web-based services, e.g., Biblioteksvagten.dk/Ask-a-librarian, Litteratursiden.dk, SpørgOlivia (Ask Olivia).

In 2007, the Danish municipal structure was changed from 275 to 98 municipalities, which led to the merging of many public libraries. One hundred and thirty-six branches were closed that year culminating a decade of closures of almost 500 out of more than 1000 libraries. In

2007, there were 550 public libraries. The closures are seen as part of a restructuring of the libraries to accommodate the needs of the knowledge society. The remaining libraries are extending their opening hours and services, and work is going on to find alternatives to the small local branch, e.g., cooperation with school libraries, self-service branches, flexible mobile libraries, and delivery of library materials. The total budget for public libraries is 2.75 billion krone DKK (Danish crowns), which means a per capita expenditure of 502 DKK per year (2007) (Fig. 4).

There is a decrease in the loan of traditional library materials, but an increase in the use of new digital services. The average loan figure per citizen is 13 (2007). The government's strategy for the development of public libraries features three main tracks:

- Continuous development of digital services.
- Changing the physical library from storehouse to a learning, meeting, and experience space.
- Innovative thinking in terms of outreach library service.

One example of a new digital service is the loan of music files from home via the library that clears the use with the rights owners. All recorded Danish music is digitized and forms part of this agreement together with a large part of foreign music.

Outreach library service is partly Web-based and partly directed toward various target groups. Kindergarten libraries and targeted early initiatives concerning children in ghettos in the shape of bookstart programs are examples.

SCHOOL LIBRARIES

School libraries are obligatory in the Folkeskole where they have status as pedagogical service centers. Thus, they are integrated into the school and are run by teachers who have supplemented their training with a school librarian course (diploma program). The school library makes available all types of educational materials for teaching and provides books and other materials for the pupils' leisure reading. There are 1929 school libraries, and most pupils use them; 75% of pupils visit the library at least once a week. The school library forms a central part of the school's learning environment and acts as the school's innovative, mediatory, and pedagogical learning center. It supports the aims of the Folkeskole and contributes to realizing the school's fundamental values, learning targets, and action lines.

There is no statutory requirement for libraries in secondary schools. About 75% of the nearly 250 secondary schools, however, do have a library with instruction in information literacy as a central feature. Upper-secondary school libraries support the pupils' learning environment

Fig. 4 Interior of children's library at Hjoerring Public Library.
Source: Photo Fjord and Bosch by Laura Stamer.

and study competence, and studies show that traditional library service is heading toward a new form of learning and knowledge center. Focus is directed at interdisciplinarity, and many places are working intensively on introducing a new project culture. In 2007, the upper secondary schools were changed from being county institutions to private institutions. Beginning in 2009, these schools will be included in Denmark's Electronic Research Library.

School libraries are supported by 16 government centers for educational services. These centers offer information on and loan of educational materials, pedagogical advice, and guidance to teachers, assistance with the production of educational materials, and educational programs, such as instruction in IT application.

Library and Information Science Education

The Royal School of Library and Information Science (http://www.db.dk/english) was established in Copenhagen in 1956 as a professional school with 4-year educational programs. In 1973, a branch was established in Aalborg in Jutland. Until the late 1960s, research and academic libraries offered a program for library assistant, which then became a 4-year education program at research and academic libraries. In the mid-1980s, the two programs merged into one.

In 1999, the school became an institution of higher education with bachelor's, master's, and Ph.D. programs (3 + 2 + 3) and a diploma program which consists of a 1-year advanced level program following a bachelor's degree. The school also offers a number of diploma and master's programs. Prior to the school's change to university status, an assessment was carried out according to American Library Association Standards for accreditation of Master's Programmes in Library and Information Studies with a very gratifying result.

A research evaluation, carried out by five recognized international and national researchers in 1999 concluded that the school's research was at the highest level. The school employs about 100 researchers with a broad spectrum of research fields. It has made its mark internationally through research within information retrieval, domain analysis, and knowledge organization. Several Danish universities have conducted information scientific research projects and established educational programs bordering on information science.

The educational programs at the Royal School of Library and Information Science are directed at tasks in both public and research libraries, public administration, organization, and private businesses. Students trained at the school are increasingly being employed in all types of knowledge-based institutions. Both the classical library services and the rapidly growing digital services play an ever-increasing role: organization, mediation, and sharing of knowledge are of fundamental importance to society's economic and cultural development and cohesion. About half of the school's graduates are employed outside the library sector. The school has close to 1000 students, about 200 in Aalborg, and 800 in Copenhagen.

The Royal School of Library and Information Science has a Department of Continuing Education and Consultancy, which is responsible for continuing education and deals with advice and development tasks. The Department of Continuing Education and Consultancy is visited annually by about 5000 course participants and arranges about 300 courses a year.

Associations

The association, "Danmarks Folkebogsamlinger," was founded in 1905 and was merged with the Danish Library Association in 1920. The aim of the association was to further the library cause in Denmark, and for more than 50 years it represented all library interests in the country. Today, the association membership includes local authorities responsible for cultural affairs and institutions as well as personal members, primarily among library staff. It lobbies for the continuous development of public libraries and publishes the journal *Danmarks Biblioteker* (http://www.dbf.dk/Default.aspx?ID=4126).

In 1969, library employees broke away from the association and formed The Danish Union of Librarians, which represents the interests of professionally trained librarians. Today, the union has 5500 members and publishes the journal *Bibliotekspressen* (http://www.bf.dk/Service/English.aspx).

Research libraries broke away in 1978 and formed the Danish Association of Research Librarians, a professional organization for research libraries and their employees (http://www.dfdf.dk/uk.php).

The Municipal School Library Association dates from 1919 and organizes municipalities and their politicians with particular interest in school libraries, http://www.ksbf.dk/page/foreningen.html while school librarians have their own association, the Association of School Librarians (http://www.emu.dk/gsk/skolebib/).

Danish public library directors are organized into the Association of Library Directors. http://www.biblioteksle-derforeningen.dk/, while the libraries' clerical staff and library assistants are organized in HKstate (http://www.hk.dk/stat/landssammenslutninger/statslige_biblioteker_og_arkiver) and HK Municipal Library Committee (http://www.hkkommunal.dk/sw30576.asp). These associations' homepages are only available in Danish.

Since 1989, all of the Danish associations have collaborated in the Library Umbrella, just as most of them are members of the European library associations, EBLIDA (European Bureau of Library, Information and Documentation Associations), and IFLA (International Federation of Library Associations).

ARCHIVES AND ARCHIVAL SCIENCE

Legislation

The Danish Archives Act regulates preservation and disposal of public records, the public archives' activities, and the public's access to records. It states that public archives must:

- Ensure the preservation of records of historical value or that serve as documentation of conditions of important administrative or legal importance to citizens or authorities.
- Guarantee the possibility of disposing of non-preservation-worthy public records in cooperation with those authorities affected by the law.
- Make records available to citizens and authorities, including for research purposes.
- Instruct citizens and authorities in the use of records.
- Do research and spread the knowledge about research results.

The Danish Archives Act is administered by the State Archives, a government agency under the Ministry of Culture that determines the detailed rules for preservation and disposal of public records. Municipalities and regions may choose to establish their own archives for the preservation of their records. The State Archives are obliged to cooperate with these regional or local archives. Government authorities must transfer their records before they are 30 years old. Special rules apply to digital records.

The Archives Act defines the rules for accessibility to public records. Public records are normally freely available when they are 20 years old. Records that contain information about an individual's private, personal, or financial, situation are only available after 75 years. There are a number of regulations about accessibility to specific types of records. In special cases, authorities transferring records can, in cooperation with the State Archives, determine accessibility deadlines for specific archive groups. The Act states that it is possible to seek access to records that are not immediately accessible. In such cases, the State Archives, possibly in collaboration with the relevant public authorities, decide whether special permission may be granted. The State Archives can collect and make available private records from individuals, associations, organizations, and companies. In such cases, agreements must be made on accessibility between the transferring party and the State Archives.

National, Regional, and Local Archives

"The State Archives," consists of the Danish National Archives, the Regional Archives of Zealand, Regional Archives of Funen, Regional Archives of Southern Jutland, Regional Archives of Northern Jutland, the Danish Data Archives, and Danish Business Archives. The State Archives altogether employ about 300 people.

The Danish National Archive in Copenhagen is the central administration's archive and collects and stores records from all Danish central authorities—ministries, government agencies, and the armed forces—and from private individuals and organizations. The National Archive contains about 168,000 shelf meters of records that are made available to the public in the reading rooms of the State Archives. The reading rooms have about 17,000 visitors each year, principally genealogists, researchers, and students.

The public archives in Denmark are quite professionalized, partly because they are administered under the authority of the State Archives. The State Archives' dual function as an agency for the administration of the Archives Act and as a cultural institution for the preservation, accessibility, and mediation of records has proved to be effective. As opposed to many other national archives, the State Archives no longer have a backlog. With the prospect of new, climate-regulated stacks that can accommodate the entire collection a volume of almost 400,000 shelf meters, the State Archives find themselves in an extremely favorable situation.

Denmark also has a number of "Regional Archives" that collect and store records from public regional authorities, primarily regions, and municipalities. These include:

- The Regional Archives of Zealand, Lolland-Falster, and Bornholm are also situated in Copenhagen.
- The Regional Archives of Zealand contain about 69,000 shelf meters of records and are visited by about 18,000 people each year in their reading rooms.
- The Regional Archives of Funen in Odense collect and store records from public regional authorities, primarily regions, and municipalities.
- The Regional Archives of Funen contain about 20,000 shelf meters of records and annually welcome about 9000 visitors to their reading rooms.
- The Regional Archives of Southern Jutland in Aabenraa collect and store records from public regional authorities, primarily regions, and municipalities.
- The Regional Archives of Southern Jutland contain about 18,000 shelf meters of records and have about 4000 visitors each year in their reading rooms.
- The Regional Archives of Northern Jutland in Viborg collect and store records from public regional authorities, primarily regions, and municipalities.
- The Regional Archives of Northern Jutland contain about 62,000 shelf meters of records and about 11,500 visit the reading rooms each year. Here you also find the State Archives' Filming Centre, which does microfilming and digitization of the records kept in the State Archives.

The Danish National Business Archives is a research institution that collects and preserves important historical source material about the development of Danish business life and makes it available to the public. The Business Archives also act as archive for Aarhus municipality. They contain about 50,000 shelf meters of records and

about 3500 visitors find their way each year to the reading rooms.

Danish Data Archives in Odense collect, preserve, and deliver digital research data from social science, medical science, and history. Quantitative research data in the form of questionnaires make up most of the collection. Danish Data Archives' material is available via search catalog on their homepage. The State Archives' collections are searchable via the database DAISY, which is available online. Digital historical data in the shape of archiving versions are available via the database SOFIA.

Separate from the State Archives are a number of municipal archives. Among the largest are Copenhagen City Archives, Aalborg Municipal Archives, Vejle Townhistorical and Municipal Archives, and Frederiksberg Municipal Archives. State archives typically offer search in special databases. Finally, there is DANPA, Denmark's National Private Archive Database where one can search registrations of private archives from most large archives in Denmark.

College and University Archives

The archives of Danish institutions of higher education are to be found in the State Archives. The archives of Copenhagen University, Technical University of Denmark, and the Aarhus University School of Education are placed in the Danish National Archive. The archives of Aarhus University and Aalborg University are placed in the Regional Archives of Northern Jutland, those of the University of Southern Denmark in the Regional Archives of Funen and Roskilde University archives in the Regional Archives of Zealand.

The State Media Collection, part of the State and University Library, collects, preserves, and mediates Danish TV and radio broadcasts, commercials and sound recordings from parliamentary debates, news bulletin manuscripts and Danish video releases. Researchers (including journalists) and students/lecturers at institutions of higher education can borrow the TV and radio broadcasts. Everyone can use the audiovisual collections in the library, even the legal deposit material, since they cannot be loaned to other libraries or to private individuals.

According to the Film Act, the Danish Film Institute is obliged to ensure the preservation of films and documentation material about films, to collect film and TV literature, to do research and to make the collections available to the public. The archives of the Film Institute hold more than 30,000 titles and contain all kinds of films shown in Danish cinemas from the beginning of the history of film in 1896 to the most recent films that are legally deposited with the archives. The film archives work actively for preventative preservation, conservation, and digital preservation/conversion. The Institute's films are available online in the database "Danmarks Nationalfilmografi."

Data–Dewey

DR Archives and Research is part of Denmark's Radio and contain archives and library. Apart from servicing the employees at DR, it sells archival and research services to external stakeholders. DR Archives and Research does not lend from its archival collections with TV broadcasts, but it is possible via the country's libraries—for research purposes—to use TV materials.

DRs Radio Archives file and maintain the broadcasts that must be preserved for posterity. The radio broadcasts go back to the 1930s and cover recent Danish history politically, socially, and in societal terms. Add to this radio dramas, montages, and recitals. There is no public access to the collections of radio broadcasts, but it is possible to buy individual broadcasts. Radio materials from the State Media Collection can be used for research purposes.

Other Archives and Repositories

The Labor Movement's Library and Archives in Copenhagen contain a large collection of archival material concerning the history of the labor movement in Denmark. The Danish Emigration Archives in Aalborg are The National Collection of records on the history of emigration in Denmark. The Map and Land Registry Agency contains previously valid cadastral maps, cadastral protocols, and registered cadastral cases, including surveying information. The collections cover the period from 1844 to the present. For information on Greenland and the Faroe Islands, see National Museum of Greenland and Archives and the Faroese National Archives.

Digital Archival Collections and Finding Aids

Cf. the Archives Act, the State Archives collect, store, and make available Danish authorities' digital records. Development of search tools for the digital collections is undergoing a tremendous process of change. The database SOFIA, which contains the authorities' digital archival version, as of 2008 was only available in the reading rooms of the State Archives. An online solution is expected to be implemented soon.

Archival Science as a Discipline and Profession

Archivistics, as profession and discipline, has emerged in Denmark mainly under the auspices of the State Archives and to a lesser extent the municipal archives. The State Archives employ about 200 archivists, providing a professional archive environment. Extensive Nordic collaboration is going on with expert seminars, Nordic Archives Academy, exchange of staff and the Nordic Archive Days. The central publication relating to archives and archivistics in the North is *Nordisk Arkivnyt*, published four times a year.

Education for archivists and records managers

Denmark has no actual archivist training course. However, Aalborg University, together with Aalborg Municipal Archives, has established a training program in information administration that includes courses such as archive theory, databases and communication, and a final project. The program, first offered in 2008, runs for two semesters. A student enrolled both terms can earn 60 points European Credit Transfer and Accumulation System. In addition, the State Archives offer a number of internal courses for their archive professional staff.

Professional associations

There are four major associations related to archives and archivistics.

1. *The Organization Danish Archives (ODA)* works to increase public awareness of the importance of Danish Archives and also attempts to promote collaboration, coordination and other kinds of activities that can enhance Denmark's archival cultural heritage.
2. *Forum for Knowledge, Information, Documentation, and Archives (VIDA)* is an association whose aim is to encourage rational archival organization, particularly in the corporate sector. Here companies, organizations, and individuals are gathered together, who have journalizing, electronic document management as areas of responsibility, occupation, or interest.
3. *The Archives Association* arranges functions open to anyone interested in archive professional issues, or who just has a general historical interest. There are 6–8 functions a year.
4. *The Association of Local Archives (SLA in Danish)* brings together people with archival interests in Denmark in a common endeavor to heighten the quality in the work with preservation of the cultural heritage. The association has more than 400 members, distributed on 13 districts that each covers one of the former counties. Members of the association profit from each other's experiences and expertise and from the development work carried out by SLA's committee.

Electronic Records as Archival Documents

The Archives Acts does not differentiate between electronic/digital records and paper records. The State Archives thus have the obligation of collecting, storing, and making available all records whatever the medium and format. The State Archives have collected electronic/digital records since the early 1970s.

In order to preserve and make available electronic/digital records, the State Archives conducted a large conversion project during the past few years where electronic/

digital records of older formats are recorded on DVD in a searchable format. The project ended in 2008, and from now on focus will be placed on accessibility of the collection of electronic/digital records.

Preservation

The State Archives do not perform actual conservation of its collections. For the purpose of conservation, a professional consultant is employed who monitors the collections and decides which records should be conserved. The conservation process is outsourced to The Royal Library's Preservation Department.

The State Archives are in the process of introducing climate control regulations for all new stacks, to ensure that a stable, low temperature and stable, low, relative humidity will inhibit the deterioration paper records. In addition, the State Archives stores the majority of its collection in acid-free, bar-coded boxes.

Conservation and preservation of digital records take place as mentioned above in a special format and structure conversion project.

MUSEUMS AND MUSEOLOGY

Introduction—The Danish Museum Sector

The Danish museum sector covers a broad and varied spectrum of institutions and subjects. The major institutions share the same legal framework—The Danish Museum Act—and receive funding or subsidies from the Ministry of Culture. Almost 100 museums cover cultural history, another 35 focus on art, and three specialize in natural history (geology, zoology, and botany).

The number of visitors at Danish museums has been stable for the past 10 years, totaling approximately 10 million visitors a year. In 2006, the state-owned and state-subsidized museums introduced free access for people under age 18. At the National museum and "Statens Museum for Kunst—The Danish National Gallery," free access is also given to adults. Since 2006, there has been a 2% yearly increase in the number of visitors. In 2007, the total number was 10.8 million. That is the equivalent of two museum visits a year per inhabitant in Denmark.

Total public spending on the museum sector is approximately DKK 1.1260 million a year, of which the State's share is DKK 716 million (2006). There are eight state-owned museums that are fully funded by the central government, and 123 others that are approved by the State and receive partial funding.

The state-subsidized museums are owned by local authorities, by independent institutions or by an association whose objective is to run the museum. These three forms of ownership are equally prevalent. The central government's share of funding for state-subsidized museums is approximately 35% of their total expenses. There are 19 state-subsidized museums that receive extra State funding, because they have special research and/or dissemination activities. Some of these museums also handle tasks at the national level.

Legal Framework

The state-owned and state-recognized museums are regulated by the Museum Act, passed in 2001.

According to the law, the general purpose of the museums is to safeguard Denmark's cultural and natural heritage and secure access to and knowledge about this heritage and its interaction with the world around us. The purpose is realized through the five key function that constitute the tasks of the museum: collecting, registering, preserving, researching, and disseminating information. The act identified three types of museums: 1) natural history museums; 2) art museums; and 3) cultural history museums. The 2006 revision of the act introduced free access for children and made some changes related to the reform of the Danish municipalities.

Heritage Agency of Denmark

This agency promotes collaboration between museums and supports the development of individual museums. It makes recommendations to the Minister of Culture about which museums are to be recognized by the State and thus eligible for state subsidies. It also administers state subsidies for these museums. Other tasks include listing buildings of national significance and the protection of ancient sites and monuments, and of the archaeological excavations undertaken by Danish museums. The Heritage Agency also administers various funds for which both state-owned and state-subsidized museums can apply annually. Such state grants provide support for research projects, study trips, purchases, publication of books.

In addition to the Heritage Agency, certain museums have special roles in regard to other museums. The National Museum of Denmark, "Statens Museum for Kunst—the Danish National Gallery" and the Danish Museum of Natural History are the principal museums for cultural history, history of art, and natural history, respectively. These three museums have a special status and offer expert advice to other museums in Denmark.

Museums of Art

There are three state-owned art museums. The Danish national "Statens Museum for Kunst—the Danish National Gallery," is according to the museum law, given has the responsibility of illustrating Danish and foreign visual arts, primarily from the western world after 1300 A. D. The museum's collections constitute almost 9000 paintings and sculptures, more than 240,000 works of art on paper as well as more than 2600 plaster casts of figures from ancient times, the Middle Ages, and the Renaissance. The major part of the museum's older collections comes from the art collections of Danish kings.

The two other State art museums are the Ordrupgaard Collection and the Hirschsprungske Collection. The former is named after the village of Ordrupgaard, which lies just outside Copenhagen. Its collection features nineteenth-century French and Danish art, including works by important Romantic, Realist, and Impressionist painters. The Hirschsprungske Collection owes it name to Pauline and Heinrich Hirschsprung, who donated their comprehensive collection of nineteenth century Danish art to the Danish State in 1902.

Among the 35 art museums are the ARoS (formerly Aarhus Art museum), which was established in 1859 and opened in a new building in 2004. It offers Denmark's largest art collection outside Copenhagen and has notable collections of Danish art that span 300 years as well as exhibitions of contemporary international art. The Ny Carlsberg Glyptotek in Copenhagen is one of Denmark's most popular museums. It houses more than 10,000 works divided into two principal collections. One is devoted to the Mediterranean cradle of Western culture and the other to Danish and French art from the nineteenth and twentieth centuries.

Outside Copenhagen are two museums of twentieth century art. The Arken Museum of Modern Art, which was opened in 1996, collects Danish, Nordic, and international art with special emphasis on work from 1990 to the present. The Louisiana Museum of Modern Art offers a collection of more than 3000 works, produced primarily after 1945, that concentrates on more compact groups of works and artists.

Cultural History Museums

The Museum Act states: "The cultural history museums illustrate change, variation, and continuity in the living conditions of human beings from prehistoric times to the present." The National Museum of Denmark is the country's principal cultural history museum. Its responsibility is to illustrate Denmark's culture and the interdependence of all the world's cultures.

In addition to exhibitions of Denmark from prehistory through the Middle Ages and the Renaissance to modern times, the museum houses exhibitions from the ancient cultures of Greece, Italy, the Near East, and Egypt. It is also in charge of some of the archaeological investigations that the Museum Act specifies as important in securing the cultural and natural heritage.

Denmark has three additional cultural history museums. The Danish Defence Museum has two exhibitions: The Royal Danish Arsenal Museum, which exhibits the development of small arms and edged weapons during the last 500 years, and the Royal Danish Naval Museum,

which presents naval models and marine paintings. The Defence Museum also exhibits historic warships, which include the frigate, Peder Skram, the last Danish submarine, Sælen, and the fast attack boat, Sehested.

The Danish Agriculture Museum illustrates farming and the life of farming families from the Late Stone Age through the agricultural reforms that took place from the late eighteenth century to the present day. The collection contains approximately 70,000 items, some of which are extremely large. The museum's buildings extend over approximately 24,000 m^2, including 8000 m^2 of exhibition space.

The Danish Museum of Hunting and Forestry is one of the largest of its kind in Europe. With 3000 m^2 of exhibition space, the museum presents the history of hunting and forestry in Denmark from the Stone Age to the present day.

Danish history from the Stone Age and Iron Age can be experienced at several other places. The Prehistoric Museum, Moesgaard, near Aarhus in Jutland, offers a wealth of relics from prehistoric Denmark to the Viking Age, including a large collection of runic stones. On the border between museums and experience centers, Hjemsted Oltidspark in southern Jutland and Lejre Experimental Centre near Roskilde, are worth mentioning.

Natural History Museums

The natural history museums illustrate nature, its development, contemporary environment, and the way it's related to human beings. In 2004, four institutions were merged to create The Natural History Museum, which is responsible for maintaining and building up natural history collections, for carrying out research in the natural sciences, and for presenting the current state of knowledge about natural history to the general public. The four merged institutions, the Botanic Garden, the Botanical Museum and Library, the Geological Museum, and the Zoological Museum, are now a department of the University of Copenhagen. The museum's exhibitions play an important role in teaching and public outreach.

The Ministry of Culture grants subsidies to four natural history museums. The Natural History Museum in Aarhus, the second largest of its kind in Denmark in both size and exhibition area, contains more than 5000 different species of animals from all over the world. Svendborg Zoological Museum (naturama) focuses on mammals and birds whereas the Mid-South Jutland Museum exhibits primarily fossils collected in the Gram Clay Pits (Gram Lergrav), which have fossils as much as 8 million years old. The Fur Museum contains a unique collection of 54 million-year-old fossils.

Digital Museum Exhibits and Services

The Heritage Agency coordinates registration of the museum's collections. The cataloging system Regin was made available to the museums in 2003, and the data are presented on the Internet at http://www.kulturarv.dk/mussam. With this service, it is possible to get an overview and search the collections of the cultural heritage museums.

A similar service is available for the arts museums. The central register of works of art in Danish museums and collections was founded in 1985 and went online in 1996. The register holds information on approximately 39,000 works by Danish and international artists. It is available at: http://www.kulturarv.dk/kid/Forside.do. In addition, there is the possibility of searching for museums and institutions by geography, subject, or collection at: http://www.dmol.dk/engelsk/start.asp.

A 2006 ministerial report recommended an increased focus on digital mediation and increased cooperation and knowledge sharing, and it proposed a specific focus on mediation for children in a digital environment. It also highlighted some of the many services and projects developed by the museums themselves. A good example is http://www.kongedragter.dk/ where it is possible to study the clothing of Danish monarchs. At Zoom Ordrupgaard (http://www.zoomo.dk) the public can experience close ups of pictures, compare pictures, and get tips on analyzing them. Another example of digital mediation is http://www.absalon.nu, which is a collaboration between the local library, archive, and museum presenting the history of Copenhagen on the Web. At http://www.tilbygningen.dk (the annex), audiences can experience a virtual addition to Thorvaldsens Museum and take a trip around the collections. The museums are continuously developing new digital exhibitions and services, frequently with funding from the Kulturnet Danmark funding pool. One such example is http://www.vildmedwillumsen.dk.

Another kind of service presented by Danish institutions in arts, design, and architecture is a joint portal http://www.arkade.dk, which offers a collection of links, the possibility of cross-searching the institution's catalogs and access to other digital information resources.

Two initiatives seem to hold interesting prospects for future mediation. One is http://www.emuseum.dk where the museum's collections and mediation is directly linked to teaching. The other is http://www.danskkulturarv.dk which is a pilot project that attempts to show how digitization and, in particular, mediation can be cross-institutional and bridge the traditional division between archives, libraries, museums, and other institutions, such as the Danish Broadcasting Cooperation.

Museology as a Discipline and Profession

The universities have a long history of offering education in museology as subjects in arts history and ethnography, but there was no coherent education specifically focused on museology until 1977 when it was established as an interdisciplinary, optional course at the Department of Art History at Aarhus University. In 2001, museology was offered as a supplementary program at the University of Aarhus, and in 2002, museology was integrated in the B.A. program at the University of Copenhagen. In 2005, a master in museology was established at the University of Aarhus. The latter program is divided into four modules: international museum theories and methods, organizational museum theories and methods, museum communication, and finally a master's project. Additional teaching study in museology is offered at the University of Roskilde and at The Royal School of Library and Information Science.

Training for curatorship and museum administration

For a number of years, The Museumshøjskolen (a folk high school) was an important center for the development of museology in Denmark. The school offered further education to employees at Danish museums. In 2006, the Museumshøjskolen was merged with the Association of Danish Museums, which offers a number of shorter courses as well as further education. For example, the training in museum administration and management is offered at the diploma level.

The School of Conservation, part of The Royal Danish Academy of Fine Arts, was established in 1973. The education as conservator is a 3 year bachelor degree followed by 2 years of graduate studies. After 5 years of study, the student earns the degree Cand.Scient.Cons. The school also offers a 3 year research program (Ph.D.).

Professional associations for curators and museum administrators

The Association of Danish Museums, which covers almost all Danish museums, organizes a number of different subject-based informal networks. One of these is a museology researcher's network, which has evolved into at more permanent organization with regular meetings.

Key contemporary issues—preservation, access, educational role

The growing importance of museology as a profession, the Museum Act of 2001 and the establishment of the National Heritage Agency all signal a new and more visible profile for Danish museums. The Danish reform of municipalities and counties has entailed new funding structures, and some mergers in the museum sector. These issues have dominated the debate for the past few years.

These developments have also served as a catalyst for a debate on the concept and functions of the museum. There is a growing emphasis on the educational and interpretive role of the museum in relation to the other four functions (collecting, registering, preserving, researching). Mediation is seen as increasingly important as the museums try

Data–Dewey

to contribute to other societal goals, such as education, tourism, social inclusion, and economic development. This has sparked a debate on whether museums risk becoming mere entertainment, like the Tivoli amusements, or whether, according to new theories of learning, entertainment, and education can be combined in innovative ways. At the same time, digital development challenges the traditional concept of museums as dependent on collections and highlights the possibilities of cross-institutional cooperation.

CONCLUSION

Danish libraries, museums, and archives are highly advanced and are undergoing rapid transformation as a result of the knowledge society's new standards for hybrid institutions. Although the library, archives, and museum sectors are formally separated and each has its central state agency, the fundamental objectives, and conditions for the institutions are similar.

All knowledge and culture institutions are facing a radical digital challenge that has to do with the materials and services of the institutions, their service to the users, their organization, and expertise.

For a number of years, work has been going on locally as well as centrally concerning cooperative digital projects between the three types of institution. Nationally, work has centered around an adaptation of search systems to make it possible to search in all collections at the same time. Locally, focus has been on the work with joint Web presentations with local history subjects or themes of common interest.

The Danish Ministry of Culture is preparing a national strategy for digitization of cultural heritage materials. The existing interim report reveals the desire for interdisciplinary presentation of digital cultural heritage based on user needs. It also points out that consolidated solutions for preservation and mediation will reduce costs in connection with digitization and stresses the need for a consolidated data warehouse. Finally, functional division of labor with a few centers of expertise is contemplated.

Confronted by new challenges libraries, archives, and museums are all moving toward a realignment of their institutional culture, going from a collection orientation to a user-centered orientation. The need for this can be most clearly observed in work with children and young adults. Particularly in libraries and museums, there have been increased efforts to establish new modes for communication and interaction based on Web 2.0, inclusion, and active participation. The importance of keeping the interest of children and young as users of cultural institutions is underscored by an increasing political understanding of the importance of culture- and knowledge-institutions in increasing social cohesion and stimulating collective innovation.

WEB LINKS

- Danish Agency for Libraries and Media. Available at http://www.bs.dk/default.aspx?lang=en
- Nordic Public Libraries in the Knowledge society. Available at http://www.bs.dk/publikationer/english/nnpl/index.htm
- Act Regarding Library Services. Available at http://www.bs.dk/publikationer/english/act/index.htm
- Danish library policy. Available at http://www.bs.dk/publikationer/english/library_policy/index.htm
- Danish library statistics. Available at Statistics:http://www.bs.dk/publikationer/english/statistics/2006/index.htm
- Svane-Mikkelsen, J. *The Library System in Denmark*; Royal School of Library and Information Science: Copenhagen, Denmark, 1997. Extracts available at http://www.bibliotekshistorie.dk/sektion14.lasso?-database=bibdan.docs2&-layout=document&-response=sektion14.lasso&refID=263&-search&-token.level=2
- Heritage Agency of Denmark. Available at http://www.kulturarv.dk/english/about_us/index.jsp
- Museum Act. Available at http://www.kum.dk/sw4497.asp
- The Danish State Archives. Available at http://www.sa.dk/content/us/about_us
- Danish Archives Act. Available at http://www.kum.dk/graphics/kum/English%20website/Legislation/Promulgation_ of_the_Danish_Archives_Act.pdf

Descriptive Cataloging Principles

Elena Escolano Rodríguez
National Library of Spain, Madrid, Spain

Abstract

This entry explains the international standard that guides bibliographic description, the International Standard Bibliographic Description (ISBD) that contains the principles of descriptive cataloging. The standard will be analyzed by giving its definition, purposes, principles, and objectives; and by explaining its structure, uses, and acceptance around the world. Its need will be justified by providing a short history of the background and evolution of the publication, ending with the current version of the consolidated ISBD that integrates the description of all types of resources that had been covered by specialized ISBDs.

INTRODUCTION

Bibliographic description is done in order to identify and retrieve resources. The descriptive part of a bibliographic record represents a substitution for the resource, a kind of surrogate. It helps general users identify and select resources, but it is especially useful for librarians, because it allows them to perform many collection development tasks without needing to recall volumes from the stacks. In addition, it is useful for library inventory. Bibliographic descriptions also can be adapted to meet the needs of specific types of users.

To standardize means to bring conformity with "something established by authority, custom or general consent."[1] The International Standard Bibliographic Description (ISBD) is the international standard approved by IFLA for bibliographic description.

The International Standard Bibliographic Description (ISBD) was recommended by the ISBD Review Group, and approved by the Standing Committee of the IFLA Cataloguing Section. Preliminary consolidated ed.; München: Saur, 2007. This work is cited as "ISBD, 2007" hereafter in this text. Per the IFLA Web page (http://www.ifla.org/III/index.htm, accessed November 2007): "The International Federation of Library Associations and Institutions (IFLA) is the leading international body representing the interests of library and information services and their users."

The ISBD is the standard that determines the data elements to be recorded or transcribed in a specific sequence as the basis of the description of the resource being cataloged. In addition, it employs prescribed punctuation as a means of recognizing and displaying these data elements and making them understandable independently of the language of the description.

PURPOSE

The ISBD *aims* to

- "make records from different sources interchangeable, so that records produced in one country can be easily accepted in library catalogs or other bibliographic lists in any other country" (*ISBD*, 2007; 0-1). It has furthered cooperative activities and projects such as interlibrary loan, shared catalogs, and networks at national and international levels. Given the huge number of cooperative projects, a high level of standardization is needed to be effective.

- "assist in the interpretation of records across language barriers, so that records produced for users of one language can be interpreted by users of other languages" (*ISBD*, 2007; 0-1). This supposes a *lingua franca* among librarians.

- "assist in the conversion of bibliographic records to electronic form;

- "enhance interoperability with other content standards" (*ISBD*, 2007; 0-1).

It is important to highlight that the ISBD is addressed to national bibliographic agencies that have the responsibility to contribute to Universal Bibliographic Control (UBC). UBC is the IFLA's program for promotion of a world-wide system for the control and exchange for bibliographic information. "National bibliographic agencies are called on to accept responsibility of creating the definitive record for each resource issued in that country. It is therefore recommended that descriptions prepared by them contain all the mandatory elements set out in the ISBD insofar as the information is applicable to the resource being described" (*ISBD*, 2007; 0-2); that is why

Data-Dewey

Encyclopedia of Library and Information Sciences, Fourth Edition DOI: 10.1081/E-ELIS4-120044427

the ISBD establishes if the element is mandatory, optional, or conditional, to accomplish the objective that the description aims to identify the resource. Although intended for national bibliographic agencies, the ISBD application is also recommended for libraries that share bibliographic data with others because normalization improves cooperation.

Originally the development of the ISBDs was pushed by the automation of bibliographic control as well as the economic necessity of sharing cataloging. Nevertheless, the ISBD is independent of any specific electronic format for information. It is useful and applicable for bibliographic descriptions of all kinds of bibliographic resources in any kind of catalog, whether Online Public Access Catalogs or catalogs less technologically advanced.[2]

The intention and objective of the International Federation of Library Associations and Institutions (IFLA) have always been to support the continuing development of library activities, and at the same time to help all countries to incorporate such developments. "IFLA is the global voice of the library and information profession … help libraries and information services to fulfil their purposes and to shape responses to the needs of clients in a rapidly changing global environment." (In IFLA Web site: http://www.ifla.org/III/index.htm (accessed October 2007)). Therefore, a standard from IFLA such as the ISBD must take into account all library situations.

The previous statement, in conjunction with the need for the standard, cannot be better explained than with the director of the IFLA International Office for UBC, Dorothy Anderson's words in 1974, which in spite of the passage of time are still current:

> In a world which is unevenly composed of over-privileged and under-privileged countries, where economic resources rest unequally and what in one country seems commonplace—computers, typewriters, copying machines—in another may seem a far distant and impossible dream, yet the objective of international standards rests firm with or without computer. All countries can participate as the component parts of a world wide UBC system if their contribution follows patterns and standards that are universal; and equally can receive.[3]

Today all kinds of resources coexist with direct access resources: books, printed serials, etc. sharing space with remote-access resources. Description, as made traditionally, provides basic and brief information of resources to enable identification of the document, to select or disregard it, and to give access to electronic resources through links.

That is why the ISBD is the agreed-upon standard, on which the descriptive portion of the bibliographic record should be based. This consensus is reflected in the Statement of International Cataloging Principles that is being developed through a series of regional IFLA Meetings of Experts on an International Cataloging Code (IME ICC) (http://www.d-nb.de/standardisierung/pdf/imeicc-statement_of_principles-2008.pdf).

The ISBDs have guided the work of national cataloging committees in updating their codes to promote internationally accepted practices. This is a point underscored by the compilations of practices by various rules that were prepared for these IFLA Meetings of Experts on an International Cataloguing Code. (IME ICC Web page, available at http://www.d-nb.de/standardisierung/afs/imeicc_index.htm (accessed October 2007). http://www.d-nb.de/news/pdf/code_comp_2003_europe_2.pdf (accessed October 2007) and http://www.loc.gov/loc/ifla/imeicc/source/code-comparisons_final-summary.pdf (accessed October 2007)). From these overviews, the general impression is overall compliance and considerable harmony among the national codes and with IFLA's recommended stipulations in the ISBDs. From the regional meetings we know

- Europe has the greatest number of cataloging codes in use, and one of them is AACR2.[4]

> Regarding the ISBD, it was acknowledged as a great achievement of international standardization for descriptive cataloging that requires the transcription of identifying information from the item at hand to create the standardized areas of description and ISBD goes on to state the basic elements to include in such descriptions, the order of those elements, and the prescribed punctuation, so the resulting records are understandable worldwide, regardless of language or script.

For IME ICC1, rule makers in Europe were asked to compare their codes and 18 reports on their cataloging codes were received. In their overviews were two questions related to ISBD acceptance and the general outcome was that all codes were based on ISBD.

Results of rule comparisons on ISBD from First IFLA Meeting of Experts on an International Cataloguing Code, Frankfurt, Germany, July 28–30, 2003. (Web site, available at http://www.d-nb.de/standardisierung/pdf/code_comp_2003_europe_2.pdf (accessed October 2007)). From the 18 responses 15 were affirmative, and from the three left it can be deduced also to be based on ISBD, although the libraries did not answer in the same way, resulting in a wrong interpretation on the comparison. This can be deduced by the second answer to 2.2: KBRSM (Lithuania), did not answer to the question 2.1, but in the answer to the 2.2 (http://www.d-nb.de/standardisierung/pdf/code_lithuania.pdf) it was confirmed "Our rules of description are based fully on ISBD. No different rules are applied." Also KSB (Sweden) recognizes, in the same document page 1 when citing their code (http://www.d-nb.de/standardisierung/pdf/code_comp_2003_europe_2.pdf) that the code is translation of AACR2, which is the first one in recognizing it. And finally the last code not cited in the question 2.1, is the RAK (Germany) in which question 2.2 (http://www.d-nb.de/standardisierung/pdf/code_rak.pdf) says: "The cataloging code RAK is principally based on ISBD for rules for description. RAK-WB was based on ISBD (M) edition 1974. For the special codes of RAK, other ISBDs were partly, but not thoroughly used."

- The IME ICC for South America was structured a little differently from the European meeting. Unlike Europe, where there are several rule-making bodies and different cataloging rules, Latin American and Caribbean countries typically follow the *Anglo-American Cataloguing Rules* or the Spanish rules, *Reglas de catalogación*. These codes were already compared in IME ICC1 and their basis on ISBD was confirmed.[5]
- "The Middle East has no rule making bodies and the countries typically follow the *Anglo-American Cataloguing Rules*."[6]
- From IME ICC for Asia reports, it is known that "China, Japan, and Korea have a history of rule making bodies ... Many other countries in Asia follow the *Anglo-American Cataloging Rules* or have a local set of rules based on AACR2."[7] So they recognized their rules are based on and consistent with ISBD.
- From IME ICC for Africa, of 29 countries, there were 19 responses. Twelve responded that they apply the ISBD directly while the rest apply codes already revised which were based on ISBD, such as AACR2 and AFNOR rules.
- International Standards used in Sub-Sahara Africa. In *Fifth IFLA Meeting of Experts on an International Cataloguing Code*, Pretoria, Durban, South Africa, August 14–15, 2007. Available at http://www.imeicc5.com/download/InternStand_Sub-SaharaAfrica.doc (accessed October 2007).

The IME ICCs have been very useful for the ISBD revision work, as there have been many suggestions to be considered in the future. Suggestions have come from the recognition of the different languages and scripts and also "cultural" patterns of publications that will be taken into account in the continued revision, and that will help to improve the ISBD and its interpretation.

OBJECTIVES AND PRINCIPLES

In order to know and understand this document language that is the ISBD, it is necessary to keep in mind the underlying objectives and principles.

The objectives are to assist in finding, identifying, selecting, and acquiring a resource, and to assist in navigating among resources. But to explain more in-depth the actual consolidated ISBD, it is necessary to address the objectives that guided its development (*ISBD*, 2007; vii—viii):

- "To prepare a consolidated, updated ISBD from the specialized ISBDs in order to meet the needs of catalogers and other users of bibliographic information."—

here has been added cataloger's convenience to stress that not only the final user is concerned, but also that catalogers represent a large part of users with special needs to carry out their tasks, and this must be taken into account.

- "To provide consistent stipulations for the description of all types of resources to the extent that uniformity is possible, and specific stipulations for specific types of resources as required to describe those resources." This objective represents the practical application of what has been called the Principle of integration by which the description of all types or resources must be based in one set of rules in a uniform manner.

Uniformity in describing bibliographic entities, irrespective of the medium in which they are embodied, is desirable for several reasons: it serves the objectives of the catalog, particularly the collocating objective; it serves user convenience in providing a common interface to bibliographic information; and it serves the principle of parsimony in achieving economy of expression. ... Early in the 1970s reaction set in, and a swing began away from specialization and toward integration.[8]

The principles are

- "The primary purpose of the ISBD is to provide the stipulations for compatible descriptive cataloging worldwide in order to aid the international exchange of bibliographic records throughout the international library and information community (e.g., including producers and publishers)." This is the principle of standardization. It supposes the most important achievement of the twentieth century, the IFLA *lingua franca* between libraries that is ISBD, necessary for communication and cooperative projects. The specific "goal of reducing bibliographic effort so that one item need be described only once worldwide necessarily assumes adherence to a uniform level of description ..."[9]
- "Different levels of cataloging will be accommodated, including those needed by national bibliographic agencies, national bibliographies, universities, and other research collections." Although intended largely for national libraries or national bibliographic agencies, it is also addressed to university and research libraries, and can be used by other types of libraries and collections that have a wider choice and do not have the same responsibility of describing the national output or of sharing records. The ISBD aims to standardize the description and to be useful for all kinds of bibliographic communities at different levels of compliance. The standardization admits levels of degree. The international exchange of bibliographic information requires and takes benefits from maximum standardization of bibliographic description, but it could be considered excessive in some situations in which it is in conflict with the principle of user convenience. That is the

reason why the standardization must be flexible to adapt to the users of different types of libraries and also to local culture and script situations.

- "The descriptive elements needed to identify and select a resource are to be specified."—This means that the description should include the elements that are significant to allow these actions and objectives. The principle requires a bibliographic description to be full enough to meet the objectives of a system for organizing information and, at the same time, allows other data elements to be optional. This principle could be considered sometimes to be against the principle of representation of the prescribed source that was the common practice of strict adherence to the title page until the revolution that represented the ideas of Lubetzky. He defended the logic of working having in mind the objectives that would determine the description:

our practice represents the result of an effort to preserve the integrity of the title-page and an inability to do so. Such effort may be justified in the cataloging of early books, where a difference in the title-page reflects a difference of edition, or in the cataloging of rare books, where the title-page has an interest of its own. It serves no purpose in the cataloging of modern books ... In the cataloging of modern books the aim of the cataloger should be not to point out the differences of the title-pages but the identity of the books under them, so when a reader has reference to a given issue which may not be available he could safely be served by any other issue of the same edition.[10]

This principle supposes a limit to a standardization that could be excessive. It is a practical action that reduces the needs for identification and selection of resources, and it was Cutter "one of the first to face the problem of necessary versus unnecessary data elements. He viewed appropriate fullness of description as a variable, depending on local needs and circumstances, such as library size ... to the present day, but is becoming less useful as global cataloging renders distinctions based on library size irrelevant."[9]

- "The set of elements of information rather than their display or use in a specific automated system will provide the focus." This principle represents the evolution of ISBD and the change of objectives since the beginning. It represents an intention of ensuring the interoperability with other systems' displays. ISBD has been adapted to the current time, where many display formats coexist, usually locally developed. Some of them are suited to local users' habits as it is the labeled display that is the most common and clear display for general end users in one language. ISBD, in addition to presenting an internationally understandable display, has introduced the necessary changes to allow consistency in other displays.

- "Cost effective practices must be considered in developing the stipulations." This is the principle of economy by which, when there are alternative ways of achieving a goal, the less complicated one and the one requiring less time and effort will be preferred.

Although not specifically mentioned as a principle, the whole ISBD is a contribution to a principle of representation. "The distinctive feature of the ISBDs—that is, that the descriptive information is taken from the item itself in the form in which it is presented in that item—has been recognized as the most economical and more certain way of ensuring compatibility in bibliographic recording."[11] This representation principle does not necessarily mean transcription that is only required in area 1 with phrases such as "in the form in which it appears on the prescribed source of information," or in area 2 or in area 6 including information not found on the prescribed source in square brackets (see section General Structure of ISBD for explanation of areas). The rest of the areas leave the cataloger the possibility of selection of elements in order to better achieve this representative description. At the same time it is necessary to ensure the accuracy of description and "to prevent idiosyncratic descriptions," just in case this principle of representation if "carried too far would result in bibliographic descriptions that individually are correct but when taken collectively are inconsistent. It would go against the principle of user convenience ..."[12] If the information that is going to be transcribed could result in ambiguous, unintelligible, or incorrect data, this assessment must be explained and corrected, within brackets depending on the kind of information, to identify the resource clearly.

BASIS FOR DESCRIPTION: SOURCES OF INFORMATION

The data elements can be found in different places on a particular resource and can take different forms. Therefore, to reach consistency in description requires prescribing exactly where the elements can be taken from. Accurate description depends on the order of preference of sources of information on the resource, which means agreement on the specification of locations where an entity can represents itself.

The determination of sources varies depending on the type of material, but there are common characteristics for the determination: comprehensiveness, proximity, and persistence. This is clearly established in ISBD 0.4.1 Basis of the description: "For all types of material the resource itself constitutes the basis of the description" but specifically the criteria to determine a source of information is cited in 0.4.2.1 of ISBD. Although this stipulation is related to printed resources, it can be extrapolated to all: "The selection of the source to be treated as title-page substitute is determined by considering which source has the fullest information, with preference given to a source that is part of the resource over sources outside the resource." There is more reliability to internal sources than external ones that could be separated, modified, or lost. When use of internal sources is not possible, these criteria of persistence guide us to choose sources permanently associated with the resource.

Depending on the types of resources, with different physical characteristics, the sources will be different. In addition, the same works or content can be published in different physical formats, for example an e-book that is also in a format of a printed text, or can be published in more than one physical medium as kits or sharing characteristics of more than one, for example serially issued maps in electronic form. To solve this situation better and to accomplish one of the basic purposes of the ISBD, that is to facilitate record exchange, the ISBD urges national bibliographic agencies and libraries participating in networks to create separate bibliographic descriptions for works issued in multiple formats. Other libraries may select a single-record approach if they wish to do so.

Therefore, "the ISBD is applied to describe manifestations, by means of description of the item in hand as an exemplar of the entire manifestation, using *Functional Requirements for Bibliographic Records* (FRBR) terminology" (*ISBD*, 2007; viii). That conforms to the recommendation of the Statement of International Cataloging Principles:

2.1.1. Bibliographic records should typically reflect manifestations. These manifestations may embody a collection of works, an individual work, or a component part of a work.

Manifestations may appear in one or more physical units.

In general, a separate bibliographic record should be created for each physical format (manifestation).[13]

GENERAL STRUCTURE OF ISBD

The ISBD is structured in eight areas with different kinds of content and with different interrelated data elements sequentially ordered. This arrangement corresponds to the order of relative importance of information that usually follows the order presented in the main sources of information. Its origin is the traditional organization that was found in the main resources at that time, books, and this was the order in which the information is presented on the title-page. The structure was accepted and standardized internationally because there was not much difference in such information in international practices, as many conferences on Universal Bibliographic Control would demonstrate. It was also accepted and adapted to other types or resources, as the publication patterns are common for the

majority of types of resources. The intention of arrangement of information following the patterns usually appearing in the resources is also for the users' convenience, as it is the order in which they are accustomed to finding them. But at one time following the strict order of presentation on the main source, the transcription of the title page was expanded and was no longer helpful for the order of the catalog. Seymour Lubetzky well expressed that, "The problem with strict adherence to title-page sanctity in the organization of a bibliographic description is that it does not make for helpful order within a catalog. A well-arranged or integrated catalog requires that similar data elements appear in similar locations in bibliographic records."[14] This is accomplished with the logical and relative importance structure of the ISBD with the following areas:

Area 1—Title and statement of responsibility area
This area covers several data elements:

Title proper:

This consists of

the title of the resource in the form in which it appears on the prescribed sources of information for the title and statement of responsibility area. It includes alternative titles and the conjunction linking an alternative title with the first part of the title proper.

It can consist of a common title and a dependent title when a section, supplement, part, etc., has a title or designation insufficient to identify it without the inclusion of the common title or the title of the main resource.
(*ISBD*, 2007; 1.1-1.)

There are many stipulations to standardize the form of recording the title proper, or the selection of title proper when two or more titles appear on the prescribed source of information or when there is more than one prescribed source of information, about resources with two or more works with a collective title, or without a collective title, about resources that are part of another resource.

General material designation:

"The purpose of the general material designation is to indicate, in general terms and at an early point in the description, the class of material to which the resource belongs" (*ISBD*, 2007;. 1.2-1). But to decide the class of material it is necessary to speak about the medium in which the manifestation is published, which is very important for organizing the collection. It is necessary to say whether it is computer-readable, microform, printed, etc.; and it is also necessary to indicate the way of perception by the user, tactile, three-dimensional form, etc.; and content characteristics, such as music or cartographic. An attempt has been made to address all these characteristics with a common terminology used by the final user to categorize the resources, and much investigation on it is being made nowadays.

Parallel title:

"A parallel title consists of a title in another language and/or script than the title proper and presented as an equivalent of the title proper on the prescribed source(s) of information" (*ISBD*, 2007; 1.3-1).

Other title information:

"Other title information consists of a word or phrase, or a group of characters, appearing in conjunction with and subordinate to the title proper, parallel title(s) or titles of individual works contained in the resource" (*ISBD*, 2007; 1.4-1).

Statement of responsibility:

"A statement of responsibility consists of name(s), phrase(s), or group(s) of characters relating to the identification and/or function of any persons or corporate bodies responsible for or contributing to the creation or realisation of the intellectual or artistic content of a work contained in the resource described" (*ISBD*, 2007; 1.5-1). This information helps in the identification of the responsible entities of the work or expression, and at the same time reflects the relationship of those entities with the work or expression.

There has always been criticism against repetition of the author's name in the statement of responsibility in addition to its access point as the principal entry, but already in 1943 there were authors who defended that. "They maintain that a knowledge of the usage of the author's name on the title-page is sometimes helpful in the identification."[15] This reason continues to be equally important nowadays, because some usage forms are not clear enough to avoid the wrong attribution by the cataloger, in spite of the normalization of access points today which tends to accept the usage of authors. This mistake could not be mended without an accurate transcription of the statement of responsibility of the work as it appears in the resource.

Elaine Svenonious speaks about controlled versus uncontrolled vocabulary, the latter being "those that are derived as-is from documents containing information," and the former "those that are assigned" and are controlled access points. "The dual representation serves to facilitate two different approaches to information: a keyword approach useful for identification and finding and a controlled-vocabulary approach required for collocation."[16]

The ISBD deals both with one statement of responsibility and with more than one statement of responsibility.

All these elements from area 1 are addressed in ISBD with its casuistry and stipulations relative to a transcription from sources of information for each element are given.

Area 2—Edition area

The edition statement is necessary for identification of the manifestation of a work. As said in the definition of the area "An edition includes all copies of a resource produced from substantially the same original input and issued by the same agency or group of agencies or a person. An edition may be identified by an edition statement on the resource or by information provided by the publisher" (*ISBD*, 2007; 2-1). We have to take into account the distinct publication patterns among countries in deciding when we have a real edition statement and not a reprint of the edition.

The edition area consists of the following data elements: the edition statement; the parallel edition statement, statements of responsibility relating to the edition; the additional edition statement and finally the statements of responsibility following an additional edition statement.

Area 3—Material or type of resource-specific area

This area is specific for particular classes of materials devoted to recording information that it is not possible to give in other areas because the data elements are different. Specifically it is to record information on the special music format; or mathematical data on scales, projection and coordinates and equinox for cartographic resources; and the numbering and dates of coverage of serials. As is explained above, nowadays there are resources that share characteristics from more than one type of resource, as for example a map serially issued, so this area is repeatable to allow giving the different data elements for specific resources.

Area 4—Publication, production, distribution, etc. area

The term "publication, production or distribution" is intended to cover all types of publication, production, distribution, issuing and release activities connected with resources (ISBD, 2007; 4-1).

In this area, with the issuing activities are recorded those data elements referring to activities of the process of physical manufacturing of the resource that can be developed by a different or by the same entity; in the last case only one statement is given. This area represents the integration of the common responsibilities of publication and of printing resources with financial and administrative responsibilities. But beyond, the activities of production include responsibilities of organization of the resource, fixing the data, and creative aspects, which are more common within electronic resources, motion pictures and sound recordings processes; and activities on making available the resource, i.e. its distribution.

The information recorded in this area has been related to, and considered representative of, the reputation of the resource, as the editor or producer is a guarantee of the physical quality of the resource and "the name of a professional or scientific organization is an endorsement of the authenticity of the subject treatment."[15]

Therefore the data elements provided in this area to identify the entity that carries out this function are place of publication, production and/or distribution; name of publisher, producer and/or distributor; the statement of function of a distributor if required; date of publication, production and/or distribution; if printing information is given it is also necessary to give the place of printing, manufacture or engraving, the name of the printer, manufacturer or engraver and/or other printing information, followed by the date of printing or manufacture.

For those data elements the ISBD provides stipulations for cases when the information is in the resource and for cases when it is not in the resource. Stipulations for resources published in multiple issues or parts, or stipulations for procedures when there are irregularities in dates are given, because this information is very important for identification and selection.

Area 5—Physical description area

This area is reserved to describe the physical carrier of the resource, that is, to describe the copy in hand that we have as representative of the manifestation. But if for any reason these physical characteristics have been modified by any circumstances, the physical description continues referring to the manifestation that can be accessed not only in the collection of the library but also in other libraries or bookshops, etc., and the special peculiarities of the item in the collection should be explained in notes.

The detailed physical description has always been criticized as not necessary and less economic, but it is important information for library activities such as storage, circulation, and conservation.

In this area the data elements given are:

The specific material designation and extent: The specific format that belongs to the medium has been categorized in the GMD (General Material Disignation) but here it is possible to use the more specific term best suited to the users. For this data element it is necessary to give stipulations when the resource is in one physical unit or when it is in more than one, or when it is a multimedia resource or kit. If the physical carriers can be counted, the number of units is given with the specific term for the carrier. It is followed by the extent, that is, the number of pieces it is composed of or the playing time. Extent-specific stipulations are given for specific types of resources.

Other data elements refer to other physical characteristics related to the method of production, illustrations, color, material from which the resource is made, etc. details that are not related to dimensions, which is the next data element defined, very useful for the management of space in the stacks, and can be used to help finding a resource being sought.

Finally an accompanying material statement can be added when appropriate. It represents a separate physical unit independent of the main carrier, and that is published jointly with the resource as part of the manifestation but with a secondary role to the main work.

Area 6—Series area

"The series area is used when the resource being described belongs to a larger bibliographic resource: series, subseries or multipart monographic resource" (*ISBD*, 2007; 6-1). It represents the granularity in description. The resource as a whole could be described with the title of the series and the specific title proper of parts could be given in a contents note, or each part could be described by its title proper giving the "common title" of the work to which it belongs in the series statement in area 6. This convertibility is why this area and area 1 are so related, having almost the same data elements:

Title proper of series, subseries, or multipart monographic resource; parallel title of series, subseries, or multipart monographic resource; other title information of series, subseries, or multipart monographic resource; statements of responsibility relating to series, subseries, or multipart monographic resource. Because the resources belonging to series or subseries can be continuing resources, the data element of International Standard Serial Number of series or subseries is added. Finally the numbering of the separate resources within the series, subseries, or multipart monographic resource is included.

Area 7—Note area

The note area contains any descriptive information that has not been given in other areas of the description but that is considered to be important to users of bibliographic records. Notes qualify and amplify the description in areas 1–6 and can deal with any aspect of a resource. Notes may also give the bibliographic history of the resource and indicate relationships to other resources. (*ISBD*, 2007; 7-1.)

Most of the notes are optional and their use depends on the depth of description the library wants to make. But some of them are mandatory because they are fundamental for user access to the resource. An example would be the notes that specify the method of access to electronic resources. When the resource is direct access, the system requirements are specified, and when it is remote access the mode of access is specified, if possible providing the link Another very important note for librarians looking for consistency in description is the one that specifies where exactly the title proper information has been taken from when the source is different from the prescribed source of information.

The notes are organized according to the ISBD areas, but in addition there can be other interesting notes not related to these areas but to description, bibliographic history, attribution of the work or expression, etc.

Area 8—Resource identifier and terms of availability area

A resource identifier is any number or alphanumeric designation associated with a resource according to an international standard, such as an International Standard

Book Number (ISBN) or an International Standard Serial Number (ISSN), or a designation assigned by a publisher. (*ISBD*, 2007; 8-1.)

The area is repeatable because one resource can have more than one identifier. For example in the case of multipart resources, each part can have its own identifier, and the whole resource can have another identifier.

In this area the following data elements are recorded when available: The resource identifier transcribed preceded, as appropriate, by letters that identify the standard; the key title assigned by the ISSN Network when the resource that is being described is a continuing resource; the terms of availability and/or price. When the identifier or the terms of availability or price need supplementary information, qualifications are given.

HISTORY AND RECENT DEVELOPMENT OF THE ISBD

Historically catalogs were lists of information to find a book in collections that essentially consisted of such types of resources. That is why the title page was used as the basis for cataloging, and the description of other types of materials had to fit into the book patterns.

Because the most important thing for finding a resource was to provide information on the author, the cataloger then gave more attention to find the authorship. The cataloging rules until the beginning of the twentieth century were mainly stipulations related to authorship. The other part of the cataloging was the description, but it was considered less important. First it was necessary to find, then it was possible to identify if the resource found was meeting the requirements that were looked for. As collections were growing, the identification needs were more important. This identification was only possible by means of the description of the resource. At this time the card catalog was considered a necessary intermediate tool. The rules for description had been influenced by the bibliographers who were developing their techniques for the description of older books, where the description should be as accurate as possible with close transcription of the title page from top to bottom. This exaggerated reverence for the title page did not allow catalogers to use a commonsense approach to late nineteenth century and twentieth century printed books.

Seymour Lubetzky was a figure who influenced many at this time presenting a

systematic approach, which took its departure from the assumption that before describing a book it is necessary first to be aware of the objectives that description is to serve. Only then is it clear what is and what is not to be included in a bibliographic record... Basically their import was that a bibliographic description served first to identify a book and, secondly, to characterize its contents.

Data elements on a title page that did not further either of these objectives were to be excluded... On the other hand, data elements that did not appear on a title page, yet were necessary to meet one or the other of the stated objectives of description, were to be included in a bibliographic record.[17]

At this time, in the 1950s there was an unprecedented boom in book production. Trying to find a centralized solution to world bibliographic control, "UNESCO's work was more realistically directed, based on two fundamental criteria, the first, concern for fundamental study and research, the second, reliance on national activities: 'it is unrealistic to think progress in bibliographic control at the international level can be achieved even if national conditions are ignored....'"[18]

In 1958 the Symposium of National Libraries in Europe held in Vienna settled the basis for defining the role of the national library and its contribution to national bibliographic control by means of developing the current national bibliography.

According to the self-criticism environment on cataloging practices in the library community, IFLA (formerly International Federation of Library Associations) organized the International Conference on Cataloging Principles, in Paris in 1961. Preparatory to this conference, an examination of the problems relating to bibliographic control through the analysis of national cataloging codes was made. The conference supposed a landmark that had as a result an international agreement that influenced the cataloging codes world wide until today. But the principles accepted were again focused or centered mainly on access points, revealing the main concern at this time was not on description as the differences between countries were not considered important.

Eva Verona, Yugoslav librarian well known internationally for her work and her chairmanship of various IFLA committees and working groups, recognized this lack in her comments on the principles:

It might be argued that the list of elements specifying a particular book as given in section 2.1, and amplified in section 3.2 and section 6.4, is not complete. A complete list should necessarily include those particulars which enable the user of the alphabetical catalog to distinguish various editions of the same work.... It is thus made quite clear that the Statement is aware of the importance of such particulars in the alphabetical catalog. The fact that those particulars are not mentioned in section 2.1 in connection with the first basic function of the alphabetical catalog may be accounted for by the limitation of the Statement to problems concerning the choice and form of elements determining the order of entries.[19]

But three things changed minds in 1960s: One was shared cataloging projects on a large scale; the other, the arrival of the computer.

As long as libraries were using computers solely for processing their own records there was no problem, but as soon as they began to exchange machine-readable records and tried to use those received from other agencies in their systems, the need for standardization became clear. Computers demand standards: standards for electronic storage and transmission, standards for the formats within which the data would be recorded and (to some extent) for the data content itself. The third factor was, oddly, a by-product of the International Conference on Cataloging Principles... the agreed text of the principles accompanied by full examples to illustrate them. Originally, the examples showed an embarrassing variety of descriptive practice beneath the agreed headings....[20]

Work was started to prepare the second major cataloging conference of the period, the International Meeting of Cataloging Experts held in Copenhagen in 1969 at which was established the basis toward creating a system for the international exchange of information: The standard bibliographic description of each publication developed and distributed by a national agency in the country of origin of the publication, which will be responsible for creating records in such standardized conditions. The effectiveness of the system was dependent on the maximum standardization of the bibliographic description.

The study of the rules in use until that time revealed that there was sufficient similarity in the descriptive part of the catalog record as all the stipulations on description were to transcribe the title page. The main goal was, and continues to be, to offer consistency when sharing bibliographic information:

Under the title Universal Bibliographic Control (UBC) IFLA is proposing that UNESCO adopts as a major policy objective the promotion of a world-wide system for the control and exchange for bibliographic information. The purpose of the system is to make universally and promptly available, in a form which is internationally acceptable, basic bibliographic data on all publications issued in all countries.[21]

In the promulgation of the UBC program three international organizations have played a major part: IFLA; the UNESCO General Information Programme (PGI); and the International Organization for Standardization (ISO). The international office for UBC was created, and it gave support at a variety of levels to projects directed toward its development. In so doing it has provided support to IFLA working groups and to experts engaged in particular bibliographic projects. Nowadays it has been supplanted by ICABS IFLA-CDNL Alliance for Bibliographic Standards. (ICAB's Web page, available at http://www.ifla.org/VI/7/icabs.htm (accessed October 2007). The National Library of Australia, the Library of Congress, The British Library, the Koninklijke Bibliotheek, and Die Deutsche Bibliothek have agreed to participate in a joint alliance together with the Biblioteca Nacional de Portugal, IFLA and CDNL to assure ongoing coordination, communication

and support for key activities in the areas of bibliographic and resource control for all types of resources and related format and protocol standards.)

Its objectives at that time were not much different from objectives today (related above):

1. The interchange of bibliographic records.
2. Interpretation of records from foreign sources and ability to identify the parts of the record, independent of the language and script.
3. Conversion of manual records to electronic form.

There were three methods to achieve these: definition of elements, organization into a structure in eight areas, and identification of each element by a symbol of punctuation.

IFLA's special contribution to the concept of UBC is its firm belief that every country can become a component part of the UBC system, that each has a contribution to make. It accepts that contributions may vary considerably in quantity between developed and developing countries...[22]

Among the requirements to achieve UBC there were the establishment of the national bibliographic agency in charge of preparing the authoritative bibliographic record for each new publication issued in the country and collected in national bibliographies; the record's acceptance at an international level; and also an international standard for creating the bibliographic records. That standard must take into account: (1) its contents: the elements to be included in the authoritative record; the order of those elements; the means of distinguishing the elements and their functions; and (2) its physical form; compatibility of machine-readable records; standardization of catalog cards.

The basic premise for establishing UBC has been set out thus: that the comprehensive bibliographic record of a publication is made once in a country of its origin, in accordance with international standards which are applicable in both manual and mechanized systems; and that record is then available speedily, in a physical form which is also internationally acceptable.

The detailed elements that make up that comprehensive and authoritative bibliographic record include all the information about the publication which may be required to fulfill any of the functions of library or information services. The selection of these elements and the way in which they are presented have evolved from careful work of experts... there are still areas of national bibliographic traditions evolving from language and culture.[23]

This is mainly the reason why the ISBD was designed primarily for national bibliographic agencies that are responsible for creating descriptions with all the defined mandatory elements, as was explicitly said in the introduction. But this practice is also recommended for libraries that exchange bibliographic records. Other libraries can use the ISBD, and it is recommended that they do, but they can adapt it to their needs, selecting the elements to be described. The reason is that the ISBDs were intended to serve as a principal component of IFLA's program to promote UBC.

The first of the ISBDs to be published was the International Standard Bibliographic Description for Monographic Publications (ISBD(M)), which appeared in 1971, with a revised text published in 1974 as the "first standard edition." It was clearly based on traditional descriptions of monographs found on printed catalog cards. Other ISBDs subsequently appeared for specific types of resources: ISBD(S) for serials was also published in 1974; ISBD (CM) for cartographic materials and ISBD(NBM) for nonbook materials were both first published in 1977; ISBD(A) for older monographic publications (antiquarian) and ISBD(PM) for printed music first editions were published in 1980; and the ISBD(CF) for computer files, first edition, was published in 1990. Along the way, the need was felt for a general framework to which all the ISBDs would conform, resulting in production of the ISBD(G) published in 1977; the primary utility of the ISBD(G) was that of ensuring harmony among the other ISBDs. For article-level publications, *Guidelines for the application of the ISBDs to the description of component parts* was issued in 1988. For a more detailed introduction to the ISBDs, see Byrum.[24]

It was necessary to normalize the description of each type of material, but today the borders are not so clear.

At the IFLA World Congress in Brussels, held in August 1977, the Standing Committee of the IFLA Section on Cataloging made important new decisions in relation to IFLA's program of ISBDs. It was decided that all ISBD texts would be fixed to a life of five years, after which revision would be considered for all texts or for particular texts.

More pragmatically, they have been revised as the need has arisen, to implement general applicable changes or by the evolution of library materials, such as those that resulted in publication of the ISBD for electronic resources and, more recently, the ISBD for serials and other continuing resources.

Although some ISBDs have been developed or revised to meet particular needs, there have been two overall revision projects affecting the entire family of ISBDs.

First General Review Project

Consequent to the decision taken in 1977, mentioned above, the initial overall revision resulted in the creation of the ISBD Review Committee, which first met in August 1981.

The committee established three major objectives for the first general review project:

1. To harmonize provisions, achieving increased consistency.

2. To improve examples.
3. To make the provisions more applicable to catalogers working with materials published in non-roman scripts.

In addition, two narrower objectives motivated this particular revision effort:

1. To review the use of the equals sign (as its use in bibliographic descriptions had been the source of some controversy).
2. To remove coverage of machine-readable materials from the ISBD for nonbook materials.[25]

By the early 1990s the revised edition of the ISBDs had been published:

- The standard for monographic publications ISBD(M) previously revised in 1978, was revised again in 1987.
- Cartographic materials ISBD(CM) was revised in 1987.
- Nonbook materials ISBD(NBM) was revised in 1987.
- Serials ISBD(S) was revised in 1988.
- Printed music ISBD(PM) was revised in 1989.
- ISBD(G) was revised in 1992.
- In addition, a separate ISBD was published for computer files (1990), which, due to the rapid advances in technology, was soon superseded by creation of an ISBD for electronic resources (1997). (The entire list of ISBDs is available at http://www.ifla.org/VI/3/nd1/isbdlist.htm, (accessed October 2007).

Second General Review Project

In the early 1990s, the section on cataloging in cooperation with other sections set up the Study Group on the Functional Requirements for Bibliographic Records (FRBR). One immediate consequence of this development was the decision to suspend most revision work on the ISBDs while the FRBR Study Group pursued its charge to "recommend a basic level of functionality and basic data requirements for records created by national bibliographic agencies." This decision resulted in the permanent suspension of a project to identify the components of a "Concise ISBD(M)," because it was expected that FRBR's findings would, in effect, provide such a baseline. In 1998, the FRBR Study Group published its final report,[26] and the ISBD Review Group was reconstituted to initiate a full-scale review of the ISBDs in order to implement FRBR's recommendations for a basic level national bibliographic record[27] and ensure conformity between the provisions of the ISBDs and FRBR's data requirements.

To facilitate the work of national bibliographic agencies of preparing the definitive description containing the mandatory elements, the ISBDs designate as "optional" those data elements that are not mandatory when applicable or as "conditional" those data elements that are needed in certain circumstances but may otherwise be considered optional. Therefore, the main task in pursuing the second general review entailed a close look at the ISBD data elements that were now mandatory in order to ensure that no element that was mandatory in FRBR was optional in the ISBDs.

Another important task was consideration of the adaptation of ISBD terminology to FRBR's terms "work," "expression," "manifestation," and "item" to determine if they should be introduced in place of terms such as "publication" or "item." The Review Group concluded that it was essential for IFLA to clarify the relationship between the ISBDs and the FRBR model. The group encountered difficulties in trying to achieve that alignment, in large part because the terms used in FRBR were defined in the context of an entity-relationship model conceived at a higher level of abstraction than the stipulations for the ISBDs. While the entities defined in the FRBR model are clearly based on the elements forming an ISBD description,[28] the relationships are too complex to be conveyed through a simple substitution of terminology. Taking into consideration Patrick Le Boeuf's advice at the Frankfurt IME ICC (International Meeting of Experts on an International Cataloging Code) in his paper on "Brave new FRBR world":[29] "FRBR terminology should not be merely incorporated such as it stands into the ISBDs and cataloging rules, but [these] should keep their own specific terminology, and provide accurate definitions showing how each term in this specific terminology is conceptually related to the FRBR terminology." The Review Group thus decided that the development of a table to detail the relationship of each of the elements specified in the ISBDs to its corresponding entity, attribute or relationship as defined in the FRBR model, would satisfy the need to make clear that the ISBDs and FRBR themselves enjoy a harmonious relationship.[30]

Nevertheless, the ISBD Review Group did decide to introduce some changes in terminology, beginning with the recently revised ISBD(G). Among them is the use of the term "resource" rather than "item" or "publication." This decision was taken because the use of the term "item" in the ISBD was different from the term "item" as used in FRBR, and it is difficult not to confuse them.

Some of the ISBDs (G, M, CR, ER, CM, and A) went through this revision process, but the process was interrupted before being finished, as work on the consolidated ISBD began.

Reasons for a Consolidated ISBD

There had been seven specialized ISBDs, plus the General ISBD. These ISBDs have been revised and published at various times, with no method for incorporating changes made in newer texts that affect all the ISBDs into the older texts. For example, when it was decided to incorporate decisions on which data elements should remain mandatory in the ISBDs based on those required in FRBR, these changes were incorporated into the ISBD(M) and the ISBD(CR) that were issued in 2002, and the ISBD(G) in 2004 although they applied to all of the ISBDs.

In addition to this situation, publications that show characteristics of more than one format require the application of stipulations from more than one ISBD. Because the ISBDs themselves had some inconsistencies, this brought major difficulties that caused the ISBD Review Group to decide in 2003 that consolidation of the ISBDs was feasible, and work was started on preparing a definitive text.

The work received ICABS support for a first merger of the text of the seven ISBDs. Project money was also granted by the IFLA Professional Committee.

A "final" version was sent to the IFLA Cataloging Section's Standing Committee, which voted for acceptance before the end of March of 2007. The consolidated ISBD replaces the specialized ISBDs.

In the integration of information from all types of resources, agreement was reached on the general outline to be followed for each area. In addition, it was decided to recommend that:

- The structure should be changed to a new structure of areas where general stipulations that apply to all types of resources are given first, followed by exceptions or additional stipulations that are needed for specific types of resources.
- Present stipulations should fit into the new structure; therefore, the order of stipulations has also been modified to make the text more logical and consistent.
- Some changes should be made to generalize wording and to match wording as much as possible, also taking into account the stipulations that were considered mandatory, conditional, or optional in the already-revised ISBDs.
- The GMD should be moved from after the title proper to another location.
- Further changes to stipulations can be made at a later stage.[31]

The focus has been on the set of elements of information rather than their display, and looking for interoperability with other systems and display formats, the punctuation has been slightly changed. Although the importance that ISBD punctuation has had in the past and continues to have in the context of different languages and scripts is recognized, the presentation of information is a secondary objective. In local catalogs the labeled display is now the most common and clear display for many users, that is why punctuation is not as essential as before but continues being recommended for international understanding.

CONCLUSION

The UBC concept continues to provide a foundation for the international and national organization of the creation of bibliographic data. "Among the characteristics of a national bibliography are that it provides a current, timely, comprehensive, and authoritative list of all titles published in a country, it provides a record of their existence, and it identifies them unambiguously."[32] The ISBD helps in providing authoritative bibliographic records, but the ISBD has spread far beyond because in the management process of our collections it is easy and cheap to copy bibliographic records or download them from other databases and use them with scarcely a need to make changes. For this reason and because the process of reviewing the ISBD will continue to keep it updated to take account of new developments, the ISBD will continue to be the standard for definition elements and descriptive content of bibliographic records.

ACKNOWLEDGMENT

The author acknowledges Dorothy McGarry for her assistance.

REFERENCES

1. Svenonius, E. *The Intellectual Foundation of Information*, MIT Press, cop.: Cambridge, MA 2000; 80.
2. Escolano, E. McGarry, D. Consolidated ISBD: A step forward *Presentation to the World Library and Information Congress*, 73rd IFLA General Conference and Council Durban, South Africa August, 19–23, 2007 2. Available at http://www.ifla.org/IV/ifla73/papers/145-Escolano Rodriguez_McGarry-en.pdf (accessed October 2007).
3. Anderson, D. *Universal Bibliographic Control: A Long Term Policy, a Plan for Action*, Verlag Dokumentation: Pullach, Germany, 1974; 19.
4. Tillet, B. Report of the 1st IFLA Meeting of Experts on an International Cataloguing Code Frankfurt, Germany July, 28–30, 2003 2. Available at http://www.d-nb.de/standardisierung/pdf/ime_icc_report_berlin.pdf (accessed October 2007).
5. Tillet, B. Report of IME ICC2 Meeting Buenos Aires, Argentina August, 17–18, 2004 7.Available at http://www.loc.gov/loc/ifla/imeicc/source/IMEICC2-report_IFLA-BA_2004.pdf (accessed October 2007).
6. Tillet, B.B. Report on the IME ICC3 Meeting Cairo, Egypt December, 12–14, 2005 2. Available at http://www.loc.gov/loc/ifla/imeicc/pdf/Report-IMEICC3_brief.pdf (accessed October 2007).
7. Lee, J. Report on the IME ICC4 Meeting Seoul, Korea August, 16–18, 2006 2. Available at http://www.nl.go.kr/icc/paper/report_1.pdf (accessed October 2007).
8. Svenonius, E. *The Intellectual Foundation of Information*, MIT Press, cop.: Cambridge, MA 2000; 82.
9. Svenonius, E. *The Intellectual Foundation of Information*, MIT Press, cop.: Cambridge, MA 2000; 76.
10. Lubetzky, S.In *Seymour Lubetzky: Writings on the Classical Art of Cataloging*; Svenonius, E., McGarry, D., Eds.; Libraries Unlimited: Englewood, CO, 2001; 54.
11. Anderson, D. *UBC: A Survey of Universal Bibliographic Control*, IFLA International Office for UBC: London, U.K., 1982; 18. Occasional Papers, no. 10.
12. Svenonius, E. *The Intellectual Foundation of Information*, MIT Press, cop.: Cambridge, MA2000; 74.
13. IFLA Cataloguing Principles: Steps Towards an International Cataloguing Code Report from the 1st IFLA Meeting of Experts on an International Cataloguing Code Frankfurt 2003 Saur: München, Germany 2004; 2.
14. Lubetzky, S. In *Seymour Lubetzky: Writings on the Classical Art of Cataloging*; Svenonius, E., McGarry, D., Eds.; Libraries Unlimited: Englewood, CO, 2001; 49.
15. Lubetzky, S. In *Seymour Lubetzky: Writings on the Classical Art of Cataloging*; Svenonius, E., McGarry, D., Eds.; Libraries Unlimited: Englewood, CO, 2001; 52.
16. Svenonius, E. *The Intellectual Foundation of Information*, MIT Press, cop.: Cambridge, MA 2000; 88.
17. Lubetzky, S. In *Seymour Lubetzky: Writings on the Classical Art of Cataloging*; Svenonius, E., McGarry, D., Eds.; Libraries Unlimited: Englewood, CO, 2001; 48.
18. Anderson, D. *UBC: A Survey of Universal Bibliographic Control*, IFLA International Office for UBC: London, U.K., 1982; 1. Occasional Papers, no. 10.
19. Statement of principles International Conference on Cataloguing Principles Paris October, 1961; Verona, E., Kaltwasser, F.G., Lewis, P.R., Pierrot, R., Eds.; IFLA Committee Cataloguing: London, 1971; 7 adopted at the.
20. Curwen, A.G. International standard bibliographic description. *Standards for the International Exchange of Bibliographic Information*; The Library Association: London, 1991; 75.
21. Anderson, D. *Universal Bibliographic Control: A Long Term Policy, a Plan for Action*, Verlag Dokumentation: Pullach bei München, Germany, 1974; 11.
22. Anderson, D. *Universal Bibliographic Control: A Long Term policy, a Plan for Action*, Verlag Dokumentation: Pullach, München, Germany 1974; 18.
23. Anderson, D. *UBC: A Survey of Universal Bibliographic Control*, IFLA International Office for UBC: London, U.K., 1982; 13–14 Occasional Papers, no. 10.
24. Byrum, J. The birth and re-birth of the ISBDs: Process and procedures for creating and revising the International Standard Bibliographic Descriptions. Presentation at 66th IFLA Council and General Conference, Jerusalem, Israel, 2000. Available at http://www.ifla.org/IV/ifla66/papers/118-164e.htm (accessed October 2007).
25. Byrum, J. IFLA's ISBD programme: Purpose, process, and prospects Presented to the Second IFLA Meeting of Experts on an International Cataloguing Code Buenos Aires, Argentina August, 17–18, 2004 3. Available at http://www.loc.gov/loc/ifla/imeicc/source/papers-byrum.pdf (accessed October 2007).
26. Functional Requirements for Bibliographic Records—Final Report. Available at http://www.ifla.org/VII/s13/frbr/frbr.htm.
27. Byrum, J. IFLA's ISBD programme: Purpose, process, and prospects Presented to the Second IFLA Meeting of Experts on an International Cataloguing Code August, 2004 3. Available at http://www.loc.gov/loc/ifla/imeicc/source/papers-byrum.pdf (accessed October 2007).

28. Functional Requirements for Bibliographic Records—Final Report. Available at http://www.ifla.org/VII/s13/frbr/frbr.htm. (accessed October 2007).

29. Le Boeuf, P. Brave new FRBR world IFLA Cataloguing Principles: Steps Towards an International Cataloguing Code Frankfurt, Germany July, 28–30, 2003 K.G. Saur: München, 2004; 3. Report from the 1st IFLA Meeting of Experts on an International Cataloguing Code Available at http://www.d-nb.de/standardisierung/pdf/papers_leboeuf.pdf (accessed October 2007).

30. Mapping ISBD Elements to FRBR Entity Attributes and Relationships on July 9, 2004. Available at http://www.ifla.org/VII/s13/pubs/ISBD-FRBR-mappingFinal.pdf .

31. Escolano, E. McGarry, D. Consolidated ISBD: A step forward*Presentation to the World Library and Information Congress*, 73rd IFLA General Conference and Council Durban, South Africa August, 19–23, 2007 10. Available at http://www.ifla.org/IV/ifla73/papers/145-EscolanoRodriguez_McGarry-en.pdf (accessed October 2007).

32. Parent, I. The importance of National Bibliographies in the Digital Age*Presentation to the World Library and Information Congress*, 73rd IFLA General Conference and Council Durban, South Africa 2007 4. Available at http://www.ifla.org/IV/ifla73/papers/089-Parent-en.pdf (accessed October 2007).

Design Science in the Information Sciences

Judith Weedman
School of Library and Information Science, San Jose State University, Fullerton, California, U.S.A.

Abstract
Design is a core professional responsibility in the information professions as in others. It may be local and idiosyncratic, or it may be the focus of a major research project. Design researchers have argued that there are fundamental design problems and design solutions that cross scale and domain boundaries; if this is so, then design science, the study of design, should build knowledge both about particular domains and also about what is true across domains. This entry examines design science in several fields to indicate where it might inform design in the library and information sciences. It concludes with two examples from the information sciences, one a design science study of vocabulary design and one a design research project, in which the research consisted of design of an information retrieval system.

INTRODUCTION

Design is a central professional task in the library and information science (LIS). Patrick Wilson wrote in 1996 that information science inhabits two fields, engineering research and development (R&D) and social/behavioral/ humanistic studies. In R&D, Wilson included both the design of material technologies for information retrieval and the design of intellectual technologies such as metadata systems and strategies for searching information retrieval systems. Thirty years earlier, Herbert Simon, in his influential *Sciences of the Artificial*,[1] wrote that design is the core responsibility in all professions. Simon defined design as taking a problematic situation and transforming it into a desirable situation. Management decision-making, strategic planning, psychotherapy, and other nonmaterial problem-solving are thus included as design work, along with material design such as engineering, sculpture, and architecture.

Design science is the study of the work of design—how designers make decisions, use tools, manage problems, and think about their work, and what the characteristics of that work are. Research methods include interviews, surveys, ethnographic techniques, introspection, and philosophical investigations. One area of design science has been referred to as "design research" (or sometimes "design science" or "design science research"); this refers to the practice of design in which novel and important design is undertaken for the combined purposes of creation of the artifact and contribution to the professional knowledge base of the field.[2]

Design is under-theorized in the library and information sciences. On the R&D side of the disciplines, there is a well-developed line of research in which information retrieval design is treated as an as an experimental science (thanks in large part to the efforts of Gerard Salton). However, there is little or no theory about the work of design

itself. The social science side of LIS has concentrated on users of information systems—information-seeking behavior, user satisfaction, search behaviors of experts and novices, sociotechnical studies of digital library use, etc. Although the understanding of the technical differences between information retrieval (IR) systems is important to understanding differences in user behavior, the characteristics of IR systems has rarely been an independent variable in research. Nor has the social science tradition in LIS often studied the processes by which technical systems are designed. The presence of both research traditions within the field could provide a "home field advantage" over disciplines where a social understanding of technical systems requires either importing ideas from outside the domain proper or the importing of social scientists themselves. Use of design science as a social science approach could create interesting connections between the social science and engineering sides of the discipline, as well as adding a dimension to the study of how information and social systems interact. Conceptualizing the sum of the design work undertaken in our field as "design research" could add dimensions interesting from both social science and technical design standpoints.

Buchanan[3] notes that each of the fields that have studied their own design work has tended to regard it "as an applied version of its own knowledge, methods, and principles" (1995a, p. 18). The various literatures have had little cross-boundary interaction; the notable exceptions are Simon (artificial intelligence) and Alexander (architecture). There is a growing belief, however, that there are similarities in design problems and solutions that cross domains, and some research to determine whether that is in fact the case.[4] Thomas and Carroll argue that design is a way of looking at a problem and is therefore not exclusive to a particular kind of problem; they found that "activities as diverse as software design, architectural design, naming, and letter-writing appear to have much in common."[5] Nigel Cross, who has

Encyclopedia of Library and Information Sciences, Fourth Edition DOI: 10.1081/E-ELIS4-120043534

written extensively about design methodology and design theory, also asserts that design is at least partially independent of the profession in which it is undertaken and that there exists a form of knowledge which is a "designerly way of knowing." In 1982, Cross[6] called for the construction of a way of conversing about design that is domain independent. It is in this spirit that this entry will draw attention to several strands of literatures from various disciplines. The goal is to highlight themes and approaches that may be of use to researchers or practitioners interested in applying them in the library and information sciences.

In everyday conversation, "design" is often equated with "style"—extra, nonfunctional aspects of a product that make it attractive or fashionable or characteristic of a particular approach; this is not the meaning used here. Design in this entry refers to the professional or research activity that results in a plan for a product or service that will be or could be instantiated in the world to solve a problem. Designing often includes the actual creation of the product or service, but as Schon notes,[4] designers often create blueprints or sketches or combinations of functions which someone else will turn into a building or landscape or software code. In some fields the distinction between design and making is theoretically important, with design as an intellectually different activity from that of instantiating the design.

Design takes place in a range of professions and a range of venues. Buchanan,[7] for instance, divides the "design professions" into four general groups: 1) those that design symbolic and visual communications (graphics, books and magazines, film, computer display, etc.); 2) those that design material objects (clothing, tools, instruments, machinery); 3) those that design activities and organized services (management functions of logistics, decision making, strategic planning); and 4) those that design systems or environments (systems engineering, software design, architecture, and urban planning). Information professionals and researchers work in all four of these categories.

Two assumptions underlie this entry. The first is that there is indeed some "designerly way of knowing" that crosses disciplinary and professional boundaries. The second is that every design context is different, with unique interactions between context and process. The uncertainty in design is a constant in design theory. After an exploration of this core concept, the following seven sections address additional aspects of design work that seem to be independent of the particular physical or intellectual artifact being designed. An example of design science and an example of design research in library and information science are then described.

UNCERTAINTY

That design practice is inherently uncertain because it involves changing potential into actuality is a key factor addressed by most design theories. In this entry, it is given pride of place, discussed first and then pervading discussion of other aspects of design.

Historically, two responses have been made to uncertainty, attempts to remove it from design or acknowledgment of it as an inherent part of the creative process. The first, in part a reaction to an earlier tendency to romanticize inspiration and individual creativity, was to find objective and rational techniques that would remove uncertainty and allow the development of methods that would give reliable results. The second, in part a reaction to the rationalists, was to acknowledge that uncertainty is not removable and to embrace it as a part of the creative process. The first philosophy can be traced back to the logical positivists, the second to the constructivism of John Dewey and Charles Sanders Peirce.

The movement to develop design techniques that removed the mysterious, inexact, intuitive component and make design more like science began in the early twentieth century. The term "design science" itself is a direct descendent of this attempt, though it is also used today by those who reject the desirability of objective, rationalist methodologies. The architect and urban planner Le Corbusier was a pioneer in developing Modern Architecture theory for the building of spaces; he began his work during the First World War, when the traditional European city was showing the destructive effects of the Industrial Revolution. Believing that improving living spaces would allow people themselves to improve, he sought techniques that would create both harmony and efficiency in the built environment. Harmony could be achieved by the application of Leonardo da Vinci's golden ratio which based building proportions on the proportions of the human body and by the incorporation of concepts about the mathematical order of the universe. Uncertainty was addressed with techniques based on the objective, rational industrial management ideas of F. W. Taylor and Henry Ford. "The use of the house consists of a regular sequence of definite functions. The regular sequence of these functions is a traffic phenomenon. To render that traffic exact, economical and rapid is the key effort of modern architectural science" (Le Corbusier, cited by Cross).[8]

Like Le Corbusier, Buckminster Fuller believed that design of buildings and spaces based on rational principles rather than aesthetic inspiration would solve many contemporary problems. He is thought to have originated the term "design science," which he defined as "effective application of the principles of science to the conscious design of our total environment in order to help make the Earth's finite resources meet the needs of all humanity without disrupting the ecological processes of the planet."[9] He declared the years between 1965 and 1975 the Design Science Decade, and urged a retooling for schools of architecture around the world, to use scientific methods to "measure, observe, and improve solutions until solutions are developed that will work not just once, but over and over, and in a variety of situations."[10]

The architect Christopher Alexander[11] also sought to develop systematic design methods that would give reliable outcomes; he explored the use of logic and mathematics, and later computers, to analyze the uncertainty out of design problems. While he saw a role for intuition, he argued that many had made a fetish of it, and that too much emphasis on intuition and artistry prevented the designer from asking reasonable questions and employing systematic processes. The increasing complexity of design problems required rational methods. A design problem "has requirements which have to be met and there are interactions between the requirements, which makes the requirements hard to meet. . . . Each of the issues interacts with several of the others . . . [In large design problems], each issue is itself a vast problem; and the pattern of interactions is vastly complicated."

In his 1964 book *Notes on the Synthesis of Form*, Alexander[12] asserts that most design problems are so complex that the designer cannot see the solution. Therefore, the architectural designer should start by listing all of the requirements and their interactions with each other. Once this is done, the requirements can be broken down into subrequirements; the solutions for each of the subrequirements will then be easier to determine, and from the set of solutions to the subrequirements, the final form can be synthesized. Thus the process is to apply the logic of analysis first, to determine all the parts of the whole, followed by applying the logic of synthesis to combine the solutions. In *A Pattern Language*,[13] Alexander and five coauthors systematically analyze common problems in design and then describe the core of the solution to each problem, providing patterns that can be combined and recombined to solve architectural problems ranging from the level of climbing plants, doors, windows, and duct space through the level of rooms and foundations to entire buildings, towns, and the distribution of towns. Over time, as his ideas and others of the rationalist approach became more widely accepted, Alexander came to feel that just as people had made a fetish of individual intuition in design, so they were now making a fetish of a rationalistic methods. Disavowing what he described as a "painful and drawn-out misunderstanding" of his work, he disassociated himself from the use of method for its own sake, which he felt had become desiccated, dried up, and senseless.

Herbert Simon is the most-quoted and most influential rationalist, objectivist theorist today. In his 1969 book *The Sciences of the Artificial*,[14] he argues that design is a process of decomposition; the problem is defined, alternatives are generated, and the alternatives are tested against an array of requirements and constraints, often in nested series of cycles. Much like Alexander, he argued in "The Structure of Ill-Structured Problems,"[15] written for the artificial intelligence community, that large, ill-structured problems can be broken down into smaller problems which are structured and therefore solvable.

In the reaction against the rational approach and attempts to decompose messy problems into solvable ones, one of the most influential writers has been Horst Rittel. He began developing the concept of "wicked problems" in the mid-1960s. Rittel took the phrase from Karl Popper, but used it differently. Wicked problems are ill-defined, and Rittel denies that they can be analyzed into smaller, well-structured problems. Published in an urban policy journal, Rittel and Webber's "Dilemmas in a General Theory of Planning"[16] defined wicked problems as those which are ill-defined, messy, circular, and aggressive. "Tame" problems are definable and separable and may have solutions that are findable; in addition, it can be determined whether or not the problem has been solved. Chess, puzzle-solving, and math are examples of tame problems. With wicked problems, "one of the most intractable problems is that of defining the problem (of knowing what distinguishes an observed condition from a desired condition) and of locating problems (finding where in the complex causal networks the trouble really lies). In turn, and equally intractable, is the problem of identifying the actions that might effectively narrow the gap between what-is and what-ought-to-be."[17] Rittel and Webber list ten distinguishing properties of wicked problems:

1. There is no definitive formulation of a wicked problem.
2. Wicked problems have no stopping rule.
3. Solutions to wicked problems are not true-or-false, but good-or-bad.
4. There is no immediate and no ultimate test of a solution to a wicked problem.
5. Every solution to a wicked problem is a "one-shot operation"; because there is no opportunity to learn by trial-and-error, every attempt counts significantly.
6. Wicked problems do not have an enumerable (or an exhaustively describable) set of potential solutions, nor is there a well-described set of permissible operations that may be incorporated into the plan.
7. Every wicked problem is essentially unique.
8. Every wicked problem can be considered to be a symptom of another problem.
9. The existence of a discrepancy representing a wicked problem can be explained in numerous ways. The choice of explanation determines the nature of the problem's resolution.
10. The planner has no right to be wrong.

Today many design theorists see the unexpected as the source of, or opportunity for, creativity. Donald Schon, a philosopher who developed an epistemology of professional practice, accused rationalist theories of being radically incomplete. He studied six different professions for his 1983 book, *The Reflective Practitioner*:[4] architecture, clinical psychology, engineering, scientists designing equipment to test their hypotheses, city planning, and management. Like Simon, he saw design as the core of professional practice, but when he actually studied professionals at work he found that they were not carrying out series of logical transformations until the problems were solvable, but rather making and remaking entire design structures. Well-formed problem-solving of the sort advocated by Simon occurred only in later stages, after the design structure had stabilized. In the early stages, he found very fluid activities which often resulted in surprise and learning. A second problem that Schon found with the rationalist tradition was that it could not account for this kind of learning, which often results in reframing the problem itself. The third problem was that Simon and others tend to regard rational decision as a process that occurs within the mind of an individual; Schon observed, to the contrary, that designing is almost always a social process, with constraints and affordances arising from colleagues, the customer or imagined user, funding agencies, management structures, designers of the technologies the designer uses, distributors of materials, and so on.

Other researchers have supported the idea that the presence of the unexpected benefits design as well as creating problems. Bucciarelli,[4] writing of product engineering, found that uncertainty actually allowed participants to exercise their creativity, that a variation untried before or challenging an assumption or constraint took engineers into unknown areas, where outcomes were unpredictable. Organizational war stories and jokes about Murphy's law reflect a design culture's realization that in design there is always disorder, chance, the creative, surprise—the unknown. Gasser,[18] in a forum on management as design, wrote that

> randomness is a natural consequence of engagement with the world. The more engaged an actor is, the more apparent randomness, uniqueness, or 'situatedness' he or she experiences. To be engaged in a present experience means to be able to differentiate that present experience from another–to experience its uniqueness, its lack of pattern with respect to other situations. ... Deliberate injection of randomness can be a powerful tool for analysis and even for improving efficiency of certain activities and processes.

PROBLEM SETTING

Simon's[15] argument that design problems which are ill-defined in the beginning can be broken down into smaller well-defined problems is undermined by many authors' descriptions of the problem-setting process. Rittel and Webber begin defining wicked problems with the characteristic that "there is no definitive formulation" of the problem. Others argue that it is not just wicked problems for which this is true, but that in fact all true design shares this characteristic. Lave,[19] writing of problem-solving in general, argues that problems are generated in relation to the particular setting within which the practitioner is working, and that problem solvers choose "whether to have a problem or not, and the specification of what constitutes the problem." Even in an engineering firm where the task is to design to client specifications, Bucciarelli asserts, they are negotiating the nature of the problem with the specifications themselves, with the suppliers of materials, with the nature of the tools they have available, and with others on the design team, and of course with the clients.

There is a large literature on client or user participation in design and the difficulties in such collaboration. Many authors of works on information systems have discussed the problem of obtaining useful information from potential users about what the problem is and what the solution should be—much of users' knowledge is tacit, and they lack the design and technical knowledge to understand the kind of information that designers need; designers, on the other hand, often lack thorough understanding of users' work and workflow despite time spent in requirements elicitation.[20] Thus the negotiation about what the artifact will be has many dimensions and generally goes through many iterations; it is frequently the case that users and designers think they agree, only to discover later that words had disguised the tacit understandings of each side and that in fact they were operating under very different assumptions. In addition, design projects are often set in motion by the supervisors of those who will actually use the artifact to accomplish their work, which adds additional layers of definition which affect the understanding of the need the project addresses.

Boland[21] stresses the impact of language on problem definition; writing of business managers as designers, he says "Good designers are aware of their own vocabulary and what it does to their work...How we describe what a manager is and what he should do, what a problem is and how it should be approached, and what a good and true course of action is and how it is to be achieved, are all dependent upon our vocabulary." Schon[22] similarly argues that "When we set the problem, we select what we will treat as the 'things' of the situation, we set the boundaries of our attention to it, and we impose upon it a coherence" 1983, p. 39.

One of the sources of uncertainty at the stage of problem definition is constraints—how needs will be ascertained, with whom, how they will be understood and then translated into design concepts, what materials and processes are both available and judged appropriate, which outcomes are required and which are secondary. The definition of constraints contributes to how a design problem is defined and therefore to how it is solved. Vincenti[23] studied events in the history of aeronautical

Data-Dewey

engineering; he asserts that although most of the work is done at the lower levels of design, the top level of problem definition, which is where the problems are primarily conceptual and unstructured, is where knowledge growth occurs in engineering.

CONVERSATIONS WITH MATERIALS

Some of the uncertainty of design results from the interaction between designer and the materials of design. Wagner[24] says that architects "meander" between seeing specifications and fixed elements of a solution precisely, and seeing them as partial and preliminary, still in formation. Schon[4] calls this a "conversation with the materials" of design, in which the designer makes a move and the materials "talk back." The designer then adapts as she sees how the materials respond to her, and they in turn respond to her adaptation. Keller and Keller[25] in an essay titled "Thinking with Iron," describe the way that a blacksmith takes an action with the fire and metal and the iron responds; the blacksmith then responds to that result, undoing the action or deciding what next action the response has made appropriate. Through this conversation, the design emerges. Although the blacksmith has begun with a general plan, the specific actions and the plan itself become fluid and may change as his actions change the situation.

Often the early conversations are carried out in "virtual reality."[4] Rather than jumping directly into the creation, designers often test their ideas using sketches, computer graphics programs, conversations, and other substitutes for the actual materials. As noted above, it is critical that the virtual medium be sufficiently indeterminate to allow surprises to occur, for the designer to learn from the actions he takes. Art historian Rudolf Arnheim quotes Goldschmidt as describing sketching as a dialectic process. Sketches are not just a representation on paper of the images in the designer's mind; rather, they are an oscillation of arguments and the responses of the sketch, in which the sketch supplies essential new food for the arguments.[26]

Another representation of this process is as experiments testing hypotheses, each of which is evaluated for fit and misfit, and changes the context in which the next hypothesis and test will be carried out.[27] Similarly, Wagner[24] describes this oscillation as the underpinning "for the passage from possibility to actuality which is the work of design."

Rationalist theorists of design have described such tests as running a maze, with the assumption that although many trials may be dead ends, eventually the correct path will be found and design will proceed. Schon, however, asserts that a designer can never make a move which has exactly the intended results, and that her knowledge about what is possible and desirable evolves as the materials of

the situation talk back to her. It is as though the process of running the maze *changes* the maze.

CONSTRAINTS

Constraints enable the definition of a problem and the range of solutions, and also limit them. Standards, codes (such as construction codes), consideration of "best practices," textbooks, and other formal sources of professional knowledge provide guidance. Current consensus about good design stimulates and provides direction to creative ideas. Codes are interpreted and conformed to in different ways; relationships between stakeholders are defined and redefined as the design situation evolves. Experience with a standard can be fed back into the system and the standard be rewritten.

Other constraints arise from the specifications for a project, as noted above. Time and money also influence design decisions. Organizational culture about how projects should be carried out may determine the approaches at both unconscious and conscious levels.

The materials of design, both the tools and the "raw material" also provide opportunities and limitations. Architects work explicitly with the constraints provided by land, soil type, and climate conditions. Schon[28] quotes an instructor in a school of architecture as advising a student to "let the land generate some sub-ideas" (p. 89). Reciprocal transformations between the designer and the field of constraints give shape to a design project.

TOOLS

Traditionally, the tools of design have often been ignored or seen simplistically as enabling or imposing limitations on the process. However, theorists in sociotechnical studies emphasize the importance of paying serious scholarly attention to *all* of the elements of a research (or design) situation if we are to eventually understand the process. Clarke and Fujimura[29] explore the idea of "the right tool for the job." Griesemer[30] in that volume makes the point that the tools the scientist understands to be appropriate shape the problem as well as the solution. Collopy[31] notes that an important difference between expert and novice designers is that novices do not fully understand the control that they could have over the design environment itself. Experts have learned how to design tools that help them to think of things that they would not normally; tools are tools for thought as well as for material actions. Wagner[24] describes ways in which design labs are often constructively cluttered, filled with toys, gadgets, interesting shapes, all tossed around somewhat arbitrarily; unfamiliar juxtapositions of objects can give rise to creative leaps, juxtaposing ideas about the artifact in ways that give new direction.

Schon[4] gives special attention to the tools that create what he calls virtual worlds—these include maquettes, scale models, rehearsals, improvisations, computer simulations, and so on. He identifies this process in architectural design studies where sketching is the basis for communication between student and instructor and also in the relationship between a psychologist and patient where transference and counter-transference serve as a substitute for firsthand experience, a virtual world which represents the patient's other relationships and which can be analyzed to understand the meanings and effects of action. Boland and Collopy[32] describe an architect's model as a tool for thinking, a stimulus and a way to explore ideas, not as a representation of a future reality. They argue that in management, models are taken too seriously, as a kind of compressed truth, and urge managers to break loose from "decision attitudes" and foster instead "design attitudes."

Henderson[33] found in an ethnographic study of industrial engineers that use of computer graphics in design often could not accommodate uncertainty, and too quickly drove the engineer to settle on an approach. Therefore engineers often mixed paper practices with their electronic practices to protect the cognitive spaces where creativity took place. Creative design work is based, she found, on unarticulated knowledge, often visual in format; and this knowledge is recalcitrant to incorporation into computer graphic systems. Attfield et al.[34] note similar phenomena, and add that uncertainty is particularly important during the early stages of the design process. Boland and Collopy[32] as well describe an architect shaping his design ideas with his hands and materials, and using software only much later. The value of virtual worlds is in their malleability; when they remove uncertainty prematurely, they limit the range of potential problem solutions.

DESIGN FAILURE

One of the consequences of the presence of the unexpected, of course, is failure. According to David Pye (cited by Petroski,)[35] there is always compromise in design.

> The requirements for design conflict and cannot be reconciled. All designs for devices are in some degree failures, either because they flout one or another of the requirements or because they are compromises, and compromise implies a degree of failure. ... All designs for use are arbitrary. The designer or his client has to choose in what degree and where there shall be failure. ... It is quite impossible for any design to be 'the logical outcome of the requirements,' simply because, the requirements being in conflict, their logical outcome is an impossibility (pp. 217–218).

And, somewhat paradoxically, failure is a major contributor to the reduction of the unexpected. Henry

Petroski,[35] writing about structural engineering, points out that all possible uses of a structure under all possible conditions can never be anticipated. Structural engineering is hypothesizing, testing one's expectations of how things will work. Engineering design is revising, analyzing by questioning the behaviors of the parts under the imagined conditions of use, discovering problem areas, redesigning, and then analyzing the new design. Prototyping is one method of hypothesizing, allowing the designer to "fail early," and without consequence. The process continues until the designer can imagine no possible way in which the structure can fail under the anticipated use. But the uncertainty is always present. The less like the past the future is, the less likely that the engineer's hypotheses will be correct; and the object itself changes the future. Although an incorrect hypothesis may hold for a long time without discovery under certain conditions, if those conditions are no longer met, the conditions under which the hypothesis fails may be revealed.

"The well prepared engineer can and does build beyond experience."[36] Copying structures which have stood the test of time is engineering work that holds no distinction; Petroski compares engineers with artists: "just as the great writers are those who have given us unique and daring experiments that have worked, so it is that the great engineers are those who have given us their daring and unique structural experiments that have stood the test of time."[37] An engineer designing beyond his knowledge or ability is violating ethical principles, with potentially catastrophic results; but "failure in innovation should be no more opprobrious to the engineer who has prepared himself as well as he could for his attempt to build a longer bridge than to a pole vaulter who fails to make a record vault after practicing his event and using his pole to its capacity."[35]

Although failure of an engineered structure can be tragic in its consequences, it is also an important component of the growth of knowledge. Structural failure, not success, improves the safety of future generations of a design. A failed structure is a counterexample to the engineer's hypothesis and shows what cannot be done; a structure that stands without incident often conceals whatever lessons it might hold for the next generation of engineers. For these reasons, Petroski argues that design literature needs to incorporate descriptions of failures.

DESIGN AS INTELLECTUAL WORK

This entry is based on the premise that the literature of design from other disciplines is relevant to the library and information sciences. Words frequently used in descriptions of a "designerly way of thinking" are creativity, fluidity, rationality, intuition, emotion, reflection, confidence, and taste. While these characteristics certainly apply in other kinds of work as well, in the practice of design they take on a unique character in relation to pervasive uncertainty.

Before discussing the elements of design thinking that are thought to be common across boundaries, it may be useful to consider what does not cross the boundaries. In Schon's 1983 study[38] of six professions, he identified four areas where each had unique elements: (1) the media, languages, and repertoires [of action] that practitioners use to describe reality and conduct experiments; (2) the appreciative systems [values] they bring to problem setting, to the evaluation of inquiry, and to reflective conversation; (3) the overarching theories by which they make sense of phenomena; and (4) the role frames within which they set their tasks . These more stable elements of the situation give the practitioner relatively solid references from which she can work to address the unknowns of the design; they provide a base for reflection in action. It is in the constantly evolving confrontation with uncertainty, ironically, that designers have most in common.

Creativity has been described in this entry as being the necessary response to conditions of uncertainty. It is required in the initial work of setting a problem out of a fluid problem space. And, as Lave[39] says, one does not have a problem without a sense of a resolution space as well. David Kelley, founder of the widely recognized design firm IDEO, emphasizes that successful design depends on being open to multiple possibilities and being ready "to take risks in a creative leap into possibilities that are not yet defined and whose consequences are not yet visible."[40]

Wagner[24] similarly describes an architect's ability to perceive "the novel within the familiar, to discover relations between seemingly incongruent objects and notions, to relate the unrelatable." She describes designing as an informal, fluent process, simultaneously focusing on floating concepts, preliminary specifications, and contradiction and constraints. The process she describes is closely related to Schon's[4] description of the path from initial idea to final design as unpredictable, emerging out of a conversation in which the materials "talk back" in response to each decision made by the designer.

This fluidity in thinking, closely related to creativity, is important in the intellectual work in design. A designer must be able to keep seeing a problem from new perspectives, avoiding filters that make everything conform to that filter. Designers must first look as broadly as they can at the universe of possible solutions; then they can feel more comfortable narrowing. It is important that hypotheses be formulated, tested, discarded, and revised; understanding of the problem, the tools, and the materials of the situation changes as the three interact.

It is often stressed that designers need to be able to live with pervasive uncertainty. "The typical design situation requires doing something that you don't yet know how to do."[41] In addition, it is never possible to be certain that one has done it in the best possible way; there may always be a new, better solution that one stopped just before reaching.

Rationality was the central concern of designers early in this century, and is certainly not dismissed by contemporary theorists. Intuition is fed by experience. Solid disciplinary knowledge is a prerequisite to meaningful creativity. If one does not understand the formal properties of the tools and materials, then there is no basis for the deeper insights that can come from failures. *The Structural Engineer*,[42] the official journal of the British Institution of Structural Engineers, defines structural engineering as "the science and art of designing and making...." Petroski argues that design is first articulated by the engineer as artist, and then analyzed by the engineer as scientist.

Intuition is another dimension of the work of design. "Creative leaps" can be based on intuition about what will work, the sense of a resolution space, as can be the hypotheses tested in building models.

Emotion in design takes various forms. Designers have been compared to athletes; they want to design the best thing they possibly can. There are no professional rewards for copying existing designs, although that work is likely to solve problems safely. Kelley,[43] says "the designer has a passion for doing something that fits somebody's needs, but that is not just a simple fix. The designer has a dream that goes beyond what exists, rather than fixing what exists. ... there is a satisfaction in addressing problems at a deep level." Surprise is a frequent emotion in good design, because of the indeterminacy of the work. At times commitment to an organization or a social goal is a strong motivator, and an additional source of satisfaction in success. A sense of play is emphasized in some design organizations, because it opens up new approaches which might not be considered otherwise. Design teams often keep an assortment of gadgets around to stimulate play and exploration that can lead to innovative work.[44]

Taking a risk in design means making a decision to create something that is not proven to be what is needed to solve that problem. Kelley asserts that even the most flexible people are uncomfortable with this kind of risk taking, but learn to live with that discomfort. Emotion, if it takes the form of commitments to particular ways of doing things or avoidance of uncertainty, will constrict design work.

Design requires confidence, the ability to make a creative leap and follow a path which doesn't yet exist. According to Kelley, a good designer creates beyond what the problem calls for, to create a solution that fits in a deeper situational or social sense. Kelley sees the designer's approach to a problem situation as dramatically different from that of an engineer, whose solution is based on mathematics and certainty. "A good problem in design is one for which you aren't sure that there *is* a right answer."[45]

Related to confidence is a designer's ability to tell when she's got something that's good, an inner gyroscope that allows her to evaluate her own work.

DESIGN RESEARCH

"Design research" is a term used in some fields for design that is undertaken for the explicit purpose of extending the knowledge base; it may be instantiated to solve a particular problem, or its purpose may be proof of concept, demonstrating that a particular solution is possible. Design is considered research rather than practice on the basis of its greater novelty and difficulty, its significance to a research community, there being a serious question about how to solve it and its being "rigorously defined, formally represented, coherent, and internally consistent."[2] Hevner et al.[2] broaden the requirement of significance in information systems work to include social analysis of the design in use, with information provided to managers about the best deployment of the artifact. Design research takes place primarily in corporate laboratories and universities, thus having some characteristic differences from design in the field, notably in problem definition and constraints.

In a corporation, design is a strategic competency;[46] a good problem is one that will contribute to the trajectory of the company's competitive strength. Teece et al.[47] argue that a firm's previous investments and the repertoire of routines it has established create its current position, and that the current position is the primary constraint determining the paths available ahead. Learning tends to be local, and opportunities in the neighborhood of a firm's prior research are the paths most available. A company's history thus shapes and constrains its problem definition, and even what is recognized as a problem. A research culture develops that defines the optimum amount of novelty, and the levels of difficulty and uncertainty that are acceptable. Research cultures change over time, as may be seen in the fact that since the 1990s, U.S. R&D programs have shortened their focus, de-emphasizing basic research, and companies have favored design problems with a clear line-of-sight to market.[48]

In universities, disciplinary value systems dominate, shaping and sometimes overriding the goals of university administrations.[49] Disciplinary value systems emphasize theory and original contributions to knowledge. The significance of research questions is defined by the discipline, embodied in scholarly journals' decisions about what is important enough to publish and what is not. Problem setting is always influenced by the tension between the need to produce new knowledge and the risks of working outside the established disciplinary boundaries.[20,50] This tension is passed on by dissertation committees and tenure committees taking seriously their responsibility to socialize new members into the academic culture. Weedman,[49] in a study of a design research project, found that students and junior faculty were advised away from problems that lay outside disciplinary boundaries.

The national emphasis on direct applicability has affected university design research as well as corporate laboratories. In the 1980s and 1990s, federal funding for basic research decreased, generating attempts to make "theory" more "relevant" in several disciplines. Addressing computer science and engineering (CS&E) in 1992, for instance, the National Research Council called for these disciplines to focus on "substantive research problems in the context of their application in and relevance to other domains."[51] They urged collaborative projects between researchers in CS&E and client disciplines who would be the users of the designed artifact. Recognizing the tension between the scholarly requirements of a discipline and the practical requirements of users, the NRC anticipated that CS&E could "thus be framed simultaneously as a discipline with its own deep intellectual traditions, as well as one that is applicable to other problem domains. CS&E [could] thus be an engine of progress and conceptual change in these other domains, even as they contribute[d] to the identification of new areas of [scholarly] inquiry" (p. 65). This approach turned out to be fraught with problems, as the incentive structures of both the design and the client disciplines worked against mutual problem definition.[20,49]

A special section in *MIS Quarterly* in 1999[52] made similar recommendations, framing the tension as rigor vs. relevance. Overemphasis on rigor was seen as posing a danger of irrelevance, because of the need to formalize the problem, removing considerable sources of uncertainty present in design in the field. Several authors argued for the importance of combining relevance and rigor: rigor provided by building on the research knowledge base and relevance provided by selecting problems that would lead to the design of artifacts for specific situations. Benbasat and Zmud[53] asserted a symbiotic relationship between researchers and information systems practitioners: "Theories and models are judged on their predictive power for guiding practitioners, the quality of theories are enhanced by testing and revising them with data from the world of practice, and the cues and insights offered by practitioners are assessed through rigorous examination across a variety of contexts." They note that much of the perceived irrelevance of research to the field may be the result of the way it is reported; to be useful, research reports must be shaped for the needs and concerns and rhetorical styles of the different audiences. Hevner et al.[2] define design science problems as dual problems requiring dual reports, one scholarly for other researchers and one for business managers who need to understand the role of information systems and specific features in achieving their company's goals. The research problem is defined as a problem in the field as well as a disciplinary problem.

Not all researchers perceive an opposition between relevance and rigor; Lyytinen,[54] for instance, wrote that many authors seemed to believe that there is a law that reads "rigor will always replace relevance if there are no powers to stop it." He argued for more reflectiveness about the concept of relevance and the assumption made by many that relevance means rigor watered down or simplified, something that can be read and learned in an afternoon. He notes that relevance does not preclude research reports from being difficult, theoretical, and challenging, thus resolving the double vision of dual problem definitions.

There are also constraints unique to design research. Researchers in professional schools are often expected to fulfill obligations to the field for which they are preparing their students at the same time that they adhere to norms of the academic discipline. Practitioners or the clients for design projects often believe that design done as research is not relevant to actual needs in the field. Research may be perceived as too far in advance of practice to be applicable in "the real world" or as lagging behind practice, starting from scratch to develop proof of concept for something that has been done in the field (perhaps on a smaller scale) already. Formalized, mess-free designs often cannot be instantiated in actual work sites, or the cutting-edge theoretical problems that researchers need to address may not be perceived as problems in the field. An inability to satisfy both sets of constraints can lead to great frustration in a design research project.[49]

Another set of constraints unique to design research is the relationship between standards and novelty. Design research requires novelty, yet a design must be standards compliant if it is to be built and used. Codified knowledge represents virtuoso performances within established boundaries; formal standards such as those issued by the American National Standards Institute cannot anticipate all future design situations. Bucciarelli[55] writes that "a code is a historical statement based on experience and testing, but mostly on experience. Design is design of the new and the untried, the unexperienced, the ahistorical." The constraints of university research require that design be novel, and therefore often outside established boundaries. Yet if it is to be used, a system needs to conform to the constraints created by technical standards. Goals to design an interesting research system that is also standards compliant must meet sometimes antithetical constraints.

DESIGN SCIENCE IN THE LIBRARY AND INFORMATION SCIENCES

Two examples suggest ways in which design science might be incorporated into the library and information sciences. One is a study of designers of controlled vocabularies for local use in image collections; the other is an ongoing design research project using probabilistic information retrieval systems.

Design Science: Local Vocabularies for Image Collections

In LIS, design work related to knowledge organization is carried out simultaneously at multiple levels—in the devising of national standards for design such as the National Information Standards Organization (NISO) *Guidelines for the Construction, Format, and Management of Monolingual Thesauri*, in the maintenance of major vocabularies such as the Library of Congress' *Thesaurus for Graphic Materials*, in the design of vocabularies intended to be diffused widely such as the *Art & Architecture Thesaurus*, and at the local level in the creation of descriptors or classification systems for individual collections of materials.

This study[56] consisted of a survey of individuals who had created or worked with locally designed vocabularies for image collections, and interviews with the respondents who had participated in the creation of a vocabulary. In the interviews, open-ended questions were asked in order to elicit description of the process—the work—of vocabulary design. Transcripts of the interviews were then coded and analyzed to ascertain whether or not concepts taken from design literature such as those discussed in this entry were applicable to design in this area of library and information science. The 2004 report was based on the first six interviews to be conducted. The sites included a collection of urban photographs, a historical site containing many objects as well as photographs, a collection of illustrated medieval manuscripts, a collection of magazine photographs illustrating mid-twentieth century culture, the photograph collection of a medical research center, and the visual resources collection of a university art department.

Uncertainty was pervasive in the work of vocabulary design. The uncertainty of language is said to plague information retrieval, with its synonyms, homonyms, nuances, and context-dependent meanings; Morville,[57] for instance, calls language "the questionable foundation upon which information retrieval is built." However, it was not language that caused the most uncertainty for the respondents. In information retrieval, language creates relationships between documents—identifying shared attributes that will aggregate some images and discriminate them from others. It was the relationships themselves about which the vocabulary designers rarely felt comfortable. The establishment of these relationships, though informed by the discipline or setting of the collection and the anticipated needs of users of the collection, was still, ultimately, a creative act by the designer, for which there was no ultimate test of correctness. The most uncertainty of all was felt about the breadth and specificity of the relationships—how broadly the aggregating attribute should be defined, whether the images it would bring together would constitute the most useful grouping, whether the entities that could be brought into that relationship should be. The designers reported that it was these relationships, not the words used to express them, that were the source of the worst uncertainty in their vocabulary design.

Conversations with the materials of design did occur. Most frequently they took the form of arranging and rearranging terms to see the relationships which resulted. Adding a new image to those previously included in a category often changed the earlier the relationship, requiring different configurations to accommodate new possibilities. Even using terms that were well established in the domain did not solve the problem of which relationships to create and which to leave invisible; an established term would create one relationship, but then some items would need to be disaggregated because they differed in some critical dimension. Designers often considered the effects of using one term or set of terms to express relationships, then changed the terms and relationships to see what the result was. Creation of a new term could affect the scope of the first. "You have to be willing to mess with things." One respondent said that he designed vocabularies in the same way that he baked bread, through experimentation— "I try things and then respond in accordance with what's happening."

There are, of course, various constraints on the work of vocabulary design. The existence of standardized structures is one constraint; one designer compared a sense of structure to a painter's understanding of oil and canvas, and said that if one didn't fully understand the nature of structure, the designer could be "misled by content." Time and money were common constraints that shaped the final vocabulary. The size of one of the older vocabularies was determined by the computer available for use and the size of its memory. In an art history library, the decision about whether a vocabulary should capture literal objects in an image or their symbolic meaning was determined by the fact that the actual indexing would be done by students who had taken not more than one art history class. User warrant, literary warrant, and the warrant of standard vocabularies such as the *Art & Architecture Thesaurus* are other forms of constraint that influence design work.

Problem setting was influenced by these constraints and other factors. In no case was the problem that gave rise to the creation of a vocabulary simply the need to provide intellectual access to the image collection, even when that was given as the initial problem statement. In the case of the urban photographs, providing intellectual access was first described as "trimming down" the descriptive terms assigned by the photojournalists, despite their unsuitability for information retrieval; this turned out to mean bringing consistency to the terms while preserving them as part of the intellectual whole of the photographs and their descriptions, to be followed by the design of an independent vocabulary for information retrieval when the collection was merged with others. In the case of the illustrated manuscripts, the general goal of providing

intellectual access turned out at its core to mean relating the illustrations to the part of the story they depicted, so that different versions of the same work could be compared by a professor and his graduate students whose research centered on this one work. The vocabulary would be useful for others doing the same kind of research, but not for individuals studying the work in different ways. An initial problem description of designing a vocabulary in one situation turned into "find something you can do NOW," bypassing the content management vocabulary for the Web site which had run more than a year beyond its deadline. For the historic site, the problem was defined both as providing computer access so that users could find things on their own, and as bringing together the materials that were all related to the same story. Doing good in the world was another problem definition that emerged well into an interview.

The designers interviewed were employed as librarians, metadata specialists, curators, or in other positions; vocabulary design was only one of many responsibilities. All said that they saw the design work as different in nature from other parts of their jobs. They saw it as requiring more creativity, making something that hadn't existed before. Some of the creativity was in the act of putting oneself in the minds who would be using the images. One designer captured the role of constraint in novelty when he commented that "when you understand your audience you can be creative." The importance of seeing things (in images) in relation to one another was strongly emphasized. They cited an intuitive dimension, a sense of how things should go together and of when a relationship wasn't right. Emotion was also present in the work, sometimes unexpectedly, as in the discovery of slave records in the historical site. There was an emotional connection with design work that took the form of curiosity about "how things could be brought together into a structure." Enjoyment of "pulling things apart and putting them back together" was important to one of the designers. Emotion was also cited as a negative factor; one's response to images could get in the way of subject analysis.

Themes taken from the study of design in other professions provided a useful frame in this study for exploring design practice in the library and information sciences. Discussions of uncertainty, problem setting, the conversation with materials, and other concepts provided a different set of insights into vocabulary design than is gained from other research approaches.

Design research: Cheshire

The development of the Cheshire information retrieval system, begun in 1990, is an ongoing design research project. Cheshire was developed by Ray Larson at the University of California, Berkeley. I interviewed him in 2007, again with the goal of determining whether concepts from the design literature of other disciplines would be echoed in descriptions of design work in the library and information sciences. The initial question was very broad; "tell me about the history of Cheshire—how it started, how it changed and why, why you made the decisions you did." The questions that followed focused on the actual work performed by Larson; what kinds of things he did, how he made decisions, and so on.

The history of Cheshire over 17 years illustrates many ways that uncertainty, problem setting, conversations with materials, constraints, the role of tools, and failure play out in design research in LIS. In a large project of long duration, none of these factors come into play only once. They interweave in various ways throughout the life of the project.

Problem setting is required at many stages of design research—in the development of Cheshire, the initial problem was redefined to take advantage of opportunities, in response to the tools available, to accommodate the unexpected, and to address subparts of the problem more specifically.

Larson began defining the problem during his dissertation work, a computer performance evaluation of the UC systemwide library catalog, when one of his findings was that users experienced subject searching as very difficult, often learning to avoid it as much as possible. At this time, the commercial search engines were entirely Boolean. Ranked retrieval appeared as the alternative to explore; William Cooper, with whom Larson had studied, argued that ranked retrieval was the optimum way to do subject searches, and W. E. Maron, with whom Larson had also studied, argued that probability theory provided the best foundation for ranked retrieval. There were two major theoretical approaches for providing relevance ranking of results, neither of which had been instantiated in full working systems because of their computational requirements. The first was that of W. E. Maron and J. L. Kuhns, who had published "On relevance, probabilistic indexing, and information retrieval" in *Journal of the ACM* in 1960,[58] and the second was the vector space model, Gerard Salton's SMART system.[59] Although Larson initially framed the problem as a need for probabilistic retrieval for subject searching, none of the computers available could carry out the computationally intense procedures; the early experiments leading to Cheshire, then, were carried out with the vector space model.

Because of his dissertation work and the availability of the library's records, Larson began with the MARC (Machine Readable Cataloging) format, but in a graduate class that gave his students the opportunity to build an IR system from the ground up, Larson and the students realized that the MARC format imposed too many constraints and that a more generalized markup language was needed. This led, after investigation, to a new subproblem, conversion to SGML (Standard Generalized Markup Language), and the system designed in the class became the first Cheshire.

The problem definition shifted again—back to probability theory as the design model—when Larson joined a multimillion dollar research project on data management in the earth sciences that made state-of-the-art computers available to the investigators. Cheshire then became Cheshire II.

The chance to build probability algorithms into a working system exposed a set of unanticipated problems—the formal results differed from the way that code actually behaved. Problem definition shifted to address differences between the model and the instantiation. Then the problem definition changed again and became how to incorporate the relevance feedback on which the probability model depends. The solution was to employ logistic regression on samples of documents for which human relevance judgments had been made, to determine which of their characteristics would predict that someone would judge the document to be relevant. The statistics from this sample are then used as the basis for the relevance ranking in the rest of the database.

Cheshire3, developed together with investigators in England, will be the next generation. A part of the problem set for Cheshire3 is to have it search multiple collections and determine the best one in which to carry out a given query; this problem definition is made possible by the fact that many of England's archival databases use Cheshire II search engines, allowing them to be used as test sites.

Larson describes his work process as starting with a vision of what he would like to have the system be able to do, and then discovering "all the little details" that are needed to make it happen. Conversations with materials often led to increasingly complex and convoluted code, until suddenly Larson would see a different way of solving the particular subproblem that would be more direct. The module would then be rebuilt. The process of creating Cheshire II contained many of these long conversations and sudden insights.

Larson described the path between "I'd like it to do this" and the point where the search engine *does* "this" as "a combination of pondering, visualization, imagining, and 'how could one...'?" The questions are "what data do I need to give it so it can do this? How do I get that data and how would I need to process it in order to make the outcomes be what I want them to be?"

Fluidity is the greatest when something is partially working. At that point there is design room for experimentation. Things can be tried to see what happens, then dropped or modified. The history of the conversations with materials can be traced in what Larson refers to as an "archeology of code." Some unused appendixes couldn't be removed because of shared variables, so they were left. Other obsolete pieces were left because it takes longer to remove code than it does to write it in the first place. So working code exists in layers over, and intertwined with, old code. A designer works down through that archeology when the addition of a new feature involves rewriting a dozen or more modules, because making one sort of change at the top level often requires that you change other things that interact with it layers down. Having written the largest share of code himself, Larson speaks of his intimate relationship with it, knowing not just where everything is but how its particular form is the result of design paths begun and abandoned, unanticipated modifications and their unanticipated results on existing code, fixes, and then fixes to fixes.

The material with which the designer conducts a conversation is not, Larson stressed, the code itself. The conversation occurs when he runs the program and looks at the data that results, and the "back talk" is the appearance of needless duplications or errors in the way that the data comes out. The designer isn't having a conversation with the underlying algorithms per se; but he has to find where in the code the problem is located to try to fix it. Finding out if he has indeed fixed it requires another conversation.

Intuition and insights are part of the intellectual work of this kind of design. Sudden insights sometimes occur after a fruitless struggle with a problem that seems impossibly difficult, or doable but not in any reasonable amount of time; it's not unusual to wake up in the middle of the night with "oh!—wait a minute, wait a minute!—I can do it *that* way!"

As other designers have described fluidity of thinking and the importance of unexpected juxtapositions, Larson has found that when a problem or approach seems insoluble, it's instructive to "turn it on its side or turn it on its head or turn it around completely, turn it backwards, and see what happens." And very often the different perspective makes visible (or discoverable) a better way of doing it.

An example is the design problem of including functionality for geographic retrieval in Cheshire3. Study of searchers shows that they scan through all the possible items until they find the one that would serve their purposes, which would be impossible in a large-scale system. R-trees in computer science are used for searching regions, but would have been "horrendously" complex to implement in the system. Larson describes spending a great deal of work on how to incorporate R-trees before asking what *else* could be done. Software developed within another Berkeley research project, Berkeley DB, gives access to the underlying index structure of a database. The techniques of Berkeley DB plus some middle-of-the-night inspirations led to a method that will in effect create R-trees but with the technique of creative scanning of the indexes. This turned out to be a solution that works accurately and very quickly.

Larson describes design as a cognitive process, with no emotional input except a desire to avoid approaches that have failed to work in the past. Emotions do accompany the cognitive process, however. Negative emotions are most often evoked not by the problem itself, but by technical limitations or some other external factor. The frustration is not a productive part of the design process; rather, it's a sign that it's time to do something else for awhile. Positive emotions are feelings of accomplishment evoked by the sudden insights into solutions, the satisfaction of something working the way that it was expected to, and the elation that follows a middle-of-the-night insight, when "you can't wait to get up and go in to try it out and see if it works."

Standards are constraints that both enable and limit design work. The value of working with standards is that it's possible to build for the existing infrastructure. Because of its use of XML, Cheshire can search any database that has an XML structure. Use of a standard may permit unexpected novel results as well. The Z39.50 protocol is an information retrieval standard used to extract data from different collections and build an index of the combined elements; any database that supports Z39.50 for querying or SRW (Search/Retrieve Webservice) and SRU (Search/Retrieval via URL) protocols can be harvested. When Z39.50 was built, it included common operators such as the "equal to" relationship, "greater than" or "less than," truncation, and so on. One of the operators was named "relevance." Some investigation revealed that no one had used that operator anywhere. What it does is direct the server to do relevance matching. This obscure operator allows Cheshire to search any server built on its model and direct it to rank the results for relevance.

Standards also provide the basis for the status quo; and as knowledge progresses, it diverges from the status quo. Forward-looking standards cannot anticipate all directions of development. Thus there is always a tension between infrastructure and change. Design research, because of its inherent novelty, puts pressure, small or large, on standards. The result in the short term is a proliferation of work-arounds, such as ways to bypass the preset record formats established by servers or by the Z39.50 protocols and request other formats. In the long term, standards change.

Problem setting is often affected by factors external to the project itself. The initial ability to do probabilistic retrieval, for instance, came from funding for a project focused on technology for global change research. Sometimes it comes from another interest of a researcher that can be blended into the design project; data mining capabilities were built into Cheshire3 as a result of one of the researchers' interests in that area. Development of the UTF-8 encoding scheme for Unicode made it possible create cross-language retrieval. That led to the need for various tools, usually open source, to be incorporated, for example, a snowball stemmer that can be given a training data set that configures it for a particular language and from it create a stemmer for that language. Cheshire now has stemmers for all major European languages.

Problem setting in a university, as discussed above, has to respond to the norm of knowledge generation. When ranked retrieval systems existed only as algorithms in the 1960s, Gerard Salton framed the field of information retrieval as an experimental science. The problem definition of Cheshire, Cheshire II, and Cheshire3 as practical application of theory in production environments resulted in both relevance and rigor as defined by the discipline;[2] in both socially useful artifacts and articles reporting the theory and experimental research, comparing the base algorithms to other well-known information retrieval algorithms in terms of the standard measures of precision and recall.

This long-term design research project, then, does illustrate a "designerly way of knowing" in common with other forms of design. While primarily cognitive, there are elements of creativity, inspiration, and emotion. The conversation with materials plays an important role in the final form of the artifact, as does response to the fertile mix of challenges and constraints.

CONCLUSION

Although design is an important part of professional and research practice in the library and information sciences, it is at present undertheorized. Schools of LIS teach Web design, thesaurus design, management, public services, system analysis, interface design, XML, and other classes that have a strong design component. Our social science traditions provide strengths in understanding the use of systems, their integration into work life, and how users evaluate results; these traditions could usefully be expanded to study design as professional practice.

There are two potential benefits to studying our own design. One is that it may give rise to increased knowledge of and thereby improvement of design practice. Boland and Collopy[32] write that the awareness of one's own profession's design practices enables discussion across professional boundaries, which can lead to new insights and "design attitude." The other is the value of knowing for its own sake; the design that we do is important work, and understanding it is interesting. The review provided here of the "designerly way of knowing" in the information sciences indicates that there is a great deal of interest that could be done.

REFERENCES

1. Simon, H.A. *The Sciences of the Artificial*, 3rd Ed.; MIT Press: Cambridge, MA, 1996; (1st Ed., 1969).
2. Hevner, A.R.; March, S.T.; Park, J.; Ram, S. Design science in information systems research. MIS Quart. **2004**, *28*(4), 75–105.
3. Buchanan, R. Myth and maturity: Toward a new order in the decade of design. In *The Idea of Design*; Margolin, V.,

Buchanan, R., Eds.; MIT Press: Cambridge, MA, 1995; 75–85.
4. Schon, D.A. *The Reflective Practitioner: How Professionals Think in Action*, Basic Books: New York, 1983.
5. Cross, N. *Developments in Design Methodology*, John Wiley & Sons: New York, 1984; 172.
6. Cross, N. Designerly ways of knowing. Des. Stud. **1982**, *3*(4), 221–227.
7. Buchanan, R. Myth and maturity: Toward a new order in the decade of design. In *The Idea of Design*; Margolin, V., Buchanan, R., Eds.; MIT Press: Cambridge, MA, 1995; 18.
8. Cross, N. Designerly ways of knowing: Design discipline versus design science. Des. Issues. **2001**, *17*(3), 49.
9. Davies A. (n.d.). Design technology department. Association of Teachers' Websites n.d. Available at http://www. design-technology.org/page1.htm.
10. Salsbury P.G. Comprehensive anticipatory design science: An introduction; 2000. Available at http://www.sculptors. com/~salsbury/Articles/Design-Science-proposal.txt Salsbury P.G. Comprehensive anticipatory design science: An introduction; 2000.
11. Alexander, C. *Notes on the Synthesis of Form*, Harvard University Press: Cambridge, MA, 1964; 2–3.
12. Alexander, C. *Notes on the Synthesis of Form*, Harvard University Press: Cambridge, MA, 1964.
13. Alexander, C.; Ishikawa, S.; Silverstein, M. *A Pattern Language: Towns, Buildings, Construction*, Oxford University Press: New York, 1977.
14. Simon, H.A. *The Sciences of the Artificial*, 3rd Ed. MIT Press: Cambridge, MA, 1996.
15. Simon, H.A. The structure of ill structured problems. Artif. Intell. **1973**, *4*(3–4), 181–201.
16. Rittel, H.W.J.; Webber, M.M. Dilemmas in a general theory of planning Working Paper Presented at the Institute of Urban and Regional Development; University of California: Berkeley, CA, 1972.
17. Rittel, H.; Webber, M. Dilemmas in a general theory of planning. Policy Sci. **1973**, *4*(2), 159.
18. Gasser, L. Chance, encounter, design, and community knowledge Managing as Designing: Creating a Vocabulary for Management Education and Research; Case Western Reserve University: Cleveland, OH, paragraph 13, 2002. Available at http://design.cwru.edu/2002workshop/Positions/ boland.doc (accessed March 2004).
19. Lave, J. *Cognition in Practice*, Cambridge University Press: Cambridge, MA, 1988; 42.
20. Weedman, J. The structure of incentive: Design and client roles in application-oriented research. Sci. Technol. Hum. Values. **1998**, *23*(3), 315–345.
21. Boland, D. Design in the punctuation of management action Managing as Designing: Creating a Vocabulary for Management Education and Research; 2002 Case Western Reserve University: Cleveland, OH, paragraph 3, 2002. Available at http://design.cwru.edu/2002workshop/Positions/boland.doc (accessed March 2004).
22. Schon, D.A. *The Reflective Practitioner: How Professionals Think in Action*, Basic Books: New York, 1983; 39.
23. Vincenti, W.G. *What Engineers Know and How They Know It*, Johns Hopkins University Press: Baltimore, MD, 1990.

24. Wagner, I. 'Open Planning'—A reflection on methods and innovative work practices in architecture Managing as Designing: Creating a Vocabulary for Management Education and Research; 2000 Case Western Reserve University: Cleveland, OH, 2000. Available at http://design.cwru.edu/2002workshop/Positions/ (accessed March 25, 2004).

25. Keller, C.; Keller, J.D. Thinking and acting with iron. In *Understanding Practice: Perspectives on Activity and Context*; Chaiklin, S., Lave, J., Eds.; Cambridge University Press: Cambridge, MA, 1993; 125–141.

26. Arnheim, R. Sketching and the psychology of design. In *The Idea of Design*; Margolin, V., Buchanan, R., Eds.; MIT Press: Cambridge, MA, 1995; 70, citing Goldschmidt.

27. Schon, D.A. The design process. In *Varieties of Thinking: Essays from Harvard's Philosophy of Education Research Center*; Howard, V.A., Ed.; Routledge: New York, 1990; 110–141.

28. Schon, D.A. *The Reflective Practitioner: How Professionals Think in Action*, Basic Books: New York, 1983; 89.

29. Clarke, A.E. Fujimura, J.H. What tools? Which jobs? Why right?. In *The Right Tools for the Job*; Clarke, A.E., Fujimura, J.H., Eds.; Princeton University Press: Princeton, NJ, 1992; 3–44.

30. Griesemer, J.R. The role of instruments in the generative analysis of science. In *The Right Tools for the Job*; Clarke, A.E., Fujimura, J.H., Eds.; Princeton University Press: Princeton, NJ, 1992; 47–76.

31. Collopy, F. Shaping the decision (nee design) environment Managing as Designing: Creating a Vocabulary for Management Education and Research; Case Western Reserve University: Cleveland, OH, 2002. Available at http://design.cwru.edu/2002workshop/Positions/ (accessed March 2004).

32. Boland, R.; Collopy, F. *Managing as Designing*, Stanford Business Books: Stanford, CA, 2004.

33. Henderson, K. *On Line and on Paper: Visual Representations, Visual Culture, and Computer Graphics in Design Engineering*, MIT Press: Cambridge, MA, 1999.

34. Attfield, S.; Blandford, A.; Dowell, J. Information seeking in the context of writing: A design psychology interpretation of the 'problematic situation.'. J. Doc. **2003**, *59*, 430–453.

35. Petroski, H. *To Engineer is Human; The Role of Failure in Successful Design*, Random House: New York, 1982.

36. Petroski, H. *To Engineer is Human; The Role of Failure in Successful Design*, Random House: New York, 1982; 223.

37. Petroski, H. *To Engineer is Human; The Role of Failure in Successful Design*, Random House: New York, 1982; 79–80.

38. Schon, D.A. *The Reflective Practitioner: How Professionals Think in Action*, Basic Books: New York, 1983; 270.

39. Lave, J. *Cognition in Practice*, Cambridge University Press: Cambridge, MA, 1988.

40. Winograd, T. *Bringing Design to Software*, ACM Press: New York, 1996.

41. Kelley, D.; Hartfield, B. The designer's stance. In *Bringing Design to Software*; Winograd, T., Ed.; ACM Press: New York, 1996; 163.

42. The Structural Engineer. Available at http://www.istructe.org/thestructuralengineer/DB/7.asp. The Structural Engineer.

43. Kelley, D.; Hartfield, B. The designer's stance. In *Bringing Design to Software*; Winograd, T., Ed.; ACM Press: New York, 1996; 153.

44. Kelley, D.; Littman, J. *The Art of Innovation*, Doubleday: New York, 2001.

45. Kelley, D.; Hartfield, B. The designer's stance. In *Bringing Design to Software*; Winograd, T., Ed.; ACM Press: New York, 1996; 157.

46. Blaich, R. Blaich, J. *Product Design and Corporate Strategy: Managing the Connection for Competitive Advantage*, McGraw-Hill: New York, 1993.

47. Teece, D.J.; Pisano, G.; Shuen, A. Dynamic capabilities and strategic management. In *The Nature and Dynamics of Organizational Capabilities*; Dosi, G., Nelson, R.R., Winter, S.G., Eds.; Oxford University Press: Oxford, U.K., 2000.

48. Destler, B. A new relationship. Nature. **2008**, *453*, 853–854.

49. Weedman, J. Client as designer in collaborative design science research projects: What does social science design theory tell us?. Eur. J. Info. Syst. **2008**, *17*, 476–488.

50. Applegate, L.M. Rigor and relevance in MIS research: Introduction. MIS Quart. **1999**, *23*(1), 1–2.

51. National Research Council. *Computing the Future: A Broader Agenda for Computer Science and Engineering*; National Academy Press: Washington, DC, 1992; 65.

52. Applegate, L.M. Special section on rigor and relevance in information systems (IS) research. MIS Quart. **1999**, *23*(1), 1–33.

53. Benbasat, I.; Zmud, R.W. Empirical research in information systems: The practice of relevance. MIS Quart. **1999**, *23*(1), 3–16.

54. Lyytinen, K. Empirical research in information systems: On the relevance of practice in thinking of IS research. MIS Quart. **1999**, *23*(1), 25–58.

55. Bucciarelli, L.L. *Designing Engineers*, MIT Press: Cambridge, MA, 1994; 135.

56. Weedman, J. The Practice of design: Creating local vocabularies for images Proceedings of 15th Workshop of the American Society for Information Science and Technology; Breitenstein, M., Ed.; Special Interest Group in Classification Research: Providence, RI, 2004. Available at http://dlist.sir.arizona.edu/1769/ (accessed January 2, 2008).

57. Morville, P. *Ambient Findability*, O'Reilly: Sebastopol, CA, 2005.

58. Maron, M.E.; Kuhns, J.L. On relevance, probabilistic indexing and information retrieval. J. ACM. **1960**, *7*(3), 216–244.

59. Salton, G. *A Flexible Automatic System for the Organization, Storage, and Retrieval of Language Data (SMART)*, Report ISR-5, sec. I.; Harvard Computational Laboratory: Cambridge, MA, 1964.

Dewey Decimal Classification (DDC)

Joan S. Mitchell
Diane Vizine-Goetz
OCLC Online Computer Library Center, Inc., Dublin, Ohio, U.S.A.

Abstract

This entry discusses the Dewey Decimal Classification's value proposition as a general knowledge organization system in terms of basic design, history, ongoing development, translations, mappings, applications, and research. The authors conclude with prospects for use of the DDC inside and outside of libraries.

INTRODUCTION

The Dewey Decimal Classification (DDC)[1] system is a general knowledge organization system that is continuously revised to keep pace with knowledge. The DDC is used around the world in 138 countries; over 60 of these countries also use Dewey to organize their national bibliographies. Over the lifetime of the system, the DDC has been translated into more than 30 languages.

The system has value because of its well-defined categories, well-developed hierarchies, rich network of relationships among topics, worldwide use, and language-independent representation of concepts. The existence of interoperable translations, mappings to other subject schemes, and the large amount of categorized content already associated with the system also contribute to Dewey's value proposition.

BASIC DESIGN

Structure and Notation

The DDC structures knowledge by disciplines or fields of study in a general-to-specific arrangement in well-developed hierarchies. At the top level, the DDC includes 10 main classes:

000	Computer science, information and general works
100	Philosophy and psychology
200	Religion
300	Social sciences
400	Language
500	Science
600	Technology
700	Arts and recreation
800	Literature
900	History and geography

Each main class is divided into 10 divisions, and each division is divided into 10 sections (some numbers in the divisions and sections have not been used—these are marked as "Unassigned"):

500	Science	
510	Mathematics	
	510	Mathematics
	511	General principles of mathematics
	512	Algebra
	513	Arithmetic
	514	Topology
	515	Analysis
	516	Geometry
	517	[Unassigned]
	518	Numerical analysis
	519	Probabilities and applied mathematics
520	Astronomy	
530	Physics	
540	Chemistry	
550	Earth sciences and geology	
560	Fossils and prehistoric life	
570	Life sciences; biology	
580	Plants (botany)	
590	Animals (zoology)	

The top-levels of the DDC—the main classes, divisions, and sections—are known collectively as the "DDC Summaries."

Arabic numerals treated like decimal fractions are used to represent each class in the DDC. In other words, main class 500 Science is really .5 Science. The main class, divisions, and sections are usually represented as three digits (extra zeros are added as needed). A decimal point (a punctuation device without mathematical significance) follows the third digit in a DDC number, after which division of the class continues by specific enumeration and/or notational synthesis. For example, 006 Special computer methods is divided into six subclasses: 006.3 Artificial intelligence, 006.4 Computer pattern recognition,

Encyclopedia of Library and Information Sciences, Fourth Edition DOI: 10.1081/E-ELIS4-120043240

006.5 Digital audio, 006.6 Computer graphics, 006.7 Multimedia systems, and 006.8 Virtual reality. All but the last are further subdivided. In addition, each of these classes (including the last) can be further extended by general notational synthesis rules as well as instructions in specific classes.

Classes 000–999 are known collectively as "the schedules"; there are also six auxiliary tables (Tables 1 through 6) that support notational synthesis:

Table 1	Standard subdivisions
Table 1	Standard subdivisions
Table 2	Geographic areas, historical periods, persons
Table 3	Subdivisions for the arts, for individual literatures, for specific literary forms
Table 4	Subdivisions of individual languages and language families
Table 5	Ethnic and national groups
Table 6	Languages

Notation in tables is represented in the print edition with an em dash followed by the number, e.g., —624 Sudan is the Table 2 number for the country of Sudan. In the Relative Index in the print edition, and throughout the current Web version, the same number is represented by T2—624. The prefix for the table number and the em dash are removed when the notation is appended to another number (see the section "Notational Synthesis").

The schedules and tables also include some numbers enclosed in square brackets and parentheses. Numbers in square brackets are not in current use. Numbers in parentheses are optional numbers—alternate notation for a concept. Optional numbers are provided to give emphasis to a topic not given preferred treatment in the standard notation.[2] For example, Library and Archives Canada routinely prefaces the notation for American literature in English and French literature with "C" to represent Canadian literature, e.g., C813.6 is the optional number for 21st century Canadian fiction in English; 813.6 is the standard number for the same concept.

Accompanying the schedules and tables are the Manual and the Relative Index. The Manual provides extended discussions on choices among related numbers, and on classification in complicated areas of the tables and schedules. The Manual was first published in 1982 as a supplement to DDC 19;[3] it was fully integrated into the system with the publication of DDC 20.[4]

The DDC is indexed by a unique tool known as the "Relative Index." The index is so named because it shows the relationship between subjects and the disciplines (or in some cases, the various aspects within disciplines) in which they appear. For example, the Relative Index entries for Garlic are as follows:

Garlic	641.3526
Garlic—botany	584.33
Garlic—cooking	641.6526
Garlic—food	641.3526
Garlic—garden crop	635.26
Garlic—pharmacology	615.32433

Within 641 food and drink, garlic appears in food (641.3526), and cooking (641.6526). Garlic also appears in botany (584); as a garden crop in agriculture (635.26); and in a subfield of medicine, pharmacology (615.32433). The interdisciplinary number for garlic is the one that appears opposite the unsubdivided entry for garlic (641.3526).

The Relative Index has been a feature of the DDC since the first edition of the system, and is considered one of Melvil Dewey's unique contributions. Miksa[5] traces the history of the Relative Index through the 22 full editions of the DDC with special attention to its nature as a conceptual indexing system, the conceptual contexts provided by Relative Index, and its treatment of concepts resident in internal tables. Green[6] investigates the explicit and implicit relationships between Relative Index terms and topics in the schedules and tables.

Classes, Hierarchies, and Relationships

Each class in the DDC is defined by its position in a hierarchy, notes within the class, and a rich network of relationships with other classes. Relationships may be explicitly stated within the class itself, within other classes, and inherited through hierarchical relationships.

Entries in the schedules and tables have two main components—a DDC number and a heading (caption) describing the number. The entry may also contain notes that further describe the class, provide instruction for notational synthesis, or define its relationships with other classes.

796.932　Cross-country skiing
　　　　　Including biathlon
　　　　　Class here Nordic combination, Nordic skiing
　　　　　For jumping, see 796.933

Hierarchy in the DDC is expressed through structure and notation. The DDC organizes knowledge first by discipline and then by subject in a hierarchical structure in which topics progress from the general to the specific. Each of the classes subordinate to the 10 main classes needs to be considered in terms of the hierarchy. Notes with "hierarchical force" regarding the nature of a class at any point in the hierarchy also apply to subordinate classes and to referenced classes.

The hierarchy is largely expressed through the notation. For a class within a given hierarchy, the next broader topic will generally be represented by a number one digit shorter, and subordinate topics will generally be one digit longer. Coordinate topics are usually represented by the same number of digits. For example, here are several specific ice and snow sports shown in the context of their complete hierarchy.

700	Arts and recreation
790	Recreational and performing arts
796	Athletic and outdoor sports and games
796.9	Ice and snow sports
796.91	Ice skating
796.92	Snowshoeing
796.93	Skiing and snowboarding

The classes 796.91, 796.92, and 796.93 are coordinate classes—they are directly subordinate to class 796.9 Ice and snow sports, which in turn is subordinate to section 796 Athletic and outdoor sports and games. Section 796 is part of division 790 Recreational and performing arts, which is part of main class 700 Arts and recreation.

General Rules for Classifying with the DDC

The general rules for classifying with Dewey are set forth in the introduction to the DDC.[7] Additional instructions are found in the beginning of Tables 1 through 6 (in the electronic version, the instructions can be found in the "0" record associated with each table, e.g., T1—0), in individual schedule and table records, and in the Manual notes associated with selected entries.

Since Dewey was originally developed to order physical materials, the instructions are geared toward the selection of a single number to represent any document-like object. The rules for choice of a single number also facilitate sharing of Dewey numbers among users, e.g., through bibliographic cooperatives such as Online Computer Library Center's (OCLC's) WorldCat. In the electronic environment, additional full and partial numbers may be assigned for access (see the section "Applications and Research").

The guiding principle is to classify a topic within its disciplinary context. For topics scattered across the DDC, an interdisciplinary number is often identified. Within a discipline, a comprehensive number might be identified if there are aspects of a topic further developed in the discipline. For example, holidays may be examined from the perspectives of customs, law, religion, etc. The numbers for holidays will vary from each of these perspectives, e.g., 394.26 (Holidays—customs), 344.091 (Holidays—law), and 203.6 (Holidays—religion). The class 394.26 is designated the interdisciplinary number for holidays. It is also the comprehensive number for holidays in customs—there is a substantial development for holidays under

394.26 for secular and religious holidays, plus provision in 394.25 for Carnival and Mardi Gras.

Notational Synthesis

The DDC schedules enumerate only a fraction of the possible numbers that can be used to represent concepts. Often, a number must be synthesized (built) to express a particular concept. Numbers can be synthesized using notation in Tables 1 through 6, notation from other parts of the schedules, or notation from add tables that appear in the schedules. Any number can be extended by notation from Table 1, known collectively as "standard subdivisions," unless there are instructions to the contrary.

Number building from the Tables 2 through 6, other parts of the schedules, and add tables can only be initiated upon instruction.

Here are some examples of notational synthesis in Dewey:

Journal of Topology	514.05

(514 Topology + notation 05 Serial publications from Table 1)

The Internet in Africa	004.678096

(004.678 Internet + notation 09 Geographic treatment from Table 1 + notation 6 Africa from Table 2)

Medical journalism	070.44961

(070.449 Journalism in specific subjects + notation 61 from 610 Medicine and health [it is a convention in Dewey to drop the final zero after the decimal point])

Elementary mathematics curricula	372.7043

(372.7 Elementary education in mathematics + notation 043 Curricula from the add table under 372.3–372.8 Elementary education in specific subjects)

HISTORY

The DDC was conceived by Melvil Dewey in 1873 and first published in 1876.[8] Dewey developed the system as an economical alternative to the practice of organizing books first in broad categories, then by a fixed location within each category representing a physical shelf location. There were no relationships built within the categories except for order of acquisition. Dewey decided to use decimal numbers to represent the subject of books—under his system, books would be numbered according to their subject content instead of physical location. The system gets its name from Dewey's surname plus the decimal element in its design. Wiegand,[9] Comaromi,[10] and Miksa[11] discuss the early history of the DDC and influences on Melvil Dewey in his development of the system; Comaromi and Miksa also discuss the development and features of subsequent editions of the DDC through DDC 18 and DDC 21, respectively.

Editions

The system is published in full and abridged editions, and in electronic and print versions. The DDC databases associated with the full and abridged editions are also available to licensees as an XML data file.

DDC 22, the latest English-language full edition of the DDC, was published in print in 2003;[12] Abridged Edition 14, an abridged version of the full edition, was published the following year.[13] The current full edition database contains nearly 27,000 numbers enumerated in the schedules, plus more than 13,000 additional synthesized numbers in the index. There are over 9000 table numbers listed in Tables 1 through 6; an additional 600 synthesized table numbers are included in the index.[14] As mentioned previously, additional notation beyond that explicitly provided in the schedules, tables, and index can be synthesized to reflect a particular aspect of a topic.

The abridged edition is a logical truncation of the notational and structural hierarchy of the corresponding full edition. It is much smaller than the full edition—in print, it is one volume instead of four, and is aimed at collections of 20,000 titles or less. It also contains fewer tables than the full edition—Tables 1 through 4 instead of Tables 1 through 6. There are still opportunities for notational synthesis, but they are more limited than the full edition provisions for number building. The current abridged edition database contains nearly 5000 numbers enumerated in the schedules, plus an additional 400 synthesized numbers in the index. There are over 500 table numbers listed in Tables 1 through 4, plus nine additional synthesized table numbers in the index.[15]

Electronic Versions of the DDC

The conversion of DDC to electronic form began in 1979 with the use of a computer-based photocomposition system to produce DDC 19. Five years later in 1984, Forest Press commissioned Inforonics, Inc., to develop a database and online system to support the continuing development and publication of the DDC.[16] The project and resulting system become known as the Editorial Support System, or ESS. John Finni, the chief programmer from Inforonics, and Peter Paulson, the executive director of Forest Press from 1985 to 1998, envisioned that DDC data would also be used in classifier-assistance tools and in end-user retrieval systems. In 1989, the ESS was used by the Dewey editorial team to produce DDC 20. Electronic Dewey was released by OCLC Forest Press 4 years later. Electronic Dewey marked the start of classifier access to machine-readable classification data. The software ran on a personal computer and provided access to the schedules, tables, Relative Index, and Manual of DDC 20 on CD-ROM. For schedule numbers, Electronic Dewey also provided up to five frequently used Library of Congress subject headings (LCSH) and a sample bibliographic record for the most frequently occurring heading.

A new Microsoft Windows®-based version of the software, Dewey for Windows, was released in mid-1996 at the same time as the publication of DDC 21. Dewey for Windows was based on the DDC 21 database and included significant enhancements to the user interface.[17] The Windows version included statistically mapped LCSH and selected LC SH editorially mapped to DDC numbers. Dewey for Windows was issued annually through 2001.

In June 2000, WebDewey, a Web-based version of DDC 21, was released by OCLC as part of the Cooperative Online Resources Catalog (CORC) system. The CORC project grew out of the work of OCLC researchers to develop automated tools for finding, harvesting, and classifying electronic resources. In 2002, WebDewey and Abridged WebDewey, the latter a Web-based version of Abridged 13, became available in the OCLC Connexion cataloging service. These services replaced Electronic Dewey and Dewey for Windows.

The latest full and abridged versions of the DDC are available in the Connexion service. WebDewey and Abridged WebDewey incorporate all changes to the print editions, plus additional index terms and built numbers, and many other enhancements.

WebDewey features[18] include:

- Regular database updates incorporating the latest changes to the DDC (new developments, new built numbers, and additional electronic index terms).
- Updated mappings to DDC 22 from the OCLC publication, *People, Places & Things*.[19]
- Thousands of LCSH that have been statistically mapped to Dewey numbers from records in WorldCat or intellectually mapped to Dewey numbers by the DDC editors.
- Thousands of Relative Index terms and built numbers not available in print.
- Links from mapped LCSH to the LCSH authority records.
- Selected mappings from Medical Subject Headings (MeSH).

Abridged WebDewey features[20] include:

- All content from Abridged Edition 14, including regular updates.
- LCSH that have been intellectually mapped to Dewey numbers by DDC editors, including mappings from the OCLC publication, *Subject Headings for Children*[21]
- Links from mapped LCSH to the LCSH authority records.

- Mappings between abridged Dewey numbers and subject headings from H.W. Wilson's *Sears List of Subject Headings*.[22]

One by-product of the development of the DDC Web-based versions was the generation of a suite of XML representations of DDC data. The XML representations are used by OCLC in products and services and distributed to translation partners, research partners, and other licensed users. The proprietary XML representations are scheduled to be replaced by ones based on the MARC 21 formats for Classification and Authority data. The conversion is being undertaken in conjunction with the development of a new version of the ESS. In the new ESS, the record format used for schedule, table, and Manual data will be based on an enhanced version of the MARC 21 Format for Classification Data. The record format used for Relative Index headings and for mapped headings from other vocabularies will be based on an enhanced version of the MARC 21 Format for Authority Data. The MARC 21 representations of the files will also be available in XML.

Emerging data models for representing knowledge organizations schemes, e.g., Simple Knowledge Organization System (SKOS), may provide new opportunities for publishing, linking, and sharing classification data on theWeb. Panzer[23,24] identifies several issues that must be addressed before the DDC can be transformed fully into a Web information resource, including the design of Uniform Resource Identifiers and modeling DDC in SKOS.

DEVELOPMENT

Since July 29, 1988, OCLC has owned all copyright rights in the DDC and funds the ongoing development of the system. The Dewey editorial office has been headquartered at the Library of Congress since 1923, and is physically located in the Dewey Section.[25] Dewey numbers have been assigned to works cataloged by the Library of Congress since 1930; classifiers in the Dewey Section are the primary assigners of Dewey numbers at the Library of Congress. Having the editorial office in close proximity to a key user group assists the editors in detecting emerging topics and shifts in viewpoints and terminology.

The DDC is continuously developed and updated by an editor in chief and four assistant editors. The editors study the distribution of topics in WorldCat to determine literary warrant (the existence of a certain level of literature on a topic) for updates—they also monitor the subject literature, news feeds, and other information resources, plus consult with users.

All changes to the DDC are reviewed by the Decimal Classification Editorial Policy Committee (EPC), a 10-member international advisory board whose main function is to advise the DDC editors and OCLC on matters relating to changes, innovation, and the general development of the DDC. The committee is a joint committee of the American Library Association and OCLC and has been in continuous existence in its present form since the early 1950s. Current EPC members represent academic, national, public, school, and special libraries and come from Australia, Canada, South Africa, the United Kingdom, and the United States. In addition, current translation partners serve as corresponding members of EPC—they receive all draft proposals for comment at the same time as EPC members.

TRANSLATIONS

Over the life of the system, the DDC has been translated into over 30 languages. Translation activities and international use prior to acquisition of Forest Press by OCLC in 1988 are summarized in Downing and Yelland[26] and Holley;[27] later activities are discussed by Chan and Mitchell,[28] Beall and Couture-Lafleur,[29] Knutsen,[30] Heiner-Freiling,[31] and Beall.[32] Since 1988, authorized translations of the full and abridged editions of the DDC have been published in the following languages: Arabic, French, German, Greek, Hebrew, Icelandic, Italian, Norwegian, Russian, Spanish, Turkish, and Vietnamese. MelvilClass, the German counterpart to WebDewey, is an up-to-date version of the German translation of DDC 22. Other Web versions are currently under study. Current versions of the top-level summaries of the DDC have been translated into Arabic, Chinese, Czech, French, German, Hebrew, Italian, Norwegian, Portuguese, Russian, Spanish, Swedish, and Vietnamese. A project is under way in South Africa to translate the DDC Summaries into the ten official languages of South Africa besides English.

OCLC enters into agreements with recognized bibliographic agencies around the world to produce localized representations of the DDC in which classes remain interoperable with the English-language edition on which the translation is based. Translations are localized with examples and terminology appropriate to the country/language group, and are often supplemented by interoperable expansions (e.g., a deeper representation of a geographic area than found in the English-language full edition).

The following example illustrates the principle of interoperable expansions. The German translation of Table 2 contains expansions for several areas; the expansion for— 43551 Regierungsbezirk Köln is shown below. The English-language version of the development for — 43551 Regierungsbezirk Köln is a logical abridgment of the German version. In the English-language version of Table 2, only the categories shown in bold are listed.

—43551	**Regierungsbezirk Köln**	
—435511	**Aachen**	
—435512	Kreise Aachen, Heinsberg, Düren, Euskirchen	
—4355122		Kreis Aachen
—4355124		Kreis Heinsberg
—4355126		Kreis Düren
—4355128		Kreis Euskirchen
—435513	Rhein-Erft-Kreis	
—435514	**Köln**	
—435515	Leverkusen	
—435516	Rheinisch-Bergischer-Kreis, Oberbergischer Kreis	
—4355163		Rheinisch-Bergischer-Kreis
—4355167		Oberbergischer Kreis
—435518	**Bonn**	
—435519	Rhein-Sieg-Kreis	

Research projects are under way on models for mixed Norwegian-English and Swedish-English translations of the DDC,[33] and on multilingual presentations of the DDC.[34]

Translations enrich the terminological base of the DDC, and extend the specificity of the system in the form of interoperable expansions and additional synthesized numbers. Translations also spur additional categorized content being associated with the DDC.[35] Translation partners bring a rich diversity of viewpoint to the DDC that often results in improvements to the English-language standard edition.[36]

MAPPINGS

Mappings between Dewey and other knowledge organization systems enrich the vocabulary associated with DDC numbers, and permit the use of the DDC as a switching system. Current services plus a host of research projects make use of such mappings for a variety of applications.

The electronic versions of the DDC contain selected mappings between Dewey numbers and three standard subject headings lists—LCSH, MeSH, and H.W. Wilson's *Sears List of Subject Headings*. The last represents the longest continuous mapping between the DDC and a subject heading systems. Dewey numbers first appeared in the 4th Ed. of Sears in 1939.[37] They were dropped in the 9th Ed. of Sears,[38] reappeared again in the 11th Ed.,[39] and have continued through the 19th Ed.[40] The mappings between abridged Dewey numbers and Sears headings are created at H.W. Wilson under an agreement with OCLC, and are included in various products and services offered by OCLC and H.W. Wilson.

The Dewey editors have long consulted LCSH and MeSH as sources of terminology for the DDC; terminology from both systems is also mapped to the DDC. The OCLC publications *Subject Headings for Children* and *People, Places & Things* are lists of LC subject headings with corresponding DDC numbers. The publications function as tools for end users and catalogers and supply

vocabulary for the DDC database. Both include subject heading-DDC number pairs statistically derived from WorldCat. Vizine-Goetz[41] describes the general processes used to map LCSH terminology, including statistical mapping. Ongoing access to LCSH mappings is through WebDewey services.

In 2008, the Dewey editors began a project to map DDC numbers to the BISAC (Book Industry Standards and Communications) subject headings.[42] The project is part of OCLCs Next Generation Cataloging pilot, which captures publisher and vendor metadata and enhances it for the mutual benefit of library and publishing industry partners.[43] The mappings are used to add Dewey numbers to publisher metadata records that contain BISAC codes, and BISAC subject headings to bibliographic records that contain DDC numbers.

Translation partners and other groups are also linking general terminology lists with the DDC.–> In the CrissCross project, headings from Schlagwortnormdatei (SWD), the German subject heading authority file, are being mapped to Dewey numbers (to date, 58,000 headings have been mapped).[44] At the Italian National Central Library in Florence, work is under way to map Dewey numbers to Nuovo Soggettario, the Italian subject heading list.[45,46] The Spanish translation of *Sears List of Subject Headings* also includes mapped Dewey numbers.[47]

There are also concordances being developed between Dewey and other classification systems. The Library of Congress's Classification Web system includes statistical correlations among LCSH, Library of Congress Classification (LCC), and DDC based on the co-occurrence of the three in Library of Congress bibliographic records. The National Library of Sweden has developed a mapping between Sveriges Allmanna Biblioteksförening (SAB), the Swedish classification system, and the DDC as part of an exploration to consider a Swedish translation of the DDC.[48]

Several concordances between the Universal Decimal Classification (UDC) and the DDC have been developed. For example, the Czech National Library has built a concordance between UDC and DDC for the purposes of collection assessment.[49] McIlwaine and Mitchell are experimenting with a concordance between the Class 2 Religion in the UDC and 200 Religion in the DDC as a method of presenting a chronological/regional view of religion in the DDC similar to the updated one found in the UDC.[50]

APPLICATIONS AND RESEARCH

The DDC is perhaps most familiar to users as the classification portion (Arabic numerals punctuated by a decimal point after the first three digits) of a call number used to label physical objects in libraries. The classification portion of a call number is one manifestation of Dewey; the underlying DDC data and associated terminologies are used for a variety of applications beyond physical shelf location.

The first and most well-known research effort to incorporate DDC data into an end user retrieval system was the DDC Online Project led by Markey.[51] Markey's team built an experimental online catalog, Dewey Online Catalog (DOC), that included data from the DDC schedules and Relative Index. The DOC system provided new subject searching capabilities not available in online catalogs, e.g., subject indexes enriched with terminology from the DDC schedules and Relative Index, and features to broaden or narrow searches using the DDC hierarchy. Other notable research projects that use DDC-based search strategies are the Renardus Service[52] and the High Level Thesaurus (HILT) project.[53]

The Renardus project developed a pilot Web-based service that enabled searching and browsing of subject gateway services from Denmark, Finland, Germany, the Netherlands, Sweden, and the United Kingdom. To enable browsing across the gateways, the local classification systems used in the gateways were mapped to a common classification system that could function as a switching language and browsing structure. The DDC was chosen as the common scheme. The project developed a mapping tool that allowed the participating gateways to specify the level of match between the local scheme and DDC.

Like Renardus, the HILT project is investigating and developing solutions for subject searching and browsing across multiple schemes and information environments. The DDC is used as a central spine to which collection descriptions are mapped. In the HILT II pilot service, user queries are matched to DDC captions, Relative Index terms, and mapped terminology; DDC caption hierarchies are displayed in search results to provide context for matched terms. When a user selects a result, the service returns a list of collections to search.

These systems are exceptional in their integration of DDC data into the search process. As Markey notes, "To this day, the only way in which most online catalog users experience classification online is through their OPACs shelflist browsing capability."[54] Even so, the value of classification-based browsing has not gone unnoticed by users and developers of online catalogs. Many online catalog redesign projects include a requirement for a virtual shelf-browsing feature.

The approval of additional MARC 21 fields for DDC numbers in the bibliographic format may provide new opportunities for using DDC data in end-user and classifier systems. The 083 field (Additional DDC Number) can be used to code additional DDC numbers, including internal and external table numbers, for subject access.[55] The 085 field (Synthesized Classification Number Components) traces the components of a synthesized number. Beall[56] gives several examples of 083 and 085 fields and

discusses how the data can help libraries make full use of the DDC for retrieval.

Liu[57] investigated the feasibility of decomposing DDC synthesized numbers in the 700s. He concludes that synthesized numbers can be decomposed automatically in all DDC classes and suggests that bibliographic records could be enhanced with additional indexing vocabulary based on the component parts of a number. Following Lui, Reiner[58] is developing software to decompose DDC numbers assigned by the German National Library. The German National Library began assigning Dewey numbers to resources in its collection in 2004. The goal of this research is to develop software to automatically assign class numbers. It remains to be seen whether the MARC 085 field will stimulate new investigations into decomposition and automated number assignment.

The Library of Congress is employing a semi-automated approach for DDC number assignment. The "AutoDewey" software takes advantage of places where the LCC and DDC schedules for literature are similar enough to facilitate mapping between the two schemes. The software suggests DDC numbers based on the LCC number chosen by the cataloger for the work in hand.[59] Where one-to-one mapping is possible, AutoDewey assigns DDC numbers automatically, based on the LCC number. When direct mapping is not possible, the cataloger must often choose a literary form (poetry, drama, and fiction); when the literary periods of LCC and DDC do not match, the cataloger must also choose a literary period. Almost 2400 DDC numbers were assigned in 2007 using AutoDewey, and 5105 numbers were assigned in 2008. The software was developed by the Library of Congress.

OCLC has taken a different approach with the beta service Classify.[60] The service provides summaries of classification data (DDC, LCC, and NLM) for FRBR-based groups of WorldCat records. All summaries include the most frequently used number based on holdings and the most recently assigned class number based on OCLC record number; many also include Dewey edition information. The service supports the assignment of classification numbers for books, DVDs, CDs, and many other types of materials. Classification data is accessible through a user interface and a Web service.

Previously, in the research phase of the CORC project, OCLC introduced tools to help users assign DDC class numbers. The tools, now available in Connexion, consist of software that automatically generates DDC numbers for Web resources and a feature to apply authority control to Dewey numbers. Despite attempts to optimize the content of classification records for automated classification using the Scorpion software, fully automatic classification remains an unrealized goal.[61,62]

The DDC is also being used for collection analysis and assessment. In the WorldCat Collection Analysis service, DDC numbers are mapped to the OCLC conspectus to enable libraries using multiple classification schemes to analyze their collections as a whole.[63] At the British Library, the DDC has been used in a pilot project to assess the library's collections in support of higher education in the United Kingdom.[64]

CONCLUSION

A rich set of tools is critical for knowledge representation and access in an information environment in which information flows freely in all formats across national and linguistic boundaries. Knowledge organization systems such as the DDC have a yet-to-be-fully-exploited role to play in the current and future environment. The Dewey Decimal Classification—with its well-defined categories, well-developed hierarchies, rich network of relationships among topics, worldwide use, language-independent representation of concepts, interoperable translations, and mappings to other subject schemes, plus the large amount of categorized content already associated with the system—holds promise in a variety of applications beyond its familiar role as a shelf location device. The success of Dewey as a tool in current and future environments will depend on ubiquitous and convenient availability of the system in a variety of formats for experimentation and use, continued (direct and automatic) application of Dewey numbers to content, aggressive association of the system with a wide variety of terminological resources, and continuous updating and development of the system by the editorial team in partnership with the worldwide community of Dewey users.

ACKNOWLEDGMENTS

The authors thank the following colleagues for their advice and assistance in preparing this paper: Julianne Beall (Library of Congress), Bob Bolander (OCLC), George Buzash (OCLC), Libbie Crawford (OCLC), Tam Dalrymple (OCLC), Rebecca Green (OCLC), Giles Martin (OCLC), Winton Matthews (Library of Congress), Joseph Miller (H.W. Wilson), Larry Olszewski (OCLC), Michael Panzer (OCLC), Federica Paradisi (Italian National Central Library, Florence), and David Williamson (Library of Congress). All opinions expressed and any omissions or errors remain the responsibility of the authors.

REFERENCES

1. Connexion, *DDC, Dewey, Dewey Decimal Classification*, WebDewey, and WorldCat are registered trademarks of OCLC Online Computer Library Center, Inc: Dublin, OH.

2. Mitchell, J.S. Options in the Dewey Decimal Classification system: The current perspective. In *Classification: Options and Opportunities*; Thomas, A., Ed.; Haworth Press: Binghamton, New York, 1995; 89–103 Co-published simultaneously in Cataloging Classif. Quart. **1995**, *19*(3/4), 89–103.

3. Comaromi, J.P. Warren, M.J. *Manual on the Use of the Dewey Decimal Classification System, Edition 19* Forest Press: Albany, NY, 1982.

4. Dewey, M. Manual. *Dewey Decimal Classification and Relative Index*, 20th Ed.; Comaromi, J.P., Beall, J., Matthews, W.E., Jr., New, G.R., Eds.; OCLC Forest Press: Albany, NY, 1989; Vol. 4, 731–969.

5. Miksa, F.L. The DDC Relative Index. In *Moving Beyond the Presentation Layer: Context and Content in the Dewey Decimal Classification (DDC) System*; Mitchell, J.S., Vizine-Goetz, D., Eds.; Haworth Press: Binghamton, NY, 2006; 65–95 Co-published simultaneously in Cataloging Classif. Quart. **2006**, *42*(3/4), 65–95.

6. Green, R. Making visible hidden relationships in the Dewey Decimal Classification: how Relative Index terms relate to DDC classes *Culture and Identity in Knowledge Organization*, Proceedings of the Tenth International ISKO Conference Montréal, Canada August 5–8, 2008; Arsenault, C., Tennis, J.T., Eds.; Ergon: Würzburg, Germany, 2008; 8–14. Updated presentation available at http://www.oclc.org/dewey/news/conferences/isko_02_green.ppt. (accessed November 2008).

7. Dewey, M. Introduction to the Dewey Decimal Classification. *Dewey Decimal Classification and Relative Index*, 22nd Ed.; Mitchell, J.S., Beall, J., Martin, G., Matthews, W.E., Jr., New, G.R., Eds.; OCLC: Dublin, OH, 2003; Vol. 1, xxxvii–lxiii http://www.oclc.org/dewey/versions/ddc22print/intro.pdf (accessed November 2008).

8. Dewey, M. *A Classification and Subject Index for the Cataloguing and Arranging the Books and Pamphlets of a Library*, Lockwood & Brainard Company: Amherst, MA, 1876. Printed by the Case, Reprinted as *Dewey Decimal Classification, Centennial 1876–1976*, by Forest Press Division; Lake Placid Education Foundation. Kingsport Press: Kingsport, TN, 1976.

9. Wiegand, W.A. *Irrepressible Reformer: A Biography of Melvil Dewey*, American Library Association: Chicago, IL, 1996.

10. Comaromi, J.P. *The Eighteen Editions of the Dewey Decimal Classification*, Forest Press: Albany, NY, 1976.

11. Miksa, F.L. *The DDC, the Universe of Knowledge, and the Post-Modern Library*, Forest Press: Albany, NY, 1998.

12. Dewey, M. *Dewey Decimal Classification and Relative Index*, 22nd Ed.; Mitchell, J.S., Beall, J., Martin, G., Matthews, W.E., Jr., New, G.R., Eds.; OCLC: Dublin, OH, 2003; Vol. 4.

13. Dewey, M. *Abridged Dewey Decimal Classification and Relative Index*, 22nd Ed.; Mitchell, J.S., Beall, J., Martin, G., Matthews, W.E., Jr., New, G.R., Eds.; OCLC: Dublin, OH, 2004.

14. Statistics provided by Giles Martin on November 12, 2008, from the September 2008 archived DDC 22 database.

15. Statistics provided by Giles Martin on November 12, 2008, from the September 2008 archived Abridged Edition 14 database.

16. Finni, J.J.; Paulson, P.J. The Dewey Decimal Classification enters the computer age: Developing the DDC database and editorial support system. Int. Cataloguing October/December **1987**, *16*, 46–48.

17. Vizine-Goetz, D. Bendig, M. Dewey for windows. In *Planning and Implementing Technical Services Workstations*; Kaplan, M., Ed.; American Library Association: Chicago, IL, 1997; 103–120.

18. http://www.oclc.org/us/en/dewey/versions/webdewey/.

19. *People, Places & Things: A List of Popular Library of Congress Subject Headings with Dewey Numbers*, Forest Press: Dublin, OH, 2001.

20. http://www.oclc.org/us/en/dewey/versions/abridgedwebdewey/.

21. *Subject Headings for Children: A List of Subject Headings Used by the Library of Congress with Abridged Dewey Numbers Added*, 2nd Ed.; Winkel, L., Ed.; Forest Press: Albany, NY, 1998.

22. *Sears List of Subject Headings*, 18th Ed.; Miller, J., Goodsell, J., Eds.; H.W. Wilson: NY, 2004.

23. Panzer, M. Cool URIs for the DDC: towards web-scale accessibility of a large classification system *Metadata for Semantic and Social Applications*, Proceedings of the International Conference on Dublin Core and Metadata Applications Berlin, Germany, September 22–26, 2008; Greenburg, J., Klas, W., Eds.; Dublin Core Metadata Initiative and Universitätsverlag Göttingen: Göttingen, Germany, 2008; 183–190.

24. Panzer, M. DDC, SKOS, and linked data on the web Presentation at OCLC/ISKO-NA Preconference to the 10th International ISKO Conference Université de Montréal, Canada: Montreal, Ontario, Canada August, 5, 2008. Available at http://www.oclc.org/us/en/news/events/presentations/2008/ISKO/20080805-deweyskos-panzer.ppt (accessed November 2008).

25. As part of the reorganization of the Acquisitions and Bibliographic Access Directorate at the Library of Congress in October 2008, the Decimal Classification Division became the Dewey Section of the U.S. General Division.

26. *Dewey, International: Papers Given at the European Centenary Seminar on the Dewey Decimal Classification, Banbury, England, September 26–30,*; Downing, J.C., Yelland, M., Eds.; Library Association: London, U.K., 1977l;976.

27. *Dewey: An International Perspective*; Holley, R.P., Ed.; K. G. Saur: Munich, Germany, 1991; Papers from a Workshop on the Dewey Decimal Classification and DDC 20 Presented at the General Conference of the International Federation of Library Associations and Institutions (IFLA), Paris, France, August 24, 1989;.

28. *Dewey Decimal Classification: Edition 21 and International Perspectives*; Chan, L.M., Mitchell, J.S., Eds.; OCLC Forest Press: Albany, NY, 1997 Papers from a Workshop Presented at the General Conference of the International Federation of Library Associations and Institutions (IFLA), Beijing, China, August 29, 1996;.

29. *Dewey Decimal Classification: Francophone Perspectives*; Beall, J., Couture-Lafleur, R., Eds.; OCLC Forest Press: Albany, NY, 1999 Papers from a Workshop Presented at the General Conference of the International Federation of Library Associations and Institutions (IFLA), Amsterdam, the Netherlands, August 20, 1998;.

30. Knutsen, U. Working in a distributed electronic environment: experiences with the Norwegian edition Paper presented at the World Library and Information Congress (69th IFLA General Conference and Council) Berlin, Germany, August 1–9, 2003. Available at http://www.ifla.org/IV/ifla69/papers/122-Knutsen.pdf (accessed November 2008).

31. Heiner-Freiling, M. DDC German—The project, the aims, the methods: New ideas for a well-established traditional classification system. In *Moving Beyond the Presentation Layer: Context and Content in the Dewey Decimal Classification (DDC) System*; Mitchell, J.S., Vizine-Goetz, D., Eds.; Haworth Press: Binghamton, NY, 2006; 147–162 Co-published simultaneously in Cataloging Classif. Quart. **2006**, *42*(3/4), 147–162.

32. Beall, J. Approaches to expansions: Case studies from the German and Vietnamese translations Paper presented at the World Library and Information Congress (69th IFLA General Conference and Council) Berlin, Germany, August 1–9, 2003. Available at http://www.ifla.org/IV/ifla69/papers/123e-Beall.pdf (accessed November 2008).

33. Mitchell, J.S. Rype, I. Svanberg, M. Mixed translation models for the Dewey Decimal Classification (DDC) system Culture and Identity in Knowledge Organization, Proceedings of the Tenth International ISKO Conference Montréal, Canada August 5–8, 2008; Arsenault, C., Tennis, J.T., Eds.; Ergon: Würzburg, Germany, 2008; 98–104. Updated presentation available at: http://www.oclc.org/dewey/news/conferences/isko_11_mitchell_et_al.ppt (accessed November 2008).

34. Panzer, M. From heteroglossia to polyglottism: Multilingual MelvilClass Presentation at meeting, Dewey Breakfast/Update, ALA Annual Meeting Anaheim July 3, 2008. Available at http://www.oclc.org/dewey/news/conferences/multilingual_melvil_class.pdf (accessed November 2008).

35. For example, as of November 14, 2008, there were 233,300 bibliographic records in WorldCat with numbers assigned from the German translation of DDC 22.

36. For examples of updates proposed by translation partners, see "EPC makes Dewey history," *025.431: The Dewey blog* Available at http://ddc.typepad.com/025431/2007/11/epc-makes-dewey.html (accessed November 16, 2007).

37. *List of Subject Headings for Small Libraries, Including Practical Suggestions for the Beginner in Subject Heading Work*, 4th Ed.; Sears, M.E., Ed.; H.W. Wilson: NY, 1939 rev., with the additions of Decimal Classification numbers by Monro, I.S.

38. *Sears List of Subject Headings*, 9th Ed.; Westby, B.M., Ed.; H.W. Wilson: New York, 1965.

39. *Sears List of Subject Headings*, 11th Ed.; Westby, B.M., Ed.; H.W. Wilson: New York, 1977.

40. *Sears List of Subject Headings*, 19th Ed.; Miller, J., Bristow, B.A., Eds.; H.W. Wilson: New York, 2007.

41. Vizine-Goetz, D. Dewey in CORC: Classification in metadata and pathfinders. In *CORC: New Tools and Possibilities for Cooperative Electronic Resource Description*; Calhoun, K., Riemer, J.J., Eds.; Haworth Press: Binghamton, NY, 2001; 67–80 Also published in J. Internet Cataloging **2001**, *4*(1/2), 67–80.

42. http://www.bisg.org/bisac/subjectcodes/index.html.

43. http://www.oclc.org/partnerships/material/nexgen/nextgencataloging.htm.

44. http://www.fbi.fh-koeln.de/institut/projekte/CrissCross/SWD-DDC-Mapping_en.html.

45. *Nuovo Soggettario: Guida al Sistema Italiano di Indicizzazione per Soggetto: Prototipo del Thesaurus*. Editrice Bibliografica: Milano, Italy, 2006; 175–177.

46. Paradisi, F. Linking DDC numbers to the new "Soggettario Italiano." Presentation at Dewey Translators Meeting, World Library and Information Congress (72nd IFLA General Conference and Council) Seoul, Korea August 23, 2006. Available at http://www.oclc.org/dewey/news/conferences/ddc_and_soggetario_ifla_2006.ppt (accessed November 2008).

47. *Sears Lista de Encabezamientos de Materia: Nueva Traddución y Adaptación de Lista Sears*; Calimano, I.E., García, A., Eds.; H.W. Wilson: New York, 2008.

48. Svanberg, M. Mapping two classification schemes—DDC and SAB. *New Perspectives on Subject Indexing and Classification: International Symposium in Honour of Magda Heiner-Freiling*, Deutsche Nationalbibliothek: Leipzig, Frankfurt am Main: Berlin, Germany, 2008; 41–51.

49. Balíková, M. UDC in Czechia Proceedings of the International Seminar "Information Access for the Global Community," The Hague, June 4–5 2007 Extensions and Corrections to the UDC **2007**, *29*, 191–227. Available at http://dlist.sir.arizona.edu/2379/01/MBalikova_UDC_Seminar 2007.pdf (accessed November 2008).

50. McIlwaine, I.C. Mitchell, J.S. The new ecumenism: exploration of a DDC/UDC view of religion Knowledge Organization for a Global Learning Society, Proceedings of the Ninth International ISKO Conference Vienna, Austria July 4–7, 2006 Budin, G., Swertz, C., Mitgusch, K., Eds.; Ergon: Würzburg, Germany, 2008; 323–330.

51. Markey, K. Demeyer, A.N. *Dewey Decimal Classification Online Project: Evaluation of a Library Schedule and Index Integrated into the Subject Searching Capabilities of an Online Catalog*, OCLC/OPR/RR-86/1; OCLC: Dublin, OH, 1986.

52. Koch, T. Neuroth, H. Day, M. Renardus: Cross-browsing European subject gateways via a common classification system (DDC). In *Subject Retrieval in a Networked World*; Proceedings of the IFLA Satellite Meeting held in Dublin, OH, August 14–16, 2001; McIlwaine, I.C., Ed.; K.G. Saur: München, Germany, 2003; 25–33.

53. Nicholson, D.M. Dawson, A. Shiri, A. HILT: A pilot terminology mapping service with a DDC spine. In *Moving Beyond the Presentation Layer: Context and Content in the Dewey Decimal Classification (DDC) System*; Mitchell, J.S., Vizine-Goetz, D., Eds.; Haworth Press: Binghamton, NY, 2006; 187–200 Co-published simultaneously in Cataloging Classif. Quart. **2006**, *42*(3/4), 187–200.

54. Markey, K. Forty years of classification online: final chapter or future unlimited?. In *Moving Beyond the Presentation Layer: Context and Content in the Dewey Decimal Classification (DDC) System*; Mitchell, J.S., Vizine-Goetz, D., Eds.; Haworth Press: Binghamton, NY, 2006; 45–46 Co-published simultaneously in Cataloging Classif. Quart. **2006**, *42*(3/4), 45–46.

55. http://www.loc.gov/marc/marbi/2008/2008-01.html.

56. Beall, J. Representation of DDC in MARC 21. *New Perspectives on Subject Indexing and Classification: International*

57. Liu, S. Decomposing DDC synthesized numbers Paper presented at the 62nd IFLA General Conference and Council Beijing, China, August 25–31, 1996. Available at http://www.ifla.org/IV/ifla62/62-sonl.htm (accessed November 2008).

58. Reiner, U. DDC-based search in the data of the German National Bibliography. *New Perspectives on Subject Indexing and Classification: International Symposium in Honour of Magda Heiner-Freiling*, Deutsche Nationalbibliothek; Leipzig, Frankfurt am Main: Berlin, Germany, 2008; 121–129.

59. Beall, J. Literary authors: AutoDewey and LC name authority file Presentation at meeting, Dewey Breakfast/Update, ALA Midwinter Meeting Philadelphia, PA Jan 12, 2008. Available at http://www.oclc.org/dewey/discussion/papers/literary_authors.ppt (accessed November 2008).

60. http://www.oclc.org/research/researchworks/classify/.

61. Vizine-Goetz, D. Beall, J. Using literary warrant to define a version of the DDC for automated classification services. In *Knowledge Organization and the Global Information Society*; Proceedings of the Eighth International ISKO Conference, London, U.K., July 13–16, 2004; McIlwaine, I.C., Ed.; Ergon: Würzburg, Germany, 2004; 147–152. Available at http://www.oclc.org/research/publications/archive/2004/vizine-goetz-beall.pdf (accessed November 2008).

62. Thompson, R. Shafer, K. Vizine-Goetz, D. Evaluating Dewey concepts as a knowledge base for automatic subject assignment Proceedings of the Second ACM International Conference on Digital Libraries Philadelphia, PA July 23–26, 1997; Allen, R.B., Rasmussen, E., Eds.; Association for Computing Machinery: New York, 1997; 37–46.

63. http://www.oclc.org/collectionanalysis/support/.

64. Kent, C. Deliot, C. Martyn, C. Management information from classification—Methods of collection analysis using DDC. *New Perspectives on Subject Indexing and Classification: International Symposium in Honour of Magda Heiner-Freiling*, Deutsche Nationalbibliothek; Leipzig, Frankfurt am Main: Berlin, Germany, 2008; 115–119.

BIBLIOGRAPHY

1. *025.431:* The Dewey blog. Available at http://ddc.typepad.com/ (accessed November 2008).

2. Chan, L.M. Mitchell, J.S. *Dewey Decimal Classification: Principles and Application*, 3rd Ed. OCLC: Dublin, OH, 2003.

3. Comaromi, J.P. *The Eighteen Editions of the Dewey Decimal Classification*, Forest Press Division, Lake Placid Education Foundation: Albany, NY, 1976.

4. Dewey Services. Available at http://www.oclc.org/dewey/ (accessed November 2008).

5. Miksa, F.L. *The DDC, the Universe of Knowledge, and the Post-modern Library*, Forest Press: Albany, NY, 1998.

6. Mitchell, J.S. Relationships in the Dewey Decimal Classification system. In *Relationships in the Organization of*

Knowledge; Bean, C.A., Green, R., Eds.; Kluwer Academic Publishers: Dordrecht,the Netherlands, 2001; 211–226.

7. In *Moving beyond the Presentation Layer: Context and Content in the Dewey Decimal Classification (DDC) System*; Mitchell, J.S., Vizine-Goetz, D., Eds.; Haworth Press: Binghamton, NY, 2006. Co-published simultaneously in Cataloging Classif. Quart. **2006**, *42* (3/4).

Digital Content Licensing

Paul D. Callister
Kathleen Hall
Leon E. Bloch Law Library, University of Missouri-Kansas City School of Law, Kansas City, Missouri, U.S.A.

Abstract

Content licensing primarily concerns the licensing of property, and impacts legal rights under diverse bodies of local, national, foreign, and international law. Besides copyright law, content licensing may concern, depending upon the jurisdiction, the author or creator's "moral rights," "neighbor rights," lender's rights, defamation, privacy, publicity, pornography and obscenity, international trade, exports and technology transfer, privacy, trademark, commercial codes, and employment law, etc. Commercial or contract law enters in as well in connection with such issues as formation, interpretation, warranties, and remedies for breach. Choice of law and choice of forum are issues as well in our present global marketplace. Thus, content licensing is a complex legal subject necessitating review of the applicable law both creating intellectual property rights and governing contractual agreements and licensing.

INTRODUCTION

Content licensing primarily concerns the licensing of property, which itself consists of certain legal rights. Besides copyright law, content licensing takes place within the context of rights and obligations stemming from an array of local, national, foreign, and international laws. Such law may concern author or creator's "moral rights," "neighbor rights," lender's rights, defamation, privacy, publicity, pornography and obscenity, international trade, exports and technology transfer, privacy, trademark, commercial codes, and employment and contract law, etc.

To understand content licensing, copyright and other law must be juxtaposed with the law governing the formation, interpretation, warranties, and remedy for breach of contract. The issues are complicated by choice of applicable commercial law. While it is always prudent to consult an attorney with respect to negotiating, drafting, and litigating any contract, this is especially true with respect to the technical field of copyright law. Consequently, the topics and issues discussed in this entry are for informational purposes only and should not be relied upon in lieu of consultation with competent legal counsel.

WHAT IS A LICENSE?

A license is a contract, not necessarily in writing, in which one party (the licensor) transfers rights to use certain property to a user (the licensee) for some limited period of time or until some event. A permanent transfer of rights is an assignment or sale, even when the licensor retains other related rights (e.g., the transfer of rights to publish in print but not in any electronic medium). With respect to intellectual property, a licensor may, but need not be, the creator, or even the owner, of the work being transferred.

By entering into license agreements, the parties seek to establish a mutually beneficial relationship in which they exchange certain promises or consideration (payment), set forth their respective rights and obligations, and provide for redress in the event of breach (i.e., a failure of one or more of the parties to meet their obligations). Besides license to use property for a given term, the licensee may seek certain warranties (guarantees) from the licensor, that the person has title or the rights to the content being licensed, and that additional payments or liability to third parties will not result from licensee's use of the property. As used in this entry, content licensing refers to license agreements affecting informational content and the software necessary to access that content.

One principal difference between licensing content and purchasing information in a print publication is that the "first sale" doctrine generally does not apply.[1] The first sale doctrine cuts off the right of owners to seek additional remuneration each time a work is subsequently sold or lent to another.[2]

WHAT RIGHTS MAY BE ADDRESSED IN A LICENSE AGREEMENT?

Although it may be said that all property consist of rights, in the case of intellectual property ([2] at 813) such property owes its existence to rights enumerated in the law, and often by statute. The right to license intellectual property interests may potentially originate in the law of copyright, neighboring rights, moral rights, and electronic rights, etc. Several of these respective sources of

Digital–Disaster

intellectual property rights frequently addressed in content licensing agreements are considered below.

Copyright Law

In the United States, such rights are found in Title 17 of the United States Code (USC) § 106 and include rights to:

1. Reproduction;
2. Adaptation (or "derivative works");
3. Distribution (including "sale or other transfer of ownership, or by rental, lease, or lending");
4. Public performance (limited to "literary, musical, dramatic, and choreographic works, pantomimes, and motion pictures and other audiovisual works");
5. Public display (limited to "literary, musical, dramatic, and choreographic works, pantomimes, and pictorial, graphic, or sculptural works, including the individual images of a motion picture or other audiovisual work"); and
6. Digital audio transmission (limited to sound recordings).

In addition, 17 USC § 201 (c), sets forth rights of publishers of "collective works" in relation to the rights of contributing authors. Specifically, publishers of collective works have the right to publish contributed articles in "revisions" of the original collected work (e.g., a second edition of the same encyclopedia) and in any "later collective work in the same series" (e.g., a subsequent reprint of an article in the *same* journal). In the European Union, the EU Database Directive provides protections for publishers of databases.[3]

Enumerated rights, such as those expressed in U.S. federal copyright law, form the basis for property rights assigned pursuant to licensing agreements. Similar rights may also be found in the common law of the various U.S. states and the law of foreign nations. Each of these rights may serve as the basis for an assignable property right and may further be limited in seemingly infinite variations by terms set forth in the licensing agreement (by time, jurisdiction, medium, types of uses, etc.).

Neighboring Rights

Besides copyright law, additional rights affecting licensing agreements stem from other law, including state law and the laws of foreign nations. For instance, many civil law jurisdictions such as France (and California, alone among U.S. jurisdictions), provide for neighboring rights (*droit de suite*), or rights designed to compensate artists for subsequent resale and reproduction of their works (traditionally, the law presumed that the reproduction rights to the works of fine artists had been transferred to the buyer of that painting, sculpture, etc., whereas the rights to literary works had not).[4] In California, *droit de suite* is

applied through the California Resale Royalties Act.[5] The Berne Convention, which was adopted by the United States in 1989, recognizes *droit de suite*. Unlike many other rights protected by the treaty, *droit de suite* requires that an author's country recognizes the right. In addition the convention's provision recognizing the right may not be "self-executing" under U.S. law (i.e., applicable without enabling legislation).[6]

As a result of neighboring rights, licensees often seek express warranties in licensing agreements whereby the licensor warrants that the person not only has the right to lease or title to the licensed property, but that licensed use (or acquisition) of such property by the licensee (or purchaser) will not result in liability as the result of neighboring rights that any third (noncontracting) party may have. In addition, licensees often require an indemnification clause in the agreement whereby the licensor agrees to fully compensate the licensee as a result of liability to third parties.

Moral Rights

In many countries, under the Berne Convention, and to some extent in the United States, but only with respect to visual artists, there is a distinctive category of rights known as "moral rights" or *le droit moral*. This bundle of rights varies by legal jurisdiction, but can generally be enumerated:

1. Attribution or paternity (including the rights to be identified as the author, free from false attribution, and to publish anonymously or pseudonymously);
2. Integrity (to prevent derogatory substantive changes to the work);
3. Disclosure (or nondisclosure), reconsideration, and withdrawal (from circulation); and
4. Association (or disassociation of the work from products or institutions distasteful to the author or artist).[7]

In many jurisdictions, moral rights are noneconomic rights. Whether or not such rights in property can be alienated, waived, or can survive their authors and creators depends upon the law of the jurisdiction being applied. The Berne Convention recognizes rights of attribution and integrity, but it leaves it up to signatory members how to protect such rights. Furthermore, the convention does not require such rights to be inalienable, "unwaivable," or to survive the death of the author or creator.[8] Under the convention, foreign authors and artists enjoy the same rights as native citizens in nations adhering to the convention.

Under the U.S. Visual Artists Rights Acts of 1990, now 17 USC § 106A, moral rights are addressed with respect to "visual art," but only with respect to rights of attribution and integrity. In addition to U.S. federal law, several states have adopted moral rights, but to the extent such rights concern the attribution and integrity rights of visual artists, state law is preempted by the federal statute.[9]

France and Germany each represent yet two different conceptions of moral rights (in addition to the U.S. viewpoint). In France, moral rights are separate from economic rights, and consequently, cannot be alienated, and have no set term.[10] In Germany, the duality of rights (economic and moral) is not recognized. Rather the approach is to prohibit the complete assignment or transfer of rights, and the term of the rights is set by statute.[11]

The impact of moral rights on licensing agreements, to some extent, depends upon whether such rights may be waived, assigned, or limited under applicable law. Regardless of the validity of such limitations, however, licensees seek warranties that the licensor has not infringed upon any third party's rights and that the intended use per the agreement will not infringe upon such rights. In addition, the licensor may seek similar assurances that the licensee will not infringe upon any third party's moral rights (e.g., by removing attribution information, etc.). Per an indemnification clause, each party may also seek compensation for any liability resulting from infringements by the other.

E-Rights

With the development of the Internet and other information technologies, some have questioned whether "e-rights" constituted a new class of rights. While the U. S. Supreme Court decision in *New York Times v. Tasini* found that e-rights (in that case rights to republish the work of freelance journalists in a searchable database) do not automatically vest with print publishers, a closer reading reveals the real issue decided by the Court. That issue was whether, in that instance, the electronic database constituted a revision of the earlier collective, print work (which would favor the publisher, as an exception to infringement for "collective works" under 17 USC § 201 (c)), or a new work (which would favor the freelance journalists). Under 17 USC § 201(c), publishers of "collective works" acquire the right to reproduce and distribute a "particular collective work, any revision of that collective work, and any later collective work in the same series." The Supreme Court found that the database, which included many collective works (and not just a digital version of the original collective work), and provided access to each freelance article individually and separately, was indeed a new work.[12] Thus, under *Tasini*, the issue is not whether e-rights are distinctive, but whether a database is considered a "revision," or falls within another exception for publishers of previous collective works under 17 USC § 201(c).

The Second, Ninth, and Eleventh Circuits have followed *Tasini*'s lead in utilizing traditional copyright analysis to determine rights in e-content. For example, in

Faulkner v. National Geographic Enterprises, Inc.,[13] plaintiff authors sued National Geographic when it published a compilation of all previous issues in CD-ROM format, through which the original content appeared in its original context, albeit in a different medium. Like the *Tasini* court, the Second Circuit focused on whether the CD-ROM constituted a compilation, or a revision of a compilation, within the meaning of § 201(c) of the Copyright Act. Because the CD-ROM presented the "underlying works ... in the same context as they were presented ... in the original versions," which had not been the case in *Tasini*, the Second Circuit held that the CD-ROM was a "privileged revision" ([13] at 38). In similar litigation also involving National Geographic, the Eleventh Circuit very recently reached the same result using a § 201(c) analysis.[14] The Ninth Circuit looked to §§ 101 and 106 of the Copyright Code in *Perfect 10 v. Amazon.com*, which involved slightly different, but similar, issues arising out of thumbnail images and redirected access to copyrighted images through Google's Image Search feature.[15] Using traditional analysis, the court found that thumbnail images were "fair use." Thus, these post-*Tasini* courts have not treated e-rights as separate or distinct, but have continued to apply traditional copyright analysis.

E-rights, to the extent that they represent rights in media created by new technologies, serve as a reminder of the importance of carefully identifying (with the assistance of competent legal counsel) what rights are subject to a licensing or assignment agreement. Careful attention needs to be given to new and unforeseen media that may result from new technologies. It follows that the greater the breadth of rights being licensed or assigned, the greater the compensation that may be expected. To assure the rights are being discretely bargained for, and thus do not include non-enumerated rights, each right or use should be identified with corresponding consideration, and a statement as to who holds the unnamed rights (including rights in any new media) should be included ([7] at 103–104).

APPLICATION OF COMMERCIAL LAW

In addition to law governing the creation of intellectual property rights (such as copyright), licensing transactions are governed by commercial law (i.e., law governing contracts). Other law may apply as well, such as consumer protection statutes, labor relations codes, professional codes of conduct, bankruptcy and debtor–creditor law, and trade law. Because it is generally in the interest of commercial transactions to promote predictability and uniformity, uniform and model commercial codes are important as sources for law governing licensing transactions.

Digital–Disaster

What Law Applies

In the United States, state law largely governs contract and commercial law through a series of uniform acts known as the Uniform Commercial Code (UCC), promulgated by the National Conference of Commissioners of Uniform State Laws (NCCUSL). For transactions involving "computer information," a special uniform or model act was prepared in 1999, known as the Uniform Computer Information Transactions Act (UCITA). Amendments to UCITA were introduced and considered in 2000 and 2001; in 2002, NCCUSL approved the final revisions and amendments to UCITA and recommended it for enactment in all the states.[16] As of summer 2007, only Maryland and Virginia have adopted the act.[17] UCITA is controversial, and Iowa, North Carolina, West Virginia, Idaho, Vermont, and New York have passed or introduced legislation refusing to apply UCITA to contracts with their citizens.[18] In addition, a committee of the ABA has recommended that UCITA be rewritten.[19] In spite of UCITA's widespread rejection, given the need for a uniform law and the impact of the UCC, not only in the United States, but also on commercial codes throughout the world, UCITA (or its progeny) may yet become an important source for the construction and interpretation of digital licensing agreements throughout the world. If nothing else, UCITA represents an important effort to address the multitude of issues pertaining to content licensing and computer information transactions.

To the extent that a U.S. state has not adopted UCITA, then often UCC Article 2 applies. In varying degrees, state courts in Connecticut, Kansas, Massachusetts, Georgia (applying Michigan law), Nebraska, New York, and Tennessee have applied UCC Article 2 to computer software licenses. Likewise, federal courts in California, Florida, New Hampshire, New Jersey, and Pennsylvania have interpreted the laws of their respective states to apply UCC Article 2, and federal courts in Michigan and Kansas have applied Illinois and Wisconsin UCC law, respectively.[20] Because many software licenses involve the licensing of both goods (the software product) and services (technical, customer support, and client-specific programming), many courts weigh whether the services or the goods predominate.[21] The question of whether software has been designed as a service (to which UCC Article 2 has been found not to apply)[22] or whether it is a product customized for a particular user or includes installation and other services (to which the UCC has been applied)[23] is one that requires careful weighing of all the pertinent facts. In addition to UCC Article 2, Article 2A, governing leases, has been adopted in 49 states and the District of Columbia. The sole state yet to adopt Article 2A is Louisiana, which has also declined to adopt Article 2.[24] Because of the similarity of leases to licenses in terms of transfers of rights or use and possession, but not ownership, one may speculate that UCC Article 2A will become the dominant law governing content licensing agreements (assuming UCITA is not widely adopted).

In August of 2002, proposals to amend Articles 2 and 2A of the UCC to exclude "information" from the definition of "goods" were submitted to the NCCUSL.[25] Such a definition of "goods" would mean that neither Article 2 nor 2A would apply to most information transactions. Somewhat surprisingly given the historical resistance of UCC Article 2 to amendment, the proposed changes were adopted in 2003. Currently, in defining "goods," Articles 2 and 2A both specify that "[t]he term does not include information."[26] The Official Comment to Article 2 acknowledges, however, that transactions often include both goods *and* information, and that it will ultimately be up to courts to determine whether, and to what extent, Article 2 should apply.[27] As of summer 2007, Oklahoma is the only state that has incorporated this change into its commercial code.[28]

At present there is no treaty or convention expressly addressing computer information transactions in the same manner as UCITA. The European Union's EC Legal Advisory Board has expressed considerable hesitation and reluctance to fashion their own law after UCITA. Principally, concern has been expressed over whether UCITA, even if adopted, will be done so on a uniform basis because of some of its controversial provisions and approach: acceptance of click-wrap agreements (via electronic agents), choice of law, focus on software (rather than other forms of intellectual property), and the acceptance of denial of access and electronic self-help as remedies for breach.[29]

The UNCITRAL Model Law on Electronic Commerce addresses admissibility of electronic documents, electronic signatures, and "data messages" pertaining to the sale of goods, but not on the licensing of copyright. Another law that may apply is the Convention on Contracts for the International Sale of Goods (CCISG) (however, unlike the UCC, the convention does not apply to "goods purchased for consumer purposes" meaning for "personal, family, or household use").[30] In addition, the European Directive on Unfair Terms in Consumer Contracts,[31] the European Data Directive,[32] and the European Directive on Legal Protection of Databases may also apply.[33]

Writing Requirement and Requirements of Formation

Under UCITA § 201, the licensing of digital rights for transactions involving payment of $5000 or more generally requires written agreement. With respect to transfers in ownership, U.S. federal copyright law under 17 USC § 204(a) requires written contracts. UCITA § 201 provides for exceptions to the written requirement, which exceptions are common to commercial contract law. Generally, no writing is needed when

1. The contract term is one year or less;
2. Performance has been tendered and accepted;
3. Such agreement has been admitted under oath;
4. Written confirmation of a contract is received between merchants and no objection is made within a reasonable time.

In addition to the requirement that certain contracts be in writing, there are other requirements to the formation of a valid license agreement:

1. Parties intent and basis for remedy;[34]
2. Agreement as to material terms;[35]
3. When applicable, a valid offer and acceptance.[36]

Official Comment 5 of UCITA § 202 clarifies that if there is disagreement as to the "scope" of the license, there is no contract.

Because of the utilization of "shrink-wrap" and "click-wrap" agreements" (i.e., agreements that are accepted by clicking "yes" on prompted display of a license agreement as part of the loading or use of software or a computer service), UCITA devotes considerable attention to the use of "electronic agents" to manifest acceptance of an agreement. Sections 107, 112, 207, and 208, recognize shrink- or click-wrap agreements. Click-wrap agreements are recognized through electronic agents, which are defined under § 102(a)(27) as "a computer program, or electronic or other automated means, used independently to initiate an action, or to respond to electronic messages or performances, on the person's behalf without review or action by an individual at the time of the action or response to the message or performance." In other words, it is possible to manifest assent or acceptance of an agreement through automated means without written signature. An example of acceptance by electronic agent is found in Official Comment 4 of UCITA § 206: "Officer dials the telephone information system using the company credit card. A computerized voice states: 'If you would like us to dial your number, press "1"; there will be an additional charge of $1.00. . . .'"

Shrink-wrap or click-wrap agreements are permitted under UCITA §§ 112, 113, 208, and 209 under the following conditions:

1. The parties had reason to know at the outset that terms would be proposed for later agreement.
2. There is an opportunity to review the terms before assent is given (this may be after payment is tendered).
3. There will be assent involving acts or inaction taken with reason to know that it will create an inference of assent.
4. If the party does not assent, it has a right to a return and refund of any price paid, which right is cost free in a mass-market case.

5. In a mass-market case, the terms are produced and assented to at or before the time of initial use of the software.

Notwithstanding the validity of shrink-wrap and click-wrap agreements or acceptance by electronic agents, UCITA § 206(a) does grant courts discretion to fashion a remedy where the acceptance resulted from "fraud, electronic mistake, or the like."

Some state consumer protection statutes may differ from UCITA in terms of their signature or record-keeping requirements. UCITA does not alter these requirements, but rather provides states the latitude to specify which such statutes are to prevail over UCITA provisions in case of a conflict.[37] State consumer laws enjoy special status (for preempting terms of licensing agreements) under UCITA.

Other laws may also recognize shrink- or click-wrap agreements. While UCC § 2-204(1) provides that "a contract for sale of goods may be made in any manner sufficient to show agreement, including... conduct by both parties which recognizes the existence of such a contract...," U.S. courts are divided as to whether shrink-wrap agreements are enforceable.[38] UCC § 2A-204(1), governing leases, contains an almost identical provision to Article 2. The CCISG permits electronic agreements (without a writing) unless one of the contracting states specifically mandates a writing requirement by excluding the applicable provision of the convention.[39]

Finally, although yet to be ratified by any country, the Hague Convention for Choice of Court Agreements (CCCA), provides a liberal standard of contract formation: "by any ... means of communication which renders information accessible so as to be usable for subsequent reference."[40] Under this standard, almost any "click-" or "shrink-wrap agreement" concluded pursuant to the law of a signatory nation would be enforceable.[41] However, the CCCA exempts contracts entered into for personal or household purposes ([41] at Art. 2(1)).

Enforceability of Contractual Terms against a Fundamental Public Policy or Conflicting with Other Law

The Eighth, Ninth, and Federal circuits have recently looked at the enforceability of "no reverse engineering" clauses included in shrink-wrap or click-wrap agreements. Faced with claims that such terms violate public policy in that they prohibit fair use, courts have generally held that those who agree to such license terms are bound by them.[42] Courts have also rejected the argument that "no reverse engineering" clauses are preempted by the Copyright Act, finding that the mutual assent and consideration required by a contract claim provide an "extra element" that makes the right asserted qualitatively different from the rights protected under the Copyright Act.[43] Absent a license term that prohibits it, however, the Ninth Circuit has held that reverse engineering constitutes fair use, privileged under § 107, when "there is good reason for studying or examining the unprotected aspects of a copyrighted computer program."[44]

Under UCITA, a license agreement (or other contract) in which any term "violates a fundamental public policy" may result in the court finding that the contract is unenforceable or limiting enforcement to the remainder of the contract.[45] In Official Comment 3 to UCITA § 105, a "shrink-wrap license" prohibiting the licensee from ever criticizing the software is seen as problematic. On the other hand it is expressly noted that such a provision might be accepted in a negotiated license where the license pertained to software in the early stages of development, which had not been released to the general market-place.[46] In addition, courts may refuse to enforce or limit the enforcement of contracts or terms that are unconscionable (generally, terms that are very "one-sided").[47]

Besides considering public policy, UCITA provides for the preemption of federal law and state consumer protection statutes.[48] Other state law does not preempt private license agreements (unless explicitly considered by the state when it enacts UCITA). This is important because copyright and other rights contained in state law, which may be broader than federal copyright law, consequently do not preempt contractual agreements under UCITA.

Of particular concern is whether licensors of digital content can extend their rights that would otherwise be limited with respect to applicable federal copyright law (state law, except for consumer law, is granted a lesser standing to preempt terms of the license agreement under UCITA § 105). The act attempts to balance a fundamental policy of contract law to enforce contractual agreements with "public interest in assuring that information in the public domain is free for all to use from the public domain and in providing access to information for public purposes such as education, research, and fair comment."[49] Having said this, there is no question that UCITA fundamentally advocates the enforceability of license agreements. "[I]t is clear that limitations on the information property rights of owners that may exist in a copyright regime, where rights are good against third parties, may be inappropriate in a contractual setting where the courts should be reluctant to set aside terms of a contract."[50] Indeed, courts are particularly reluctant to set aside negotiated (as opposed to "mass-market," "shrink-" or "clip-wrap") agreements.[51]

With respect to "mass-market" transactions, Official Comment 3 of UCITA § 105 suggests that license terms prohibiting the making of multiple copies, use of information for commercial purposes, limiting the number of authorized users, or modification of the software or content are generally enforceable.[52] However, terms in a "mass-market" agreement that "prohibit persons from observing the visible operations or visible characteristics of software and using the observations to develop noninfringing commercial products, that prohibit quotation of limited material for purposes of education or criticism, or that preclude a nonprofit library licensee from making an archival (backup) copy would ordinarily be invalid in the absence of a showing of significant commercial need."[53] Additional provisions are suggested for the circumvention of technical measures protecting copyright for purposes of checking security and to provide for the "interoperability of computer programs." Finally, "to the extent that Congress has established policies on fair use, those can be taken into consideration under [UCITA § 105]."[54] Consequently, policy articulated in the legislative history of the fair use provisions of 17 USC § 107 may have bearing on the enforceability of terms in license agreements that otherwise restrict the application of "fair use."

Like UCITA, UCC Article 2 has a section addressing "unconscionable contracts."[55] It does not, however, have a specific section addressing conflict with fundamental public policies or consumer protection statutes. However, the UCC does not necessarily restrict claims of aggrieved parties to breach of contract under the UCC. For example, it is possible to bring a claim for breach of warranty under the UCC in the same action as claims based upon violation of a consumer protection statute provided that the consumer protection claim is not simply a restatement of the breach of warranty claim.[56] Likewise, UCC Article 2A, governing leasing, and now adopted in 49 states, addresses consumer protection statutes but does not conflict with "fundamental public policy."[57] Article 2A also addresses "unconscionable" leases and terms.[58] The CCISG, unless otherwise noted therein, expressly does not address the "validity of the contract or any of its provisions...."[59] Consequently, enforceability of terms that may be in violation of a fundamental public policy or unconscionable is a matter to be determined under national or local law pursuant to choice of law rules.

Choice of Law and Forum

Choice of law and forum matter because the outcome of a particular dispute may rest on the discrepancies of the law between jurisdictions. Under UCITA § 109, the law governing any agreement is generally the law selected by the parties per the agreement. However, this does not apply to "consumer contracts" (i.e., between a licensed merchant and consumer) to the extent that this would affect the application of any state law (such as consumer law) pursuant to choice of law rules under UCITA (assuming the absence of agreement as to choice of law).

If the parties have not specified what law applies by agreement, then the law of the licensor's jurisdiction applies if the contract called for electronic delivery of the product or information, and the law of the licensee's jurisdiction applies if a delivery was designated by a tangible medium. In any other instance, the law of the jurisdiction with the "most significant relationship to the transaction applies." As a final caveat, for an international transaction in which choice of law has not been determined per the agreement, the law of a jurisdiction outside the United States only applies if a party located in the United States would have "substantially similar protections and rights" to those found under UCITA. As indicated in Official Comment 5, this does not mean "merely that the foreign law is different," but rather the "differences must be substantial and adverse." Under UCITA § 110, choice of forum, the place where litigation of a dispute will take place, is also left up to the parties unless the choice is "unreasonable and unjust." Official Comment 3 indicates:

> "Terms may be unreasonable in that they have no commercial purpose or justification … and their impact may be unjust if the term unfairly harms the other party. … On the other hand, an agreed choice of forum based on a valid commercial purpose is not invalid simply because it adversely affects one party, even if bargaining power was unequal."

In essences valid commercial purposes, such as a party's location, will justify choice of a particular forum.

For those states that do not adopt NCCUSL's recently changed definition of "goods," which now excludes "information" (see [25] and accompanying text), UCC Article 2 applies Article 1, § 1-301, to determine choice of law for digital content agreements. Like UCITA, the UCC distinguishes consumer from other types of transactions, but otherwise gives deference to the choice of the parties regardless of whether the jurisdiction selected has a "reasonable relation" to the transaction. However, for consumer transactions, the selected jurisdiction must bear a "reasonable relation" to the transaction, and may not deprive a consumer of any protection under their applicable consumer protection law. Regardless of whether the transaction is a consumer transaction, per § 1-301, a choice of law clause is "not effective to the extent that application of the law of the State or country designated would be contrary to a fundamental policy of the State or country" whose law would otherwise apply.

In the absence of UCITA, and once again assuming that "information" is not excluded from the definition of "goods," UCC Article 2A may become the preferred uniform law for interpreting content licenses. Under Article 2A, choice of law and forum clauses for consumer leases are limited:

1. If the law chosen by the parties to a consumer lease is that of a jurisdiction other than a jurisdiction in which the lessee resides at the time the lease agreement becomes enforceable or within 30 days thereafter or in which the goods are to be used, the choice is not enforceable.

2. If the judicial forum chosen by the parties to a consumer lease is a forum that would not otherwise have jurisdiction over the lessee, the choice is not enforceable.[60]

Consequently, under either UCC Article 2 or 2A, applicable consumer law of the party who is a consumer will generally always apply. Indeed, under Article 2A, the law of the party who is a consumer will always apply.

Although only applying to commercial (and not consumer) transactions, the CCISG, applies if both of the parties (which must be in different countries) are located in contracting states (to the CCISG), or if the law of a contracting state applies through choice of law rules.[61] Having said this, parties may, per the agreement, elect out of the application of the convention.[62] Since the convention neither applies to consumer transactions nor addresses the validity or enforceability of contractual terms,[63] choice of law rules of the jurisdiction where the dispute is adjudicated have to be applied for many issues relating to international transactions. For U.S. courts, choice of law questions are increasingly decided based upon "significant relationship" of the jurisdiction to the transaction (even if the UCC is not considered). Certain factual contacts are weighed to determine if such a relationship exists:

- The place of contracting;
- The place of negotiation of the contract;
- The place of performance;
- The location of the subject matter of the contract; and
- The domicile, residence, nationality, place of incorporation, and place of business of the parties.[64]

In addition several policy considerations are weighed:

- Maintenance of interstate and international order;
- Relevant policies and government interests of the forum;
- Relevant policies of other interested states;
- Relevant interests of those states in the determination of the particular issue;
- Protection of justified expectations (of the parties);
- Basic policies underlying the particular field of law;
- Certainty, predictability and uniformity of result;
- Simplification of the judicial task; and
- Application of the better rule of law.[65]

For EU countries, the issue of choice of law is governed by the Convention on the Law Applicable to Contract Obligations (adopted in 1960), which generally honors the choice of the contracting parties.[66] If no choice has been made by the parties, the law of the country "most closely connected" which usually defaults to the domicile or place of business of the party "who is to effect the performance" (i.e., deliver the licensed product) ([66] at Art. 4). Once again, certain exceptions are made for consumer contracts (defined as pertaining to goods or services outside of the buyer's profession ([66] at Art. 5).

Warranties

Warranties are additional promises made by the parties, usually pertaining to ownership of/or rights to the property being licensed, capacity to contract, outstanding claims for infringement, etc. Warranties may be specified by contract, but there are always certain warranties addressed in the applicable governing law on contracts. Under UCITA § 401(a), a licensor, who is "a merchant regularly dealing in information of the kind warrants that the information will be delivered free of the rightful claim of any third person by way of infringement or misappropriation...." For other licensors (although also applying to merchants who deal in information), the warranty is limited: "no person holds a rightful claim to, or interest in, the information which arose from an act or omission of the licensor, other than a claim by way of infringement or misappropriation, which will interfere with the licensee's enjoyment of its interest... ."[67] Additional warranties (that the information is not in the public domain and that no other party shares in rights to the information) are made in the event that an exclusive license is granted.[68] Warranties are not made with respect to the infringement of rights pertaining to collective administration (e.g., rights obtained through collective bargaining), or with respect to compulsory rights (certain limitations on copyright under U.S. law).[69] Neither do UCITA's § 401 warranties apply to informational rights arising under foreign law (unless the contract expressly provides for warranties under the laws of other countries *and* the rights originate in countries "under a treaty or international convention to which the country and the United States are signatories").[70]

The warranties set forth in UCITA § 401 can be waived or modified by agreement, but only if by "specific language or by circumstances that give the licensee reason to know that the licensor does not warrant that competing claims do not exist or that the licensor purports to grant only the rights it may have."[71] In an electronic or automated transaction, the language has to be "conspicuous."[72] Merchants have the option of "quitclaiming" rights without any warranty.[73]

UCITA also applies for express warranties (additional promises made by the licensor)[74] and, with respect to software, an implied warranty of merchantability (i.e., "fit for the ordinary purpose for which programs of that description are used").[75]

For content licensing agreements, a key issue is always whether there is a warranty as to the accuracy of information. UCITA § 404 distinguishes between licensors who are merchants "in a special relationship of reliance with a licensee," who collect and compile previously non-published information, and other kinds of licensors (editors or "conduits" for informational content). Essentially, the former are required to exercise "reasonable care." In determining whether a "special relationship of reliance" exists, several requirements are articulated in the Official Comments to § 404, which comments attempt to capture doctrines already set forth in U.S. case law:

- Licensor possesses "unique or specialized expertise;"
- Licensor is in a "position of confidence and trust with the licensee such that reliance on the inaccurate information is justified;"
- Licensor is in the business of providing the type of information that is the subject of the transaction;
- Information is personally tailored to the needs of the licensee.[76]

In addition, to the UCITA warranties for accuracy, other duties may be imposed on professionals (lawyers, physicians, etc.) based upon the law of the respective jurisdictions of their practice. The exclusion from warranty under § 404(b)(1) is for "published informational content," which is "informational content made available to the public as a whole or to a range of subscribers on a standardized, not a personally tailored, basis."[77] The policy behind this exclusion is discussed on Official Comment 3. b. Regardless of UCITA or the UCC, claims brought against information and news services have been made under negligence rather than contractual warranty theory, and courts have found First Amendment reasons for not imposing liability.[78]

Published informational content is the subject matter of general commerce in ideas, political, economic, entertainment or the like, whose distribution engages fundamental public policy interests in supporting and not chilling this distribution by creating liability risks. This Act treats published informational content that is computer information analogously to print newspapers or books which are not exposed to contractual liability risks based on mere inaccuracy; treating the computer informational content differently would reject the wisdom of prior law. Creating greater liability risk in contract would place an undue burden on the free flow of information. Once again, UCITA attempts to capture existing law as defined in the courts.[79]

In addition to warranties concerning noninfringement, express warranties, and accuracy of information, UCITA also addresses implied warranties for compatibility with computer systems dependent upon whether the licensor "has reason to know any particular purpose for which the computer information is required...."[80]

Like UCITA, both UCC Articles 2 and 2A provide for warranties from infringement, express warranties and implied warranties of merchantability. Instead of providing for an implied warranty addressing system integration,

UCC Articles 2 and 2A each have an implied warranty for a "particular purpose."[81] However, there is a material difference with respect to UCC Articles 2 and 2A pertaining to warranties from infringement. Generally, Article 2 just warrants "rightful" title, and freedom from security interests, encumbrances, and liens.[82] Article 2A, pertaining to leases grants freedom from interference with enjoyment (otherwise known as "the warranty of quiet enjoyment") resulting from "a claim to or interest in the goods not attributable to the lessee's own act or omission..."[83] The distinction is that "quiet enjoyment" includes the right to *use* and possess property without infringing upon third parties, whereas good title only refers to infringement as a result of the transfer of ownership (e.g., a transfer of title to a car may legitimately transfer ownership without guaranteeing that the car may be driven on state roads). This is a clear instance in which UCC Article 2A favors licensees. One can imagine litigation over whether Article 2A should apply to a transaction because the licensee argues that a particular use of the licensed information is covered under § 2A-211's warranty of enjoyment. Like UCC Article 2, the CCISG requires transfer of good title (for intellectual property this warranty is limited to infringements of which the licensor knew or should have known),[84] but there is no reference to a warranty for quiet enjoyment.

Like UCC Article 2A, UCITA warrants the "enjoyment" of the licensee's interest from competing interests or claims "which arose from an act or omission of the licensor...."[85] Merchants who "regularly deal[] in information" have an unrestricted warranty of delivery that is free of third party claims for infringement or misappropriation (i.e., the infringement does not have to result from acts or omissions of the licensor). However, this higher standard for certain merchants does not encompass warranties of quiet enjoyment (which, for such merchants, still requires acts or omissions on their part).[86]

However, since UCITA does not limit the warranty on merchants who "regularly deal[] in information" to their infringements resulting from *their own acts and omissions*, it provides better protection in some instances for licensees than Article 2A, but without explicit reference to enjoyment. Consequently, whether UCITA, the CCISG, UCC Article 2, or UCC Article 2A applies can have significant impact on the outcome of a dispute.

To illustrate this difference, imagine that a business subscribes to a database of fine art images from a commercial vendor who regularly sells databases of images from art museums and galleries. The license agreement says nothing about permissible uses of the images, and the initial subscription or access to images does not constitute infringement. The subscribing business uses an image as a background for the Web pages of its Web site. The owner of the image, a museum, informs the subscribing business that it is infringing on the museum's rights by using the image on its Web site. Apparently, the museum had licensed the images to the database vendor for educational purposes only, and the vendor was expressly obligated under its agreement with the museum to place a statement as to the educational limitation in any sublicense agreements, such as the one with the business (but failed to do so). The subscribing business to the database seeks redress from the database vendor for breach of implied warranty. Under UCITA § 401(b) and UCC § 2A-211(a), the database vendor may be held in breach of his warranty for quiet enjoyment. However, under both UCC § 2-312 and the CCISG Article 42, the database vendor is only in breach if it does not have good title, and it is unclear in this instance whether the database vendor's failure to notify the subscribing business of any limitations for "educational purpose" constitutes failure of good title, especially since there are other permissible uses for the database. Since this section of UCC Article 2 has been applied to software,[87] a legitimate issue is raised as to the potential for disparate treatment under the different uniform laws. This disparity may lead to "forum shopping" and greater use of contractual provisions that select the applicable law.

Remedies—Electronic Self-Help and Denial of Access

Although UCITA generally avoids functioning as a consumer protection statute, it does, in its final draft, completely ban the licensor's use of electronic disabling devices or "self-help."[88] Termination of access for access contracts is permissible upon "material breach" of the agreement or "if the agreement so provides" without any other limitation under UCITA.[89] Other remedies are available under UCITA including damages, cancellation, withholding payments, discontinuing access (for access contracts), repossession of all copies of the licensed information, etc.[90]

UCITA's use of electronic "self-help" (in early drafts where it was permitted) is really a reflection of UCC Article 9, pertaining to secured transactions, specifically the repossession of collateral.[91] However, no analogous provision exists in UCC Article 2 or 2A or the CCISG. The propriety of such action is uncertain under case law. For example, a Minnesota case on the subject discusses claims (or counterclaims) against those invoking electronic deactivation of software; the court basically found that deactivation was appropriate because it comported with license terms to which the parties had agreed.[92] In another case (although unpublished), claims based upon breach of warranty and the Computer Fraud and Abuse Act (CFAA)[93] survived a summary judgment motion to dismiss.[94] Subsequent case law ruled that the CFAA applies not just to hackers but to computer manufacturers as well.[95] In yet another instance, a "drop dead" software device was found "void as a matter of public policy."[96]

Digital–Disaster

Without the blessing of a uniform law such as UCITA, utilization of electronic self-help remedies such software deactivation and "drop dead" devices may subject licensors to liability. Even with UCITA, a significant legal issue is raised as to whether federal statutes such as CFAA or state or federal consumer protection statutes are superseded by UCITA with respect to electronic self-help.

As a kind of self-help remedy, termination of access, as provided for under UCITA § 814, does not have the same stringent requirements for exercise as electronic measures embedded in software under UCITA § 816. However, even the exercise of this remedy may be problematic if it conflicts with federal statutes or state consumer law.[97] Nonetheless, the apparent greater latitude available for the termination of access remedy may propel vendors into exclusively providing content via online services.

CONCLUSION

Content licensing is a complex legal subject necessitating review of the applicable law both creating intellectual property rights and governing contractual agreements and licensing. In addition, consumer protection and other law may impact the transaction. Because of the nature of information transactions to involve a wide array of jurisdictions, choice of law has to be carefully considered with respect to international, foreign, and domestic (both state and federal) law. To add yet an additional layer of complexity, UCITA, a uniform law governing computer information transactions has evoked widespread opposition, and significant disharmony among jurisdictions. Nonetheless, UCC Articles 2 and 2A (and potentially, on a limited basis, the CCISG) may, on an increasing basis, fill some of the void left by UCITA. This is especially true of Article 2A, governing leases, assuming UCITA fails and that states decline to redefine their codifications of Article 2A to exclude information transactions.

Principal among the issues addressed by the various commercial codes and conventions are issues of formation, unenforceability, warranties, and available remedies in the event of breach. Particularly noteworthy (and worthy of scrutiny) are the attempts of such uniform laws to resolve issues surrounding shrink-wrap, click-wrap, mass-market transactions, and the validity of provisions conflicting with copyright law (including the interest of the public in "fair use"); other state and foreign intellectual property rights (which may be broader than, for instance, U.S. federal law); and state consumer laws. In addition, the enforceability and desirability of choice of law and forum provisions, the scope and validity of both implied and explicit warranties, and the potential for abuse and disruption potentially caused by remedies such as denial of access and electronic self-help through means such as disabling devices in software need to be resolved.

REFERENCES

1. U.S. *v.* Wise, 550 F.2d 1180, 1190 (9th Cir. 1977).
2. *Black's Law Dictionary* 651 (7th ed. 1999).
3. Nimmer, R.T. *1 Information Law*—§ 3.45 (available through WL Infolaw, database updated May 2007) (citing Directive on Legal Protection of Databases, 96/9/EC, O.J. 77 (March 27, 1996)).
4. Nimmer, M.B.; Nimmer, D. 2 *Nimmer on Copyright*, § 8C.04[A][1] (August 2004).
5. Cal. Civ. Code § 986 (West Supp. 2007).
6. 2 *Nimmer on Copyright,* Ref. [4], at § 8C.04[A][2] (August 2004).
7. Harris, L.E. *Digital Property: Currency of the 21st Century*; 1998; 127–129.
8. 3 *Nimmer on Copyright,* Ref. [4], at § 8D.01[B] (August 2004).
9. 3 *Nimmer on Copyright,* Ref. [4], at § 8D.01[B] (August 2004)., at § 8D. [02][A] and [B] (August 2004), and § 8D.06[F][1] (December 1999).
10. Geller, P.E.; Nimmer, M.B. 1 *International Copyright Law and Practice*; France § 1[3] (available through LexisNexis, database updated regularly).
11. 2 *International Copyright Law and Practice,* Ref. [10] at § 7[1] and [3] (available through LexisNexis, database updated regularly).
12. NY Times Co. v. Tasini., 533 U.S. 483, 121 S.Ct. 2381, 150 L. Ed. 2d 500 (2001).
13. 409 F.3d 26, *cert. den. sub nom.* Faulkner v. National Geographic Soc., 546 U.S. 1076 (2005).
14. Greenberg v. National Geographic Society, 533 F.3d 1244 (9th Cir. 2008), *cert. denied,* 129 S. Ct. 727 (2008) (freelance photographer sued over an electronic collection of past magazine issues in which plaintiff's copyrighted photographs had appeared).
15. 487 F.3d 701 (9th Cir. 2007).
16. The final version of UCITA may be viewed at http://www.law.upenn.edu/bll/archives/ulc/ucita/2002final.htm.
17. Md. Code Ann. Com. Law. § 22-101 (2000), Va. Code Ann. § 59.1-501.1 (2001).
18. Iowa Code § 554D.125 (2004), (transferred from § 554D.104 4. (2002) (act amended indicating intention to consider adoption of UCITA, see 2001 IA HF 2446), N. C. Gen. Stat. § 66-329 (2001), W. Va. Code § 55-8-15 (2001), Idaho Code Ann. § 29-116 (2007), Vermont Stat. Ann. Comm. and Trade, § 2463a (2004), A.B. 7902, 224th Sess. (NY 2001). Similar legislation has been introduced in Ohio and Washington. H.B. 287, 124th Gen. Assem., Reg. Sess. (OH 2001) and SB 6314, 57th Leg., 1st Reg. Sess. (WA 2002).
19. American Bar Association Working Group Report on the Uniform Computer Information Transactions Act ("UCITA") (2002), http://www.abanet.org/leadership/ucita.pdf.
20. Sand, S.J. *Validity, Construction, and Application of Computer Software Licensing Agreements*, 38 ALR 5th, 20–21 (1996 and Supp. 2007). See also Micro Data Base Sys. v. Dharma Sys., Inc., 148 F.3d 649, 654–55 (7th Cir. 1998)(applying New Hampshire law), NMP Corp. v. Parametric Tech. Corp., 958 F. Supp. 1536, 1542 (N.D. Okla. 1997)(applying Massachusetts law) and Systems

Design & Mgmt. Info, Inc. v. Vogel, 1991 U.S. Dist. LEXIS 10079, at *17-*20 (W.D. Mich. 1991)(applying Illinois law).

21. Micro Data Base Systems, Inc. v. Dharma Systems, Inc., 148 F. 3d 649, 654–655 (7th Cir. 1998), NPM Corp. v. Parametric Technology Corp., 958 F. Supp. 1536, 1542 (N.D. Okla. 1997), Colonial Life Ins. Co. v. Electronic Data Sys. Corp., 817 F. Supp. 235 (D.N.H. 1993), and Dahlmann v. Sulcus Hospitality Technologies, Corp., 63 F. Supp. 2d 772, 775 (E.D. Mich. 1999).

22. Micro-Managers, Inc. v. Gregory, 434 N.W. 2d 97 (Wis. Ct. App. 1988), State v. Lockheed Martin IMS, 2002 WL 99554 (Cal. Ct. App. 2002) (non-published, non-citable).

23. Micro Data Base Systems, Inc. v. Dharma Systems, Inc., 148 F. 3d 649, 654 (7th Cir. 1998) and RRX Industries, Inc. v. Lab-Con, Inc., 772 F. 2d 543, 546–547 (9th Cir. 1985).

24. Uniform Commercial Code Reporting Service, State UCC Variations, Thomson-West, Louisiana 1 (2007).

25. Draft for Approval Proposed Amendments to Uniform Commercial Code Article 2 Sales § 2-103(l) (July 26-August 2, 2002 annual meeting), at http://www.law.upenn.edu/bll/archives/ulc/ucc2/annual2002.htm; Draft for Approved Proposed Amendments to Uniform Commercial Code Article 2A Leases § 2A-103(o) (July 26–August 2, 2002 annual meeting), http://www.law.upenn.edu/bll/archives/ulc/ucc2a/annual2002.htm.

26. U.C.C. § § 2-103(1)(k) and 2A-103(1)(n) (2007).

27. U.C.C. § 2-103 cmt. 7.

28. Okla. Stat. Ann. tit. 12A, § 2-105(1)(West 2007), Okla. Stat. Ann. tit. 12A, § 2A-103(1)(h)(West 2007).

29. Legal Advisory Board, Directorate-General Information Society, European Commission, Agenda Brussels, 7–9, May 18, 2000, http://europa.eu.int/ISPO/legal/en/lab/000518/LAB180500-3.pdf.

30. 2 *Information Law,* Ref. [3], § 12.12 (citing Convention Article 2 (a))(available through Westlaw Infolaw, database updated May 2007).

31. Council Directive 93/13/EEC of 5 April 1993 on unfair terms in consumer contracts, 1993 O.J. (L95) 29–34; available online at http://eurlex.europa.eu.

32. Directive 95/46/EC of the European Parliament and of the Council of 24 October 1995 on the protection of individuals with regard to the processing of personal data and on the free movement of such data, 1995 O.J. (L 281) 31–50; available online at http://eur-lex.europa.eu.

33. Directive 96/9/EC of the European Council and of the Council of 11 March 1996 on the legal protection of databases, 1996 O.J. (L 77) 20–28; available online at http://eur-lex.europa.eu.

34. UCITA § 202(c) (amended 2002). All citations to UCITA herein are to the 2002 amendment. See Ref. [16].

35. UCITA § 202(d).

36. UCITA § 202 (a), § § 203-206.

37. UCITA § 105 cmt. 6.

38. ProCD, Inc. v. Zeidenberg, 86 F. 3d 1447 (7th Cir. 1996) (shrink wrap contract is enforceable under UCC), Hill v. Gateway 2000, Inc., 105 F. 3d 1147 (7th Cir. 1997) (followed ProCD), Klocek v. Gateway, Inc., 104 F. Supp. 2d 1332 (D. Kan. 2000) (declined to follow ProCD), Specht v. Netscape Communications Corp., 150, F. Supp. 2d 585 (S.D.N.Y. 2001) (declined to follow ProCd).

39. United Nations Convention on Contracts for the International Sale of Goods (hereinafter CCISG), April 11, 1980, S. Treaty Doc. No. 9, 98, 19 I.L.M. 668 (1980), Articles 11, 12, and 96, available at http://fletcher. tufts.edu/multi/texts/BH775.txt.

40. Hague Convention for Choice of Courts Agreements, concluded June 30, 2005, Art. 3(c)(ii) available at http://www.hcch.net/index_en.php (follow the "conventions" hyperlink; then follow "all conventions"; then follow "Convention of 30 June 2005 on Choice of Court Agreements").

41. Hague Convention, Ref. [43], Art. 8.

42. Davidson & Assoc. v. Jung, 334 F. Supp.2d 1164, 1180–81 (E.D. Mo. 2004), aff'd 422 F.3d 630 (8th Cir. 2005) (defendants waived their "fair use" right to reverse engineer by agreeing to the license terms); Bowers v. Baystate Tech., Inc., 320 F.3d 1317, 1325–1326 (Fed. Cir. 2003), cert. denied, 539 U.S. 928 (2003)(parties are free to contractually forego the limited ability to reverse engineer a software product under the exemptions of the Copyright Act).

43. Meridian Project Sys., Inc. v. Hardin Constr. Co., 426 F. Supp.2d 1101, 1109 (E.D. Cal. 2006)(to the extent that the license agreement prohibits reverse engineering, breach of contract claim is not preempted because the contract protects a qualitatively different right than those protected by the Copyright Act). See also *Information Law,* Ref. [3], at § 2:18, and 4 *Nimmer on Copyright,* Ref. [4], at § 13.05[D] [4] (August 2005).

44. Sega Enter., Ltd. v. Accolade, Inc., 977 F.2d 1510, 1520 (9th Cir. 1993). The Ninth Circuit has followed its own precedent in regards to reverse engineering cases where no license terms are involved. See Sony Computer Entm't, Inc. v. Connectix Corp., 203 F.3d 596 (9th Cir. 2000). In DSC Communications Corp. v. DGI Technologies, Inc., 898 F. Supp. 1183, 1189 (N.D. Tx. 1995), the Northern District of Texas followed *Sega* in holding that reverse engineering, when engaged in for purposes of studying unprotected aspects of a copyrighted program, constitutes fair use; as in *Sega,* no license terms prohibited reverse engineering.

45. UCITA § 105 (b).

46. UCITA § 105 cmt. 3.

47. UCITA § 111 (including cmt. 2).

48. UCITA § 105 (a) and (e).

49. UCITA § 105 cmt. 1.

50. UCITA § 105 cmt. 1.

51. Man O War Restaurants, Inc. v. Martin, 932 S.W. 2d 366 (Ky. 1996.). See also UCITA § 105 cmt. 3 ("Where parties have negotiated terms in their agreement, courts should be even more reluctant to set aside terms of the agreement.").

52. UCITA § 105 cmt. 3.

53. UCITA § 105 cmt. 3.

54. UCITA § 105 cmt. 3.

55. UCC § 2-302 (as amended 2003).

56. Winter Panel Corp. v. Reichhold Chemicals, Inc., 823 F. Supp. 963 (D. Mass. 1993).

57. UCC § 2A-104 (as amended 2003).

58. UCC § 2A-108 (as amended 2003).

59. CCISG, Ref. [39], Article 4a.

60. UCC § 2A-106 (as amended 2003).

61. CCSIG, Ref. [39], Article 1.

62. CCISG, Ref. [39], Art. 6.

63. CCISG, Ref. [39], Arts. 2(a) and 4(a).

64. *Restatement (Second) of Conflict of Laws* § 188(2) (1969) and 16 Am. Jur 2d § 87 (1998).

65. 16 *Am. Jur* 2d § 88 (1998).

66. Convention on the Law Applicable to Contract Obligations, June 19, 1980, Art. 3, available at http://fletcher.tufts.edu/multi/texts/BH784.txt.

67. UCITA § 401(b)(1).

68. UCITA § 401(b)(2) and cmt. 4.

69. UCITA § 401(c)(1).

70. UCITA § 401(c)(2).

71. UCITA § 401(d).

72. UCITA § 401(d).

73. UCITA § 401(e).

74. UCITA § 402.

75. UCITA § 403 and cmt. 3(a).

76. UCITA § 404, cmt. 3(a)(citing *Restatement (Second)* of Torts § 552 (1965), Murphy v. Kuhn, 90 N.Y. 2d 266, 682 N.E. 2d 972 (N.Y. 1997), A.T. Kearney v. IBM, 73 F. 3d 238 (9th Cir. 1997), and Picker International, Inc. v. Mayo Foundation, 6 F. Supp. 2d 685 (N.D. Ohio 1998)).

77. UCITA § 404 cmt. 3(b) (citing Cubby, Inc. v. CompuServe, Inc., 3 CCH Computer Cases 46,547 (S.D.N.Y. 1991), Daniel v. Dow Jones & Co., Inc., 520 N.Y.S. 2d 334 (N.Y. City Ct. 1987), and Great Central Insurance Co. v. Insurance Services Office, Inc., 74 F. 3d 778 (7th Cir. 1997)). See also Ginsberg v. Agora, Inc. 915 F.Supp. 733 (D.Md. 1995), Gutter v. Dow Jones, Inc. 490 N.E. 2d 898 (S.Ct. Ohio 1986).

78. See *Daniel*, 520 N.Y.S. 2d 334, *Ginsberg*, 915 F.Supp. 733, and *Gutter*, 490 N.E. 2d 898. However, for instance where liability was found based upon futures trading regulations, see R&W Technical Services Ltd. v. Commodity Futures Trading Commission, 205 F.3d 165 (5th Cir. 2000).

79. UCITA § 404 cmt. 3(b)(citing *Cubby*, 3 CCH Computer Cases 46,547 (S.D.N.Y. 1991), Daniel, 520 N.Y.S. 2d 334, and *Great Central Insurance Co.*, 74 F. 3d 778).

80. UCITA § 405.

81. *Compare* UCC § 2-315 with § 2A-213.

82. UCC § 2-312 (1).

83. UCC § 2A-211 (as amended 2003 and 2005).

84. CCISG, Ref. [39], Art. 42.

85. UCITA § 401(b) and (b)(1).

86. UCITA § 401(a) and (b).

87. Camara v. Hill, 596 A. 2d 349, 157 Vt. 156 (Vt. 1991).

88. UCITA § 816(b).

89. UCITA § 814.

90. UCITA §, § 802, 808, 809, 810, 814, and 815.

91. UCC § 9-609.

92. American Computer Trust Leasing v. Jack Farrell Implement Co., 763 F. Supp. 1473 (D. Minn. 1991), *aff'd* American Computer Trust Leasing v. Boerboom Intern., Inc., 967 F. 2d 1208 (8th Cir. 1992) (this case presented many claims, which unsuccessfully incorporated a variety of legal theories including fraud, RICO conspiracy, extortion, consumer debt protection statutes, trespass, nuisance, violations of the federal wiretapping statute, violations of the Electronic Communications Decency Act, breach of contract, fraud, and theft).

93. 18 U.S.C. § 1030 (2002).

94. North Tex. Preventive Imaging v. Eisenberg, 1996 U.S. Dist. LEXIS 19990 (C.D. Cal. 1996).

95. Shaw v. Toshiba Am. Info. Sys., 91 F. Supp. 2d 926 (E.D. Tex. 1999). See also In re AOL, Inc. Version 5.0 Software Litig., 168 F. Supp. 2d 1359 (S.D. Fl. 2001).

96. Franks & Sons v. Information Solutions, 1988 U.S. Dist. LEXIS 18646 (N.D. Okla.) (order clarified in 1988 U.S. Dist. LEXIS 19356 (N. D. Okla)).

97. UCITA § 105(a) and (c).

Digital Divide and Inclusion

Mark Warschauer
School of Education, University of California, Irvine, CA, U.S.A.

Melissa Niiya
Portland Public Schools, Portland, Oregon, U.S.A.

Abstract

The term "digital divide" is used to describe unequal access to computers, the Internet, and online information, whether among individuals, communities, or countries. Originally targeted at issues of physical access, such as whether people had a computer or Internet account at home, the concept is increasingly used to incorporate related issues, such as whether people have the skills and knowledge required to make effective use of digital media and information. A variety of initiatives have been taken within the United States and internationally to try to combat the digital divide.

INTRODUCTION

The term "digital divide" refers to the gap between those with access to computers, the Internet, and online information and those who lack such access. The digital divide has been discussed in relation to income group, race, ethnicity, age, gender, and language status among people within a community or country. Used internationally, it is often used to refer to gaps between countries that overall have greater access to information and communication technology (ICT) and countries with lesser access.

The term was originally used to refer to inequality in physical access, as represented by ownership of a home computer or having broadband Internet access. Soon thereafter, the term began to include other factors that enabled them to effectively use new technology, such as skills, knowledge, and social support.

This article will introduce the origin of the term in the 1990s and examine how the concept has evolved since it first emerged. It will review key facts about inequality in access to ICT, both within the United States and internationally, and discuss important individuals, organizations, and initiatives that have responded to this inequality.

HISTORICAL CONTEXT

Though the online communication dates back to the late 1960s, the Internet first became widely popular following the introduction of World Wide Web browsers in the 1990s. With this growing popularity, both officials and activists became increasingly concerned about the consequences of unequal access to ICT. In the mid-1990s, journalists and government officials in the United States began to describe this unequal access as a "digital divide." *New York Times* writer Gary Andrew Poole used the term in several articles in late 1995 and early 1996,[1] and then both Al Gore and Bill Clinton used it in a speech in Knoxville, Tennessee.[2] That same year, sociologist Manuel Castells published the first of three volumes on the information age.[3] Castells' three-volume work laid out the most compelling analysis to date of the critical role of information technology access and use in generating wealth, power, and knowledge in the current era.

Beginning in the mid-1990s, the term was used regularly by Clinton administration officials, especially by Larry Irving, Assistant Secretary of Commerce and Director of the National Telecommunications and Information Administration (NTIA). The NTIA published national studies in 1995, 1998, 1999, 2000, 2002, 2004, 2007, 2010, 2011, 2013, and 2014 that attempted to measure technological inequality in the thorough analysis of U.S. census data on computer ownership and Internet access as differentiated by race/ethnicity, income, gender, employment status, disability status, and urban/rural location.[4] These research efforts were backed by policy initiatives, including the E-Rate program, which has provided funding to assist Internet connectivity in schools and libraries since 1996, the Federal Community Technology Centers Program, which provided substantial funding for local technology training and access in fiscal years 2000 and 2001, and later the National Broadband Plan, which aimed to use stimulus funds to bring broadband connectivity and technology education to underserved populations, particularly in rural areas in 2009–2010.

Just as steps were being taken to address the digital divide in the United States, international leaders and organizations became increasingly concerned about a global digital divide between rich and poor countries. The Group of 8 (G8) formed a Digital Opportunity Task Force in 2000 that brought together teams from government, the private sector, and nonprofit organizations in developed

Encyclopedia of Library and Information Sciences, Fourth Edition DOI: 10.1081/E-ELIS4-140000153

1279

Digital–Disaster

and developing countries to identify ways to spread the benefits of the digital revolution more broadly.[5] The following year, the United Nations Information and Communication Technologies Task Force was launched with a similar mission.[6] The U.N. task force, still in existence today, organizes awareness programs, develops stakeholder networks, assists countries and regional groups with strategy development, supports broadened international participation in policy development, works to improve Internet connectivity around the world, and promotes efforts to support local content and application creation.

CONCEPTIONS OF THE DIGITAL DIVIDE

Early conceptions of the digital divide focused on a binary distinction between those who had and did not have access to ICT as indicated by availability of an Internet-connected computer. However, these conceptions soon came under criticism on several levels. First, since people access and use ICT in a wide variety of locations and contexts, the notion of a binary divide, rather than a complex continuum, was portrayed as simplistic, and one that could lead to failure to recognize the diverse ways that different individuals and groups do connect to digital information. Second, ICT access does not have a one-way relationship causal to individual and social development, but rather two-way; higher levels of development enable more ICT access, and ICT access can enhance developmental processes. Finally, the focus on physical access to technology was seen as too narrow since there are many other factors, such as language and literacy ability, computer skills, suitability of online content, and availability of instruction or social support that enable or constrain meaningful ICT use; any efforts to overcome inequity related to technology thus need to take these broader factors into account, rather than merely supplying additional hardware.[7,8]

Today, there is broad recognition that the digital divide must be understood as incorporating a broad range of variables. A number of models have been developed to portray the factors involved in meaningful technology access and use, such as the one by Warschauer seen in Fig. 1.[9]

Finally, some prominent individuals and groups have downplayed the notion of a digital divide. Michael Powell, chairman of the U.S. Federal Communications Commission from 2001 to 2004, compared the digital divide to a "Mercedes divide," suggesting that ICT represented a consumer product that people could purchase or not depending on their wealth and desire and that government had little interest in promoting equitable ICT access.[10] This view was echoed by the U.S. Heritage Foundation, which claimed that the free market will rapidly erase any digital divide in the United States and that government action would thus be counterproductive.[11]

MEASURING THE U.S. DIVIDE

A variety of approaches have been developed for measuring the digital divide, both within and across countries. Within the United States, the early standards on this issue were largely set by the NTIA, whose national reports were broadly seen as the authoritative source of information on the topic. The reports were based on the Current Population Surveys (CPS) of about 50,000 U.S. households conducted by the Bureau of Labor Statistics and the U.S. Census Bureau. The CPS collect general demographic data on a monthly basis and supplement that with specialized data at different times; supplemental data on computer and Internet access were collected on six occasions between 1994 and 2003 and formed the basis of the NTIA reports.[12]

The 1995 NTIA report focused on the question of whether U.S. households had either 1) a computer (i.e., *computer access*) or 2) a computer, a modem, and subscription to an online service (i.e., *Internet access*).[13] Computer and Internet access were then compared by

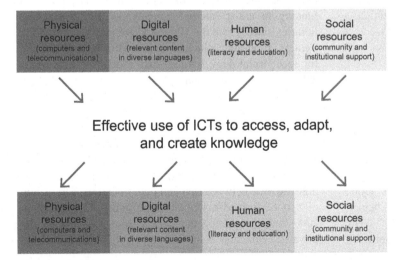

Fig. 1   A model of factors affecting technology access and use.

geographic region and by the income, race, age, and educational attainment of the head of household. The 1998[14] and 1999[15] reports used a similar methodology, though the latter also added an additional variable of having an e-mail account (i.e., *e-mail access*).

The 2000 NTIA report continued to include comparative household data, but also included for the first time data on individual use, again compared by demographic variables. This shift represented an emerging recognition that any true measure of the digital divide needed to account for not only whether one had physical access to the technology but also whether one actually used it. Also for the first time, the 2000 NTIA report included the category of disabled status, thus drawing attention to an important dimension of the digital divide.[16]

As home computer and Internet access continued to expand, the NTIA further de-emphasized household access and instead discussed individual use in more detail. For example, the 2002 report compared different types of Internet use (e.g., finding health information, finding financial information, entertainment-oriented activity) by the gender, age, race, and income of users; began to investigate who had broadband access to the Internet (though differentiated only by urban/rural location); examined types of computer use at work by the occupation of the user; compared amount of Internet and e-mail use at work by occupation and by gender; looked at whether diverse groups of children used computers at home, school, and other locations; and examined Internet use among particular categories of the disabled (e.g., blind, deaf, difficulty walking).[17] The 2004 report indicated Internet use in relationship to broadband access and other demographic factors (e.g., gender, race/ethnicity, employment, income, education, age, and particular types of disabilities).[18]

Beginning in 2013, the U.S. Census Bureau collected data on ownership of computers, smartphones, and other devices, as well as Internet access and type (e.g., broadband, dial-up, fiber optic), and has since provided these data on a yearly basis at the national, state, and, in some cases, city-specific level.[19] These census data have revealed smaller gaps across race in terms of Internet use on smartphones.

Other groups have collected a range of data on Internet use that is helpful for understanding technology and equity. The most important of these groups is the Pew Research Center's Internet & American Life Project, which conducts random digit-dial telephone surveys on a wide variety of topics related to Internet use. Topics addressed by the Pew project include home broadband adoption, the use of the Internet for particular kinds of pursuits (election news and activity, health information), typologies of Internet users, and uses of the Internet by particular demographic groups (see Table 1).[20] Data from NTIA, Pew, and others thus presents the following overview of the digital divide in the United States in relationship to particular demographic groups.

Table 1 Demographics of U.S. Internet users

	Use the Internet (%)
Total adults	88
Women	86
Men	89
Age	
18–29	99
30–49	96
50–64	87
65+	64
Race	
Caucasian, non-Hispanic	88
African-American, non-Hispanic	85
Hispanic	88
Geography	
Urban	89
Suburban	90
Rural	81
Household income	
Less than $30,000/yr	79
$30,000–$49,999	90
$50,000–$74,999	95
$75,000+	98
Educational attainment	
Less than high school graduate	68
High school graduate	81
Some college	94
College +	98

Source: Pew Research Group, Internet/Broadband Fact Sheet. http://www.pewinternet.org/fact-sheet/internet-broadband/ (accessed May 22, 2017).

Gender: Differential computer and Internet access by gender had disappeared in the United States by 1997, and women and men continue to access the Internet to about the same degree. However, women receive only 18.2% of the computer science bachelor's degrees in the United States and encompass only 24.5% of professionals in information technology industries.[21,22] These facts have led many groups to be concerned about the types of early experiences girls have with technology and whether these experiences are helping them develop the skills, knowledge, and attitudes to become leaders in technology-oriented careers.

Race/ethnicity: The race/ethnicity gap in Internet use has lessened over time, but it is unclear exactly how much. According to the most recent published U.S. Census Bureau information, 82.5% of Caucasian and 89.9% of Asian individuals live in a house with at least some Internet access, whereas only 71.1% of Hispanic and 67.3% of African-American households had an Internet connection.[23] Pew Internet reports much smaller gaps, with a similar proportion of Caucasian (88%), African-American (85%), and Hispanic (88%) adults using the Internet, which could be due to the more recent dates of the data gathered (Pew in 2016 vs. Census surveys in 2013), or differences in methodology, with the Census data based on in-person visits to households and the Pew data based on telephone surveys.[20] In addition to different rates of Internet access, there appear to be differences in how different racial groups make use of digital media and the Internet, with African-Americans and Latinos disproportionate uses of social media and video streaming sites and Caucasians and Asians reporting more frequent use of the Internet for interest-driven content production practices.[24–26]

Age: While the gap in Internet use between older and younger Americans is declining, age continues to be an important factor in the digital divide, with only 64% of U.S. seniors aged 65 or older using the Internet.[20] Research suggests that income, cognitive ability, and the availability of relatives to help with technology are all factors correlated with whether and how seniors access the Internet.[27]

Geography: Urban and suburban residents access the Internet to equal degrees. The gap between them and rural users has lessened in recent years and appears to be due in part to lesser access to broadband in rural U.S. areas; however, initiatives such as the Broadband Technology Opportunities Program have targeted these populations for increased broadband connectivity and education.[28] Most recent data indicate that 81% of the rural population has broadband access compared to 89% of the urban population.[29]

Income: Though all income groups have expanded their access to the Internet in recent years, income remains a major factor, with only 79% of those with household incomes under $30,000 using the Internet compared to 98% of those with household incomes over $75,000.[20] Differences in quality of use are likely as well, due to the higher likelihood among families of having up-to-date computers, multiple computers, and broadband Internet connections than low-income families.

Education: Educational attainment is one of the most prominent factors of the digital divide, with 68% of those with less than a high school diploma or less education using the Internet and 98% of college graduates using the Internet.[30] Differences in types of usage are also strongly correlated with education, with college graduates far more likely than others to use the Internet to enhance their productivity or manage digital content.[31]

Disability: Disability status is also strongly correlated with Internet use, with only 62.5% of people with disabilities using the Internet.[23] Limited mobility, limited income, and the high cost of specialized adaptive technology are all barriers toward people with disabilities using computers. Inconsistent implementation of accessibility standards in the design of online content also makes it difficult for people with certain disabilities, such as visual impairment, to make effective use of the Internet.

MEASURING THE INTERNATIONAL DIVIDE

Assessments of the international digital divide are usually made at the level of countries, or groups of countries,

Table 2 World Internet usage

Region	Percent of population using the Internet (%)	Usage growth, 2000–2016 (%)
Africa	28.7.3	7,488.8
Asia	45.6	1,515.2
Europe	73.9	485.2
Middle East	57.4	4,207.4
North America	89.0	196.1
Latin America/ Caribbean	61.5	2,029.4
Oceania/ Australia	73.3	261.4
World total	50.1	918.3

Source: Internet World Stats. Internet Usage Statistics. http://www. internetworldstats.com/stats.htm (accessed January, 2017).

rather than individuals. Indicators that are taken into account include the number of computers, Internet subscribers, or Internet users as a percentage of the population. Countries are then often aggregated by either region or continent for comparison purposes. For example, as seen in Table 2, dramatic differences exist between regions of the world in Internet penetration. Though regions with the least Internet access are expanding the fastest rate, it will still take a long time for them to catch up.

The international digital divide is also reflected in production of Internet content. An earlier study demonstrated that Internet domains are overwhelmingly concentrated in certain countries (e.g., the United States, Germany, and United Kingdom) and in major cities within those countries; follow-up studies have not been conducted to show how these trends may have changed over time.[32]

The International Telecommunications Union (ITU) has attempted to develop a more complete measure of the international divide using a wide variety of indicators measuring network infrastructure (e.g., international Internet bandwidth), individual use (e.g., Internet users per 100 inhabitants), individual access (e.g., broadband subscribers per 100 inhabitants), and skills that enable computer and Internet use (e.g., adult literacy rates). It then brings this data together into an ICT Development Index (IDI) and groups countries based on this index into high, upper, medium, and lower levels. The ITU study found a huge gap between these different levels, with the divide steadily increasing further between the high and low extremes from 2001 to 2004. In 2004, the divide between high- and low-IDI countries began to decrease, suggesting the beginning of a small catch-up effect in overcoming the international digital divide. By 2007, IDIs had increased across all countries, and the gap between high- and low-IDI countries had slightly decreased, only to widen again in the subsequent 2011 reports.[33,34] However, the gaps between developed and developing countries are now decreasing once again according to the groups' most recent report.[35]

Researchers have also investigated the social, economic, and political factors that tend to correlate with the digital divide internationally. Studies suggest that general developmental level, amount of political openness and democracy, mass education, the presence of a sizeable service sector in the economy, and flexible telecommunication policy are all factors that correlate with Internet diffusion in particular countries.[36,37]

The availability of mobile Internet connections has also contributed to increased Internet access and use. Some 95% of the global population lives within reach of mobile-cellular signal.[35]However, the cost of mobile connectivity remains high in developing nations and is a major barrier to mobile phone ownership.[35] Whereas about 80% of the world's population is using mobile phones, this falls to less than 60% in large developing economies such as Bangladesh, India, Indonesia, and Pakistan.[35]

THE EDUCATIONAL DIVIDE

A good deal of attention on the digital divide has focused on the role of schools. Within the United States, for example, the National Center for Educational Statistics has carried out national studies since 1998 measuring Internet and computer access in public schools throughout the country. Though gaps between the number of Internet-connected computers in high-person of color (POC) schools (i.e., with 50% or more of their students being racial or ethnic minorities) and low-POC schools (i.e., with fewer than 6% of their students being racial or ethnic minorities) steadily fell from 1998 to 2002, it remained steady thereafter (see Fig. 2). In 2005, a study indicated that there were 3.0 students per Internet-connected computer in low-POC schools and 4.1 students per such computers in high-minority schools.[38] More recent figures in 2009 suggest that on average there are 1.7 students per computer that can be brought into the classroom (such as via a shared laptop cart), with a slightly lower ratio in schools with less than 35% of students on free or reduced-price lunch (1.5 students per computer) and slightly higher in schools serving 50% or more students eligible for free or reduced-price lunch (1.8 students per computer).[39] Though current data is not available, the widespread diffusion of low-cost Chromebooks is likely bringing these numbers down further. The digital divide in schools goes beyond the availability of computers and extends to how technology is used. African-Americans, Hispanics, and low-income students have been shown to disproportionately use computers for drills, remediation, and vocational education, whereas Caucasians, Asians, and high-income students more frequently use computers for advanced simulations and research.[40] These differences are due to a number of factors, including the different levels of background, skill, and knowledge that

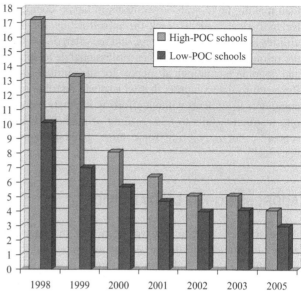

Fig. 2 Number of Internet-connected computers per student in high-POC and low-POC U.S. K-12 schools, 1998–2005.
Source: Wells et al.[38]

students have; the differential amounts of technology they have at home (that may help them prepare for more advanced uses at school); and the different levels of skill and experience among teachers in low-income versus high-income neighborhood schools.[39]

On the international level, little data exists as to the number of computers or Internet connections in schools around the world; however, obvious differences in these measures exist between developed and developing countries. Many developing countries think of schools as a critically important arena for overcoming the digital divide and are thus making efforts to outfit schools with computers and Internet access.

Schools have been a major focus for overcoming the digital divide. In the United States, the federal program known as E-Rate has made use of the Universal Service fee charged to telecommunication companies to distribute funds for schools and libraries to obtain affordable telecommunications and Internet access. Renewed in 2014 as the E-Rate Modernization Order, this program has expanded its goals to include provision of high-speed broadband, particularly Wi-Fi, in schools and libraries.[41] Internationally, a number of countries, including Portugal, Peru, Uruguay, and Thailand, have carried out widespread distribution of individual laptops or tablets to children to attempt to increase technology access and educational equity.[42–45] A number of prominent programs in this regard have been organized by the U.S.-based One Laptop Per Child (OLPC) program.[46] Though OLPC extended computer access to the poor in a number of countries, it has also been criticized by some who believe that developing countries have more pressing educational priorities than making large-scale investments in laptop computers for individual students, lack the infrastructure for basic utilities let alone Internet access, and too often do not have the resources to include teacher professional development and ongoing technological support for such initiatives.[47] Research to date suggests that widespread distribution of computers to students without efforts to integrate their use into instruction fails to raise reading or mathematics test scores[48] but may bring some more general cognitive benefits.[42,49]

ADDRESSING THE DIGITAL DIVIDE

A number of programs have been put in place for addressing the digital divide. At the infrastructural level, programs have been launched to reduce the cost of computers or Internet connectivity for low-income citizens, for example, through providing free municipal wireless access. Other programs, such as the aforementioned OLPC initiative, seek to develop special versions of hardware or software that are both lower in cost and more suitable for use among the urban and rural poor.

As regards content, advocacy groups work to create online materials that reflect the economic or social needs (e.g., information about health care for low-income residents in the United States or local crop prices for rural farmers in India) and are available in multiple languages and dialects and at reading levels suitable for mass access. The development of technologies that enable self-publishing and collective content creation (e.g., wikis, blogs, and social media) has also enabled advocacy groups to work with underserved populations to promote inclusive participation in digital media production and to generate community-relevant educational materials.

As regards human capital development, initiatives have focused on making computers and the Internet more affordable to schools and for developing curricular and pedagogical approaches that ensure that all students have equal access to advanced forms of learning with new technology.

Finally, as regards social support, a number of governmental and nongovernmental organizations have promoted the availability of online population- and community-targeted resources for digital literacy education and to boost participation in digital media.[50] Additionally, populations previously underrepresented in digital access and use have more and more been able to participate via mobile devices.[51–53] However, some argue that lack of cultural capital means that—like computers and the Internet—access to mobile broadband alone is not enough to bridge the digital divide.[53]

A number of grassroots groups attempt to coordinate information and organize, aimed at tackling the digital divide. Among these is the Digital Inclusion Network,[54] which includes discussion lists, blogs, and event announcements for educators, activists, policy makers, and others concerned with technology and social inclusion. Additionally, the Digital Media + Learning Central blog publishes case studies, articles, blogs, and educational resources promoting digital inclusion and ICT equity among global communities.[55] A growing information and communications technologies for development (ICT4D) or development informatics community currently explores strategies for implementing information technologies as a means for spurring national development (e.g., see).[56]

CONCLUSION

In the 1990s, governments and organizations around the world became concerned about unequal access to new technologies, whether among individuals or nations. Labeling this unequal access a *digital divide* helped draw attention to the issue. Since that time, the concept has broadened to address not only physical access to computers and the Internet but also the kinds of knowledge, skills, online content, and social support necessary to make such access meaningful. In that sense, there is not one digital divide but many, and diverse efforts on many fronts are needed to overcome them.

REFERENCES

1. Poole, G.A. A new gulf in American education, the digital divide. *New York Times*, January 29, 1996; 1.
2. National Telecommunications and Information Administration. Remarks by the president and the vice president to the people of Knoxville, 1996. http://www.ntia.doc.gov/legacy/ntiahome/101096clinton.htm (accessed November 2014).
3. Castells, M. *The Rise of the Network Society*; Blackwell: Malden, MA, 1996.
4. National Telecommunications and Information Administration. Data central, 2014. http://www.ntia.doc.gov/data (accessed November 2014).
5. http://www.g7.utoronto.ca/summit/2002kananaskis/dotforce_reportcard.pdf (accessed November 2014).
6. http://www.unicttaskforce.org/ (accessed August 2007).
7. Warschauer, M. *Technology and Social Inclusion: Rethinking the Digital Divide*; MIT Press: Cambridge, MA, 2003.
8. Hargittai, E. The digital divide and what to do about it. In *New Economy Handbook*; Jones, D.C., Ed.; Academic Press: San Diego, CA, 2003; 822–841.
9. Warschauer, M. Reconceptualizing the digital divide. First Monday **2002**, *7* (7), http://www.firstmonday.org/issues/issue7_7/warschauer/ (accessed November 2014).
10. http://www.wired.com/politics/law/news/2001/04/43349 (accessed August 2007).
11. http://www.heritage.org/Research/InternetandTechnology/BG1361.cfm (August 2007).

12. http://www.bls.census.gov/cps/computer/computer.htm (accessed August 2007).

13. http://www.ntia.doc.gov/ntiahome/fallingthru.html (accessed November 2014).

14. http://www.ntia.doc.gov/ntiahome/net2/ (accessed August 2007).

15. http://www.ntia.doc.gov/ntiahome/fttn99/contents.html (accessed August 2007).

16. http://www.ntia.doc.gov/ntiahome/fttn00/contents00.html (accessed August 2007).

17. http://www.ntia.doc.gov/opadhome/digitalnation/index_2002.html (accessed August 2007).

18. http://www.ntia.doc.gov/reports/anol/NationOnlineBroadband04.html (accessed August 2007).

19. http://www.census.gov/hhes/computer/files/2012/Computer_Use_Infographic_FINAL.pdf (accessed November 2014).

20. http://www.pewinternet.org/ (accessed January 2017).

21. http://www.nsf.gov/statistics/wmpd/2013/pdf/tab5-1_updated_2014_05.pdf (accessed November 2014).

22. http://www.aauw.org/files/2013/02/position-on-STEM-education-111.pdf (accessed November 2014).

23. http://www.census.gov/content/dam/Census/library/publications/2014/acs/acs-28.pdf(accessed November 2014).

24. http://kaiserfamilyfoundation.files.wordpress.com/2013/04/8010.pdf (accessed November 2014).

25. Attewell, P.; Winston, H. Children of the digital divide. Disadvantaged Teens and Computer Technologies. 2003; 117–136.

26. Warschauer, M.; Matuchniak, T. New technology and digital worlds: Analyzing evidence of equity in access, use, and outcomes. Rev. Res. Edu. **2010**, *34* (1), 179–225.

27. Freese, J.; Rivas, S.; Hargittai, E. Cognitive ability and Internet use among older adults. Poetics **2006**, *34* (4), 236–249.

28. http://www2.ntia.doc.gov/ (accessed November 2014).

29. http://www.ntia.doc.gov/files/ntia/publications/exploring_the_digital_nation_americas_emerging_online_experience.pdf (accessed November 2014).

30. http://www.pewinternet.org (accessed November 2017).

31. http://www.pewinternet.org/pdfs/PIP_ICT_Typology.pdf (accessed August 2007).

32. Zook, M.A. Old hierarchies or new networks of centrality?: The global geography of the Internet content market. Am. Behav. Sci. **2001**, *44* (10), 1679–1696.

33. http://www.itu.int/ITU-D/ict/publications/idi/material/2009/MIS2009_w5.pdf (accessed November 2014).

34. http://www.itu.int/en/ITU-D/Statistics/Documents/publications/mis2012/MIS2012_without_Annex_4.pdf (accessed November 2014).

35. https://www.itu.int/en/ITU-D/Statistics/Documents/publications/misr2016/MISR2016-w4.pdf (accessed January 2017).

36. Robison, K.K.; Crenshaw, E.M. Post-industrial transformations and cyber-space: A cross-national analysis of Internet development. Soc. Sci. Res. **2002**, *31* (3), 334–363.

37. Hargittai, E. Weaving the Western Web: Explaining differences in Internet connectivity among OECD countries. Telecommun. Policy **1999**, *23* (10/11), 701–718.

38. Wells, J.; Lewis, L.; Greene, B. *Internet Access in U.S. Public Schools and Classrooms: 1994–2005*; National Center for Educational Statistics: Washington, DC, 2006.

39. http://nces.ed.gov/pubs2010/2010003.pdf (accessed November 2014).

40. Warschauer, M.; Knobel, M.; Stone, L.A. Technology and equity in schooling: Deconstructing the digital divide. Edu. Policy **2004**, *18* (4), 562–588.

41. http://www.fcc.gov/page/summary-e-rate-modernization-order (accessed November 2014).

42. Cristia, J.; Ibarrarán, P.; Cueto, S.; Santiago, A.; Severín, E. *Technology and Child Development: Evidence from the One Laptop per Child Program*; Inter-American Development Bank: Washington, DC, 2012.

43. http://www.economist.com/node/21556940 (accessed November 2014).

44. Kraemer, K.L.; Dedrick, J.; Sharma, P. One laptop per child: Vision vs. reality. Commun. ACM **2009**, *52* (6), 66–73.

45. Severin, E.; Capota, C. *One-to-One Laptop Programs in Latin America and the Caribbean: Panorama and Perspectives*; Inter-American Development Bank: Washington, D.C., 2011.

46. http://one.laptop.org/ (accessed November 2014).

47. http://timesofindia.indiatimes.com/articleshow/msid-1698603,curpg-1.cms (accessed September 2008).

48. de Melo, G.; Machado, A.; Miranda, A.; Viera, M. *Profundizando en los efects del Plan Ceibal*; Instituto de Economía: Mexico, 2013.

49. Malamud, O.; Pop-Eleches, C. *The Effect of Computer Use on Child Outcomes*; Harris School of Public Policy/University of Chicago: Chicago, IL, 2008.

50. http://www.dcenr.gov.ie/NR/rdonlyres/54AF1E6E-1A0D-413F-8CEB-2442C03E09BD/0/NationalDigitalStrategy-forIreland.pdf (accessed November 2014).

51. Brown, K.; Campbell, S.W.; Ling, R. Mobile phones bridging the digital divide for teens in the US?. Future Internet **2011**, *3* (2), 144–158.

52. Srinuan, C.; Srinuan, P.; Bohlin, E. An analysis of mobile Internet access in Thailand: Implications for bridging the digital divide. Telematics Inform. **2012**, *29* (3), 254–262.

53. Wijetunga, D. The digital divide objectified in the design: Use of the mobile telephone by underprivileged youth in Sri Lanka. J. Comput. Mediated Commun. **2014**, *19* (3), 712–726.

54. http://forums.e-democracy.org/groups/inclusion (accessed November 2014).

55. http://dmlcentral.net/ (accessed November 2014).

56. Silva, L.; Westrup, C. Development and the promise of technological change. Inform. Technol. Dev. **2009**, *15*, 59–65.

FURTHER READING

1. Hargittai, E. The digital divide and what to do about it. In *New Economy Handbook*; Jones, D.C., Ed.; Academic Press: San Diego, CA, 2003; 822–841.

2. Warschauer, M. *Technology and Social Inclusion: Rethinking the Digital Divide*; MIT Press: Cambridge, MA, 2003.

3. Warschauer, M. Demystifying the digital divide. Sci. Am. **2003**, *289* (2), 42–27.

Digital Humanities

Julia Flanders
Elli Mylonas
Brown University, Providence, Rhode Island, U.S.A.

Abstract

Digital humanities is a recent and rapidly evolving field. It includes the range of activities and projects associated with the use of digital technologies for humanities research. Its roots lie in the 1960s with early work on digital texts and text corpora. With the emergence of desktop computing, use of computers for humanities research expanded in the 1980s, followed by the development of standards and the rapid growth of digital research projects and academic centers. In the 1990s, the rise of the World Wide Web made digital forms of publication increasingly common, and placed new emphasis on the value of networked information and online patterns of usage. The modern field of digital humanities has multiple forms of institutional presence, and embraces a range of characteristic methods, questions, and topics including information modeling, pattern discovery, standardization, and metadata.

INTRODUCTION

The field of digital humanities is a recent and rapidly moving target. There are several reasons for this: first, the fact that both of its putative two "sides" (humanities and digital technology) are themselves evolving swiftly, responding to cultural pressures and also to their own inner developmental logic. But in addition, their relationship is evolving. As digital technology moves into essential scholarly systems such as libraries, research and instructional tools, and methods of communication, the institutional juxtaposition of digital technology to the humanities disciplines has shifted. Where three decades ago, the technological infrastructure was housed and managed with visible and impressive separateness (and rarely used by humanists), it is now pervasive and unremarkable. Digital technology is no longer positioned as "science" or as "machine" but rather as media, as access, as enhanced modes of instruction, as a medium of collaboration.

The desktop revolution has made all of this possible by making digital technology cheap, user-friendly, and appealing to consumers. The ubiquitous connectivity of the Internet has also introduced new types of interaction and new participants in the humanities discourse. But this prompts an important question: how is digital humanities distinguishable from the routine (and expanding) use of desktop computing technology and the Internet for ordinary workday tasks? How does it differ from publications and research by nontraditional scholars and the general public? Is one doing digital humanities when one uses a word processor, or uses Flickr, or registers for an online seminar? If there is a clear difference, then it should be possible to describe—for funding agencies, for university administrations, and even ultimately for professional assessment—where that difference lies. It now appears that digital humanities together with its various cognates is emerging as a distinct field of study – as suggested by the rise of departments, professorships and national funding programs using "digital humanities," "humanities computing," "humanities informatics," and similar terms. If digital humanities, together with its various cognates, is to be considered an emerging field of study, then how can we most usefully characterize it and identify its boundaries?

This entry begins by providing a definition of digital humanities and a brief history, followed by a discussion of digital humanities in its institutional contexts, its relationship with digital libraries and finally, a short introduction to characteristic methodologies.

DEFINITION

Digital humanities can be understood both as a field in its own right and as a way of identifying digital research and project development efforts in specific humanities fields. More broadly, it also refers to any digital activity that furthers research in the humanities, or assists in the scholarly activities of its practitioners. Some of these activities may operate outside of any particular humanities field: for example, digital publishing or digital libraries.

As a discrete field, digital humanities studies the intersection of humanities ideas and digital methods, with the goal of understanding how the use of digital technologies and approaches alters the practice of humanities scholarship. In this sense it is concerned with studying the emergence of scholarly disciplines and communicative practices at a time when those are in flux, under the influence of rapid technological, institutional, and cultural change.

Encyclopedia of Library and Information Sciences, Fourth Edition DOI: 10.1081/E-ELIS4-120043527

Digital–Disaster

As a way of identifying digital interests and efforts within traditional humanities fields, the term "digital humanities" identifies, in general terms, any kind of critical engagement with digital tools and methods in a humanities context. This includes the creation of digital editions and digital text or image collections, and the creation and use of digital tools for the investigation and analysis of humanities research materials. It also includes the aggregation and arrangement of digital resources and tools in order to present humanities material to students, and other forms of broader dissemination. Finally, the term can be used to refer to tools, processes, and projects that expand access to the source materials of scholarship and teaching such as primary source texts, images, representations of artifacts, objects of study, and secondary source materials. In many cases, these expanded forms of access closely resemble their traditional counterparts, albeit with improvements of speed, accessibility, scope, and flexibility of use. These aspects of digital humanities can be expressed through conventional publication. But humanities researchers, accustomed to studying discursive modes, have also begun to seek experimental ways of embodying their work in new forms of digital publication. Examples include journals like *Vectors* and experiments with new models of scholarly publication such as *Hypertext in American Studies*, supported by *American Quarterly* and the Center for History and New Media.[1,2]

It is useful to identify what we mean by "critical engagement" with digital tools a little more precisely. When an experimental digital tool first enters humanities practice, its methods of operation require significant user knowledge and are also subjected to critical scrutiny. However, as digital tools enter the realm of routine utilities, and develop surfaces that permit shallow rather than deep configuration, they become optimized for the most common uses. This optimization limits opportunities for critical engagement, by limiting access to information about their internal processes. In effect, as they become normalized and predictable, they become more like black boxes. This evolution mirrors the development of consumer tools in other technological areas. For example, automotive technology initially required the driver to have a detailed working knowledge of engines and to perform all configurations and repairs, thereby permitting the expert user to optimize the vehicle's behavior (but also permitting mistakes and disasters). Modern vehicles allow the knowledgeable driver to make improvements and repairs, but do not assume this as a common practice. We can envision that the cars of the near future will be extremely high function, but only within the limits of the standard design, with no user-serviceable systems at all. Different digital humanities tools are at different stages in this evolution. Systems for authoring and publishing XML documents are just starting to enter the second phase, permitting but not requiring user configuration and expertise, whereas word processing systems have been at this stage for over a decade. Some kinds of digital scholarly tools will probably never reach this point, but will always require significant levels of intervention from the responsible (and necessarily expert) user.

The question is whether this kind of engagement is, *ipso facto*, meaningful in a critical sense—in the sense of yielding important levels of disciplinary insight into methodology and process—or whether it merely seems meaningful at this incunabular stage of digital tool development because of the novelty of these processes. It is useful to recall in this context the intellectual significance Douglas Engelbart attached in the early 1960s to what we now regard as commonplace editorial functions like copying and pasting. The full description of the copy/paste process is worth quoting in full for its reminder of the historical distance traversed: "Adding one more light-pen pointing to what it took to delete an arbitrary string of symbols, Joe could direct the computer to move that string from where it was to insert it at a new point which his light pen designated. Again it would disappear instantaneously from where it had been, but now the modified display would show the old text to have been spread apart just enough at the indicated point to hold this string. The text would all still look as neat as if freshly retyped. With similar types of keyset and light-pen operations, Joe could change paragraph break points, transpose two arbitrary symbol strings (words, sentences, paragraphs, etc., or fragments thereof), readjust margins of arbitrary sections of text—essentially being able to affect immediately any of the changes that a proofreader might want to designate with his special marks, only here the proofreader is always looking at clean text as if it had been instantaneously retyped after each designation had been made."[3] Similarly, the use of online reference sources and journals is now taken for granted in humanities scholarship. The immediacy and comprehensiveness of these sources arguably has had a transformative effect on humanities research, but it would be harder to argue that it now has a significant effect on the intellectual or methodological content of that research.

There may thus be a critical window during which new tools expose their methodological significance to us, before they respond to the pressure toward commodification and the seamless interface required for general use. This would suggest that as digital humanities becomes established as a field, it will embrace both humanists for whom the use of digital tools is central to their regular research practice, and those for whom the exploration of tools and their impact on research methodology is itself of critical interest.

John Unsworth has suggested a definition which addresses this question from a different angle: digital humanities involves activities "in which the computer is used as tool for modeling humanities data and our understanding of it, and that activity is entirely distinct from using the computer when it models the typewriter, or the telephone, or the phonograph, or any of the many other things it can be."[4] This formulation usefully relocates the idea of "meaningful engagement" away from the tool itself and onto the modeling activity the tool enables. It is not a question, in other words, of whether the tool itself resembles a modern automobile, but rather of whether our use of it resembles our use of the automobile: of whether we are capable of taking it apart and reassembling it as a spacecraft or a work of art. Tools and methods that look unscholarly or purely utilitarian at one point may over time be appropriated for scholarship in unanticipated ways; for instance, we are now beginning to see techniques from social networking sites such as del.icio.us and Flickr being incorporated into the design of scholarly digital publications. Examples include the experiment in folksonomic museum cataloging being undertaken at http://www.steve.museum, the ThoughtMesh project, and also the work of the NINES project.[5,6]

The term "digital humanities" has emerged at least partly as a gesture of inclusion and an attempt to define a broader domain than was suggested by earlier terms such as "humanities computing." But there are also several closely related fields which, though they share methods, interests, and populations with the digital humanities, can nonetheless be usefully distinguished from it. One of these is the field of new media (also, media studies), which contextualizes an interest in the digital within a broader set of concerns about media more generally. New media often combines a more strongly theoretical approach with a practical interest in multimedia production, and the field also engages more directly with domains like the visual arts and the performing arts. A second neighboring field is digital libraries,[7] which sets shared interests (in metadata, digital representation, and humanities content) within the context of library science issues such as information retrieval, knowledge representation, classification and cataloging methods. Digital libraries approaches are also framed by institutional priorities such as long-term sustainability, scalability, standard work flows, and cost-effectiveness.

HISTORY

Computing in the humanities began as a specialized practice which required access to scarce equipment. It was originally practiced by individual scholars who used it to perform their own research on literary or historical questions, and who published their disciplinary results in conventional venues. Subsequently, humanities computing became less concerned with the purely technical aspects of digitizing and analyzing digitized materials, and focused more on the preparation and representation of text collections and other objects of study. As this knowledge left the exclusive province of researchers and became a component of scholarly infrastructure like the library,

digital humanities has moved on to grapple with the social and collaborative aspects of computing, while continuing to explore aspects of text representation and text analysis. As it has matured, digital humanities has evolved from "humanities computing" which was defined by its reliance on and interaction with a computer to "digital humanities" which is concerned more broadly with media and methods in a digital context.

The earliest known use of technology to advance a discipline in the humanities was in 1949, when Father Roberto Busa approached IBM for help in creating a print concordance of the works of Thomas Aquinas and related texts.[8–10] This was characteristic of early humanities computing, which replicated well-understood existing scholarly technologies such as concordances and dictionaries, but made their preparation faster, more accurate, and less tedious. There were no standards specifying how to encode a text for machine processing, which programming language to use, or even which hardware. Concordance programs had to be developed from the ground up, and although methodology was published and shared, the specifics of each implementation were unique.

Early humanities computing focused on indexing and analyzing texts, as the limitations of computers in the 1960s privileged character-based data. Early digitized text collections were usually small, and were not designed to be read online or disseminated electronically. Instead they represented a data set for processing: one step in the process of preparing a particular scholarly product. However, it was a natural progression to apply quantitative analysis to these data sets of literary and historical texts. This also fit into the data processing paradigm of computing that was prevalent at the time. Apart from Father Busa's corpus of Aquinas, which took decades to be completed, most early humanities computing projects were applied to individual texts, and addressed specialized problems, for a single researcher. (In 1967, *Computers and the Humanities* listed 120 such projects under the category "Literature."[11]) Their results were published in conventional venues, books, and journals, and the "computerized" materials were not easily reusable by other scholars. Examples of this kind of processing were indexes, stylistic analysis, bibliographic compilations, and authorship studies.

By the late 1960s, we begin to see the appearance of journals and newsletters that document computer projects in the humanities (for example *Computers and the Humanities*, first published in 1966) followed soon thereafter by the founding of conferences and professional organizations (for example, the Association for Literary and Linguistic Computing was founded in 1973, and the Association for Computers and the Humanities was founded in 1978) that provided venues for sharing information, providing support, and creating the beginnings of a disciplinary identity. This increased sense of professional interconnection reflected important changes in the scale and collaborative nature of digital projects. As computers became more standardized, centralized computer facilities appeared on campuses which allowed broader access and it became possible to acquire programs and materials created elsewhere. This made it feasible to justify paying for the development of larger corpora by pointing out the value of shared access to materials that could not be created for the use of a single researcher. Projects like the *Thesaurus Linguae Graecae* were initially funded by private donors, and were concerned from the outset with justifying the basis on which they selected texts and the ways in which they encoded them, so as to be acceptable to their destined audience in classics.[12,13] Although not exclusively, work sprang from the disciplines with the most preexisting scholarly apparatus and with well-defined corpora of manageable size: religious studies, classics, Old English, and linguistics. Such disciplines were early users of computational tools to mediate their interaction with textual materials, partly because these tools reproduced and enhanced the utility of traditional research tools such as concordances and critical apparatus and perhaps partly because these fields are more hospitable to quantitative and empirical approaches to textual study. As computational tools elicited stronger mathematical forms of quantitative analysis, methodological disagreements (which had already separated the more philologically oriented field of Old English from the more critically oriented field of English literature) became more acute, alienating more traditional humanists from humanities computing.[14]

Computerized texts also made it possible to print editions, concordances, and dictionaries more accurately and more efficiently. In the 1970s, with the development of corpora and the ability to output to typesetting equipment, it was possible to avoid rekeying texts with difficult formatting and unfamiliar character sets.[15] Individual scholars and professional organizations like the Society for Biblical Literature developed specialized knowledge about fonts and typesetting, which was a digital extension of the scholarly apparatus they already applied to their discipline. Computerized texts could be repurposed, and used not only for generating indexes, but also for wholesale printing of new editions.

In the early 1980s, this emerging emphasis on large-scale shared corpora and text processing tools was joined by a complementary trend: the emergence of desktop computing, with the introduction of the IBM PC (1981) and the Apple Macintosh (1984). The introduction of the graphical user interface helped to broaden the scope of humanities computing by making it possible to show images and display non-ASCII character sets. Specialized knowledge was no longer necessary to interact with a computer—word processing, and somewhat later e-mail, became part of the daily work of every scholar. The term "computing humanist" began to shift: from describing any scholar using a computer to perform research in the humanities, to referring solely to those creating technology for the use of their colleagues in the humanities, or themselves exploring applications of technology in the humanities. As more scholars had access to computing, efforts were made to bring existing searching and analysis tools to the desktop [for example, tools like MicroOCP (Micro-OCP User Manual, Oxford University Computing Service: Oxford, 1988) and Conc (http://www.sil.org/computing/conc/)] as well as specialized word processing and textual editing software, targeted at the scholar, that mimicked the production of scholarly print editions.[16] These tools did not form the mainstream of scholarly computing: they tended to be very specialized, with nonstandard formats and user interfaces, and were difficult to share between different hardware and software platforms. However, by broadening the accessibility of scholarly computing, they helped to create an environment in which digital humanities methods could be discussed not merely as a novelty but as an emerging set of shared methods and practices. At the same time, they revealed a set of new opportunities and challenges. The overhead of having to prepare one's own text for analysis, the difficulty of finding texts prepared by others, and the challenges of dealing with idiosyncratic markup systems were a substantial obstacle to scholars whose primary interest lay with the text and not with the digital methods themselves. On the other hand, the knowledge that scholars could make use of digital texts and other information at their desk, as they did conventional reference material, coupled with the graphical user interface, opened new horizons for translating conventional scholarly publication into richly linked, multimedia hypertexts.

In response to these limitations and challenges, two important developments emerged in the late 1980s and became more firmly entrenched in the 1990s. First, leading computing humanists who had been writing software and performing analyses on digitized texts, and who were aware of the lost opportunities and wasted effort due to the widely varying encodings applied to digital texts, gathered in Poughkeepsie, New York in 1987 to call for a standard encoding scheme for scholarly documents. This turned into the Text Encoding Initiative (TEI), which issued its first draft set of *Guidelines for Electronic Text Encoding and Interchange* in 1990, with the first major release in 1993. The guidelines were based on SGML, an emerging international standard, and have since evolved into one of the most influential components of digital humanities work. The process of developing the TEI Guidelines, and their application in specific projects, brought a wider range of humanities scholars into the field of humanities computing and opened up opportunities for digital text representation and analysis that went beyond the purely quantitative early approaches. It also raised issues of the relationship between language and its representation in text giving rise (perhaps for the first time) to theoretical questions about digital text itself, which contributed importantly to the emergence of humanities computing as a research field rather than a way of getting things done.[17–20] At roughly the same time as the development of the TEI *Guidelines*, other standards for humanities text encoding and metadata (such as EAD in the mid-1990s, to be followed by METS (Metadata Encoding and Transmission Standard) and related standards in the early 2000s) laid the groundwork for large-scale text digitization projects based on SGML and designed on a platform-independent and interoperable basis. Early examples include the Women Writers Project, the Victorian Women Writers Project, the Perseus Project, the Oxford Text Archive, the Canterbury Tales Project, the Piers Plowman Archive.

The other development was the dissemination of the work of Douglas Engelbart at Stanford and the writings of Ted Nelson on hypertext and hypertextual structures of information, and their application to knowledge work.[21,22] Hypertext arose as a research area in Computer Science, and was implemented in several commercial and widely available software applications that ran on personal computers, the best known of which were Hypercard (Apple, 1987), SuperCard (Silicon Beach Software, 1989), and Guide (Owl, 1987). These applications allowed technical neophytes to create small, interlinked systems that could be used by their students and their colleagues. The parallelism of hypertextual structures with the literary theories of intertextuality and deconstruction resonated with scholars and instructors, and encouraged experiments in building self-contained hypertexts around particular areas of study: for example, Context 32, which turned into the Victorian Web (http://www.victorianweb .org/), and the Shakespeare Project developed by Larry Friedlander at Stanford University. The emergence of image and early multimedia capability on personal computers also permitted the use of non-textual materials. Projects like the IRIS Intermedia project at Brown University and the Perseus Project at Harvard University created multimedia digital content that could be used by other scholars and students. Several such projects are described in Delany.[23] Although there was still no standardization of formats or software, humanities computing was now concerned not only with databases and textual analysis, but also digital dissemination and publication.

The World Wide Web, which was introduced in 1989, but whose potential became evident with the release of the Mosaic browser (1993), allowed all humanists with an Internet connection to be computing humanists by providing access to searchable corpora that were seamlessly linked to other relevant work. The WWW might be said to have made hypertext so common that it became invisible. Although the underlying structures and the linking mechanisms of the WWW were less powerful than what was available on desktops and in research software, they had several important effects: scholars, authors, and software developers were able to rely on a uniform infrastructure that allowed them to focus their efforts on their own

materials and presentation, the WWW's reliance on standards encouraged the development of standards in other areas, and the ability to link easily across Web sites and topic areas introduced the concept of collaboration as a scholarly tool.

The 1990s and the early part of the twenty-first century have seen both consolidation and further advances in all these tools and methods: a mixture of advanced experiments in desktop hypertext, scholarly editing, large corpus building and the increasing development and adoption of standards and guidelines such as SGML (which became XML in 1997),[24] TEI,[25] METS, and EAD,[26] and the technologies that are based on them. At the same time, literary and media theorists have begun to engage with digital humanities projects, and have generated an increased awareness of digital art which tests the tropes of digital rhetoric. This has brought to the forefront a new research domain, the problematization of digital methods and systems. Heretofore, theoretical concerns had been situated in traditional disciplinary issues of scholarly editing, and analysis. Starting in the 1990s, media theory and critical theory find themselves sharing concerns.[27–29] Finally, there has been a rise in international collaboration and the development of very large-scale digital infrastructure for humanities research.[30]

INSTITUTIONAL LOCATIONS

What is suggested but not fully revealed in this history, as the field of humanities computing and digital humanities takes shape, is the important role of institutional location and funding models. Digital humanities projects find an institutional home in a variety of different contexts, and it is often these contexts that determine their scale, research agenda, personnel, and practical outcomes. For this reason, classification of digital humanities projects and work models can be a useful way of understanding the terrain. One such classification was developed in 2003 by Willard McCarty and Matthew Kirschenbaum and published by the Association for Literary and Linguistic Computing.[31] This was repeated and expanded by the Centernet classification.[32] It emphasizes the functional role of the various institutional centers: whether they provide teaching, research, collegial support, or technical support, or several of these in combination.

This classification leaves out some important sites of digital humanities activity (for instance, digital publication projects and individual research projects), and it also elides some useful distinctions. The category of "library-based units," for example, includes both large-scale digitization efforts located within libraries, library units focused on managing electronic resources for patrons, and library projects with a more specific scholarly focus. This is not a failing in the classification itself but an expression of its intended purpose: to create a classificatory matrix that can accommodate all humanities computing projects. But for purposes of understanding the broad outlines of the field and its evolution over time, we suggest an alternative classification that illuminates the most significant types of projects and takes into account the kind of intellectual product that motivates their design and activity. Naturally a given entity may occupy multiple spaces in this classification. The significant terms in this classification might be as follows:

- Digital library projects and centers which undertake the digitization of library collections on a large scale.
- Faculty support centers in which the goal is to enable humanities faculty (typically nontechnical or at least technically not self-sufficient) to use digital humanities technologies and approaches in teaching and/or research. Examples include the Institute for Advanced Technology in the Humanities (http://www.iath.virginia.edu/), HUMLAB (http://www.humlab.umu.se/), Maryland Institute for Technology in the Humanities (http://www.mith2.umd.edu/), Oxford University Computing Services (http://www.oucs.ox.ac.uk/), and the Scholarly Technology Group (http://www.stg.brown.edu).
- Digital humanities research units in which central questions in digital humanities and its constitutive fields (human–computer interaction, digitization standards and practices, text encoding theory, new media theory, etc.) are pursued as the central activity; publications, projects, and funding initiatives emerge from this agenda. Examples include the Center for Research in Digital Humanities (http://cdrh.unl.edu/), CTB at the Royal Dutch Academy (http://www.kantl.be/ctb/), SpecLab (http://www.speculativecomputing.org), STG, Women Writers Project (http://www.wwp.brown.edu), and the Center for History and New Media (http://chnm.gmu.edu).
- Digital humanities programs and departments in which digital humanities is the subject being taught (and where research is conducted as part of that effort). Examples include the Centre for Computing in the Humanities at King's College, London (http://www.kcl.ac.uk/cch; English and Film Studies at University of Alberta (http://www.arts.ualberta.ca/efs/research/dhrc.php); TextTechnologie Department at Bielefeld, Germany (http://coli.lili.uni-bielefeld.de/).
- Digital publication projects, organized around the creation of a specific digital publication (often a scholarly edition or thematic research collection). Examples include NINES (http://www.nines.org), WWP, and the Walt Whitman Archive (http://www.whitmanarchive.org).

Some important relationships between these terms deserve closer attention. First, there are developmental processes by which one type of group will evolve into another.

Digital humanities research units, as they mature, may begin to resemble academic departments, particularly because the personnel they attract are already hybrids: technologists with advanced degrees in humanities fields or humanities faculty on a temporary detour from standard teaching jobs. This process in some cases results in a formal institutional transformation (for instance, the Centre for Computing in the Humanities at King's College London was converted from a support center into an academic department in 2006), and sometimes produces a group in which personnel occupy a dual role (for example, the senior staff of the Maryland Institute for Technology in the Humanities at the University of Maryland and at the Institute for Advanced Technology in the Humanities at the University of Virginia hold faculty positions). Digital publication projects may evolve into digital humanities research units, by attracting personnel for whom the research problems attendant upon the publication become an interest in themselves and provide an agenda that extends beyond the bounds of the original publication. Examples include the Women Writers Project at Brown University, which was originally founded to create digital anthologies of early women's writing but has evolved into a digital humanities research group; and the Walt Whitman Archive, which began as an electronic edition of Whitman's writings but similarly has gained critical mass in digital humanities research more generally. It now undertakes significant research on metadata usage and text encoding standards and has become the nucleus of a Center for Research in the Digital Humanities at the University of Nebraska. The reverse is also the case: research units and faculty support units often engender digital publication projects by providing support and impetus for faculty to undertake scholarly publication in digital modes. Finally, digital library centers often produce digital publication projects focusing on individual collections or authors of particular significance. Examples include the Robert Graves Diary at the University of Victoria (http://graves.uvic.ca/), the Chymistry of Isaac Newton at Indiana University (http://webapp1.dlib.indiana.edu/newton/), the New York Public Library's Digital Schomburg collection (http://digital.nypl.org/schomburg/images_aa19/), and numerous others.

There are also important structural alliances arising between entities in this list. Digital library centers and faculty support centers often find themselves in complementary (or potentially competing) roles in responding to faculty needs for digital materials. Depending on where digital services first arise in a given institution, facilities such as digital course reserves, digitization services, and support for digital publications or scholarly digital projects based on library collections may fall within the purview of either type of group. A clear mutual articulation of responsibility can be crucial in avoiding duplication, gaps in service, and territorial disputes. Along different lines, digital publication projects and faculty support centers often depend on digital library centers for essential infrastructure, both technical and intellectual: metadata, cataloging, and digitization services, long-term archiving and digital repository management, and expertise in rights management and best practices.

DIGITAL HUMANITIES FROM A LIBRARY PERSPECTIVE

Thus far, we have been considering the field of digital humanities more or less as it considers itself. But from the perspective of the library community, the field presents a few specific faces of particular significance.

First of all, a very large proportion of large-scale digitization efforts in North America are being undertaken in libraries, or in partnership with libraries. The library community and in particular the academic library community are thus the places where attention is being paid to ways of making the resulting collections usable in a digital humanities context. Digital library staff are typically those charged with developing and implementing best practices for the use of metadata standards, and with producing and maintaining interfaces that permit these collections to be used effectively by readers. Already, experimentally, this use may include the ability to build new projects that draw and recombine materials from large digital collections, together with project-specific commentary or more specialized interface tools. And as we have already observed, a substantial number of digital humanities projects actually arise within libraries, arising either from faculty interests or from specific library collections (or both).

More importantly, though, libraries play a crucial role in the larger life cycle of the digital humanities. As we noted earlier, digital humanities tools and methods are constantly evolving from early experimental forms into routinized practices; as this happens, the kinds of support and implementation they require undergo significant changes. A digital tool or process in the incipient stages is initially adopted experimentally by a few adventurous practitioners; the required tools are installed as prototypes on a development server and programmers explore configurations, make optimizations, and work closely with faculty to develop cutting-edge projects that innovate both technically and intellectually. The results are often published as demonstrations of the potentially transformative effect the tool in question will have on humanities research. These activities typically take place within a digital humanities research group or faculty support center: groups devoted to small-scale, custom approaches that need not operate at scale to be effective as investigations. However, once the process in question is working smoothly and no longer requires attention (or poses interesting problems), such groups need to move on: their funding and institutional mandate require them to tackle new tools and processes, not to maintain well-established

projects at a production level, or to undertake their long-term preservation. As projects and processes enter a mature phase of active operation, a new set of needs arise: for the articulation of best practices, for cost-effective methods of executing work processes consistently and at scale, for anticipation of future needs such as forward migration of data, and for the provision of sustainable approaches to preservation and long-term access. These needs are entirely consonant with the traditional mission of libraries and it is in digital library centers that these needs are now typically being met. Because the library community is already primed to be aware of the importance of standards and best practices, they have led the digital humanities world in advocating, developing, adopting, and documenting standards and best practices in all areas of digitization.

Among these standards and practices a few of the most significant deserve specific mention:

- Metadata standards and specifically METS,[33] MODS (Metadata Object Description Schema),[34] EAD (Encoded Archival Description), the various name authority formats (MADS,[35] etc.), and controlled vocabularies which form the basis for large-scale data management and retrieval. While these are typically not used directly by digital humanities projects, they provide an infrastructure on which many digital humanities projects rely at some point in their life cycle: for instance, when they enter a digital repository, or when they draw on digital materials from a digital library collection.
- Digitization methods such as digital imaging, OCR, automated scanning and markup technologies. Advances in this area are often driven by digital library needs, which are on a larger scale than other typical digital humanities projects.
- Aggregation and federation of data to permit cross-collection searching and other forms of functionality such as metadata harvesting. These are complicated infrastructural systems that can only be implemented by libraries, but they can be (and increasingly are) used by digital humanities projects and activities.
- Intellectual property rights management, and reciprocally the issues surrounding digital publication and the licensing of research materials such as online journals. Libraries have traditionally acted as institutional agents in these realms and continue to do so in the digital arena; additionally, however, as libraries play an increasing role as publishers of digital information, they also play a potentially transformative (or disruptive) role in the publication ecology and its cost structures.[30]
- Information retrieval and knowledge representation, as these affect the design and implementation of large-scale systems for aggregating, processing, and using digital information in scholarly research. The field of

information science is merging into library science, specifically on the terrain of digital research materials. While these issues are by no means limited to the humanities, humanities data poses distinctive challenges and research requirements.

Finally, the rise of digital humanities activity and the increased resources that are being devoted to digital humanities projects mean that sustainability and long-term preservation of digital resources are rapidly becoming far from academic. Libraries are typically the place where digital repositories are being developed and housed, and the library world is the institutional space where issues of long-term archiving, metadata management, and forward migration are being tackled.

CHARACTERISTIC METHODS, PRACTICES, AND QUESTIONS

Modularity

The idea of a modular toolset or "scholar's workbench" has preoccupied the digital humanities community for decades[36] and has led to an interest in identifying the essential intellectual components of humanities scholarship and research. In a November 1995 posting to Humanist, Willard McCarty called for "a basic set of primitives" and a corresponding set of "component-packages"; "It seems to me that the most broadly useful invention would be a set of components the 'garden-variety' humanist could assemble quickly into a process." (Humanist 9.301 http://www.digitalhumanities.org/humanist/Archives/Virginia/v09/0278.html.) Perhaps in recognition of the tendency noted earlier—by which methods and tools become "black-boxed" as they attain routine status—modularity of design has become an important paradigm for the digital humanities at a fundamental level. Its corollary is the concept of the application programming interface: the exposure of processes, of inputs and outputs, so that modules can be developed independent of one another and assembled by the practitioner in whatever combinations suit the task at hand. Its underlying logic is that of the open source, in which a published specification and open architecture permit extension and experimentation without artificial dependency or limitation.

For digital humanists, this modularity has two important goals. The first is, practically, to be able to model or represent these components in a combinatorial way in the digital arena; in other words, rather than prepackaging them in arbitrary and immutable combinations, to provide more granular or elemental tools which can then be used in whatever combinations scholars need. The second, more theoretically, is to be able to work on the difficult task of modeling these primitives themselves digitally: not so much with the intention of producing tools, but rather of understanding the activities themselves more deeply.

The first goal has been tackled by digital humanities software developers. Willard McCarty gives as a notable example, the case of the Tübingen System of Text Processing Programs (TUSTEP),[37] which provides for a sequenced set of tasks which are taken as fundamental to certain types of digital text processing: "capture, retrieval, collation, analysis, sorting, rule-based manipulation and output in digital or printed form."[38] But as he points out, the second goal is more challenging; mapping functional modularity onto the "functional primitives of scholarship" is not straightforward and in fact they do not correspond directly. These functional primitives actually turn out to require a different kind of modularization from what is in evidence in current tools. John Unsworth suggests what these might be: "discovering, annotating, comparing, referring, sampling, illustrating, representing."[4] Unsworth explicitly proposes these as a basis for a "useful tool-building exercise in humanities computing." But as his subsequent discussion makes clear, the tools that arise to serve these needs are not focused in any simple way on sequencing these tasks or fulfilling them through a direct, modular implementation. On the contrary, he presents complex interfaces that integrate these functions as essential but not necessarily separable dimensions. In other words, modularity operates usefully at a conceptual level to help us understand the activities being supported or modeled, but at the level of implementation the units of modularization may be quite different.

Representation

Digital humanities as a field is deeply concerned with questions of representation, particularly as these impinge both on the digital representation "under the hood," and on the way source material is offered for use to the reader. These questions sometimes loom as large theoretical problems. For instance, through what kinds of information structures can a digital object represent a material object or a time-based object? How do we measure the adequacy of a representation: through qualities like visual fidelity, or informational richness, or retrievability, or tractability to analysis?[39,40] Does the form of the digital representation itself even matter, as long as its effects for the reader are serviceable? From another angle, the questions are methodological. What are the appropriate or strategically useful levels of granularity at which to represent data? What are the appropriate descriptive vocabularies and what are their characteristics? What is the strategically appropriate balance between, as Willard McCarty puts it, the "complexity and ambiguity" of the cultural source material, and the "mechanically rigorous" demands of computational form?[41]

We can usefully identify several distinct (and often complementary) approaches to the representation of digital humanities information.

The first of these is modeling, which McCarty describes as the "performative" building of "hypothetical constructs" (p. 53)[41] through which we can "make new knowledge" (p. 71);[41] a process of "purposeful simplification" (p. 52).[41] Modeling is thus an intellectual process which is not necessarily or even primarily digital, but which digital research methods bring to the fore. In this respect modeling recapitulates the relationship of critical engagement with the method that we observed earlier. McCarty notes the "mediating role and ternary relationship modeling establishes between the knower and known: the directed, vector-like engagement of the inquirer's attention, through the model he or she has made to the object of study, and the model's consequent function as an artificial agent of perception and instrument of thought" (p. 38).[41] One measure of success here is the sophistication of the questions the model permits us to entertain, and its horizon of usefulness. Do we exhaust its intellectual potential and its ability to sustain questions immediately or over a longer period of time? Another measure is the range of different kinds of questions the model permits. Digital modeling technologies are typically those that permit complex data representation: databases, XML structures like TEI, METS, or SVG, metadata of various sorts, and data formats that represent spatial information such as GIS or CAD.

An opposed, or at least complementary approach, is what we might term the "facsimile": representations that seek to reproduce the source more and more exactly according to some metric of fidelity. These metrics include, for instance, exactness of color duplication, granularity of visual detail, or fineness of sampling rate. Typically facsimiles appeal directly to some human sense: most frequently sight or sound, but we can imagine others becoming relevant with the advent of different output technologies catering to other senses. The measure of success for a facsimile is typically a level of accuracy, exactness of duplication, or sensory indistinguishability, rather than function. More precisely, the facsimile's accuracy supports high function in the human brain through the human analytic processes that it enables, rather than functionality within the digital system.[42]

The most common examples of facsimile approaches to digital representation are found in digital library collections that have been digitized as page images, often with metadata but without a corresponding transcription (either for reasons of cost or of transcriptional difficulty). In these cases, the facsimile simply offers an affordable way of providing basic access to rare or otherwise inaccessible materials for which transcription would be prohibitively expensive. However, for some projects the facsimile carries specific methodological merit as a way of representing visual (or other non-textual) information that

cannot yet be usefully modeled. The most vivid examples are the archives of visual artists such as William Blake or Dante Gabriel Rossetti, both of whom have prompted digital publications that not only rely on high-quality facsimile representations but also argue the limitations of modeling.[42]

These arguments also reflect an increasing interest in the materiality of media and in particular of the source materials that are the objects of scholarly research. The modeling approach involves the complete absorption and transfiguration of the source's informational content into a representation that is oriented toward some specific research problem. The facsimile approach suggests instead that there is an irreducible and resistant "thingness" to texts and artifacts that requires a more direct sensory interaction. The digital representation necessarily intervenes in this interaction (through sampling and the other reductions that take place in digitization) but it may do so to enhance some dimensions while it reduces in others. A good example is the work that has been done at the University of Kentucky's *Electronic Beowulf*,[43] where images of the damaged manuscript have been digitally processed so as to reconstruct damaged pages and make visible letters that could not otherwise be read. Processes such as digital flattening of folded or crumpled pages too brittle to be moved,[44] or magnification and special lighting to reveal nearly invisible marks, suggest the ways in which a researcher's apprehension of the material text itself is oddly more immediate and vivid—in some dimensions—when digitally mediated.

A third predominant form of digital representation is metadata, and in this category we can usefully also include the more traditional scholarly domain of commentary and contextualization. In an important sense, metadata is a more structured form of commentary: a way of formalizing our knowledge about an object and associating it with that object in a durable way. Under this informational rubric there is considerable variety. Some types of metadata are embedded within the digital object itself, such as EXIF or XMP data in a digital image file, or the TEI header in a TEI document. Other kinds stand outside the digital object and serve to catalog, manage, or situate it within a larger collection, or to manage information about some dimension of its content. Examples include METS, MODS, and the numerous formal standards for authority control. As the uses of metadata change with the growing importance of aggregation and cross-collection functionality, metadata is increasingly being managed apart from the digital object, pointing to it rather than being embedded within it, so that the distinction between embedded and independent metadata is less clear and less important.

Metadata plays a crucial role in the digital humanities, and particularly in projects and research tools in which scale is a critical component. For individual digital projects (such as a scholarly exploration of a single poem, or a multimedia installation, or an edition of a single text) the need for metadata is minimal, and is focused on the requirement that such digital objects should carry with them basic information about their creation and status as publications, much as a book carries a title page and publication information. Best practice suggests that such objects should also carry further information about their preparation: the editorial principles that guided their creation, the relevant digitization standards, and methods of capture. This information, while not always strictly necessary for a reader, is probably useful for most critical readers. It serves the role of the discussion of methods that accompanies scholarly editions, and also serves the crucial purpose of facilitating future support or archiving of the digital object by an IT support group or a digital repository. Indeed, as soon as the object finds its way into institutional structures like these, it no longer functions in isolation but has to take its place in collections (increasingly large ones) in which its effective functioning will depend greatly on what kinds of metadata it carries or has added to it as part of its acquisition.

This transition illustrates an important tension in how metadata functions within the digital ecology. To the extent that the digital humanities domain aspires toward effects of scale (interinstitutional collaboration, large-scale aggregation of resources, cross-collection searching, reliable retrieval, analysis) it anticipates the value of metadata and invests significant resources in creating it, typically through partnerships with libraries or organizations devoted to creating standards and metadata aggregations (e.g., OAI). At the same time, as digital humanities reaches the scholarly desktop and no longer requires large-scale funding or groups of people to implement digital humanities projects, digital humanities activities resemble individual monographic publications, but without the publication infrastructure through which metadata in the print world has traditionally been supplied. In addition, the structure and even the medium of many digital humanities projects and publications leaves little space for metadata. For this reason, many of the digital scholarly products of the current era find themselves in publication (via the Web) without the levels of formal metadata control that were commonplace in print.

Pattern Discovery and Visualization

There has been increased interest in a new breed of text analysis tools which emphasize dynamic manipulation and pattern discovery rather than hypothesis testing and scientific approaches.[45–49] The value of interactive systems was recognized much earlier; see for example Ben Shneiderman's 1983 discussion of "direct manipulation" which he defined as systems whose key features are "visibility of the object of interest; rapid, reversible, incremental actions; and replacement of complex command language syntax by direct manipulation of the object of interest."[50] In the same vein, John Bradley contrasts what he calls the "deterministic-transformational" approach to text analysis with approaches that consider "the effect of the machine on the development of a critic's *mental model* of the text" (187, emphasis in the original). McCarty, commenting on this entry, observes further that "Criticism is ... poorly supported by batch-orientated software, which being a 'black box' is by nature peripheral to what the scholar actually does" (219).

This emphasis on text analysis has led to significant research efforts in two directions: first, a resurgence of interest in large data sets that will permit meaningful literary text analysis, but with some differences from earlier corpus-building approaches: whole texts rather than samples; texts that are of significance to scholarship; markup used to represent genres and textual structures. And second, there has been a strong interest in developing tools that draw on data mining technologies drawn from the sciences and financial analysis to permit very large-scale pattern discovery. Currently the most prominent example of humanities data mining is the MONK Project (http://www.monkproject.org). These efforts are still nascent, but they offer significant potential to respond to real scholarly needs in the humanities rather than overlaying scientific investigative techniques onto literary content.

In concert with the development of the back end software and substantial corpora for analysis, visualization tools are also emerging as a crucial component of modern text analysis, but they have also arisen on their own as part of the fascination with Web 2.0 styles of graphical display and aggregations of data. From a digital humanities perspective, visualization tools fit well with the prevailing interest in modeling, since they provide ways of creating visual analogues to the representational models operating within the data itself, or within the researcher's own mind. Digital humanities visualization tools draw techniques from a wide array of sources: knowledge management tools, mapping, social networking tools, medical and scientific imaging, and virtual reality tools.

Future Trends

The developmental tendencies for the digital humanities field seem to run both toward increased disciplinary consolidation (through the emergence of departments, faculty, and degree programs) and also, ironically, toward disciplinary dispersal as digital techniques penetrate the humanities more and more broadly. It is thus difficult to predict whether in 20 years the field will have created very clear boundaries for itself, or on the contrary will simply have become synonymous with "the humanities" and perhaps have disappeared altogether. However, beyond its impact on the practice of traditional humanities disciplines, perhaps the clearest indication of its influence is the emergence of new humanities fields in which digital media are themselves the focus of attention. We have already mentioned new media studies, the study (as Janet

Murray puts it in her introduction to the *New Media Reader*) of "the computer as an expressive medium." Adjoining this field are two others of note: first, game studies, which takes the same approach but with a close focus on computer games and the expressive logic of the game form. The second is digital aesthetics, not yet perhaps a field but certainly a research domain, again attending to the expressive potential of the digital realm but with an emphasis on specifically aesthetic questions and problems. These three fields which represent visible nodes in an intellectual continuum that is still in the process of coagulating, all take the computer itself, and the digitally networked systems that arise from it and depend on it, as having pervasive cultural significance—not because of their novelty, but because of the distinctiveness of the intervention they are making in our cultural and intellectual habits. The complex relationship between digital information and human cognition, which could be characterized as augmentative, complementary, frictional, or mutually antagonistic seems to reveal problems and questions of deep and lasting significance which we need new tools and approaches to study. Digital humanities may prove to be the durable locus of that study, or it may turn out to be a temporary phase through which these studies are passing on their way to a more tightly defined disciplinary focus.

REFERENCES

1. Vectors: Journal of Culture and Technology in a Dynamic Vernacular University of Southern California http://www.vectorsjournal.org.
2. Hypertext in American Studies http://chnm.gmu.edu/aq/.
3. Engelbart, D.C. *Augmenting Human Intellect: A Conceptual Framework*, Summary Report AFOSR-3223 under Contract AF 49(638)-1024, SRI Project 3578 for Air Force Office of Scientific Research section III.B.2 Stanford Research Institute: Menlo Park, CA, 1962 http://www.bootstrap.org/augdocs/friedewald030402/augmentinghumanintellect/3examples.html#B.
4. Unsworth, J. *Scholarly Primitives: What Methods Do Humanities Researchers have in Common, and how Might Our Tools Reflect this?*, King's College: London, U.K., May 13, 2000 http://www3.isrl.uiuc.edu/~unsworth/Kings.5-00/primitives.html (accessed February 2008).
5. Ippolito, J.; Dietrich, C. ThoughtMesh. Vectors **2007**, *3* (1) http://www.vectorsjournal.org/index.php?page=7&projectId=84 (accessed February 2008).
6. NINES http://www.nines.org.
7. http://www.diglib.org/about/dldefinition.htm.
8. Busa, R. Complete index verborum of the works of St Thomas. Speculum **1950**, *25*, 424–425.
9. *Index Thomisticus: Sancti Thomae Aquinatis operum indices et concordantiae.* Frommann-Holzboog: Stuttgart, Germany, 1974–1979; 49 vols.
10. Busa, R. *Thomæ Aquinatis opera omnia cum hypertextibus in CD-ROM*, Editoria Elettronica Editel: Milano, 1992.
11. *Directory of Scholars Active.* CHum **1967**, *1* (5), 178–241.
12. Brunner, T.F. Classics and the computer. The history of a relationship. In *Accessing Antiquity. The Computerization of Classical Studies*; Solomon, J., Ed.; University of Arizona Press: Tucson, AZ, 1993; 10–33.
13. Luci Berkowitz, L.; Squitier, K.A. *Thesaurus Linguae Graecae Canon of Greek Authors and Works*, 3rd Ed.; Oxford University Press: Oxford, 1990.
14. Hockey, S. The history of humanities computing. *A Companion to Digital Humanities*; Blackwell: Oxford, 2004; 10.
15. Hockey, S. *A Guide to Computer Applications in the Humanities*; The Johns Hopkins Press: Baltimore and London, 1980; 34–36, 75.
16. *Nota Bene*, Dragonfly Software, 1982.
17. DeRose, S.J.; Durand, D.G.; Mylonas, E.; Renear, A.H. What is text, really?. J. Comput. Higher Educ. **1990**, *2* (1), 3–26.
18. Renear, A.H.; Mylonas, E.; Durand, D.G. Refining our notion of what text really is: The problem of overlapping hierarchies Research in Humanities Computing 4: Selected Papers from the ALLC/ACH Conference Christ Church Oxford April, 1992; Hockey, S., Ide, N., Eds.; Oxford University Press: Oxford, 1996; 263–280.
19. Renear, A. The descriptive/procedural distinction is flawed. Markup Languages Theory Practice **2001**, *2* (4), 411–420.
20. Renear, A.; Phillippe, C.; Lawton, P.; Dubin, D. An XML document corresponds to which FRBR group 1 entity? Proceedings of Extreme Markup Languages Montréal, Québec August, 4–8, 2003; Usdin, B.T., Newcomb, S.R., Eds.; 2005 http://www.idealliance.org/papers/extreme03/xslfo-pdf/2003/Lawton01/EML2003Lawton01.pdf (accessed February 2008).
21. Engelbart, D.C. Augmenting Human Intellect: A Conceptual Framework Summary Report AFOSR-3223 under Contract AF 49(638)-1024, SRI Project 3578 for Air Force Office of Scientific Research Stanford Research Institute Menlo Park, CA 1962.
22. Nelson, T.H. *Literary Machines. The Report on, and of, Project Xanadu Concerning Word Processing, Electronic Publishing, Hypertext, Thinkertoys, Tomorrow's Intellectual... Including Knowledge, Education and Freedom*, Mindful Press: Sausalito, CA, 1981.
23. Delany, P.; Landow, G. *Hypermedia and Literary Studies*; MIT Press: Cambridge, MA, 1991.
24. http://www.w3.org/XML/.
25. http://www.tei-c.org.
26. Encoded Archival Description. Available at http://www.loc.gov/ead/.
27. Bolter, J.D. *Writing Space. The Computer, Hypertext, and the History of Writing*, L. Erlbaum Associates: Hillsdale, NJ, 1991.
28. 28.Landow, G.P., Ed. *Hyper/Text/Theory*; Johns Hopkins University Press: Baltimore, MD, 1994.
29. Ulmer, G.L. *Heuretics: The Logic of Invention*, Johns Hopkins University Press: Baltimore, MD, 1994.
30. *Our Cultural Commonwealth, The Report of the American Council of Learned Societies Commission on Cyberinfrastructure for the Humanities and Social Sciences*, ACLS: New York, 2006; 30. Available at http://www.acls.org/cyberinfrastructure/OurCulturalCommonwealth.pdf (accessed February 2008).

31. http://www.allc.org/content/pubs/imhc/imch.html.
32. http://digitalhumanities.pbwiki.com/.
33. Metadata Encoding & Transmission Standard. Available at http://www.loc.gov/standards/mets/.
34. Metadata Object Description Standard. Available at http://www.loc.gov/standards/mods/.
35. Metadata Authority Description Standard. Available at http://www.loc.gov/standards/mads/.
36. http://www.iath.virginia.edu/lists_archive/Humanist/v09/0278.html.
37. http://www.zdv.uni-tuebingen.de/tustep/tustep_eng.html.
38. McCarty, W. *Humanities Computing*; Palgrave: London and New York, 2005; 217.
39. Renear, A. Out of praxis: Three (meta)theories of textuality. In *Electronic Text: Investigations in Method and Theory*; Sutherland, K., Ed.; Oxford University Press: Oxford, 1997; 107–126.
40. Lavagnino, J. Completeness and adequacy in text encoding. In *The Literary Text in the Digital Age*; Finneran, R., Ed.; University of Michigan Press: Ann Arbor, 1996; 63–76.
41. McCarty, W. *Humanities Computing*; Palgrave: London and New York, 2005; 122.
42. Viscomi, J. Digital facsimiles: reading the William Blake Archive. CHum **2002**, *36*, 27–48.
43. http://beowulf.engl.uky.edu.
44. Seales, W.B.; Griffioen, J.; Kiernan, K.; Yuan, C.J.; Cantara, L. The digital atheneum: New technologies for restoring and preserving old documents. Comput. Libr. **2000**, *20* (2), 26–30. Available at http://www.infotoday.com/cilmag/feb00/seales.htm (accessed February 2008).
45. Bradley, J. Finding a middle ground between 'determinism' and 'aesthetic indeterminacy': A model for text analysis tools. LLC **2003**, *18* (2), 185–207.
46. Rockwell, G. What is text analysis, really?. LLC **2003**, *18* (2), 209–219.
47. Ramsay, S. Reconceiving text analysis: toward an algorithmic criticism. LLC **2003**, *18* (2), 167–174.
48. Sinclair, S. Computer-assisted reading: Reconceiving text analysis. LLC **2003**, *18* (2), 175–184.
49. Siemens, R. A new computer-assisted literary criticism?. CHum **2002**, *36* (3), 259–267.
50. Shneiderman, B. Direct manipulation: A step beyond programming languages. IEEE Comput. **1983**, *16* (8), 57–69.

BIBLIOGRAPHY

Books

1. McCarty, W. *Humanities Computing*, Palgrave: Basingstoke, 2005. Includes a very good bibliography.
2. Schreibman, S., Siemens, R., Unsworth, J., Eds.; *A Companion to Digital Humanities;* Blackwell: Oxford, 2002. Available at http://www.digitalhumanities.org/companion/. Each section provides a list of sources for further reading.
3. Siemens, R., Schreibman, S., Eds. *A Companion to Digital Literary Studies*; Blackwell: Oxford, 2007.
4. Wardrip-Fruin, N., Montfort, N., Eds. *The New Media Reader*; MIT: Cambridge, MA, 2003. This extensive documentary history of new media also illuminates an important dimension of the early history of digital humanities. Each article is accompanied by a list of sources for further reading.

Journals

1. Computers and the Humanities (CHum) Kluwer **1966–2005**. The official journal of the Association for Computers and the Humanities until 2004.
2. Digital Humanities Quarterly (DHQ). ACH and ADHO **2006–present**. The digital journal of the Alliance of Digital Humanities Organizations. Available at http://www.digitalhumanities.org/dhq/.
3. Literary and Linguistic Computing (LLC). Oxford **1986–present**. The official journal of the Association for Literary and Linguistic Computing until 2004, and subsequently the journal for the Alliance of Digital Humanities Organizations.

Sites and Online Resources

1. Arts and Humanities Data Service. Although no longer active, the Web site has a collection of articles on best practices in digital humanities that are very valuable. Available at http://ahds.ac.uk/.
2. ICT Methods Network. Another currently active site that collects resources and best practices for digital humanities. As it is in the United Kingdom, this site provides information on European projects. Available at http://www.methodsnetwork.ac.uk.
3. Intute: Arts and Humanities (formerly the Humbul Humanities Hub). A comprehensive portal with annotated listings for over 21,000 Web resources in the arts and humanities.
4. Humanist is an ongoing international "electronic seminar" on the application of computers to the humanities that began in 1987 (http://www.princeton.edu/humanist/).
5. Liu, A. Ed. *The Voice of the Shuttle;* A very extensive annotated listing of online digital humanities sites, projects, and resources. Available at http://vos.ucsb.edu/ .
6. NINCH Guide to Good Practice in the Digital Representation and Management of Cultural Heritage Materials NINCH 2002. Available at http://www.nyu.edu/its/humanities/ninchguide/ (accessed February 2008).
7. The Web sites of the digital humanities professional organizations are a good way to learn about conferences and resources. The Alliance of Digital Humanities Organizations (http://www.digitalhumanities.org) is an umbrella organization for the European Association for Literary and Linguistic Computing (ALLC) (http://www.allc.org) the American Association for Computers and the Humanities (ACH) (http://www.ach.org), and the Canadian The Society for Digital Humanities/Société pour l'étude des médias interactifs (SDH-SEMI) (http://www.sdh-semi.org).

Digital Humanities and Academic Libraries

Bobby Smiley
Vanderbilt University, Heard Libraries, Nashville, Tennessee, U.S.A.

Michael Rodriguez
Michigan State University Libraries, East Lansin, Michigan, U.S.A.

Abstract

This entry opens by defining and outlining digital humanities as an academic enterprise and exploring the intellectual and institutional connections between digital humanities and libraries. Through an examination of the major publications on the subject, the theory and concepts of digital humanities as a field of inquiry are explored, and how those theories and concepts are possibly mapped to academic library traditional collections and services. The majority of the narrative is then dedicated to focusing on the nature of the work being done in these areas by academic libraries and librarians and the issues and challenges they encounter surfacing in that work.

INTRODUCTION

"[O]f all scholarly pursuits," the literary scholar Stephen Ramsey relates, "Digital Humanities most clearly represents the spirit that animated the ancient foundations at Alexandria, Pergamum, and Memphis, the great monastic libraries of the Middle Ages, and even the first research libraries of the German Enlightenment." For Ramsey, digital humanities (DH) "is obsessed with varieties of representation, the organization of knowledge, the technology of communication and dissemination, and the production of useful tools for scholarly inquiry." These sentiments underline an enduring connection between DH work and librarians, accenting a shared investment in information organization, discovery and access, outreach, and collection development. Indeed, sites of DH research, Ramsey contends, enable "scholars to act more like librarians, and . . . librarians to act more like scholars."[1]

Ramsey's remarks highlight a growing consensus among librarians and DH scholars about the place of the library in DH, and DH in libraries. With expertise in metadata, knowledge of digital collections, and familiarity with the operational side of digital projects—whether sourcing, preparing, and manipulating data; digitization and analysis of text, moving images, or other audiovisual material, information architecture, and user experience; or instruction about tools and techniques—librarians have played an important role in promoting and integrating DH in universities.[2] At the same time, librarians have also generated DH scholarship, such as leading the large Text Encoding Initiative (TEI), and data and text mining projects, which, inter alia, helps efface and complicate the implied division of labor that often surfaces between librarians and digital humanists.[3] That librarians are integral participants in conversations about DH *as* digital humanists is a perspective embraced by many working in the field.[4]

And while DH labs and centers have been well established and based in libraries (such as the Center for Digital Research in the Humanities at the University of Nebraska), more libraries have begun to investigate different ways of initiating or formalizing their work in DH and are considering the place of the library in the institutional development of DH programs in universities and the attendant difficulties inherent in establishing infrastructure and support for library-led DH initiatives.[5] But the opportunities offered and the questions raised by this relationship are manifold, and all parties—librarians, professors, and administrators—also understand how indispensable collaboration is in fostering and sustaining successfully digitally oriented research endeavors in the humanities and social sciences.[6]

This entry opens by defining and outlining DH as an academic enterprise and exploring the intellectual and institutional connections between DH and libraries. The majority of the narrative is dedicated to focusing on the nature of the work being done in these areas by libraries and librarians, by librarians working with academic faculty, and the issues and challenges they encounter surfacing in that work.

DIGITAL HUMANITIES

One of the principal problems for anyone interested in DH is the vexed question of definition. Whether made capacious or narrowly drawn, definitions for DH often reflect the research interests and work of persons proffering definitions. At a talk in 2010, Johanna Drucker, observed in jest that the heterogeneous nature of DH—filled with librarians, information scientists, and scholars working in disparate fields of the humanities—resembled the variegated extraterrestrial crowd at the Mos Eisley Cantina from the original *Star Wars* film.[7] And, to be sure, this heterogeneity is reflected in the Whitman's sampler of methodological approaches employed by numerous scholars from the various fields doing original work in the DH: network analysis, algorithmic criticism (topic modeling, word frequency analysis, large-scale text analysis), preparation and analysis of linguistic corpora, digital media archeology, spatial humanities (geo-analysis), data visualization, instructional design and pedagogy, and locating and assembling humanities data sets—to name only a few.

In view of this, when venturing a definition, a more functionalist approach that examines scholarly activities or modalities related to DH is probably most appropriate. For Josh Honn, a Digital Scholarship Librarian at Northwestern University, the work that shapes what is classed as DH falls into five, nonmutually exclusive categories:

1. Scholarship presented in digital form(s)
2. Scholarship enabled by digital methods and tools
3. Scholarship about digital technology and culture
4. Scholarship building and experimenting with digital technology
5. Scholarship critical of its own digitalness[8]

What Honn means by each speaks (in a disciplinary manner) ecumenically to DH's computational, experimental, cultural, and deeply self-reflexive humanist academic origins. Beginning with Father Roberto Busa's enlistment of IBM in 1949 to help develop the *Index Thomisticus* (often adduced as the first DH project), DH work has been characterized by the engagement of information technology and methods, questions, and content culled from diverse scholarly fields and a concomitant reflection on the use of that technology in that engagement.

By this reckoning, DH is not so much a distinct, intellectually autonomous disciplinary field, but rather as John Unsworth contends, "a method of reasoning."[9] What this means for librarians is that DH librarianship does not necessarily have to be tethered to the kind of single subject specialization associated with subject librarianship (expressed most frequently by additional disciplinary degrees). Instead, DH furnishes powerful digital tools and interdisciplinary methodologies to gather data, analyze them in ways previously unused/underused in humanities research (for instance, network analysis), and take the results thereof to draw novel conclusions and pose original research questions. This understanding of DH, with its accent on critical, interdisciplinary openness, affords librarians greater purchase, both intellectually and procedurally, in skilling up for, participating in, or overseeing DH enterprises—whether as extensions of library-focused work (using DH methods for collections analysis), as collaborations with disciplinary faculty (procuring data for research), or building digital projects.

LIBRARIES AND DH: THEORY AND PRACTICE

Theory

The current scholarship on DH and libraries theoretically and conceptually places libraries within the DH more as collaborative entities and having a greater role in faculty scholarship endeavors. As the title of the 2015 Association of College and Research Libraries (ACRL) publication *Digital Humanities in the Library*: *Challenges and Opportunities for Subject Specialists* suggests, DH and libraries has now in great part wrested with subject librarians and collections specialists. In collaboration with other campus entities (mainly faculty, but also grad students), libraries and librarians can offer "partner relationships, becoming embedded in the mission-critical aspects of higher education—research, teaching, and learning—and infusing librarians particular expertise, collections and values into new types of research..." (Forward, X).[10] This ACRL publication does well to combine many of the "core" publications on libraries and DH that came before it—especially Issue 53 of the *Journal of Library Administration*, the Association of Research Libraries (ARL) SPEC Kit 326, and the Ithaka report on *Sustaining the Digital Humanities*: *Host Institution Support Beyond the Start-Up Phase*—by giving an overview of the state of scholarship in the field as pertains to libraries, while simultaneously demonstrating best-case scenarios and real-world solutions to DH-generated problems. Most recently, *Laying the Foundation*: *Digital Humanities in Academic Libraries* does well illustrating how "librarians are critical partners in DH instruction and inquiry and that libraries are essential for publishing, preserving, and making accessible digital scholarship" (xii). Along the 2016 SPEC Kit 350 on *Supporting Digital Scholarship*, these publications (among many others) form a core of titles around which to explore three areas of theoretical encounters: 1) how libraries enact and engage DH, 2) how libraries understand and relate to DH, and 3) how libraries can sustain, foster, and facilitate DH.

How libraries enact and engage DH

The first to appear of the "core" publications on the subject was the 2011 ARL SPEC Kit 326: *Digital Humanities*, which was made to answer the question of whether and which libraries offered centers or services that support DH work. Its stated purpose was "to provide a snapshot of research library experiences in these centers...and the benefits and challenges of hosting them" (p. 10). By way of survey, the SPEC Kit identifies major trends of libraries supporting DH and estimates levels of project staffing, services and support, hardware and software, (the range of) service users, actual project workspace, funding sources, policies and procedures, sustainability (through project preservation), partnerships, and whether these efforts were undergoing assessment. The survey recognizes the relative prevalence of "bricks and mortar" DH centers (as opposed to a more general digital scholarship center) and how great the overall effort of a library team (with other units such as metadata and preservation units) being involved is. The remainder of the SPEC Kit delineates findings from the survey instrument, and then provides representative documents (mostly screen captures) attached to the DH-related units who responded. Especially useful are the conclusions that libraries are most useful (and are considered that way by scholars) at the starting and ending phases of a DH project because they provide knowledge of various information technologies and collections, and because libraries have knowledge of metadata and preservation.

In 2016, ACRL released another SPEC Kit (350) on *Supporting Digital Scholarship* that surveyed and updated much of the same terrain as the earlier publication. That these volumes bore a remarkable similarity in content yet were branded differently could serve an informal index of how ACRL envisions how libraries enact and engage DH. Using Abby Smith Rumsey's definition for digital scholarship, this SPEC Kit understands library engagement as the "use of digital evidence and method, digital authoring, digital publishing, digital curation and preservation, and digital use and reuse of scholarship."[11] For librarians, what this engagement includes are varied activities and support services within the library, such as digitizing and reformatting analog media, metadata creation, building digital collections and exhibits, digital publishing support, database support, software development, interface design, and consulting on geospatial information (GIS) and digital mapping projects, doing text encoding and analysis. Indeed, the move toward "digital scholarship" elicits questions about what, if anything, is distinctive about "digital humanities" librarianship. *Supporting Digital Scholarship* does not discuss or acknowledge a distinction (nor does it use "digital humanities" in its executive summary). Given the list of duties detailed in the report, an emphasis on generating original scholarship, or acting as research partners, is comparatively not stressed.[12] Whatever "digital scholarship" is for libraries engaging in DH, it remains undetermined whether the term functions as simply rebranding, implies a discrete set of duties that principally accent service and support, or extends librarians' work in DH to other disciplines as library-led scholarship.

How libraries understand and relate to DH

In 2013, the *Journal of Library Administration* devoted an entire issue to addressing the nexus of DH and libraries—what was currently being done and what the future was. Chris Alen Sula's article on *Digital Humanities and Libraries: A Conceptual Model* for the first time presents

a "cultural informatics model of libraries and digital humanities, and (situates) DH work with the user-centered paradigm of library and information science."[13] By doing so, Sula conjoins DH and libraries and how the two can be operationalized through collaboration—both within the library (between library units) and across campus. This model places emphasis on relevancy rather than sustainability, which is a slight departure from the scholarship on the subject previously. Potential collaboration between DH scholars and librarians then "offer(s) an important opportunity to provide renewed support for the humanities and to bring library resources across the board up to speed with digital scholarship for the 21st century." Others within the *JAL* issue pick up the mantel of collaboration: Jennifer Vinopal and Monica McComick suggest that "New models for librarian-scholar collaboration include much more librarian engagement with the entire research process than ever before," including "grant-seeking, project planning, data collection and organization, and metadata creation," as well as "data analysis and visualization, content dissemination, and long-term archiving."[14] And this range of work is reflected in the multi-institution survey results from librarians reporting about the variety of work they do published the 2016 ACRL SPEC Kit on digital scholarship:

- (90–95%) making digital collections, creating metadata, and offering data curation and management support
- (85%) creating exhibits and project planning
- (81%) GIS and digital mapping
- (79%) digitization
- (76%) digital publishing
- (72%) project management
- (38%) developing DS software[12]

How libraries can sustain, foster, and facilitate DH

The Ithaka report on *Sustaining the Digital Humanities: Host Institution Support Beyond the Start-Up Phase* combines the theoretical with the practical, demonstrates what libraries are doing with DH, and points out possible success scenarios for the future—in part answering the mythic question of "If I/we build it will they come?"[15] Though the study focused on a small but tidy group of ARL institutions that had established DH "centers" within their libraries, many other administrators, librarians, and scholars were interviewed around questions having to do with sustainability, investment in resources, and expected outcomes. For libraries, the report is important for its insistence on institutional ("top level") support from university administrations and provides several frameworks for gap analysis surveys to be done on campuses. Once it has been decided upon whether to start a DH center, and the answer is "to build," then there is a practical road map in the section on "Success Factors and Examples of Good Practice" by keeping the following in mind while visualizing and operationalizing a DH center:

1. Knit deep partnerships among campus units (library, IT, digital labs).
2. Rationalize support and manage faculty expectations.
3. Figure out how to use scale solutions, without overly limiting the creativity and research aims of project leaders.
4. Clearly communicate pathways and expectations to faculty.
5. Measure and communicate impact.

The report goes beyond previous theoretical models and suggests the "Comprehensive System" for creating the DH center through

1. A clear starting point for any faculty or staff developing digital projects
2. An "intake" process that allows an important screening process
3. Regular communication among those units on campus with human or infrastructure capacity to share
4. Establishment of measures for success
5. Bring(ing) in new partners to the digital life cycle to support dissemination activities
6. Documentation that spells out the process to all faculty and staff members

The Ithaka report is heavy on institutional collaboration for the success of a DH unit, as are most of the advisory takeaways from the scholarship on the subject. So in answer to the question "If I/We build it will they come?" the answer is, "Only if you build it in partnerships and collaboration with other campus entities."

The subtext of the Ithaka report also suggests an emphasis on new skills and ways approaching the profession for librarians of the twenty-first century. Preceding Ithaka was a 2012 report released by Research Libraries United Kingdom (RLUK) that broadly redefined roles for subject librarians.[16] Entitled *Re-skilling for Research*, the report accented the growing importance of equipping academic and research librarians with a large swath of technical skills associated with data analysis and curation, in addition to further training in grant writing and soliciting funding for projects. The recommendations in *Re-skilling* for subject and liaison librarians in academic and research institutions conclude by emphasizing how these librarians have effectively created and curated metadata in the past, and will be required to do more of the same in the future.[16] Librarians must evince "knowledge to advocate, and advise on, the use of metadata," as well as possess "[s]kills to develop metadata schema, and advise on discipline/subject standards and practices, for individual research projects." This emphasis on training is also outlined by Alix Keener in her study of DH scholars and academic librarians within the Center for Institutional Cooperation (CIC) network of institutions, where she urges "libraries … [to] address internal issues, such as training and re-skilling librarians as necessary," in order to help "make the library an active and equal partner in research."[17]

Practice

Owing to its relative, more formalized newness in libraries, steps for practical implementation of library-led DH initiatives have only recently begun to be discussed. As a template based on their own experiences, Katie Gibson, Marcus Ladd, and Jenny Presnell have outlined a tiered commitment level description of how librarians can start building DH capacity through outreach, instruction, and self-education:

- *Low commitment*: connect with graduate students, explore other DH sites and projects, and learn about institutional technological infrastructure, preservation formats and standards, and altmetrics.
- *Moderate commitment*: host DH symposium with external participants, collaborate on designing curriculum for courses, provide workshops, and seek opportunities to learn DH tools and how to code.
- *Intensive commitment*: build new DH projects with materials sourced from library's unique holdings.[18]

As indicated, skilling up for DH work (learning code, tools, methodologies, data manipulation, different application programming interfaces [APIs]) composes an essential component at all stages, and beyond self-paced websites (e.g., Codecademy) or MOOCs, options are limited for professional development—and are often pitched to those already working in allied, tech-heavy areas. Some institutions have developed in-house initiatives designed to equip subject librarians the "hard" technological skills often needed for DH projects. For instance, informed by *Re-skilling for Research*'s conclusions about the future import of DH, the humanities and history librarians at Columbia University formed the Developing Librarian Project, a 2 yr hands-on effort to learn-by-doing that required them to design and build a digital project ab initio. But, explains Miriam Posner, the coordinator and core faculty in Digital Humanities Program at the University of California, Los Angeles, "much of the discussion about building a DH-friendly library environment leans too hard on individual librarians, without taking into account the set of institutional supports, incentives, and rewards that will allow DH to flourish in a sustained way."[19] In addition to these concerns, Posner emphasizes several practical problems library-based DH work can encounter, and ones that might stymie any level of commitment investment; these include limited training opportunities, "lack of support for librarian-conceived initiatives," innumerable tasks with limited time, "lack of authority to marshal the appropriate resources," "inflexible infrastructure," "lack of incentive," concerns working with faculty, "diffusion of effort," and "lack of a real institutional commitment." By drawing attention to these issues, Posner urges consideration not only of the substance of DH library work but also how necessary the material conditions and institutional commitments are to enable and sustain its possibility.

For librarians just beginning to establish or build out DH work in the library, more sensitive, existential, and political questions surface concerning their role in that work. If there are librarians doing DH work, asks Dot Porter, the curator for Digital Research Services at the University of Pennsylvania, then "what the heck is a DH academic?"[20] In high-level discussions of DH in the library, there is often an implied division invoked between "librarians" and "DH scholars/academics" and an argument for understanding the role of "librarians as digital sherpas" or for separating out the work of the "DH skilled-librarians" from "DH academics."[21] And, to be sure, such a perspective is in consonant with the traditional service orientation of library work, which accents librarians' role in providing critical and often necessary support and guidance for DH projects. Without library expertise, for instance, in furnishing metadata or sourcing data sets, DH projects that rely on these indispensable library services would most likely flounder or stall. But as Alix Keener explains, while "scholars appreciate the specialized expertise of librarians" (such as metadata and special collections work), librarians at the same time should "take a more active stance in utilizing current library resources or vocalizing their needs for other resources."[17]

All the same, as Trevor Muñoz, assistant dean for Digital Humanities Research at the University of Maryland Libraries, contends, "[d]igital humanities in libraries isn't a service and libraries will be more successful at generating engagement with digital humanities if they focus on helping librarians lead their own DH initiatives and projects."[4] While these two approaches are not mutually exclusive, they do suggest the charged valence that often slots digital humanists working in the library into a category that is distinct from colleagues stationed in other campus units. "It doesn't make sense to measure the digital humanist-ness of someone," Porter advances, "based on their current post (especially as digital humanists tend to be fairly fluid, moving between posts inside and outside of the library)." And to militate against these concerns, Bethany Nowviskie, director of the Digital Library Federation and director of Digital Research and Scholarship at the University of Virginia Library, proposes embracing a collaborative model that emphasizes independence and parity, the "Skunk Works." Taken from a Lockheed-Martin working group, the term skunk works "describes a small and nimble technical team, deliberately and self-

consciously and (yes) quite unfairly freed from much of the surrounding bureaucracy of the larger organization in which it finds itself."[22] For building DH projects that involve participants across university units (including the library), skunk works are premised on marking out inventive spaces for digital humanists—irrespective of job title—to collaborate as research and development peers in generating original research. As Harriet Green argues, only by "engaging in radical collaborations and pursuing new reconfigurations of library engagement and services, librarians can become even more embedded in the research workflow and engage researchers as partners."[23]

With these practical—and at times abstract—considerations informing the library environment for DH work, the operational side for the library resembles the recommendations of the tiered commitment model outlined by Gibson, Ladd, and Presnell. Working from those recommendations and expanding its scope, a more generic set of terms to group the elements described can be divined that characterizes the broad areas of work DH librarians do: instruction, consultation and collaboration, and collection. While many librarians do work in these areas (in the case of the subject specialists, usually all four), these terms take on a special, practically oriented valance when used in a DH context.

Instruction

For many librarians, instruction often entails teaching information literacy, or providing demonstrations of print and electronic resources or discovery systems, like the library catalog. While this variety of teaching falls within the purview of librarians whose work might encompass DH, instruction for DH librarians frequently emphasizes two ways that extend traditional library teaching: pedagogical collaboration with teaching faculty and leading workshops and boot camps.[24] Ideally, informing instruction in these settings is a holistic understanding of digital pedagogy that helps facilitate digital literacy, that is, as Anita Say Chan and Harriet Green explain, these are pedagogical approaches that "connect digital tools to research practices linked to course content."[25]

Library-led curriculum support in DH can range from working with instructors to developing assignments that introduce DH tools and methods, making available data sets for analysis (whether sourced from the library's own collection or available elsewhere), or leading sessions that introduce tools or being an embedded presence providing specific assistance for DH class projects. Successful pedagogical collaborations between librarians and teaching faculty, Zoe Borovsky and Elizabeth McAulay argue, usually involve making "subject matter . . . the central concern of the course rather than digital methodology."[26] In other words, these collaborations can help cultivate digital literacy (for instance, evaluating different digital tools and methods) from grounding in and speaking through disciplinary knowledge. Another common area of instruction for DH librarians are workshops or boot camps, which pivot around introducing DH tools and methods in a manner often similar to information literacy sessions, albeit without the disciplinary focus. There are efforts to explore to use the unique affordances of library instruction to teach DH through information and data literacy principles, as well as disciplinary expectations, but much of the teaching remains tool focused.[27] Whether course based or workshop introduced, Adeline Koh has identified four general types of projects best suited to library-led DH instruction: digital mapping, text analysis, multimedia websites/online exhibits, and Wikipedia editing.[28] These types of projects can both complement disciplinary instruction as well as serve as a single session in a workshops series. In all instances, library-led DH instruction incorporates traditional elements of library pedagogy (information literacy, one-shot sessions) but entails greater collaboration and co-presence with teaching faculty.

Consultation and collaboration

Like instruction, consultation for DH librarians builds upon the principles of the reference interview and an understanding of information seeking behavior but is also frequently augmented by counsel, partnership/collaboration on grant writing, research data management, technical advice, and project management. With its stress on collaboration, DH consultations in the library can (or in some cases are designed to) become equal partnerships on projects or initiatives. Elizabeth Lorang and Kathleen A. Johnson particularize elements that can be read as project consultation that evolves into (or is in its conception) a successful DH collaboration.[29] Their inventory of requirements includes articulating clearly the project's research question and the scholarly conversation being entered, researching other projects with similar research aims or methodologies, defining the scope of the project, developing a communication plan, investigating issues regarding intellectual property, developing a project work plan and a data management plan, providing regular assessment of project development, and documenting project work (among several others).

Much has already been discussed here about collaboration—both as intralibrary initiatives that take advantage of existing collections and services and also between faculty and librarians. Collaboration between faculty and librarians arises in part because of a fundamental shift in the world of academic publishing, which has made academics turn to libraries as partners in their endeavors. Open-access publishing has created new methods of disseminating scholarship, and libraries have now found themselves in the middle of this new and challenging landscape, at least in part due to the rise of institutional repositories (which are often administered by academic libraries).

Many institutions have mandated open-access scholarship and simultaneously mandated that libraries become repositories for data and the publications that arise from research. A "Research Data Management Plan" became mandatory for the National Institutes of Science Education and Research grants in 2013 and the mandate became a requirement for the National Endowment for the Humanities shortly thereafter, which was important for those doing DH projects. When scholars turned to libraries for help with managing, housing, and providing access to data, and even with publishing research, the open-access movement began to take shape within libraries. So we must now add to the role of an academic library (in addition to the traditional roles of acquisition, organization, and preservation of information) the roles of curation and publishing. This is significant to DH practitioners when they realize that libraries have long been the curators and preservationists for digital collections, understand digital publishing issues, and serve as natural collaborators for DH projects. In addition to the roles of acquiring, curating, and disseminating DH projects, subject librarians can also be the natural collaborating partners for the teaching of workshops and instruction sessions for combining digital collections with the DH project management (see the *Instruction* part of this article). The list of DH projects that have academic libraries as their center abound: ARC (NINES, 18th Connect, MESA, and others, now centered at Texas A&M: http://idhmc.tamu.edu/arcgrant/), the Text Creation Partnership (centered at the University of Michigan: http://www.textcreationpartnership.org/tcp-texts/), to name but a few.

Collections

Traditional collection management responsibilities, such as purchasing monographs or databases, building subject-specific collection strength, or even negotiating with vendors, are situated in an expanded field when considering DH in a library context. Evaluating what constitutes of the components of what is collected, what formats—or how many, and how they are made accessible, uniquely DH collection practices are broadened to include to what can be termed, in this context, humanities data, whether these data are textual or audiovisual, but always in a digital form. Like traditional collection management, the way in which these data are accessed, stored, and made discoverable are paramount questions, but they are also ones made more complicated when curating with born-digital materials.

For Miriam Posner, the idea of humanities data is "a necessary contradiction."[30] Indeed, humanities scholars often find it difficult to reimagine books, photographs, and film, among other formats (including born-digital ones, like websites), as agglomerations of discrete data points. But when rendered digitally (or already digital), the possibilities of analysis at scale, or working with metadata about a text (whether descriptive, technical, or administrative metadata), are opened in ways not previously countenanced. With this in mind, Devin Higgins and Thomas Padilla define humanities data as "organized difference presented in a form amenable to computation [and] put into the service of humanistic inquiry."[31] For instance, a scholar could use the API of the Digital Public Library of America to retrieve, en masse, a subset of bibliographic metadata in JSON for a distant reading project. The metadata harvested and transformed constitute humanities data sets, drawn from a larger universe of humanities data, and formatted for computational analysis. Because of its unique affordances, that humanities data are available digitally is what enables novel forms of analysis.

Humanities data, like research data or other data available digitally, requires curation. Julia Flanders and Trevor Muñoz describe the principal purpose of humanities data curation as "ensur[ing] that the representations of objects of study in the humanities functions effectively as data."[32] What they mean by this is that humanities data curation maintains data for computational analysis and keeps it interoperable across systems and format migration "while still retaining provenance and complex layers of meaning." Often questions of curation fall outside the ambit of collections, but recognizing humanities data unique characteristics, such as the features of scholarly editions, text with markup (like TEI), textual corpora (and the fonds thereof), or other annotated data accompanying analysis, can afford a better perspective on how these data are collected and used.

For libraries, the challenges of working with humanities data can be complex. While there are manifold online repositories (the Internet Archive and HathiTrust, among many others), the rationale for libraries to collect one variety of humanities data over another can be a confusing proposition. In many instances, humanities data are digital versions of analog material (and by being rendered digital are thus freighted with additional metadata in order to be made available for the possibility of computational analysis), and this can generate concerns about collection duplication, and item reproduction. If an item is made available in one digital format, is there argument it should be available in another? And, if so, what copyright issues will need to be addressed in producing an additional digital access copy for computational analysis? For librarians thinking about DH in their collection management decisions, addressing the unique affordances of humanities data will be an intellectual and operational challenge, but a necessary one for fostering DH scholarship at their institutions.

CONCLUSION

"Libraries and digital humanities have the same goals. Stop asking if the library has a role, or what it is, and start getting involved in digital projects that are already happening. Advocate for new expanded roles and responsibilities to be able to do this. Become producers/creators in collaboration with scholars rather than servants to them."

In his article from *In the Library With a Lead Pipe*, Micah Vandergrift, echoing Matthew Kirschenbaum's "What Is Digital Humanities and What's it Doing in English Departments," gets to the point quickly that DH is something that libraries have in a less unified form been doing for quite some time, though they may have been calling it something else (digitization projects, metadata, curation of digital projects, etc.).[33] Libraries that have actually named DH units in order to keep up with the prevailing parlance of academia are reimaging already existing services and collections, leveraging their knowledge of metadata and familiarity with digital project management, while adding to that existing knowledge and resource base the sourcing, preparing, and manipulation of data, and analysis of digitized text, image, and audio for both themselves as a campus unit and for the patrons they serve. Most of these DH units are based around the following areas: collections (to build and/or enhance collections amenable to computational analysis, enable new modes of discovery and access to collections, acquire and/or condition data to support pursuit of DH research questions), collaboration (to partner on DH research, develop tools, convene events, symposia, and colloquia), consultation (to aid with text analysis, network analysis, image analysis, visualization, digital preservation, data curation, grant application process), and instruction (in method, tool, and technique lectures and workshops). As libraries reskill and transition to new ways of supporting patron teaching and research, they also find themselves in new roles because of the changing landscape of academic publishing—and because of repositories, librarians find themselves at the nexus of curation, consultation, and collaboration in the publication of research. So whether or not scholars agree on what DH means and what forms it takes (or should take), the practice of DH looks to remain core to the mission of academic libraries well into the future.

REFERENCES

1. Ramsey, S. Centers of Attention (personal blog) April 2010. http://stephenramsay.us/text/2010/04/27/centers-of-attention/ (accessed December 2015).
2. Vandegrift, M.; Varner, S. Evolving in common: Creating mutually supportive relationships between libraries and the digital humanities. J. Libr. Admin. **2013**, *53* (1), 67–78.
3. Green, H.E. Facilitating communities of practice in digital humanities: Librarian collaborations for research and training in text encoding. Libr. Quart. **2014**, *84*, 219–234, http://acrl.ala.org/dh/2014/02/12/what-if-we-do-in-fact-know-best-a-response-to-the-oclc-report-on-dh-and-research-libraries/ (accessed December 2015).

4. Muñoz, T. Digital humanities in the library isn't a service. (personal blog) August 2012. https://gist.github.com/3415438 (accessed December 2015).

5. Posner, M. No half measures: Overcoming common challenges to doing digital humanities in the library. J. Libr. Admin. **2013**, *53* (1), 43–52.

6. Cunningham, L. The lbrarian as digital humanist: The collaborative role of the research library in digital humanities projects. Faculty Info. Quart **2010**, *2* (2), 1–11; Kretzschmar, W. A.; Gray Potter, W. Library collaboration with large digital humanities projects. LLC **2010** *25* (4), 439–445.

7. Drucker, J. SpecLab's experiment: The humanist, the library, and the digital future of cultural materials and their interpretation. 2010, http://youtu.be/RgsyWKgmaSA (accessed December 2015).

8. Honn, J. Never neutral: Critical approaches to digital tools & culture in the humanities. Digital Humanities Speaker Series, Univ. West Ontario. October 2013. (speech) https://figshare.com/articles/Never_Neutral_Critical_Approaches_to_Digital_Tools_Culture_in_the_Humanities/1101385 (accessed May, 2017).

9. Unsworth, J. What is humanities computing and what is not? Forum Computerphilologie. November 2002 (online). http://computerphilologie.uni-muenchen.de/jg02/unsworth.html (accessed December, 2015).

10. Hartsell-Gundy, A.; Braunstein, L.; Golomb, L., Ed. *Forward in Digital Humanities in the Library: Challenges and Opportunities for Subject Specialists*; ACRL: Washington, DC, 2015.

11. Mulligan, R. *Association for Research Libraries (ARL) Spec Kit 350: Supporting Digital Scholarship*; ARL: Washington, DC, May 2016, 2.

12. Mulligan, R. *Association for Research Libraries (ARL) Spec Kit 350: Supporting Digital Scholarship*; ARL: Washington, DC, May 2016, 4.

13. Sula, C.A. Digital humanities and libraries: A conceptual model. J. Libr. Admin. **2013**, *53* (1), 10–26.

14. Vinopal, J.; McCormick, M. Supporting digital scholarship in research libraries: Scalability and sustainability. J. Libr. Admin. **2013**, *53* (1), 27–42.

15. Marion, N.L.; Pickle, S. *Sustaining the Digital Humanities: Host Institution Support beyond the Start-Up Phase*; Ithaka S+R: New York, 2014, http://www.sr.ithaka.org/wp-content/mig/SR_Supporting_Digital_Humanities_20140618f.pdf (accessed December 2015).

16. RLUK: Research Libraries United Kingdom. Re-skilling for research: investigating the needs of researchers and how library staff can best support them. 2012, http://www.rluk.ac.uk/wp-content/uploads/2014/02/RLUK-Re-skilling.pdf (accessed December 2015).

17. Keener, A. The arrival fallacy: Collaborative research relationships in the digital humanities. Dig. Human. Quart. **2015**, *9*(2), http://www.digitalhumanities.org/dhq/vol/9/2/000213/000213.html.

18. Gibson, K.; Ladd, M.; Presnell, J. Traversing the gap: Subject specialists connecting humanities researchers and digital scholarship centers. In *Digital Humanities in the Library: Challenges and Opportunities for Subject Specialists*; Hartsell-Gundy, A., Braunstein, L., Golomb, L., Eds.; ACRL: Washington, DC, 2015; 15.

19. Posner, M. No half measures: Overcoming common challenges to doing digital humanities in the library. J. Libr. Admin **2013**, *53* (1), 44.

20. Porter, D. What if we do, in fact, know best?: A Response to the OCLC Report on DH and Research Libraries. dh+lib (blog). http://acrl.ala.org/dh/2014/02/12/what-if-we-do-in-fact-know-best-a-response-to-the-oclc-report-on-dh-and-research-libraries/ (accessed December 2015).

21. Alexander, L.; Case, B.; Downing, K.; Gomis, M.; Maslowski, E. Librarians and scholars: Partners in Digital Humanities. Edu. Rev. Online 2014; 14–16, http://er.educause.edu/articles/2014/6/librarians-and-scholars-partners-in-digital-humanities (accessed December 2015); Schaffner, J.; Erway, R. *Does Every Research Library Need a Digital Humanities Center*; OCLC: Dublin, OH, 2014; 14–16, http://www.oclc.org/content/dam/research/publications/library/2014/oclcresearch-digital-humanities-center-2014.pdf (accessed December 2015).

22. Nowviskie, B. Skunks in the library: A path to production for scholarly R&D. J. Libr. Admin. **2013**, *53* (1), 33–56.

23. Green, H. Breaking down the desk: Librarians engaging researchers in the new scholarly landscape. Parameters (blog), November 2016. Social Science Research Council (SSRC). http://parameters.ssrc.org/2016/11/breaking-down-the-desk-librarians-engaging-researchers-in-the-new-scholarly-landscape/ (accessed February, 2017).

24. Stewart, V. Library instruction for digital humanities Pedagogy in undergraduate classes. In *Laying the Foundation: Digital Humanities in Academic Libraries*; John, W., Gilbert, Heather Eds.; Purdue University Press: West Lafayette, IN, 2016; Miriam Posner, "Here and There: Creating DH Community" (blog post), http://miriamposner.com/blog/here-and-there-creating-dh-community/.

25. Anita, S.C; Harriet, G. Practicing collaborative digital Pedagogy to foster digital literacies in humanities classrooms. Edu. Rev. October 2014, www.educause.edu/ero/article/practicing-collaborative-digital-pedagogy-foster-digital-literacies-humanities-classrooms.

26. Borovsky, Z.; McAulay, E. Digital humanities curriculum support inside the library. In *Digital Humanities in the Library: Challenges and Opportunities for Subject Specialists*; Hartsell-Gundy, A., Braunstein, L., Golomb, L., Eds.; ACRL: Washington, DC, 2015.

27. Rosenblum, B.; Devlin, F.; Albin, T.; Garrison, W. Collaboration co-teaching: Librarians teaching digital humanities in the classroom. In *Digital Humanities in the Library: Challenges and Opportunities for Subject Specialists*; Hartsell-Gundy, A., Braunstein, L., Golomb, L., Eds.; ACRL: Washington, DC, 2015; 151–176. Mooney, H.; Miller, S. D.; Padilla, T. G.; Smiley, B.L. Modeling approaches to library-led DH Pedagogy, 2015: Global Digital Humanities Conference, July 2015.

28. Koh, A. Introducing digital humanities work to undergraduates an overview. Hybrid Pedagogy, August 14, 2014, www.hybridpedagogy.com/journal/introducing-digital-humanities-work-undergraduates-overview.

29. Lorang, E.; Johnson, K.A. A checklist for digital humanities scholarship. In *Digital Humanities in the Library: Challenges and Opportunities for Subject Specialists*; Hartsell-Gundy, A., Braunstein, L., Golomb, L., Eds.; ACRL: Washington, DC, 2015; 83–102.

30. Posner, M. Humanities data: A necessary contradiction. June 2015 (personal blog). http://miriamposner.com/blog/humanities-data-a-necessary-contradiction/ (accessed December 2015).

31. Padilla, T.G.; Higgins, D. Library collections as humanities data: The facet effect. Pub. Ser. Quart. **2014**, *10* (4), 324–35.

32. Flanders, J., Muñoz, T. An introduction to humanities data curation. DH curation guide, (online). https://web. archive.org/web/20170126012445/http://guide.dhcuration. org/contents/intro/ (accessed May, 2017).

33. Vandergrift, M. What is digital humanities and what's it doing in the library? In the library with a lead pipe. 2012, http://www.inthelibrarywiththeleadpipe.org/2012/dhandthe lib/ (access December 2015).

Digital Images

Melissa Terras
UCL Department of Information Studies, UCL Centre for Digital Humanities, University College London, London, U.K.

Abstract

Although the technologies that underpin digital imaging have been in development for a surprisingly long time, recent developments in computing and networking technologies mean that digital images have recently become the dominant means to create and share photographic material. The Library and Archive sector were early adopters of these technologies, with many and various digitization projects being undertaken to produce digital images of important holdings, which is now an expected practice across the heritage sector. Best practice guidelines have been produced to provide technical and managerial recommendations for those wishing to undertake digitization projects. However, due to the increase in digital images in general society, the information professional also has role in educating industry and the public regarding issues in the long-term preservation of this medium, and we are now at a juncture where cultural and heritage institutions have to explore how best to interact with the general public effectively via digital images.

INTRODUCTION

Images are an integral part of human history, culture, and society. From daubing on rocks, to inventing printing and photographic techniques, humans have continually improved the technology available that enables them to create, share, and disseminate visual information. The way we produce, manipulate, disseminate, and comment on visual imagery has changed considerably since the closing parts of the last millennium. Recent developments in digital imaging, personal computing, and networking technologies have led to an exponential increase in image-based material, from both the personal and public sectors. Digital images are now the dominant, and pervasive, medium used to create, display, and share photographic images, and photographic reproductions of objects and artifacts. The library, archive, museum, and cultural sector were quick to embrace these technologies to increase access to collections through digitization: creating digital representations, usually images, of holdings, predominantly for distribution via the Internet. Various guidelines and recommendations are now in place to ensure best practice in creating digital image surrogates for memory institutions, although concerns regarding benchmarking, quality, management, and long-term preservation remain. Questions regarding use and usefulness are also being raised: does the evidence of use match the investment required to create such representations? Additionally, the pervasive use of digital imaging technology by the general public presents novel and immediate concerns for information professionals.

THE HISTORY OF DIGITAL IMAGES

Visual imagery is a powerful communicator, and the development of digital imaging technologies is tied to the development of communications technology, itself dependent on complex relationships between various scientific discoveries and the culture that encouraged them. Digital photography did not just materialize in the late twentieth century: scientists and technologists had been working for over a hundred years to understand how to use the power of electricity to communicate across long distances and how to use automated computational power to carry out mathematical analysis, eventually finding ways of capturing, distributing, then storing and processing digital information, including images. In turn, the growth in information communications technologies has led to the increased production and use of digital images in all areas of life and culture in the developed world.

Shortly after the first telegraph message was sent in 1837 (2 years before the "discovery" of photography), inventors aimed to transmit drawings via this new technology, with a working system in operation by 1851.[1] By the mid-1860s, the Victorian world possessed the understanding and the means to enable an image to be scanned in, distributed, and reproduced electronically, in a precursor to facsimile, or fax, technology. Photographic images were first sent by fax in the 1890s, and by the late 1900s, with the discovery of silicon's conductive properties, technological advances meant automated light-sensitive scanning was available. By using such optical technology to analyze an image broken up into discreet sections, or pixels, and by sending these encoded signals over the

Encyclopedia of Library and Information Sciences, Fourth Edition DOI: 10.1081/E-EISA-120053300

wire, digital scanning, encoding, and reproduction of photographs was possible. This was established in 1920 with the Bartlane system, named after its British inventors, H. G. Bartholomew and M. L. MacFarlane. Many early transatlantic news images appeared in newspapers after being delivered via this system, cutting down transmission time from a week (the time it took a ship to cross from the United States to the United Kingdom) to a couple of hours. By the 1930s, the transmission of images by digital fax was commonplace, with many commercial news organizations owning scanners and networks throughout the world, yet although the digital fax converted images into digital signals by breaking them into refined units, and expressing these units numerically, it was missing vital elements of image processing and electronic storage: digital representations could be created, distributed, then printed, but computing technologies did not yet exist to store or manipulate them.

It was over 35 years later that computers could be powerful enough to store or manipulate digital image representations: in 1957, a drum scanner was used to input image data into a SEAC 1500 word memory computer.[2] Advances in computing and digital imaging technologies were many and varied in the Cold War years (NASA invested large sums to investigate the use of digital image technologies as a means of defense). However, it was not until the 1980s when the falling costs of computer components, and rising storage and processing capacities of computers, meant that access to computational power became more commonplace, allowing (and requiring) research and development to be carried out on the intricacies of picture-generating software and systems. By the close of the twentieth century, most basic, affordable personal computing systems were able to handle standard full-color images and were capable of running sophisticated photo-manipulation software that allowed digital manipulation that rivaled the accuracy and resolution of traditional photographic darkrooms.[3] Image capture peripheral devices also became increasingly available (scanners, digital cameras, mobile phones incorporating digital camera technology, printers) in cheaper and smaller incarnations, encouraging users to abandon traditional film-based photographic technology.

Alongside these developments, engineers and computer scientists were also busy constructing networks that would allow computers to source and exchange information. The Internet, and its subset, the World Wide Web, is the perfect vehicle for the distribution of both professional and user-created digital content: having a reliable, and fast, networked environment that can act as a way to share, disseminate, and view digital information has encouraged the creation of both digital versions of analogue material (through digitization) and digital-born media. The role of the Internet in encouraging the uptake of digital image technology should not be underestimated, and digital images of artifacts, objects, people, and places are often the central focus of information available online. Various online communities now exist around image-sharing sites, including the photo-sharing site Flickr.com, the lifestyle imagery site Pinterest.com, the photo-sharing and -filtering site Instagram.com, and the image-based blog site Tumblr.com.

The history of digital imaging is rooted in the Victorian era but was only toward the end of the twentieth century that it has existed as a practical technology, due to converging developments in communications technology and the networked environment, increased access to cheaper and faster computers, and the lowering cost and improving performance of the peripherals that create digital images, all encouraging the production and use of digital images, by both individuals and institutions. This has been followed by a corresponding rise in user expectations regarding the quality and amount of digital image information that should be able to be produced by desktop machines, or be available online. The recent rapid uptake of digital imaging, and the growing provision of services and online tools, means it appears to be, and functions as, a new medium, changing the information environment and creating new concerns for those working in the information professions.

DIGITAL IMAGE FUNDAMENTALS

There are two distinct classes of digital images: vector graphics (which use a series of geometric drawing commands, such as lines, curves, or shapes and solid or graduated color, to represent an image), and bitmap or raster images (where an image is broken into a grid by the capture device, with the light value (lightness, darkness or color) of each piece of the grid—an individual pixel—recorded individually. The term *raster* stems from the Latin, to rake). Bitmaps are relatively easy to implement, and, within limits, work for any image: they can record just about any conceivable image or view of a scene since any image can be broken up into a grid, and as far as the human eye is concerned, if that grid is small enough we see it as a continuous tone image. Vector graphics are predominantly used in graphic design, and computer-aided design systems for engineering and architecture: neither bitmap or vector graphics methods are better than the other: they simply have different functions and uses. Digitization projects and cultural and heritage institutions will be most likely to produce and deal with bitmapped images, although as Digital Humanities techniques become more widespread, images are also increasingly used alongside other types and formats of data such as marked up text, large textual repositories, or geographically encoded data (see Schreibman et al.[4] for an overview of different commonly used approaches to information generated from the digitization process).

The term "pixel" has been used to describe the individual points of a bitmapped image since the 1960s, being an abbreviated form of "picture element." Each pixel contains complete information about a particular point of an image, detailing the color (hue, lightness, and saturation) and place of the individual pixel within the grid. From a mathematical point of view, this array is merely a collection of numbers that may be transformed and manipulated in a wide variety of ways. Such an array is called a bitmap—a representation of the image data that parallels the manner in which it is stored in computer memory. Bitmap image pixels are generally square, but pixel size is variable depending on the size of the grid chosen to display or output them. The number of pixels in a given area is described as the *resolution* of the image. The amount of color information stored for each individual pixel is determined by *bit depth* (Fig. 1).

Resolution is usually denoted by a measurement such as pixels, or points per inch (ppi: measuring the number of pixels in an image within a linear one-inch space), dots per inch (dpi: measuring the number of individual dots of ink a printer can produce), or lines per inch (lpi: used to denote how close together lines are in halftone printing, the method commonly used in newspapers and magazines where images are represented by a series of dots of different size and density). The terms are often used interchangeably when talking about image resolution, dpi being the most common, and conventionally understood to cover different media. (For cameras, resolution is stated differently. Rather than the number of pixels in an inch, the resolution given is usually the maximum resolution a digital sensor at the back of the camera can achieve, normally expressed as the absolute number of pixels in the grid, rounded up to one decimal place.) The topic of resolution can be confusing because it isn't fixed and immutable. If you change the size of a digital image without changing the number of pixels within it, you change its resolution: the size of the grid has changed without changing the individual elements within it. Interpolation—the term given to the mathematical creation of missing data—is often used to create new pixels to insert into, or choose which pixels to delete from, a resized image, in order to maintain image resolution and to ensure that the image does not become visibly disrupted, or pixelated. The ideal resolution at which to capture or store an image depends on the purpose of the image: resolution for online display, for example, is much lower than that needed for print or archival purposes. Digitization guidelines (see section "Use of Digital Images in the Library and Archive Sector") provide guidance in this area (Fig. 2).

Bit depth describes the number of bits of memory that are available to describe the color of each pixel of the image. The greater number of bits assigned to each pixel, the greater number of colors the image can have. The simplest type of image, black and white, sometimes referred to as a binary image, has a bit depth of 1, as each pixel is either black or white (0 or 1). Grayscale images are 8 bit—capable of describing 256 difference shades of gray.

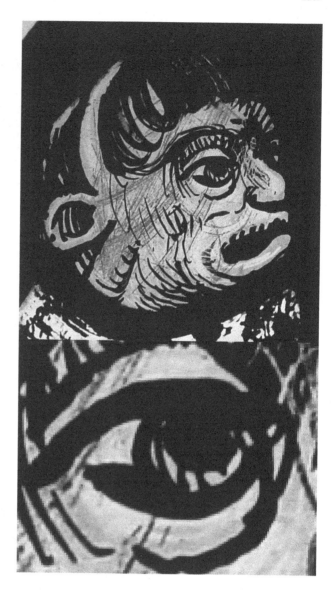

Fig. 1 A digital image of a Mediaeval stained glass window. At the viewing resolution, pixels cannot normally be seen, but when magnified, such as the lower section featuring the devil's eye, the underlying matrix containing pixels of individual color become apparent. Being able to see pixels within an image under normal viewing conditions is termed "pixelation."

24-bit and 32-bit colors are capable of describing millions of different permutations of color information for each pixel. 48-bit color is capable of describing billions of different colors (more than the human eye can discern, and only used for specialist systems). The amount of color information created, sampled, or stored regarding an image depends on the images purpose: for some images, such as representations of black and white newspapers, color brings little to the image, whereas for others, such as images of mediaeval manuscripts, color may hold intrinsic information regarding the object. Digitization guidelines provide guidance regarding the bit depth suitable for different media (Fig. 3).

(a)   (b)   (c)

Fig. 2 A section of an image of a Mediaeval stained glass window captured at different resolutions. (A) At 30 pixels per inch, the size of the pixels is above the threshold of human vision, and the image is pixelated. (B) At 72 dots per inch, the image is suitable for online display, and we see it as a continuous tone image, but some detail is lacking. (C) At 300 dots per inch, the level of detail captured makes the image a more accurate representation of the object.

Creating accurate representations of objects and artifacts using digital imaging technologies requires attention to detail: photographing objects at high resolution and normally, now, at full color (over the past few years, the sector has moved away from scanning, and black and white capture, as Digital SLR cameras and the cost of data storage have come down in cost). However, the more samples captured, and the more detailed the color information captured, the larger the file size of a resulting digital image. There is a playoff between representing detail and the ability to manipulate, display, and disseminate images efficiently. Smaller file sizes are required, for example, for delivery via the Internet. Compression techniques are often used to reduce the number of bytes required to represent a data set: some techniques are designed to store information efficiently, while others store the data set accurately. Lossless compression ensures that an image viewed and decompressed will be identical to its state before being compressed (but although the image is stored accurately, it is difficult to reduce the file size significantly using lossless compression). Lossy techniques eliminate information from the pre-compressed state, the amount of detail discarded can usually be adjusted to change as little of the visible detail in an image as possible. Lossy compression can achieve significant storage savings and is ideal for creating images for display on the Internet; however, once the information is gone, the original image cannot be recreated. It is important to use lossless

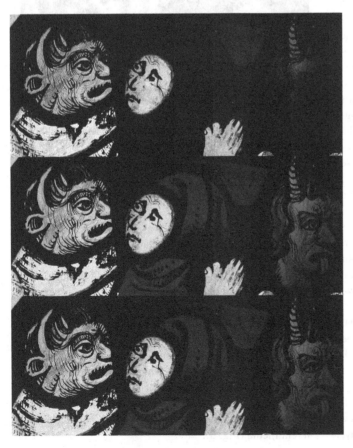

Fig. 3 A section of an image of a Mediaeval stained glass window captured at different bit depth. The top section is bitonal, being only black and white, and although the resulting file size is small, much of the detail is lost. The middle section demonstrates the same image section in grayscale: 256 different shades of gray, which is much more effective in capturing detail. The final section, in 24-bit color, contains much more information, demonstrating that the provision of color information can be important when providing images of originals that rely on vivid color themselves.

compression for images that are to be stored long term, such as master files resulting from digitization projects, to ensure that all information possible is preserved for future use.

Further information and introductions to the basic infrastructure of digital images specifically targeted for librarians and information professionals are available,[5–10] with many digitization projects using the Library of Congress "Technical Standards for Digital Conversion of Text and Graphic Materials" as a base.[11] The Jisc Digital Media service (formerly the Technical Advisory Service for Images) provides many up-to-date online guides to digital imaging at http://www.jiscdigitalmedia.ac.uk/. A detailed introduction to the fundamental physics, mathematics, and perceptual phenomena behind digital images, covering optics, electronics, photography, and semiconductor technology is also available.[12]

IMAGE FILE FORMATS

Image formats are files that store any type of persistent graphical data (as opposed to text, spreadsheet, or numerical information) that is intended for eventual rendering and display. There are now over one hundred image formats in existence[13] and that number continues to grow: different applications use different types of data in different ways to satisfy different user needs. A cultural and heritage digitization project will mostly work on creating two-dimensional representations of artifacts and documents, or bitmap graphics, and use commonly available formats to facilitate interoperability and information exchange of digital image data. Using recommended, commonly available, documented formats also ensures that the information should be accessible when technology advances, and formats change and become obsolete. File formats can be converted from one to another. This can be useful if the organization of the data stream is incompatible with the requirements of a particular device or application, or if the original format is not one suited for, say, online delivery, long-term storage, or interoperability.

Although there are many different image file formats, most work in a broadly similar way. Most typical data sets consist of a linear list of data values, commonly referred to as a data stream. The entire data stream makes up the file. The difference between individual image files formats lies in the details: what type of data is stored, if it is compressed, and how it is encoded. A typical structure of an image data stream may be: File Signature (declaring which format the data are stored in), Image Header (containing technical information that describes the image, such as pixel dimensions, image height and width, and bit depth), perhaps a Color Palette (a means of storing color information effectively), then the individual pixel color data (the major part of a data stream for a bitmapped image, storing individual pixel color values, usually in display order: this is the part of the file that can be compressed), and finally a File Closing Marker (marking the end of the data stream, and so the end of the file). Disruption to this datastream generally means that the file cannot be read at all.

The most popular image formats that an information professional may come across are GIF, PNG, JPEG, and TIFF. GIF, PNG, and JPEG files are commonly used to save images that need to be compressed in order to be delivered easily across a network, such as the Internet. GIF files have a limited color palette and use a compression algorithm that is suited to compressing areas of the same color, meaning they are suitable for logos, graphics, and buttons. The PNG format is becoming more popular for this purpose: it was designed to improve the GIF specification and to avoid any of the licensing issues that plagued GIF toward the close of the last century. JPEG is actually a method of file compression specifically designed to cope with complexity of photographic images, and the file format developed to incorporate this technique is now the most common format for storage and interchange of digital photographs, although it is a very lossy format. TIFF files are one of the most useful formats for the capture, storage, and exchange of high-quality digital image data. Since the early 1990s, TIFF has been embraced as an archival digital image format by the library and archive community and is now also in common use as an output format from professional-level digital cameras. It is recommended that the capture of archival and library material is done "once for all purposes": creating a high-resolution TIFF file of an object will allow lower resolution and compressed image files in different formats to be generated from the master file, while creating a digital surrogate for long-term preservation and access, and limiting the handling of the object experiences.[14] However, many digitization studios are now also maintaining the RAW files that come directly from a Digital SLR sensor, allowing further tonal adjustments at a later stage, although these can be very large. In addition, there is a growing interest in the JPEG2000 format, which allows more sophisticated image compression and storage possibilities than either existing JPEG or TIFF. Again, digitization guidelines can provide guidance in this area, and the recommendations and documentation on a working group on the use of JPEG2000 in the heritage sector are also available at http://wiki.opf-labs.org/display/JP2/Home.

USE OF DIGITAL IMAGES IN THE LIBRARY AND ARCHIVE SECTOR

The Information, Culture, and Heritage sectors were quick to embrace the potential of imaging technologies as they became available, primarily to facilitate access to items in collections by providing them in electronic format, allowing a broader audience to use and appreciate the objects. Additionally, collections can be enhanced through the provision of digital representations: gaps in collections can be filled or material that has been geographically dispersed between institutions (such as manuscript material) can be virtually reunited. Early projects believed that digitization of artifacts could also be a form of preservation: this is only the case when the medium of the original is deteriorating, as digital information and media have relatively short life spans themselves; but digitization can also be perceived as a form of preservation when access to the original is restricted and users directed to the digital version of the artifact to reduce the stress of repeated handling on an object. Digitization projects often raise the profile of an institution, showcasing their collections, allowing detailed research to be undertaken, and encouraging outside funding to invest in their infrastructure.[15]

Many early projects, coming from a long tradition of microfilming, showed initial interests in digitizing text, with the hope the Optical Character Recognition technologies would be able to convert the images into moveable type. In the 1980s, small-scale, in-house projects of limited scope and interest were undertaken, but toward the end of the decade large-scale projects were launched, including pilot projects aiming to investigate the appropriation of digital technologies to the handling of large volumes of information, such as those carried out at the Library of Congress, Cornell University (both the United States), and the Archivo General de Indias (in Spain), sometimes in partnership with commercial computing companies.[10] The 1990s were termed the "decade of digitization"[7] as the lowering costs of equipment and storage, and the increased networking possibilities, encouraged most institutions to create digital representations of at least some of their holdings themselves for online display. This was also fostered by many funding opportunities arising around the Millennium, such as that provided by the New Opportunities Fund in the United Kingdom, specifically for the purposes of digitization. Growing user expectations encouraged libraries, museums, and archives to provide images (and related records and metadata) of their material online. Since then, digitization efforts for individual institutions have slowed somewhat, as funding becomes harder to come by, and questions have been raised regarding the costs of digitization and the resulting benefits to institutions. It is all very well to provide images of a medieval manuscript in glorious full color, at great cost, online, but if only three or four scholars in the world are actually interested in looking at it in any great detail, could the money be spent in other ways that are more beneficial to the institution? Questions are now being asked about how we understand value and worth of digitized content.[16,17] In the early twenty-first century, digital imaging activities have moved beyond digitization of the treasures held in special collections in libraries and archives, back to large-scale commercial partnerships for mass digitization of more general collections to

enable (and experiment with) information searching and retrieval. Industry partners (such as Google or Microsoft) pay for the digitization, getting access to the information in return, and such digitization projects promise to make information available to all via the Internet. However, there is consternation in the publishing industry and the library world regarding issues such as copyright, licensing, and information quality, unanswered questions about technical and managerial procedures, and a fear that such large-scale commercial digitization has a potential to misrepresent, or even damage, the world's cultural heritage.[18] We are also only beginning to understand use and usage of large-scale digitized content.[19] It is now difficult to remember a time when institutions did not provide digital representations of the important materials held in their collection: a recent survey of 1400 European galleries, libraries, archives, and museums showed that 87% of them now have a digital collection,[20] a rise of 4% since 2012. However, far from everything is available online: on average at time of writing, 17% of collections are digitized across Europe, with further plans to digitize another 52% of institutional holdings across the sector.

Producing digital image versions of holdings through digitization has become an industry in itself, and there is much research devoted to producing guides to best practice in undertaking the digitization of library and archive material. Many early projects were, in effect, experimental case studies, exploring the best way in which to appropriate digital imaging technologies for the Library and information sector. Nowadays, however, guidelines are in place covering all aspects of the digitization process: creating a digital image of an object is just one step in a long chain of procedures that enable digital access to an object, including collections management, object selection, preservation issues, copyright and rights management, technical issues, managing the digital workflow, quality assurance, production of metadata and associated records to allow searching and retrieval, delivering images to users, usability testing, accessibility legislation, and beyond.[6–8,15]

The need for technical digitization guidelines was highlighted by early projects in the library and archive sector. Given that technologies, standards, and recommendations are constantly changing, the best place to find up-to-date recommendations regarding the technical aspects of digitization is from the online documentation provided by trusted and well-known institutions, such as the frequently updated "Library of Congress Technical Standards for Digital Conversion of Text and Graphic Materials":[11] those produced by national bodies such as the U.S. National Archives and Records Association:[14] those produced by University Libraries, such as the guides available at the California Digital Library (www.cdlib.org/) and the standards advocated by the Digital Library Federation (www.diglib.org/); guides to good practice created and pointed to by the United Kingdom's Digital

Curation Centre (http://www.dcc.ac.uk/); and resources produced by the Jisc Digital Media service (http://www.jiscdigitalmedia.ac.uk/), which remains a comprehensive source for all aspects of digitization and digital imaging. Most guides and recommendations are meant to be informative rather than prescriptive, and many cover areas such as management, workflow, delivery, and quality control, as well as providing an insight into up-to-date technical specifications for the production of digital images.

However, although these has been much investment into digital imaging in the Library and Archive sector, there still remain unresolved issues regarding both technical and usability aspects. Benchmarking image quality is difficult as the human visual system varies from operator to operator, and likewise, color management and fidelity is difficult to quantify and manage. Questions still remain about the long-term preservation of digital image files and the resources required to maintain digital image collections in the long term.[21] The searching and retrieval of digital images is still computationally complex: most systems require adequate metadata regarding the content and provenance of images to be provided, and this can be costly. Evidence of value and levels of use of digitized resources is also scant.[10,16,17] There are also benefits and opportunities that remain to be explored in using digitized collections further, via "crowdsourcing" of labor to help sort, tag, identify, label, and transcribe images:[22] how we can best use all this digital image information, now we have it, remains a large issue.

PERSONAL DIGITAL IMAGE COLLECTIONS AND THE LIBRARIAN

Due to the pervasive nature of digital imaging technologies, and the ease with which images can be taken, manipulated, and shared, personal photography has now become vastly more popular than it ever was, and been transformed from a private to a community experience. The online storage and organization of personal digital image collections, often made available to the general public, and made more searchable through the use of tagging, metadata, and online (and mobile phone based) sharing platforms, has been one of the success stories of Web 2.0 (the growing online phenomenon of websites that are community driven, service based, with high-level tools that also harness the collective intelligence of large groups of users). Online services such as Yahoo/Flickr, Google/Picasa, Photobucket, Instagram, Tumblr, Pinterest, and Facebook host hundreds of millions of photographs posted by millions of users. An expanding service industry is growing alongside the user-generated content, providing, for example, online services for ordering digital prints, and facilities for digital photographers to sell or license their images for advertising purposes. Such industries are

undermining traditional photography manufacturers and photo-stock agencies.

Yet users seem to know little about how to archive, preserve, or maintain their personal image data despite photographic industry initiatives such as "Save my Memories."[23] Concerns about digital preservation are not only limited to institutional requirements: a child born today may be the most photographed of any generation, but without careful consideration of how these image files are stored, the chances of them being able to see their baby photos in 20 or 30 years are slim. Home computers tend to be seldom backed up or maintained beyond their short lifespan: digital images are emailed and shared online, but seldom printed and stored in archival conditions, meaning loss of the hardware they are stored on means permanent loss of the images themselves. Further research is needed into how digital imaging technology has transformed user habits, and although the industry has started to provide advice for users regarding the long-term preservation and access to their data,[23] there is increasing concern from the information profession regarding the potential loss of decades of digital images, and any personal digital data, for future use, never mind future generations.[24–26] To that end, the Library of Congress has recently established a "Personal Archiving" section to give advice to the public about "Preserving your Digital Memories,"[27] using digital outreach methods to reach as wide audience an as possible to highlight these issues, such as regular guest blog posts in sites that have a large audience.[28] In the United Kingdom, the Digital Preservation Coalition recently reported on "Personal Digital Archiving," providing advice for both individuals and information professionals on how to tackle this growing issue.[29] Other public engagement initiatives undertaken by information professionals, such as the Society of Georgia Archivists' "Everyday Digital Archives" campaign,[30] provide a model as to how institutions can inform, educate, and help the general public in both understanding the need for personal archiving of photographic (and other) data, but also how to do so, to ensure their digital photographs are available for future generations. With the rise of social media and image-sharing sites such as Flickr and Instagram, it is also important that people understand issues of privacy and ownership of digital content, and the information community can have an advocacy role in encouraging engagement with the like of the Creative Commons framework[31] to increase the information literacy[32] of a wider audience in these increasingly complex areas.

The pervasive nature of digital imaging technologies in the developed world has also led to recent changes in news coverage as the general public can now capture an immediate and personal response to subjects and events that would traditionally be covered by news agencies, often before traditional media outlets are aware of the incident or able to dispatch reporters. This can aid police in their investigations, and calls for the public to submit such eyewitness material are now commonplace (as is the creation of user-generated video and pictures that counteract official records of events and happening). User generation of digital content is set to become ever more common, and important, blurring the distinction between professional and amateur, democratizing news reporting, and providing historical and judicial evidence. The maintenance and preservation of such digital material for future users, historians, and investigators is the responsibility of the professionals within the media and information environment, and the library and archive sector have role and opportunity in educating the public and media regarding the importance of preserving this information for future generations.

CONCLUSION

Digital imaging technologies, and related advanced in Internet technologies, have changed the way we produce and disseminate visual information, leading to an exponential increase in visual material available in recent years. The Library and Information sector has, through trial and error, developed best practice procedures for the creation of digital image representations of documents and artifacts, and many institutions have undertaken digitization projects to increase access to their holdings. Although successful projects have been undertaken, delivering much image-based content to the user, questions remain regarding the cost, long-term viability, and usefulness of digitized collections. Additionally, the role of the librarian and information professional does not stop at the institution's door: issues regarding the preservation of digital information created by general society, including digital images, are becoming increasingly pressing.

REFERENCES

1. McConnell, K.; Bodson, D.; Urban, S. *FAX: Facsimile Technology and Systems*, 3rd Ed.; Artech House: London, U.K., 1999.
2. Kirsch, R.L.; Cahn, L.C.; Ray, G.H. In *Urban experiments with processing pictorial information with a digital computer, 1957*, Proceedings of the Eastern Joint Computer Conference, December 9–13, 1957. Institute of Radio Engineers and Association of Computing Machinists: New York. pp. 221–229.
3. Lipkin, J. *Photography Reborn, Image Making in the Digital Era*; Harry N. Abrams: New York, 2005.
4. Schreibman, S.; Siemens, R.; Unsworth, J., Eds. *New Companion to Digital Humanities*; Wiley-Blackwell: Oxford, U.K., 2016.
5. Besser, H.; Trant, J. *Introduction to Imaging, Issues in Constructing an Image Database*; The Getty Art History Information Program: Santa Monica, CA, 1995.
6. Kenney, A.R.; Reiger, O.Y. *Moving Theory into Practice: Digital Imaging for Libraries and Archives*; Research Libraries Group: Mountain View, CA, 2000.
7. Lee, S.D. *Digital Imaging: A Practical Handbook*; Facet Publishing: London, U.K., 2000.
8. Cornell University Library. Moving theory into practice: digital imaging tutorial, 2003. http://www.library.cornell.edu/preservation/tutorial/index.html (accessed February 28, 2016).
9. Besser, H. *Introduction to Imaging*; Getty Research Institute: Los Angeles, CA, 2004. http://www.getty.edu/research/conducting_research/standards/introimages/ (accessed February 28, 2016).
10. Terras, M. *Digital Images for the Information Professional*; Ashgate: London, U.K., 2008.
11. Library of Congress. Federal Agencies Digitization Guidelines Initiatives. Technical guidelines for digitizing cultural heritage materials, 2015. http://www.digitizationguidelines.gov/guidelines/digitize-technical.html (accessed February 28, 2016).
12. Graham, R. *The Digital Image*, 2nd Ed.; Whittles Publishing Ltd: Caithness, U.K., 2005.
13. Murray, J.D.; van Ryper, W. *Encyclopedia of Graphics File Formats*, 2nd Ed.; O'Reilly & Associates, Inc.: Sebastopol, CA, 1996.
14. NARA. Technical guidelines for digitizing material for electronic access: creation of production of master files—Raster Images, 2004. http://www.archives.gov/preservation/technical/guidelines.pdf (accessed February 28, 2016).
15. Hughes, L. *Digitizing Collections: Strategic Issues for the Information Manager*; Facet Publishing: London, U.K., 2004.
16. Hughes, L. *Evaluating and Measuring the Value, Use and Impact of Digital Collections*; Facet: London, U.K., 2011.
17. Tanner, S. Measuring the impact of digital resources: the balanced value impact model, 2012. http://www.kdcs.kcl.ac.uk/fileadmin/documents/pubs/BalancedValueImpact-Model_SimonTanner_October2012.pdf (accessed February 28, 2016).
18. Jeanneney, J.-N. *Google and the Myth of Universal Knowledge: a View from Europe*; University of Chicago Press: London, U.K., 2007.
19. Gooding, P.; Terras, M.; Warwick, C. The myth of the new: mass digitization, distant reading, and the future of the book. Lit. Linguist. Comput. **2013**, *28* (4), 629–639.
20. Stroeker, N.; Vogels, R. *Survey Report on Digitisation in European Cultural Heritage Institutions 2014*. ENUMERATE Thematic Network Report, January 2014. http://www.enumerate.eu/en/surveys/core_survey_2/ (accessed February 28, 2016).
21. van Horik, R. *Permanent Pixels: Building Blocks for the Longevity of Digital Surrogates of Historical Photographs*. DANS studies in Digital Archiving 1. Data Archiving and Networked Services: The Hague, the Netherlands, 2005.
22. Ridge, M., Ed. *Crowdsourcing our Cultural Heritage*; Ashgate: Farnham, U.K., 2014.
23. Save My Memories. "Are Your Memories Safe?," 2007; International Imaging Industry Association, http://www.savemymemories.org/ (accessed February 28, 2016).
24. Beagrie, N. Plenty of room at the bottom? Personal digital libraries and collections. D-Lib **2005**, *11*, 6. http://www.dlib.org/dlib/june05/beagrie/06beagrie.html (accessed February 28, 2016).

Digital–Disaster

25. Beagrie, N. Digital curation for science, digital libraries, and individuals. Int. J. Digit. Curation, **2006**, *1*, 3–16.

26. Lee, C. *I, Digital: Personal Collections in the Digital Era*; Society of American Archivists: Chicago, IL, 2011.

27. Library of Congress (n. d.). Personal archiving, preserving your digital memories, http://digitalpreservation.gov/personalarchiving (accessed February 28, 2016).

28. Public Libraries Online. Posts tagged 'Personal Digital Archiving', http://publiclibrariesonline.org/tag/personal-digital-archiving/ (accessed February 28, 2016).

29. Redwine, G. *Personal Digital Archiving*. Digital Preservation Coalition Technology Watch Report; Digital Preservation Coalition: Glasgow, Scotland. 2015. http://dx.doi.org/10.7207/twr15-01 (accessed February 28, 2016).

30. Society of Georgia Archivists (2014). Announcing the everyday digital archives outreach campaign. Tuesday April 15. http://georgiaarchivists.blogspot.co.uk/2014/04/announcing-everyday-digital-archives.html (accessed February 28, 2016).

31. Creative Commons. https://creativecommons.org/ (accessed February 28, 2016).

32. Antonio, A.B.; Tuffley, D. Promoting information literacy in higher education through digital curation. M/C J **2015**, *18*(4), http://www.journal.media-culture.org.au/index.php/mcjournal/article/viewArticle/987 (accessed February 28, 2016).

FURTHER READING

A variety of both online and print material exists specifically for the Information professional wishing to know more about digital imaging, and undertaken digitization projects. Print materials such as Besser and Trant,[5] Kenney and Reiger,[6] Lee,[7] Besser,[9] Terras[10] are good starting points for those wishing to know more about the technical underpinnings of image files and formats, with a much more detailed account available in Graham[12] (although this may be a little too technical for those starting out). Online materials, such as Cornell University Library,[8] Besser,[9] Library of Congress[11] and the resources available at the Jisc Digital Media service (http://www.jiscdigitalmedia.ac.uk/), also provide good resources regarding all aspects of imaging for the LIS sector. Management issues are dealt with in Lee,[7] Hughes,[15] van Horik[21] raises interesting issues about longevity of digital images and image surrogates and Hughes[16] covers issues on the impact of digitized content, and what we know of its use. Outreach and public engagement by the sector regarding personal archiving of digital photography collections is covered in Save My Memories,[23] Library of Congress,[27] Society of Georgia Archivists,[30] Public Libraries Online,[28] Redwine,[29] and Creative Commons.[31].

Digital Millennium Copyright Act of 1998

Jonathan A. Franklin
Gallagher Law Library, University of Washington, Seattle, Washington, U.S.A.

Abstract

The Digital Millennium Copyright Act (DMCA) was the most important amendment to U.S. copyright law during the 1990s. Unlike other amendments that altered small but important pieces of the copyright law, the DMCA created an entirely new form of protection that will have wide-ranging effects and has even caused some to suggest it could be the death of copyright. The DMCA was passed by the U.S. Congress and signed by President Clinton in 1998. It amended the U.S. Code, primarily Title 17 of the U.S. Code, part of the federal law that deals with copyright law. The DMCA includes a cluster of discrete copyright-related issues that were combined in one substantial piece of legislation. It covers a wide range of topics, including limiting Internet service provider (ISP) liability, the scope of exclusive rights in ephemeral sound recordings, and protecting boat hull designs. One of the most important sections—the circumvention prohibition—forbids circumvention of technological measures that prevent access to a work.

INTRODUCTION

The Digital Millennium Copyright Act (DMCA) was the most important amendment to U.S. copyright law during the 1990s. Unlike other amendments that altered small but important pieces of the copyright law,[1] the DMCA created an entirely new form of protection that will have wide-ranging effects and has even caused some to suggest it could be the death of copyright.[2–4]

The DMCA was passed by the U.S. Congress and signed by President Clinton in 1998.[5] It amended the U.S. Code, primarily Title 17 of the U.S. Code, part of the federal law that deals with copyright law.[6] The text of the DMCA and the copyright laws is available online at the Library of Congress Copyright Office.[7] The DMCA includes a cluster of discrete copyright-related issues that were combined in one substantial piece of legislation. It covers a wide range of topics, including limiting Internet service provider (ISP) liability,[8] the scope of exclusive rights in ephemeral sound recordings,[9] and protecting boat hull designs.[10] One of the most important sections—the circumvention prohibition—forbids circumvention of technological measures that prevent access to a work.[11] The Act is 58 pages long and divided into five topical sections, or titles. Each title of the DMCA has its own background, history, and implications, and each title is discussed separately below. Two important topics that were in early versions of the bills that became the DMCA, database legislation and parallel import legislation, were excluded from the final version.

TITLE I. WORLD INTELLECTUAL PROPERTY ORGANIZATION TREATIES IMPLEMENTATION

Title I of the DMCA is the enabling legislation for two World Intellectual Property Organization (WIPO) treaties

that were drafted in 1996.[12] The WIPO is an intergovernmental organization under the United Nations umbrella. It is based in Geneva, Switzerland, and is responsible for the administration of various multilateral intellectual property treaties, including the Berne Convention.[13] There are over 150 WIPO member states that take part in negotiations on a broad array of intellectual property topics, from protection of folklore to database protection.

There is no such thing as international copyright law. Therefore, once a copyright treaty is finalized, each member state that wants to join that treaty must ratify it and amend its own national laws to conform to the substantive and procedural terms of the treaty. This means that each nation must pass "enabling legislation" to amend its national copyright laws.

Under the U.S. Constitution, the President can negotiate a treaty. However, the President needs the Senate to reject, approve, or conditionally approve a treaty. After two-thirds of the Senate ratifies a treaty, the President deposits it with the originating organization, in this case WIPO. Ideally, the implementing legislation, which goes through both the House and the Senate, should be completed prior to depositing the treaty.

For the same treaty, one jurisdiction might have only minor amendments, while another jurisdiction joining the same treaty might have to rewrite large portions of its copyright laws to conform to the new instrument. It is important to remember that these treaties serve to establish minimum standards, and, as discussed below, countries may amend their national laws to protect copyrights well beyond the terms of the treaty.

The two treaties enabled by the DMCA are the WIPO Copyright Treaty (WCT)[14] and the WIPO Performances and Phonographs Treaty (WPPT).[15] The WCT implemented several relatively noncontroversial legal

Encyclopedia of Library and Information Sciences, Fourth Edition DOI: 10.1081/E-ELIS4-120044854

requirements, including recognizing that authors have the right to control the distribution of their works (with first sale exceptions being determined on a national basis), providing for exclusive rental rights for certain types of works, and increasing the term of protection for photographic works to 50 years.[16] The WPPT covered the rights of performers and music producers in their creations. These issues had already been largely addressed in U.S. copyright law.

Title I of the DMCA amends the copyright law to include a section prohibiting circumvention of access controls.[17] Access controls are technological locks that prevent users from copying the underlying digital information. For example, CDs do not have any access controls, and hence can easily be copied. DVDs, on the other hand, have access controls that prevent the user from skipping certain portions of the introductory content and copying the disc. This section of the DMCA also includes a section that prevents tampering with copyright management information, such as digital identifiers of the title of the work, the author of the work, and relevant licensing terms.[18] It also includes civil and criminal penalties for violations of the copyright management information tampering provisions and the anticircumvention provisions. The maximum penalty on the criminal conspiracy charge is 5 years of imprisonment and a $500,000 fine;[19] the maximum penalty for each of the civil charges is 5 years of imprisonment and a $250,000 fine.[20]

Anticircumvention

The most important section of the WCT, from the perspective of U.S. copyright law, is Article 11, the rationale for the important anticircumvention provisions of the DMCA.

Article 11 states:

Contracting Parties shall provide adequate legal protection and effective legal remedies against the circumvention of effective technological measures that are used by authors in connection with the exercise of their rights under this Treaty or the Berne Convention and that restrict acts, in respect of their works, which are not authorized by the authors concerned or permitted by law.[14]

Article 18 of the WPPT includes virtually the same language.[15] Although some have suggested that existing U.S. law was sufficient to meet the requirements of Article 11,[21] industries concerned with the distribution of their digital content lobbied for a new form of protection in U.S. law.[22] This protection is based not on copyright (i.e., the right to copy), but on the right of access (i.e., the right to read, view, or experience the work in the first place).[23,24]

Access rights

Section 1201(1)(a) of the copyright law as added by the DMCA states: "No person shall circumvent a technological measure that effectively controls access to a work protected under this title."[25] A technological measure "[e]ffectively controls access to a work … if the measure, in the ordinary course of its operation, requires the application of information, or a process or a treatment, with the authority of the copyright owner, to gain access to the work."[26] In other words, if the copyright owner or representative has supplied a mathematical formula or code to make a video readable by the video-playing machine, the work is effectively controlled. There is the potential for substantial litigation about the word "effectively," because some types of encryption, whether pig Latin or a simple mathematical transposition, are arguably ineffective, even though they are required in the ordinary course of operation. If, and only if, access to the work is "effectively controlled" does the second phrase, "circumvent a technical measure," become relevant. "Circumvent a technological measure … means to descramble a scrambled work, to decrypt an encrypted work, or otherwise avoid, bypass, remove, deactivate, or impair a technological measure, without authority of the copyright owner."[27] Thus, if a user circumvents an effective access control, regardless of intent, there has been a violation of this section. Notice that this section requires that the work be "protected under this title." It is possible that this clause will be used by courts in the future to limit the scope of the DMCA to only those works that are currently protected by copyright.

There are a few narrow exceptions to the anticircumvention provisions, notably for law enforcement, reverse engineering, and encryption research.[28] For example, reverse engineering of software is permitted if certain conditions are met and if the sole purpose of the circumvention is to achieve interoperability.[29] The exception for nonprofit libraries, archives, and educational institutions permits access "to make a good faith determination of whether to acquire a copy of the work."[30] There is also a triennial rule-making mechanism, discussed below, that can result in additional exceptions.

It is important that the technological measure control "access," not "copying." Even though the DMCA amends the copyright law, the anticircumvention provisions of the DMCA, sometimes called paracopyright,[31] are fundamentally different from the rest of the copyright law. Copyright is a constitutionally mandated legal balance between the interests of creators of protected works and society. The U.S. Constitution states: "Congress shall have the power …[t]o promote the progress of science and useful arts, by securing for limited times to authors and inventors the exclusive right to their respective writings and discoveries."[32] This is achieved by granting creators specific exclusive rights to control certain aspects of their work for a limited time, after which the work becomes part of the public domain, and the exclusive rights cease to exist. In contrast to the balance between the incentive to create and the benefit to society found in copyright law, the anticircumvention provisions have no such balance. If a technological measure effectively controls access to a work, there is no time period after which there is a right to decrypt it or any fair use right that trumps the anticircumvention provisions.[33]

Access controls prevent the user from using the work, including viewing it. Copy controls prevent the user, who can view the work, from copying it. The important distinction is that the DMCA permits circumvention of a measure that prevents copying, but not circumvention of a measure that prevents access. It states "[n]othing in this section shall affect rights, remedies, limitations, or defenses to copyright infringement, including fair use, under this title."[34] If you can legitimately gain access, then you can still exercise your fair use rights and other rights embodied in traditional copyright law. However, because you cannot copy what you cannot access, and content providers know access controls cannot be circumvented, there is great incentive for content providers to use technological measures to limit access, thereby preventing potential copiers from ever reaching the work. To restore the balance of copyright law to the access rights, scholars opposed to the DMCA have proposed expanding fair use to include access rights or creating a new right of access.[24] For other articles discussing the relationship between the DMCA and public interest concerns, see Cohen[35] and Samuelson.[36] For a different perspective, see Ginsburg.[37]

Device trafficking

Along with the prohibition of circumvention in most cases, one cannot "manufacture, import, offer to the public, provide, or otherwise traffic" in devices or methods if they are primarily designed or produced to circumvent; they have only limited commercially significant purpose or use other than to circumvent; or they are marketed for use in circumventing.[38] Additionally, users cannot avoid, bypass, remove, deactivate, or otherwise impair a technological measure that effectively protects a right of a copyright owner under Title 17. Finally, they cannot traffic in devices that bypass technological measures.[39] Together, these device trafficking prohibitions are much like prohibiting the sale of lock-picking tools if those tools have no other purpose. However, most prohibitions against lock-picking tools require the owner to have some level of intent to use them in an illegal way. To the extent that fair use is extended to access rights, there will need to be legal mechanisms that permit the distribution of devices to facilitate legitimate circumvention. Otherwise, only the technological elite will be able to avail themselves of these access rights. Both device trafficking sections require that the works be "protected under this title," suggesting that perhaps devices that are designed in large part to circumvent access controls blocking access to public domain works or uses are permissible.

"Particular Class" Rule Making

The DMCA also requires the Librarian of Congress to conduct rule making 2 years after enactment, and every 3 years thereafter, to define "particular classes" to exclude from the anticircumvention provisions.[40] The rules can only permit circumvention of access to a defined class of works by all users, rather than permit access by the type of use or user. This means that the rule making would have to justify permitting access to the least favorable user, e.g., a direct competitor or consumer in the marketplace, rather than permitting access exclusively to researchers or for educational purposes. The narrow constraints of the rule-making framework minimize the potential for them to ameliorate the more socially detrimental aspects of the DMCA. The first rule making defined only two exempted classes, lists of blocked Web sites and literary works rendered unusable due to inoperative control devices.[41] More recent rule making has created exceptions that permit circumvention in other cases, such as circumventing DVD copy protection systems to create clip reels, circumventing digital locks in cell phones that prevent the user from changing carriers, and circumventing the access controls on e-books if there is no version that permits them to be read aloud.[42]

The scope of the rule making is limited by the DMCA to address anticircumvention, not device trafficking. By excluding devices from the scope of the review, even if an access right is recommended, each individual exercising that right would need to achieve the technological sophistication to circumvent the controls without the assistance of a distributed device, an extremely unlikely scenario.

Section 104 Report

The anticircumvention and antitrafficking sections of the DMCA did not become effective until 2 years after passage of the Act. The DMCA also required the drafting of a report that addressed the relationship between the DMCA and parts of the copyright law, notably section 109,[43] the first sale doctrine, and section 117,[44] the section that permits the making of archival copies of computer programs. The Librarian of Congress, based on the recommendations of the Register of Copyrights and the Assistant Secretary of Commerce, issued the report in 2001.[45]

The report addresses three proposals: creation of a "digital first sale doctrine," creation of an exemption for the making of certain temporary incidental copies, and the expansion of the archival copying exemption for computer programs in section 117 of the Act.[45] The comments related to the first sale doctrine discuss whether the societal benefits of the first sale doctrine should be carried over into the digital realm, where the "loan" of a digital work is really the making of a copy and the concurrent deletion of the original.[45] The concern of opponents is that this would lead to widespread piracy and destruction of the market for the legitimate original if the originals are not deleted.[45] This is a particular concern for digital works, because, unlike analog works, there is no degradation of quality when a copy is copied.

There is substantial scholarship on trusted systems,[46–49] systems that automatically delete the original when sending the copy. In light of the infancy of such systems, the report concluded, "Given the relative infancy of digital rights management, it is premature to consider any legislative change at this time. Should this practice become widespread, it could have serious consequences for the operation of the first sale doctrine, although the ultimate effect on consumers is unclear."[50] An additional concern was the effect of anticircumvention legislation on the creation of archival copies of software.[50] The report addressed that point as well, stating:

> The library community has raised concerns about how the current marketing of works in digital form affects libraries with regard to five specifically enumerated categories: interlibrary loans, off-site accessibility, archiving/preservation, availability of works, and use of donated copies. Most of these issues arise from terms and conditions of use, and costs of license agreements. One arises because, when the library has only online access to the work, it lacks a physical copy of the copyrighted work that can be transferred.

These issues arise from existing business models and are therefore subject to market forces. We are in the early stages of electronic commerce. We hope and expect that the marketplace will respond to the various concerns of customers in the library community. However, these issues may require further consideration at some point in the future. Libraries serve a vital function in society, and we will continue to work with the library and publishing communities on ways to ensure the continuation of library functions that are critical to our national interest.[50]

Cases

Several cases have dealt with the issues raised by anticircumvention provisions of the DMCA. One recent District Court opinion rejected the argument that there was a fair use right to access.[35] The most important cases attempt to invalidate the anticircumvention sections on Constitutional grounds and are discussed in the following sections.

Two important types of challenges to the anticircumvention provisions of the DMCA are likely. The first challenge will be claims that by preventing circumvention of access controls when the underlying works are partially or completely in the public domain, the DMCA oversteps the authority granted by Congress in

the Patent and Copyright Clause of the U.S. Constitution. The intent of the Patent and Copyright Clause is to create an incentive for creators to create; thereby subsequently benefiting all of society after the limited term of the exclusive rights comes to an end. Since the term of protection for public domain works has expired, Congress may lack the authority to protect them further.[34,51,52] Because Congress is only granted the power to secure exclusive rights for a limited time, the anticircumvention provisions arguably exceed the scope of the powers of Congress by permitting the encryption of public domain material without a right of circumvention. It is possible that the DMCA could survive this Constitutional challenge, either because a court determines it does not exceed the scope of that clause or because the DMCA is considered within the scope of Congressional power under another Constitutional clause, such as the Commerce Clause.[53]

The second challenge will be that the DMCA is unconstitutional, because it is in conflict with the First Amendment. The success of Constitutional challenges to the DMCA will largely hinge on the level of scrutiny the court applies. Even if a court decides that the prevention of copyright piracy is an "important or substantial governmental interest,"[54,55] the DMCA could be declared unconstitutional, because the DMCA cannot "burden substantially more speech than necessary."[55] The court would then have to determine if less restrictive means could reach the same end, such as preventing copying, but not blocking access. Whether the court would consider the technological feasibility of the alternatives as of the time of passage of the DMCA or as of the time of lawsuit raises interesting issues and, if the latter, suggests that subsequent attacks on the DMCA might be successful, even if earlier ones failed. What follows is a discussion of several recent cases that touch on the relationship between the First Amendment and the DMCA.

DeCSS case (*MPAA v. Corley*)

DVD discs include a content scrambling system (CSS).[56] DVD players include chips that permit them to play DVDs that use the CSS. Without "decoding" the DVDs, the content on them is not viewable. A program was written, called DeCSS, which makes DVDs playable on devices other than licensed DVD players, including computers running the Linux operating system. To achieve this goal, the program decrypts the CSS on the DVD and uses the information to make the content on the DVD viewable on unlicensed players that lack the special chip.[57] Although DVDs can be copied without breaking the CSS, so long as the CSS is not circumvented, the content cannot be viewed, except on licensed players. The CSS is a type of access control.

The DeCSS case arose when an online magazine posted the DeCSS program and hyperlinked to other sites that posted the DeCSS program.[58] There are two issues in the DeCSS case: whether, under the DMCA, Web sites can be liable for posting the code to decrypt the DVDs; and whether Web sites can be liable for knowingly linking to sites that post the code to decrypt the DVDs. The Web sites raised constitutional First Amendment concerns, because a limitation on posting programs or linking to programs limits the ability of the Web site owner to communicate, and hence free speech.

To address these questions, the court determined that CSS was "effective" and that decrypting CSS to play DVDs on unlicensed players, such as computers running Linux, was not within the interoperability exception.[58] In addressing the free speech issue, the court applied the O'Brien test, because the DMCA targeted functional speech, rather than expressive speech, and the speech limitation was considered content neutral, meaning that it did not attempt to discriminate against certain types of content.[58] The court upheld the constitutionality of the DMCA in both the posting and linking scenarios. It found that in the context of the DMCA, there was an "important or substantial governmental interest" and that the DMCA avoided burdening substantially more speech that is necessary to further the government's legitimate interests.[58] In the context of linking, it upheld the District Court's linking test that found that limiting some acceptable speech was Constitutionally acceptable, even though the alternative of limiting less speech and tolerating some decryption would have reduced the burden on speech, but at the cost of the potential for widespread piracy.[58]

Felten case (*Felten v. RIAA*)

Professor Edward Felten of the Computer Science Department at Princeton University researched music samples distributed by the Secure Digital Music Initiative (SDMI).[59] These samples included watermarks that could be detected by players or recorders to prevent duplication. The challenge was to remove the watermarks without overly degrading the sound quality.[60] After Professor Felten's group achieved this goal, they wanted to present their results. In a complicated set of facts, SDMI and others suggested that presenting their results might violate the licensing agreement Professor Felten had agreed to prior to receiving the samples or might violate the DMCA, because their research could help others defeat the watermarking system, which was already in public use outside the challenge.[60] Professor Felten sued to be able to present his results. After initially not presenting their results, his research team did so at a subsequent conference, with the permission of SDMI and others. After presenting his results at a conference, but arguing that there was still a controversy because future research would be chilled, a court determined that the issue was moot, because there was no continuing controversy.[61] Along with threat of DMCA and breach of contract claims, the Felten litigation team raised First Amendment

free speech claims, suggesting that the DMCA was being used to censor discussions about encryption research.[62]

The Felten case highlights two important effects of the DMCA: the potential chilling effect of such broad legislation and the role of contracts in potentially preventing access to both copyright-protected and public domain content. Professor Felten received e-mail that suggested he might face liability if he presented his paper. Even though he subsequently presented it, the threat of liability might stifle research in the encryption and computer security areas. The concern is that this would be detrimental to the U.S. economy, because there would then be reliance on systems that are not secure. The counter to this argument is that the process of encrypting content and unauthorized decryption will lead to a great deal of wasted effort spent trying to encrypt and decrypt content and that it is better that those efforts be spent in other areas. This argument is put forth along with the suggestion that the exemptions within the DMCA are sufficient for research in these areas.[63]

The Felten case is also different from the DeCSS case in that Professor Felten agreed to contractual terms prior to receiving the SDMI samples. Contracts, particularly nonnegotiable shinkwrap or clickwrap licenses, are the legal equivalents of the technological access controls in the DMCA. If a nonnegotiable clickwrap agreement is a contract, then the agreeing party will be bound by the terms of the contract. Although there are certain exceptions, the drafters of these licenses to circumvent the balance in copyright law by eliminating the acquirer's first sale and fair use rights, just the way access controls can technologically prevent exercise of first sale and fair use rights.

The 104 Report addressed this point:

> On the other hand, the movement at the state level toward resolving questions as to the enforceability of non-negotiated contracts coupled with legally-protected technological measures that give right holders the technological capability of imposing contractual provisions unilaterally increases the possibility that right holders, rather than Congress, will determine the landscape of consumer privileges in the future. Although market forces may well prevent right holders from unreasonably limiting consumer privileges, it is possible that at some point in the future a case could be made for statutory change.[64]

The Court dismissed the case as moot after the RIAA promised not to sue Professor Felten for publicly presenting his research.[65]

Sklyarov case (*U.S. v. ElcomSoft*)

The third important DMCA case is the case of the Russian programmer, Dmitry Sklyarov, who was arrested in the United States while attending a conference on e-books.[66,67] The Sklyarov case was notable, because it was a criminal prosecution, unlike the other two cases, which were civil cases for monetary damages. Dmitry Sklyarov works for ElcomSoft, a Russian company that creates and sells software that circumvents access controls on e-books. This is a legal product in Russia but not in the United States, due to the DMCA. After a substantial period of detention in the United States, Sklyarov was released in late 2001 on the condition that he testifies against his employer, ElcomSoft.[68] A U.S. jury subsequently cleared ElcomSoft on all charges.[69]

Arguably, the Sklyarov scenario is precisely the reason the DMCA was passed, but it also highlights the complexity of enforcing laws in an area where the laws and norms vary widely from country to country. In fact, the European equivalent of the DMCA has numerous provisions that differ substantially from the DMCA.[70] Given that circumvention of access controls and distribution of software devices that circumvent access controls are facilitated by Internet access, issues of jurisdiction and enforcement of judgments are likely to become more important in the coming decades.

Lexmark case (*Lexmark Int'l v. Static Control Components, Inc.*)

Lexmark sold laser printers and toner cartridges. The toner cartridges had a chip in them that enabled them to work with their printers. Competitors could not sell replacement toner cartridges because without the chip, the printer would not operate. The defendant manufactured chips that would enable non-Lexmark toner cartridges to work with Lexmark printers. Lexmark sued, claiming a DMCA violation and won at the District Court.[71] The Court of Appeals subsequently reversed the District Court's opinion.[72] The case is notable because it prevented the scope of the DMCA from expanding into a realm where interoperability and competition would be hampered by permitting manufacturers to use the DMCA to block competition in areas approaching patent law. For a related case regarding garage door openers, see Chamberlain v. Skylink.[73]

DVDXCopy case (*321 Studios v. Metro-Goldwyn-Mayer Studios, Inc.*)

DVDXCopy, produced by 321 Studios, was software that permitted users to copy their DVDs. 321 Studios was sued because the software circumvented the access controls on the DVD. Even though the end users could do what the software permitted them to do, the District Court held that 321 Studios was still liable for selling the tool that permitted the end user to decrypt the DVD.[74] This case highlights that even if tech-savvy end users can legally do certain things, those who lack the savvy will not be able to take advantage of the rights that they do have. In

addition, 321 Studios made certain constitutional arguments that the court largely rejected.

Bnetd case (*Davidson & Associates v. Jung*)

Blizzard created Battle.net as a server-based application that would permit players of Blizzard games to find each other online players and play online.[75] Among other things, it checked to see if the user's copy of the software was legal. Bnetd.org was designed to serve the same purpose as Battle.net, but lacked some features, such as the authentication of the user's copy of the software. When Blizzard sued bnetd, part of bnetd's defense relied on analogizing to the Lexmark Case. The court rejected that analogy, suggesting that the difference between the two is that the acquisition of the printer provides access to the relevant programs, while in the bnetd case, no one ever gets access to the Battle.net code, so the DMCA does apply. In addition, the court stated that the interoperability exception did not apply, suggesting that the lack of a check that the user's software was legal made a substantial difference.

TITLE II. ONLINE COPYRIGHT INFRINGEMENT LIABILITY LIMITATION

Title II of the DMCA addresses the twin concerns of content providers and ISPs.[76] Prior to the DMCA, content providers were concerned that, without the threat of liability, ISPs would facilitate the distribution of pirated digital content. ISPs were concerned that they would be liable for money damages for infringing copyrights by distributing or hosting protected content. Because copyright law grants creators exclusive display and performance rights, ISPs might be directly, contributorily, or vicariously infringing the owner's rights. The ISPs were particularly concerned, because the person who actually posted the content would probably not be as well off as the ISP, would be harder to trace, and might be a more sympathetic defendant, leaving the ISP to become the primary defendant in online copyright suits.

A compromise was struck wherein Title 17 of the U.S. Code, the copyright law, was amended by adding a new section 512. It set forth that ISPs would not be liable for hosting or transmitting content so long as they had registered contact information, had no actual knowledge of copyright infringements, and cooperated with processes to disable access and limit the harm to the copyright owner following a valid notification of a violation.[77] Section 512 is extraordinarily detailed. It lays out an elaborate roadmap for ISPs wishing to avoid liability for caching, storage, and transmission of protected works.

In the Napster case, dealing with whether the decentralized file sharing service that did not host any information itself could be found liable for secondary copyright infringement, one of the issues in the Napster case was whether Napster could invoke this liability limitation.[78] Napster was a service in which a server indexed music files on users' computers and facilitated users copying files from other users' personal computers. Napster was not an intermediary in the copying of files. Although the Napster model could be used to distribute public domain content, most of the content distributed via Napster was protected content.[78] On appeal, the court suggested that this section of the DMCA was intended to provide relief to vicarious infringers in some contexts but did not opine on whether such an analysis would include Napster.[78] Other cases have confirmed that companies like Amazon[79] and eBay[80] are able to take advantage of this limitation. The issue of whether search engines, such as Google, are able to take advantage of section 512 is currently being litigated.[81]

More recently, the major case law has involved service provider liability for repeat infringement by users.[82]

TITLE III. COMPUTER MAINTENANCE AND REPAIR COPYRIGHT EXEMPTION

This section, also know by its short title, the "Computer Maintenance Competition Assurance Act" amends section 117 of the copyright law to overrule a case that held that if software was licensed and a service company came to maintain the computer, by turning the computer on, the party servicing the computer was creating an illegal copy of the program in the memory of the computer.[83] This section permits the making of a copy in the memory of the computer if the purpose of the use is to repair or maintain the hardware.[84] This section does not apply to software to the extent that the exemption does not apply if the copy is made when the software is "not necessary for that machine to be activated."[85]

TITLE IV. MISCELLANEOUS PROVISIONS

Title IV amends various parts of the copyright law to address issues related to distance education, libraries, and ephemeral recordings, among other things. Due to the concerns of educators, the DMCA required the Register of Copyrights to issue a report on how to promote distance education through digital technologies.[86] After an intense 6 mo review, the report suggested nine changes:

1. Clarify the meaning of transmission to include both digital and analog.
2. Expand coverage of rights to the extent technologically necessary.
3. Emphasize the concept of mediated instruction. Ensure that the performance or display is analogous to the type of performance or display that would take place in a live classroom setting, rather than a substitute for the original.
4. Eliminate the requirement of a physical classroom, but substitute the requirement of official enrollment to limit abuses of distance education.
5. Add new safeguards to counteract new risks, such as using technological measures to control unauthorized use and educating students and faculty on copyright law.
6. Maintain existing standards of eligibility.
7. Expand categories of works covered.
8. Require use of lawful copies.
9. Add new ephemeral recording exemption.[86]

Section 404 of the DMCA updates the library exemption, section 108 of the copyright law,[87] to meet current archival needs and standards. This section permits archives to make three copies of archival works, one as the master, one as the archival copy, and one as the use copy. Additionally, the copy no longer has to be a facsimile, but it can reform the content. Libraries cannot distribute digital content in the same way that they are permitted to distribute the analog facsimiles. Although print works could become damaged or stolen, existing section 108 did not address the library's needs when the digital format was unreadable. This section of the DMCA added that archival copies could be made when the format became obsolete. Obsolete is defined as "if the machine or device necessary to render perceptible a work stored in that format is no longer manufactured, or is no longer reasonably available in the commercial marketplace."[88] Finally, if no notice of copyright appears on the work, the library can state that the work "may be protected by copyright."[89]

Sections 402 and 405 of the DMCA address the issue of ephemeral recordings and reconcile previous copyright legislation and the anticircumvention provisions with the need for broadcast organizations to make ephemeral copies of their programming. Another section defined the scope of exclusive rights in sound recordings as they pertain to ephemeral recordings.[90]

TITLE V. PROTECTION OF CERTAIN ORIGINAL DESIGNS

Title V, also known by its short title, "Vessel Hull Design Protection Act," protects boat hull designs for 10 yr.[91] There is a long and contentious history of protection of boat hull designs.[92] Boat hull designs, like digitized music, can be very hard to create and very easy to copy. In the context of boat hulls, they are copied through the use of plug molds. To qualify for protection, the design has to be registered, and notice of protection would be required.[93] The section includes exceptions for educational uses, independent creation, and liability for resellers if there was no notice of protection.[94]

REFERENCES

1. No Electronic Theft Act, Pub. L. No. 105–147 (1998) and the Sonny Bono Copyright Term Extension Act, Pub. L. No. 105–298 (1998).
2. Lunney, G.S., Jr. The death of copyright: Digital technology, private copying, and the digital millennium copyright act. Va. Law Rev. **2001**, *87*, 813.
3. Denicola, R.C. Mostly dead? Copyright law in the new millennium. J. Copyr. Soc. U.S.A. **2000**, *47*, 193.
4. Crawford, M.D. *Modern Technology and the Death of Copyright.* Available at http://www.goingware.com/comments/2000/feb/05top.html (accessed February 5, 2000).
5. PL 105–304, 112 Stat. 2860 (1998).
6. Title 17 of the United States Code, often abbreviated 17 U.S.C.
7. http://www.loc.gov/copyright/.
8. Title II of the DMCA (Sections 201–203); see text accompanying notes 75–79.
9. Part of Title IV of the DMCA (Sections 402, 405); see text accompanying note 88.
10. Title V of the DMCA (Sections 501–505); see text accompanying notes 89–92.
11. Part of Title I of the DMCA (Section 103); see text accompanying notes 11–74.
12. Title I of the DMCA (Sections 101–105).
13. The Berne Convention for the Protection of Literary and Artistic Works, opened for signature July 24, 1971, 25 U.S.T. 1341. Available at http://www.wipo.int/treaties/en/ip/berne/index.html.
14. World Intellectual Property Organization (WIPO) Copyright Treaty, December 20, 1996, WIPO Doc. CRNR/DC/94. Available at http://www.wipo.int/treaties/en/ip/wct/.
15. WIPO Performances and Phonograms Treaty, December 20, 1996, WIPO Doc. CRNR/DC/95. Available at http://www.wipo.int/treaties/en/ip/wppt/.
16. Section 102 of the DMCA.
17. 17 United States Code 1201.
18. 17 United States Code 1202.
19. 17 United States Code 1204.
20. 17 United States Code 1203.
21. Lipton, J. Copyright in the digital age: A comparative survey. Rutgers Comput. Technol. Law J. **2001**, *27*, 333–360.
22. Manz, W.H. *Federal Copyright Law: The Legislative Histories of the Major Enactments of the 105th Congress*, William S. Hein: Buffalo, NY, 1999.
23. Litman, J. The exclusive right to read. Cardozo Arts Entertain. Law J. **1994**, *13*, 29.
24. Litman, J. *Digital Copyright*, Prometheus Books: Amherst, NY, 2001; 183–184.
25. 17 United States Code 1201 (a)(1)(A).
26. 17 United States Code 1201 (b)(3)(B).
27. 17 United States Code 1201 (b)(3)(A).
28. 17 United States Code 1201 (d)–(j).
29. 17 United States Code 1201 (f).
30. 17 United States Code 1201 (d).
31. Letter Dated September 16, 1997 from 62 law professors, cited at H.R. Rep. No. 105–551, pt. 2, at 24 (1998).
32. Article I, Section 8, Clause 8 of the United States Constitution.
33. RealNetworks, Inc. v. Streambox Inc., 2000 U.S. Dist. LEXIS 1889 (W.D. WA 1-18-00).
34. 17 United States Code 1201 (c)(1).
35. Cohen, J. WIPO treaty implementation in the United States: Will fair use survive?. Eur. Intellect. Prop. Rev. **1999**, *21*(5), 236.
36. Samuelson, P. Intellectual property and the digital economy: Why the anti-circumvention regulations need to be revised. Berkeley Technol. Law J. **1999**, *14*, 519, 562–564.
37. Ginsburg, J.C. Copyright legislation for the Digital Millennium. Columbia-VLA J. Law Arts **1999**, Spring *23*(2), 137.
38. 17 United States Code 1201(a)(2).
39. 17 United States Code 1201(b).
40. 17 United States Code 1201(a)(1)(C).
41. Library of Congress, Exemption to Prohibition on Circumvention of Copyright Protection Systems for Access Control Technologies, 65 Federal Register 64555 (October 28, 2000), codified at 37 C.F.R. 201.40.
42. Library of Congress, Exemption to Prohibition on Circumvention of Copyright Protection Systems for Access Control Technologies, 71 Federal Register 68472 (November 27, 2006), codified at 37 C.F.R. 201.40 http://www.copyright.gov/1201/ (accessed December 2007).
43. 17 United States Code 109.
44. 17 United States Code 117.
45. Study required by Section 104 of the Digital Millennium Copyright Act [electronic resource]/U.S. Copyright Office, Library of Congress; Washington, D.C.: The Office, 2001 [hereinafter 104 Report], http://www.loc.gov/copyright/reports/studies/dmca/dmca%5Fstudy.html.
46. Gimbel, M. Some thoughts on the implications of trusted systems for intellectual property law. Stanford Law Rev. **1998**, *50*, 1671.
47. Stefik, M. Shifting the possible: How trusted systems and digital property rights challenge us to rethink digital publishing. Berkeley Technol. Law J. **1998**, *12*, 137, 152–153, 155–156.
48. Burk, D.L.; Cohen, J.E. Fair use infrastructure for copyright management systems. Harv. J. Law Technol. **2001**, 41–84.
49. Stefik, M.; Silverman, A. The bit and the pendulum: Balancing the interests of stakeholders in digital publishing. Comput. Law **1997**, *16*, 1.
50. 104 Report at xvi. xxi, 60–66, 148–162i.
51. http://eon.law.harvard.edu/openlaw/golanvashcroft/.
52. Nimmer, D. A riff on fair use in the digital millennium copyright act. Univ. PA. Law Rev. **2000**, *148*, 673, 681–682.
53. Article I, Section 8, clause 2 of the U.S. Constitution, stating "Congress shall have the power … [t]o regulate commerce with foreign nations, and among the several states, and with the Indian tribes."
54. Turner Broad. Sys., Inc. v. FCC, 512 U.S. 622, 662 (1994) (quoting United States v. O'Brien, 391 U.S. 367, 377 (1968)).
55. Netanel, N. Weinstock locating copyright within the first amendment skein. Stanford Law Rev. **2001**, *54*, 1 74–181.
56. Universal Studios v. Corley, 273 F.3d 429 (2d Cir. 2001).
57. http://cryptome.org/cryptout.htm#DVD-DeCSS.
58. Corley, 273 F.3d at 439, 444, 454–458.
59. Felten v. Recording Industry Association of America Inc, No. 01-CV-2669 (D.N.J., November 28, 2001).

Available at http://www.linuxtoday.com/news_story.php3? ltsn=2001-06-06-008-20-NW-CY.

60. Department of Justice's Motion to Dismiss. Available at http://www.eff.org/Legal/Cases/Felten_v_RIAA/ 20010925_doj_mtd_memo.html.

61. Court Dismisses Computer Scientists' Challenge to DMCA, 3 No. 4 Andrews E-Bus. L. Bull. 3 (January 2002).

62. Electronic Frontier Foundation Reply Brief. Available at http://www.eff.org/Legal/Cases/Felten_v_RIAA/ 20011025_eff_felten_ opp_brief.pdf.

63. 104 Report at 164–165.

64. 104 Report at xxxi–xxxii.

65. http://www.wired.com/politics/law/news/2001/11/48726.

66. Sklyarov Documents. Available at http://www.eff.org/IP/ DMCA/US_v_ Sklyarov/.

67. Sklyarov Indictment. Available at http://w2.eff.org/IP/ DMCA/US_v_Elcomsoft/20010828_sklyarov_elcomsoft _indictment.html.

68. U.S. Attorney's Press Release. Available at http://w2.eff. org/IP/DMCA/US_v_Elcomsoft/20011213_usatty_pr.html (accessed February 2002).

69. http://www.wired.com/techbiz/media/news/2002/12/ 56894.

70. Directive 2001/29/EC of the European Parliament and of the Council of 22 May 2001 on the Harmonisation of Certain Aspects of Copyright and Related Rights in the Information Society, 2001 O.J. (L 167) 10.

71. Lexmark International, Inc. v. Static Control Components, Inc, 253 F. Supp. 2d 943 (E.D. Ky. 2003).

72. Lexmark International, Inc. v. Static Control Components, Inc., 387 F.3d 522 (6th Cir. 2004).

73. Chamberlain v. Skylink, 381 F.3d 1178 (Fed. Cir. 2004).

74. 321 Studios v. Metro-Goldwyn-Mayer Studios, Inc., 307 F. Supp. 2d 1085 (N.D. Cal. 2004).

75. Davidson & Associates v. Jung, 422 F.3d 630 (8th Cir. 2005).

76. Title II of the DMCA (Sections 201–203).

77. 17 United States Code 512.

78. A&M Records v. Napster, 239 F.3d 1004, 1025 (9th Cir. 2001).

79. Corbis v. Amazon.com, 351 F. Supp. 2d 1090 (W.D. Wash. 2004).

80. Hendrickson v. eBay, Inc., 165 F. Supp. 2d 1082, 1087 (C.D. Cal. 2001).

81. Perfect 10, Inc. v. Amazon.com, Inc., 487 F.3d 701 (9th Cir. 2007) (as amended December 3, 2007).

82. Nimmer, D. Repeat infringers. J. Copyright Soc. **2005**, *52*, 167.

83. MAI v. Peak, 991 F.2d 511 (9th Cir. 1993).

84. 17 United States Code 117.

85. 17 United States Code 117(c)(2).

86. Report on Copyright and Digital Distance Education. Available at http://www.copyright.gov/disted/.

87. 17 United States Code 108.

88. 17 United States Code 108(c).

89. 17 United States Code 108(a)(3).

90. Section 405 of the DMCA, amending 17 United States Code 114.

91. Section 502 of the DMCA, adding 17 United States Code 1301, et seq.

92. Vessel Hull Design Protection Act, H. Rep. No. 105–436, 105th Cong., 2d Sess. (March 11, 1998).

93. 17 United States Code 1306.

94. 17 United States Code 1309(b),(c),(g).

Digital Object Identifier (DOI®) System

Norman Paskin
Tertius Ltd., Oxford, U.K.

Abstract

The Digital Object Identifier (DOI®) System is a managed system for persistent identification of content on digital networks. It can be used to identify physical, digital, or abstract entities. The identifiers (DOI names) resolve to data specified by the registrant, and use an extensible metadata model to associate descriptive and other elements of data with the DOI name. The DOI system is implemented through a federation of registration agencies, under policies and common infrastructure provided by the International DOI Foundation which developed and controls the system. The DOI system has been developed and implemented in a range of publishing applications since 2000; by early 2009 over 40 million DOIs had been assigned. The DOI system provides identifiers which are persistent, unique, resolvable, and interoperable and so useful for management of content on digital networks in automated and controlled ways.

IDENTIFIER CONCEPTS

An identifier is a concise means of referencing something. The term "identifier" can mean several different things:

- A "string," typically a number or name, denoting a specific entity (the referent of the identifier string). For example, the identifier ISBN 978-0-00-721331-3 denotes the book "Francis Crick" by Matt Ridley.
- A "specification," which prescribes how such strings are constructed. For example, the ISO standard ISO 2108:2005[1] is the current specification of the ISBN numbering system; but having that standard alone will not enable someone to construct and register a new valid ISBN.
- A "scheme," which implements such a specification. For example, the ISBN International Agency[2] implements the ISBN standard in an implemented scheme, by assigning ISBN prefixes to publishers, registering specific ISBNs (strings); providing rules on use of the ISBN (such as the incorporation of the ISBN as a bar code on the cover of a book). Typically, such schemes provide a managed registry of the identifiers within their control, in order to offer a related service.

Some important concepts relating to identifiers are "uniqueness," "resolution," "interoperability," and "persistence."

Uniqueness is the requirement that one string denotes one and only one entity (the "referent"). Note that the converse is not a logical consequence: it is not necessary that an entity have only one identifier. For example, a book may have an ISBN and also an LCCN. An identifier scheme may even allow multiple identifiers for one entity, though usually these are deprecated.

Resolution is the process in which an identifier is the input to a service to receive in return a specific output of one or more pieces of current information related to the identified entity. For example, a bar code ISBN in a bookshop is scanned by a bar code reader and resolves to some point of sale information, such as title and price. Note that resolution depends on a particular application: while a bar code in a bookshop may resolve to price, the same bar code in a warehouse application might resolve to current stock number, or pallet position. Another familiar example of resolution is the Internet Domain Name System (DNS) which resolves a domain name address (URL) to a file residing on a specific host server machine.

Interoperability denotes the ability to use an identifier in services outside the direct control of the issuing assigner: identifiers assigned in one context may be encountered in another place or time without consulting the assigner. This requires that the assumptions made on assignment will be made known in some way. For example, a customer may order a book from a bookseller or a library system by quoting its ISBN, without consulting the publisher who assigned the number.

Persistence is the requirement that once assigned, an identifier denotes the same referent indefinitely. For example, ISBNs, once assigned, are managed so as to reference the same book always (and are not reassigned). Persistence can be considered to be "interoperability with the future."

The management of content on digital networks requires identifiers to be persistent, unique, resolvable, and interoperable. As an example, URLs do not identify content but a file location: using them as a substitute for such identifiers is not sustainable for reliable automation. The content may be removed ("404 not found"), or changed (not being the same as the user anticipated, or the user being unaware of such change). There have been a number of efforts to address the need for such reliable identifiers, notable among them URN[3] and

Encyclopedia of Library and Information Sciences, Fourth Edition DOI: 10.1081/E-ELIS4-120044418

URI[4] specifications; however these do not of themselves provide an implemented managed scheme and registry for specific content sector applications. Such full schemes require more: a model for identifiers and their management; shared, standards-based, persistent identifier management infrastructure; support for adoption of persistent identifiers and services, and a plan for sustainable shared identifier infrastructure.[5,6] The Digital Object Identifier (DOI®) system is such a managed system for persistent identification of content on digital networks, using a federation of registries following a common specification.

The uncapitalized term "digital object identifier" may be used nonspecifically to describe a number of varied technologies concerned with the identification of entities in a digital environment. The capitalized term "Digital Object Identifier" refers to one specific system defined and managed by the International DOI Foundation,[7] which provides an infrastructure for persistent unique identification of entities (here termed "objects") on digital networks deployed in a number of content-related applications.

DOI SYSTEM: OUTLINE

DOI is an acronym for Digital Object Identifier. The DOI system provides for unique identification, persistence, resolution, metadata, and semantic interoperability of content entities ("objects"). Information about an object can change over time, including where to find it, but its DOI name will not change.

The DOI system brings together

- A syntax specification, defining the construction of a string (a DOI name)
- A resolution component, providing the mechanism to resolve the DOI name to data specified by the registrant
- A metadata component, defining an extensible model for associating descriptive and other elements of data with the DOI name
- A social infrastructure, defining the full implementation through policies and shared technical infrastructure in a federation of registration agencies

More detail on each of these aspects is given later in this entry.

The DOI system operates through a tiered structure:

- The International DOI Foundation is the umbrella organization defining the rules and operation of the system. It is a non-profit member-funded organization.
- Registration agencies are all members of the International DOI Foundation, and have a contractual

arrangement with the Foundation including a license to operate the DOI system. They provide defined services in specific sectors or applications. DOI registration is normally only a part of the service such an organization offers, since assignment of an identifier is usually done for the purpose of a specific initial service or application. An example is the CrossRef registration agency,[8] which provides services to publishers for linking reference citations in articles based on DOI-identified articles. Registration agencies may collaborate, or remain relatively autonomous.

- DOI names are registered by clients via a registration agency (e.g., in the case of the CrossRef agency, individual publishers are clients using the CrossRef service). Part of this process may be undertaken by the registration agency, as part of its service offering. If a suitable registration agency cannot be found for a certain sector, the International DOI Foundation will seek to appoint one.

DOI is a registered trademark of the International DOI Foundation, Inc. (abbreviated to IDF). The preferred usage, to avoid ambiguity, is with a qualifier to refer to either specific components of the DOI system (e.g., "DOI name": the string that specifies a unique referent within the DOI system); or the system as a whole ("DOI system": the functional deployment of DOI names as the application of identifiers in computer-sensible form through assignment, resolution, referent description, administration, etc.).

SCOPE

The term "Digital Object Identifier" is construed as "digital identifier of an object," rather than "identifier of a digital object": the objects identified by DOI names may be of any form—digital, physical, or abstract—as all these forms may be necessary parts of a content management system. The DOI system is an abstract framework which does not specify a particular context of its application, but is designed with the aim of working over the Internet.[9]

A DOI name is permanently assigned to an object, to provide a persistent link to current information about that object, including where it, or information about it, can be found. The principal focus of assignment is to content-related entities; that term is not precisely defined but is exemplified by text documents; data sets; sound carriers; books; photographs; serials; audio, video, and audiovisual recordings; software; abstract works; artwork, etc., and related entities in their management, for example, licenses or parties. A DOI name is not intended as a replacement for other identifier schemes, such as those of ISO TC46/SC9[10] ISBN, ISSN, ISAN, ISRC, etc., or other commonly recognized identifiers: if an object is already identified with another identifier string, the character string of the other identifier may be integrated into the DOI name syntax, and/or carried in DOI metadata, for use in DOI applications.

A DOI name may be assigned to any object whenever there is a functional need to distinguish it as a separate entity. Registration agencies may specify more constrained rules for the assignment of DOI names to objects for DOI-related services (e.g., a given registration agency may restrict its activities to one type of content or one type of service).

SYNTAX

A DOI name is the string that specifies a unique object (the referent) within the DOI system. The DOI syntax (standardized as ANSI/NISO Z39.84-2005)[11] prescribes the form and sequence of characters comprising any DOI name. The DOI syntax is made up of a "prefix" element and a "suffix" element separated by a forward slash. There is no defined limit on the length of the DOI name, or of its prefix or its suffix elements. The DOI name is case-insensitive and may incorporate any printable characters from the Unicode Standard.

- Example: a DOI name with the prefix element "10.1000" and the suffix element "123456": 10.1000/123456

The combination of a unique prefix element (assigned to a particular DOI registrant) and a unique suffix element (provided by that registrant) is unique, and so allows the decentralized allocation of DOI numbers. The DOI name is an opaque string for the purposes of the DOI system: no definitive information should be inferred from the specific character string of a DOI name. In particular, the inclusion in a DOI name of any registrant code allocated to a specific organization does not provide evidence of the ownership of rights or current management responsibility of any intellectual property in the referent. Such information can be asserted in the associated DOI metadata.

The DOI prefix has two components: a "Directory" indicator followed by a "Registrant" code, separated by a full stop (period) (e.g., 10.1000). The directory indicator is always "10" and distinguishes the entire set of character strings (prefix and suffix) as DOIs within the wider Handle System® used for resolution. The registrant code is a unique alphanumeric string assigned to an organization that wishes to register DOI names (four digit numeric codes are currently used though this is not a compulsory syntax). The registrant code is assigned through a DOI registration agency, and a registrant may have multiple-registrant codes. Once a DOI name is assigned the string should not be changed, regardless of any changes in the ownership or

management of the referent object; if an object is withdrawn from digital access, its DOI name should still resolve to some appropriate message to this effect.

The DOI suffix may be a sequential number, or it may incorporate an identifier generated from or based on another system used by the registrant (e.g., ISBN, ISSN, ISTC). In such cases, the existing system may specify its own preferred construction for such a suffix:

- Example: a DOI suffix using an ISSN: 10.1038/issn.0028-0836.

When displayed on screen or in print, a DOI name is normally preceded by a lowercase "doi": unless the context clearly indicates that a DOI name is implied.

- Example: the DOI name 10.1006/jmbi.1998.2354 is displayed as doi:10.1006/jmbi.1998.2354.

The use of lowercase string "doi" follows the specification for representation as a URI (as for e.g., "ftp:" and "http:").

DOI names may be represented in other forms in certain contexts. For example, when displayed in Web browsers the DOI name itself may be attached to the address for an appropriate proxy server (e.g., http://dx.doi.org/ resolves DOIs in the context of Web browsers using the Handle System resolution technology) to enable resolution of the DOI name via a standard Web hyperlink.

- Example: the DOI name 10.1006/jmbi.1998.2354 would be made an active link as http://dx.doi.org/10.1006/jmbi.1998.2354.

DOI names so represented in a URL and transported by the HTTP protocol are constrained to follow standard IETF guidelines for URI representations. The syntax for URIs is more restrictive than the syntax for DOIs; some characters are reserved and will need encoding (the NISO Z39.84 DOI syntax standard provides more detail). Certain client or server software may be able to handle DOIs using native handle resolution technology (where doi:10.1006/jmbi.1998.2354 would be understood by the browser and automatically resolved without the addition of the proxy server address). DOI names may also be represented in other schemes, for example, in the info URI schema[12,13] as info:doi/10.1006/jmbi.1998.2354.

RESOLUTION

A DOI name can, within the DOI system, be resolved to values of one or more types of data relating to the object identified by that DOI name, such as a URL, an e-mail address, other identifiers, and descriptive metadata (or any additional types defined extensibly by the registration agency). Resolution is the process of submitting a specific

DOI name to the DOI system (e.g., by clicking on a DOI in a Web browser) and receiving in return the associated values held in the DOI resolution record for one or more of those types of data relating to the object identified by that DOI name. Since the referent objects referred to by DOI names may be of various types (including abstractions as "works," physical "manifestations," performances), they may or may not be directly accessible in the form of a digital file or other manifestation; hence the resolution may or may not return an instance of the object.

The initial implementation of DOI system was that of persistent naming: a single redirection from a DOI name to a digital location (URL) of the entity (Fig. 1).

A significant DOI function is the capability for multiple resolution, that is, delivering more than one value back from a resolution request. The values are grouped into defined types, which can form the basis of services (Fig. 2). An example of current usage of this facility is resolution to a specific local copy of an article, determined by combining the resolution result (several URLs) and local information about the user's location (from the user's browser application).

Objects (identified by DOI names) which have common behavior (defined by metadata) can be grouped, using DOI application profiles; these application profiles can in turn be associated with one or more services applicable to that group of DOI names (see Fig. 3).

The Handle System,[14] the resolution component used in the DOI system, is a general-purpose distributed information system designed to provide an efficient, extensible, and secure global name service for use on networks such as the Internet. The Handle System includes an open set of protocols, a namespace, and a reference implementation of the protocols. The DOI system is one implementation of the Handle System; hence a DOI name is a "Handle." DOI names are distinguished from other handles by additional "metadata" and "policy." The Handle System enables entities to be assigned first-class names, independent of domain names and other location-specific information, which can then be resolved (redirected) to appropriate locations: since the resolution destination is managed and can be changed, this provides a tool for persistence, avoiding "404 not found" and similar problems with URLs. The Handle System is used in a variety of applications such as the Content Object Repository Discovery and Resolution Architecture (CORDRA) of the U.S. Department of Defense (DoD) Advanced Distributed Learning initiative; The Library of Congress National Digital Library Program; and applications in grid computing and advanced future Internet architectures. The Handle System also includes several features not currently used in the DOI system, such as trusted resolution using public key infrastructure.

The Handle System is part of a wider Digital Object Architecture;[15] that architecture specifically deals only with digital objects with identifiers (Handles). There is no conflict in these two views, since any non-digital entity may be reified (or represented) as a corresponding digital object for the purposes of digital object management

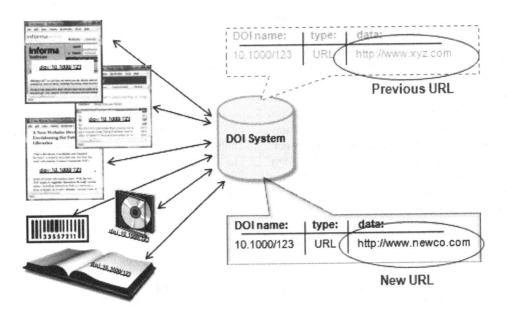

Fig. 1 The role of the DOI system as a persistent identifier. A DOI name (10.1000/123) has been assigned to a content entity; the DOI system provides resolution from that name to a current URL. When the content, previously at URL xyz.com, is moved to a new URL newco.com, a single change in the DOI directory is made: all instances of the DOI name identifying that content (even if already recorded in print, as bookmarks, etc.) will resolve to the new URL, without the user having to take any action or be aware of the change. Note that the DOI name is persistent, i.e., remains unchanged.
Source: From International DOI Foundation.

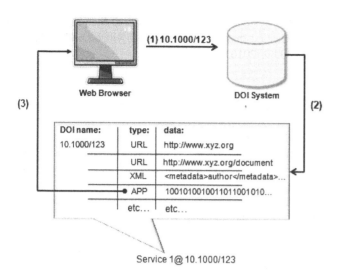

Fig. 2 Multiple resolution. A Web browser is running an application "Service 1." That service resolves DOI name 10.1000/123 to the DOI system (1) where it finds four values within the relevant DOI record (2): here, two are of the type URL, one is XML, and one is a conjectural application. Service 1 selects one of these results (in this case, the APP value) on the basis of combining information provided in the resolution result and the local application.
Source: From International DOI Foundation.

(though some care is needed in the definition of such objects and how they relate to non-digital entities).

METADATA

The object associated with a DOI name is described unambiguously by DOI metadata, based on an extensible data model to support interoperability between DOI applications. Assignment of a DOI name requires the registrant to record metadata describing the object to which the DOI name is being assigned. The metadata describes the object to the degree that is necessary to distinguish it as a separate entity within the DOI system.

A minimum set of such metadata, the DOI kernel, is specified by the IDF. This includes elements such as "other identifier(s) commonly referencing the same referent (e.g., ISBN, ISRC)," and the name by which the referent is usually known (e.g., title). This minimum kernel may be enhanced by registration agencies through the development of specific application profiles with metadata elements appropriate to a particular application or set of applications. The IDF also specifies the template for the exchange of metadata between DOI registration agencies to support their service requirements, and specifies a Data Dictionary as the repository for all data elements and allowed values used in DOI metadata specifications.

The basis of the metadata scheme and extensions used in the DOI system is the indecs (interoperability of data in

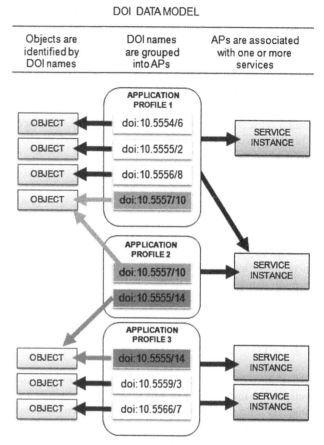

DOI DATA MODEL

Objects are identified by DOI names	DOI names are grouped into APs	APs are associated with one or more services

Fig. 3 DOI data model: the Application Profile Framework. DOI names (identifying the entities on the left) are grouped into application profiles. Any single DOI name can be a member of multiple application profiles (e.g., DOI 10.5557/10 is shown here in two). Each application profile can similarly be associated with one or more services: each service can be made available in multiple ways. This makes it possible to make a new service applicable to many DOI names, simply by adding that service to the relevant application profile(s).
Source: From International DOI Foundation.

e-commerce systems) project.[16] This contextual ontology approach to interoperability is shared by a number of significant content sector activities.[17,18] This allows the use of a variety of existing metadata schemes with DOI names in a common framework.

The use of these tools for DOI metadata has been limited in initial applications, but more applications are emerging as the sophistication of content management on digital networks and the need for interoperability increases.

SOCIAL INFRASTRUCTURE

DOI names are intended to be persistent identifiers: no time limit for the existence of a DOI name is assumed in any assignment, service, or DOI application. A DOI name and its referent are unaffected by changes in the rights associated with the referent, or changes in the management responsibility of the referent object. Since such persistence requires a social infrastructure, policies as well as technical infrastructure need to be defined and implemented. The IDF develops and implements policies such as rules for transfer of management responsibility between registration agencies, requirements placed on registration agencies for maintenance of records, default resolution services, and technical infrastructure resilience. These are codified in a formal agreement between the IDF and each of the registration agencies.

The DOI system is not a means of archival preservation of identified entities; it does not store the identified objects themselves; nor does the central DOI Directory store comprehensive metadata (only pointers to the registration agency or other source of such data). The system provides a means to continue interoperability through exchange of meaningful information about identified entities through at minimum persistence of the DOI name and a description of the referent.

HISTORY

The DOI system was the result of a publishing industry initiative in the late 1990s, which recognized the need to uniquely and unambiguously identify content entities, rather than refer to them by locations, and commissioned a study to specify an appropriate technical solution, selected if possible from one or more existing technologies rather than developing a new system. The International DOI Foundation was incorporated in 1998 to develop the system; where possible, existing technologies and standards were adopted for the implementation of the DOI system. The first DOI registration agency began in 2000; by early 2009 around 40 million DOI names had been assigned through eight registration agencies. The most widely known application of the DOI system is the Crossref cross-publisher citation linking service which allows a researcher link from a reference citation directly to the cited content on another publisher's platform, subject to the target publisher's access control practices. Other applications include government documentation, books, and data; further applications are under development.

The development of the DOI system has proceeded through three parallel tracks:

- An initial implementation of persistent naming: a single redirection from a DOI name to a digital location (URL) of the entity or information about it.
- The development of more sophisicated means of management such as contextual resolution, where the result of a redirection is also a function of some additional information such as local holdings information.
- Collaboration with other standards activities in the further development of tools for managing entities in a digital environment.

The DOI System is a Draft International Standard of ISO, it is expected that the final standard will be published in late 2009 or 2010.

RELATED ACTIVITIES

The DOI system is associated with two independent technical activities which it has used as components of DOI implementations: the Handle System and the series of contextual ontology initiatives derived from the indecs project. Each is used in other non-DOI applications (an aim of the International DOI Foundation was to use existing solutions where available and proven to be useful). Either of these components could be replaced in the DOI system by other technologies offering similar features in the future if necessary.

The International DOI Foundation, particularly through its registration agency CrossRef, has also been closely involved in the development of the OpenURL, a mechanism for transporting metadata and identifiers describing a publication for the purpose of context-sensitive linking. The DOI system is now widely implemented using OpenURL by many libraries: further information on this topic is available from the Crossref Web site. The use of open URL was the first widespread example of more sophisticated means of content management through contextual resolution.

The expertise of the International DOI Foundation in issues such as resolution and semantic interoperability has also led to some IDF members being active participants in discussions of further identifier scheme development such as the International Standard Text Code (ISTC) numbering system for the identification of textual works, and identifiers for parties (persons and organizations), and licenses.

REFERENCES

1. ISO 2108:2005 Information and documentation—International standard book number (ISBN), http://www.iso.org/iso/iso catalogue/catalogue tc/catalogue detail.htm?csnumber=36563 (accessed July 2009).
2. The International ISBN Agency web site: International Standard Book Number System for Books, Software, Mixed Media etc. in Publishing, Distribution and Libraries. http://www.isbn-international.org/ (accessed July 2009).
3. Sollins, K.; Masinter, L. 1994. Functional Requirements for Uniform Resource Names. Internet Engineering Task Force (IETF) Request for Comments (RFC) 1737, December 1994. http://tools.ietf.org/html/rfc1737 (accessed July 2009).
4. Berners-Lee, T.; Fielding, R.; Masinter, L. Uniform Resource Identifiers (URI): Generic Syntax. Internet Engineering Task Force (IETF) Request for Comments (RFC) 3986, January 2005. http://www.ietf.org/rfc/rfc3986.txt (accessed July 2009).

5. Dyson, E. Online Registries: The DNS and Beyond. Release 1.0, Volume 21, Number 8, 16 September 2003. http://doi.contentdirections.com/reprints/dyson_excerpt.pdf (accessed July 2009).

6. PILIN team: Persistent Identifier Linking Infrastructure Project Report December 2007. https://www.pilin.net.au/Closure_Report.pdf (accessed July 2009).

7. The DOI system web site: http://www.doi.org (accessed July 2009).

8. CrossRef web site: http://www.crossref.org (accessed July 2009).

9. Kahn, R.E.; Cerf, V.G. *What is the Internet (And What Makes It Work)*; Internet Policy Institute, December 1999. http://www.cnri.reston.va.us/what_is_internet.html (accessed July 2009).

10. ISO (International Organization for Standardization) TC 46 (Technical Committee for information and documentation standards SC9 (Subcommittee on the identification and description of information resources). http://www.iso.org/iso/iso_catalogue/catalogue_tc/catalogue_tc_browse.htm?commid=48836&published on (accessed July 2009).

11. ANSI/NISO Z39.84 (2005): Syntax for the Digital Object Identifier. http://www.niso.org (accessed July 2009).

12. Van der Sompel, H.; Hammond, T.; Neylon, E.; Weibel, S. The info URI Scheme for Information Assets with Identifiers in Public Namespaces. Internet Engineering Task Force (IETF) Request for Comments (RFC) 4452, April 2006. http://www.ietf.org/rfc/rfc4452.txt.

13. About INFO URIs: Frequently Asked Questions, http://info-uri.info/registry/docs/misc/faq.html (accessed July 2009).

14. The Handle System, http://www.handle.net/ (accessed July 2009).

15. Kahn, R.; Wilensky, R. A framework for distributed digital object services. Int. J. Digital Libr. April **2006**, *6*(2). [doi:10.1007/s00799–005–0128-x] (First published by the authors in May 1995.) Reproduced at http://www.doi.org/topics/2006_05_02_Kahn_Framework.pdf with permission of the publisher (accessed July 2009).

16. Rust, G.; Bide, M. The <indecs> Metadata Framework: Principles, model and data dictionary. 2000. http://www.doi.org/topics/indecs/indecs_framework_2000.pdf (accessed July 2009).

17. Paskin, N. Identifier interoperability: A report on two recent ISO activities. D-Lib Mag. April **2006**, *12*(4). http://www.dlib.org/dlib/april06/paskin/04paskin.html (accessed July 2009).

18. Dunsire, G. Distinguishing content from carrier: The RDA/ONIX framework for resource categorization. D-Lib Mag. January **2007**, *13*(1). http://www.dlib.org/dlib/january07/dunsire/01dunsire.html (accessed July 2009).

Digital Preservation

Jacob Nadal
ReCAP: The Research Collections and Preservation Consortium, Princeton, New Jersey, U.S.A.

INTRODUCTION

Digital preservation can be viewed as a set of strategies or methods used for preserving information in a certain format and also as a means for preserving information using digital systems. In the first usage, digital preservation is one aspect of preservation writ large, a companion to preservation practices for paper, film, and all the other media of art and expression that libraries collect. In the second usage, digital preservation is closely linked to digitization, the reformatting processes used to create digital surrogates for works that were issued in various nondigital formats. Most professional bodies are careful to make a distinction between digitization as a method of reformatting, and digital preservation, the ensuing process and relevant technologies for keeping the resulting digital content viable over time.

The Association of Library Collections and Technical Services defines digital preservation in process-oriented terms, as the "policies, strategies and actions that ensure access to digital content over time," focusing on digital collections as objects that require preservation effort and in turn, describing the work that must be done to maintain them.[1] Libraries have also recognized that digitization and digital libraries can serve as valuable preservation methods themselves. Just as printed books serve to preserve information, but also require libraries to provide preservation support and conservation intervention to keep them usable and available, digital objects can preserve information, provided they are supported by the right systems and practices, and use appropriate technologies to realize the library's preservation goals.

FRAMEWORKS AND METHODOLOGIES

Digital preservation has developed rapidly, the internet and digital tools themselves providing a platform for the exchange of ideas among practitioners and researchers in libraries and a variety of allied sectors. Even though particular efforts of government or economic boundaries on philanthropy have led to many digital preservation projects, platforms, and technologies that have a strong national or regional association, there are certain frameworks and methodologies that are shared across the globe. These frameworks serve an important role in digital preservation, guiding the development of particular technologies in the present while also preparing libraries to move from one specific system to another as technologies develop and supersede one another.

The Open Archival Information System Reference Model

The Open Archival Information System Reference Model (OAIS) has achieved near-universal acceptance as the canonical model of a digital preservation system.[2] The OAIS describes three zones of activity relevant to digital preservation. Although the core of the OAIS addresses management of the archive itself, the framing activities of submission and dissemination are important preservation concepts in the OAIS. In particular, the dissemination activities are coupled to a Designated Community, and the use-cases associated with the Designated Community have a reciprocal effect on the way that the OAIS framework is implemented.

In the OAIS model, preservation begins when Submission Information Packages (SIP) are taken into the archive in a process called Ingest. Ingest associates preservation metadata with the SIP to create an Archival Information Package (AIP). This set of data and metadata is often referred to as a Digital Object among digital preservation practitioners. The core of the OAIS, Management, has two streams of activity. One, roughly analogous to systems administration or core IT activities, is Administration. This set of activities provides archival storage of the AIP, through storage and database maintenance, backup and redundancy measures, and protection of the archive against disasters or threats. The other, Preservation Planning, includes the data management and reporting operations that are necessary to monitor the status of the archive and determine when preservation actions are required, as well as to take in materials from producers and prepare them for the archives as AIPs, and then distribute them to consumers, a process called Dissemination. This involves querying the archive for results sets describing the archive's contents, and then ordering a Dissemination Information Package (DIP), consisting of some derivative form of the AIP intended for end-users. The DIP could be identical to the AIP, or it could contain alternate versions of the AIP content, perhaps a lower-resolution copy for faster transmission over the network or a version in an alternate file format, when the original format is obsolete.

Encyclopedia of Library and Information Sciences, Fourth Edition DOI: 10.1081/E-ELIS4-120050527

Deposit Systems for Electronic Publications

Although the OAIS has been accepted as the common reference framework for the digital preservation community in its widest sense, embracing not just libraries, but archives, museums, research centers, and more, the Deposit Systems for Electronic Publications (DSEP) deserves some attention for libraries, specifically.[3] This model was developed by the Networked European Deposit Library (NEDLIB), one of the host archives for the Portico and JSTOR projects, and reflects an integration of library-specific practice into the OAIS model. Of particular note is the inclusion of numerous sources and recipients for a variety of bibliographic metadata, including publishers and external bibliographic utilities, as well as the relationships mapped between internal preservation functions.

Trustworthy Repositories

The OAIS model is central to ongoing efforts to develop audit and certification processes for trustworthy digital archives. These efforts were initiated in response to an RLG-OCLC report, "Trusted Digital Repositories: Attributes and Responsibilities," published in 2002.[4] The audit process couples an assessment of OAIS compatibility with a broader institutional assessment intended to ascertain whether a digital preservation effort has addressed all of the potential hazards in preserving materials, has sufficient technical capability to execute its plans, and has the financial resources and institutional resilience needed to remain in business and capable of responding to future developments. Two prominent efforts that have emerged from the trustworthy repositories: the Trusted Repositories Audit Checklist (TRAC), the related ISO/DIS 16363 standard, and the Trusted Digital Repositories Checklist (TDR).

Program Development

There is an ongoing effort to educate practitioners, so that digital preservation efforts can commence in a variety of institutional contexts. These programs use a variety of frameworks to help practitioners perform needs assessments in order to select appropriate technologies and process changes to advance their digital preservation goals. Where TRAC and related efforts tend to be used for large scale assessments of entire institutions, these program development models can be applied at a small scale, within a single department or subprogram. They share the OAIS reference model as a point of agreement, however, and can be seen as a system of needs assessment aimed toward fuller or improved OAIS compatibility, that might in turn be evaluated or audited through TRAC or TDR.

The longest-standing development program is the Digital Preservation Management (DPM) Workshop, started by Anne R. Kenney and Nancy Y. McGovern with support from the National Endowment for the Humanities and hosted at Cornell University (2003–2006), the ICPSR (2007–2012), and now at MIT Libraries since 2012.[5] The DPM model is often described as "Five stages and the Three-legged stool," for its framework of three categories of activity—policy and planning, technological infrastructure, and content and use—and five stages of program development within them:[6]

- Acknowledge: Understanding that digital preservation is a local concern
- Act: Initiating digital preservation projects
- Consolidate: Segueing from projects to programs
- Institutionalize: Incorporating the larger environment
- Externalize: Embracing inter-institutional collaboration and dependency

These concepts influence a set of activities hosted by the Library of Congress Office for Strategic Initiatives and funded by the National Digital Information Infrastructure and Preservation Program (NDIIPP). The National Digital Stewardship Alliance (NDSA) and the Digital Preservation Outreach and Education (DPOE) program both promote progressive frameworks, with the assumption that libraries were starting with little or no digital preservation capacity. The NDSA describes four levels of competency in each of five functional areas: (1) storage and geographic location; (2) file fixity and data integrity; (3) information security; (4) metadata; and (5) file formats. The DPOE identifies six core areas of digital preservation activity and trains practitioners to identify, select, store, protect, manage, and provide digital content to their designated communities.

METHODOLOGIES

Digital preservation efforts employ a variety of technical methods to ensure that the data stored in an archive can be rendered in the ways that are useful to the Designated Community. These methods respond to two broad classes of preservation problems: (1) obsolescence and (2) damage. Damage includes any number of events that cause data loss, through failures of media or computing systems; errors in transmission, synchronization, or duplication of data; deliberate sabotage; or a myriad of other possible accidents.

In instances of obsolescence, the bitstream itself may be undamaged, even though the digital object cannot be rendered on a particular system. This is frequently attributed to the changes in the prevailing technologies in use. Examples include the release of a new application software that lacks compatibility with files produced by older versions, file formats that cease to be supported or developed, or broader shifts within an industry or other group from one preferred technology to another.

Bit Preservation

The baseline for all digital preservation efforts is maintaining data integrity. Bit preservation, also referred to as refreshing, uses a variety of approaches to ensure that data are unaltered across time. This includes the maintenance of multiple copies of data so that they can be compared for discrepancies and the periodic copying of data from one physical storage medium to another, to avoid data loss from damaged or decaying media. Bit preservation is usually tested by mathematical derivatives, called checksums or hashes, which can be computed against a particular set of data to show if any bits have changed. A variety of algorithms can be used to compute fixity indicators, but all have in common the property of generating a different value if any bit in the data has altered. Fixity tools do not themselves provide a way to correct damaged data, a process called error-correction. Comparing fixity indicators over time allows digital preservation managers to determine when data were altered and which copies are intact and should be used as the canonical version of the data going forward.

Emulation

Emulation consists in creating a virtual computing system that offers the necessary and significant functions required to execute code from one platform on a different, generally newer and more powerful, platform. Universal Turing machine theory and Moore's law make emulation both possible and practical. All discreet computing systems are logically equivalent, that is, they all perform the same set of logical operations that were initially defined by Alan Turning in his paper *"On Computable Numbers, with an Application to the Entscheidungsproblem."*[7] This logical equivalency has a valuable practical outcome. Intel founder Gordon Moore observed that improvements in manufacturing were enabling manufacturers to improve the complexity or circuit density of their chips "at a rate of roughly a factor of two per year," effectively doubling the processing power.[8] Because computer systems have been rapidly increasing in computational power, more recent computers can not only perform every function of an earlier system, as a matter of logical equivalency, but they can also perform those functions at roughly the same speed of the original system.

Emulation has been subjected to some criticism for its apparent complexity, since modeling a physical computer in software is a nontrivial task, and can be more laborious than defining a crosswalk between two formats and writing code to replicate that translation, the strategy used in migration. This potential complexity has been offset in practice by the widespread value derived from emulators. Testing and prototyping of systems and networks in software is much less expensive than doing the same work in hardware for instance, and, because a single emulator can often be reused for many applications, the initial cost of development can be spread over many uses. Emulation has been widely adopted in some areas of digital

preservation, especially for multimedia and interactive systems, such as games and computer art. In these instances, the nature of the work itself requires complex code execution and may also have an important esthetic dimension that could be lost by migration to an alternate format or design.

Migration

Migration addresses the problem of obsolescence by converting from one format or encoding to another. This could mean a change from one file type to another (e.g., migrating an image from TIFF to JPEG2000) or from one method of encoding data to another (e.g., from ASCII text to UTF-8), or both. Migration can be seen as the digital preservation instance of a preservation practice called reformatting, where obsolete or damaged media or formats are transcribed onto or translated into contemporary formats. This approach has the benefit of allowing for easy integration of the resource's informational content into the libraries' current systems and processes. The core disadvantages of migration, as with all reformatting strategies, is that the new format may differ from the original format in ways that preclude certain uses of the information or require additional metadata creation and management to document provenance and significant differences. For many file types or encodings, however, migration is a widely used and easy-to-implement approach to keeping information available.

Forensics and Conservation

In some instances, digital preservation relies on the maintenance of original systems, especially original hardware, to render data. Digital forensics primarily deals with the recovery of data from damaged or obsolete systems, usually by creating a bit-perfect replica of stored data, so that the copy can be examined or altered without risking change to the original. Because the systems in question may be obsolete, digital forensics intersects with conservation through the maintenance of older computing hardware as a means to keep data available. In addition, conservation of computing hardware is done for reasons of material culture preservation, to make the tools and technology of different eras available in present-day curatorial programs or research efforts. Maintaining and repairing these computing systems, as well as the specific knowledge required to use them, mirrors the practices of other branches of conservation practiced in libraries, archives, and museums.

DIGITIZATION

In the late twentieth and early twenty-first century, libraries often centered digital preservation activities around digital libraries created by digitization of their physical resources: (1) books; (2) journals; (3) photographs; and

(4) recorded sound, video, and motion pictures. This focus on digitization as a type of preservation reformatting led to an ongoing emphasis on the creation of high quality digital objects, often referred to as preservation masters. A number of projects exist to promulgate standards for digitization, specifying resolution and bit depth requirements for various media types and desirable formats for storing digital information. In general, these standards emphasized digitization that captures more data than the human eye or ear can perceive, and storing data in file formats that are uncompressed and not encumbered by any proprietary or for cost licenses. These digitization projects tend to be driven by highly specific selection criteria and focus on creating a high-fidelity surrogate of the original items, serving a dual purpose of creating a high-quality preservation master while improving access to library collections, often through curated presentations of materials accompanied by secondary scholarship or other contextual information to create a specific collection in the context of a digital library.

In counterpoint to this approach, a large-scale digitization initiative (LSDI) converts a massive quantity of information into digital forms. Several LSDIs for library print collections were started in the first part of the twenty-first century. The Google Books Project and the Internet Archive's digitization efforts are the largest of these, and were the primary impetus for the creation of the HathiTrust, an organization that operates a preservation repository for the output of LSDI projects and works with its member libraries to develop digital library services and collection management projects built around this corpus of materials. Other LSDI projects are notable, as well, including Microsoft's Live Search and the Million Books Project and, arguably, publisher efforts to convert their catalogs to e-book formats.

BORN-DIGITAL WORKS

Despite the early emphasis on digitization, the largest groups of digital materials in libraries are "born-digital" works. These have no direct analog source, and are often created through entirely digital production processes. The best practice that has emerged for these materials is to accept them as they come to the repository and retain their original format, and then to normalize, migrate, or emulate data and systems to allow access as needed.

Electronic Publications

E-journal preservation is probably the most active area of born-digital preservation, especially when it is combined with e-publications as a whole, including serials, monographs, and published datasets. Libraries subscribe to a large amount of digital content, and have launched cooperative projects to ensure that this content remains available in the future. Although the process and technology

differs between these efforts, they share the common features of a present-day intake mechanism to build an archive, based on an agreement between the publisher and a third-party repository that, in turn, manages permissions based on the subscription profiles of libraries, and provides authorized libraries with post-cancellation access (PCA) to the archive in response to certain trigger events, usually the cessation of business by a publisher or the end of publisher support for a particular title.

Two of the most extensive and long-standing digital preservation efforts have their roots in the e-journal preservation challenge. The oldest of these is called LOCKSS, an acronym for "Lots of Copies Keeps Stuff Safe." This project was started at Stanford University by Victoria Reich and David Rosenthal and has developed into a series of related projects that rely on a peer-to-peer network of many devices to compare multiple instances of a given work and then repair any damage detected. LOCKSS was initially an e-journal preservation effort, but has developed a wider range of services under the auspices of the LOCKSS alliance, including controlled and private LOCKSS systems that allow for the management of a variety of digital content. Portico was also started as an e-journal preservation service, focusing on the content in JSTOR, but has quickly grown by expanding the scope of publishers involved and the types of content maintained in the service. Portico uses a different technical infrastructure than LOCKSS, relying on a smaller number of copies of the entire archive in geographically separated data centers. These mirrors of the archives are in turn monitored for integrity and completeness on a regular cycle.

Institutional Repositories

Institutional repositories have been developed as a way to preserve a variety of born-digital materials, including pre- and post-prints, working papers, student work, ports, datasets, and gray literature. These systems perform the administrative tasks of identifying and documenting works, keeping digital objects organized, and placing objects into reliable storage systems. DSpace, EPrints, BePress, and OPUS were all developed in the late 1990s or early 2000s in close alignment with the Open Access movement, as a way to provide unrestricted online access to peer-reviewed scholarly research. In terms of the OAIS model, these systems control the Ingest, archival management, and dissemination of information. To provide a complete digital preservation solution, they must be connected to reliable archival storage and supported by ongoing preservation management efforts.

Digital art and multimedia works have presented a particular challenge for born-digital preservation, because artworks may be closely tied to obsolescent computing platforms and multimedia works may combine elements with vastly different risks and requirements for preservation. Many preservation efforts in this area focus on metadata creation to document the as-built state of the work, with the assumption that this will facilitate preservation efforts in the future. Emulation has received substantial attention for this reason, as well, since sufficiently detailed documentation of the system alongside maintenance of its component parts can allow for its emulation on a later computing platform.

Web archiving projects collect websites available over the internet for later access. These efforts face difficulties similar to collecting multimedia work, since the web provides a disparate set of born-digital materials, but the standardizing pressure of network protocols, the HMTL specifications, and related technologies mitigates the risks somewhat. Two major difficulties for web archiving are deciding how far to follow hyperlinks in the interest of creating a useful archive, and problems in collecting dynamically generated web pages, since content that is created on the fly from a database or content management system has no single, fixed form that can be treated as a definitive copy of record.

Data management includes elements that align with born-digital preservation, as well. These include the promulgation of standards and the best practices for creating and managing data, which entails making choices about the format and encoding of data and their related rendering software, as well as the creation of metadata that will be needed for the future interpretation and reuse of data. Data management plans are often required by research-funding agencies, and this has led to the creation of tools to assist in data management planning and helped to align data management with related efforts such as institutional repository development.

DIGITAL CURATION AND DIGITAL STEWARDSHIP

The terms "digital curation" and "digital stewardship" have become strongly associated with digital preservation. These ideas place digital preservation within a larger context of selection and appraisal of materials and of providing access to them. These practices are implicit in many digital preservation models, and explicit in others. The OAIS reference model, for example, uses the concept of a Designated Community that receives a DIP as a way of framing access to the archive, and the first two stages of the DPOE model are "identify" and "select," which focus on determining what content is appropriate for the archive.

The digital curation movement builds on this, however, to encompass many ways of understanding the way technology is used and interpreted in a variety of contexts and to create and manage data in such a way that they can be reused in future research. The Digital Curation Centre, for example, describes eleven steps in their digital curation life cycle,[9] while the University of North Carolina, Chapel Hill, School of Information and Library Science's DigCCurr project proposed 39 elements of "knowledge and competency" in their matrix of digital curation.[10]

Digital preservation and the core practices associated with it—safe storage, migration, and emulation of data and systems, and forensic and conservation practices—exist as key subsidiary elements of these digital curation models. Digital curation, in turn, is an overarching set of activities that comprise the whole life cycle of materials in libraries and archives, predicated on their continued availability due to sound preservation efforts.

CONCLUSION

Digital Preservation, to borrow the definition of the American Library Association, "combines policies, strategies and actions to ensure access to reformatted and born digital content regardless of the challenges of media failure and technological change." At present, this area of librarianship is enacted through numerous tools addressed to specific technical issues and a variety of widely accepted frameworks for evaluating preservation efforts and outcomes. In counterpoint to this maturity though, digital preservation efforts are always engaged in adaptation to developments in technology.

Computers and computing have been active fields for decades and if one counts from Turing's papers, the centenary of digital computing is just a few decades away. In that time, many technologies have proven stable and reliable, but others have been short-lived and problematic from a preservation viewpoint. As of this writing, the text and image data that make up the bulk of library and archive collections are supported by formats and encoding that have been stable for multiple decades, as has digital audio preservation. Video, datasets, and 3-D models all present preservation challenges, however, as do the processes for preserving systems and interactive works, like social media, video games, and websites.

Libraries have adopted, developed, and now depend upon a wide range of technologies, making digital preservation an intrinsic part of library science. Although digital preservation emerged from the problems associated with novel technologies prone to obsolescence, there is substantial evidence of libraries' success and capability in resolving digital preservation problems, shown by the wide acceptance of certain technologies and frameworks.

ACKNOWLEDGMENTS

I am grateful to the Indiana University Library and their Digital Library Program, where I had my first practical opportunities to work on these issues, and to UCLA and the California Digital Library. I also wish to thank the Library of Congress' Office of Strategic Initiatives for the opportunities to work on the Digital Preservation

Outreach and Education Program and the National Digital Stewardship Residency, and the Pratt Institute School of Information and Library Science for the opportunity to refine my understanding of preservation by teaching it to smart students. Finally, Anne Kenney, Nancy McGovern, and the Cornell Digital Preservation Management Workshop deserve special recognition for giving me and so many others our first deep dive into the then-new ideas of digital preservation management that underpin much of the work we do today.

REFERENCES

1. ALCTS Preservation and Reformatting Section. Working Group on Defining Digital Preservation. Definitions of Digital Preservation; American Library Association: Chicago, IL, 2007. http://www.ala.org/alcts/resources/preserv/defdigpres0408 (accessed July 2015).
2. Consultative Committee for Space Data Systems. Reference Model for an Open Archival Information System (OAIS). CCSDS Secretariat: Washington, DC, 2012. http://public.ccsds.org/publications/archive/650x0m2.pdf (accessed July 2015).
3. Van der Werf, T. *The Deposit System for Electronic Publications: A Process Model*; Koninklijke Bibliotheek: The Hague, the Netherlands, 2000. https://www.kb.nl/sites/default/files/docs/DSEPprocessmodel.pdf (accessed July 2015).
4. Research Libraries Group. *Trusted Digital Repositories: An RLG-OCLC Report*; RLG: Mountain View, CA, 2002. http://www.oclc.org/content/dam/research/activities/trustedrep/repositories.pdf?urlm=161690 (accessed July 2015).
5. Cornell University Library; ICPSR; MIT Libraries. Digital Preservation Management: Implementing Short-Term Strategies for Long-Term Solutions. Online Tutorial Developed for the Digital Preservation Management Workshop, MIT Libraries: Cambridge, MA. http://www.dpworkshop.org/ (accessed July 2015).
6. Kenney, A.R.; McGovern, N.Y. The five organizational stages of digital preservation. In *Digital Libraries: A Vision for the Twenty-first Century, a Festschrift to Honor Wendy Lougee*, Available from the University of Michigan Scholarly Monograph Series, 2003.
7. Turing, A. On computable numbers, with an application to the Entscheidungsproblem. Proc. Lond. Math. Soc. **1937**, *2* (42), 230–265; On Computable Numbers, with an application to the Entscheidungsproblem: A correction. Proc. Lond. Math. Soc. **1937**, *2* (43), 544–546.
8. Moore, G.E. Cramming more components onto integrated circuits. Electronics **1965**, *38* (8), 114–117.
9. Digital Curation Centre. What is digital curation. 2015. http://www.dcc.ac.uk/digital-curation/what-digital-curation (accessed July 2015).
10. Lee, C. Mandates, Values and Principles: Dimension 1 of Matrix of Digital Curation Knowledge and Competencies (Version 17). School of Information and Library Science, University of North Carolina: Chapel Hill, NC. 2009. http://www.ils.unc.edu/digccurr/digccurr-principles.html (accessed July 2015).

BIBLIOGRAPHY

1. Arthur, K.; Byrne, S.; et al. *Recognizing Digitization as a Preservation Reformatting Measure.* Assoc. of Research Libraries: Washington, DC, 2004. http://old.arl.org/bm~doc/digi_preserv.pdf (accessed July 2015).
2. California Digital Library. Digital File Format Recommendations. 2011. http://www.cdlib.org/gateways/docs/cdl_dffr.pdf (accessed July 2015).
3. Ceruzzi, P. *A History of Modern Computing*; MIT Press: London, U.K., 2003.
4. Gleick, J. *The Information: A History, a Theory, a Flood*; Pantheon Books: New York, 2011.
5. Library of Congress. *Sustainability of Digital Formats.* Library of Congress, Washington, DC, 2013. http://www.digitalpreservation.gov/formats/ (accessed July 2015).
6. Rieger, O. *Preservation in the Age of Large-Scale Digitization: A White Paper*; Washington, DC: CLIR, 2008. http://www.clir.org/pubs/reports/pub141 (accessed July 2015).
7. Rosenthal, D. Format Obsolescence: Assessing the threat and the defenses. Libr. Hi Tech. **2010**, *28* (2), 195–210.
8. Ross, S.; Gow, A. *Digital Archaeology: Rescuing Neglected and Damaged Data Resources*; Humanities Advanced Technology and Information Institute: Glasgow, Scotland, 1999. http://www.ukoln.ac.uk/services/elib/papers/supporting/pdf/p2.pdf (accessed July 2015).
9. Rothenberg, J. *Avoiding Technological Quicksand: Finding a Viable Technical Foundation for Digital Preservation*; CLIR: Washington, DC, 1999. http://www.clir.org/pubs/reports/rothenberg/ (accessed July 2015).
10. Schumacher, J.; Thomas, L.; VandeCreek, D. *From Theory to Action: Good Enough Digital Preservation for Under-Resourced Cultural Heritage Institutions* Northern Illinois University: DeKalb, IL, 2014. http://commons.lib.niu.edu/handle/10843/13610 (accessed July 2015).
11. Task Force on Archiving of Digital Information. *Preserving digital information report of the Task Force on Archiving of Digital Information*; Commission on Preservation and Access: Washington, DC, 1996. http://www.oclc.org/research/activities/digpresstudy.html (accessed July 2015).

Digital–Disaster

Diplomatics

Luciana Duranti
School of Library, Archival and Information Studies, University of British Columbia,
Vancouver, British Columbia, Canada

Abstract

This entry presents the science of diplomatics, briefly describing its history, its theoretical content, and its methodology. Comparing classic diplomatics with modern diplomatics, it discusses the concepts of authenticity, originality, and record. Then, it outlines the building blocks of the diplomatic body of knowledge, that is, the context, the act, the persons, the procedure, the documentary form, and the archival bond and comments on the process of diplomatic criticism and on the usefulness of diplomatics as a discipline.

INTRODUCTION

Diplomatics is a science that was developed in France in the seventeenth century for the purpose of ascertaining the provenance and authenticity of records that attested to patrimonial rights and later grew into a legal, historical, and philological discipline, as it came to be used by lawyers to resolve disputes, by historians to interpret records, and by editors to publish medieval deeds and charters. Its name comes from the Latin term *diploma*—derived from the Greek words διπλοω, meaning I fold, and διπλωμα, meaning doubled or folded—which was used in ancient Rome to refer to documents written on two tablets attached with a hinge and later to any recorded deed, and it means "about records." However, over the centuries, its focus has expanded from its original concern with medieval deeds to an all-encompassing study of any document produced in the usual and ordinary course of activity as a means for it and a residue of it.

This entry briefly outlines the history of diplomatics; presents its purpose, object, and fundamental tenets, including the concepts of record, authenticity, and originality; describes the concepts that constitute the building blocks of diplomatic analysis, including those of person, procedure, and form; and discusses diplomatic methodology and its usefulness. In the process, classic and modern diplomatics will be constantly compared to show their relationship and interplay.

THE HISTORY OF DIPLOMATICS

The history of diplomatics is directly linked to the so-called "diplomatic wars" (*bella diplomatica*), judicial controversies over political or religious claims based on records of disputed origin, which, in the seventeenth century, especially in Germany and France, assumed a doctrinal character and prepared the ground for a scientific debate between the Benedictines of the Congregation of Saint-Maur in France and the Jesuits organized by Jean Bolland in a scientific society in Antwerp (Bollandists). In 1675, the second volume of the *Acta Sanctorum*, an analysis of the lives of saints published in several tomes by the Bollandists, was released, with an introduction by Daniel Van Papenbroeck, which outlined the general principles and methods for assessing the authenticity of medieval records. In the text, the author, applying his analysis to the records of Frankish kings, declared a diploma issued by Dagobert I to be a forgery, thereby discrediting all Merovingian diplomas, on which most patrimonial rights of the French Benedictines rested.

The Benedictines answered Van Papenbroeck 6 yr later, in 1681, with a treatise in six parts written by Dom Jean Mabillon and called *De Re Diplomatica Libri VI* [1], p. 37]. The treatise analyzed about 200 documents by comparing the material support, seals, ink, script, punctuation, abbreviations, formulas, discourse, types of subscriptions, etc. and, on the basis of this study, established a method of criticism of records whose validity was recognized throughout Europe. Several works followed Mabillon's and contributed to a further development of the discipline. Among them, the most notable are the *Nouveau traite de diplomatique* by Rene Prosper Tassin and Charles Toustain, published in Paris between 1750 and 1765, which, by comparing records of different geographical origin, on one hand, demonstrated the validity of diplomatics across contexts and, on the other hand, gave origin to the idea of a special diplomatics for records of the same provenance, and *Beitrage zur Diplomatik I-VIII*, by Theodor von Sickel, in *Sitzungsberichte der Kaiserlichen Akademie der Wissenschaften*, published in Vienna between 1861 and 1882, which linked the assessment of the authenticity of records to the analysis of their procedure of creation. Although mostly regarded as an

Encyclopedia of Library and Information Sciences, Fourth Edition DOI: 10.1081/E-ELIS4-120053296

auxiliary science of history since the middle of the nineteenth century, diplomatics was included in the body of knowledge required for archivists since the first half of that century in all European archival programs of education and later on in all programs influenced by the European tradition in other continents. As a consequence, diplomatics concepts and methodology became in most parts of the world an integral part of archival science and of the intellectual armor of the archival profession [[2], pp. 3–5].

THE OBJECT OF DIPLOMATICS

When discussing diplomatics, it is useful to distinguish "classic diplomatics" from "modern diplomatics," the reason being that these two branches of the discipline do not represent a natural evolution of the latter from the former, but exist in parallel and focus on different objects of study. Classic diplomatics uses the concepts and methodologies developed by diplomatists living between the seventeenth and the twentieth centuries and studies medieval charters, instruments, and deeds; modern diplomatics has adapted, elaborated, and developed the core concepts and methodology of classic diplomatics in order to study modern and contemporary records of all types. Among the key distinctions between the two branches of the discipline are the concept of record and that of diplomatics. According to classic diplomatics, a record is a document (i.e., information affixed to a medium) that constitutes "the written evidence of a fact having a juridical nature, compiled in compliance with determined forms, which are meant to provide it with full faith and credit" [[3], p. 18]. Therefore, classic diplomatics only studies documents that are meant to have legal consequences and therefore require specific documentary forms and is defined as the knowledge of the formal rules that apply to legal records [[4], p. 1; [5], p. 32; [6], p. 4]. According to modern diplomatics, a record is a document created (i.e., made or received and set aside for action or reference) in the course of activity as an instrument and by-product of it [[7], p. 604; [8], p. 667]. Therefore, modern diplomatics is concerned with all documents that are created in the course of affairs of any kind and is defined as "the discipline which studies the genesis, forms, and transmission" of records and "their relationship with the facts represented in them and with their creator in order to identify, evaluate, and communicate their true nature" [[1], p. 45; [9], p. 28].

THE APPROACH AND PURPOSE OF DIPLOMATICS

Although the primary focus of both classic and modern diplomatics is to assess the trustworthiness of records, the former establishes it retrospectively, looking at

records issued several centuries ago, while the latter is concerned not only with establishing the trustworthiness of existing records but also with ensuring the trustworthiness of records that have yet to be created, thereby taking a prospective approach as well as a retrospective one. Additionally, classic diplomatics identifies trustworthiness with authenticity, while modern diplomatics distinguishes several aspects of trustworthiness. To classic diplomatists, trustworthy records are authentic records, that is, documents "written according to the practice of the time and place indicated in the text, and signed with the name(s) of the person(s) competent to create them" [[1], p. 46]. This is far too simplistic a concept for the variety of records that modern diplomatics aims to evaluate and the time span of their creation (from the sixteenth to the twenty-first century), especially in consideration of the fact that its concern is the entire life cycle of records, from creation to permanent preservation. Thus, modern diplomatics defines and assesses four aspects of trustworthiness: reliability, authenticity, accuracy, and authentication.

Reliability

Reliability is the trustworthiness of a record content and is defined as the trustworthiness of a record as a statement of fact. It is assessed on the basis of the *completeness* of the record, that is, the presence of all the formal elements required by the administrative–legal system for that specific record to be capable of achieving the purposes for which it was generated and of the *controls exercised on the process of creation* of the record, among which are included those exercised on the author of the record, who must be the person competent, that is, having the authority and the capacity, to issue it. The reliability of a record is the exclusive responsibility of its creator, that is, of the person or organization that made or received it and maintained it with its other records.

Authenticity

Authenticity is the trustworthiness of a record as a record and is defined as the fact that a record has not been tampered with or corrupted, either accidentally or maliciously. An authentic record is one that preserves the same *identity* it had when first generated and can be presumed or proven to have maintained its *integrity* over time. The identity of a record is constituted of those characteristics that, together, distinguish it from any other record (e.g., the names of its author and its addressee, the date of its compilation, its title, its classification code, or its register number) and is assessed on the basis of the formal elements on the face of the record and/or its attributes, as expressed, for example, in a register entry or as metadata. The integrity of a record is linked to its ability to convey the message it was intended to communicate when generated. Thus, it does not matter if the ink is fading, the medium (i.e., the material support) is falling apart, or the bit stream is not the same as in the first manifestation of the record, as long as the content is readable and is the same as it was originally intended, the medium does not have missing parts, or the manifestation we see on the computer screen is the same as it was the first time the record was saved. The integrity of a record is inferred not only from its appearance, which might be deceiving in the case of good forgeries, but also from the circumstances of its maintenance and preservation: An unbroken chain of responsible and legitimate custody is considered an insurance of integrity till proof to the contrary. The authenticity of a record is a movable responsibility, as it shifts from the creator, who needs to guarantee it for as long as the record is in its custody, to the preserver, who guarantees it for as long as the record exists.

Accuracy

Accuracy is the trustworthiness of the data (i.e., the smallest meaningful indivisible piece of information) within a record and is defined as their truthfulness, exactness, precision, or completeness and usually presumed for reliable records as well as for authentic records. However, in the digital environment, it is necessary to consider and assess accuracy as a separate quality of a record because of the easiness with which data can be corrupted during transmission across space (between persons and/or systems) and time (when digital systems are upgraded or records are migrated to a new system). Consequently, accuracy also is a shifting responsibility that moves over time from the creator to the preserver.

Authentication

Traditionally, the most trustworthy records are those that are declared to be so by a person who is given such responsibility in a formal way. Authentication is defined as a declaration of authenticity made by a competent officer and consists of a statement or an element, such as a seal, a stamp, or a symbol, added to the record after its completion. It is not to be identified with authenticity—which is a quality of the record that accompanies it for as long as it exists—in that it only guarantees that a record is authentic at one specific moment in time, when the declaration is made or the element is affixed.

STATUS OF TRANSMISSION

Although it is a general assumption that an original record is a trustworthy record, simply because it presents all the possible elements that allow for an assessment of trustworthiness, it is obvious to all diplomatists, classic and modern, that originality has no relationship with

trustworthiness. Rather, it is one of three possible statuses of transmission of a record, that is, it relates to the degree of perfection of a record. An *original record* is the first record generated in a complete form that is capable of reaching the consequences wanted by its author. Thus, an original has the qualities of *primitiveness*, *completeness*, and *effectiveness*. With records that are meant for transmission across space, the original is the document received by the addressee, while with records that are only intended to be transmitted through time (i.e., internal records), the original is the document kept by the author. In the digital environment, the original is the first manifestation of either the received record or the saved record, depending on whether we have an external or an internal record. We have multiple originals when the same record is issued at the same time to multiple recipients, such as a contract (e.g., indenture), a treaty, an invitation, or a directive.

The other two possible statuses of transmission are the *draft* and the *copy*. A draft is a document prepared for purposes of correction and is meant to be provisional, temporary. A draft may have various levels of completion, but it is never an effective or a legal document, and, if kept, it is intended to stay with the author; thus it may be transmitted through time but not across space. If a draft is electronically circulated, the document received by each recipient is an original as to "status of transmission"—having been communicated to an addressee in the intended status of completion and having been the first capable of reaching its purpose of being examined by the person receiving it—and it is a draft only as to content, therefore as type of document (e.g., an ISO draft standard circulated for comments to the ISO members). A copy is a reproduction of another document, which may be an original, a draft, or another copy. Classic diplomatists study the sequence of copies over time to assess the probability of trustworthiness of a text that has been transmitted through the centuries by copying it. The most trustworthy copy is the copy in the form of the original, which is identical to the original in all respects, including holographic signatures, if required, but is issued after the original. Equally trustworthy is the authentic copy, which is declared to conform to the original by an official entrusted with such responsibility. Imitative copies (e.g., photocopies) reproduce both the form and the content of the record; simple copies only transcribe the record content; and inserts (also called *vidimus* or *inspeximus*) are original records containing a copy of another record or a part of it. The study of copies, their process of creation, and their trustworthiness is becoming increasingly relevant in the digital environment as we will no longer have originals on which to assess the authority of records.[10]

THE BUILDING BLOCKS OF DIPLOMATICS

Diplomatics saw the documentary world as a system and built a system to understand and explain it. Early diplomatists rationalized, formalized, and universalized document creation by identifying within it the relevant elements, extending their relevance in time and space, eliminating their particularities, and relating the elements to each other and to their ultimate purpose. These elements are building blocks that have an inherent order: in fact, they can be analyzed in sequence from the general to the specific, following a natural method of inquiry [[1]], p. 107].

The building blocks used by classic diplomatists were the *juridical system*, which is the context of records creation; the *act*, which is the reason for records creation; the *persons*, which are the agents; the *procedures*, which guide the actions and determine their documentary residue; the *documentary form*, which reflects the act and allows it to reach its purpose; and the *archival bond*, which reveals the relationship of a record with all the other records in the same aggregation.

THE CONTEXT OF RECORDS CREATION

As a consequence of its definition of record, classic diplomatics identified the *juridical system* as the only relevant context of records creation and defined it as a social group organized according to shared principles and values that allow it to establish and recognize a body of rules and to give institutions the power to enforce them. Thus, a juridical system is constituted of a community, its institutions, and its legal system. The legal system comprises positive law and all the other conceptions of binding law (e.g., natural law, ethics, custom) that are held by a community.

Modern diplomatics, having extended the concept of record, has redefined the context of records creation as the framework of action in which the record participates and has identified five relevant contexts, proceeding from the general to the specific. They are 1) the juridical–administrative context, that is, the legal and organizational system in which the record-creating body belongs, as indicated by laws, regulations, etc.; 2) the provenancial context, that is, the record-creating body, its mandate, structure, and functions, as indicated in organizational charts, annual reports, the classification scheme, etc.; 3) the procedural context, that is, the business procedure in the course of which the record is created, which, in the modern environment, is often integrated with documentary procedures, as indicated by workflow rules, codes of administrative procedure, classification schemes, etc.; 4) the documentary context, that is, the archival fonds to which the record belongs and its internal structure, as indicated by classification schemes, record inventories, indexes, registers, etc.; and 5) the technological context, that is, the characteristics of the technical components of the record system in which the record is created [[11], p. 18].

ACTS

An act is defined as an exercise of will that aims to produce determined effects. Acts are distinguished in mere acts and transaction. Whereas a mere act is an act whose purpose is the accomplishment of the act itself, a transaction is an act that aims to create, modify, maintain, or extinguish relationships between two or more physical or corporate persons. Some acts, especially transactions, occur in writing, thereby resulting in records. Classic diplomatics categorizes those records according to their relationship with the acts that caused their creation. It calls *notitia* a record that was meant to provide evidence of an act that came into existence and was complete before being manifested in writing, while it calls *charta* a record that was meant to put the act into being and was therefore the essence and substance of the act. In modern English, we call the former *probative* records and the latter *dispositive* records. Examples of probative records are certificates, registrations, transcripts, and receipts. Examples of dispositive records are contracts, grants, applications, and money orders. These types of records have all in common the fact that their existence and written form are required by the juridical–administrative system within which they are created, and therefore they are all legal records. They do encompass all the types of documents that classic diplomatics defines as records.

However, modern diplomatics has a much broader focus, and its object of inquiry—what it calls records—is constituted not only of documents whose written form is required, but also of documents whose existence is not required by the juridical–administrative system and the written form of which is discretionary. These nonlegal records can be distinguished in two categories: *supporting* records, whose function is to support the activity in which they take part, and *narrative* records, whose function is one of free-form communication of information. While both categories of records participate in some kind of act, neither is able to provide evidence of such act by itself or to carry it out. Examples of supporting documents are teaching notes and maps, and examples of narrative documents are informal correspondence, discretionary reports, and accounts of events. In the digital environment, two additional categories of records have been identified: *instructive* records and *enabling* records. The former indicate the form in which external data are to be presented (e.g., regulations, manuals of procedure, instructions for filling out forms), and the latter enable performance of artworks (e.g., software patches), execution of business transactions (e.g., interacting business applications), conduct of experiments (e.g., workflows generated and used to carry out the experiment of which it is instrument, by-product, and residue), or analysis of observational data (e.g., interpreting software). The salient characteristic of these two categories of digital records is that the record as it is stored differs from the record as it is manifested on the computer screen [[10], pp. 49–52].

PERSONS

In diplomatics, as well as in law, persons are the subjects of rights and duties, that is, they are entities recognized by the juridical system as capable of acting. This means not only that a person in a given juridical system may not be considered a person in another one but also that the same entity in the same juridical system may be a person with respect to a type of act and not a person with respect to another (e.g., in the past, women have been persons in regard to being paid for a job, but nonpersons in regard to owning real estate). Persons can be *physical*, that is, individual human beings, or *juridical*, that is, collections of human beings (e.g., an organization, a committee) or successions of human beings (e.g., a position, a title).

Classic diplomatics posits that, for a record to come into existence, three persons are necessary: the author, the writer, and the addressee. The *author* is the person having the competence (i.e., the authority and the capacity) of issuing a record, which is made by it, in its name, or by its order (e.g., the testator in a last will, the university in a letter of appointment of a professor, the king in a proclamation). The *writer* is the person competent for the articulation of the discourse in the record. It might be the same as the author or may not, as is the case when the author is an abstract entity, such as a corporation. The *addressee* is the person for whom the record is intended in its documentary form. It may coincide with the recipient of the record and may not, as is the case when a second original of a letter of appointment whose addressee is the appointed person is sent to the financial office responsible for paying the salary, which is therefore the recipient.

Modern diplomatics, which tends to focus on aggregations of records, rather than on individual items, identifies a fourth person necessary to the existence of a record, the *creator*, that is, the person in whose fonds or archives a record exists as an item or as part of a file and/or a series. In the digital environment, it is important to identify a fifth person, the *originator*, that is, the person responsible for the electronic account or space in which the record is generated or from which the record is sent [[12], pp. 51–52]. Persons are the primary diplomatic criterion for determining the public or private nature of a record. Thus, a record is *public* if issued by a public person, that is, a physical or juridical person who, by performing functions considered to be public by the juridical system in which the person acts, is invested with the exercise of some form of sovereignty. A record is *private* when its author is a person "deprived" of public function. In situations in which the wills of a public person and a private person meet in the same record (e.g., a contract between a government and a contractor, or an income tax return), the record acquires the nature of the person who dictates the form and the procedure of creation of the record.

PROCEDURE

A procedure is the formal sequence of steps or phases whereby a transaction is carried out. It is different from a process, which is the series of motions by which a person prepares to carry out the acts involved in a procedure. In relation to each record, classic diplomatics identifies two distinct types of procedures: the procedure governing the act and the procedure governing its documentation. The first type is further distinguished in two categories: the procedures that are the initiative of the persons who carry them out and the procedures that result from an external initiative. The procedures included in the former category consist only of the decisional moment, the *iussio*, while those included in the latter begin with the *petition* to the authority or request to accomplish some action and proceed with the *intercession*, or recommendation of persons close to the authority; the *intervention*, or permission of the persons who are affected by the consequences of the requested action; and the *iussio*, or command to create the record enacting the act or providing evidence of it. After the procedure controlling the action is concluded, the procedure controlling the production of the related documentation begins. Its phases are the *compilation of the draft*; the *preparation of the fair copy*; the unabridged or abridged *registration*; the *validation* through signatures or affixing of stamps, seals, etc.; the *computation of the taxes* for the issuing of the record; and the *delivery* of the record.

Modern diplomatics, having moved the focus of study from medieval to modern and contemporary records, has observed an increasing integration of the procedures for acting and the procedures for creating the record, as over time the acts have begun to be carried out by writing records, and indeed several records for each procedure, not just one, as it used to be. Thus, modern diplomatists have identified for each procedure six typical integrated phases. They are the *initiative*, constituted by the acts that initiate a procedure and producing records such as applications and claims; the *inquiry*, consisting of the collection of the information necessary to evaluate the situation and producing records such as surveys and estimates; the *consultation*, consisting of the collection of opinion and advice based on the information accumulated and producing records such as minutes and discussion papers; the *deliberation*, or final decision-making, resulting in records such as appointments or contracts; the *deliberation control*, exercised by a person different from the author of the record embodying the transaction on the substance and form of the deliberation and the form of the record resulting from it; and the *execution*, constituted by all the actions that give formal character to the transaction and resulting in the final record of the transaction, plus letters of transmissions, registrations, etc. [[1], pp. 115–119; [9], pp. 47–63]. In the digital environment, the same fundamental structure has to date proven to be valid and easy to embed in a workflow.

DOCUMENTARY FORM

Form is the whole of the rules of representation by which an act is documented or a message is conveyed in writing. It comprises all those characteristics of a record that can be separated from the determination of the particular subjects, persons, or places the record is about. The fundamental idea of the early diplomatists was that all records are similar enough that it is possible to conceive of one typical ideal documentary form, a template, which encompasses all the possible characteristics of a record, and which can be used to analyze existing records for the purpose of determining their nature, provenance, and trustworthiness. Thus, they built this ideal documentary form as follows. First they distinguished the formal characteristics that determine the appearance of the record and make it effective from those that represent the articulation of the discourse and make the record complete. They called the former extrinsic elements and the latter intrinsic elements. Classic diplomatics has continued over the past three centuries in this tradition, and modern diplomatics has only introduced a few new elements; therefore, the formal elements of the record are presented here in their logical sequence, with some reflection on their variations over time as appropriate.

Extrinsic Elements of Form

The extrinsic elements of form are the medium, the script, the language, the special signs, the seals, and the annotations. The *medium* is the physical carrier of the record, of which diplomatists study the material, the way it is prepared, the watermark, the shape and size, the edging, rulings, etc. With modern records and the increasing standardization of supporting media, this element has lost importance as it is no longer itself imbued with meaning and a key factor in the assessment of the authority and authenticity of the record. Furthermore, in the digital environment, the medium is no longer to be considered part of the record, although it is still necessary to its existence, as a record that is not affixed to a medium does not exist.

The *script* is not analyzed paleographically, but in terms of layout, paragraphing, punctuation, abbreviations, or initialisms. The *language* is studied in terms of the style, formulas, and tenor of the discourse. *Special signs* are symbols identifying the persons involved with the record, like logos, heraldic images, mottos, stamps, or drawings, and are key to the identification of the record provenance. *Seals* are examined as to their material, size, shape, typology, legend, and the method of affixing or appending them, and they are also indicators of the origin of the record and of its authority.

Annotations are additions made to the record after its completion. They can be distinguished in three types: the annotations that are added to the record at the conclusion of the procedure generating the record itself, those added to the record in the course of the procedure in which it participates after its creation, and those added to the record in the course of recordkeeping activities. The annotations of the first type, added during the execution phase of the integrated business and documentary procedure, include the mention of the registration of the record in a register or book, with identification of the latter and of the relevant page and date, and the authentication of the record, of signatures on the record, of the identity of persons participating in the issuing of the record, or of the act referred to in the record, such as an oath of office. The annotations of the second type, added in the course of handling the matter in which the record participates, include mention of the decision made or further actions to be carried out, dates of hearings or readings, and locutions such as "urgent" or "bring forward." The annotations of the third type, added in the course of managing the record, include a registry number, a classification code, and the endorsement of docket-style folded records. In the digital environment, the latter also include the record profile, that is, the metadata schema that is attached to the record for the purposes of declaring and maintaining its identity and protecting its integrity.

Intrinsic Elements of Form

The study of a large number of records of different times and provenance has shown that the intrinsic elements of form, those that are meant to convey the action or message and its context, do not appear in a simple sequence, even if an ordered one, but tend to gather in groups, to be in some relation of subordination to each other, thereby forming sections, each of which comprises several of them [[6], p. 527]. Thus, it is fair to say that all records present an ideal structure and an ideal substructure, which is constituted of three sections, each of which has a clear purpose. The first section is called *protocol* and contains the administrative context of the action, that is, the place, date, and subject of the record, and the persons who have participated in its creation; the second section is called *text* and contains the action or message, including its motivation, circumstances, or conditions; and the third section is called *eschatocol* and contains the validation of the record, including the mention of the means used to validate it, the signature of the author, and those of witnesses and countersigners.

The elements that follow will be identified by the English version of their name, except for the few that only exist in medieval records and have retained their Latin name. Classic diplomatists, however, tend to use exclusively the Latin name of the formal elements of records. Thus, for the elements that existed in medieval records, the English name will be accompanied in brackets by its Latin version, as given by the *Encyclopaedia Britannica*[13].

Digital–Disaster

The intrinsic elements that usually appear in the protocol of a record are the *entitling*, or letterhead, comprising the name, title, capacity, and address of the physical or juridical person issuing the record or of which the author of the document is an agent; the *title* of the record; the *topical date*, that is, the place where the record was issued; the *chronological date* (*actum*, for the date of the act, and *datum*, for the date of the record); the *invocation*, that is, the mention of the entity in whose name the act is made (e.g., God, the Republic, the People, the Law); the *superscription* (*intitulatio*), that is, the name of the author of the record and/or the act; the *inscription* (*inscriptio*), that is, the name of the addressee of the record and/or the act; the *salutation* (*salutatio*), which is usually a formula of greeting; the *subject*, that is, a statement signifying what the record is about; the *formula perpetuitatis*, which is a sentence declaring that the rights given by the record are valid forever (*in perpetuum*, *ad perpetuam rei memoriam*, *pp.*); and the *apprecatio*, that is, a prayer for the realization of the content of the record (*feliciter*, *amen*).

The intrinsic elements that usually appear in the text are the *preamble* (*arenga*), which expresses the ideal motivation of the act or the principles inspiring the message; the *notification* (*promulgatio*), a formula stating that the record is communicated to all those concerned, who therefore must be aware of it; the *exposition* (*narratio*), which explains the concrete circumstances and motivation for the creation of the record; the *disposition* (*dispositio*), that is, the act or message that the record is intended to carry out or convey; and various *clauses* expressing the obligation of those concerned to respect the will of the author (*of injunction*), the prohibition to violate the act or oppose it (*of prohibition*), the obligation to respect the act notwithstanding other orders or decisions contrary to it (*of derogation*), situations or conditions that constitute exceptions (*of exception*), the obligation to respect the act for one's heirs or successors (*of obligation*), the consent to give up a right or a claim (*of renunciation*), a threat of punishment should the act be violated (*of warning* or *sanctio*), or the promise of a prize (*promissory*). Sometimes the *apprecatio* concludes the text, or begins the eschatocol.

The intrinsic elements that usually appear in the eschatocol are the *corroboration* (*corroboratio*), a clause that states the means used to validate the record (e.g., "signed and sealed," or "I have hereunto set my Hand and Seal of Office"), normally followed by the topical and chronological date; the *complimentary clause*, which is a brief formula expressing respect (e.g., "Yours truly"); the *attestation* (*subscriptio*), that is, the subscription of those who took part in the issuing of the record (author, writer, countersigner) or of witnesses to the enactment or to the subscription; the *qualification of signature*, that is, the mention of the title and capacity of each signer; and the *secretarial notes*, such as initials of the secretary, indication of enclosures, or indication of additional recipients of the record.

ARCHIVAL BOND

The concept of archival bond is unknown to classic diplomatics because of its focus on medieval records, the main characteristic of which was the fact that each incorporated the entire act as carried out through the acting procedure and the subsequent documentary procedure. The focus of modern diplomatics on modern records meant that one of its main concerns had to be the interrelationship that each modern record has with the previous and subsequent records that participate in the same act and/or integrated business and documentary procedure. This interrelationship, following archival theory, was by modern diplomatists called the archival bond and was configured as an incremental network of relationships that links all the records of the same file and/or the same series and the same archival fonds. The archival bond is *originary*, that is, it exists from the moment a record is created; *necessary*, that is, there is no record without it; and *determined*, that is, uniquely defined by the function of the record in the business activity in which it participates. Besides determining the whole structure of the archival fonds, the archival bond is the primary identifier of each modern record and is usually made explicit by a classification code. While in a traditional paper environment the archival bond is implicit in the physical location of the record in the aggregation in which it belongs, in the digital environment it must be made explicit and expressed among the metadata; otherwise, according to the archival postulate that a record is made up of a document and the whole of its relationship, we are unable not only to identify the record but to have a record altogether [12], pp. 53–54].

DIPLOMATIC CRITICISM

The structure of diplomatic analysis, or criticism, as it is called by classic diplomatists, is rigorous and systematic and may proceed from the general to the specific or vice versa, depending on the available information. The early diplomatists first separated the record from the world and then put them into relation trying to understand the world through the record. Thus, they began analyzing the formal elements of the records, and, from the results of such analysis, they reached conclusions about procedures, persons, acts, and contexts. They firmly believed in the possibility of discovering a consistent, underlying truth about the nature of a record and of the act producing it through the use of a scientific method for analyzing its various components.

The diplomatic analysis of the elements of a record is a process of abstraction and systematization, the aim of which is to identify the essential attributes of a record and make them transportable to different historical and documentary contexts. By decontextualizing and generalizing the essential attributes of a record, the original diplomatists were able to recognize and evaluate records created over several centuries and across different juridical systems. The overarching thesis of contemporary archival diplomatics is that it will enable archivists to recognize and identify electronic records created in a variety of administrative contexts and in different hardware and software environments [[14], p. 209].

Indeed, modern diplomatics has gone much further than that: Using its century-old understanding of the nature of records and of their necessary characteristics, it has attempted to design record-making and recordkeeping systems and to determine at the outset the documentary form of the records resulting from specific acts. This proactive stance is still experimental and it has mostly been developed in the course of two research endeavors called "The UBC Project" and InterPARES [[14], p. 199]. However, irrespective of its success as a designing instrument, diplomatics remains a fundamental component of the intellectual armor of every record professional.

Diplomatics has long been recognized as a formative discipline, which develops analytical ability by making explicit the set of principles by which a record is created, and its form is shaped by defining its elements by their meaning and function, their order, and their consequences and by naming them in a consistent and meaningful way. In addition, it enables record professionals to work with a heuristic device, a diagnostic tool for establishing the meaning of the phenomenon under investigation, thereby making possible the understanding of unprecedented manifestations of records, the assessment of the trustworthiness of records that come to us at the end of several reproduction processes (in this regard, it is complementary to Digital Records Forensics[15]), and the identification of what needs to be protected and how to ensure that a trace of our actions will be carried into the future. Finally, the capacity of diplomatic analysis to uncover the interrelationships of records focusing on context over content and on purpose over use makes of it the most useful instrument for carrying out all archival functions, from appraisal to arrangement and description and from preservation to communication.

CONCLUSION

This entry has outlined the origin, purpose, object, and content of a three-century-old science, diplomatics, which has been used by several disciplines—such as jurisprudence, philology, history, and archival science—primarily, as an instrument of inquiry, a tool for analysis, but which has a substantial body of knowledge of its own, especially in its conceptualization of the record, and should be studied on its own merit by all those who either manage records or use them as sources.

The discussion of the concepts has been carried out comparing the perspective of classic and modern

diplomatics. The reason is that modern diplomatics does not replace classic diplomatics but adapts and elaborates the same body of core knowledge to make it applicable to modern records. Thus, we have two branches of one science that coexist and are equally important. While classic diplomatists, being persons of our times, need to gain an understanding of contemporary records by accepting modern diplomatics, modern diplomatists could never grasp the depth of diplomatic concepts without learning first classic diplomatics. The profound understanding of the nature of records that both classic and modern diplomatics provide is a vital component of the intellectual armor of every record professional and, like in Europe, it should be an integral part the curricula of graduate education for all records, archives, and information specialists.

REFERENCES

1. Duranti, L. *Diplomatics: New Uses for an Old Science*; Scarecrow Press: Lanham, MD/London, U.K., 1998.
2. Duranti, L. Archival science. In *Encyclopedia of Library and Information Science*; Kent, A., Ed.; Marcel Dekker, Inc.: New York, 1997; Vol. 59, Suppl 22; 3–5.
3. Paoli, C. *Diplomatica*, 2nd Ed.; Sansoni: Firenze, Italy, 1942.
4. Bresslau, H. *Handbuch der Urkundenlehre für Deutschland und Italien*. 2 vols., 1889 and Leipzig, 1912–1931; de Gruyter: Berlin, Germany, 1968.
5. De Boüard, A. *Diplomatique Générale*; Editions Auguste Piscard: Paris, France, 1929.
6. Giry, A. *Manuel de diplomatique: Diplomes et chartes Chronologie technique: Éléments critiques et parties constitutives de la teneur des chartes Les chancelleries*. Les actes privés. 1893; Burt Franklin: New York, 1964.
7. Duranti, L. Pour une diplomatique des documents electroniques. Bibliotheque de L'École des Chartes **2003**, *161*, 604.
8. Tessier, G. Diplomatique. In *L'Histoire et ses méthodes*; Samarin, C., Ed.; Librarie Gallimard: Paris, France, 1961; 633–676.
9. Carucci, P. *Il Documento Contemporaneo*; La Nuova Italia Scientifica: Roma, Italy, 1987.
10. Duranti, L.; Thibodeau, K. The concept of record in interactive, experiential and dynamic environments: The view of InterPARES. Arch. Sci. **2006**, *6* (1), 13–68. (Online: http://dx.doi.org/10.1007/s10502-006-9021-7).
11. Duranti, L.; Eastwood, T.; MacNeil, H. *Preservation of the Integrity of Electronic Records*; Kluwer Academic Publishers Group: Dordrecht, the Netherlands, 2002.
12. Duranti, L.; MacNeil, H. The preservation of the integrity of electronic records: An overview of the UBC-MAS research project. Archivaria, **1996**, *42*, 46–67.
13. Encyclopaedia Britannica Inc *Encyclopaedia Britannica*, 11th Ed.; Encyclopaedia Britannica Inc.: New York, 1910, s.v. diplomatics 300–306.
14. MacNeil, H. Contemporary archival diplomatics as a method of inquiry: Lessons learned from two research projects. Arch. Sci. **2004**, *4* (3–4), 199–232.

15. Duranti, L. From digital diplomatics to digital records forensics. Archivaria **2009**, *68*, 39–66.

BIBLIOGRAPHY

1. Barbiche, B. Diplomatics of modern official documents (sixteenth–eighteenth centuries): Evaluation and perspectives. Am. Arch. **1996**, *59*, 422–436.
2. Duranti, L. The Return of Diplomatics as a Forensic Discipline. Beihefte of the Archiv für Diplomatik Fall **2013**; 89–98.
3. Encyclopaedia Britannica Inc *Encyclopaedia Britannica*, 11th Ed.; Encyclopaedia Britannica Inc.: New York, 1910, s.v. diplomatics 300–306.
4. Gatterer, J.C. *Elementa artis diplomaticae universalis*; Apvd Vidvam V. Vandenhoeckii: Gottingen, Germany, 1765.
5. Guyotjeannin, O.; Pycke, J.; Tock, B.M. *Diplomatique medieval*; Brepols: Paris, France, 1993.
6. Guyotjeannin, O. The expansion of diplomatics as a discipline. Am. Arch. **1996**, *59*, 414–421.
7. Guyotjeannin, O., Ed. Exportations de la diplomatique, I, Mondes anciens. Bibliothèque de l'École des chartes **2002**, *160*, 475–564.
8. Guyotjeannin, O., Ed. Exportations de la diplomatique, II, Documents contemporains. Bibliothèque de l'École des chartes **2003**, *161*, 493–623.
9. Hall, H. *A Formula Book of English Official Historical Documents*. 2 vols. 1908–1909, Burt Franklin, New York, 1969.
10. Mabillon, J. *De re diplomatica*, Paris, France, 1681.
11. MacNeil, H. *Trusting Records: Legal, Historical and Diplomatic Perspectives*; Kluwer Academic: Dordrecht, the Netherlands, 2000.
12. MacNeil, H. Providing grounds for trust: Developing conceptual requirements for the long-term preservation of authentic electronic records. Archivaria **2000**, *50*, 52–78.
13. MacNeil, H. Trusting records in a postmodern world. Archivaria **2001**, *51*, 36–47.
14. MacNeil, H. Providing grounds for trust II: The findings of the authenticity task force of InterPARES. Archivaria **2002**, *54*, 24–58.
15. Petrucci, A. The illusion of authentic history: Documentary evidence. In *Writers and Readers in Medieval Italy*; Radding, C.M., Ed.; Yale University Press: New Haven, CT, 1995; Vol. 59, 236–250.
16. Pratesi, A. *Elementi di diplomatica generale*; Adriatica Editrice: Bari, Italy, n.d.
17. Tessier, G. *Diplomatique royale frarnyaise*; A et J. Picard: Paris, France, 1962.
18. Herde, P. *The New Encyclopaedia Britannica Macropedia*, 15th Ed., Preece, W.E., Ed.; Chicago, IL, 1974; s.v. diplomatic 807–813.

Disaster Planning and Recovery for Cultural Institutions

Sheryl Davis
University Library, University of California, Riverside, Riverside, California, U.S.A.

A. Patricia Smith-Hunt
Science Library, Preservation Services, University of California, Riverside, Riverside, California, U.S.A.

Kristen Kern
Portland State University, Portland, Oregon, U.S.A.

Abstract

Disaster planning is the ongoing process by which cultural institutions (libraries, museums, archives, etc.) seek to prevent loss of collections using data gathered to identify and mitigate risks; prepare and revise the written Disaster Plan; and train staff in response procedures.

This entry briefly discusses disasters of the last few decades, which have led to today's understanding of disaster planning. The majority of the text discusses the major components of a disaster plan and the requisite steps for achieving an effective plan.

DISASTER-DRIVEN: HOW DISASTERS HAVE LED TO IMPROVEMENTS IN DISASTER PLANNING

Disasters to repositories of cultural materials (libraries, museums, etc.) have always happened. Acts of nature and of man have taken their toll ever since man assembled the first collection—each loss resulted in an irreplaceable loss of cultural memory.

Thus, it is surprising that it was not until the mid-twentieth century that disaster planning and prevention efforts by libraries and other cultural institutions gained momentum.

The beginnings of modern disaster planning for cultural institutions can be traced to the 1966 flooding of Florence, Italy when the Arno River rose 22 ft, covering millions of books, manuscripts, and works of art in water, mud, oil, and sewage in numerous libraries, churches, archives, and rare bookshops. Conservators from all over the world sped to aid these institutions. The Florence flood heightened awareness of the incalculable loss that major disasters can inflict upon the world's cultural legacy and the enormous resources needed to recover from them.

In the months and years following the Florence flood, much was learned about how to effectively treat wet materials. For example, when the disaster first happened, freezing was not accepted nor was there sufficient technical support to use it as a means of preventing mold growth and stabilizing the materials. But by the 1990s freezing most materials, to buy time, had become the first step in recovering water damaged collections. Through the cooperative efforts of conservators, and many others from all over the world, major improvements to conserving and restoring wet objects were made. British conservator Peter Waters (later head of the Library of Congress' Preservation Office), who worked on-site in Italy, drew on his experiences in his *Procedures for Salvage of Water Damaged Library Materials*,[1] a preservation resource which is still highly regarded today. Hilda Bohem's 1978 work, *Disaster Prevention and Disaster Preparedness*[2] was the first to describe the elements of a disaster plan and how an institution might organize the work to achieve it.

A few examples of some of the advances in response and recovery that have come out of experiencing disasters follow.

Water Damage

While the Florence flood taught much about cleaning and air drying wet materials, in the late 1970s, speculation began on how to dry large quantities of objects more efficiently. Options for drying treatments that would not distort the materials, especially when large quantities were involved, were extremely limited. However, following the Stanford University Library Flood, in 1979, vacuum freeze-drying was used for the first time and eventually became the preferred method to dry paper, especially for books printed on coated paper. Although the vacuum freeze-drying process is still undergoing refinement, there is no doubt that it has saved numerous collections from irretrievable loss. Other mass drying methods such as freeze-drying (done with heat) and dehumidification are used to a lesser extent.

In 2000, the European Space Agency (ESA) began to offer satellite images of environmental disasters in Europe adding a new source of information on the extent of damage from natural disasters.[3] In 2002, the waters of the

Encyclopedia of Library and Information Sciences, Fourth Edition DOI: 10.1081/E-ELIS4-120044077

Elbe rose to record highs affecting primarily Germany, Austria, and the Czech Republic. Early warnings allowed for evacuation of some cultural artifacts in Prague and Dresden[4] but, "in general the water was just too high for all materials to be moved...a number of libraries, archives, and art museums had their basements and ground floor completely flooded...It is estimated that one million volumes were under water, 800,000 in the Czech Republic alone and the majority of them are lost."[5] The Elbe River rose to record high level's again in Northern Germany in 2006.

Earthquakes

Understanding how to withstand sudden and unpredictable earthquake damage to buildings which house collections is a significant challenge to cultural stewards, architects, engineers, geologists, contractors, and first responders (personnel trained to react to emergencies such as: firemen, police, and facilities staff).

In earthquake-prone California, the California State Library recommended seismic safety standards for library shelving due, in part, to the effects of the 1971 San Fernando earthquake (6.6 on the Richter scale) which included the collapse of a hospital which had just been built as "earthquake resistant."[6]

In 1989, an earthquake of 6.9 was centered near the Loma Prieta peak in the Santa Cruz, California mountains, approximately 14 km (9 mi) northeast of Santa Cruz and 96 km (60 mi) south-southeast of San Francisco.[7] The unbraced stacks of the University of California campus library located there collapsed. In 1990 and again in 1991,

other southern California cultural institutions whose stacks and storage areas were seismically braced proved that the bracing standards needed improvement (see Fig. 1).[8] [See also Library Stacks and Shelving. created by Earl Siems and Linda Demmers and provided through the Libris Design Project (http://www.librisdesign.org), http://www.librisdesign.org/docs/ShelvingforLibraries.pdf (accessed May 2008).] Subsequently new standards were adopted by the *Uniform Building Code-California Additions*.

The fact that properly braced shelving can survive was borne out in the earthquake that devastated the California State University, Northridge, January 1994. Even though 600,000 books required reshelving, this process was less costly in terms of time and money than replacing broken shelving as had been the case following the San Fernando quake. While anticipated damage to structural concrete, drywall and nonstructural ceiling tiles occurred, the Northridge calamity provided an unexpected education on steel frame buildings. Construction with steel framing to withstand earthquakes did not work in this case. The four-story high girders in the library's wings cracked at the 4 ft thick steel base fastened to the foundation. Microform storage units also proved dangerous, resulting in the cabinets shifting and falling over and the self-locking drawers opening from the force of the ground swell. This led to new recommendations on seismic retrofitting to fasten cabinets to walls and each other.

Fires

Similar to seismic and structural guidelines, fire safety is also covered by a variety of building codes[9] and the

Fig. 1   Failed seismic bracing.

National Fire Protection Association.[10] Concern for having fire codes rose to a panic level in the nineteenth century following the Chicago Fire and other tragedies and ultimately led to improved codes for building materials.

Fire resulting from defective electrical, heating, or photocopying machines, arson, construction, lightening, and other causes is still a prime threat to all cultural institutions; as is the combustion level of historic buildings. For many years there were debates about the destructive power and incinerating effects of fire and heat versus, the damaging effects of water used to arrest the spread of fire and the accompanying smoke damage.

The fire detection and suppression industry, however, has adhered to rigorous standards and in doing so has made strides to improve the precision and timeliness of detecting fires and alerting potential victims and responders. Most of this progress is a result of new technology such as fine mist sprayers. Advances in technology have also led to fewer instances of indiscriminate and inadvertent release of water from sprinkler systems, and the availability of a number of choices for water delivery. When appropriate fire suppression is employed, results can be positive as illustrated by the Historic Fourth Ward School Museum fire on February, 2008 in Virginia City, Nevada. In that case, the 20 year old sprinkler system saved the building and minimized damage to the collection.[11]

The Los Angeles Central Library arson fire of 1986 also demonstrated the importance of fire detection and suppression. An effective smoke alarm system and evacuation procedures saved staff and patrons. However, the lack of a sprinkler system and fire doors, combined with an open flue-like stacks configuration of the old Carnegie building resulted in $18 million worth of damage and destruction to the collection (400,000 books burned and 500,000 were damaged by heat and smoke).

In 1988, the damages from a fire at the Academy of Sciences Library in Leningrad, Russia surpassed those of the Los Angeles Public Library. Again, 400,000 books were destroyed by fire but an additional 2–3 million were damaged by heat and smoke, and 1 million items were damp and wet. In this case, the library had no disaster plan or, it seems, any other type of preparation. While at first the authorities tried to suppress information and minimize reports of damage, eventually, they invited consultants from the Los Angeles Library fire and other countries for advisement.

An article in the 1991 *Book and Paper Group Annual* reports on the progress of the recovery and the many techniques tried and some promising new techniques developed.[12]

Useful Tool: Barclay Ogden's 2004 publication, *Collection Preservation in Library Building Design*, does an excellent job of incorporating preservation and disaster concerns in building design and interior space intended to minimize risk and harm.[13]

Civil Unrest, Armed Conflicts

Three sets of international treaties form the framework for protecting cultural heritage in time of war and its aftermath. These are The Hague Conventions of 1899 and 1907; the Geneva Convention of 1949 and its two Protocols; and the Hague Convention of 1954 and its two Protocols. Together, they respond to four threats to cultural heritage: deliberate attack, incidental damage, pillage, and outright theft.[14]

Museums, libraries, and archives are particularly vulnerable in times of armed conflict. With the culminating recognition that cultural property was entitled to protection from outright acts of war and associated risks, a treaty to address the protection of both moveable and immovable cultural property was realized in "The 1954 Hague Convention on the Protection of Cultural Property in the Event of Armed Conflict" developed under the auspices of the United Nations Educational Scientific and Cultural Organization (UNESCO). This convention was strengthened in 1999 with the issuing of the "Second Protocol" particularly in the recognition of explicit crimes in relation to breaches of cultural protection and permanent institutional arrangements including meetings and an elected Committee. Moreover, the International Committee of the Blue Shield was established in 1996 to work to protect the world's cultural heritage threatened by wars and natural disasters, and its constituent "civil" organizations have standing advisory roles in relation to The Hague's Committee. In addition to The Hague Convention, other international conventions address terrorism and the illicit traffic of cultural property. Sadly, the world continues to witness the threat to institutions from civil wars, ethnic conflicts, and terrorism as demonstrated in Iraq, Croatia, Bosnia, and elsewhere.

Avoiding all disasters is impossible because there will always be hurricanes, floods, fires, and wars. However, being prepared with a plan is crucial to ensuring optimal response. Disaster planning today goes beyond the preparations that individual institutions make, and includes collaborative planning on local, regional, national, or even international levels as The Hague Convention advises. A significant event can serve as the catalyst for developing cooperative emergency preparedness networks. Such was the case in the devastating Los Angeles Central Library fire in 1986 that inspired formation of the Inland Empire Libraries Disaster Response Network in southern California, which in turn led to similar networks in California and elsewhere. Similarly, the Heritage Emergency National Task Force—Alliance for Response[15] initiative builds partnerships in cities across the United States between cultural heritage stewards and first responders to help emerging networks become cooperative models. The Task Force's "Lessons Applied"[16] initiative assists members with developing and implementing projects to address issues raised by hurricane Katrina in 2005, and provide tools useful for disaster planning.

Digital–Disaster

Since Italy's 1966 flood, the concept of disaster planning has broadened to include all stages of planning and preparation. Cultural stewards are making better use of expertise and practices from other industries and occupations, and more cooperation is in evidence between those responsible for heritage collections and emergency management professionals. In addition, professional recovery services with experience in libraries, archives, and museums are more widely available as well as national and international preservation initiatives and collaborations have increased.[17]

ACHIEVING A DISASTER PLAN AND A PREPARED STAFF

It is a common axiom that disasters only occur on holidays, evenings, and weekends and one might add "when under construction." This refinement of the Murphy's Law adage should be firmly in mind when preparing the disaster plan and when training staff.

The purpose of this section is to highlight important preliminary steps in disaster preparedness, such as risk assessment and mitigation, collections assessment, and setting collections priorities. We also discuss several basic components of a typical disaster plan, such as: packing out instructions; insurance considerations; staff training; response actions; salvaging, building concerns and the like from other countries.

The goal of a disaster response strategy is to plan for and ensure the protection and/or salvaging of collections. A well-conceived disaster plan replaces chaos with thoughtful, deliberate response and recovery guidelines. In doing so, it increases the speed and efficiency of response, while minimizing damage, saving money, and decreasing the amount of time service is disrupted. While institutions always hope such a plan will never be necessary, advance preparation for a disaster is an inexpensive form of insurance when compared with the daunting challenge of salvaging and—if even possible—replacing huge segments of the collection.

While a written disaster plan is important, the need to familiarize staff with these guidelines, and train them in response tactics cannot be stressed enough. When disasters strike, time is critical; therefore having both a plan of action and first responders who are trained and prepared to jump into action is much more efficient than trying to bring them up to speed while dealing with threats to the collections.

Whatever the size or manifestation of a disaster, keepers of cultural heritage have learned that no institution is immune. They have also learned that emergencies of any size may result in the disruption of services, as well as a loss to cultural memory. Most importantly, experiences have taught that preparation, by way of an organized and coordinated response strategy, is essential.

The first activity in developing a plan is to gather information on an institution's current risks.

Useful Tools: dPlan, a free online disaster writing template is posted on the Northeast Document Conservation Center (NEDCC) Web-site (http://www.dplan.org/aboutdplan.asp):

Enter information about the institution using the comprehensive fill-in-the-blank template. The template guides the writer through the steps necessary for effective disaster planning. Once completed, dPlan generates a printed disaster plan specific to the institution. The resulting plan contains contact information for staff and key personnel, preventive maintenance checklists, salvage techniques, and much more. dPlan can be updated continuously to reflect the changes that occur.[18]

Conservation OnLine (CoOL) is a great tool for all areas of preservation and conservation. Its "Disaster Planning and Response" section has good examples of disaster plans that can be used as models. http://palimpsest.stanford.edu/bytopic/disasters/.[19]

Assessment of Risks

Before an institution can successfully articulate preventive measures, the hazards and/or situations that are potentially damaging to collections must be identified.

As mentioned earlier, emergency situations often result from a combination of forces including natural and/or manmade threats, faulty mechanical systems, weakened physical storage structures, and the collections themselves (such as nitrate negatives). The most effective method of minimizing or, even better, eliminating these risks is through a comprehensive risk survey. This important first step in long-term planning and preventive maintenance includes close examination of geographic, climatic, structural, and interior hazards that pose potential threats to cultural collections. For example, is the building susceptible to damage from natural disasters such as hurricanes, tornadoes, or earthquakes? Or, is it located in a flood plain? Does the structure have a flat roof or a very old roof? Basically, the comprehensive risk assessment requires a thorough survey of both the exterior of the storage facility as well as the interior's structural and nonstructural elements.

When surveying the interior of the building note the availability and location of fire suppression systems, alarm systems, water sources and the condition of plumbing. Consider past events. Where have there been problems in the past and what caused them? Is there a bathroom with constant plumbing problems or a leaky air conditioner? Shelving for the collections is also important and must be examined for location and stability.

Ultimately, the risk assessment seeks to provide the best possible picture of exactly what hazards may threaten the storage facility, and the collections they house.

Prevention/Mitigation

Once the data has been collected and analyzed, strategies to mitigate the potential risks need to be mapped out. Some hazards may be minimized or prevented by the facilities staff doing regular building inspection (e.g., clean leaves from gutters and check drainage around building in fall and spring). Certain "fixes" may require more labor-intensive or costly strategies (such as a new roof or a new heating, ventilation, air conditioning (HVAC) system) If, however, "all improvements cannot be undertaken at once, make a schedule and follow it."[20] In the meantime, list the actions that should be taken when there is a threat (i.e., when a storm is predicted put plastic sheeting over objects and shelving areas where the roof is known to leak). Regular inspections will catch new problems before they become hazardous.

Preparation Activities

The purpose of this set of activities is to gather information which results in documentation, instructions, policies and procedures, and assigning responsibilities; each of which become part of the Disaster Plan.

Assessing collections assets and setting priorities

If the entire building was under water and everything in it was wet, what assets should be saved first? This is one eye-opening approach to establishing salvage priorities.

When responding to disasters, working quickly will lessen damage; therefore, immediate access to information that articulates what item(s) or collection(s) to salvage first is critical to a successful recovery. Determining collection salvage priorities during the Preparation phase can save valuable time during an emergency situation.

Normally, priority for salvage is given to those records and collections that are not backed up elsewhere and (1) have information needed to either establish or continue operations, including administrative records necessary to pay staff, responders, and vendors; (2) have the highest value; and (3) assist in fulfilling the requirements of the insurance company in order to file a claim. Early determination of salvage priorities save valuable time during an emergency situation and should therefore should be done early in the Preparation process.

What is the emphasis of the collection? What is the greatest current need to support the institution's programs? How difficult is the material to replace and/or how costly? What type of formats are included in the collections, and to what are they most vulnerable? Can the material be frozen? Can it be air-dried? Knowledge of this information may change its priority on the list. Being aware of the vulnerability of the collections' format is important, and may result in moving some collections to a higher priority. An excellent document to both assist with prioritizing and to place in the disaster plan is "Salvage at a Glance" by Betty Walsh.[21]

The highest priority collections will be the first items packed out it if they are damaged or the threat of damage is imminent. If these items are not in immediate danger, or are impossible or too dangerous to reach, then the next highest priority would become the focus for salvage. Consider the circumstances and limiting factors (time, access to materials, availability of resources, etc.) which may require deviations from the plan.

In large institutions, especially libraries, priorities are usually assessed by groups of materials or subject classification rather than item-by-item. Individual items which have extremely high value might, however, be listed separately. One thing is certain: running around a building during the crisis, gathering an item here and there is an inefficient way to salvage any collection.

Instead, salvage priorities should be documented and added to the Disaster Plan. In addition, the location of high priority items and/or collections should be clearly marked on the Floor Maps used by staff and other rescue workers.

Pack-out instructions

What will be the packing techniques to remove items from the building safely? Having just determined the salvage priorities, this is an opportune time to proceed with developing instructions on how to safely pack-out the different formats, whether wet or dry. Will there be a staging area to transport the material to or will the wet items be so delicate that they must be packed in place rather than handled a second time? With large-scale book disasters, packing books into boxes often happens right in the book stack aisles where the only sorting is between wet and dry. Other times a staging area is set up and the books are brought to it on book carts where they are sorted by wet, damp, and dry; might have freezer paper placed around every other or every one; and where more precise inventory control can be carried out. These instructions are added to the Disaster Plan.

Staff training

Staff training has already been mentioned a few times in this entry and its importance cannot be overstated. Clarifying roles and responsibilities and periodically practicing salvage techniques gives staff confidence and teaches success. Training can also reveal weaknesses in the Disaster Plan. Are there gaps in resources, for example? Does communication and coordination need improvement? Do staff members know the chain of command and have copies of contact lists? Do they even know where to find a copy of the Disaster Plan?

Training exercises should be as realistic as possible. Wet materials are extremely fragile so all staff should be given hands-on experience with carrying and packing all the major formats collected by the institution. Libraries, which regularly deaccession books, can provide a ready resource for experimentation and training. Deaccessioned items can be wet in order to train staff in the proper way to remove materials from a shelf and how to box them. This exercise can be paired with having each staff member take a wet book and learning to air-dry it.

One way to teach damage assessment is to design a scenario that simulates wet and/or fire damaged material in storage areas. This can be signaled easily with crepe paper streamers (e.g. black crepe for burned; blue for wet books). Have the assessment teams take pictures, mark damage on the floor maps and estimate the number of damaged items.

Other exercises may be done sitting around a table and describing a situation and walking it through with the Disaster Plan.

It is good to work with local emergency responders involving them in drills and training whenever possible. Making them aware of the salvage priorities as well as walking them through the building is also a good preparation step.

Useful Tools: *The California Preservation Program has a Web site with several useful documents in the section on "Emergencies Preparedness and Response." In addition to an elaborate tabletop exercise there is a "fill-in-the-blank" disaster plan workbook and templates (*http://calpreservation.org/disasters/index.html*)*.[22]

Supplies, suppliers, service vendors, and consultants

The Preparation phase is a great time to purchase and distribute supplies to have on hand to aid in immediate response for small and moderate disasters, and to also list the response supplies and equipment in the building. Compile contact lists of suppliers and vendors in the surrounding area who would be able to provide the amount of supplies necessary to respond to any large size disaster. Another important contact list to generate is for disaster services vendors as well as recovery and conservation experts. These lists of in-house supplies and equipment, suppliers and vendors, and potential consultants are invaluable components of the Disaster Plan. The locations of in-house supplies should be clearly marked on the Floor Maps.

Useful Tool: *A useful Web site to consult for supplies, suppliers, and experts is The Disaster Mitigation Planning Assistance Web site (*http://matrix.msu.edu/~disaster/*)*.[23]

Finances

Procedures on accessing funds and finances should be added to the Disaster Plan. One of the many roadblocks that can slow down recovery is how does the institution pay for what is needed? While an important part of being prepared is to buy and store supplies before they are needed the amounts are limited by the building's capacity

to store them. In most cases, the supplies in storage would be expended quickly in a major disaster. Another example: workers must be fed regularly and take-out restaurants are unlikely to accept institutional purchase orders. Thus, the cash on hand at the institution on an average day should be taken into consideration. Are there institutional credit cards and, if so, who is authorized to use them? Can purchase order information be set up with local vendors ahead of an event? If staff members pay for something related to the recovery, how quickly can they be reimbursed?

Insurance

Another area that must be investigated during the Planning or Preparation Phase is the insurance policy. Find out how the institution contents are insured and learn the policy's exclusions. Meet with the risk manager and/or insurance representative to review coverage and discuss the documentation required to file a claim. What is the replacement cost per book or per object? What documentation does the insurer require in order for the institution to begin salvage efforts immediately without waiting for a company representative? For rare and valuable items a special policy, often called a "fine arts" insurance policy, covers each piece individually against all risks. This list must be updated annually and the items should be given a high salvage priority.

Once the information is gathered, develop a document for the Disaster Plan that succinctly gives instructions on how to file a claim. In addition, the contact information for the insurance company is added to the appropriate contact list in the Disaster Action Plan. Claim forms and instructions can become one of the plan's appendices.

Note about FEMA: Federal Emergency Management Association funds are difficult to get. It pays, therefore, to file as soon as possible, document everything and take extensive pictures.

Chain of command, communication, and contact information

There are many steps needed to achieve a successful recovery from a disaster. The most important may be in the assigning of responsibilities and ensuring those duties are clearly understood and practiced *before* an emergency occurs. Setting up a clear chain of command and reporting relationships that are understood by all staff is particularly essential.

In the Planning and Preparation phases, staff members' roles during disaster response and recovery should be clearly defined and extensive training implemented in order to teach them how to fulfill their responsibilities. The Appendix lists many of the tasks that need to be assigned for a successful response and recovery. It pays to assign each responsibility to the appropriate staff member. For example, a cataloger might be assigned to maintain inventory control, and track the materials either moved to other sites or sent to commercial drying companies. Once these roles are assigned, the next step is to put the information in writing and compile the contact lists that are needed for the Response section of the Disaster Plan.

Upper management level staffs, together with certain additions such as the facilities manager, preservation specialist, personnel representative, and budget/finance person oversee the entire Response and Recovery phases. Once called to report to the Command Center (a group of individual staff members who have been assigned key responsibilities in responding to disaster) each member assumes his or her role as operations director, recovery coordinator, risk management/insurance, finance person, personnel, public relations and communications, facilities, disaster coordinator, etc (see Appendix).

The next level of staff consists of the individuals who have been designated and trained to deal with a disaster of any type. This group is often called the "Disaster Response Team" or "Disaster Action Team" and may include some members of the Command Center Team as well as department heads and supervisors. The primary purpose of this group is to deal with the day-to-day issues of getting the work done, such as leading work teams in packing out, monitoring supplies, inventory control, and training other staff members and volunteers in proper salvage procedures.

Remaining staff make up the disaster work teams, or if physically unable to do the packing out duties, they help with inventory control, phone calls, refreshments, screening volunteers, etc.

Useful Tool: *The Council of State Archivists (CoSA) has developed a "Pocket Response Plan (PReP)" one side of which is an Emergency Communication Directory, with contact information for staff, first responders, emergency services, utilities, vendors and suppliers, disaster teams, etc. The other side contains an Emergency Response and Checklist for Collections Recovery that lists actions that should be taken in the first 24–72 hr following a disaster.*[24]

Management issues

To manage a disaster response and recovery operation effectively requires access to a variety of ways to communicate including cell phones, walkie-talkies, e-mail, and even people to serve as "runners." While remaining on-site is the best option for the Command Center Team to manage the operations and may also be the best psychologically for the staff, it can be a problem if electricity is not available. Ideally, several areas within the building will have been planned to become the designated Command Center, and hopefully one of them is actually accessible and has electricity. If this is not possible, the institution should consider renting a modular unit with a generator parked near the building or space in a nearby building.

Other areas that should be identified before they are needed are those areas in the building that could serve as staging areas to triage materials and properly pack items being sent out of the building.

Among the many other duties, someone, on the Command Center Team should have responsibility for keeping staff informed of progress, perhaps with briefings at the beginning of shifts or as staff exit and enter the operation. Even if it is only a series of handwritten notes posted and updated regularly, it will reduce the sense of isolation that staff feel when working "in the trenches."

A brief description of the responsibilities, along with contact information for the person assigned to them, should be documented and added to the Response section of the Disaster Plan. Any contact list should list all the ways each person (staff, vendor, suppliers, custodians, safety, etc.) can be reached, including on evenings, weekends, and holidays.

Another vital contact list is the "First Response Emergency Contact List." As any staff member might be the person who discovers an emergency situation; he or she needs to know how to respond. A brief set of instructions to ensure the staff member's safety and a short list of whom to call to report the problem needs to be assembled. These instructions should be given to every staff member, and posted by every work phone. To be truly effective this document will need to be reviewed and updated on a regular basis and, similarly, staff members should be reminded of its existence every few months.

After identifying the nature of the emergency, the person who discovers it should be able to determine what type of emergency responder is needed. In other words, is this something that may easily be handled by custodial staff, or should they call either the fire or police departments? The next step should be for the staff person to contact their supervisor, the building manager, the director or whomever protocol dictates. In some circumstances, it might require staff to evacuate the building. Fig. 2 is an example of a first responder instruction sheet as used by the University of California Riverside. (For another approach, see CalPreservation's website.[25])

Security

When assessing risks it is important to evaluate the current status of security and determine what extra measures are needed both before an emergency and during disaster response and recovery. This is especially true of areas that store high value items.

During the Response and Recovery, the building and collections will need to be secured from unauthorized entry. Volunteers and workers should be screened and proper documentation filed. Media and crowds may need to be controlled. Is there adequate key or access card control?

REPORTING AN EMERGENCY

The following is a list of the 4 calls the person discovering an emergency situation must make. If you are the first person on the scene, determine the nature of the emergency and make the appropriate calls. Ensure your own safety first!

1st Call:	For FIRE - PEOPLE PROBLEMS-POLICE WATER OR ELECTRICAL Emergency (Day) Evenings/Weekends	_____ _____ _____
2nd Call:	Library Administration (Day) Evenings/Weekends	_____ _____
3nd Call:	PEOPLE PROBLEMS, Circulation Dept. BUILDING DAMAGE, Facilities Manager (Day) Evenings/Weekends Cell Phone COLLECTION DAMAGE, Preservation Librarian Evenings/Weekends Cell Phone	_____ _____ _____ _____ _____ _____ _____
4th Call:	Your Immediate Supervisor (Day) Evenings/Weekends Cell Phone	_____ _____ _____

Note: In some emergencies you may need to locate a single line phone or use a cell phone to make the necessary calls or send runners. Refer to page_____ in the Disaster Plan for the list of single line phones and their locations.

Fig. 2 Reporting an emergency.

Are there alarms and are they monitored by an entity outside the building? Are there security personnel patrolling, even when the building is closed? Are the items tagged in some way to set off an alarm if taken from the building without authorization? The findings should be analyzed and developed into an action plan and filed in the Disaster Plan.

Floor maps

Almost all facilities, which are open to the public, have the "You Are Here" floor maps. These usually show the main features of the interior of the building such as rooms, stairs, elevators, emergency exits, restrooms, etc.

A disaster response and recovery floor map should have all of this and much more, and because of this should probably not be posted publicly. This "emergency map" should be an accurate representation of storage areas (for example, book storage areas should accurately reflect the number of ranges of book stacks), the location of disaster supplies, and as already mentioned, the priorities of the various collections as well as the location of fire alarms and extinguishers; The maps should also note the location of water cutoff valves to the building and electrical panels. It also makes sense to include projected area for the Command Center and potential sites for the staging areas for triage and pack out.

The detailed floor map prepared in the Preparation phase has many uses when an emergency is discovered. First, it is used to direct fire, police, and custodial personnel to the correct location. (Library of Congress call numbers and other classification systems usually mean nothing to non-library personnel.) Second, these maps are used by staff doing assessment of damage. And third, when damaged areas are correctly marked on an accurate map it is easy to visualize the extent of the affected areas and start planning for response and recovery.

Response Actions

In order to respond efficiently, the Response section of a Disaster Plan contains information and actions needed to respond to an emergency situation in order to lessen the effects, as well as protect property and save lives. It also includes actions necessary to evacuate or retrieve collections and property from damaged areas and "first-aid" measures to stabilize collections.

Useful Tool: *"The Detailed Building and Site Assessment," available on the National Center for Preservation Technology & Training Web site, is a "three-page form that may be used to make a more intensive survey of damaged properties after natural or manmade disasters. The form requires some knowledge of architectural history and survey techniques in order to produce the most accurate results. It is intended for use by preservation professionals.*"[26]

Damage assessment

Keep in mind that when cultural collections are damaged or at risk of damage, time is of the essence. In fact, the first 48–72 hours, following a disaster are usually considered the most critical for the long-term viability of the collections. Depending upon the size, extent, and type of the disaster, access to the storage environment may not be possible. While the inability to see the condition of the collections can be very stressful, it is vital to refrain from entering the damaged areas until the fire marshal, police, or other official has declared it safe to do so. Regardless of the collections' value, the safety of staff and patrons safety should never be compromised. As this may be the only "slow" period before the staff is immersed in the recovery process, it makes sense to start preparing. For example, is the area that was planned to become the base of operations for the Command Center still usable? If not, what else is available that has electrical power and access to phones and computers? Call all members of the Command Center Team to meet and start the planning. If safety personnel can estimate the approximate time the area will be accessible, this would be the time to inform staff who are on-site and not part of the Command Center to go home and wait to be called or to report back at a specified time. Contact should also be made with staff not on the premises to alert them as to when they might be needed. Review the Disaster Plan and Salvage Priorities, and assemble in-house disaster supplies.

Once the building or storage area has been declared safe to enter, proceed with caution. Assessors should enter in pairs, rather than alone, wearing protective clothing, footwear, and carry a means of communication such as a cellular phone or walkie-talkie. Document the damage with pictures and/or videos. Take copies of the floor maps to mark the damage to help visualize the scope of the disaster as described in the Floor Map section. Not only will photographic documentation assist in determining treatment needs, but it also fulfills requirements for insurance coverage and FEMA. Remember "even things which seem insignificant now may prove to be very important as you negotiate with insurance adjusters" (SOLINET, "Actions for the first day after").[27]

In some situations, only a limited number of persons may be allowed entry into the building or must be escorted by police or fire safety personnel. Whatever the case, the goal of the assessment is to determine the scope of the damage. Where exactly is the damaged area? Is it confined to one particular area? Has it affected the floor below or above? Estimate how many items are damaged and/or threatened. Are there different formats involved? In a disaster, a quick response is critical and valuable time

may have already been lost during the time the building was inaccessible. Time lost may increase the likelihood of a mold outbreak. Therefore, the damage assessment must be as efficient and timely as possible.

Assessors should note additional hazards or areas that need to be stabilized. "It is essential that whatever damage there is to collections be limited at this time."[28] If possible, "create an inventory of found items, dislodged architectural features, decorative fragments, furnishings, collections. DO NOT THROW AWAY MATERIALS AT WILL. Many items may prove salvageable as the restoration and rehabilitation projects proceed."[29] Assessment of the disaster site will yield useful information for determining whether additional, external, assistance is required. It also allows staff to obtain a more realistic sense of what additional supplies may be required and for what purpose. Visual documentations will inform the decisions that are to follow. Other questions for consideration include: whether or not recovery can be done in-house with staff; whether wet materials should be shipped off-site to a commercial freezer or be sent immediately to a vacuum freeze-drying facility or some other process; whether a consultant will be necessary; whether to use a commercial disaster recovery firm; whether to store dry materials out of the building? Keep in mind that even with this preliminary data the salvage plan may need to be revised during the actual salvaging process so it should be as flexible as possible.

Once the damage assessment has been completed, and the area declared safe to work in, the next step should focus on salvaging and/or retrieving those resources fundamental to the mission and operation of the organization. In other words, what collections and other resources are needed, and what steps need to be taken to have the facility operational again? Of course, resources will vary dependent upon the facility, extent of the damage, and availability of responders.

As the immediate threat of a disaster begins to dissipate, the first thought is to begin the salvage process as quickly as possible. While a fast response time is vital be aware that "during this phase, many historic structures and properties are needlessly lost and damaged through hasty clean-up procedures."[30] Therefore, the need to proceed with care and caution—and yes, patience—cannot be stressed enough.

Salvage

Starting with the highest level priority that is accessible, carefully transport materials to the staging/triage areas where, while keeping some type of inventory control (with barcodes or numbers, etc), items are sorted by their condition (wet, damp, dry) and packed using the instructions written during the Preparation phase. During a large disaster is not the time to decide whether an individual item needs to be kept or discarded. Those decisions can be made when the items are returned to the building after drying. Materials with any sign of mold should be isolated from other items as soon as possible.

Recovery Phase

After the damaged and threatened assets have been moved from the building, either to a freezer or drying facility or, if dry, to store in another part of the building or off-site, it is time to prepare the building for their return and reopening to the public. Documentation regarding actions to take after an emergency, in order to rehabilitate the materials, building and storage areas, and return to full operations should be in the Disaster Plan.

Building concerns

Before the materials are returned to the building, several issues must be addressed. First, the facility must be declared ready for occupancy. Did the after-the-disaster building assessment include examining and addressing the building's structure, such as walls and the roof? Are there holes in the physical structure of the facility, for example, which may place the already damaged collections at further risk?

Is the Heating, Ventilation, Air Conditioning (HVAC) system fully operational? Has it been examined by a qualified technician? Have the vents and air ducts been checked for mold and/or soot? Do the filters need replacing? Is the security system operational? Have the facility's fire detection and extinguishing systems been thoroughly examined and reset by the fire department, and determined to be working at full capacity?

The conditions of the storage areas are equally important. Having salvaged, cleaned and stabilized the collections it would be counterproductive to place them in an unclean or unsafe storage environment. Therefore, before relocating the materials "check every shelf, drawer and surrounding floors and areas" to be sure that the requisite cleaning has actually been completed.[31] If yes, are all surfaces completely dry? If left unchecked, excess moisture in the environment may result in mold growth; therefore, double-checking to make certain that the area is completely dry will save both time and the health of the collections and staff.

Returning collections to the building

If accurate inventory control was maintained during the removal of items from the building then the staff should know the location of each item. This provides an opportunity to return things to the building in a logical manner and reintegrate them into the rest of the collection. If not, the result can be chaos.

If possible, the dried and/or restored items should be unpacked in an isolated area with ample space for the material to be spread out for examination, sorted by

format and later, put into a logical order for return to storage or display. This makes it easier to maintain accurate records of materials and the decisions made about them. This organized, systematic approach allows trained staff and consultants to assess material for specialized conservation treatment, withdrawal, replacement, or repair. What can be repaired in-house? Which need a conservation specialist? Are there items that are damaged beyond repair? Should they be discarded? Another reason for the items to be isolated before reshelving is that an insurance claim settlement cannot be completed until loss-evaluation is completed.

Once the treatment needs are determined, the remaining materials can be returned to permanent shelving/storage. However, even after the materials are returned to their permanent location, spot-checks for mold should continue to be done regularly for at least 6 months.

Debriefing, revision, and more training

Every disaster plan needs to be established according to the needs and demands of the institution that it is meant to serve. In addition, it is very important that the disaster plan cover all types of disasters, big and small, with clear instruction on what needs to be done. The plan must be reviewed frequently so that any necessary changes and updates can be made.

Throughout the disaster, debriefing sessions should be held so as not to lose any information that will help improve future response. The Command Center Team should have a simple list that can help them to make a final assessment of how well (or not) they responded to and dealt with the disaster. How did staff perform? In what areas could they benefit from more training? Were supplies adequate? What about communication and cooperation between departments, divisions, and outside help? Was record keeping accurate? How efficiently were things handled? What were the unexpected problems and their solutions?

CONCLUSION

The topics discussed in this entry deal with some of the most important factors to consider when charting a plan of action for preparing for and responding to threats to our cultural heritage. Even though the hope is that we will never have a need to use the disaster plan, it pays to be prepared. Making sure that information is accurate and current, staff trained, and emergency supplies readily available will place us in a far stronger and more prepared position to respond to a disaster—should it happen!

Every cultural institution needs a Disaster Plan that is subject to continual review and revision. The most effective plans cover every likely contingency and involve as many of staff as possible in the planning and training phase. A well-informed and well-trained staff can help with every step from planning and preparation to rapid response. A plan written by one or two specialists soon becomes a dusty, forgotten plan; a plan produced and practiced by an entire institution is the strongest defense against incalculable damage and irretrievable loss.

ACKNOWLEDGMENTS

The writers gratefully acknowledge editorial advice from the following:

Dr. Melissa Conway (UC Riverside), Karen Mokrzycki (UC Santa Cruz), Barbara Schader (UC Riverside), and Barbara Glendenning (UC Berkeley, retired).

APPENDIX:

RESPONSIBILITIES FOR DISASTER RESPONSE AND RECOVERY

There are many responsibilities that must be assigned to a group or specific staff to make a successful response and recovery. Doing this in the Preparation stage of disaster planning and making sure everyone is clear on their assignments will eliminate lost time. It is recommended that each person have two backup people trained in the performance of the same duties.

Management

Responsible for overall management of recovery and salvage operation (often a team of upper management personnel called the Command Center)
Determines the kind of salvage necessary based upon assessment and collection priorities
Determines when to begin salvage after consulting emergency personnel and Facilities Management
Determines the type and level of preservation response
Determines timetable for recovery
Receives reports and analyzes progress; makes adjustments accordingly
Designates treatment area(s)
Decides on restoration of services
Secures information needed to establish replacement costs for damaged or destroyed

Communications

Notifies and assembles the members of the Command Center Team
Notifies with staff workers who have been trained in packing our procedures (often called the Disaster Action Team)

Receives reports from Team members
Communicates with the other members of the staff keeping them informed of the status of the recovery progress
Responsible for public relations with media and is the only person to officially speak for the institution
Interacts with the organization to which the entity reports
Works with emergency responders (Fire, Police, custodial staff)
Tells library staff and volunteers where to report on the advice of the Disaster Response Director
Contacts Insurance Company or Risk Manager and fills out required forms.

Personnel Issues

Provides up-to-date information on how to reach staff members
Deals with union contract issues
Health, safety, and comfort (physical and emotional) concerns
Screens volunteers

Assessment and Documentation

Ensures proper documentation of damage (pictures, video, etc.) to building, furniture, and collections
Estimates the type and extent of the damage
Reviews the collections priorities list and confirms or adjusts it based upon the assessment of damage
Estimates number of personnel needed to complete the work and how long clean up will take
Evaluates and recommends whether or not recovery can be done in house with staff; will involve shipping material off-site to a commercial freezer of a vacuum freeze drying process; the need to bring in consultant(s); use a commercial disaster recovery firm; storage of dry materials out of the building; decision to store wet materials in a freezer or send immediately for vacuum freezing drying
Identifies locations for storing materials out of building if a commercial disaster recovery firm is not going to be used
Formulates logistics for packing out and moving materials out of the building if a commercial disaster recovery firm is not going to be used
Keeps inventory control of items being removed, discarded, etc.
Records all major decisions and a chronology of events
Keep records of materials moved to other sites

Security

Secures and protect the building's contents

Financial Issues

Figures the monetary impact of all decisions

Arranges for funds necessary to buy supplies, equipment, food, etc.

Salvage Operations

Trains and supervises work teams in proper packing and personal safety

Schedules and deploys work teams

Prepares regular reports on work team progress for the Command Center

Transportation and relocation activities

Arrangements for removing books from site

Arrangements for equipment and supplies

Responsible for handling and treatment of materials from the time they are removed until they are reshelved

Supplies and Equipment

Contacting outside agencies for services and supplies

Responsible for ordering, delivery, and dispersal of sufficient quantities of the right materials for packing out

Responsible for ordering, delivery, and dispersal of sufficient quantities of food, water, and other comfort items for the workers

Transportation of supplies and materials and the movement of damaged collections

Building Issues

All issues leading up to the eventual restoration of the building to normal

Organizes the orderly return of materials to approved shelving

Identification of locations for response and recovery activities

Supervises in-house cleaning and drying

Recovery Operations

Works with appropriate bibliographers and serves as liaison to cataloging and acquisitions to record destroyed items and to arrange for replacement copies

Prepares report for the Command Center, including photographic record, on the rehabilitation process and unsalvageable materials

Acknowledges and thanks people who have participated in the recovery

Rewrites the disaster plan in light of lessons learned

User Issues

Where can we refer our users until we can open again?

Can we establish some basic services for users in some part of the building or nearby?

REFERENCES

1. Waters, P. *Procedures for Salvage of Water-Damaged Library Materials*, Library of Congress: Washington, DC, 1979.
2. Bohem, H. *Disaster Prevention and Disaster Preparedness*, University of California: Berkeley, CA, April 1978, Office of the Assistant Vice President—Library Plans and Policies, System wide Administration.
3. http://www.esa.int/esaEO/SEMRPVNFGLE_environment_0.html#subhead1.
4. http://palimpsest.stanford.edu/byorg/abbey/an/an26/an26-2/an26-202.html.
5. Peterson, M. 2009. E-mail correspondence dated June 25.
6. http://earthquake.usgs.gov/regional/states/events/1971_02_09.php.
7. http://earthquake.usgs.gov/regional/nca/1989/index.php US Geological Survey.
8. Shelton, J.A. *Manual of Recommended Practice, Seismic Safety Standards for Library Shelving*, California State Library Foundation: Sacramento, CA, 1990.
9. University of California, Berkeley, Environmental Design Library. Building Codes & Regulatory Resources. Available at http://www.lib.berkeley.edu/ENVI/Codes.html.
10. http://www.nfpa.org/aboutthecodes/list_of_codes_and_standards.asp.
11. http://www.nevadaappeal.com/article/20080205/NEWS/537274652.
12. http://aic.stanford.edu/sg/bpg/annual/v10/bp10-18.html.
13. http://www.librisdesign.org/docs/.
14. Nafziger, J.A.R. Protection of Cultural Heritage in Time of War and Its Aftermath, International Foundation for Art Research. Available at http://www.ifar.org/heritage/htm (accessed June 2009).
15. http://www.heritagepreservation.org/programs/AFRmain.HTM.
16. http://www.heritagepreservation.org/lessons/index.html.
17. Wellheiser, J. Scott, J. *An Ounce of Prevention: Integrated Disaster Planning for Archives, Libraries and Record Centers*, 2nd Ed. Scarecrow Press: Lanham, MD. 2002; 3.
18. http://www.dplan.org/aboutdplan.asp NEDCC (Northeast Document Conservation Center).
19. http://palimpsest.stanford.edu/bytopic/disasters/.
20. Lindblom, B. Motylewski, K. Disaster planning for cultural institutions. In *Preservation of Library & Archival Materials: A Manual*; Ogden, S., Ed.; Northeast Document Conservation Centre: Andover, MA, 1993, (Disaster Planning, 1–6).
21. Walsh, B. Salvage operations for water damaged archival collections: A second glance and salvage at a glance. WAAC Newsl. **1997**, *19* (2), 12–23. Available at http://palimpsest.stanford.edu/waac/wn/wn19/wn19-2/wn19-207.html (accessed June 2009).
22. http://www.CalPreservation.org.
23. http://matrix.msu.edu/disaster/.
24. http://www.statearchivists.org/prepare/framework/prep.htm.
25. http://calpreservation.org/disasters/generic/unit2.html#sect1.

26. http://www.ncptt.nps.gov/Disaster-Recovery/Default.aspx.

27. http://www.solinet.net/Preservation/Disaster%20Resources.aspx.

28. http://www.lyrasis.org/Preservation/Disaster%20Resources/Actions%20for%20the%20First%20Day%20After.aspx.

29. http://cool-palimpsest.stanford.edu/byorg/nps/npsafter.html.

30. U.S. National Park Service, Preservation Assistance Division. After the Flood: Emergency Stabilization and Conservation Measures. Available at http://cool-palimpsest.stanford.edu/byorg/nps/npsafter.html (accessed January 2009).

31. Library of Congress, Emergency preparedness for Library of Congress Collections Appendix 2. Activities for Alarm Alert Communication System. Available at http://www.loc.gov/preserv/pub/seibert/app2.html.

Document Information Systems

K. van der Meer
Faculty of Electrical Engineering, Mathematics and Computer Science, Delft University, the Netherlands; Information and Library Science, IOIW, Antwerp University, Belgium; and D-CIS, Delft, The Netherlands

Abstract

From characteristics of information, documents and document information systems (document IS), motives to use document IS are described. A few cases are presented.

The functional aspects of document IS are described, derived from ISO standard 15489 on records management and the Sarbanes–Oxley law, and made operational in MoReq and DoD standard 5015.2. Explicit attention is given to related subjects from a viewpoint of document management: information sharing (workflow, knowledge management), and interoperability of Information and Communication Technology (ICT) tools; authenticity because of the possible evidential value of documents; and digital longevity because of the possible long-time function of archival documents.

The technical aspects answer functional demands; important information science standards, and standard components for 12 characteristics of document IS are described, among others ODMA, the XML family, OAIS, and metadata schemes.

The design methodological aspects answer functional demands and technical possibilities. Models are introduced and the way of working of, e.g., a digitization project is described.

INTRODUCTION

In the past, information was scarce and precious. (Information denotes in this entry an entity from the series data-information-knowledge-wisdom. Information should be recorded, have meaning, and be able to change a person's knowledge: "Information is a body of data on a semantic level.") Information was a matter to be preserved carefully. But today people are drowning in information.[1] All civilized people are "dataholics." Everyone has to cope with the information overload. And still users are thirstier for information and knowledge than ever; one cannot afford to be ill informed. Information is rated ever higher, "the fourth production factor, the essence of economy, and the fundament of human culture."

Information is a strange commodity. Information can easily be multiplied and spread once it is generated. Information does not vanish when it is being used. Information can be reused and inserted in new documents, without glue, seam, or welding. Information is not an object, but a representation of an existing or intended reality.

Documents contain information. (Due to Information and Communication Technology (ICT), the word document is not used for hardcopies only. A document is defined as "any object which has the purpose, or to which the purpose is given, to serve for the perusal of the data of which it is the carrier." The object may be a book, report, journal article, form, contract, letter, etc.; the data carrier may be paper, CD-ROM disk, microfiche, etc.) The information in documents is ill-structured; its semantics depends upon a context. Ill-structured information is more difficult to handle for a computer than well-structured data, but it has become feasible. So, there are document information systems (document IS) to keep document information for all those documents that need to be read if necessary, to support our memory, and to serve as witnesses of transactions, and perhaps even to give evidence of today's circumstances in a distant future. The two seemingly conflicting views, information overload and information requirements at the same time, are resolved by document IS to handle, consult, share, draw attention, store, reuse, and discard information—the tasks of librarians, archivists, record managers, document managers, and knowledge managers. (A document IS is defined simply as an information system of which the data is of document nature. The database of a document IS contains references to documents, and it may contain (parts of) documents in the form of texts and/or document images.)

Former ideals of the paperless office have vanished. Paper books, documents, reports, and records have their advantages: they are common, cheap, easy to use, and legally accepted. Electronic documents have other advantages. They can bring savings in the document sector—the economic motive. Without ICT support, control of the mass of electronic documents is impracticable—the manageability motive. Documents have moving pictures and sometimes sounds, or spreadsheets and dynamic links—the presentation motive. Organizations face increasing quality requirements of their products and services, and thus have increased quality needs of document

Encyclopedia of Library and Information Sciences, Fourth Edition DOI: 10.1081/E-ELIS4-120043914

Document–Engineering

information and information retrieval facilities—the quality motive. Documents are open to support collaborative authoring, and they can be used everywhere and at all times—the usability motive. These and others motives call for document IS.

If someone still thinks a document IS is a luxury, one may recommend trying to do without. A nasty example of what that means was seen after the destruction of the World Trade Center on September 11, 2001. The memory of many organizations in the Towers had been destroyed. They had to try to reconstruct their organization's transactions and assets when much of the paper was gone, the servers that stored all electronic information were gone, and many employees did not survive either. Resulting ideas on the value of document management have been described by Cox et al.[2]

This entry starts with a few cases. Then, in the section on the functional requirements for document IS, ISO standard 15489 and the Sarbanes–Oxley law are presented, two firmly established foundations, as well as the resulting software requirements in MoReq and the DoD 5015.2-STD. Explicit attention is given to related subjects from a viewpoint of document management: information sharing (workflow, knowledge management) and interoperability of ICT tools; authenticity because of the possible evidential value of documents; and digital longevity because of the possible long-time function of archival documents. Then, in the section on the technical aspects answering the functional demands, standards, and standard components of document IS are discussed. Examples are the Open Document Management API (ODMA) for information interchange between applications; the eXtensible Markup Language (XML) syntactical data model family; the Reference Model for an Open Archival Information System (OAIS) for preservation of digital information objects that have to be kept for a long-term; metadata schemes for information retrieval; and others. The section on design methodology, as an answer to functional and technical demands, focuses primarily on models of documents, information, users, and usage; and on design questions in, for example, a digitization project.

A FEW CASES

From a few practical cases the highlights are concisely presented.

1. A medium-sized industrial firm wanted to reduce the costs of document information handling (No increase in the number of document managers anymore). The organization wanted to control the design process: each phase of the project needed approval. The functions this firm wanted were common to document management software: they were equivalent to the Model Requirements for the management of electronic records (MoReq) scheme. The document usage and working time spent on documents were thoroughly investigated. A classification structure was designed. The economic aspects of the document IS were carefully studied. Part of the process was outsourced, for which a request for proposal was written. Business Process Redesign was postponed.

2. A consultancy firm wanted to facilitate reuse of its projects reports by other team members. The needs and wants of the organization were investigated; they were to make reports easily accessible, draw attention to relevant items, ensure security of the report, and guarantee that expertise of consultants is maintained in case of job hopping. It required the prescription of a standard for the reports of the consultants, which took several iterations. The document IS was to be made available in an intranet; it is an internal Web application.

    In the design phase, the setup and tools were demonstrated, and in a short course the ICT and the corresponding procedures were discussed. The consultants have been encouraged to share experiences. The document IS was a start to knowledge management, which was indeed one of the purposes of the project.

3. A ministry has an investigation service for environmental frauds. In the research stages, a wide range of information sources is used and produced. The document IS should improve the level of document management support, make the status of each process clear, and guard time limits. The main technical requirements were control of documents, folders, and user's rights; control of descriptors for information retrieval; control of the applications accessing the document repository; compatibility with the software already in use; and document data conversion. This is quite a list, but even more effort was needed to bring around the change of work: the employees had to change profoundly their way of working with documents; the records management unit had to change from routine "information handling" to "organizing document management."

4. A Royal Library, having its own collection but also responsible for preservation of all publications of the country, wanted to renew its information infrastructure. The data structures and software should enable interoperability for services and data from its own collection, its national task for publications and other collections. The infrastructure encompasses XML as an information structure, Web services based on XML and the eXtensible Stylesheet Language (XSL) and the HyperText Transfer protocol (http), facilities for query languages, the use of a standard metadata scheme (Extended Dublin Core), Digital Object Identifiers, and the use of the redirect facility OpenURL.

5. A University wanted to build trusted digital repositories. What technology exists to ensure trust? One answer is: make XML containers, store the original bitstream, zero or more bitstreams in a converted format (!), and the metadata in an XML container, use a digital signature and use a persistent identifier. For harvesting the Open Archives Initiative–Protocol for Metadata Harvesting (OAI–PMH) was used. The use of open standards is stressed. Other organizations, among others a city archive and an institute for historical information, came to the same setup as the University.

In all these cases expertise is needed both from document management, information retrieval, collection management, and knowledge management and from the ICT domain.

The cases differ with respect to the problems, the goals, the project plan, and the type and size of costs and benefits. That is on purpose. There is a wealth of problems in practice. Many cases could be added. Due to their differences, it is no use to write a cookbook. However, functional and technical requirements and design issues can be discerned and best practices and guidelines can be given.

FUNCTIONAL ASPECTS OF DOCUMENT IS

Procedures

Document IS starts by proper document management procedures.

The ISO standard for records management, ISO standard 15489, describes "best practices" for records management. The standard is partly based on the older Australian AS 4390 standard. It states economic and legal reasons for records management, strategies, and operational guidelines for best practices; and actions to be taken: management, responsibilities, education (!), control, ICT infrastructure, records ingest, metadata, access, and security. This influential standard is in a way the best thing that happened to records management for a century.

Another way to draw attention to records management procedures is the U.S. Sarbanes–Oxley Act, in effect since 2002. This Act, often abbreviated as the SOX Act, has a profound impact by its legal character. U.S. businesses legally need to manage, control, and preserve their information. Every company has to control the management and procedures of information and management, the executive control of the records management program, and the technical environment of their records. It is considered to be a crime to delete information with the purpose to obstruct inquiries into proper management.

Of course, ISO standard 15489 and Sarbanes–Oxley did not come out of the blue. They reflect a modern view on centuries of filing and archival practices and proper business management practices. But currently, ISO standard 15489 and Sarbanes–Oxley are a concrete-based foundation of document IS.

Software

Document management has close relations to other requirements. It makes no sense to file and archive documents if you cannot find them, so retrieval must be supported. It makes no sense to store documents if someone else cannot access them (if that person had the right to access it); this leads to the demand of information sharing, workflow management, knowledge management through groupware, and also the important demand of technical interoperability. For these functions, separate software exists, that may be connected to document management software.

One can distinguish the following types of software applications:

- Document management software, emphasizing document capture, control tools, folder management, version management, and security facilities.
- Information storage and retrieval software, with metadata bases and elaborate ranking.
- Library document management, with retrieval and loan facilities.
- Workflow management, with business process building facilities, document routing, item status facilities, and time control.
- Information sharing and knowledge management packages; groupware.

Records Management Software Functions

The "Model requirements for the management of electronic records" (MoReq) is a "standard" used all over Europe.[3] In the United States, the U.S. Department of Defense (DoD) 5015.2-STD is used.[4] The National Archives and Records Administration (NARA) endorsed this DoD standard to all federal agencies. Both MoReq and DoD 5015.2 state the functionality for applications for electronic records management. Records management has a wide scope. All kinds of people create, receive, and retrieve records as part of their daily work, and they need all kind of operations. That work is supported by records managers and archivists and by the records management application. As a consequence of the many types of operations, the functionality is extended.

Operations, demands, and facilities have been prescribed for functions such as process control, security, classified marking and declassification, retention and disposal, retrieval and rendering records, administrative functions such as changing and deleting records, metadata requirements, and nonfunctional requirements such as performance, system availability, and legislative requirements.

Interoperability

All kinds of organizations face the demand of interoperability. There is a mass-document information exchange between governmental levels; between businesses for reasons of e-commerce; and for common catalogs like Picture Australia.[5] Picture Australia offers an online portal with search facilities to find digital photos that are not owned by themselves but stored in repositories all over Australia. With a click on a thumbnail you get the whole photo. Picture Australia is an archive without an own collection, all photos reside at the participating organizations. That is an extreme example of interoperability!

The demand on interoperability is a response to the trend to globalization, enabled by ICT. Networked organizations have developed; loosely coupled, seemingly independent organizations without much common authority. Memory organizations like archives, libraries, and museums, and businesses form electronic networked organizations, as well as businesses that collaborate via electronic documents. They share electronic information, exchange information, and reuse each other's information. Interoperability has become an enormous important aspect of document IS.

The participating organizations may be more or less alike, partly colleagues and partly competitors, with horizontal connections, characterized by common or mutual information use. In other cases suppliers and customers of information can be discerned, with vertical connections. The cooperation is based on information exchange. Establishing functional requirements for common document IS for a networked organization consisting of memory institutions (or businesses) without much common authority is difficult for the following reasons:

- There is a problem (for instance, poor service, poor coordination, high costs of the end product, long delivery times of products or services), but the fact that there is a problem does not by itself lead to collaboration.
- The necessary conceptual and empirical model of the new situation at business level is not shaped.
- As a consequence, at employee level it cannot be predicted how the new situation will work out, so that no one can tell senior staff and personnel exactly how their work is going to change. This leads to organizational fuzz.
- It takes time to realize good cooperation with another organization (do not underestimate the *time* needed to realize good cooperation between organizations).
- Insufficient knowledge of ICT issues for common use of document IS.

Authenticity

For document information, three types of values can be distinguished:

- Informational value: the document describes an existing or intended reality.
- Evidential value: the document is a witness of a decision or a transaction.
- Cultural-historical value: the document describes a historical reality.

Most people have for documents only the informational value in mind and realize their evidential, legal value only if they need proof. The evidential value must not be neglected! A document can have evidential value only if it is authentic (if the document is what it purports to be). The content, structure, layout, context, and (if applicable) behavior of the document must be proven to be identical to what it was like in the past.

Authenticity is for an electronic record in a document information system a more difficult item than for a paper record. The fact that a bitstream has to be rendered in order to be readable brings about the questions: what do we mean by authenticity in this case and how to realize authenticity of digital documents.

International Research on Permanent Authentic Records in Electronic Systems (InterPARES) is the major initiative to bring the concept of authenticity applicable to our electronic era.[6] The InterPARES 1 project resulted, among others, in terms of assessment of authenticity. To assess the authenticity of an electronic record, the InterPARES report states the preserver must be able to establish its *identity*, i.e., the attributes of the record that uniquely characterize it and distinguish it from other records; and demonstrate its *integrity*, i.e., the record is complete, whole, sound and uncorrupted. Next to an overview of the custody—who kept this record and how—this means that the records need a quality check before they are transferred to the document information system where they will be kept, and the records must be maintained after transfer.

Gladney and Bennett studied the authenticity and trustworthiness and genuineness for derivates for digital objects and transformed text, and also for a broader domain: analog signals, performances, artifacts, and natural entities.[7] As a result of this work they propose the definition: something is an authentic copy if it is a *sufficiently faithful* derivative with true *provenance*.

Authenticity should be either 1 or 0; a document is either authentic or it is not. The finding of Gladney and Bennett (*sufficiently faithful*) is not at ease with the demand of either 1 or 0.

Hedstrøm and Lampe investigated the result of various forms of preservation (migration and emulation) of Chuckie egg, a game.[8] The game has been migrated and emulated and users played the original and a preserved game. As a result, the game is supposed to be authentic if there is no longer a difference in playing the original and the preserved game, although the software is different! So, evidently, for a given user group a *test* can tell the authenticity of a digital object upon change in the ICT infrastructure.

OAIS states that an information object in a document IS will be preserved for a designated community. The designated community must be defined in order to predict what the document should be used for. So, the community and the foreseen use define the measures to keep the document authentic and this defines the test setup to decide whether the document is still authentic in the future.

Next to the demand to describe the designated community, OAIS defines a Preservation Description Metadata scheme with four types of metadata: reference information, context information, provenance information, and fixity information. The reference information is meant to define the identity, the provenance information must provide the demanded true provenance (custody!), and the fixity information must indicate the data integrity. That could function as a solution for the demands that InterPARES disclosed.

Digital Longevity

Due to the urge of ICT innovation, the life time of digital information objects that are represented by bitstreams that have to be rendered, is small. The average maximum life time of a digital information object, a program, or digital document, may be 5 years. In sharp contrast to the short life time of digital objects, an archive demands many of its information objects, digital or no, to have lifetimes that may easily exceed a century.

The changes in ICT within the time of even one generation are such that within a few generations we can foresee a big "Byte out of history" from our times.[9] Content, structure, lay-out, context, and/or behavior of digital information objects are at risk by the urge of ICT innovations.

In order to preserve electronic records, the refreshing strategy will periodically be necessary: all data on a medium are transferred to fresh media so that the bits are "square and fair" at a new copy of the same type of medium. If the medium is becoming obsolete, the data will be transferred to a more modern type of medium, the strategy of migration. A study of ICT standards, the building blocks of our digital information objects, in time, shows that they are aging fast. The data format and application type get obsolete, too. In that case, the bit stream is "converted" to a more modern standard, data type, or application type (in computer science the term porting is used for this strategy). In cases like this, an audit is necessary to be able to ensure that the result conforms to archival demands.

In the emulation strategy, a new computer system "behaves" like an old one. The Universal Virtual Computer (UVC) emulator, based on a minimal and future-proof computer instruction set, has been developed by Van der Hoeven.[10] Kol showed, that it takes a computer scientist no more than two hours to express an existing data format to a future-proof instruction set (in UVC terms: a logical data schema) that can be executed in a distant future.[11] This seems to be a solution to ensure longevity for digital records in the very long run.

TECHNICAL ASPECTS OF DOCUMENT IS: STANDARDS AND STANDARD COMPONENTS

The technical aspects for document IS start from functional requirements of document IS, that have been stated in ISO standard 15489 and Sarbanes–Oxley; to which demands for search and retrieval, sharing information, and possible long-time storage have been added.

The hardware for a document IS is well known from other ICT applications: servers, storage device, monitors, scanning equipment, storage media readers and burners, printers, and telecom. For software, there is a growing number of (information science) standards and standard components for document IS. Some important ones are discussed here.

Storage Media

It has long been recognized that standards for exchangeable data carriers are indispensable. The ISO standard 9660 for CD-Rom and ISO standard 11560 for a common type of Worm disk were the first well known standardized media. From a standardization viewpoint, storage media standardization is a success story. There is a list of some 150 standards for data storage on the Web site for Interchangeable Media for Mass Computer Storage.[12] They enable ubiquitous media use!

Software Selection

The choice depends on the type of support that is needed, of course. Overviews for package selection containing detailed descriptions help to draw a short-list.

Tailor-made adjustments to software are often needed. Reasons for those demands can be summarized as: we are different, we know better, we cannot wait, and we want to be on our own. These reasons have been put forward for 20 years now. Although additions and adjustments can be useful and necessary, a warning is in place to be careful with them. Every addition carries the burdens of increasing ICT service costs, continuing difficulties to upgrade existing software, and making work procedures more rigid.

ODMA

The ODMA[13] enables applications to interface seamlessly with a document management client. ODMA offers the support to create, edit, revise, and manage documents. ODMA is very successful, to be judged from the fact that most document management packages are ODMA compliant. ODMA's website[13] also gives a list of ODMA-compliant packages.

Persistent Identifiers

A persistent identifier is a unique label that is assigned to an information object and that identifies and locates that object forever. By using persistent identifiers, one hopes to avoid dead links (http code 404) and related problems. But it is also avoided that, in order to make electronic documents accessible, someone must maintain the data locations or update the references upon every change. Instead, indirect links to the resources are maintained using a persistent identifier on the one side that is coupled to an updatable reference to the location on the other side. The principle of persistent identifier is based on the redirect principle: the persistent identifier is sent to a resolver that "knows" the address of the demanded document. The Digital Object Identifier (DOI) system is an example of a persistent identifier mechanism. An example of a DOI is the Web address doi:10.1177/0165551504045850. If recognized as a link, in Microsoft Word® or PowerPoint® the cursor is drawn over the identifier, the window shows http://dx.doi.org/10.1177/0165551504045850. dx/doi/org indicates a "resolver," the DOI naming authority [in this case identified by 1177, which knows what Uniform Resource Locator (URL) is indicated by 0165551504045850] returns the useable URL and the result of these actions is that the Web page with the current URL is sent to the requestor.

XML Syntactic Data Model Family

The Office Document Architecture (ODA, ISO standard 8613) was never used much. The Standard Generalized Markup Language (SGML, ISO standard 8879) was more popular from 1990 by publishers and by constructors of complex technical equipment (medical photo cameras, airplane engines). The XML is a data model that is an advanced version of SGML that is commonly used, especially for Web-based document IS. XML itself describes the syntactic data model, the Document Type Definition (DTD) or XML Schema describes the "grammar" of the XML syntactic data model, the Extensible Stylesheet Language (XSL) or rather the XSL Transformations (XSLT) describes the lay-out structure, XPath enables to navigate through XML documents, and XQuery is a query language for XML collections. W3Schools Online Web Tutorials are an introduction into all XML family members.[14]

OAIS

The Reference Model for an OAIS[15] is ISO standard 14721. OAIS is used by many digital archives that are meant for long-term preservation of digital information objects. OAIS contains important principles. It gives a high-level overview of the handling of the bitstream and the metadata of the bitstream upon ingest, keeping, and consumer request; and allows the description of a workflow for object handling in the archive. OAIS distinguishes the Submission Information Package (SIP) from the Archival Information Packages (AIP) and the Dissemination Information Package (DIP): the information object submitted to the archive by an author may be repackaged by the archive for keeping purposes and it may be tailored to the user's demands upon request! Moreover, OAIS demands to define a "designated community" for which the information objects are kept, influencing which documents shall be kept, and what should be possible with the document in the future, influencing how it shall be kept and preserved, as a result of the (sometimes anticipated) demands of future "consumers" (users)!

OAI-PMH and OAI-ORE

The OAI-PMH is a protocol to harvest metadata of other institutions.[16] Especially in the document sector, collaboration is necessary; no one organization can afford to use solely its own documents. So, it may become useful to share repositories. Organizations that are willing to give access to parts of their documents or their collections can implement software to handle OAI-PMH requests. They become data providers. A service provider acts as data publisher having a harvester, an application that handles OAI-PMH requests like "listRecords" to get the metadata, builds a database with metadata of the data providers and offers that to the companies that collaborate or top the general public. The original exemplar of the latter is Picture Australia.[5] A follow-up standard exists: the Open Archives Initiative-Object Reuse and Exchange (OAI-ORE) standard. OAI-ORE is more ambitious than OAI-PMH; it is meant to describe tools for richer services, even Web 2.0-like services, based on digital objects in distributed repositories.

Metadata

The access structure to document information is another main reason for the use of ICT. On the one hand, the flood of documents leads to ever-increasing demands on sophisticated tools to separate the necessary from the unwanted documents. On the other hand, and not less important, increasing quality requirements of the company lead to increasing needs for information retrieval. We refer to situations like "We have had a similar situation before, how did we react to it?" In the past, if the pertinent documents could not be found quickly they were not searched for at all. Such a question would be answered from memory, and not always precisely. The enhanced quality that is required nowadays by every business and government body is precisely the reason that these questions have to be answered correctly from the relevant documents.

It may be necessary to find the pertinent documents, but the possibilities of finding a document needle in the information universe haystack are poor. Reuse of information objects is furthered by the intrinsic interoperability in standard metadata sets. The following standard metadata tag libraries are often used.

a. Dublin Core, "DC", ISO standard 15836, is the best known metadata element set.[17] It consists of 15 elements. The Qualified Dublin Core, DCQ, adds to DC the possibility to use refinement to the metadata elements, encoding schemes, and extra metadata fields from a small expansion list. Dublin Core is a common tool in digital libraries.

b. The General International Standard Archival Description [ISAD(G)] was developed in the archival world.[18] It contains 26 fields, of which reference, title, archive creator, date, size, and level of description (record, record group, collection, etc.) are obligatory. Next to it is the International Standard Archival Authority Record for Corporate Bodies, persons, and Families [ISAAR (CPF)], describing persons and organizations.

c. The Encoded Archival Description (EAD) is the successor of ISAD(G) for electronic collections.[19] Like Dublin Core, it has the form of an XML tag library. An EAD record consists of three parts: <eadheader> describes the archival description or finding aid, <frontmatter> describes information that could have been stated on a title page of the electronic record, and <archdesc> contains the archival description itself.

d. Metadata for records, ISO standard 23081, is a metadata scheme for "document management" records. As of mid-2007 only part 1, principles, has been published; the other parts, more explanatory and providing practical guidelines, will follow. The standard prescribes metadata on the description and the accessibility of records, about the business rules and the business processes, and metadata about records management processes. This metadata element set indeed corresponds to ISO standard 15489 for records management. It is likely to become important.

e. OAIS describes electronic information packages. The information packages have metadata for packaging information: content information about the content information object, i.e., bitstream, as well as the associated representation information needed to make the bitstream understandable; as well as Preservation Description Information (PDI). The PDI encompasses: reference, the identifier of the bitstream; provenance, the source of the bitstream, who had custody, and its history; context, stating for instance how this bitstream relates to other ones (e.g., "reply"); and the fixity, that makes alteration in the bitstream perceivable. The OAIS metadata add well to the original Dublin Core.

f. PREservation Metadata: Implementation Strategies (PREMIS) is meant for digital objects. The PREMIS data dictionary[20] contains the information a repository uses to support the preservation process of the digital objects. The viability, renderability, understandability, authenticity, and identity of digital objects must be protected on preservation; also digital provenance and relations between digital objects should be preserved. PREMIS builds upon OAIS and uses XML Schema.

Content Representation

Both classification and thesauri are used in the content representation section of the metadata sections. For thesauri, ISO standard 2788 has been developed; ISO standard 5964 was meant for multilingual thesauri. Collaboration between organizations led to the demand for semantics on information exchange. In order to enable interoperability on the World Wide Web, a computer must be able to identify exactly the subject. As ever more document IS are being Web-accessible, this development is important for document IS as well. Ontologies are being developed and implemented. In an ontology the Resource Definition Framework (RDF) is a tool to define a lemma; RDF Schema [RDF(S)] to define relations between lemmas; and the Ontology Interference Language (OIL) and the Web Ontology Language (OWL) are the richest tools to define an ontology. RDF, RDFS, OIL, and OWL are W3C (World Wide Web Community) standards and XML-based.

Checksums

For data integrity a checksum can be used. Entlich describes how checksums are used to determine whether the bitstream in a document IS is still identical to the original bitstream.[21] A well-known checksums algorithm for this purpose is the Message Digest Algorithm 5 (MD-5). The Secure Hash Algorithm 1 (SHA-1) is more extended than MD-5, SHA-1 may be more common in the future. In order to be able to prove the document has not been changed, in the fixity metadata field of an OAIS-AIP (document), the type of algorithm and the checksum value must be stored, preferably with date and time when it was computed. This is part of the proof of authenticity.

Query Language

Many libraries have used the Z39.50 query language protocol for information retrieval in distributed environments.[22,23] It enables the client to request that the server searches databases for information that meets specified criteria, and to retrieve some or all of the identified information. It is meant to control the search session as well. Z39.50 is also known as ISO standard 23950. The Z39.50 standard has port number 210; and the world is adopting the http protocol, port 80, for this purpose. Search/Retrieve via URL and Search/Retrieve via Web Service (SRU/SRW) is a port 80 protocol with Z39.50 semantics. The W3C defined XQuery for the query language for XML repositories.

Data Formats

Adobe Portable Document Format (PDF) must be regarded as the factual standard; PDF/A is a part of PDF for stills, without encryption, private fonts, and patented compression, that is an ISO standard (ISO standard 19005) and suitable for long-time storage (probably much longer than 10 years). The HyperText Markup Language (HTML, ISO standard 15445) is a presentation structure compliant to XML to represent XML in a browser. HTML (and XML documents that are transformed to HTML) and PDF are different types of solutions to the way a bitstream can be presented in a browser. Kasdorf compares PDF and XML; they are complementary and can both be necessary.[24]

The Tagged Image File Format (TIFF, ISO standards 12234 and 12639), and JPEG 2000 (cf. the Joint Photographers Expert Group; ISO standard 15444) are two more examples of frequently used format standards for visual materials with good prospects to longevity.

The list of information science standards and standard components for document IS could be expanded with items that are not yet common and stable. It can be foreseen that this list will gradually, slowly, be expanded with items that are stable and have been accepted worldwide. There are also ICT standards from outside the document area. They are outside the scope of this entry.

Awareness of standards and standard components is something different from using them without second thoughts. Their use takes time and costs effort. In every case, it is recommended to study whether the advantages to use them match the drawbacks.

Finally, we draw attention to the fact that such an authoritative list of commonly-used standards and standard components could not have been drawn a decade ago. Evidently, document IS have come of age and it is not only necessary, but now also possible to draw up such a list.

DESIGN METHODOLOGICAL ASPECTS OF DOCUMENT IS

The design of an information system for document information requires building upon the functional requirements and technical tools and craftsmanship.

The design means finding a balance between specific needs and wants and profits of an organization on the one hand and ICT possibilities on the other. This balance is important. Too little attention to organizational requirements will generally result in systems that have limited value to the problem-owner; too little attention to ICT may lead to unrealistic and expensive demands on technology. IS design surely is an engineering process![25,26]

The benefit is difficult to predict. We found for evaluation of the benefits of document IS, that an ex ante representation of the benefits is rarely fully correct, even if the costs and benefits have been properly calculated. Often, during the design and implementation of the document IS or immediately afterwards, personnel came up with ideas for modification, new developments, task restructuring, or new services. Of course, the original goal was adapted. So, the benefits are partly ascribed to other circumstances. But for measurements on the benefits, then, it is not clear *what* to measure.

Moreover, the increased use of ICT is a step in the development path of an organization. The ability to grow and to change with help of ICT is a vital condition for an organization. (Less kind but more succinctly: an expanding document IS is only a battle in a war.) The problem with benefit measurements, then, is *when* to measure.

There are different types of users. "A good document information system" contains aspects of economic and managerial nature on the one hand and quality and usability aspects on the other hand. Not surprisingly, the aspects of an economic and managerial nature are of more interest to the executive staff, the management level of an organization. The quality and usability aspects refer to the personnel who will be using the document IS every day, the employee level. Important at the employee level is that users will be happy to work with the document IS if it is functioning well. Most employees in an organization will be proud to perform good quality work, and the challenge for the information system designer is to enable them to do so.

For the design of any IS, other than a very simple one, a design methodology is used. (A methodology is defined as a coherent collection of methods and techniques to solve a class of practical problems.) There are advantages to use a design methodology.

Firstly, the experiences of expert designers are used, one can use tested and proven ways to describe an organization (top-down, bottom-up, processes, actors); there are checklists; there is less chance that vital parts of significant organizational and technical problems or solutions are overlooked. Secondly, communication is enabled, there are rules to make representations, documentation and software can be shown in a standardized way to the customers, to problem-owners, and to other members of the design team; communication enables to share work among colleagues.

The use of a design methodology has disadvantages as well. Methodologies are made for problem solving in general, for a class of practical problems. But in practice each design problem is different. Whatever methodology is chosen, it will miss views and tools on some of the problems; some actions will be described too globally and other actions receive needlessly much attention. A methodology will not do the work! A methodology is just a toolbox in the hands of a designer, who does need an open eye for actual circumstances.

The design methodologies differ considerably. The elements of one design methodology may even have no counterpart in another methodology. This leads to the question what kind of elements exist and what elements should be provided to ensure that a document IS can be effectively designed. The Delft framework is used to adjust theoretical views to practical needs. It characterizes design methodologies by the following ways.

- Way of thinking (the "Weltanschauung"—the perspective on the problem domain—from which among others can be derived what objects are pertinent).
- Way of modeling (what conceptual models are made and what are their mutual relations).
- Way of working (what steps and actions must be taken by the designer).
- Way of control (what successive stages are distinguished in the progress of the design and what happens after each stage).
- Way of support (what electronic diagram and scheme tools will be used for the models, the way of working and the way of control). The way of support is the least interesting one. All kinds of tools are available to support representations of static models that are used for document IS. For dynamic situations (like process models and document routing), excellent results have been reported with simulation and animation techniques for dynamic modeling. They need not be discussed here.

These ways may eventually be added to any methodology that is used by or known to the organization for which the document IS is meant.

Way of Thinking

The objects that are pertinent for the document IS are documents, information, users, and usage. These four terms will appear in a document that describes its purpose or for instance from the result of a Balanced Scorecard approach. They then must be the main objects in the methodology and in the actual design. Other terms that can be found occasionally here are: time to complete, action sequence, and queuing. In these cases, document routing and workflow management play a role.

Way of Modeling

A model is a representation by reduction of an all-too-rich and heterogeneous reality (an existing or an intended reality) to something that can easier be understood. Modeling is thus "the science and art of leaving out." Top management, department managers, employees, ICT management, and others all have their own views on their own relevant parts of reality. Therefore, the relations between models are as important as the models themselves. The way of modeling is a part of the core of expertise of the designer.

Models of document IS will refer to the documents, the information, the users, and the usage.

- Examples of document models: document types, readiness level (under construction, ready, published), and classification level.
- Examples of information models: its (analytical) components: content, structure, lay-out, context, and behavior (for dynamic information); and information quality: correctness, preciseness, timeliness, completeness, and controllability of the information; next to that information relevance to a topic should be modeled.
- Examples of user models: role-based user models, indicating which users have access to the IS; expertise models, distinguishing novice users from experts; and personalization models, for instance the habit to adapt the lay-out of information if it was shown to that user before.
- Example of usage models: processes to which the document belong, document management leads to requirements on, for instance, version management of documents, folder management, appraisal procedures, removal of documents that are no longer needed, selection of documents for transfer to the static archives. Frequency of document use is another example.

In the design phase the attention is usually directed to the new situation, however, one needs a valid and easy but sufficiently detailed description (a model) of the current situation. This is necessary for a proper problem-solving cycle that exists of conceptualization, validation, and verification of a problem situation. Only after the current situation has been described, one or more models of new situations with consequences and benefits can be compared to the current situation.

Modeling is difficult. It takes students a lot of time to learn to model sensibly. A problem and one or more solutions, new situations have to be modeled. The current and new, foreseen situation must be conceptually modeled and represented. It is difficult to make one's new view explicit, to make choices, to think through a new situation.

Way of Working

The way of working indicates the steps and actions that have to be taken to solve the ill-structured problem of the design of a document IS. This is part of the core of the expertise of the designer.

1. In order to get an impression of the sizes and amounts the document IS will contain, an inventory must be made up of the document data.
   a. Data on the static document database (numbers, sizes, requirements on document colors, document storage space, index storage space).
   b. Data on the dynamic requirements (numbers of incoming documents per day, period of record keeping, printing capacities).
   c. The technical infrastructure (server requirements, work stations, printers, other peripherals, network requirements for data communication).
   d. The index structures.
2. Man–machine interaction aspects form an important part of usability. Surprisingly, this aspect still does not always get the necessary attention. The usability of document IS is often not satisfactory. The meaning of document data depends on the context and structure, which is only partly visible on a computer screen with its limited size.

   The dialogues should contain command shortcuts and adaptive responses for experienced users, informative feedback during an operation (for instance "please wait"), closed dialogues, and simple error messages.
3. Communication to users and training of users. Users differ in their level of education, their familiarity with computers, and in the frequency they will use the document IS, but they are the ones that decide on its success. This also holds true if the users are the general public. In one case announcements of the automation project were given, a formal introduction, informal demonstrations, and tests with users to find out whether the system is foolproof. Communicative talents of the designer are extremely valuable.

   More formally, three consecutive stages are distinguished.
   a. Communication before the document IS will be built (give an introductory course, ask users who will want to participate some time in the design stages).
   b. Communication during the design and development (manage participation, present reports on the progress, show a prototype, let users work with an experimental IS).
   c. Communication afterwards (training, courseware, help desk).
4. Digitization
   Papers arrive in the mailroom. Here, it is decided by selection which documents will be put into machine-readable form. The images are put on temporary magnetic media until they are indexed and it is decided for how long they will be kept; then they are put on permanent media. The end users index incoming documents but, even so, information management (the

responsibility for the documents and the index terms) remains centralized. Digitization of documents is costly.

The following design questions are characteristic for a digitization project:
   a. Which documents to convert: digitization of all documents may be costly; but that part that is not digitized loses part of its value, even if it is indicated that there are folders and collections present that have not been digitized.
   b. The quality of the metadata (indexes): if they have to be modernized, corrected, or adapted to the ideas of some cooperative body, they will be very expensive.
   c. The resolution of the images: it seems attractive to make high-resolution scans, but the scan of an A4 page at 300 dpi (dots per inch) results in some 8.7 million pixels (picture elements), the scan of an A4 page at 1600 dpi will need far more, some 250 million pixels. Storage space is cheap but not for free.
   d. Compression of the images: lossless compression is attractive, as original details can always be restored, but lossy compression is stronger. LZW, ZIP, and JPEG2000 can be used in a lossless way. Present and future compression algorithms may bring about that a dead (flipped) pixel results in a dead image, a feature that may be chosen to be avoided.
   e. The color in the images: color schemes that are used most are RGB (Red, Green, Blue); CMYK (Cyan, Magenta, Yellow, and Black); and HSL (Hue, Saturation, Lightness). The standard technology of RGB will result in 24 bits to represent one pixel, each color is represented by 8 bits or 256 possible "color intensities" for that pixel.
   f. The format of the images: next to PDF, TIFF, JPEG 2000, and sometimes HTML other formats are met: BMP, GIF, JPEG, PNG, and others.
   g. Image correction is technically easy; improve contrast, color correction, despecle by removal of surface pollution.
5. The aspect of digital document longevity, digital archiving and preservation is important. There is no experience with the behavior of electronic document repositories over the ages. Important standards are referred to in the section of Technical aspects.
6. For management purposes it must be possible to obtain static and dynamic data from the document IS. Document use and process control to have a managerial dimension. The need to generate management information, however, is not limited to *document* IS.
7. A complex document IS is expensive to design and expensive to maintain. Therefore, possibilities to reduce complexity must always be kept in mind. An example to reach this is downsizing, and if necessary data interchange between modules. Guarding clear

Document–Engineering

responsibilities of personnel is one more principle. Reduction of complexity is not a problem to *document* IS design only. We refer to standard works on IS design.

8. Both in the design and in the deployment of document IS, tasks can be outsourced. The advantages of outsourcing are the availability of manpower, expertise, and infrastructure. Outsourcing, however, does not mean that the stakeholder gets rid of all responsibilities. An outsourcing situation or a quotation request for outsourcing demands clear statements of the problem-owner on the purpose of the services, the way of collaboration of the partners, the technical situation (hardware, software, functionality, availability, support), the management, the costs, and the legal aspects; the number of legal suits has spectacularly grown. There is much experience on outsourcing document IS, but also on other IS. It is an important issue for which we refer to standard works on outsourcing.

9. For implementation there is a choice between a phased, controlled growth path, and a big bang approach, in which a complete information system is put into use at once. A strong argument for a controlled growth path is the limited predictability of a new system. One should always be prepared for unprepared setbacks. A strong argument for a big bang approach is of economic nature, the big bang approach will bring benefits soon after the complete document IS has been installed, while in a controlled growth path the benefits will evolve only gradually. In practice document IS tend to be complex. That may be the reason that most organizations choose for a gradual growth path.

Way of Control

The way of control indicates how the design process should be managed and controlled. Overall, this is an important issue. A change in document information provision affects an organization so pervasively that organizational understanding and rethinking are vital. Information is a primary production factor, after all. Organizational aspects are a main feature rather than of secondary importance.

1. User acceptance is too weak an approach for the design of document IS. On the design of a document IS user participation or user centered design should be required rather than mere user acceptance. There is a group of design methodologies based on Rapid Application Design (RAD). They adhere to the principle of participation. In fact, the document sector has been aware for a long time of the need to let users participate and contribute to the design and realization process. Mumford's design methodology ETHICS, a thoroughly participative methodology, published

already around 1980, was based on experiences in the document sector.

The flow of phases in projects in this area is something like Joint Requirements Planning—Architecture definition—One prototype (specify functions and construct)—One more prototype—Just one more prototype—Integration of the software with other present software—Cutover (i.e., deployment).

2. Cascade control models flow such as: requirement engineering—global functional design—technical design—programming—testing—implementation.
This approach is used if a document IS must fit in a rigid architecture.

3. Extreme Programming, XP, is meant to investigate the ICT possibilities for a domain. The XP way of control is not used too often.

4. In most cases, standard tested and proven document IS applications can be bought and tailored. In automation of document information, software engineering and the quality of the software is important but not the main concern in the realization. There are other points demanding much attention.

CONCLUSION

Document IS are used for reasons of economy, manageability, presentation, quality and usability. This entry contains an overview of functional, technical, and design methodological aspects on document IS.

The functional aspects of document IS derive from ISO standard 15489, with best practices and guidelines for good document management, and the U.S. Sarbanes–Oxley Act, stating legal demands on document management that are impracticable without document IS. They are answered in the descriptions of functions for software for records management that have been established in MoReq and in the DoD 5015.2-STD. There is an increasing demand to find information while an increasing amount is sent every day; there is an increasing demand to share information; there is awareness that in some future a small part of the documents of today may still be used. So, these functions are demanded of document IS, too.

The nature of document use calls for the document being unchanged over time. So, the demands and possibilities to ensure authenticity of electronic documents have been discussed. The UVC approach, based on a minimal and future-proof instruction set, seems to guarantee digital longevity of document information that is represented by a bitstream.

Technical aspects refer to building blocks like standards and standard components for document IS. Some 12 of them are stable and used worldwide. We draw attention to the fact that such a list of standards and standard components, as described in this entry, can be written down; this is a witness that the field of document IS has come of age.

Design methodological aspects are building upon functional demands and technical possibilities. Most interesting here are models. A model, a representation by reduction of an all-too-rich and heterogeneous reality (an existing or an intended reality) to something that can easier be understood, is in the case of a document IS made for documents, for information, for users, and/or for usage. Examples of models are given. Moreover, the steps and actions to be taken to realize a document IS are indicated, for instance in case of a digitization project.

Document IS being of age does not imply there will be no developments anymore. The increasing value of information is one reason for future changes in document IS; the demand to standardize technical components to use them as standard building blocks or as Web services in applications is a second one; developments in semantics, so that computers will "understand" the information they handle is a third reason for future changes. The author does not contradict the opinion that the development in semantics is a bit further away.

REFERENCES

1. Königer, P.; Janowitz, K. Drowning in information, but thirsty for knowledge. Internat. J. Inform. Manage. **1995**, *15*(1), 5–16.

2. Cox, R.J.; Biagini, M.K.; Carbo, T.; Debons, T.; Detlefsen, E.; Griffiths, J.M.; King, D.; Robins, D.; Thompson, R.; Tomer, C.; Weiss, M. The day the world changed: Implications for archival, library, and information sciences by first Monday. December **2001**, *6*(12), http://firstmonday.org/issues/issue6_12/cox/index.html (accessed August 3, 2007).

3. *Model requirements for the management of electronic records: Moreq specification.* March 2001, http://www.digitaleduurzaamheid.nl/bibliotheek/docs/moreq.pdf.

4. *Design Criteria Standard for Electronic Records Management Applications.* DoD 5015.2-STD. http://jitc.fhu.disa.mil/recmgt/.

5. *Picture Australia.* http://www.pictureaustralia.org/.

6. *International Research on Permanent Authentic Records in Electronic Systems InterPARES.* http://www.interpares.org/.

7. Gladney, H.M.; Bennett, J.L. What do we mean by authentic? What is the real McCoy?. D-Lib Mag. **2003**, *9*(7/8), http://www.dlib.org/dlib/july03/gladney/07gladney.html (accessed August 3, 2007).

8. Hedstrom, M.; Lampe, C. Migration vs. emulations: Do users care?. RLG Diginews **2001**, *5*(6), http://www.rlg.org/preserv/diginews/diginews5-6.html#feature1 (accessed August 3, 2007).

9. Taking a byte out of history: The archival preservation of federal computer records. US Congress. GPO, 1990.

10. van der Hoeven, J.R.; van Diessen, R.J.; van der Meer, K. Development of a Universal Virtual Computer for long-time preservation of digital objects. J. Inform. Sci. **2005**, *31*(3), 196–208.

11. Kol, N.J.C.; van Diessen, R.J.; van der Meer, K. An improved Universal Virtual Computer approach for long-time preservation of digital objects. Inform. Services Use **2006**, *26*, 283–291.

12. *ISO standards: Interchangeable Media for Computer Mass Storage.* http://www.mscience.com/iso.html.

13. *Open Document Management API, ODMA.* http://odma.info/.

14. *W3Schools Online Web Tutorials.* http://www.w3schools.com/.

15. *Reference Model for an Open Archival Information System (OAIS).* CCSDS Blue Book 651.0-B-1. January 2002. http://public.ccsds.org/publications/archive/650x0b1.pdf.

16. Lagoze, C.; Van de Sompel, H. *The Open Archives Initiative Protocol for Metadata Harvesting,* OAI-PMH. http://www.openarchives.org/OAI/openarchivesprotocol.html.

17. *Dublin Core Metadata Initiative: Dublin Core Metadata Set.* http://dublincore.org/.

18. *ISAD(G): General International Standard Archival Description,* 2nd Ed. http://www.ica.org/en/node/30000.

19. <ead> *Encoded Archival Description, EAD.* http://www.loc.gov/ead/.

20. *PREMIS Data Dictionary for Preservation Metadata.* http://www.loc.gov/standards/premis/v2/premis-2-0.pdf.

21. Entlich, R. A little bit'll do you (in): Checksums to the rescue. RLG Diginews **2005**, *9*(3), http://www.rlg.org/en/page.php?Page_ID = 20666#article3 (accessed August 3, 2007).

22. St. Pierre, M. Z39.50 for Full-Text Search and Retrieval. In *Z39.50 Implementation Experiences. NIST Special Publication 500–229*; Over, P., Moen, W.E., Denenberg, R., Stovel, L., Eds.; U.S. Department of Commerce, NIST: Gaithersburg, MD, 1995; 1–9.

23. *Information Retrieval (Z39.50): Application Service Definition and Protocol Specification Z.39.50.* http://www.loc.gov/z3950/agency/..

24. Kasdorf, B. SGML and PDF: Why we need both. J. Electron. Publ. **1998**, *3*(4), http://www.press.umich.edu/jep/03-04/kasdorf.html (accessed August 3, 2007).

25. Saiedian, H. Information systems design is an engineering process. Enc. Libr. Inform. Sci. **1997**, *60*, 120–133.

26. van der Meer, K. *Documentaire informatiesystemen,* 4th revised Ed. Biblion: The Hague, the Netherlands, 2002; (in Dutch).

Document Theory

Niels Windfeld Lund
Roswitha Skare
Institute of Culture and Literature, UiT The Arctic University of Norway, Tromsø, Norway

Abstract

This entry provides an overview about the historical development of theoretical reflections on documents and formulation of document theories. Starting out with its Latin predecessor documentum and the use of the conception in the European state bureaucracy from the seventeenth century, the first interest for document theory was a professional one and can be observed at the beginning of the twentieth century, closely connected with names like Paul Otlet and Suzanne Briet. While the notion of document and documentation was well established around 1930, it was replaced by the notion of information after World War II, at least in the Anglophone community. Nevertheless, at the same time, a new kind of document theory was emerging, a critical one connected to names like Michel Foucault, Harold Garfinkel, and Dorothy E. Smith. While the "professional" document theory developed by Otlet and others was focused on the knowledge more or less inherent in the documents and to make documents *about* something, then the general document theory developed by critical social scientists such as Foucault is much more about what the documents *are* and *do*. Since the 1990s, there has been a growing interest in general in the notion of document and documentation as well as inside Library and Information Science (LIS). Together with a growing interest in digital documents, document theorists around the world are emphasizing the complexity in document theory and a need of a complementary approach to document theory connecting physical, social, and cultural dimensions in how documents are and do.

INTRODUCTION

An interest in a document approach within the Library and Information Science (LIS) has varied from time to time. Since the late 1980s, there seems to have been an increased emphasis on a document perspective in LIS as well as in society in general. The reasons may be very diverse, depending on the different contexts for using the notion of document.

If one begins tracing the use of the word *document* through history and making a kind of conceptual archeology, one will realize that *document* has been understood in many different ways throughout history. The word *document* and its Latin predecessor, *documentum*, was from its beginnings in antiquity not only something to be held in hand or a piece of written evidence. It was primarily related to teaching and instruction. In 1214, the Latin form *documentum* was registered as meaning example, model, lecture, teaching, and demonstration. The word *document* until the seventeenth century meant *primarily* "ce qui sert à instruire, enseignement, leçon" (something serving the act of instruction, teaching, and giving a lecture).[1] An oral lecture or instruction could be a document and may indeed have been the norm and prototype of a document. This oral document tradition oriented toward educational purposes is almost forgotten today, and many would think of the legal conception of the document as being its original one dating back to antiquity. However, this conception is more related

to the emergence of the European state bureaucracy from the seventeenth century and onward. In France, it was first found in 1690 in the combination of "titres et documents."[1] It is defined as "écrit servant de preuve ou de renseignement"[1] or "something written, inscribed, etc. which furnishes evidence or information upon any subject, as a manuscript, title-deed, tombstone, coin, picture, etc."[2] From the beginning of European modernity and enlightenment, a document is first and foremost a written object stating and proving transactions, agreements, and decisions made by citizens. It was an essential part of the creation of a public bureaucracy across and independent of local customs based on a "droit coutumier" contrary to "droit écrit," laws and rules varying from place to place, being oral or gestural like handshaking agreements on a market place. Second, documents became a matter of proof, a question of whether the statements in the documents were true or not; the authenticity of the documents became crucial. Many court trials have been and are still dealing with exactly this issue. Third, the document is still an issue of "renseignement," of delivering information partly drawing on the earlier educational concept of document. It is a piece of writing which tells you something. These three characteristics can be merged into one central phenomenon in the modern society: written, true knowledge. During the eighteenth century, an essential part of the development of modern bourgeois society and especially its public sphere was that the legitimacy of politics,

Encyclopedia of Library and Information Sciences, Fourth Edition DOI: 10.1081/E-ELIS4-120053306

Document–Engineering

economy, the court, and science became increasingly dependent on one's ability to document one's rights and claims.

Following the legal tradition, in the late eighteenth century science began to be a question of empirical proof and thus "appuyer (une thèse) par des documents (1876)."[1] During the nineteenth century, the noun *documentation*, created from the verb *to document*, became a key word in administration as well as in science. From now on, the quality of scientific work depended on the documentation that the researcher could present to his colleagues and the public. It was no longer enough to make a good narrative or to present good logical arguments without empirical evidence. Scientists as well as humanists, especially historians, from then on had to demonstrate true positive knowledge by either making controlled experiments or collecting documents which demonstrated that they had empirical proof as basis for their arguments. This created the perfect setting for the first explicit document theory to be articulated as part of what has been called the first documentation movement, first and foremost led by the Belgian lawyer Paul Otlet (1868–1944).

PROFESSIONAL INTEREST FOR DOCUMENT THEORY

About 100 years ago, around 1900, many European scholars worked together in creating environments and tools for international collaboration among scholars. Many scientific associations as well as international journals were founded. This created also an urgent need for tools by which to find work by colleagues, to locate the publications, and to use the collections of data, collected by scholars. This was the background for the work started by Henri La Fontaine, who within the Society for Social and Political Studies created the bibliographic section of the Society. Together with his younger colleague, Paul Otlet, in 1893, he opened the International Office of Sociological Bibliography. Very soon, in 1895, this was extended to be the International Institute of Bibliography (IIB), being the center for international cooperation able to create its catalog, Repertoire Bibliographique Universel (RBU), organized by an elaborated version of Dewey classification scheme resulting in the Universal decimal classification (UDC). All this was being done for practical reasons, in order to provide useful tools for scholars. Neither Otlet nor Fontaine were theoretical people. For Otlet, the main purpose was the organization of documentation on an increasingly comprehensive basis in an increasingly practical way in order to achieve for the intellectual worker the ideal of a "machine for exploring time and space."[3]

But in order to realize his ideal and improve the practical organization of documentation, he had to define what is meant by document. For that purpose, he needed a new science of bibliography:

The Science of Bibliography can be defined as that science whose object of study is all questions common to different kinds of documents: production, physical manufacture, distribution, inventory, statistics, preservation, and use of bibliographic documents; that is to say, everything which deals with editing, printing, publishing, bookselling, bibliography, and library economy. The scope of this science extends to all written or illustrated documents which are similar in nature to books: printed or manuscript literary works, books, brochures, journal articles, news reports, published or manuscript archives, maps, plans, charts, schemas, ideograms, diagrams, original or reproductions of drawings, and photographs of real objects.[3]

Otlet developed a very broad concept of document while he also kept a bias toward printed texts, toward books. He always talked about "books and documents" as well as "bibliography and documentation." He developed a document theory for libraries, not for social life in general. While the spoken word is the primary focus for linguists, it is the written sources which are of interest for Otlet and his fellows in IIB:

Today Documentation is understood to mean bringing into use all of the written or graphic sources of our knowledge as embodied in documents of every kind, though chiefly printed texts. [...] Knowledge and impressions would last for only a limited time without the help of graphic documents to capture and hold them fast because *memory* alone is insufficient for recollection.[4]

Even if Otlet acknowledged oral communication as having some value, for him it is graphic documentation that ensures the memory of humanity. Otlet was also realistic about the inevitable diversity of documents:

Individual publications will continue to appear quite independently of each other. They will retain their characteristics of being separate, idiosyncratic, and poorly related to the whole body of knowledge itself.[5]

But he was very optimistic about the possibilities for and advantages of a *Universal Book*. He strongly emphasized the technical possibilities of new media at the time for realizing the Universal Book as one large *hyper-book*. This book should be created by the so-called monographic principle. It was a question of isolating each *fact* by pulling apart all documents and make a card or sheet for each *fact* by cutting out the original documents and pasting the isolated fact-card into an order, creating a coherent cosmos out of the chaos of idiosyncratic documents. While this method of *codification* could be fatal in an analog environment, destroying the original document for ever, Otlet envisioned the possibilities for a digital *hyper-book*, in which you can cut and paste without destroying the original document. Otlet thought a great deal about how to solve this problem and was inspired by H.G. Wells' ideas about a World Brain.

Even if Otlet primarily was interested in the written documents, he was in principle open for other kinds of documents: not only images and sound recordings, but also natural objects, models, games, etc.[6] In this way, he went beyond the graphic universe and the library model to the idea of Palais Mondial or Mundaneum as a kind of complete worldwide documentation including all kinds of documents, transgressing the traditions of libraries, archives, and museums.

While there were others besides Otlet who considered the theoretical issues regarding documents, like Walter Schürmeyer and Donker Duyvis, the most important person regarding theoretical discussions on documents is without any doubt Suzanne Briet (1894–1989), the French documentalist and author of many articles on documentation.

Like Otlet, Briet was also mostly engaged in practical documentation and not theoretical questions. At the same time, she was very conscious about what she was trying to accomplish. In order to promote her vision of a new professional field, she wrote a small pamphlet, a manifesto, in 1951, on the basic question: "Qu'est-ce que la documentation?" (What is documentation?), naturally including the question of what constitutes a document. She starts referring to a very general definition: "A document is a proof in support of a fact,"[7] and to the "official" definition of the French Union of Documentation Organizations from 1935, "all bases of materially fixed knowledge, and capable of being used for consultation, study and proof."[8]

At the same time, Briet acknowledges that there may be some theoretical problems related to this pragmatic kind of definition of a document, saying:

> This definition has often been countered by linguists and philosophers, who are, as they should be, infatuated with minutia and logic. Thanks to their analysis of the content of this idea, one can propose here a definition, which may be, at the present time, the most accurate, but is also the most abstract, and thus, the least accessible.[8]

Unfortunately, Briet did not specify her sources and references in this discussion and analysis, but we may be able to identify some of the sources by reading her following proposal of definition:

> any concrete or symbolic indexical sign [indice], preserved or recorded toward the ends of representing, of reconstituting, or of proving a physical or intellectual phenomenon.[8]

It appears to be in accordance with the semiotics of Charles S. Peirce (1839–1914) and the theory of three basic kinds of signs: iconic, indexical, and symbolic signs.

From this, one may see why Briet claims that documents primarily are indexical signs compared to the quality of symbolic signs.

This is illustrated in her following paragraph:

Is a star a document? Is a pebble rolled by a torrent a document? Is a living animal a document? No. But the photographs and the catalogs of stars, the stones in a museum of mineralogy, and the animals that are cataloged and shown in a zoo are documents.[8]

The major difference between the two kinds of objects is that the star and other objects named are concrete objects unconnected with any specific sign, while the photograph, catalog, etc. are specifically intended to represent something like stars, a special kind of mineral, or a special animal specimen such as a new kind of antelope, which Briet uses as an example of the relationship between document and the whole process of documentation. They are initial documents distinguished from what she calls secondary documents. She describes how new documents are created as derivatives or secondary documents, from the antelope considered as the initial document and being the basis for a whole complex of documents like catalogs, sound recordings, monographs about antelopes, articles for encyclopedia about antelopes, and so on, all together creating a new kind of culture for scientists, centers of documentation conducted by documentalists "performing the craft of documentation," using a new cultural technique of documentation:

> The proper job of documentation agencies is to produce secondary documents, derived from those initial documents that these agencies do not ordinarily create, but which they sometimes preserve. [...] We are now at the heart of the documentalists' profession. These secondary documents are called translations, analyses, documentary bulletins, files, catalogs, bibliographies, dossiers, photographs, microfilms, selections, documentary summaries, encyclopedias, and finding aids.[9]

Like Otlet, the document theory presented by Briet is a very specific theory on documents with the aim of promoting a new professional field defining the role of libraries as centers of documentation in a very proactive sense.

Both Otlet and Briet played a key role in the international community of documentation, and it was indeed international. It was the foundation for a movement across the continents making it possible to talk about "fifty years of documentation," as Samuel Bradford did in 1948 working within the international organization of International Federation for Information and Documentation (FID). In 1924, The Association of Special Libraries and Information Bureaux (ASLIB) was created and they founded the *Journal of Documentation* (which is still running). In 1931, L'UFOD, Union française des organismes de documentation, was founded. In 1937, the American Documentation Institute came into existence with a journal, *American Documentation*, and a similar French comité of documentation was created. International cooperation has continued since then, but an important difference between the Anglo-American and francophone worlds began slowly, but steadily to emerge due to two distinctive traditions for libraries in North America and continental Europe.

While the North American library tradition is focused on the user of the library trying to provide all relevant materials in the most convenient way for the user, the continental European, not least the French library tradition is much more a matter of preserving and taking care of the materials in the library, the documents, and keeping them in a secure distance from the user inside the walls of the libraries.[10] In a paradoxical way, this difference may explain some part of the decision of the American Documentation Institute in 1968 to change its name into American Society for Information Science.[11]

GENERAL SCIENTIFIC INTEREST FOR DOCUMENT THEORY

In the late 1960s and 1970s, professional document theory lost power, especially in the Anglophone world, in favor of information theory as the basis for the transformation of the sciences of documentation into information science. However at the same time, a new kind of document theory was emerging, a critical document theory. It was developed primarily within the critical and Marxist traditions of philosophy, sociology, and anthropology.

The French philosopher Michel Foucault states the following about documents in the introduction to the *Archeology of Knowledge*:

> [...] ever since a discipline such as history has existed, documents have been used, questioned, and have given rise to questions; scholars have asked not only what these documents meant, but also whether they were telling the truth, [...] all this critical concern, pointed to one and the same end: the reconstitution, on the basis of what the documents say, and sometimes merely hint at, [...] the document was always treated as the language of a voice since reduced to silence, its fragile, but possibly decipherable trace.[12]

From this case of the discipline of history, Foucault develops a general document theory turning the focus away from the assumed content or message of the document to the very material and active role of documents as bricks or parts in the construction of a historical totality. In his later book on the emergence of the prison, *Discipline and Punish*: *The Birth of the Prison*, he demonstrates how this document theory not only can be used in historical studies, but also as a critical analytical tool in relation to the modern society in general. This is a fundamental critique of the belief that a document contains a message in itself, as if a book is a document per se. It is only when a particular material thing such as a printed book becomes a part of a constructed totality, such as the literary world, that it becomes a document. When one compares this conception of document to the concept of a documentary

culture by Briet, there actually seems not to be a big difference between Foucault and Briet. However, one may argue that Foucault's critique of the assumption of an inherent content in documents challenges the belief of Otlet of the possibility of making a hyper-organization of knowledge with a lot of cards with facts.

It was not only Michel Foucault who understood documents as material building bricks in the social construction of the world. In the late 1960s and during the 1970s, American sociologists like Harold Garfinkel and Dorothy E. Smith developed similar theories about documentary practices and developed methods for studying these practices. These methodologies, the so-called ethnomethodology and documentary interpretation, were to a large degree based on the German sociologist Karl Mannheim, who formulated what he called "documentary or evidential meaning."[13] The *documentary meaning* is the meaning the document reveals "unintentionally," which might be the meaning in a larger social context, or in other words, the documentary interpretation deals with the social role of the document which is not explicitly expressed in the document but nevertheless demonstrated by its place in the construction of a social world as a whole. Inspired by Garfinkel, Foucault, and others, the French sociologist Bruno Latour made similar studies of how scientific facts were constructed in the laboratory and has demonstrated this in several works, notably by the work together with Steve Woolgar from 1979. Latour and Woolgar made anthropological fieldwork in a scientific laboratory in California observing how *scientific facts* were constructed by making documents of different sorts, articles, monographs, diagrams, photos, etc. Since then a large field of science studies has emerged based on the same general document theory, stressing "[d]ocuments of various kinds come into play, but their connection with human agency varies according to the particular instance of interaction."[14]

While the "professional" document theory developed by Otlet and others was focused on the knowledge more or less inherent in the documents and to make documents *about* something, then the general document theory developed by critical social scientists such as Foucault is much more about what the documents *are* and *do*.

This general approach to documents is followed by John Seely Brown and Paul Duguid in an essay from 1996. Here they presented a social theory of documents based on their own document oriented readings of a number of theorists in sociology, communication, and media studies.

They start out with questioning the "the widely held notion of the document as some sort of paper transport carrying preformed 'ideas' or 'information' through space and time" based on the "conduit" metaphor and belief of "information as 'in' books, files, or databases as if it could just as easily be 'out' of them." Brown and Duguid say:

> As new technologies take us through major transformations in the way we use documents, it becomes

increasingly important to look beyond the conduit image. We need to see the way documents have served not simply to write, but also to underwrite social interactions; not simply to communicate, but also to coordinate social practices.[15]

The research Brown and Duguid are using comprises works primarily by authors like Anselm Strauss, Benedict Anderson, Stanley Fish, and Bruno Latour. It is interesting to notice that apart from Latour, these scholars very little, if at all, use the notion of document in their writings. Brown and Duguid translate a number of related theories of social life into one theory of the role of documents in social life. These related theories are all characterized by an interest in how worlds, communities, and networks of humans and objects are created and constructed through shared documents.

Brown and Duguid develop a general document theory claiming that it is up to humans to discuss and decide if anything is a document. The Italian philosopher Maurizio Ferraris goes even further in his book on documentality,[44,45] drawing on the works of Derrida and Foucault, presenting a whole document oriented philosophy, an ontology of documentality, claiming that the whole social world is based on documents and that there is nothing social outside texts or one may say documents. Ferraris says that social objects are made by acts of inscription, acts of registration. When you marry, it is being registered and people will know you are married. When you make a piece of art, it is registered either for yourself or for the public as a piece of art and you can look at it as art. Each certificate of marriage and each piece of art are characterized by an element of individuality (the names of the persons or the style) as well as by an element of regularity (standards and traditions).

DOCUMENT THEORY: A PART OF A MATERIALISTIC CRITIQUE OF LIS

One of the main arguments for leaving the documentation approach in the 1960s in the documentation/library field was that it was believed that when one got the computer, it was possible to go beyond physical barriers directly into cyberspace independent of time and place, having realized the Otletian dream of a world brain having everything in one place, in one format. In principle, this gives a possibility of focusing almost only on the user and his or her needs of information. It became a matter of formulating the information needs of the users, or in other words of observing how users thought, of getting a hold on their cognitive structures in order to match them with data structures in the computer.

While many definitions of document stress the physicality of the document, some might think that the document approach will become outdated when everything becomes digital and gathered together into one big database. The reality is that the digital documents are no less physical than printed documents, but their type of physicality differs.

Following the historical approach, Michael Buckland has in a number of articles focused on the physical dimension, notably in the article "Information as thing" (1991). Buckland makes a distinction between "information-as-process," "information-as-knowledge," and "information-as-thing." Buckland believes that "'information-as-thing,' by whatever name, is of especial interest in relation to information systems because ultimately information systems, including 'expert systems' and information retrieval systems, can deal directly with information *only* in this sense."[16] Buckland tells us that he deals with the ultimate condition for information, thingness, or material conditions for information. He wants to "clarify its meaning," "affirm the fundamental role of 'information-as-thing'" and by that "bringing theoretical order to the heterogeneous, ill-ordered fields associated with 'information science.'[16] In this context, the notion of "document" is discussed as a possible concept for the "informative thing," being the core object for the whole field drawing very much on the contributions by Otlet and Briet.

In the classic article "What is a document" (1997), Buckland reviews a number of definitions of a document. Most authors, except for the Indian S.R. Ranganathan, are in fact in favor of a very broad definition of a document such as the general international definition from 1937: "Any source of information, in material form, capable of being used for reference or study or as an authority."[17]

So one may ask whether the most important question is how far you can push the notion of document or whether it is the questions of the defining properties that may divide people. This brings us to another important issue, which Buckland brings up in his concluding comments:

> One difference between the views of the documentalists discussed above and contemporary views is the emphasis that would now be placed on the social construction of meaning, on the viewer's perception of the significance and evidential character of documents.[18]

This shifts the focus from being on the materiality of the document to a focus on the social and perceptual dimensions of a document, moving back to the semiotic tradition of "object-as-sign." After being told in the beginning that the materiality/physicality is the ultimate condition for dealing with information, it is surprising to read that one should not focus so much on the physical form but give more priority to the social function and how it is perceived by people in different social settings. According to Buckland, this must be seen in the light of the digital technology:

> any distinctiveness of a document as a physical form is further diminished, and discussion of "What is a digital

document?" becomes even more problematic unless we remember the path of reasoning underlying the largely forgotten discussions of Otlet's objects and Briet's antelope.[19]

This apparent paradox of where to put emphasis in document theory can be understood better when we see the work by Buckland not only as a materialistic critique of the dominating information paradigm in LIS, but also as part of several attempts to formulate one or more socially and culturally oriented alternatives in LIS since the early 1990s. In addition to Buckland, this has been dealt with by North American scholars like Ronald E. Day and Bernd Frohmann, and Scandinavian scholars like Birger Hjørland and Vesa Suominen.

Drawing on many general theories from philosophy, especially Benjamin, Foucault, Derrida, Deleuze, Peirce, etc. it has been a major theme for Ronald Day in several of his works to demonstrate the metaphysical character of the dominating information paradigm, which perceives the idea of information as something abstract, existing in our heads or in the air, and thus ignoring the objects, the "information-as-things" as the material basis for information. At the same time, Day has shown how the material qualities are dependent on their cultural and social conditions and cannot be separated from them. In this perspective, the notion of document and the works by Otlet and Briet become essential.

Bernd Frohmann started out in the early 1990s by making a number of critical inquiries on some of the dominant paradigms, in order to present the alternative paradigm of a materialist approach to documentary systems formerly known as information systems. Frohmann established this as his major field through several contributions.

Like Day, Frohmann draws on several larger theories not only to make a critique of the information paradigm, but also to present a paradigmatic alternative. In an article from 2000, Frohmann argues in favor of using the ideas of Foucault regarding materiality providing a possibility for studying what documents do in social life.[20]

The most important contribution by Frohmann is his monograph from 2004, where he manages to present a full-scale paradigmatic alternative to the dominating LIS paradigms, based on a complex document theory. Frohmann defines documents as "different material kinds of temporally and spatially situated bundles of inscriptions embedded in specific kinds of cultural practices."[21] What interests Frohmann is how documents work in different situations, how they function as stabilizing factors in social communities, like the role of scientific journals in scientific communities. In this way, he follows the document theory developed by Foucault and other critical philosophers and social scientists like Garfinkel, Smith and so on as has been mentioned above.

A similar approach has been taken by a number of Scandinavian scholars. Birger Hjørland recommends that "the

object of study [changed] from mental phenomena of ideas, facts and opinion, to social phenomena of communication, documents and memory institutions."[22] Hjørland claims that the most important thing is that "the intrinsic natures of these objects are relatively irrelevant."[22] They only become documents once they are assigned an informative value by a collective or domain, as Hjørland has called the communities involved in the decision whether a thing becomes a document or not. Here we are told that documents are used as stabilizing means in our society, being "relatively stable forms of practice"[23] creating a sociocultural document theory along the lines of the work by Ron Day, Vesa Suominen, and notably Bernd Frohmann.

The Danish scholar Jack Andersen attempts to develop a theory of the social organization of documents and knowledge in society, and it is the German social theorist, Jürgen Habermas, who functions as Andersen's primary theoretical background, especially his work on the Public Sphere. The theory of the Public Sphere can be considered a social theory stressing the role of various communication media in the organization and transformation of modern societies, in the formation of public opinion and how it relates to the capitalist mode of production.[24] This understanding enables Andersen to translate the theory of public sphere into a theory of the social organization of documents and knowledge in society. In this way, it creates the basis for saying:

> What is crucial about this variety of document genres operating in society and state is that they organize the communicative activities of the various spheres and domains. The spheres generate documents in order to act within and in-between the particular spheres and are thus forming a communicative action.[25]

Therefore, the theory of the social organization of documents in society as formulated by Andersen explains the need for and potential advantages of the diversity of documents, in contrast to Otlet's interest in bringing all documents of the world into one format.

THEORIES ON DOCUMENTS IN A DIGITAL AGE

David Levy, who already in 1988 launched the idea of having a large program for document research, wrote in 2001 about how documents may make sense in a digital age. According to Levy, documents "are, quite simply, talking things. They are bits of the material world—clay, stone, animal skin, plant fiber, sand—that we've imbued with the ability to speak."[26] Levy relates this function to the theory by Bruno Latour on delegation of responsibility not only to other humans through networks, but also to inanimate objects.

After having presented a very broad definition of documents, David Levy wants to look more closely "at the nature of digital documents" with the hope of sorting out what is new and what is not.[27] He says: "Digital materials are made up of both the *digital representation* and the *perceptible forms* produced from it."[28]

As a result of all these threads of invention and adaption, a global infrastructure for the production, distribution, and consumption of digital documents is now emerging.[29]

This leads to one of the important issues: "How to guarantee fixity and permanence?"

One may ask: What is meant by being the same, How do you identify the likeness of two documents? This is a theme that has attracted a number of scholars and which leads to a number of questions concerning the nature of a document. If you identify two documents as being alike, you must be able to define the criteria for them being the same. In the article "Towards identity conditions for digital documents," Allen Renear and David Dubin deal exactly with this problem, wondering why so little has been done in document theory since it is crucial for dealing with digital documents.

> As a result, not only is this critical concept under-theorized, but progress on a number of important problems— including preservation, conversion, integrity assurance, retrieval, federation, metadata, identifiers—has been hindered. The development of identity conditions for a particular kind of entity is not something separate from, let alone subsequent to, defining that entity, so we cannot *begin* our development of identity conditions with an explicit definition of what we mean by "document". [...] By *document*, then, we refer to the abstract symbolic expression that may be physically instantiated repeatedly and in various media. This use corresponds more or less to the FRBR term "expression"[17] and has the colloquial synonym "text." Although now fairly common, this sense of "document" does compete with another well established and closely related use of the term [...] to the physical carrier with its instantiated inscription.[5] Terminological choices in this area are difficult, but we believe our usage is consistent with common and emerging practice in publishing and information science.[30]

They touch one of the core issues in document theory regarding competing use of the notion of a document as referring either to the physical instantiation or the abstract expression and one could add the understanding of a document as a sociocultural construction.

This theoretical challenge has been dealt with in one of the largest theoretical projects regarding document theory, the French network-based project, RTP-doc: Recherche thematique pluridisciplinaire (http://rtp-doc.enssib.fr/). It illustrates that the document approach has survived more prominently in the Francophone world, in contrast to the Anglophone world. The group consists of scholars from many different disciplines enabling an interdisciplinary project on document theory. It was decided to approach the concept of document from three angles: first,

a document as form, emphasizing the materiality of document. The second perspective was to see the document as a sign, focusing on the way the document may make sense, being meaningful, and being based on an intention. The third approach concerns how a document is a social object, depending on its position in a social context.[31]

GENERAL INTEREST FOR DOCUMENT THEORY: A COMPLEMENTARY APPROACH TO DOCUMENT THEORY

In 1996, a program in documentation studies at the University of Tromsø, Norway was established on all levels from an undergraduate to Ph.D. program.

Before the program started, a committee of librarians and faculty members from different disciplines formulated the general conceptual framework for the program, at this point not knowing very much about Otlet or Briet. The main reason for choosing the name documentation studies was not based on a theoretical interest in making a new paradigm within LIS, but on a much more pragmatic and general political interest in relation to the establishment of a National Library in Norway in 1989 and at the same time the launching of a very broadly defined act of legal deposit in Norway, including documents of all kinds, printed matter, broadcast television, radio and movies, and last but not least including the new digital documents on the Web changing all the time! One may say that it made the Otletian ideal explicit and challenged the Norwegian Library system in two fundamental ways, regarding open and free access and preservation. One challenge was posed by the complicated copyrights connected to interests of users as well as producers of all the documents and the other challenge was no less than about the "intrinsic" nature of the documents, how to preserve the documents making them available at the right time for any user in all future.

This practical challenge called for a so-called complementary approach to document theory formulated by Niels Windfeld Lund.[32,33] It is not a question of making a synthesis, but to view the document from three complementary angles, all together making a complete description. That means that the document does not partly carry one of these three features, but it is 100% a physical phenomenon, 100% a social phenomenon, and 100% a mental phenomenon. Any document is a physical object as well as a social and mental object. The core issue is how these dimensions are interacting with each other in different ways, depending on the physical, social, and mental environments in which documentation takes place, for example, health care, the arts, business, local as well as virtual subcultures, politics, and so on.[34] Instead of a belief in making one format for documentation, document theorists today are focusing on the diversity of documents and studying the wide range of problems related to processes of documentation and the resulting documents posed by concepts of "authorship," "identity," "intellectual property," as well as by document retrieval, annotation, principles of preserving digital documents, multimedia documents, politics of documentation, and many more.[31]

Since 2003, The Annual Meeting of the Document Academy, DOCAM,[35] has been one of the main fora for the "neo-documentalist movement."[36] The Document Academy is an international organization discussing document theory as well as presenting a diversity of document-oriented studies in their annual meetings. One of the key discussions has been where and how far can you take and apply the document approach: does it cover orality,[37,38] literature and movies,[39,40] and museums[41]?

Another recent tendency is that the notion of document is being used as concept and focus in other disciplines than Library and Information Science like anthropology,[42] medical informatics/telemedicine,[43] and philosophy.[44]

REFERENCES

1. Rey, A.; Tomi, M.; Horé, T.; Tanet, Ch. *Dictionnaire historique de la langue française sous la direction d'Alain Rey, édition enrichie par Alain Rey et Tristan Hordé*; Dictionnaires Le Robert: Paris, France, 1992–1998; 620.

2. Simpson, J.A.; Weiner, E. *The Oxford English Dictionary*, 2nd Ed.; Clarendon Press: Oxford, U.K., 1989; Vol. IV, 916.

3. Otlet, P. *International Organisation and Dissemination of Knowledge. Selected Essays of Paul Otlet*; Rayward, B.W., Ed.; Elsevier: Amsterdam, the Netherlands, 1990; 86.

4. Otlet, P. *International Organisation and Dissemination of Knowledge. Selected Essays of Paul Otlet*; Rayward, B.W., Ed.; Elsevier: Amsterdam, the Netherlands, 1990; 105.

5. Otlet, P. *International Organisation and Dissemination of Knowledge. Selected Essays of Paul Otlet*; Rayward, B.W., Ed.; Elsevier: Amsterdam, the Netherlands, 1990; 83.

6. Otlet, P. *Traité de Documentation*; Editions Mundaneum: Brussels, Belgium, 1934; 217, IIB Publication No. 197.

7. Briet, S. *What Is Documentation? English Translation of the Classic French Text*; Day, R.E., Martinet, L., Anghelescu, H.G.B., Eds.; The Scarecrow Press, Inc.: Lanham, MD, 2006; 9.

8. Briet, S. *What is Documentation? English Translation of the Classic French Text*; Day, R.E., Martinet, L., Anghelescu, H.G.B., Eds.; The Scarecrow Press, Inc.: Lanham, MD, 2006; 10.

9. Briet, S. *What Is Documentation? English Translation of the Classic French Text*; Day, R.E., Martinet, L., Anghelescu, H.G.B., Eds.; The Scarecrow Press, Inc.: Lanham, MD, 2006; 25–26.

10. Meyriat, J. Un siècle de documentation. La chose et le mot. Documentaliste-Science de l'information **1993**, *30* (4–5), 192–198.

11. Farkas-Conn, I.S. *From Documentation to Information Science: The Beginnings and Early Development of the American Documentation Institute-American Society for Information Science*; Greenwood Press: New York, 1990.

12. Foucault, M. *Archeology of Knowledge*; London/New York: Routledge, 2002; 6–7.

13. Mannheim, K. *Essays on the Sociology of Knowledge*; Routledge & Kegan Paul/LTD: London, U.K., 1952; 44.

14. Lynch, M.; Woolgar, S. *Representation in Scientific Practice*; The MIT Press: Cambridge, MA/London, U.K., 1990; 133.

15. Brown, J.S.; Duguid, P. The social life of documents. First Monday **1996**. http://firstmonday.org/ojs/index.php/fm/article/view/466/820 (accessed October 2014).

16. Buckland, M.K. Information as thing. J. Am. Soc. Inf. Sci. Technol. **1991**, *42* (5), 351–360, 352.

17. Buckland, M.K. What is a "document?" J. Am. Soc. Inf. Sci. Technol. **1997**, *48* (9), 804–809, 805.

18. Buckland, M.K. What is a "document?" J. Am. Soc. Inf. Sci. Technol. **1997**, *48* (9), 804–809, 807.

19. Buckland, M.K. What is a "document"? J. Am. Soc. Inf. Sci. Technol. **1997**, *48* (9), 808.

20. Frohmann, B. Discourse and documentation: some implications for Pedagogy and research. J. Educ. Libr. Inf. Sci. **2000**, *42*, 13–28.

21. Frohmann, B. *Deflating Information: From Science Studies to Documentation*; University of Toronto Press: Toronto, Ontario, Canada/Buffalo, NY/London, U.K., 2004; 137.

22. Hjørland, B. Documents, memory institutions and information science. J. Document. **2000**, *56* (1), 27–41, 39.

23. Fjordback Søndergaard, T.; Fjordback Søndergaard, T.; Andersen, J.; Hjørland, B. Documents and the communication of scientific and scholarly information. Revising and updating the UNISIST-model. J. Document. **2003**, *59* (3), 278–320, 310.

24. Andersen, J. *Analyzing the Role of Knowledge Organization in Scholarly Communication: An Inquiry into the Intellectual Foundation of Knowledge Organization*; Department of Information Studies, Royal School of Library and Information Science: Copenhagen, Denmark, 2004; 72.

25. Andersen, J. *Analyzing the Role of Knowledge Organization in Scholarly Communication: An Inquiry into the Intellectual Foundation of Knowledge Organization*; Department of Information Studies, Royal School of Library and Information Science: Copenhagen, Denmark, 2004; 75.

26. Levy, D.M. *Scrolling Forward. Making Sense of Documents in the Digital Age*; Arcade Publishing: New York, 2001; 23.

27. Levy, D.M. *Scrolling Forward. Making Sense of Documents in the Digital Age*; Arcade Publishing: New York, 2001; 137.

28. Levy, D.M. *Scrolling Forward. Making Sense of Documents in the Digital Age*; Arcade Publishing: New York, 2001; 138.

29. Levy, D.M. *Scrolling Forward. Making Sense of Documents in the Digital Age*; Arcade Publishing: New York, 2001; 151.

30. Renear, A.; Dubin, D. Towards identity conditions for digital documents. In *Proceedings of the 2003 Dublin Core Conference*; Sutton, S., Ed.; University of Washington:

Seattle, WA, October 2003. http://dcpapers.dublincore.org/pubs/article/view/746/742 (accessed October 2014).

31. Pédauque, R.T. *Le document à la lumière du numérique-forme, texte, medium: comprendre le rôle du document numérique dans l'émergence d'une nouvelle modernité*; C & F editions: Caen, France, 2006.

32. Lund, N.W. Documentation in a complementary perspective. In *Aware and responsible: Papers of the Nordic-International Colloquium on Social and Cultural Awareness and Responsibility in Library, Information and Documentation Studies (SCARLID)*; Boyd, R.W., Ed.; The Scarecrow Press: Lanham, MD, 2004; 93–102.

33. Lund, N.W. Document, text and medium: concepts, theories and disciplines. J. Document. **2010**, *66* (5), 734–749.

34. Skare, R.; Lund, N.W.; Vårheim, A. A Document Return. Contributions from a Research Field in Transition. Peter Lang: Frankfurt, Germany, 2007.

35. Document Academy proceedings. http://ideaexchange.uakron.edu/docam/ (accessed in October 2014).

36. Buckland, M.K.; Lund, N.W.; Rayward, B. Documentation and information science. Libr. Trends **2013**, *62*(2) (*Essays in Honor of W. Boyd Rayward*; Part I, Black, A., van den Heuvel, C. Eds.), 302–310; The John Hopkins University Press: Baltimore, MD, 2013.

37. Turner, D. Oral documents in concept and in situ, part I: managerial decrees. J. Document. **2012**, *68* (6), 852–863.

38. Turner, D. Oral documents in concept and in situ, part II: managerial decrees. J. Document. **2012**, *68* (6), 864–881.

39. Skare, R. Nanook of the North (1922)—On the role of paratextual elements for the understanding of the film. Neohelicon **2010**, *37* (1), 231–246.

40. Skare, R. *Christa Wolfs "Was bleibt". Kontext - Paratext - Text*; LIT Verlag: Münster, Germany, 2008.

41. Latham, K.F. Museum object as document: Using Buckland's information concepts to understand museum experiences. J. Document. **2012**, *68* (1), 45–71.

42. Riles, A. *Documents: Artifacts of Modern Knowledge*; University of Michigan Press: Ann Arbor, MI, 2006.

43. Olsen, B.I.; Lund, N.W.; Ellingsen, G.; Hartvigsen, G. Document theory for the design of socio-technical systems: a document model as ontology of human expression. J. Document. **2012**, *68* (1), 100–126.

44. Ferraris, M. Documentality: *Why It Is Necessary to Leave Traces*. Translated by Richard Davies, Fordham University Press: New York, 2013..

45. The Monist. *Documentality*. Oxford University Press: Oxford, United Kingdom, **2014**, 97, 2.

Document Type Definition (DTD)

Judith Wusteman
*School of Information and Communication Studies, University College Dublin,
Dublin, Ireland*

Abstract
Document Type Definitions (DTDs) are schemas that describe the structure and, to a limited extent, the
content of XML and SGML documents. At its inception, the XML standard inherited the DTD from
SGML as its only schema language. Many alternative schema languages have subsequently been developed for XML and are widely used in data-centric applications. But the DTD is still alive and actively used
to define some narrative-based document types, particularly journal articles. This entry describes the basic
syntax of the DTD and compares it to its two main rivals: W3C XML Schema and RELAX NG.

INTRODUCTION

Despite their names, Extensible Markup Language (XML)
[ref XML entry] and its predecessor, Standard Generalized
Markup Language (SGML) [ref Markup languages entry],
are not languages *per se*. Rather, they are systems for
creating customized markup languages. As XML is a subset of SGML, many of the comments made in this entry
will be relevant to both. However, given that the SGML
standard has now been largely superseded by XML, this
entry will concentrate on XML. Some examples of XML
languages of particular interest to the Library and Information Science community are listed in Table 5.

The set of rules that defines an XML or SGML language is called a schema. Schemata describe the structure
and, to a varying extent, the content and semantics of
documents that conform to specific languages. For example, a schema for XHTML 1.0 Strict, would, among other
things, identify which elements and attributes are allowed
or required in an XHTML 1.0 Strict document.

There are several common formats used to express schemata; such formats are referred to as schema languages.
The schema language designed to express SGML schemata
was the Document Type Definition (DTD). At its inception,
the XML standard inherited the DTD as its only method of
defining schemata. Many alternative methods have subsequently been developed for XML, the most influential of
these being the W3C XML Schema Definition (XSD)[1]
and RELAX NG.[2] These latter two schema languages are
widely used in data-centric applications. However, despite
its rivals, and continuous predictions of its demise, the
DTD is still alive and actively used to define narrative-
based document types, such as e-journal articles, prose,
poetry, and archival finding aids, as is illustrated in Table 5.

This entry describes the basic syntax of the DTD
and explains some of its more common features,
such as elements, attributes, and entities. Methods of
associating DTDs with XML documents are mentioned,
along with an explanation of the function of validating
parsers. This is followed by a comparison of the DTD
with its two main rivals: W3C XML Schema and
RELAX NG. Sample XML languages that employ each
of these schema languages are listed. They demonstrate
how the DTD has been losing ground to its rivals but
also that it is still an important schema definition format
in some domains.

VALIDATING XML INSTANCES

XML documents are commonly referred to as XML
instances. The software that reads and interprets these
instances is called an XML parser. The parser may be
contained within another piece of software, such as a
browser or an editor, or it may exist independently.
Parsers come in two main varieties: nonvalidating and
validating. Nonvalidating parsers simply check whether
XML instances are well formed, that is, whether they obey
basic constraints such as including a document element
(previously known as a root element) that contains all
other elements [ref XML entry]. Validating parsers also
check whether instances are valid, that is, whether they
conform to the rules of a schema, for example, a DTD.

DTD SYNTAX

Fig. 1 illustrates an example of a well-formed XML
instance, prefaced by the relevant DTD (within square
brackets). This simple DTD comprises a series of element
and attribute declarations. The first thing to notice is that a
DTD is not written using XML document syntax; rather, it
uses a distinctive syntax of its own.

Encyclopedia of Library and Information Sciences, Fourth Edition DOI: 10.1081/E-ELIS4-120053413

```
<?xml version="1.0" encoding="UTF-8"?>
<!DOCTYPE catalogue [
<!ELEMENT catalogue (entry)+>
<!ELEMENT entry (authors , title , publisher? , isbn+ , notes* , related, location)>
<!ATTLIST entry id ID #REQUIRED>
<!ELEMENT authors (#PCDATA)>
<!ELEMENT title (#PCDATA)>
<!ELEMENT publisher (#PCDATA)>
<!ELEMENT isbn (#PCDATA)>
<!ATTLIST isbn version (isbn-10 | isbn-13) "isbn-10">
<!ELEMENT notes (#PCDATA | reference)*>
<!ELEMENT reference (#PCDATA)>
<!ELEMENT related EMPTY>
<!ATTLIST related related-ids IDREFS #IMPLIED>
<!ELEMENT location (shelved-at | url)>
<!ELEMENT shelved-at (#PCDATA)>
<!ELEMENT url EMPTY>
<!ATTLIST url href CDATA #REQUIRED>
]>
<catalogue>
 <entry id="X123">
  <authors> St.Laurent, Simon </authors>
  <title>Inside XML DTDs</title>
  <publisher>Osborne/McGraw-Hill,U.S.</publisher>
  <isbn version="isbn-13">978-0071346214</isbn>
   <notes>Includes bibliographical references
<reference>(p.100-120)</reference> and
    <reference> index</reference>.
  </notes>
  <!-- These IDs are in other catalog entries-->
  <related related-ids="X345 X456 X567"/>
  <location>
   <url href="http://www.location.com"/>
  </location>
 </entry>
 …
</catalogue>
```

Fig. 1 An XML instance of a simplified book catalogue entry plus DTD.

Elements

The basic structure of an element declaration is as follows:

`<!ELEMENT elementName (content model)>`

Note that reserved words, such as ELEMENT, must appear in upper case. The right-hand side of the element declaration, referred to as the content model, details what combinations of child elements and plain text (indicated by #PCDATA) are permitted to appear in the element in question and in what order they may appear.

Sequence within the content model is indicated by the comma. For example, in the following element declaration, the *authors* element is followed by *title*, which is followed by an optional *publisher* element, and so on:

```
<!ELEMENT entry (authors, title, pub-
lisher?, isbn+, notes*, related,
location)>
```

The occurrence indicators +, ?, and *, listed in Table 1, define how many times an element (or a more complex pattern within parentheses) can be repeated. For example, an *entry* may include

- One optional *publisher*
- At least one *isbn*, but it can have any number
- Any number of *notes* or none at all.

Options are indicated by a vertical bar. For example, in the following element declaration, the *location* element may contain either the *shelved-at* or the *url* element, but not both.

`<!ELEMENT location (shelved-at | url)>`

Mixed Content

When an element can contain a mixture of plain text and child elements, the content is referred to as "mixed." For example:

`<!ELEMENT notes (#PCDATA | reference)*>`

Table 1 Occurrence indicators.

Occurrence indicator	Meaning
?	Optional
+	Must appear one or more times
*	Can appear 0 or more times
(no indicator)	Must appear once

Document–Engineering

Here, the *notes* element may contain any number of *reference* elements interspersed with the plain text. In the sample instance, it contains two *reference* elements. The plain text comprises the words "Includes bibliographic references," "and," and a full stop.

SGML allowed a range of mixed content types. However, as part of a concerted effort to make the XML standard as simple as possible, there is only one form of mixed content allowed in XML. The basic structure is as follows:

```
<!ELEMENT elementName (#PCDATA | childElementA
| childElementB | ...)*>
```

Limitations of the Element Declaration

Some grammatical expressions are not easily expressible via a DTD. For example, number ranges and unordered content may require complex or inelegant element declarations, as illustrated by the following examples.

Indicating a number range

To define the *authors* element as having between one and five child elements called *name*:

```
<!ELEMENT authors (name, name?, name?,
name?, name?)>
```

Indicating unordered content

To imply that the child elements *authors*, *title*, and *publisher* must all appear in element *entry* but can appear in any order:

```
<!ELEMENT entry ((authors, title, pub-
lisher) |
        (authors, publisher, title) |
        (title, publisher, authors) |
        (title, authors, publisher) |
        (publisher, authors, title) |
        (publisher, title, authors))>
```

In the real world, this would probably be modeled as

```
<!ELEMENT (authors | title | publisher)+>
```

which allows the unordered nature of the content model to be validated. The numerical aspect (one of each and only one), however, would need to be enforced via an additional schema or programming language, such as Schematron.

Attributes

Attributes appear within element start tags and supply additional information, or metadata, about the element that is not part of normal document content. Since the inception of SGML, there has been heated discussion concerning when to use elements and when to use attributes. There are no fixed rules, but Ogbugi[3] provides some useful guidelines.

Table 2 Attribute types.

Attribute type	Explanation of attribute value
CDATA	Character Data is plain text, that is, text that does not contain markup
Enumerated list of form (x | y | z)	One of a predefined set of values
ID	A unique identifier
IDREF	Reference to a unique identifier
IDREFS	List of references to unique identifiers
ENTITY	An entity
ENTITIES	A list of entities
NMTOKEN	A valid XML name
NMTOKENS	A list of valid XML names
NOTATION	The name of a notation

The general structure of a declaration for one attribute is as follows:

```
<!ATTLIST element-name attribute-name attribute-type
default-value>
```

One attribute declaration may be used to define any number of attributes relating to a single element. For example, if two attributes were to be defined for one element, the format would be

```
<!ATTLIST element-name attribute-name attribute-
type default-value attribute-name attribute-type default-
value>
```

Table 2 lists all of the allowable types of attribute. CDATA is probably the most commonly used attribute type; enumerated lists, ID, IDREF, and IDREFS are also common. Possible *default values* for attributes are listed in Table 3.

Examples

Attribute of type CDATA

In DTD:

```
<!ELEMENT url EMPTY>
<!ATTLIST url href CDATA #REQUIRED>
```

In instance:

```
<url href="http://www.location.com"/>
```

An empty element, indicated by the */* at the end of the tag, has no content, thus no close tag. The sole function of an empty element is often to be the placeholder for an

Table 3 Attribute default value types.

Default-value	Explanation
Value	Attribute has specified default value
#REQUIRED	Attribute must always be included
#IMPLIED	Attribute is optional
#FIXED *value*	Attribute must always have specified value

attribute, as in this example. The #REQUIRED default value for attribute *href* indicates that this attribute is compulsory for the *url* element. There could be no sensible default value for *href* but the DTD author still wants to force the attribute to be present.

Attribute of type enumerated list
In DTD:

```
<!ATTLIST isbn version (isbn-10 | issb-13)
"isbn-10">
```

In instance:

```
<isbn  version="isbn-13">978-0071346214
</isbn>
```

The attribute declaration indicates that the default value of attribute *version* is *isbn-10*. Defaults may be left out in the document instance. Thus,

```
<isbn>007134621X</isbn>
```

has the same meaning as

```
<isbn  version=  "isbn-10">  007134621X
</isbn>
```

Attributes of type ID and IDREFS
In DTD:

```
<!ATTLIST entry id ID #REQUIRED>
<!ATTLIST  related  related-ids  IDREFS
#IMPLIED>
```

In instance:

```
<entry id= "X123">
<related related-ids = "X345 X456 X567"/>
```

Attribute type ID facilitates attribute values that are unique and nonrepeatable throughout an XML instance. In the example, each entry is given a unique identifier via the *id* attribute. It is common, but not compulsory, to use *id* as the name of an attribute of type ID.

The attribute *related-ids* lists the identifiers of all entries related to the current entry. The identifiers listed in an attribute of type IDREF or IDREFS must appear within the current instance. Thus, this instance would only be valid if the three entries, referenced by identifiers *X345, X456,* and *X567,* were listed in the same document as entry *X123.*

An entry may not have any related entries; thus, the use of the default value #IMPLIED. The latter implies that the inclusion of an attribute value in the document instance is optional.

Entities

The basic concept of an entity is simple: it is shorthand for a larger piece of text or an alias for some other form of data, for example, a special character. When an XML parser comes across a reference to an entity, the reference is replaced with what it represents. Entities can be divided into two main groups: general entities, which provide short cuts for use within an XML instance, and parameter entities, which perform the same function for use within a DTD. An entity must be defined in the DTD before any reference is made to it. Because of this, it is good practice to place all entity declarations at the beginning of the DTD.

General entities

There are three types of general entity: internal parsed, external parsed, and external unparsed.

Internal parsed general entities: The data referenced by the entity is internal to the DTD. For example:

```
<!ENTITY rights "All rights reserved">
```

The inclusion of the entity reference *&rights;* in a document instance results in the text "All rights reserved" being placed in the text at that point when the instance is parsed.

External parsed general entities: The data referenced by the entity is in a file external to the DTD, as indicated by the reserved word, SYSTEM. For example:

```
<!ENTITY rights SYSTEM "rights.txt">
```

The inclusion of *&rights;* has a similar effect as in the previous example, but in this case, the contents of the file *rights.txt* is placed in the text.

External unparsed general entities: These entities enable the embedding of non-XML content in XML documents. For example, such an entity could be used to include a movie file in a document instance. Such entities are described as "unparsed" because the XML parser does not look at their contents.

Using general entities to represent special characters. Unicode provides a unique number for each text character in most of the world's writing systems. For example, the character â is represented by the number 226.

To include a Unicode character that cannot be typed directly via the keyboard, an internal parsed general entity reference may be used in the XML instance. For example, the character â may be represented by the entity reference *â*. Given that the latter refers to a specific character, it is described as a character entity reference. Assuming that a character set containing the glyph is available on the computer in question, this will result in the character â being placed in the text when the instance is parsed.

The general entity reference *â* does not need to be defined in the DTD because all XML processors are required to support Unicode. However, if, instead of this numeric reference, the use of a mnemonic character entity reference such as *â* is preferred, the latter should be defined in the DTD using an internal parsed general entity as follows:

```
<!ENTITY acirc "&#226;">
```

Table 4 Built-in general entities.

Built-in entity	Character represented
&lt;	<
&gt;	>
&amp;	&
&quot;	"
&apos;	'

There are five mnemonic character entities that do not have to be declared in the DTD because they form part of the definition of XML. They are listed in Table 4.

Parameter entities

Parameter entities are similar to general entities but are for use in the DTD itself. As with general entities, parameter entities can be internal or external but, unlike general entities, they are always parsed. In the real world, complex DTDs are rarely presented as a simple list of element and attribute declarations as illustrated in Fig. 1. Rather, a combination of internal and external parameter entities are used to modularize the DTDs.

Internal parameter entities: These can be useful if an element or attribute content model is repeated regularly or if the model is complex. The following entity declaration is taken from the ANSI/NISO Z39.96-2012 JATS: Journal Article Tag Suite (JATS):[4]

```
<!ENTITY % app-model "(%sec-model;,
permissions?)">
```

This defines a parameter entity describing the content model for the appendix of a journal article. Note that the syntax for parameter entity declarations is the same as for general entities, with the addition of a % symbol after the reserved word ENTITY. The parameter entity *app-model* is subsequently used in the element declaration for the appendix. Again, the syntax for parameter entity references is similar to that for general entity references but includes % instead of &.

```
<!ELEMENT app %app-model;>
```

In this example, the value of the parameter entity itself includes a reference to another parameter entity: *%sec-model;*. The use of nested parameter entity references is a common method of modularizing large DTDs.

External parameter entities: External parameter entities are also used to modularize DTDs. For example, the following declaration occurs near the beginning of the XHTML 1.0 DTD:

```
<!ENTITY % HTMLlat1 PUBLIC "-//W3C//
ENTITIES Latin 1 for XHTML//EN"
"xhtml-lat1.ent">
```

The keyword PUBLIC indicates that what follows is the formal public identifier for the entity. This identifier is followed by the name of the file containing the entity's content, namely *xhtml-lat1.ent*. In the XHTML 1.0 DTD, this entity declaration is immediately followed by an invocation of the entity:

```
%HTMLlat1;
```

As a result, when the DTD is parsed, the contents of the file *xhtml-lat1.ent* are placed at this point within the DTD.

The file *xhtml-lat1.ent* contains declarations for several dozen mnemonic character entities, for example:

```
<!ENTITY Agrave "&#192;">
<!ENTITY Aacute "&#193;">
<!ENTITY Acirc "&#194;">
<!ENTITY yen "&#165;">
```

Thus, by using the parameter entity, all the mnemonic character entities defined in file *xhtml-lat1.ent* are available for use within document instances. Incorporating external files of general entity declarations that define useful mnemonic character entities is a common use of parameter entities.

Readability

If the reader is familiar with basic DTD syntax, a well-written DTD can be relatively simple to interpret. Good human readability is one of the advantages that DTDs have over schema languages such as the W3C XML Schema and is one of the reasons why the DTD has not yet been superseded. It is therefore important to ensure that DTDs are as readable as possible, for example, by using meaningful element and attribute names and including a liberal number of comments. In fact, many DTDs contain far more comments than code. The syntax for comments is as follows:

```
<!- Comments go here ->
```

Apart from listing entities before using them, there are no rules concerning the order of declarations in DTDs. However, authors should attempt to ensure that DTDs are clear and logical to human readers.

DOCUMENT TYPE DECLARATIONS

A DTD is associated with an XML instance via a Document Type Declaration (DOCTYPE). The latter is placed after the XML declaration at the beginning of the XML file, as illustrated in Fig. 1.

The most widely recognized DOCTYPEs are those related to HTML as they appear—or should appear—at the start of every HTML file. Because HTML5 is not an XML language and so not definable by a DTD, its DOCTYPE is very simple:

```
<!DOCTYPE html>
```

Table 5 Sample XML languages of particular interest to the Library and Information Science community.

Language	Original format	Definitive form	Other formats available	Comments	Website
NISO Journal Article Tag Suite (JATS)	DTD	DTD	XSD RELAX NG	Almost everyone is still using the DTD for production and publishing[a]	http://jats.nlm.nih.gov/
Text Encoding Initiative (TEI)	DTD	ODD (One Document Does it all)	ODD can be compiled into DTD XSD RELAX NG	DTD use gradually giving way to RELAX NG and XSD	http://www.tei-c.org/
Encoded Archival Description (EAD)	DTD	DTD	XSD Relax NG	Some migrated away from DTDs, but they are still widely used	http://www.loc.gov/ead/
CrossRef	DTD	XSD			http://www.crossref.org/
Metadata Encoding and Transmission Standard (METS)	XSD	XSD		Based on (The Making of America II, MOA2) DTD	http://www.loc.gov/standards/mets/
Metadata Object Description Schema (MODS)	XSD	XSD			http://www.loc.gov/standards/mods/
ETD-MS: Electronic Theses, and Dissertations Metadata Standard	XSD	XSD			http://www.ndltd.org/standards/metadata
Visual Resources Association (VRA) Core	XSD	XSD			http://www.loc.gov/standards/vracore/
Docbook	DTD	RELAX NG (with integrated Schematron rules)	DTD XSD		http://www.docbook.org/
OASIS Darwin Information Typing Architecture (DITA)	DTD	DTD	XSD RELAX NG		http://dita.xml.org/
XHTML 1.0	DTD	DTD	XSD RELAX NG	XHTML 2.0 abandoned at Working Draft stage in favor of HTML5	http://www.w3.org/TR/xhtml1

Key: XSD, W3C XML Schema.

[a]See http://www.niso.org/workrooms/sts/for ongoing efforts at standardization.

Document-Engineering

```
<?xml version="1.0"?>
<!DOCTYPE catalogue SYSTEM "http://www.catalogue.com/catalogue.dtd"
[
<!ENTITY Acirc "&#194;">
<!ENTITY Atilde "&#195;">
<!ENTITY Ccedil "&#199;">
]>
XML instance follows
```

Fig. 2   An XML instance with internal and external DTD subsets.

XHTML 1.0 Transitional, on the other hand, is an XML language and the structure of its DOCTYPE reflects this:

```
<!DOCTYPE html PUBLIC "-//W3C//DTD
XHTML 1.0 Transitional//EN"
"http://www.w3.org/TR/xhtml1/DTD/
xhtml1-transitional.dtd">
```

In this latter DOCTYPE, *html* is the DTD's document element, that is, the element that must contain all other elements in documents that conform to this DTD. The document element is followed by the keyword PUBLIC, then the formal public identifier, and, finally, a Uniform Resource Identifier locating the DTD. As can be seen, there are parallels between the structure of document type declarations and external parameter entities.

In this example, the DOCTYPE simply identifies the document element and provides information to identify and locate the relevant DTD. It is also possible for the DOCTYPE to include the DTD, or an *internal subset* of the DTD. In Fig. 1, the DTD is included within the DOCTYPE between square brackets. In Fig. 2, the main DTD, referred to as the *external subset*, is in file *catalogue.dtd* at http://www.catalogue.com/. An internal subset, comprising three mnemonic character entity declarations, is contained within the DOCTYPE. The declaration of mnemonic character entities is a common use of an internal subset within an XML file. As this method is recognized by all schema languages, this limited use of DTDs is often used in conjunction with other schema languages.

VALIDATING PARSERS

It is compulsory to include a DTD with every SGML instance. With XML, it is optional; many XML documents are not related to any form of schema. This is appropriate for some uses of XML, particularly one-off machine-to-machine communications that are not meant to be archived. But it is not appropriate for documents that require consistency of markup. In addition, it is important to note that DTDs often do more than provide validation rules for XML instances. They may also add to the document's information set, or *infoset*, that is, the information provided by the document. For example, they may define entity references or provide default values for attributes.

Parsers vary as to how they deal with internal and external DTD subsets. Although nonvalidating parsers do not check documents for validity, some do read the external subset of the DTD, process default attributes, and expand entities. And all conforming parsers should do this for internal subsets. When receiving a document from a third party, it is preferable to use a parser that performs all of these tasks. However, when authoring documents, it is prudent to assume that the receiving parser may not read the DTD. Thus, the DTD should not be used to add to the infoset.[5]

ALTERNATIVE SCHEMA LANGUAGES

W3C XML Schema Language

SGML and the DTD were designed to enable the markup of document-centric applications: full-text documents such as technical manuals, journal articles, prose, poetry, and drama. They were not designed for data-centric documents. XML was intended to be a simplified web-enabled version of SGML. When XML became a W3C standard in 1998, the DTD was adopted as XML's only schema language.

However, it soon became clear that the most widespread use of XML would be in data-centric applications such as eCommerce and Web Services. And, for XML to achieve its full potential in such applications, a more data-centric method of describing document validity was required. In particular, finer control was needed over the validity of element content and, to a lesser extent, of attribute content.

So, in 2001, the W3C XML Schema language, commonly, if confusingly, known as XML Schema, became a W3C standard. One of the two main advantages of XML Schema is the powerful data typing facilities for element and attribute values. There are 40 two different types that can be assigned to an attribute or element, including integer, date, string, qualified name, positive integer, and so on. Users can also define their own types, for example, currencies, colors, phone numbers, and so on. The other main advantage of XML Schema over DTDs is the support for namespaces, which is a method for avoiding naming conflicts when more than one XML language is used in the same instance. Datatype declarations and namespaces were both added to DTDs as part of the

Document Schema Definition Languages (DSDL).[6] However, no developer of XML software has ever showed an interest in implementing these aspects of DSDL.[7]

The W3C XML Schema language has come in for criticism due to its verboseness and its lack of human readability. But, at this stage, it is well established and well supported by XML software. Further, the schemata of many data-centric applications are not primarily intended for human consumption but for machine-to-machine communication, thus human readability is not paramount. For such applications, software-generated graphical views of XML Schemas are generally sufficient for the end user.

RELAX NG

Whereas the use of XML Schemas is currently best practice for data-centric applications, best practice for narrative-centered applications is far less clear. The main contender, RELAX NG (which stands for REgular LAnguage for XML Next Generation and is pronounced "relaxing") is widely regarded as technically superior to DTDs. It can do almost everything that DTDs can do (apart from defining entities and notations), almost everything that XML Schemas can do (apart from defining its own data types) and quite a few things that XML Schemas cannot do. What is more, RELAX NG schemas are easy to read, easy to write, and easy to extend. They can represent more powerful content models than can DTDs and, unlike the latter, they support namespaces.

However, RELAX NG has not yet displaced the DTD in some domains, for example, the publishing industry. This is due to a combination of reasons. Because RELAX NG is not a W3C standard, it has not received the same level of support as XML Schema. Tool support, although growing, is not yet adequate for some industries to consider its use. There is also the issue of legacy data and whether the advantages of RELAX NG constitute a good enough reason for a potentially costly migration.

Using More Than One Schema Language

The validation of XML documents is too diverse to rely on a single schema language across all domains. It is likely that the medium term future will see the use of a range of schema languages, particularly XML Schema, RELAX NG, DTDs, each potentially in combination with Schematron.[8] Increasingly, applications do not rely on one document model to provide all the information necessary for validation. For example, DTDs may provide the tag set but additional rules about how these tags may be used is enforced via another schema language, such as Schematron, or via a traditional programming language

such as Perl, JavaScript, XSLT, Python, Java, C#, C++, or Ruby.

Table 5 lists some sample XML languages of particular interest to the Library and Information Science community, along with their normative, or definitive, schema form and any other schemas available. The trend of using one schema language to produce the normative version of a schema and then auto-generating other versions from it is likely to increase. For example, both JATS and Encoded Archival Description [ref EAD entry] are available in DTD, XML Schema, and RELAX NG versions. In both cases, the DTD is the normative form.

It is interesting to note that, although the DTD was the original schema language for many applications, the normative version is now often in an alternative schema language. For example, the master version of the Text Encoding Initiative (TEI) [ref TEI entry] is now in ODD (One Document Does it all) format. This may be compiled into schemas in DTD, W3C XML Schema, or RELAX NG format as required. Rahtz[9] summarizes the position of the competing schemas in TEI (as of August 2014) as follows: "Periodically, the TEI Technical Council asks itself "do we need to maintain TEI DTDs any more? doesn't everyone use RELAX NG or W3C Schema now?." The answer is (usually) always "yes, we do, some people have DTD technology embedded in their workflow."

Tables 6 and 7, respectively, summarize the advantages and disadvantages of DTDs.

Table 6   Advantages of the DTD.

A simple, mature, robust, well-tested standard
An integral part of the XML recommendation, so wide tool support
Includes entity definition (not available in RELAX NG and XML Schema)
Supports widely used practices in industries such as publishing
Easy to author and maintain
Most appropriate for narrative documents, particularly those with considerable mixed content
Designed for human consumption; easy to read
Good support for validation of element and attribute structures
Easily modularized
Considerable legacy data exists

Table 7   Disadvantages of the DTD.

Non-XML syntax
No data typing for element content
Limited data typing for attribute content
No *implemented* support for namespaces
No support for newer features of XML (i.e., constraining the number of element occurrences)
Some common grammatical expressions are not easily expressible

CONCLUSION

The DTD schema defines the structure and, to a limited extent, the content of conforming XML documents. At the turn of the twenty-first century, it appeared that DTDs would soon be obsolete, to be imminently superseded by W3C XML Schema and RELAX NG. However, this did not happen. The move away from DTDs has been significant, particularly for data-centric applications, where the W3C XML Schema language has all but won the day. But the move has not been universal. Although alternative schemas may now be made available for many document-centric XML applications, this does not mean that users are actually employing them. In the medium term, it is likely that DTDs will come to be regarded as a legacy technology in many domains. But, in some industries, the DTD will continue to be widely used for some time to come.

ACKNOWLEDGMENTS

Thanks to Deborah Aleyne Lapeyre (Mulberry Technologies) for her meticulous proofreading and helpful advice. Thanks also to B. Tommie Usdin (Mulberry Technologies, Inc.) and Bruce D. Rosenblum (Inera Inc.) for their insightful comments.

REFERENCES

1. W3C XML Schema, http://www.w3.org/XML/Schema (accessed August 2014).

2. RELAX NG, http://relaxng.org/ (accessed August 2014).

3. Ogbuji, U. XML design principles for form and function, IBM developerWorks, March 4, 2004, http://www.ibm.com/developerworks/library/x-eleatt/ (accessed August 2014).

4. ANSI/NISO Z39.96–2012 JATS, Journal Article Tag Suite (JATS), http://jats.nlm.nih.gov/ (accessed August 2014).

5. Harold, E.R. Structure. In *Effective XML: 50 Specific Ways to Improve your XML*; Addison Wesley Professional: Boston, MA, 2003; 59–154.

6. ISO/IEC 19757-9:2008: Information technology—Document schema definition languages (DSDL)—Part 9: namespace and datatype declaration in Document Type Definitions (DTDs), http://www.iso.org/iso/catalogue_detail.htm?csnumber=41009 (accessed August 2014).

7. Brown, A. Personal communication, August 2014.

8. Schematron. http://www.schematron.com/ (accessed August 2014).

9. Rahtz, S. *TEI and paramterized DTDs*, tei-l@listserv.brown.edu Archive, 3 August 2014.

BIBLIOGRAPHY

1. Goldberg, K.H. *XML: Visual QuickStart Guide*, 2nd Ed.; Peachpit Press/Pearson Education: Boston, MA, 2008.

2. The XML FAQ. http://xml.silmaril.ie/faq.html (accessed August 2014).

3. XML 1.0 Syntax Quick Reference, http://www.mulberrytech.com/quickref/XMLquickref.pdf (accessed August 2014).

Dublin Core Metadata Initiative (DCMI): A Personal History

Stuart L. Weibel
Office of Research and Special Projects, OCLC Research, Dublin, Ohio, U.S.A.

Abstract

This entry is a personal remembrance of the emergence and evolution of the Dublin Core Metadata Initiative from its inception in a 1994 invitational workshop to its current state as an international open standards community. It describes the context of resource description in the early days of the World Wide Web, and discusses both social and technical engineering brought to bear on its development. Notable in this development is the international character of the workshop and conference series, and the diverse spectrum of expertise from many countries that contributed to the effort. The Dublin Core began as a consensus-driven community that elaborated a set of resource description principles that served a broad spectrum of users and applications. The result has been an architecture for metadata that informs most Web-based resource description efforts. Equally important, the Dublin Core has become the leading community of expertise, practice, and discovery that continues to explore the borders between the ideal and the practical in the description of digital information assets.

IN THE BEGINNING

In 1994, Internet search engines were virtually unknown, "resource description" meant library catalogers in technical services departments, and the idea of harvesting and indexing billions of pages of electronic resources was too fantastic for most people to contemplate. Information assets, if they were cataloged at all, were described using a collection of library content and format standards known as MARC, and even the description of traditional paper resources was typically backlogged in overburdened cataloging departments.

Web-scale harvesting and indexing has long since carried the burden of open online search, but many electronic resources (e.g., images, services, or applications) have no suitable harvestable surrogates. Metadata—information about other information resources—is intended to fill this gap, providing explicit descriptions to support many administrative, commercial, and management needs. Governments use metadata to connect legislative mandates and citizens, and target services to those who need them. Electronic commerce requires metadata to match search queries with products. Publishers need metadata to create product catalogs and manage rights. Corporations use metadata to organize and integrate documentation, business processes, reporting requirements, and products. Thus, descriptive metadata remains a key aspect of resource management, on the open Web as well in organizational intranets. As the importance of images grows in online media, so too does the metadata that describes such images. Normally-sighted people need image metadata to search for images. For the visually impaired, an image without a description is worse than no image at all—an unfulfilled promise of inaccessible content.

As the Web exploded on our desktops, it was evident that MARC of electronic resources would be too complex and costly, and might not be suitable for many electronic resources in any case. Might there be a simpler alternative for describing Web assets that does not require the experience of expert catalogers?

That was the question posed over coffee between sessions at the Second International World Wide Web meeting in Chicago in October of 1994. Joseph Hardin, Yuri Rubinski, Eric Miller, Stuart Weibel, and Terry Noreault were bemoaning the fact that it was difficult to find a given item among the nearly 500,000 addressable resources on the World Wide Web (never mind how many single sites of that size there are now). Joseph Hardin was leader of the software development team at the National Center for Super Computer Applications (NCSA) that developed Mosaic, the first cross-platform Web browser. The late Yuri Rubinski founded SoftQuad, and is credited with popularizing SGML, the precursor to XML. Terry Noreault was then director of the OCLC (Online Computer Library Center) Office of Research, and Eric and I were colleagues in the Office of Research. Why not convene a group to look at the question systematically? Eric Miller and I spent the next few months organizing such a meeting, driven by the timeline of the next Web conference to be held the following April in Darmstadt, Germany.

THE OCLC–NCSA METADATA WORKSHOP

The OCLC and NCSA (the National Center for Super Computer Applications at the University of Illinois) cosponsored this first meeting. We invited people from

Encyclopedia of Library and Information Sciences, Fourth Edition DOI: 10.1081/E-ELIS4-120043530

Document–Engineering

three general categories: content specialists, Internet technologists, and librarians (later we thought of these groups affectionately as the "freaks, the geeks, and the people with sensible shoes"). Fifty-two people attended that first two and a half day workshop in March of 1995. We started with the notion of "document-like object (DLOs)" on the Web—something familiar to give us a mental image without being too precise about what we might want to describe. This vagueness was comforting in our early, unbounded expectations, but sometimes confounded later efforts to bring description standards to bear in actual applications. We stopped talking much about *DLOs* and often struggled with the differences among Web resources and how they should be characterized to enhance their discoverability.

What we hoped to do was to characterize conventions for resource description—to give people (authors, Web site managers, content providers) a set of common descriptive metadata elements for describing electronic assets on the Web. We hoped that a relatively simple set of descriptors could be widely applied so the task of traversing silos of information would become easier on the Web than it has been in the physical world.

Dublin, Ohio, (OCLC's headquarters, and location for the first workshop), gave us the name for the original set of 13 metadata elements—attributes of our document-like-objects that would help others locate and categorize them. We called this set of elements the "Dublin Core" or simply "DC" for short. Our objective, naïve in some respects, was to balance practicality and complexity, aiming for descriptions that untrained users might construct reliably, and which would make resources more findable. We created something that had some traction in the loose, fast-moving community of the early Web, something that attracted consensus from content specialists, Web technologists, and librarians. Bottom-up consensus building was, and remains, an essential attribute of what evolved into the Dublin Core Metadata Initiative (DCMI).

The name of the element set, in addition to reflecting its geographic patrimony, captures the notion that DC is a starting place (a core). It has always been an expectation that DC would be a kernel around which other metadata would grow. That first meeting generated basic principles that continue to guide DC development: Elements would be:

- Intrinsic (describe one thing)
- Extensible (modular, easily expanded)
- Syntax Independent (keep syntax and semantics separate)
- Optional (use only the elements you need)
- Repeatable (as many instances of a given attribute as appropriate)
- Modifiable (element "refinements" could be used to sharpen descriptions)

We wrote up the report,[1] and published a synopsis in the first issue of *DLib Magazine*.[2] Eric and I felt like we'd launched something of interest, but neither of us knew what to do next. We hoped a path would reveal itself, and in fact it did, in the person of Lorcan Dempsey, then leader of the United Kingdom Office of Library Networking (UKOLN) in Bath, United Kingdom.

THE WARWICK METADATA WORKSHOP[3]

Lorcan suggested we might extend the reach of the original effort through a follow-on event in the United Kingdom. Thus did our one-off effort acquire a trajectory. The University of Warwick had a perfect conference venue for the sort of meeting we envisioned: good meeting rooms, all accommodations onsite, and a great bar that stayed open late.

Each of the early workshops had a tight-wire feel about it, a sense that what we were doing was fragile, and to emerge from a workshop without a major step forward would be fatal. The major result of the Warwick meeting was what came to be known as the "Warwick Framework,"[4] a conceptual architecture for metadata that recognized the requirement for modular, extensible metadata. The ideas articulated in the Warwick Framework helped us decide what should be part of the Dublin Core and what might be borrowed from metadata element sets designed by others. The infrastructure scarcely existed to support deployment in those days, but the idea survived the intervening years of change, slowly morphing into what we today refer to as "application profiles"—hybrid schemas comprised of elements drawn from some number of metadata sets.[5] These ideas hold up well in the current world of metadata, as long as the element sets can be declared within a common data model, a proviso that has been a sticking point for interoperability from the very beginning.

DC-3: OCLC–CNI WORKSHOP ON IMAGE DESCRIPTION[6]

At this point in 1996, we still didn't have a strong sense of where we were going. In fact the third "DC workshop" wasn't chartered as such at all. It was co-sponsored by the Coalition for Networked Information (CNI), one of the last major efforts of Paul Evan Peters prior to his untimely death. Eric Miller did most of the organizational work, building on our experiences with the first two DC workshops. We didn't announce it as part of the series, but the subtext of the meeting was basically: Can a simple DC element set be used effectively to describe images? The consensus of the group was yes, though there was a strong sense that the 13 elements needed to be augmented with two additions: "Rights" and "Description." We declared, somewhat belatedly, that this workshop was the third in the DC series.

The group felt fairly strongly that without the means to determine intellectual property rights (IPR) associated with an image, just finding it was inadequate. History tells us otherwise. The use of the "Rights" element remains marginal at best, largely because it is a difficult problem, with many infrastructural and legal dimensions that are not easily dealt with in a simple declarative metadata element. Nonetheless, it at least has provided for simple declarations about IPR, and a convenient hook for future deployment.

The "Description" element was brought into being because conferees felt that the "Subject" element did not encompass the notion of an image description sufficiently well, and that a separate element was necessary. One may argue such distinctions forever—I would probably resist this element more strongly today. It is easy enough to condense these two elements as "aboutness." But DC was then, and continues, to be a consensus activity: a roughly-right solution that attracts usage is to be preferred over perfection that never arrives.

At this point it was clear we had a workshop series on our hands, and the acronym DCMI—Dublin Core Metadata Initiative—came into use. One memorable moment, which reinforced this sense of impact, came at a metadata interoperability workshop held near Bonn, Germany, late in 1996.[7] I attended this small workshop to learn that a group in Osnabrück, Germany had launched a digital library effort that harvested metadata for mathematical preprints. Judith Plümer reported on work she and Roland Schwänzl had led using Dublin Core metadata. It was the first time I encountered people who had not been active in the DC effort, but had simply recognized it as something of use to them and deployed it. Roland later became an enthusiastic DCMI contributor until his death in 2004.

DC-4: SURFACING DOWN UNDER[8]

We certainly thought of ourselves as working on a problem of international scope, and we wanted the venues of the workshop series to reflect that. Australia was actively shaping a government metadata standard based on Dublin Core. Renato Iannella, then of the Distributed Systems Technology Centre in Brisbane, Australia and Warwick Cathro, of the National Library of Australia in Canberra, had attended the Warwick Workshop (DC-2, if you will), and were enthusiastic about broadening the geographic scope of the effort. The National Library of Australia offered to host the meeting. We wondered how we could manage to get people (especially public sector people, who rarely benefit from international travel support) to attend. Australia is a long way from both Europe and the Americas. But it is the "World-Wide Web," not the U.S. Web or the European Web, and we felt it was important to

reflect that global perspective in our efforts. This approach remains central to choosing locations for DC conferences, rotating venues among Europe, the Americas, and Asia.

We enlisted the support of the National Science Foundation, attracting small amounts of funding that we shared with applicants to help make their trips look (financially) more like domestic travel. No one got a free ride, but rather these funds helped to keep travel costs manageable. "DC-Down Under" helped consolidate the work that we'd done to date, and resulted, in part, in the first adoption of DC as a national information standard. This precedent continues today—adoption and localization. Australia was then, and continues to be, an important locale for the advancement of information description standards, and their hosting of DC-4 was a convincing testament to the international character of the effort.

Discussions at DC-4 raised the specter of "creeping elegance" within the community. We all want simple…but exactly the right degree of simple. The functional requirements differ from application to application and domain to domain. For the first time we tried to instantiate notions articulated in the Warwick Framework—modular and extensible metadata. The so-called "Canberra qualifiers" emerged—a first attempt to provide the extensibility that developers wanted to meet the local requirements in their applications. One may cavil about complexity and simplicity, and where the right balance lies, but that balance point is found in applications rather than theory.

Thus were element refinements born. We agreed that the basic fifteen "buckets" could be refined in order to sharpen the description. A date might be a date of publication, a date of copyright, a date of availability, or something else. It is permissible to refine or qualify the basic date field so as to make explicit the character of the instance.

But what if people use different refinements? The "dumb-down principle" emerged as (an unfortunately named) rule of thumb, decreeing that applications that lacked knowledge of a given refinement could simply ignore them. Some information may be lost, but the user will be no worse off than having had unrefined elements in the first place.

The "one to one principle" emerged in Canberra as well: in Erik Jul's paraphrase of Ranganathan: "to each resource, its [own] description." Why is this not obvious? Once again, the tension between alluring simplicity and tempting complexity arises. In the ideal world, all descriptions should be as discrete as their referents. "Stuart Weibel" is the author of this history, but his email address has nothing more than an accidental relationship to it. Still, I might want to have it in the document. Is it metadata? About what? Certainly not the document, though readers may find it handy to have it. It is metadata (contact information) pertaining to a "person," not an "information asset." "One to one," then, is a many-headed-snake, and it has bitten us often over the years.

There was one other advance at DC-4: the workshop T-shirt. Lynn Marko, of the University of Michigan, arrived with her husband, Ken, then of Ford Motor Company. Unfortunately, Ken's luggage didn't make it. We gave him a couple of T-shirts to tide him over. Ken repaid the kindness many times, sponsoring several future workshop T-shirts.

DATA MODELS: WHENCE THE DEVIL RESIDES

While it is useful to recount DCMI history in the rhythm of its annual workshops, a good deal of activity took place outside as well. Workshops begat working groups, tasked with specific objectives, and laden with sunset provisions (working groups were chartered with specific objectives and expired at the following conference). Among the most difficult of objectives was the evolution of a data model for the Dublin Core. No experience of my professional life has been as contentious as these meetings. They were so singularly disruptive that we changed the names of the working groups to protect the guilty and innocent alike. Initially we had a Data Model group, and later an Architecture group, and the name of the outcome evolved from data model to abstract model. (More on this topic follows).

The early DC workshops were about broad consensus, and they were fiery experiences. Those early "bun fights" revealed a pattern of rising expectations, followed by a rapid slide into a trough of contentious argumentation before we "bounced" to find a plateau of consensus that moved us forward. In Canberra we had to push beyond the surface of simple descriptive metadata to the rather more complicated underpinnings necessary to achieve interoperable metadata systems. This realization paralleled similar recognition elsewhere in the Web. Protocols were evolving, new standards, both formal and informal, were emerging. DC at this stage was far from a standard, but certainly there was recognition that it needed to be if it were to take root.

Somewhere in this interval, Bill Arms, then of the Coalition for National Research Initiatives (CNRI), arranged a meeting that would help jumpstart the formulation of the Resource Description Framework (RDF) working group at the World Wide Web Consortium (W3C). Political pressure to support filtering of content so as to avoid the inadvertent exposure of minors to pornography had led to something called PICS (Platform for Internet Content Selection). PICS was a bit of *ad hocery* born of expedience without great forethought, and did little but provide a sense that someone was at least working on the problem. Recognizing that PICS was a rather-too-specialized solution, W3C folks had it in mind to generalize it as a platform for formalized semantics—metadata. Tim Berners-Lee is credited with originating the notion of the Semantic Web, and RDF would become a key enabling technology to support it.

Jim Miller, then of the W3C, Dan Connolly, also and still of the W3C, Bill Arms, and myself met to discuss the idea of an open community working group to address the issue. I was there largely as a prospective consumer of the results (that is, as leader of a community that could both use such a technology and provide practical functional requirements). Thus began DCMI's tightly coupled relationship to the beginnings of the Semantic Web. Key DCMI participants have been intimately involved in Semantic Web activities in the W3C and the wider community since that time. Indeed, my colleague at OCLC, Eric Miller, would eventually move to the W3C and become the Semantic Web Lead.

THE UNFINISHED CACOPHONY: DC-5— HELSINKI AND THE FINNISH FINISH[9]

Early DC workshops were hosted by the players: the organizations and people with a stake in the effort. Juha Hakala of the National Library of Finland stepped to the line for DC-5, hosting the meeting in Helsinki. We stayed in a wonderful hotel on the waterfront, within easy striking distance of the herring boats and an urban architecture evocative of Tolstoy.

Resource Description Framework (RDF) was a hot topic in Helsinki, held high by some participants as the answer to the infrastructure impediments holding back metadata applications. Others grumbled, eyes narrowed with skepticism, concerned that RDF was immature and over-hyped. But everyone was eager to find solutions, and knots of conferees could be found huddled over laptops in the lobby at 2 A.M or with laptops open on restaurant tables sorting through problems of syntax and semantics. The stamina, good will, and collective work done at these workshops remain for me the epitome of professional dedication, as well as foundations of lifelong friendships.

As for elements and refinements, our slogan was the "Finnish finish..." the equivalent of the "Mission Accomplished" banner on the aircraft carrier of metadata. While it is true that no elements have been added since DC-2, and a number of element qualifiers were in use, there were yet plenty of arguments to be heard.

Among the DC geezers, people still talk of the tar ice cream served at the conference dinner in Helsinki...a crystalline, ice-white concoction that, paradoxically, evoked tar and freshness at once. The flavor of pine tar and peppered strawberries defines my memory of this great northern city. The T-shirt was great, too...we had a Dublin Core World Tour T-shirt with the element set in three languages on one side, and the stops and dates of the global tour on the other. The listing embodied at least three variant syntaxes for dates, and some of us imagined mischievous intent in Juha's grin. T-shirts, and now, too, a song. The workshop came to a close with a group sing-along, a characterization of workshop achievements superior in brevity and eloquence to the workshop report. I confess having been taken somewhat aback at this development. At a followup meeting soon after, I asked Roland Schwänzl, our German Mathematician-cum-metadata wonk..."Is this sort of thing common in Europe...a song of summary after a workshop?" Roland seemed surprised at my question..."Ja Ja!"

GROWING PAINS AND CONSOLIDATION: DC-6 (DC:DC)[10]

Our premature declaration of success from Helsinki was not long un-tattered. The DC Tour traveled next to the Library of Congress in Washington, D.C. The meeting included representatives of the INDECS project (a metadata activity focused on rights declarations), who felt we'd gotten a few things wrong. Of course, we had. The tension between INDECS and DC is classically a top-down/bottom-up conflict. DC evolved by consensus and the judgment of practitioners, INDECS by deductive inference. Each model has strengths, and each has weaknesses. To quote Marshall Rose:

> The distance between theory and practice is always smaller in theory, than in practice.

We had hopes of finding the means to bring the two efforts closer together, and I think both activities would have benefited. DC and INDECs supporters collaborated on a paper in an effort to promote this convergence,[11] but in the long run our differences were too great. One proposal motivated in part by this hope of consolidation, and in part by an ongoing recognition that simplification of the set would be a benefit in the long run, became known as the "secret agent proposal." The notion of consolidating Publisher, Contributor, and Creator into a single element ("Agent," or "Names" perhaps) was floated quietly among some DC participants. The idea never got to the point of serious open consideration, as there was strong opposition based on breaking legacy applications. This was perhaps the first time we were aware that DC *was* a legacy system. We weren't engaging in an intellectual exercise in resource description: people cared, and systems depended on stability. The outcome of this attempt at reconciliation was almost certainly impaired as well by a sense of hostile intent between the two camps. This was, I believe, an unfortunate interpretation of the very natural inclination to cling to one's own ideas. The clarity of hindsight leaves me with regret that we did not accomplish this simplification of model and application.

In this same vein, the RDF proponents lobbied hard to make this syntax the preferred encoding of DC metadata instances. There was strong pushback by others, who judged that simpler encodings (embedded HTML metatags for example) were being deprecated in favor of what they judged to be an over-elaborated and unproven technology that mere mortals found hard to grasp. The practitioners reined in the wild-eyed theoreticians with a "Now just hold on!" Those of us who believed in the value of RDF (I count myself among them) had to acknowledge that we weren't marching inexorably toward a single, coherent deployment strategy, but that various paths would persist, progressing at their own speeds, indefinitely. DCMI needed to support each of these paths. It still does.

Hindsight may be 20/20 vision, but I am still blind on this one. On the one hand, a single deployment path would have greatly simplified the onerous task of syntax support, and consolidated more effort around reference code. This would have been helpful (still would be, for all that). On the other hand, the Web teaches us that technology deployment in the early twenty-first century is riverine and decentralized. Attempts to channel and coerce are rarely successful. As I write this, nearly a decade later, RDF struggles on, seemingly gaining momentum, but the tools and techniques we expected to catch fire have mostly smoldered. Timing is everything, and we may have been ahead of the curve, or perhaps off in the weeds. The last chapters are yet unwritten.

The conference dinner for DC:DC was held in what was once the library for the Smithsonian Institution—a large and lovely hall in the Smithsonian's "castle," its first building. On the way into the dinner, there were Buddhist monks engaged in the composition of a sand Mandela. These meticulously wrought sand paintings take many hours on the part of several monks, and at the end, the visual esthetic, created as an act of prayer, is swept away. Standards creation is a bit like this, a kind of hopefulness that is inevitably short lived, but may nonetheless result in an abstraction of intent that reverberates in many ways through its practitioners and community.

That dinner was a great one, and fomented another workshop sing-along. I do not know all the details of its genesis, but I am given to understand that Diann Rusch-Feja and Godfrey Rust of the INDECS project were co-conspirators. The lyrics, sung to the tune of "Both Sides Now," were, as in Helsinki, a far more succinct summary of the workshop than any reports could have captured. I hope someone still has the lyrics.

THE BIG VOTE

The instability of consensus regarding qualifiers led to a formal voting procedure in 2000 that marked an inflection point for DCMI, creating for the first time a structured (if yet messy) procedure for decision-making. We subsequently borrowed governance methods where we could find them—the Internet Engineering Task Force (IETF), MARBI (the community that looks after the MARC standards), the W3C, and others. From these, we crafted procedures to make evident a commitment to open, public processes to manage the element sets in our care.

The DC Advisory Committee, made up of working group chairs and invited experts, agreed to vote on proposed qualifiers. The results of this vote comprised the first formal approval of terms beyond the basic 15, and what we learned in the process informed the next stage of formal procedures, which remain largely intact today. This vote, contentious though it was in certain respects, marks the maturing of the Dublin Core from a group of metadata enthusiasts to a formal standards community. The character of the meetings changed at about this time as well, evolving away from contentious passions to a more business-like collegiality.

DC-7 FRANKFURT

Die Deutsche Bibliothek hosted the next workshop in their splendid facility in Frankfurt, Germany in 1999. The tenor and scope of the workshops evolved towards a stronger educational and informational tone, leaving behind us the sense of "we'll-die-if-we-fail" and strengthening the recognition that DC had a strong foothold that wasn't going to evaporate. There were, of course, myriad details of contention and ambiguity that required attention. But the approach was workman-like and deliberate, with a confidence born of more stable ground beneath our feet.

DC-8, OTTAWA, AND LOM[12]

The following year we returned to North America for DC-8 at the National Library of Canada in Ottawa. One of the important developments that emerged at this meeting was a closer alignment between the Learning Object Metadata (LOM) community and the DC community. LOM embraces both descriptive metadata for resources, based on Dublin Core semantics, as well as a variety of other classes of metadata intended to support management and use of educational resources.

Unfortunately, the two initiatives evolved in different directions structurally, a problem that plagues the technical implementation of metadata to this day. In Ottawa, DCMI and LOM agreed on a Memorandum of Understanding that has helped to guide a slow process of convergence. One of the deliverables of that agreement remains an important articulation of common principles that should be useful to many communities: "Metadata Principles and Practicalities," co-a by principals of both initiatives.[13]

The enduring lesson of the long history between DCMI and LOM is that without a common underlying data model, sharing metadata becomes difficult, imprecise, and (perhaps most crippling) expensive. I've drawn an analogy elsewhere to the incompatibilities between railway gages.[14] Different underlying rail gages force the unpacking and reloading of cargo, whether bales of cotton or metadata. The lack of a common underlying metadata model remains, in my estimation, a major impediment to broad cross-disciplinary metadata interoperability.

DCMI COMES OF AGE

In 2001, the DCMI community transitioned from workshops to conferences. In addition to the working group meetings, we offered a tutorial track and a refereed conference paper track. The National Institute for Information (NII) in Tokyo hosted the meeting in their beautiful facility a short walk from the Imperial Palace. We marked this transition in the names of the conferences, using years to distinguish them. The transition from a standards creation activity to a standards maintenance activity was taking place as well, and much more of the effort involved sharing of practice, through tutorials, plenary lectures, conference papers, and poster sessions. The locations of the conferences, listed in Table 1, are testament to the ongoing commitment of DCMI to its international foundations.

Behind the public face of the Initiative, much work was still underway to strengthen the procedures necessary to support an evolving standard. We reorganized the structure and procedures of the initiative, to include:

- A Board of Trustees: distinguished representatives of sectors and regions with experience and commitment to the advancement of the Dublin Core, and metadata in general.
- The DCMI Directorate: administrative staff to manage the activities of the Initiative.
- A Usage Board: recognized experts in the field who would review and guide proposed additions or changes in the standard.
- An Affiliate Program: Institutional sponsors for DCMI in various countries around the world to promote and support DCMI activities.
- An Advisory Board: (successor to the original Advisory Committee) Working group chairs that have been involved in the evolution of DCMI and other invited experts who provide consultation and advice.

Table 1 The Dublin core conference series.

DC-2001	Tokyo, Japan
DC-2002	Florence, Italy
DC-2003	Seattle, WA, United States
DC-2004	Shanghai, China
DC-2005	Madrid, Spain
DC-2006	Colima, Mexico
DC-2007	Singapore
DC-2008	Berlin, Germany

Building an organizational structure for the initiative also exposed issues of ownership and sponsorship. OCLC generously paid most of DCMI's bills for more than the first decade of its evolution, but certainly never owned or directed its development. OCLC's role as host was a side effect of the organizational involvement of myself and Eric Miller and the willingness of OCLC management to support our efforts. Subsequently, the formal link between OCLC and DCMI has been (amicably) severed, DCMI having been established as a limited liability company under the auspices of the National Library of Singapore; DCMI's formal organizational structure now reflects what was always operationally true—a genuine operational independence befitting a community-based initiative.

As the need for managerial capacity evolved, Makx Dekkers and Tom Baker were enlisted as members of the DCMI Directorate. Tom had been an active contributor to DC since the second workshop, and has authored many papers and DCMI documents that are milestones of DC development. His knowledge of languages and linguistics have been particularly valuable. I have been privileged to have shared with him many wonderful brainstorming sessions about metadata. Two particularly memorable experiences—developing notions of metadata grammar atop a sunlit tower in Lucca, overlooking the Tuscan hills, and a middle of the night Japanese "onsen" (hot springs bath)—rank among the most pleasurable of work experiences. Makx, also a long time DC participant, brought to the initiative strong project managerial skills and experiences in the European standards world.

My own role in the Dublin Core began to decline during this period. Start-up and sustenance require different skill sets. Separating from guidance and management of DCMI was both difficult and right (for the Initiative and for myself). But surely surviving its founders is an important measure of success for any organization!

STANDARDIZATION STRATEGIES

For most countries and many large organizations, information management practices must be built around formal standards. Our approach was to transition DC from simpler to more formal efforts. We started with an IETF RFC (request for comments). The IETF route had two advantages: many of our anticipated adopters came from the Internet culture, and establishing an RFC was relatively simple. An informational RFC is little more than a public declaration of an approach, useful for informing others of what has been done and why it is the right thing to do. It requires a minimum of external review or persuasion. Publication of RFC 2413 in 1998[15] constituted the initial stake in the ground for standardization of DC metadata (this RFC was updated as RFC 5013 in 2007[16]).

Subsequently DCMI embarked upon standardization in the National Information Standards Organization (NISO)

in the United States. NISO approval was seen as a step to international standardization in ISO, as NISO is a U.S. organizational member of ISO. NISO standardization proved challenging, both because DCMI encountered political opposition in various quarters, and because we were the initial use case for a "fast-track" approval process intended to reduce the latency of standardization activities in a rapidly changing Web environment. Pat Harris, then director of NISO, skillfully negotiated the minefields, and helped DCMI achieve this important imprimatur, and DC metadata was standardized as ANSI/NISO Z39.85 in 2001. Once DC metadata became a NISO standard, ratification as ISO 15836 followed relatively easily.

THE DCMI ABSTRACT MODEL AND INTEROPERABILITY

As alluded to earlier, data modeling has from the start been problematic for DCMI. In pre-Web days, it was less important to have a formal model for metadata. MARC standards, for example, have never benefited from an underlying data model, and yet have enjoyed wide adoption and usefulness. As infrastructural boundaries between domains have dissolved in the universal solvent of Web protocols, the need for agreements about syntax and structure increased. While humans readily distinguish nuances of meaning and structure, machines do not.

The formal emergence of a data model for DC took a decade. The final breakthrough was spearheaded by Andy Powell and Mikael Nilsson, following on Tom Baker's exposition of DC grammar[17] (and a decade of vociferous argumentation from many quarters). The DCMI Abstract Model (DCAM)[18] abstracts the basic metadata entities used in DC metadata and specifies their expression in RDF.

Sharing metadata requires agreements on a variety of levels. Some of the salient issues:

- What is the meaning conveyed in metadata assertions? Meaning, of course, resides in the minds of people, not machines. The focus of the Dublin Core was initially on promoting common meanings and making them sharable on the Web.
- How are metadata assertions packed so that one machine can send them to another without changing their meaning?
- How can metadata be structured so as to assure consistent and unambiguous interpretation? Reliable syntax encoding requires consistent data structures. The sorts of things that must be specified in a well-structured metadata assertion include:
  — The boundaries of a set of assertions (what constitutes a record)
  — Cardinality: can an element be repeated, and if so, is there a limit on the number of repetitions?

— How is a name structured? What is the delimiter separating elements of a compound name ("Prince" and "Bono" excepted, most names are compound structures, many with surprising and confounding complexity).

— At what granularity are descriptions associated with resources? How is nesting managed for hierarchical resources?

— How are dates encoded? YYYY-MM-DD? DD-MM-YYYY? MM-DD-YYYY?

— How does one identify an encoding scheme that specifies the above question?

— How are character encodings declared?

— How does one identify a value-encoding scheme (e.g., LCSH, MeSH, Dewey...) from which metadata values can be chosen? Are such schemes required or optional?

— Are metadata values specified by reference (URI) or by value (literal strings)?

It is in these details that the success or failure of interoperability is written; understanding and declaration of these details remains incomplete.

Current thinking among DCMI metadata architects suggests it is useful to distinguish four levels of interoperability, each characterized by a set of choices, costs, and benefits:[19]

Level 1: Informal interoperability: A vocabulary of concepts expressed in natural languages that support sharing of meaning among people. Metadata terms can be described as informally interoperable with Dublin Core if their natural language representations can be mapped to the 15 legacy DC elements. There is no requirement for DCAM conformance, and values for metadata are expressed as human-readable strings. Prospects for machine-to-machine interoperability at this level are low.

Level 2: Semantic interoperability: Metadata that can be accurately and completely expressed using RDF formalisms, but which is not conformant with additional structures elaborated in the DCAM.

Level 3: Syntactic interoperability based on the DCMI abstract model: RDF-compatible metadata that conforms to all elements of the DCAM (in particular, "bounded descriptions"—a collection of metadata assertions bound together and identified as what is thought of as a "record" in traditional bibliographic practice).

Level 4: Singapore Framework Interoperability: Conformance to a complete specification of functional requirements, a domain model, and description set profile.[20]

Levels 1 and 2 roughly define the divide between human-sharable and machine-processable metadata strategies of the first decade of DC's existence. Level 3 promises a higher level of interoperability through conformance to abstract metadata structures that are defined in the DCAM (in particular, bounded records which can be identified using URIs). The benefits of these additional structures accrue to managing and validating metadata collections.

If Level 4 seems vague, it is perhaps a reflection of yet-poorly understood requirements for bringing together large aggregations of heterogeneously managed metadata collections. This remains an area of active exploration.

At this writing, metadata modeling experts do not agree on the finality of the DCAM, or its general usefulness for all metadata. It is currently the closest approximation of a generalized data model for metadata in a Web environment, and is one of the most important contributions of the Dublin Core to the larger metadata community, the result of many years of grappling with a difficult problem.

SUMMARY

The protocols and standards that underpin our digital lives are, in the long term, as ephemeral as the sand mandelas of the monks. The understanding that emerges from their creation, however, is part of a more persistent trajectory. The Dublin Core marks its 15th year in 2009, arising and co-evolving with the Web itself. The conference series remains the preeminent venue for defining and deploying structured description on the Web. Its practitioners are found in 50 or more countries, and its descriptions are quietly at work in applications that serve literally billions of people over a range of domains that includes the latest media formats, government publications, scientific data, Internet syndication feeds, image collections, and many more.

The architecture and details of DCMI metadata have evolved over its lifetime. Its practitioners have labored together in meetings in 30 countries or more. Notable venues for DC events include the rolling hills of Kataminga, outside Melbourne, Australia (the first DC-Education meeting), the magnificent National Museum of Art in Canada (DC-8 conference dinner, Ottawa), the splendid conference hall in the National Institute for Information in Tokyo (DC-2001), the Shanghai Library (DC-2004) and perhaps most spectacular of all, the Hall of the 500 in the Palazzo Vecchio in Florence (DC-2002 conference dinner). The privilege of working and socializing in such places (and so many others, too numerous to mention), have left rich imprints on participants and the work alike.

The principles and practices elaborated in DCMI reverberate throughout the metadata community and provide a useful framework for metadata now and into the future. That this is so is a credit to the many people who have contributed their time, their expertise, and their passion to its evolution. These efforts are an important and lasting contribution to the digital future.

Document–Engineering

REFERENCES

1. Weibel, S.; Godby, J.; Miller, E.; Daniel, R. 1995; OCLC/ NCSA Metadata Workshop Report. Available at http:// dublincore.org/workshops/dc1/report.shtml.
2. Weibel, S. Metadata: The foundations of resource description. *D-Lib Magazine*, July 1995. Available at http://www. dlib.org/dlib/July95/07weibel.html.
3. Dempsey, L.; Weibel, S.L. The Warwick metadata workshop: A framework for the deployment of resource description. *D-Lib Magazine*, July/August 1996. ISSN 1082-9873. Available at http://www.dlib.org/dlib/july96/07weibel. html.
4. Lagoze, C. The Warwick framework: A container architecture for diverse sets of metadata. *D-Lib Magazine*, July/ August 1996. ISSN 1082-9873. Available at http://www. dlib.org/dlib/july96/lagoze/07lagoze.html.
5. Heery, R.; Patel, M. Application profiles: Mixing and matching metadata schemas. Ariadne. September 25, 2000. Available at http://www.ariadne.ac.uk/issue25/app-profiles/.
6. Weibel, S.; Miller, E. Image description on the Internet: A summary of the CNI/OCLC image metadata workshop. *D-Lib Magazine*, January 1997. ISSN 1082-9873. Available at http://www.dlib.org/dlib/january97/oclc/01weibel.html.
7. Metadata and interoperability GMD (The second DELOS workshop). Bonn, Germany, October 7–8, 1996. Available at http://www.iei.pi.cnr.it/ErcimDL/second-DELOS-workshop/hall.html.
8. Weibel, S.; Iannella, R.; Cathro, W. The 4th Dublin core metadata workshop report. *D-Lib Magazine*, June 1997. ISSN 1082-9873. Available at http://www.dlib.org/dlib/ june97/metadata/06weibel.html.
9. Weibel, S.; Hakala, J. DC-5: The Helsinki metadata workshop: A report on the workshop and subsequent developments. *D-Lib Magazine*, February 1998. ISSN 1082-9873. Available at http://www.dlib.org/dlib/february98/02weibel. html.
10. Weibel, S. The state of the Dublin core metadata initiative. *D-Lib Magazine*, April 5, 1999 (4). ISSN 1082-9873. http://www.dlib.org/dlib/april99/04weibel.html.
11. Bearman, D.; Miller, E.; Rust, G.; Trant, J.; Weibel, S. A common model to support interoperable metadata: Progress report on reconciling metadata requirements from the Dublin core and INDECS/DOI communities. *D-Lib Magazine*, January 5, 1999 (1). ISSN 1082-9873. Available at http://www.dlib.org/dlib/january99/bearman/01bearman .html.
12. Weibel, S.L.; Koch, T. The Dublin core metadata initiative: Mission, current activities, and future directions. *D-Lib Magazine*, December 6, 2000 (12). ISSN 1082-9873. http://www. dlib.org/dlib/december00/weibel/12weibel.html.
13. Duval, E.; Hodgins, W.; Sutton, S.; Weibel, S.L. Metadata principles and practicalities. *D-Lib Magazine*, April 8, 2002 (4). ISSN 1082-9873. Available at http://www.dlib. org/dlib/april02/weibel/04weibel.html.
14. Weibel, S.L. Border crossings: Reflections on a decade of metadata consensus building. *D-Lib Magazine*, July/ August 11, 1999 (7/8). ISSN 1082-9873. Available at http://www.dlib.org/dlib/july05/weibel/07weibel.htm.
15. Weibel, S.; Kunze, J.; Lagoze, C.; Wolf, M. Dublin core metadata for resource discovery. IETF Informational Request for Comments: 2413, September 1998. Available at http://www.ietf.org/rfc/rfc2413.txt.
16. Kunze, J.; Baker, T. The Dublin core metadata element set. IETF Informational Request for Comments: 5013, August 2007. Available at http://www.ietf.org/rfc/rfc5013.txt.
17. Baker, T. A grammar of Dublin core. *D-Lib Magazine*, October 6, 2000 (10). ISSN 1082-9873. Available at http://www.dlib.org/dlib/october00/baker/10baker.html.
18. Powell, A.; Nilsson, M.; Naeve, A.; Johnston, P.; Baker, T. DCMI abstract model. 6 DCMI Web site. Available at http://dublincore.org/documents/2007/06/04/abstract-model/.
19. Nilsson, M.; Baker, T.; Johnston, P. DCMI architecture wiki: Interoperability levels. DCMI architecture working group wiki. Available at http://dublincore.org/architecturewiki/InteroperabilityLevels.
20. Nilsson, M.; Baker, T.; Johnston, P. The Singapore framework for Dublin core application profiles. January 2008. 14 DCMI Web site, Available at http://dublincore.org/ documents/singapore-framework/.

Economics Literature: History *[ELIS Classic]*

Arthur H. Cole
Laurence J. Kipp
Harvard University, Cambridge, Massachusetts, U.S.A.

Abstract
One of the objectives of the information disciplines is to study the universe of recorded information—that is, to study the documentary products of domains of human activity—and to come to understand such bodies of literature as social and historical phenomena in and of themselves. Cole and Kipp describe the development of the literature—including periodicals—of economics from the Renaissance to the twentieth century. The development of economic theory and understanding is discussed in relation to the development of the literature of the field.

—ELIS Classic, from 1972

INTRODUCTION

This survey aims to consider the printed materials dealing with economic and business activities in Western Europe and the United States, with some reference to publications emanating elsewhere. It seems appropriate to handle all economic and business printed literature as a single whole, for when the entirety of this literature is examined, one finds no clearly marked dividing lines. All items can be regarded as falling in a spectrum, extending perhaps from a mathematical formulation of international trade to a flyer in Canadian uranium stocks. The differences are notable at the extremes, but there are no sharp breaks in the succession of types.

Nearly all economic and business literature is purposeful, intended by its authors to be of use in modifying public policies, improving business performance, informing the youth or the general public, and providing other than amusement or aesthetic enjoyment. This review of economic and business literature, therefore, seeks to determine how it has served its purposes. It is also necessary to determine whether the materials for the formation of public policies has changed over the centuries. If so, how and when? More in some countries than in others? It is also pertinent to inquire whether economic theorizing has improved over the centuries, i.e., can economists be said now to think better than those of 100 or of 200 years ago? And do economist and businessmen think differently from their predecessors of 1850 or 1750? If so, in what ways? and as result of what forces?

Concepts are slippery things and seem often to have gotten into the literature only with difficulty. This study of economic and business literature, therefore, attempts to reflect the process and the timing whereby and when concepts important in this area were introduced into printed form, repeated in other printed items, and incorporated into libraries where the policy makers or the research members of their staffs could gain access to them and use them.

The centuries since Gutenberg seem divisible, as far as economic and business literature is concerned, into four periods of somewhat variant length—one lasting until the latter half of the seventeenth century, another extending thence until the closing years of the eighteenth, a third from then until about 1880, and a fourth extending to the present. These are set off by more than one phenomenon in all cases, and the dividing dates become rather fuzzy. However, the periods have distinctive characteristics.

HISTORY

The First Period

The first period was one of mixed movements, extending from the invention of printing with movable type to the latter decades of the seventeenth century. Within it, there was an extension of themes from preprinting days; there were new themes that failed to persist, as if lacking in pertinence; and there were other new themes that gained the strength to spill over into subsequent periods.

The publications of the earlier portion of this period, and to some extent throughout it, reflect considerations or controversies of pre-Gutenberg days. There were the treatises and tracts pertaining to usury and incunabula, such as the booklet by Consobrinus, and as late as 1634 John Braxton's *Usury Condemned*. Books on agriculture also kept appearing all through these centuries—and of course have never ceased appearing. The classical writers on agriculture were frequently reprinted in the early decades of printing: *Scriptores Rei Rusticae*, among the incunabula; the collection called *Geoponica* somewhat later; plus

Encyclopedia of Library and Information Sciences, Fourth Edition DOI: 10.1081/E-ELIS4-120008984

Document—Engineering

individual Latin authors, often also in translation, rather thickly down through the middle of the sixteenth century. Overlapping with them and continuing later were the books by such authors as Estienne, Heresbach, Markham, and Tusser.

There was a third type of continuing item: compilations and treatises upon commercial law. They appear in the fifteenth century and continue like the books on agriculture. In some measure there was change here over time. For example, the "Consulate of the Sea" type of compilation reaches back into pre-Gutenberg days, but they became infrequent after about the middle of the sixteenth century. And then there is the case of Malynes. His *Consuetudo, vel, Lex Mercatoria*, the leading English specimen of its genus, first published in 1622, went through a growth that seems to mirror the changing business world. By 1656, appendices had been added in which the exchange of money by bills was "anatomized," and the "ordering and keeping" of merchants' accounts were explained. Knowledge of the law was apparently moving over to give place to knowledge of business practices.

In these decades, there were some literary occurrences that stirred no immediate continuing developments. One is the Malynes-Misselden debate over the effects of the exchange rates. Their contentious pamphlets flew back and forth in the early 1620s and then everyone appears to have forgotten about the matter. There was a considerable number of items pertaining to money in the sixteenth century, including Jean Bodin's famous *Apologie*, but then little was published again until the eighteenth century. Finally, one may note the tracts of the Levellers, especially Gerrard Winstanley, in the Commonwealth period, expounding communistic ideas that were not to become common for another couple of centuries.

On the other hand, some novel developments may be recorded. One is the rise of the controversial pamphlet related to secular affairs. This was something new in the world. The outpouring was much the greatest in England. The names of Sir Dudley Digges, Thomas Mun, and many others will occur to students of the history of economic thought. There were some comparable items of Continental origin, such as those of Laffemas in France or of Pieter de la Court in Holland. On the whole, however, the Continent remained an inhospitable area for publications of this type, even to the end of our next time period, the close of the eighteenth century, except for the Netherlands and Sweden. With all due allowance for these countries, England provided the richest and most productive soil for this form of literature.

The period also brings the first calls to make money. The oldest book on retail selling, William Scott's *Essay of Drapery* (1635) seems to take a stand with one foot in the Middle Ages and one in the modern world. As early as 1558, Roger Bieston had been willing to argue that money was "a necessary mean to mayntayne a vertuous quiet lyfe" in his *Bayte and Snare of Fortune*. Gervase Markham

thought it advantageous—presumably in keeping with the spirit of the times—to label a book on agriculture practices *A Way to Get Wealth* in 1625. So uninhibited had the sponsors of wealth seeking become by 1684 that a volume with the gay title of *The Pleasant Art of Money Catching* could be published.

There were also the first publications of types that have since blossomed luxuriantly. One may note two subvarieties of manuals: one with a geographical and another with a technical base. The former type existed as early as the fourteenth century. There were specialized printed specimens devoted to the moneys of various regions, appearing as early as 1530 in Antwerp, and in Vienna in 1563 (which had progressed to being a reckoning book). Books of broader coverage were soon to be issued: one in 1576 out of London, which gave data on "the most famous cities in Europe," their "trade and traficke," "their coynes and the places of their mynts," to be followed half a century later (1638) by Lewes Roberts' famous *Merchants Mappe of Commerce*. This extensive folio manual went through at least four editions, the last appearing in 1700.

The other subvariety includes books of arithmetic and ready reckoning, compounded particularly for the use of merchants, the expositions of bookkeeping such as Ympyn's *Nieuwe Instructie* published in Antwerp in 1543, together with volumes of applied science, which may perhaps be considered to begin with Schopper's illustrated book on mechanical arts, printed in Frankfurt in 1574.

A second general type of literature with a modern flavor is that stimulated or issued by individual companies. John Wheeler wrote his *Treatise of Commerce* (1601) in support of the Company of Merchant Adventurers; Sir Dudley Digges addressed his *Defence of Trade* (1615) to the governor of the East India Company; and Thomas Mun composed his *Discourse of Trade* (1621) in defense of that Company. Before 1680, quite a flock of pamphlets had been printed about enterprises from the "West-Indische Compaignie" of Holland to the "Company of Royal Adventurers of England Trading into Africa." Sometime in the 1650s, if not indeed earlier, such enterprises commenced to issue material on their own initiative, e.g., *The Advantages of the Kingdome of England* from the operations of the "Fellowship of the Merchant's-Adventurers of England" (c. 1650), which looks very much like a "public relations" piece or minutes of meetings of the general court of the English East India Company.

Despite these new sorts of items and despite the issue and reissue of divers books on agriculture, the general impression of the literature of this whole period is that of discontinuity and some naivete.

The Second Period

The second period was characterized by enhanced continuity, by the beginnings of measurement, and by the development of integration—a period extending from the late seventeenth to the late eighteenth century.

The "continuity" is evident on various sides. The effort of the Parisian Académie des Sciences to prepare and issue its *Description des arts et métiers* is a case in point. The original idea was broached as early as the 1660s, it recurred fitfully in the next few decades, a more formal start was made in the 1730s, and the volumes appeared from the 1760s to 1788. The successive editions of Savary's *Parfait négotiant* from 1675 to 1763, of Ricard's *Traité générale de commerce* from 1706 to a fifth edition in 1732, or of Thomas Mortimer's *Every Man His Own Broker*, first published in 1761 and reaching its twelfth edition in 1798, yield the same picture—there was a persistent interest in the particular line of thought. Publishing houses were increasing within the economic and business field.

However, institutional connection was not essential. Continuity begins now to be more clearly apparent in the evolution of economic thought. Some such condition is evident in English mercantilist thought, especially after Mun; but it takes a more creative turn on the Continent. In France, there was the development of speculative ideas in Boisguilbert, Cantillon, Quesnay, and Dupont de Nemours, resulting in the advent of an informal group that promoted discussions and supported journals of communications. In Germany, one can find a persistent growth of cameralistic thought, beginning actually a little earlier than physiocratic ideas or preliminary notions, namely, with the publication of Becher's *Politische Discurs* in 1668. Here, evolution took the road leading into administration and education. Officials of Austria and the German states were intimately connected with the development. And Hermann Conring (1606–1681), Gottfried Achenwall (1719–1772), and many other professors gave lectures that by and large were presentations of economic data relevant to public administration. This concentration of economic thought, teaching, and governmental activity persisted into the nineteenth century.

Continuity in the area of business communication presents a curiuos but intriguing picture. During the seventeenth and eighteenth centuries, merchants dominated the business communities of all countries; and merchants have always been interested in changes in commodity prices, movements of ships, and alterations in the course of exchange rates in about that order of declining values. A natural evolution in instrumentalities, once the volume and diversity of business required more than the partial picture conveyed by private letters from agents and correspondents, was that an entrepreneur would set up a reporting agency to serve a given community. Thus began *Oram's New York Price Current and Marine Register* (1798–1804) and *Ming's New York Price Current* (1805–1813, 1815–1817), which would be displaced in time by a newspaper of broader coverage—in this New York case, by the *Shipping and Commercial List and New York Price Current*, which in fact ran continuously (with only one minor change in title) from 1815 to 1861.[1] At other places, a mercantile journal carried current commodity price quotations as a regular portion of its news; this "prices current" section was reprinted on a flyer, sometimes with a merchant's name added as a running head, and merchants distributed copies of these prices–currents to their correspondents.

Neither of these sequences occurred in the Netherlands and in England. In the one case, printed lists of commodity prices began to appear in the first years of the seventeenth century. They were soon compiled under regulations of the city and may have been printed by various booksellers for distribution. They continued to be issued up into the first part of the nineteenth century, and no general commercial journal seems to have blossomed on this stem. In the case of England, supposedly the "land of shopkeepers," the story is one of unexpected deficiencies. Some privately printed merchants' price lists appeared in 1670 and thereafter, but only intermittently until the first decades of the succeeding century. The only periodical that carried such price data seems to have been John Houghton's *Collection of Letters for the Improvement of Husbandry and Trade*, which ran from 1692 till 1703. For 30 years or so after 1715, there appears to have been no public or semipublic commodity price reporting; then perhaps some specializing sheets; and not until 1775 and the launching of Prince's *London Price–Current* can one grasp commodity price reporting that persisted into modern times in some form, if under various aspects.[2]

In the meantime, to be sure, there had come periodicals that reported on financial affairs and on shipping: the semiweekly called *The Course of the Exchange* begun by John Castaing at almost the peak of the South Sea speculation, specifically in 1719, but carried on by him and his successors continuously ever since; and *Lloyd's List*, which, starting in 1734, gave news of ship movements, share prices, and some general matters of commerce.

The eighteenth century has been referred to as the "era of political arithmetic," and surely measurement became a more widely recognized desideratum. Doubtless, Sir William Petty should be canonized as the patron saint of modern economics. Writing of his "Method," he stated that, "instead of using only comparative and superlative Words, and intellectual Arguments," he had taken the course of expressing himself "in terms of Number, Weight, or Measure." It is the creative ideas that are important: that in economic affairs, one might emulate the practices of the natural scientist; and from measurements one might derive apparent uniformities in economic life. Already John Graunt had seized upon London's "bills of mortality"—perhaps the only good result of the plague—and had laid the first bricks in demographic studies and actuarial science. Graunt was followed by Halley, de Moivre, Price, and a continuing band of students and writers in England; and by an equally notable, if not really superior chain of successors on the Continent.

Document—Engineering

Other seventeenth and eighteenth century English writers in various fields of economics adopted the Petty approach. Arthur Young wrote a *Political Arithmetic* of his own, devoted largely to agricultural problems of his times. There was a new stress on "experience" and "experiments," as in William Harte's *Essays on Husbandry* (1764). In the meantime, too, the British government had seemingly become infected. Governmental reports began to be issued, often largely statistical in character, on the course of trade, the activities of the East India Company, public finance, and the like. These reports were generally irregular, but they laid the basis for the series that in 1801 began as the Parliamentary Papers.

In other countries, the zeal for measurement burned with variant brightness. In France, the impact appears not to have been great in this period though Vauban, Deparcieux, and few others were influenced. On the other hand, "political arithmetic" appears to have been quite congenial to cameralism. Johann Peter Süssmilch (1708–1767) became an exponent of the "method" in his own right. His *Göttliche Ordnung*, published in 1742, was noteworthy for its contributions to the study of what came to be called "vital statistics." His contemporary, Gottfried Achenwall, was the first person to use the term "statistics." Actually the word then signified general description of economic phenomena, not specifically quantified measurements and statement.

The notion of a census of population has been traced back to Bodin and Montchrétien. And certain censuses of population were taken in the eighteenth century: Sweden from the middle of the century onward; Austria in 1753, 1762, and 1777; not to mention certain Canadian provinces even in the seventeenth century. However, in Europe, population data were not broadly published until the nineteenth century; military rivalry was too severe.

The evolution of syntheses seems a third feature of this period. One aspect of this trend was the compilation of dictionaries or collections of information on various subjects—not merely merchants' *vade mecums* such as Savary's and Ricard's but more specialized, topical affairs, such as the *London and Country Brewer* (1736), or Duhamel du Monceau's six volumes on fishes and fishing (1769–1782). The Germans were particularly given to such compilations. Another type can be represented by *Select Essays on Husbandry* printed in Edinburgh in 1767 or John Almon's *Collection of Tracts, on the Subjects of Taxing the British Colonies in America, and Regulating their Trade* published in 1773.

More noteworthy yet were the efforts of theorists Quesnay, Sir James Steuart, and particularly Adam Smith to describe or analyze economic systems. Professor Schumpeter speaks of "quasi-systems" in earlier times. By this Schumpeter seems to mean partial views of the whole economy, from which one may properly infer that their authors possessed quite surely a sound concept of the whole.[3] There can be less doubt of the physiocrats, Steuart, and the "father of political economy."

Smith's *Wealth of Nations* illustrates the importance of conceptualization. It has been said of Smith's book that, like the American Constitution, there is little that is original in it, and what is original isn't very good. However, Schumpeter—curiously reluctant to see virtue in "A. Smith"—does assert:

> We know that the skeleton of Smith's analysis hails from the scholastics and the natural-law philosophers...They had worked out all the elements of such a scheme, and Smith was no doubt equal to the task of co-ordinating them without further help from anyone.[3]

The leading features of this period may be embraced under the general term "increased sophistication." The developments of the decades after 1660 reveal a level of thought hitherto unattained in the economic and business field. Other phenomena lend support to this contention. One is the awakening of a historical sense, at least in this field of thought and publication.

The eighteenth century is noteworthy for the increase in number and the extension in variety of historical studies. Interest in coinage of the past was very early evoked (e.g., in Occo's survey of Roman coins, published first in 1579). However, much more substantial works in this area were produced two centuries later (e.g., those of Leake and Snelling in England). And now appeared also such items as Madox's *History and Antiquities of the Exchequer of the Kings of England* (1711), Raynal's famous *Histoire philosophique et politique des établissements & du commerce des Européens dans les deux Indes (1770)*, even such a piece of business history as Henning Calvör's *Historische Nachricht von der Unter und Gesamten Ober Harzischen Bergwerke* (1765). Also not to be overlooked is the launching of effort in the area of price history—surely a "sophisticated" realm [e.g., Bishop Fleetwood's innovating volume entitled *Chronicon Preciosum: or, An Account of English Money, the Price of Corn, and Other Commodities, for the Last 600 Years* (1707)].

Data of a somewhat different sort are supplied by the reprintings of earlier materials. Among those were John Smith's *Chronicon Rusticum-Commerciale; or, Memoirs of Wool* (1747) and Robert Vansittart's *Certain Ancient Tracts Concerning the Management of Landed Property Reprinted* (1767). The tracts were reproduced, not primarily because they would presumably be of utility in practical affairs, but seemingly because they were interesting in themselves; the wisdom of earlier times should not be forgotten, even if not immediately applicable to contemporary problems.

The increased sophistication, the rise of a historical sense, and the power of cameralistic thinking were responsible for another important development: the creation of bibliographies of economic literature. According to Kenneth E. Carpenter:

The first bibliography of economics was J. B. von Rohr's *Compendieuse Hausshaltungs Bibliotheck* (first ed., 1716). For each of the subjects covered—"Cammeralwesen", agriculture, commerce, mining, etc.—Rohr provides a kind of encyclopedia article, with comments on books, which are in most of the languages of western Europe. Rohr disclaims any attempt at completeness, but as a classified bibliography, it is perhaps still useful for some purposes.

In his *Hausshaltungs Bibliotheck*, Rohr added his voice to that of numerous advocates of university chairs of Cameralism. The first in Europe was founded at Halle in 1727, and others in Germany soon followed. It is probably to this early recognition of economics as an academic subject that we owe a long series of German bibliograhies.[4]

Carpenter identifies other bibliographies of the period:

Two unusual and very definitely usable items are J.J. Moser's *Bibliothec von Oeconomischen-Cameral-Policey-Handlungs-Manufactur-Mechanischen und Bergwercks Gesetzen, Schrifften und Kleinen Abhandlungen* (1758) and J.H.L. Bergius' *Cameralism Bibliothek* (1762). They are essentially indexes to periodicals and laws and can make available much detailed information.

These were published "prior to the work which has generally been considered the first bibliography of economic literature—the 34-page 'Catalogue d'une bibliothèque d'économie politique formée pour le travail du nouveau dictionnaire de commerce' in Mollet's *Prospectus d'un nouveau dictionnaire de commerce* (Paris, 1769)."[4]

However, lest the element of sophistication be overemphasized, Professor Edwin F. Gay made a considerable reputation for himself by controverting statistically certain allegations of sixteenth century writers on the extent of the contemporary enclosures; and Professor Brebner has remarked that economic history writing of these centuries should generally be examined with much care; much of it was compounded to prove a case of some sort or another.

The use of earlier materials and of libraries was limited. One of the first notes about economic and business literature is contained in John Houghton's *Husbandry and Trade Improved* (1728).[5] He lists what looks like 35 titles: something like 20 in Latin, of which 6 or 8 are reproductions of classical authors; 2 in Italian; 3 or 4 about trees; 2 or 3 about fishes; 1 about gardens; and More's *Utopia*.

It is recognized that the *Wealth of Nations* was not composed with a wealth of citations. It had not become the prevailing practice among scholars of Smith's time to acknowledge sources, but it is significant that in Smith's collection of books and pamphlets aggregating approximately 1600 items, there are scarcely 150 that could be labeled economic.[6]

In the case of David Ricardo, there was apparently slight interest in predecessors. Despite Smith and Malthus and a few others, writers in the field were not generally learned.

Any impression that all proceeded smoothly in the evolution of economic and business literature is erroneous. Generally, the most advanced thinkers of given periods are taken to represent those decades. This, of course, is not a satisfactory procedure if one is interested in this literature as a vehicle of the formation of public opinion and public policy. Some attention to the irregularities or bulges from any trend line is justified. There was the Cromwellian period in England, with its enhancement of volume and its manifestation of new idea through its John Lilburne, Gerrard Winstanley, Henry Parker, Henry Robinson, Thomas Violet, William Potter, and others. There was also the peculiarly interesting period between Robert Murray's *Corporation Credit* (1682) and the early years of the next century. The volume of economic writing expanded now, especially in the 1690s, and particularly with the first sizeable crop of anonymous pamphlets, but it is also interesting how many writers of note from Nicholas Barbon to John Briscoe, and from Daniel Defoe to Sir Humphrey Mackworth fall into these decades.

In the meanwhile, cameralistic writings had flourished rather extraordinarily in greater Austria, if one may use that term. After Becher came his brother-in-law, Philipp Wilhelm von Hörnigk, with his *Oesterreich über Alles, wenn es nur will*, which went through 13 editions in the course of a century; Wilhelm von Schröder's *Fürstliche Schatz- und Rentkammer*, which enjoyed 6 editions between 1686 and 1752; and scores of lesser writers. There was also the especially interesting phenomenon of Paul Jacob Marperger (1656–1730). Perhaps he should be recorded as the first full-time economist; some 90 separate publications may be credited to him, running literally into thousands of pages. He did not really rise to the level of theory, yet Marperger did not publish trash. He represents at least a bulge from any general trend line, greater than that produced by Defoe, or earlier Samuel Hartlib or Gervase Markham.

A bulge of a different type centers in the South Sea and Mississippi Bubbles. This movement may be measured in the numbers of items recorded in the Kress Library printed catalog which lists 524 titles published in the years 1720 and 1721, compared with 128 in the years 1719 and 1722.

In Holland, this "bulge" seems to have flooded Amsterdam with scores of satirical prints. Several plays and several poems were also prepared relative to the speculation in shares. These and other documents pertaining to actual company ventures were gathered up and issued as a warning in a thick folio volume entitled *Het Groote Tafereel der Dwaashied* (or "The Great Mirror of Foolishness").

Similar deluges were to accompany later periods of excitement: the controversy of England with her colonies in America; in France, the problems of the new government after 1789, especially those of currency, taxes, and the disposition of the lands of the Church and nobility; shortly thereafter in England and Ireland, the question of union between the two islands; and later still the "bullion controversy."

The Third Period

The third period, from the late eighteenth to the late nineteenth century, was marked by the efflorescence of printed matter and by the very considerable spread of organization within the business world.

Professor Innis has posited a hypothesis that media of communication succeed one another as the arteries of business are lengthened geographically and the pulse of business quickens. Oral communication was feasible when merchants could make frequent journeys in promotion of their enterprises, although each journey might run into months. As a second stage, correspondents kept in touch with their principals by letter. This latter system must have been quite unsatisfactory and could not function adequately in such a trade as that which New York, Salem, and other American towns initiated with China after 1790.

The long period of wars between 1790 and 1815, with the uncertainties and changing demands that war always brings, seems to have stirred all segments of Western societies to cast aside the slow, private means of communication, to seek by political means an increase in the volume of governmental publication and to stimulate, by means of subscription payments to venturesome entrepreneurs, the expansion of commercial vehicles.

The British Parliamentary Papers began to be issued regularly in 1801; by the 1840s, 50 folio tomes were required, and by the 1880s, 90–100. The publication activity of the U.S. government kept close pace with that of the British. Regularity was imparted to the *Congressional Documents* only with the Fifteenth Congress (1819–1820), but many statistical and other materials were printed as individual *Documents* in the preceding 30 years.

In Canada, a documentary series of the Dominion began in 1841 and one of the province of Quebec in 1869. France and Germany have contented themselves with the publication of the reports of Enquêtes and Ausschusses and with that of special series, e.g., the French *Catalogue* and successive reports on inventions from 1791 onward or its *Tableaux généraux du commerce* in 1818 and later years.

A considerable proportion of this governmental activity may be attributed to the desire for measurement that arose in the late seventeenth century. The United States was a leader in statistical developments. The census of population of 1790 was the earliest to be published; in 1810 and 1820 the federal government made some effort to secure data on manufacturing facilities as well as population; and the reports on manufactures in the 1850, 1860, and 1880 censuses were more extensive than any elsewhere in the world.

Some of the American states became active in collecting data on population and in other lines: New York and Massachusetts, manufactures; Maine, ownership of bank stocks; and the like. There was the famous (if not too thorough) survey of manufactures and their likelihood of growth made by Hamilton, the better inquiry made by McLane in 1833, useful reports on various industries that accompanied the censuses of 1860, and 1880, and essays on such topics as coal measures or movement of tobacco accompanying that of the later date. The annual statistical reports, such as those on commerce and navigation (regularized in 1820), and some special reports such as that of I. DeW. Andrews on the commerce of the Great Lakes, or on internal commerce of the country (1876–1891), produced notably useful data.

Quantitative reports also appeared in such periodicals as Niles's *Weekly Register, Hazard's Register of Pennsylvania, DeBow's Review*, and Hunt's *Merchants' Magazine*. Two other private statistical publications not seen duplicated in any other country for some decades appeared: Benton and Barry's *Statistical View of the Number of Sheep* [in northwestern United States]; *And an account of the Principal Woolen Manufactures in said States* (1837); and the other is William H. Sumner's *Statistics of the Woollen Manufactories of the United States* (1845). But the major private efforts come a bit later with the quantitative reporting of the *Commercial and Financial Chronicle*, including its annual *Investors' Supplement* volume of many years after 1875, and *Poor's Manual of Railroads*, of which a historical volume appeared in 1860 and regular annual ones after 1868.

In Europe (probably with the exception of Germany over the last decade or two of the period), the developments were less pervasive and somewhat more scholarly. There were published censuses of population, as in England in 1802 (and later decades), Sweden 1811, etc., but no industrial or agricultural censuses. Europe's principal contributions fell elsewhere.

"Statistical" activity in the sense of descriptive economics there was, and especially noteworthy examples pertain to agriculture in the British Isles, perhaps attributable to the influence of Arthur Young. The agricultural surveys of English, Scottish, and Irish counties were made between 1790 and 1815 or thereabouts. Those related to the British countries were prepared under the auspices of the semiofficial Board of Agriculture and Internal Improvement, some of them composed by Arthur Young. They number nearly 90 and were published between 1793 and 1800. Another series ran to more than 60 volumes and appeared between 1804 and 1815. Between 1801 and 1812, the Royal Dublin Society published surveys of 21 Irish counties (three others being published later: 1824, 1832, and 1833) with the slightly variant titles of a "general view of the agriculture and manufactures" of a given county, or "statistical observations" of the same.

More important was another contribution, namely, what Funkhouser describes as "the gradual merging of political arithmetic and the theory of probabilities in the science of statistics." Funkhouser traces the evolution of probability theory back to Pascal and Fermat working in the middle of the seventeenth century and notes that de Moivre discovered the formula for the normal probability curve in 1733, that J.B.J. Fourier drew the curve in 1821, and that de Morgan first made published use of the curve in 1838.[7]

There was a third contribution from Europe: new organizations in the field of statistics. The Statistischer Verein for the Kingdom of Saxony began publishing in 1831, the London Statistical Society was founded as early as 1825 and was publishing its own *Journal* in 1837, and the corresponding Dublin society followed somewhat later (1855). Shortly after the middle of the century, specifically in 1853, a series of International Statistical Congresses were launched, largely as a result of the initiative of Adolphe Quetelet, that until 1876 convened pretty regularly in alternate years in some European city. Their proceedings were published.

Another aspect of the increasing quantity of literature is the marked growth of periodicals. Before this period, journals that could be called professional were few and short-lived, although the *Leipziger Sammlungen von Wirtschafftlichen-policey-cammer-und finantz-sachen* was published from 1744 to 1761 and the *Ephémérides du citoyen*, published in Paris and carrying the discussion of the physiocrats, was maintained from 1765 to 1772 and from 1774 to 1776 under the title *Nouvelles éphémérides economiques*. A German endeavor to sustain publication of similar materials, issued under the title *Ephemeriden der Menschheit*, carried action along to 1782. If we look on the *Journal économique* (1751–1772) and the *Gazette d'agriculture, commerce, arts et finances* (1776–1781) as in part supplementing the *Ephémérides*, it is obvious that professional publications did flourish for a quarter of a century in France's *ancien regime*.

Thereafter came a considerable hiatus. The *Journal of the London Statistical Society* was one of the first items in the new crop: the semiprofessional *Journal des économiques* and London *Economist* were launched in the early 1840s, the publication activity of the American Social Science Association started in the middle 1860s, Conrad's *Jahrbücher für Nationalokonimie und Statistik* began in 1863, and the *Jahrbuch für Gesetzgebung, Verwaltung und Rechtspflege* (which later became *Schmoller's Jahrbuch*) in 1877. However, organized professional publication in the English-speaking world had by and large to wait until the decade of the 1880s and later years.

One phenomenon in the 1785–1885 century marked that century as at least quantitatively unique: the reprinting of earlier materials. The Italians provided the startling example. Beginning in 1803 and continuing through 1816, they produced an amazing 50 volumes that they entitled *Scrittori classici italiani di economia politica*. A sequence of reprinting and translation efforts which took place after 1850 produced five more series with 71 volumes. Between 1840 and 1848, a *Collection des principaux économistes* was published in France, running to 16 volumes, whereas in England, McCulloch edited a half-dozen volumes of "early" or "scarce and valuable" tracts on "economical" subjects. A German, Reinhold Pauli, unearthed and published *Drei volkwirtschaftliche Denkschriften aus der Zeit Heinrichs VIII* in 1878. The background was being laid for professional economics.

Carpenter has pointed out that "not until the nineteenth century is well along does one find bibliographies compiled by historians for historians." He then identifies several landmark bibliographies. The first general bibliography of economic literature of this period is John Ramsey McCulloch's *The Literature of Political Economy: a Classified Catalogue* (1845), based on his own library.

The first attempt at a comprehensive historical bibliography of a nation's economists was Manual Colmeiro's *Biblioteca de los economistas españoles de los siglos XVI, XVII, XVIII* (1880), [while] Luigi Cossa's *Saggi bibliografici di economia politica* (1891–1990, reprinted 1963) made a good start at doing for Italian economic literature what Colmeiro did for Spanish.[4]

In these same decades, the volume of business publication increased rapidly in the United Sates to cover a great geographical spread and the lack of any predominant city as in England or France. The start came in the form of prices currents, but not long thereafter arose journals of wider characters, such as the *General Shipping and Commercial List* at New York, soon the *Shipping and Commercial List and Price-Current* (from 1815 onward), the New York *Journal of Commerce* (1827 onward), even the *New Orleans Price Current* (1822 onward) despite its name. These were followed by specializing periodicals: the *American Railroad Journal* and *Advocate of Internal Improvements* (1832–1838 and succeeded by organs of somewhat similar titles); the *Banker's Magazine* (founded in 1846); before the Civil War, a number of peculiarly American aids to the businessman, banknote detectors; but also journals that pertained to mining, iron manufacture, and shoes and leather, beyond Hunt's *Merchants' Magazine*, already cited.

Activity in England was much more limited and still less considerable on the Continent. England did have agricultural journals, Herepath's and other railway periodicals, a *Mining Journal and Commercial Gazette* that began in 1835, and a *Bankers' Magazine* that started 2 years prior to the American one of similar name. Perhaps the localization of merchants in specific regions in London— Mark Lane, Mincing Lane, etc.—was adequate for much communication; and mercantile newsrooms may have helped. Perhaps commodity bourses on the Continent served similar purposes.

For the most part, a single agricultural journal served England; but the United States had a journal for nearly every region: the *New England Farmer* (1822 onward); the *New York Farmer* (after 1828); the *Southern Farmer* and the *Prairie Farmer* (launched in 1840 and 1841, respectively); and others.

Two developments in the decades between 1780 and 1880 were of great magnitude: the rapid expansion of materials published by new organizations and the increase in the international flow of ideas.

Note has already been made of the East India Company, the Board of Agriculture and Internal Improvement, and the like. The number of such organizations was greater in the United States than in any other country. Societies for the promotion of agriculture were soon joined by those devoted to the promotion of manufacturing and the "useful arts." There were the private corporations (turnpike, canal, and railroad, particularly) that sought to keep in touch with their stockholders and with customers. By 1880 the volume of publications produced by American railroads was already considerable: not only annual reports, but indentures, leases, and other financial documents; freight tariffs; timetables; advertisements of lands for sale; even occasional public relations pieces. There were the periodicals stimulated by private enterprise, and there were publications flowing from trade associations, chambers of commerce, stock exchanges, labor unions, credit reporting agencies, and other bodies.

A start in company histories had been made in the decades before 1780, but the period between that date and 1880 witnessed a significant expansion of output. Occasionally, these documents arose from conditions of distress, as when Caleb Eddy wrote a sketch of the Middlesex Canal in 1846, when the enterprise was suffering from competition of the Boston and Lowell Railroad. Usually, they were sponsored—at least blessed—by individual firms as a tribute to their successful existence over a substantial period of years. Such were Ludwig Wachler's *Geschichte des ersten Jahr-hunderts der Königlichen Eisenhütten-werke in Malapane* (1851) or Henry Domett's *Bank of New York* (1884). Historical accounts prepared by competent scholars who endeavored to write objectively were yet to appear.

Somewhat the same can be said of businessmen's biographies and autobiographies which were usually efforts at praise or self-justification. Such were Stephen Simpson's *Biography of Stephen Girard* (1832) or Bethel Henry Strousberg's document, *Dr. Strousberg und sein Wirken* (1876). There was quite a rash of such biographies in France: biographies of Laffitte (1884), several on the Rothschilds (1846, 1847, 1868, and 1869), François de Wendel (1851), Casimir Périer (1858), and a dozen others. The flow diminished after 1870 and has never really

increased much in later decades. Businessmen's biographies have never amounted to much in England; they were infrequent in the United States before 1890. An interesting number of collected biographies, written generally in a popular vein, did appear; e.g., Smiles's lives of George Stephenson (1868) or Boulton and Watt (1865), and the collection entitled *Men of Invention and Industry* (1884) in England; Otto Spamer's *Buch berühmter Kaufleute* (two series, 1868 and 1869); and Freeman Hunt's *Lives of American Merchants* (1858) in America. Perhaps again the ground was being laid for higher grade performances later.

The international movement of ideas and materials had been indicated by the acceptance by German scholars of Petty's "political arithmetic," or the Italian translation and publication of works of non-Italian authors. However, movement in the nineteenth century appears to have been much enhanced. Relative to Swedish economic development of that century, e.g., Professor Heckscher stated that "perhaps the most fundamental change of all was the tremendous increase in the international exchange of scientific and technological information."[8]

There had been occasional translations of economic and business items in the earlier centuries, especially the eighteenth: Garzoni's *Piazza universale* (1st Italian, 1585; German edition, 1619); Savary's *Parfait négociant* (1st French, 1675; German, 1676); Savary des Bruslons' *Dictionnaire universal de commerce* (1st French, 1723–1730; English, 1751–1755; Italian, 1770–1771); Mandeville's *Fable of the Bees* (1st English, 1714; French, 1740); or Arthur Young's *Political Arithmetic* (1st English, 1774; French, 1775). Such movement was slow, with more international movement of items at the business end of the spectrum than at the economics end.

Adam Smith was important in helping to break down international barriers. Steuart's *Inquiry into the Principles of Political Economy* (1767), to be sure, was translated into the German promptly, appearing in 1769–1770. Smith's contacts were closer to France, at the time a more advanced country than Germany. Smith brought a foreign body of thought into English economic thinking for the first time in history. His *Wealth of Nations* was especially welcome in France. Before the end of the century, nine editions had been published in French, and editions had appeared in the United States, Ireland, Italy, Germany, Switzerland, Spain, France, Denmark, and the Netherlands. Excerpts appeared in Sweden in 1799 and a translation appeared in Russia in 1802–1806. Ricardo seems not to have been influenced by non-English ideas, but communication did increase more or less steadily in the decades between 1780 and 1880.

One vehicle of that communication was the international congress, which not only provided for verbal exchanges of ideas during its sessions but also left behind published proceedings or other documents. There was a "Congrès des économistes" in 1847, one on "réformes douanières" in 1856, one on "propriété littéraire et artistique" in 1859, meetings of the International Association for Social Progress in 1862–1865, an International Commercial Convention in 1868, and a series on "Sunday rest" beginning in 1876.

Another vehicle of communication among countries was the international exhibition. Elkanah Watson was the "father" of our agricultural fairs, which were initiated in 1810. Customarily, a report of some sort was issued covering the awards. Fairs are alleged to have been organized earlier, but little is known about them. Quite surely they produced no published residuum. One held in France in 1798, organized by M. de Neufchateau and devoted to French industrial productions, did yield a report, drafted by M. Chaptal. And there was a succession of such exhibits until the eleventh in 1849.

The Grand Exhibition of 1851 in London in the Crystal Palace was truly international in scope and set the pattern for Philadelphia in 1876 and Chicago in 1893. These gatherings with their displays of machinery and products did much to promote industrial communication and left behind a considerable literature in the reports of judges and in the findings of delegations from foreign countries. Documents published on Philadelphia's Centennial Exposition of 1876 ran to more than 20 volumes.

Two features of the decades between 1780 and 1880 pertain to quality of output. One might be construed as a development from "political arithmetic," the graphic presentation of statistical data. The innovator was William Playfair, who in 1786 published his *Commercial and Political Atlas*, which was followed in 1801 by his *Statistical Breviary*. In these and other works of Playfair, one finds several varieties of diagram: line, bar, and pie.

The employment of diagrams expanded rather slowly, however, and their popularity came more in France than in their country of origin. Playfair's first book was translated into French, where it appeared under the title of *Tableaux d'arithmétique linéaire*, almost as if it were a study in method rather than a "commercial and political atlas" of England. Quetelet and other French vital statisticians made use of graphs and so did the French government engineers having to do with public works and with transportation. C.J. Minard composed the first memoir on the graphic method in 1861, and E.J. Marey composed a notable text on *La Méthode graphique* 1878. Funkhouser calls the period from 1860 to 1890 "the golden age of graphics...marked by the unrestrained enthusiasm, not only of statisticians, but of government and municipal authorities."[7]

The other qualitative change in the 1780–1880 period is that of economic thought. What Adam Smith had started, the generation of Ricardo, Malthus, James Mill, and Jean-Baptiste Say advanced further. As Professor Rogin put it, "Ever since the advent of economic science as a separate academic discipline there has existed an impulse to model it in the alleged image of an exact natural science and thus to evade both the intractability of history and disagreement as to values." From the physiocrats and Smith came the competitive equilibrium; and this provided the basis of abstract elaboration of principles in the nineteenth century, especially the roles of the different factors of production.[9] Already in the first quarter of the century, Say was complaining of his contemporary, Ricardo, that the latter was "drawing all his results from a small number of principles, putting or leaving aside all others." He thought his case to be all the stronger because he believed Ricardo through his method "arrived at results different from the real state of the case."[10] Also it may be significant that in the generation after Ricardo and James Mill, economists began to be concerned with their own procedures. John Stuart Mill published in 1843 his *Logic* in which he exposed "the methods of physical sciences as the proper models for the political"; John Elliot Cairnes wrote his *Character and Logical Method of Political Economy* in 1857; meanwhile, the "historical school" in Germany had begun its creative response to the intellectual methods of the English proponents of political economy; and as late as 1891, John Neville Keynes, the father of John Maynard, issued a well-received volume on the *Scope and Method* of his subject. And in the 1870s and 1880s appeared the first substantial group of histories of economic thought—books that, unlike Blanqui's of 1842, dealt almost wholly with the abstractions and concepts that had sprung up in the preceding century.

These changes in the intellectual apparatus of economists apparatus of economists indicated an enhanced sophistication. In the eighteenth century and earlier, political economy had been largely a set of rather specific rules, not very broadly entertained, all more or less slanted toward spelling out the roles that individuals could play in the promotion of a richer, somehow better economy. In the nineteenth century, more and more came the increased regard for imponderable, impersonal forces—maximization of profits, the interest rate, demand and supply, etc.—with at least an implied dichotomy between political and business economy. By reason of the change in the quality of political economy in the nineteenth century, a professional literature evolved within those decades—in the era, say, between David Hume and Alfred Marshall.

The Fourth Period

The final period, extending from about 1885 to the present, has been marked by a greatly increased volume of publication in the field, by enhanced professionalization in the ranks of economists, and by a revolution in the area of business administration and its literature.

The extraordinary enlargement of economic and business literature in the last century has resulted from the operation of many forces: the alterations in printing technology; the changes in the publishing world; growth in the field of communication commanded by governments;

increase in the number and variety of private organizations active in publication performance; and transformations of thought within both economics narrowly construed and business administration similarly viewed. There has also been a geographical expansion. Countries such as Canada, Australia, or Sweden were publishing relatively little in the field in the 1880s.

Publishing houses have contributed to the whole movement through their creative activities. Institutions, such as McGraw-Hill or Simmons-Boardman, were set up originally by innovating entrepreneurs. It was to the advantage of the publishing concerns to have more readers and the information they purveyed proved to be advantageous to the readers. Improved operations of business institutions, higher profits of the purchasers, meant in turn greater demand for the publisher's products. Beyond this, publishers were frequently creative by virtue of the missionary zeal for reform. Henry Varnum Poor waged almost continuous war against evils or in advocacy of reform while he was editor of the *American Railroad Journal*. The Simmons-Boardman Company promoted through its periodicals such improvements as standardized threads for bolts and nuts and standardized design for automatic coupling for railroad vehicles. The *American Journal of Mining* sponsored the American Bureau of Mines. This was good business for the economy as a whole, and it helped to swell persistently the volume of business literature.[11]

The change from laissez-faire to welfare government meant a tremendous increase in governmental production of literature concerned with economic and business affairs. Particularly pertinent is the conversion of occasional investigatory efforts into persisting regulatory ones, with a marked enhancement of literary output. Already this change had occurred in England relative to railroads. It came in the United States primarily after 1880. The Windom and Cullom Committees that inquired respecting railroads were followed by the Interstate Commerce Commission. The Aldrich Committee of 1891–1893 and the National Monetary Commission of 1909–1910 were succeeded by the Federal Reserve Board. In the end, the country possessed not merely these agencies of regulation but the Federal Trade Commission, the United States Tariff Commission, and numerous others equally well staffed and equally capable of issuing orders and regulations and special reports as well as the stock annual ones.

National governments have also become "service" states, assuming an obligation to provide freely, or at low cost, data essential or convenient for policy formation in agriculture and business, for public appraisal of economic and business affairs, etc. Such data are useful to various federal governmental agencies, but chiefly it has value to economists and businessmen scattered over the county. This is true of much work performed by the Bureau of Standards, the Department of Agriculture, and the Library of Congress. The American state governments have been equally active, or nearly so.

The enlargement of the flow of literature from private institutions has been particularly great in the United States. The decades since 1880 have witnessed notable increases in the number of trade associations, chambers of commerce, cooperatives, produce exchanges, and the like. But now international chambers of commerce, organizations of bondholders or taxpayers, and many other new institutions issue publications, especially periodicals or other serials.

Important with respect to volume and quality have been the new professional organizations and educational institutions. To the local statistical societies above noted were now added national economic and statistical associations in many countries: the Nationalekonomiska Föreningen (or Economic Society) launched in Sweden in 1877, the Royal Economic Society set up in England in 1888, the American counterpart founded the next year, down to the International Economic Association organized subsequent to World War II. In the field of business the launching of new institutions has been even more noteworthy, especially in the United States: the American Association of Public Accountants in 1887, the National Association of Credit Men in 1896, the Advertising Federation of America in 1905—and on down through the decades organizations of industrial advertisers and controllers, of sales executives and management engineers.

Schools of business have also manifested a capacity for publication. The area of business management possessed few established facts when the first schools of business were established. The Bureau of Business Research set up by the Harvard School and the Department of Industrial Research launched by the Wharton School were early responses to this situation.

Note should be taken of corporate research agencies, organized separate from governmental or educational institutions, and the financial foundations that have promoted research in the economic and business field. Both are largely the children of twentieth century United States. The research agencies have been varied in character. One early group (rather loosely organized) was devoted to the promotion of a series of studies in American economic history. The financial support came from the Carnegie Corporation of Washington, and the studies were published by it—of which the best known are Victor S. Clark's three volumes on our manufacturing industries and L.C. Gray's two volumes on Southern agriculture before 1860. Somewhat later came the International Committee on Price History, financed by the Rockefeller Foundation and constituted of representatives from several interested countries under the chairmanship of Sir William Beveridge. Institutions with centralized research staffs have arisen: the National Bureau of Economic Research, the Commonwealth Fund, and the like. Some are loosely connected with educational institutions as the Food Research Institute at Stanford or the Scripps Foundation for population research at Miami University.

Their publications bear the implied and sometimes the explicit indication that the specific item has been developed with aid from the whole body of scholars attached to the institution and perhaps issued only after criticism by another body of scholars. The day of the individual scholar has not passed, but such institutionalized research was unknown a half century earlier.

As for the financial foundations, all that one need note is that the funds supplied by the Rockefeller, Carnegie, Ford, and other such bodies have permitted and stimulated research and publication in a measure undreamed of prior to World War I. The impact has been largely in this country, but more recently moneys for these purposes have gone abroad from the same foundations.

Not only has the volume of economic and business literature expanded in an extraordinary degree, but the general complexion of that literature has undergone revolutionary changes.

In some measure, to be sure, there was persistence of trends, such as in the matter of continuity or accumulation. By the later decades of the nineteenth century, it had become an almost universal practice for writers in the economic and business field to consult previous writings. By the twentieth century, it had become a test of scholarly quality that a man remember whence he had borrowed significant ideas or important statements of fact. The growth of national libraries, such as the British Museum or The Library of Congress, and of university and large public libraries, comes chiefly in the past three quarters of the century, especially in the United States. Cumulation has been promoted by large bibliographical works such as Gregory's *Union List of Serials*, Stammhammer's bibliography of socialism and communism, or Daniel C. Haskell's "check-list" of early European railroad literature. Cumulation has also been fostered by service departments of national governments or private research organizations. Information is collected and hoarded in such governmental agencies as the American Bureau of Labor Statistics or Bureau of Agricultural Economics. It is also assembled and hoarded by organizations such as the National Bureau of Economic Research or the Brookings Institution. Now no one on its staff launching work on almost any historical theme need really "start from scratch."

There was also continuity from past eras in the persisting effort at measurement. The statistical work of governments increased, and there was marked enlargement of activities on the part of private organizations. Here again the United States has taken the lead with such reporting agencies as Dodge on building construction, Cram on automobile production, Dun & Bradstreet on business failures, or Dow-Jones on stock market movements. The measurements recorded by the quasi-private, quasi-public Federal Reserve Banks make the expansion of recent decades even more striking.

Changes in the character of economic and business literature since 1880 may also be pictured correctly as proceeding from tranquility to profound disturbance. Optimism, general agreement on principles, calmness of exposition—this was the economists' "era of good feeling." Something of this spilled over into the twentieth century in the writing of such an economist as Thomas Nixon Carver. In the meantime, business had settled into a belief in the necessity of learning only by doing; experience was not merely the "best," but really the only teacher.

Of course, troubles of various sorts were already brewing. Marx and Engels had formulated their "manifesto," and Marx was busy writing in the British Museum. More immediately important, Jevons, Walras, and Menger were introducing ideas of marginal utility. And still more unsettling, at least over the intermediate future, Walras was hatching his general equations, and with Pareto was introducing mathematics into the previously common-sense field of economic theory. In the same years, "practical" problems were causing controversy: bimetallism, the return of protectionism, social insurance, regulation of railroads, spread of labor unionism, and the like. The world of economics seemed to grow ever more complex.

Efforts to solve some of these problems gave encouragement to the advocates of measurement and to those who were moved to improve the science of statistics. On the whole, the protectionist-free trade controversy and that surrounding monetary affairs did not lend themselves to much quantitative handling. The field of social insurance was also somewhat infertile in this regard. However, the governmental bureaus charged with the supervision of railways in England and on the Continent collected statistical data with avidity. Some of the earliest treatises in the field, such as Gerstner's out of Austria or Audiganne's out of France, displayed a considerable bias toward quantification. And the Interstate Commerce Commission was issuing statistical volumes with its formation in 1887.

Sometimes a measurement-resisting subject would yield indirectly at least to quasi-statistical treatment in the hands of an intellectual innovator such as Professor Taussig who spoke of the "verification" of the theory of international trade under the "abnormal" conditions of dealings between a gold-standard and a paper- or silver-using country.

The study of business cycles represented most clearly the convergence of trends. Juglar demonstrated the existence of cycles in his examination of bank data from France and England (1860) in quantitative data. Subsequently, the tendency in the treatment of the subject—by Jevons in 1875, the American Frederick B. Hawley, Hull in his handling of building cost data, and preeminently Wesley C. Mitchell in his pathbreaking volume of 1913—was for an ever-increasing reliance on measurement. The literature concerned directly or indirectly with the business cycle would cover many running feet of library shelving, constituting a "bulge" from the trend line for this period.

Concurrently with the study of the business cycle had gone a considerable expansion in the exploration of population trends and of the associated field of actuarial science. International congresses, professional journals, a series of examinations for advanced standing, and the like have created a literature within a literature.

Not least important has been the development over the past few decades of statistical inference—with its literary products. The advances here have been linked closely with the name of R.A. Fisher of England, whose *Statistical Methods for Research Workers* (1925) and *Design for Experiments* (1935) led the way. Fisher asked what could be learned about a "universe" or aggregate from a sample out of it and whether a sample could be selected out of the universe that would display the characteristics of the whole, or characteristics with recognized deviations from the whole. Out of this line of thought has grown quality control in business, opinion research in business and elsewhere, and the like—with another sizeable addition to the volume of economic–business literature.

In the area of economic theory a noteworthy change has occurred—especially as far as the English-speaking world is concerned. In the preceding period, Cournot, Walras, and Pareto emphasized that the ideas of the theorists could be expressed clearly and precisely in mathematical language. Marshall, Edgeworth, Irving Fisher, and Pigou helped to introduced this language into England and the United States, whereas more recently still, the developments in this area and in statistics have coalesced to produce econometrics, and these three in turn, with the ideas on national income stemming from Keynes, to yield model building, linear programming, and the like. By a more direct route from the mathematical "fathers" has come Professor Leontief's input-output analysis and the work that this innovation has promoted.

Twentieth century bibliographies in this field, Carpenter states, "have been compiled [to] cover all the subjects generally falling under the heading economics, rather than just the writings of economists or the literature of public finance [with] a greater emphasis on the ephemeral literature."[4] Henry Higgs, setting himself the goal of listing books in all Western languages, produced the important *Bibliography of Economics, 1751–1775* (1935). Magdalene Humpert's *Bibliographic der Kamerelwissenschaften* followed in 1937 and a major French work, *Economie et population, les doctrines francaises avant 1800; bibliographie générale commentée*, was issued by the Institut national d'études démographiques in 1956. L.W. Hanson's *Contemporary Printed Sources for British and Irish Economic History, 1701–1750* (1963), reaches a new height in economic bibliographies, according to Carpenter.

Another significant aid to scholars is the *Catalogue of the Kress Library of Business and Economics at the Harvard Business School*, which has been issued in four volumes between 1940 and 1967.

A novel development of the era since the 1880s is the publication of "festschriften." Action of this sort suggests respect for the subject of the honor and a high appraisal of

the results of research. Such publications began to appear in Germany in the latter half of the nineteenth century, and the example was followed in Italy, Scandinavia, the Low Countries, the United States, and less so in France and England.

A second novelty was the publication of manuscript material. There had been printing of governmental materials for some time—national and local, administrative and legal—and some of the first publications in our field were so constituted, or were largely so, e.g., documents in Schmoller's study of the Strassburg cloth gild (1879), Hintze's compilation relative to the Prussian silk industry (3 vols., 1892), Hayem's *Mémoires et documents pour servir a l'histoire du commerce et de l'industrie en France* (12 series, 1911–1929), even Bland, Brown, and Tawney's *Select Documents* (1914). The publication of private papers has come chiefly through the printing of documents from the archives of such historic institutions as the East India Company and the Hudson's Bay Company.

Literature which pertains specifically to the operation of business institutions had in these decades since 1880 been going through no less extraordinary an experience. There had been manuals that told the merchants how things *are* done—what weights, what types of money, what procedures, and the like; and occasionally a manual as to how things *should* be done. In the latter category would fall the books that linked religion with business activities. As early as the sixteenth century, John Browne's *Merchants Avizo* (1588) had given instructions to young merchants going to Spain and Portugal. Soon there were the manuals of Savary and Kruse, of Malachy Postlethwayt and Wyndham Beawes, descriptions of what was done and sometimes advice on the best among several possible practices. Even in the nineteenth century, with Babbage and Freedly and others of the midcentury, there was very limited conceptualization of business functions.

A break appears to have come in the 1880s. We know that Henry Varnum Poor and some of the American railroad executives had had ideas relative to their industry as far back as the 1850s. A new, broader, more vigorous start came in the 1880s, largely through the American Society of Mechanical Engineers. From this background came Frederick M. Taylor and what in 1905 rose to be labeled "scientific management." In these years, too, books of a new character were beginning to appear in England. There was J. Slater Lewis' *Commercial Organization of Factories* (1896), F.G. Burton's *Commercial Management of Engineering Works* (1899), and somewhat later, E.J. Elbourne's *Factory Administration and Accounts* (1914). In general, the English approach was more largely accounting and commercial control than the American. In France, Faye was making a major contribution in his materials on the functional organization of business operations. And the Germans made at least an indirect contribution in the "line" and "staff" organization of their army.

These steps represented a forthright belief that generalizations, abstractions, perhaps "principles," were possible with respect to business structures and performances. The abstractions were those of business functions (marketing, production, finance, etc.), which tended to make all business institutions into an "extended kinship group," if not into one closely knit family.

In step with the changing climate of opinion in the business world, there was the initiation of specialized training in business at the college and university level: the Wharton School of Finance at Pennsylvania, the Amos Tuck School at Dartmouth, and that on Business Administration at Harvard—with a rapid increase in popularity at other universities in the years after World War I. And a specialized literature began to flourish. Mr. Arch W. Shaw had launched *System, Business*, and other publications in the field. Other publishers kept close pace and books of professional character began to appear: Hatfield's quasi-classic *Modern Accounting* (1909), P.T. Cherington's *Advertising as a Business Force* (1913), and a small flood of items on scientific management.

Business literature has flourished most luxuriantly in the United States. Germany has been a rather distant second, although vigorous in the theoretical phases of the field, with England, France, and other countries less involved. The general attitude in England has been that one could not learn business out of books.

In the United States, the growth of the literature has been notable for its increased sophistication and its changed time perspectives. Business literature reveals an increasing concern with the future. The introduction of budgeting, of market analysis, of employee training or executive development, etc., has turned businessmen's eyes increasingly toward the future; and a whole new stream of literature reflects this change. The field of business has also developed a sophisticated *historical* interest. Histories of individual business units and business functions had appeared intermittently over past centuries, but the conscious effort to create a new branch of historical study and writing relative to the operation of individual business enterprises may be regarded as a contribution of Dean Wallace B. Donham of the Harvard Business School (who brought Professor N.S.B. Gras to that institution to implement his ideas) and their imitators and admirers of that period. An almost contemporary development—seemingly independent—occurred in Germany under the inspiration of Professor Kurt Wiedenfield of Cologne.

A number of factors have encouraged the preparation of histories of companies: increasing longevity, which makes possible semicentennial or other anniversary volumes; an improved sense of public relations; sometimes the aroused curiosity of scholars; sometimes the letter of the tax laws, etc. Increasingly, at any rate, the flow of company histories has broadened and the quality risen. Nor is the enhancement in volume and quality restricted to merely the United States and Germany. By and large, England and France have lagged behind (except for histories of banking institutions in the former), but to their output must be added quite a flood from the Netherlands and Scandinavia.

Beyond businessmen's biographies there have been studies of business practices and institutions other than individual houses: methods of dealing in foreign exchange, the commercial paper market, trade associations, and the like—even the businessman as a social creature.

CONCLUSION

This survey of the evolution of economic and business literature suggests that a narrowness in the concept has dominated the histories of economic thought. The wide-ranging literature reflects, for the Western world as a whole, the changes in the entrepreneurial and governmental systems over the centuries. Economic and business literature constitutes a connecting link between economic and business performance and the realm of ideas. It throws light, too, on the formation of public opinion and the relation of that opinion to social action. The differences in rates of economic change among nations are of increasing interest among scholars, and here, too, a study of economic and business literature may prove of value. There is recognition that economic sophistication is a prerequisite to forward-looking public administration and that there are forces and conditions in business life not adequately taken care of in the economists' abstractions. Again, the materials for a history of economic and business literature are those also for a history of economists, or of explorers and innovators among economic historians. No less than in medicine or natural science, this literature seems to manifest a tremendous increase in the volume of communication, an evolution and testing of new ideas, and a marked advance in sophistication.

The above article draws heavily upon a longer consideration of the topic by Arthur H. Cole, which was published first under the title "Conspectus for History of Economic and Business Literature" in the *Journal of Economic History*, **17**(3), (September 1957) and, in a slightly revised version, under the title *The Historical Development of Economic and Business Literature* (Publication #12 of the Kress Library of Business and Economics, Graduate School of Business, Harvard University, Boston, 1957).

REFERENCES

1. Forsyth, D.P. *The Business Press in America*, Chilton: Philadelphia, PA, 1964.
2. Price, J.M. Notes on some London price-currents, 1667–1715. Economic History Rev. **1954–1955**, *7*(2), 240–250.
3. Schumpeter, J.A. *History of Economic Analysis*, Oxford University Press: New York, 1954; 183, 194–199.
4. Carpenter, K.E. *An Exploration in Bibliographies of Economics...*, Bulletin #6 Kress Library of Business and

Economics, Graduate School of Business Administration, Harvard University: Boston, MA, 1970; April 1, 2; 4–5.

5. Houghton, J. *Husbandry and Trade Improved*, 2nd Ed. Woodman and Lyon: London, U.K., 1728; 4–6.

6. Mizuta, H. *Adam Smith's Library, a Supplement to Bonar's Catalogue with a Checklist of the Whole Library*, University Press for the Royal Economics Society: Cambridge, MA, 1967.

7. Funkhouser, H.G. Historical development of the graphical representation of statistical data. Osiris **1937**, November, *3*, 292, 330.

8. Heckscher, E.F. *An Economic History of Sweden*, Harvard Univ. Press: Cambridge, MA, 1954; 212.

9. Rogin, L. *The Meaning and Validity of Economic Theory: A Historical Approach*, Harper & Brothers: New York, 1956; 11.

10. Palgrave, R.H.I. *Dictionary of Political Economy*, Macmillan: London, U.K., Vol. 3, 358.

11. Flynn, M.B. Development of Business Papers in the United States. New York University Graduate School of Business Administration, 1944, PhD Thesis; 29, 33, 62.

Electronic Records Preservation

Robert P. Spindler
Department of Archives and Manuscripts, Arizona State University, Tempe, Arizona, U.S.A.

Abstract

The need to preserve electronic records and publications has been expressed in archival and library literature, but analysis of the challenges and development of strategies for achieving reliable retention are in their infancy. Many archivists and librarians perceive that information created in or converted to electronic form is at risk as a result of several notable losses of important electronic information like National Aeronautics and Space Administration's electronic files from the 1976 Viking mission to Mars, pre-1997 e-mail communications of U.S. Vice President Al Gore, and photographic image files damaged by the "I Love You" virus in 2000.

WHAT IS AN ELECTRONIC RECORD?

Electronic records can include information originally created in an electronic format or information created in hard copy or analog format and subsequently digitized through use of digital imaging, optical character recognition technologies or direct analog to digital conversion for audio and video information. Electronic records can include digital image files, audio files, and geographic information system files, as well as the more common documents produced by word processing or e-mail. Compound documents may include several of the above technologies in a single product.

An electronic record is a form of information produced in the course of an event or a routine activity by an individual or an organization. Electronic records are created and retained as specially designed output from an information system or personal computer. They may be selected for retention because of their comprehensiveness and portability, or they may not be retained since other forms of the same information (e.g., hard copy, microfilm) may be preferable for personal use, acceptable as evidence, or retained at lower cost. Most files output or saved from information systems or personal computers are not electronic records. Simple backups or downloads usually do not contain sufficient contextual information to authenticate and verify the accuracy of the content.

Connecting Content and Context

For many years, archivists have struggled to understand and explain the difference between an electronic record and electronic information or data. Archivists have made important distinctions between the content of information and its context, since elements of the context of information creation can certify the accuracy and authenticity of information content. Context is also essential for documenting how and when content changes have been made over time. Electronic records must have content *and* context in order to successfully document an event, an activity, or a business transaction.

Electronic publications often serve as a record of an activity or transaction since they generally are presented with attributions of authorship and sources. They are often granted the status of records because authors, footnotes, and bibliographies provide sufficient context for readers to have confidence in the accuracy and authenticity of the information presented. Other electronic information products such as specially formatted output from a large information system are intended to serve as records, but often that output does not include the contextual information necessary to be considered a reliable record of an event or transaction. Much of the research in electronic record preservation has centered on identifying the contextual information necessary to authenticate the content of an electronic record.

History of Electronic Records Preservation

Early attempts to collect and preserve electronic records began with the establishment of data libraries that supported social science research in the 1970s. These projects generally concentrated on retaining textual and numeric research data in a software-neutral form for access and reuse. Although certain quality control tests were conducted and error logs were investigated, it was the mission of these institutions to retain data derived from specific research projects to facilitate subsequent reuse and research replication. Contextual information about the data was generally retained in separate data dictionaries and codebooks that described the functions and allowable data values for specific pieces or fields of information.

The U.S. National Archives received its first accession of electronic records in 1970, and this function was retained through several reorganizations to this day. The current

Document–Engineering

Center for Electronic Records physically acquires and preserves similar textual and numeric data sets produced by government agencies and does not generally retain electronic records in software-dependent formats. The center and its predecessors developed and implemented standards for selecting and accessioning electronic records, conducting quality control tests, and establishing public access services.

As more electronic content was produced with the advent of inexpensive personal computers and mainframes in the 1980s, computing professionals established facilities and routines for system backups. They generally did not consider long-term retention other than content presented in computer output microfilm (COM). Quite often the labeling on COM sets and backup tapes was not sufficient to describe the scope or age of the content within. At the end of this decade, electronic reformatting technologies such as digital imaging became widely available and many institutions implemented imaging to reduce paper record storage costs. Legal standards were soon established for certifying the accuracy of digitally reformatted content, but these standards generally focused on documenting imaging and quality control as routine business practices for litigation defense support.

In the 1990s, e-mail and word processing became essential features of business and personal life, and questions of the accuracy and authenticity of electronic records began to emerge in highly publicized cases of fraud and unauthorized system security breaches.

The landmark 1993 U.S. Court of Appeals decision in Armstrong versus Executive Office of the President highlighted the challenges of increasing government efficiency through technology, while retaining citizens' right to access government records. The decision confirmed that, in this case, e-mail did constitute a federal record that must be retained or destroyed in accordance with the Federal Records Act. The court also ruled that printouts of White House e-mails did not contain sufficient structural and contextual information to authenticate the communications and that the electronic version of the communications needed to be retained to satisfy federal record-keeping requirements.

In the next few years, widespread availability of digitization technologies and production of electronic books, journals, and indexes enabled the development of digital libraries that presented locally owned and commercially licensed content made accessible through the Internet. The opportunity for development of digital libraries caused librarians to take a more active interest in preservation for electronic publications and establishment of metadata standards to support Internet resource discovery.

In 1997, the Virginia Institute of Technology (Virginia Tech) initiated the first university program to accept electronic theses and dissertations. This project highlighted the similarities between librarians' concerns for preserving electronic publications and archivists' interest in preserving electronic records. Theses and dissertations are simultaneously considered a publication and also a student record. As a result of the Virginia Tech initiative and in response to the 1996 Research Libraries Group report *Preserving Digital Information*, archivists and librarians began to study the relationships between content and context. Academic research on these issues emerged with the support of the National Historical Publications and Records Commission, a division of the National Archives and Records Administration that made electronic records research a funding priority throughout the 1990s.

Beginning in 1989, Luciana Duranti of the University of British Columbia published a series of articles in the journal *Archivaria* that examined the applicability of diplomatics for modern record-keeping practices. Diplomatics was a mid-seventeenth-century discipline that viewed the character and content of individual documents, as well as the organizational context of document production, as indicators of document integrity and authenticity. Intrinsic and extrinsic elements of particular documentary forms are cataloged and used as tests of authenticity. Extrinsic elements included medium used, script, language, seals, and annotations, while intrinsic elements included document protocol, actions taken or described in the document, and final responsibility for the content.

In 1994, Duranti's interest in diplomatics and document authentication led her and colleague Terry Eastwood to establish the "University of British Columbia (UBC) Project," which defined requirements for creating, handling, and preserving reliable and authentic electronic records in active record-keeping systems. Duranti and Eastwood then collaborated with the U.S. Department of Defense to set standards for record management system requirements that are used for certifying software vendors and their products. A planned second phase of the UBC Project was intended to address long-term preservation of inactive electronic records, but the scope of such a project required a larger and more diverse research team. As a result, the "InterPARES" (International Research on Permanent Authentic Records in Electronic Systems) project was launched in 1999, an international research initiative in which archivists, computer engineers, national archival institutions, and private industry representatives are working to develop the theoretical and methodological knowledge required for the permanent preservation of authentic electronic records.

Meanwhile, in 1991, the Minnesota Historical Society hosted the "Working Meeting on Research Issues in Electronic Records," which established the National Historical Publications and Records Commission's research agenda for electronic record keeping. In response to this agenda, Richard Cox of the University of Pittsburgh launched a three-year project, beginning in 1993, to establish functional requirements for record keeping in electronic information systems. The project also investigated several related topics including organizational culture, technical capabilities of existing software, utility of standards and policies for satisfying archival requirements, and evaluation of technology and policy strategies.

The "Pittsburgh Project" resulted in dissemination of lists of functional requirements for record keeping, an analysis of tactics for implementing record-keeping systems, and an assessment of variables that may affect the use and implementation of those systems. In 1994, project consultant David Bearman of *Archives and Museum Informatics* and project researcher Ken Sochats asserted that the functional record-keeping requirements could be converted into formal requirements for specific metadata elements. In 1995, Philip Bantin of Indiana University began testing this model in an analysis of records systems for the Financial Management Support and Enrollment Services offices at that institution. More recently, the Australian Recordkeeping Metadata Research Project has made substantial progress on metadata issues, with record-keeping metadata standards issued by the Commonwealth, Victorian, and New South Wales governments between 1998 and 2001.

The search for electronic record preservation strategies also led to attempts to enunciate the competencies necessary for archivists, records managers, and librarians to participate in electronic preservation projects. In 1993, the Committee on Automated Records and Techniques of the Society of American Archivists established the Automated Records and Techniques Curriculum Project, and this work also resulted in the publication of a special edition of *The American Archivist* dedicated to electronic records case studies.

In addition, two annual national conferences on electronic records preservation were established. Cohasset Associates, a Chicago consulting firm established the MER: Managing Electronic Records conference in 1993, which serves as a forum for presentation of emerging preservation strategies that is widely attended by corporate and government organizations. In 1999, Arizona State University established ECURE: Preservation and Access for Electronic College and University Records, which focuses on the special record-keeping needs of colleges and universities and is dedicated to the critical analysis and dissemination of practical strategies for electronic records access and preservation.

Advanced technologies are now being applied to electronic preservation issues. In 1999, the Distributed Object Computation Testbed project was established as a partnership between the U.S. Patent and Trademark Office, the National Archives and Records Administration, and the San Diego Supercomputer Center. The test bed was developed to store complex documents on geographically distributed data archives and systems using the processing power of supercomputers to implement preservation strategies from the digital library, archival, and computing communities. Brewster Kahle's Internet Archive established technology that finds and stores snapshots of websites from around the world in an attempt to comprehensively document the Internet. Both the National Archives and the Library of Congress recently implemented programs to collect archival snapshots of selected web pages, but none of these projects have fully addressed the potential software incompatibility and proprietary markup issues related to websites.

At the beginning of the twenty-first century, implementation of new technologies continues to advance as archivists, librarians, and technology professionals continue to work on several aspects of the electronic records preservation challenges. The Government Paperwork Elimination Act of 1998 and the Electronic Records and Signatures in Global and National Commerce Act of 2000 (known as E-Sign) mandated widespread implementation of electronic government services and electronic signatures. Similar legislation has been adopted in several state governments.

Interactive Internet technologies and the advent of virtual reality and desktop videoconferencing are increasing the complexity of electronic record keeping. Electronic content is increasingly software dependent so that long-term retention of products may require continued support for obsolete software and operating systems, active migration of records to new software, or development of emulation hardware and software. Increasing data storage capacities and the fast development and implementation of proprietary compression and backup technologies are hastening the obsolescence and increasing the incompatibility and interoperability of data storage media and systems. Widely distributed computing facilities and multi-institutional or multinational collaborations make retention and appropriate deletion of electronic records much more difficult than before. Distributed computing places greater pressure on policy, procedure development, and oversight since file maintenance is no longer centralized.

Preserving Electronic Information

Thirty years of work in acquiring and retaining electronic content has not resulted in complete solutions for electronic record preservation, but researchers have started to identify and catalog the major barriers to successful electronic record keeping. A successful electronic record preservation strategy requires attention to seven major challenges (Table 1).

Storage media

Storage media is often used to support backups, off-line storage, or distribution of electronic content. These challenges have received a great deal of attention in the popular media and the professional literature, but they are the easiest to manage since estimates of the reliable shelf life of various media and interoperability of certain media

Table 1 Seven challenges of electronic record preservation.

Challenge	Example
1. Physical degradation of storage media	CD does not read anymore since the recording surface has been degraded by air pollutants.
2. Physical obsolescence of storage media	5.25 inch floppy disc does not fit in CD-R drive.
3. Incompatibility/ noninteroperability of storage media	One manufacturer's DVD disc will not play in DVD players produced by a different manufacturer.
4. Software, operating system, or encoding incompatibility/ noninteroperability	New software release will not run file from old release. New software release opens old file, but contents are corrupted. Software is not compatible with operating system. Product designed for display with one Internet browser does not look the same in a different browser. Proprietary backup software and storage format not compatible with new release or other backup software. Proprietary codes from HTML editing packages do not convert to XML.
5. Human error/vandalism	Accidental or malicious deletion. Website is vandalized.
6. Backups and snapshots	Backups lost or overwritten. Wrong files backed up. Incomplete snapshot: Video server backed up, Web server not backed up. Snapshots of different servers not contemporaneous.
7. Metadata	Insufficient context to verify source and authenticate content.

formats like CD-R are available. We can project the expected physical life of the media, track changing format standards for media players, and plan to move the information to new media based on the expected physical shelf life and availability of new formats and players. The generally accepted reliable shelf life of compact discs for example is 5–100 years, depending on several factors, including manufacturer, production materials used, storage conditions, level of use, etc. However, many experts believe that physical obsolescence and incompatibility and noninteroperability of storage media occur faster than the media can physically degrade. One source reports that media players are becoming obsolete every 2 to 5 years. It is critically important to move electronic content from old storage media to newer media before the old media player fails or becomes unavailable. Commercial data conversion and recovery services and

some archival repositories retain and maintain some obsolete media players, but the usable life of this equipment is unknown.

Software and document encoding issues

Software incompatibility or noninteroperability results in files that will not open at all or documents that are corrupted and must be repaired if possible (usually through comprehensive manual reentry or manual editing and correction of content). The two major strategies for addressing software incompatibility and noninteroperability issues are known as emulation and migration.

The emulation concept proposed by Jeff Rothenberg of the Rand Corporation involves writing new software that mimics the appearance and functionality of old software. Recently, experts in this area have challenged emulation, suggesting that efforts to write emulation software solutions have not resulted in exact reproductions of appearance or function. Approximate reproductions of appearance or function might be sufficient for some record-keeping applications, provided that the information content is accurate and can be authenticated.

Migration tends to be the more widely accepted preservation strategy, in which files are regularly saved to new releases of the same software as they become available or are converted to new software produced by another manufacturer. Migration is not always successful, as conversion programs do not always have full "backward compatibility" that results in "clean" conversions between old and new software releases. Many electronic document managers are selecting ubiquitous software packages, relying upon a large "installed base" in the hope that that the manufacturer will survive for many years and that future releases will have complete backward compatibility. In addition, software manufacturers have not always supported "interoperability" by including reliable conversion programs for moving files between their own products and those of other manufacturers without corruption. Manufacturers are increasingly including backward compatibility and limited interoperability into their product designs, but, for now, migration cannot be considered a fully reliable preservation strategy.

When electronic information is encoded to support electronic publication or display on the Internet, the selection of encoding syntax or language is an important issue. Although standards for encoding electronic documents such as SGML (standard generalized markup language), HTML (hypertext markup language) and XML (extensible markup language) have been established, software developers have not always complied with the standard, introducing proprietary codes in their document-editing software. These are codes that may be misinterpreted or cannot be read by other software packages, resulting in data-processing errors or changes of document color or formatting. Color or formatting may not be essential elements of a textual electronic record but may be significant components of multimedia presentations that incorporate graphic or video content. Proprietary codes can sometimes be replaced with their standardized equivalents but the appearance and functionality of the document could be changed as a result.

Human error and vandalism

Human interaction with electronic information presents important challenges for electronic records preservation. At a very basic level, the culture of technology transfer, adoption, and implementation makes preservation more difficult since our faith in new technology sometimes precludes critical analysis of its effectiveness. Those who would champion system design changes that support effective record keeping often are met with resistance since record keeping is often not valued as highly as fast implementation. One result of our culture is that although sound data management practices are available, systems managers for large enterprise level systems or users of desktop personal computers do not always rigorously follow them.

Electronic records can also be intentionally compromised through actions of individuals who have access to the content or have learned to circumvent data security measures. Records can also be corrupted as an intended or unintended consequence of a computer virus infection. An individual can compromise any encryption and security technology with access to specialized expertise and high-performance computing facilities. Often, violations of system security are undetected until damaged content or other evidence of the violation is subsequently discovered. These threats to electronic record keeping can be minimized through the retention and maintenance of off-line backups.

Backups and snapshots

Reliable backups of electronic records are essential for successful short-term retention since data can easily be deleted or corrupted with the push of a button. Redundancy has always been a very successful preservation strategy and inexpensive data storage can make redundancy cost effective. Backups are intended to support recovery from disasters, system failures, or human error, but many data losses can be attributed to improperly managed backups.

Backup failures can result from of improper backup system configuration, lack of quality control, failure to migrate the content before backup system failure, incompatibility with new backup systems, or simple operator command error. Most backup systems use proprietary compression and software that has a very high degree of noninteroperability and incompatibility. In addition, the rapid increases in storage technology capacity and the increasing frequency of new backup software releases make long-term survival of backups unlikely. Accurate file backups must be made to a nonproprietary and compressionless environment, and they must be effectively migrated or emulated for successful long-term preservation. The timing and scope of backups should be established in advance, rigorously followed, and tested for accuracy and completeness. Many experts believe that given the risks, backups are not effective for record keeping. Migration of records to a specially designed record-keeping system or redundant live-server storage may be more reliable, especially for long-term retention.

Specially designed downloads of websites known as "snapshots" are key issues for preserving a record of an interactive website since their scope and timing are critical for capturing a "record" of the changing content. Many complex Web products are now stored on a number of different servers to facilitate efficient retrieval and display. The products themselves only exist for a moment in time on a patron's computer screen, but the sources of the content are distributed. All the source files of product components must be included in the snapshot so that the record of the website is complete, unless certain parts of the content are deemed "nonrecord," such as the chat room attached to an electronic college course.

The timing of snapshots is also important since an interactive website may have certain components that are static and others changing. Snapshot timing needs to be established with some attention to the rate and nature of change in the website. Ideally, the snapshot of the record components across a series of servers should be done contemporaneously so an accurate record of the components and their relationships can be retained.

Metadata and retention of context

The essential difference between data or electronic information and an electronic record is that electronic records have information content *and* specific pieces of contextual information that authenticate or explain the content. This contextual information is called "metadata."

In general, metadata tags or "metatags" are elements of textual information inserted into the header of an electronic file to enable automated searching, retrieval, and use of the content within the file. In the record-keeping context, metadata is divided into two types: descriptive metadata and administrative metadata.

Descriptive metadata is generally used for describing or indexing the content of an electronic file. The Dublin Core is recognized as the most commonly used structure for presenting metadata, and the development of this standard and other descriptive metadata standards is driven by the need to support Internet commerce or other business applications. Dublin Core does contain elements that support retention of some but not all of contextual information necessary for effective record keeping.

Administrative metadata addresses more of the contextual information necessary to understand the accuracy and authenticity of the content. It also can facilitate management and preservation of the electronic file over time. Administrative metadata can document such attributes as document version, software and hardware requirements, location and availability of other metadata such as software documentation, location and availability of backup files, and migration history. Establishing and implementing administrative metadata standards would greatly improve the prospects for electronic record preservation in the future.

BIBLIOGRAPHY

General Research Reports

1. CENSA *Titanic 2020 (Press Release and Research Report)*, 1999. Available at http://www.censa.org/html/Press-Releases/Titanic2020.htm (accessed February 9, 2001).
2. Research Libraries Group. *Preserving Digital Information: Report of the Task Force on Archiving of Digital Information*, Research Libraries Group: Mountain View, CA, 1996. Available at http://lyra.rlg.org/ArchTF/tfadi.index.htm (accessed February 9, 2001).

Electronic Signatures

1. National Archives and Records Administration. *Records Management Guidance for Agencies Implementing Electronic Signature Technologies*, 2001. Available at http://www.nara.gov/records/policy/gpea.html (accessed February 9, 2001).

Encoding/Markup Standards

1. World Wide Web Consortium Homepage with links to HTML standard and verification service. Available at http://www.w3.org (accessed February 9, 2001).

Metadata and Authentication

1. Dublin Core Metadata Initiative Homepage. Available at http://purl.org/dc/ (accessed February 9, 2001).
2. Gilliland-Swetland, A. Introduction to Metadata (Presentation Abstract and Bibliography). ECURE: Preservation and Access for Electronic College and University Records, Tempe, AZ, October, 7–8, 1999. Available at http://www.asu.edu/it/events/ecure/ecure1999/gilliland-swetland-present.html (accessed February 9, 2001).
3. InterPARES Project Homepage. Available at http://www.interpares.org/ (accessed February 9, 2001).
4. State Records, New South Wales. *New South Wales Recordkeeping Metadata Standard (draft)*, 2001. Available at http://www.records.nsw.gov.au/publicsector/erk/metadata/rkmeta data.htm (accessed February 9, 2001).
5. University Archives, Indiana University Bloomington Libraries, Indiana University Electronic Records Project *Metadata Specifications*, 1998. http://www.indiana.edu/~libarche/metadataspecifications.html (accessed February 9, 2001).

Migration and Preservation Cost Analyses

1. Balough, A. The true cost of electronic documents. Rec. Inf. Manag. Q. **1998**, *14*(1), 1.

Recordkeeping System Design Projects

1. San Diego Supercomputer Center, Distributed Object Computation Testbed Homepage. Available at http://www.sdsc.edu/DOCT/ (accessed February 9, 2001).

Software Migration/Emulation Strategies

1. Bearman, D. Reality and chimeras in the preservation of electronic records. D-Lib Mag. April **1999**, *5*(4). Available at http://www.dlib.org/dlib/april99/bearman/04bearman.html (accessed February 9, 2001).
2. Rothenberg, J. *Avoiding Technological Quicksand: Finding a Viable Technical Foundation for Digital Preservation*, Council on Library and Information Resources: Washington, DC, 1999. Available at http://www.clir.org/pubs/reports/rothenberg/contents.html (accessed February 9, 2001).

Web Site Preservation

1. National Library of Australia. *Safeguarding Australia's Web Resources: Guidelines for Creators and Publishers*, 2001. Available at http://www.nla.gov.au/guidelines/2000/webresources.html (accessed February 9, 2001).
2. Spindler, R. Preserving Web-Based Records ECURE: Preservation and Access for College and University Electronic Records Conference, Tempe, AZ, 1999. Available at http://www.asu.edu/it/events/ecure/ecure1999/spindler-presentation.html (accessed February 9, 2001).

Electronic Resources & Libraries (ER&L)

Jesse Koennecke
Cornell University Library, Cornell University College of Arts and Sciences, Ithaca, New York, U.S.A.

Abstract
The annual Electronic Resources & Libraries conference (ER&L) was first held in 2006 to bring people together to focus directly on the trends, workflows, and technologies involved in managing electronic resources within the library community. Attendees gather, both in person and online, to find common ground, learn, and have an impact on their profession.

INTRODUCTION

The Electronic Resources & Libraries conference, or ER&L, is an annual international library conference focused on trends, workflows, and technologies involved in the management, maintenance, and accessibility of electronic resources in libraries. ER&L's stated mission and purpose, as found on http://electroniclibrarian.org/about/, focus on the need for communication and collaboration to enable individuals that deal with electronic resources to keep up in a quickly evolving environment. With these in mind, attendees gather annually both in person and online to learn from one another, make connections, and develop a better understanding of how to go about their work.

Mission: ER&L facilitates the communication and collaboration for information professionals around issues related to managing electronic resources in the digital world.

Purpose: The goal of the ER&L conference is to bring together information professionals from libraries and related industries to improve the way we collect, manage, maintain, and make accessible electronic resources in an ever-changing online environment. We do this once a year at an in-person conference. In addition, sessions are recorded and made available in an online conference. ER&L allows for cross-pollination of ideas across fields of librarianship not often brought together in traditional public services or technical services conferences.

HISTORY AND GROWTH

ER&L was first conceived by Bonnie Tijerina, a librarian at the Georgia Institute of Technology (Georgia Tech) at the time. Tijerina attended a conference where someone presented on a survey they conducted with a new area of the profession called e-resources librarianship. The results of the survey indicated people working primarily with electronic resources felt isolated and overwhelmed. Survey respondents said their colleagues didn't understand what they did and that there was a lack of standard practices across library vendors. In an e-mail interview, Tijerina recalled, "While I attended the session I thought that if a lot of the librarians from across the country could get together, they could build community, share best practices, and work closely with vendors to communicate the needs of the library community." She put out a call to the broader community, asking a few questions about what conferences cover e-resources professional development and if a new conference was needed. Getting a lot of positive responses, as well as volunteers to help, she set about organizing a conference.

What was to become the first annual ER&L was held March 23–26, 2006, in Atlanta, Georgia, on the Georgia Tech campus. Featuring two keynote speakers and 33 sessions spread across 10 tracks, the conference drew approximately 100 attendees. The opening keynote by Robert McDonald, associate director of Libraries for Technology & Research at Florida State University at the time, set a tone that has continued to drive the forward thinking nature of the ER&L conference since. He applied the concept of Internet 2.0 to libraries, using the term Library 2.0 to illustrate how library systems and services could develop in the coming years. The presentation tracks from the first ER&L reflected the broad topics that staff working with electronic resources were wrestling with, mostly on their own.

> *First ER&L Conference Tracks*
>
> *Organizational Change*
> *Access*
> *Electronic Resource Management*
> *Partnerships*
> *Consortia*
> *Usage Data*
> *Workflow*
> *Licensing*
> *Resources*
> *Technology*

Encyclopedia of Library and Information Sciences, Fourth Edition DOI: 10.1081/E-ELIS4-120053104

Document–Engineering

From that first event to celebrating its 10th annual in 2015, ER&L has changed location several times and grown considerably. In addition, the organizers and volunteers have continued to adjust their plans to ensure the conference evolves and continues to meet its mission and purpose in the changing world of electronic resources.

ER&L remained in Atlanta then moved to Los Angeles in 2009. As of 2010, ER&L has had a regular home in the early spring on the University of Texas at Austin campus.

Throughout this time, Tijerina has continued to serve as the conference coordinator, assisted by numerous regular volunteers. Among these volunteers are several that have been key to ER&L since the beginning. Elizabeth Winter (Georgia Tech) has been the chair of program planning committee, managing the process of reviewing and finalizing the extensive set of presentations that are at the primary content of ER&L. Jill Emery (Portland State University) has filled many different roles including program planning, engaging sponsors, communication, and social media. As of 2015, there are dozens of individuals involved in planning the conference and dozens more that volunteer on-site to help keep everything running smoothly.

Since 2009, Tijerina has relied on the advice and business skills of her sister, Sandy Tijerina, who in 2012 became ER&L's first and only full-time paid employee. As sponsorship and communications director, Sandy handles the logistics for the conference planning as well as the physical conference itself. She also coordinates the vendor exhibits and sponsorship activities that are a major part of sustaining ER&L.

Attendance has grown steadily from those initial 100 in 2006. By 2010, the number had reached 400, then up to 650 on-site in 2015. Although the vast majority of attendees come from the United States, a growing number are travelling from abroad with representation from 22 countries across 6 continents.

Beginning in 2011, ER&L introduced an online conference option, recording and streaming select sessions to an online audience. Since 2014, the online conference has streamed most of the live sessions and keynote speakers. This has allowed participation in the conference to grow further, enabling people to attend the conference after the attendance cap has been reached or if they are unable to travel to Austin in person. In addition to the on-site attendees in 2015, another estimated 450 joined via the online option. A group rate makes it more affordable for several individuals from an institution to take advantage of the online conference. Presenters, in-person attendees who pay to add online access, and all online attendees are able to access the recorded sessions to cover any that they missed or wish to review.

In addition to examples like the online conference, ER&L continues to innovate to keep ahead of trends and to push boundaries of what people who work with e-resources consider important to their work and

profession. This can be seen in the topics that the keynote speakers address, in the focus of the presentation sessions in any given year, and in the nature of the related events (see the following text) that have emerged out of ER&L.

Keynote speakers over the history of ER&L have been invited specifically to provide insight into the broader world of libraries and beyond. A few examples from past ER&L conferences illustrate how the keynotes can serve as bridges to topics that are not traditionally associated directly with electronic resource management in libraries. In 2013, Michael Eisenberg, dean emeritus of the Information School at the University of Washington, presented "Listening to Users: What the 'Google Generation' Says About Using Library & Information Collections, Services, and Systems in the Digital Age," sharing how young users do research and what they think of the library. That same year, Rachel Frick, director of the Digital Library Federation (DLF) at the time, gave an inspirational talk titled "The Courage of Our Connections: thoughts on professional identities, organizational affiliations and common communities," about the increased role librarians can play in the networked world. In her 2014 talk "Freeing Knowledge: A Values Proposition," Barbara Fister, a librarian at Gustavus Adolphus College and blogger for *Inside Higher Ed* (https://www.insidehighered.com/), spoke about library values, the open movement, and how libraries could lead in developing an open network. These and other ER&L keynote addresses are available to the public on the ER&L website.

The selection of concurrent presentation sessions and longer workshops changes from year to year, as new topics emerge in the world of electronic resources. ER&L's program planning committee sorts through submissions and hosts an online community voting process to finalize the slate of presentations. This allows the community to have a direct impact on the upcoming conference to make it as relevant and timely as possible. These sessions are supplemented by informal activities like lightning talks and roundtables to provide opportunities for people to actively discuss ideas that may not have been previously proposed.

Throughout its first 10 years, the organizers for ER&L have actively worked to increase the social aspects of the conference. In addition to being a useful networking opportunity for people working with electronic resources and library vendors, ER&L includes a number of social and entertainment opportunities to give attendees a chance to connect outside of conference presentations. Early on, these included organized dining events, tours, networking sessions, and receptions. Recently, organizers have held a Battledecks competition and a gaming night.

ER&L had benefited from sponsorship since its inception. Growing from 11 sponsors in 2006 to 56 in 2015, the conference draws interest and support from publishers, library content and service vendors, and related organizations. Sponsors support ER&L by hosting luncheons and receptions, providing scholarships, and helping to cover the costs of the conference services such as A/V technology.

ER&L TODAY

Planning and organizing ER&L occurs throughout the year, coordinated by both Bonnie and Sandy Tijerina. They are in communication regularly with the host site, sponsors, and volunteers during the lead up to the actual conference. As of the 2016 conference, the planning committee consists of the following subcommittees and functions: program planning, fellowship, fun and games, grants, sponsorship, social media, web, workshop, and local logistics.

The typical calendar for conference planning begins 6–8 months before the conference and includes

- Keynote speakers identified and invited
- Sponsors recruited on an ongoing basis
- Call for workshops in early fall
- Call for concurrent session proposals in the fall
- Community voting several months before the conference
- Notifications of acceptance by late fall or early winter
- Developing the official schedule
- Conference typically held in late March/early April

As with many conferences, individual sessions are assigned to a track to help attendees identify a focused group of session to attend. The focus of the conference tracks change over time as the nature of the library electronic resource world changes. The tracks from 2016 conference website are as follows:

Managing e-resources and licensing: Managing electronic resources is a challenge, whether you're new to it or have been engaged in it for years. Which systems and tools can be used to manage electronic resources more effectively? What kinds of challenges are new formats posing? How are we rearranging our workflows to find solutions to e-resources problems? What can we achieve through more thoughtful licensing? How can standards and best practices assist our efforts?

Collection development and assessment: How do we demonstrate value to our larger organizations? Are our collection and analytic processes as efficient as they could be? Can collecting data be easier? How can we best analyze what we collect?

Organizational strategies: Our organizations regularly evolve due to changes in leadership and strategic vision, budget constraints, user needs, and the simple fact that so many of our resources are now online. All of these impact the way we manage e-resources. What type of leadership has helped create positive change? What are some examples of beneficial organizational shift and improved communication? Where are there opportunities for internal collaboration? Where do we still need to open up communications?

External relationships: In the digital world, libraries don't stand alone. They work closely with consortia, vendors, other libraries, and intermediaries. Are all these relationships working? Are we getting the most out of our relationships with other organizations or groups? How can we improve our external relationships?

User experience: Libraries exist in large part to support our users. How can we better serve our user populations? What kinds of communications will help us reach them when so much is competing for their attention? How can we demonstrate to users the value of libraries and create a better user experience?

Scholarly communication: How do we deal with new models of scholarship that are emerging? How do we accommodate new forms of content? What can we do to facilitate knowledge sharing and access?

Library as publisher: What role can the library play in the creation and distribution of the products of scholarship and creativity?

Emerging technologies and trends: So much of what we do in libraries today is driven by technology, and so many of the problems we face can be solved, at least in part, by employing or developing new technologies. How are current technologies being used? What emerging technologies are on the horizon? How can we employ them effectively to meet the information needs of the library, internally and externally?

RELATED EVENTS

Library Idea Drop House—(http://electroniclibrarian.org/ideadrop/): Starting in 2012, Tijerina hosted the Library #IdeaDrop House, inviting speakers from the SXSW Interactive Conference to discuss topics of interest to libraries in a small, relaxed setting. Partnering with regular ER&L sponsor, ProQuest, the IdeaDrop House has continued annually to offer conversations about libraries, data, privacy, and other topics.

UX Day: Andrea Resmini, information architect and a teacher and researcher at Jönköping University in Sweden, was an ER&L keynote speaker in 2012. He spoke about cross-channel experience for our users and how the information and services they utilize from a library's digital space is one of many facets of the larger information landscape they interact with in their daily lives. This concept led to a user experience or UX Day at ER&L 2014 with the goal, as expressed on its website (http://electroniclibrarian.org/erlplus/uxday/), "to educate and expose librarians and other information professionals to colleagues working on user experience, discovery, usage and usability projects in libraries and professionals working in user experience outside of libraries." The concept of UX Day was to concentrate on user experience–related sessions, speakers, and workshops. Invited presenters included Susie Herbstritt, senior interaction designer for Dell; Brian Taylor, senior user experience researcher and designer for Dell; and Matt Franks, professor at the Austin Center for Design and product owner and lead interaction designer at MyEdu. UX for Good founders, Jason Ulaszek and Jeff Leitner, and TEDxAustin Executive Producer Nancy Giordano led a hands-on workshop. ER&L attendees could attend the UX Day and individuals could register separately to join the UX Day on its own.

Designing for Digital: The success of UX Day led Tijerina to start Designing for Digital (http://www.designingfordigital.com/), a separate conference immediately following ER&L in 2015. Designing for Digital is held in the same location as ER&L, allowing interested people to attend both without additional travel, while it provides a robust enough conference experience to draw additional attendees that are specifically working on user experience, discovery, design, and usability projects inside and outside of libraries. Tijerina is joined by UX designer, Judy Siegel, to coordinate Designing for Digital.

Library Publishing Unconference: An example of how ER&L fosters innovative ideas, ER&L hosted a Library Publishing Unconference in 2013. A regular attendee, Amy Buckland (McGill University), proposed the idea and was encouraged to go ahead and organize it with the support of ER&L. The announcement for the Unconference encouraged attendees to come with their own questions, ideas, and enthusiasm to discuss issues around open access publishing, how the library can support and/or supplement the university press, and how to help faculty comply with open access guidelines.

AWARDS AND SCHOLARSHIPS

DLF/CLIR + ER&L Cross-Pollinator Travel Award (2013–): Cosponsored by ER&L and the DLF, this grant was introduced to provide an opportunity to a library professional who might not normally attend ER&L, but whose work might align well with the goals of ER&L. As a cross-pollinator, the grantees bring perspectives from the DLF, connecting ideas from the broader library profession to the core ER&L mission. The travel grant includes a conference registration, air travel costs, and housing.

Taylor & Francis Group Student Travel Grant (2013–): Taylor & Francis Group has offered an annual scholarship for two aspiring e-resource librarians to support their travel, registration, and lodging at the ER&L conference. This scholarship was introduced in an effort to promote and increase opportunities for students to attend the conference. Applicants must be currently enrolled students from anywhere in the world. They are required to answer questions in writing about how ER&L can help them meet their professional goals.

CONCLUSION

ER&L arose in response to a vacuum of resources and support for those who manage electronic resources in libraries. Over its first 10 years, the conference and community has filled this gap and innovated to keep at the forefront of this continually changing area of the field. ER&L offers professional growth opportunities for new librarians and information professionals, those who are new to electronic resources, and to those who have been involved for many years. It was founded on the principle that by coming together as a community, ER&L participants can find common ground with each other to learn and have an impact on their profession.

ER&L can be found on
The web at http://electroniclibrarian.org/
Twitter as @ERandL

Encoded Archival Description

Daniel Pitti
*Alderman Library, Institute for Advanced Technology in the Humanities, University
of Virginia, Charlottesville, Virginia, U.S.A.*

Michael Rush
Beinecke Rare Book and Manuscript Library, Yale University, New Haven, Connecticut, U.S.A.

Abstract

Encoded Archival Description (EAD) is an international standard based on Extensible Markup Language
(XML) for encoding descriptions of archival records. People living their lives as individuals, as members
of families, and as members of corporate bodies create and assemble records that serve as instruments for
carrying out or documenting the performance of activities. Based on the archival principles of *respect des
fonds* (or provenance) and original order, archivists traditionally have treated all of the records created and
assembled by one individual, family, or corporate body as a collection or *fonds*. Archivists describe records
as an essential part of their responsibility for preserving and facilitating access to and use of archives.
Archival description provides information essential for establishing the authenticity and completeness of
fonds and serves effective administration, discovery, access, and understanding of records. Traditionally,
archivists have described each *fonds* hierarchically in a single apparatus commonly called a finding aid.
Until the advent of computing, finding aids were typically in printed form. In the 1990s, archivists created
EAD, an encoding standard for archival description that made it possible to derive online and print finding
aids from the same structured data. EAD is based technologically on XML and intellectually on *General
International Standard Archival Description* (*ISAD(G)*), a descriptive framework developed by the International Council of Archives (ICA). The third version of the standard, EAD3, will be released in 2015 and
will continue to develop in the future. Future changes to EAD will be influenced by ICA descriptive
standards, in particular the conceptual model and ontology for archival description to be developed by the
Experts Group on Archival Description, and related encoding standards. This entry is organized into six
sections: introduction, archival records, archival description, EAD, history, and future.

INTRODUCTION

Encoded Archival Description (EAD) is an international
standard for encoding descriptions of archival records.
An individual archival description is commonly called a
finding aid, archival guide, handlist, inventory, or register.
Though these terms cover a wide variety of apparatus,
they most commonly refer to a hierarchical description
of records that share a common origin or provenance.
A collection of records sharing a common provenance is
called a *fonds* or simply a collection. The hierarchical
description begins with a description of all records in a
fonds and then proceeds to a description of components,
typically identified by the activity or function that they
document (for example, correspondence or minutes of
meetings). These components and components of components, and so on, may be analyzed and described, with the
hierarchical analysis and description terminating in the
description of a file or an item. The depth of analysis is
determined by both intellectual criteria and available time
and resources.

EAD is a standard for communicating archival descriptions and is not itself a standard for the content of the
descriptions. The general standard for descriptive content
is *General International Standard Archival Description
(ISAD(G))*,[1] developed by the International Council on
Archives (ICA). *ISAD(G)* provides general guidance on
the composition of archival descriptions and serves as the
basis of national standards such as the Society of American Archivist's *Describing Archives: A Content Standard*
(DACS).[2] As a communication standard, EAD has a
number of interrelated purposes. In conjunction with complementary content standards, it is intended to promote the
regularization of description in order that the data are
consistent and readily understood by users across archives.
Regularized description and encoding enables intelligent
searching, rendering, navigation, access, and use of archival materials. And since EAD is based on Extensible
Markup Language (XML), a widely used and supported
standard for developing encoding schemas, it provides
reasonable assurance that the data will endure changes in
hardware and software. Finally, standardized description
enables the repurposing of archival description, including
its eventual migration into successor encodings, and
aggregation of descriptions across repositories to provide
union access to distributed archival resources.

Encyclopedia of Library and Information Sciences, Fourth Edition DOI: 10.1081/E-ELIS4-120053313

Document–Engineering

The Society of American Archivists (SAA) is responsible for the maintenance and development of EAD and the Library of Congress hosts the standard and official documentation. Within SAA, the Technical Subcommittee for Encoded Archival Description (TS-EAD) is responsible for the intellectual and technical content of the standard. The members of the Technical Subcommittee reflect the international nature of the standard, with members from the United Kingdom, Germany, France, the Netherlands, Sweden, Italy, Canada, and the United States.

The standard was first released in 1998. It was revised in 2002 and a third version—EAD3—will be released in 2015. The first two versions of the standard were in the form of an XML Document Type Definition (DTD) with an accompanying Tag Library. In 2007, EAD was released in the form of a schema, an alternative syntax for defining the standard. EAD3 will be maintained as a Relax NG schema but will also be available as a W3C schema and a DTD. The schemas and DTD provide the formal semantic and structural requirements of the standard and are used by software to validate encoded instances of archival descriptions. The Tag Library provides guidance on the use of the elements and attributes prescribed in the schemas and DTD and used to encode descriptive data.

ARCHIVAL RECORDS

Archival records are created and assembled by people living their lives as individuals, as members of families, and as members of corporate bodies. The creation of records is typically not the objective of the activities, but rather the records serve as instruments for carrying out or documenting the performance of activities. Archival records thus document people and organizations performing activities or functions, and as such, may serve as legal evidence and historical evidence. By contrast, the books and journals that constitute the bulk of most library collections are the objectives of the activities that created them. To illustrate this difference, it is useful to look at the creation of an encyclopedia.

At the beginning, the editors have the objective of publishing an encyclopedia. They correspond with a publisher with the proposal. Or perhaps the publisher conceives of the encyclopedia and contacts one or more editors. In either case, through a series of exchanges the publisher and editors negotiate the scope and content of the encyclopedia, the form or forms of publication, financial arrangements, methods for soliciting authors and editing entries, and so on. In turn authors for entries are solicited and a series of exchanges take place between the editors, authors, and publisher. Various agreements are formally made and signed. The authors are given formal instructions and deadlines. The authors create and submit drafts of articles to the editors, and after another series of exchanges, the authors submit entries to the publisher for publication. At each stage, the participants in the creation and publication of the encyclopedia generate and maintain copies of the correspondence, agreements, instructions, drafts, financial transactions, and so forth. All of these documents serve the dual purpose of creating and publishing the encyclopedia and documenting the activities that lead to its publication. Each document is not an objective in itself but an instrument by which the objective is realized.

The participants' involvement in the creation of the encyclopedia constitutes only one set of activities over the course of their existence. The authors and the editors have both professional and personal lives. The publishing company publishes more than one book. Each participant generates and accumulates records over the course of a lifetime or existence. Many of these records will be kept for legal reasons, such as financial accounting and reporting, as proof of responsibilities performed, or perhaps self-consciously as records documenting a life or the history of a business. All of the records generated or accumulated by an individual, family, or corporate body, collectively serve as documentation of the life of the individual, or the history of the family or organization. When they are assembled and preserved, they are archival records. Each collection of records generated and accumulated by one individual, family, or organization is called a *fonds*. The items in a *fonds* share a common origin or provenance.

When considered individually, records frequently make little sense and thus have little value. It is only when individual records are considered in context, in relation to other records that document a network of interrelated transactions or series of transactions carrying out a particular function, that they can be understood. In this way, archival records are quite different from books and journals, as the latter are intended to function independently. This statement ignores the issue of intertextuality, which is beyond the scope of present considerations. Archival records are by and large unique. In this respect, archival records again differ fundamentally from books. Books and journals are not unique, at least not in ways that would be of interest to most users. Typically, books and journals exist in many copies, and any one copy will serve as well as any other.

Archival records are varied in both content and format, and the number of items in any given *fonds* may be quite large. While many records are exclusively or primarily textual, these may be in the form of handwritten, typed, printed, or digital. The content may be minutes of a meeting, a marriage license, receipts, a report card, correspondence, and so on. Sound, photographic, and audiovisual records may be in any format used for recording each of these forms. Content again will be varied, depending upon the context and the purpose of the recording. Maps, similar to textual records, may be hand-drawn, printed, or in digital form, as images, graphics, or as geographic information system (GIS) data. While a *fonds* may contain exclusively one form or content, it is more likely, in particular with respect to personal and family records, that both the form and content of the records will be diverse. In addition to a variety of form and content, the number of items in any given *fonds* may be quite large. The administrative records of Tom Bradley, who served as the mayor of Los Angeles from 1973 to 1993, are stored in 4253 boxes occupying 2101.5 linear feet of shelf space.[3]

ARCHIVAL DESCRIPTION

Archival description reflects the nature of archival records and the mission of the archival institutions into which their care and management is placed. Like museums and libraries, archives have a responsibility to remember on behalf of others. Preservation is the first essential responsibility, for without the physical preservation, memory fails. Equally important though is a description of archival records that provides information essential for establishing their authenticity and completeness and serves effective administration, discovery, access, and understanding. Archival preservation and description make the remembering as trustworthy, reliable, and thorough as possible. To serve these objectives, archival description has traditionally focused on the *fonds* as the fundamental unit of description rather than the individual items, as is the common practice in libraries and museums. While there is an obvious savings of time and effort in collection-level description, this descriptive practice is based on the nature of archival records and the objectives to be served.

Archival description rests on two fundamental principles, *respect des fonds* and principle of original order. *Respect des fonds* is frequently also called the principle of provenance. While understanding of this principle has undergone ongoing interpretation since its articulation by French archivists in the early nineteenth century, its fundamental meaning has remained unchanged. Archivists must honor the origin and integrity of records generated or accumulated by an individual, family, or corporate body. The records generated or accumulated by a single source are intricately related to that source, whether it is a corporate body performing the functions with which it is charged or an individual pursuing personal and occupational activities. Given this intimate relationship, records cannot be understood apart from their origin. From this follows the archival practice of treating all records with a common provenance as a group.

The principle of original order addresses the arrangement of the archival records. The concept of original order is frequently conflated with the physical arrangement of records as received by the archive, though it is better understood as an intellectual arrangement that reflects the purpose and use of the records by the creating entity.[4] Commonly, particularly with records deriving from and maintained within a corporate body (such as a government agency or business), records have been arranged and maintained to support the functions and related transactions performed by the body. In such cases, the physical order reflects the purpose and use of the records. It is quite common, though, that the arrangement of the records as received by the archive does not reflect a discernable order, and it is incumbent on the archivist to analyze and arrange the records to reflect their understood purpose and use.

Based on the application of the principle of *respect des fonds* and the principle of original order, archivists maintain and describe all records in a *fonds* together, physically arranged to reflect the original order. A description of a *fonds* begins with a description of the whole and, through a progressive, hierarchical analysis, describes components of the whole based on a shared characteristic or characteristics, which may in turn be analyzed into components and described. The analysis and description can progress to the item level, though frequently do not. Each level of description has a formal designation based on the nature of the shared characteristics that identify them as a coherent group: *fonds*, series, file, and item. Series and files may have intervening levels. The depth of the description is based on both intellectual and economic considerations. While it may seem counterintuitive, excessive analysis and description may hinder rather than facilitate the discovery, identification, and use of archival records, a phenomenon known as "getting lost in the details."

Archival hierarchical analytic or multilevel description is shaped in part on two rules. First, the description of a component at any given level applies exclusively to that component (including its hierarchical descendants). Second, the description of a given component inherits the description of its parent, including any description the parent inherits from its parent, and so on up to the top level. A number of distinctive features follow from these two rules. Typical finding aids begin at the top level with several descriptive components, many of which may comprise detailed prose. At each successive level, the number of descriptive components and the amount of data supplied decrease. It is quite typical for the top level of description to provide lengthy narrative description, while an item-level description may be no more than a title or a date. Viewed from the perspective of the entire archival description, though, the item inherits all of the description back to the top level.

A third rule governing archival description dictates that all components of description are available at each level of description. This rule addresses the fact that individual archival collections are each unique, as they each reflect the lives and activities of individuals, families, or corporate bodies in particular places and times. They also vary greatly in the forms and quantity of records. In principle, all elements of description may be appropriate at any level of description. In practice, though, given inheritance and progression from general to specific, both the elements and quantity of description typically follow common patterns.

In a typical description, the top- or *fonds*-level contains information about the entire collection. The following information is typically given succinctly:

- Identifier or designation that is unique within the repository
- Title of the *fonds*
- Date range giving the earliest and latest dates of creation, frequently with a second range for the dates within which the bulk of the materials was created
- Provenance or creator information
- Extent of the collection, typically given in linear units of shelf space occupied and number of boxes
- Repository holding the collection
- Language or languages represented in the content

Information generally provided in brief text form at the top level includes the following:

- Restrictions on physical access to the materials
- Copyright restrictions
- Scope and content or biography/administrative history abstract
- Preferred form of citation
- Processing and acquisitions information
- Related and separated materials

Finally, the following information is commonly given in expansive text form:

- Biographical/administration history
- Scope and content
- Overview of the arrangement of the materials

The detailed analysis of the *fonds* into components follows. The form of this analysis varies considerably from description to description, and sometimes within a single description from component to component. Some patterns of analysis, though, are prevalent: *Fonds*-series-file, *fonds*-series-subseries-file, *fonds*-series-file-item, and *fonds*-series-subseries-file-item. The pattern of the hierarchical analysis is not prescribed but is determined by the judgment of the archivists analyzing and processing the collection.

Series and subseries descriptions frequently include the following information:

- Title
- Dates range giving the earliest and latest dates of creation
- Extent
- Scope and content
- Arrangement

File or item information commonly includes the following:

- Title
- Date or date range
- Container information

Container information or storage location is provided at the terminal node of description, which corresponds to the most specific intellectual unit that can be requested for use. In the scenario described earlier, this may be an item or file; though when the description terminates at the series or subseries level, container information will be provided at these levels.

ENCODED ARCHIVAL DESCRIPTION

Technical Foundation

Traditionally, archival description was typescript and then later printed using word processors and to a lesser extent, database software. With the emergence of markup technologies in the middle to late 1980s, it became possible to create machine-readable findings that were descriptively encoded and thereby supported a much broader range of functional possibilities. Standard Generalized Markup Language (SGML) was first issued as a formal standard in 1986 by the International Standards Organization (ISO). In the early 1990s, the Hypertext Transfer Protocol (HTTP) and an accompanying document encoding standard, Hypertext Markup Language (HTML), became the foundation of the rapidly emerging World Wide Web (WWW). The success of HTTP and HTML gave rise to the World Wide Web Consortium (W3C), which turned its attention to the development of standards. While remarkably successful, HTML was insufficient for secure, flexible, semantically rich exchange of information, and SGML, though supporting flexible, semantically rich exchange, was difficult to process. As an alternative to both SGML and HTML, the W3C developed XML, releasing version 1.0 in 1998. Among the key features of both SGML and XML was the ability to develop community-based rules or schemas to govern the encoding of specific kinds of documents, employing a semantics that reflected the nature of the document and the professional language of the community. The archival community was one of the first to employ XML.

The archivists developing EAD chose XML as the best available technology for developing a communication standard for archival description for a number of reasons. Markup and database technologies are the two prevailing techniques for representing textual data in forms that support complex, multipurpose processing. While they have some overlapping functionalities, each is optimized to support specific and distinct kinds of data. Markup technologies support traditional documents, such as books, journals, and journal articles, where the order of components and unbounded component hierarchies are prevalent. Database technologies support information with complex many-to-many relations, and the particular order of data elements has minimal if any significance. Archival description can best be characterized as occupying a middle ground, having structurally different data components that map well to one or the other technology. For the purposes of communicating information, as opposed to its creation and maintenance, XML is the superior representation, as it will accommodate native XML data and data derived from databases.

In addition to its representational capability, XML also offers other attractive features. Since its release in 1998, XML has been widely adopted and supported, not only by the original document community where SGML had had reasonably good success, but also by the database development community. As a widely used and supported standard for developing encoding schemas, XML provides reasonable assurance that the data will endure changes in hardware and software, an essential concern because digital data are absolutely dependent on computers for retrieval and rendering into human readable form. The semantically and structurally rich descriptive encoding made possible by XML also enables multiple uses of the data: a wide range of alternative renderings for onscreen presentation and printing, in-depth and descriptive component-specific indexing and retrieval, and, when a successor to XML emerges, migration into a successor digital representation.

There are several apparatus for a defining rule-based encoding for a particular class or kind of documents, including DTD, ISO Relax NG Schema, and W3C Schema. EAD exists in all three forms. The semantics and structure of each are the same, although the schemas add compliance with other XML and descriptive markup schemas, constraints on some data values, and the option to embed XML objects defined according to external rules.

Semantics and Structure: Top Level

In EAD3, the new version to be released in 2015, EAD (<ead>) comprises two main sections: Control (<control>) and Archival Description (<archdesc>). The <archdesc> contains the archival description itself, while the <control> contains control information about the description. Both <control> and <archdesc> are required. For detailed information on the semantics and structure of EAD versions 1.0 and 2002, see the Society of American Archivists, and Library of Congress[5] and Ruth.[6] When it is published, the EAD3 Tag Library will be hosted at the Library of Congress.

While an EAD document provides information describing and documenting archival materials, it is itself a resource that must be maintained and managed. The <control> section contains information that facilitates control of the resource. It contains the following sections:

Record Identifier (<recordid>): a unique designation for identifying and tracking the EAD instance.

Other Record Identifier (<otherrecordid>): an alternate designation for identifying and tracking the EAD instance.

Representation (<representation>): a link to a deliverable version of the description.

File Description (<filedesc>): title, edition, publication, series, and notes describing the description.

Maintenance Status (<maintenancestatus>): enumerated values indicating the drafting status of the EAD instance.

Publication Status (<publicationstatus>): enumerated values indicating the publication status of the EAD instance.

Maintenance Agency (<maintenanceagency>): the institution responsible for the creation, maintenance, or dissemination of the Encoded Archival Context—Corporate bodies, Persons, and Families (EAC-CPF) instance.

Language Declaration (<languagedeclaration>): declaration of the language used in the EAD instance.

Convention Declaration (<conventiondeclaration>): declaration of the rules or conventions, including authorized controlled vocabularies and thesauri, applied in creating the EAD instance.

Local Type Declaration (<localtypedeclaration>): declaration of any local conventions used in the local type attribute in the EAD instance.

Local Control (<localcontrol>): additional control entries necessary to accommodate local practice.

Maintenance History (<maintenancehistory>): information on the history of the creation and maintenance of the EAD instance.

Sources (<sources>): the sources used for the description of the records in the EAD instance.

Of these sections, <recordid>, <filedesc>, <maintenancestatus>, <maintenanceagency>, and <maintenancehistory> are required.

The section dedicated to an archival description is <archdesc>. The <archdesc> is probably best understood as representing the logical semantics and structure of archival description, with additional semantics and structure that facilitate navigable and intelligible rendering for those seeking archival records. These additional structures enable labeling sections or descriptive components and rendering them in forms that are readily understood. An example of the former is Head (<head>), which enables the archivist to supply section titles, and an example of the latter is Paragraph (<p>), which enables rendering of prose description. The primary focus of <archdesc>, though, is the hierarchical description itself.

The first component of the archival description is Descriptive Identification (<did>). The <did> is intended to succinctly provide all of the information

Document-Engineering

necessary to uniquely identify the collection and make a competent first-pass judgment of its relevancy. The information is succinctly stated and collocated in order to function as a summary surrogate for the complete description, in particular in retrieval sets in union archival description systems (such as those used by state and regional consortia, and archival gateways). Archivists have identified the following descriptive elements to support these objectives:

Unit Identifier (<unitid>): unique identifier of the *fonds*, including a national identifier and repository identifier.

Unit Title (<unittitle>): title of the *fonds*.

Unit Date (<unitdate>) or Unit Date Structured (<unitdatestructured>): date range of the earliest and latest creation, frequently with a second range for the dates within which the bulk of the materials was created.

Origination (<origination>): Provenance or creator information.

Physical Description (<physdesc>) or Physical Description Structured (<physdescstructured>): description usually of the extent of the materials described, either in terms of the space occupied (e.g. linear feet), carriers (e.g. number of boxes), or material types (e.g. a count of photographs).

Repository (<repository>): archival institution holding the collection.

Language of the Materials (<langmaterial>): Languages or scripts represented in the content, with languages provided in Language (<language>) and scripts provided in Script (<script>).

Abstract (): summary of either or both the scope and content, or biography or administrative history.

Following the summary description of the *fonds*, several components already described in summary form are described in more detail. In addition, some new descriptive elements that are not considered essential to the objectives of the summary description but are essential or at least useful for fully understanding and using the collections are provided. Expanded descriptions are commonly provided for Scope and Content (<scopecontent>) and Biography or History (<bioghist>), both of which may have been provided in summarized form in the in the <did>. Further information may be provided in the following descriptive components:

Arrangement (<arrangement>): information on the intellectual analysis and arrangement of the records, reflecting, in principle, the original order and the hierarchical analysis reflected in the description.

Access Restrictions (<accessrestrict>): information concerning limitations on physical access to the records because of privacy, agreements with donors, or other reasons.

Use Restrictions (<userestrict>): information concerning copyright restrictions.

Acquisition Information (<acqinfo>): information on the immediate source of the records and the circumstances of the acquisition.

Controlled Access (<controlaccess>): controlled personal name, family name, corporate name subject, genre or form, function or activity, geographic, title, and other headings under authority control.

Preferred Citation (<prefercite>): information on the preferred form of citation of the records in referencing or citing publications.

Processing Information (<processinfo>): information on archival record processing activities applied to the records such as accessioning, describing, preserving, and storing.

Related Material (<relatedmaterial>): information, usually in the form of a citation, on intellectually related records (though not related by provenance).

Separated Material (<separatedmaterial>): information, usually in the form of a citation, on publications and artifacts in a collection, or archival records that have been separated from the *fonds*, frequently for curatorial reasons.

Accruals (<accruals>): information about anticipated additions to the materials, including (when available) information indicating the quantity and frequency of additions.

Several additional descriptive components are available. This additional information is provided when it is appropriate and available. When copies of the records, such as microfilm copies or digital facsimiles are available, this is typically noted. The corollary is also true, that is, in the description of copies of archival records, information about the originals is provided. If there is more than one description of a *fonds*, each description will reference the alternative description. For example, predominately French-language *fonds* may be held by an institution that prepares descriptions in English. A French translation of the original English description would function as an alternative finding aid.

EAD attempts to be comprehensive in accommodating accepted components of archival description. Due to the nature and complexity of archival records and the *fonds* within which they are interrelated, descriptive information deemed essential or at least useful may not be accommodated within an existing element. EAD accommodates such information with the Other Descriptive Data (<odd>). It is similar to the use of a general note in bibliographic description.

Semantics and Structure: Hierarchical Analysis

The EAD apparatus used in the hierarchal analysis is the Description of Subordinate Components (<dsc>). The key element within the <dsc> is the Component, which comes in two forms, simple and enumerated. To enable hierarchical description, each Component is recursive, which is to say, it is available within itself. The simple form is called <c>, and the enumerated form is called <c01>, <c02>, through <c12>. The major difference between the two forms is that the <c> permits unlimited recursion or depth of analysis, and the enumerated limits depth of analysis to 12 levels. Because more than 12 levels of analysis is rare, choosing which form of the Component to use is primarily a decision based on ease of use and processing, usually influenced by the software chosen for processing.

Each <c> or <c01> through <c12> contains all of the descriptive components available in the <archdesc>, beginning with the <did>. This availability reflects a rule governing archival description described earlier, that all components of description are available at each level of descriptive analysis. Thus all of the <did> contained elements are available, as are <scopecontent>, <arrangement>, and so on. While all of the components are available throughout the hierarchy, because of the inheritance of description both the number of elements employed and the quantity of description contained in them typically decrease through each descending level of analysis.

In order to understand the way in which the hierarchical analysis unfolds as reflected in the EAD structure, it is useful to translate common patterns of analysis. The following examples exclude the *fonds* description, as it has been covered immediately above.

Fonds-series-file (3 levels including *fonds*)

```
<c01 level="series">
 [description]
  <c02 level="file">
   [description]
  </c02>
</c01>
```

Fonds-series-subseries-file (4 levels including *fonds*)

```
<c01 level="series">
 [description]
  <c02 level="subseries">
   [description]
    <c03 level="file">
```

```
     [description]
    </c03>
  </c02>
</c01>
```

Fonds-series-file-item (2 levels including *fonds*)

```
<c01 level="series">
 [description]
  <c02 level="file">
   [description]
    <c03 level="item">
     [description]
    </c03>
  </c02>
</c01>
```

Fonds-series-subseries-file-item (5 levels including *fonds*)

```
<c01 level="series">
 [description]
  <c02 level="subseries">
   [description]
    <c03 level="file">
     [description]
      <c04 level="item">
       [description]
      </c04>
    </c03>
  </c02>
</c01>
```

It is very important to note that <c01> through <c12> are not to be equated with the level of analysis. The <c01> places the description within a hierarchy but does not itself indicate the level of analysis. The level of analysis is rather indicated through the use of a Level attribute on the tag, for example, <c01 level="series">. Note that in example 1 mentioned earlier, <c02> has the Level attribute value "file," while in example 2, the <c02> has the Level attribute value "subseries." This is further complicated by the fact that even within one series, for example, the Level attribute values of the same subordinate Component may change, depending on the arrangement of the records.

Following the same pattern as the <archdesc>, the first and required descriptive element in each descriptive component is <did>. Typically, each <did>, no matter what the level of analysis (*fonds*, series, subseries, file, item), will contain a <unittitle>, a <unitdate>, or <unitdatestructured>, and often a <physdesc> or <physdescstructured>. For series and subseries analysis, the <did> is generally augmented with a <scopecontent> and an <arrangement>.

When a user identifies records of interest, the archival staff and the user need to know in what box and folder or folders the records will be found (or other container types, as appropriate to the nature of the records). The organization of records in storage containers has its own inherent physical logic and structure, independent of the intellectual arrangement of the records. EAD privileges the intellectual arrangement in the single hierarchy that XML supports, and thus information on the physical organization and storage is subordinate to the intellectual arrangement. Information about the box and folder or other medium of storage is given in Container (<container>), an element contained in the <did>. Container information is most appropriately supplied at the deepest or terminal components of description. Following this practice, in the hierarchies illustrated earlier, <container> would appear within the <did> in the following component descriptions:

```
1.  <c02 level="file">
2.  <c03 level="file">
3.  <c03 level="item">
4.  <c04 level="item">
```

Access to archival records can also be facilitated via the Digital Archival Object (<dao>) element. Like <container>, <dao> provides necessary information for the retrieval and delivery of records, but in the form of a link to an online resource rather than a box or folder number.

In order to complete our understanding of how the hierarchical descriptive apparatus works in EAD, it is necessary to understand one additional feature of the use of Component. Not only are the Component elements recursive, they are also repeatable. Thus, at the top level of analytic description, the <c01> is repeated. A *fonds* comprising four series will have a sequence of four <c01>s, one for each series. Within a series, a series containing 12 files will begin with a <c01>, and within it, a sequence of 12 <c02>s, one for each file. While the order of the sequence (arrangement) may not always be significant, in many and perhaps most descriptions it is important, such as, when a sequence of files is arranged chronologically by date of creation or alphabetically by title.

Repeating <c01> components

```
<c01 level="series">
  [description of series 1]
</c01>
<c01 level="series">
  [description of series 2]
</c01>
<c01 level="series">
  [description of series 3]
</c01>
```

HISTORY

Work on an encoding standard for archival description began in 1992 at the University of California, Berkeley.

In the early 1980s, archivists developed the MARC AMC (MAchine-Readable Cataloging for Archives and Manuscript Control) format that enabled archivists to make collection-level summary descriptions available in online catalogs. While representing a major improvement in archival access, the full, detailed descriptions found in finding aids remained available only in printed forms. There was a widespread perception in the archival community that a method for making the full descriptions Internet-accessible was needed. Many archivists experimented with the use of database technologies as a solution. The complex, unbounded hierarchical descriptions found in finding aids, however, were not easily accommodated using database technology. The Berkeley effort was initiated by Timothy Hoyer in the Bancroft Library, who recruited Daniel Pitti to work on the problem. With a grant from the U.S. Department of Education, Pitti developed a prototype SGML DTD based on representative sample finding aids contributed by archivists at collaborating institutions in the United States. The FindAid DTD, as the prototype was called, served to demonstrate the feasibility and utility of using markup technologies, rather than MARC or database technologies, to develop an encoding method that would enable Internet-accessible finding aids.

At the conclusion of the Berkeley project, the Commission on Preservation and Access sponsored a conference in Berkeley to bring together archivists, librarians, and technologists to evaluate the results. With encouragement from the participants at this conference, Pitti applied for and was awarded a Bentley Historical Library fellowship that brought together seven archival description experts, Pitti, and Steve DeRose, a systems designer and developer at Electronic Book Technologies. The description experts were Jackie M. Dooley (University of California, Irvine), Michael J. Fox (Minnesota Historical Society), Steven L. Hensen (Duke University), Kris Kiesling (Harry Ransom Center), Janet E. Ruth (Library of Congress), Sharon Gibbs Thibodeau (National Archives and Records Administration), and Helena Zinkham (Library of Congress). The team met for one week in summer, 1995, in Ann Arbor, MI. Based on experience with the FindAid prototype, the team substantially revised the underlying conceptual model, in part in reference to *ISAD(G)*. The prototype standard that emerged from this meeting was renamed EAD.

Subsequent to the Ann Arbor meeting, the Library of Congress and the SAA agreed to share responsibility for further development and maintenance of the emerging standard. SAA formally charged the EAD Working Group (EADWG) in August 1995 with overseeing the ongoing development of the standard. With support from the Library of Congress National Digital Library Program, Delmas Foundation, and Council on Library Resources (now Council on Library and Information Resources), the EADWG met several times from 1995 to 1998 to further revise the conceptual model, and review and revise first the alpha and then the beta versions of the EAD DTD and Tag Library. Version 1.0 of the EAD DTD and Tag Library were released in summer 1998. The version 1.0 DTD was compliant with both SGML and XML.

Subsequent to the release of EAD version 1.0, there were developments in both technological and descriptive standards that led the EADWG to begin revising EAD. Released in early 1998 by the W3C, XML was quickly embraced by both developers and users. The availability of software for the editing, validation, and processing of XML made it possible for users of EAD to make a transition from SGML to XML. The ICA also completed its review and revision of *ISAD(G)* in 2000. With funding from the National Historical Publications and Records Commission (NHPRC), the EADWG began revision of EAD in 2000. Based on comments and suggestions solicited from the EAD user community and the second edition of *ISAD(G)*, EAD 2002 was developed and released. Following the release of version 2002, responding to the emergence of schemas as an alternative to DTDs, the EADWG released two schema versions of the 2002 DTD in early 2008, one in the Relax NG Schema syntax and the other in W3C Schema syntax. Funding for this work was again provided by NHPRC.

By 2010, 8 years after the release of EAD 2002, significant developments in both archival description and information technologies made a second revision of EAD necessary, in particular the release of EAC-CPF[7] in 2010, the development of collection management systems such as Archivists' Toolkit and Archon, and the emergence of Linked Open Data. The SAA Standards Committee charged a new group, the Technical Subcommittee for Encoded Archival Description (TS-EAD) to replace the EAD Working Group, and tasked it to complete a revision of EAD within 5 years. Funding for the revision was provided by the Gladys Krieble Delmas Foundation, the National Endowment for the Humanities, and the Nationaal Archief of the Netherlands. The revision process encompassed four public comment periods and three draft releases, and the resulting version—EAD3—will be released officially in 2015. EAD3 is a significant revision of the standard, with many changes intended to achieve greater conceptual and semantic consistency, make it easier to exchange or incorporate data maintained according to other protocols, and better support multilingual description.

Since its release in 1998, adoption and use of EAD by institutions with archival holdings has increased steadily. While only a few institutions employed EAD in the first year or two after its release, today EAD is used around the world by scores of academic research libraries, business archives, historical societies, museums, national libraries and archives, and other archival repositories. State and regional consortia in the United States have formed to provide union access to the archival holdings of members.

Similar regional, national, and international consortia have formed in Europe and elsewhere. The EAD Tag Library has been translated into Spanish, Greek, Chinese, French, German, Italian, and Russian. Reflecting the internationalization of EAD, the members of the TS-EAD represent seven countries.

FUTURE

Paralleling the ever increasing utility of computer and network technologies, archival descriptive practice has been undergoing a transition from the printed finding aid to an integrated archival description system. This transition is at least in part inspired by the advancements in the technology. Particularly important have been database technologies, in particular relational and object-relational databases, and markup technologies. Each of these technologies is optimized to represent and facilitate the maintenance and use of distinct data structures. Many real world data structures, however, are not wholly of one type or the other, which has required those promoting automation to make difficult compromises when choosing which technology to use. But there are indications that this situation is changing. Many of the major developers of database technologies, responding to real world data structures and needs, are exploring the integration of database and markup technologies. If these efforts are successful, archivists will no longer have to choose between the two technologies and will be able to take advantage of the strengths of each.

In a world dominated by print technologies, archivists have generally employed a single apparatus, the finding aid, to describe all of the records created by a single person, family, or corporate body. For a given *fonds*, the finding aid brought together information describing the creator, the functions performed by the creator, the records that facilitated or documented the performance of the functions, and the archival institution responsible for the records. Since at least the early 1980s, archivists have been discussing "relational" archival systems that enable creating and maintaining each of these fundamental components of description separately and bringing them together dynamically upon user request. Such an approach not only has economic advantages, but also supports more flexible and accurate description, and greatly enhanced access.

The ICA has supported the development of four standards for the components of archival description. The first of these standards, *ISAD(G)*, addresses the description of archival records and was first released in 1993. A second edition was released in 2000. Following *ISAD(G)* was *International Standard Archival Authority Control for Corporate Bodies, Persons, and Families (ISAAR(CPF))* in 1996, with a second edition in 2003.[8] The third and fourth standards, *International Standard for Describing*

Functions (ISDF)[9] and International Standard for the Description of Institutions with Archival Holdings (ISDIAH),[10] were released in 2007 and 2008, respectively. Each of these standards provides a framework for the intellectual content of the four areas of description: records, creators, functions, and repositories. All are intended to function together in a complete archival description. In order to be realized in a dynamic archival description system, though, communication standards for each are necessary.

EAD was originally designed as a communication standard for archival description as represented in finding aids. As such, the four descriptive components were and continue to be interleaved in EAD. Separate, dedicated, and detailed encoding standards for each are necessary, however, to achieve the goal of dynamic and efficient archival description. EAC-CPF is the communication standard for ISAAR(CPF), and preliminary work to develop a communication standard for ISDF is under way. A future version of EAC-CPF will likely serve as the communication standard for ISDIAH. In addition to communication standards, however, it is necessary to formalize and express in consistent terminology how the components of archival description relate to each other. Toward that end, ICA charged the Experts Group on Archival Description for a term spanning 2012–2016 with the goal of developing a formal conceptual model for archival description and an accompanying ontology.[11] Future versions of EAD will be heavily influenced by the conceptual model developed by the EGAD and will further integrate with the related communication standards for archival description.

REFERENCES

1. International Council on Archives. *ISAD(G): General International Standard Archival Description*, 2nd Ed.; International Council on Archives: Ottawa, ON, 2000. http://www.ica.org/10207/standards/isadg-general-international-standard-archival-description-second-edition.html (accessed November 2, 2014).

2. Society of American Archivists. *Describing Archives: A Content Standard*, 2nd Ed.; Society of American Archivists: Chicago, IL. http://www2.archivists.org/standards/DACS (accessed November 2, 2014).

3. Online Archive of California. *Mayor Tom Bradley Administrative Papers 1973–1993*; Online Archive of California: Oakland, CA. http://www.oac.cdlib.org/findaid/ark:/13030/kt4489n8jd/.

4. Fox, M.J. *Introduction to Archival Organization and Description*; Getty Information Institute: Los Angeles, CA, 1998.

5. Society of American Archivists, and Library of Congress. *Encoded Archival Description Tag Library*; Society of American Archivists: Chicago, IL, 2002. version 2002; EAD technical document, no. 2. http://www.loc.gov/ead/tglib/index.html (accessed November 2, 2014).

6. Ruth, J. The development and structure of the encoded archival description (EAD) document type definition. J. Internet Catalog. **2001**, *4* (3), 27–61. [Taylor & Francis Online], [CSA].

7. Society of American Archivists; Staatsbibliothek zu Berlin. *Encoded Archival Context—Corporate bodies, Persons and Families (EAC-CPF) Tag Library*; Society of American Archivists: Chicago, IL, 2010, version 2014. http://eac.staatsbibliothek-berlin.de/fileadmin/user_upload/schema/cpfTagLibrary.html (accessed November 2, 2014).

8. International Council of Archives. *ISAAR(CPF): International Standard Archival Authority Control for Corporate Bodies, Persons, and Families*, 2nd Ed.; International Council of Archives: Ottawa, ON, 2003. http://www.ica.org/10203/standards/isaar-cpf-international-standard-archival-authority-record-for-corporate-bodies-persons-and-families-2nd-edition.html (accessed November 2, 2014).

9. International Council on Archives. *ISDF: International Standard for Describing Functions*; International Council on Archives: Ottawa, ON, 2008. http://www.ica.org/10208/standards/isdf-international-standard-for-describing-functions.html (accessed November 2, 2014).

10. International Council on Archives. *ISDIAH: International Standard for Describing Institutions with Archival Holdings*; International Council on Archives: Ottawa, Ontario, Canada, 2008. http://www.ica.org/10198/standards/isdiah-international-standard-for-describing-institutions-with-archival-holdings.html (accessed November 2, 2014).

11. International Council on Archives. *ICArchives: The Experts Group on Archival Description: About the EGAD*; International Council on Archives: Ottawa, Ontario, Canada. http://www.ica.org/13799/the-experts-group-on-archival-description/about-the-egad.html (accessed November 2, 2014).

Engineering Literatures and Their Users *[ELIS Classic]*

Thomas E. Pinelli
*Langley Research Center, National Aeronautics and Space Administration (NASA) Hampton,
Virginia, U.S.A.*

Ann P. Bishop
*Graduate School of Library and Information Science, University of Illinois at Urbana-
Champaign, Urbana, Illinois, U.S.A.*

Rebecca O. Barclay
Rensselaer Polytechnic Institute, Troy, New York, U.S.A.

John M. Kennedy
Indiana University, Bloomington, Indiana, U.S.A.

Abstract

Research on the information seeking of engineers over decades has found—despite the many changes in
information technologies—on the whole, relatively stable behaviors. This ELIS Classic article from 1993
is written by several people who have been at the forefront of research in this area for some time.

—*ELIS Classic, from 1993*

INTRODUCTION

Engineers are an extraordinarily diverse group of professionals, but an attribute common to all engineers is their
use of information. Engineering can be conceptualized as
an information processing system that must deal with
work-related uncertainty through patterns of technical
communications. Throughout the process, data, information, and tacit knowledge are being acquired, produced,
transferred, and utilized. (See Entry 2, "Technology Policy and the Technology Base" in *Beyond Spinoff: Military
and Commercial Technologies in a Changing World*, by
John A. Alic et al. for an in-depth discussion of "tacit"
knowledge.) The fact that these data, information, and
tacit knowledge deal with hard technologies or may be
"physically or hardware encoded"[1] should not detract
from the observation that engineering is fundamentally an
information processing activity. The engineer can be
viewed as the center of that information processing system. According to Sayer:[2]

> Engineering is a production system in which data, infor-
> mation, and knowledge are new materials. Whatever the
> purpose of the engineering effort, the engineer is an infor-
> mation processor who is constantly faced with the prob-
> lem of effectively acquiring, using, producing, and
> transferring data, Information, and knowledge.

While acknowledging that other models exist (see
Wilkins[3] for a discussion of other models), we have
chosen to view the information-seeking behavior of engineers within a conceptual framework of the engineer as an
information processor. This article uses the chosen framework to discuss information-seeking behavior of engineers, reviewing selected literature and empirical studies
from library and information science, management, communications, and sociology. The article concludes by proposing a research agenda designed to extend our current,
limited knowledge of the way engineers process
information.

BACKGROUND

Stevens[4] and Paisley[5] provide useful discussions of
information in terms of history, definitions, and frameworks for analysis. The concept of information-seeking is
imbedded in studies of users, use, and uses. These studies
constitute "one of the most extensive and amorphous areas
of research in library and information sciences over the
better part of four decades."[6] (See the *Annual Review of
Information Science and Technology* for reviews of information needs and use). The majority of the studies, and
certainly the early studies, concentrated on the uses of
scientific and technical information (STI). In the majority
of these STI usage studies however, scientists, not engineers, were the subjects of investigation.

The literature regarding the information-seeking
behavior of engineers is fragmented and superficial. The
results of these studies have not accumulated to form a
significant body of knowledge. The difficulty in applying
the results of these studies has been attributed to the lack
of a unifying theory, standardized methodology, and

common definitions. With specific reference to engineers, the difficulty may be attributed to the failure of researchers to take into account the essential difference between science and technology and, similarly, between engineers and scientists.[7] This fundamental difference is emphasized by Vincenti[8] in his analysis of the role of knowledge in technological developments.

Engineering is a process dominated by engineers and technology as opposed to scientists and science. As Joenk points out, this fact "leads to different philosophies, habits, and behaviors not only about contributing to the technical literature but also to using the technical literature and other sources of information."[9] Recent interest in the information-seeking behavior of engineers corresponds to rising interest and concerns regarding industrial competitiveness and technological innovation. Consequently, an understanding of the information-seeking behavior of engineers is essential to predicting information use and to planning, developing, and implementing engineering information systems. Such an understanding is also critical to enhancing economic competitiveness, improving productivity, and maximizing the process of technological innovation.

THE WORLD OF ENGINEERING

According to the U.S. Bureau of Labor Statistics, engineers held almost 1,411,000 jobs in 1988. About half of these jobs were located in manufacturing industries: about 511,000 were located in nonmanufacturing industries; and about 185,000 were employed by federal, state, and local governments. About one-third of these jobs (439,000) were held by electrical engineers followed, in decreasing order of frequency, by mechanical (225,000), civil (186,000), and industrial (132,000) engineers. A bachelor's degree in engineering from an accredited engineering program is generally acceptable for beginning engineering jobs. Most engineering degrees are granted in branches such as electrical, chemical, or nuclear engineering. Within these branches, most engineers specialize; more than 25 major specialties are recognized by professional societies. *The Occupational Outlook Handbook*[10] lists and discusses the ten branches of engineering: aerospace; chemical; civil; electrical and electronics; industrial; mechanical; metallurgical, ceramic, and materials; mining; nuclear; and petroleum.

Formal registration is a requirement in the United States for engineers whose work may affect life, health, or property, or who offer their services to the public. Registration generally requires, in addition to a degree from an engineering program accredited by the Accreditation Board for Engineering and Technology (ABET), four years of relevant work experience and satisfactory performance on a state examination.

The engineering profession cannot be described fully without reference to the nature of engineering work, knowledge, and communication. These three areas are also important in establishing the conceptual framework of the engineer as an information processor.

ENGINEERING WORK

What is engineering work like? What tasks and activities are performed by engineers on a day-to-day basis? Florman,[11] an engineer who has written extensively on the nature of the professional, proclaims that

> the essence of engineering lies in its need and willingness to embrace opposites. Empiricism and theory, craftsmanship and science, workshop and laboratory, apprenticeship and formal schooling, private initiative, and government venture, commerce and independent professionalism, military necessity and civic benefit—all of these and more have their place.[11]

In trying to sort out the diversity of engineering, Adams notes that it may be categorized according to, among other things, particular industries, fields, disciplines, job functions, and end products. He concludes that engineering is interlocked with science, mathematics, and business in a complex environment that "requires a multidimensional map for understanding."[12]

The characteristic activity of engineers is making things. Expressed more formally, engineering is usually defined as the application of scientific knowledge to the creation or improvement of technology for human use.[13] The term "technology" as used in the context of describing engineering work encompasses products, systems, structures, and processes. Engineering work is often described as a process that originates with the first idea for a new or improved technology that is put into use. The National Research Council, for example, describes what it calls "the product realization process" as extending "over all phases of product development from initial planning to customer follow-up."[14] Phases in this process include: definition of customer needs and product performance requirements, planning for product evolution, planning for design and manufacturing, product design, manufacturing process design, and production.

Engineering work can also be described in terms of the kinds of tasks and activities that engineers perform on a day-to-day basis. Because of the multidimensional nature of engineering work and the extensiveness of the product development process, engineers perform a wide variety of tasks. Engineering work involves cognitive activities and physical tasks that include the technical and the nontechnical, the routine and the creative, the rational and the serendipitous. According to Ritti,[15] engineering work consists of scientific experimentation, mathematical analysis, design and drafting, building and testing of prototypes, technical writing, marketing, and project management. Murotake calls attention to the nontechnical elements of engineering work: "the process of engineering work is not only a technical one, but a social one in which management, communication, and motivation influence the efficiency, quality, and innovativeness of the project team's work."[16] If the characteristic physical activity of engineering is making things, the characteristic cognitive activity is problem-solving. Laudan notes that "change and progress in technology is achieved by the selection and solution of technological problems, followed by choice between rival solutions."[17]

The great variety in the nature of the tasks and activities that comprise engineering work is often reflected in the individual engineer's work, as well. Kemper notes that the typical engineer is likely to define problems, come up with new ideas, produce designs, solve problems, manage the work of others, produce reports, perform calculations, and conduct experiments.[13] Hollister also describes the work of an engineer as multifaceted: "He begins with an idea, a mental conception. He conducts studies, and when necessary, research into the feasibility of this idea. He directs the building and operation of what he has planned."[18] Mailloux highlights the centrality of knowledge production and transfer to engineering work. She reports that about

> 20% of an engineer's time is spent in the intellectual activities of engineering—conceiving, sketching, calculating, and evaluating—with the remaining 80% spent on activities associated with creating, accessing, reviewing, manipulating, or transferring information.[19]

Although engineers perform many tasks independently, most products result from team effort, requiring engineers to share their knowledge and the result of their work with others.[20] For complex products, teamwork is required at each stage of the engineering process. The literature on concurrent engineering indicates that teamwork is a natural requirement of the need to integrate the various stages of the engineering process. (see, e.g., Stoll[21]). Bringing a high-quality product to market in an efficient manner often requires, for example, that design engineers communicate with managers, manufacturing and marketing staff within their firm as well as with people outside their organizations, such as clients, funders, and suppliers.

Engineering work takes place in a variety of environments, depending not only on the nature of the product being developed and the stage of product development, but also on the type of employing organization. Organizations employing engineers include universities, research centers, government laboratories and agencies, and private sector manufacturers and consulting firms. The basic goal of engineering is to produce usable products in the shortest possible time at the lowest possible cost. This goal drives the work and communication activities of virtually all engineers, but it is manifested to a different degree in different employment settings.

ENGINEERING KNOWLEDGE

What kinds of knowledge do engineers need to perform the tasks and activities described above? How is knowledge acquired? Engineering work and knowledge are so closely intertwined, that it is difficult to discuss one without the other. As noted by Vincenti, "... engineering knowledge cannot—and should not—be separated from engineering practice. The nature of engineering knowledge, the process of its generation, and the engineering activity it serves form an inseparable whole."[8] Engineering practice, in other words, involves both knowing and doing. Even the popular literature suggests the wide variety of knowledge needed by engineers, due to the diversity of their work:

> [The engineer's] task is not alone that of contrivance with material things, for which he must possess an extensive working knowledge of scientific principles and facts. He must also thoroughly understand the functions to be performed by the projected work when it is completed, the methods of its manufacture and construction, and the economics that govern its use. He must have an understanding of the crafts that are to be used and of the organization of the work. It is his responsibility to coordinate and guide the contributions of labor, machines, money, and ideas, and to exert the control necessary to attain his objectives within the prescribed limits of time, cost, and safety.[18]

Scholarly literature on the nature and generation of engineering knowledge reinforces such popular accounts. Donovan asserts that the range of scientific and technical knowledge used by engineers includes "not only the more formal types of experimental and theoretical knowledge but also all forms of practical skill and tacit understanding as well ...."[22]

Schön rejects the model of technical rationality which is typically applied to scientific and technical professions and paints instead a different picture of engineering knowledge. He argues that the situations encountered by practicing professionals are increasingly characterized by "complexity, uncertainty, instability, uniqueness, and value conflicts";[23] such situations require intuitive, artistic, and ethical responses in addition to purely technical and rational ones. Schön labels this model of professional work "tacit knowing-in-action"[23] and describes the development of a new process to produce a desired gunmetal color to illustrate his argument. He represents the activities of the mechanical engineers involved in this project as "a reflective conversation with the materials of the situation ... [that] wove its way through stages of diagnosis, experiment, pilot process, and production design."[23] Throughout this process, experiments are used to explore puzzling phenomena, test the applicability of potentially useful theories, or achieve particular technological effects. These experiments, however, often produce unanticipated phenomena and outcomes, which then trigger new hypotheses, questions, and goals.[23] Schön's analysis of this and other examples suggests that the knowledge required to reach a technological solution is derived from the integration of intuition, past experience, creativity (often in the form of analogy development), theory, experimentation, and reflective thinking that occur in a particular problematic situation. He also argues that engineering solutions incorporate social and ethical considerations.

As these accounts suggest, the notion of tacit knowledge permeates discussions of engineering work. Tacit knowledge is knowledge that cannot be articulated. Polanyi describes tacit knowledge—part experience, part intuition, part tactile sensation—as combining "knowing what" and "knowing how" and declares that it is expressed in such actions as expert diagnoses, the performance of skills, and the use of tools.[24] Another important type of engineering knowledge, visual information, is also expressed in a nonverbal manner. The importance of visual information in technological work is the subject of a paper by Ferguson and is also discussed by Breton.[25] Layton[26] describes this phenomenon, too: "technologists display a plastic, geometrical, and to some extent nonverbal mode of thought that has more in common with that of artists than that of philosophers."[26] The importance of these two nonverbal modes of thought is rooted in the essence of engineering as the production of physically encoded knowledge. Engineers must know how to make things, and the results of this knowledge are, first and foremost, encoded in the technologies produced. Engineers rely heavily on nontextual information, such as interpersonal communication, drawings, and the examination of physical objects, to acquire the knowledge they need to perform their work.

Holmfeld found three common mechanisms for generating needed knowledge in engineering work. Engineers rely on the "cut and try" method to refine and fine tune.[20] They also frequently search their memories for familiar concepts and designs in order to increase their confidence in some new variation.[20] Finally, they make use of that scientific knowledge which they deem to be relevant and readily applicable. This knowledge is often in the form of a simple fact, such as the optimum hole size or speed rotation, resulting from scientific work.[20] A number of other writers also note that engineers adopt, at times, the methods used by scientists to generate knowledge. Florman describes engineering work as encompassing both theory and empiricism.[11] Ziman writes that

technological development itself has become 'scientific': it is no longer satisfactory, in the design of a new automobile, say, to rely on rule of thumb, cut and fit, or simple trial and error. Data are collected, phenomena are observed, hypotheses are proposed, and theories are tested in the true spirit of the hypothetico-deductive method.[27]

Constant presents a detailed history of the origin of the modern jet engine, a revolutionary technological advance. He presents a "variation-retention" model of technological change that is based on the process of random variation and selective retention that occurs in biological organisms. Technological conjecture, which can occur as a result of knowledge gained from either scientific theory or engineering practice, yields potential variations to existing technologies. These variations are subsequently tested, and successful variations are retained.[28] In the case of the turbojet revolution, technological conjecture was based on engineers' knowledge of scientific theories. The design, development, and testing of systems that resulted in the retention of the most successful variation involved, on the other hand, the technical and craft knowledge needed to carry out those tasks.

Vincenti traces five "normal" (as opposed to revolutionary) developments in the history of aerospace engineering to detail what he calls "the anatomy of engineering design knowledge."[8] His examples reveal that technological developments require a range of scientific, technical and practical knowledge as well as information about social, economic, military, and environmental issues. Vincenti conducts three important analyses of engineering knowledge. The first involves his own elaboration of the variation-selection model of the growth of technological knowledge. Vincenti concludes, after examining numerous examples from history, that the mechanisms for producing variations in engineering design include three types of cognitive activities:[8] searching past experience to find knowledge that has proved useful, including the identification of variations that have not worked; incorporating novel features thought to have some chance of working; and "winnowing" the conceived variations to choose those most likely to work. Vincenti notes that these activities occur in an interactive and disorderly fashion. Selection occurs through physical trials such as everyday use, experiments, simulations (e.g., the use of wind tunnels), or analytical tests such as the production of sketches of proposed designs, calculations, and other means of imagining the outcome of selecting a proposed variation.[8]

Vincenti also proposes a schema for engineering knowledge that categorizes knowledge as either descriptive (factual knowledge), prescriptive (knowledge of the desired end), or tacit (knowledge that cannot be expressed in words or pictures but is embodied in judgment and skills). Descriptive and prescriptive knowledge are explicit; tacit knowledge is implicit. Both tacit and prescriptive knowledge are procedural and reflect a "knowing how."[8] Finally, Vincenti enumerates and defines specific engineering knowledge categories: fundamental design concepts, criteria and specifications, theoretical tools (i.e., mathematical methods and theories and intellectual concepts), quantitative data, practical considerations, and design instrumentalities (i.e., procedural knowledge and judgmental skills).[8] He then presents a matrix that details how each type of knowledge is acquired. The possible sources of engineering knowledge that he describes include transfer from science or generation by engineers during invention, theoretical and experimental engineering research, design practice, production, or direct trial and operation.[8]

Communications and management studies confirm the findings of historical and sociological research about the range of knowledge, information, and data needed in engineering work. Ancona and Caldwell investigated the tasks and communication of new product development teams in high technology companies. The authors note that such teams

> are responsible not only for the specific technical design of a product, but also for coordinating the numerous functional areas and hierarchical levels that have information and resources necessary to make the new product a success.[29]

Ancona and Caldwell found that new product teams progress through three phases of activity: creation, development, and diffusion. The communication- and information-intensive tasks that accompany these phases include:[29]

- Getting to know and trust team members
- Determining the availability of resources
- Understanding what other functional groups think the product can should be
- Investigating technologies for building the product
- Exploring potential markets
- Solving technical problems
- Coordinating the teams' work internally and externally
- Keeping external groups informed
- Building relationships with external groups that will receive the team's output
- Promoting the product with manufacturing, marketing, and service groups.

Ancona and Caldwell conclude that information systems designed to support these changing activities must be flexible and support the team's need to identify and contact relevant external groups, generate and evaluate ideas, and coordinate work. Barczak and Wilemon also look at the communication patterns of new product development teams and find a similar range of communication purposes: to discuss product features, technical issues, customer needs, manufacturing issues, schedules and timing, financial issues, managerial issues, and resources issues.[30]

THE ENGINEERING COMMUNITY

Engineering work and communication are rooted in the concept of "community." A community is a group of people who maintain social contact with each other and who exhibit common interests, goals, norms of behavior, and knowledge. As members of a profession, engineers share a common knowledge base and set of espoused values. The profession prescribes its own approach to work behavior. Engineering is also a social activity; most work is accomplished as a result of group effort and requires extensive interpersonal communication.

Studies of scientific communities look at the values, norms, knowledge, methods, reward system, and culture shared by community members and frequently underscore the role of interpersonal communication in defining the community and holding it together. (see e.g., Barber–Kuhn[31–33]). This type of investigation has not often been performed in relation to engineering communities. Gaston notes that "[the problem of the internal workings of the technological community] is virtually unexplored. . . . In contrast to the sociology of the scientific community, little is known about the sociology of the technological community."[34] Constant also notes the lack of research on technological communities. He writes that "While extensive research has been done on 'invisible colleges,' research fronts, and the community structure of science, there has been little analogous [sic] sociological or historical investigation of technological practice."[35] Rothstein, pointing to the diversity inherent in engineering, warns that defining the entire profession of engineering as a single community provides a model that is inadequate to describe engineering behavior. He argues that the huge variety of occupations and disciplines in engineering demonstrates that there is no such thing as a single engineering community. Further, he contends that most discussions of professional communities fail to direct enough attention to the nature of professional knowledge and its influence on behavior. He contends that the heterogeneity, rate of change, and degree of specialization of engineering knowledge also lead to the emergence of specific communities in engineering.[36]

Some work has begun to explore the extent to which members of engineering communities share similar work tasks, goals, and methods; are governed by shared social and technical norms; and engage in extensive informal information exchange among themselves. Laudan finds justification for this approach in that

> cognitive change in technology is the result of the purposeful problem-solving activities of members of relatively small communities of practitioners, just as cognitive change in science is the product of the problem-solving activities of the members of scientific communities.[17]

Layton also contends that "... the ideas of technologists cannot be understood in isolation; they must be seen in the context of a community of technologists . . . ."[27] Donovan notes that "the study of engineering knowledge must not be divorced from the social context of engineering" and suggests that "the interplay of social values and theoretical understanding in the evolution of scientific disciplines certainly has its analogues in engineering, although the values and knowledge involved are often quite different."[22]

Rosenthal discusses the design-manufacturing team in new product development. He says that such teams represent "a community of interest" with a shared commitment to the group effort. The group shares information and advice, as well as instructions and decisions.[37] He describes the difficulties in merging these two subcommunities or cultures, because design and manufacturing engineers have developed their own "tacit understandings built up through years of working on particular problems with special points of view."[37]

The notion of an engineering community has also been addressed in connection with aerospace work. Vincenti describes informal communities of practitioners as the most important source of knowledge generation and means of knowledge transfer in aerospace. He defines a community as those involved in work on a particular aerospace development or problem (e.g., fasteners, airfoils, or propellers). Vincenti attributes several functions to these engineering communities. Competition between members supplies motivation, while cooperation provides mutual support. The exchange of knowledge and experience generates further knowledge, which is disseminated by word of mouth, publication, and teaching and is also incorporated into the tradition of practice. The community also plays a significant role in providing recognition and reward. Vincenti describes the particular roles of important types of aerospace engineering institutions, such as government research organizations, university departments, aircraft manufacturers, military services, airlines, professional societies, government regulatory agencies, and equipment and component suppliers."[8] He concludes, however, that

> formal institutions do a complex multitude of things that promote and channel the generation of engineering knowledge. They do not, however, constitute the locus for that generation in the crucial way that informal communities do. Their role... is to supply support and resources for such communities.[8]

Constant also describes aerospace communities as the central locus of technological cognition. He notes that the aeronautical community is, in fact, composed of a multilevel, overlapping hierarchy of subcommunities and he argues that technological change is better studied at the community as opposed to the individual, firm, national, or industry level. Constant describes the community as the embodiment of traditions of practice.[28]

> [Technological traditions of practice] define an accepted mode of technical operation, the conventional system of accomplishing a specified technical task. Such traditions encompass aspects of relevant scientific theory, engineering design formulae, accepted procedures and methods, specialized instrumentation, and, often, elements of ideological rationale. A tradition of technological practice is proximately tautological with the community which embodies it; each serves to define the other. Traditions of practice are passed on in the preparation of aspirants to community membership. A technological tradition of practice has, at minimum, a knowledge dimension, including both software and hardware, and a sociological dimension, including both social structure and behavioral norms.

Constant discusses further the importance of community norms in engineering. He alleges that, at least in connection with complex systems, there are "fundamental social norms governing the behavior of technological practitioners which are very close in structure, spirit, and effect to the norms governing the behavior of scientists."[28] Such norms guide the development of techniques and instruments and the reporting of data. Constant also argues for the existence of "counternorms" in engineering that are similar to those attributed to scientists by Mitroff.[38] Constant explains that

> Technological practitioners are required to be objective, emotionally neutral, rational, and honest. Yet technological practitioners often are—and protagonists of technological revolution usually are—passionate, determined, and irrationally recalcitrant in the face of unpleasant counter evidence bearing on their pet ideas.[28]

These descriptions of the world of engineering indicate that the activities performed by engineers are diverse and multifaceted. Engineering is defined as the creation or improvement of technology; as such, it clearly encompasses both intellectual and physical tasks, i.e., both knowing and doing. Engineering work is fundamentally both a social and a technical activity. It is a social activity in that it often involves teamwork, as individuals are required to coordinate and integrate their work. It is also a social activity in that the production of the final product depends on the ability to maintain successful social relationships (e.g., negotiate with vendors, maintain smooth personal relations among members of a work group).

The nature of engineering work suggests that engineers require access to a variety of tools and information resources. Further, the use of these tools and resources and the way they are integrated into engineering work may be planned in some cases and ad hoc in other situations. The engineering community, although it has received little attention from researchers, clearly plays an important role in the conduct of engineering work and the generation and transfer of engineering knowledge, information, and data. From this depiction of the engineering profession, we now move to the establishment of a broader conceptual framework for our model of engineers as information processors.

TOWARD A CONCEPTUAL FRAMEWORK FOR INVESTIGATING THE INFORMATION BEHAVIOR OF ENGINEERS

Engineers are not scientists. Arguments that a scientist is a more generic term merely implies that the two are one and the same. They are not. The practice of lumping the two groups [engineers and scientists] together is self-defeating in information behavior studies because confusion over the characteristics of the sample has led to conflicting results and to a greater difficulty in developing normative measures for planning, developing, and implementing information systems and policy in either science or technology.

Further, the terms "engineer" and "scientist" are not synonymous. Although the previous section has made it clear that many engineers—especially in high tech branches such as aerospace—perform a variety of empirical and theoretical tasks, the differences in work environment and personal/professional goals between the engineer and scientist prove to be an important factor in determining their information-seeking behavior. The following sections explore the science/technology and scientist/engineer dichotomy.

THE NATURE OF SCIENCE AND TECHNOLOGY

The relationship between science and technology is often expressed as a continuous process or normal progression from basic research (science) through applied research (technology) to development (utilization). This relationship, which is illustrated in Fig. 1, is based on the widely held assumption that technology grows out of or is dependent upon science for its development. This "assumed" relationship is the foundation upon which U.S. science policy is based and may help to explain the use of the conventional phrase "scientists and engineers."

However, the belief that technological change is somehow based on scientific advance has been challenged in recent years. Technological change has been increasingly seen as the adaption of existing technological concepts in response to demand.[41] Moreover, several years of study that attempted to trace the flow of information from science to technology have produced little empirical evidence to support the relationship.[40–41] Price, for example, claims.[42]

> The naive picture of technology as applied science simply will not fit the facts. Inventions do not hang like fruits on a scientific tree. In those parts of the history of technology where one feels some confidence, it is quite apparent that most technological advances are derived immediately from those that precede them.

The single-tree concept, shown in Fig. 2, is often used to illustrate the relationship between science and technology as a continuous process. Shapley and Roy argue that such a metaphor is historically inaccurate. In their case for a reorientation of American science policy, they argue that the two-tree concept, which is shown in Fig. 3, is a more accurate metaphor and is much more useful in developing science policy.[43]

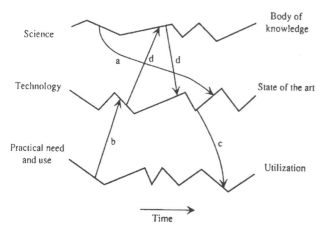

Fig. 1 The progression from science through technology to development as a continuous process.

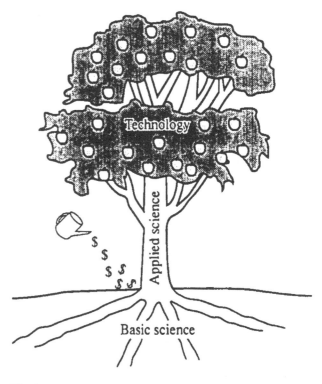

Fig. 2 Science and technology as a single tree.

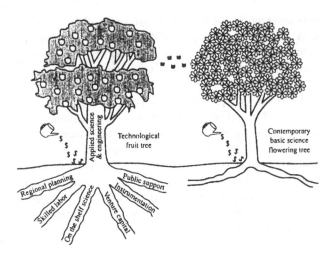

Fig. 3 Technology and science as separate trees.

Shapley and Roy contend that a normal progression from science to technology does not exist, nor is there direct communication between science and technology.[43] Allen's 1977 study of transfer of technology and the dissemination of technological information in R&D organizations found little evidence to support the relationship between science and technology as a continuous relationship. Allen concludes that the relationship between science and technology, which is depicted in Fig. 4, is best described as a series of interactions that are based on need rather than on a normal progression.[44]

According to Allen,[44] (a) the results of science do progress to technology in the sense that some sciences such as physics are more closely connected to technologies such as electronics, but (b) overall a wide variation exists between science and technology. The need for a (c) device, technique, or scientific understanding influences technology. Technology, in turn, (d) responds to a need and, in doing so, may generate the need for an understanding of certain physical phenomena.[44] A direct communication system between science and technology does not exist to the extent that communication between science and technology is restricted almost completely to that which takes place through the process of education.

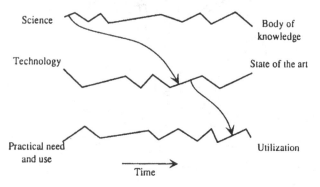

Fig. 4 The progression from science through technology to development as a series of interactions.

Price concludes that science and technology progress independently of one another. Technology builds upon its own prior developments and advances in a manner independent of any link with the current scientific frontier and often without any necessity for an understanding of the basic science underlying it.[42]

In summarizing the differences between science and technology, Price makes the following 12 points. (1) Science has a cumulating, close-knit structure; that is, new knowledge seems to flow from highly related and rather recent pieces of old knowledge, as displayed in the literature. (2) This property is what distinguishes science from technology and from humanistic scholarship. (3) This property accounts for many known social phenomena in science and also for its surefootedness and high rate of exponential growth. (4) Technology shares with science the same high growth rate, but it shows quite complementary social phenomena, particularly in its attitude to the literature. (5) Technology therefore may have a similar, cumulating, close-knit structure to that of science, but the structure is of the state of the art rather than of the literature. (6) Science and technology each therefore have their own separate cumulating structures. (7) A direct flow from the research front of science to that of technology, or vice versa, occurs only in special and traumatic cases since the structures are separate. (8) It is probable that research-front technology is strongly related only to that part of scientific knowledge that has been passed down as part of ambient learning and education, not to research-front science. (9) Research-front science is similarly related only to the ambient technological knowledge of the previous generation of students, not to the research front of the technological state of the art and its innovation. (10) This reciprocal relation between science and technology, involving the research front of one and the accrued archive of the other, is nevertheless sufficient to keep the two in phase in their separate growths within each otherwise independent cumulation. (11) It is naive to regard technology as applied science or clinical practice as applied medical science. (12) Because of this, one should be aware of any claims that particular scientific research is needed for particular technological breakthroughs, and vice versa. Both cumulations can only be supported for their own separate ends.[42]

Allen states that the independent nature of science and technology (S&T) and the different functions performed by engineers and scientists directly influence the flow of information in science and technology.[44] Science and technology are ardent consumers of information. Engineers and scientists both require large quantities of information to perform their work. At this level, there is a strong similarity between the information input needs of engineers and scientists. However, the difference between engineers and scientists in terms of information processing becomes apparent upon examination of their outputs.

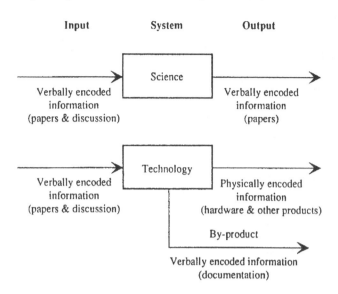

Fig. 5 Information processing in science and technology.

Information processing in S&T is depicted in Fig. 5 in the form of an input-output model.[44] Scientists use information to produce information. From a system standpoint, the input and output, which are both verbal, are compatible. The output from one stage is in a form required for the next stage. Engineers use information to produce some physical change in the world. Engineers consume information, transform it, and produce a product that is information bearing; however, the information is no longer in verbal form. Whereas scientists consume and produce information in the form of human language, engineers transform information from a verbal (or often visual or tacit) format to a physically encoded form. Verbal information is produced only as a byproduct to document the hardware and other physical products produced.

According to Allen, there is an inherent compatibility between the inputs and outputs of the information-processing system of science. He further states that since both are in a verbal format, the output of one stage is in the format required for the next stage.[44] The problem of supplying information to the scientist becomes a matter of collecting and organizing these outputs and making them accessible. Since science operates for the most part on the premise of free and open access to information, the problem of collecting outputs is made easier.

In technology, however, there is an inherent incompatibility between inputs and outputs. Since outputs are usually in a form different from inputs, they usually cannot serve as inputs for the next stage. Further, the outputs are usually in two parts, one physically encoded and the other verbally encoded. The verbally encoded part usually cannot serve as input for the next stage because it is a byproduct of the process and is itself incomplete. Those unacquainted with the development of the hardware or physical product therefore require some human intervention to supplement and interpret the information contained

in the documentation. Since technology operates to a large extent on the premise of restricted access to information, the problem of collecting the documentation and obtaining the necessary human intervention becomes difficult.

DISTINGUISHING ENGINEERS FROM SCIENTISTS

Engineers and scientists exhibit important differences other than the evident differences in education (degree), technical discipline, and type of work/activity. They share such common psychological needs as survival, security, self-esteem, self-expression, belonging, opportunity for growth, and self-determination. The strength of these needs varies from person to person and fluctuates over time. In a collective sense, engineers and scientists share the following attitudes that are conducive to high productivity:[45]

- effective communication
- optimum salary band benefits
- freedom and authority
- optimum utilization

There are also differences that tend to create sharp distinctions between the two groups. At the risk of inviting a charge of "overgeneralization," Peake offers the list of differences shown in Table 1.

Danielson investigated engineers and scientists in an attempt to identify those characteristics that affect their motivation and utilization. He concluded that there are recognizable differences between the two groups. He concluded that engineers and scientists are fundamentally different in terms of how they approach their job, the type and amount of supervision required, the type of recognition desired, the personality traits exhibited, and the differences in their goals.[46]

In their study of the values and career orientation of engineering and science undergraduate students, Krulee and Nadler found that engineering and science students have certain aspirations in common: to better themselves and to achieve a higher socioeconomic status than that of their parents. They report that science students place a higher value on independence and on learning for its own sake, while engineering students are more concerned with success and professional preparation. Many engineering students expect their families to be more important than their careers as a source of satisfaction, but the reverse pattern is more typical for science students.[47]

Krulee and Nadler also determined that engineering students are less concerned than science students with what one does in a given position and more concerned with the certainty of the rewards to be obtained. They report that, overall, engineering students place less emphasis on independence, career satisfaction, and the inherent interest their specialty holds for them and place more

Table 1 Peake's list of differences between engineers and scientists

Most engineers	Most scientists
Do development, design or applications work	Do research, basic or applied
Apply scientific knowledge	Seek new knowledge
Have engineering degree	Have science degree
Recognize managerial authority	Respect "colleague" authority
Want assignments to good, challenging projects	Want freedom to select their own projects
Like a company with a good record of engineering accomplishment	Like a company with a reputation for scientific advancement
Are hardware oriented	Are software oriented
Dislike preparing talks and publications	Insist on freedom to publish their work
are company oriented (i.e., committed to a variety of work areas, tasks, positions)	Are career oriented (i.e., committed to limited kinds of work areas, tasks, positions)
Dislike ambiguous, uncertain situations	Can work effectively with ambiguity, uncertainty
Are interested in processes, results, realizations	Are interested in concepts, meanings, abstractions
Believe in equalitarian group practices	Believe in authoritarian group practices
Expect to be faced with work schedules, deadlines, constrained resources	Abhor schedules, believe schedules should be self-determined, desire autonomy

Source: H. J. Peake, Technical and Management Notes: Difference Between Engineers and Scientists, *IEEE Transact, Eng. Mgt.*, EM-15, 50–53 (February 1969). p. 52.

value on success, family life, and avoiding a low-level job. Engineering students appear to be prepared to sacrifice some of their independence and opportunities for innovation in order to realize their primary objectives. Engineering students are more willing to accept positions that will involve them in complex organizational responsibilities and they assume that success in such positions will depend upon practical knowledge, administrative ability, and human relations skills.[47]

In his study of engineers in industry, Ritti found marked contrast between the work goals of engineers and scientists. Ritti draws the following three conclusions from his study: (1) the goals of engineers in industry are very much in line with meeting schedules, developing products that will be successful in the marketplace, and helping the company expand its activities; (2) while both engineers and scientists desire career development or advancement, for the engineer advancement is tied to activities within the organization, while advancement for the scientist is dependent upon the reputation established outside of the organization; and (3) while publication of results and professional autonomy are clearly valued goals of the Ph.D. scientist, they are clearly the least valued goals of the baccalaureate engineer.[15]

Allen states that the type of person who is attracted to a career in engineering is fundamentally different from the type of person who pursues a career as a scientist. He writes that

> perhaps the single most important difference between the two is the level of education. Engineers are generally educated to the baccalaureate level; some have a master's degree while some have no college degree. The research scientist is usually assumed to have a doctorate. The long, complex process of academic socialization involved in obtaining the Ph.D. is bound to result in persons who differ considerably in their lifeviews.

According to Allen, these differences in values and attitudes toward work will almost certainly be reflected in the behavior of the individual, especially in their use and production of information.[5]

According to Blade, engineers and scientists differ in training, values, and methods of thought. Further, Blade states that the following differences exist in their individual creative processes and in their creative products: (1) scientists are concerned with discovering and explaining nature; engineers use and exploit nature; (2) scientists are searching for theories and principles; engineers seek to develop and make things; (3) scientists are seeking a result for its own ends; engineers are engaged in solving a problem for the practical operating results; and (4) scientists create new unities of thought; engineers invent things and solve problems. Blade states that "this is a different order of creativity."[48]

INFLUENCE ON INFORMATION BEHAVIOR

Communications in engineering and science are fundamentally different. Communication patterns differ because of the fundamental differences between engineering and sciences and because of the social systems associated with the two disciplines. Holmfeld offers the following examples of how the social systems affect the communication behavior of engineers and scientists.[20]

Engineer

- Contribution is [technical] knowledge used to produce end items or products
- New and original knowledge is not a requirement
- Reward is monetary or materialistic and serves as an inducement to continue to make further contributions to technical knowledge

- Seeking rewards that are not part of the social system of technology is quite proper and also encouraged
- The value of technical knowledge lies in its value as a commodity of indirect exchange
- Exchange networks found in the social system of technology are based on end-item products, not knowledge
- Strong norms against free exchange or open access to knowledge with others outside of the organization exist in the social system of technology
- Restriction, security classification, and proprietary claims to knowledge characterize the social system of technology

Scientist

- Contribution is new and original knowledge
- Reward is social approval in the form of professional [collegial] recognition
- Recognition is established through publication and claim of discovery
- A well-developed communication system based on unrestricted access is imperative to recognition and claim of discovery
- Since recognition and priority of discovery are critical, strong norms against any restriction to free and open communication exist in the social system of science
- Seeking rewards that are not part of the social system of science in return for scientific contribution is not considered proper within the social system of science
- Exchange networks commonly referred to as "invisible colleges" exist in the social system of science; in these networks the commodities are knowledge and recognition.[49–50]

Taylor,[51] who quotes Brinberg,[52] offers the following characteristics for engineers and scientists:

> Unlike scientists, the goal of the engineer is to produce or design a product, process, or system; not to publish and make original contributions to the literature. Engineers, unlike scientists, work within time constraints; they are not interested in theory, source data, and guides to the literature nearly so much as they are in reliable answers to specific questions [39–40].

Anthony et al. suggest that engineers may have psychological traits that predispose them to solve problems alone or with the help of colleagues rather than finding answers in the literature. They further state that

> engineers like to solve their own problems. They draw on past experiences, use the trial and error method, and ask colleagues known to be efficient and reliable instead of searching or having someone search the literature for them. They are highly independent and self-reliant without being positively anti-social.[53]

According to Allen,

> engineers read less than scientists, they use literature and libraries less, and seldom use information services which are directly oriented to them. They are more likely to use specific forms of literature such as handbooks, standards, specifications, and technical reports.[44]

What an engineer usually wants, according to Cairns and Compton, is "a specific answer, in terms and format that are intelligible to him—not a collection of documents that he must sift, evaluate, and translate before he can apply them."[54] Young and Harriott report that

> the engineer's search for information seems to be based more on a need for specific problem solving than around a search for general opportunity. When engineers use the library, it is more in a personal-search mode, generally not involving the professional (but nontechnical) librarian.[55]

Young and Harriot conclude by saying that

> when engineers need technical information, they usually use the most accessible sources rather than searching for the highest quality sources. These accessible sources are respected colleagues, vendors, a familiar but possibly outdated text, and internal company [technical] reports. He [the engineer] prefers informal information networks to the more formal search of publicly available and cataloged information.[55]

MAJOR EMPIRICAL STUDIES OF ENGINEERING INFORMATION BEHAVIOR

Studies concerned with the information-seeking behavior of engineers were reviewed by Pinelli[56] to further develop the conceptual framework. Table 2 lists those major research studies deemed significant to this topic and which are discussed in this section.

HERNER[57]

Herner's work is one of the first "user" studies specifically concerned with "differences" in information-seeking behavior. He reports significant differences in terms of researchers performing "basic and applied" research, researchers performing "academic and industry" type duties, and their information-seeking behavior. Herner states that researchers performing "basic or academic" duties make greater use of formal information channels or sources, depend mainly on the library for their published material, and maintain a significant number of contacts outside of the organization.

Table 2 Overview of Engineering Information Behavior Studies.

Year	Principal Investigator	Research Method	Population	Sample Frame	Sample Design	Sample Size	Percentage Response Rate (number responding)	Description
1954	Herner[57]	Structured interview	All scientific and technical personnel at Johns Hopkins	Unknown	Unknown	600	100	Survey to determine the information-gathering methods of scientific and technical personnel at Johns Hopkins
1970	Rosenbloom and Wolek[58]	Self-administered questionnaire	Members of 5 industrial R&D organizations Members of 4 IEEE interest groups	2430 Unknown	Census Probability	2430 Unknown	71 (1735) Unknown (1034)	Survey to determine how engineers and scientists in industrial research and development organizations acquire STI
1977	Allen[44]	Record analysis Self-administered questionnaire	Unknown	Unknown	Unknown	Unknown	Unknown (1153)	Survey to determine technology transfer and the dissemination of technological information in research and development organizations
1980	Kremer[57]	Self-administered questionnaire	All design engineers at one engineering design firm	73	Census	73	82 (60)	Survey to identify and evaluate the information channels used by engineers in a design company
1981	Shuchman[60]	Structured interview Self-administered questionnaire	Engineers in 89 R&D and non-R&D organizations	14797	Probability	3371	39 (1315)	Survey to determine information used and production in engineering
1983	Kaufman[61]	Self-administered questionnaire	Engineers in six technology-based organizations	147	Census	147	100 (147)	Survey to determine the use of technical information in technical problem solving

Researchers performing "applied or industry" duties make greater use of informal channels or sources, depend on their personal collections of information and colleagues for information, make significantly less use of the library than do their counterparts, and maintain fewer contacts outside of the organization. Applied or industry researchers make substantial use of handbooks, standards, and technical reports. They also read less and do less of their reading in the library than do their counterparts.

ROSENBLOOM AND WOLEK[58]

In 1970, Rosenbloom and Wolek published the results of one of the first "large-scale" industry studies that was specifically concerned with the flow of STI within R&D organizations. They report three significant and fundamental differences between engineers and scientists: (1) engineers tend to make substantially greater use of information sources *within* the organization than do scientists; (2) scientists make considerably greater use of the professional (formal) literature than do engineers; and (3) scientists are more likely than engineers to acquire information as a consequence of activities directed toward general competence rather than a specific task.

In terms of interpersonal communication, the engineers in the Rosenbloom and Wolek study recorded a higher incidence of interpersonal communication with people in other parts of their own corporation, whereas scientists recorded a greater incidence of interpersonal communication with individuals employed outside their own corporation. When using the literature, the engineers tended to consult in-house technical reports or trade publications, while the scientists made greater use of the professional (formal) literature.

Rosenbloom and Wolek also report certain similarities between engineers and scientists. The propensity to use alternative types of technical information sources is related to the purposes that will give meaning to the use of that information. Work that has a professional focus draws heavily on sources of information external to the user's organization. Work that has an operational focus seldom draws on external sources, relying heavily on information that is available within the employing organization. Those engineers and scientists engaged in professional work commonly emphasize the simplicity, precision, and analytical or empirical rigor of the information source. Conversely, those engineers and scientists engaged in operational work typically emphasize the value of communication with others who understand and are experienced in the same real context of work.

ALLEN[44]

Allen's study of technology transfer and the dissemination of technological information within the R&D organization is the result of a 10-year investigation. Allen describes the study, which began as a "user study," as a systems-level approach to the problem of communication in technology. Many information professionals consider his work to be the seminal research on the flow of technical information within R&D organizations. Allen was among the first to produce evidence supporting different information-seeking behaviors for engineers and scientists. These differences, Allen notes, lead to different philosophies and habits regarding the use of the technical literature and other sources of information by engineers. The most significant of his findings is the relative lack of importance of the technical literature in terms of generating new ideas and in problem definition, the importance of personal contacts and discussions between engineers, the existence of technological "gatekeepers," and the importance of the technical report. Allen states that "the unpublished report is the single most important informal literature source; it is the principal written vehicle for transferring information in technology."[44]

KREMER[57]

Kremer's study was undertaken to gain insight on how technical information flows through formal and informal channels among engineers in a design company. The engineers in her study were not involved in R&D. The reason given most frequently to search for information is problem solving; colleagues within the company are contacted first for needed information, followed by colleagues outside of the company. In terms of the technical literature, handbooks are most important, followed by standards and specifications. Libraries are not important sources of information and are used infrequently by company engineers.

Regardless of age and work experience, design engineers demonstrate a decided preference for internal sources of information. They consult personal files for needed information. The perceived accessibility, ease of use, technical quality, and amount of experience a design engineer has had with an information source strongly influence the selection of an information source. Technological gatekeepers exist among design engineers; they are high technical performers and a high percentage are first line supervisors.

SHUCHMAN[60]

Shuchman's study is a broad-based investigation of information transfer in engineering. The respondents represent 14 industries and the following major disciplines: civil, electrical, mechanical, industrial, chemical and environmental, and aeronautical. Seven percent, or 93 respondents, were aeronautical engineers. The engineers, regardless of discipline, display a strong preference for informal sources of information. Further, these engineers rarely find all the information they need for solving technical problems in one source; the major difficulty engineers encounter in finding the information they need to do their job is identifying a specific piece of missing data and then learning who has it.

In terms of information sources and solving technical problems, Shuchman reports that engineers first consult their personal store of technical information, followed in order by informal discussions with colleagues, discussions with supervisors, use of internal technical reports, and contact with a "key" person in the organization who usually knows where the needed information may be located. A small proportion of the engineering profession uses technical libraries and librarians.

In general, Shuchman finds that engineers do not regard information technology as an important adjunct to the process of producing, transferring, and using information. While technological gatekeepers appear to exist across the broad range of engineering disciplines, their function and significance are not uniform; considering the totality of engineering, gatekeepers account for only a small part of the information transfer process.

KAUFMAN[61]

Kaufman's study is concerned with the factors relating to the use of technical information by engineers in problem solving. The study reported that, in terms of information sources, engineers consult their personal collections first, followed by colleagues and then by formal literature sources. In terms of the formal literature sources used for technical problem solving, engineers use technical reports, followed in order by text books, and technical handbooks.

Most sources of information, according to Kaufman, are found primarily through an intentional search of written information, followed by personal knowledge and then by asking someone. The criteria used in selecting all information sources, in descending order of frequency, are accessibility, familiarity or experience, technical quality, relevance, comprehensiveness, ease of use, and expense. Engineers use various information sources for specific purposes. They primarily utilized librarians and information specialists are to find leads to information sources. Engineers used online computer searches primarily to define the problem and technical literature to learn techniques applicable to dealing with the problem. They rely primarily on personal experience to find solutions to the problem.

Kaufman reports that the criteria used in selecting the most useful information sources, in descending order of frequency, are technical quality or reliability, relevance, accessibility, familiarity or experience, comprehensiveness, ease of use, and expense. In terms of the effectiveness, efficiency, and usefulness of the various information sources, personal experience is rated as the most effective in accomplishing the purpose for which it is used; librarians and information specialists receive the lowest rating for efficiency and effectiveness. Most engineers use

several different types of information sources in problem solving; however, engineers do depend on their personal experience more often than on any single specific information source.

ENGINEERS AS INFORMATION PROCESSORS

To establish a specific conceptual and organizing framework for further research on information use by engineers, engineering can be viewed as an information processing system that must deal with work-related uncertainty through patterns of technical communications. Throughout the process, data, information, and knowledge are being acquired, produced, transferred, and used. The fact that these data, information, and knowledge may be physically or hardware encoded should not detract from the observation that the process of engineering is fundamentally an information processing activity.

The concept of engineering as an information processing entity represents an extension of the arguments developed by Tushman and Nadler.[62] The concept has its roots in open systems theory developed by Katz and Kahn.[63] The major work on organizations and work-related uncertainty can be traced to, among others, Galbraith and Duncan,[64] who have conceptualized organizations as information processing systems.

Uncertainty, defined as the difference between information possessed and information required to complete a task, is central to the concept of engineering as an information processing activity. Rogers[65] states that coping with uncertainty is the central concept in information behavior. The process of engineering is one of grappling with the unknown. These unknowns or uncertainties may be technical, economic, or merely the manifestations of personal and social variables. When faced with uncertainty, engineers typically seek data, information, and knowledge. In other words, data, information, and knowledge are used by engineers to moderate technical uncertainty. Because engineering always entails coping with a relatively high degree of uncertainty, engineering can certainly be viewed as an informational process. Consequently, information behavior and patterns of technical communication cannot be ignored when studying engineers.

AN ORGANIZING MODEL FOR RESEARCH

The conceptual framework, shown in Fig. 6, represents an extension of Orr's scheme of the engineer as an information processor. The framework focuses on information-seeking and assumes that, individual differences notwithstanding, an internal, consistent logic governs the information-seeking behavior of engineers.[66]

A project, task, or problem that precipitates a need for information is central to the conceptual framework for this

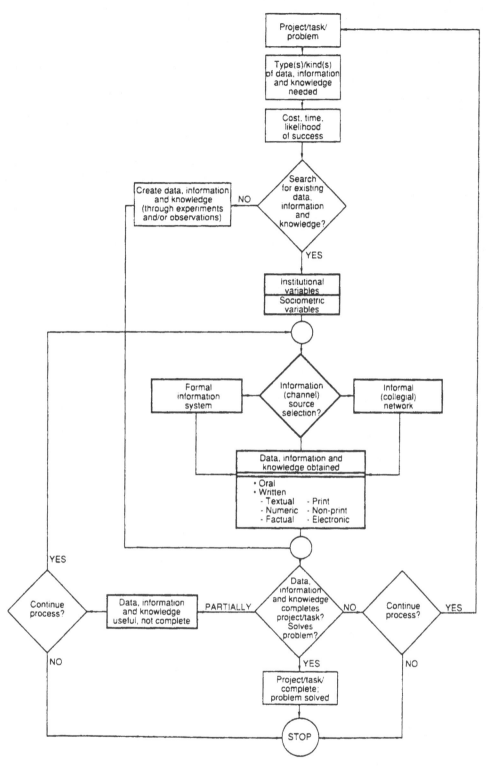

Fig. 6 The engineer as an information processor: A structure analysis with data on variables related to information-seeking behavior.

research. This need for information may, in turn, be *internally* or *externally* induced and is referred to by Orr as *inputs* or *outputs*, respectively. Orr,[66] who cites the work of Voight,[67] Menzel,[68] Storer,[69] and Hagstrom,[70] states that inputs originate within the mind of the individual engineer and include data, information, and knowledge needed to keep up with advanced in one's profession, to perform one's professional duties to interact with peers, colleagues, and coworkers, and to obtain stimulation and feedback from them.

Document–Engineering

Outputs frequently, but not exclusively, result from an external stimulus or impetus. Outputs serve a variety of functions, including responding to a request for information from a supervisor, a coworker, peer, or colleague; reporting progress; providing advice; reacting to inquiries; defending; advocating; and proposing. Inputs and outputs require the use of specific kinds and types of data, information, and knowledge.[66]

The conceptual framework for this research assumes that, in response to a project, task, or problem, specific kinds or types of data, information, and knowledge are needed. In response to this scenario, engineers are confronted with two basic alternatives: they can create the information through experimentation or observation or they can search the existing information. If they act rationally, the decision to "make or buy" the information will depend upon their subjective perception of the relative likelihood of success in acquiring the desired information by these two alternatives with an acceptable time, and on their perception of the relative cost [money and/or effort] of these alternatives.

If a decision is made to search the existing information, engineers must choose between two information channels. One is the *informal or collegial network*, which is characterized by interpersonal (oral) communications with peers, coworkers, colleagues, gatekeepers, vendors, consultants, "key" personnel, and supervisors and by personal collections of information. The other is the *formal information system*, which includes libraries, technical information centers, librarians and technical information specialists, information products and services, and information storage and retrieval systems. It is assumed that the decision to choose a particular information channel is influenced by institutional and sociometric variables operating within the previously identified systems. Gerstberger and Allen,[71] Rosenberg,[72] and Orr[66] theorize that certain sociometric variables influence information source and product selection.

More recent work highlights the value of exploring contextual and situational variables related to information-seeking and use. Taylor's theoretical investigation of information use environments emphasizes the importance of understanding the context in which information is sought, conveyed, and applied. Context for professional groups, including engineers, is defined as a combination of the nature of work problems, solutions, and settings associated with particular types of jobs. Taylor assumes, in other words, that members of a profession share tasks, goals, and needs in a way that influences their use of information. Taylor's analysis recognizes, as Fig. 6 shows, that information-seeking and use is determined by the nature of the particular project, task, problem at hand.[73]

A shift in emphasis toward the study of cognitive and situational variables surrounding information-seeking and use, and away from users' personal characteristics and specific systems features, has been advocated by a number of communications and information science researchers, most notably Dervin and Nilan (see *Annual Review of Information Science and Technology*, 21, 1986). They devote special attention to understanding what there is about a particular situation that encourages an individual to use networks in fulfilling an information need. In Fig. 6, the subjective perception of cost, time, and likelihood of success may often be situationally driven.

The resulting data, information, and knowledge are evaluated subjectively. The engineer as an information processor faces three possible courses of action. *First*, if the acquired-obtained data, information, and knowledge complete the project or task or solve the problem, the process is terminated. *Second*, if the acquired-obtained, data, information, and knowledge are useful but only partially complete the project or task or solve the problem, a decision is made either to continue the process by reevaluating the information source selection or to terminate the process. *Third*, if the acquired-obtained data, information, and knowledge are not applicable to or do not complete the project or task or solve the problem, a decision is made either to continue the process by redefining the project, task, or problem or to terminate the process.

An Empirical Study: The Aerospace Knowledge Diffusion Research Project

We noted earlier that the literature regarding the information-seeking behavior of engineers is fragmented and superficial and that the results have not accumulated to form a significant body of knowledge. The inability to apply these findings is attributable to the lack of a unifying theory, standardized methodology, and common definitions. The simple truth is that little is known about the information-seeking behavior of engineers generally. Further, there is little evidence that addresses differences that may exist among various engineering branches or specialities. We have little knowledge of whether the attributes and information-seeking behaviors associated with engineers in one discipline (e.g., civil) are transferable to engineers in another discipline (e.g., nuclear).

The authors are involved in a research project currently underway that is investigating the production, transfer, and use of federally funded aerospace R&D by aerospace engineers from the perspective of the model presented in Fig. 6. This four-phase project is providing descriptive and analytical data regarding the diffusion of aerospace knowledge at the individual, organizational, national, and international levels. It is examining both the channels used to communicate and the social system of the aerospace knowledge diffusion process. Phase 1 investigates the information-seeking behavior of U.S. aerospace engineers and scientists and places particular emphasis on their use of federally funded aerospace R&D and U.S. government technical reports. Phase 2 examines the industry-government interface and places special emphasis on the role of information intermediaries in the aerospace knowledge diffusion process. Phase 3 concerns the academic-government interface and places specific emphasis on the information intermediary-faculty-student relationship. Phase 4 explores the information seeking behavior of non-U.S. aerospace engineers and scientists in selected countries. Another portion of the project looks specifically at the use of electronic networks by U.S. aerospace engineers.[74]

Over the long term, the project findings will provides an empirical basis for understanding the aerospace knowledge diffusion process itself and its implications at the individual, organizational, national, and international levels. The results of the project should provide useful information to R&D managers, information managers, and others concerned with improving access to, the quality of, and the utilization of federally funded aerospace R&D.[75] Selected descriptive results from this research, as it pertains to the information-seeking behavior of aerospace engineers, are reported in this section.

Patterns of technical communication

The communication of technical information (e.g., producing written materials or oral discussions) is an important aspect of aerospace engineering. Based on a 40-hour week, aerospace engineers spend an average $(\overline{X})$ of 8.7 hours per week writing technical information and 10.3 hours per week communicating technical information orally. Combining these means shows that aerospace engineers spend an average of 19 hours per week communicating in written and oral form. On average, aerospace engineers spend more time per week communicating technical information $(\overline{X} = 19.06)$ to others than they do working with technical information received from other $(\overline{X} = 14.64)$. As their years of work experience increase and as they advance professionally, so too does the amount of time they spend communicating (i.e., producing and using) technical information.

On average, the majority of aerospace engineers prepare written technical communications alone. Of the approximately 22% who write with a group of engineers, about 40% write with the same group of engineers. The average size $(\overline{X})$ of the group is 5.75 people. Of those who write in or with a group, about 22% indicated that doing so made them more productive than writing alone, and 21% indicated that doing so made them less productive than writing alone. Letters and memos were the technical information products most frequently prepared alone. Drawings/specifications were the technical information product most frequently prepared in a group. Drawings/specifications were the most frequently used technical information product.

Patterns of technical information use and problem solving

Aerospace engineers use a variety of technical information sources when solving technical problems. In general, aerospace engineers are not interested in guides to the literature nearly so much as they are interested in reliable answers to specific questions. They prefer informal sources of information, especially conversations with individuals within their organization. Aerospace engineers may also have psychological traits that predispose them to solve problems alone or with the help of colleagues rather than seeking answers in the literature. When they use libraries, they tend to use them in a self-help mode. When they use them, aerospace engineers tend to turn to librarians and library services for assistance only after they have consulted their personal store of information, talked to co-workers and colleagues, consulted a "key" person, and used a library in a personal search mode. Having failed to that point, aerospace engineers search or have a database searched and/or seek the assistance of a librarian or technical information specialist.

The role of the library

Regardless of their relative position in the problem solving process, libraries and librarians provide an important link in the aerospace engineer's quest for information. Overall, libraries and technical information centers are important $(\overline{X} = 3.8$ with 5 being most important) to aerospace engineers in performing their professional duties. Statistically, academically-affiliated aerospace engineers assign a higher rating of importance to libraries and technical information centers than do their counterparts in government and industry. Academically-affiliated aerospace engineers also tend to use libraries and technical information centers more often than do government- and industry-affiliated aerospace engineers.

Why do aerospace engineers not use libraries and technical information centers? The primary reasons include "no information needs" and "information needs met some other way." There also appears to be a positive correlation between "use" by aerospace engineers and "physical distance." In other words, the closer the aerospace engineer resides to the library, the greater the probable use of the library or technical information center.

Factors affecting use of technical information

The relevant literature overwhelmingly favors accessibility as the single most important (variable) determinant of use. Gerstberger and Allen reported that among R&D engineers, accessibility rather than technical quality influences use.[71] Allen[44] stated, "There is apparently some relationship between the perceptions of technical quality and channel accessibility, but it is the accessibility component that almost exclusively determines frequency of use".[44] Rosenberg in a study of research and non-research personnel in industry and government found that both groups exhibited similar information-seeking behavior. Of the eight variable investigated by Rosenberg, both groups indicated that accessibility had the greatest influence on information use.[72] Orr, on the other hand, disagreed, stating that quality of information was the most important consideration in selecting/using an information product.[66] Our results indicate that accessibility influences the use of information products by aerospace engineers. However, accessibility does not "exclusively" determine information use. Relevance and technical quality, together with accessibility, are the factors that affect the use of information products by aerospace engineers.

Use of Information Technology

In Shuchman's investigation[60] of information transfer in engineering, aeronautical engineers made greater use of information technologies, including computers, than did engineers in other disciplines (see Bishop[76] and Pinelli[77] for an overview of recent literature on the use of information technology in aerospace engineering). Study data indicate that aerospace engineers tend to use many forms of information technology and that they are likely to use information if accessible via a computer. Approximately half of all aerospace engineers have access to and use electronic networks. Electronic networks are used by aerospace engineers for various purposes including online database searching; communicating via electronic mail, bulletin boards or conferencing systems; logging into remote computers to run programs; and exchanging data and other files.

The need for theory-based practice

With its contribution to trade, its coupling with national security, and its symbolism of U.S. technological strength, the U.S. aerospace industry holds a unique position in the nation's industrial structure. However, this industry, in particular the commercial aviation sector, is in the midst of profound change and now faces a significantly more challenging competitive and global environment. To remain a world leader in aerospace, the U.S. must improve and maintain the professional competency of its engineers and scientists, increase the R&D knowledge base, improve productivity, and maximize the integration of recent technological developments into the R&D process. How well these objectives are met, and at what cost, depends on a variety of factors, but largely on the ability of U.S. aerospace engineers and scientists to acquire and process the results of aerospace R&D. Hence, an understanding of the information-seeking behavior of aerospace engineers

would offer valuable insight for maintaining U.S. supremacy in aerospace.

Despite the expenditure of considerable effort, there is no generally accepted or systematically acquired body of research that can accurately describe or explain information-seeking behavior or predict the use of information by engineers in general and aerospace engineers in particular other than at the most elementary levels. A variety of environmental and structural changes, including the growth of computer and information technology, combine to significantly weaken the relevance and reliability of this research. Hence there is the need for a modestly constructed engineering-oriented research agenda.

ENGINEERING INFORMATION-SEEKING BEHAVIOR: DEVELOPING A RESEARCH AGENDA

Considerable research and numerous user studies have been conducted over the past 25 years. The generally held beliefs are that (1) the results of this research and these studies have not accumulated to form a significant body of knowledge that can be used by information professionals and (2) the results that are usable have been virtually ignored by those concerned with the design and provision of information policy, products, services, and systems.

An acquired body of research is vital to the development of theory and the solution of professional problems, to the formation of tools and methods for analyzing organizations, services, environments, and behaviors, to determining the cost and benefits of information products, services, and systems, to establishing and developing theories upon which to base practice, and to contributing paradigms, models, and radically new conceptualizations of information-seeking behavior. The following outline suggests the directions that continued research should take.

1. Previous research regarding the information-seeking behavior of engineers is noncumulative, has been variously criticized, and has largely been dismissed on the basis of research and scholarship.

    A. Conduct a "critical" review, analysis, and evaluation of previous research, identity and remove spurious research findings, and establish a starting point or foundation for "what is known and accepted as fact" vis-a-vis engineering information-seeking behavior.
    B. Identify the criticisms and deficiencies of previously used research designs and methodologies and compile a list of "lessons learned" to guard against committing the same or similar mistakes.
    C. Consider the lessons learned in the context of existing research designs and methodologies and identify those that correct or compensate for previous mistakes.

2. Previous research regarding the information-seeking behavior of the engineer has been limited to a particular system, product, or service in a particular organization or environment. Hence, the results are often confusing, conflicting, and not sufficient to form the basis for the development of theory.

   A. Develop standard definitions, terms, and terminologies.

   B. Develop, test, and validate research tools, instruments, and techniques.

   C. Develop a standard set of variables.

     1. Types of Users
       a. Engineers
       b. Scientists
       c. Intermediaries
       d. Gatekeepers
       e. Managers

     2. Types of Organizations
       a. Academic
       b. Government
       c. Industry

     3. Size of Organization
       a. Small
       b. Medium
       c. Large

     4. Types of Environment
       a. Research
       b. Development
       c. Design
       d. Manufacturing
       e. Production
       f. Test and Evaluation
       g. Marketing and Sales
       h. Service and Maintenance
       i. Management

     5. Types of Knowledge
       a. Tacit knowledge
       b. Information
       c. Data

     6. Types of Product/Service
       a. Print
       b. Nonprint
       c. Electronic

     7. Types of Engineering Discipline
       a. Civil
       b. Electrical
       c. Mechanical

   D. Determine which variable(s) (institutional and situational) best describe and explain the use of information by engineers in a variety of environments.

3. What is known about the information-seeking behavior of engineers seems not to explain information use and nonuse. Hence, there is little knowledge that can be used for testing existing and developing new paradigms.

   A. Conduct engineering information-seeking behavior research within a conceptual framework that embraces the production, transfer, use, and management of information. One possible outcome could be the identification of barriers that prohibit or restrict the use of information by engineers.

   B. Seek to understand the diffusion of engineering knowledge as a precursor to describing and explaining the information-seeking behavior of engineers.

   C. Develop and test hypotheses, the results of which, can lead to the formation of theory that can be used to predict the use of information by engineers.

   D. Develop a series of experiments, the results of which will lead to the formation of paradigms, models, and radically new conceptualizations of library and information science phenomena.

4. Conventional wisdom states that a "disconnect" exists between researchers and practitioners in the field of library and information science.

   A. Develop a mechanism that couples the results of basic and applied research with users in the field.

   B. Develop the means by which researchers and practitioners have greater opportunities for interaction.

Determining what we know and where we are will provide a starting point to formulate the questions that must be asked. The answers to these questions will form the elements of a basic research program and lead to the development of theory-based practice. Applied research can then be used to test and validate these theories. Tests and validation will lead to the identification of spurious findings and eventually to the accumulation of a significant body of knowledge that can be used by information professionals to design aerospace information policy, products, services, and systems.

REFERENCES

1. Allen, T. J. *Managing the Flow of Technology: Technology Transfer and the Dissemination of Technological Information within the R & D Organization*, MIT Press: Cambridge, MA, 1984.
2. Sayer, J. Do present information services serve the engineer. Data Proc. **1965**, *7*(2), 24–25 64–65.
3. Wilkins, A. Personal roles and barriers in information transfer. In *Advances in Librarianship*; Voight, M. J., Harris, M. H., Eds.; Academic Press: New York, 1977; Vol.7, 257–297.

4. Stevens, N. D. The history of information. In *Advances in Librarianship*; Simonton, W., Ed.; Academic Press: New York, 1986; Vol.14, 1–48.

5. Paisley, W. J. Information and Work. In *Progress in Communication Sciences*; Dervin, B., Voight, M. J., Eds.; Ablex Press: Norwood, NJ, 1980.

6. Rhode, N. F. Information Needs. *Ref. 4*, 1–48.

7. Allen, T. J. Distinguishing engineers from scientists. In *Managing Professionals in Innovative Organizations*; Katz, R., Ed.; Ballinger Publishing: Cambridge, MA, 1988; 3–18.

8. Vincenti, W. G. *What Engineers Know and How They Know It: Analytical Studies from Aeronautical History*, Johns Hopkins University Press: Baltimore, MD, 1990.

9. Rudy, Joenk J. Engineering text for engineers. In *Technology of Text: Vol. 11, Principles for Structuring, Designing, and Displaying Text*; David, Jonassen, H., Ed.; Educational Technology Publications: Englewood Cliffs, NJ, 1985; 346–369.

10. U.S. Department of Labor, Professional Specialty Occupations—Engineers. *Occupational Outlook Handbook 1990-91 Edition*; U.S. Government Printing Office: Washington, DC, 1990; 62–70.

11. Florman, S. C. *The Civilized Engineer*, St. Martin's Press: New York, 1987.

12. Adams, J. L. *Flying Buttresses, Entropy, and O-rings: The World of an Engineer*, Harvard University Press: Cambridge, MA, 1991; 38.

13. Kemper, J. D. *Engineers and Their Profession*, 4th Ed. W. B. Saunders: Philadelphia, PA, 1990; 2–3.

14. National Research Council. *Improving Engineering Design: Designing for Competitive Advantage*; National Academy Press: Washington, DC, 1991; 17.

15. Ritti, R. R. *The Engineer in the Industrial Corporation*, Columbia University Press: New York, 1971.

16. Murotake, D. K. *A Double-Edged Sword: Relationships Between the Engineering Use of Computer Tools and Project Performance*, MIT, Cambridge, MA, 1990; 20, PhD diss., (Not available from UMI.).

17. In *Introduction. In The Nature of Technological Knowledge: Are Models of Scientific Change Relevant?*; Laudan, R., Ed.; D. Reidel: Boston, MA, 1984; 1–26, 84.

18. Hollister, S. C. *Engineer: Ingenious Contriver of the Instruments of Civilization*, Macmillan: New York, 1966; 18.

19. Mailloux, E. N. Engineering Information Systems. In *Annual Review of Information Science and Technology*; Williams, M. E., Ed.; Elsevier Science Publishers: Amsterdam, the Netherlands, 1989; Vol. 24, 239–266.

20. Holmfeld, J. D. *Communication Behavior of Scientists and Engineers*, Case Western Reserve University, Cleveland, OH, 1970, PhD Diss., UMI 70-25874.

21. Stoll, H. W. In *Managing the Design-Manufacturing Process*; Ettlie, J. E., Stoll, H. W., Eds.; McGraw-Hill: New York, 1990; 73–119.

22. Donovan, A. Thinking about engineering. Technol. Cult. **1986**, *27*, 674–678.

23. Schön, D. A. *The Reflective Practitioner: How Professionals Think in Action*, Basic Books: New York, 1983.

24. Polanyi, M. *The Tacit Dimension*, University of Chicago Press: Chicago, IL, 1966; 6–7.

25. Breton, E. J. Why engineers don't use databases: Indexing techniques fail to meet the needs of the profession. ASIS Bull. **1981**, *7*(6), 20–23.

26. Layton, E. T. Technology as knowledge. Technol. Cult. **1974**, *15*(1), 31–37.

27. Ziman, J. *An Introduction to Science Studies: The Philosophical and Social Aspects of Science and Technology*, Cambridge University Press: Cambridge, U.K., 1984.

28. Constant, E. W., II *The Origins of the Turbojet Revolution*, The Johns Hopkins University Press: Baltimore, MD, 1980.

29. Ancona, D. G.; Caldwell, D. F. Information technology and work groups: The case of new product teams. In *Intellectual Teamwork: Social and Technical Foundations of Cooperative Work*; Galagher, J., Kraut, R. E., Egido, C., Eds.; Lawrence Earlbaum: Hillsdale, NJ, 1990; 173–190.

30. Barczak, G.; Wilemon, D. Communication patterns of new product development team leaders. IEEE Trans. Eng. Mgt. **1991**, *38*(2), 101–109.

31. Barber, B. *Science and the Social Order*, Rev. Ed. Collier Books: New York, 1962.

32. Doty, P.; Bishop, A. P.; McClure, C. R. Scientific norms and the use of electronic research networks ASIS'91, Proceedings of the 54th ASIS Annual Meeting, 1991; 28, 24–29.

33. Kuhn, T. *The Structure of Scientific Revolutions*, 2nd Ed. University of Chicago Press: Chicago, IL, 1970, expanded.

34. Gaston, J. Sociology of science and technology. In *A Guide to the Culture of Science, Technology and Medicine*; Durcan, P. T., Ed.; Free Press: New York, 1980; 495.

35. Constant, E.W. II. Communities and hierarchies: Structure in the practice of science and technology. In *The Nature of Technological Knowledge: Are Models of Scientific Change Relevant?*; Rachel, Lauden, Ed.; D. Reidel: Boston, MA, 1984; 27–46.

36. Rothstein, W. G. Engineers and the functionalist model of professions. In *The Engineers and the Social System*; Pericci, R., Gerstl, J. E., Eds.; Wiley: New York, 1969; 73–97.

37. Rosenthal, S. R. Bridging the cultures of engineers: Challenges in organizing for manufacturable product design. In *Managing the Design-Manufacturing Process*; Ettlie, J.E. E., Stool, H.W., Eds.; McGraw-Hill: New York, 1990; 21–51.

38. Mitroff, I. Norms and counter-norms in a select group of the Apollo Moon Scientists: A case study of the ambivalence of scientists. Am. Sociol. Rev. **1974**, *34*, 579–595.

39. Langrish, J.; Gibbons, M.; Evans, W. G.; Jevons, F. R. *Wealth From Knowledge: A Study of Innovation in Industry*, Wiley: New York, 1972.

40. Illinois Institute of Technology. *Technology in Retrospect and Critical Events in Science*; National Science Foundation: Washington, DC, 1968. AKA Project TRACES, (Available from NTIS, Springfield, VA: PB-234 767.).

41. U.S. Department of Defense, Office of the Director of Defense Research and Engineering. *Project Hindsight*; U.S. Department of Defense: Washington, DC, October 1969 (Available from NTIS, Springfield, VA: AD-495 905.).

42. de Solla Price, D. J. Is technology historically independent of science. Technol. Cult. **1965**, *6*(3), 553–578.

43. Shapley, D.; Roy, R. *Lost at the Frontier: U.S. Science and Technology Policy Adrift*, ISI Press: Philadelphia, PA, 1985.

44. Allen, T. J. *Managing the Flow of Technology: Technology Transfer and the Dissemination of Technological Information within the R&D Organization*, MIT Press: Cambridge, MA, 1977.

45. Peake, H. J. Technical and management notes: Difference between engineers and scientists. *IEEE Trans. Eng. Mgt.*, February 1969,50–53, EM-15.

46. Danielson, Lee E. *Characteristics of Engineers and Scientists: Significant for Their Utilization and Motivation*, University of Michigan Press: Ann Arbor, MI, 1960; 11.

47. Krulee, G. K.; Nadler, E. B. Studies of education for science and engineering: Student values and curriculum choice. *IRE Trans. Eng. Manage.* 1960, 7.4, 149–151, 157–158.

48. Blade, M.-F. Creativity in engineering. In *Essays on Creativity in the Sciences*; Coler, M. A., Ed.; New York University Press: New York, 1963; 110–122.

49. Crane, D. *Invisible Colleges: Diffusion of Knowledge in Scientific Communities*, University of Chicago Press: Chicago, IL, 1972.

50. de Solla Price, D. J. *Science Since Babylon*, Yale Press: New Haven, CT, 1961.

51. Taylor, R. S. *Value-Added Processes in Information Systems*, Ablex Press: Norwood, NJ, 1986.

52. Brinberg, H. R. The contribution of information to economic growth and development Paper Presented at the 40th Congress of the International Federation for Documentation Copenhagen, Denmark, 1980.

53. Anthony, L. J.; East, H.; Slater, M. J. The growth of the literature of physics. *Rep. Progr. Phys.* 1969, *3*, 709–767.

54. Cairns, R. W.; Compton, B. E. The SATCOM report and the engineer's information problem. *Eng. Educ.* 1970, *60*, 375–376.

55. Young, J. F.; Harriott, L. C. The changing technical life of engineers. *Mech. Eng.* 1979, *101*(1), 20–24.

56. Pinelli, T. E.; Kennedy, J. M.; Barclay, R. O. The NASA/DoD aerospace knowledge diffusion research project. *Gov. Inform. Quart.* 1991, *8*(2), 219–233.

57. Herner, S. Information gathering habits of workers in pure and applied science. *Ind. Eng. Chem.* 1954, *46*(1), 228–236.

58. Rosenbloom, R. S.; Wolek, F. W. *Technology and Information Transfer: A Survey of Practice in Industrial Organizations*, Harvard University Press: Boston, MA, 1970.

59. Kremer, J. M. *Information Flow Among Engineers in a Design Company*, University of Illinois at Urbana-Champaign, Champaign , IL, 1980, PhD diss., UMI 80-17965.

60. Shuchman, H. L. *Information Transfer in Engineering*, The Futures Group: Glastonbury, CT, 1981.

61. Kaufman, H. G. *Factors Related to Use of Technical Information in Engineering Problem Solving*, Polytechnic Institute of New York: Brooklyn, NY, 1963.

62. Tushman, M. L.; Nadler, D. A. Communication and technical roles in R&D laboratories: An information processing model. In *Management of Research and Innovation*; Dean, B. V., Goldhar, J. L., Eds.; North-Holland Publishing Company: New York, 1980; 91–112.

63. Katz, D. Kahn, R. L. *The Social Psychology of Organizations*, Wiley: New York, 1966.

64. Galbraith, J. K. *Designing Complex Organizations*, Addison-Wesley: Reading, MA, 1973.

65. Rogers, E. M. Information exchange and technological innovation. In *The Transfer and Utilization of Technical Knowledge*; Sahal, D., Ed.; D.C. Health: Lexington, MA, 1982; 105–123.

66. Orr, R. H. The scientist as an information processor: A conceptual model illustrated with data on variables related to library utilization. In *Communication Among Scientists and Engineers*; Nelson, C. E., Pollack, D. K., Eds.; D.C. Heath: Lexington, MA, 1970; 143–189.

67. Voight, M. J. *Scientists' Approaches to Information*, American Library Association: Chicago, IL, 1960, ACRL Monograph, No. 24.

68. Menzel, H. The information needs of current scientific research. *Libr. Quart.* 1964, *34*(1), 4–19.

69. Storer, N. W. *The Social System of Science*, Holt, Rinehart and Winston: New York, 1966.

70. Hagstrom, W. O. *The Scientific Community*, Basic Books: New York, 1965.

71. Gerstberger, P. G.; Allen, T. J. Criteria Used by Research and development engineers in the selection of an information source. *J. Appl. Psychol.* 1968, *52*(4), 272–279.

72. Rosenberg, V. Factors affecting the preferences of industrial personnel for information gathering methods. *Inform. Storage Retr.* 1967, July 3, 119–127.

73. Taylor, R. S. Information user environments. *Progress in Communication Sciences*; Ablex Press: Norwood, NJ, 1991; Vol.10, 217–255.

74. Pinelli, T. E.; Kennedy, J. M.; Barclay, R. O.; Bishop, A. P. Computer and information technology and aerospace knowledge diffusion. Paper Presented at the Annual Meeting of the American Association for the Advancement of Science The Hyatt Regency Hotel: Chicago, IL, February 8, 1992 (Available from NTIS, Springfield, VA; 92N28211.).

75. Pinelli, T. E. The information seeking habits and practices of engineers. *Sci. Technol. Libr.* 1991, *11*(3), 5–25.

76. Bishop, A. P. Electronic communication in engineering work. In *Proceedings of the 55th Annual Meeting of the American Society for Information Sciences*; Shaw, D., Ed.; Learned Information: Medford, NJ, 1992; Vol. 29, 193–205.

77. Pinelli, T. E.; Barclay, R. O.; Bishop, A. P.; Kennedy, J. M. Information technology and aerospace knowledge diffusion: Exploring the intermediary-end user interface in a policy framework. *Electron. Netw. Res. Applica. Policy* 1992, *2*(2), 31–49.

Index

A

building competitive edge
    challenges, 1102–1103
    customer intimacy, 1102
    for-profit sector, 1102
  communication, 1101–1102
  general services, 1100
  organization, impact and strategic positioning
    budgets, 1101
    costs and productive time, 1100
    placement, 1100
  professional development, 1096–1097
  service specialization
    alerting (current awareness) service, 1094
    Deutsche Bank (see Deutsche Bank, CIC)
    information technology company, 1095
    law firm, 1096
    public libraries, 1094
  special libraries, 1096
  staff qualifications, 1096–1097
  strategic planning, 1102
  subject specialization
    Nike Design Library, areas of, 1094–1095
    textile company, 1094
  user, 1095
Corporate libraries, 4374
Corporate mentality, 1089–1090
Corporate portals, 2893
Corporate records management programs
  active records management
    components, 1107
    document management systems, 1108
    ECM systems, 1108
    electronic records management, 1108–1109
    equipment costs and use office space, 1107
    filing system, 1107
    imaging program, 1108
  audits, 1111–1112
  California Public Records Act, 1105
  "cradle-to-grave" management, 1104–1105
  elements, 1105
  external requirements, 1104
  FOIA, 1105
  good corporate citizen, 1104
  government agencies, 1105
  inactive records management, 1109–1110
  internal requirements, 1104
  mergers, acquisitions and divestitures,
    1110–1111
  records management placement, 1111
  records retention
    appraisal, 1105
    legal environment and compliance,
      1106–1107
    litigation, legal holds, and discovery, 1107
    records series, 1105
    risk management, 1105–1106
  standards, 1111
  storage formats, 1104
  vital records protection program, 1110
Corporation Credit, 1403
Corporation for Public Broadcasting (CPB),
  1014, 1579
Correspondence approach, 2612
Cosijn model, 4875
Cosine correlation, 2203–2204
Cosmographia, 494
Cosmographia universalis, 1685

Cost and benefit attributes, 2294
Cost per thousand model (CPM), 2522
Cosway bindings, 541
Cougar, 2630
Council for Higher Education Accreditation
  (CHEA), 18–19
Council of Australian University Librarians
  (CAUL), 384
Council of Provincial and Territorial Archivists
  (CPTA), 666
Council of Scientific and Industrial Research
  (CSIR), 2002–2003
Council of State Archivists (CoSA), 3319
Council on Library and Information Resources
  (CLIR), 368
Council on Library Resources (CLR), 988, 2873,
  2963–2964
COUNTER, 413
Counting Online Usage of Networked Electronic
  Resources (COUNTER) Project, 4146
Country code top level domain (ccTLD) system,
  780
County Library Authority, 1839
COUPERIN, 2826
The Course of the Exchange, 1401
Covers common foreign and security policy
  (CFSP), 2140
CPLEX, 1196
CQL, see Contextual Query Language
Cranfield model of information retrieval (IR),
  4872
Cranfield paradigm, 4554
Cranfield tests, 2222–2223
Create Change Web site, 367
Credentialed librarians, 4777
Credibility
  definition
    expertise, 1113–1114
    trustworthiness, 1113–1114
  historical development, 1114
  process, 1117–1118
  typology of, 1115
Credit reports, 639
Crelle's Journal, 3024, 3026
Crestadoro, Andres, 761
CRG, see Classification Research Group
Crime fiction, 3701–3702
Crimestat, 1676
Criminal network analysis, 2402
Critical discourse analysis (CDA), 1664–1665
Critical incidence technique, 4531
*Criticas: An English Speaker's Guide to the
  Latest Spanish-Language Titles*, 2699
CRL, see Center for Research Libraries
Croatia
  archives
    Croatian State Archives, 1127–1128
    historical overview, 1126–1127
    legislation, 1127
    National Film Archives, 1128
    publishing and professional associations,
      1128
    specialized archives, 1128
  historical development, 1121
  literacy, books, and libraries
    academic, research, and special libraries,
      1125

Church libraries, 1126
  diocese libraries, 1122–1123
  in fifteenth and sixteenth centuries, 1123
  Glagolitic and Cyrillic alphabets,
    1121–1122
  Latin language, 1121
  legislation, 1124
  library and information science education,
    1126
  monastery libraries, 1122
  national and university library, 1124–1125
  professional associations, 1126
  public and school libraries, 1125–1126
  reading rooms, 1123
  in seventeenth century, 1123
  in twentieth century, 1123–1124
  location, 1121
  map of, 1121–1122
  museums
    history, 1129
    legislation and organization, 1129–1130
    publishing, staff, and professional associa-
      tion, 1130
  National Programme for the Digitisation of
    Archival, Library and Museum Records,
    1130
Croatian Academic Research Network
  (CARNET), 1125, 2828
Croatian Archival Council, 1127
Croatian Archivist Association, 1128
Croatian Library Association, 1126
Croatian Library Council, 1124
Croatian Museum Association, 1130
Croatian National and University Library,
  1124–1125
Croatian National Film Archives, 1128
Croatian State Archives, 1127–1128
CrossCheck, 1137
Cross-correlation, 4421
Cross-disciplinary faculty teaching, 2771
Cross-domain linking, 3294
Cross-genre phenomenon, 3706–3707
Cross-Language Evaluation Forum (CLEF),
  3143
Cross-lingual information retrieval (CLIR),
  2222, 2402, 3140
CrossRef publisher linking network
  cited-by linking, 1137
  CrossCheck, 1137
  CrossRef metadata services, 1137
  database, 1133
  distributed integration, 1138
  DOI, 1133–1134
  endeavor, 1133
  history, 1132–1133
  impacts
    on intermediaries, 1137
    on libraries, 1136–1137
    on publishers, 1136
    on researchers, 1137
  initiative, 1133
  interlinking, 1138
  metadata, 1133
  mission, 1132
  working process
    citation submission, 1134
    DOI registration, 1134

Functional retention schedules, 3893

Fund-raising, academic libraries, *see* Academic libraries, fund-raising and development

Furner, Jonathan, 2060

Fussler, Herman H., 497–498, 502, 506

Fuzzy set theory, information retrieval
  associative retrieval mechanisms
    clustering techniques, 1622, 1633
    compatible purposes, 1631
    ontologies, 1622
    pseudothesauri, 1622, 1631–1632
    thesauri, 1631–1633
  Boolean retrieval model, 1621–1622
  cross language retrieval, 1619
  document indexing
    generalized Boolean indexing, 1622–1623
    HTML document, weighted representation of, 1625–1626
    probabilistic models, 1622
    structured documents, representation of, 1623–1624
    techniques for, 1621
    term significance, 1624–1625
    vector space model, 1622
  flexible query languages, 1618
    definition of, 1621–1622, 1627–1628
    linguistic query weights, 1629–1630
    query evaluation mechanism, 1027–1028
    query weights, 1628–1629
    selection conditions, linguistic quantifiers, 1630–1631
  imprecision, vagueness, uncertainty, and inconsistency, 1619–1621
  knowledge-based models, 1621
  MCDM activity, 1618
  multicriteria decision-making activity, 1618
  multimedia document, 1619
  OCAT methodology, 1621
  relevance, concept of, 1619
  representation of documents, 1619
  research trends, 1619
  retrieval status value, 1633–1634
  semantic web, 1619

F-value, 419–420

G

Gabor-based features, 4424

Gallery of the Serbian Academy of Science and Arts, 4134

Gallica, 1604

Game Making Interes Group, 1641

Games and gaming
  game, definition of, 1636–1637
  in library
    academic libraries, 1639–1640
    ALA, GameRT, 1637
    benefits, 1637
    collections, 1637
    computer and console games, 1636–1637
    as cultural significance, 1637
    digital preservation, 1640
    for instructional purposes, 1641
    for outreach purposes, 1640–1641
    publc libraries, 1638
    school libraries, 1638–1639

tabletop games, 1637
video games, 1637

Games and Gaming Round Table (GameRT), 1637

Game theory, 1198

Garfield, Eugene, 502–503, 506

Gary Klein's sensemaking, 4116–4117

Gateway page, 4035

Gaussian distribution, 494

Gay, Lesbian, Bisexual Transgender (GLBT) Historical Society, 4760

Gaylord Award, 2777

Gender and sexuality archives
  Cornell Human Sexuality Project, 4760
  GBLT historical society, 4760
  Kinsey Institute, 4760
  Lesbian Herstory Archives, 4760
  National Gay & Lesbian Archives, 4760–4761

Genealogical Library, 1649

Genealogical literature
  compiled sources, 1651–1652
    biographies, 1652, 1654
    family histories and genealogies, 1654, 1656
    local histories, 1656
    pedigree chart, 1656
    Query services, 1656
    society and association resources, 1656
  definitions, 1644
  genealogical research
    classification and evaluation of, 1650–1651
    steps in, 1650
  genealogy, interest in, 1644
  history
    antiquity, 1645
    genealogical research, 1646
    historical associations, 1645
    Internet and digitization, 1646–1648
    modern genealogy, 1646
    new genealogy, characteristics of, 1646
    record keeping, 1645
    scientific genealogy, 1645–1646
  library catalogs and classification, use of, 1649
  news and networking sources, 1657, 1660
  original sources, 1653–1654, 1656–1659
  periodical sources, 1657
    non-society periodicals, 1659
    periodical indexes, 1660
    society periodicals, 1659
  reference tools, 1655–1656, 1659
  users of, 1648–1649

Gene ontology, 4087

General Archives of the Nation (AGN), 3096

General comparative research methodology, 2407

General Information Program (PGI), 2312, 4656–4657

General International Standard Archival Description (ISAD-G), 1366, 1593

Generality (G), 3945

Generalized Markup Language (GML)
  applications, 3075
  descriptive markup, 3074–3075

Generalized Retrieval and Information Processing for Humanities Oriented Studies (GRIPHOS), 3179

Generalized systems of order in museum, 1817

General Material Disignation (GMD), 1235

General Research Library, 1697

General-specific-sparse search strategy, 2213–2214

General State Archives (GSA), 1736

General systems theory, 3514

The General Theory of Employment, Interest and Money, 647

Generic ontologies, 3457

Generic Record Syntax (GRS), 2186

Genesis, 2068

Genetic Algorithms (GA), 274

Genetic flow line, 2058

Genetic information, 2058

Genetic programming, 274

Gennadius library, 1732

Genocide, 4400

Genocide Institute and Museum, 236–237

Genre
  definition, 1662

Genreflecting: A Guide to Reading Interests in Genre Fiction, 3856

Genre/form terms, 2856–2864

Genre repertoire, 2504, 2506

Genres
  commercial, 2504
  definition, 1662, 2503
  documents, 2509–2510
    automated classification, 2510–2512
    communication, 2504–2505
    educational genres, 2509
    genre chain, 2504
  environmental impact statements, 2503
  Internet
    business and academic e-mail messages, 2507
    classifications, 2507–2509
    evolution of, 2506–2507
    information access, 2509
    non-textual documents, 2507
    personal home pages, 2507
    unsolicited commercial e-mail, 2507
    Web communication, 2505–2506
    Weblog/blog, 2507
    World Wide Web, 2505
  journalistic genres, 2504
  learning theories, 1669
  popular literature
    adventure, 3701
    appeal characteristics, 3700
    "chick lit," 3705–3706
    collection arrangement, 3700
    crime fiction, 3701–3702
    cross-genre phenomenon, 3706–3707
    fantasy, 3702
    historical fiction, 3702–3703
    horror, 3703
    narrative nonfiction, 3705
    reading interests, 3706
    romance, 3703–3704
    science fiction, 3704–3705
    slipstream, 3706
    street lit/urban fiction, 3706
    westerns, 3705
  recurrent communicative situations, 2503
  research in linguistics, 1664–1665

in United States (*see* United States, public
   libraries)
urban libraries, 1848
users needs, 3784
value, 3794–3795
Venezuelan libraries, 4890
Public Libraries and Museums Act 1964, 4720
Public Library Act of 1919, 1839
Public Library Association (PLA), 74–75, 335,
   3783
   ALA, 3801
   CPLA program, 3804
   eight special-interest sections, 3801
   grant projects, 3804
   mangement, publications, 3803
   member-driven organization, 3801
   membership, 3802
   National Conference, 3804
   new clusters, 3802
   organization, 3802–3803
   preconferences and workshops, 3803
   presidents, 3805
   priority concerns, 3802
   Public Libraries magazine, 3803
   Public Library Data Service, 3803
The Public Library Inquiry, 2769–2770,
   3775–3776
Public Library Manifesto, 3774
Public Library Movement, 888
Public Library of Science (PLoS), 557,
   3468–3469
*Public Library Service: A Guide to Evaluation
   with Minimum Standards*, 1846
Public machine bureaucracies, 3512
Public metadata creators, 3067
Public museums
   Milwaukee Public Museum, 3164
   in Moldova, 3121
   purpose-designed public museum, 3150
   in United Kingdom, 4716
Public Participation GIS (PPGIS), 1672–1673
Public patent databases on Internet
   CIPO, 3568
   EPO, 3569
   FreePatentsOnline, 3570
   Google Patents, 3570
   JPO, 3569–3570
   Patent Lens, 3570–3751
   proliferation, 3567
   USPTO, 3568–3569
   WIPO, 3570
Public policy advocacy, 347
Public portals, 2893
Public Record Office (PRO), 108
Public Record Office (PRO) Act 1838,
   4732–4733
Public Record Office of Great Britain, 1792
Public Record Office of Northern Ireland
   (PRONI), 4734
Public Records Act, 183, 2012, 4733–4734
Public Relations and Marketing (PRMS), 2842
Public services, academic libraries, 4–5, 7–8
Public service special collections professionals,
   4349
Published informational content, 1274
Publishing histories, 1861
PubMed, 819, 1878

PubMed Central® (PMC), 3338
PubMed database, 1765, 1767
PubScience, 1555
Pugillares, 542
Punctuational markup, 3073
Pura Belpre Award, 334
Purdue University Research Repository
   (PURR), 2902
Pythagorean theorem, 3020
Python spatial analysis library (PySal), 1676

Q

Qayrawan Grand Mosque, 4626
Quai Branly Museum, 1596–1597
QuakeNet, 1049
Qualified Dublin Core (DCQ), 1366
Qualisigns, 4098
Qualitative research, 3807–3810
   methods and tools, 3813–3816
   principles, 3810–3813
   semiotics, 3816
Quality improvement, 568, 1179–1180, 1517,
   1874, 1889
Quality of service (QoS), 1056
Quality Oversight Organizations (QOO), 1889
Quantitative models, 1192–1193
Quantitative structure-activity relationships
   (QSAR), 836
Quarterly of Applied Mathematics, 3027
Quasi nongovernmental organization
   (QUANGO), 3380
Quasi-official press, 3738–3739
Queensland Art Gallery, 389
Queen Sofia Center of Art National Museum,
   4332
Query languages, 1366–1367, 1621–1622
Questia service, 985
Question-answering, NLP, 3353
Question-answering (QA) systems, 1903, 4574
Questionnaires, 4530–4531, 4798–4799
QuestionPoint, 3398–3399
Quetelet, Adolph, 495

R

Radio, 1572–1573
Radio broadcast libraries, 3277
Radio Corporation of America (RCA), 1015
Radio frequency identification (RFID), 921,
   2924
Radio stations, 998–999
Raisig, L. Miles, 496, 498
Rajput School of painting, 1957
Randomized controlled trials (RCTs), 1519
Random network, 1039
Random variables, information theory
   mutual information, 2351–2353
   unpredictability, 2350
   varying probabilities and entropy measure,
   2351
Ranganathan, S.R., 1534, 1536
Ranked half-life (RHL), 1902
Rapid automatized naming (RAN), 3842, 3845
Rare book collections, 3726
   access points, 3825–3826
   colleges and universities, 3822

deaccessioning, 3825
determination of, 3821–3822
digitization, 3828
donations, 3822–3823
environmental issues, 3826
exhibitions, 3828
growth of
   gifts, 3824
   purchase of materials, 3823–3824
   transfers, 3824–3825
independent rare book libraries, 3822
institutional support, 3827–3828
librarians, responsibilities of, 3823
national libraries, 3822
origins of, 3820
public libraries, 3822
public/quasi-public collections, 3823
restrictions, 3823
security, 3826–3827
Rare Books and Manuscripts Librarianship
   (RBML), 355
Rare Books and Manuscripts Section (RBMS),
   4336, 4338, 4344
Rare books, provenance of, *see* Provenance of
   rare books
Rare manuscript libraries, United Kingdom,
   4738
RASKE modeling, 3109
Raster images, 1308
Rathgen, Friedrich, 1069
Rationalism, 3625–3626
Ratzel, Friedrich, 1687
RDA, *see* Resource, Description and Access
RDF, *see* Resource Description Framework
rdfs:label property, 3964
rdfs:seeAlso property, 3964
Reaction searching, 825–826
Reactive strategies, 2241
A Reader in Art Librarianship, 249
ReaderMeter, 47
Readers' advisory, 3914
Readex United Nations Documents Collections,
   1724
Reading disorders
   adults, 3843
   causes of
      genetic factors, 3846
      language processes, 3845
      linguistic coding, 3844
      memory, 3845
      naming speed, 3845
      neurological basis, 3845–3846
      phonological coding, 3844
      semantic coding, 3844
      syntactic coding, 3844
      visual coding, 3844
      word recognition, 3844
   difficulties, 3841
   historical trends, 3842
   impairments, 3841
   intrinsic disorders, 3841
   learning disabilities, 3843–3844
   scientifically based interventions, 3846–3848
   subgroups of, 3842–3843
Reading interests
   advisory and appeal factors, 3857
   boredom, 3854–3855

Tasman, Abel, 1685
Tatomir Accessibility Checklist, 3578
"Taxidermy and Plastic Art" teaching lab and
    course, 3216
Taximetrics, *see* Numerical taxonomy
Taxonomic Databases Working Group
    (TDWG), 3311
Taxonomy
    classical taxonomy, 4538–4539
    classification, 4537
    contemporary taxonomy
        AI ontology, 4540
        classificatory structures, 4539
        information access systems, 4540–4541
        object-oriented programming, 4540
    definition, 4537
    history, 4538
    methodology and practices, 4543–4544
    numerical taxonomy, 4539
    organization, 4538
    theory and principles, 4541–4543
Taxpayer Return on Investment in Florida Pub-
    lic Libraries study, 3795
Tax-supported public libraries, 3774
Taylor and Fayol's scientific approach, 142
Taylor & Francis Group Student Travel Grant,
    1422
Taylorism, 2065
Taylor's information need model, 2118–2119
Taylor Society, 651
Teach Act, 1472
Teaching hospital library, 1872
Team computing, 1054
TeamWare, 1062
Technical Center for Agricultural and Rural
    Cooperation (CTA), 2312
Technical Chamber of Greece (TEE), 1732
Technical Committee 8 (TC8), 2276
Technical libraries, 4009
Technical Library of Lithuania, 2953
Technical metadata creators, 3066
Technical Report Archive and Image Library
    (TRAIL), 791, 4012
Technical services (TS)
    academic libraries, 4–5, 8–9
    acquisitions, 2918–2919
    cataloging, 2918, 2920–2924
    collections management, 2918, 2924
Technical Subcommittee for Encoded Archival
    Description (TS-EAD), 1424, 1431
Technical writing
    audience analysis, 4547
    composition, 4548
    documentation, 4547–4550
    field of study
        early history, 4549
        new millennium, 4551–4552
        twentieth century, 4549–4551
    information architecture, 4552
    information design and architecture, 4548
    nonacademic writing, 4547
    professional communication, 4547
    professional writing, 4547, 4549
    research, 4548
    rhetoric and writing programs, 4548
    technical communication, 4547–4548, 4552
    writing studies, 4548, 4552

Techniques in Electronic Resource Management
    (TERMS), 414
Techno-economic paradigm, 2254
Technological Educational Institutions (TEIs),
    1731
Technological Institute of Higher Education
    Studies in Monterrey (ITESM), 3086
Technological scarcity argument, 1017
Technology, 4978
    economy, 2308
    knowledge, 2275
Technology Opportunities Program (TOP),
    1028–1029
Technoscapes, 2124
Teeple Scholarship, 81
TEI P1, 4566
TEI P2, 4566
TEI P3, 4566
TEI P4, 4566
TEI P5, 4567
Telecommunications and Information
    Infrasture Assistance Program (TIIAP),
    1028
Telecoms Package, 2141–2142
TelegraphCQ, 2631
Television, 999, 1573–1574
Television archives, *see* International Federation
    of Television Archives
Television Studies Commission, 2468–2469
TEMPUS program, 2827, 2954
Term frequency–inverse document frequency
    (TFIDF) weights, 2204
Test collections
    available, 4557
    construction, 4556–4557
Texas State Archives, 4385
Text analysis, 2930
Text encoding initiative (TEI), 3075
    character encoding, 4559
    Consortium, 4559
    ground rules
        customization files, 4564
        guidelines, 4561–4562
        modules, 4562–4564
        structural grammars, 4564
        text structure, 4562
    Guidelines, 1289–1290
    history, 4565–4567
    humanities
        data representation, 4559
        flags, 4560
        markup languages, 4560–4561
Text generation, *see* Natural language
    generation
Text mining, 2401–2402
Text planning, 432
TExtract, 1987
Text retrieval conference (TREC), 482, 484,
    1904, 2175–2176, 2223, 3932, 4557
    historical context, 4569–4570
    test collections, 4570–4571
    tracks, 4571–4572
Text schemas, 437
Textual bibliography, 478
Thales of Miletus, 1683
Theatrum Orbis Terrarum, 1685
The European Library (TEL), 3331, 3682

Theft, vandalism and security
    ABAA, 4578
    Antiquarian Booksellers database, 4576
    archival repositories, 4580
    BAMBAM, 4578
    basic security and preservation policies, 4580
    bomb threats, 4580
    book theft, 4579
    communication among librarians, 4587–4588
    communication, book dealers, 4581–4582
    digital recordings, 4579
    electronic articles, 4579
    ideological vandalism, 4580
    library crimes, 4578
    Library Proxy Server, 4580
    lobby state legislatures, 4586
    MARC format, 4578
    missing treasures, Library of Congress,
        4582–4583
    in museums
        definitions, 4593–4594
        history, 4594
        prevention, 4598–4600
    OCLC database, 4578
    paging slips, 4580
    play vandalism, 4580
    preventions
        consistent security procedures, 4584–4585
        mark materials and use colored photocopy
            paper, 4585–4586
        microfilming, 4585
        security systems and trust no one,
            4583–4584
    replevin, 4577, 4583
    security devices, 4586–4587
    stolen/mutilated library books, replacement
        of, 4577
    tactical vandalism, 4580
    vindictive vandalism, 4580
The information literacy tutorial (TILT), 3440
The Joint Commission on Accreditation of
    Healthcare Organizations (JCAHO),
    1874
Thema–nomen conceptual model, 4066
Thematic wayfinding, 4958
The National Archives (TNA), 111, 4733,
    4735
Theodor Seuss Geisel Award, 335
Theological librarianship
    ATLA, 4606–4608
    European library, 4605
    international association, 4608–4609
    North American experience, 4605–4606
    origins, 4604–4605
    professional associations support, 4608
    today, 4609–4610
Theophrastes, 1683
Theoretical Economics, 3468
Theoretical knowledge, 2267–2269
Theory of action, 4806–4807
Theory of forms, 2094
Recuyell of the Histories of Troy, 1973
Thesauri, 1984–1986
Thesaurofacet, 589
Thesaurus, 1076, 1537–1538
    BC2, 589
    definition, 4673